McGraw Hill Education create™

AF861223

Course	Intermediate Accounting Ninth Edition Volume 2
rse Number	**with Connect**
	VIRGINIA TECH
	ACIS 3116

McGraw Hill Education create™

http://create.mheducation.com

ISBN-10: 1309090432 ISBN-13: 9781309090435

Contents

Credits

Online Supplements

About the Authors

DAVID SPICELAND

David Spiceland is professor of accounting at the University of Memphis, where he teaches intermediate accounting and other financial accounting courses at the undergraduate and master's levels. He received his BS degree in finance from the University of Tennessee, his MBA from Southern Illinois University, and his PhD in accounting from the University of Arkansas.

Professor Spiceland's primary research interests are in earnings management and educational research. He has published articles in a variety of journals, including *The Accounting Review, Accounting and Business Research, Journal of Financial Research,* and *Journal of Accounting Education,* and is an author of McGraw-Hill's *Financial Accounting* with Wayne Thomas and Don Herrmann. Professor Spiceland has received university and college awards and recognition for his teaching, research, and technological innovations in the classroom.

MARK NELSON

Mark Nelson is the Anne and Elmer Lindseth Dean and Professor of Accounting at Cornell University's S. C. Johnson Graduate School of Management. He received his BBA degree from Iowa State University and his MA and PhD degrees from The Ohio State University. Professor Nelson has won ten teaching awards, including an inaugural Cook Prize from the American Accounting Association.

Professor Nelson's research focuses on decision making in financial accounting and auditing. His research has been published in the *Accounting Review;* the *Journal of Accounting Research; Contemporary Accounting Research; Accounting, Organizations and Society;* and several other journals. He has received the American Accounting Association's Notable Contribution to Accounting Literature Award, as well as the AAA's Wildman Medal for work judged to make a significant contribution to practice.

Professor Nelson served three terms as an area editor of *The Accounting Review* and is a member of the editorial boards of several journals. He also served for four years on the FASB's Financial Accounting Standards Advisory Council.

WAYNE THOMAS

Wayne Thomas is the John T. Steed Chair and Professor of Accounting at the University of Oklahoma's Price College of Business. He received his BS degree from Southwestern Oklahoma State University and his MS and PhD from Oklahoma State University. He has received teaching awards at the university, college, and departmental levels, and has received the Outstanding Educator Award from the Oklahoma Society of CPAs. He is an author of McGraw-Hill's *Financial Accounting* with David Spiceland and Don Herrmann.

His research focuses on various financial reporting issues and has been published in *The Accounting Review, Journal of Accounting Research, Journal of Accounting and Economics, Contemporary Accounting Research, Review of Accounting Studies, Accounting Organizations and Society,* and others. He has served as an editor for *The Accounting Review* and has won the American Accounting Association's Competitive Manuscript Award and Outstanding International Accounting Dissertation.

Professor Thomas enjoys various activities such as tennis, basketball, golf, and crossword puzzles, and most of all, he enjoys spending time with his wife and kids.

Intermediate Accounting Ninth Edition:

Welcome to the fastest-growing learning program in intermediate accounting! Instructors recognize the "Spiceland advantage" in content that's intensive and thorough, as well as in writing that's fluid and precise—together, these combine to form a resource that's rigorous yet readable. By blending a comprehensive approach, clear conversational tone, current updates on key standards, and the market-leading technological innovations of Connect®, the Spiceland team delivers an unrivaled experience. As a result of Spiceland's rigorous yet readable learning system, students develop a deeper and more complete understanding of intermediate accounting topics.

> "The chapters are well written in a style that makes difficult materials approachable for students."
>
> **—Kathy Hsiao Yu Hsu, *University of Louisiana–Lafayette***

The *Intermediate Accounting* learning system is built around four key attributes: current, comprehensive, clear, and Connect®

Current: Few disciplines see the rapid changes that accounting experiences. The Spiceland team is committed to keeping instructors' courses up to date. The ninth edition fully integrates the latest FASB updates, including:

- **NEW** Chapter 15, covering the latest standard on leases (ASU No. 2016–02, Leases (Topic 842)).
- ASU No. 2016–01, Financial Instruments—Overall (Subtopic 825–10): Recognition and Measurement of Financial Assets and Financial Liabilities
- ASU No. 2016–013, Financial Instruments—Credit Losses (Topic 326) on "Current Expected Credit Loss" (CECL) model for accounting for credit losses, as well as current GAAP requirements for recognizing impairments of investments.
- ASU No. 2015–17, Income Taxes (Topic 740): Balance Sheet Classification of Deferred Taxes
- ASU No. 2015–03, Interest—Imputation of Interest (Subtopic 835–30)
- ASU No. 2016–10, Revenue from Contracts with Customers: Identifying Performance Obligations and Licensing (Topic 606)
- ASU No. 2016–09, Improvements to Employee Share-Based Payment Accounting, which amends ASC Topic 718, Compensation—Stock Compensation.

Current events regularly focus public attention on the key role of accounting in providing information useful to financial decision makers. The CPA exam, too, has changed to emphasize the professional skills needed to critically evaluate accounting method alternatives. *Intermediate Accounting* provides a **decision makers' perspective,** highlighting the professional judgment and critical thinking skills required of accountants in today's business environment.

> "The *Spiceland Intermediate Accounting* provides a truly up to date view of financial reporting. The authors explain complex topics in a very relevant, engaging, easy to follow approach for students with excellent examples and illustrations."
>
> **— Celina Jozsi, *Florida Southern University***

Comprehensive: The Spiceland team ensures comprehensive coverage and quality throughout the learning system by building content and assets with a unified methodology that meets rigorous standards. Students are challenged through diverse examples and carefully crafted problem sets which promote in-depth understanding and drive development of critical-thinking skills.

The author team is committed to providing a learning experience that fully prepares students for the future by solidifying core comprehension and enabling confident application of key concepts. Students can feel confident that the conceptual underpinnings and practical skills conveyed in the ninth edition will prepare them for a wide range of real world scenarios.

Rigorous yet readable

Clear: Reviewers, instructors, and students have all hailed *Intermediate Accounting's* ability to explain both simple and complex topics in language that is coherent and approachable. The author team's highly acclaimed conversational writing style establishes a friendly dialogue—establishing the impression of a conversation with students, as opposed to lecturing at them.

This tone remains consistent throughout the learning system, as authors Spiceland, Nelson, and Thomas write not only the primary content, but also every major supplement: study guide, instructor's resource manual, solutions manual, and test bank. All end-of-chapter material, too, is written by the author team and tested in their classrooms. *Intermediate Accounting* is written to be the most complete, coherent, and student-oriented resource on the market.

"This textbook is written in a way that is easy to read, provides clear examples, includes thorough coverage of necessary topics, and provides ample opportunity for practice and mastery of the material through end of chapter problems."

—Terra Brown, *University of Texas–Arlington*

Connect: Today's accounting students expect to learn in multiple modalities. As a result, the ninth edition of Spiceland's learning system features the following: Connect, SmartBook's adaptive learning and reading experience, **NEW** Concept Overview Videos, Guided Examples, **NEW** Excel® simulations, and General Ledger problems.

Quality assessment continues to be a focus of Connect, with over **2,500 questions** available for assignment, including more than 1,125 algorithmic questions.

McGraw-Hill Education is continually updating and improving our digital resources. To that end, we have a new partnership with Roger CPA, providing multiple choice practice questions directly within our Connect banks, as well as links to the Roger CPA site for complementary selected simulations.

"Connect is a great resource for any course, but the new updates to the General Ledger and Excel Simulations allow this package to go above and beyond; students will exit the intermediate series with a strong foundation in Excel and the accounting cycle."

—Joshua Neil, *University of Colorado–Boulder*

Spiceland's Financial Accounting Series

Intermediate Accounting forms a complete learning system when paired with *Financial Accounting* by authors David Spiceland, Wayne Thomas, and Don Herrmann. Now in its fourth edition, *Financial Accounting* uses the same proven approach that has made *Intermediate Accounting* a success—a conversational writing style with real-world focus and author-prepared supplements, combined with Connect's market leading technology solutions and assessment.

"If you like Spiceland's intermediate text, you will be thrilled with the financial accounting text. It is written in the same conversational style, addresses topics directly and clearly, and the illustrations are terrific too."

—Nancy Snow, *University of Toledo*

What Keeps SPICELAND Users Coming Back?

Where We're Headed

These boxes describe the potential financial reporting effects of many of the FASB and IASB joint projects intended to further align U.S. GAAP and IFRS, as well as other projects the Boards are pursuing separately. Where We're Headed boxes allow instructors to deal with ongoing projects to the extent they desire.

Where We're Headed

In 2004, the FASB and IASB began working together on a project, Financial Statement Presentation, to establish a common standard for presenting information in the financial statements, including classifying and displaying line items and aggregating line items into subtotals and totals. This project could have a dramatic impact on the format of financial statements. An important part of the proposal involves the organization of elements of the balance sheet (statement of financial position), statement of comprehensive income (including the inc
classifications.
Progress was
concentrate on
FASB's agenda.
all of the financi
FASB issued an

"Where We're Headed boxes allow the students to be updated with the most current accounting changes without inundating them with needless technical specifications. A perfect balance!"

—Cheryl Bartlett, *Indiana University—South Bend*

Financial Reporting Cases

Each chapter opens with a Financial Reporting Case that places the student in the role of the decision maker, engaging the student in an interesting situation related to the accounting issues to come. Then, the cases pose questions for the student in the role of decision maker. Marginal notations throughout the chapter point out locations where each question is addressed. The case questions are answered at the end of the chapter.

Financial Reporting Case Solution

© goodluz/123RF

1. **What purpose do adjusting entries serve?** *(p. 63)* Adjusting entries help ensure that all revenues are recognized in the period goods or services are transferred to customers, regardless of when cash is received. In this instance, for example, $13,000 cash has been received for services that haven't yet been performed. Also, adjusting entries enable a company to recognize all expenses incurred during a period, regardless of when cash is paid. Without depreciation, the friends' cost of using the equipment is not taken into account. Conversely, without adjustment, the cost of rent is overstated by $3,000 paid in advance for part of next year's rent.

With adjustments, we get an accrual
measure of a company's operating perfo
operating cash flows. Similarly, the bal
of assets and liabilities as sources of futu

"The case at the beginning of each chapter is very captivating. After I read the case, I wanted to get paper and pencil and answer the questions."

—Carol Shaver, *Louisiana Tech University*

Decision Makers' Perspective

These sections appear throughout the text to illustrate how accounting information is put to work in today's firms. With the CPA exam placing greater focus on application of skills in realistic work settings, these discussions help your students gain an edge that will remain with them as they enter the workplace.

Decision Makers' Perspective

Cash often is referred to as a *nonearning* asset because it earns no interest. For this reason, managers invest idle cash in either cash equivalents or short-term investments, both of which provide a return. Management's goal is to hold the minimum amount of cash necessary to conduct normal business operations, meet its obligations, and take advantage of opportunities. Too much cash reduces profits through lost returns, while too little cash increases risk. This trade-off between risk and return is an ongoing choice made by management (internal decision makers). Whether the choice ma
by investors and creditors (external decis
A company must have cash available
previous section as well as for planned di
and financing cash flows. However, becau
amounts, a company needs an additional
events. The size of the cushion depends o

"This is an excellent feature of the book. It is so important to know why and how information is used and not just memorizing the 'right' answers."

—Jeff Mankin, *Lipscomb University*

In talking with so many intermediate accounting faculty, we heard more than how to improve the book—there was much, much more that both users and nonusers insisted we not change. Here are some of the features that have made Spiceland such a phenomenal success in its previous editions.

Additional Consideration

Discounts in Contracts with Multiple Performance Obligations. Note that Illustration 5–7 shows that Tri-Box systems are sold at a discount—TrueTech sells the system for a transaction price ($250) that's less than the $300 sum of the stand-alone selling prices of the Tri-Box module ($240) and the subscription to Tri-Net ($60). Because there is no evidence that the discount relates to only one of the performance obligations, it is spread between them in the allocation process. If TrueTech had clear evidence from sales of those goods and services that the discount related to only one of them, the entire discount would be allocated to that good or service.

"This is a good technique that I actually use in my class and it's good to see it in a book!"

—Ramesh Narasimhan, *Montclair State University*

Ethical Dilemma

You recently have been employed by a large retail chain that sells sporting goods. One of your tasks is to help prepare periodic financial statements for external distribution. The chain's largest creditor, National Savings & Loan, requires quarterly financial statements, and you are currently working on the statements for the three-month period ending June 30, 2018.

During the months of May an
TV advertising campaign. The $
as well as the radio and TV time
charged to advertising expense
to prepare a June 30 adjusting
set up an asset called *prepaid a*
that "This advertising campaign
will continue to bring in custome
an asset, we can match the cost
we expense the advertising in M

"Having ethical dilemma boxes in every chapter is much more significant than having a separate chapter devoted to ethics. Students can relate to the importance of being ethical in every aspect of business dealings."

—Gloria Worthy, *Southwest Tennessee Community College*

Broaden Your Perspective

Apply your critical-thinking ability to the knowledge you've gained. These cases will provide you an opportunity to develop your research, analysis, judgment, and communication skills. You also will work with other students, integrate what you've learned, apply it in real-world situations, and consider its global and ethical ramifications. This practice will broaden your knowledge and further develop your decision-making abilities.

Judgment Case 4–1
Earnings quality
● LO4–2, LO4–3

The financial community in the United States has become increasingly concerned with the quality of reported company earnings.

Required:

1. Define the term
2. Explain the dis

"I think students would benefit tremendously from the cases."

—Joyce Njoroge, *Drake University*

Additional Consideration Boxes

These are "on the spot" considerations of important, but incidental or infrequent, aspects of the primary topics to which they relate. Their parenthetical nature, highlighted by enclosure in Additional Consideration boxes, helps maintain an appropriate level of rigor of topic coverage without sacrificing clarity of explanation.

Ethical Dilemmas

Because ethical ramifications of business decisions impact so many individuals as well as the core of our economy, Ethical Dilemmas are incorporated within the context of accounting issues as they are discussed. These features lend themselves very well to impromptu class discussions and debates.

Broaden Your Perspective Cases

Finish each chapter with these powerful and effective cases, a great way to reinforce and expand concepts learned in the chapter.

Star Problems

In each chapter, particularly challenging problems, designated by a ★, require students to combine multiple concepts or require significant use of judgment.

McGraw Hill Education connect®

Required=Results

©Getty Images/iStockphoto

McGraw-Hill Connect®
Learn Without Limits

Connect is a teaching and learning platform that is proven to deliver better results for students and instructors.

Connect empowers students by continually adapting to deliver precisely what they need, when they need it, and how they need it, so your class time is more engaging and effective.

Connect's Impact on Retention Rates, Pass Rates, and Average Exam Scores

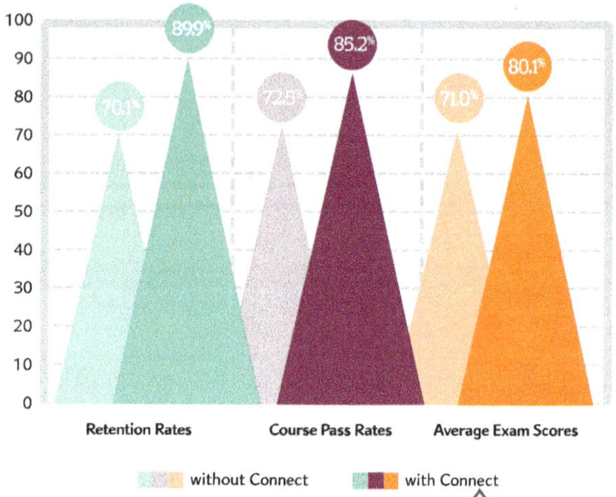

Using **Connect** improves retention rates by **19.8%**, passing rates by **12.7%**, and exam scores by **9.1%**.

73% of instructors who use **Connect** require it; instructor satisfaction **increases** by 28% when **Connect** is required.

Analytics

Connect Insight®

Connect Insight is Connect's new one-of-a-kind visual analytics dashboard that provides at-a-glance information regarding student performance, which is immediately actionable. By presenting assignment, assessment, and topical performance results together with a time metric that is easily visible for aggregate or individual results, Connect Insight gives the user the ability to take a just-in-time approach to teaching and learning, which was never before available. Connect Insight presents data that helps instructors improve class performance in a way that is efficient and effective.

Impact on Final Course Grade Distribution

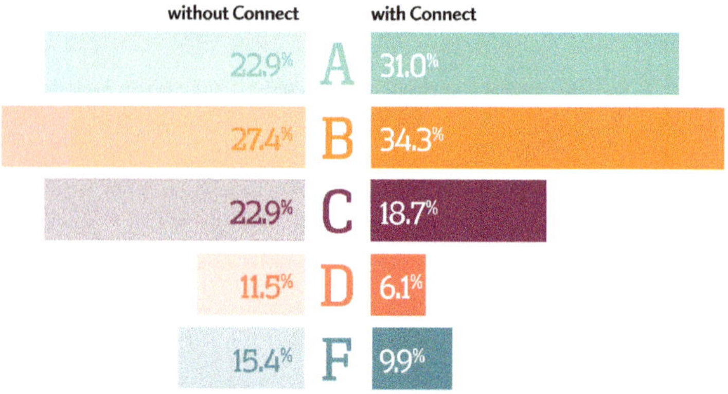

Adaptive

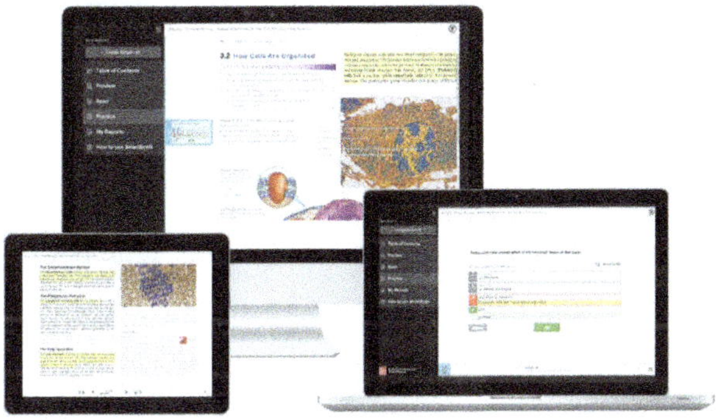

THE **ADAPTIVE READING EXPERIENCE** DESIGNED TO TRANSFORM THE WAY STUDENTS READ

More students earn **A's** and **B's** when they use McGraw-Hill Education **Adaptive** products.

SmartBook®

Proven to help students improve grades and study more efficiently, SmartBook contains the same content within the print book, but actively tailors that content to the needs of the individual. SmartBook's adaptive technology provides precise, personalized instruction on what the student should do next, guiding the student to master and remember key concepts, targeting gaps in knowledge and offering customized feedback, and driving the student toward comprehension and retention of the subject matter. Available on tablets, SmartBook puts learning at the student's fingertips—anywhere, anytime.

Over **8 billion questions** have been answered, making McGraw-Hill Education products more intelligent, reliable, and precise.

STUDENTS WANT

SMARTBOOK®

95% of students reported **SmartBook** to be a more effective way of reading material.

100% of students want to use the Practice Quiz feature available within **SmartBook** to help them study.

100% of students reported having reliable access to off-campus wifi.

90% of students say they would purchase **SmartBook** over print alone.

95% of students reported that **SmartBook** would impact their study skills in a positive way.

Mc Graw Hill Education

*Findings based on 2015 focus group results administered by McGraw-Hill Education

www.mheducation.com

ONLINE ASSIGNMENTS

Connect helps students learn more efficiently by providing feedback and practice material when they need it, where they need it. Connect grades homework automatically and gives immediate feedback on any questions students may have missed. The extensive assignable, gradable end-of-chapter content includes a general journal application that looks and feels more like what you would find in a general ledger software package. Also, select questions have been redesigned to test students' knowledge more fully. They now include tables for students to work through rather than requiring that all calculations be done offline.

End-of-chapter questions in Connect include:

- Brief Exercises
- Exercises
- Problems

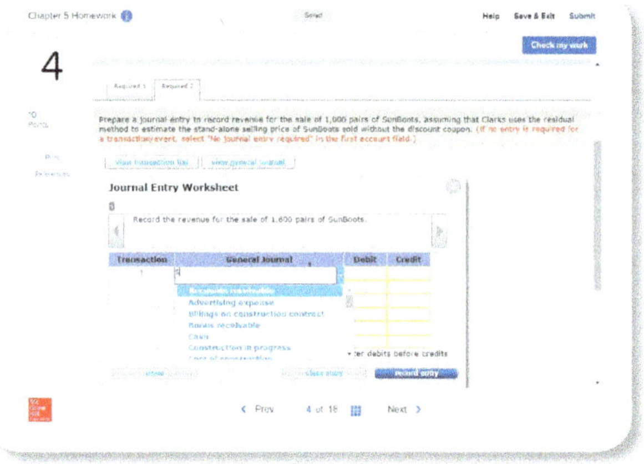

> "The textbook's General Ledger, Concept Overview Videos, and Excel Simulations are outstanding. "
>
> **—Professor Kaye Sheridan, *Troy University***

NEW! GENERAL LEDGER PROBLEMS

New **General Ledger Problems** provide a much-improved student experience when working with accounting cycle questions, offering improved navigation and less scrolling. Students can audit their mistakes by easily linking back to their original entries and can see how the numbers flow through the various financial statements. Many General Ledger Problems include an analysis tab that allows students to demonstrate their critical thinking skills and a deeper understanding of accounting concepts.

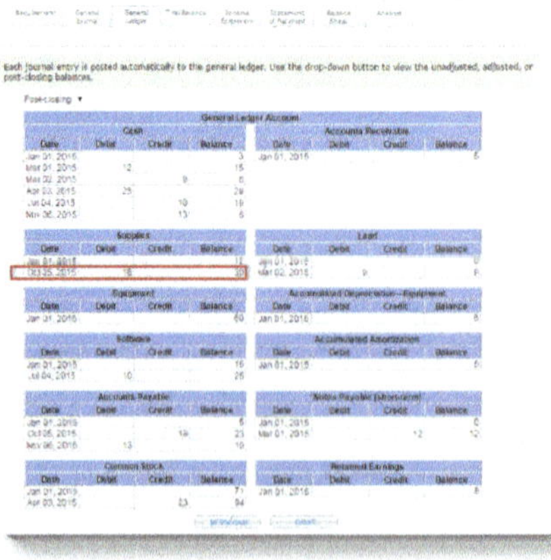

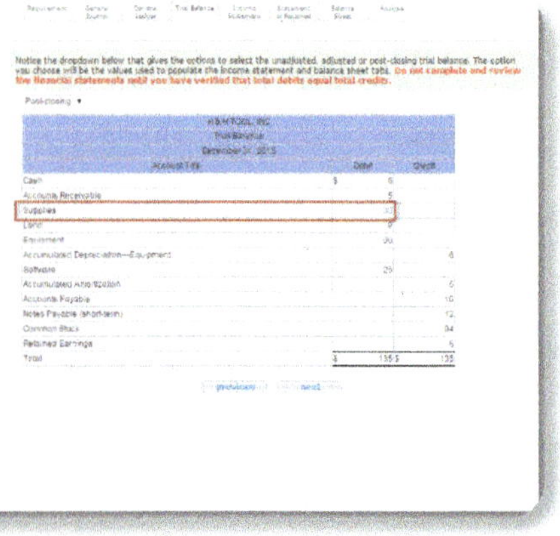

NEW! CONCEPT OVERVIEW VIDEOS

The **Concept Overview Videos** provide engaging narratives of key topics in an assignable and interactive online format. They follow the structure of the text and are organized to match the specific learning objectives within each chapter of *Intermediate Accounting.* The Concept Overview Videos provide additional explanation and enhancement of material from the text chapter, allowing students to learn, study, and practice with instant feedback, at their own pace.

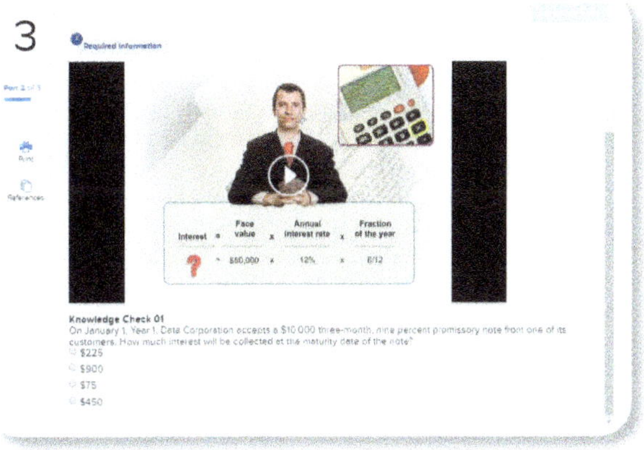

NEW! EXCEL SIMULATIONS

Simulated Excel Questions, assignable within Connect, allow students to practice their Excel skills—such as basic formulas and formatting—within the content of financial accounting. These questions feature animated, narrated Help and Show Me tutorials (when enabled), as well as automatic feedback and grading for both students and professors.

GUIDED EXAMPLES

The **Guided Examples** in Connect provide a narrated, animated, step-by-step walk-through of select exercises similar to those assigned. These short presentations can be turned on or off by instructors and provide reinforcement when students need it most.

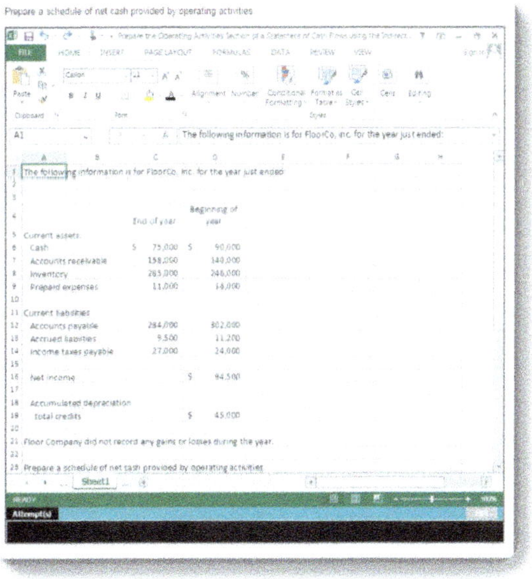

"As a student I need to interact with course material in order to retain it, and **Connect** offers a perfect platform for this kind of learning. Rather than just reading through textbooks, **Connect** has given me the tools to feel engaged in the learning process."

—**Jennah Epstein Kraus, student, *Bunker Hill Community College***

CPA SIMULATIONS

McGraw-Hill Education has partnered with Roger CPA Review, a global leader in CPA Exam preparation, to provide students a smooth transition from the accounting classroom to successful completion of the CPA Exam. While many aspiring accountants wait until they have completed their academic studies to begin preparing for the CPA Exam, research shows that those who become familiar with exam content earlier in the process have a stronger chance of successfully passing the CPA Exam. Accordingly, students using these McGraw-Hill materials will have access to sample CPA Exam Multiple-Choice questions and Task-based Simulations from Roger CPA Review, with expert-written explanations and solutions. All questions are either directly from the AICPA or are modeled on AICPA questions that appear in the exam. Task-based Simulations are delivered via the Roger CPA Review platform, which mirrors the look, feel and functionality of the actual exam. McGraw-Hill Education and Roger CPA Review are dedicated to supporting every accounting student along their journey, ultimately helping them achieve career success in the accounting profession. For more information about the full Roger CPA Review program, exam requirements and exam content, visit www.rogercpareview.com.

> "*Intermediate Accounting* is current, complete, well written, and highly detailed. It belongs in the library of anyone who is preparing for the CPA exam."
>
> **—Barbara K. Parks, *American Intercontinental University—Online***

Other Student Supplements

Study Guide

Volume 1: ISBN-13: 9781260030259 (MHID: 1260030253)

Volume 2: ISBN-13: 9781260030266 (MHID: 1260030261)

The Study Guide, written by the text authors, provides chapter summaries, detailed illustrations, and a wide variety of self-study questions, exercises, and multiple-choice problems (with solutions).

ALEKS®

ALEKS ACCOUNTING CYCLE

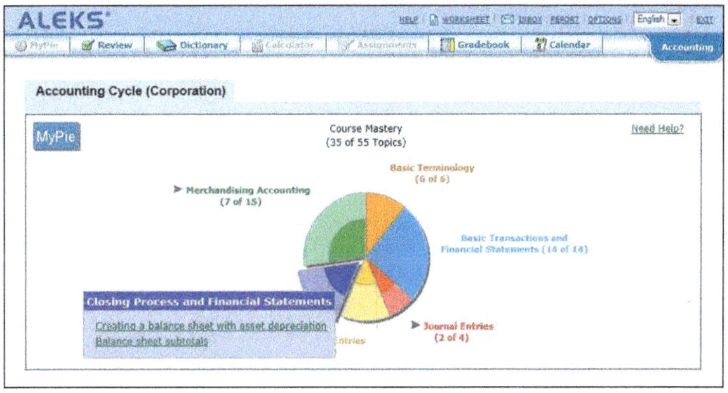

ALEKS Accounting Cycle is a web-based program that provides targeted coverage of prerequisite and introductory material necessary for student success in Intermediate Accounting. ALEKS uses artificial intelligence and adaptive questioning to assess precisely a student's preparedness and deliver personalized instruction on the exact topics the student is **most ready to learn.** Through comprehensive explanations, practice, and immediate feedback, ALEKS enables students to quickly fill individual knowledge gaps in order to build a strong foundation of critical accounting skills. Better prepared students saves you valuable time at the beginning of your course!

Use ALEKS Accounting Cycle as a pre-course assignment or during the first three weeks of the term to see improved student confidence and performance, as well as fewer drops.

ALEKS Accounting Cycle Features:

- **Artificial Intelligence:** Targets Gaps in Prerequisite Knowledge
- **Individualized Learning and Assessment:** Ensure Student Preparedness
- **Open-Response Environment:** Avoids Multiple-Choice and Ensures Mastery
- **Dynamic, Automated Reports:** Easily Identify Struggling Students

For more information, please visit: www.aleks.com/highered/business.

Read ALEKS Success Stories: www.aleks.com/highered/business/success_stories.

"With ALEKS, the issues that our finance majors were having with *Intermediate Accounting* have practically disappeared."

—**Eric Kelley,** ***University of Arizona***

INSTRUCTOR LIBRARY

The Connect Instructor Library is a repository for additional resources to improve student engagement in and out of class. You can select and use any asset that enhances your lecture. The Connect Instructor Library includes:

- Presentation slides
- Animated PowerPoint® exercises
- Solutions manual
- Test bank available in Connect and TestGen
    - TestGen is a complete, state-of-the-art test generator and editing application software that allows instructors to quickly and easily select test items from McGraw Hill's test bank content. The instructors can then organize, edit, and customize questions and answers to rapidly generate tests for paper **or online administration.** Questions can include stylized text, symbols, graphics, and equations that are inserted directly into questions using built-in mathematical templates. TestGen's random generator provides the option to display different text or calculated number values each time questions are used. With both quick-and-simple test creation and flexible and robust editing tools, TestGen is a complete test generator system for today's educators.
- Instructor's resource manual
- Instructor Excel templates. Solutions to the student Excel Templates used to solve selected end-of-chapter exercises and problems. These assignments are designated by the Excel icon.

MCGRAW-HILL EDUCATION CUSTOMER EXPERIENCE GROUP CONTACT INFORMATION

At McGraw-Hill Education, we understand that getting the most from new technology can be challenging. That's why our services don't stop after you purchase our products. You can contact our Product Specialists 24 hours a day to get product training online. Or you can search the knowledge bank of Frequently Asked Questions on our support website. For Customer Support, call **800-331-5094,** or visit www.mhhe.com/support. One of our Technical Support Analysts will be able to assist you in a timely fashion.

ASSURANCE OF LEARNING READY

Many educational institutions today are focused on the notion of *assurance of learning,* an important element of some accreditation standards. *Intermediate Accounting* is designed specifically to support your assurance of learning initiatives with a simple, yet powerful solution.

Each test bank question for *Intermediate Accounting* maps to a specific chapter learning objective listed in the text. You can use Connect to easily query for learning outcomes/objectives that directly relate to the learning objectives for your course. You can then use the reporting features of Connect to aggregate student results in a similar fashion, making the collection and presentation of assurance of learning data simple and easy.

AACSB STATEMENT

McGraw-Hill Education is a proud corporate member of AACSB International. Understanding the importance and value of AACSB accreditation, *Intermediate Accounting* recognizes the curricula guidelines detailed in the AACSB standards for business accreditation by connecting selected questions in the test bank to the eight general knowledge and skill guidelines in the AACSB standards.

The statements contained in *Intermediate Accounting* are provided only as a guide for the users of this textbook. The AACSB leaves content coverage and assessment within the purview of individual schools, the mission of the school, and the faculty. While *Intermediate Accounting* and the teaching package make no claim of any specific AACSB qualification or evaluation, within the Test Bank to accompany *Intermediate Accounting* we have labeled selected questions according to the eight general knowledge and skill areas.

What's New in the Ninth Edition?

Revising a program as successful as *Intermediate Accounting* takes careful consideration and a strong vision for how the print and digital content work together to provide a robust learning solution. The Spiceland team only implements changes that constitute real improvements as identified through extensive research with users. The result is a program that never loses its original strengths, continuing to gain usefulness and flexibility with each revision.

Pervasive changes throughout the program include the following:

- **Updated content to reflect the latest GAAP and Accounting Standards Updates including:**
  - **Leases**
  - **Coverage of financial instruments**
  - **Revenue recognition**
- **New partnership with Roger CPA Review,** with new assignable multiple-choice CPA Exam Review questions in Connect and access to CPA simulations.
- Updated and revised all real-world illustrations, amounts, and discussions.
- **Revised** Air France–KLM IFRS case to reflect financial statements for the year ended December 31, 2015.
- Added a **new Continuing Case featuring Target Corporation** and a variety of characteristics of financial statements prepared using U.S. GAAP. A comprehensive version of the case is available in Appendix B.
- Reviewed, updated, and introduced new end-of-chapter material in each chapter to support new topics and learning objectives.
- Incorporated the latest technology, including a **new Connect interface for students,** along with **Connect Insight for students,** an updated SmartBook, and **new Connect problem formats** include **General Ledger Problems** that auto-post from journal entries to T-accounts to trial balances, **Excel Simulations,** and **Concept Overview Videos.**

Chapter 1

ENVIRONMENT AND THEORETICAL STRUCTURE OF FINANCIAL ACCOUNTING

- Changed opening case to introduce Target, and featured Target throughout the chapter.
- Added Pathways visualization "THIS is accounting!" and related discussion.
- Improved discussion of cash basis vs. accrual basis accounting.
- Enhanced description of IFRS organizational structure and convergence process.
- Added a Where We're Headed box regarding the FASB's materiality exposure draft.

Chapter 2

REVIEW OF THE ACCOUNTING PROCESS

- Replaced all CPA Exam Questions with current ones from Roger CPA Review.
- Added a Target case.
- Added an Air France case.

Chapter 3

THE BALANCE SHEET AND FINANCIAL DISCLOSURES

- Revised introduction to include reference to SEC's EDGAR filing system.
- Added reference to the accounting equation in Illustration 3–1.
- Updated discussion of assets, liabilities, and shareholders' equity to include those of Nike.
- Updated discussion of operating cycle to include distinction between merchandising and manufacturing company.
- Revised discussion of categories of long-term assets, including consideration of management intent.
- Added discussion and key term for accumulated other comprehensive income component of shareholders' equity.
- Revised discussion of auditors' report to clearly distinguish the different report types.
- Moved discussion of management compensation to be included with other management-related disclosures.

Chapter 4

THE INCOME STATEMENT, COMPREHENSIVE INCOME, AND THE STATEMENT OF CASH FLOWS

- Revised introduction to make clear the difference in reporting perspective for the balance sheet (point in time) versus the income statement and statement of cash flows (interval of time).
- Revised discussion of earnings quality, income smoothing, and classification shifting.
- Revised section on "Operating Income and Earnings Quality" to include analysis of The Hershey Company.
- Created separate section on non-GAAP earnings, discussing HP.
- Clarified discussion of what constitutes of a discontinued operation.
- Clarified discussion and added new Additional Consideration box on presentation of discontinued operations.
- Added discussion of the modified retrospective approach for accounting changes.
- Revised introduction to the discussion of earnings per share.
- Provided additional discussion of comprehensive income.
- Moved discussion of profitability analysis from chapter 5 to chapter 4, including all related end-of-chapter material.

Chapter 5

REVENUE RECOGNITION

- Added learning objective regarding differences between U.S. GAAP and IFRS, IFRS boxes that meet the objective, and related end-of-chapter material.
- Changed discussion of identifying separate performance obligations to incorporate ASU 2016–10.
- Added Additional Consideration for shipping costs to incorporate ASU 2016–10.
- Changed discussion of licenses to incorporate ASU 2016–10.
- Added IFRS box discussing differences in licensing criteria.

- Moved discussion of Profitability Analysis and related end-of-chapter material to Chapter 4 to focus Chapter 5 more tightly on revenue recognition.
- Added significant new end-of-chapter material to incorporate ASU 2016–10 and various IFRS differences.

Chapter 6

TIME VALUE OF MONEY CONCEPTS

- Replaced all CPA Exam Questions with current ones from Roger CPA Review.
- Added a Target case.
- Added an Air France case.

Chapter 7

CASH AND RECEIVABLES

- Added new opening case: Community Health Systems.
- Completely revised coverage of initial and subsequent valuation of accounts receivable, including discussions of time value of money, discounts, sales returns, accounting for bad debts, and accounting for notes receivable, to tie coverage more tightly to revenue recognition and impairment recognition criteria and practice.
- In chapter, as well as Appendix 7B, included coverage of ASU 2016–013's CECL model for accounting for credit losses, as well as current GAAP requirements for recognizing impairments of receivables.
- Revised Illustration 7–24 and related discussion of analysis of accounts receivable.
- Added or updated cases relevant to Microsoft, Nike, Avon Products, Tyson Foods, and Pilgrim's Pride Corp.

Chapter 8

INVENTORIES: MEASUREMENT

- Changed feature story to Kroger Company.
- Revised discussion of goods in transit.
- Revised discussion of accounting for transactions that affect net purchases related to freight-in, returns, and discounts, including revisions to Illustration 8–6.
- Incorporated beginning inventory into Illustration 8–7 to clarify calculation of goods available for sale and to better link to Illustrations 8–7B through 8–7H.
- Revised discussion of the LIFO reserve adjustment.
- Clarified discussion and added calculation to demonstrate dollar-value LIFO.

Chapter 9

INVENTORIES: ADDITIONAL ISSUES

- Revised section on subsequent measurement of inventory to include both lower of cost or market (LCM) and lower of cost or net realizable value (LCNRV).
- Clarified discussion of which companies are required to use LCNRV versus LCM.
- Added new end-of-chapter material for LCM – BE 9–3, BE 9–4, E 9–4, E 9–5, E 9–6, E 9–7, P 9–3, and P 9–4.

Chapter 10

PROPERTY, PLANT, AND EQUIPMENT AND INTANGIBLE ASSETS: ACQUISITION

- Moved discussion of asset dispositions and related end-of-chapter material to chapter 11.
- Moved discussion of noncash acquisitions (deferred payments, stock issuances, and donations) to Part B with nonmonetary exchanges.
- Added Illustration 10–16 to summarize effects of different types of nonmonetary exchanges.
- Provided additional discussion to clarify accounting for software development costs.
- Reorganized section on R&D to include more real-world examples and clarification of which R&D-type costs are capitalized.
- Added end-of-chapter material for fixed asset turnover (BE 10–9), software development costs (BE 10–17), various types of research and development costs (BE 10–18), and start-up costs (BE 10–19 and E 10–33).

Chapter 11

PROPERTY, PLANT, AND EQUIPMENT AND INTANGIBLE ASSETS: UTILIZATION AND DISPOSITION

- Revised discussion of the conceptual meaning of cost allocation.
- Added Illustration 11–3A and related discussion of depreciation expense versus accumulated depreciation.
- Added discussion and illustrations of asset dispositions, as well as related end-of-chapter material from chapter 10.
- Added a Decision Maker's Perspective box to explain in more detail the interpretation of gains and losses on the sale of depreciable assets.
- Modified Illustration 11–12 to include disposal of an intangible asset.
- Revised discussion of intangible assets not subject to amortization.
- Revised discussion of two-step process for goodwill impairment.
- Added a Where We're Headed box to explain the FASB's current proposal to simplify measurement of goodwill impairment.

Chapter 12

INVESTMENTS

- Reorganized Chapter to include Part A (Accounting for Debt Investments) and Part B (Accounting for Equity Investments).
- Revised coverage of debt investments, including improved treatment of trading securities and available-for-sale investments to enhance student understanding and better reflect practice and the ASC.
- Revised coverage of equity investments to incorporate ASU 2016–01 (prohibiting AFS treatment and requiring "fair value through net income" treatment of most insignificant-influence investments).
- Revised coverage of the equity method to enhance and clarify examples.
- Revised IFRS boxes for differences between IFRS and U.S. GAAP.
- In chapter, as well as Appendix 12B, included coverage of ASU 2016–013's CECL model for accounting for credit losses, as well as current GAAP requirements for recognizing impairments of investments.
- Revised end-of-chapter material to incorporate ASU 2016–013's CECL model for accounting for credit losses.

Chapter 13

CURRENT LIABILITIES AND CONTINGENCIES

- Updated General Mills example used in Illustration 13–1 and throughout the chapter.
- Added Additional Consideration box regarding escheatment laws relevant to gift cards.
- Updated contingent liability examples.
- Added new Trueblood cases.

Chapter 14

BONDS AND LONG-TERM NOTES

- Revised discussion of debt issue costs to conform with Accounting Standards Update 2015–03, *Interest—Imputation of Interest* (Subtopic 835–30).
- Added and revised end-of-chapter material pertaining to debt issue costs.

Chapter 15

LEASES

- Rewrote the entire chapter to conform to Accounting Standards Update 2016–02, *Leases* (Topic 842).
- Created a Chapter Supplement—Leases: GAAP in Effect Prior to ASU No. 2016–02.
- Developed all-new ancillaries (Connect, Test bank, Instructors' resource manual, Solutions manual, PowerPoint presentations, and videos) to conform to the new Leases standard.

Chapter 16

ACCOUNTING FOR INCOME TAXES

- Added new version of Real World "Shoe Carnival" case covering linkage between tax expense journal entry and changes in deferred tax assets, liabilities, and the valuation allowance.
- Revised coverage of balance sheet presentation of deferred tax accounts to incorporate ASU 2015–17.
- Added or modified end-of-chapter material to incorporate ASU 2015–17.

Chapter 17

PENSIONS AND OTHER POSTRETIREMENT BENEFIT PLANS

- Added a Real World Case involving Microsoft's pension plan.
- Added discussion of new FASB requirement to report service cost separate from other components of pension expense.

Chapter 18

SHAREHOLDERS' EQUITY

- Replaced all CPA Exam Questions and Simulation with current ones from Roger CPA Review.
- Revised Research Case involving Cisco's accumulated other comprehensive income in its balance sheet as a component of shareholders' equity.

Chapter 19

SHARE-BASED COMPENSATION AND EARNINGS PER SHARE

- Revised discussion and illustration of graded vesting stock options.
- Revised discussion of forfeitures of stock options and restricted stock to conform with Accounting Standards Update No. 2016–09, Compensation—Stock Compensation (Topic 718): Improvements to Employee Share-Based Payment Accounting.
- Added and revised end-of-chapter material pertaining to forfeitures of stock options and restricted stock.
- Revised discussion of tax issues related to share-based compensation to conform with Accounting Standards Update No. 2016–09—Compensation—Stock Compensation (Topic 718): Improvements to Employee Share-Based Payment Accounting.
- Revised end-of-chapter material pertaining to tax issues related to share-based compensation.

Chapter 20

ACCOUNTING CHANGES AND ERROR CORRECTIONS

- Revised discussion of approaches to account for accounting changes to include the modified retrospective approach.

Chapter 21

STATEMENT OF CASH FLOWS REVISITED

- Revised a CVS Caremark Corp illustration of presenting cash flows from operating activities by the direct method.
- Added an enhanced Additional Consideration box on reporting bad debt expense in the SCF.
- Added a Toys "R" Us illustration of presenting cash flows from operating activities by the indirect method.
- Revised a Research Case related to FedEx's investing and financing activities.
- Added a Real World Case on Staples reporting of its SCF.

Appendix A

DERIVATIVES

- Revised a Real World Case related to the Chicago Mercantile Exchange.
- Revised a Johnson & Johnson Real World Case on hedging transactions.

Acknowledgments

Intermediate Accounting is the work not just of its talented authors, but of the more than 750 faculty reviewers who shared their insights, experience, and insights with us. Our reviewers helped us to build *Intermediate Accounting* into the very best learning system available. A blend of Spiceland users and nonusers, these reviewers explained how they use texts and technology in their teaching, and many answered detailed questions about every one of Spiceland's 21 chapters. The work of improving *Intermediate Accounting* is ongoing—even now, we're scheduling new symposia and reviewers' conferences to collect even more opinions from faculty.

We would like to acknowledge and highlight the Special Reviewer role that Ilene Leopold Persoff of Long Island University (LIU Post) took on the ninth edition. Utilizing her accounting and reviewing expertise, Ilene verified the accuracy of the manuscript and promoted our efforts toward quality and consistency. Her deep subject-matter knowledge, keen eye for detail, and professional excellence in all aspects were instrumental in ensuring a current, comprehensive, and clear edition. Her contributions are deeply appreciated.

In addition, we want to recognize the valuable input of all those who helped guide our developmental decisions for the ninth edition.

Noel Addy, *Mississippi State University*

Naser Albarghouthi, *Hudson County Community College*

Elizabeth Almer, *Portland State University*

Matthew Anderson, *Michigan State University*

Ryan Anthony, *University of Washington*

Sidney Askew, *Borough of Manhattan Community College*

Lynn Bible, *Fayetteville State University*

John Borke, *University of Wisconsin, Platteville*

Salem Boumediene, *Montana State University–Billings*

Brian Bratten, *University of Kentucky, Lexington*

Alisa Brink, *Virginia Commonwealth University*

Kevin Brown, *Wright State University*

Esther Bunn, *Stephen F. Austin State University*

Linda Carrington-Duvall, *Sam Houston State University*

Mary Ellen Carter, *Boston College*

Meghann Cefaratti, *Northern Illinois University*

Kam Chan, *Pace University*

Nandini Chandar, *Rider University*

Shannon Charles, *University of Utah*

Cheryl Corke, *Genesee Community College*

Marc Cussatt, *Washington State University*

Judy Daulton, *Piedmont Technical College*

Denise De La Rosa, *Grand Valley State University*

David Deboskey, *San Diego State University–San Diego*

Marcus Doxey, *University of Alabama*

Amie Dragoo, *Edgewood College*

Barbara Durham, *University of Central Florida*

Kathryn Easterday, *Wright State University*

David Emerson, *Salisbury University*

James Emig, *Villanova University*

Denise English, *Boise State University*

Caroline Falconetti, *Nassau Community College*

Dov Fischer, *Brooklyn College*

Mitchell Franklin, *Lemoyne College*

Laurel Franzen, *Loyola Marymount University*

Lori Fuller, *West Chester University*

Gregory Gaynor, *University of Baltimore*

Hubert Glover, *Drexel University*

Sunita Goel, *Siena College*

Ying Guo, *California State University–East Bay*

Joohyung Ha, *University of San Francisco*

Lizhong Hao, *California State University–Fresno*

Don Herrmann, *Oklahoma State University*

Dana Hollie, *Louisiana State University–Baton Rouge*

Pei Hui Hsu, *California State University–East Bay*

Kathy Hsiao Yu Hsu, *University of Louisiana–Lafayette*

Xuerong Huang, *Ball State University*

Ying Huang, *University of Louisville*

Stacie Hughes, *Athens University*
Paul Hutchison, *University of North Texas*
Mark Jackson, *University of Nevada, Reno*
John Jiang, *Michigan State University*
Kevin Jones, *University of California–Santa Cruz*
Robert L. Kachur, *Richard Stockton College of New Jersey*
Julia Karcher, *University of Louisville*
Sergey Komissarov, *University of Wisconsin–La Crosse*
Lisa Kutcher, *Colorado State University*
Richard Lahijani, *Queens College*
Marco Lam, *Western Carolina University*
Melissa Larson, *Brigham Young University*
Charles Leflar, *University of Arkansas–Fayetteville*
Charles Lewis, *Houston Community College*
Shu Lin, *California State University–Fresno*
Lin Liu, *California State University–Dominguez Hills*
Ricki Livingston, *University of Connecticut*
Ming Lu, *Santa Monica College*
Mostafa Maksy, *Kutztown University of Pennsylvania*
Nancy Mangold, *California State University–East Bay*
Christina Manzo, *Queensborough Community College*
Joshua Neil, *University of Colorado–Boulder*
Kelly Noe, *Stephen F. Austin State University*
Shailendra Pandit, *University of Illinois–Chicago*
Veronica Paz, *Pennsylvania State University*
Aimee Pernsteiner, *University of Wisconsin–Eau Claire*
Mikhail Pevzner, *University of Baltimore*
Eric Press, *Temple University*
Dirk Pruis, *Calvin College*
K.K. Raman, *University of Texas–San Antonio*
K. Ramesh, *Rice University*
Arundhati Rao, *Towson University*
Barbara Reider, *University of Montana*
Douglas Smith, *Dalton State College*
Kevin Smith, *Utah Valley University*
Sheldon Smith, *Utah Valley University*
Dennis Stovall, *Grand Valley State University*
Joel Strong, *Saint Cloud State University*
C. Daniel Stubbs, *Rutgers University–Newark*
Ronald Stunda, *Valdosta State University*
Amy Sun, *University of Houston*
Jenny Teruya, *University of Hawaii–Manoa*
Paula B. Thomas, *Middle Tennessee State University*
Robin Thomas, *North Carolina State University–Raleigh*
John Trussel, *University of Tennessee–Chattanooga*
Ingrid Ulstad, *University of Wisconsin–Eau Claire*
Huishan Wan, *University of Nebraska*
Barbara White, *University of West Florida*
Jan Williams, *University of Baltimore*
Donald Wygal, *Rider University*
Yan Xiong, *California State University–Sacramento*
Jing-Wen Yang, *California State University–East Bay*
Jian Zhang, *San Jose State University*

We Are Grateful

We would like to acknowledge and thank the following individuals for their contributions in developing, reviewing. and shaping the extensive ancillary package: Kim Fatten, *Capital College;* Jeannie Folk, *College of DuPage;* Burch Kealey, *University of Nebraska–Omaha;* Mark McCarthy, *East Carolina University;* Barbara Muller, *Arizona State University;* Helen Roybark, *Radford University;* Kevin Smith, *Utah Valley University;* Emily Vera, *University of Colorado–Denver;* Beth Woods of Accuracy Counts; and Teri Zuccaro, *Clarke University,* who contributed new content and accuracy checks of Connect and LearnSmart. We greatly appreciate everyone's hard work on these products!

We are most grateful for the talented assistance and support from the many people at McGraw-Hill Education. We would particularly like to thank Tim Vertovec, managing director; Natalie King, marketing director; Rebecca Olson, executive brand manager; Rebecca Mann, senior product developer; Randall Edwards, product developer; Zach Rudin, marketing manager; Peggy Hussey, director of digital content; Xin Lin, digital product analyst; Daryl Horrocks, program manager; Pat Frederickson, lead content project manager; Angela Norris, senior content project manager; Laura Fuller, buyer; Matt Diamond, senior designer; and Melissa Homer and Lori Slattery, content licensing specialists.

Finally, we extend our thanks to Roger CPA Review for their assistance developing simulations for inclusion in the end-of-chapter material, as well as Target and Air France–KLM for allowing us to use their Annual Reports throughout the text. We also acknowledge permission from the AICPA to adapt material from the Uniform CPA Examination, and the IMA for permission to adapt material from the CMA Examination.

David Spiceland *Mark Nelson* *Wayne Thomas*

Liabilities and Shareholders' Equity

CHAPTER

13 Current Liabilities and Contingencies

OVERVIEW

Chapter 13 is the first of five chapters devoted to liabilities. In Part A of this chapter, we discuss liabilities that are classified appropriately as current. In Part B we turn our attention to situations in which there is uncertainty as to whether an obligation really exists. These are designated as loss contingencies. Some loss contingencies are accrued as liabilities, but others only are disclosed in the notes.

LEARNING OBJECTIVES

After studying this chapter, you should be able to:

- **LO13–1** Define liabilities and distinguish between current and long-term liabilities. (*p. 716*)
- **LO13–2** Account for the issuance and payment of various forms of notes and record the interest on the notes. (*p. 718*)
- **LO13–3** Characterize accrued liabilities and liabilities from advance collection and describe when and how they should be recorded. (*p. 721*)
- **LO13–4** Determine when a liability can be classified as a noncurrent obligation. (*p. 727*)
- **LO13–5** Identify situations that constitute contingencies and the circumstances under which they should be accrued. (*p. 730*)
- **LO13–6** Demonstrate the appropriate accounting treatment for contingencies, including unasserted claims and assessments. (*p. 731*)
- **LO13–7** Discuss the primary differences between U.S. GAAP and IFRS with respect to current liabilities and contingencies. (*pp. 729, 739,* and *740*)

© Rob Daly / age fotostock

FINANCIAL REPORTING CASE

Debbie's Dad

"My dad is confused," your friend Debbie Hirst proclaimed at the office one morning. "You see, we're competing against each other in that investment game I told you about, and one of his hot investments is Syntel Microsystems. When he got their annual report yesterday afternoon, he started analyzing it, you know, really studying it closely. Then he asked me about this part here." Debbie pointed to the current liability section of the balance sheet and related disclosure note:

SYNTEL MICROSYSTEMS, INC.
Balance Sheet
December 31, 2018 and 2017
($ in millions)

Current Liabilities	**2018**	**2017**
Accounts payable	$233.5	$241.6
Short-term borrowings (Note 3)	187.0	176.8
Accrued liabilities	65.3	117.2
Accrued loss contingency	76.9	—
Other current liabilities	34.6	45.2
Current portion of long-term debt	44.1	40.3
Total current liabilities	$641.4	$621.1

Note 3: Short-Term Borrowings (in part)

The components of short-term borrowings and their respective weighted average interest rates at the end of the period are as follows:

	2018		**2017**	
($ in millions)	**Amount**	**Average Interest Rate**	**Amount**	**Average Interest Rate**
Commercial paper	$ 34.0	5.2%	$ 27.1	5.3%
Bank loans	218.0	5.5	227.7	5.6
Amount reclassified to long-term liabilities	(65.0)	—	(78.0)	—
Total short-term borrowings	$187.0		$176.8	

The Company maintains bank credit lines sufficient to cover outstanding short-term borrowings. As of December 31, 2018, the Company had $200.0 million fee-paid lines available. At December 31, 2018 and 2017, the Company classified $65.0 million and $78.0 million, respectively, of commercial paper and bank notes as long-term debt. The Company has the intent and ability, through formal renewal agreements, to renew these obligations into future periods.

Note 6: Contingencies (in part)

Between 2016 and 2017, the Company manufactured cable leads that, the Company has learned, contribute to corrosion of linked components with which they are installed. At December 31, 2018, the Company accrued $132.0 million in anticipation of remediation and claims settlement deemed probable, of which $76.9 million is considered a current liability.

"So, what's the problem?" you asked.

"Well, he thinks I'm some sort of financial wizard because I'm in business."

"And because you tell him so all the time," you interrupted.

(continued)

(continued)

"Maybe so, but he's been told that current liabilities are riskier than long-term liabilities, and now he's focusing on that. He can't see why some long-term debt is reported here in the current section. And it also looks like some is reported the other way around; some current liabilities reported as long term. Plus, the contingency amount seems like it's not even a contractual liability. Then he wants to know what some of those terms mean. Lucky for me, I had to leave before I had to admit I didn't know the answers. You're the accounting graduate; help me out."

QUESTIONS

By the time you finish this chapter, you should be able to respond appropriately to the questions posed in this case. Compare your response to the solution provided at the end of the chapter.

1. What are accrued liabilities? What is commercial paper? (*p. 721*)
2. Why did Syntel Microsystems include some long-term debt in the current liability section? (*p. 727*)
3. Did they also report some current amounts as long-term debt? Explain. (*p. 728*)
4. Must obligations be known contractual debts in order to be reported as liabilities? (*p. 731*)
5. Is it true that current liabilities are riskier than long-term liabilities? (*p. 742*)

PART A

Current Liabilities

Liabilities and owners' equity accounts represent specific sources of a company's assets.

Before a business can invest in an asset it first must acquire the money to pay for it. This can happen in either of two ways—funds can be provided by owners or the funds must be borrowed. You may recognize this as a description of the basic accounting equation: Assets = Liabilities + Owners' Equity. You studied assets in the chapters leading to this one and you will study owners' equity later. This chapter and the next four describe the various liabilities that constitute creditors' claims on a company's assets.

Characteristics of Liabilities

Most liabilities obligate the debtor to pay cash at specified times and result from legally enforceable agreements.

● LO13–1

Some liabilities are not contractual obligations and may not be payable in cash.

You already know what liabilities are. You encounter them every day. If you are paying for a car or a home with monthly payments, you have a personal liability. Similarly, when businesses issue notes and bonds, their creditors are the banks, individuals, and organizations that exchange cash for those securities. Each of these obligations represents the most common type of liability—one to be paid in cash and for which the amount and timing are specified by a legally enforceable contract.

However, to be reported as a **liability**, an obligation need not be payable in cash. Instead, it may require the company to transfer other assets or to provide services. A liability doesn't have to be represented by a written agreement nor be legally enforceable. Even the amount and timing of repayment need not be precisely known.

From a financial reporting perspective, a liability has three essential characteristics. Liabilities:

1. Are *probable, future* sacrifices of economic benefits.
2. Arise from *present* obligations (to transfer assets or provide services) to other entities.
3. Result from *past* transactions or events.[1]

Notice that the definition of a liability involves the past, the present, and the future. It is a present responsibility to sacrifice assets in the future because of a transaction or other event that happened in the past.

[1]"Elements of Financial Statements," *Statement of Financial Accounting Concepts No. 6* (Stamford, Conn.: FASB, 1985), par. 38.

What Is a Current Liability?

In a classified balance sheet, we categorize liabilities as either current liabilities or long-term liabilities. We often characterize current liabilities as obligations payable within one year or within the firm's operating cycle, whichever is longer. This general definition usually applies. However, a more discriminating definition identifies current liabilities as those expected to be satisfied with *current assets* or by the creation of other *current liabilities.*[2]

Current liabilities are expected to require current assets and usually are payable within one year.

Classifying liabilities as either current or long term helps investors and creditors assess the risk that the liabilities will require expenditure of cash or other assets in the near term. Is the due date years in the future, permitting resources to be used for other purposes without risking default? Or, will payment require the use of current assets and reduce the amount of liquid funds available for other uses? If so, are sufficient liquid funds available to make necessary payments of liabilities in addition to meeting current operating needs, or must additional funds be obtained by raising capital? The answers to these questions can have significant implications. For example, a major factor contributing to the collapse of the financial giant Bear Stearns in 2008 was its reliance on short-term liabilities that it couldn't refinance when lenders, clients, and trading partners grew concerned about the quality of Bear's investments.[3]

Classifying liabilities as either current or long term helps investors and creditors assess the relative risk of a business's liabilities.

Conceptually, liabilities should be recorded at their present values. In other words, the amount recorded is the present value of all anticipated future cash payments resulting from the debt (specifically, principal and interest payments).[4] However, in practice, liabilities payable within one year ordinarily are recorded instead at their maturity amounts.[5] This inconsistency usually is inconsequential because the relatively short-term maturity of current liabilities makes the interest or time value component immaterial.

Current liabilities ordinarily are reported at their maturity amounts.

The most common obligations reported as current liabilities are accounts payable, notes payable, commercial paper, income tax liability, dividends payable, and accrued liabilities. Liabilities related to income taxes are the subject of Chapter 16. We discuss the others here.

Before we examine specific current liabilities, let's use the current liability section of the balance sheet of General Mills, Inc., and related disclosure notes to provide perspective on some of the liabilities we discuss (Illustration 13–1). General Mills' presentation and supplemental footnote disclosures are fairly typical.

We'll refer back to portions of Illustration 13–1 as corresponding liabilities are described later in the chapter.

Open Accounts and Notes

Many businesses buy merchandise or supplies on credit. Most also find it desirable to borrow cash from time to time to finance their activities. In this section we discuss the liabilities these borrowing activities create: trade accounts and trade notes, bank loans, and commercial paper.

Accounts Payable and Trade Notes Payable

Accounts payable are obligations to suppliers of merchandise or of services purchased on *open account.* Most trade credit is offered on open account. This means that the only formal credit instrument is the invoice. Because the time until payment usually is short (often 30, 45, or 60 days), these liabilities typically are noninterest-bearing and are reported at their face amounts. As shown in Illustration 13–1, General Mills' accounts payable in 2015 was $1,684 million. The key accounting considerations relating to accounts payable are determining their existence and ensuring that they are recorded in the appropriate accounting period. You studied these issues and learned how cash discounts are handled during your study of inventories in Chapter 8.

Buying merchandise on account in the ordinary course of business creates *accounts payable.*

[2]FASB ASC Master Glossary (previously Committee on Accounting Procedure, American Institute of CPAs, *Accounting Research and Terminology Bulletin, Final Edition (New York: AICPA, August 1961), p. 21).*
[3]William D. Cohan, *House of Cards: A Tale of Hubris and Wretched Excess on Wall Street* (New York: Doubleday, 2009).
[4]The concepts of the time value of money and the mechanics of present value calculations are covered in Chapter 6.
[5]In fact, those arising in connection with suppliers in the normal course of business and due within a year are specifically exempted from present value reporting by FASB ASC 835–30–15–3: Interest–Imputation of Interest–Scope and Scope Exceptions (previously "Interest on Receivables and Payables," *Accounting Principles Board Opinion No. 21* (New York: AICPA, August 1971), par. 3).

Illustration 13–1

Current Liabilities—General Mills

Real World Financials

GENERAL MILLS, INC.
Excerpt from Consolidated Balance Sheets
May 31, 2015 and May 27, 2014

Liabilities	($ in millions)	
Current Liabilities	**2015**	**2014**
Accounts payable	$1,684.0	$1,611.3
Current portion of long-term debt	1,000.4	1,250.6
Notes payable	615.8	111.7
Other current liabilities	1,589.9	1,449.9
Total current liabilities	$4,890.1	$4,423.5

Note 8. Debt

Notes Payable The components of notes payable and their respective weighted-average interest rates at the end of the periods were as follows:

	2015		**2014**	
Dollars in Millions:	**Note Payable**	**Weighted Average Interest Rate**	**Note Payable**	**Weighted Average Interest Rate**
U.S. commercial paper	$432.0	0.3%	$1,007.6	0.2%
Financial institutions	183.8	9.5	104.1	12.1
Total notes payable	$615.8	3.0%	$1,111.7	1.3%

To ensure availability of funds, we maintain bank credit lines sufficient to cover our outstanding notes payable. Commercial paper is a continuing source of short-term financing. We have commercial paper programs available to us in the United States and Europe. We also have uncommitted and asset-backed credit lines that support our foreign operations. The following table details the fee-paid committed and uncommitted credit lines we had available as of May 31, 2015:

Dollars in Billions:	**Facility Amount**	**Borrowed Amount**
Credit facility expiring:		
April 2017	$1.7	$ –
May 2019	1.0	–
June 2019	0.2	0.1
Total committed credit facilities	2.9	0.1
Uncommitted credit facilities	0.5	0.1
Total committed and uncommitted credit facilities	$3.4	$0.2

Trade notes payable differ from accounts payable in that they are formally recognized by a written promissory note. Often these are of a somewhat longer term than open accounts and bear interest.

Short-Term Notes Payable

LO13–2

The most common way for a corporation to obtain temporary financing is to arrange a short-term bank loan. When a company borrows cash from a bank and signs a promissory note (essentially an IOU), the firm's liability is reported as *notes payable* (sometimes *bank loans* or *short-term borrowings*). About two-thirds of bank loans are short term, but because many are routinely renewed, some tend to resemble long-term debt. In fact, in some cases we report them as long-term debt (as you'll see later in the chapter).

Very often, smaller firms are unable to tap into the major sources of long-term financing to the extent necessary to provide for their working capital needs. So they must rely heavily on short-term financing. Even large companies typically utilize short-term debt as a significant and indispensable component of their capital structure. One reason is that short-term funds usually offer lower interest rates than long-term debt. Perhaps most importantly, corporations desire flexibility. Managers want as many financing alternatives as possible.

CREDIT LINES. Usually short-term bank loans are arranged under an existing line of credit with a bank or group of banks. A line of credit is an agreement to provide short-term financing, with amounts withdrawn by the borrower only when needed. Even though the loans are short-term, with amounts borrowed and repaid frequently, the agreement to provide a line of credit typically lasts several years. Lines of credit can be noncommitted or committed. A *noncommitted* line of credit is an informal agreement that permits a company to borrow up to a prearranged limit without having to follow formal loan procedures and paperwork. Banks sometimes require the company to maintain a compensating balance on deposit with the bank, say, 5% of the line of credit.[6] A *committed* line of credit is a more formal agreement that usually requires the company to pay a commitment fee to the bank to keep a credit line amount available to the company. A typical annual commitment fee is ¼% of the total committed funds, and may also require a compensating balance. A recent annual report of IBM Corporation illustrates noncommitted lines of credit (Illustration 13–2).

A line of credit allows a company to borrow cash without having to follow formal loan procedures and paperwork.

Note J. Borrowings (in part)

LINES OF CREDIT: In 2015, the company extended the term of its five-year, $10 billion Credit Agreement (the "Credit Agreement") by one year to November 10, 2020. The total expense recorded by the company related to this global credit facility was $5.3 million in 2015, $5.4 million in 2014, and $5.4 million in 2013. The Credit Agreement permits the company and its Subsidiary Borrowers to borrow up to $10 billion on a revolving basis. Borrowings of the Subsidiary Borrowers will be unconditionally backed by the company. . . . As of December 31, 2015, there were no borrowings by the company, or its subsidiaries, under the Credit Agreement.

Illustration 13–2

Disclosure of Credit Lines—IBM Corporation

Real World Financials

General Mills' disclosure notes that we looked at in Illustration 13–1 indicate that the company has both noncommitted and committed lines of credit.

INTEREST. When a company borrows money, it pays the lender interest in return for using the lender's money during the term of the loan. You might think of the interest as the "rent" paid for using money. Interest is stated in terms of a percentage rate to be applied to the face amount of the loan, which makes this an interest-bearing note. Because the stated rate typically is an annual rate, when calculating interest for a short-term note we must adjust for the fraction of the annual period the loan spans. Interest on notes is calculated as:

Face amount × Annual rate × Time to maturity

This is demonstrated in Illustration 13–3.

On May 1, Affiliated Technologies, Inc., a consumer electronics firm, borrowed $700,000 cash from First BancCorp under a noncommitted short-term line of credit arrangement and issued a six-month, 12% promissory note. Interest was payable at maturity.

May 1		
Cash	700,000	
Notes payable		700,000
November 1		
Interest expense ($700,000 × 12% × 6/12)	42,000	
Notes payable	700,000	
Cash ($700,000 + 42,000)		742,000

Illustration 13–3

Note Issued for Cash

Sometimes a bank loan assumes the form of a so-called noninterest-bearing note. Obviously, though, no bank will lend money without interest. Noninterest-bearing loans actually do bear interest, but the interest is deducted (or discounted) from the face amount to

[6]A compensating balance is a deposit kept by a company in a low-interest or noninterest-bearing account at the bank. The required deposit usually is some percentage of the committed amount or the amount used (say, 2% to 5%). The effect of the compensating balance is to increase the borrower's effective interest rate and the bank's effective rate of return.

determine the cash proceeds made available to the borrower at the outset. For example, the preceding note could be packaged as a $700,000 noninterest-bearing note, with a 12% discount rate.[7] In that case, the $42,000 interest would be discounted at the outset, rather than explicitly stated:[8]

The proceeds of the note are reduced by the interest in a noninterest-bearing note.

May 1		
Cash (difference)	658,000	
Discount on notes payable ($700,000 × 12% × 6/12)	42,000	
Notes payable (face amount)		700,000
November 1		
Interest expense	42,000	
Discount on notes payable		42,000
Notes payable (face amount)	700,000	
Cash		700,000

Notice that the amount borrowed under this arrangement is only $658,000, but the interest is calculated as the discount rate times the $700,000 face amount. This causes the *effective* interest rate to be higher than the 12% stated rate:

When interest is discounted from the face amount of a note, the effective interest rate is higher than the stated discount rate.

$$\frac{\$42{,}000 \text{ Interest for 6 months}}{\$658{,}000 \text{ Amount borrowed}} = 6.38\% \text{ Rate for 6 months}$$

To annualize:

$$6.38\% \times 12/6 = 12.76\% \text{ Effective interest rate}$$

We studied short-term notes from the perspective of the lender (note receivable) in Chapter 7.

Inventory or accounts receivable often are pledged as security for short-term loans.

SECURED LOANS. Sometimes short-term loans are *secured,* meaning a specified asset of the borrower is pledged as collateral or security for the loan. Although many kinds of assets can be pledged, the secured loans most frequently encountered in practice are secured by inventory or accounts receivable. For example, Smithfield Foods, Inc., disclosed the secured notes described in Illustration 13–4.

Illustration 13–4

Disclosure of Notes Secured by Inventory—Smithfield Foods, Inc.

Real World Financials

Note 7: Debt (in part)

Working Capital Facilities

The obligations under the Inventory Revolver Credit Agreement are guaranteed by substantially all of our subsidiary guarantors' personal property, including accounts receivable (other than those sold and financed pursuant to the Securitization Facility), inventory, cash and cash equivalents, deposit accounts, intercompany notes, intellectual property and certain capital stock and interests pledged by us and our subsidiary guarantors, and all proceeds thereof.

[7]Sometimes the terms *discount rate* and *effective interest rate* are used interchangeably, so don't be confused by the different use of the term *discount rate* with respect to noninterest-bearing notes. Here *discount rate* refers only to a rate that is multiplied by the face amount of the note (in Affiliated's case, $700,000) to calculate how much interest is included in the note (in Affiliated's case, $42,000). That discount rate is different from the *effective interest rate* that Affiliated pays on the outstanding payable balance, and that Affiliated would use to calculate the present value of future cash flows.

[8]Be sure to understand that we are actually recording the note at 658,000, *not* 700,000, but are recording the interest portion separately in a contra-liability account, *discount on notes payable.* The entries shown reflect the gross method. By the net method, the interest component is netted against the face amount of the note as follows:

May 1		
Cash	658,000	
Notes payable		658,000
November 1		
Interest expense ($700,000 × 12% × 6/12)	42,000	
Notes payable	658,000	
Cash		700,000

When accounts receivable serve as collateral, we refer to the arrangement as *pledging* accounts receivable. Sometimes, the receivables actually are sold outright to a finance company as a means of short-term financing. This is called *factoring* receivables.[9]

Commercial Paper

Some large corporations obtain temporary financing by issuing **commercial paper**, often purchased by other companies as a short-term investment. Commercial paper refers to unsecured notes sold in minimum denominations of $25,000 with maturities ranging from 30 to 270 days (beyond 270 days the firm would be required to file a registration statement with the SEC). Interest often is discounted at the issuance of the note. Usually commercial paper is issued directly to the buyer (lender) and is backed by a line of credit with a bank. This allows the interest rate to be lower than in a bank loan. Commercial paper has become an increasingly popular way for large companies to raise funds, the total amount having expanded over fivefold in the last decade.

Large, highly rated firms sometimes sell *commercial paper* to borrow funds at a lower rate than through a bank loan.

Illustration 13–5 includes a disclosure note from the 2015 annual report of Comcast Corporation that describes Comcast's commercial paper program.

Illustration 13–5

Disclosure of Commercial Paper—Comcast Corporation

Real World Financials

Note 9: (in part)

Commercial Paper Program

Our commercial paper programs provide a lower-cost source of borrowing to fund our short-term working capital requirements. . . . The maximum borrowing capacity under the Comcast commercial paper program is $6.25 billion, and it is supported by the Comcast and Comcast Cable Communications, LLC $6.25 billion revolving credit facility due June 2017 ("Comcast revolving credit facility")

The name *commercial paper* refers to the fact that a paper certificate traditionally is issued to the lender to signify the obligation, although there is a trend toward total computerization so that no paper is created. Since commercial paper is a form of notes payable, recording its issuance and payment is exactly the same as our earlier illustration.

In a statement of cash flows, the cash a company receives from using short-term notes to borrow funds as well as the cash it uses to repay the notes are reported among cash flows from financing activities. Most of the other liabilities we study in this chapter, such as accounts payable, interest payable, and bonuses payable, are integrally related to a company's primary operations and thus are part of operating activities. We discuss long-term notes in the next chapter.

FINANCIAL Reporting Case

Q1, p. 716

Accrued Liabilities

● LO13–3

Accrued liabilities represent expenses already incurred but not yet paid (accrued expenses). These liabilities are recorded by adjusting entries at the end of the reporting period, prior to preparing financial statements. Common examples are salaries and wages payable, income taxes payable, and interest payable. Although recorded in separate liability accounts, accrued liabilities usually are combined and reported under a single caption or perhaps two accrued liability captions in the balance sheet. General Mills includes accrued liabilities in other current liabilities (totaling $1,589.9 million as of May 31, 2015).

Liabilities accrue for expenses that are incurred but not yet paid.

Accrued Interest Payable

Accrued interest payable arises in connection with notes payable (as well as other forms of debt). For example, to continue Illustration 13–3, let's assume the fiscal period for Affiliated Technologies ends on June 30, two months after the six-month note is issued. The issuance of the note, intervening adjusting entry, and note payment would be recorded as shown in Illustration 13–6.

[9]Both methods of accounts receivable financing are discussed in Chapter 7, "Cash and Receivables."

Illustration 13–6
Note with Accrued Interest

Issuance of Note on May 1		
Cash	700,000	
Note payable		700,000
Accrual of Interest on June 30		
Interest expense ($700,000 × 12% × $^2/_{12}$)	14,000	
Interest payable		14,000
Note Payment on November 1		
Interest expense ($700,000 × 12% × $^4/_{12}$)	28,000	
Interest payable (from June 30 accrual)	14,000	
Note payable	700,000	
Cash ($700,000 + 42,000)		742,000

At June 30, two months' interest has accrued and is recorded to avoid misstating expenses and liabilities on the June 30 financial statements.

Salaries, Commissions, and Bonuses

Compensation for employee services can be in the form of hourly wages, salary, commissions, bonuses, stock compensation plans, and pensions.[10] Accrued liabilities arise in connection with compensation expense when employees have provided services but have not yet been paid as of a financial statement date. These accrued expenses/accrued liabilities are recorded by adjusting entries at the end of the reporting period, prior to preparing financial statements.

VACATIONS, SICK DAYS, AND OTHER PAID FUTURE ABSENCES. Suppose a firm grants two weeks of paid vacation each year to nonsalaried employees. Some employees take their vacations during the year in which the vacations are earned and are compensated then. Some wait. Should the firm recognize compensation expense during the year for only those employees who actually are paid that year for their absence? When you recall what you've learned about accrual accounting, you probably conclude otherwise.

An employer should accrue an expense and the related liability for employees' compensation for future absences (such as vacation pay) if the obligation meets *all* of the four conditions listed in Illustration 13–7.

Illustration 13–7
Conditions for Accrual of Paid Future Absences

1. The obligation is attributable to employees' services already performed.
2. The paid absence can be taken in a later year—the benefit vests (will be compensated even if employment is terminated) or the benefit can be accumulated over time.
3. Payment is probable.
4. The amount can be reasonably estimated.

If these conditions look familiar, it's because they are simply the characteristics of a liability we discussed earlier, adapted to relate to a potential obligation for future absences of employees. Also, these conditions are consistent with the requirement that we accrue loss contingencies only when the obligation is both (a) probable and (b) can be reasonably estimated, as discussed in Part B of this chapter.

The liability for paid absences usually is accrued at the existing wage rate rather than at a rate estimated to be in effect when absences occur.[11] So, if wage rates have risen, the difference between the accrual and the amount paid increases compensation expense that year. This situation is demonstrated in Illustration 13–8, in which vacation time carried over from 2018 is taken in 2019 and the actual amount paid to employees is $5,700,000.

[10] We discuss pensions in Chapter 17 and share-based compensation plans in Chapter 19.

[11] Actually, FASB ASC 710–10–25: Compensation–General–Overall–Recognition (previously *SFAS 43,* "Accounting for Compensated Absences") is silent on how the liability should be measured. In practice, most companies accrue at the current rate because it avoids estimates and usually produces a lower expense and liability. Then, later, they remeasure periodically at updated rates.

Illustration 13–8

Paid Future Absences

Davidson-Getty Chemicals has 8,000 employees. Each employee earns two weeks of paid vacation per year. Vacation time not taken in the year earned can be carried over to subsequent years. During 2018, 2,500 employees took both weeks' vacation, but at the end of the year, 5,500 employees had vacation time carryovers as follows:

Employees	Vacation Weeks Earned But Not Taken	Total Carryover Weeks
2,500	0	0
2,000	1	2,000
3,500	2	7,000
8,000		9,000

During 2018, compensation averaged $600 a week per employee.

When Vacations Were Taken in 2018

Salaries and wages expense (2,500 × 2 weeks × $600) + (2,000 × 1 week × $600	4,200,000	
Cash (or wages payable)		4,200,000

December 31, 2018 (adjusting entry)

Salaries and wages expense (9,000 carryover weeks × $600)	5,400,000	
Liability—compensated future absences		5,400,000

When the necessary conditions are met, compensated future absences are accrued in the year the compensation is earned.

Company policy and actual practice should be considered when deciding whether the rights to payment for absences have been earned by services already rendered. For example, scientists in a private laboratory are eligible for paid sabbaticals every seven years. Should a liability be accrued at the end of a scientist's sixth year? No—if sabbatical leave is granted only to perform research beneficial to the employer. Yes—if past practice indicates that sabbatical leave is intended to provide unrestricted compensated absence for past service and other conditions are met.

Customary practice should be considered when deciding whether an obligation exists.

When Year 2018 Vacations Are Taken in 2019

Liability—compensated future absences (account balance)	5,400,000	
Salaries and wages expense (difference)	300,000	
Cash (or salaries and wages payable) (given)		5,700,000

Custom and practice also influence whether unused rights to paid absences expire or can be carried forward. Obviously, if rights vest (payable even if employment is terminated), they haven't expired. But holiday time, military leave, maternity leave, and jury time typically do not accumulate if unused, so a liability for those benefits usually is not accrued. On the other hand, if it's customary that a particular paid absence, say holiday time, can be carried forward—if employees work on holidays, in this case—a liability is accrued if it's probable that employees will be compensated in a future year.

Interestingly, sick pay quite often meets the conditions for accrual, but accrual is not mandatory because future absence depends on future illness, which usually is not a certainty. Similar to other forms of paid absences, the decision of whether to accrue nonvesting sick pay should be based on actual policy and practice. If company policy or custom is that employees are paid sick pay even when their absences are not due to illness, it's appropriate to record a liability for unused sick pay. For example, some companies routinely allow unused sick pay benefits to be accumulated and paid at retirement (or to beneficiaries if death comes before retirement). If each condition is met except that the company finds it impractical to reasonably estimate the amount of compensation for future absences, a disclosure note should describe the situation.

Accrual of sick pay is not required, but may be appropriate in some circumstances.

ANNUAL BONUSES. Sometimes compensation packages include annual bonuses tied to performance objectives designed to provide incentive to executives. The most common

Bonuses sometimes take the place of permanent annual raises.

performance measures are earnings per share, net income, and operating income, each being used by about a quarter of firms having bonus plans. Nonfinancial performance measures, such as customer satisfaction and product or service quality, also are used.[12] Annual bonuses also are popular, not just for executives, but for nonmanagerial personnel as well. Unfortunately for employees, bonuses often take the place of annual raises. This allows a company to increase employee pay without permanently locking in the increases in salaries. Bonuses are compensation expense of the period in which they are earned.

Liabilities from Advance Collections

Liabilities are created when amounts are received that will be returned or remitted to others. Deposits and advances from customers and collections for third parties are cases in point.

Deposits and Advances from Customers

Collecting cash from a customer as a refundable deposit or as an advance payment for products or services creates a liability to return the deposit or to supply the products or services.[13]

REFUNDABLE DEPOSITS. In some businesses it's typical to require customers to pay cash as a deposit that will be refunded when a specified event occurs. You probably have encountered such situations. When apartments are rented, security or damage deposits often are collected. Utility companies frequently collect deposits when service is begun. Similarly, deposits sometimes are required on returnable containers, to be refunded when the containers are returned. That situation is demonstrated in Illustration 13–9.

Illustration 13–9

Refundable Deposits

Rancor Chemical Company sells combustible chemicals in expensive, reusable containers. Customers are charged a deposit for each container delivered and receive a refund when the container is returned. Deposits collected on containers delivered during the year were $300,000. Deposits are forfeited if containers are not returned within one year. Ninety percent of the containers were returned within the allotted time. Deposits charged are twice the actual cost of containers. The inventory of containers remains on the company's books until deposits are forfeited.

When Deposits Are Collected		
Cash	300,000	
Liability—refundable deposits		300,000
When Containers Are Returned*		
Liability—refundable deposits	270,000	
Cash		270,000
When Deposits Are Forfeited*		
Liability—refundable deposits	30,000	
Revenue—sale of containers		30,000
Cost of goods sold	15,000	
Inventory of containers		15,000

*Of course, not all containers are returned at the same time, nor does the allotted return period expire at the same time for all containers not returned. These entries summarize the several individual returns and forfeitures.

A customer advance produces an obligation that is satisfied when the product or service is provided.

ADVANCES FROM CUSTOMERS. At times, businesses require advance payments from customers that will be applied to the purchase price when goods are delivered or services provided. Gift certificates, magazine subscriptions, layaway deposits, special order deposits, and airline tickets are examples. These customer advances, also called *deferred revenue* or *unearned revenue,* represent liabilities until the related product or service is provided. For instance, the

[12]C. D. Ittner, D. F. Larcker, and M. V. Rajan, "The Choice of Performance Measures in Annual Bonus Contracts," *The Accounting Review,* vol. 72, No. 2 (April, 1997), pp. 231 –255.

[13]*SFAC 6* specifically identifies customer advances and deposits as liabilities under the definition provided in that statement. "Elements of Financial Statements," *Statement of Financial Accounting Concepts No. 6* (Stamford, Conn.: FASB, 1985), par. 197.

New York Times Company reports deferred revenue from unexpired subscriptions of over $60 million in its 2015 balance sheet. Advances are demonstrated in Illustration 13–10.

Illustration 13–10
Customer Advance

Tomorrow Publications collects magazine subscriptions from customers at the time subscriptions are sold. Subscription revenue is recognized over the term of the subscription. Tomorrow collected $20 million in subscription sales during its first year of operations. At December 31, the average subscription was one-fourth expired.

	($ in millions)	
When Advance Is Collected		
Cash	20	
Deferred subscriptions revenue		20
When Product Is Delivered		
Deferred subscriptions revenue	5	
Subscriptions revenue		5

This illustration highlights that deferred revenue gets reduced when the revenue associated with the advance has been recognized, either because the seller has delivered the goods or services as promised or because the buyer has forfeited the advance payment (for example, not redeeming a gift certificate before it expires). Less often, deferred revenue is reduced when an advance payment is returned by the seller to the buyer because the seller didn't deliver the goods or services as promised. This should sound familiar—recall from Chapter 5 that revenue recognition must be delayed until the seller has fulfilled its performance obligation. When revenue recognition is delayed, but some advanced payment is received, the seller reports a deferred revenue liability until delivery has occurred.

Additional Consideration

Accounting for Interest on Advances from Customers. Earlier in this chapter you saw that we calculate interest expense on "noninterest-bearing" notes. After all, there is a "time value of money," and nobody is willing to loan money for free. The same reasoning suggests that companies should calculate interest expense when a customer pays far in advance of delivery of a product or service. As indicated in Chapter 5, that's what GAAP for revenue recognition requires.[14]

For example, assume that on January 1, 2018, Lewis Manufacturing Co. enters into a contract to deliver equipment to Williams Surgical Supply, Inc., on December 31, 2019. Williams pays $907 (in thousands) to Lewis at the start of the contract (January 1, 2018). In this arrangement, Williams pays Lewis significantly in advance of delivery, so Williams can be viewed as loaning money to Lewis, and Lewis should recognize interest expense on the loan. Assuming an effective interest rate of 5%, Lewis would recognize interest expense on its deferred revenue liability as follows:

January 1, 2018		
When prepayment occurs:		
Cash	907*	
Deferred revenue		907

*$907 = $1000 × 0.90703 (present value of $1, n = 2, I = 5%; from Table 2)

December 31, 2018		
Accrual of year 1 interest expense:		
Interest expense ($907 × 5%)	45	
Accrued interest payable		45

(continued)

[14]FASB ASC 606-10-32-16: Revenue from Contracts with Customers – Overall – Measurement – The Existence of a Significant Financing Component in the Contract (previously "Revenue from Contracts with Customers (Topic 606)" *Accounting Standards Update 2014-09* (Norwalk, Conn: FASB, 2014)).

(concluded)

December 31, 2019

When subsequent delivery occurs:

Interest expense (($907 + 45) × 5%)	48	
Accrued interest payable	45	
Deferred revenue	907	
Revenue		1,000

Lewis recognizes revenue of $1,000 rather than $907 because that is the fair value it received from Williams, including the $907 received up front and $45 + $48 = $93 of interest that Williams is allowing Lewis to not pay. Put differently, the equipment must be worth $1,000 for Williams to be willing to accept it in exchange for giving up $907 cash and $93 of interest it is owed by Lewis.

As discussed in Chapter 5, companies can ignore the interest component of advance payments if it is not significant, which is assumed to be the case if the period between payment and delivery is less than one year.

Gift Cards

Gift cards or gift certificates are particularly common forms of advanced payments. As indicated in Chapter 5, when a company sells a gift card, it initially records the cash received as deferred revenue, and then recognizes revenue either when the gift card is redeemed or when the probability of redemption is viewed as remote (called *gift card breakage,* and based on expiration or the company's experience). The amounts involved can be significant. For example, Best Buy's 2016 annual report lists a $409 million liability for unredeemed gift cards and $65 million of income from gift card breakage. Illustration 13–11 shows the journal entries used to account for gift cards.

Illustration 13–11

Accounting for Gift Cards

During May 2018, Great Buy, Inc., sold $2 million of gift cards. Also during May, $1.5 million of gift cards sold in May and in prior periods were redeemed by customers, and $1 million of gift cards sold in prior periods expired and unused. Great Buy would make the following journal entries:

To record sale of gift cards		
Cash	2,000,000	
Deferred gift card revenue		2,000,000
To record redemption of gift cards (ignoring entries to inventory and cost of sales)		
Deferred gift card revenue	1,500,000	
Revenue—gift cards		1,500,000
To record expiration of gift cards		
Deferred gift card revenue	1,000,000	
Revenue—gift cards		1,000,000

Liabilities for deferred revenue are classified as current or long-term depending on when the obligation is expected to be satisfied.

Collections for Third Parties

Companies often make collections for third parties from customers or from employees and periodically remit these amounts to the appropriate governmental (or other) units. Amounts collected this way represent liabilities until remitted.

An example is sales taxes. For illustration, assume a state sales tax rate of 4% and local sales tax rate of 3%. Adding the tax to a $100 sale creates a $7 liability until the tax is paid:

Sales taxes collected from customers represent liabilities until remitted.

Cash (or accounts receivable)	107	
Sales revenue		100
Sales taxes payable [(4% + 3%) × $100]		7

Additional Consideration

Escheatment laws specify the rights of a state to claim abandoned property. Unused gift cards are a type of abandoned (or unclaimed) property. While most states exempt gift cards from escheatment laws, some do not. In those states where gift cards are subject to escheatment laws, after a period of three to five years, retailers are required to turn over all or part of the unredeemed value of gift cards to the state. To see how this works, let's modify Illustration 13–11 and assume that Great Buy is subject to an escheatment law that requires payment of 100% of unredeemed gift cards to the state in which Great Buy is incorporated. The third journal entry of Illustration 13–11 would be modified as follows:

To record expiration of gift cards		
Deferred gift card revenue (amount of expired gift cards)	1,000,000	
Cash (to balance)		1,000,000

Payroll-related deductions such as withholding taxes, Social Security taxes, employee insurance, employee contributions to retirement plans, and union dues also create current liabilities until the amounts collected are paid to appropriate parties. These payroll-related liabilities are discussed further in the appendix to this chapter.

Amounts collected from employees in connection with payroll represent liabilities until remitted.

A Closer Look at the Current and Noncurrent Classification

LO13–4

Given a choice, do you suppose management would prefer to report an obligation as a current liability or as a noncurrent liability? Other things being equal, most would choose the noncurrent classification. The reason is that in most settings outsiders (like banks, bondholders, and shareholders) consider debt that is payable currently to be riskier than debt that need not be paid for some time, because the current payable requires the company to be able to access the necessary cash relatively soon. Also, the long-term classification enables the company to report higher working capital (current assets minus current liabilities) and a higher current ratio (current assets/current liabilities). Working capital and the current ratio often are explicitly restricted in loan contracts. As you study this section, you should view the classification choice from this perspective. That is, a manager might not so much ask the question "What amount should I report as a current liability?" but rather "What amount can I exclude from classification as a current liability?"

Current Maturities of Long-Term Debt

Long-term obligations (bonds, notes, lease liabilities, deferred tax liabilities) usually are reclassified and reported as current liabilities when they become payable within the upcoming year (or operating cycle, if longer than a year). For example, a 20-year bond issue is reported as a long-term liability for 19 years but normally is reported as a current liability on the balance sheet prepared during the 20th year of its term to maturity.[15] General Mills reported $1,000.4 million of its long-term debt as a current liability in 2015 (see Illustration 13–1).

FINANCIAL Reporting Case

Q2, p. 716

Obligations Callable by the Creditor

The requirement to classify currently maturing debt as a current liability includes debt that is *callable* (in other words, due on demand) *by the creditor* in the upcoming year (or operating cycle, if longer), even if the debt is not expected to be called. The current liability classification also is intended to include situations in which the creditor has the right to demand payment because an *existing violation* of a provision of the debt agreement makes it callable (say, working capital has fallen below a minimum covenant specified by a debt agreement). This also includes situations in which debt is not yet callable but will be callable within the

The currently maturing portion of a long-term debt must be reported as a current liability.

[15]Debt to be refinanced is an exception we discuss later.

year if an existing violation is not corrected within a specified grace period (unless it's probable the violation will be corrected within the grace period or waived by the creditor).[16]

When Short-Term Obligations Are Expected to Be Refinanced

FINANCIAL Reporting Case

Q3, p. 716

Reconsider the 20-year bond issue we discussed earlier. Normally we would reclassify it as a current liability on the balance sheet prepared during its 20th year. But suppose a second 20-year bond issue is sold specifically to refund the first issue when it matures. Do we have a long-term liability for 19 years, then a current liability in year 20, and then another long-term liability in years 21 and beyond? Or, do we have a single 40-year, long-term liability? If we look beyond the outward form of the transactions, the substance of the events obviously supports a single, continuing, noncurrent obligation. The concept of substance over form influences the classification of obligations expected to be refinanced.

Short-term obligations can be reported as noncurrent liabilities if the company (a) *intends* to refinance on a long-term basis and (b) demonstrates the *ability* to do so by a refinancing agreement or by actual financing.

Short-term obligations (including the callable obligations we discussed in the previous section) that are expected to be refinanced on a long-term basis can be reported as noncurrent, rather than current, liabilities only if two conditions are met:

(1) the firm must intend to refinance on a long-term basis, and

(2) the firm must actually have demonstrated the ability to refinance on a long-term basis.

Ability to refinance on a long-term basis can be demonstrated by either an existing refinancing agreement or by actual financing prior to the issuance of the financial statements.[17] Illustration 13–12 provides an example.

Illustration 13–12

Short-Term Obligations that Are Expected to Be Refinanced on a Long-Term Basis

Brahm Bros. Ice Cream had $12 million of notes that mature in May 2019 and also had $4 million of bonds issued in 1989 that mature in February 2019. On December 31, 2018, the company's fiscal year-end, management intended to refinance both on a long-term basis.

On February 7, 2019, the company issued $4 million of 20-year bonds, applying the proceeds to repay the bond issue that matured that month. In early March, prior to the actual issuance of the 2018 financial statements, Brahm Bros. negotiated a line of credit with a commercial bank for up to $7 million any time during 2019. Any borrowings will mature two years from the date of borrowing. Interest is at the prime London interbank borrowing rate.*

	December 31, 2018 ($ in thousands)
Classification	
Current Liabilities	
Notes payable	$5,000
Long-Term Liabilities	
Notes payable	$7,000
Bonds payable	4,000

Management's ability to refinance the $4 million of bonds on a long-term basis was demonstrated by actual financing prior to the issuance of the financial statements. Management's ability to refinance $7 million of the $12 million of notes was demonstrated by a refinancing agreement. The remaining $5 million must be reported as a current liability.

*This is a widely available rate often used as a basis for establishing interest rates on lines of credit and often abbreviated as LIBOR.

If shares of stock had been issued to refinance the bonds in the illustration, the bonds still would be excluded from classification as a current liability. The specific form of the long-term refinancing (bonds, bank loans, equity securities) is irrelevant when determining the appropriate classification. Requiring companies to actually demonstrate the ability to refinance on a long-term basis in addition to merely intending to do so avoids intentional or unintentional understatements of current liabilities.

[16]FASB ASC 470–10–45: Debt–Overall–Other Presentation Matters (previously "Classification of Obligations That Are Callable by the Creditor," *Statement of Financial Accounting Standards No. 78* (Stamford, Conn.: FASB, 1983)).

[17]FASB ASC 470–10–45–14: Debt–Overall–Other Presentation Matters (previously "Classification of Obligations Expected to Be Refinanced," *Statement of Financial Accounting Standards No. 6* (Stamford, Conn.: FASB, 1975)).

It's important to remember that several weeks usually pass between the end of a company's fiscal year and the date the financial statements for that year actually are issued. Events occurring during that period can be used to clarify the nature of financial statement elements at the reporting date. Here we consider refinancing agreements and actual securities transactions to support a company's ability to refinance on a long-term basis. Later in the chapter we use information that becomes available during this period to decide how loss contingencies are reported.

International Financial Reporting Standards

Classification of Liabilities to be Refinanced. Under U.S. GAAP, liabilities payable within the coming year are classified as long-term liabilities if refinancing is completed before the date of issuance of the financial statements. Under IFRS, refinancing must be completed before the balance sheet date.[18]

● LO13–7

Concept Review Exercise

CURRENT LIABILITIES

The following selected transactions relate to liabilities of Southern Communications, Inc., for portions of 2018 and 2019. Southern's fiscal year ends on December 31.

Required:

Prepare the appropriate journal entries for these transactions.

2018

July 1	Arranged an uncommitted short-term line of credit with First City Bank amounting to \$25,000,000 at the bank's prime rate (11.5% in July). The company will pay no commitment fees for this arrangement.
Aug. 9	Received a \$30,000 refundable deposit from a major customer for copper-lined mailing containers used to transport communications equipment.
Oct. 7	Received most of the mailing containers covered by the refundable deposit and a letter stating that the customer will retain containers represented by \$2,000 of the deposit and will forfeit that amount. The cost of the forfeited containers was \$1,500.
Nov. 1	Borrowed \$7 million cash from First City Bank under the line of credit arranged in July and issued a nine-month promissory note. Interest at the prime rate of 12% was payable at maturity.
Dec. 31	Recorded appropriate adjusting entries for the liabilities described above.

2019

Feb. 12	Using the unused portion of the credit line as support, issued \$9 million of commercial paper and issued a six-month promissory note. Interest was discounted at issuance at a 10% discount rate.
Aug. 1	Paid the 12% note at maturity.
12	Paid the commercial paper at maturity.

2018

July 1
No entry is made for a line of credit until a loan actually is made. The existence and terms of the line would be described in a disclosure note.

August 9

Cash	30,000	
Liability—refundable deposits		30,000

October 7

Liability—refundable deposits	30,000	
Cash		28,000
Revenue—sale of containers		2,000
Cost of goods sold	1,500	
Inventory of containers		1,500

[18]"Presentation of Financial Statements" *International Accounting Standard No. 1* (IASCF), as amended effective January 1, 2016.

November 1		
Cash	7,000,000	
Notes payable		7,000,000
December 31		
Interest expense ($7,000,000 × 12% × 2/12)	140,000	
Interest payable		140,000

2019

February 12		
Cash [$9,000,000 − ($9,000,000 × 10% × 6/12)]	8,550,000	
Discount on notes payable (difference)	450,000	
Note payable		9,000,000
Note that the effective interest rate is [($9,000,000 × 10% × 6/12) ÷ $8,550,000] × 12/6 = $450,000 ÷ $8,550,000 × 2 = 10.53%		
August 1		
Interest expense ($7,000,000 × 12% × 7/12)	490,000	
Interest payable (from adjusting entry)	140,000	
Note payable (face amount)	7,000,000	
Cash ($7,000,000 + $630,000)		7,630,000
August 12		
Interest expense ($9,000,000 × 10% × 6/12)	450,000	
Discount on notes payable		450,000
Note payable (face amount)	9,000,000	
Cash ($8,550,000 + $450,000)		9,000,000

PART B

Contingencies

The feature that distinguishes the loss contingencies we discuss in this part of the chapter from the liabilities we discussed previously is uncertainty as to whether an obligation really exists. The circumstance giving rise to the contingency already has occurred, but there is uncertainty about whether a liability exists that will be resolved only when some future event occurs (or doesn't occur).

Loss Contingencies

LO13–5

General Motors Company's 2015 financial statements indicate a variety of potential obligations, as shown in Illustration 13–13.

Illustration 13–13

Disclosure of Potential Contingent Losses—General Motors Company

Real World Financials

17. Commitments and Contingencies (in part)

Various other legal actions, governmental investigations, claims and proceedings are pending against us including matters arising out of alleged product defects; employment-related matters; governmental regulations relating to safety, emissions and fuel economy; product warranties; financial services; dealer, supplier and other contractual relationships; tax-related matters not recorded pursuant to ASC 740, "Income Taxes" (indirect tax-related matters) and environmental matters.

These "legal actions, governmental investigations, claims and proceedings" all relate to situations that already have occurred. However, it isn't clear that these situations have given rise to liabilities, because GM doesn't know if it will have to make future payments. How likely is an unfavorable outcome, and how much will GM have to pay if an unfavorable outcome occurs?

A *loss contingency* arises when there is uncertainty about whether a past event will result in a future loss. The uncertainty will be resolved only when some future event occurs.

A loss contingency is an existing, uncertain situation involving potential loss depending on whether some future event occurs. Whether a contingency is accrued and reported as a liability depends on (a) the likelihood that the confirming event will occur and (b) what can be determined about the amount of loss. For example, consider lawsuits filed against GM by customers who allege they suffered injuries as a result of faulty ignition switches in GM cars that were recalled in 2014. GM's note 17 discloses much information about such claims, including 121 class-action lawsuits and 235 personal-injury lawsuits filed against it, as of January 27, 2016. It may take several years for those lawsuits to be settled or litigated. When considering how to account for those lawsuits prior to their resolution, GM must assess the likelihood that it eventually will have to pay damages, and if so, what the amount of those damages will be.

Note that we only account for a loss contingency when the event that gave rise to it occurred before the financial statement date. Otherwise, regardless of the likelihood of the eventual outcome, no liability existed at the statement date. Remember, one of the essential characteristics of a liability is that it results from past transactions or events. In our GM example, GM previously sold the cars to customers, so the event giving rise to potential litigation losses has occurred. The uncertainty relates not to that past event, but to the potential litigation losses that could occur in the future.

Generally accepted accounting principles require that the likelihood that the future event(s) will confirm the incurrence of the liability be (somewhat arbitrarily) categorized as probable, reasonably possible, or remote:[19]

FINANCIAL Reporting Case

Q4, p. 716

Probable	Confirming event is likely to occur.
Reasonably possible	The chance the confirming event will occur is more than remote but less than likely.
Remote	The chance the confirming event will occur is slight.

● LO13–6

Also key to reporting a contingent liability is its dollar amount. The amount of the potential loss is classified as either known, reasonably estimable, or not reasonably estimable.

A liability is accrued if it is both probable that the confirming event will occur and the amount can be at least reasonably estimated. A general depiction of the accrual of a loss contingency is:

Loss (or expense)	x,xxx	
Liability		x,xxx

If one amount within a range of possible loss appears better than other amounts within the range, that amount is accrued. When no amount within the range appears more likely than others, the minimum amount should be recorded and the possible additional loss should be disclosed.[20]

As an example, consider the following disclosure note from Merck & Co.'s 2015 financial statements (Illustration 13–14).

Illustration 13–14

Accrual of a Loss Contingency—Merck & Co.

Real World Financials

10. Contingencies and Environmental Liabilities (in part)

In management's opinion, the liabilities for all environmental matters that are probable and reasonably estimable have been accrued and totaled $109 million and $125 million at December 31, 2015 and 2014, respectively. Although it is not possible to predict with certainty the outcome of these matters, or the ultimate costs of remediation, management does not believe that any reasonably possible expenditures that may be incurred in excess of the liabilities accrued should exceed $57 million in the aggregate.

Consistent with GAAP, Merck accrued and disclosed the $109 million loss that is probable and reasonably estimable, and then only disclosed the $57 million estimated range of reasonably possible losses above that amount.

[19]Because FASB ASC 740–10–25: Income Taxes–Overall–Recognition (previously "Accounting for Uncertainty in Income Taxes," *FASB Interpretation No. 48* (Norwalk, Conn.: FASB, 2006)) provides guidance on accounting for uncertainty in income taxes, FASB ASC 450–10: Contingencies–Loss Contingencies (previously *SFAS No. 5*) does not apply to income taxes. GAAP regarding uncertainty in income taxes changes the threshold for recognition of tax positions from the most probable amount to the amount that has a "more likely than not" chance of being sustained upon examination. We discuss accounting for uncertainty in income taxes in Chapter 16.

[20]FASB ASC 450–20–30: Contingencies–Loss Contingencies–Initial Measurement (previously "Reasonable Estimation of the Amount of the Loss," *FASB Interpretation No. 14* (Stamford, Conn.: FASB, 1976)).

It is important to note that some contingent losses don't involve liabilities at all. Rather, these contingencies, when resolved, cause a noncash asset to be impaired, so accruing the contingency means reducing the related asset rather than recording a liability:

Loss (or expense)	x,xxx	
Asset (or valuation account)		x,xxx

The most common loss contingency of this type is an uncollectible receivable. You have recorded these before without knowing you were accruing a loss contingency (*Debit:* bad debt expense; *Credit:* allowance for uncollectible accounts).[21]

A loss contingency is disclosed in notes to the financial statements if there is at least a reasonable possibility that the loss will occur.

Not all loss contingencies are accrued. If one or both criteria for accrual are not met, but there is at least a reasonable possibility that a loss will occur, a disclosure note should describe the contingency. It also should provide an estimate of the potential loss or range of loss, if possible. If an estimate cannot be made, a statement to that effect is needed.

As an example of only disclosing a contingent loss, consider a disclosure note accompanying a 2015 annual report of U.S. Steel Corporation. As shown in Illustration 13–15, U.S. Steel considered it to be impossible to estimate its potential environmental liability associated with previously sold properties and businesses, and so only disclosed that contingent loss.

Illustration 13–15
Disclosure of Loss Contingency—U.S. Steel

Real World Financials

Note 20: Contingencies and Commitments (in part)

Throughout its history, U. S. Steel has sold numerous properties and businesses and many of these sales included indemnifications and cost sharing agreements related to the assets that were divested. . . . The amount of potential environmental liability associated with these transactions and properties is not estimable due to the nature and extent of the unknown conditions related to the properties divested and deconsolidated.

Illustration 13–16 highlights the appropriate accounting treatment for each possible combination of (a) the likelihood of an obligation being confirmed and (b) the determinability of its dollar amount.

Illustration 13–16
Accounting Treatment of Loss Contingencies

	Dollar Amount of Potential Loss		
Likelihood	**Known**	**Reasonably Estimable**	**Not Reasonably Estimable**
Probable	Liability accrued and disclosure note	Liability accrued and disclosure note	Disclosure note only
Reasonably possible	Disclosure note only	Disclosure note only	Disclosure note only
Remote	No disclosure required*	No disclosure required*	No disclosure required*

*Except for certain guarantees and other specified off-balance-sheet risk situations discussed in the next chapter.

Product Warranties and Guarantees

Most consumer products are accompanied by a guarantee.

MANUFACTURER'S QUALITY-ASSURANCE WARRANTY. Satisfaction guaranteed! Your money back if not satisfied! If anything goes wrong in the first five years or 100,000 miles . . .! Three-year guarantee! These and similar promises accompany most consumer goods. In Chapter 5 we called this sort of guarantee a *quality-assurance warranty*. When this type of warranty is included in a contract between a seller and a customer, it isn't a

[21]FASB ASC 310–10–35–7: Receivables–Overall–Subsequent Measurement–Losses from Uncollectible Receivables (previously "Accounting for Contingencies" *SFAS No. 5*, Norwalk, Conn: FASB 1975, par. 22).

separate performance obligation for the seller. Rather, it is a guarantee by the seller that the customer will be satisfied with the goods or services that the seller provided.

Why do sellers offer quality-assurance warranties? To boost sales. It follows, then, that any costs of making good on such guarantees should be estimated and recorded as expenses in the same accounting period the products are sold (matching expenses with revenues). Also, it is in the period of sale that the company becomes obligated to eventually make good on a guarantee, so it makes sense that it recognizes a liability in the period of sale. The challenge is that much of the cost of satisfying a guarantee usually occurs later, sometimes years later. So, this is a loss contingency. There may be a future sacrifice of economic benefits (cost of satisfying the guarantee) due to an existing circumstance (the guaranteed products have been sold) that depends on an uncertain future event (customer claim).

The costs of satisfying guarantees should be recorded as expenses in the same accounting period the products are sold.

The criteria for accruing a contingent loss (rather than only disclosing it) almost always are met for product warranties (or product guarantees). While we usually can't predict the liability associated with an individual sale, reasonably accurate estimates of the *total* liability for a period usually are possible, because prior experience makes it possible to predict how many warrantees or guarantees (on average) will need to be satisfied. Illustration 13–17 demonstrates accrual of the contingent liability for warranties in the reporting period in which the product under warranty is sold.

The contingent liability for quality-assurance warranties almost always is accrued.

Illustration 13–17

Product Warranty

Caldor Health, a supplier of in-home health care products, introduced a new therapeutic chair carrying a two-year warranty against defects. Estimates based on industry experience indicate warranty costs of 3% of sales during the first 12 months following the sale and 4% the next 12 months. During December 2018, its first month of availability, Caldor sold $2 million of chairs.

During December

Cash (and accounts receivable)	2,000,000	
Sales revenue		2,000,000

December 31, 2018 (adjusting entry)

Warranty expense [(3% + 4%) × $2,000,000]	140,000	
Estimated warranty liability		140,000

When customer claims are made and costs are incurred to satisfy those claims, the liability is reduced (let's say $61,000 in 2019):

Estimated warranty liability	61,000	
Cash, wages payable, parts and supplies, etc		61,000

Estimates of warranty costs cannot be expected to be precise. However, if the estimating method is monitored and revised when necessary, overestimates and underestimates should cancel each other over time. The estimated liability may be classified as current or as part current and part long-term, depending on when warranty claims are expected to be satisfied.

EXPECTED CASH FLOW APPROACH. In Chapter 6, you learned of a framework for using future cash flows as the basis for measuring assets and liabilities, introduced by the FASB in 2000 with *Statement of Financial Accounting Concepts No. 7,* "Using Cash Flow Information and Present Value in Accounting Measurements."[22] The approach described in the Concept Statement offers a way to take into account *any uncertainty concerning the amounts and timing of the cash flows.* Although future cash flows in many instances are contractual and certain, the amounts and timing of cash flows are less certain in other situations, such as warranty obligations.

SFAC No. 7 provides a framework for using future cash flows in accounting measurements.

As demonstrated in Illustration 13–17, the traditional way of measuring a warranty obligation is to report the "best estimate" of future cash flows, ignoring the time value of money on the basis of immateriality. However, when the warranty obligation spans more than one year and we can associate probabilities with possible cash flow outcomes, the approach

[22]"Using Cash Flow Information and Present Value in Accounting Measurements," *Statement of Financial Accounting Concepts No. 7* (Norwalk, Conn.: FASB, 2000). Recall that Concept Statements do not directly prescribe GAAP, but instead provide structure and direction to financial accounting.

described by *SFAC No. 7* offers a more plausible estimate of the warranty obligation. This "expected cash flow approach" incorporates specific probabilities of cash flows into the analysis. In Chapter 6, we discussed the expected cash flow approach to determining present value. Illustration 13–18 provides an example.

Illustration 13–18

Product Warranty

Probabilities are associated with possible cash outcomes.

The probability-weighted cash outcomes provide the expected cash flows.

The present value of the expected cash flows is the estimated liability.

Caldor Health, a supplier of in-home health care products, introduced a new therapeutic chair carrying a two-year warranty against defects. During December of 2018, its first month of availability, Caldor sold $2 million of the chairs. Industry experience indicates the following probability distribution for the potential warranty costs:

Warranty Costs	Probability
2019	
$50,000	20%
$60,000	50%
$70,000	30%
2020	
$70,000	20%
$80,000	50%
$90,000	30%

An arrangement with a service firm requires that costs for the two-year warranty period be settled at the end of 2019 and 2020. The risk-free rate of interest is 5%. Applying the expected cash flow approach, at the end of the 2018 fiscal year, Caldor would record a warranty liability (and expense) of $131,564, calculated as follows:

2019	$50,000 × 20% =	$10,000	
	60,000 × 50% =	30,000	
	70,000 × 30% =	21,000	
		$61,000	
		× 0.95238*	$ 58,095
2020	$70,000 × 20% =	$14,000	
	80,000 × 50% =	40,000	
	90,000 × 30% =	27,000	
		$81,000	
		× 0.90703†	73,469
			$131,564

*Present value of $1, $n = 1$, $i = 5\%$ (from Table 2)
†Present value of $1, $n = 2$, $i = 5\%$ (from Table 2)

December 31, 2018 (adjusting entry)		
Warranty expense	131,564	
Estimated warranty liability (calculated above)		131,564

EXTENDED WARRANTY CONTRACTS. It's difficult these days to buy a computer, a digital camera, a car, or almost any durable consumer product without being asked to buy an extended warranty agreement. An extended warranty provides warranty protection beyond the manufacturer's original warranty. As discussed in Chapter 5, because an extended warranty is priced and sold separately from the warranteed product, it constitutes a separate performance obligation. So, rather than only worrying about how to recognize the contingent liability associated with an extended warranty, we face another accounting question: When should the revenue from the sale of an extended warranty be recognized?

Revenue is recognized when performance obligations are satisfied, not necessarily when cash is received. Because an extended warranty provides coverage over a period of time, these arrangements typically qualify for revenue recognition over the period of coverage. However, cash typically is received up front, when the extended warranty is sold. Similar to other advanced payments for future products and services, revenue from extended warranty contracts is not recognized immediately, but instead is recorded as a deferred revenue liability at the time of sale and recognized as revenue over the contract period, typically on a straight-line basis. We demonstrate accounting for extended warranties in Illustration 13–19.

Illustration 13–19

Extended Warranty

Brand Name Appliances sells major appliances that carry a one-year manufacturer's warranty. Customers are offered the opportunity at the time of purchase to also buy a three-year extended warranty for an additional charge. On January 3, 2018, Brand Name sold a $60 extended warranty, covering years 2019, 2020, and 2021.

January 3, 2018		
Cash (or accounts receivable)	60	
Deferred revenue—extended warranties		60
December 31, 2019, 2020, 2021 (adjusting entries)		
Deferred revenue—extended warranties	20	
Revenue—extended warranties ($60 ÷ 3)		20

The costs incurred to satisfy customer claims under the extended warranties also will be recorded during the same three-year period. That way, net income in each year of the extended warranty will reflect both the warranty revenue recognized and the costs associated with that revenue.

Additional Consideration

Accounting for Rebates, Premiums, and Coupons. Sometimes a company promotes its products in ways that obligate the company to do something in the future. For example, at the time of a sale, customers obtain cash register receipts, bar codes on the product, or other proofs of purchase that later can be mailed to the manufacturer for *cash rebates*. Also, customers sometimes can show proof of purchase to obtain noncash items (called *premiums*), like toys, small appliances, or dishes. Companies may also mail out *coupons*, which entice customers to buy a company's products and services at a discounted price at some point in the future. How should we account for the future obligations created by these promotions?

Until very recently, all of these promotions were viewed as creating a contingent liability. After all, they obligate the seller to transfer some uncertain amount of cash, goods, or services at a future date. However, with recent changes in accounting for revenue recognition, the accounting in this area has changed. Now we view promises to provide rebates and premiums to be part of agreements between sellers and customers. This means we account for them using the revenue recognition process we learned about in Chapter 5.

Cash rebates are an obligation to return cash in the future, so they represent a reduction in the net amount paid by the customer. To record these, we estimate the amount of cash rebates that customers will take and reduce revenue by the amount of that estimate in the period revenue is recognized. We also recognize a liability for the estimated rebate, similar to how we recognize a refundable deposit.

Premiums obligate a company to provide noncash items and are treated as separate performance obligations. We allocate a portion of the original sales price to the premiums (based on their relative stand-alone selling prices), record that amount as deferred revenue, and recognize that portion as revenue when premiums are delivered. No contingent liability is recognized because, as with extended warranties, we recognize the cost of premiums in the period in which we deliver them and recognize revenue.

Coupons that aren't offered as part of a sales contract aren't accounted for as part of revenue recognition. Instead, issuing coupons creates a contingent liability that is recognized in the period the coupons are issued. In practice, firms typically either (a) recognize the entire expense associated with estimated coupon redemptions in the period the coupons are issued, or (b) recognize no liability in the period the coupons are issued and instead record the expense when coupons are redeemed. The difference between these approaches typically is not viewed as material.

Litigation Claims

Pending litigation is not unusual. In fact, as you saw for GM, the majority of medium and large corporations annually report multiple loss contingencies due to litigation.

In practice, accrual of a loss from pending or ongoing litigation is rare. Can you guess why? Suppose you are chief financial officer of Feinz Foods. Feinz is the defendant in a $44 million class-action suit. The company's legal counsel informally advises you that the chance the company will win the lawsuit is quite doubtful. Counsel feels the company might lose $30 million. Now suppose you decide to accrue a $30 million loss in your financial statements. Later, in the courtroom, your disclosure that Feinz management feels it is probable that the company will lose $30 million would be welcome ammunition for the opposing legal counsel. Understanding this, most companies rely on the knowledge that in today's legal environment the outcome of litigation is highly uncertain, making likelihood predictions difficult.

Therefore, while companies may accrue estimated lawyer fees and other legal costs, they usually do not record a loss until after the ultimate settlement has been reached or negotiations for settlement are substantially completed. While companies should provide extensive disclosure of these contingent liabilities, they do not always do so in practice.[23] In 2010, the SEC began pressuring firms for more complete disclosure of litigation, including better descriptions of the range of losses that are reasonably possible to occur. As an example, Illustration 13–20 provides a few excerpts from the eight pages of litigation note appearing in JP Morgan Chase & Company's 2015 annual report.

Illustration 13–20

Disclosure of Litigation Contingencies—JP Morgan Chase & Company

Real World Financials

Note 31: Litigation (in part)

As of December 31, 2015, the Firm and its subsidiaries are defendants or putative defendants in numerous legal proceedings, including private, civil litigations and regulatory/government investigations. . . . The Firm believes the estimate of the aggregate range of reasonably possible losses, in excess of reserves established, for its legal proceedings is from $0 to approximately $3.6 billion at December 31, 2015. This estimated aggregate range of reasonably possible losses is based upon currently available information for those proceedings in which the Firm believes that an estimate of reasonably possible loss can be made. For certain matters, the Firm does not believe that such an estimate can be made.

Even after a firm loses in court, it may not make an accrual. As you can see in Illustration 13–21, the Las Vegas Sands Corporation, in its 2015 annual report, disclosed but did not accrue damages from a lawsuit it lost, because the company was appealing the verdict.

Illustration 13–21

Disclosure of a Lawsuit—Las Vegas Sands Corporation

Real World Financials

Note 13: Commitments and Contingencies (in part): Litigation

The Company believes that it has valid bases in law and fact to appeal these verdicts. As a result, the Company believes that the likelihood that the amount of the judgments will be affirmed is not probable, and, accordingly, that the amount of any loss cannot be reasonably estimated at this time. Because the Company believes that this potential loss is not probable or estimable, it has not recorded any reserves or contingencies related to this legal matter.

Subsequent Events

Several weeks usually pass between the end of a company's fiscal year and the date the financial statements for that year actually are issued or available to be issued.[24] As shown on the following time line, events occurring during this period can be used to clarify the nature of financial statement elements at the report date.

[23]For research indicating incomplete disclosure of litigation-related contingent liabilities, see R. Desir, K. Fanning, and R. Pfeiffer, "Are Revisions to SFAS No. 5 Needed?" *Accounting Horizons* 24(4): December, 2010: 525–546.

[24]Financial statements are viewed as *issued* if they have been widely distributed to financial statement users in a format consistent with GAAP. Some entities (for example, private companies) do not widely distribute their financial statements to users. For those entities, the key date for subsequent events is not the date of issuance but rather the date upon which the financial statements are *available to be issued*, which occurs when the financial statements are complete, in a format consistent with GAAP, and have obtained the necessary approvals for issuance. Entities must disclose the date through which subsequent events have been evaluated (FASB ASC 855: Subsequent Events (previously "Subsequent Events," *Statement of Financial Accounting Standards No. 165* (Stamford, Conn.: FASB, 2009)).

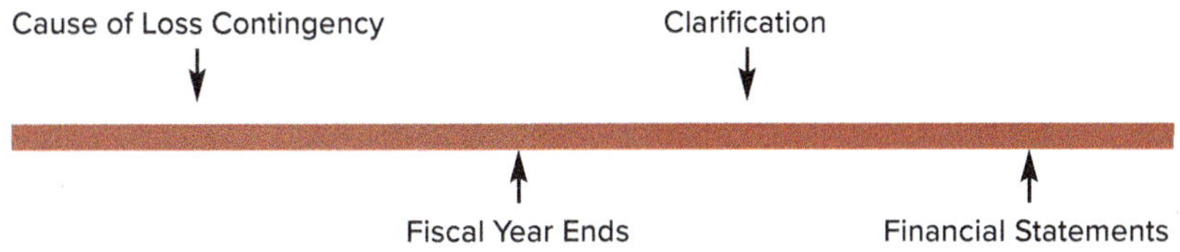

When the cause of a loss contingency occurs before the year-end, a clarifying event before financial statements are issued can be used to determine how the contingency is reported.

If information becomes available that sheds light on a claim that existed when the fiscal year ended, that information should be used in determining the probability of a loss contingency materializing and in estimating the amount of the loss.

The settlement of a lawsuit after **Starbucks**' September 29, 2013, fiscal year ended apparently influenced its accrual of a loss contingency (Illustration 13–22).

Illustration 13–22

Accrual of Litigation Contingencies—Starbucks

Real World Financials

Note 15: Commitments and Contingencies (in part)

Legal Proceedings

On December 6, 2010, Kraft commenced a federal court action against Starbucks, entitled Kraft Foods Global, Inc. v. Starbucks Corporation, in the U.S. District Court for the Southern District of New York. On November 12, 2013, the arbitrator ordered Starbucks to pay Kraft $2,227.5 million in damages plus prejudgment interest and attorney's fees. We have estimated prejudgment interest, which includes an accrual through the estimated payment date, and attorneys' fees to be approximately $556.6 million. As a result, we recorded a litigation charge of $2,784.1 million in our fiscal 2013 operating results.

For a loss contingency to be accrued, the cause of the lawsuit must have occurred before the accounting period ended. It's not necessary that the lawsuit actually was filed during that reporting period.

Sometimes, the cause of a loss contingency occurs after the end of the year but before the financial statements are issued:

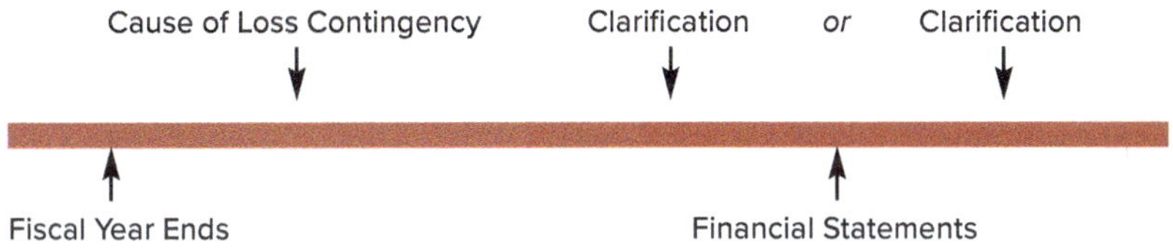

If an event giving rise to a contingency occurs after the year-end, a liability should not be accrued.

When a contingency comes into existence after the company's fiscal year-end, a liability cannot be accrued because it didn't exist at the end of the year. However, if the failure to disclose the possible loss would cause the financial statements to be misleading, the situation should be described in a disclosure note, including the effect of the possible loss on key accounting numbers affected.[25]

In fact, *any* event occurring after the fiscal year-end but before the financial statements are issued that has a material effect on the company's financial position must be disclosed in a subsequent events disclosure note. Examples are an issuance of debt or equity securities, a business combination, and discontinued operations.

A disclosure note from the **Coca-Cola Company**'s 2015 annual report is shown in Illustration 13–23 and describes events that occurred in the first quarter of 2016.

Illustration 13–23

Subsequent Events—Coca-Cola Company

Real World Financials

Note 21: Subsequent events (in part)

In February 2016, additional territories in North America met the criteria to be classified as held for sale. Therefore, we are required to record the related assets and liabilities at the lower of carrying value or fair value less any costs to sell based on the estimated sale price, which will result in a noncash loss of $296 million in 2016.

[25]FASB ASC 450–20–50v9: Contingencies–Loss Contingencies–Disclosure (previously "Accounting for Contingencies," *Statement of Financial Accounting Standards No. 5* (Stamford, Conn.: FASB, 1975), par. 11).

Additional Consideration

Contingent liabilities that a company takes on when it acquires another company may be treated differently from those that arise during the normal course of business. If the acquirer can determine the fair value of a contingent liability, the liability is measured at fair value. For example, the acquisition-date fair value of a warranty obligation often can be determined. If the acquirer cannot determine the fair value, then the acquirer uses the normal criteria that apply to contingent liabilities. That is, the contingent liability is accrued if (1) available information indicates that it is probable a liability has been incurred as of the acquisition date, and (2) the amount of the liability can be reasonably estimated. In periods subsequent to the acquisition, GAAP is vague about how the acquirer should account for these contingent liabilities, indicating that "An acquirer shall develop a systematic and rational basis for subsequently measuring and accounting for assets and liabilities arising from contingencies depending on their nature."[26] This lack of clear guidance suggests that there could be a lack of comparability between firms in how they account for acquired contingent liabilities.

Unasserted Claims and Assessments

It must be probable that an unasserted claim or assessment will be asserted before considering whether and how to report the possible loss.

Even if a claim has yet to be made when the financial statements are issued, a contingency may warrant accrual or disclosure. In this case, a two-step process is involved in deciding how the unasserted claim should be reported:

1. Is it probable that a claim will be asserted? If the answer to that question is "no," stop. No accrual or disclosure is necessary. If the answer is "yes," go on to step 2.
2. Treat the claim as if the claim has been asserted. That requires evaluating (a) the likelihood of an unfavorable outcome and (b) whether the dollar amount of loss can be estimated, just as we already have discussed for other loss contingencies for which a claim has already been asserted.

For example, suppose a trucking company frequently transports hazardous waste materials and is subject to environmental laws and regulations. Management has identified several sites at which it is or may be liable for remediation. For those sites for which no penalties have been asserted, management must assess the likelihood that a claim will be made, and if so, the likelihood that the company actually will be held liable. If management feels an assessment is probable, an estimated loss and contingent liability would be accrued only if an unfavorable outcome is probable and the amount can be reasonably estimated. However, a disclosure note alone would be appropriate if an unfavorable settlement is only reasonably possible or if the settlement is probable but cannot be reasonably estimated. No action is needed if chances of that outcome occurring are remote.

As described in a December 31, 2015, disclosure note (see Illustration 13–24), **Union Pacific** concluded that some unasserted claims met the criteria for accrual under this two-step decision process.

Illustration 13–24

Unasserted Claims—Union Pacific Corporation

Real World Financials

15. Commitments and Contingencies (in part)

Asserted and Unasserted Claims—Various claims and lawsuits are pending against us and certain of our subsidiaries. We cannot fully determine the effect of all asserted and unasserted claims on our consolidated results of operations, financial condition, or liquidity. To the extent possible, we have recorded a liability where asserted and unasserted claims are considered probable and where such claims can be reasonably estimated.

Notice that the treatment of contingent liabilities is consistent with the accepted definition of liabilities as (a) probable, future sacrifices of economic benefits (b) that arise from present obligations to other entities and (c) that result from past transactions or

[26] FASB ASC 805-20-25: Business Combinations–Identifiable Assets and Liabilities, and Any Noncontrolling Interest–Recognition (previously "Accounting for Assets Acquired and Liabilities Assumed in a Business Combination that Arise from Contingencies," FASB Staff Position *No. 141R-1* (Norwalk, Conn.: FASB, 2009)).

events.[27] The inherent uncertainty involved with contingent liabilities means additional care is required to determine whether future sacrifices of economic benefits are probable and whether the amount of the sacrifices can be quantified.

International Financial Reporting Standards

Loss Contingencies. Accounting for contingencies is part of a broader international standard, *IAS No. 37,* "Provisions, Contingent Liabilities and Contingent Assets." Overall, accounting for contingent losses under IFRS is quite similar to accounting under U.S. GAAP. A contingent loss is accrued if it's both probable and can be reasonably estimated, and disclosed if it's of at least a remote probability. However, there are some important differences:

● LO13–7

- IFRS refers to accrued liabilities as "provisions," and refers to possible obligations that are not accrued as "contingent liabilities." The term "contingent liabilities" is used for all of these obligations in U.S. GAAP.
- IFRS requires disclosure (but not accrual) of two types of contingent liabilities: (1) possible obligations whose existence will be confirmed by some uncertain future events that the company does not control, and (2) a present obligation for which either it is not probable that a future outflow will occur or the amount of the future outflow cannot be measured with sufficient reliability. U.S. GAAP does not make this distinction but typically would require disclosure of the same contingencies.
- IFRS defines "probable" as "more likely than not" (greater than 50%), which is a lower threshold than typically associated with "probable" in U.S. GAAP.
- If a liability is accrued, IFRS measures the liability as the best estimate of the expenditure required to settle the present obligation. If there is a range of equally likely outcomes, IFRS would use the midpoint of the range, while U.S. GAAP requires use of the low end of the range.
- If the effect of the time value of money is material, IFRS requires the liability to be stated at present value. U.S. GAAP allows using present values under some circumstances, but liabilities for loss contingencies like litigation typically are not discounted for time value of money.[28]
- IFRS recognizes provisions and contingencies for "onerous" contracts, defined as those in which the unavoidable costs of meeting the obligations exceed the expected benefits.[29] Under U.S. GAAP we generally don't disclose or recognize losses on such money-losing contracts, although there are some exceptions (for example, losses on long-term construction contracts are accrued, as are losses on contracts that have been terminated).

Here's a portion of a note from the 2015 financial statements of Vodafone, which reports under IFRS:

Note 17: Provisions (in part)

Provisions are recognised when the Group has a present obligation (legal or constructive) as a result of a past event, it is probable that the Group will be required to settle that obligation and a reliable estimate can be made of the amount of the obligation. Provisions are measured at the Directors' best estimate of the expenditure required to settle the obligation at the reporting date and are discounted to present value where the effect is material.

Where We're Headed

The controversy over accounting for contingencies and the mixture of approaches is likely to continue. The FASB recently removed from its agenda a project to reconsider the recognition and measurement of contingent losses, and has postponed further work on a project intended to enhance note disclosures of contingent losses. The IASB has a project ongoing, but progress on this project has been slow as the IASB has focused on more pressing projects.

[27] "Elements of Financial Statements," *Statement of Financial Accounting Concepts No. 6* (Stamford, Conn.: FASB, 1985).

[28] See, for example, FASB ASC 410–30–35–12: Asset Retirements and Environmental Obligations–Environmental Obligations–Subsequent Measurement.

[29] Paragraph 10 of "Provisions, Contingent Liabilities and Contingent Assets", *International Accounting Standard 37* (London, UK: IASB, 2008).

Gain Contingencies

Gain contingencies are not accrued.

LO13–7

A gain contingency is an uncertain situation that might result in a gain. For example, in a pending lawsuit, one side—the defendant—faces a loss contingency; the other side—the plaintiff—has a gain contingency. As we discussed earlier, loss contingencies are accrued when it's probable that an amount will be paid and the amount can reasonably be estimated. However, gain contingencies are not accrued. The nonparallel treatment of gain contingencies is an example of conservatism, following the reasoning that it's desirable to anticipate losses, but recognizing gains should await their realization.

Though gain contingencies are not recorded in the accounts, material ones are disclosed in notes to the financial statements. Care should be taken that the disclosure note not give "misleading implications as to the likelihood of realization."[30]

International Financial Reporting Standards

Gain Contingencies. Under U.S. GAAP, gain contingencies are never accrued. Under IFRS, gain contingencies are accrued if their future realization is "virtually certain" to occur. Both U.S. GAAP and IFRS *disclose* contingent gains when future realization is probable, but under IFRS "probable" is defined as "more likely than not" (greater than 50 percent), and so has a lower threshold than it does under U.S. GAAP.

Additional Consideration

Accounting for contingencies is controversial. Many accountants dislike the idea of only recognizing a liability for a contingent loss when it is probable, and then reporting the liability at the best estimate of the future expenditure. The obvious alternative is fair value, which does not incorporate probability into determining whether to *recognize* a loss but rather considers probability when *measuring* the amount of loss. Recent changes in GAAP have adopted fair value approaches for some types of events that are contingent losses (or appear to be close relatives). Consider the following examples:

- Illustration 13–18 uses a discounted expected cash flow approach to measure the contingent liability associated with a warranty. That approach approximates fair value.
- Recall from Chapter 10 that asset retirement obligations are recorded at fair value when an asset is acquired. The offsetting liability is similar to a contingent liability because it is an uncertain future amount arising from the past purchase of the asset but is recorded at fair value.
- Sometimes a company provides a guarantee that may require it to make payment to another party based on some future event. For example, a company might guarantee the debt of an affiliated company to make it easier for the affiliate to obtain financing. GAAP views this sort of guarantee as having two parts: (1) a certain "stand ready obligation" to meet the terms of the guarantee, and (2) the uncertain contingent obligation to make future payments depending on future events (for example, the affiliate defaulting on their debt). The "stand ready obligation" is recorded initially at fair value, while the contingent obligation is handled as an ordinary contingent loss.[31]

---

[30]FASB ASC 450–30–50: Contingencies–Gain Contingencies–Disclosure (previously "Accounting For Contingencies," *Statement of Financial Accounting Standards No. 5* (Stamford, Conn.: FASB, 1975), par. 17).

[31]FASB ASC 460–10–25: Guarantees–Overall–Recognition (previously "Guarantor's Accounting and Disclosure Requirements for Guarantees, Including Indirect Guarantees of Indebtedness of Others," *FASB Interpretation No. 45* (Stamford, Conn.: FASB, 2002)).

Concept Review Exercise

CONTINGENCIES

Hanover Industries manufactures and sells food products and food processing machinery. While preparing the December 31, 2018, financial statements for Hanover, the following information was discovered relating to contingencies and possible adjustments to liabilities. Hanover's 2018 financial statements were issued on April 1, 2019.

a. On November 12, 2018, a former employee filed a lawsuit against Hanover alleging age discrimination and asking for damages of $750,000. At December 31, 2018, Hanover's attorney indicated that the likelihood of losing the lawsuit was possible but not probable. On March 5, 2019, Hanover agreed to pay the former employee $125,000 in return for withdrawing the lawsuit.

b. Hanover believes there is a possibility a service provider may claim that it has been undercharged for outsourcing a processing service based on verbal indications of the company's interpretation of a negotiated rate. The service provider has not yet made a claim for additional fees as of April 2019, but Hanover thinks it will. Hanover's accountants and legal counsel believe the charges were appropriate but that if an assessment is made, there is a reasonable possibility that subsequent court action would result in an additional tax liability of $55,000.

c. Hanover grants a two-year warranty for each processing machine sold. Past experience indicates that the costs of satisfying warranties are approximately 2% of sales. During 2018, sales of processing machines totaled $21,300,000. 2018 expenditures for warranty repair costs were $178,000 related to 2018 sales and $220,000 related to 2017 sales. The January 1, 2018, balance of the warranty liability account was $250,000.

d. Hanover is the plaintiff in a $600,000 lawsuit filed in 2017 against Ansdale Farms for failing to deliver on contracts for produce. The suit is in final appeal. Legal counsel advises that it is probable that Hanover will prevail and will be awarded $300,000 (considered a material amount).

Required:

1. Determine the appropriate reporting for each situation. Briefly explain your reasoning.
2. Prepare any necessary journal entries and state whether a disclosure note is needed.

Solution:

a. This is a loss contingency. Hanover can use the information occurring after the end of the year in determining appropriate disclosure. The cause for the suit existed at the end of the year. Hanover should accrue the $125,000 loss because an agreement has been reached confirming the loss and the amount is known.

Loss—litigation	125,000	
Liability—litigation		125,000

A disclosure note also is appropriate.

b. At the time financial statements are issued, a claim is as yet unasserted. However, an assessment is probable. Thus, (a) the likelihood of an unfavorable outcome and (b) whether the dollar amount can be estimated are considered. No accrual is necessary because an unfavorable outcome is not probable. But because an unfavorable outcome is reasonably possible, a disclosure note is appropriate.

Note: If the likelihood of a claim being asserted is not probable, disclosure is not required even if an unfavorable outcome is thought to be probable in the event of an assessment and the amount is estimable.

c. The contingency for warranties should be accrued because it is probable that expenditures will be made and the amount can be estimated from past experience. When customer claims are made and costs are incurred to satisfy those claims the liability is reduced.

Warranty expense (2% × $21,300,000)	426,000	
Estimated warranty liability		426,000
Estimated warranty liability ($178,000 + 220,000)	398,000	
Cash, wages payable, parts and supplies, etc		398,000

The liability at December 31, 2018, would be reported as $278,000:

Warranty Liability
($ in thousands)

		250	Balance, Jan. 1
		426	2018 expense
2018 expenditures	398		
		278	Balance, Dec. 31

A disclosure note explaining the contingency also is appropriate.

d. This is a gain contingency. Gain contingencies cannot be accrued even if the gain is probable and reasonably estimable. The gain should be recognized only when realized. It can be disclosed, but care should be taken to avoid misleading language regarding the realizability of the gain.

Decision Makers' Perspective

Current liabilities impact a company's liquidity. Liquidity refers to a company's cash position and overall ability to obtain cash in the normal course of business. A company is said to be liquid if it has sufficient cash (or other assets convertible to cash in a relatively short time) to pay currently maturing debts. Because the lack of liquidity can cause the demise of an otherwise healthy company, it is critical that managers as well as outside investors and creditors maintain close scrutiny of this aspect of a company's well-being.

A risk analyst should be concerned with a company's ability to meet its short-term obligations.

Keeping track of the current ratio is one of the most common ways of doing this. The current ratio is intended as a measure of short-term solvency and is determined by dividing current assets by current liabilities.

FINANCIAL Reporting Case

Q5, p. 716

A manager should actively monitor a company's liquidity.

When we compare liabilities that must be satisfied in the near term with assets that either are cash or will be converted to cash in the near term, we get a useful measure of a company's liquidity. A ratio of 1 to 1 or higher often is considered a rule-of-thumb standard, but like other ratios, acceptability should be evaluated in the context of the industry in which the company operates and other specific circumstances. Keep in mind, though, that industry averages are only one indication of adequacy and that the current ratio is but one indication of liquidity.

We can adjust for the implicit assumption of the current ratio that all current assets are equally liquid. The acid-test, or quick, ratio is similar to the current ratio but is based on a more conservative measure of assets available to pay current liabilities. Specifically, the numerator, quick assets, includes only cash and cash equivalents, short-term investments, and accounts receivable. By eliminating current assets such as inventories and prepaid expenses that are less readily convertible into cash, the acid-test ratio provides a more rigorous indication of a company's short-term solvency than does the current ratio.

A liquidity ratio is but one indication of a company's liquidity.

If either of these liquidity ratios is less than that of the industry as a whole, does that mean that liquidity is a problem? Not necessarily. It does, though, raise a red flag that suggests caution when assessing other areas. It's important to remember that each ratio is but one piece of the puzzle. For example, profitability is probably the best long-run indication of liquidity. Also, management may be very efficient in managing current assets so that some current assets—receivables or inventory—are converted to cash more quickly than they otherwise would be and are more readily available to satisfy liabilities. The turnover ratios discussed in earlier chapters help measure the efficiency of asset management in this regard.

Some companies maintain relatively high current liabilities as part of a cash-management strategy.

In fact, some companies view their accounts payable as a free loan from their suppliers, just as they view their accounts receivable as a free loan to their customers. These companies tend to pressure their customers to pay quickly, but try to obtain more extended terms with their suppliers. Although this would produce relatively low current assets and high current liabilities, and therefore a lower current ratio, it could be a very intelligent way to manage cash and decrease the overall amount of capital needed by the company to finance operations.

Given the actual and perceived importance of a company's liquidity in the minds of analysts, it's not difficult to adopt a management perspective and imagine efforts to manipulate the ratios that measure liquidity. For instance, a company might use its economic muscle or persuasive powers to influence the timing of accounts payable recognition by asking suppliers to change their delivery schedules. Because accounts payable is included in the denominator in most measures of liquidity, such as the current ratio, the timing of their recognition could mean the difference between an unacceptable ratio and an acceptable one, or between violating a debt covenant and compliance. For example, suppose a company with a current ratio of 1.25 (current assets of $5 million and current liabilities of $4 million) is in violation of a debt covenant requiring a minimum current ratio of 1.3. By delaying the delivery of $1 million of inventory, the ratio would be 1.33 (current assets of $4 million and current liability of $3 million).

Analysts should be alert for efforts to manipulate measures of liquidity.

It is important for creditors and analysts to be attentive for evidence of activities that would indicate timing strategies, such as unusual variations in accounts payable levels. You might notice that such timing strategies are similar to earnings management techniques we discussed previously—specifically, manipulating the timing of revenue and expense recognition in order to "smooth" income over time.

Finally, all financial statement users need to keep in mind the relation between the recognition of deferred revenue associated with advance payments and the later recognition of revenue. On the one hand, increases in deferred revenue can signal future revenue recognition because the deferred revenue likely will eventually be recognized as revenue. On the other hand, research suggests that some firms that report deferred revenue may manipulate the timing of revenue recognition to manage their earnings.[32]

Changes in deferred revenue provide information about future revenue, and may be used to manipulate it.

In the next chapter, we continue our discussion of liabilities. Our focus will shift from current liabilities to long-term liabilities in the form of bonds and long-term notes. ●

Financial Reporting Case Solution

© Rob Daly / age fotostock

1. **What are accrued liabilities? What is commercial paper?** *(p. 721)* Accrued liabilities are reported for expenses already incurred but not yet paid (accrued expenses). These include salaries and wages payable, income taxes payable, and interest payable. Commercial paper is a form of notes payable sometimes used by large corporations to obtain temporary financing. It is sold to other companies as a short-term investment. It represents unsecured notes sold in minimum denominations of $25,000 with maturities ranging from 30 to 270 days. Typically, commercial paper is issued directly to the buyer (lender) and is backed by a line of credit with a bank.
2. **Why did Syntel Microsystems include some long-term debt in the current liability section?** *(p. 727)* Syntel Microsystems did include some long-term debt in the current liability section. The currently maturing portion of a long-term debt must be reported as a current liability. Amounts are reclassified and reported as current liabilities when they become payable within the upcoming year.
3. **Did they also report some current amounts as long-term debt? Explain.** *(p. 728)* Yes they did. It is permissible to report short-term obligations as noncurrent liabilities if the company (a) intends to refinance on a long-term basis and (b) demonstrates the ability to do so by a refinancing agreement or by actual financing. As the disclosure note explains, this is the case for a portion of Syntel's currently payable debt.

(continued)

[32]Marcus Caylor, "Strategic Revenue Recognition to Achieve Earnings Benchmarks," *Journal of Accounting and Public Policy*, January-February 2010, pp. 82-95.

(concluded)

4. **Must obligations be known contractual debts in order to be reported as liabilities?** *(p. 731)* No. From an accounting perspective, it is not necessary that obligations be known, legally enforceable debts to be reported as liabilities. They must only be probable and the dollar amount reasonably estimable.
5. **Is it true that current liabilities are riskier than long-term liabilities?** *(p. 742)* Other things being equal, current liabilities generally are considered riskier than long-term liabilities. For that reason, management usually would rather report a debt as long term. Current debt, though, is not necessarily risky. The liquidity ratios we discussed in the chapter attempt to measure liquidity. Remember, any such measure must be assessed in the context of other factors: industry standards, profitability, turnover ratios, and risk management activities, to name a few.

The Bottom Line

- **LO13–1** Liabilities are present obligations to sacrifice assets in the future because of something that already has occurred. Current liabilities are expected to require current assets (or the creation of other current liabilities) and usually are payable within one year. *(p. 716)*
- **LO13–2** Short-term bank loans usually are arranged under an ongoing line of credit with a bank or group of banks. When interest is discounted from the face amount of a note (a type of noninterest-bearing note), the effective interest rate is higher than the stated discount rate. Large, highly rated firms sometimes sell commercial paper directly to the buyer (lender) to borrow funds at a lower rate than through a bank loan. *(p. 718)*
- **LO13–3** Accrued liabilities are recorded by adjusting entries for expenses already incurred, but for which cash has yet to be paid (accrued expenses). Familiar examples are salaries and wages payable, income taxes payable, and interest payable. (*p.* 721)
- **LO13–4** Short-term obligations can be reported as noncurrent liabilities if the company (a) intends to refinance on a long-term basis and (b) demonstrates the ability to do so by actual financing or a formal agreement to do so. *(p. 727)*
- **LO13–5** A loss contingency is an existing, uncertain situation involving potential loss depending on whether some future event occurs. Whether a contingency is accrued and reported as a liability depends on (a) the likelihood that the confirming event will occur and (b) what can be determined about the amount of loss. It is accrued if it is both probable that the confirming event will occur and the amount can be at least reasonably estimated. *(p. 730)*
- **LO13–6** A clarifying event before financial statements are issued, but after the year-end, can be used to determine how a contingency is reported. An unasserted suit, claim, or assessment warrants accrual or disclosure if it is probable it will be asserted. A gain contingency is a contingency that might result in a gain. A gain contingency is not recognized until it actually is realized. *(p. 731)*
- **LO13–7** IFRS and U.S. GAAP are relatively similar with respect to current liabilities and contingencies. Relatively minor differences relate to when financing must be in place for a liability expected to be refinanced to be classified as long term. Also, with respect to contingent losses, IFRS defines "probable" at a lower threshold, requires the accrual of the expected value of loss, and requires the use of present values when measuring amounts to be accrued. Contingent gains are not accrued under U.S. GAAP, but are accrued under IFRS when they are considered to be virtually certain to occur. *(pp. 729, 739,* and *740)*

APPENDIX 13 Payroll-Related Liabilities

All firms incur liabilities in connection with their payrolls. These arise primarily from legal requirements to withhold taxes from employees' paychecks and from payroll taxes on the firms themselves. Some payroll-related liabilities result from voluntary payroll deductions of amounts payable to third parties.

Employees' Withholding Taxes

Employers are required by law to withhold federal (and sometimes state) income taxes and Social Security taxes from employees' paychecks and remit these to the Internal Revenue Service.

The amount withheld for federal income taxes is determined by a tax table furnished by the IRS and varies according to the amount earned and the number of exemptions claimed by the employee. Also, the Federal Insurance Contributions Act (FICA) requires employers to withhold a percentage of each employee's earnings up to a specified maximum. Both the percentage and the maximum are changed intermittently. As this text went to print, the deduction for Social Security was 6.2% of the first $118,500 an employee earns, and this ceiling amount changes each year for cost-of-living adjustments. Additionally, a deduction for Medicare tax is 1.45% with no limit on the base amount. The employer also must pay an equal (matching) amount on behalf of the employee. Self-employed persons must pay both the employer and employee portions (12.4% for Social Security and 2.9% for Medicare).

Voluntary Deductions

Besides the required deductions for income taxes and Social Security taxes, employees often authorize their employers to deduct other amounts from their paychecks. These deductions might include union dues, contributions to savings or retirement plans, and insurance premiums. Amounts deducted this way represent liabilities until paid to the appropriate organizations.

Employers' Payroll Taxes

One payroll tax mentioned previously is the employer's matching amount of FICA taxes. The employer also must pay federal and state unemployment taxes on behalf of its employees. The Federal Unemployment Tax Act (FUTA) requires a tax of 6.0% of the first $7,000 earned by each employee. This amount is reduced by a 5.4% (maximum) credit for contributions to state unemployment programs, so the net federal rate often is 0.6%.[33] In many states, the state rate is 5.4% but may be reduced if the employer maintains relatively low employee turnover.

Fringe Benefits

In addition to salaries and wages, withholding taxes, and payroll taxes, many companies provide employees a variety of fringe benefits. Most commonly, employers pay all or part of employees' insurance premiums and/or contributions to retirement income plans.

Representative payroll-related liabilities are presented in Illustration 13A–1.

As you study the illustration, you should note the similarity among all payroll-related liabilities. Amounts withheld from paychecks—voluntarily or involuntarily—are liabilities until turned over to appropriate third parties. Payroll taxes and expenses for fringe benefits are incurred as a result of services performed by employees and also are liabilities until paid to appropriate third parties.

Illustration 13A–1
Payroll-Related Liabilities

Crescent Lighting and Fixtures' payroll for the second week in January was $100,000. The following deductions, fringe benefits, and taxes apply:

Federal income taxes to be withheld	$20,000
State income taxes to be withheld	3,000
Medical insurance premiums (Blue Cross)—70% paid by employer	1,000
Employee contribution to voluntary retirement plan (Fidelity Investments)—contributions matched by employer	4,000
Union dues (Local No. 222)—paid by employees	100
Life insurance premiums (Prudential Life)—100% paid by employer	200
Social Security tax rate	6.2%
Medicare tax rate	1.45%
Federal unemployment tax rate (after state deduction)	0.60%
State unemployment tax rate	5.40%

(continued)

[33]All states presently have unemployment tax programs.

Amounts withheld from paychecks represent liabilities until remitted to third parties.

The employer's share of FICA and unemployment taxes constitute the employer's payroll tax expense.

Fringe benefits are part of salaries and wages expense and represent liabilities until remitted to third parties.

(concluded)

Crescent's journal entries to record payroll:

Salaries and wages expense (total amount earned)	100,000	
Withholding taxes payable (federal income tax)		20,000
Withholding taxes payable (state income tax)		3,000
Social Security taxes payable (employees' portion, 6.2%)		6,200
Medicare taxes payable (employees' portion, 1.45%)		**1,450**
Payable to Blue Cross (employee's portion of insurance premiums—30%)		300
Payable to Fidelity Investments (employees' investment)		**4,000**
Payable to Local No. 222 (union dues)		100
Salaries and wages payable (net pay)		64,950
Payroll tax expense (total)	13,650	
Social Security taxes payable (employer's matching amount)		6,200
Medicare taxes payable (employer's matching amount)		**1,450**
FUTA payable (federal unemployment tax: 0.6%)		600
State unemployment tax payable (5.4%)		5,400
Salaries and wages expense (fringe benefits)	4,900	
Payable to Blue Cross (insurance premiums—70%)		700
Payable to Fidelity Investments (employer's matching amount)		**4,000**
Payable to Prudential life (insurance premiums)		200

Questions For Review of Key Topics

Q 13–1 What are the essential characteristics of liabilities for purposes of financial reporting?

Q 13–2 What distinguishes current liabilities from long-term liabilities?

Q 13–3 Bronson Distributors owes a supplier $100,000 on open account. The amount is payable in three months. What is the theoretically correct way to measure the reportable amount for this liability? In practice, how will it likely be reported? Why?

Q 13–4 Bank loans often are arranged under existing lines of credit. What is a line of credit? How does a noncommitted line of credit differ from a committed line?

Q 13–5 Banks sometimes loan cash under noninterest-bearing notes. Is it true that banks lend money without interest?

Q 13–6 How does commercial paper differ from a bank loan? Why is the interest rate often less for commercial paper?

Q 13–7 Salaries of $5,000 have been earned by employees by the end of the period but will not be paid to employees until the following period. How should the expense and related liability be recorded? Why?

Q 13–8 Under what conditions should an employer accrue an expense and the related liability for employees' compensation for future absences? How do company custom and practice affect the accrual decision?

Q 13–9 How are refundable deposits and customer advances similar? How do they differ?

Q 13–10 How do companies account for gift cards?

Q 13–11 Amounts collected for third parties represent liabilities until remitted. Provide several examples of this kind of collection.

Q 13–12 When companies have debt that is not due to be paid for several years but that is callable (due on demand) by the creditor, do they classify the debt as current or as long-term?

Q 13–13 Long-term obligations usually are reclassified and reported as current liabilities when they become payable within the upcoming year (or operating cycle, if longer than a year). So, a 25-year bond issue is reported as a long-term liability for 24 years but normally is reported as a current liability on the balance sheet prepared during the 25th year of its term to maturity. Name a situation in which this would not be the case.

IFRS **Q 13–14** How do IFRS and U.S. GAAP differ with respect to the classification of debt that is expected to be refinanced?

Q 13–15 Define a loss contingency. Provide three examples.

Q 13–16 List and briefly describe the three categories of likelihood that a future event(s) will confirm the incurrence of the liability for a loss contingency.

Q 13–17 Under what circumstances should a loss contingency be accrued?

IFRS **Q 13–18** What is the difference between the use of the term *contingent liability* in U.S. GAAP and IFRS?

Q 13–19 Suppose the analysis of a loss contingency indicates that an obligation is not probable. What accounting treatment, if any, is warranted?

Q 13–20 Name two loss contingencies that almost always are accrued.

Q 13–21 Distinguish between the accounting treatment of a manufacturer's warranty and an extended warranty. Why the difference?

Q 13–22 At December 31, the end of the reporting period, the analysis of a loss contingency indicates that an obligation is only reasonably possible, though its dollar amount is readily estimable. During February, before the financial statements are issued, new information indicates the loss is probable. What accounting treatment is warranted?

Q 13–23 After the end of the reporting period, a contingency comes into existence. Under what circumstances, if any, should the contingency be reported in the financial statements for the period ended?

IFRS **Q 13–24** How do U.S. GAAP and IFRS differ in their treatment of a range of equally likely losses?

IFRS **Q 13–25** How do U.S. GAAP and IFRS differ in their use of present values when measuring contingent liabilities?

Q 13–26 Suppose the Environmental Protection Agency is in the process of investigating Ozone Ruination Limited for possible environmental damage but has not proposed a penalty as of December 31, 2017, the company's fiscal year-end. Describe the two-step process involved in deciding how this unasserted assessment should be reported.

Q 13–27 You are the plaintiff in a lawsuit. Your legal counsel advises that your eventual victory is inevitable. "You will be awarded $12 million," your attorney confidently asserts. Describe the appropriate accounting treatment.

IFRS **Q 13–28** Answer Q 13-27, but assume that you report under IFRS.

Brief Exercises

connect

BE 13–1
Bank loan; accrued interest
● LO13–2

On October 1, Eder Fabrication borrowed $60 million and issued a nine-month, 12% promissory note. Interest was payable at maturity. Prepare the journal entry for the issuance of the note and the appropriate adjusting entry for the note at December 31, the end of the reporting period.

BE 13–2
Non-interest-bearing note; accrued interest
● LO13–2

On October 1, Eder Fabrication borrowed $60 million and issued a nine-month promissory note. Interest was discounted at issuance at a 12% discount rate. Prepare the journal entry for the issuance of the note and the appropriate adjusting entry for the note at December 31, the end of the reporting period.

BE 13–3
Determining accrued interest
● LO13–2

On July 1, Orcas Lab issued a $100,000, 12%, eight-month note. Interest is payable at maturity. What is the amount of interest expense that should be recorded in a year-end adjusting entry if the fiscal year-end is (a) December 31? (b) September 30?

BE 13–4
Commercial paper
● LO13–2

Branch Corporation issued $12 million of commercial paper on March 1 on a nine-month note. Interest was discounted at issuance at a 9% discount rate. Prepare the journal entry for the issuance of the commercial paper and its repayment at maturity.

BE 13–5
Non-interest-bearing note; effective interest rate
● LO13–2

Life.com issued $10 million of commercial paper on April 1 on a nine-month note. Interest was discounted at issuance at a 6% discount rate. What is the effective interest rate on the commercial paper?

BE 13–6
Advance collection
● LO13–3

On December 12, 2018, Pace Electronics received $24,000 from a customer toward a cash sale of $240,000 of diodes to be completed on January 16, 2019. What journal entries should Pace record on December 12 and January 16?

BE 13–7
Advance collection
● LO13–3

In Lizzie Shoes' experience, gift cards that have not been redeemed within 12 months are not likely to be redeemed. Lizzie Shoes sold gift cards for $18,000 during August 2018. $4,000 of cards were redeemed in September 2018, $3,000 in October, $2,500 in November, and $2,000 in December 2018. In 2019 an additional $1,000 of cards were redeemed in January and $500 in February. How much gift card revenue associated with the August 2018 gift card sales would Lizzie get to recognize in 2018 and 2019?

BE 13–8
Sales tax
● LO13–3

During December, Rainey Equipment made a $600,000 credit sale. The state sales tax rate is 6% and the local sales tax rate is 1.5%. Prepare the appropriate journal entry.

BE 13–9
Classifying debt
● LO13–4

Consider the following liabilities of Future Brands, Inc., at December 31, 2018, the company's fiscal year-end. Should they be reported as current liabilities or long-term liabilities?

1. $77 million of 8% notes are due on May 31, 2022. The notes are callable by the company's bank, beginning March 1, 2019.
2. $102 million of 8% notes are due on May 31, 2023. A debt covenant requires Future to maintain a current ratio (ratio of current assets to current liabilities) of at least 2 to 1. Future is in violation of this requirement but has obtained a waiver from the bank until May 2019, since both companies feel Future will correct the situation during the first half of 2019.

BE 13–10
Refinancing debt
● LO13–4

Coulson Company is in the process of refinancing some long-term debt. Its fiscal year ends on December 31, 2018, and its financial statements will be issued on March 15, 2019. Under current U.S. GAAP, how would the debt be classified if the refinancing is completed on December 15, 2016? What if instead it is completed on January 15, 2019?

BE 13–11
Refinancing debt
● LO13–4, LO13–7
IFRS

Fleener Company is in the process of refinancing some long-term debt. Its fiscal year ends on December 31, 2016, and its financial statements will be issued on March 15, 2019. Under current IFRS, how would the debt be classified if the refinancing is completed on December 15, 2016? What if instead it is completed on January 15, 2019?

BE 13–12
Warranties
● LO13–5, LO13–6

Right Medical introduced a new implant that carries a five-year warranty against manufacturer's defects. Based on industry experience with similar product introductions, warranty costs are expected to approximate 1% of sales. Sales were $15 million and actual warranty expenditures were $20,000 for the first year of selling the product. What amount (if any) should Right report as a liability at the end of the year?

BE 13–13
Product recall
● LO13–5, LO13–6

Consultants notified management of Goo Goo Baby Products that a crib toy poses a potential health hazard. Counsel indicated that a product recall is probable and is estimated to cost the company $5.5 million. How will this affect the company's income statement and balance sheet this period?

BE 13–14
Contingency
● LO13–5, LO13–6

Skill Hardware is the plaintiff in a $16 million lawsuit filed against a supplier. The litigation is in final appeal and legal counsel advises that it is virtually certain that Skill will win the lawsuit and be awarded $12 million. How should Skill account for this event?

BE 13–15
Contingency
● LO13–5, LO13–6

Bell International can estimate the amount of loss that will occur if a foreign government expropriates some company property. Expropriation is considered reasonably possible. How should Bell report the loss contingency?

BE 13–16
Contingencies
● LO13–5, LO13–6

Household Solutions manufactures kitchen storage products. During the year, the company became aware of potential costs due to (1) a recently filed lawsuit for patent infringement for which the probability of loss is remote and damages can be reasonably estimated, (2) another recently filed lawsuit for food contamination by the plastics used in Household Solutions' products for which a loss is probable but the amount of loss cannot be reasonably estimated, and (3) a new product warranty that is probable and can be reasonably estimated. Which, if any, of these costs should be accrued?

BE 13–17
Contingencies
● LO13–5, LO13–6, LO13–7
IFRS

Quandary Corporation has a major customer who is alleging a significant product defect. Quandary engineers and attorneys have analyzed the claim and have concluded that there is a 51% chance that the customer would be successful in court and that a successful claim would result in a range of damages from $10 million to $20 million, with each part of the range equally likely to occur. The damages would need to be paid soon enough that time-value-of-money considerations are not material. Would a liability be accrued under U.S. GAAP? Under IFRS? If a liability were accrued, what amount would be accrued under U.S. GAAP? Under IFRS?

BE 13–18
Unasserted assessment
● LO13–5, LO13–6

At March 13, 2019, the Securities Exchange Commission is in the process of investigating a possible securities law violation by Now Chemical. The SEC has not yet proposed a penalty assessment. Now's fiscal year ends on December 31, 2018, and its financial statements are published in March 2019. Management feels an assessment is *reasonably possible,* and if an assessment is made, an unfavorable settlement of $13 million is *probable.* What, if any, action should Now take for its financial statements?

Exercises

connect

E 13–1
Bank loan; accrued interest
LO13–2

On November 1, 2018, Quantum Technology, a geothermal energy supplier, borrowed $16 million cash to fund a geological survey. The loan was made by Nevada BancCorp under a noncommitted short-term line of credit arrangement. Quantum issued a nine-month, 12% promissory note. Interest was payable at maturity. Quantum's fiscal period is the calendar year.

Required:

1. Prepare the journal entry for the issuance of the note by Quantum Technology.
2. Prepare the appropriate adjusting entry for the note by Quantum on December 31, 2018.
3. Prepare the journal entry for the payment of the note at maturity.

E 13–2
Determining accrued interest in various situations
LO13–2

On July 1, 2018, Ross-Livermore Industries issued nine-month notes in the amount of $400 million. Interest is payable at maturity.

Required:

Determine the amount of interest expense that should be recorded in a year-end adjusting entry under each of the following independent assumptions:

	Interest Rate	Fiscal Year-End
1.	12%	December 31
2.	10%	September 30
3.	9%	October 31
4.	6%	January 31

E 13–3
Short-term notes
LO13–2

The following selected transactions relate to liabilities of United Insulation Corporation. United's fiscal year ends on December 31.

Required:

Prepare the appropriate journal entries through the maturity of each liability.

2018	
Jan. 13	Negotiated a revolving credit agreement with Parish Bank that can be renewed annually upon bank approval. The amount available under the line of credit is $20 million at the bank's prime rate.
Feb. 1	Arranged a three-month bank loan of $5 million with Parish Bank under the line of credit agreement. Interest at the prime rate of 10% was payable at maturity.
May 1	Paid the 10% note at maturity.
Dec. 1	Supported by the credit line, issued $10 million of commercial paper on a nine-month note. Interest was discounted at issuance at a 9% discount rate.
31	Recorded any necessary adjusting entry(s).
2019	
Sept. 1	Paid the commercial paper at maturity.

E 13–4
Paid future absences
LO13–3

JWS Transport Company's employees earn vacation time at the rate of 1 hour per 40-hour work period. The vacation pay vests immediately (that is, an employee is entitled to the pay even if employment terminates). During 2018, total wages paid to employees equaled $404,000, including $4,000 for vacations actually taken in 2018 but not including vacations related to 2018 that will be taken in 2019. All vacations earned before 2018 were taken before January 1, 2018. No accrual entries have been made for the vacations. No overtime premium and no bonuses were paid during the period.

Required:

Prepare the appropriate adjusting entry for vacations earned but not taken in 2018.

E 13–5
Paid future absences
LO13–3

On January 1, 2018, Poplar Fabricators Corporation agreed to grant its employees two weeks of vacation each year, with the stipulation that vacations earned each year can be taken the following year. For the year ended December 31, 2018, Poplar Fabricators' employees each earned an average of $900 per week. Seven hundred vacation weeks earned in 2018 were not taken during 2018.

Required:

1. Prepare the appropriate adjusting entry for vacations earned but not taken in 2018.
2. Suppose that, by the time vacations actually are taken in 2019, wage rates for employees have risen by an average of 5 percent from their 2018 level. Also, assume wages earned in 2019 (including vacations earned and taken in 2019) were $31 million. Prepare a journal entry that summarizes 2019 wages and the payment for 2018 vacations taken in 2019.

E 13–6
Customer advances; sales taxes
● LO13–3

Bavarian Bar and Grill opened for business in November 2018. During its first two months of operation, the restaurant sold gift certificates in various amounts totaling $5,200, mostly as Christmas presents. They are redeemable for meals within two years of the purchase date, although experience within the industry indicates that 80% of gift certificates are redeemed within one year. Certificates totaling $1,300 were presented for redemption during 2018 for meals having a total price of $2,100. The sales tax rate on restaurant sales is 4%, assessed at the time meals (not gift certificates) are purchased. Sales taxes will be remitted in January.

Required:

1. Prepare the appropriate journal entries (in summary form) for the gift certificates sold during 2018 (keeping in mind that, in actuality, each sale of a gift certificate or a meal would be recorded individually).
2. Determine the liability for gift certificates to be reported on the December 31, 2018, balance sheet.
3. What is the appropriate classification (current or noncurrent) of the liabilities at December 31, 2018? Why?

E 13–7
Customer deposits
● LO13–3

Diversified Semiconductors sells perishable electronic components. Some must be shipped and stored in reusable protective containers. Customers pay a deposit for each container received. The deposit is equal to the container's cost. They receive a refund when the container is returned. During 2018, deposits collected on containers shipped were $850,000.

Deposits are forfeited if containers are not returned within 18 months. Containers held by customers at January 1, 2018, represented deposits of $530,000. In 2018, $790,000 was refunded and deposits forfeited were $35,000.

Required:

1. Prepare the appropriate journal entries for the deposits received and returned during 2018.
2. Determine the liability for refundable deposits to be reported on the December 31, 2018, balance sheet.

E 13–8
Various transactions involving advance collections
● LO13–3

The following selected transactions relate to liabilities of Interstate Farm Implements for December 2018. Interstate's fiscal year ends on December 31.

Required:

Prepare the appropriate journal entries for these transactions.

1. On December 15, received $7,500 from Bradley Farms toward the purchase of a $98,000 tractor to be delivered on January 6, 2019.
2. During December, received $25,500 of refundable deposits relating to containers used to transport equipment parts.
3. During December, credit sales totaled $800,000. The state sales tax rate is 5% and the local sales tax rate is 2%. (This is a summary journal entry for the many individual sales transactions for the period).

E 13–9
Gift cards
● LO13–3

CircuitTown commenced a gift card program in January 2018 and sold $10,000 of gift cards in January, $15,000 in February, and $16,000 in March 2018 before discontinuing further gift card sales. During 2018, gift card redemptions were $6,000 for the January gift cards sold, $4,500 for the February cards, and $4,000 for the March cards. CircuitTown considers gift cards to be "broken" (not redeemable) 10 months after sale.

Required:

1. How much revenue will CircuitTown recognize with respect to January gift card sales during 2018?
2. Prepare journal entries to record the sale of January gift cards, redemption of gift cards (ignore sales tax), and breakage (expiration) of gift cards.
3. How much revenue will CircuitTown recognize with respect to March gift card sales during 2018?
4. What liability for deferred revenue associated with gift card sales would CircuitTown show as of December 31, 2018?

E 13–10
FASB codification research
● LO13–3, LO13–4, LO13–5

Access the *FASB Accounting Standards Codification* at the FASB website (www.fasb.org).

Required:

Determine the specific citation for accounting for each of the following items:

1. If it is only reasonably possible that a contingent loss will occur, the contingent loss should be disclosed.
2. Criteria allowing short-term liabilities expected to be refinanced to be classified as long-term liabilities.
3. Accounting for the revenue from separately priced extended warranty contracts.
4. The criteria to determine if an employer must accrue a liability for vacation pay.

E 13–11
Current–noncurrent classification of debt; Sprint Corporation
● LO13–1, LO13–4

An annual report of **Sprint Corporation** contained a rather lengthy narrative entitled "Review of Segmental Results of Operation." The narrative noted that short-term notes payable and commercial paper outstanding at the end of the year aggregated $756 million and that during the following year, "This entire balance will be replaced by the issuance of long-term debt or will continue to be refinanced under existing long-term credit facilities."

Required:

How did Sprint report the debt in its balance sheet? Why?

E 13–12
Current–noncurrent classification of debt; Sprint Corporation
● LO13–1, LO13–4, LO13–7
IFRS

Consider the information presented in E 13–11.

Required:

1. How would Sprint report the debt in its balance sheet if it reported under IFRS? Why?
2. Would your answer to requirement 1 change if Sprint obtained its long-term credit facility after the balance sheet date? Why?

E 13–13
Current–noncurrent classification of debt
● LO13–1, LO13–4

At December 31, 2018, Newman Engineering's liabilities include the following:

1. \$10 million of 9% bonds were issued for \$10 million on May 31, 1999. The bonds mature on May 31, 2029, but bondholders have the option of calling (demanding payment on) the bonds on May 31, 2019. However, the option to call is not expected to be exercised, given prevailing market conditions.
2. \$14 million of 8% notes are due on May 31, 2022. A debt covenant requires Newman to maintain current assets at least equal to 175% of its current liabilities. On December 31, 2018, Newman is in violation of this covenant. Newman obtained a waiver from National City Bank until June 2019, having convinced the bank that the company's normal 2 to 1 ratio of current assets to current liabilities will be reestablished during the first half of 2019.
3. \$7 million of 11% bonds were issued for \$7 million on August 1, 1989. The bonds mature on July 31, 2019. Sufficient cash is expected to be available to retire the bonds at maturity.

Required:

What portion of the debt can be excluded from classification as a current liability (that is, reported as a noncurrent liability)? Explain.

E 13–14
FASB codification research
● LO13–5
CODE

Access the *FASB Accounting Standards Codification* at the FASB website (www.fasb.org).

Required:

1. Obtain the relevant authoritative literature on recognition of contingent losses. What is the specific citation that describes the guidelines for determining when an expense and liability should be accrued for a contingent loss?
2. List the guidelines.

E 13–15
Warranties
● LO13–5, LO13–6

Cupola Awning Corporation introduced a new line of commercial awnings in 2018 that carry a two-year warranty against manufacturer's defects. Based on their experience with previous product introductions, warranty costs are expected to approximate 3% of sales. Sales and actual warranty expenditures for the first year of selling the product were:

Sales	Actual Warranty Expenditures
\$5,000,000	\$37,500

Required:

1. Does this situation represent a loss contingency? Why or why not? How should Cupola account for it?
2. Prepare journal entries that summarize sales of the awnings (assume all credit sales) and any aspects of the warranty that should be recorded during 2018.
3. What amount should Cupola report as a liability at December 31, 2018?

E 13–16
Extended warranties
● LO13–5, LO13–6

Carnes Electronics sells consumer electronics that carry a 90-day manufacturer's warranty. At the time of purchase, customers are offered the opportunity to also buy a two-year extended warranty for an additional charge. During the year, Carnes received \$412,000 for these extended warranties (approximately evenly throughout the year).

Required:

1. Does this situation represent a loss contingency? Why or why not? How should it be accounted for?
2. Prepare journal entries that summarize sales of the extended warranties (assume all credit sales) and any aspects of the warranty that should be recorded during the year.

E 13–17
Contingency; product recall
● LO13–5, LO13–6

Sound Audio manufactures and sells audio equipment for automobiles. Engineers notified management in December 2018 of a circuit flaw in an amplifier that poses a potential fire hazard. An intense investigation indicated that a product recall is virtually certain, estimated to cost the company $2 million. The fiscal year ends on December 31.

Required:

1. Should this loss contingency be accrued, only disclosed, or neither? Explain.
2. What loss, if any, should Sound Audio report in its 2018 income statement?
3. What liability, if any, should Sound Audio report in its 2018 balance sheet?
4. Prepare any journal entry needed.

E 13–18
Impairment of accounts receivable
● LO13–5, LO13–6

The Manda Panda Company uses the allowance method to account for bad debts. At the beginning of 2018, the allowance account had a credit balance of $75,000. Credit sales for 2018 totaled $2,400,000 and the year-end accounts receivable balance was $490,000. During this year, $73,000 in receivables were determined to be uncollectible. Manda Panda anticipates that 3% of all credit sales will ultimately become uncollectible. The fiscal year ends on December 31.

Required:

1. Does this situation describe a loss contingency? Explain.
2. What is the bad debt expense that Manda Panda should report in its 2018 income statement?
3. Prepare the appropriate journal entry to record the contingency.
4. What is the net accounts receivable value Manda Panda should report in its 2018 balance sheet?

E 13–19
Unasserted assessment
● LO13–6

At April 1, 2019, the Food and Drug Administration is in the process of investigating allegations of false marketing claims by Hulkly Muscle Supplements. The FDA has not yet proposed a penalty assessment. Hulkly's fiscal year ends on December 31, 2018. The company's financial statements are issued in April 2019.

Required:

For each of the following scenarios, determine the appropriate way to report the situation. Explain your reasoning and prepare any necessary journal entry.

1. Management feels an assessment is *reasonably possible,* and if an assessment is made, an unfavorable settlement of $13 million is *reasonably possible.*
2. Management feels an assessment is *reasonably possible,* and if an assessment is made, an unfavorable settlement of $13 million is *probable.*
3. Management feels an assessment is *probable,* and if an assessment is made, an unfavorable settlement of $13 million is *reasonably possible.*
4. Management feels an assessment is *probable,* and if an assessment is made, an unfavorable settlement of $13 million is *probable.*

E 13–20
Various transactions involving contingencies
● LO13–5, LO13–6

The following selected transactions relate to contingencies of Classical Tool Makers, Inc., which began operations in July 2018. Classical's fiscal year ends on December 31. Financial statements are issued in April 2019.

Required:

Prepare the year-end entries for any amounts that should be recorded as a result of each of these contingencies and indicate whether a disclosure note is indicated.

1. Classical's products carry a one-year warranty against manufacturer's defects. Based on previous experience, warranty costs are expected to approximate 4% of sales. Sales were $2 million (all credit) for 2018. Actual warranty expenditures were $30,800 and were recorded as warranty expense when incurred.
2. Although no customer accounts have been shown to be uncollectible, Classical estimates that 2% of credit sales will eventually prove uncollectible.
3. In December 2018, the state of Tennessee filed suit against Classical, seeking penalties for violations of clean air laws. On January 23, 2019, Classical reached a settlement with state authorities to pay $1.5 million in penalties.
4. Classical is the plaintiff in a $4 million lawsuit filed against a supplier. The suit is in final appeal and attorneys advise that it is virtually certain that Classical will win the case and be awarded $2.5 million.
5. In November 2018, Classical became aware of a design flaw in an industrial saw that poses a potential electrical hazard. A product recall appears unavoidable. Such an action would likely cost the company $500,000.
6. Classical offered $25 cash rebates on a new model of jigsaw. Customers must mail in a proof-of-purchase seal from the package plus the cash register receipt to receive the rebate. Experience suggests that 60% of the rebates will be claimed. Ten thousand of the jigsaws were sold in 2018. Total rebates to customers in 2018 were $105,000 and were recorded as promotional expense when paid.

E 13–21
Various transactions involving contingencies
● LO13–5, LO13–6

The following selected circumstances relate to pending lawsuits for Erismus, Inc. Erismus's fiscal year ends on December 31. Financial statements are issued in March 2019. Erismus prepares its financial statements according to U.S. GAAP.

Required:

Indicate the amount of asset or liability that Erismus would record, and explain your answer.

1. Erismus is defending against a lawsuit. Erismus's management believes the company has a slightly worse than 50/50 chance of eventually prevailing in court, and that if it loses, the judgment will be $1,000,000.
2. Erismus is defending against a lawsuit. Erismus's management believes it is probable that the company will lose in court. If it loses, management believes that damages could fall anywhere in the range of $2,000,000 to $4,000,000, with any damage in that range equally likely.
3. Erismus is defending against a lawsuit. Erismus's management believes it is probable that the company will lose in court. If it loses, management believes that damages will eventually be $5,000,000, with a present value of $3,500,000.
4. Erismus is a plaintiff in a lawsuit. Erismus's management believes it is probable that the company eventually will prevail in court, and that if it prevails, the judgment will be $1,000,000.
5. Erismus is a plaintiff in a lawsuit. Erismus's management believes it is virtually certain that the company eventually will prevail in court, and that if it prevails, the judgment will be $500,000.

E 13–22
Various transactions involving contingencies; IFRS
● LO13–5, LO13–6, LO13–7
IFRS

[This exercise is a variation of E 13–21 focusing on reporting under IFRS]. Refer to the circumstances listed in E 13–21, but assume that Erismus prepares its financial statements according to International Financial Reporting Standards.

Required:

For each circumstance, indicate the amount of asset or liability that Erismus would record, and explain your answer.

E 13–23
Disclosures of liabilities
● LO13–1 though LO13–6

Indicate (by letter) the way each of the items listed below should be reported in a balance sheet at December 31, 2018.

Item	Reporting Method
_____ 1. Commercial paper	N. Not reported
_____ 2. Noncommitted line of credit	C. Current liability
_____ 3. Customer advances	L. Long-term liability
_____ 4. Estimated quality-assurance warranty cost	D. Disclosure note only
_____ 5. Accounts payable	A. Asset
_____ 6. Long-term bonds that will be callable by the creditor in the upcoming year unless an existing violation is not corrected (there is a reasonable possibility the violation will be corrected within the grace period)	
_____ 7. Note due March 3, 2019	
_____ 8. Interest accrued on note, December 31, 2018	
_____ 9. Short-term bank loan to be paid with proceeds of sale of common stock	
_____ 10. A determinable gain that is contingent on a future event that appears extremely likely to occur in three months	
_____ 11. Unasserted assessment of back taxes that probably will he asserted, in which case there would probably be a loss in six months	
_____ 12. Unasserted assessment of back taxes with a reasonable possibility of being asserted, in which case there would probably be a loss in 13 months	
_____ 13. A determinable loss from a past event that is contingent on a future event that appears extremely likely to occur in three months	
_____ 14. Note payable due April 4, 2021	
_____ 15. Long-term bonds callable by the creditor in the upcoming year that are not expected to be called	

E 13–24
Warranty expense; change in estimate
● LO13–5, LO13–6

Woodmier Lawn Products introduced a new line of commercial sprinklers in 2017 that carry a one-year warranty against manufacturer's defects. Because this was the first product for which the company offered a warranty, trade publications were consulted to determine the experience of others in the industry. Based on that experience, warranty costs were expected to approximate 2% of sales. Sales of the sprinklers in 2017 were $2.5 million. Accordingly, the following entries relating to the contingency for warranty costs were recorded during the first year of selling the product:

Accrued liability and expense		
Warranty expense (2% × $2,500,000)	50,000	
Estimated warranty liability		50,000
Actual expenditures (summary entry)		
Estimated warranty liability	23,000	
Cash, wages payable, parts and supplies, etc		23,000

In late 2018, the company's claims experience was evaluated and it was determined that claims were far more than expected—3% of sales rather than 2%.

Required:

1. Assuming sales of the sprinklers in 2018 were $3.6 million and warranty expenditures in 2018 totaled $88,000, prepare any journal entries related to the warranty.
2. Assuming sales of the sprinklers were discontinued after 2017, prepare any journal entry(s) in 2018 related to the warranty.

E 13–25
Change in accounting estimate
● LO13–3

The Commonwealth of Virginia filed suit in October 2016 against Northern Timber Corporation, seeking civil penalties and injunctive relief for violations of environmental laws regulating forest conservation. When the 2017 financial statements were issued in 2018, Northern had not reached a settlement with state authorities, but legal counsel advised Northern Timber that it was probable the ultimate settlement would be $1,000,000 in penalties. The following entry was recorded:

Loss—litigation	1,000,000	
Liability—litigation		1,000,000

Late in 2018, a settlement was reached with state authorities to pay a total of $600,000 to cover the cost of violations.

Required:

1. Prepare any journal entries related to the change.
2. Briefly describe other steps Northern should take to report the change.

E 13–26
Contingency; Dow Chemical Company disclosure
● LO13–5, LO13–6
Real World Financials

The Dow Chemical Company provides chemical, plastic, and agricultural products and services to various consumer markets. The following excerpt is taken from the disclosure notes of Dow's 2015 annual report:

> In total, the Company's accrued liability for probable environmental remediation and restoration costs was $670 million at December 31, 2015, compared with $706 million at the end of 2014. This is management's best estimate of the costs for remediation and restoration with respect to environmental matters for which the Company has accrued liabilities, although it is reasonably possible that the ultimate cost with respect to these particular matters could range up to approximately two and a half times that amount.

Required:

Does the excerpt describe a loss contingency? Under what conditions would Dow accrue such a contingency? What journal entry would Dow use to record this amount of provision (loss)?

E 13–27
Payroll-related liabilities
● Appendix

Lee Financial Services pays employees monthly. Payroll information is listed below for January 2018, the first month of Lee's fiscal year. Assume that none of the employees exceeded any relevant wage base.

Salaries	$500,000
Federal income taxes to be withheld	100,000
Federal unemployment tax rate	0.60%
State unemployment tax rate (after FUTA deduction)	5.40%
Social Security tax rate	6.2%
Medicare tax rate	1.45%

Required:

Prepare the appropriate journal entries to record salaries and wages expense and payroll tax expense for the January 2018 pay period.

Problems

connect

P 13–1
Bank loan; accrued interest
● LO13–2

Blanton Plastics, a household plastic product manufacturer, borrowed $14 million cash on October 1, 2018, to provide working capital for year-end production. Blanton issued a four-month, 12% promissory note to L&T Bank under a prearranged short-term line of credit. Interest on the note was payable at maturity. Each firm's fiscal period is the calendar year.

Required:

1. Prepare the journal entries to record (a) the issuance of the note by Blanton Plastics and (b) L&T Bank's receivable on October 1, 2018.
2. Prepare the journal entries by both firms to record all subsequent events related to the note through January 31, 2019.
3. Suppose the face amount of the note was adjusted to include interest (a noninterest-bearing note) and 12% is the bank's stated discount rate. (a) Prepare the journal entries to record the issuance of the noninterest-bearing note by Blanton Plastics on October 1, 2018, the adjusting entry at December 31, and payment of the note at maturity. (b) What would be the effective interest rate?

P 13–2
Various transactions involving liabilities
● LO13–2 through LO13–4

Camden Biotechnology began operations in September 2018. The following selected transactions relate to liabilities of the company for September 2018 through March 2019. Camden's fiscal year ends on December 31. Its financial statements are issued in April.

2018

a. On September 5, opened checking accounts at Second Commercial Bank and negotiated a short-term line of credit of up to $15,000,000 at the bank's prime rate (10.5% at the time). The company will pay no commitment fees.
b. On October 1, borrowed $12 million cash from Second Commercial Bank under the line of credit and issued a five-month promissory note. Interest at the prime rate of 10% was payable at maturity. Management planned to issue 10-year bonds in February to repay the note.
c. Received $2,600 of refundable deposits in December for reusable containers used to transport and store chemical-based products.
d. For the September–December period, sales on account totaled $4,100,000. The state sales tax rate is 3% and the local sales tax rate is 3%. (This is a summary journal entry for the many individual sales transactions for the period.)
e. Recorded the adjusting entry for accrued interest.

2019

f. In February, issued $10 million of 10-year bonds at face value and paid the bank loan on the March 1 due date.
g. Half of the storage containers covered by refundable deposits were returned in March. The remaining containers are expected to be returned during the next six months.

Required:

1. Prepare the appropriate journal entries for these transactions.
2. Prepare the current and long-term liability sections of the December 31, 2018, balance sheet. Trade accounts payable on that date were $252,000.

P 13–3
Current–noncurrent classification of debt
● LO13–1, LO13–4

The balance sheet at December 31, 2018, for Nevada Harvester Corporation includes the liabilities listed below:

a. 11% bonds with a face amount of $40 million were issued for $40 million on October 31, 2009. The bonds mature on October 31, 2029. Bondholders have the option of calling (demanding payment on) the bonds on October 31, 2019, at a redemption price of $40 million. Market conditions are such that the call is not expected to be exercised.
b. Management intended to refinance $6 million of its 10% notes that mature in May 2019. In early March, prior to the actual issuance of the 2018 financial statements, Nevada Harvester negotiated a line of credit with a commercial bank for up to $5 million any time during 2019. Any borrowings will mature two years from the date of borrowing.
c. Noncallable 12% bonds with a face amount of $20 million were issued for $20 million on September 30, 1996. The bonds mature on September 30, 2019. Sufficient cash is expected to be available to retire the bonds at maturity.
d. A $12 million 9% bank loan is payable on October 31, 2024. The bank has the right to demand payment after any fiscal year-end in which Nevada Harvester's ratio of current assets to current liabilities falls below a

contractual minimum of 1.7 to 1 and remains so for six months. That ratio was 1.45 on December 31, 2018, due primarily to an intentional temporary decline in inventory levels. Normal inventory levels will be reestablished during the first quarter of 2019.

Required:

1. Determine the amount that can be excluded from classification as a current liability (that is, reported as a noncurrent liability) for each. Explain the reasoning behind your classifications.
2. Prepare the liability section of a classified balance sheet and any necessary note disclosure for Nevada Harvester at December 31, 2018. Accounts payable and accruals are $22 million.

P 13–4
Various liabilities
● LO13–1 through LO13–4

The unadjusted trial balance of the Manufacturing Equitable at December 31, 2018, the end of its fiscal year, included the following account balances. Manufacturing's 2018 financial statements were issued on April 1, 2019.

Accounts receivable	$ 92,500
Accounts payable	35,000
Bank notes payable	600,000
Mortgage note payable	1,200,000

Other information:

a. The bank notes, issued August 1, 2018, are due on July 31, 2019, and pay interest at a rate of 10%, payable at maturity.

b. The mortgage note is due on March 1, 2019. Interest at 9% has been paid up to December 31 (assume 9% is a realistic rate). Manufacturing intended at December 31, 2018, to refinance the note on its due date with a new 10-year mortgage note. In fact, on March 1, Manufacturing paid $250,000 in cash on the principal balance and refinanced the remaining $950,000.

c. Included in the accounts receivable balance at December 31, 2018, were two subsidiary accounts that had been overpaid and had credit balances totaling $18,000. The accounts were of two major customers who were expected to order more merchandise from Manufacturing and apply the overpayments to those future purchases.

d. On November 1, 2018, Manufacturing rented a portion of its factory to a tenant for $30,000 per year, payable in advance. The payment for the 12 months ended October 31, 2019, was received as required and was credited to rent revenue.

Required:

1. Prepare any necessary adjusting journal entries at December 31, 2018, pertaining to each item of other information (a–d).
2. Prepare the current and long-term liability sections of the December 31, 2018, balance sheet.

P 13–5
Bonus compensation; algebra
● LO13–3

Sometimes compensation packages include bonuses designed to provide performance incentives to employees. The difficulty a bonus can cause accountants is not an accounting problem, but a math problem. The complication is that the bonus formula sometimes specifies that the calculation of the bonus is based in part on the bonus itself. This occurs any time the bonus is a percentage of income because expenses are components of income, and the bonus is an expense.

Regalia Fashions has an incentive compensation plan through which a division manager receives a bonus equal to 10% of the division's net income. Division income in 2018 before the bonus and income tax was $150,000. The tax rate is 30%.

Required:

1. Express the bonus formula as one or more algebraic equation(s).[34]
2. Using these formulas, calculate the amount of the bonus.
3. Prepare the adjusting entry to record the bonus compensation.
4. Bonus arrangements take many forms. Suppose the bonus specifies that the bonus is 10% of the division's income before tax, but after the bonus itself. Calculate the amount of the bonus.

P 13–6
Various contingencies
● LO13–5, LO13–6

Eastern Manufacturing is involved with several situations that possibly involve contingencies. Each is described below. Eastern's fiscal year ends December 31, and the 2018 financial statements are issued on March 15, 2019.

a. Eastern is involved in a lawsuit resulting from a dispute with a supplier. On February 3, 2019, judgment was rendered against Eastern in the amount of $107 million plus interest, a total of $122 million. Eastern plans to appeal the judgment and is unable to predict its outcome though it is not expected to have a material adverse effect on the company.

[34] Remember when you were studying algebra and you wondered if you would ever use it?

b. In November 2017, the State of Nevada filed suit against Eastern, seeking civil penalties and injunctive relief for violations of environmental laws regulating hazardous waste. On January 12, 2019, Eastern reached a settlement with state authorities. Based upon discussions with legal counsel, the Company feels it is probable that $140 million will be required to cover the cost of violations. Eastern believes that the ultimate settlement of this claim will not have a material adverse effect on the company.

c. Eastern is the plaintiff in a $200 million lawsuit filed against United Steel for damages due to lost profits from rejected contracts and for unpaid receivables. The case is in final appeal and legal counsel advises that it is probable that Eastern will prevail and be awarded $100 million.

d. At March 15, 2019, Eastern knows a competitor has threatened litigation due to patent infringement. The competitor has not yet filed a lawsuit. Management believes a lawsuit is reasonably possible, and if a lawsuit is filed, management believes damages of up to $33 million are reasonably possible.

Required:

1. Determine the appropriate means of reporting each situation. Explain your reasoning.
2. Prepare any necessary journal entries and disclosure notes.

P 13–7
Various liabilities
● LO13–4, LO13–5, LO13–6, LO13–7
IFRS

HolmesWatson (HW) is considering what the effect would be of reporting its liabilities under IFRS rather than U.S. GAAP. The following facts apply:

a. HW is defending against a lawsuit and believes it is virtually certain to lose in court. If it loses the lawsuit, management estimates it will need to pay a range of damages that falls between $5,000,000 and $10,000,000, with each amount in that range equally likely.

b. HW is defending against another lawsuit that is identical to item (a), but the relevant losses will only occur far into the future. The present values of the endpoints of the range are $3,000,000 and $8,000,000, with the timing of cash flow somewhat uncertain. HW considers these effects of the time value of money to be material.

c. HW is defending against another lawsuit for which management believes HW has a slightly worse than 50/50 chance of losing in court. If it loses the lawsuit, management estimates HW will need to pay a range of damages that falls between $3,000,000 and $9,000,000, with each amount in that range equally likely.

d. HW has $10,000,000 of short-term debt that it intends to refinance on a long-term basis. Soon after the balance sheet date, but before issuance of the financial statements, HW obtained the financing necessary to refinance the debt.

Required:

1. For each item, indicate how treatment of the amount would differ between U.S. GAAP and IFRS.
2. Consider the total effect of items a–d. If HW's goal is to show the lowest total liabilities, which set of standards, U.S. GAAP or IFRS, best helps it meet that goal?

P 13–8
Expected cash flow approach; product recall
● LO13–6

The Heinrich Tire Company recalled a tire in its subcompact line in December 2018. Costs associated with the recall were originally thought to approximate $50 million. Now, though, while management feels it is probable the company will incur substantial costs, all discussions indicate that $50 million is an excessive amount. Based on prior recalls in the industry, management has provided the following probability distribution for the potential loss:

Loss Amount	Probability
$40 million	20%
$30 million	50%
$20 million	30%

An arrangement with a consortium of distributors requires that all recall costs be settled at the end of 2019. The risk-free rate of interest is 5%.

Required:

1. By the traditional approach to measuring loss contingencies, what amount would Heinrich record at the end of 2018 for the loss and contingent liability?
2. For the remainder of this problem, apply the expected cash flow approach of *SFAC No. 7*. Estimate Heinrich's liability at the end of the 2018 fiscal year.
3. Prepare the journal entry to record the contingent liability (and loss).
4. Prepare the journal entry to accrue interest on the liability at the end of 2019.
5. Prepare the journal entry to pay the liability at the end of 2019, assuming the actual cost is $31 million. Heinrich records an additional loss if the actual costs are higher or a gain if the costs are lower.

P 13–9
Subsequent events
● LO13–6

Lincoln Chemicals became involved in investigations by the U.S. Environmental Protection Agency in regard to damages connected to waste disposal sites. Below are four possibilities regarding the timing of (A) the alleged damage caused by Lincoln, (B) an investigation by the EPA, (C) the EPA assessment of penalties, and (D) ultimate settlement. In each case, assume that Lincoln is unaware of any problem until an investigation is begun. Also assume that once the EPA investigation begins, it is probable that a damage assessment will ensue and that once an assessment is made by the EPA, it is reasonably possible that a determinable amount will be paid by Lincoln.

Required:

For each case, decide whether (1) a loss should be accrued in the financial statements with an explanatory note, (2) a disclosure note only should be provided, or (3) no disclosure is necessary.

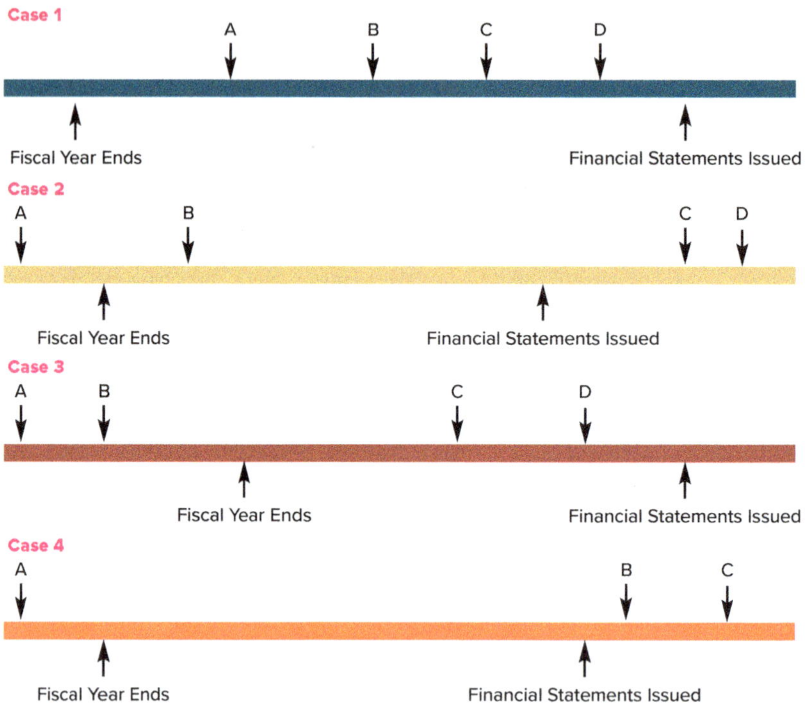

P 13–10
Subsequent events; classification of debt; loss contingency; financial statement effects
● LO13–4, LO13–5

Van Rushing Hunting Goods' fiscal year ends on December 31. At the end of the 2018 fiscal year, the company had notes payable of $12 million due on February 8, 2019. Rushing sold 2 million shares of its $0.25 par, common stock on February 3, 2019, for $9 million. The proceeds from that sale along with $3 million from the maturation of some 3-month CDs were used to pay the notes payable on February 8.

Through his attorney, one of Rushing's construction workers notified management on January 5, 2019, that he planned to sue the company for $1 million related to a work-site injury on December 20, 2018. As of December 31, 2018, management had been unaware of the injury, but reached an agreement on February 23, 2019, to settle the matter by paying the employee's medical bills of $75,000.

Rushing's financial statements were finalized on March 3, 2019.

Required:

1. What amount(s) if any, related to the situations described should Rushing report among current liabilities in its balance sheet at December 31, 2018? Why?
2. What amount(s) if any, related to the situations described should Rushing report among long-term liabilities in its balance sheet at December 31, 2018? Why?
3. How would your answers to requirements 1 and 2 differ if the settlement agreement had occurred on March 15, 2019, instead? Why?
4. How would your answers to requirements 1 and 2 differ if the work-site injury had occurred on January 3, 2019, instead? Why?

P 13–11
Concepts; terminology
● LO13–1 through LO13–4

Listed below are several terms and phrases associated with current liabilities. Pair each item from List A (by letter) with the item from List B that is most appropriately associated with it.

List A	List B
______ 1. Face amount × Interest rate × Time	a. Informal agreement
______ 2. Payable with current assets	b. Secured loan
______ 3. Short-term debt to be refinanced with common stock	c. Refinancing prior to the issuance of the financial statements
______ 4. Present value of interest plus present value of principal	d. Accounts payable
______ 5. Noninterest-bearing	e. Accrued liabilities
______ 6. Noncommitted line of credit	f. Commercial paper
______ 7. Pledged accounts receivable	g. Current liabilities
______ 8. Reclassification of debt	h. Long-term liability
______ 9. Purchased by other corporations	i. Usual valuation of liabilities
______10. Expenses not yet paid	j. Interest on debt
______11. Liability until refunded	k. Customer advances
______12. Applied against purchase price	l. Customer deposits

P 13–12
Various liabilities; balance sheet classification; prepare liability section of balance sheet; write notes
● LO13–4, LO13–5

Transit Airlines provides regional jet service in the Mid-South. The following is information on liabilities of Transit at December 31, 2018. Transit's fiscal year ends on December 31. Its annual financial statements are issued in April.

1. Transit has outstanding 6.5% bonds with a face amount of $90 million. The bonds mature on July 31, 2027. Bondholders have the option of calling (demanding payment on) the bonds on July 31, 2019, at a redemption price of $90 million. Market conditions are such that the call option is not expected to be exercised.
2. A $30 million 8% bank loan is payable on October 31, 2024. The bank has the right to demand payment after any fiscal year-end in which Transit's ratio of current assets to current liabilities falls below a contractual minimum of 1.9 to 1 and remains so for six months. That ratio was 1.75 on December 31, 2018, due primarily to an intentional temporary decline in parts inventories. Normal inventory levels will be reestablished during the sixth week of 2019.
3. Transit management intended to refinance $45 million of 7% notes that mature in May 2019. In late February 2019, prior to the issuance of the 2018 financial statements, Transit negotiated a line of credit with a commercial bank for up to $40 million any time during 2019. Any borrowings will mature two years from the date of borrowing.
4. Transit is involved in a lawsuit resulting from a dispute with a food caterer. On February 13, 2019, judgment was rendered against Transit in the amount of $53 million plus interest, a total of $54 million. Transit plans to appeal the judgment and is unable to predict its outcome though it is not expected to have a material adverse effect on the company.

Required:

1. How should the 6.5% bonds be classified by Transit among liabilities in its balance sheet? Explain.
2. How should the 8% bank loan be classified by Transit among liabilities in its balance sheet? Explain.
3. How should the 7% notes be classified by Transit among liabilities in its balance sheet? Explain.
4. How should the lawsuit be reported by Transit? Explain.
5. Prepare the liability section of a classified balance sheet for Transit Airlines at December 31, 2018. Transit's accounts payable and accruals were $43 million.
6. Draft appropriate note disclosures for Transit's financial statements at December 31, 2018, for each of the five items described.

P 13–13
Payroll-related liabilities
● Appendix

Alamar Petroleum Company offers its employees the option of contributing retirement funds up to 5% of their wages or salaries, with the contribution being matched by Alamar. The company also pays 80% of medical and life insurance premiums. Deductions relating to these plans and other payroll information for the first biweekly payroll period of February are listed as follows:

Wages and salaries	$2,000,000
Employee contribution to voluntary retirement plan	84,000
Medical insurance premiums	42,000
Life insurance premiums	9,000
Federal income taxes to be withheld	400,000
Local income taxes to be withheld	53,000
Payroll taxes:	
Federal unemployment tax rate	0.60%
State unemployment tax rate (after FUTA deduction)	5.40%
Social Security tax rate	6.20%
Medicare tax rate	1.45%

Required:

Prepare the appropriate journal entries to record salaries and wages expense and payroll tax expense for the biweekly pay period. Assume that no employee's cumulative wages exceed the relevant wage bases for Social Security, and that all employees' cumulative wages do exceed the relevant unemployment wage bases.

Broaden Your Perspective

Apply your critical-thinking ability to the knowledge you've gained. These cases will provide you an opportunity to develop your research, analysis, judgment, and communication skills. You also will work with other students, integrate what you've learned, apply it in real-world situations, and consider its global and ethical ramifications. This practice will broaden your knowledge and further develop your decision-making abilities.

Research Case 13–1
Bank loan; accrued interest
● LO13–1, LO13–2
CODE

A fellow accountant has solicited your opinion regarding the classification of short-term obligations repaid prior to being replaced by a long-term security. Cheshire Foods, Inc., issued $5,000,000 of short-term commercial paper during 2017 to finance construction of a plant. At September 30, 2018, Cheshire's fiscal year-end, the company intends to refinance the commercial paper by issuing long-term bonds. However, because Cheshire temporarily has excess cash, in November 2018 it liquidates $2,000,000 of the commercial paper as the paper matures. In December 2018, the company completes a $10,000,000 long-term bond issue. Later during December, it issues its September 30, 2018, financial statements. The proceeds of the long-term bond issue are to be used to replenish $2,000,000 in working capital, to pay $3,000,000 of commercial paper as it matures in January 2019, and to pay $5,000,000 of construction costs expected to be incurred later that year to complete the plant.

You initially are hesitant because you don't recall encountering a situation in which short-term obligations were repaid prior to being replaced by a long-term security. However, you are encouraged by a vague memory that this general topic is covered by GAAP literature you came across when reading an Internet article.

Required:

Determine how the $5,000,000 of commercial paper should be classified by consulting the authoritative GAAP literature and citing the appropriate location in the FASB Codification. Before doing so, formulate your own opinion on the proper treatment.

Real World Case 13–2
Returnable containers
● LO13–1, LO13–3
Real World Financials

The Zoo Doo Compost Company processes a premium organic fertilizer made with the help of the animals at the Memphis Zoo. Zoo Doo is sold in a specially designed plastic pail that may be kept and used for household chores or returned to the seller. The fertilizer is sold for $12.50 per two-gallon pail (including the $1.76 cost of the pail). For each pail returned, Zoo Doo donates $1 to the Memphis Zoo and the pail is used again.[35]

Required:

The founder and president of this start-up firm has asked your opinion on how to account for the donations to be made when fertilizer pails are returned. (Ignore any tax implications.)

Research Case 13–3
Relationship of liabilities to assets and owners' equity
● LO13–1

SFAC No. 6, "Elements of Financial Statements," states that "an entity's assets, liabilities, and equity (net assets) all pertain to the same set of probable future economic benefits." Explain this statement.

Judgment Case 13–4
Paid future absences
● LO13–3

Cates Computing Systems develops and markets commercial software for personal computers and workstations. Three situations involving compensation for possible future absences of Cates's employees are described below.

a. Cates compensates employees at their regular pay rate for time absent for military leave, maternity leave, and jury time. Employees are allowed predetermined absence periods for each type of absence.
b. Members of the new product development team are eligible for three months' paid sabbatical leave every four years. Five members of the team have just completed their fourth year of participation.
c. Company policy permits employees four paid sick days each year. Unused sick days can accumulate and can be carried forward to future years.

Required:

1. What are the conditions that require accrual of an expense and related liability for employees' compensation for future absences?

[35]Case based on Kay McCullen, "Take The Zoo Home With You!" *Head Lions,* July 1991; and a conversation with the Zoo Doo Compost Company president, Pierce Ledbetter.

2. For each of the three situations, indicate the circumstances under which accrual of an expense and related liability is warranted.

Ethics Case 13–5
Outdoors R Us
● LO13–1

Outdoors R Us owns several membership-based campground resorts throughout the Southwest. The company sells campground sites to new members, usually during a get-acquainted visit and tour. The campgrounds offer a wider array of on-site facilities than most. New members sign a multiyear contract, pay a down payment, and make monthly installment payments. Because no credit check is made and many memberships originate on a spur-of-the-moment basis, cancellations are not uncommon.

Business has been brisk during its first three years of operations, and since going public in 2005, the market value of its stock has tripled. The first sign of trouble came in 2018 when new sales dipped sharply.

One afternoon, two weeks before the end of the fiscal year, Diane Rice, CEO, and Gene Sun, controller, were having an active discussion in Sun's office.

Sun: I've thought more about our discussion yesterday. Maybe something can be done about profits.
Rice: I hope so. Our bonuses and stock value are riding on this period's performance.
Sun: We've been recording deferred revenues when new members sign up. Rather than recording liabilities at the time memberships are sold, I think we can justify reporting sales revenue for all memberships sold.
Rice: What will be the effect on profits?
Sun: I haven't run the numbers yet, but let's just say very favorable.

Required:

1. Why do you think liabilities had been recorded previously?
2. Is the proposal ethical?
3. Who would be affected if the proposal is implemented?

Trueblood Case 13–6
Contingencies
● LO13–5

CODE

The following Trueblood case is recommended for use with this chapter. The case provides an excellent opportunity for class discussion, group projects, and writing assignments. The case, along with Professor's Discussion Material, can be obtained from the Deloitte Foundation at its website: www.deloitte.com/us/truebloodcases.

Case 13–8: Accounting for a Loss Contingency for a Verdict Overturned on Appeal
This case gives students the opportunity to apply GAAP regarding accrual and disclosure of contingencies with respect to a complex lawsuit. As an addition to the case, students should cite the appropriate location of relevant GAAP in the FASB Codification.

Communication Case 13–7
Exceptions to the general classification guideline; group interaction
● LO13–4

Domestic Transfer and Storage is a large trucking company headquartered in the Midwest. Rapid expansion in recent years has been financed in large part by debt in a variety of forms. In preparing the financial statements for 2019, questions have arisen regarding the way certain of the liabilities are to be classified in the company's classified balance sheet.

A meeting of several members of the accounting area is scheduled for tomorrow, April 8, 2019. You are confident that that meeting will include the topic of debt classification. You want to appear knowledgeable at the meeting, but realizing it's been a few years since you have dealt with classification issues, you have sought out information you think relevant. Questionable liabilities at the company's fiscal year-end (January 31, 2019) include the following:

a. \$15 million of 9% commercial paper is due on July 31, 2019. Management intends to refinance the paper on a long-term basis. In early April 2019, Domestic negotiated a credit agreement with a commercial bank for up to \$12 million any time during the next three years, any borrowings from which will mature two years from the date of borrowing.
b. \$17 million of 11% notes were issued on June 30, 2016. The notes are due on November 30, 2019. The company has investments of \$20 million classified as "available for sale."
c. \$25 million of 10% notes were due on February 28, 2019. On February 21, 2019, the company issued 30-year, 9.4% bonds in a private placement to institutional investors.
d. Recently, company management has considered reducing debt in favor of a greater proportion of equity financing. \$20 million of 12% bonds mature on July 31, 2019. Discussions with underwriters, which began on January 4, 2019, resulted in a contractual arrangement on March 15 under which new common shares will be sold in July for approximately \$20 million.

In order to make notes to yourself in preparation for the meeting concerning the classification of these items, you decide to discuss them with a colleague. Specifically, you want to know what portion of the debt can be excluded from classification as a current liability (that is, reported as a noncurrent liability) and why.

Required:

1. What is the appropriate classification of each liability? Develop a list of arguments in support of your view prior to the class session for which the case is assigned.

2. In class, your instructor will pair you (and everyone else) with a classmate (who also has independently developed a position). You will be given three minutes to argue your view to your partner. Your partner likewise will be given three minutes to argue his or her view to you. During these three-minute presentations, the listening partner is not permitted to speak.
3. Then after each person has had a turn attempting to convince his or her partner, the two partners will have a three-minute discussion to decide which classifications are more convincing. Arguments will be merged into a single view for each pair.
4. After the allotted time, a spokesperson for each of the four liabilities will be selected by the instructor. Each spokesperson will field arguments from the class as to the appropriate classification. The class then will discuss the merits of the classification and attempt to reach a consensus view, though a consensus is not necessary.

Communication Case 13–8
Various contingencies
● LO13–5, LO13–6

"I see an all-nighter coming on," Gayle grumbled. "Why did Mitch just now give us this assignment?" Your client, Western Manufacturing, is involved with several situations that possibly involve contingencies. The assignment Gayle refers to is to draft appropriate accounting treatment for each situation described below in time for tomorrow's meeting of the audit group. Western's fiscal year is the calendar year 2018, and the 2018 financial statements are issued on March 15, 2019.

1. During 2018, Western experienced labor disputes at three of its plants. Management hopes an agreement will soon be reached. However negotiations between the Company and the unions have not produced an acceptable settlement and, as a result, strikes are ongoing at these facilities since March 1, 2019. It is virtually certain that material costs will be incurred but the amount of possible costs cannot be reasonably ascertained.
2. In accordance with a 2016 contractual agreement with A. J. Conner Company, Western is entitled to $37 million for certain fees and expense reimbursements. These were written off as bad debts in 2017. A. J. Conner has filed for bankruptcy. The bankruptcy court on February 4, 2019, ordered A. J. Conner to pay $23 million immediately upon consummation of a proposed merger with Garner Holding Group.
3. Western warrants most products it sells against defects in materials and workmanship for a period of a year. Based on their experience with previous product introductions, warranty costs are expected to approximate 2% of sales. A warranty liability of $39 million was reported at December 31, 2017. Sales of warranted products during 2018 were $2,100 million and actual warranty expenditures were $40 million.
4. Western is involved in a suit filed in January 2019 by Crump Holdings seeking $88 million, as an adjustment to the purchase price in connection with the Company's sale of its textile business in 2018. The suit alleges that Western misstated the assets and liabilities used to calculate the purchase price for the textile division. Legal counsel advises that it is reasonably possible that Western could end up losing an indeterminable amount not expected to have a material adverse effect on the Company's financial position.

Required:
1. Determine the appropriate means of reporting each situation.
2. In a memo to the audit manager, Mitch Riley, explain your reasoning. Include any necessary journal entries and drafts of appropriate disclosure notes.

Judgment Case 13–9
Loss contingency and full disclosure
● LO13–5, LO13–6

In the March 2019 meeting of Valleck Corporation's board of directors, a question arose as to the way a possible obligation should be disclosed in the forthcoming financial statements for the year ended December 31. A veteran board member brought to the meeting a draft of a disclosure note that had been prepared by the controller's office for inclusion in the annual report. Here is the note:

> On May 9, 2018, the United States Environmental Protection Agency (EPA) issued a Notice of Violation (NOV) to Valleck alleging violations of the Clean Air Act. Subsequently, in June 2018, the EPA commenced a civil action with respect to the foregoing violation seeking civil penalties of approximately $853,000. The EPA alleges that Valleck exceeded applicable volatile organic substance emission limits. The Company estimates that the cost to achieve compliance will be $190,000; in addition the Company expects to settle the EPA lawsuit for a civil penalty of $205,000 which will be paid in 2019.

"Where did we get the $205,000 figure?" he asked. On being informed that this is the amount negotiated last month by company attorneys with the EPA, the director inquires, "Aren't we supposed to report a liability for that in addition to the note?"

Required:
Explain whether Valleck should report a liability in addition to the note. Why or why not? For full disclosure, should anything be added to the disclosure note itself?

Communication Case 13–10
Change in loss contingency; write a memo
● LO13–5, LO13–6

Late in 2018, you and two other officers of Curbo Fabrications Corporation just returned from a meeting with officials of the City of Jackson. The meeting was unexpectedly favorable even though it culminated in a settlement with city authorities that required your company pay a total of $475,000 to cover the cost of violations of city construction codes. Jackson had filed suit in November 2016 against Curbo, seeking civil penalties and injunctive relief for violations of city construction codes regulating earthquake damage standards. Alleged violations involved several construction projects completed during the previous three years. When the financial statements were issued in 2017, Curbo had not reached a settlement with state authorities, but legal counsel had advised the Company that it was probable the ultimate settlement would be $750,000 in penalties. The following entry had been recorded:

Loss—litigation	750,000	
Liability—litigation		750,000

The final settlement, therefore, was a pleasant surprise. While returning from the meeting, your conversation turned to reporting the settlement in the 2018 financial statements. You drew the short straw and were selected to write a memo to Janet Zeno, the financial vice president, advising the proper course of action.

Required:

Write the memo. Include descriptions of any journal entries related to the change in amounts. Briefly describe other steps Curbo should take to report the settlement.

Research Case 13–11
Researching the way contingencies are reported; retrieving information from the Internet
● LO13–5, LO13–6

EDGAR (Electronic Data Gathering, Analysis, and Retrieval system) performs automated collection, validation, indexing, acceptance, and forwarding of submissions by companies and others who are required by law to file forms with the U.S. Securities and Exchange Commission (SEC). All publicly traded domestic companies use EDGAR to make the majority of their filings. Form 10-K, which includes the annual report, is required to be filed on EDGAR. The SEC makes this information available on the Internet.

Required:

1. Access the *FASB Accounting Standards Codification* at the FASB website (www.fasb.org). Identify the authoritative literature that provides guidance on accounting for contingent losses, and indicate the specific citations that describe the guidelines for determining when an expense and liability associated with a contingent loss should be accrued versus only disclosed in the notes?
2. Access EDGAR on the Internet at: www.sec.gov.
3. Search for a public company with which you are familiar. Access its most recent 10-K filing. Search or scroll to find the financial statements and related notes.
4. Specifically, look for any contingency(s) reported in the disclosure notes. Identify the nature of the contingency(s) described and explain the reason(s) the loss or losses was or was not accrued.
5. Repeat requirements 2 and 3 for two additional companies.

Communication Case 13–12
Accounting changes
● LO13–5, LO13–6

Kevin Brantly is a new hire in the controller's office of Fleming Home Products. Two events occurred in late 2018 that the company had not previously encountered. The events appear to affect two of the company's liabilities, but there is some disagreement concerning whether they also affect financial statements of prior years. Each change occurred during 2018 before any adjusting entries or closing entries were prepared. The tax rate for Fleming is 40% in all years.

- Fleming Home Products introduced a new line of commercial awnings in 2017 that carry a one-year warranty against manufacturer's defects. Based on industry experience, warranty costs were expected to approximate 3% of sales. Sales of the awnings in 2017 were $3,500,000. Accordingly, warranty expense and a warranty liability of $105,000 were recorded in 2017. In late 2018, the company's claims experience was evaluated and it was determined that claims were far fewer than expected—2% of sales rather than 3%. Sales of the awnings in 2018 were $4,000,000 and warranty expenditures in 2018 totaled $91,000.
- In November 2016, the State of Minnesota filed suit against the company, seeking penalties for violations of clean air laws. When the financial statements were issued in 2017, Fleming had not reached a settlement with state authorities, but legal counsel advised Fleming that it was probable the company would have to pay $200,000 in penalties. Accordingly, the following entry was recorded:

Loss—litigation	200,000	
Liability—litigation		200,000

Late in 2018, a settlement was reached with state authorities to pay a total of $350,000 in penalties.

Required:

Kevin's supervisor, perhaps unsure of the answer, perhaps wanting to test Kevin's knowledge, e-mails the message, "Kevin, send me a memo on how we should handle our awning warranty and that clean air suit." Wanting to be accurate, Kevin consults his reference materials. What will he find? Prepare the memo requested.

Real World Case 13–13
Lawsuit settlement; Morgan Stanley
● LO13–5, LO13–6

Real World Financials

Morgan Stanley is a leading investment bank founded in 1935. The company's fiscal year ends December 31, 2013, and it filed its financial statements with the SEC on February 25, 2014. On February 5, 2014, *Bloomberg* reported that Morgan Stanley would make a $1.25 billion settlement with the Federal Housing Finance Agency:

> Morgan Stanley said yesterday it reached a $1.25 billion deal to end Federal Housing Finance Agency claims the bank sold faulty mortgage bonds to Fannie Mae (FNMA) and Freddie Mac (FMCC) before the firms' losses pushed them into U.S. conservatorship. . . . Morgan Stanley, which disclosed its settlement in a regulatory filing yesterday, was among 18 banks sued by the FHFA in 2011. Authorities sought to recoup some losses taxpayers covered when the government took control of the failing mortgage-finance companies in 2008.

Required:

1. From an accounting perspective, how should Morgan Stanley have treated the settlement?
2. Relying on the information provided by the news article, re-create the journal entry Morgan Stanley recorded for the settlement. Assume it had not made any prior liability accrual with respect to this litigation.
3. Suppose the settlement had occurred after February 25, 2014. How should Morgan Stanley have treated the settlement?

Ethics Case 13–14
Profits guaranteed
● LO13–5

This was Joel Craig's first visit to the controller's corner office since being recruited for the senior accountant position in May. Because he'd been directed to bring with him his preliminary report on year-end adjustments, Craig presumed he'd done something wrong in preparing the report. That he had not was Craig's first surprise. His second surprise was his boss's request to reconsider one of the estimated expenses.

S & G Fasteners was a new company, specializing in plastic industrial fasteners. All products carry a generous long-term warranty against manufacturer's defects. "Don't you think 4% of sales is a little high for our warranty expense estimate?" his boss wondered. "After all, we're new at this. We have little experience with product introductions. I just got off the phone with Blanchard (the company president). He thinks we'll have trouble renewing our credit line with the profits we're projecting. The pressure's on."

Required:

1. Should Craig follow his boss's suggestion?
2. Does revising the warranty estimate pose an ethical dilemma?
3. Who would be affected if the suggestion is followed?

IFRS Case 13–15
Current liabilities and contingencies; differences between U.S. GAAP and IFRS
● LO13–4, LO13–5, LO13–7

IFRS

As a second-year financial analyst for A.J. Straub Investments, you are performing an initial analysis on Fizer Pharmaceuticals. A difficulty you've encountered in making comparisons with its chief rival is that Fizer uses U.S. GAAP and the competing company uses International Financial Reporting Standards. Some areas of concern are the following:

1. Fizer has been designated as a potentially responsible party by the United States Environmental Protection Agency with respect to certain waste sites. These claims are in various stages of administrative or judicial proceedings and include demands for recovery of past governmental costs and for future investigations or remedial actions. Fizer accrues costs associated with environmental matters when they become probable and reasonably estimable. Counsel has advised that the likelihood of payments of about $70 million is slightly more than 50%. Accordingly, payment is judged reasonably possible and the contingency was disclosed in a note.
2. Fizer had $10 million of bonds issued in 1990 that mature in February 2019. On December 31, 2018, the company's fiscal year-end, management intended to refinance the bonds on a long-term basis. On February 7, 2019, Fizer issued $10 million of 20-year bonds, applying the proceeds to repay the bond issue that matured that month. The bonds were reported in Fizer's balance sheet as long-term debt.
3. Fizer reported in its 2018 financial statements a long-term contingency at its face amount rather than its present value even though the difference was considered material. The reason the cash flows were not discounted is that their timing is uncertain.

Required:

If Fizer used IFRS as does its competitor, how would the items described be reported differently?

Analysis Case 13–16
Analyzing financial statements; liquidity ratios
● LO13–1

IGF Foods Company is a large, primarily domestic, consumer foods company involved in the manufacture, distribution and sale of a variety of food products. Industry averages are derived from Troy's *The Almanac of Business and Industrial Financial Ratios*. Following are the 2018 and 2017 comparative balance sheets for IGF. (The financial data we use are from actual financial statements of a well-known corporation, but the company name used is fictitious and the numbers and dates have been modified slightly.)

IGF FOODS COMPANY
Comparative Balance Sheets Years Ended
December 31, 2018 and 2017
($ in millions)

	2018	2017
Assets		
Current assets:		
Cash	$ 48	$ 142
Accounts receivable	347	320
Marketable securities	358	—
Inventories	914	874
Prepaid expenses	212	154
Total current assets	$1,879	$1,490
Property, plant, and equipment (net)	2,592	2,291
Intangibles (net)	800	843
Other assets	74	60
Total assets	$5,345	$4,684
Liabilities and Shareholders' Equity		
Current liabilities:		
Accounts payable	$ 254	$ 276
Accrued liabilities	493	496
Notes payable	518	115
Current portion of long-term debt	208	54
Total current liabilities	$1,473	$ 941
Long-term debt	534	728
Deferred income taxes	407	344
Total liabilities	$2,414	$2,013
Shareholders' equity:		
Common stock	180	180
Additional paid-in capital	21	63
Retained earnings	2,730	2,428
Total shareholders' equity	$2,931	$2,671
Total liabilities and shareholders' equity	$5,345	$4,684

Liquidity refers to a company's cash position and overall ability to obtain cash in the normal course of business. A company is said to be liquid if it has sufficient cash or is capable of converting its other assets to cash in a relatively short period of time so that currently maturing debts can be paid.

Required:

1. Calculate the current ratio for IGF for 2018. The average ratio for the stocks listed on the New York Stock Exchange in a comparable time period was 1.5. What information does your calculation provide an investor?
2. Calculate IGF's acid-test or quick ratio for 2018. The ratio for the stocks listed on the New York Stock Exchange in a comparable time period was .80. What does your calculation indicate about IGF's liquidity?

Trueblood Case 13–17
Accounting for litigation contingencies
● LO13-5, LO13-6, LO13-7

CODE

The following Trueblood case is recommended for use with this chapter. The case provides an excellent opportunity for class discussion, group projects, and writing assignments. The case, along with Professor's Discussion Material, can be obtained from the Deloitte Foundation at its website: www.deloitte.com/us/truebloodcases.

Case 15-02: Burying the Hatchet: A Litigation Settlement with a Customer
This case gives students an opportunity to apply the accounting for contingencies guidance to a complex legal settlement. It also raises issues of substance over form and income statement classification.

Real World Case 13–18
Contingencies
● LO13–5
Real World Financials

The following is an excerpt from *USAToday.com:*

> Microsoft (MSFT) on Thursday extended the warranty on its Xbox 360 video game console and said it will take a charge of more than $1 billion to pay for "anticipated costs." Under the new warranty, Microsoft will pay for shipping and repairs for three years, worldwide, for consoles afflicted with what gamers call "the red ring of death." Previously, the warranty expired after a year for U.S. customers and two years for Europeans. The charge will be $1.05 billion to $1.15 billion for the quarter ended June 30. Microsoft reports its fourth-quarter results July 19.

Required:

1. Why must Microsoft report this charge of over $1 billion entirely in one quarter, the last quarter of the company's fiscal year?
2. When the announcement was made, analyst Richard Doherty stated that either a high number of Xbox 360s will fail or the company is being overly conservative in its warranty estimate. From an accounting standpoint, what will Microsoft do in the future if the estimate of future repairs is overly conservative (too high)?

Real World Case 13–19
Contingencies
● LO13–5
Real World Financials
IFRS

Reporting requirements for contingent liabilities under IFRS differ somewhat from those under U.S. GAAP.

Required:

For each of the following, access the online version of the indicated financial report and answer the question. Also compare reporting under IFRS to similar reporting under U.S. GAAP.

1. AU Optronics (Form 20-F, filed 3/21/2016): Where there is a continuous range of possible outcomes, with each point in the range as likely as any other, what amount is accrued as the estimate of the obligation?
2. B Communications LTD (Form 20-F, filed 4/19/2016): With respect to legal claims, at what probability level would B Communications accrue a liability for a possible litigation loss?

Real World Case 13–20
Contingencies and Subsequent events
● LO13–5, LO13–6
Real World Financials

The following events are indicated in note 15 of J. Crew's 10-K annual report for the fiscal year ended January 29, 2011, and its 10-K was filed on March 21, 2011.

> **Acquisition**
> On November 23, 2010, the Company entered into an Agreement and Plan of Merger (the "Merger Agreement") with Chinos Holdings, Inc., a Delaware corporation ("Parent"). . . . At a special meeting of shareholders held in March 1, 2011, our shareholders voted to approve the Acquisition, and Parent acquired us on March 7, 2011 through a reverse subsidiary merger with J. Crew Group, Inc. being the surviving company. . . .
>
> **Litigation**
> In connection with the Acquisition, between November 24, 2010 and December 16, 2010, sixteen purported class action complaints were filed against some or all of the following: the Company, certain officers of the Company, members of the Company's Board of Directors, Holdings, the Issuer, TPG, TPG Fund VI and LGP. The plaintiffs in each of these complaints allege, among other things, (1) that certain officers of the Company and members of the Company's Board breached their fiduciary duties to the Company's public stockholders by authorizing the Acquisition for inadequate consideration and pursuant to an inadequate process, and (2) that the Company, TPG and LGP aided and abetted the other defendants' alleged breaches of fiduciary duty. The purported class action complaints sought, among other things, an order enjoining the consummation of the Acquisition or an order rescinding the Acquisition and an award of compensatory damages. Although the Company, the Company's Board, TPG, and LGP have entered into a memorandum of understanding to settle the actions filed in Delaware, they believe that the claims asserted in that action, as well as the claims asserted in New York and Federally, are without merit and intend to defend against the actions vigorously. The Company has notified its insurers of the actions and believes that any and all costs, expenses, and/or losses associated with the lawsuits are covered by its applicable insurance policies. The Company has recorded a reserve for litigation settlement of $10 million in the consolidated financial statements as of and for the fiscal year ended January 29, 2011.

Required:

1. Is the acquisition a subsequent event? What are J. Crew's responsibilities in its financial statements with respect to disclosing it?
2. With respect to litigation:

a. Has J. Crew recorded any journal entry with respect to the litigation associated with the acquisition? If so, prepare the journal entry.

b. Do you believe that there is some amount associated with the litigation that J. Crew considers to be probable and reasonably estimable? What about reasonably possible, or probable but not reasonably estimable? Explain your reasoning.

Trueblood Case 13–21
Subsequent Events
● LO13–5

CODE

The following Trueblood case is recommended for use with this chapter. The case provides an excellent opportunity for class discussion, group projects, and writing assignments. The case, along with Professor's Discussion Material, can be obtained from the Deloitte Foundation at its website: www.deloitte.com/us/truebloodcases.

Case 12-02: To Recognize or Not to Recognize, That is the Question
This case gives students the opportunity to apply GAAP regarding recognition of subsequent events. As an addition to the case, students should cite the appropriate location of relevant GAAP in the FASB Codification.

Continuing Cases

Target Case
● LO13–1, LO13–3, LO13–5

Target Corporation prepares its financial statements according to U.S. GAAP. Target's financial statements and disclosure notes for the year ended January 30, 2016, are available Connect. This material also is available under the Investor Relations link at the company's website (www.target.com).

Required:

1. Target's Consolidated Statement of Financial Position (its balance sheet) discloses its current assets and current liabilities.
   a. What are the four components of Target's current liabilities?
   b. Are current assets sufficient to cover current liabilities? What is the current ratio for the year ended January 30, 2016? How does the ratio compare with the prior year?
   c. Why might a company want to avoid having its current ratio be too low? Too high?
2. Disclosure Note 2 discusses Target's accounting for gift card sales. Disclosure Note 18 indicates the amount of gift card liability that is recognized in Target's balance sheet.
   a. By how much did Target's gift card liability change between January 30, 2016 and January 31, 2015?
   b. How would the following affect Target's gift card liability (indicate "increase," "decrease," or "no change" for each):
      i. Sale of a gift card
      ii. Redemption of a gift card (the holder using it to acquire goods or services)
      iii. Increase in breakage estimated for gift cards already sold
3. Disclosure Note 19 discusses Target's accounting for a data breach in 2013, when "an intruder stole certain payment card and other guest information from our network."
   a. What is Target's approach for accruing losses for litigation claims associated with the data breach? Is their approach appropriate?
   b. Prepare a journal entry to record Target's recognition of new expenses associated with the data breach litigation for the fiscal year ended January 30, 2016.
   c. Prepare a journal entry to record Target's reduction of its liability associated with the data breach litigation for the fiscal year ended January 30, 2016.

Air France–KLM Case
● LO13–7

IFRS

Air France-KLM (AF), a Franco-Dutch company, prepares its financial statements according to International Financial Reporting Standards. AF's financial statements and disclosure notes for the year ended December 31, 2015, are available in Connect. This material is also available under the Finance link at the company's website (www.airfranceklm.com).

Required:

1. Read Notes 4.6 and 35. What do you think gave rise to total deferred income of €249 as of the end of fiscal 2015? Would transactions of this type be handled similarly under U.S. GAAP?
2. Is the threshold for recognizing a provision under IFRS different than it is under U.S. GAAP? Explain.
3. Note 32 lists "other provisions."
   a. Do the beginning and ending balances of total provisions and retirement benefits shown in Note 32 for fiscal 2015 tie to the balance sheet? By how much has the total amount of the AF's "other provisions" increased or decreased during fiscal 2015?

b. Prepare journal entries for the following changes in the litigation provision that occurred during fiscal 2015, assuming any amounts recorded on the income statement are recorded as "provision expense," and any use of provision is paid for in cash. In each case, provide a brief explanation of the event your journal entry is capturing.

   i. New provision

   ii. Use of provision

c. Is AF's treatment of its litigation provision under IFRS similar to how it would be treated under U.S. GAAP?

4. Note 32.2 lists a number of contingent liabilities. Are amounts for those items recognized as a liability on AF's balance sheet? Explain.

CPA Exam Questions and Simulations

ROGER CPA Review

Sample CPA Exam questions from Roger CPA Review are available in Connect as support for the topics in this chapter. These Multiple Choice Questions and Task-Based Simulations include expert-written explanations and solutions, and provide a starting point for students to become familiar with the content and functionality of the actual CPA Exam.

CHAPTER

14 Bonds and Long-Term Notes

OVERVIEW

This chapter continues the presentation of liabilities. While the discussion focuses on the accounting treatment of long-term liabilities, the borrowers' side of the same transactions is presented as well. Long-term notes and bonds are discussed, as well as the extinguishment of debt and debt convertible into stock.

LEARNING OBJECTIVES

After studying this chapter, you should be able to:

- **LO14–1** Identify the underlying characteristics of debt instruments and describe the basic approach to accounting for debt. (*p. 771*)
- **LO14–2** Account for bonds issued at face value, at a discount, or at a premium, recording interest using the effective interest method or using the straight-line method. (*p. 773*)
- **LO14–3** Characterize the accounting treatment of notes, including installment notes, issued for cash or for noncash consideration. (*p. 784*)
- **LO14–4** Describe the disclosures appropriate to long-term debt in its various forms and calculate related financial ratios. (*p. 788*)
- **LO14–5** Record the early extinguishment of debt and its conversion into equity securities. (*p. 793*)
- **LO14–6** Understand the option to report liabilities at their fair values. (*p. 798*)
- **LO14–7** Discuss the primary differences between U.S. GAAP and IFRS with respect to accounting for bonds and long-term notes. (*pp. 775* and *795*).

© Klaus Vedfelt/Getty Images

FINANCIAL REPORTING CASE

Service Leader, Inc.

The mood is both upbeat and focused on this cool October morning. Executives and board members of Service Leader, Inc., are meeting with underwriters and attorneys to discuss the company's first bond offering in its 20-year history. You are attending in the capacity of company controller and two-year member of the board of directors. The closely held corporation has been financed entirely by equity, internally generated funds, and short-term bank borrowings.

Bank rates of interest, though, have risen recently and the company's unexpectedly rapid, but welcome, growth has prompted the need to look elsewhere for new financing. Under consideration are 15-year, 6.25% first mortgage bonds with a principal amount of $70 million. The bonds would be callable at 103 any time after June 30, 2020, and convertible into Service Leader common stock at the rate of 45 shares per $1,000 bond.

Other financing vehicles have been discussed over the last two months, including the sale of additional stock, nonconvertible bonds, and unsecured notes. This morning *The Wall Street Journal* indicated that market rates of interest for debt similar to the bonds under consideration are about 6.5%.

QUESTIONS

By the time you finish this chapter, you should be able to respond appropriately to the questions posed in this case. Compare your response to the solution provided at the end of the chapter.

1. What does it mean that the bonds are "first mortgage" bonds? What effect does that have on financing? *(p. 772)*
2. From Service Leader's perspective, why are the bonds callable? What does that mean? *(p. 773)*
3. How will it be possible to sell bonds paying investors 6.25% when other, similar investments will provide the investors a return of 6.5%? *(p. 773)*
4. Would accounting differ if the debt were designated as notes rather than bonds? *(p. 784)*
5. Why might the company choose to make the bonds convertible into common stock? *(p. 793)*

The Nature of Long-Term Debt

● LO14–1

A company must raise funds to finance its operations and often the expansion of those operations. Presumably, at least some of the necessary funding can be provided by the company's own operations, though some funds must be provided by external sources. Ordinarily, external financing includes some combination of equity and debt funding. We explore debt financing first.

Liabilities signify *borrowers'* interests in a company's assets.

In the present chapter, we focus on debt in the form of bonds and notes. The following three chapters deal with liabilities also, namely those arising in connection with leases (Chapter 15), deferred income taxes (Chapter 16), and pensions and employee benefits (Chapter 17). Some employee benefits create equity rather than debt, which are discussed in Chapter 19. In Chapter 18, we examine shareholders' interests arising from external *equity* financing. In Chapter 21, we see that cash flows from both debt and equity financing are reported together in a statement of cash flows as "cash flows from financing activities."

As you read this chapter, you will find the focus to be on the liability side of the transactions we examine. Realize, though, that the mirror image of a liability is an asset (bonds payable/investment in bonds, note payable/note receivable, etc.). So as we discuss accounting for debts from the viewpoint of the issuers of the debt instruments (borrowers), we also will take the opportunity to see how the lender deals with the corresponding asset. Studying the two sides of the same transaction in tandem will emphasize their inherent similarities.

A note payable and a note receivable are two sides of the same coin.

Accounting for a liability is a relatively straightforward concept. This is not to say that all debt instruments are unchallenging, "plain vanilla" loan agreements. Quite the contrary, the financial community continually devises increasingly exotic ways to flavor financial instruments in the attempt to satisfy the diverse and evolving tastes of both debtors and creditors.

Periodic interest is the effective interest rate times the amount of the debt outstanding during the interest period.

Packaging aside, a liability requires the future payment of cash in specified (or estimated) amounts, at specified (or projected) dates. As time passes, interest accrues on debt. As a general rule, the periodic interest is the effective interest rate times the amount of the debt outstanding during the period. This same principle applies regardless of the specific form of the liability—note payable, bonds payable, lease liability, pension obligation, or other debt instruments. Also, as a general rule, long-term liabilities are reported at their present values. The present value of a liability is the present value of its related cash flows (principal and/or interest payments), discounted at the effective rate of interest at issuance.

We begin our study of long-term liabilities by examining accounting for bonds. We follow that section with a discussion of debt in the form of notes in Part B. It's important to note that, although particulars of the two forms of debt differ, the basic approach to accounting for each type is precisely the same. In Part C, we look at various ways bonds and notes are retired or converted into other securities. Finally, in Part D we discuss the option companies have to report liabilities at their fair values.

PART A

Bonds

A company can borrow cash from a bank or other financial institution by signing a promissory note. We discuss notes payable later in the chapter. Medium- and large-sized corporations often choose to borrow cash by issuing bonds to the public. In fact, the most common form of corporate debt is bonds. A bond issue, in effect, breaks down a large debt (large corporations often borrow hundreds of millions of dollars at a time) into manageable parts—usually $1,000 or $5,000 units. This avoids the necessity of finding a single lender who is both willing and able to loan a large amount of money at a reasonable interest rate. So rather than signing a $400 million note to borrow cash from a financial institution, a company may find it more economical to sell 400,000 $1,000 bonds to many lenders—theoretically up to 400,000 lenders.

A bond issue divides a large liability into many smaller liabilities.

Bonds obligate the issuing corporation to repay a stated amount (variously referred to as the *principal, par value, face amount,* or *maturity value*) at a specified *maturity date.* Maturities for bonds typically range from 10 to 40 years. In return for the use of the money borrowed, the company also agrees to pay *interest* to bondholders between the issue date and maturity. The periodic interest is a stated percentage of face amount (variously referred to as the *stated rate, coupon rate,* or *nominal rate*). Ordinarily, interest is paid semiannually on designated interest dates beginning six months after the day the bonds are "dated."

Corporations issuing bonds are obligated to repay a stated amount at a specified *maturity date* and periodic *interest* between the issue date and maturity.

The Bond Indenture

The specific promises made to bondholders are described in a document called a **bond indenture**. Because it would be impractical for the corporation to enter into a direct agreement with each of the many bondholders, the bond indenture is held by a trustee, usually a commercial bank or other financial institution, appointed by the issuing firm to represent the rights of the bondholders. If the company fails to live up to the terms of the bond indenture, the trustee may bring legal action against the company on behalf of the bondholders.

A *bond indenture* describes the specific promises made to bondholders.

FINANCIAL Reporting Case

Q1, p. 771

Most corporate bonds are debenture bonds. A **debenture bond** is secured only by the "full faith and credit" of the issuing corporation. No specific assets are pledged as security. Investors in debentures usually have the same standing as the firm's other general creditors.

So in case of bankruptcy, debenture holders and other general creditors would be treated equally. An exception is the subordinated debenture, which is not entitled to receive any liquidation payments until the claims of other specified debt issues are satisfied.

A mortgage bond, on the other hand, is backed by a lien on specified real estate owned by the issuer. Because a mortgage bond is considered less risky than debentures, it typically will command a lower interest rate.

Today most corporate bonds are registered bonds. Interest checks are mailed directly to the owner of the bond, whose name is registered with the issuing company. Years ago, it was typical for bonds to be structured as coupon bonds (sometimes called *bearer bonds*). The name of the owner of a coupon bond was not registered. Instead, to collect interest on a coupon bond the holder actually clipped an attached coupon and redeemed it in accordance with instructions in the indenture. A carryover effect of this practice is that we still sometimes see the term *coupon rate* in reference to the stated interest rate on bonds.

Most corporate bonds are callable (or redeemable). The call feature allows the issuing company to buy back, or call, outstanding bonds from bondholders before their scheduled maturity date. This feature affords the company some protection against being stuck with relatively high-cost debt in the event interest rates fall during the period before maturity. The call price must be pre-specified and often exceeds the bond's face amount (a call premium), sometimes declining as maturity is approached.

FINANCIAL Reporting Case

Q2, p. 771

For example, financial statements of Emhart Corporation included this disclosure note:

> The Company's 9¼% (9.65% effective interest rate, after discount) sinking fund debentures are callable at prices decreasing from 105% of face amount currently to 100%.

Real World Financials

"No call" provisions usually prohibit calls during the first few years of a bond's life. Very often, calls are mandatory. That is, the corporation may be required to redeem the bonds on a prespecified, year-by-year basis. Bonds requiring such sinking fund redemptions often are labeled *sinking fund debentures.*

Mandatory sinking fund redemptions retire a bond issue gradually over its term to maturity.

Serial bonds provide a more structured (and less popular) way to retire bonds on a piecemeal basis. Serial bonds are retired in installments during all or part of the life of the issue. Each bond has its own specified maturity date. So for a typical 30-year serial issue, 25 to 30 separate maturity dates might be assigned to specific portions of the bond issue.

Convertible bonds are retired as a consequence of bondholders choosing to convert them into shares of stock. We look closer at convertible bonds a little later in the chapter.

Recording Bonds at Issuance

● LO14–2

Bonds represent a liability to the corporation that issues the bonds and an asset to an investor who buys the bonds as an investment. Each side of the transaction is the mirror image of the other.[1] This is demonstrated in Illustration 14–1.

Most bonds these days are issued on the day they are dated (date printed in the indenture contract). On rare occasions, there may be a delay in issuing bonds that causes them to be issued between interest dates, in which case the interest that has accrued since the day they are dated is added to the bonds' price. We discuss this infrequent event in Appendix 14A to this chapter.

Determining the Selling Price

The price of a bond issue at any particular time is not necessarily equal to its face amount. The $700,000, 12% bond issue in the previous illustration, for example, may sell for more than face amount (at a premium) or less than face amount (at a discount), depending on how the 12% *stated* interest rate compares with the prevailing *market* or *effective rate* of interest (for securities of similar risk and maturity). For instance, if the 12% bonds are

FINANCIAL Reporting Case

Q3, p. 771

[1]You should recall from Chapter 12 that investments in bonds that are to be held to maturity by the investor are reported at amortized cost, which is the method described here. However, also remember that investments in debt securities *not* to be held to maturity are reported at the fair value of the securities held, as described in Chapter 12, with the interest determined by the effective interest method.

Illustration 14–1

Bonds Sold at Face Amount

On January 1, 2018, Masterwear Industries issued $700,000 of 12% bonds. Interest of $42,000 is payable semiannually on June 30 and December 31. The bonds mature in three years (an unrealistically short maturity to shorten the illustration). The entire bond issue was sold in a private placement to United Intergroup, Inc., at the face amount.

At Issuance (January 1)

Masterwear (Issuer)		
Cash	700,000	
Bonds payable (face amount)		700,000
United (Investor)		
Investment in bonds (face amount)	700,000	
Cash		700,000

competing in a market in which similar bonds are providing a 14% return, the bonds could be sold only at a price less than $700,000. On the other hand, if the market rate is only 10%, the 12% stated rate would seem relatively attractive and the bonds would sell at a premium over face amount. The reason the stated rate often differs from the market rate, resulting in a *discount* or *premium,* is the inevitable delay between the date the terms of the issue are established and the date the issue comes to market.

Other things being equal, the lower the perceived riskiness of the corporation issuing bonds, the higher the price those bonds will command.

In addition to the characteristic terms of a bond agreement as specified in the indenture, the market rate for a specific bond issue is influenced by the creditworthiness of the company issuing the bonds. To evaluate the risk and quality of an individual bond issue, investors rely heavily on bond ratings provided by **Standard & Poor's Corporation** and by **Moody's Investors Service, Inc.** See the bond ratings in Illustration 14–2.

Illustration 14–2

Bond Ratings*

	S&P	Moody's
Investment Grades:		
Highest	AAA	Aaa
High	AA	Aa
Medium	A	A
Minimum investment grade	BBB	Baa
"Junk" Ratings:		
Speculative	BB	Ba
Very speculative	B	B
Default or near default	CCC	Caa
	CC	Ca
	C	C
	D	

*Adapted from Moodys.com and SPRatings.com.

A bond issue will be priced by the marketplace to yield the market rate of interest for securities of similar risk and maturity.

Forces of supply and demand cause a bond issue to be *priced to yield the market rate.* In other words, an investor paying that price will earn an effective rate of return on the investment equal to the market rate. The price is calculated as the present value of all the cash flows required of the bonds, where the discount rate used in the present value calculation is the market rate. Specifically, the price will be the present value of the periodic cash interest payments (face amount × stated rate) plus the present value of the principal payable at maturity, both discounted at the market rate.

Bonds priced at a discount are described in Illustration 14–3.

The calculation is illustrated in Illustration 14–4.

Although the cash flows total $952,000, the present value of those future cash flows as of January 1, 2018, is only $666,633. This is due to the time value of money. These bonds are issued at a discount because the present value of the cash flows is less than the face amount of the bonds.

Illustration 14–3

Bonds Sold at a Discount

On January 1, 2018, Masterwear Industries issued $700,000 of 12% bonds, dated January 1. Interest of $42,000 is payable semiannually on June 30 and December 31. The bonds mature in three years. The market yield for bonds of similar risk and maturity is 14%. The entire bond issue was purchased by United Intergroup, Inc.

Calculation of the Price of the Bonds

		Present Values
Interest	$ 42,000 × 4.76654* =	$200,195
Principal	$700,000 × 0.66634† =	466,438
Present value (price) of the bonds		$666,633

*Present value of an ordinary annuity of $1: $n = 6$, $i = 7\%$ (Table 4).
†Present value of $1: $n = 6$, $i = 7\%$ (Table 2).
Because interest is paid semiannually, the present value calculations use: (a) one-half the stated rate (6%) to determine cash payments, (b) one-half the market rate (7%) as the discount rate, and (c) six (3 × 2) semiannual periods.
Note: Present value tables are provided at the end of this textbook. If you need to review the concept of the time value of money, refer to the discussions in Chapter 6.
Rounding: Because present value tables truncate decimal places, the solution may be slightly different if you use a calculator or Excel.

Using a calculator:
Enter: N 6 I 7
PMT −42000
FV −700000
Output: PV 666,634

Using Excel, enter:
=PV(.07,6,−42000,
−700000)
Output: 666,634

Illustration 14–4

Cash Flows from a Bond Issue

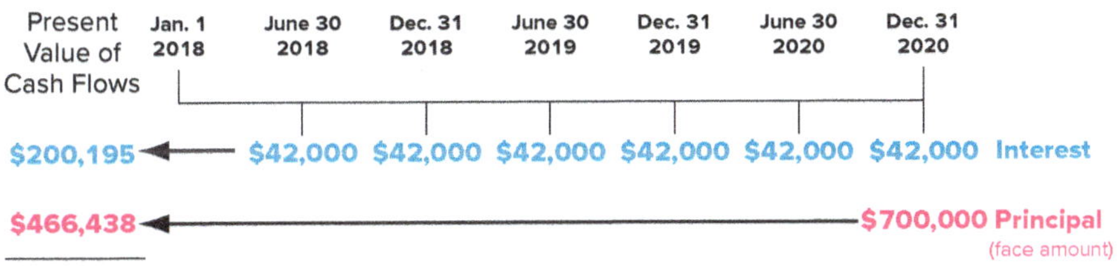

$666,633 Present value of interest and principal

Journal Entries at Issuance—Bonds Sold at a Discount

Masterwear (Issuer)		
Cash (price calculated above)	666,633	
Discount on bonds payable (difference)	33,367	
Bonds payable (face amount)		700,000
United (Investor)		
Investment in bonds (face amount)	700,000	
Discount on bond investment (difference)		33,367
Cash (price calculated above)		666,633

Note: A sometimes-used alternative way to record bonds is the "net method," shown next, in which the discount is included directly in the book value.

Masterwear (Issuer)		
Cash	666,633	
Bonds payable		666,633
United (Investor)		
Investment in bonds	666,633	
Cash		666,633

When bond prices are quoted in financial media, they typically are stated in terms of a percentage of face amounts. Thus, a price quote of 98 means a $1,000 bond will sell for $980; a bond priced at 101 will sell for $1,010.

● LO14–7

Determining Interest—Effective Interest Method

The *effective interest* on debt is the market rate of interest multiplied by the outstanding balance of the debt.

Interest accrues on an outstanding debt at a constant percentage of the debt each period. Of course, under the concept of accrual accounting, the periodic effective interest is not affected by the time at which the cash interest actually is paid. Recording interest each period as the *effective market rate of interest multiplied by the outstanding balance of the debt* (during the interest period) is referred to as the **effective interest method**. Although giving this a label—the effective interest method—implies some specialized procedure, this simply is an application of the accrual concept, consistent with accruing all expenses as they are incurred.

Continuing our example, we determined that the amount of debt when the bonds are issued is $666,633. Since the effective interest rate is 14%, interest recorded (as expense to the issuer and revenue to the investor) for the first six-month interest period is $46,664:

$666,633	×	(14% ÷ 2)	=	$46,664
Outstanding balance		Effective rate		Effective interest

However, the bond indenture calls for semiannual interest payments of only $42,000—the *stated* rate (6%) times the *face amount* ($700,000). The remainder, $4,664, increases the liability and is reflected as a reduction in the discount (a contra-liability account). This is illustrated in Illustration 14–5.

Illustration 14–5

Change in Debt When Effective Interest Exceeds Cash Paid

The difference between the effective interest and the interest paid increases the existing liability.

			Account Balances		
	Outstanding Balance		**Bonds Payable (face amount)**		**Discount on Bonds Payable**
January 1	$666,633	=	$700,000	less	$33,367
Interest accrued at 7%	46,664				
Portion of interest paid	(42,000)				(4,664)
June 30	$671,297	=	$700,000	less	$28,703

Interest expense (issuer) and revenue (investor) are calculated on the outstanding debt balance at the effective (or market) rate. Interest *paid* is the amount specified in the bond indenture—the *stated* rate times the face amount. These amounts and the change in the outstanding debt are recorded as follows:

Journal Entries—The Interest Method

The effective interest is calculated each period as the market rate times the amount of the debt outstanding during the interest period.

At the First Interest Date (June 30)		
Masterwear (Issuer)		
Interest expense (effective rate × outstanding balance)	46,664	
Discount on bonds payable (difference)		4,664
Cash (stated rate × face amount)		42,000
United (Investor)		
Cash (stated rate × face amount)	42,000	
Discount on bond investment (difference)	4,664	
Interest revenue (effective rate × outstanding balance)		46,664

In this example and others in the chapter we look at the investor's entries as well as the issuer's to see both sides of the same transactions.

Because the balance of the debt changes each period, the dollar amount of interest (balance × rate) also will change each period. To keep up with the changing amounts, it usually is convenient to prepare a schedule that reflects the changes in the debt over its term to maturity. An amortization schedule for the situation under discussion is shown in Illustration 14–6.

Amounts for the journal entries each interest date are found in the second, third, and fourth columns of the schedule. The essential point to remember is that the effective interest method is a straightforward application of the accrual concept, whereby interest expense (or revenue) is accrued periodically at the effective rate. We record that amount of interest expense or revenue accrued even though the cash interest is a different amount.

Determining interest in this manner has a convenient side effect. It results in reporting the liability at the present value of future cash payments—the appropriate valuation method

Illustration 14–6

Amortization Schedule—Discount

Date	Cash Interest	Effective Interest	Increase in Balance	Outstanding Balance
	(6% × Face amount)	(7% × Outstanding balance)	(Discount reduction)	
1/1/18				666,633
6/30/18	42,000	0.07 (666,633) = 46,664	4,664	671,297
12/31/18	42,000	0.07 (671,297) = 46,991	4,991	676,288
6/30/19	42,000	0.07 (676,288) = 47,340	5,340	681,628
12/31/19	42,000	0.07 (681,628) = 47,714	5,714	687,342
6/30/20	42,000	0.07 (687,342) = 48,114	6,114	693,456
12/31/20	42,000	0.07 (693,456) = 48,544*	6,544	700,000
	252,000	**285,367**	**33,367**	

*Rounded

for any liability. This is obvious at issuance; we actually calculated the present value to be $666,633. What perhaps is not quite as obvious is that the outstanding amount of debt each subsequent period (shown in the right-hand column of the amortization schedule) is still the present value of the remaining cash flows, discounted at the original rate. The outstanding amount of the debt is its book value, sometimes called carrying value or carrying amount, which is the face amount minus the balance in the discount.

Before moving on, notice some key characteristics of the amortization schedule. As mentioned earlier, the unpaid interest each period ($4,664 the first period) adds to the balance. Since this happens each period, the balance continually increases, eventually becoming the face amount at maturity. Conveniently, that's the amount to be paid at maturity. Also, because the balance increases each period, so does the effective interest. That's because effective interest is the same percentage rate times a higher balance each period.

Now look at the column totals. The total interest expense (from the issuer's perspective) is equal to the sum of the total cash interest plus the total change in the balance (the discount). One way we might view this is to say the total interest paid ($285,367) is the $252,000 cash interest paid during the term to maturity plus the "extra" amount paid at maturity. That $33,367 amount is extra in the sense that, by selling the bonds, we borrow $666,633 but must repay $700,000 at maturity. That's why the effective interest on the bonds is 14% even though the cash interest is only 12% annually; the extra interest at maturity makes up the difference.

Additional Consideration

Although the reported amount each period is the present value of the bonds, at any date after issuance this amount is not necessarily equal to the market value (fair value) of the bonds. This is because the market rate of interest will not necessarily remain the same as the rate implicit in the original issue price (the effective rate). Of course, for negotiable financial instruments, the issue price is the market price at any given time. Differences between market values and present values based on the original rate are holding gains and losses. If we were to use the market rate to revalue bonds on each reporting date—that is, recalculate the present value using the market rate—the reported amount always would be the market value. As we will see later, companies have the option to report their liabilities at fair value.

Zero-Coupon Bonds

A zero-coupon bond pays no interest. Instead, it offers a return in the form of a "deep discount" from the face amount. For illustration, let's look at the zero-coupon bonds issued by General Mills, Inc. Two billion, two hundred thirty million dollars face amount of the

20-year securities sold for one billion, five hundred one million dollars. As the amortization schedule in Illustration 14–7 demonstrates, they were priced to yield 2%.[2]

Illustration 14–7

Zero-Coupon Securities—General Mills, Inc.

Real World Financials

($ in millions)	Cash Interest	Effective Interest	Increase in Balance	Outstanding Balance*
	(0% × Face amount)	(2% × Outstanding debt)	(Discount reduction)	
				1,501
2002	0	0.02 (1,501) = 30	30	1,531
2003	0	0.02 (1,531) = 31	31	1,561
2004	0	0.02 (1,561) = 31	31	1,593
◆	◆	◆	◆	◆
◆	◆	◆	◆	◆
◆	◆	◆	◆	◆
2021	0	0.02 (2,143) = 43	43	2,186
2022	0	0.02 (2,186) = 44	44	2,230
		729	729	

*Some numbers appear not to total because the underlying calculations are not rounded. Note that the final number in the schedule ($2,230 million) is the face amount payable at maturity.

Zero-coupon bonds provide us with a convenient opportunity to reinforce a key concept we just learned: that we accrue the interest expense (or revenue) each period at the effective rate regardless of how much cash interest actually is paid (zero in this case). An advantage of issuing zero-coupon bonds or notes is that the corporation can deduct for tax purposes the annual interest expense (see schedule) but has no related cash outflow until the bonds mature. However, the reverse is true for investors in "zeros." Investors receive no periodic cash interest, even though annual interest revenue is reportable for tax purposes. So those who invest in zero-coupon bonds usually have tax-deferred or tax-exempt status, such as pension funds, individual retirement accounts (IRAs), and charitable organizations. Zero-coupon bonds and notes have popularity but still constitute a relatively small proportion of corporate debt.

Bonds Sold at a Premium

In Illustration 14–3, Masterwear Industries sold the bonds at a price that would yield an effective rate higher than the stated rate. The result was a discount. On the other hand, if the 12% bonds had been issued when the market yield for bonds of similar risk and maturity was *lower* than the stated rate, say 10%, the issue would have been priced at a *premium*. Because the 12% rate would seem relatively attractive in a 10% market, the bonds would command an issue price of more than $700,000, calculated in Illustration 14–8.

Illustration 14–8

Bonds Sold at a Premium

Because interest is paid *semiannually*, the present value calculations use:

a. one-half the stated rate (6%),
b. one-half the market rate (5%), and
c. 6 (3 × 2) semiannual periods.

On January 1, 2018, Masterwear Industries issued $700,000 of 12% bonds, dated January 1. Interest of $42,000 is payable semiannually on June 30 and December 31. The bonds mature in three years. The market yield for bonds of similar risk and maturity is 10%. The entire bond issue was purchased by United Intergroup, Inc.

Calculation of the Price of the Bonds

	Present Values
Interest	$42,000 × 5.07569* = $213,179
Principal	$700,000 × 0.74622† = 522,354
Present value (price) of the bonds	$735,533

*Present value of an ordinary annuity of $1: $n = 6$, $i = 5\%$.
†Present value of $1: $n = 6$, $i = 5\%$.

[2]The present value of $2,230M, discounted at 2% for 20 years, is $1,501M.

Interest on bonds issued at a premium is determined in precisely the same manner as on bonds issued at a discount. Again, interest is the effective interest rate applied to the debt balance outstanding during each period (balance at the end of the previous interest period), and the cash paid is the stated rate times the face amount, as shown in Illustration 14–9. The difference between the two is the reduction (amortization) of the premium.

Journal Entries at Issuance—Bonds Sold at Premium

Masterwear (Issuer)		
Cash (price calculated above)	735,533	
Bonds payable (face amount)		700,000
Premium on bonds payable (difference)		35,533
United (Investor)		
Investment in bonds (face amount)	700,000	
Premium on bond investment (difference)	35,533	
Cash (price calculated above)		735,533

Illustration 14–9

Amortization Schedule—Premium

Date	Cash Interest	Effective Interest		Decrease in Balance	Outstanding Balance
	(6% × Face amount)	(5% × Outstanding balance)		(Premium reduction)	
1/1/18					735,533
6/30/18	42,000	0.05 (735,533) =	36,777	5,223	730,310
12/31/18	42,000	0.05 (730,310) =	36,516	5,484	724,826
6/30/19	42,000	0.05 (724,826) =	36,241	5,759	719,067
12/31/19	42,000	0.05 (719,067) =	35,953	6,047	713,020
6/30/20	42,000	0.05 (713,020) =	35,651	6,349	706,671
12/31/20	42,000	0.05 (706,671) =	35,329*	6,671	700,000
	252,000		**216,467**	**35,533**	

*Rounded

Since *more* cash is paid each period than the effective interest, the debt outstanding is reduced by the overpayment.

Notice that the debt declines each period. As the premium is reduced by amortization, the book value of the bonds declines toward face value. This is because the effective interest each period is less than the cash interest paid. Remember, this is precisely the opposite of when the bonds are at a discount, when the effective interest each period is more than the cash paid. As the discount is reduced by amortization, the book value of the bonds increases toward face value. This is illustrated in Illustration 14–10.

Whether bonds are issued at a premium or a discount, the outstanding balance becomes zero at maturity.

Illustration 14–10

Premium and Discount Amortization Compared

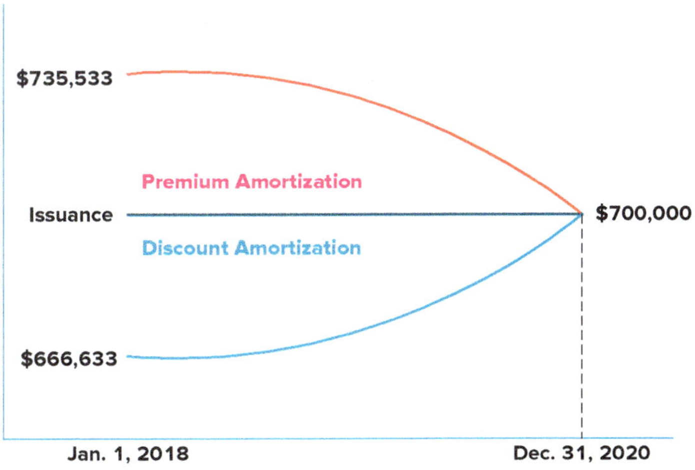

In practice, corporate bonds rarely are issued at a premium.[3] Because of the delay between the date the terms of the bonds are established and when the bonds are issued, it's difficult to set the stated rate equal to the ever-changing market rate. Knowing that, for marketing reasons, companies deliberately set the terms to more likely create a small discount rather than a premium at the issue date. Some investors are psychologically prone to prefer buying at a discount rather than a premium even if the yield is the same (the market rate).

Additional Consideration

The preceding illustrations describe bonds sold at a discount and at a premium. The same concepts apply to bonds sold at face amount. But some of the procedures would be unnecessary. For instance, calculating the present value of the interest and the principal always will give us the face amount when the effective rate and the stated rate are the same:

Calculation of the Price of the Bonds

	Present Values
Interest	$ 42,000 × 4.91732* = $206,528
Principal	$700,000 × 0.70496† = 493,472
Present value (price) of the bonds	$700,000

*Present value of an ordinary annuity of $1: $n = 6$, $i = 6\%$.
†Present value of $1: $n = 6$, $i = 6\%$.

Any interest that has accrued since the last interest date must be recorded by an adjusting entry prior to preparing financial statements.

When Financial Statements are Prepared between Interest Dates

When an accounting period ends between interest dates, it is necessary to record interest that has accrued since the last interest date. As an example, refer again to Illustration 14–3. If the fiscal years of Masterwear and United end on October 31 and interest was last paid and recorded on June 30, four months' interest must be accrued in a year-end adjusting entry. Because interest is recorded for only a portion of a semiannual period, amounts recorded are simply the amounts shown in the amortization schedule (Illustration 14–6) times the appropriate fraction of the semiannual period (in this case 4/6).

Adjusting Entries—To Accrue Interest

To avoid understating interest in the financial statements, four months' interest is recorded at the end of the reporting period.

At October 31

Masterwear (Issuer)		
Interest expense (4/6 × 46,991)	31,327	
Discount on bonds payable (4/6 × 4,991)		3,327
Interest payable (4/6 × 42,000)		28,000
United (Investor)		
Interest receivable (4/6 × 42,000)	28,000	
Discount on bond investment (4/6 × 4,991)	3,327	
Interest revenue (4/6 × 46,991)		31,327

Two months later, when semiannual interest is paid next, the remainder of the interest is allocated to the first two months of the next fiscal year—November and December:

Of the six months' interest paid December 31, only the November and December interest is expensed in the new fiscal year.

At the December 31 Interest Date

Masterwear (Issuer)		
Interest expense (2/6 × 46,991)	15,664	
Interest payable (from adjusting entry)	28,000	
Discount on bonds payable (2/6 × 4,991)		1,664
Cash (stated rate × face amount)		42,000

[3]Only about 1% of corporate bonds are issued at a premium. Amiram, Dan, A. Kalay, and B Ozel, "The Bond Discount Puzzle," *Financial Accounting eJournal*, March 25, 2013.

United (Investor)		
Cash (stated rate × face amount)	42,000	
Discount on bond investment (2/6 × 4,991)	1,664	
Interest receivable (from adjusting entry)		28,000
Interest revenue (2/6 × 46,991)		15,664

The Straight-Line Method—A Practical Expediency

In some circumstances the profession permits an exception to the conceptually appropriate method of determining interest for bond issues. A company is allowed to determine interest indirectly by allocating a discount or a premium equally to each period over the term to maturity—if doing so produces results that are not materially different from the usual (and preferable) interest method. The decision should be guided by whether the straight-line method would tend to mislead investors and creditors in the particular circumstance.

By the straight-line method, the discount in Illustration 14–3 and Illustration 14–6 would be allocated equally to the six semiannual periods (three years):

$33,367 ÷ 6 periods = $5,561 per period

Journal Entries—Straight-Line Method

By the straight-line method, interest (expense and revenue) is a plug figure, resulting from calculating the amount of discount reduction.

At Each of the Six Interest Dates		
Masterwear (Issuer)		
Interest expense (to balance)	47,561	
Discount on bonds payable (discount ÷ 6 periods)		5,561
Cash (stated rate × face amount)		42,000
United (Investor)		
Cash (stated rate × face amount)	42,000	
Discount on bond investment (discount ÷ 6 periods)	5,561	
Interest revenue (to balance)		47,561

Allocating the discount or premium equally over the life of the bonds by the straight-line method results in a constant dollar amount of interest each period. An amortization schedule, then, would serve little purpose. For example, if we prepared one for the straight-line method in this situation, it would provide the same amounts each period as shown in Illustration 14–11.

Illustration 14–11

Amortization Schedule—Straight-Line Method

By the straight-line method, the amount of the discount to be reduced periodically is calculated, and the recorded interest is the plug figure.

	Cash Interest	Recorded Interest	Increase in Balance	Outstanding Balance
	(6% × Face amount)	(Cash + Discount reduction)	($33,367 ÷ 6)	
1/1/18				666,633
6/30/18	42,000	(42,000 + 5,561) = 47,561	5,561	672,194
12/31/18	42,000	(42,000 + 5,561) = 47,561	5,561	677,755
6/30/19	42,000	(42,000 + 5,561) = 47,561	5,561	683,316
12/31/19	42,000	(42,000 + 5,561) = 47,561	5,561	688,877
6/30/20	42,000	(42,000 + 5,561) = 47,561	5,561	694,438
12/31/20	42,000	(42,000 + 5,561) = 47,561	5,561	700,000*
	252,000	285,366	33,366	

*Rounded

Remember, constant dollar amounts are not produced when the effective interest method is used. By that method, the dollar amounts of interest vary over the term to maturity because the percentage rate of interest remains constant but is applied to a changing debt balance.

Also, be sure to realize that the straight-line method is not an alternative method of determining interest in a conceptual sense. Instead, it is an application of the materiality concept, by which an appropriate application of GAAP (e.g., the effective interest method) can be

Determining interest by allocating the discount (or premium) on a straight-line basis is a practical expediency permitted in some situations by the materiality concept.

bypassed for reasons of practical expediency in situations when doing so has no material effect on the results. Based on the frequency with which the straight-line method is used in practice, we can infer that managers very frequently conclude that its use has no material impact on investors' decisions.

Concept Review Exercise

ISSUING BONDS AND RECORDING INTEREST

On January 1, 2018, the Meade Group issued $8,000,000 of 11% bonds, dated January 1. Interest is payable semiannually on June 30 and December 31. The bonds mature in four years. The market yield for bonds of similar risk and maturity is 10%.

Required:

1. Determine the price these bonds issued to yield the 10% market rate and record their issuance by the Meade Group.
2. Prepare an amortization schedule that determines interest at the effective rate and record interest on the first interest date, June 30, 2018.

Solution:

1. Determine the price these bonds sold for to yield the 10% market rate and record their issuance by the Meade Group.

Calculation of the Price of the Bonds

There are eight semiannual periods and one-half the market rate is 5%.

Interest	$ 440,000 × 6.46321* =	$2,843,812
Principal	$8,000,000 × 0.67684† =	5,414,720
Present value (price) of the bonds		$8,258,532

*Present value of an ordinary annuity of $1: $n = 8$, $i = 5\%$.
†Present value of $1: $n = 8$, $i = 5\%$.

Journal Entries at Issuance

Cash (price calculated above)	8,258,532	
Bonds payable (face amount)		8,000,000
Premium on bonds payable (difference)		258,532

2. Prepare an amortization schedule that determines interest at the effective rate and record interest on the first interest date, June 30, 2018.

Amortization Schedule

Date	Cash Interest	Effective Interest	Decrease in Balance	Outstanding Balance
	(5.5% × Face amount)	(5% × Outstanding balance)	(Premium reduction)	
1/1/18				8,258,532
6/30/18	440,000	0.05 (8,258,532) = 412,927	27,073	8,231,459
12/31/18	440,000	0.05 (8,231,459) = 411,573	28,427	8,203,032
6/30/19	440,000	0.05 (8,203,032) = 410,152	29,848	8,173,184
12/31/19	440,000	0.05 (8,173,184) = 408,659	31,341	8,141,843
6/30/20	440,000	0.05 (8,141,843) = 407,092	32,908	8,108,935
12/31/20	440,000	0.05 (8,108,935) = 405,447	34,553	8,074,382
6/30/21	440.000	0.05 (8,074,382) = 403,719	36,281	8,038,101
12/31/21	440,000	0.05 (8,038,101) = 401,899*	38,101	8,000,000
	3,520,000	3,261,468	258,532	

*Rounded

More cash is paid each period than the effective interest, so the debt outstanding is reduced by the "overpayment."

Interest expense (5% × $8,258,532)	412,927	
Premium on bonds payable (difference)	27,073	
Cash (5.5% × $8,000,000)		440,000
To record interest for six months.		

Debt Issue Costs

Rather than sell bonds directly to the public, corporations usually sell an entire issue to an underwriter who then resells them to other security dealers and the public. By committing to purchase bonds at a set price, investment banks such as JPMorgan Chase and Goldman Sachs are said to underwrite any risks associated with a new issue. The underwriting fee is the spread between the price the underwriter pays and the resale price.

Alternatively, the issuing company may choose to sell the debt securities directly to a single investor (as we assumed in previous illustrations)—often a pension fund or an insurance company. This is referred to as *private placement.* Issue costs are less because privately placed securities are not subject to the costly and lengthy process of registering with the SEC that is required of public offerings. Underwriting fees also are avoided.[4]

When issuing bonds or notes, the issuing company will incur costs, such as legal and accounting fees, printing costs, and registration and underwriting fees. These costs are recorded by combining them with any discount (or subtracting them from any premium) on the debt. The combined valuation account is reported in the balance sheet as a direct deduction from the liability and then amortized over the life of the debt.[5]

Costs of issuing debt securities are called "debt issue costs" and are accounted for the same way as bond discount.

This approach has the appeal of reflecting the effect that debt issue costs have on the effective interest rate. Debt issue costs reduce the cash proceeds from the issuance of debt, so it makes sense that they should reflect a higher cost of borrowing. By deducting debt issue costs, we lower the carrying amount of the debt, which effectively increases the interest rate on that debt. In other words, with debt issue costs, the net amount borrowed is less, but interest payments are the same, so the effective rate of borrowing is higher.

For example, let's assume that in Illustration 14–11, we had debt issue costs of $14,000. The debt issue costs reduce the net cash the issuing company receives from the issuance of the bonds. The entry for the issuance would reflect the lower net cash proceeds and the higher valuation account for the discount and the debt issue costs:

Masterwear (Issuer)		
Cash ($666,633 price minus $14,000 issue costs)	652,633	
Discount and debt issue costs (difference)	47,367	
Bonds payable (face amount)		700,000

The price discount and the debt issue costs reduce the cash proceeds from the issuance of the bonds.

Interest expense is determined in the usual way; that is, the effective interest rate times the outstanding balance. The outstanding balance is the "net" liability, the face amount reduced by the discount and debt issue costs ($652,633 for the first interest period).[6] The debt issue costs of $14,000 have the effect of increasing the effective rate from 7% semiannually (as in Illustration 14–4) to 7.4389% semiannually (rounded). To see how the effective rate is determined, see the next Additional Consideration box. The first semiannual interest payment would be recorded as follows:

Interest expense (652,633 × 7.4389%)	48,549	
Discount and debt issue costs (difference)		6,549
Cash ($700,000 × 6% stated rate)		42,000

The corporate bond is the basic long-term debt instrument for most large companies. But for many firms, the debt instrument often used is a *note.* We discuss notes next.

[4]Rule 144A of the Securities Act of 1933, as amended, allows for the private resale of unregistered securities to "qualified institutional buyers," which are generally large institutional investors with assets exceeding $100 million.

[5]Accounting Standards Update 2015-03: "Interest–Imputation of Interest (Subtopic 835-30) Simplifying the Presentation of Debt Issuance Costs," FASB, April 2015. This approach is consistent with the treatment of issue costs when equity securities are sold. You will see in Chapter 18 that the effect of share issue costs is to reduce the amount credited to stock accounts. It also is consistent with IFRS.

[6]If we have a premium instead of a discount, the valuation account is the premium reduced by the debt issue costs.

Additional Consideration

One important effect of the debt issue costs is that they reduce the amount of cash Masterwear is borrowing with the bond issuance (from $666,633 to $652,633). A lower (net) amount is borrowed at the same cost, making the *effective* interest rate higher than it would be without the debt issue costs. Previously, in Illustration 14–4 when we had no debt issue costs, the effective (market) rate was 14% (7% semiannually). That was the discount rate that caused the present value of the six interest payments and the maturity amount of $700,000 to be $666,633. Now, though, the effective rate is the one that would cause the present value of the six interest payments and the maturity amount of $700,000 to be $652,633. That annual rate is 14.8778% instead of 14%, and thus is a semiannual rate of 7.4389%, up from 7%. The following amortization schedule demonstrates this:

Cash Payments	Effective Interest	Increase or (decrease) in Balance	Balance
6.0%	7.4389%		
			652,633
42,000	7.4389% × (652,633) = 48,549	6,549	659,182
42,000	7.4389% × (659,182) = 49,036	7,036	666,218
42,000	7.4389% × (666,218) = 49,559	7,559	673,777
42,000	7.4389% × (673,777) = 50,122	8,122	681,898
42,000	7.4389% × (681,898) = 50,726	8,726	690,624
42,000	7.4389% × (690,624) = 51,376*	9,376	700,000

*Rounded

PART B

Long-Term Notes

● LO14–3

FINANCIAL Reporting Case

Q4, p. 771

When a company borrows cash from a bank and signs a promissory note (essentially an IOU), the firm's liability is reported as a *note payable.* Or a note might be issued in exchange for a noncash asset—perhaps to purchase equipment on credit. In concept, notes are accounted for in precisely the same way as bonds. In fact, we could properly substitute notes payable for bonds payable in each of our previous illustrations. For comparison, we continue to also present the lenders' entries (in blue) in the illustrations to follow.

As we discuss accounting for the borrower's notes *payable,* we also will consider the lender's perspective and look at notes *receivable* at the same time. By considering both sides of each transaction at the same time, we will see that the two sides are essentially mirror images of one another. This coverage of long-term notes complements our Chapter 7 discussion of *short-term* notes receivable.

Note Issued for Cash

The interest rate stated in a note is likely to be equal to the market rate because the rate usually is negotiated at the time of the loan. So discounts and premiums are less likely for notes than for bonds. Accounting for a note issued for cash is demonstrated in Illustration 14–12.

Note Exchanged for Assets or Services

Occasionally the *stated* interest rate is not indicative of the *market* rate at the time a note is negotiated. The value of the asset (cash or noncash) or service exchanged for the note establishes the market rate.[7] For example, let's assume Skill Graphics purchased a package-labeling machine from Hughes–Barker Corporation by issuing a 12%, $700,000, three-year note that requires interest to be paid semiannually. Let's also assume that the machine could have been purchased at a cash price of $666,633. You probably recognize this numerical situation

[7]If the debt instrument is negotiable and a dependable exchange price is readily available, the market value of the debt may be better evidence of the value of the transaction than the value of a noncash asset, particularly if it has no established cash selling price. The value of the asset or the debt, whichever is considered more reliable, should be used to record the transaction.

Illustration 14–12

Note Issued for Cash

On January 1, 2018, Skill Graphics, Inc., a product-labeling and graphics firm, borrowed $700,000 cash from First BancCorp and issued a three-year, $700,000 promissory note. Interest of $42,000 was payable semiannually on June 30 and December 31.

At Issuance

Skill Graphics (Borrower)		
Cash	700,000	
Notes payable (face amount)		700,000
First BancCorp (Lender)		
Notes receivable (face amount)	700,000	
Cash		700,000

At Each of the Six Interest Dates

Skill Graphics (Borrower)		
Interest expense	42,000	
Cash (stated rate × face amount)		42,000
First BancCorp (Lender)		
Cash (stated rate × face amount)	42,000	
Interest revenue		42,000

At Maturity

Skill Graphics (Borrower)		
Notes payable	700,000	
Cash (face amount)		700,000
First BancCorp (Lender)		
Cash (face amount)	700,000	
Notes receivable		700,000

as the one used earlier to illustrate bonds sold at a discount (Illustration 14–3). Reference to the earlier example will confirm that exchanging this $700,000 note for a machine with a cash price of $666,633 implies an annual market rate of interest of 14%. That is, 7% is one-half the discount rate that yields a present value of $666,633 for the note's cash flows (interest plus principal):

	Present Values
Interest	$ 42,000 × 4.76654* = $200,195
Principal	$700,000 × 0.66634† = 466,438
Present value of the note	$666,633

*Present value of an ordinary annuity of $1: $n = 6$, $i = 7\%$.
†Present value of $1: $n = 6$, $i = 7\%$.

This is referred to as the **implicit rate of interest**—the rate implicit in the agreement. It may be that the implicit rate is not apparent. Sometimes the value of the asset (or service) is not readily determinable, but the interest rate stated in the transaction is unrealistic relative to the rate that would be expected in a similar transaction under similar circumstances. Deciding what the appropriate rate should be is called *imputing* an interest rate.

A basic concept of accounting is *substance over form.*

For example, suppose the machine exchanged for the 12% note is custom-made for Skill Graphics so that no customary cash price is available with which to work backwards to find the implicit rate. In that case, the appropriate rate would have to be found externally. It might be determined, for instance, that a more realistic interest rate for a transaction of this type, at this time, would be 14%. Then it would be apparent that Skill Graphics actually paid less than $700,000 for the machine and that part of the face amount of the note in effect makes up for the lower than normal interest rate. You learned early in your study of accounting that the economic essence of a transaction should prevail over its outward appearance. In keeping with this basic precept, the accountant should look beyond the *form* of this transaction and record its *substance.* The amount actually paid for the machine is the present value of the cash flows called for by the loan agreement, discounted at the market rate—imputed in this case to be 14%. So both the asset acquired and the liability used to purchase it should be recorded at the real cost, $666,633.

Additional Consideration

For another example, let's assume the more realistic interest rate for a transaction of this type is, say, 16%. In that case we would calculate the real cost of the machine by finding the present value of both the interest and the principal, discounted at half the 16% rate (because interest is paid semiannually):

	Present Values
Interest	$ 42,000 × 4.62288* = $ 194,161
Principal	$700,000 × 0.63017† = 441,119
Present value of the note	$ 635,280

*Present value of an ordinary annuity of $1: $n = 6$, $i = 8\%$.
†Present value of $1: $n = 6$, $i = 8\%$.

Both the asset acquired and the liability used to purchase it would be recorded at $635,280.

The accounting treatment is the same whether the amount is determined directly from the market value of the machine (and thus the note) or indirectly as the present value of the note (and thus the value of the asset):[8]

Journal Entries at Issuance—Note with Unrealistic Interest Rate

Skill Graphics (Buyer/Issuer)		
Machinery (cash price)	666,633	
Discount on notes payable (difference)	33,367	
Notes payable (face amount)		700,000
Hughes-Barker (Seller/Lender)		
Notes receivable (face amount)	700,000	
Discount on notes receivable (difference)		33,367
Sales revenue (cash price)		666,633

Likewise, whether the effective interest rate is determined as the rate implicit in the agreement, given the asset's market value, or whether the effective rate is imputed as the appropriate interest rate if the asset's value is unknown, both parties to the transaction should record periodic interest (interest expense to the borrower, interest revenue to the lender) at the effective rate, rather than the stated rate.

Journal Entries—The Interest Method

The effective interest (expense to the issuer; revenue to the investor) is calculated each period as the effective rate times the amount of the debt outstanding during the interest period.

At the First Interest Date (June 30)		
Skill Graphics (Borrower)		
Interest expense (effective rate × outstanding balance)	46,664	
Discount on notes payable (difference)		4,664
Cash (stated rate × face amount)		42,000
Hughes-Barker (Seller/Lender)		
Cash (stated rate × face amount)	42,000	
Discount on notes receivable (difference)	4,664	
Interest revenue (effective rate × outstanding balance)		46,664

[8]The method shown is the *gross method.* Alternatively, the *net method* can be used as follows:

Skill Graphics (Buyer/Issuer)		
Machinery (cash price)	666,633	
Notes payable		666,633
Hughes-Barker (Seller/Lender)		
Notes receivable	666,633	
Sales revenue (cash price)		666,633

Under the net method, the note is recorded at the face amount reduced by the discount on notes payable, which is the difference between face value and present value. As cash interest is paid, the note balance increases by the difference between the cash interest payment and the interest revenue (and interest expense). After the last payment, the note account balance will be equal to the face amount of the note.

The interest expense (interest revenue for the lender) varies as the balance of the note changes over time. See the amortization schedule in Illustration 14–13.[9] Be sure to notice that this amortization schedule is identical to the one in Illustration 14–6 for bonds issued at a discount.

Illustration 14–13
Amortization Schedule—Note

Date	Cash Interest	Effective Interest	Increase in Balance	Outstanding Balance
	(6% × Face amount)	(7% × Outstanding balance)	(Discount reduction)	
1/1/18				666,633
6/30/18	42,000	0.07 (666,633) = 46,664	4,664	671,297
12/31/18	42,000	0.07 (671,297) = 46,991	4,991	676,288
6/30/19	42,000	0.07 (676,288) = 47,340	5,340	681,628
12/31/19	42,000	0.07 (681,628) = 47,714	5,714	687,342
6/30/20	42,000	0.07 (687,342) = 48,114	6,114	693,456
12/31/20	42,000	0.07 (693,456) = 48,544*	6,544	700,000
	252,000	285,367	33,367	

*Rounded

Since less cash is paid each period than the effective interest, the unpaid difference (the discount reduction) increases the outstanding balance (book value) of the note.

Installment Notes

You may have recently purchased a car, or maybe a house. If so, unless you paid cash, you signed a note promising to pay a portion of the purchase price over, say, five years for the car, or 30 years for the house. Car and house notes usually call for payment in monthly installments rather than by a single amount at maturity. Corporations, too, often borrow using installment notes. Typically, installment payments are equal amounts each period. Each payment includes both an amount that represents interest and an amount that represents a reduction of the outstanding balance (principal reduction). The periodic reduction of the balance is sufficient that at maturity the note is completely paid. This amount is easily calculated by dividing the amount of the loan by the appropriate discount factor for the present value of an annuity. The installment payment amount that would pay the note described in the previous section is:

$666,633	÷	4.76654	=	$139,857
Amount of loan		(from Table 4 $n = 6, i = 7.0\%$)		Installment payment

Consider Illustration 14–14.

Illustration 14–14
Amortization Schedule—Installment Note

Date	Cash Payment	Effective Interest	Decrease in Debt	Outstanding Balance
		(7% × Outstanding balance)		
1/1/18				666,633
6/30/18	139,857	0.07 (666,633) = 46,664	93,193	573,440
12/31/18	139,857	0.07 (573,440) = 40,141	99,716	473,724
6/30/19	139,857	0.07 (473,724) = 33,161	106,696	367,028
12/31/19	139,857	0.07 (367,028) = 25,692	114,165	252,863
6/30/20	139,857	0.07 (252,863) = 17,700	122,157	130,706
12/31/20	139,857	0.07 (130,706) = 9,151*	130,706	0
	839,142	172,509	666,633	

*Rounded

Each installment payment includes interest on the outstanding debt at the effective rate. The remainder of each payment reduces the outstanding balance.

[9] The creation of amortization schedules is simplified by an electronic spreadsheet such as Microsoft Excel.

For installment notes, the outstanding balance of the note does not eventually become its face amount as it does for notes with designated maturity amounts. Instead, at the maturity date the balance is zero. The procedure is the same as for a note whose principal is paid at maturity, but the periodic cash payments are larger and there is no lump-sum payment at maturity. We calculated the amount of the payments so that after covering the interest on the existing debt each period, the excess would exactly amortize the debt to zero at maturity (rather than to a designated maturity amount).

Consequently, the significance is lost of maintaining separate balances for the face amount (in a note account) and the discount (or premium). So an installment note typically is recorded at its net book value in a single note payable (or receivable) account:

Journal Entries at Issuance—Installment Note

Skill Graphics (Buyer/Issuer)		
Machinery	666,633	
Note payable		666,633
Hughes-Barker (Seller/Lender)		
Note receivable	666,633	
Sales revenue		666,633

At the First Interest Date (June 30)

Each payment includes both an amount that represents interest and an amount that represents a reduction of principal.

Skill Graphics (Borrower)		
Interest expense (effective rate × outstanding balance)	46,664	
Notes payable (difference)	93,193	
Cash (installment payment calculated above)		139,857
Hughes-Barker (Seller/Lender)		
Cash (installment payment calculated above)	139,857	
Notes receivable (difference)		93,193
Interest revenue (effective rate × outstanding balance)		46,664

Additional Consideration

You will learn in the next chapter that the liability associated with a lease is accounted for the same way as this installment note. In fact, if the asset described above had been leased rather than purchased, the cash payments would be designated lease payments rather than installment loan payments, and a virtually identical amortization schedule would apply.

The reason for the similarity is that we view a finance lease as being, in substance, equivalent to an installment purchase of the right to use an asset. Naturally, then, accounting treatment of the two essentially identical transactions should be consistent. Be sure to notice the parallel treatment as you study leases in the next chapter.

Financial Statement Disclosures

● LO14–4

In the balance sheet, long-term debt (liability for the debtor; asset for the creditor) typically is reported as a single amount, net of any discount or increased by any premium, rather than at its face amount accompanied by a separate valuation account for the discount or premium. Any portion of the debt to be paid (received) during the upcoming year, or operating cycle if longer, should be reported as a current amount.

Note disclosure is required of the fair value of bonds, notes, and other financial instruments.

The fair value of financial instruments must be disclosed either in the body of the financial statements or in disclosure notes.[10] These fair values are available for bonds and other securities traded on market exchanges in the form of quoted market prices. On the other hand, financial instruments not traded on market exchanges require other evidence of market value. For example, the market value of a note payable might be approximated by the

[10]FASB ASC 825–10–50–10: Financial Instruments–Overall–Disclosure (previously "Disclosures About Fair Values of Financial Instruments," *Statement of Financial Accounting Standards No. 107* (Norwalk, Conn.: FASB, 1991)).

present value of principal and interest payments using a current discount rate commensurate with the risks involved.

The disclosure note for debt includes the nature of the company's liabilities, interest rates, maturity dates, call provisions, conversion options, restrictions imposed by creditors, and any assets pledged as collateral. For all long-term borrowings, disclosures also should include the aggregate amounts payable for each of the next five years. To comply, Microsoft's annual report for the fiscal year ended June 30, 2015, included the disclosure shown in Illustration 14–15.

Maturities of our long-term debt for each of the next five years and thereafter are as follows:

Year Ending June 30,	($ in millions)
2016	$ 2,500
2017	0
2018	1,050
2019	2,250
2020	1,500
Thereafter	23,163
Total	$30,463

Illustration 14–15

Debt Disclosures—Microsoft Corporation

Real World Financials

In a statement of cash flows, issuing bonds or notes are reported as cash flows from financing activities by the issuer (borrower) and cash flows from investing activities by the investor (lender). Similarly, as the debt is repaid, the issuer (borrower) reports a financing activity while the investor (lender) reports an investing activity. However, because both interest expense and interest revenue are components of the income statement, both parties to the transaction report interest among operating activities. We discuss the cash flow reporting process in more depth in Chapter 21.

Borrowing is a financing activity; lending is an investing activity.

Paying or receiving interest is an operating activity.

Decision Makers' Perspective

Business decisions involve risk. Failure to properly consider risk in those decisions is one of the most costly, yet one of the most common mistakes investors and creditors can make. Long-term debt is one of the first places decision makers should look when trying to get a handle on risk.

In general, debt increases risk. As an owner, debt would place you in a subordinate position relative to creditors because the claims of creditors must be satisfied first in case of liquidation. In addition, debt requires payment, usually on specific dates. Failure to pay debt interest and principal on a timely basis may result in default and perhaps even bankruptcy. The debt to equity ratio, total liabilities divided by shareholders' equity, often is calculated to measure the degree of risk. Other things being equal, the higher the debt to equity ratio, the higher the risk. The type of risk this ratio measures is called *default risk* because it presumably indicates the likelihood a company will default on its obligations.

Generally speaking, debt increases risk.

Debt also can be an advantage. It can be used to enhance the return to shareholders. This concept, known as leverage, was described and illustrated in Chapter 3. If a company earns a return on borrowed funds in excess of the cost of borrowing the funds, shareholders are provided with a total return greater than what could have been earned with equity funds alone. This desirable situation is called *favorable financial leverage.* Unfortunately, leverage is not always favorable. Sometimes the cost of borrowing the funds exceeds the returns they generate. This illustrates the typical risk-return trade-off faced by shareholders.

To evaluate a firm's risk, you might start by calculating its debt to equity ratio.

As a manager, you would try to create favorable financial leverage to earn a return on borrowed funds in excess of the cost of borrowing the funds.

Creditors demand interest payments as compensation for the use of their capital. Failure to pay interest as scheduled may cause several adverse consequences, including bankruptcy. Therefore, another way to measure a company's ability to pay its obligations is by comparing interest payments with income available to pay those charges. The times interest earned ratio does this by dividing income, before subtracting interest expense or income tax expense, by interest expense.

As an external analyst or a manager, you are concerned with a company's ability to repay debt.

Two points about this ratio are important. First, because interest is deductible for income tax purposes, income before interest and taxes is a better indication of a company's ability to pay interest than is income after interest and taxes (i.e., net income). Second, income before interest and taxes is a rough approximation for cash flow generated from operations. The primary concern of decision makers is, of course, the cash available to make interest payments. In fact, this ratio often is computed by dividing cash flow generated from operations by interest payments.

For illustration, let's compare the ratios for Coca-Cola and PepsiCo. Illustration 14–16 provides condensed financial statements adapted from 2015 annual reports of those companies.

Illustration 14–16

Condensed Financial Statements—Coca-Cola, PepsiCo

Real World Financials

Balance Sheets

	($ in millions)	
	Coca-Cola	**PepsiCo**
Assets		
Current assets	$33,395	$23,031
Property, plant, and equipment (net)	12,571	16,317
Intangibles and other assets	44,127	30,319
Total assets	$90,093	$69,667
Liabilities and Shareholders' Equity		
Current liabilities	$26,930	$17,578
Long-term liabilities	37,399	40,059
Total liabilities	$64,329	$57,637
Shareholders' equity	25,764	12,030
Total liabilities and shareholders' equity	$90,093	$69,667
Income Statements		
Net sales	$44,294	$63,056
Cost of goods sold	(17,482)	(28,384)
Gross profit	$26,812	$34,672
Operating and other expenses	(16,366)	(26,309)
Interest expense	(856)	(970)
Income before taxes	$ 9,590	$ 7,393
Tax expense	(2,239)	(1,941)
Net income	$ 7,351	$ 5,452

The debt to equity ratio is much higher for PepsiCo:

The debt to equity ratio indicates the extent of trading on the equity, or financial leverage.

$$\text{Debt to equity ratio} = \frac{\text{Total liabilities}}{\text{Shareholders' equity}}$$

$$\text{Coca-Cola} = \frac{\$64,329}{\$25,764} = 2.5$$

$$\text{PepsiCo} = \frac{\$57,637}{\$12,030} = 4.8$$

Remember, that's not necessarily a positive or a negative. Let's look closer. When the return on shareholders' equity is greater than the return on assets, management is using debt funds to enhance the earnings for shareholders. Both firms do this. We calculate return on assets for 2015 as follows:

The rate of return on assets indicates profitability without regard to how resources are financed.

$$\text{Rate of return on assets}^{11} = \frac{\text{Net income}}{\text{Total assets}}$$

$$\text{Coca-Cola} = \frac{\$7,351}{\$90,093} = 8.2\%$$

$$\text{PepsiCo} = \frac{\$5,452}{\$69,667} = 7.8\%$$

[11]A more accurate way to calculate this ratio is: Rate of return on assets = Net income + Interest expense (1 − tax rate) ÷ Average total assets. The reason for adding back interest expense (net of tax) is that interest represents a return to suppliers of debt capital and should not be deducted in the computation of net income when computing the return on total assets. In other words, the numerator is the total amount of income available to both debt and equity capital.

The return on assets indicates a company's overall profitability, ignoring specific sources of financing. In this regard, Coca-Cola's profitability is slightly higher than PepsiCo's. That advantage, though, disappears when we compare the return to shareholders:

$$\text{Rate of return on shareholder's equity} = \frac{\text{Net income}}{\text{Shareholder's equity}}$$

$$\text{Coca-Cola} = \frac{\$7{,}351}{\$25{,}764} = 28.5\%$$

$$\text{PepsiCo} = \frac{\$5{,}452}{\$12{,}030} = 45.3\%$$

The rate of return on shareholders' equity indicates the effectiveness of employing resources provided by owners.

Coca-Cola's return on assets is 5% higher than PepsiCo's, but its return on shareholders' equity is 37% less. The reason is that higher leverage has been used by Pepsi to provide a relatively greater return to shareholders. PepsiCo increased its return to shareholders 5.8 times (45.3% / 7.8%) the return on assets. Coca-Cola increased its return to shareholders 3.5 times (28.5% / 8.2%) the return on assets. Interpret this with caution, though. PepsiCo's higher leverage means higher risk as well. In down times, PepsiCo's return to shareholders will suffer proportionally more than will Coca-Cola's.

From the perspective of a creditor, we might look at which company offers the most comfortable margin of safety in terms of its ability to pay fixed interest charges:

$$\text{Times interest earned ratio} = \frac{\text{Net income plus interest plus taxes}}{\text{Interest}}$$

$$\text{Coca-Cola} = \frac{\$7{,}351 + 856 + 2{,}239}{\$856} = 12.2 \text{ times}$$

$$\text{PepsiCo} = \frac{\$5{,}452 + 970 + 1{,}941}{\$970} = 8.6 \text{ times}$$

The times interest earned ratio indicates the margin of safety provided to creditors.

In this regard, Coca-Cola provides a greater margin of safety. And, Pepsi has more debt in its capital structure relative to Coca-Cola. However, Pepsi clearly is able to pay the cost of borrowing and provide an impressive return to its shareholders. Both firms, though, trade quite favorably on their leverage.

Liabilities also can have misleading effects on the income statement. Decision makers should look carefully at gains and losses produced by early extinguishment of debt. These have nothing to do with a company's normal operating activities. Unchecked, corporate management can be tempted to schedule debt buybacks to provide discretionary income in down years or even losses in up years to smooth income over time.

Decision makers should be alert to gains and losses that have nothing to do with a company's normal operating activities.

Alert investors and lenders also look outside the financial statements for risks associated with "off-balance-sheet" financing and other commitments that don't show up on the face of financial statements but nevertheless expose a company to risk. Relatedly, most companies attempt to actively manage the risk associated with these and other obligations. It is important for top management to understand and closely monitor risk management strategies. Some of the financial losses that have grabbed headlines in recent years were permitted by a lack of oversight and scrutiny by senior management of companies involved. It is similarly important for investors and creditors to become informed about risks companies face and how well-equipped those companies are in managing that risk. The supplemental disclosures designed to communicate the degree of risk associated with the financial instruments we discuss in this chapter contribute to that understanding. We examine the significance of lease commitments in the next chapter. ●

Outside analysts as well as managers should actively monitor risk management activities.

Concept Review Exercise

NOTE WITH AN UNREALISTIC INTEREST RATE

Cameron-Brown, Inc., constructed for Harmon Distributors a warehouse that was completed and ready for occupancy on January 2, 2018. Harmon paid for the warehouse by issuing a $900,000, four-year note that required 7% interest to be paid on December 31 of each year. The warehouse was custom-built for Harmon, so its cash price was not known. By comparison with similar transactions, it was determined that an appropriate interest rate was 10%.

Required:

1. Prepare the journal entry for Harmon's purchase of the warehouse on January 2, 2018.
2. Prepare (a) an amortization schedule for the four-year term of the note and (b) the journal entry for Harmon's first interest payment on December 31, 2018.
3. Suppose Harmon's note had been an installment note to be paid in four equal payments. What would be the amount of each installment if payable (a) at the end of each year, beginning December 31, 2018? or (b) at the beginning of each year, beginning on January 2, 2018?

Solution:

1. Prepare the journal entry for Harmon's purchase of the warehouse on January 2, 2018.

	Present Values
Interest	\$ 63,000 × 3.16987* = \$199,702
Principal	\$900,000 × 0.68301† = 614,709
Present value of the note	\$814,411

*Present value of an ordinary annuity of \$1: $n = 4$, $i = 10\%$.
†Present value of \$1: $n = 4$, $i = 10\%$.

Warehouse (price determined above)	814,411	
Discount on notes payable (difference)	85,589	
Notes payable (face amount)		900,000

2. Prepare (a) an amortization schedule for the four-year term of the note and (b) the journal entry for Harmon's first interest payment on December 31, 2018.

Each period the unpaid interest increases the outstanding balance of the debt.

Dec. 31	Cash	Effective Interest	Increase in Balance	Outstanding Balance
	(7% × Face amount)	(10% × Outstanding balance)	(Discount reduction)	
				814,411
2018	63,000	0.10 (814,411) = 81,441	18,441	832,852
2019	63,000	0.10 (832,852) = 83,285	20,285	853,137
2020	63,000	0.10 (853,137) = 85,314	22,314	875,451
2021	63,000	0.10 (875,451) = 87,549*	24,549	900,000
	252,000	337,589	85,589	

*Rounded

The effective interest is the market rate times the amount of the debt outstanding during the year.

Interest expense (effective rate × outstanding balance)	81,441	
Discount on notes payable (difference)		18,441
Cash (stated rate × face amount)		63,000

Because money has a time value, installment payments delayed until the end of each period must be higher than if the payments are made at the beginning of each period.

3. Suppose Harmon's note had been an installment note to be paid in four equal payments. What would be the amount of each installment if payable (a) at the end of each year, beginning December 31, 2018? or (b) at the beginning of each year, beginning on January 2, 2018?

a.	\$814,411	÷	3.16987	=	\$256,923
	Amount of loan		(from Table 4 $n = 4$, $i = 10\%$)		Installment payment
b.	\$814,411	÷	3.48685	=	\$233,566
	Amount of loan		(from Table 6 $n = 4$, $i = 10\%$)		Installment payment

Debt Retired Early, Convertible Into Stock, or Providing an Option to Buy Stock

PART C

Early Extinguishment of Debt

● LO14–5

As we saw in the previous section, debt paid in installments is systematically retired over the term to maturity so that at the designated maturity date the outstanding balance is zero. On the other hand, when a maturity amount is specified as in our earlier illustrations, any discount or premium has been systematically reduced to zero as of the maturity date and the debt is retired simply by paying the maturity amount. Sometimes, though, companies choose to retire debt before its scheduled maturity. In that case, a gain or a loss may result.

Earlier we noted that a call feature accompanies most bonds to protect the issuer against declining interest rates. Even when bonds are not callable, the issuing company can retire bonds early by purchasing them on the open market. Regardless of the method, when debt of any type is retired prior to its scheduled maturity date, the transaction is referred to as **early extinguishment of debt**.

Any difference between the outstanding debt and the amount paid to retire that debt represents either a gain or a loss.

To record the extinguishment, the account balances pertinent to the debt obviously must be removed from the books. Of course cash is credited for the amount paid—the call price or market price. The difference between the book value of the debt and the reacquisition price represents either a gain or a loss on the early extinguishment of debt. When the debt is retired for less than book value, the debtor is in a favorable position and records a gain. The opposite occurs for a loss. Let's continue an earlier example to illustrate the retirement of debt prior to its scheduled maturity (Illustration 14–17).

Illustration 14–17

Early Extinguishment of Debt

On January 1, 2019, Masterwear Industries called its $700,000, 12% bonds when their book value was $676,288. The indenture specified a call price of $685,000. The bonds were issued previously at a price to yield 14%.

Bonds payable (face amount)	700,000	
Loss on early extinguishment ($685,000 – 676,288)	8,712	
Discount on bonds payable ($700,000 – 676,288)		23,712
Cash (call price)		685,000

For instance, in its 2015 income statement, Levi Strauss & Co. reported a $20.3 million loss on the early extinguishment of debt.

Convertible Bonds

FINANCIAL Reporting Case

Q5, p. 771

Convertible bonds can be exchanged for shares of stock at the option of the investor.

Convertible bonds have features of both debt and equity.

Sometimes corporations include a convertible feature as part of a bond offering. **Convertible bonds** can be converted into (that is, exchanged for) shares of stock at the option of the bondholder. Among the reasons for issuing convertible bonds rather than straight debt are (a) to sell the bonds at a higher price (which means a lower effective interest cost),[12] (b) to use as a medium of exchange in mergers and acquisitions, and (c) to enable smaller firms or debt-heavy companies to obtain access to the bond market. Sometimes convertible bonds serve as an indirect way to issue stock when there is shareholder resistance to direct issuance of additional equity.

Central to each of these reasons for issuing convertible debt is that the conversion feature is attractive to investors. This hybrid security has features of both debt and equity. The owner has a fixed-income security that can become common stock if and when the firm's prosperity makes that feasible. This increases the investor's upside potential while limiting the downside risk. The conversion feature has monetary value. Just how valuable it is depends on both the conversion terms and market conditions. But from an accounting perspective the question raised is how to account for its value. To evaluate the question, consider Illustration 14–18.

[12]Remember, there is an inverse relationship between bond prices and interest rates. When the price is higher, the rate (yield) is lower, and vice versa.

Illustration 14–18
Convertible Bonds

> On January 1, 2018, HTL Manufacturers issued $100 million of 8% convertible debentures due 2038 at 103 (103% of face value). The bonds are convertible at the option of the holder into no par common stock at a conversion ratio of 40 shares per $1,000 bond. HTL recently issued nonconvertible, 20-year, 8% debentures at 98.

Because of the inseparability of their debt and equity features, the entire issue price of convertible bonds is recorded as debt, as if they are nonconvertible bonds.

It would appear that the conversion feature is valued by the market at $5 million—the difference between the market value of the convertible bonds, $103 million, and the market value of the nonconvertible bonds, $98 million. Some accountants argue that we should record the value of the conversion option in a shareholders' equity account ($5 million in this case) and the debt value in the bond accounts ($100 million bonds payable less $2 million discount). However, counter to that intuitive argument, the currently accepted practice is to record the entire issue price as debt in precisely the same way as for nonconvertible bonds.[13] Treating the features as two inseparable parts of a single security avoids the practical difficulty of trying to measure the separate values of the debt and the conversion option.

Journal Entry at Issuance—Convertible Bonds

	($ in millions)	
Cash (103% × $100 million)	103	
Convertible bonds payable (face amount)		100
Premium on bonds payable (difference)		3

The value of the conversion feature is not separately recorded.

Since we make no provision for the separate value of the conversion option, all subsequent entries, including the periodic reduction of the premium, are exactly the same as if these were nonconvertible bonds. So the illustrations and examples of bond accounting we discussed earlier would pertain equally to nonconvertible or convertible bonds.

Additional Consideration

While we normally don't separate the conversion option from the debt for convertible bonds, an exception is when the conversion option is deemed to be a "beneficial conversion feature." That's the case when the conversion option has a positive "intrinsic value" at the time the bonds are issued, meaning the fair value of the stock into which the bonds are convertible exceeds the face amount of the bonds.[14] Suppose, for instance, that HTL's stock in Illustration 14–18 has a fair value of $30 per share when the bonds are issued. This implies an intrinsic value of the conversion feature of $5 per share:

Price per share to convert: $1,000 ÷ 40 shares = $25 per share	
Fair value of stock at issue date	$30
Conversion price for shares	25
Intrinsic value of beneficial conversion option per share	$ 5

Intrinsic value of beneficial conversion feature:

100,000 bonds × 40 shares = 4,000,000 shares × $5 per share = **$20,000,000**

The intrinsic value of the conversion option is recorded separately:

	($ in millions)	
Cash (103% × $100 million)	103	
Discount on bonds (to balance)	17	
Convertible bonds payable (face amount)		100
Equity—conversion option (intrinsic value)		20

[13]FASB ASC 470–20–25: Debt–Debt with Conversion Options–Recognition (previously "Accounting for Convertible Debt and Debt Issued with Stock Purchase Warrants," *Accounting Principles Board Opinion No. 14* (New York: APB, 1969)).

[14]FASB ASC 470–20–25–5: Debt–Debt with Conversion and Other Options–Recognition–Beneficial Conversion Features (previously "Accounting for Convertible Securities with Beneficial Conversion Features or Contingently Adjustable Conversion Ratios," *EITF Issue No. 98-5* (Norwalk, Conn.: FASB, 1998)).

Where We're Headed

Accounting for convertible debt is likely to change. In fact, the FASB and IASB have worked on a joint project on "Financial Instruments with Characteristics of Equity."[15] A pre-Codification FASB Staff Position gives us another hint, perhaps, of the direction the project might take. For a limited subset of convertible securities not within the scope of current GAAP—those that could possibly be settled in cash rather than shares—companies must divide the proceeds from convertible securities into its two components and record the fair value of the debt as a liability and the conversion option in an equity account. Lending credence to that projection is the fact that international standards already require that convertible debt be divided into its liability and equity elements, so moving in that direction would be a step closer to convergence of U.S. GAAP and IFRS.

International Financial Reporting Standards

Convertible bonds. Under IFRS, unlike U.S. GAAP, convertible debt is divided into its liability and equity elements. In Illustration 14–18, if HTL prepared its financial statements in accordance with IFRS, it would record the convertible bonds as follows:

Journal Entry at Issuance—Convertible Bonds

	($ in millions)	
Cash (103% × $100 million)	103	
Convertible bonds payable (value of the debt only)		98*
Equity—conversion option (to balance)		5

*Notice that the discount is combined with the face amount of the bonds. This is the "net method". Using the "gross method" we would credit Convertible bonds payable $100 and debit Discount on bonds $2.

● LO14–7

The components of compound financial instruments such as convertible bonds are valued and reported separately under IFRS.

In essence, HTL is selling two securities—(1) bonds and (2) an option to convert to stock—for one package price. The bonds represent a liability; the option is shareholders' equity. Compound instruments such as this one are separated into their liability and equity components in accordance with IAS No. 32.[16] Because the bonds have a separate fair value of $98 million, we record that amount as the liability and the remaining $5 million (the difference between the fair value of the convertible bonds, $103 million, and the $98 million) as equity. If the fair value of the bonds cannot be determined from an active trading market, that value can be calculated as the present value of the bonds' cash flows, using the market rate of interest.

When the Conversion Option Is Exercised

If and when the bondholder exercises his or her option to convert the bonds into shares of stock, the bonds are removed from the accounting records and the new shares issued are recorded at the same amount (in other words, at the book value of the bonds). To illustrate, assume that half the convertible bonds issued by HTL Manufacturers are converted at a time when the remaining unamortized premium is $2 million:

Journal Entry at Conversion

	($ in millions)	
Convertible bonds payable (½ the account balance)	50	
Premium on bonds payable (½ the account balance)	1	
Common stock (to balance)		51

[15] The Boards developed a classification model that includes consideration of which financial instruments might be divided into separate components of liabilities and equity. In its tentative decisions reached earlier, the Boards had decided that "A bond (or other debt instrument) should be separated into a liability component and an equity component if it is convertible at the option of the holder into a specified number of instruments that will be equity in their entirety when issued." That project is classified as "inactive" as of the time this textbook was printed.

[16] "Financial Statements: Presentation," *International Accounting Standard (IAS) No. 32* (IASCF) as amended effective January 1, 2016.

Additional Consideration

The method just described is referred to as the *book value method,* since the new shares are recorded at the book value of the redeemed bonds. It is by far the most popular method in practice. Another acceptable approach, the *market value* method, records the new shares at the market value of the shares themselves or of the bonds, whichever is more determinable. Because the market value most likely will differ from the book value of the bonds, a gain or loss on conversion will result. Assume for illustration that the market value of HTL's stock is $30 per share at the time of the conversion:

	($ in millions)	
Convertible bonds payable (½ the account balance)	50	
Premium on bonds payable (½ the account balance)	1	
Loss on conversion of bonds (to balance)	9	
Common stock [(50,000 bonds × 40 shares) × $30]		60

If the 50,000 convertible bonds were held by a single investor, that company would record the conversion as follows:

The 2 million shares issued are recorded at the $51 million book value of the bonds retired.

	($ in millions)	
Investment in common stock	51	
Investment in convertible bonds (account balance)		50
Premium on bond investment (account balance)		1

Induced Conversion

Investors often are reluctant to convert bonds to stock, even when share prices have risen significantly since the convertible bonds were purchased. This is because the market price of the convertible bonds will rise along with market prices of the stock. So companies sometimes try to induce conversion. The motivation might be to reduce debt and become a better risk to potential lenders or achieve a lower debt-to-equity ratio.

One way is through the call provision. As we noted earlier, most corporate bonds are callable by the issuing corporation. When the specified call price is less than the conversion value of the bonds (the market value of the shares), calling the convertible bonds provides bondholders with incentive to convert. Bondholders will choose the shares rather than the lower call price.

Any additional consideration provided to induce conversion of convertible debt is recorded as an expense of the period.

Occasionally, corporations may try to encourage voluntary conversion by offering an added inducement in the form of cash, stock warrants, or a more attractive conversion ratio. When additional consideration is provided to induce conversion, the fair value of that consideration is considered an expense incurred to bring about the conversion.[17]

Bonds with Detachable Warrants

Another (less common) way to sweeten a bond issue is to include **detachable stock purchase warrants** as part of the security issue. A stock warrant gives the investor an option to purchase a stated number of shares of common stock at a specified *option price,* often within a given period of time. Like a conversion feature, warrants usually mean a lower interest rate and often enable a company to issue debt when borrowing would not be feasible otherwise.

However, unlike the conversion feature for convertible bonds, warrants can be separated from the bonds. This means they can be exercised independently or traded in the market separately from bonds, having their own market price. In essence, two different securities—the bonds and the warrants—are sold as a package for a single issue price. Accordingly, the

[17]FASB ASC 470–20–40: Debt–Debt with Conversion Options–Derecognition (previously "Induced Conversions of Convertible Debt," *Statement of Financial Accounting Standards No. 84* (Stamford, Conn.: FASB, 1985)).

issue price is allocated between the two different securities on the basis of their fair values. If the independent market value of only one of the two securities is reliably determinable, that value establishes the allocation. This is demonstrated in Illustration 14–19.

On January 1, 2018, HTL Manufacturers issued $100 million of 8% debentures due 2022 at 103 (103% of face value). Accompanying each $1,000 bond were 20 warrants. Each warrant permitted the holder to buy one share of no par common stock at $25 per share. Shortly after issuance, the warrants were listed on the stock exchange at $3 per warrant.

	($ in millions)	
Cash (103% × $100 million)	103	
Discount on bonds payable (difference)	3	
Bonds payable (face amount)		100
Equity—stock warrants* (100,000 bonds × 20 warrants × $3)		6

*Reported as part of shareholders' equity rather than as a liability.

Illustration 14–19

Bonds with Detachable Warrants

The issue price of bonds with detachable warrants is allocated between the two different securities on the basis of their fair values.

Additional Consideration

Market imperfections may cause the separate market values not to sum to the issue price of the package. In this event, allocation is achieved on the basis of the relative market values of the two securities. Let's say the bonds have a separate market price of $940 per bond (priced at 94):

Market Values	Dollars ($ in millions)	Percent
Bonds (100,000 bonds × $940)	$ 94	94%
Warrants (100,000 bonds × 20 warrants × $3)	6	6
Total	$100	100%

Proportion of Issue Price Allocated to Bonds:

$103 million × 94% = $96,820,000

Proportion of Issue Price Allocated to Warrants:

$103 million × 6% = $6,180,000

	($ in millions)	
Cash (103% × $100 million)	103.00	
Discount on bonds payable ($100 million – $96.82 million)	3.18	
Bonds payable (face amount)		100.00
Equity—stock warrants ($103 million × 6% = $6,180,000)		6.18

Notice that this is the same approach we used in Chapter 10 to allocate a single purchase price to two or more assets bought for that single price. We also will allocate the total selling price of two equity securities sold for a single issue in proportion to their relative market values in Chapter 18.

If one-half of the warrants (1 million) in Illustration 14–19 are exercised when the market value of HTL's common stock is $30 per share, 1 million shares would be issued for one warrant each plus the exercise price of $25 per share.

	($ in millions)	
Cash (1,000,000 warrants × $25)	25	
Equity—stock warrants (1,000,000 warrants × $3)	3	
Common stock (to balance)		28

Journal Entry at Exercise of Detachable Warrants

The $30 market value at the date of exercise is not used in valuing the additional shares issued. The new shares are recorded at the total of the previously measured values of both the warrants and the shares.

Concept Review Exercise

ISSUANCE AND EARLY EXTINGUISHMENT OF DEBT

The disclosure notes to the 2018 financial statements of Olswanger Industries included the following:

NOTE 12: BONDS

On September 15, 2017, the Corporation sold bonds with an aggregate principal amount of $500,000,000 bearing a 14% interest rate. The bonds will mature on September 15, 2027, and are unsecured subordinated obligations of the Corporation. Interest is payable semiannually on March 15 and September 15. The Corporation may redeem the bonds at any time beginning September 15, 2017, as a whole or from time to time in part, through maturity, at specified redemption prices ranging from 112% of principal in declining percentages of principal amount through 2024 when the percentage is set at 100% of principal amount. The cost of issuing the bonds, totaling $11,000,000, and the discount of $5,000,000 are being amortized over the life of the bonds. Amortization of these items for the year ended December 31, 2018, was $1,212,000.

During the year ended December 31, 2018, the Corporation repurchased, in open market transactions, $200,000,000 in face amount of the bonds for $219,333,000. The unamortized cost of issuing these bonds and the unamortized discount, totaling $5,864,000 have been deducted in the current period.

From the information provided by Olswanger in Note 12, you should be able to recreate some of the journal entries the company recorded in connection with this bond issue.

Required:

1. Prepare the journal entry for the issuance of these bonds on September 15, 2017.
2. Prepare the journal entry for the repurchase of these bonds, assuming the date of repurchase was September 15, 2018. The cash paid to repurchase the bonds was $219,333,000.

Solution:

1. Prepare the journal entry for the issuance of these bonds on September 15, 2017.

	($ in thousands)	
Cash (to balance)	484,000	
Discount and debt issue costs (given in note)	16,000	
Bonds payable (face amount—given in note)		500,000

2. Prepare the journal entry for the repurchase of these bonds, assuming the date of repurchase was September 15, 2018.

	($ in thousands)	
Bonds payable (face amount repurchased)	200,000	
Loss on early extinguishment (to balance)	25,197	
Discount and debt issue costs (given in note)		5,864
Cash (given in requirement 2)		219,333

PART D

Option to Report Liabilities at Fair Value

● LO14–6

A company has the option to value financial assets and liabilities at fair value.

Companies are not required to, but have the option to, value some or all of their financial assets and liabilities at fair value.[18] In Chapter 12, we saw examples of the option applied to financial assets—specifically, companies reporting their investments in securities at fair value. Now, we see how liabilities, too, can be reported at fair value.

[18]FASB ASC 825–10–25–1: Financial Instruments–Overall–Recognition–Fair Value Option (previously "The Fair Value Option for Financial Assets and Financial Liabilities," *Statement of Financial Accounting Standards No. 159* (Norwalk, Conn.: FASB, 2007)).

How does a liability's fair value change? Remember that there are two sides to every investment. For example, if a company has an investment in General Motors' bonds, that investment is an asset to the investor, and the same bonds are a liability to GM. So, the same market forces that influence the fair value of an investment in debt securities (interest rates, credit risk, etc.) influence the fair value of liabilities. For bank loans or other debts that aren't traded on a market exchange, the mix of factors will differ, but in any case, changes in the current market rate of interest often are a major contributor to changes in fair value.

Determining Fair Value

Changes in interest rates cause changes in the fair value of liabilities.

For demonstration, we revisit the Masterwear Industries bonds that sold at a discount in Illustration 14–3. Now, suppose it's six months later, the market rate of interest has fallen to 11%, and June 30 is the end of Masterwear's fiscal year. A decline in market interest rates means bond prices rise. Let's say that checking market prices in *The Wall Street Journal* indicates that the fair value of the Masterwear bonds on June 30, 2018, is $714,943. Referring to the amortization schedule, we see that on the same date, with five periods remaining to maturity, the present value of the bonds—their price—would have been $671,297 if the market rate still had been 14% (7% semiannually).

Additional Consideration

If the bonds are not traded on an open-market exchange, their fair value would not be readily observable. In that case, the next most preferable way to determine fair value would be to calculate the fair value as the present value of the remaining cash flows discounted at the current interest rate. If the rate is 11% (5.5% semiannually),[19] as we're assuming now, that present value would be $714,943:

	Present Values
Interest	$ 42,000 × 4.27028* = $179,352
Principal	$700,000 × 0.76513† = 535,591
Present value of the bonds	$714,943

*Present value of an ordinary annuity of $1: $n = 5$, $i = 5.5\%$.
†Present value of $1: $n = 5$, $i = 5.5\%$

When the bonds were issued, Masterwear had a choice—report this liability (a) at its amortized initial measurement throughout the term to maturity or (b) at its current fair value on each reporting date. Had the company not elected the fair value option, on June 30 it would report the $671,297 we calculated earlier for the amortization schedule. On the other hand, if Masterwear had elected the fair value option, it would report the bonds at their current fair value, $714,943.

Reporting Changes in Fair Value

Electing the FVO means reporting unrealized holding gains and losses in OCI to the extent the change is due to credit risk.

If a company chooses the option to report at fair value, a change in fair value will create a gain or loss. Any portion of that gain or loss that is a result of a change in the "credit risk" of the debt, rather than a change in general interest rates, is reported, not as part of net income, but instead as other comprehensive income (OCI). Credit risk is the risk that the investor in the bonds will not receive the promised interest and maturity amounts at the times they are due. Companies can assume that any change in fair value that exceeds the amount caused by a change in the general (risk-free) interest rate is the result of credit risk changes.

In our example, Masterwear would report the increase in fair value from $666,633 to $714,943, or $48,310. Note, though, that part of the change is due to the unpaid interest we discussed earlier. Here's a recap.

[19]The current market rate would consist of the general risk-free rate at the time, increased by a risk premium for the credit risk of the bonds.

At June 30, 2018, the interest that accrued during the first six months was $46,664, but only $42,000 of that was paid in cash; so the book value increased by the $4,664 unpaid interest. We recorded the following entry:

Interest expense	46,664	
Discount on bonds payable		4,664
Cash		42,000

Amortizing the discount in this entry increased the book value of the liability by $4,664 to $671,297:

Bonds payable
Less: Discount
Book value

January 1 book value and fair value	$666,633
Increase from discount amortization	4,664
June 30 book value (amortized initial amount)	$671,297

FAIR VALUE RISES. Comparing that book value with the fair value of the bonds on that date provides the amount needed to adjust the bonds to their fair value.

June 30 fair value	$714,943
June 30 book value (amortized initial amount)	671,297
Fair value adjustment needed	$ 43,646

Rather than increasing the bonds payable account itself, though, we instead adjust it *indirectly* with a credit to a valuation allowance (or contra) account. If general interest rates have not changed, we assume the change in fair value is due to the credit risk associated with the bonds and report the loss in OCI:

When the fair value option is elected, we report changes in fair value in OCI to the extent caused by changes in credit risk.

Unrealized holding loss—OCI	43,646	
Fair value adjustment ($714,943 – 671,297)		43,646

The *credit* balance in the fair value adjustment *increases* the book value; the discount reduces it.

If any portion of the fair value change is due to a change in general interest rates, that portion would be reported in net income. For instance, if interest rate declines alone would have created a $20,000 increase in fair value, we would report $20,000 of the loss in in the income statement and $23,646 as OCI.

The new book value of the bonds is now the fair value:

Bonds payable	$700,000
Less: Discount ($33,367 − 4,664)	(28,703)
Amortization schedule value	$671,297
Plus: Fair value adjustment	43,646
Book value, June 30	$714,943

FAIR VALUE FALLS. Suppose the fair value at June 30, 2018, had been $650,000 instead of $714,943. In that case, Masterwear would record a *reduction* in the liability from $671,297 to $650,000, or $21,297. Again assuming no change in interest rates, the entry would be:

Fair value adjustment ($671,297 − 650,000)	21,297	
Unrealized holding gain—OCI		21,297

The new book value of the bonds is the fair value:

The *debit* balance in the fair value adjustment *reduces* the book value; as does the discount.

Bonds payable	$ 700,000
Less: Discount ($33,367 − 4,664)	(28,703)
Amortization schedule value	$ 671,297
Less: Fair value adjustment	(21,297)
Book value, June 30	$650,000

The outstanding balance in the last column of the amortization schedule at any date up to and including the balance at maturity will be the bonds payable less the discount (for instance $671,297 at June 30, 2018). But the amount we report in the balance sheet at any reporting date, the fair value, will be that amortized initial amount from the amortization schedule, plus or minus the fair value adjustment. That's the $714,943 or the $650,000 in the two scenarios above.

To understand why we report credit risk-related fair value changes as OCI, it's useful to consider the consequence of reporting them in the income statement, which was the prescribed treatment prior to the FASB mandating their classification as OCI beginning in 2015. Here's one example. As a result of adjusting for fair value changes in its debt, J.P. Morgan Chase & Co. reported an impressive $1.9 billion gain in its 2011 third-quarter income statement. This was reason for the company's shareholders and creditors to celebrate, right? Not so fast. It's true that the company followed the proper procedure for recording a decline in the fair value of its debt, which was to record a gain in the income statement. As it turned out, though, the reason the fair value declined was that the company's financial situation had worsened, resulting in increased credit risk, and the increased credit risk caused the fair value of liabilities to decline. This, in fact, is the reason for most if not all of J.P. Morgan's huge gain. Does it make sense to you that worsening credit ratings should result in higher net income? Most observers, including the FASB, saw that as counterintuitive, and as a result, credit risk-related fair value changes are now reported as part of OCI rather as part of net income.

Mix and Match

Companies choose which financial instruments to report at fair value.

Remember from our discussions in prior chapters that if a company elects the fair value option, it's not necessary that the company elect the option to report all of its financial instruments at fair value or even all instruments of a particular type at fair value. They can "mix and match" on an instrument-by-instrument basis. So Masterwear, for instance, might choose to report these bonds at fair value but all its other liabilities at their amortized initial measurement. However, the company must make the election when the item originates, in this case when the bonds are issued, and is not allowed to switch methods once a method is chosen.

Here's an excerpt from the notes to the financial statements of Citigroup Inc. describing its fair value option election for some of its liabilities (omitting the portion of the note related to the fair value option election for financial assets):

23. FAIR VALUE ELECTIONS (In part)

The Company may elect to report most financial instruments and certain other items at fair value on an instrument-by-instrument basis. . . . The election is made upon the initial recognition of an eligible financial asset, financial liability or firm commitment or when certain specified reconsideration events occur. The fair value election may not be revoked once made. The changes in fair value are recorded in current earnings, other than DVA [Debit Valuation Adjustments], which from January 1, 2016 is reported in AOCI.

	Changes in fair value gains (losses) for the Three Months Ended March 31,	
($ in millions)	**2016**	**2015**
Liabilities		
Interest-bearing deposits	$ (50)	$ 10
Federal funds purchased and securities loaned or sold under agreements to repurchase selected portfolios of securities	(6)	2
Trading account liabilities	94	29
Short-term borrowings	80	(1)
Long-term debt	(423)	189
Total liabilities	$(305)	$229

Financial Reporting Case Solution

© Klaus Vedfelt/Getty Images.

1. **What does it mean that the bonds are "first mortgage" bonds? What effect does that have on financing?** *(p. 772)* A mortgage bond is backed by a lien on specified real estate owned by the issuer. This makes it less risky than unsecured debt, so Service Leader can expect to be able to sell the bonds at a higher price (lower interest rate).
2. **From Service Leader's perspective, why are the bonds callable? What does that mean?** *(p. 773)* The call feature gives Service Leader some protection against being stuck with relatively high-cost debt in case interest rates fall during the 15 years to maturity. Service Leader can buy back, or call, the bonds from bondholders before the 15-year maturity date, after June 30, 2017. The call price is prespecified at 103 percent of the face value—$1,030 per $1,000 bond.
3. **How will it be possible to sell bonds paying investors 6.25% when other, similar investments will provide the investors a return of 6.5%?** *(p. 773)* Service Leader will be able to sell its 6.25% bonds in a 6.5% market only by selling them at a discounted price, below face amount. Bonds are priced by the marketplace to yield the market rate of interest for securities of similar risk and maturity. The price will be the present value of all the periodic cash interest payments (face amount × stated rate) plus the present value of the principal payable at maturity, both discounted at the market rate.
4. **Would accounting differ if the debt were designated as notes rather than bonds?** *(p. 784)* No. Other things being equal, whether they're called bonds, notes, or some other form of debt, the same accounting principles apply. They will be recorded at present value and interest will be recorded at the market rate over the term to maturity.
5. **Why might the company choose to make the bonds convertible into common stock?** *(p. 793)* Convertible bonds can be converted at the option of the bondholders into shares of stock. Sometimes the motivation for issuing convertible bonds rather than straight debt is to use the bonds as a medium of exchange in mergers and acquisitions, as a way for smaller firms or debt-heavy companies to obtain access to the bond market, or as an indirect way to issue stock when there is shareholder resistance to direct issuance of additional equity. None of these seems pertinent to Service Leader. The most likely reason is to sell at a higher price. The conversion feature is attractive to investors. Investors have a fixed-income security that can become common stock if circumstances make that attractive. The investor has additional possibilities for higher returns, with downside risk limited by the underlying debt. ●

The Bottom Line

- **LO14–1** A liability requires the future payment of cash in specified amounts at specified dates. As time passes, interest accrues on debt at the effective interest rate times the amount of the debt outstanding during the period. This same principle applies regardless of the specific form of the liability. *(p. 771)*
- **LO14–2** Forces of supply and demand cause a bond to be priced to yield the market rate, calculated as the present value of all the cash flows required, where the discount rate is the market rate. Interest expense is calculated as the effective market rate of interest multiplied by the outstanding balance (during the interest period). A company is permitted to allocate a discount or a premium equally to each period over the term to maturity if doing so produces results that are not materially different from the interest method. *(p. 773)*
- **LO14–3** In concept, notes are accounted for in precisely the same way as bonds. When a note is issued with an unrealistic interest rate, the effective market rate is used both to determine the amount recorded in the transaction and to record periodic interest thereafter. *(p. 784)*
- **LO14–4** In the balance sheet, disclosure should include, for all long-term borrowings, the aggregate amounts maturing and sinking fund requirements (if any) for each of the next five years. Supplemental disclosures are needed for (a) off-balance-sheet credit or market risk, (b) concentrations of credit risk, and (c) the fair value of financial instruments. *(p. 788)*

- **LO14–5** A gain or loss on early extinguishment of debt should be recorded for the difference between the reacquisition price and the book value of the debt. Convertible bonds are accounted for as straight debt, but the value of the equity feature is recorded separately for bonds issued with detachable warrants. *(p. 793)*
- **LO14–6** Companies are not required to, but have the option to, value some or all of their liabilities at fair value. If the option is elected, an increase (or decrease) in fair value from one balance sheet to the next is reported as a loss (or gain) as other comprehensive income to the extent it's related to credit risk. Otherwise, it's reported in net income. It's a one-time election for each liability when the liability is created. *(p. 798)*
- **LO14–7** U.S. GAAP and IFRS are generally compatible with respect to accounting for bonds and long-term notes. Some differences exist in determining which securities are reported as debt, the way convertible securities are accounted for, and when the fair value option can be elected. *(pp. 775 and 795)*.

APPENDIX 14A

Bonds Issued Between Interest Dates

In Part A of this chapter, we assumed that the bonds were issued on the day they were dated (date printed in the indenture contract). But suppose a weak market caused a delay in selling the bonds until two months after that date (four months before semiannual interest was to be paid). In that case, the buyer would be asked to pay the seller **accrued interest** for two months in addition to the price of the bonds.

When Bonds are Issued at Face Amount between Interest Dates

For illustration, assume that in Illustration 14–1, Masterwear was unable to sell the bonds in the previous example until March 1—two months after they are dated. This variation is shown in Illustration 14A–1. United would pay the price of the bonds ($700,000) plus $14,000 accrued interest:

$$\underset{\text{Face amount}}{\$700{,}000} \times \underset{\text{Annual rate}}{12\%} \times \underset{\text{Fraction of the annual period}}{2/12} = \underset{\text{Accrued interest}}{\$14{,}000}$$

All bonds sell at their price plus any interest that has accrued since the last interest date.

Illustration 14A–1
Bonds Sold at Face Amount between Interest Dates

At Issuance (March 1)		
Masterwear (Issuer)		
Cash (price plus accrued interest)	714,000	
Bonds payable (face amount)		700,000
Interest payable (accrued interest determined above)		14,000
United (Investor)		
Investment in bonds (face amount)	700,000	
Interest receivable (accrued interest determined above)	14,000	
Cash (price plus accrued interest)		714,000

When Masterwear pays semiannual interest on June 30, a full six months' interest is paid. But having received two months' accrued interest in advance, Masterwear's net interest expense will be four months' interest, for the four months the bonds have been outstanding at that time. Likewise, when United receives six months' interest—after holding the bonds for only four months—United will net only the four months' interest to which it is entitled:

Since the investor will hold the bonds for only four months before receiving six months' interest, two months' accrued interest must be added to the price paid.

At the First Interest Date (June 30)		
Masterwear (Issuer)		
Interest expense (6 mo. − 2 mo. = 4 mo.)	28,000	
Interest payable* (accrued interest determined above)	14,000	
Cash (stated rate × face amount)		42,000
		(continued)

The issuer incurs interest expense, and the investor recognizes interest revenue, for only the four months the bonds are outstanding.

United (Investor)		
Cash (stated rate × face amount)	42,000	
Interest receivable (accrued interest determined above)		14,000
Interest revenue (6 mo. − 2 mo. = 4 mo.)		28,000

*Some accountants prefer to credit interest expense, rather than interest payable, when the bonds are sold. When that is done, this entry would require a debit to interest expense and a credit to cash for $42,000. The interest expense account would then reflect the same *net* debit of four months' interest ($42,000 − $14,000).

Interest Expense

	2 months
6 months	
4 months	

Similarly, the investor could debit interest revenue, rather than interest receivable when buying the bonds.

When Bonds are Issued at a Discount between Interest Dates

All bonds sell at their price plus any interest that has accrued since the last interest date.

Our objective is the same when the bonds are not issued at their face amount. For instance, in Illustration 14–3, the $700,000 of 12% bonds were issued when the market rate was 14% and thus were priced at a discount, $666,633. If those bonds were issued March 1, two months after they are dated, the investor would pay the price of the bonds ($666,633) plus $14,000 accrued interest[20]:

Illustration 14A–2

Bonds Sold at a Discount between Interest Dates

Masterwear (Issuer)		
Cash (price plus accrued interest)	680,633	
Discount on bonds payable (difference)	33,367	
Bonds payable (face amount)		700,000
Interest payable (accrued interest determined above)		14,000
United (Investor)		
Investment in bonds (face amount)	700,000	
Interest receivable (accrued interest determined above)	14,000	
Discount on bond investment (difference)		33,367
Cash (price plus accrued interest)		680,633

By contract, a full six months' interest is paid on June 30 at the *stated* rate times the face amount. But having received two months' accrued interest in advance, Masterwear's *net* interest expense will be four months' interest, for the four months the bonds have been outstanding at that time. Interest is calculated on the outstanding debt balance at the effective (or market) rate. Interest for the first six months, then, would be $666,633 × 14% × ½ = $46,664. But because on June 30 only four months have passed, only four months' interest, 4/6 × 46,664, or $31,109, is recorded as interest expense. Similarly, the reduction of the discount, which for a full six-month interest period would be $46,664 – 42,000, or $4,664, will be only 4/6 of that amount. These amounts are recorded as follows:

Journal Entries—Interest between Interest Dates

Only four months' interest is recorded because the bonds were outstanding only four months.

At the First Interest Date (June 30)

Masterwear (Issuer)		
Interest expense (4/6 × 46,664)	31,109	
Interest payable (accrued interest determined above)	14,000	
Discount on bonds payable (4/6 × 4,664)		3,109
Cash (stated rate × face amount)		42,000
United (Investor)		
Cash (stated rate × face amount)	42,000	
Discount on bond investment (4/6 × 4,664)	3,109	
Interest receivable (accrued interest determined above)		14,000
Interest revenue (4/6 × 46,664)		31,109

[20]This assumes the price of the bonds still is $666,633, which assumes the effective market interest rate still is 7% semiannually. The proceeds will be the price of the bonds based on effective market interest rate on March 1 plus accrued interest.

APPENDIX 14B

Troubled Debt Restructuring

A respected real estate developer, Brillard Properties, was very successful developing and managing a number of properties in the southeastern United States. To finance these investments, the developer had borrowed hundreds of millions of dollars from several regional banks. For years, events occurred as planned. The investments prospered. Cash flow was high. Interest payments on the debt were timely and individual loans were repaid as they matured.

A sharp rise in debt restructurings accompanied the 2008/2009 economic crisis.

Almost suddenly, however, the real estate climate soured. Investments that had provided handsome profits now did not provide the cash flow necessary to service the debt. Bankers who had loaned substantial funds to Brillard now faced a dilemma. Because contractual interest payments were unpaid, the bankers had the legal right to demand payment, which would force the developer to liquidate all or a major part of the properties to raise the cash. Sound business practice? Not necessarily.

If creditors force liquidation, they then must share among themselves the cash raised from selling the properties—at forced sale prices. Believing the developer's financial difficulties were caused by temporary market forces, not by bad management, the bankers felt they could minimize their losses by *restructuring* the debt agreements, rather than by forcing liquidation.

When changing the original terms of a debt agreement is motivated by financial difficulties experienced by the debtor (borrower), the new arrangement is referred to as a **troubled debt restructuring**. By definition, a troubled debt restructuring involves some concessions on the part of the creditor (lender). In the first half of 2009, the economic crisis prompted nearly 40 companies to negotiate such deals with their creditors, a huge increase over the handful that normally would do so during a six-month period.[21] A troubled debt restructuring may be achieved in either of two ways:

1. The debt may be *settled* at the time of the restructuring.
2. The debt may be *continued,* but with *modified terms.*

Debt is Settled

In the situation described above, one choice the bankers had was to try to actually settle the debt outright at the time of the troubled debt restructuring. For instance, a bank holding a $30 million note from the developer might agree to accept a property valued at, let's say, $20 million as final settlement of the debt. In that case, the developer has a $10 million gain equal to the difference between the book value of the debt and the fair value of the property transferred. The debtor may need to adjust the book value of an asset to its fair value prior to recording its exchange for a debt. The developer in our example, for instance, would need to change the recorded amount for the property specified in the exchange agreement if it is carried at an amount other than its $20 million fair value. In such an instance, an ordinary gain or loss on disposition of assets should be recorded as shown in Illustration 14B–1.

In all areas of accounting, a noncash transaction is recorded at fair value.

Illustration 14B–1
Debt Settled

First Prudent Bank agrees to settle Brillard's $30 million debt in exchange for property having a fair value of $20 million. The book value of the property on Brillard's books is $17 million:

	($ in millions)	
Land ($20 million minus $17 million)	3	
Gain on disposition of assets		3
Note payable (book value)	30	
Gain on troubled debt restructuring		10
Land (fair value)		20

An asset is adjusted to fair value prior to recording its exchange for a debt.

[21]David Henry, "The Time Bomb in Corporate Debt," *BusinessWeek,* July 15, 2009.

The payment to settle a debt in a troubled debt restructuring might be cash, or a noncash asset (as in the example here), or even shares of the debtor's stock. An example of shares of stock given in exchange for debt forgiveness is the celebrated reorganization of TWA in 1992 (since acquired by American Airlines), when creditors received a 55% stake in the company's common shares in return for forgiving about $1 billion of the airline's $1.5 billion debt. In any case, the debtor's gain is the difference between the book value of the debt and the fair value of the asset(s) or equity securities transferred.

Debt Is Continued, but with Modified Terms

The book value of a debt is the current balance of the primary debt plus any accrued (unpaid) interest.

We assumed in the previous example that First Prudent Bank agreed to accept property in full settlement of the debt. A more likely occurrence would be that the bank allows the debt to continue, but modifies the terms of the debt agreement to make it easier for the debtor to comply. The bank might agree to reduce or delay the scheduled *interest payments*. Or, it may agree to reduce or delay the *maturity amount*. Often a troubled debt restructuring will call for some combination of these concessions. Distressed by the 2008/2009 economic downturn, amusement park operator Six Flags persuaded a group of creditors to trim its debt by 5%, or $130 million, a restructuring designed to give Six Flags a financial cushion going into its busy 2009 summer season and an opportunity to recover its interest-paying ability.

Let's say the stated interest rate on the note in question is 10% and annual interest payments of $3 million (10% × $30 million) are payable in December of each of two remaining years to maturity. Also assume that the developer was unable to pay the $3 million interest payment for the year just ended. This means that the amount owed—the carrying amount (or book value) of the debt—is $33 million ($30 million plus one year's accrued interest).

Two quite different situations are created when the terms of a debt are modified, depending on whether the cash payments are reduced to the extent that interest is eliminated.

The way the debtor accounts for the restructuring depends on the extent of the reduction in cash payments called for by the restructured arrangement. More specifically, the accounting procedure depends on whether, under the new agreement, total cash payments (a) are *less than* the book value of the debt or (b) still *exceed* the book value of the debt.

WHEN TOTAL CASH PAYMENTS ARE LESS THAN THE BOOK VALUE OF THE DEBT By the original agreement, the debtor was to pay at maturity the $30 million loaned, plus enough periodic interest to provide a 10% effective rate of return. If the new agreement calls for less cash than the $33 million now owed, interest is presumed to have been eliminated.

As one of many possibilities, suppose the bank agrees to (1) forgive the interest accrued from last year, (2) reduce the two remaining interest payments from $3 million each to $2 million each, and (3) reduce the face amount from $30 million to $25 million. Clearly, the debtor will pay less by the new agreement than by the original one. In fact, if we add up the total payments called for by the new agreement, the total [($2 million × 2) plus $25 million] is less than the $33 million book value. Because the $29 million does not exceed the amount owed, the restructured debt agreement no longer provides interest on the debt. Actually, the new payments are $4 million short of covering the debt itself. So, after the debt restructuring, no interest expense is recorded. All subsequent cash payments are considered to be payment of the debt itself. Consider Illustration 14B–2.

After restructuring, no interest expense is recorded. All cash payments are considered to be payment of the note itself.

When the total future cash payments are less than the book value of the debt, the difference is recorded as a gain at the date of restructure. No interest should be recorded thereafter. That is, all subsequent cash payments result in reductions of principal.

The $25 million payment at maturity reduces the note to zero.

At Each of the Two Interest Dates	($ in millions)	
Note payable	2	
Cash (revised "interest" amount)		2
At Maturity		
Note payable	25	
Cash (revised principal amount)		25

WHEN TOTAL CASH PAYMENTS EXCEED THE BOOK VALUE OF THE DEBT Let's modify the example in the previous section. Now suppose the bank agrees to delay the due

Illustration 14B–2

Cash Payments Less than the Debt

Brillard Properties owes First Prudent Bank $30 million under a 10% note with two years remaining to maturity. Due to financial difficulties of the developer, the previous year's interest ($3 million) was not paid. First Prudent Bank agrees to:

1. Forgive the interest accrued from last year.
2. Reduce the remaining two interest payments to $2 million each.
3. Reduce the principal to $25 million.

Analysis:	Book value	$30 million + $3 million =	$33 million
	Future payments	($2 million × 2) + $25 million =	29 million
	Gain		$ 4 million

	($ in millions)	
Accrued interest payable (10% × $30 million)	3	
Note payable ($30 million − 29 million)	1	
Gain on debt restructuring		4

Book Value		
Before Restr.	Adj.	After Restr.
$30	(1)	$29
3	(3)	0
$33	(4)	$29

date for all cash payments until maturity and accept $34,333,200 at that time in full settlement of the debt. Rather than just reducing the cash payments as in the previous illustration, the payments are delayed. It is not the nature of the change that creates the need to account differently for this situation, but the amount of the total cash payments under the agreement relative to the book value of the debt. This situation is demonstrated in Illustration 14B–3.

Illustration 14B–3

Cash Payments More than the Debt

Brillard Properties owes First Prudent Bank $30 million under a 10% note with two years remaining to maturity. Due to Brillard's financial difficulties, the previous year's interest ($3 million) was not paid. First Prudent Bank agrees to:

1. Delay the due date for all cash payments until maturity.
2. Accept $34,333,200 at that time in full settlement of the debt.

Analysis:	Future payments		$34,333,200
	Book value	$30 million + $3 million =	33,000,000
	Interest		$ 1,333,200

Calculation of the New Effective Interest Rate

- $33,000,000 ÷ 34,333,200 = 0.9612, the Table 2 value for $n = 2, i = ?$
- In row 2 of Table 2, the number 0.9612 is in the 2% column. So, this is the new effective interest rate.

The discount rate that equates the present value on the debt ($33 million) and its future value ($34,333,200) is the effective rate of interest.

Now the total payments called for by the new agreement, $34,333,200, exceed the $33 million book value. Because the payments exceed the amount owed, the restructured debt agreement still provides interest on the debt—but less than before the agreement was revised. No longer is the effective rate 10%. The accounting objective now is to determine what the new effective rate is and *record interest for the remaining term of the loan at that new, lower rate,* as shown in Illustration 14B–3.

As long as cash payments exceed the amount owed there will be interest—although at a lower effective rate.

Because the total future cash payments are not less than the book value of the debt, no reduction of the existing debt is necessary and no entry is required at the time of the debt restructuring. Even though no cash is paid until maturity under the restructured debt agreement, interest expense still is recorded annually—but at the new rate.

Unpaid interest is accrued at the effective rate times the book value of the note.

At the End of the First Year		
Interest expense [2% × ($30,000,000 + 3,000,000)]	660,000	
Accrued interest payable		660,000
At the End of the Second Year		
Interest expense [2% × ($30,000,000 + 3,660,000)]	673,200	
Accrued interest payable		673,200

(continued)

The book value of the debt is increased by the unpaid interest from the previous year.

The total of the accrued interest account plus the note account is equal to the amount scheduled to be paid at maturity.

(concluded)

At Maturity (End of the Second Year)

Note payable	30,000,000	
Accrued interest payable ($3,000,000 + 660,000 + 673,200)	4,333,200	
Cash (required by new agreement)		34,333,200

Additional Consideration

To keep up with the changing amounts, it may be convenient to prepare an amortization schedule for the debt.

Year	Cash Interest	Effective Interest	Increase in Balance	Outstanding Balance
		(2% × Outstanding balance)		
				33,000,000
1	0	0.02 (33,000,000) = 660,000	660,000	33,660,000
2	0	0.02 (33,660,000) = 673,200	673,200	34,333,200
	0	1,333,200	1,333,200	

An amortization schedule is particularly helpful if there are several years remaining to maturity.

In our example, the restructured debt agreement called for a single cash payment at maturity ($34,333,200). If more than one cash payment is required (as in the agreement in our earlier example), calculating the new effective rate is more difficult. The concept would remain straightforward: (1) determine the interest rate that provides a present value of all future cash payments that is equal to the current book value and (2) record the interest at that rate thereafter. Mechanically, though, the computation by hand would be cumbersome, requiring a time-consuming trial-and-error calculation. Since our primary interest is understanding the concepts involved, we will avoid the mathematical complexities of such a situation.

You also should be aware that when a restructuring involves modification of terms, accounting for a liability by the debtor, as described in this section, and accounting for a receivable by the creditor (essentially an impairment of a receivable), which was described in Chapter 7, are inconsistent. You may recall that when a creditor's investment in a receivable becomes impaired, due to a troubled debt restructuring or for any other reason, the receivable is remeasured based on the discounted present value of currently expected cash flows at the loan's original effective rate (regardless of the extent to which expected cash receipts have been reduced). For ease of comparison, the example in this chapter (Illustration 14B–3) describes the same situation as the example in Chapter 7 (Illustration 7B–2). There is no conceptual justification for the asymmetry between debtors' and creditors' accounting for troubled debt restructurings.

Questions For Review of Key Topics

Q 14–1 How is periodic interest determined for outstanding liabilities? For outstanding receivables? How does the approach compare from one form of debt instrument (say bonds payable) to another (say notes payable)?

Q 14–2 As a general rule, how should long-term liabilities be reported on the debtor's balance sheet?

Q 14–3 How are bonds and notes the same? How do they differ?

Q 14–4 What information is contained in a bond indenture? What purpose does it serve?

Q 14–5 On January 1, 2018, Brandon Electronics issued $85 million of 11.5% bonds, dated January 1. The market yield for bonds of maturity issued by similar firms in terms of riskiness is 12.25%. How can Brandon sell debt paying only 11.5% in a 12.25% market?

Q 14–6 How is the price determined for a bond (or bond issue)?

Q 14–7 A zero-coupon bond pays no interest. Explain.

Q 14–8 When bonds are issued at a premium the debt declines each period. Explain.

Q 14–9 Compare the two commonly used methods of determining interest on bonds.

Q 14–10 What are debt issue costs and how should they be reported?

Q 14–11 When a note's stated rate of interest is unrealistic relative to the market rate, the concept of substance over form should be employed. Explain.

Q 14–12 How does an installment note differ from a note for which the principal is paid as a single amount at maturity?

Q 14–13 Long-term debt can be reported either (a) as a single amount, net of any discount or increased by any premium or (b) at its face amount accompanied by a separate valuation account for the discount or premium. Any portion of the debt to be paid during the upcoming year, or operating cycle if longer, should be reported as a current amount. Regarding amounts to be paid in the future, what additional disclosures should be made in connection with long-term debt?

Q 14–14 Early extinguishment of debt often produces a gain or a loss. How is the gain or loss determined?

Q 14–15 Air Supply issued $6 million of 9%, 10-year convertible bonds at 101. The bonds are convertible into 24,000 shares of common stock. Bonds that are similar in all respects except that they are nonconvertible, currently are selling at 99 (that is, 99% of face amount). What amount should Air Supply record as equity and how much as a liability when the bonds are issued?

Q 14–16 Both convertible bonds and bonds issued with detachable warrants have features of both debt and equity. How does the accounting treatment differ for the two hybrid securities? Why is the accounting treatment different?

Q 14–17 At times, companies try to induce voluntary conversion by offering an added incentive—maybe cash, stock warrants, or a more favorable conversion ratio. How is such an inducement accounted for? How is it measured?

Q 14–18 Cordova Tools has bonds outstanding during a year in which the market rate of interest has risen. If Cordova has elected the fair value option for the bonds, will it report a gain or a loss on the bonds for the year? Explain.

IFRS **Q 14–19** If a company prepares its financial statements according to International Financial Reporting Standards, how would it account for convertible bonds it issues for $12.5 million? What is the conceptual justification?

Q 14–20 (Based on Appendix 14A) Why will bonds always sell at their price plus any interest that has accrued since the last interest date?

Q 14–21 (Based on Appendix 14B) When the original terms of a debt agreement are changed because of financial difficulties experienced by the debtor (borrower), the new arrangement is referred to as a *troubled debt restructuring*. Such a restructuring can take a variety of forms. For accounting purposes, these possibilities are categorized. What are the accounting classifications of troubled debt restructurings?

Q 14–22 (Based on Appendix 14B) Pratt Industries owes First National Bank $5 million but, due to financial difficulties, is unable to comply with the original terms of the loan. The bank agrees to settle the debt in exchange for land having a fair value of $3 million. The book value of the property on Pratt's books is $2 million. For the reporting period in which the debt is settled, what amount(s) will Pratt report on its income statement in connection with the troubled debt restructuring?

Q 14–23 (Based on Appendix 14B) The way a debtor accounts for the restructuring depends on the extent of the reduction in cash payments called for by the restructured arrangement. Describe, in general, the accounting procedure for the two basic cases: when, under the new agreement, total cash payments (a) are less than the book value of the debt or (b) still exceed the book value of the debt.

Brief Exercises

connect

BE 14–1
Bond interest
• LO14–1

Holiday Brands issued $30 million of 6%, 30-year bonds for $27.5 million. What is the amount of interest that Holiday will pay semiannually to bondholders?

BE 14–2
Determining the price of bonds
• LO14–2

A company issued 5%, 20-year bonds with a face amount of $80 million. The market yield for bonds of similar risk and maturity is 6%. Interest is paid semiannually. At what price did the bonds sell?

BE 14–3
Determining the price of bonds
• LO14–2

A company issued 6%, 15-year bonds with a face amount of $75 million. The market yield for bonds of similar risk and maturity is 6%. Interest is paid semiannually. At what price did the bonds sell?

BE 14–4
Determining the price of bonds
● LO14–2

A company issued 5%, 20-year bonds with a face amount of $100 million. The market yield for bonds of similar risk and maturity is 4%. Interest is paid semiannually. At what price did the bonds sell?

BE 14–5
Effective interest on bonds
● LO14–2

On January 1, a company issued 7%, 15-year bonds with a face amount of $90 million for $82,218,585 to yield 8%. Interest is paid semiannually. What was interest expense at the effective interest rate on June 30, the first interest date?

BE 14–6
Effective interest on bonds
● LO14–2

On January 1, a company issued 3%, 20-year bonds with a face amount of $80 million for $69,033,776 to yield 4%. Interest is paid semiannually. What was the interest expense at the effective interest rate on the December 31 annual income statement?

BE 14–7
Straight-line interest on bonds
● LO14–2

On January 1, a company issued 3%, 20-year bonds with a face amount of $80 million for $69,033,776 to yield 4%. Interest is paid semiannually. What was the straight-line interest expense on the December 31 annual income statement?

BE 14–8
Investment in bonds
● LO14–2

On January 1, a company purchased 3%, 20-year corporate bonds for $69,033,776 as an investment. The bonds have a face amount of $80 million and are priced to yield 4%. Interest is paid semiannually. Prepare the journal entry to record revenue at the effective interest rate on December 31, the second interest payment date.

BE 14–9
Note issued for cash; borrower and lender
● LO14–3

On January 1, 2018, Nantucket Ferry borrowed $14,000,000 cash from BankOne and issued a four-year, $14,000,000, 6% note. Interest was payable annually on December 31. Prepare the journal entries for both firms to record interest at December 31, 2018.

BE 14–10
Note with unrealistic interest rate
● LO14–3

On January 1, Snipes Construction paid for earth-moving equipment by issuing a $300,000, 3-year note that specified 2% interest to be paid on December 31 of each year. The equipment's retail cash price was unknown, but it was determined that a reasonable interest rate was 5%. At what amount should Snipes record the equipment and the note? What journal entry should it record for the transaction?

BE 14–11
Installment note
● LO14–3

On January 1, a company borrowed cash by issuing a $300,000, 5%, installment note to be paid in three equal payments at the end of each year beginning December 31. What would be the amount of each installment? Prepare the journal entry for the second installment payment.

BE 14–12
Early extinguishment; effective interest
● LO14–5

A company retired $60 million of its 6% bonds at 102 ($61.2 million) before their scheduled maturity. At the time, the bonds had a remaining discount of $2 million. Prepare the journal entry to record the redemption of the bonds.

BE 14–13
Bonds with detachable warrants
● LO14–5

Hoffman Corporation issued $60 million of 5%, 20-year bonds at 102. Each of the 60,000 bonds was issued with 10 detachable stock warrants, each of which entitled the bondholder to purchase, for $20, one share of $1 par common stock. At the time of sale, the market value of the common stock was $25 per share and the market value of each warrant was $5. Prepare the journal entry to record the issuance of the bonds.

BE 14–14
Convertible bonds
● LO14–5

Hoffman Corporation issued $60 million of 5%, 20-year bonds at 102. Each of the 60,000 bonds was convertible into one share of $1 par common stock. Prepare the journal entry to record the issuance of the bonds.

BE 14–15
Reporting bonds at fair value
● LO14–6

AI Tool and Dye issued 8% bonds with a face amount of $160 million on January 1, 2018. The bonds sold for $150 million. For bonds of similar risk and maturity the market yield was 9%. Upon issuance, AI elected the option to report these bonds at their fair value. On June 30, 2018, the fair value of the bonds was $145 million as determined by their market value on the NASDAQ. Will AI report a gain or will it report a loss when adjusting the bonds to fair value? If the change in fair value is attributable to a change in the interest rate, did the rate increase or decrease? Will the gain or loss be reported in net income or as OCI?

Exercises

connect

E 14–1
Bond valuation
● LO14–2

Your investment department has researched possible investments in corporate debt securities. Among the available investments are the following $100 million bond issues, each dated January 1, 2018. Prices were determined by underwriters at different times during the last few weeks.

	Company	Bond Price	Stated Rate
1.	BB Corp.	$109 million	11%
2.	DD Corp.	$100 million	10%
3.	GG Corp.	$ 91 million	9%

Each of the bond issues matures on December 31, 2037, and pays interest semiannually on June 30 and December 31. For bonds of similar risk and maturity, the market yield at January 1, 2018, is 10%.

Required:

Other things being equal, which of the bond issues offers the most attractive investment opportunity if it can be purchased at the prices stated? The least attractive? Why?

E 14–2
Determine the price of bonds in various situations
● LO14–2

Determine the price of a $1 million bond issue under each of the following independent assumptions:

	Maturity	Interest Paid	Stated Rate	Effective (Market) Rate
1.	10 years	annually	10%	12%
2.	10 years	semiannually	10%	12%
3.	10 years	semiannually	12%	10%
4.	20 years	semiannually	12%	10%
5.	20 years	semiannually	12%	12%

E 14–3
Determine the price of bonds; issuance; effective interest
● LO14–2

The Bradford Company issued 10% bonds, dated January 1, with a face amount of $80 million on January 1, 2018. The bonds mature on December 31, 2027 (10 years). For bonds of similar risk and maturity, the market yield is 12%. Interest is paid semiannually on June 30 and December 31.

Required:

1. Determine the price of the bonds at January 1, 2018.
2. Prepare the journal entry to record their issuance by The Bradford Company on January 1, 2018.
3. Prepare the journal entry to record interest on June 30, 2018 (at the effective rate).
4. Prepare the journal entry to record interest on December 31, 2018 (at the effective rate).

E 14–4
Investor; effective interest
● LO14–2

(Note: This is a variation of E 14–3 modified to consider the investor's perspective.) The Bradford Company sold the entire bond issue described in the previous exercise to Saxton-Bose Corporation.

Required:

1. Prepare the journal entry to record the purchase of the bonds by Saxton-Bose on January 1, 2018.
2. Prepare the journal entry to record interest revenue on June 30, 2018 (at the effective rate).
3. Prepare the journal entry to record interest revenue on December 31, 2018 (at the effective rate).

E 14–5
Bonds; issuance; effective interest; financial statement effects
● LO14–2

Myriad Solutions, Inc., issued 10% bonds, dated January 1, with a face amount of $320 million on January 1, 2018, for $283,294,720. The bonds mature on December 31, 2027 (10 years). For bonds of similar risk and maturity the market yield is 12%. Interest is paid semiannually on June 30 and December 31.

Required:

1. What would be the net amount of the liability Myriad would report in its balance sheet at December 31, 2018?
2. What would be the amount related to the bonds that Myriad would report in its income statement for the year ended December 31, 2018?
3. What would be the amount(s) related to the bonds that Myriad would report in its statement of cash flows for the year ended December 31, 2018?

E 14–6
Bonds; issuance; effective interest
● LO14–2

The Gorman Group issued $900,000 of 13% bonds on June 30, 2018, for $967,707. The bonds were dated on June 30 and mature on June 30, 2038 (20 years). The market yield for bonds of similar risk and maturity is 12%. Interest is paid semiannually on December 31 and June 30.

Required:

1. Prepare the journal entry to record their issuance by The Gorman Group on June 30, 2018.

2. Prepare the journal entry to record interest on December 31, 2018 (at the effective rate).
3. Prepare the journal entry to record interest on June 30, 2019 (at the effective rate).

E 14–7
Determine the price of bonds; issuance; straight-line method
● LO14–2

Universal Foods issued 10% bonds, dated January 1, with a face amount of $150 million on January 1, 2018. The bonds mature on December 31, 2032 (15 years). The market rate of interest for similar issues was 12%. Interest is paid semiannually on June 30 and December 31. Universal uses the straight-line method.

Required:

1. Determine the price of the bonds at January 1, 2018.
2. Prepare the journal entry to record their issuance by Universal Foods on January 1, 2018.
3. Prepare the journal entry to record interest on June 30, 2018.
4. Prepare the journal entry to record interest on December 31, 2025.

E 14–8
Investor; straight-line method
● LO14–2

(Note: This is a variation of E 14–7 modified to consider the investor's perspective.) Universal Foods sold the entire bond issue described in the previous exercise to Wang Communications.

Required:

1. Prepare the journal entry to record the purchase of the bonds by Wang Communications on January 1, 2018.
2. Prepare the journal entry to record interest revenue on June 30, 2018.
3. Prepare the journal entry to record interest revenue on December 31, 2025.

E 14–9
Issuance of bonds; effective interest; amortization schedule; financial statement effects
● LO14–2

When Patey Pontoons issued 6% bonds on January 1, 2018, with a face amount of $600,000, the market yield for bonds of similar risk and maturity was 7%. The bonds mature December 31, 2021 (4 years). Interest is paid semiannually on June 30 and December 31.

Required:

1. Determine the price of the bonds at January 1, 2018.
2. Prepare the journal entry to record their issuance by Patey on January 1, 2018.
3. Prepare an amortization schedule that determines interest at the effective rate each period.
4. Prepare the journal entry to record interest on June 30, 2018.
5. What is the amount(s) related to the bonds that Patey will report in its balance sheet at December 31, 2018?
6. What is the amount(s) related to the bonds that Patey will report in its income statement for the year ended December 31, 2018? (Ignore income taxes.)
7. Prepare the appropriate journal entries at maturity on December 31, 2021.

E 14–10
Issuance of bonds; effective interest; amortization schedule
● LO14–2

National Orthopedics Co. issued 9% bonds, dated January 1, with a face amount of $500,000 on January 1, 2018. The bonds mature on December 31, 2021 (4 years). For bonds of similar risk and maturity the market yield was 10%. Interest is paid semiannually on June 30 and December 31.

Required:

1. Determine the price of the bonds at January 1, 2018.
2. Prepare the journal entry to record their issuance by National on January 1, 2018.
3. Prepare an amortization schedule that determines interest at the effective rate each period.
4. Prepare the journal entry to record interest on June 30, 2018.
5. Prepare the appropriate journal entries at maturity on December 31, 2021.

E 14–11
Bonds; effective interest; adjusting entry
● LO14–2

On February 1, 2018, Strauss-Lombardi issued 9% bonds, dated February 1, with a face amount of $800,000. The bonds sold for $731,364 and mature on January 31, 2038 (20 years). The market yield for bonds of similar risk and maturity was 10%. Interest is paid semiannually on July 31 and January 31. Strauss-Lombardi's fiscal year ends December 31.

Required:

1. Prepare the journal entry to record their issuance by Strauss-Lombardi on February 1, 2018.
2. Prepare the journal entry to record interest on July 31, 2018 (at the effective rate).
3. Prepare the adjusting entry to accrue interest on December 31, 2018.
4. Prepare the journal entry to record interest on January 31, 2019.

E 14–12
Bonds; straight-line method; adjusting entry
● LO14–2

On March 1, 2018, Stratford Lighting issued 14% bonds, dated March 1, with a face amount of $300,000. The bonds sold for $294,000 and mature on February 28, 2038 (20 years). Interest is paid semiannually on August 31 and February 28. Stratford uses the straight-line method and its fiscal year ends December 31.

Required:

1. Prepare the journal entry to record the issuance of the bonds by Stratford Lighting on March 1, 2018.
2. Prepare the journal entry to record interest on August 31, 2018.
3. Prepare the journal entry to accrue interest on December 31, 2018.
4. Prepare the journal entry to record interest on February 28, 2019.

E 14–13
Issuance of bonds; effective interest
● LO14–2

Federal Semiconductors issued 11% bonds, dated January 1, with a face amount of $800 million on January 1, 2018. The bonds sold for $739,814,813 and mature on December 31, 2037 (20 years). For bonds of similar risk and maturity the market yield was 12%. Interest is paid semiannually on June 30 and December 31.

Required:

1. Prepare the journal entry to record their issuance by Federal on January 1, 2018.
2. Prepare the journal entry to record interest on June 30, 2018 (at the effective rate).
3. Prepare the journal entry to record interest on December 31, 2018 (at the effective rate).
4. At what amount will Federal report the bonds among its liabilities in the December 31, 2018, balance sheet?

E 14–14
New debt issues; offerings announcements
● LO14–2

When companies offer new debt security issues, they publicize the offerings in the financial press and on Internet sites. Assume the following were among the debt offerings reported in December 2018:

New Securities Issues

Corporate

National Equipment Transfer Corporation—$200 million bonds via lead managers Second Tennessee Bank N.A. and Morgan, Dunavant & Co., according to a syndicate official. Terms: maturity, Dec. 15, 2024; coupon 7.46%; issue price, par; yield, 7.46%; noncallable; debt ratings: Ba-1 (Moody's Investors Service, Inc.), BBB+ (Standard & Poor's).

IgWig Inc.—$350 million of notes via lead manager Stanley Brothers, Inc., according to a syndicate official. Terms: maturity, Dec. 1, 2026; coupon, 6.46%; Issue price, 99; yield, 6.56%; call date, NC; debt ratings: Baa-1 (Moody's Investors Service, Inc.), A (Standard & Poor's).

Required:

1. Prepare the appropriate journal entries to record the sale of both issues to underwriters. Ignore share issue costs and assume no accrued interest.
2. Prepare the appropriate journal entries to record the first semiannual interest payment for both issues.

E 14–15
Error correction; accrued interest on bonds
● LO14–2

At the end of 2017, Majors Furniture Company failed to accrue $61,000 of interest expense that accrued during the last five months of 2017 on bonds payable. The bonds mature in 2031. The discount on the bonds is amortized by the straight-line method. The following entry was recorded on February 1, 2018, when the semiannual interest was paid:

Interest expense	73,200	
Discount on bonds payable		1,200
Cash		72,000

Required:

Prepare any journal entry necessary to correct the errors as of February 2, 2018, when the errors were discovered. Also, prepare any adjusting entry at December 31, 2018, related to the situation described. (Ignore income taxes.)

E 14–16
Error in amortization schedule
● LO14–3

Wilkins Food Products, Inc., acquired a packaging machine from Lawrence Specialists Corporation. Lawrence completed construction of the machine on January 1, 2016. In payment for the machine Wilkins issued a three-year installment note to be paid in three equal payments at the end of each year. The payments include interest at the rate of 10%.

Lawrence made a conceptual error in preparing the amortization schedule, which Wilkins failed to discover until 2018. The error had caused Wilkins to understate interest expense by $45,000 in 2016 and $40,000 in 2017.

Required:

1. Determine which accounts are incorrect as a result of these errors at January 1, 2018, before any adjustments. Explain your answer. (Ignore income taxes.)
2. Prepare a journal entry to correct the error.
3. What other step(s) would be taken in connection with the error?

E 14–17
Note with unrealistic interest rate; borrower; amortization schedule
● LO14–3

Amber Mining and Milling, Inc., contracted with Truax Corporation to have constructed a custom-made lathe. The machine was completed and ready for use on January 1, 2018. Amber paid for the lathe by issuing a $600,000, three-year note that specified 4% interest, payable annually on December 31 of each year. The cash market price of the lathe was unknown. It was determined by comparison with similar transactions that 12% was a reasonable rate of interest.

Required:

1. Prepare the journal entry on January 1, 2018, for Amber Mining and Milling's purchase of the lathe.
2. Prepare an amortization schedule for the three-year term of the note.
3. Prepare the journal entries to record (a) interest for each of the three years and (b) payment of the note at maturity.

E 14–18
Note with unrealistic interest rate; lender; amortization schedule
● LO14–3

Refer to the situation described in E 14–17.

Required:

1. Prepare the journal entry on January 1, 2018, for Truax Corporation's sale of the lathe.
2. Prepare an amortization schedule for the three-year term of the note.
3. Prepare the journal entries to record (a) interest for each of the three years and (b) payment of the note at maturity for Truax.

E 14–19
Installment note; lender; amortization schedule
● LO14–3

FinanceCo lent $8 million to Corbin Construction on January 1, 2018, to construct a playground. Corbin signed a three-year, 6% installment note to be paid in three equal payments at the end of each year.

Required:

1. Prepare the journal entry for FinanceCo's lending the funds on January 1, 2018.
2. Prepare an amortization schedule for the three-year term of the installment note.
3. Prepare the journal entry for the first installment payment on December 31, 2018.
4. Prepare the journal entry for the third installment payment on December 31, 2020.

E 14–20
Installment note; amortization schedule
● LO14–3

American Food Services, Inc., acquired a packaging machine from Barton and Barton Corporation. Barton and Barton completed construction of the machine on January 1, 2018. In payment for the $4 million machine, American Food Services issued a four-year installment note to be paid in four equal payments at the end of each year. The payments include interest at the rate of 10%.

Required:

1. Prepare the journal entry for American Food Services' purchase of the machine on January 1, 2018.
2. Prepare an amortization schedule for the four-year term of the installment note.
3. Prepare the journal entry for the first installment payment on December 31, 2018.
4. Prepare the journal entry for the third installment payment on December 31, 2020.

E 14–21
Installment note
● LO14–3

LCD Industries purchased a supply of electronic components from Entel Corporation on November 1, 2018. In payment for the $24 million purchase, LCD issued a 1-year installment note to be paid in equal monthly payments at the end of each month. The payments include interest at the rate of 12%.

Required:

1. Prepare the journal entry for LCD's purchase of the components on November 1, 2018.
2. Prepare the journal entry for the first installment payment on November 30, 2018.
3. What is the amount of interest expense that LCD will report in its income statement for the year ended December 31, 2018?

E 14–22
FASB codification research
● LO14–2, LO14–3, LO14–4

CODE

Access the *FASB Accounting Standards Codification* at the FASB website (www.fasb.org). Determine the specific citation for accounting for each of the following items:

1. Disclosure requirements for maturities of long-term debt.
2. How to estimate the value of a note when a note having no ready market and no interest rate is exchanged for a noncash asset without a readily available fair value.
3. When the straight-line method can be used as an alternative to the interest method of determining interest.

E 14–23
Early extinguishment
● LO14–5

The balance sheet of Indian River Electronics Corporation as of December 31, 2017, included 12.25% bonds having a face amount of $90 million. The bonds had been issued in 2010 and had a remaining discount of $3 million at December 31, 2017. On January 1, 2018, Indian River Electronics called the bonds before their scheduled maturity at the call price of 102.

Required:

Prepare the journal entry by Indian River Electronics to record the redemption of the bonds at January 1, 2018.

E 14–24
Convertible bonds
● LO14–5

On January 1, 2018, Gless Textiles issued $12 million of 9%, 10-year convertible bonds at 101. The bonds pay interest on June 30 and December 31. Each $1,000 bond is convertible into 40 shares of Gless's no par common stock. Bonds that are similar in all respects, except that they are nonconvertible, currently are selling at 99 (that is, 99% of face amount). Century Services purchased 10% of the issue as an investment.

Required:

1. Prepare the journal entries for the issuance of the bonds by Gless and the purchase of the bond investment by Century.
2. Prepare the journal entries for the June 30, 2022, interest payment by both Gless and Century assuming both use the straight-line method.
3. On July 1, 2023, when Gless's common stock had a market price of $33 per share, Century converted the bonds it held. Prepare the journal entries by both Gless and Century for the conversion of the bonds (book value method).

E 14–25
IFRS; convertible bonds
● LO14–5, LO14–7

Refer to the situation described in E 14–24.

Required:

How might your solution to requirement 1 for the issuer of the bonds differ if Gless Textiles prepares its financial statements according to International Financial Reporting Standards? Include any appropriate journal entry in your response.

E 14–26
Convertible bonds; induced conversion
● LO14–5

On January 1, 2018, Madison Products issued $40 million of 6%, 10-year convertible bonds at a net price of $40.8 million. Madison recently issued similar, but nonconvertible, bonds at 99 (that is, 99% of face amount). The bonds pay interest on June 30 and December 31. Each $1,000 bond is convertible into 30 shares of Madison's no par common stock. Madison records interest by the straight-line method.

On June 1, 2020, Madison notified bondholders of its intent to call the bonds at face value plus a 1% call premium on July 1, 2020. By June 30, all bondholders had chosen to convert their bonds into shares as of the interest payment date. On June 30, Madison paid the semiannual interest and issued the requisite number of shares for the bonds being converted.

Required:

1. Prepare the journal entry for the issuance of the bonds by Madison.
2. Prepare the journal entry for the June 30, 2018, interest payment.
3. Prepare the journal entries for the June 30, 2020, interest payment by Madison and the conversion of the bonds (book value method).

E 14–27
IFRS; convertible bonds
● LO14–5, LO14–7
IFRS

Refer to the situation described in E 14–26.

Required:

How might your solution for the issuer of the bonds differ if Madison Products prepares its financial statements according to International Financial Reporting Standards? Include any appropriate journal entries in your response.

E 14–28
Bonds with detachable warrants
● LO14–5

On August 1, 2018, Limbaugh Communications issued $30 million of 10% nonconvertible bonds at 104. The bonds are due on July 31, 2038. Each $1,000 bond was issued with 20 detachable stock warrants, each of which entitled the bondholder to purchase, for $60, one share of Limbaugh Communications' no par common stock. Interstate Containers purchased 20% of the bond issue. On August 1, 2018, the market value of the common stock was $58 per share and the market value of each warrant was $8.

In February 2029, when Limbaugh's common stock had a market price of $72 per share and the unamortized discount balance was $1 million, Interstate Containers exercised the warrants it held.

Required:

1. Prepare the journal entries on August 1, 2018, to record (a) the issuance of the bonds by Limbaugh and (b) the investment by Interstate.
2. Prepare the journal entries for both Limbaugh and Interstate in February 2029, to record the exercise of the warrants.

E 14–29
Reporting bonds at fair value
● LO14–6

(Note: This is a variation of E 14–13 modified to consider the fair value option for reporting liabilities.) Federal Semiconductors issued 11% bonds, dated January 1, with a face amount of $800 million on January 1, 2018. The bonds sold for $739,814,813 and mature on December 31, 2037 (20 years). For bonds of similar risk and maturity the market yield was 12%. Interest is paid semiannually on June 30 and December 31. Federal determines interest at the effective rate. Federal elected the option to report these bonds at their fair value. On December 31, 2018, the fair value of the bonds was $730 million as determined by their market value in the over-the-counter market.

Required:

1. Prepare the journal entry to adjust the bonds to their fair value for presentation in the December 31, 2018, balance sheet. Federal determined that none of the change in fair value was due to a decline in general interest rates.
2. Assume the fair value of the bonds on December 31, 2019, had risen to $736 million. Prepare the journal entry to adjust the bonds to their fair value for presentation in the December 31, 2019, balance sheet. Federal determined that one-half of the increase in fair value was due to a decline in general interest rates.

E 14–30
Reporting bonds at fair value
● LO14–6

On January 1, 2018, Rapid Airlines issued $200 million of its 8% bonds for $184 million. The bonds were priced to yield 10%. Interest is payable semiannually on June 30 and December 31. Rapid Airlines records interest at the effective rate and elected the option to report these bonds at their fair value. On December 31, 2018, the fair value of the bonds was $188 million as determined by their market value in the over-the-counter market. Rapid determined that $1,000,000 of the increase in fair value was due to a decline in general interest rates.

Required:

1. Prepare the journal entry to record interest on June 30, 2018 (the first interest payment).
2. Prepare the journal entry to record interest on December 31, 2018 (the second interest payment).
3. Prepare the journal entry to adjust the bonds to their fair value for presentation in the December 31, 2018, balance sheet.

E 14–31
Reporting bonds at fair value; calculate fair value
● LO14–6

On January 1, 2018, Essence Communications issued $800,000 of its 10-year, 8% bonds for $700,302. The bonds were priced to yield 10%. Interest is payable semiannually on June 30 and December 31. Essence Communications records interest at the effective rate and elected the option to report these bonds at their fair value. On December 31, 2018, the market interest rate for bonds of similar risk and maturity was 9%. The bonds are not traded on an active exchange. The increase in the market interest rate was due to a 1% increase in general (risk-free) interest rates.

Required:

1. Using the information provided, estimate the fair value of the bonds at December 31, 2018.
2. Prepare the journal entry to record interest on June 30, 2018 (the first interest payment).
3. Prepare the journal entry to record interest on December 31, 2018 (the second interest payment).
4. Prepare the journal entry to adjust the bonds to their fair value for presentation in the December 31, 2018, balance sheet.

E 14–32
Accrued interest
● Appendix A

On March 1, 2018, Brown-Ferring Corporation issued $100 million of 12% bonds, dated January 1, 2018, for $99 million (plus accrued interest). The bonds mature on December 31, 2037, and pay interest semiannually on June 30 and December 31. Brown-Ferring's fiscal period is the calendar year.

Required:

1. Determine the amount of accrued interest that was included in the proceeds received from the bond sale.
2. Prepare the journal entry for the issuance of the bonds by Brown-Ferring.

E 14–33
Troubled debt restructuring; debt settled
● Appendix B

At January 1, 2018, Transit Developments owed First City Bank Group $600,000, under an 11% note with three years remaining to maturity. Due to financial difficulties, Transit was unable to pay the previous year's interest.

First City Bank Group agreed to settle Transit's debt in exchange for land having a fair value of $450,000. Transit purchased the land in 2014 for $325,000.

Required:

Prepare the journal entry(s) to record the restructuring of the debt by Transit Developments.

E 14–34
Troubled debt restructuring; modification of terms
● Appendix B

At January 1, 2018, Brainard Industries, Inc., owed Second BancCorp $12 million under a 10% note due December 31, 2020. Interest was paid last on December 31, 2016. Brainard was experiencing severe financial difficulties and asked Second BancCorp to modify the terms of the debt agreement. After negotiation Second BancCorp agreed to:

a. Forgive the interest accrued for the year just ended.
b. Reduce the remaining two years' interest payments to $1 million each and delay the first payment until December 31, 2019.
c. Reduce the unpaid principal amount to $11 million.

Required:
Prepare the journal entries by Brainard Industries, Inc., necessitated by the restructuring of the debt at (1) January 1, 2018; (2) December 31, 2019; and (3) December 31, 2020.

E 14–35
Troubled debt restructuring; modification of terms; unknown effective rate
● Appendix B

At January 1, 2018, NCI Industries, Inc., was indebted to First Federal Bank under a $240,000, 10% unsecured note. The note was signed January 1, 2014, and was due December 31, 2019. Annual interest was last paid on December 31, 2016. NCI was experiencing severe financial difficulties and negotiated a restructuring of the terms of the debt agreement. First Federal agreed to reduce last year's interest and the remaining two years' interest payments to $11,555 each and delay all payments until December 31, 2019, the maturity date.

Required:
Prepare the journal entries by NCI Industries, Inc., necessitated by the restructuring of the debt at: (1) January 1, 2018; (2) December 31, 2018; and (3) December 31, 2019.

E 14–36
FASB codification research; legal fees in a troubled debt restructuring
● Appendix B

CODE

In negotiating and effecting a troubled debt restructuring, the creditor usually incurs various legal costs. The *FASB Accounting Standards Codification* represents the single source of authoritative U.S. generally accepted accounting principles.

Required:
1. Obtain the relevant authoritative literature on the accounting treatment of legal fees incurred by a creditor to effect a troubled debt restructuring using the *FASB Accounting Standards Codification* at the FASB website (www.fasb.org).
2. What is the specific citation that describes the guidelines for reporting legal costs?
3. What is the appropriate accounting treatment?

Problems

connect

P 14–1
Determining the price of bonds; discount and premium; issuer and investor
● LO14–2

On January 1, 2018, Instaform, Inc., issued 10% bonds with a face amount of $50 million, dated January 1. The bonds mature in 2037 (20 years). The market yield for bonds of similar risk and maturity is 12%. Interest is paid semiannually.

Required:
1. Determine the price of the bonds at January 1, 2018, and prepare the journal entry to record their issuance by Instaform.
2. Assume the market rate was 9%. Determine the price of the bonds at January 1, 2018, and prepare the journal entry to record their issuance by Instaform.
3. Assume Broadcourt Electronics purchased the entire issue in a private placement of the bonds. Using the data in requirement 2, prepare the journal entry to record the purchase by Broadcourt.

P 14–2
Effective interest; financial statement effects
● LO14–2

On January 1, 2018, Baddour, Inc., issued 10% bonds with a face amount of $160 million. The bonds were priced at $140 million to yield 12%. Interest is paid semiannually on June 30 and December 31. Baddour's fiscal year ends September 30.

Required:
1. What amount(s) related to the bonds would Baddour report in its balance sheet at September 30, 2018?
2. What amount(s) related to the bonds would Baddour report in its income statement for the year ended September 30, 2018?
3. What amount(s) related to the bonds would Baddour report in its statement of cash flows for the year ended September 30, 2018? In which section(s) should the amount(s) appear?

P 14–3
Straight-line and effective interest compared
● LO14–2

On January 1, 2018, Bradley Recreational Products issued $100,000, 9%, four-year bonds. Interest is paid semiannually on June 30 and December 31. The bonds were issued at $96,768 to yield an annual return of 10%.

Required:

1. Prepare an amortization schedule that determines interest at the effective interest rate.
2. Prepare an amortization schedule by the straight-line method.
3. Prepare the journal entries to record interest expense on June 30, 2020, by each of the two approaches.
4. Explain why the pattern of interest differs between the two methods.
5. Assuming the market rate is still 10%, what price would a second investor pay the first investor on June 30, 2020, for $10,000 of the bonds?

P 14–4
Bond amortization schedule
● LO14–2

On January 1, 2018, Tennessee Harvester Corporation issued debenture bonds that pay interest semiannually on June 30 and December 31. Portions of the bond amortization schedule appear below:

Payment	Cash Payment	Effective Interest	Increase in Balance	Outstanding Balance
				6,627,273
1	320,000	331,364	11,364	6,638,637
2	320,000	331,932	11,932	6,650,569
3	320,000	332,528	12,528	6,663,097
4	320,000	333,155	13,155	6,676,252
5	320,000	333,813	13,813	6,690,065
6	320,000	334,503	14,503	6,704,568
~	~	~	~	~
~	~	~	~	~
~	~	~	~	~
38	320,000	389,107	69,107	7,851,247
39	320,000	392,562	72,562	7,923,809
40	320,000	396,191	76,191	8,000,000

Required:

1. What is the face amount of the bonds?
2. What is the initial selling price of the bonds?
3. What is the term to maturity in years?
4. Interest is determined by what approach?
5. What is the stated annual interest rate?
6. What is the effective annual interest rate?
7. What is the total cash interest paid over the term to maturity?
8. What is the total effective interest expense recorded over the term to maturity?

P 14–5
Issuer and investor; effective interest; amortization schedule; adjusting entries
● LO14–2

On February 1, 2018, Cromley Motor Products issued 9% bonds, dated February 1, with a face amount of $80 million. The bonds mature on January 31, 2022 (4 years). The market yield for bonds of similar risk and maturity was 10%. Interest is paid semiannually on July 31 and January 31. Barnwell Industries acquired $80,000 of the bonds as a long-term investment. The fiscal years of both firms end December 31.

Required:

1. Determine the price of the bonds issued on February 1, 2018.
2. Prepare amortization schedules that indicate (a) Cromley's effective interest expense and (b) Barnwell's effective interest revenue for each interest period during the term to maturity.
3. Prepare the journal entries to record (a) the issuance of the bonds by Cromley and (b) Barnwell's investment on February 1, 2018.
4. Prepare the journal entries by both firms to record all subsequent events related to the bonds through January 31, 2020.

P 14–6
Issuer and investor; straight-line method; adjusting entries
● LO14–2, Appendix A

On April 1, 2018, Western Communications, Inc., issued 12% bonds, dated March 1, 2018, with face amount of $30 million. The bonds sold for $29.3 million and mature on February 28, 2021. Interest is paid semiannually on August 31 and February 28. Stillworth Corporation acquired $30,000 of the bonds as a long-term investment. The fiscal years of both firms end December 31, and both firms use the straight-line method.

Required:

1. Prepare the journal entries to record (a) issuance of the bonds by Western and (b) Stillworth's investment on April 1, 2018.
2. Prepare the journal entries by both firms to record all subsequent events related to the bonds through maturity.

P 14–7
Issuer and investor; effective interest
● LO14–2

McWherter Instruments sold $400 million of 8% bonds, dated January 1, on January 1, 2018. The bonds mature on December 31, 2037 (20 years). For bonds of similar risk and maturity, the market yield was 10%. Interest is paid semiannually on June 30 and December 31. Blanton Technologies, Inc., purchased $400,000 of the bonds as a long-term investment.

Required:

1. Determine the price of the bonds issued on January 1, 2018.
2. Prepare the journal entries to record (a) their issuance by McWherter and (b) Blanton's investment on January 1, 2018.
3. Prepare the journal entries by (a) McWherter and (b) Blanton to record interest on June 30, 2018 (at the effective rate).
4. Prepare the journal entries by (a) McWherter and (b) Blanton to record interest on December 31, 2018 (at the effective rate).

P 14–8
Bonds; effective interest; partial period interest; financial statement effects
● LO14–2

The fiscal year ends December 31 for Lake Hamilton Development. To provide funding for its Moonlight Bay project, LHD issued 5% bonds with a face amount of $500,000 on November 1, 2018. The bonds sold for $442,215, a price to yield the market rate of 6%. The bonds mature October 31, 2038 (20 years). Interest is paid semiannually on April 30 and October 31.

Required:

1. What amount of interest expense related to the bonds will LHD report in its income statement for the year ending December 31, 2018?
2. What amount(s) related to the bonds will LHD report in its balance sheet at December 31, 2018?
3. What amount of interest expense related to the bonds will LHD report in its income statement for the year ending December 31, 2019?
4. What amount(s) related to the bonds will LHD report in its balance sheet at December 31, 2019?

P 14–9
Zero-coupon bonds
● LO14–2

On January 1, 2018, Darnell Window and Pane issued $18 million of 10-year, zero-coupon bonds for $5,795,518.

Required:

1. Prepare the journal entry to record the bond issue.
2. Determine the effective rate of interest.
3. Prepare the journal entry to record annual interest expense at December 31, 2018.
4. Prepare the journal entry to record annual interest expense at December 31, 2019.
5. Prepare the journal entry to record the extinguishment at maturity.

P 14–10
Notes exchanged for assets; unknown effective rate
● LO14–3

At the beginning of the year, Lambert Motors issued the three notes described below. Interest is paid at year-end.

1. The company issued a two-year, 12%, $600,000 note in exchange for a tract of land. The current market rate of interest is 12%.
2. Lambert acquired some office equipment with a fair value of $94,643 by issuing a one-year, $100,000 note. The stated interest on the note is 6%.
3. The company purchased a building by issuing a three-year installment note. The note is to be repaid in equal installments of $1 million per year beginning one year hence. The current market rate of interest is 12%.

Required:

Prepare the journal entries to record each of the three transactions and the interest expense at the end of the first year for each.

P 14–11
Note with unrealistic interest rate
● LO14–3

At January 1, 2018, Brant Cargo acquired equipment by issuing a five-year, $150,000 (payable at maturity), 4% note. The market rate of interest for notes of similar risk is 10%.

Required:

1. Prepare the journal entry for Brant Cargo to record the purchase of the equipment.
2. Prepare the journal entry for Brant Cargo to record the interest at December 31, 2018.
3. Prepare the journal entry for Brant Cargo to record the interest at December 31, 2019.

P 14–12
Noninterest-bearing installment note
● LO14–3

At the beginning of 2018, VHF Industries acquired a machine with a fair value of $6,074,700 by issuing a four-year, noninterest-bearing note in the face amount of $8 million. The note is payable in four annual installments of $2 million at the end of each year.

Required:

1. What is the effective rate of interest implicit in the agreement?
2. Prepare the journal entry to record the purchase of the machine.
3. Prepare the journal entry to record the first installment payment at December 31, 2018.
4. Prepare the journal entry to record the second installment payment at December 31, 2019.
5. Suppose the market value of the machine was unknown at the time of purchase, but the market rate of interest for notes of similar risk was 11%. Prepare the journal entry to record the purchase of the machine.

P 14–13
Note and installment note with unrealistic interest rate
● LO14–3

Braxton Technologies, Inc., constructed a conveyor for A&G Warehousers that was completed and ready for use on January 1, 2018. A&G paid for the conveyor by issuing a $100,000, four-year note that specified 5% interest to be paid on December 31 of each year, and the note is to be repaid at the end of four years. The conveyor was custom-built for A&G, so its cash price was unknown. By comparison with similar transactions it was determined that a reasonable interest rate was 10%.

Required:

1. Prepare the journal entry for A&G's purchase of the conveyor on January 1, 2018.
2. Prepare an amortization schedule for the four-year term of the note.
3. Prepare the journal entry for A&G's third interest payment on December 31, 2020.
4. If A&G's note had been an installment note to be paid in four equal payments at the end of each year beginning December 31, 2018, what would be the amount of each installment?
5. Prepare an amortization schedule for the four-year term of the installment note.
6. Prepare the journal entry for A&G's third installment payment on December 31, 2020.

P 14–14
Early extinguishment of debt
● LO14–5

Three years ago American Insulation Corporation issued 10%, $800,000, 10-year bonds for $770,000. American Insulation exercised its call privilege and retired the bonds for $790,000. The corporation uses the straight-line method to determine interest.

Required:

Prepare the journal entry to record the call of the bonds.

P 14–15
Early extinguishment; effective interest
● LO14–5

The long-term liability section of Twin Digital Corporation's balance sheet as of December 31, 2017, included 12% bonds having a face amount of $20 million and a remaining discount of $1 million. Disclosure notes indicate the bonds were issued to yield 14%.

Interest expense is recorded at the effective interest rate and paid on January 1 and July 1 of each year. On July 1, 2018, Twin Digital retired the bonds at 102 ($20.4 million) before their scheduled maturity.

Required:

1. Prepare the journal entry by Twin Digital to record the semiannual interest on July 1, 2018.
2. Prepare the journal entry by Twin Digital to record the redemption of the bonds on July 1, 2018.

P 14–16
Debt issue costs; issuance; expensing; early extinguishment; straight-line amortization
● LO14–2, LO14–5

Cupola Fan Corporation issued 10%, $400,000, 10-year bonds for $385,000 on June 30, 2018. Debt issue costs were $1,500. Interest is paid semiannually on December 31 and June 30. One year from the issue date (July 1, 2019), the corporation exercised its call privilege and retired the bonds for $395,000. The corporation uses the straight-line method both to determine interest expense and to amortize debt issue costs.

Required:

1. Prepare the journal entry to record the issuance of the bonds.

2. Prepare the journal entries to record the payment of interest and amortization of debt issue costs on December 31, 2018.
3. Prepare the journal entries to record the payment of interest and amortization of debt issue costs on June 30, 2019.
4. Prepare the journal entry to record the call of the bonds.

P 14–17
IFRS; transaction costs
● LO14–2, LO14–7
IFRS

Refer to the situation described in P 14–16.

Required:

How might your solution for the issuer of the bonds differ if Cupola prepares its financial statements according to International Financial Reporting Standards? Include any appropriate journal entries in your response.

P 14–18
Early extinguishment
● LO14–5

The long-term liability section of Eastern Post Corporation's balance sheet as of December 31, 2017, included 10% bonds having a face amount of $40 million and a remaining premium of $6 million. On January 1, 2018, Eastern Post retired some of the bonds before their scheduled maturity.

Required:

Prepare the journal entry by Eastern Post to record the redemption of the bonds under each of the independent circumstances below:

1. Eastern Post called half the bonds at the call price of 102 (102% of face amount).
2. Eastern Post repurchased $10 million of the bonds on the open market at their market price of $10.5 million.

P 14–19
Convertible bonds; induced conversion; bonds with detachable warrants
● LO14–5

Bradley-Link's December 31, 2018, balance sheet included the following items:

	($ in millions)
Long-Term Liabilities	
9.6% convertible bonds, callable at 101 beginning in 2019, due 2022 (net of unamortized discount of $2) [note 8]	$198
10.4% registered bonds callable at 104 beginning in 2028, due 2032 (net of unamortized discount of $1) [note 8]	49
Shareholders' Equity	
Equity—stock warrants	4

Note 8: Bonds (in part)

The 9.6% bonds were issued in 2005 at 97.5 to yield 10%. Interest is paid semiannually on June 30 and December 31. Each $1,000 bond is convertible into 40 shares of the Company's no par common stock.

The 10.4% bonds were issued in 2009 at 102 to yield 10%. Interest is paid semiannually on June 30 and December 31. Each $1,000 bond was issued with 40 detachable stock warrants, each of which entitles the holder to purchase one share of the Company's no par common stock for $25, beginning 2019.

On January 3, 2019, when Bradley-Link's common stock had a market price of $32 per share, Bradley-Link called the convertible bonds to force conversion. 90% were converted; the remainder were acquired at the call price. When the common stock price reached an all-time high of $37 in December of 2017, 40% of the warrants were exercised.

Required:

1. Prepare the journal entries that were recorded when each of the two bond issues was originally sold in 2005 and 2009.
2. Prepare the journal entry to record (book value method) the conversion of 90% of the convertible bonds in January 2019 and the retirement of the remainder.
3. Assume Bradley-Link induced conversion by offering $150 cash for each bond converted. Prepare the journal entry to record (book value method) the conversion of 90% of the convertible bonds in January 2019.
4. Assume Bradley-Link induced conversion by modifying the conversion ratio to exchange 45 shares for each bond rather than the 40 shares provided in the contract. Prepare the journal entry to record (book value method) the conversion of 90% of the convertible bonds in January 2019.
5. Prepare the journal entry to record the exercise of the warrants in December 2019.

P 14–20
Convertible bonds; zero coupon; potentially convertible into cash; FASB codification research
● LO14–5

The 2018 annual report of MLS Corporation included the following disclosure note:

> **Note 10: Borrowings (in part)**
> **Convertible Debt**
> On June 15, 2018, we issued $125 million of zero coupon convertible unsecured debt due on June 15, 2020 in a private placement offering, priced to yield 1.85%. Proceeds from the offering were $118.3115 million. Initially, each $1,000 principal amount of bonds was convertible into 30 shares of MLS common stock at a conversion price of $35 per share.
>
> The bonds are convertible at any time. Upon conversion, we will pay cash up to the aggregate principal amount of the bonds and pay or deliver cash, shares of our common stock, or a combination of cash and shares of our common stock, at our election.
>
> Because the convertible debt may be wholly or partially settled in cash, we are required to separately account for the liability and equity components of the bonds in a manner that reflects our nonconvertible debt borrowing rate when interest costs are recognized in subsequent periods. The net proceeds of $118.3 million were allocated between debt for $117.2 million and shareholders' equity for $1.1 million with the portion in shareholders' equity representing the fair value of the option to convert the debt.

Required:

1. Prepare the journal entry that was recorded when the bonds were issued on June 15, 2018.
2. What amount of interest expense, if any, did MLS record the first year the bonds were outstanding?
3. Normally under U.S. GAAP, we record the entire issue price of convertible debt as a liability. However, MLS separately recorded the liability and equity components of the notes. Why?
4. Obtain the relevant authoritative literature on classification of debt expected to be financed using the FASB's Codification Research System. You might gain access from the FASB website (www.fasb.org), from your school library, or some other source. Determine the criteria for reporting debt potentially convertible into cash. What is the specific codification citation that MLS would rely on in applying that accounting treatment?

P 14–21
Concepts; terminology
● LO14–1 through LO14–5

Listed below are several terms and phrases associated with long-term debt. Pair each item from List A with the item from List B (by letter) that is most appropriately associated with it.

List A	List B
____ 1. Effective rate times balance	a. Straight-line method
____ 2. Promises made to bondholders	b. Discount
____ 3. Present value of interest plus present value of principal	c. Liquidation payments after other claims satisfied
____ 4. Call feature	d. Name of owner not registered
____ 5. Debt issue costs	e. Premium
____ 6. Market rate higher than stated rate	f. Checks are mailed directly
____ 7. Coupon bonds	g. No specific assets pledged
____ 8. Convertible bonds	h. Bond indenture
____ 9. Market rate less than stated rate	i. Backed by a lien
____ 10. Stated rate times face amount	j. Interest expense
____ 11. Registered bonds	k. May become stock
____ 12. Debenture bond	l. Legal, accounting, printing
____ 13. Mortgage bond	m. Protection against falling rates
____ 14. Materiality concept	n. Periodic cash payments
____ 15. Subordinated debenture	o. Bond price

P 14–22
Determine bond price; record interest; report bonds at fair value
● LO14–6

On January 1, 2018, NFB Visual Aids issued $800,000 of its 20-year, 8% bonds. The bonds were priced to yield 10%. Interest is payable semiannually on June 30 and December 31. NFB Visual Aids records interest expense at the effective rate and elected the option to report these bonds at their fair value. On December 31, 2018, the fair value of the bonds was $668,000 as determined by their market value in the over-the-counter market.

Required:

1. Determine the price of the bonds at January 1, 2018, and prepare the journal entry to record their issuance.
2. Prepare the journal entry to record interest on June 30, 2018 (the first interest payment).
3. Prepare the journal entry to record interest on December 31, 2018 (the second interest payment).
4. Prepare the journal entry to adjust the bonds to their fair value for presentation in the December 31, 2018, balance sheet.

P 14–23
Report bonds at fair value; quarterly reporting
● LO14–6

Appling Enterprises issued 8% bonds with a face amount of $400,000 on January 1, 2018. The bonds sold for $331,364 and mature in 2037 (20 years). For bonds of similar risk and maturity the market yield was 10%. Interest is paid semiannually on June 30 and December 31. Appling determines interest expense at the effective rate. Appling elected the option to report these bonds at their fair value. The fair values of the bonds at the end of each quarter during 2018 as determined by their market values in the over-the-counter market were the following:

March 31	$350,000
June 30	340,000
September 30	335,000
December 31	342,000

General (risk-free) interest rates did not change during 2018.

Required:

1. By how much will Appling's comprehensive income be increased or decreased by the bonds (ignoring taxes) in the March 31 *quarterly* financial statements?
2. By how much will Appling's comprehensive income be increased or decreased by the bonds (ignoring taxes) in the June 30 *quarterly* financial statements?
3. By how much will Appling's comprehensive income be increased or decreased by the bonds (ignoring taxes) in the September 30 *quarterly* financial statements?
4. By how much will Appling's comprehensive income be increased or decreased by the bonds (ignoring taxes) in the December 31 *annual* financial statements?

P 14–24
Investments in bonds; accrued interest; sale; straight-line interest
● LO14–2, Appendix A

The following transactions relate to bond investments of Livermore Laboratories. The company's fiscal year ends on December 31. Livermore uses the straight-line method to determine interest.

2018	
July 1	Purchased $16 million of Bracecourt Corporation 10% debentures, due in 20 years (June 30, 2038), for $15.7 million. Interest is payable on January 1 and July 1 of each year.
Oct. 1	Purchased $30 million of 12% Framm Pharmaceuticals debentures, due May 31, 2028, for $31,160,000 plus accrued interest. Interest is payable on June 1 and December 1 of each year.
Dec. 1	Received interest on the Framm bonds.
31	Accrued interest.
2019	
Jan. 1	Received interest on the Bracecourt bonds.
June 1	Received interest on the Framm bonds.
July 1	Received interest on the Bracecourt bonds.
Sept. 1	Sold $15 million of the Framm bonds at 101 plus accrued interest.
Dec. 1	Received interest on the remaining Framm bonds.
31	Accrued interest.
2020	
Jan. 1	Received interest on the Bracecourt bonds.
Feb. 28	Sold the remainder of the Framm bonds at 102 plus accrued interest.
Dec. 31	Accrued interest.

Required:

1. Prepare the appropriate journal entries for these long-term bond investments.
2. By how much will Livermore Labs' earnings increase in each of the three years as a result of these investments? (Ignore income taxes.)

P 14–25
Accrued interest; effective interest; financial statement effects
● Appendix A

On March 1, 2018, Baddour, Inc., issued 10% bonds, dated January 1, with a face amount of $160 million. The bonds were priced at $140 million (plus accrued interest) to yield 12%. Interest is paid semiannually on June 30 and December 31. Baddour's fiscal year ends September 30.

Required:

1. What would be the amount(s) related to the bonds Baddour would report in its balance sheet at September 30, 2018?
2. What would be the amount(s) related to the bonds that Baddour would report in its income statement for the year ended September 30, 2018?
3. What would be the amount(s) related to the bonds that Baddour would report in its statement of cash flows for the year ended September 30, 2018?

P 14–26
Troubled debt restructuring
● Appendix B

At January 1, 2018, Rothschild Chair Company, Inc., was indebted to First Lincoln Bank under a $20 million, 10% unsecured note. The note was signed January 1, 2015, and was due December 31, 2021. Annual interest was last paid on December 31, 2016. Rothschild Chair Company was experiencing severe financial difficulties and negotiated a restructuring of the terms of the debt agreement.

Required:

Prepare all journal entries by Rothschild Chair Company, Inc., to record the restructuring and any remaining transactions relating to the debt under each of the independent circumstances below:

1. First Lincoln Bank agreed to settle the debt in exchange for land having a fair value of $16 million but carried on Rothschild Chair Company's books at $13 million.
2. First Lincoln Bank agreed to (a) forgive the interest accrued from last year, (b) reduce the remaining four interest payments to $1 million each, and (c) reduce the principal to $15 million.
3. First Lincoln Bank agreed to defer all payments (including accrued interest) until the maturity date and accept $27,775,000 at that time in settlement of the debt.

Broaden Your Perspective

Apply your critical-thinking ability to the knowledge you've gained. These cases will provide you an opportunity to develop your research, analysis, judgment, and communication skills. You also will work with other students, integrate what you've learned, apply it in real-world situations, and consider its global and ethical ramifications. This practice will broaden your knowledge and further develop your decision-making abilities.

Communication Case 14–1
Convertible securities and warrants; concepts
● LO14–5

It is not unusual to issue long-term debt in conjunction with an arrangement under which lenders receive an option to buy common stock during all or a portion of the time the debt is outstanding. Sometimes the vehicle is convertible bonds; sometimes warrants to buy stock accompany the bonds and are separable. Interstate Chemical is considering these options in conjunction with a planned debt issue.

"You mean we have to report $7 million more in liabilities if we go with convertible bonds? Makes no sense to me," your CFO said. "Both ways seem pretty much the same transaction. Explain it to me, will you?"

Required:

Write a memo. Include in your explanation each of the following:

1. The differences in accounting for proceeds from the issuance of convertible bonds and of debt instruments with separate warrants to purchase common stock.
2. The underlying rationale for the differences.
3. Arguments that could be presented for the alternative accounting treatment.

Real World Case 14–2
Zero-coupon debt; HP Inc.
● LO14–2

Real World Financials

HP Inc. (formerly Hewlett-Packard Company) issued zero-coupon notes at the end of its 1997 fiscal year that mature at the end of its 2017 fiscal year. One billion, eight hundred million dollars face amount of 20-year debt sold for $968 million, a price to yield 3.149%. In fiscal 2002, HP repurchased $257 million in face value of the notes for a purchase price of $127 million, resulting in a gain on the early extinguishment of debt.

Required:

1. What journal entry did HP Inc. use to record the sale in 1997?
2. Using an electronic spreadsheet, prepare an amortization schedule for the notes. Assume interest is calculated annually and use numbers expressed in millions of dollars; that is, the face amount is $1,800.
3. What was the effect on HP's earnings in 1998? Explain.
4. From the amortization schedule, determine the book value of the debt at the end of 2002.
5. What journal entry did HP Inc. use to record the early extinguishment of debt in 2002, assuming the purchase was made at the end of the year?
6. If none of the notes is repaid prior to maturity, what entry would HP use to record their repayment at the end of 2017?

Communication Case 14–3
Is convertible debt a liability or is it shareholders' equity? Group Interaction
● LO14–5

Some financial instruments can be considered compound instruments in that they have features of both debt and shareholders' equity. The most common example encountered in practice is convertible debt—bonds or notes convertible by the investor into common stock. A topic of debate for several years has been whether:

View 1: Issuers should account for an instrument with both liability and equity characteristics entirely as a liability or entirely as an equity instrument depending on which characteristic governs.

View 2: Issuers should account for an instrument as consisting of a liability component and an equity component that should be accounted for separately.

In considering this question, you should disregard what you know about the current position of the FASB on the issue. Instead, focus on conceptual issues regarding the practicable and theoretically appropriate treatment, unconstrained by GAAP. Also, focus your deliberations on convertible bonds as the instrument with both liability and equity characteristics.

Required:

1. Which view do you favor? Develop a list of arguments in support of your view prior to the class session for which the case is assigned.
2. In class, your instructor will pair you (and everyone else) with a classmate (who also has independently developed an argument).
   a. You will be given three minutes to argue your view to your partner. Your partner likewise will be given three minutes to argue his or her view to you. During these three-minute presentations, the listening partner is not permitted to speak.
   b. After each person has had a turn attempting to convince his or her partner, the two partners will have a three-minute discussion in which they will decide which view is more convincing. Arguments will be merged into a single view for each pair.
3. After the allotted time, a spokesperson for each of the two views will be selected by the instructor. Each spokesperson will field arguments from the class in support of that view's position and list the arguments on the board. The class then will discuss the merits of the two lists of arguments and attempt to reach a consensus view, though a consensus is not necessary.

Analysis Case 14–4
Issuance of bonds
● LO14–2

The following appeared in the October 15, 2018, issue of the *Financial Smarts Journal:*

This announcement is not an offer of securities for sale or an offer to buy securities.
New Issue October 15, 2018

$750,000,000
CRAFT FOODS, INC.
7.75% Debentures Due October 1, 2028
Price 99.57%
plus accrued interest if any from date of issuance

Copies of the prospectus and the related prospectus supplement may be obtained from such of the undersigned as may legally offer these securities under applicable securities laws.

Keegan Morgan & Co. Inc.
Coldwell Bros. & Co.
Robert Stacks & Co.
Sherwin-William & Co.

Required:

1. Explain what is being described by the announcement.
2. Can you think of a psychological reason for the securities to be priced as they are?
3. What are the accounting considerations for Craft Foods, Inc.? Describe how Craft recorded the sale.

Judgment Case 14–5
Noninterest-bearing debt
● LO14–3

While reading a recent issue of *Health & Fitness,* a trade journal, Brandon Wilde noticed an ad for equipment he had been seeking for use in his business. The ad offered oxygen therapy equipment under the following terms:

Model BL 44582
$204,000 zero interest loan
Quarterly payments of $17,000 for only 3 years

The ad captured Wilde's attention, in part, because he recently had been concerned that the interest charges incurred by his business were getting out of line. The price, though, was somewhat higher than prices for this model he had seen elsewhere.

Required:

Advise Mr. Wilde on the purchase he is considering.

Judgment Case 14–6
Noninterest-bearing note exchanged for cash and other privileges
● LO14–3

The Jaecke Group, Inc., manufactures various kinds of hydraulic pumps. In June 2018, the company signed a four-year purchase agreement with one of its main parts suppliers, Hydraulics, Inc. Over the four-year period, Jaecke has agreed to purchase 100,000 units of a key component used in the manufacture of its pumps. The agreement allows Jaecke to purchase the component at a price lower than the prevailing market price at the time of purchase. As part of the agreement, Jaecke will lend Hydraulics $200,000 to be repaid after four years with no stated interest (the prevailing market rate of interest for a loan of this type is 10%).

Jaecke's chief accountant has proposed recording the note receivable at $200,000. The parts inventory purchase from Hydraulics over the next four years will then be recorded at the actual prices paid.

Required:

Do you agree with the accountant's valuation of the note and his intention to value the parts inventory acquired over the four-year period of the agreement at actual prices paid? If not, how would you account for the initial transaction and the subsequent inventory purchases?

Communication Case 14–7
Note receivable exchanged for cash and other services
● LO14–3

The Pastel Paint Company recently loaned $300,000 to KIX 96, a local radio station. The radio station signed a noninterest-bearing note requiring the $300,000 to be repaid in three years. As part of the agreement, the radio station will provide Pastel with a specified amount of free radio advertising over the three-year term of the note.

The focus of this case is the valuation of the note receivable by Pastel Paint Company and the treatment of the "free" advertising provided by the radio station. Your instructor will divide the class into two to six groups depending on the size of the class. The mission of your group is to reach consensus on the appropriate note valuation and accounting treatment of the free advertising.

Required:

1. Each group member should deliberate the situation independently and draft a tentative argument prior to the class session for which the case is assigned.
2. In class, each group will meet for 10 to 15 minutes in different areas of the classroom. During that meeting, group members will take turns sharing their suggestions for the purpose of arriving at a single group treatment.
3. After the allotted time, a spokesperson for each group (selected during the group meetings) will share the group's solution with the class. The goal of the class is to incorporate the views of each group into a consensus approach to the situation.

Ethics Case 14–8
Debt for equity swaps; have your cake and eat it too
● LO14–5

The cloudy afternoon mirrored the mood of the conference of division managers. Claude Meyer, assistant to the controller for Hunt Manufacturing, wore one of the gloomy faces that were just emerging from the conference room. "Wow, I knew it was bad, but not that bad," Claude thought to himself. "I don't look forward to sharing those numbers with shareholders."

The numbers he discussed with himself were fourth-quarter losses which more than offset the profits of the first three quarters. Everyone had known for some time that poor sales forecasts and production delays had wreaked havoc on the bottom line, but most were caught off guard by the severity of damage.

Later that night he sat alone in his office, scanning and rescanning the preliminary financial statements on his computer monitor. Suddenly his mood brightened. "This may work," he said aloud, though no one could hear. Fifteen minutes later he congratulated himself, "Yes!"

The next day he eagerly explained his plan to Susan Barr, controller of Hunt for the last six years. The plan involved $300 million in convertible bonds issued three years earlier.

Meyer: By swapping stock for the bonds, we can eliminate a substantial liability from the balance sheet, wipe out most of our interest expense, and reduce our loss. In fact, the book value of the bonds is significantly more than the market value of the stock we'd issue. I think we can produce a profit.

Barr: But Claude, our bondholders are not inclined to convert the bonds.

Meyer: Right. But, the bonds are callable. As of this year, we can call the bonds at a call premium of 1%. Given the choice of accepting that redemption price or converting to stock, they'll all convert. We won't have to pay a cent. And, since no cash will be paid, we won't pay taxes either.

Required:

Do you perceive an ethical dilemma? What would be the impact of following up on Claude's plan? Who would benefit? Who would be injured?

Judgment Case 14–9
Analyzing financial statements; financial leverage; interest coverage
● LO14–1, LO14–4

AGF Foods Company is a large, primarily domestic, consumer foods company involved in the manufacture, distribution, and sale of a variety of food products. Industry averages are derived from Troy's *The Almanac of Business and Industrial Financial Ratios*. Following are the 2018 and 2017 comparative income statements and balance sheets for AGF. (The financial data we use are from actual financial statements of a well-known corporation, but the company name is fictitious and the numbers and dates have been modified slightly to disguise the company's identity.)

AGF FOODS COMPANY
Years Ended December 31, 2018 and 2017
($ in millions)

Comparative Income Statements	2018	2017
Net sales	$6,440	$5,800
Cost of goods sold	(3,667)	(3,389)
Gross profit	2,773	2,411
Operating expenses	(1,916)	(1,629)
Operating income	857	782
Interest expense	(54)	(53)
Income from operations before tax	803	729
Income taxes	(316)	(287)
Net income	$ 487	$ 442
Comparative Balance Sheets		
Assets		
Total current assets	$1,879	$1,490
Property, plant, and equipment (net)	2,592	2,291
Intangibles (net)	800	843
Other assets	74	60
Total assets	$5,345	$4,684
Liabilities and Shareholders' Equity		
Total current liabilities	$1,473	$ 941
Long-term debt	534	728
Deferred income taxes	407	344
Total liabilities	2,414	2,013
Shareholders' equity:		
Common stock	180	180
Additional paid-in capital	21	63
Retained earnings	2,730	2,428
Total shareholders' equity	2,931	2,671
Total liabilities and shareholders' equity	$5,345	$4,684

Long-term solvency refers to a company's ability to pay its long-term obligations. Financing ratios provide investors and creditors with an indication of this element of risk.

Required:

1. Calculate the debt to equity ratio for AGF for 2018. The average ratio for the stocks listed on the New York Stock Exchange in a comparable time period was 1.0. What information does your calculation provide an investor?
2. Is AGF experiencing favorable or unfavorable financial leverage?
3. Calculate AGF's times interest earned ratio for 2018. The coverage for the stocks listed on the New York Stock Exchange in a comparable time period was 5.1. What does your calculation indicate about AGF's risk?

Research Case 14–10
FASB codification research; researching the way long-term debt is reported; Macy's, Inc.
● LO14–1 through LO14–4
Real World Financials

EDGAR, the Electronic Data Gathering. Analysis, and Retrieval system, performs automated collection, validation, indexing, acceptance and forwarding of submissions by companies and others who are required by law to file forms with the U.S. Securities and Exchange Commission (SEC). All publicly traded domestic companies use EDGAR to make the majority of their filings. (Some foreign companies do so voluntarily.) Form 10-K, including the annual report, is required to be filed on EDGAR. The SEC makes this information available on the Internet.

Required:

1. Access EDGAR on the Internet at www.sec.gov or from Investor Relations at the Macy's, Inc. (www.macys.com).
2. Search for Macy's. Access its 10-K filing for the year ended January 30, 2016. Search or scroll to find the financial statements and related notes.
3. What is the total debt (including current liabilities and deferred taxes) reported in the balance sheet? How has that amount changed over the most recent two years?
4. Compare the total liabilities (including current liabilities and deferred taxes) with the shareholders' equity and calculate the debt to equity ratio for the most recent two years. Has the proportion of debt financing and equity financing changed recently?

5. Does Macy's obtain more financing through notes, bonds, or commercial paper? Are required debt payments increasing or decreasing over time? Is any short-term debt classified as long-term? Why?
6. **Note 6: Financing** includes the following statement: "On November 18, 2014, the Company issued $550 million aggregate principal amount of 4.5% senior notes due 2034. This debt was used to pay for the redemption of the $407 million of 7.875% senior notes due 2015 described above." Under some circumstances, Macy's could have reported the amounts due in 2015 as long-term debt at the end of the previous year even though these amounts were due within the coming year. Obtain the relevant authoritative literature on classification of debt expected to be financed using the *FASB Accounting Standards Codification*. You might gain access from the FASB website (www.fasb.org), from your school library, or some other source. Determine the criteria for reporting currently payable debt as long-term. What is the specific codification citation that Macy's would rely on in applying that accounting treatment?

Analysis Case 14–11
Bonds; conversion; extinguishment
● LO14–5

On August 31, 2015, Chickasaw Industries issued $25 million of its 30-year, 6% convertible bonds dated August 31, priced to yield 5%. The bonds are convertible at the option of the investors into 1,500,000 shares of Chickasaw's common stock. Chickasaw records interest expense at the effective rate. On August 31, 2018, investors in Chickasaw's convertible bonds tendered 20% of the bonds for conversion into common stock that had a market value of $20 per share on the date of the conversion. On January 1, 2017, Chickasaw Industries issued $40 million of its 20-year, 7% bonds dated January 1 at a price to yield 8%. On December 31, 2018, the bonds were extinguished early through acquisition in the open market by Chickasaw for $40.5 million.

Required:
1. Using the book value method, would recording the conversion of the 6% convertible bonds into common stock affect earnings? If so, by how much? Would earnings be affected if the market value method is used? If so, by how much?
2. Were the 7% bonds issued at face value, at a discount, or at a premium? Explain.
3. Would the amount of interest expense for the 7% bonds be higher in the first year or second year of the term to maturity? Explain.
4. How should gain or loss on early extinguishment of debt be determined? Does the early extinguishment of the 7% bonds result in a gain or loss? Explain.

Continuing Cases

Target Case
● LO14–4

Target Corporation prepares its financial statements according to U.S. GAAP. Target's financial statements and disclosure notes for the year ended January 30, 2016, are available in Connect. This material is also available under the Investor Relations link at the company's website (www.target.com).

Target's share-based compensation includes several long-term incentive plans.

Long-term solvency refers to a company's ability to pay its long-term obligations. Financing ratios provide investors and creditors with an indication of this element of risk.

Required:
1. Calculate the debt to equity ratio for Target at January 30, 2016. The average ratio for companies in the General Retailers industry sector in a comparable time period was 1.6. What information does your calculation provide an investor?
2. Calculate Target's times interest earned ratio for the year ended January 30, 2016. The coverage for companies in the General Retailers industry sector in a comparable time period was 10.6. What does your calculation indicate about Target's risk?

Air France–KLM Case
● LO14–7
IFRS

Air France–KLM (AF), a Franco-Dutch company, prepares its financial statements according to International Financial Reporting Standards. AF's financial statements and disclosure notes for the year ended December 31, 2015, are available in Connect. This material also is available under the Finance link at the company's website (www.airfranceklm-finance.com.)

Required:
1. Examine the long-term borrowings in AF's balance sheet and the related note (33.2.2). Note that AF has convertible bonds outstanding that it issued in 2013. Prepare the journal entry AF would use to record the issue of convertible bonds. Prepare the journal entry AF would use to record the issue of the convertible bonds if AF used U.S. GAAP.
2. AF does not elect the fair value option (FVO) to report its financial liabilities. Examine Note 36.3 "Market value of financial instruments." If the company had elected the FVO for all of its debt measured at amortized cost, what would be the balance at December 31, 2015, in the fair value adjustment account?

CPA Exam Questions and Simulations

ROGER CPA Review

Sample CPA Exam questions from Roger CPA Review are available in Connect as support for the topics in this chapter. These Multiple Choice Questions and Task-Based Simulations include expert-written explanations and solutions, and provide a starting point for students to become familiar with the content and functionality of the actual CPA Exam.

CHAPTER

15

Leases

OVERVIEW

In Chapter 14, we saw how companies account for their long-term debt. The focus of that discussion was *bonds* and *notes*. In this chapter, we continue our discussion of debt, but we now turn our attention to liabilities arising in connection with *leases*. A lease is a contract that gives a lessee (user) the right to control the use of an asset for a period of time. The lessee pays the lessor (owner) for that right, typically with a series of payments made over the lease term. The lessee initially accounts for this arrangement by recording a "right-of-use" asset and a lease liability at the beginning of the lease. Subsequent accounting depends on the nature of the lease contract. When the substance of the lease contract represents a temporary rental agreement between the lessee and lessor, we classify those as operating leases. However, in situations where the lease contract essentially represents the sale of an asset, the lessee has a finance lease, and the lessor has a sales-type lease. As we'll see in this chapter, the way we account for a lease contract depends on how the lease is classified.

LEARNING OBJECTIVES

After studying this chapter, you should be able to:

- **LO15–1** Explain the basis for each of the criteria used to classify leases. (*p. 832*)
- **LO15–2** Describe and demonstrate how the lessee accounts for a finance lease and the lessor accounts for a sales-type lease with no selling profit. (*p. 836*)
- **LO15–3** Describe and demonstrate how the lessor accounts for a sales-type lease with a selling profit. (*p. 841*)
- **LO15–4** Describe and demonstrate how the lessor and lessee account for all transactions associated with operating leases. (*p. 843*)
- **LO15–5** Explain when and how a lessee accounts for a lease by the short-cut method. (*p. 849*)
- **LO15–6** Explain the impact on lease accounting of uncertainties, including uncertain lease terms, variable lease payments, residual values, purchase options, and termination penalties. (*p. 850*)
- **LO15–7** Explain the impact on lease accounting of other payments, including nonlease payments, initial direct costs, and leasehold improvements. (*p. 861*)
- **LO15–8** Describe the impact of leases on the statement of cash flows and disclosure requirements pertaining to leases. (*p. 867*)
- **LO15–9** Discuss the primary differences between U.S. GAAP and IFRS with respect to leases. (*pp. 849* and *853*)

© Pressmaster/Shutterstock

FINANCIAL REPORTING CASE

Lease or Buy?

"The days of off-balance-sheet financing are over," said Aaron Sanchez, controller for your new employer, Higher Graphics. "Now that we have to report liabilities for both finance and operating leases, maybe we shouldn't keep limiting our leases to short-term arrangements that would be considered operating leases. In fact, maybe we should start buying our equipment rather than leasing it."

Like most companies in your industry, HG leases much of the electronic equipment it uses to develop and test the software it produces. Eager to understand the implications of your new supervisor's concerns, you turn to the Internet to bolster your knowledge of the new lease accounting standards.

QUESTIONS

By the time you finish this chapter, you should be able to respond appropriately to the questions posed in this case. Compare your response to the solution provided at the end of the chapter.

1. Are there advantages of leasing its equipment that HG should consider? *(p. 834)*
2. Would the effect on HG's income statement be the same if HG used finance leases instead of operating leases? *(p. 841)*

PART A

Accounting by the Lessor and Lessee

If you ever have leased an apartment, you know that a lease is a contractual arrangement by which a lessor (owner) provides a lessee (user) the right to use an asset for a specified period of time. In return for this right, the lessee agrees to make periodic cash payments during the term of the lease. An apartment lease is a typical rental agreement in which the fundamental rights and responsibilities of ownership are retained by the lessor; the lessee merely uses the asset temporarily. Businesses, too, lease assets under similar arrangements. These are referred to as operating leases. Many contracts, though, are formulated outwardly as leases, but in reality are installment purchases/sales. These are called finance leases by the lessee and sales-type leases by the lessor. Illustration 15–1 compares the classification possibilities.

An apartment lease is a typical rental agreement referred to as an *operating lease*.

Illustration 15–1
Basic Lease Classifications

Lessee	Lessor
• Finance lease	• Sales-type lease ➡ without selling profit ➡ with selling profit
• Operating lease	• Operating lease*

*In a very specific situation described in Part B, a lease that doesn't qualify as a sales-type lease might be classified as a "direct financing" lease rather than an operating lease.

Lease Classification

● LO15-1

A lease is accounted for in one of two ways. It is viewed as either a finance/sales-type lease (a purchase/sale accompanied by debt financing) or as an operating lease (a rental).[1] The accounting method we use hinges on the nature of the leasing contract.

Sometimes the true nature of the contract is obvious. For example, a 10-year noncancelable lease of a computer with a 10-year useful life, by which title passes to the lessee at the end of the lease term, obviously more nearly represents a purchase than a rental agreement, and should be treated as a finance lease. A 10-day rental of the same computer, with no passage of title to the lessee, obviously represents a rental and not a sale. But what about the gray area between the obvious cases? What if the terms of the contract don't transfer title, and the lease term is for only seven years of the asset's 10-year life? What if contractual terms permit the lessee to obtain title under certain prearranged conditions? What if the present value of payments provided by the lease contract is nearly equal to the value of the asset under lease? These situations are less clear-cut.

A basic concept of accounting is substance over form.

Professional judgment is needed to differentiate between leases that in essence are installment purchases/sales and those that are not. It's important to note that from an accounting perspective *legal ownership is irrelevant* in the decision. A finance lease is not the same as the purchase of an asset. The rights a lease grants a lessee under any lease, whether classified as a finance lease or an operating lease, are different from the rights transferred in the outright purchase of an asset. As one example, a lessee can't sell the leased asset.

Accounting for leases attempts to see through the legal form of the agreements to determine their economic substance.

Nonetheless, a finance lease is economically similar to a purchase of the asset because the terms of a finance lease (a) normally allow the lessee to *direct the use* of the asset in a way that the lessee receives *substantially all of the remaining benefits* from the asset and (b) creates obligations for the lessee that are similar to those that financing the purchase of an asset would impose. An operating lease lacks those characteristics. Thus, the essential question when determining lease classification is whether a particular lease arrangement has the characteristics of a finance lease.

Determining lease classification based on judgment alone is likely to lead to inconsistencies in practice. The desire to encourage consistency in practice motivated the FASB to provide guidance for distinguishing between the two fundamental types of leases. As you study the classification criteria in the following paragraphs, keep in mind that some leases clearly fit the classifications we give them, but others fall in a gray area somewhere between the two extremes. For those, we end up classifying according to the best evidence available.

CLASSIFICATION CRITERIA. We classify a lease transaction as a *finance lease* (*sales-type lease* from the lessor's perspective) if one or more of the five criteria listed in Illustration 15–2 is met. Otherwise, it is an *operating lease.*

Illustration 15–2
Criteria for Classification as a Finance Lease

1. The agreement specifies that ownership of the asset transfers to the lessee.
2. The agreement contains a purchase option that the lessee is reasonably certain to exercise.
3. The lease term is for the "major part" of the remaining economic life of the underlying asset.*
4. The present value of the total of the lease payments† equals or exceeds "substantially all" of the fair value of the underlying asset.
5. The underlying asset is of such a specialized nature that it is expected to have no alternative use to the lessor at the end of the lease term.

*If the lease begins at or near the end of the economic life of the asset, this criterion shouldn't be used for purposes of classifying the lease.
†This total includes any residual value of the asset at the end of the lease term that is guaranteed by the lessee. We discuss residual values, guaranteed and unguaranteed, later in the chapter.

[1] An "Additional Consideration" in Part B describes a very specific situation in which a lease that doesn't qualify as a sales-type lease might be classified as a "direct financing" lease rather that an operating lease.

Let's look closer at these criteria.

Criterion 1. Since our objective is to determine whether the lessor has, in substance, sold the asset to the lessee, the first criterion is self-evident. If legal title passes to the lessee during, or at the end of, the lease term, obviously ownership attributes are transferred.

Criterion 1: Transfer of ownership.

Criterion 2. A purchase option is a provision in the lease contract that gives the lessee the option of purchasing the leased property at a specified exercise price. Criterion 2 is met if the exercise price is sufficiently lower than the expected fair value of the property when the option becomes exercisable that the exercise of the option by the lessee appears "reasonably certain" at the beginning of the lease.

Criterion 2: Purchase option the lessee is reasonably certain to exercise.

For example, suppose instead of purchasing farmland for its fair value of $100,000, the farmland is leased for $20,000 per year for five years with an option at the end of the lease period to purchase it for an additional $25,000. Because $25,000 is likely to be a bargain price for the farmland in five years, the lessee is reasonably certain to exercise the purchase option, and transfer of ownership is expected.

Although the lease accounting guidance (ASC Topic 842: "Leases") does not use the term, in this chapter, we will refer to this as a "Bargain Purchase Option" (BPO). So the logic of the second criterion is similar to that of the first. Applying criterion 2 in practice, though, often is more difficult because it's necessary to make a judgment *now* about whether a *future* fair value will be sufficiently higher than the exercise price so that exercise is "reasonably certain."

Criterion 3. The third criterion considers whether the asset is leased for the "major part" of its useful life. If that criterion is met, then most of the risks and rewards of ownership are deemed to have been transferred to the lessee. The lease accounting guidance (ASC Topic 842: "Leases") suggests that one reasonable approach to assessing this criterion would be to conclude that 75% or more of the remaining economic life of the underlying asset constitutes a "major part" of the remaining economic life of that underlying asset. Note, though, that this is only one approach and not a precise indication.

Criterion 3: Lease term is for the major part of economic life.

Although the intent of this criterion is fairly straightforward, implementation sometimes is troublesome. First, the lease term may be uncertain. It may be renewable beyond its initial term. Or, the lease may be cancelable after a designated noncancelable period. If the lease includes these provisions, we need to consider whether a change in the lease term is reasonably certain to occur.

Additional Consideration

Periods covered by renewal options are not included in the lease term if a bargain purchase option (BPO) is present. This is because the lease term cannot extend beyond the date a purchase option is exercised. For example, assume a bargain purchase option allows a lessee to buy a leased delivery truck at the end of a noncancelable five-year lease term. Even if an option to renew the lease beyond that date is considered to be reasonably certain to be exercised in the event of not exercising the purchase option, that renewal period would not be included as part of the lease term. Remember, we presume the purchase option will be exercised after the initial five-year term, making the renewal option irrelevant.

A second implementation issue is estimating, at the beginning of the lease, the economic life of the leased property. This is the estimated remaining time the property is expected to be economically usable for its intended purpose, with normal maintenance and repairs. Estimates of the economic life of leased property are subject to the same uncertainty limitations of most estimates. This uncertainty presents the opportunity to arrive at estimates that cause this third criterion not to be met.

Finally, if the lease begins "at or near the end" of an asset's economic life, this third criterion does not apply. That's because most of the risks and rewards of ownership occur prior to that time.[2]

[2]ASC Topic 842: "Leases" specifies that one reasonable approach to determining whether this exception should be applied would be to conclude that a lease that commences in the final 25% of an asset's economic life is "at or near the end" of the underlying asset's economic life.

Criterion 4: Present value of payments is substantially all of fair value.

Criterion 4. The fourth criterion indicates that, if the lease payments have a total value that represents "substantially all" of the asset's fair value, it's logical to identify the lease contract as equivalent to a sale. The lease accounting guidance suggests that one reasonable approach to assessing this criterion would be to conclude that payments with a present value of 90% or more of the fair value of the underlying asset represent "substantially all" of the fair value. In general, lease payments for the purpose of classifying a lease are payments the lessee is *required* to make in connection with the lease. We look closer at the make-up of lease payments later in the chapter when we discuss various uncertainties in lease transactions in more detail.

Criterion 5: Leased asset is so specialized that it cannot reasonably be repurposed.

Criterion 5. The fifth criterion recognizes that, if the underlying asset is of such a specialized nature that it is expected to have *no alternative use* to the lessor at the end of the lease term, then only the lessee can derive the usual risks and rewards of ownership of the asset. Likewise, the lessor will achieve its desired return on investment only through the lease payments from that particular lease, indicating that the lessor intends a sale of ownership rights.

Decision Makers' Perspective—Advantages of Leasing

Consider the decision being made by each of the following three individuals.

When a young entrepreneur started a computer training center a few years ago, she had no idea how fast her business would grow. While she knows computers are needed, she doesn't know how many. Just starting out, she also has little cash with which to buy them.

The mutual funds department of a large investment firm often needs new computers and peripherals—fast. The department manager knows he can't afford to wait up to a year, the time it sometimes takes to go through company channels to obtain purchase approval.

An established computer software publisher recently began developing a new line of business software. The senior programmer has to be certain he's testing the company's products on the latest versions of computer hardware and mobile devices. And yet he views large expenditures on equipment subject to rapid obsolescence as risky business.

FINANCIAL Reporting Case

Q1, p. 831

Each of these individuals is faced with different predicaments and concerns. The entrepreneur is faced with uncertainty and cash flow problems, the department manager with time constraints and bureaucratic control systems, and the programmer with fear of obsolescence. Though their specific concerns differ, these individuals have all met their firms' information technology needs with the same solution: each has decided to lease the computers rather than buy them.

Leasing can facilitate asset acquisition.

Computers are by no means the only assets obtained through leasing arrangements. To the contrary, leasing has grown to be the most popular method of external financing of corporate assets in America. The airplane in which you last flew probably was leased, as was the gate from which it departed. Your favorite retail outlet at the local shopping mall likely leases the space in which it operates. Many companies actually exist for the sole purpose of acquiring assets and leasing them to others. This kind of leasing is a thriving industry. It is a profitable part of operations for banks and other financial institutions (Citicorp is one of the largest). Some leasing companies do nothing else. Leasing companies, like IBM Credit Corporation, often are subsidiaries of larger corporations, formed for the sole purpose of conducting financing activities for their parent corporations. And, leasing often is a primary method of "selling" a firm's products. IBM and Boeing are familiar examples.

The number one method of external financing by U.S. businesses is leasing.

In light of its popularity, you may be surprised that leasing usually is more expensive than buying. The higher apparent cost of leasing compensates the lessor for shouldering at least some of the financial and risk burdens that a purchaser normally would assume. So, why the popularity?

The lease decisions described above are motivated by operational incentives. Tax and market considerations also motivate firms to lease. Sometimes leasing offers tax savings over outright purchases. For instance, a company with little or no taxable income—maybe a business just getting started, or one experiencing an economic downturn—will get little benefit from depreciation deductions for an owned asset. But the company can benefit *indirectly* by leasing assets rather than buying. By allowing the *lessor* to retain ownership and thus benefit from depreciation deductions, the lessee often can negotiate lower lease payments. Lessees

Tax incentives often motivate leasing.

with sufficient taxable income to take advantage of the depreciation deductions, but still in lower tax brackets than lessors, also can achieve similar indirect tax benefits.

Prior to recent lease accounting guidance, another reason to lease rather than buy was to obtain "off-balance-sheet financing."[3] When funds are borrowed to purchase an asset, the liability has a detrimental effect on the company's debt to equity ratio and other quantifiable indicators of riskiness. Similarly, the purchased asset increases total assets and correspondingly lowers calculations of the rate of return on assets. To avoid looking more risky and less profitable, managers previously were able to keep assets and liabilities "off balance sheet" by leasing them rather than buying them. That way, managers could avoid surpassing contractual limits on designated financial ratios (such as the debt to equity ratio).[4] Also, despite research that indicates otherwise, some managers might have thought they were fooling the financial markets into thinking their strategies were less risky and more profitable than actually was the case. However, GAAP now requires lessees to record assets and liabilities for all but short-term leases. In fact, the primary impetus for the new guidance was to curtail off-balance-sheet financing. Still, even without the incentive of off-balance-sheet financing, when the operational, tax, and financial advantages are considered, the *net* cost of leasing often is less than the cost of purchasing, so leasing arrangements are still very popular. ●

Traditionally, leasing was used as a means of off-balance-sheet financing.

Operational, tax, and financial incentives often make leasing an attractive alternative to purchasing.

Before we apply the classification criteria to identify a finance lease, it's useful to see how accounting for a finance lease is similar to the way we accounted for installment notes in the previous chapter.

Finance Leases and Installment Notes Compared

You learned in Chapter 14 how to account for an installment note. To a great extent, then, you already have learned how to account for a finance lease. Finance leases are agreements that we identify as being formulated outwardly as leases, but which in reality are essentially installment purchases.

To illustrate, let's recall a situation described in the previous chapter. We assumed that Skill Graphics purchased a package-labeling machine from Hughes–Barker Corporation by issuing a three-year installment note that required six semiannual installment payments of $139,857 each. That arrangement provided for the purchase of the $666,633 machine as well as interest at an annual rate of 14% (7% twice each year). Remember, too, that each installment payment consisted of part interest (7% times the outstanding balance) and part payment for the machine (the remainder of each payment).

Now let's suppose that Skill Graphics instead acquired control of the package-labeling machine from Hughes–Barker Corporation under a three-year *lease* that required six semiannual lease payments of $139,857 each. The fundamental nature of the transaction remains the same regardless of whether it is negotiated as an installment purchase or as a lease. So, we account for this lease in fundamentally the same way as an installment purchase. To see this, let's first compare how we account for an installment note versus a finance lease at the beginning (or commencement) of the lease (see Illustration 15–3):

At Beginning (January 1)		
Installment Note		
Machinery	666,633	
Note payable		666,633
Finance Lease		
Leased machinery	666,633	
Lease payable		666,633

Illustration 15–3

Comparison of a Note and Finance Lease

In keeping with the basic accounting concept of substance over form, accounting for a finance lease parallels that for an installment purchase.

[3]Accounting Standards Update 2016-02: Leases (Topic 842) (Norwalk, Conn.: FASB, 2016).

[4]It is common for debt agreements, particularly long-term ones, to include restrictions on the debtor as a way to provide some degree of protection to the creditor. Sometimes a minimum level is specified for current assets relative to current liabilities, debt as a ratio of equity, return on net assets or many other financial ratios. Typically, the debt becomes due on demand when the debtor becomes in violation of such a debt covenant, often after a specified grace period.

Notice that we debit an asset account and credit a liability, regardless of whether the machinery is acquired through financing with a note payable or through a finance lease.

With each periodic payment, interest expense accrues at the effective rate times the outstanding balance, and the balance of the liability is reduced for the difference as shown in Illustration 15–3A.

Illustration 15–3A

Interest Compared for a Note and Finance Lease

Each payment includes both an amount that represents interest and an amount that represents a reduction of principal.

At the First Semiannual Payment Date (June 30)

(7% × Outstanding balance)

Installment Note		
Interest expense (7% × $666,633)	46,664	
Note payable (difference)	93,193	
Cash (installment payment)		139,857
Finance Lease		
Interest expense (7% × $666,633)	46,664	
Lease payable (difference)	93,193	
Cash (lease payment)		139,857

Because the lease payable balance declines with each payment, the amount of interest expense decreases each period. An amortization schedule is convenient to track the changing amounts as shown in Illustration 15–3B.

Illustration 15–3B

Lease Amortization Schedule

Each lease payment includes interest on the outstanding balance at the effective rate. The remainder of each payment reduces the outstanding balance.

Date	Payments	Effective Interest	Decrease in Balance	Outstanding Balance
		(7% × Outstanding balance)	(Pmt. − Interest)	
				666,633
1	139,857	0.07(666,633) = 46,664	93,193	573,440
2	139,857	0.07(573,440) = 40,141	99,716	473,724
3	139,857	0.07(473,724) = 33,161	106,696	367,028
4	139,857	0.07(367,028) = 25,692	114,165	252,863
5	139,857	0.07(252,863) = 17,700	122,157	130,706
6	139,857	0.07(130,706) = 9,151*	130,706	0
	839,142	172,509	666,633	

*Rounded

You should recognize this as essentially the same amortization schedule we used in the previous chapter in connection with our installment note example. The reason for the similarity is that we view a finance lease as being, in substance, equivalent to an installment purchase. So naturally the accounting treatment of the two essentially identical transactions should be consistent.

In the remaining sections of Part A of this chapter, we'll apply the lease classification criteria to a basic lease situation and consider, in order, (a) finance leases to the lessee/sales-type leases to the lessor and (b) operating leases.

Finance/Sales-Type Leases

LO15–2

Let's look at an example that illustrates the application of the classification criteria listed in Illustration 15–2. The earlier example in Illustration 15–3B comparing a finance lease to an installment purchase assumed lease payments at the *end* of each period. A more typical leasing contract requires lease payments at the *beginning* of each period. This more realistic payment schedule is assumed in Illustration 15–4.

Let's first think about this contract from the perspective of Sans Serif, the lessee. Because at least one of the five classification criteria is met, Sans Serif would classify the lease as a finance

Illustration 15–4

Finance Lease/Sales-Type Lease: No Selling Profit

On January 1, 2018, Sans Serif Publishers, leased printing equipment from First LeaseCorp. First LeaseCorp purchased the equipment from CompuDec Corporation at a cost of $479,079.

The lease agreement specifies six annual payments of $100,000 beginning January 1, 2018, the beginning of the lease, and at each December 31 from 2018 through 2022. The six-year lease term ending December 31, 2023, is equal to the estimated useful life of the equipment. First LeaseCorp routinely acquires electronic equipment for lease to other firms. The interest rate in these financing arrangements is 10%.

How should this lease be classified by the lessee (finance or operating)? By the lessor (sales-type or operating)? We apply the five classification criteria:

1. Does the agreement specify that ownership of the asset transfers to the lessee?	No
2. Does this agreement contain a purchase option reasonably certain to be exercised?	No
3. Is the lease term for the "major part" of the estimated economic life of the asset?	Yes (6-year lease term; 6-year life)
4. Is the present value of the lease payments equal to or greater than "substantially all" of the fair value of the asset?	Yes ($479,079 present value; $479,079 fair value) $100,000 × 4.79079* = $479,079
5. Is the asset of such a specialized nature that it is expected to have no alternative use to the lessor at the end of the lease term?	No (First LeaseCorp routinely leases this type of equipment)

Decision: Since at lease one (two in this case) of the five classification criteria is met, this is a finance lease to the lessee and a sales-type lease to the lessor.

*Present value of an annuity due of $1: $n = 6$, $i = 10\%$. Recall from Chapter 6 that we refer to periodic payments at the beginning of each period as an *annuity due*.

If at least one of the five classification criteria is met, this is a finance/sales-type lease.

lease. While Sans Serif does not have legal ownership of the printing equipment as with a typical purchase, Sans Serif did acquire the right to use the printing equipment. That's why Sans Serif records a "right-of-use asset." In addition, just as if it were an installment purchase, Sans Serif also would record a liability for the present value of the lease payments. The entry by Sans Serif to record the finance lease is shown in Illustration 15–4A.

On the flip side of the transaction, just as if it were an installment sale, First LeaseCorp records a lease receivable for the present value of the payments to be received and removes from its balance sheet (derecognizes) the asset being leased. Later, we'll look at situations in which the lease receivable (reflecting the 'selling price') exceeds the asset's carrying value, creating the need to also record a selling profit for the difference. Indeed, some lessors use leasing as an alternative way to sell their assets and have no intention of reusing or re-leasing assets leased under a sales-type lease.

In the journal entries in Illustrations 15–4A and 15–4B and throughout the chapter, we often look at the entries of the lessee and the lessor together. This way, we can be reminded that, usually, the entries for the lessor are essentially the mirror image of those for the lessee, the other side of the same coin.[5]

Recording Interest Expense/Interest Revenue

Interest accrues at the effective rate on the balance outstanding during the period.

As lease payments are made over the term of the lease, both the lessee and lessor record interest at the effective interest rate. In addition, the lessee, Sans Serif, will record amortization expense on its right-of-use asset over the term of the lease. Let's first consider interest.

As shown in Illustration 15–4B, the entire $100,000 first lease payment is applied to principal (lease payable/receivable) reduction.[6] That's because the payment occurred at the beginning of the lease, so no interest had yet accrued. Subsequent lease payments, though,

[5]We see later in the chapter that sometimes the lessee and lessor have accounting that is not a mirror image, particularly when the lease is either a sales-type lease with a selling profit or an operating lease. However, even when the two sides are not mirror images, there are many similarities, so the comparison still is helpful.

[6]Another way to view this is to think of the first $100,000 as a down payment with the remaining $379,079 financed by 5 (i.e., 6 − 1) *year-end* lease payments.

Illustration 15–4A

Finance Lease/Sales-Type Lease: No Selling Profit

Using Excel, enter:
=PV(.10,6, –100000, 1)
Output: 479079

Using a calculator, enter: BEG mode N 6
I 10
PMT – 100000 FV
Output: PV 479079

An asset and liability are recorded by the lessee at the present value of the lease payments.

Notice that the lessor's entries are the flip side or mirror image of the lessee's entries.

On January 1, 2018, Sans Serif Publishers leased printing equipment from First LeaseCorp. First LeaseCorp purchased the equipment from CompuDec Corporation at a cost of $479,079.

The lease agreement specifies six annual payments of $100,000 beginning January 1, 2018, the beginning of the lease, and at each December 31 from 2018 through 2022. The six-year lease term ending December 31, 2023, is equal to the estimated useful life of the equipment. First Lease Corp routinely acquires electronic equipment for lease to other firms. The interest rate in these financing contracts is 10%.

The price Sans Serif pays for the right to control the use of the equipment is the present value of the lease payments:

$$\underset{\text{Lease Payments}}{\$100{,}000} \times 4.79079^{*} = \underset{\text{Right-of-Use Asset}}{\$479{,}079}$$

*Present value of an annuity due of $1: $n = 6$, $i = 10\%$.

Beginning of the Lease (January 1, 2018)

Sans Serif (Lessee)		
Right-of-use asset (present value of lease payments)	479,079	
Lease payable (present value of lease payments)		479,079
First LeaseCorp (Lessor)		
Lease receivable (present value of lease payments)	479,079	
Equipment (lessor's cost: carrying amount)		479,079

include interest of 10% on the outstanding balance as well as a portion that reduces that outstanding balance. As of the second lease payment twelve months later, one year's interest of $37,908 has accrued on the $379,079 ($479,079 – 100,000) balance outstanding during 2018. After recording that interest, $62,092 of the $100,000 payment remains to reduce the outstanding balance to $316,987 ($379,079 – 62,092).

Illustration 15–4B

Journal Entries for the First and Second Lease Payment

First Lease Payment (January 1, 2018)

Sans Serif (Lessee)		
Lease payable	100,000	
Cash (lease payment)		100,000
First LeaseCorp (Lessor)		
Cash (lease payment)	100,000	
Lease receivable		100,000

Second Lease Payment (December 31, 2018)

Sans Serif (Lessee)		
Interest expense [10% × ($479,079 – 100,000)]	37,908	
Lease payable (difference)	62,092	
Cash (lease payment)		100,000
First LeaseCorp (Lessor)		
Cash (lease payment)	100,000	
Lease receivable		62,092
Interest revenue [10% × ($479,079 – 100,000)]		37,908

Lease payable/receivable

$479,079	
(100,000)	1st payment
$379,079	
(62,092)	2nd payment
$316,987	

Because the outstanding balance declines with each payment, the amount of interest decreases each period. An amortization schedule is convenient to track the changing amounts, as shown in Illustration 15–4C. That schedule shows how the lease balance and the effective interest change over the six-year lease term, using an effective interest rate of 10%. Each lease payment after the first one includes both an amount that represents interest and an amount that represents a reduction of the outstanding balance. The periodic reduction is sufficient that, at the end of the lease term, the outstanding balance is zero.

	Payments	Effective Interest	Decrease in Balance*	Outstanding Balance
		(10% × Outstanding balance)		
1/1/18				479,079
1/1/18	100,000		100,000	379,079
12/31/18	100,000	0.10 (379,079) = 37,908	62,092	316,987
12/31/19	100,000	0.10 (316,987) = 31,699	68,301	248,686
12/31/20	100,000	0.10 (248,686) = 24,869	75,131	173,555
12/31/21	100,000	0.10 (173,555) = 17,355	82,645	90,910
12/31/22	100,000	0.10 (90,910) = 9,090*	90,910	0
	600,000	120,921†	479,079	

*Payment in first column minus the interest in the second column.
†Adjusted for rounding of other numbers in the schedule.

Illustration 15–4C

Lease Amortization Schedule

The first lease payment includes no interest.

The total of the cash payments ($600,000) provides for:

1. Payment for the equipment's use ($479,079).
2. Interest ($120,921) at an effective rate of 10%.

Both the lessee and lessor would use this same amortization schedule. The lessee amortizes its lease payable and records interest *expense*. Similarly, the lessor amortizes its lease receivable and records interest *revenue,* reflecting the opposite side of the same transaction.

That's how the lessee accounts for its lease liability. Now, let's see how the lessee amortizes its right-of-use asset over the term of the lease.

Recording Amortization of the Right-of-Use Asset

Like other noncurrent assets, the lessee's right-of-use asset provides an economic benefit (the right to use a productive asset) over the period covered by the lease term. So, the lessee amortizes its right-of-use asset over the lease term. The amortization process usually is on a straight-line basis unless the lessee's pattern of using the asset is different.[7] That amortization results in an *expense* for the lessee. In Sans Serif's case, it amortizes its right-of-use asset over the six-year lease term.

December 31, 2018, and End of Next Five Years		
Amortization expense ($479,079 ÷ 6 years)	79,847	
Right-of-use asset		79,847

The lessee incurs an expense as it uses the asset.

AMORTIZATION PERIOD. The lessee normally should amortize a leased asset over the term of the lease. However, if ownership transfers, or exercise of a purchase option is reasonably certain (i.e., either of the first two classification criteria is met), the asset should be amortized over its useful life. Meeting either of those two criteria means the lessee will have the asset beyond the lease term, and thus the asset is amortized over the useful life of the asset *to the lessee* whether or not that useful life is limited by the term of the lease.

The amortization period is restricted to the lease term unless the lease provides for transfer of title or a BPO.

Concept Review Exercise

FINANCE LEASE/ SALES-TYPE LEASE: NO SELLING PROFIT

United Cellular Systems leased a satellite transmission device from Pinnacle Leasing Services on January 1, 2018. Pinnacle paid $625,483 for the transmission device. Its fair value is $625,483.

[7] Output measures such as units produced or input measures such as hours used might provide a better indication of the reduction in some leased assets.

Terms of the Lease Agreement and Related Information:	
Lease term	3 years (6 semiannual periods)
Semiannual lease payments	$120,000 at beginning of each period
Economic life of asset	3 years
Interest rate	12%

Required:

1. Prepare the appropriate entries for both United Cellular Systems and Pinnacle Leasing Services on January 1, 2018, the beginning of the lease.
2. Prepare an amortization schedule that shows the pattern of interest expense for United Cellular Systems and interest revenue for Pinnacle Leasing Services over the lease term.
3. Prepare the appropriate entries to record the second lease payment on July 1, 2018, and adjusting entries on December 31, 2018 (the end of both companies' fiscal years).

Solution:

1. Prepare the appropriate entries for both United Cellular Systems and Pinnacle Leasing Services on January 1, 2018, the beginning of the lease.

Calculation of the present value of lease payments.

Present value of periodic lease payments:

$$(\$120{,}000 \times 5.21236^{*}) = \$625{,}483$$

*Present value of an annuity due of $1: $n = 6$, $i = 6\%$.

January 1, 2018		
United Cellular Systems (Lessee)		
Right-of-use asset (calculated above)	625,483	
Lease payable (calculated above)		625,483
Lease payable	120,000	
Cash (lease payment)		120,000
Pinnacle Leasing Services (Lessor)		
Lease receivable (calculated above)	625,483	
Equipment (lessor's cost)		625,483
Cash (lease payment)	120,000	
Lease receivable		120,000

2. Prepare an amortization schedule that shows the pattern of interest expense for United Cellular Systems and interest revenue for Pinnacle Leasing Services over the lease term.

Date	Payments	Effective Interest	Decrease in Balance	Outstanding Balance
		(6% × Outstanding balance)		
1/1/18				625,483
1/1/18	120,000		120,000	505,483
7/1/18	120,000	0.06 (505,483) = 30,329	89,671	415,812
1/1/19	120,000	0.06 (415,812) = 24,949	95,051	320,761
7/1/19	120,000	0.06 (320,761) = 19,246	100,754	220,007
1/1/20	120,000	0.06 (220,007) = 13,200	106,800	113,207
7/1/20	120,000	0.06 (113,207) = 6,793*	113,207	0
	720,000	94,517	625,483	

*Adjusted for rounding of other numbers in the schedule.

3. Prepare the appropriate entries to record the second lease payment on July 1, 2018, and adjusting entries on December 31, 2018 (the end of both companies' fiscal years).

July 1, 2018		
United Cellular Systems (Lessee)		
Interest expense [6% × ($625,483 − 120,000)]	30,329	
Lease payable (difference)	89,671	
Cash (lease payment)		120,000
Pinnacle Leasing Services (Lessor)		
Cash (lease payment)	120,000	
Lease receivable (difference)		89,671
Interest revenue [6% × ($625,483 − 120,000)]		30,329
December 31, 2018		
United Cellular Systems (Lessee)		
Interest expense (6% × $415,812: from schedule)	24,949	
Interest payable		24,949
Amortization expense ($625,483 ÷ 3 years)	208,494	
Right-of-use asset		208,494
Pinnacle Leasing Services (Lessor)		
Interest receivable	24,949	
Interest revenue (6% × $415,812: from schedule)		24,949

In our illustrations above, the present value of the lease payments, or "selling price," is the same as the cost or carrying value of the asset "sold." For example, in Illustration 15–4A, we assumed that First LeaseCorp bought the equipment for $479,079 and then leased it for the same price. There was no profit on the "sale" itself. The only income derived by the lessor was interest revenue earned over the lease term. In effect, First LeaseCorp financed the acquisition of the equipment by Sans Serif Publishers.[8] That's usually the case when the lessor is a financial intermediary that provides financing by acquiring the asset and then leasing it to the lessee. In that case, the lessor records the "flip side" of the lessee's transaction. That is, the lessor records a receivable corresponding to the lessee's liability and removes the asset from its books as the lessee adds the asset to its books.

In some cases, though, the lessor is not a financial intermediary, but is a manufacturer or retailer using leases as a means of "selling" its products. In addition to interest revenue earned over the lease term, the lessor receives a selling profit on the "sale" of the asset. We look at this situation next.

Sales-Type Leases with Selling Profit

LO15–3

FINANCIAL Reporting Case

Q2, p. 831

Selling profit exists when the fair value of the asset (usually the present value of the lease payments, or "selling price") exceeds the cost or carrying value of the asset sold. In addition to interest revenue earned over the lease term, the lessor recognizes a selling profit on the "sale" of the asset. Accounting is the same as for a sales-type lease without a selling profit except that profit is recognized at the beginning.[9]

As in the sale of any product, gross profit is the difference between sales revenue and cost of goods sold. Dell, Inc. "sells" some of its products using sales-type leases and disclosed its accounting policy in a recent annual report shown in Illustration 15–5.

When there is a selling profit, all lessor entries, other than the entry at the beginning of the lease to include the selling profit, are precisely the same as the entries for a sales-type lease without a selling profit. On the other side of the transaction, accounting by the *lessee* is not affected by whether the *lessor* recognizes a profit or not. All lessee entries are exactly the same as in our previous illustration of a lessee's finance lease.

[8]Under the GAAP in place prior to ASU 2016-02, this type of lease (no selling profit) was referred to as a *direct financing lease.* While that label still exists in the new lease guidance, it now refers to a situation that happens only when the lease includes a residual value and the residual value is *guaranteed by a third party* (not the lessee). We consider guaranteed residual values later in the chapter when we look at uncertainties in lease accounting.

[9]It's possible that the asset's carrying value will exceed its fair value, in which case a selling loss should be recorded.

Illustration 15–5

Sales-Type Leases—Dell, Inc.

Real World Financials

Note 1 (in part)

Dell records revenue from the sale of equipment under sales-type leases as product revenue at the inception of the lease. Sales-type leases also produce financing income, which Dell recognizes at consistent rates of return over the lease term.

To illustrate accounting for sales-type leases with selling profit, let's modify our previous illustration. Assume all facts are the same except Sans Serif Publishers leased the equipment directly from CompuDec Corporation rather than through First LeaseCorp, the financing intermediary. Also assume that CompuDec's cost of the equipment was $300,000. If you recall that the lease payments (their present value) provide a selling price of $479,079, you see that CompuDec earns a gross profit on the sale of $479,079 – 300,000 = $179,079. This sales-type lease that provides a selling profit is demonstrated in Illustration 15–6.

Illustration 15–6

Finance Lease/Sales-Type Lease: With Selling Profit

Because the PV of lease payments > cost, the lessor has a profit that is recorded at the beginning of the lease.

Sales revenue	$479,079
– COGS	300,000
Selling profit	$179,079

Remember, no interest has yet accrued when the first payment is made at the beginning of the lease.

On January 1, 2018, Sans Serif Publishers leased printing equipment from CompuDec Corporation. The lease agreement specifies six annual payments of $100,000 beginning January 1, 2018, the beginning of the lease, and at each December 31 from 2018 through 2022. The six-year lease term ending December 31, 2023, is equal to the estimated useful life of the equipment. CompuDec manufactured the equipment at a cost of $300,000.

Using an interest rate of 10% for financing this transaction, CompuDec calculates the present value of the lease payments to be received as $479,079 ($100,000 × 4.79079*).

Beginning of the Lease (January 1, 2018)

CompuDec Corporation (Lessor)

Lease receivable (present value of lease payments)	479,079	
Cost of goods sold (lessor's cost)	300,000	
Sales revenue (present value of lease payments)		479,079
Equipment (lessor's cost)		300,000

First Lease Payment (January 1, 2018)

CompuDec Corporation (Lessor)

Cash	100,000	
Lease receivable		100,000

*Present value of an annuity due of $1: $n = 6$, $i = 10\%$.

Recording a sales-type lease is similar to recording a sale of merchandise on account:

A/R	(price)	
Sales rev		(price)
COGS	(cost)	
Inventory		(cost)

You should recognize the similarity between recording both the revenue and cost components of this "sale by lease" and recording the same components of other sales transactions. Remember, when a company sells a product on account, two entries are recorded: one to record the receivable and sales revenue, and another to record the cost of goods sold and corresponding reduction in inventory. Let's say you purchase a TV from Best Buy for $479 and pay for it with your Best Buy credit card. And, assume Best Buy paid the wholesale price of $300 to Samsung to acquire the TV. Here's the way Best Buy would record the sale to you:

Accounts receivable (price)	479	
Sales revenue (price)		479
Cost of goods sold (cost)	300	
Inventory (cost)		300

Now compare those entries to the entry to record our sale by lease. We'll reorder a few lines in the entry to make that comparison easier:

Lease receivable (price)	479,079	
Sales revenue (price)		479,079
Cost of goods sold (cost)	300,000	
Equipment (cost)		300,000

In both cases, the seller is recording revenue and cost, and gross profit from the transaction will appear on the seller's income statement. Economically, leases are just one of the arrangements that sellers can use to help customers buy their products. Sales-type leases must be separately distinguished from nonlease sales in the financial statements.

Let's turn our attention now to situations in which at least one of the classification criteria is *not* met, so that the lease is classified as an operating lease.

Operating Leases

In the finance/sales-type leases we've looked at, the lease is economically similar to the purchase of an asset, because the lessee has the ability to direct the use of the asset and obtain substantially all of its remaining benefits. If a lease doesn't meet any of the criteria for a finance/sales-type lease in Illustration 15–2, then it's considered to be more in the nature of a rental agreement for a period of time. We refer to this second type of arrangement as an **operating lease**.[10]

● LO15–4

To demonstrate accounting for operating leases, we need to change our example so none of the finance lease classification criteria in Illustration 15–2 is met. We'll do that by changing the lease term. In the previous illustrations, the lease term is equal to the expected useful life of the asset (six years). Now, in Illustration 15–7, the lease term is for only *four* years of the asset's six-year life, which is less than the "major part" of approximately 75%. Assuming none of the other criteria are met, the arrangement is classified as an operating lease. (See Illustration 15–7.)

Illustration 15–7
Operating Lease

On January 1, 2018, Sans Serif Publishers leased printing equipment from First LeaseCorp. First LeaseCorp purchased the equipment from CompuDec Corporation at a cost of $479,079. Sans Serif's borrowing rate for similar transactions is 10%.

The lease agreement specifies **four** annual payments of $100,000 beginning January 1, 2018, the beginning of the lease, and at each December 31 from 2018 through 2020. The useful life of the equipment is estimated to be six years. The present value of those four payments at a discount rate of 10% is **$348,685**.

The price Sans Serif pays for the right to control the use of the equipment is the present value of the lease payments:

$100,000 × 3.48685* = **$348,685**

Lease Payments — Lessee's cost

*Present value of an annuity due of $1: $n = 4$, $i = 10\%$.

The lease doesn't meet any of the criteria listed in Illustration 15–2, so it is accounted for as an operating lease.

Beginning of the Lease (January 1, 2018)

Sans Serif (Lessee)

Right-of-use asset (present value of lease payments)	348,685	
Lease payable (present value of lease payments)		348,685

First LeaseCorp (Lessor)

(No entry to record a receivable or to derecognize asset)

How do we account for an operating lease? The lessee still records an asset and a liability at the beginning of the lease. The reason is that Sans Serif, although not having effectively purchased the asset via the lease agreement, still has acquired the *right to use the asset* for four years of the asset's six-year useful life. Just as in the case of a finance lease, the right to use the leased asset can be a significant benefit, even if for a shorter period of time, and the promise to make the lease payments can be a significant obligation. So, just like our prior example in which the asset was leased for its entire life, Sans Serif still recognizes a right-of-use asset and lease liability. The only difference in the initial entry is that, because the lease includes fewer payments, a smaller present value is recorded at the beginning of the lease.

By signing a lease, the lessee has an obligation to make payments (a liability), and in exchange for those payments, the lessee is receiving the right to use a specified asset (a right-of-use asset).

[10]The term *operating lease* got its name long ago when a lessee routinely received from the lessor an operator along with leased equipment.

Although an operating lease liability is reported in the balance sheet of the lessee, it is designated as a "non-debt liability" in order to distinguish it from traditional liabilities, including finance lease liabilities. That separate classification is intended to prevent operating lease liabilities from causing companies to violate debt covenants, such as restrictions that the debt to equity ratio not exceed a preset limit.

The lessor does not record a lease receivable. Instead, the lessor views an operating lease as simply renting the asset to the lessee, and as we'll see next, records rent revenue on a straight-line basis over the lease term.

Recording Interest Expense/Lease Revenue

For an operating lease, the *lessee* will *report* a single lease expense. This amount includes two components that the lessee will *calculate and record* separately, and then combine for purposes of reporting. The first component is the interest expense on the lease liability and the second component is the amortization of the right-of-use asset. On the other hand, the *lessor* in an operating lease determines a single straight-line lease revenue.

Sans Serif (the lessee) determines interest expense on the lease payable in an operating lease the same way as in a finance lease, as demonstrated in Illustration 15–7A.

Illustration 15–7A

Journal Entries for the First and Second Lease Payment

Lease payable

$348,685
(100,000) 1st payment
$248,685
(75,131) 2nd payment
$173,554

The lessor earns the lease revenue during the year after it is received.

First Lease Payment (January 1, 2018)		
Sans Serif (Lessee)		
Lease payable	100,000	
Cash (lease payment)		100,000
First LeaseCorp (Lessor)		
Cash (lease payment)	100,000	
Deferred lease revenue (lease revenue in 2018)		100,000
Second Lease Payment (December 31, 2018)		
Sans Serif (Lessee)		
Interest expense [10% × ($348,685 − 100,000)]	24,869	
Lease payable (difference)	75,131	
Cash (lease payment)		100,000
First LeaseCorp (Lessor)		
Deferred lease revenue (Jan. 1 lease payment)	100,000	
Lease revenue		100,000
Cash (second lease payment)	100,000	
Deferred lease revenue (lease revenue in 2019)		100,000
Depreciation expense ($479,079 ÷ 6 years)	79,847	
Accumulated depreciation		79,847

The amortization schedule in Illustration 15–7B shows how the lease liability balance and the effective interest expense change over the four-year lease term.

Illustration 15–7B

Lease Amortization Schedule

The first lease payment includes no interest.

The total of the cash payments ($400,000) provides for:

1. Payment for the equipment's use ($348,685).
2. Interest ($51,315) at an effective rate of 10%.

	Payments	Effective Interest	Decrease in Balance	Outstanding Balance
		(10% × Outstanding balance)		
1/1/18				348,685
1/1/18	100,000		100,000	248,685
12/31/18	100,000	0.10 (248,685) = 24,869	75,131	173,554
12/31/19	100,000	0.10 (173,554) = 17,355	82,645	90,909
12/31/20	100,000	0.10 (90,909) = 9,091	90,909	0
	400,000	**51,315**	**348,685**	

Recording Amortization of the Right-of-Use Asset

In an operating lease we amortize the right-of-use asset differently from the way we amortize it in a finance lease. The disparity considers the nature of finance leases and operating leases.

We can think of lease expenses in a *finance lease* as reflecting (a) the right to use the asset (amortization) plus (b) the financing of that right (interest). On the other hand, in an *operating lease,* lease expense is recorded in a manner that is designed to mirror *straight-line rental* of the asset during the lease term. The way the lessee accomplishes that is to determine interest expense as in Illustration 15–7A and 15–7B and then to determine amortization of the right-of-use asset as the *amount needed to cause the total lease expense (interest plus amortization) to be an equal, straight-line amount over the lease term.* In other words, the lessee records interest the normal way and then "plugs" the right-of-use asset amortization at whatever amount is needed for interest plus amortization to equal the straight-line lease payment. So, in Illustration 15–7C, Sans Serif, having determined interest expense to be $24,869, plugs an amortization expense of $75,131 to cause the total of the two components of the lease expense to be $100,000.

In an operating lease, the lessee records interest the normal way and then "plugs" the right-of-use asset amortization at whatever amount is needed for interest plus amortization to equal the *straight-line* lease payment.

Interest expense	$ 24,869
Amortization expense	75,131
Lease expense	$100,000

Illustration 15–7C

Lessee Entries for the Second Lease Payment: Interest and Amortization

Second Lease Payment (December 31, 2018)		
Interest expense [10% × ($348,685 − 100,000)]	24,869	
Lease payable (difference)	75,131	
Cash (second lease payment)		100,000
Amortization expense ($100,000 − 24,869)	75,131	
Right-of-use asset		75,131

Total lease expense (amortization plus interest) for Sans Serif will equal $100,000 each year over the lease term. On the flip side of the transaction, the lessor in an operating lease does not record a lease receivable at the beginning of the lease and does not remove from its balance sheet the asset being leased. With no receivable to accrue interest, First LeaseCorp simply records straight-line revenue as a single lease revenue amount equal to the $100,000 lease payments and equal to the $100,000 amount the lessee reports as lease expense. First LeaseCorp also depreciates the asset over the asset's useful life (six years in this example), just as it would any other asset it owns and keeps on its books.

The lessor earns the lease revenue during the year for which payment is received at the beginning of the year.

Reporting Lease Expense and Lease Revenue

After recording these entries, the lessee will have two lease-related expenses—interest expense and amortization expense. However, the lessee combines these two accounts into a single *lease expense* and reports a single $100,000 amount each year in its income statement. This is in keeping with the key objective of reporting a straight-line lease expense for an operating lease. In a finance lease, the lessee will report interest expense and amortization expense separately in the income statement.

In an operating lease, the lessee combines interest expense and amortization expense to report a single lease expense in the income statement.

First LeaseCorp, the lessor, has only a single lease revenue account in an operating lease and reports that straight-line amount, $100,000, each year in its income statement. Thus, in keeping with the presumption that an operating lease is considered to be more in the nature of a rental agreement, the lessee reports ***lease expense on a straight-line basis*** and the lessor reports ***lease revenue on a straight-line basis*** over the lease term. Illustration 15–7D shows this accounting for both the lessee and the lessor over the life of the lease.

Now, let's turn to Illustration 15–8 to compare how the lessee reports its lease expense for a finance lease and an operating lease. Reflecting back to our illustrations for a finance lease, you should note that the lessee records more expense and the lessor records more revenue early in the life of a finance lease. This "front loading" of lease expense/revenue occurs due to the fact that interest is higher initially than it is in the later stages of a lease, while amortization expense for the lessee's right-of-use asset remains the same each period.[11] Operating leases avoid front loading. As you might imagine, lessees tend to prefer the operating lease classification. It defers expense recognition, making net income higher in the early years of the lease.

[11]Because the lessor, First LeaseCorp, removed the asset from its records at the beginning of the finance lease, it would not have depreciation (amortization) to record.

Illustration 15–7D Operating Lease—Determining Lease Expenses and Revenue

	Jan. 1, 2018		Dec. 31, 2018		Dec. 31, 2019		Dec. 31, 2020		Dec. 31, 2021	
Sans Serif (Lessee)										
Right-of-use asset	348,685									
Lease payable		348,685								
Interest expense	0		24,869		17,355		9,091		0	
Lease payable	100,000		75,131		82,645		90,909		0	
Cash		100,000		100,000		100,000		100,000		0
Amortization expense*			75,131		82,645		90,909		100,000	
Right-of-use asset				75,131		82,645		90,909		100,000
Total lease expenses each year =			100,000		100,000		100,000		100,000	
First LeaseCorp (Lessor)										
[No entry to record receivable or to derecognize asset]										
Cash	100,000		100,000		100,000		100,000			
Deferred revenue**		100,000		100,000		100,000		100,000		
Deferred revenue**			100,000		100,000		100,000		100,000	
Lease revenue				100,000		100,000		100,000		100,000
Depreciation expense†			79,847		79,847		79,847		79,847	
Accumulated depreciation				79,847		79,847		79,847		79,847

*Plug to cause the *total* lease expense to equal the straight-line amount: $100,000 minus interest.
**When the $100,000 is received at the beginning of the lease year, it is not yet earned and should be recorded as deferred lease revenue. When it has been earned by the end of the year, it becomes lease revenue.
†($479,079/6). Depreciation expense also is recognized in 2022 and 2023, because the asset has a six-year useful life.

Illustration 15–8 Comparison of Lessee's Expense Recognition between Finance and Operating Leases

In an operating lease, it's the *total* lease expense, not the amortization component, that's a straight-line amount.

	Finance Lease Financing Approach			Operating Lease Straight-Line Approach		
	Interest Expense	Amortization Expense	Total Expense	Interest Expense	Amortization Expense	Total Expense
2018	24,869	87,171	112,040	24,869	75,131	100,000
2019	17,355	87,171	104,526	17,355	82,645	100,000
2020	9,091	87,171	96,262	9,091	90,909	100,000
2021	0	87,171	87,171	0	100,000	100,000
	51,315	348,685*	400,000*	51,315	348,685	400,000

*Adjusted for rounding of other numbers in the schedule.

International Financial Reporting Standards

No Operating Leases for Lessees under IFRS. Under *IFRS No. 16*, all leases are accounted for as finance leases by the lessee (one-model approach). Only lessors apply the classification criteria to distinguish between finance and operating leases. Thus, even for leases that qualify under U.S. GAAP (two-model approach) as operating leases, the lessee amortizes the right-of-use asset on a straight-line basis rather than "plugging" that amount to cause the total of interest and amortization to be a straight-line amount. This means that those leases under IFRS will have a front-loaded expense profile (because interest expense is more at the beginning than at the end).

Decision Makers' Perspective—Financial Statement Impact

As indicated in the Decision Makers' Perspective at the beginning of the chapter, leasing can allow a firm to conserve assets, to avoid some risks of owning assets, and to obtain favorable tax benefits. These advantages are desirable. Accounting guidelines are designed to limit the ability of firms to obscure the realities of their financial position through off-balance-sheet financing or by avoiding violating terms of contracts that limit the amount of debt a company can have. Nevertheless, investors and creditors should be alert to the impact leases can have on a company's financial position and on its risk. Disclosure requirements include reporting finance lease liabilities and operating lease liabilities separately.

A noteworthy benefit to lessees of operating lease accounting is that expenses are recognized straight line, rather than front-loaded as in the case of finance leases for which interest expense and amortization are separately reported. In fact, the leasing industry lobbied the FASB extensively to make sure operating lease accounting was allowed. From the perspective of an analyst, though, it's unclear why expenses associated with operating leases should be treated any differently than are expenses associated with finance leases. Consequently, even though a goal of ASC Topic 842: "Leases" was to reduce the need for investors to restate financial statements "as if" leased assets and their related liabilities were on the balance sheet, it is likely that some sophisticated users now will restate financial statements to back out the straight-line recognition afforded operating leases and treat them like finance leases, similar to how they are treated under IFRS. ●

Discount Rate

An important factor in lease calculations that we've glossed over until now is the discount (interest) rate used in present value calculations. Because lease payments occur in future periods, we must consider the time value of money when evaluating their present value. The rate is important because it influences virtually every amount reported by both the lessor and the lessee in connection with the lease.

One discount rate is implicit in the lease agreement. This is the effective interest *rate of return the lease payments provide the lessor* under the lease. It is the desired rate of return the lessor has in mind when deciding the size of the lease payments. (Refer to our earlier calculations of the periodic lease payments.) If known by the lessee, the lessee also should make its calculations using the lessor's rate implicit in the lease agreement.

The lessee uses the interest rate implicit in the lease if known; otherwise the lessee uses its own incremental borrowing rate.

What if the lessee is unaware of the lessor's implicit rate? This is frequently the case in practice. This might happen, for example, if the leased asset has a relatively high residual value. As we will discuss later, if there's a residual value (guaranteed or not), it is an ingredient in the lessor's calculation of the lease payments. Sometimes it may be hard for the lessee to identify the residual value estimated by the lessor if the lessor chooses not to make it known.[12] However, as the lease term and risk of obsolescence increase, the residual value typically is less of a factor.

When the lessor's implicit rate is not known, the lessee should use its own incremental borrowing rate. This is the rate the lessee would expect to pay a bank if funds were borrowed to buy the asset.[13]

Concept Review Exercise

OPERATING LEASE

United Cellular Systems leased a satellite transmission device from Pinnacle Leasing Services on January 1, 2018. Pinnacle paid $800,000 for the transmission device. Its fair value is $800,000.

Terms of the Lease Agreement and Related Information:

Lease term	3 years (6 semiannual periods)
Semiannual lease payments	$120,000 at beginning of each period
Economic life of asset	5 years
Interest rate	12%

[12]Disclosure requirements provide that the lessor must disclose the components of its investments in nonoperating leases, which would include any estimated residual values. But the disclosures are aggregate amounts, not amounts of individual leased assets.

[13]*Incremental borrowing rate* refers to the fact that lending institutions tend to view debt as being increasingly risky as the level of debt increases. Thus, additional (i.e., incremental) debt is likely to be loaned at a higher interest rate than existing debt, other things being equal.

Required:

1. Prepare the appropriate entries for both United Cellular Systems and Pinnacle Leasing Services on January 1, 2018, the beginning of the lease.
2. Prepare an amortization schedule that shows the pattern of interest expense for United Cellular Systems and interest revenue for Pinnacle Leasing Services over the lease term.
3. Prepare the appropriate entries to record the second lease payment on July 1, 2018, and adjusting entries on December 31, 2018 (the end of both companies' fiscal years).

Solution:

1. Prepare the appropriate entries for both United Cellular Systems and Pinnacle Leasing Services on January 1, 2018, the beginning of the lease.

Present value of periodic lease payments:

Calculation of the present value of lease payments.

($120,000 × 5.21236*) = $625,483

*Present value of an annuity due of $1: $n = 6$, $i = 6\%$.

January 1, 2018		
United Cellular Systems (Lessee)		
Right-of-use asset (calculated above)	625,483	
Lease payable (calculated above)		625,483
Lease payable	120,000	
Cash (lease payment)		120,000
Pinnacle Leasing Services (Lessor)		
[No entry to record a receivable or to remove asset]		
Cash (lease payment)	120,000	
Deferred lease revenue		120,000

2. Prepare an amortization schedule that shows the pattern of interest expense for United Cellular Systems and interest revenue for Pinnacle Leasing Services over the lease term.

Date	Payments	Effective Interest	Decrease in Balance	Outstanding Balance
		(6% × Outstanding balance)		
1/1/18				625,483
1/1/18	120,000		120,000	505,483
7/1/18	120,000	0.06 (505,483) = 30,329	89,671	415,812
1/1/19	120,000	0.06 (415,812) = 24,949	95,051	320,761
7/1/19	120,000	0.06 (320,761) = 19,246	100,754	220,007
1/1/20	120,000	0.06 (220,007) = 13,200	106,800	113,207
7/1/20	120,000	0.06 (113,207) = 6,793*	113,207	0
	720,000	94,517	625,483	

*Adjusted for rounding of other numbers in the schedule.

3. Prepare the appropriate entries to record the second lease payment on July 1, 2018, and adjusting entries on December 31, 2018 (the end of both companies' fiscal years).

July 1, 2018		
United Cellular Systems (Lessee)		
Interest expense [6% × ($625,483 − 120,000)]	30,329	
Lease payable (difference)	89,671	
Cash (lease payment)		120,000
Amortization expense ($120,000 − 30,329)	89,671	
Right-of-use asset		89,671
Pinnacle Leasing Services (Lessor)		
Deferred lease revenue (Jan. 1 lease payment)	120,000	
Lease revenue		120,000
Cash (second lease payment)	120,000	
Deferred lease revenue		120,000

(continued)

(concluded)

December 31, 2018		
United Cellular Systems (Lessee)		
Interest expense (6% × $415,812: from schedule)	24,949	
Interest payable		24,949
Amortization expense ($120,000 − 24,949)	95,051	
Right-of-use asset		95,051
Pinnacle Leasing Services (Lessor)		
Deferred lease revenue (July 1 lease payment)	120,000	
Lease revenue		120,000
Depreciation expense ($800,000 ÷ 5 years)	160,000	
Accumulated depreciation		160,000

Short-Term Leases – A Shortcut Method

● LO15–5

It's not unusual to simplify accounting for situations in which doing so has no material effect on the financial statements. One such situation that permits a simpler application is a short-term lease. A lease is considered a "short-term lease" if it:

1. Has a lease term (including any options to renew or extend) of twelve months or less, *and*
2. Does not contain a purchase option that the lessee is reasonably certain to exercise, which would extend the term beyond twelve months.

The shortcut approach for short-term leases permits the lessee to choose *not* to record an asset and related liability associated with the lease at the beginning of the lease term. Instead, the lessee can simply record lease payments as rent expense over the lease term. Yes, this is the approach used by the lessor for lease revenue on the flip side of the transaction.

In a short-term lease, the lessee can elect not to record a right-of-use asset and lease payable at the beginning of the lease term, but instead to simply record lease payments as expense as they occur.

Let's look at an example that illustrates the relatively straightforward accounting for short-term leases. To do this, in Illustration 15–9 we modify Illustration 15–4A to assume the lease term is *twelve months.*

Illustration 15–9

Short-Term Lease

On January 1, 2018, Sans Serif Publishers leased printing equipment from First LeaseCorp. The lease agreement specifies four quarterly payments of $25,000 beginning January 1, 2018, the beginning of the lease, and at the first day of each of the next three quarters. The useful life of the equipment is estimated to be six years.

Beginning of the Lease (January 1, 2018)

No entry to record a right-of-use asset and liability (lease term ≤ one year)

Lease Payments (January 1, April 1, July 1, October 1, 2018)

Lease expense	25,000	
Cash		25,000

International Financial Reporting Standards

● LO15–9

Shortcut Method.
As in the case for short-term leases in U.S. GAAP, IFRS allows the lessee to elect not to record a right-of-use asset and lease payable at the beginning of the lease term, but instead to simply record lease payments as an expense as they occur. U.S. GAAP, though, defines a short-term lease as a lease that has a lease term of 12 months or less and does not include a purchase option *that the lessee is reasonably certain to exercise.* IFRS precludes a lease from being considered short term if the lease includes a purchase option regardless of whether the lessee is reasonably certain to exercise it.

In addition, though, unlike U.S. GAAP, IFRS allows "small ticket leases" also to apply this shortcut method. Small ticket leases are defined as those having a value of $5,000 or less.

PART B

Uncertainty in Lease Transactions

● LO15–6

Let's turn our attention now to several issues related to uncertainty in lease transactions that impact lessee and lessor accounting. Among those issues are variable lease terms, variable lease payments, residual values, purchase options, and termination penalties.

What if the Lease Term is Uncertain?

The lease term is the contractual lease term modified by any renewal or termination options that are reasonably certain to be exercised.

Sometimes the actual term of a lease is not obvious. Suppose, for instance, that the lease term is specified as four years, but it can be renewed at the option of the lessee for two additional years. Or, maybe either party can terminate the lease after, say, three years. In such situations, we consider the lease term to be the contractual lease term adjusted for any periods covered by options to extend or terminate the lease for which there is a significant economic incentive to exercise the options. A company adjusts the lease term for an option only if it is "reasonably certain" that the lessee will exercise the option after considering the relevant economic factors.[14] In other words, if the benefits of exercising an option are sufficiently high that we think the lessee will exercise it, we adjust the contractual term by adding the additional period of renewal, or by subtracting the period that follows a termination option.

The lease term is reassessed only when a significant event or change in circumstances indicates a change in the economic incentive for extension or termination of the lease.

REASSESSMENT OF THE LEASE TERM. Circumstances can change that require reassessment of how long the lease term will be. Reassessment requires a "triggering event" such that the lessee now has an economic incentive to exercise an option that extends or terminates the lease. For example, assume that a lessee had no significant economic incentive as of the beginning of a 6-year lease to exercise a 2-year extension option. However, by the end of the third year, the lessee has made significant improvements to the asset whose cost could be recovered only if it exercises the extension option, making extension of the lease "reasonably certain." In that case, the full term of the lease is now expected to be a total of eight years with five years remaining.

At the end of the third year, the lessee would remeasure the lease liability as the present value of the remaining five lease payments. Importantly, the discount rate for the new term is the incremental borrowing rate of the lessee using market interest rates *at the time of the reassessment,* rather than the rate used at the beginning of the lease. Assuming the present value of the remaining five lease payments totaled $400,000, while the current balance of the lease liability before remeasurement is $250,000, the lessee would make the following adjustment:

Reassessment of the Lease Term

Right-of-use asset	150,000	
Lease payable (increase in balance*)		150,000

*PV of *remaining* 5 *payments*, discounted at the *current* rate	$400,000
Liability balance after 3 years based on initial lease terms	250,000
Increase[†] in balance	$150,000

[†]In situations when the lease term is shortened (termination option), the journal entry would be reversed to reduce the account balances.

Also, when there is a change in the lease term, lessees are required to reassess the *classification* of a lease. In the current example, because, with the assumed renewal, the lease term is for the entire useful life of the asset, the lease classification might need to be changed. Suppose, for instance, that the lease had been classified initially as an operating lease. Now, with the increase in the lease term, it might meet the criteria for a finance lease rather than an operating lease as previously classified. If so, we would have had an operating lease for three years, and now have a five-year finance lease. That would mean amortizing the

[14]Reasonably certain is a high threshold, essentially the same as "reasonably assured."

right-of-use asset as a straight-line allocation of the balance in that account at this point over the next five years, rather than "plugging" amortization as we would for an operating lease.

The discussion above pertains to a lessee. A lessor is not permitted to reassess its initial determination of the lease term or discount rate.

Decision Makers' Perspective—Considering the Economic Incentive for Exercising Options

What if we did not have the requirement to consider renewal options and the economic incentive for exercising them when we determine the lease term? Management might be tempted to structure leases with artificially short initial terms and numerous renewal options as a scheme to be able to use the shortcut method (which we discussed earlier) or to reduce significantly the amount of the lease liability to be reported (off-balance-sheet financing).

What if the Lease Payments are Uncertain?

Sometimes lease payments are scheduled to be increased (or decreased) at some future date during the lease term, depending on whether or not some specified event occurs. Usually the contingency is related to revenues, profitability, or asset usage above some designated level. For example in Illustration 15–10, a recent annual report of The Gap included the following note:

Rent Expense (in part)

Certain leases provide for contingent rents that are not measurable at inception. These contingent rents are primarily based on a percentage of sales that are in excess of a predetermined level and/or rent increase based on a change in the consumer price index or fair market value. These amounts are excluded from minimum rent and are included in the determination of rent expense when it is probable that the expense has been incurred and the amount can be reasonably estimated.

Illustration 15–10

Contingent Lease Payments—The Gap

Real World Financials

Why would a lease include a contingent payment provision? It's a way for lessees and lessors to share the risk associated with the asset's productivity. For example, let's assume a store owner, like at Gap, who pays for a premium mall location is doing so anticipating higher revenue. If the mall attracts a sufficiently higher number of shoppers, the lessee pays the lessor part of the resulting higher profits, but if not, the lessee makes only the normal lease payments. This arrangement also provides the lessor an incentive to attract shoppers to the mall, which is in the lessee's best interest. Because the amounts of future lease payments are uncertain and often avoidable, we don't consider them as part of the lease payments used to calculate the lessee's lease liability and the lessor's lease receivable. If and when lease payments increase, the change in the lease payments has no effect on balance sheet accounts and simply is reported as a separate lease expense (lessee) and lease revenue (lessor).[15]

Most variable lease payments are recognized when incurred rather than being estimated at lease commencement and included in the lessee's right-of-use asset and lease liability.

There are two exceptions to not including variable payments in the calculation of the lease liability recorded at the beginning of the lease. Let's take a look at both exceptions.

WHEN VARIABLE LEASE PAYMENTS ARE IN-SUBSTANCE FIXED PAYMENTS. The first exception to not including variable payments is when apparent "variable" payments actually are in-substance fixed payments. We include these "fixed payments in disguise" as part of the lessee's lease payments. For example, assume a retail store's monthly lease payments will increase next year by the higher of $250 or 0.5% of monthly store revenue. In that case, we know that the lease payment will increase by at least $250, so those payments are deemed to be in-substance fixed payments and are included in the lease payments used in present value calculations.

If future lease payments are uncertain, we consider them as part of the lease payments only if they are "in-substance fixed payments" or if payments vary solely when an index or rate changes.

[15]The lease payment can also decrease. The decrease in the lease payments is reported as a reduction in lease expense (lessee) and a reduction in lease revenue (lessor).

WHEN VARIABLE LEASE PAYMENTS DEPEND ON AN INDEX OR RATE. Another exception to not including variable payments when initially recording the lease is when the amount of the lease payments depends on an index or a rate, such as the Consumer Price Index or current interest rates. Even though lease payments will vary in the future, we use the initial lease payment amount, based on the current index (or rate), to discount to present value when determining the right of use asset, lease liability, and lease receivable. When lease payments do change in the future (because the index or rate changes), we don't remeasure the lease liability or leased asset at that time, but simply report the additional amount as a separate lease payment that produces expense for the lessee and revenue for the lessor.

Only if the lease asset and lease liability are later remeasured for another reason will a change in payments based on the CPI or market interest rates affect the right-of-use asset and liability.

Only if and when the lessee remeasures the lease liability for reasons other than a change in the index or rate should the lessee adjust the right-of-use asset and lease liability for changes in the amount of the payments. This might happen, for example, because of a reassessment of the lease term (as described in the previous section) or a modification of the lease (as described in the next section). In that case, the leased asset and lease liability are recalculated by determining the present value of future lease payments using (a) the new lease payments as adjusted for changes in the index or rate and (b) the discount rate that applies as of the date of the reassessment.

The *lessor* never reassesses its lease receivable for variable lease payments.

What if Lease Terms are Modified?

If a modification grants the lessee an *additional right of use*, the original lease is terminated and a new lease is created based on the modified arrangement.

Sometimes the lessee and lessor will agree to modify the terms of a lease before the lease term ends. This creates two possibilities. (1) The modification might grant the lessee an *additional right of use*. This would mean terminating the original lease and accounting for the modified arrangement as a new lease. (2) The modification might *alter the lessee's right to use* the asset rather than grant an additional right of use. This would mean adjusting, adding to, or deleting what has been recorded in order to conform to the new terms of the contract (say, a change in the lease term or lease payments) and perhaps reclassifying the lease from one type to another.

Modifying lease terms sometimes requires reclassifying operating leases to finance/sales-type leases, or vice versa.

As an example, assume a four-year operating lease of equipment with a useful life of six years. Let's say that after two years, the lessee and lessor agree to extend the lease term by two years, and to alter the amount of the lease payments. The additional two years were not originally an option. In this case, the modification alters the lessee's right to use the equipment; it doesn't grant the lessee an additional right to use another asset. In addition, the modified lease term of two additional years (six years total) is now for a "major part" of the asset's six-year economic life, so classification changes from an operating lease to a finance/sales-type lease. Illustration 15–11 demonstrates how modifications to the contract would be recorded.

Sans Serif, the lessee, updates the balances of the right-of-use asset and lease liability for the increase in present value. In addition, because the lease is now classified as a finance lease, Sans Serif no longer will recognize straight-line lease expense of $100,000. Instead, at the end of each remaining year, Sans Serif will record interest expense and amortization of the right-of-use asset in the usual way for a finance lease.

First LeaseCorp, the lessor, records a lease receivable for the present value of the remaining lease payments and removes the equipment (and related accumulated depreciation) from its books. Because the sales revenue is higher than the carrying amount of the equipment, First LeaseCorp also recognizes selling profit for the difference: Sales revenue of $329,068 minus cost of goods sold of $319,386 equals $9,682. In addition, at the end of each remaining year, First LeaseCorp will record interest revenue at the now current effective rate of 9% for a sales-type lease (instead of straight-line rent revenue of $100,000 for an operating lease).

Residual Value

The residual value is an estimate of what a leased asset's commercial value will be at the end of the lease term.

The **residual value** of leased property is an estimate of what its commercial value will be at the end of the lease term. Typically, we will have a residual value in an *operating* lease because the lease term usually ends before the lease asset's value has been depleted. A residual value is less likely, but certainly not unusual, when the lease qualifies as a sales-type lease, because the lease term is for most, if not all, of the asset's life.

Illustration 15–11 Lease Modifications: Term, Payments, and Classification

On January 1, 2018, Sans Serif Publishers leased printing equipment from First LeaseCorp. First LeaseCorp purchased the equipment from CompuDec Corporation at a cost of $479,079. Sans Serif's borrowing rate for similar transactions is 10%. The lease agreement specifies four annual payments of $100,000 beginning January 1, 2018, the beginning of the lease, and at each December 31 from 2018 through 2020. The useful life of the equipment is estimated to be six years. The present value of those four payments at a discount rate of 10% is $348,685.

On January 1, 2020 (after three payments*), the lessee and lessor agreed to (1) extend the lease term by two years and (2) increase the remaining three payments from $100,000 to $130,000 each. The market rate of interest at that time has decreased from 10% to 9%. The table below summarizes the effect of four important contract modifications:

Contract	Original Lease	Modified Lease	Effect
1. Term	4 years	6 years	Increase in present value
2. Payments	$100,000	$130,000	Increase in present value
3. Discount rate	10%	9%	Increase in present value
PV on Jan. 1, 2020	$90,909**	$329,068†	**Lessee:** Increase PV balances by $238,159††
4. Classification	Operating	Finance/Sales-type	**Lessor:** Record sale of asset for $329,068 (and remove asset's carrying amount)

Modification of the Lease (January 1, 2020)

Sans Serif (Lessee)		
Right-of-use asset (present value of lease payments)	238,159	
Lease payable (present value of lease payments)		238,159
First LeaseCrop (Lessor)		
Lease receivable (PV of 3 remaining lease payments)	329,068	
Sales revenue (PV of 3 remaining lease payments)		329,068 } profit 9,682
Cost of goods sold (cost minus accumulated depreciation)	319,386	
Accumulated depreciation [($479,079 ÷ 6 years) × 2 years]	159,693	
Asset (cost)		479,079

*The modification occurs two years into the lease, but there have been three payments since payments are at the beginning of each year.

**See Illustration 15–7B.

†Present value of remaining three lease payments = $130,000 × 2.53129. (Present value of an ordinary annuity of $1: $n = 3$, $i = 9\%$.)

††$329,068 − 90,909

International Financial Reporting Standards

● LO15–9

Reassessment of the Right-of-Use Asset and Lease Liability.
Under IFRS, a lessee will remeasure the variable lease payments that depend on an index or a rate not just when the lessee remeasures the right-of-use asset and lease liability for other reasons, but also whenever there is a change in the cash flows resulting from a change in the reference index or rate.

Sometimes a lease agreement includes a guarantee by the lessee that the lessor will recover a specified residual value when custody of the asset reverts back to the lessor at the end of the lease term. This not only reduces the lessor's risk, but also provides an incentive for the lessee to exercise a higher degree of care in maintaining the leased asset to preserve the residual value. The lessee promises to return not only the property but also sufficient cash to provide the lessor with a minimum combined value.

A lessee sometimes will guarantee that the lessor will recover a specified residual value when custody of the asset reverts back to the lessor.

A residual value affects several aspects of lease accounting, including the size of the periodic lease payments, the classification of a lease, and the amounts recorded by both the lessee and lessor.

EFFECT OF A RESIDUAL VALUE ON THE SIZE OF LEASE PAYMENTS. Suppose the printing equipment leased in our finance/sales-type lease (Illustration 15–4) was expected to be worth $60,000 at the end of the six-year lease term. Should this influence the lessor's (First LeaseCorp) calculation of periodic rental payments? Yes! Here's why.

The leasing company purchased the equipment for $479,079. That's the amount the company needs to recover through the leasing contract along with interest revenue sufficient to achieve its business objectives. We are assuming that means a 10% return on investment. Where does that return come from? In some leases (our finance/sales-type lease in Illustration 15–4, for instance) the entire return comes from the lessee's lease payments, which must be enough over the lease term to pay the lessor its investment in the lease asset plus the desired amount of interest (10%).

We calculated the necessary payments by dividing the $479,079 investment by the present value of an annuity due of $1, discounted at 10% for six years. That calculation by the lessor yielded $100,000 for each of the six payments.

In that situation the lessor calculated the lease payments as:

Amount to be recovered (present value)	$479,079
	÷ 4.79079*
Lease payments at the beginning of each of the next 6 years	$100,000

*Present value of an annuity due of $1: $n = 6$, $i = 10\%$.

However, if the lessor gets the asset back at the end of the lease, and the asset has commercial value at that time, the lessor has another source of return. The value of the asset itself, the residual value, will provide another source of recovery of the lessor's investment. That reduces the amount needed from periodic lessee payments for the lessor to generate its 10% return. To see how, in Illustration 15–12 let's assume a $60,000 residual value at the end of the six-year lease term.

Illustration 15–12

Effect of Residual Value on the Calculation of Lease Payments

On January 1, 2018, Sans Serif Publishers leased printing equipment from First LeaseCorp. First LeaseCorp purchased the equipment from CompuDec Corporation at a cost of $479,079. Assume the lease includes six annual payments beginning January 1, 2018, and at each December 31 from 2018 through 2022. At the end of the six-year lease term ending December 31, 2023, the equipment is expected to have a **residual value of $60,000**. The estimated useful life of the equipment is **seven years**. If the six lease payments are of an equal amount, what payment amount would provide First LeaseCorp with a return of 10%?

Amount to be recovered* (fair value)	$479,079
Less: Present value of the residual value ($60,000 × 0.56447**)	(33,868)
Amount to be recovered through periodic rental payments	$445,211
	÷ 4.79079†
Lease payments at the beginning of each of the six years	$ 92,931††

*The amount to be recovered would also include "initial direct costs" paid by the lessor. We discuss initial direct costs in Part C of this chapter.
**Present value of $1: $n = 6$, $i = 10\%$.
†Present value of an annuity due of $1: $n = 6$, $i = 10\%$.
††For another example, recall our four-year *operating* lease (Illustration 15–7) in which the lease payments are $100,000 each. Although not stated at the time, First LeaseCorp anticipated that the fair value of the equipment at the end of the lease term (residual value) would be $190,911, which is why the lease payments were $100,000:

Amount to be recovered (fair value)	$479,079
Less: Present value of the residual value ($190,911 × 0.68301‡)	(130,394)
To be recovered through periodic lease payments (present value)	$348,685
	÷ 3.48685‡‡
Lease payments at the beginning of each of the four years	$100,000

‡Present value of $1: $n = 4$, $i = 10\%$.
‡‡Present value of an annuity due of $1: $n = 4$, $i = 10\%$.

The present value of the residual value of a lease asset is called a **residual asset**. The lessee doesn't view the residual asset as *its* asset, since the residual asset will revert to the lessor. However, from the lessor's perspective, even if a residual value is not guaranteed, the lessor still expects to receive it. So, the lessor will view the residual asset as contributing to the amount needed to recover its $479,079 investment, causing the lessee's lease payments to be $92,931 rather than $100,000. *As the expected residual value increases, the size of the lease payments decreases.*

EFFECT OF A RESIDUAL VALUE ON AMOUNTS RECORDED BY THE LESSOR.
Sales-Type Lease with Residual Value. The *lessee's accounting is unaffected* by the residual value other than its causing the payments to be lower. In the situation described in Illustration 15–12, Sans Serif, the lessee, would record a right-of-use asset and lease liability for the present value of the six lease payments ($445,211). Then, over the term of the lease, it would record interest expense and amortization in the usual way for this finance-type lease.

The *lessor's accounting is affected* by the residual value. In Illustration 15–12A we see how the lessor will record the lease introduced in Illustration 15–12.

Illustration 15–12A
Sales-Type Lease with Residual Value: Lessor

Beginning of the Lease (January 1, 2018)

First LeaseCorp (Lessor)

Lease receivable (PV of lease payments plus PV of $60,000 residual value)*	479,079	
Equipment (lessor's cost: carrying amount)		479,079

*Alternatively, the lessor could record the receivable and the residual asset separately:

Lease receivable (PV of lease payments)	445,211	
Residual asset (PV of $60,000 unguaranteed residual value)	33,868	
Equipment (lessor's cost: carrying amount)		479,079

The lessor's lease receivable includes the value of the asset expected at the end of the lease term.

Both (a) the present value of the lease payments and (b) the present value of the unguaranteed residual value combine to allow the lessor to recover its $479,079 investment and are recorded as the lease receivable at the beginning of the lease. The lessor includes the $60,000 residual value in its amortization schedule, along with the lease payments as demonstrated in Illustration 15–12B.

Illustration 15–12B
Lessor's Amortization Schedule—with Residual Value

	Receipts	Effective Interest (10% × Outstanding balance)	Decrease in Balance	Outstanding Balance
1/1/18				479,079
1/1/18	92,931		92,931	386,148
12/31/18	92,931	0.10 (386,148) = 38,615	54,316	331,832
12/31/19	92,931	0.10 (331,832) = 33,183	59,748	272,084
12/31/20	92,931	0.10 (272,084) = 27,208	65,723	206,361
12/31/21	92,931	0.10 (206,361) = 20,636	72,295	134,066
12/31/22	92,931	0.10 (134,066) = 13,407	79,524	54,542
12/31/23	60,000	0.10 (54,542) = 5,458*	54,542	0
	617,586	138,507	479,079	

*Adjusted for rounding of other numbers in the schedule.

The lessor expects to receive the residual value ($60,000) in the form of equipment at the end of the lease term.

The amortization schedule reveals several important points. First, the six periodic cash payments are now $92,931, as we calculated previously. Notice also that we now include the $60,000 residual value. Despite the different composition of the amounts the lessor will receive, their present value ($479,079) is the same as when we assumed $100,000 periodic payments and no residual value. However, a greater amount of interest revenue will be recognized over the lease term: $138,507. (It was $120,921 before.) The higher interest reflects the fact that payments are farther in the future, causing the outstanding lease balances (and interest on those balances) to be higher during the lease term. Also, note that a greater total amount of lease receipts is collected: $617,586. (It was $600,000 before.) This total is referred to as the lessor's gross investment in the lease and is included in the lessor's lease disclosure note. The present value of those same payments ($479,079) is referred to as the net investment in the lease and is the amount recorded as the lease receivable in the journal entry at the beginning of the lease.

The lessor's *gross investment in the lease* is the total of periodic lease payments and any residual value.

Remember, the final periodic cash payment on December 31, 2023, is at the beginning of the final year. Then, at the end of the year of the lease on December 31, 2023, the equipment is returned to the lessor and is reinstated on the lessor's books at its fair value, which we assume to be $60,000, the amount predicted when the lease began.

If the actual residual value at December 31, 2023, is less (or more) than $60,000, the lessor would record a loss (or gain). Notice, too, that the residual asset is returned to the lessor.

Illustration 15–12C

End of Lease Term—Actual Residual Value Equals the Estimated Amount: **Lessor**

End of the Lease (December 31, 2023)

First LeaseCorp (Lessor)

Equipment (residual value)	60,000	
Lease receivable (account balance)		54,542
Interest revenue (10% × outstanding balance)		5,458

Sales-Type Lease with Selling Profit and Residual Value. When a sales-type lease that includes a residual value also has a selling profit, we need to take that into consideration when the lease is recorded initially. Recall that the lessor records both sales revenue and cost of goods sold to account for the selling profit. The sales revenue is the present value of only the periodic lease payments, not including the residual value. To visualize this, let's assume that our sales-type lease with a selling profit (Illustration 15–6) had included a residual value of $60,000. In that case, the initial lessor entry would be modified as shown in Illustration 15–13.

Illustration 15–13

Sales-Type Lease with Selling Profit and Residual Value: Lessor

Sales revenue	$445,211
– COGS	266,132
Selling profit	$179,079

The lease provides the lessor with a selling profit if the PV of payments exceeds the asset's cost.

On January 1, 2018, Sans Serif Publishers leased printing equipment from CompuDec Corporation. The lease agreement specifies six annual payments of $92,931 beginning January 1, 2018, the beginning of the lease, and at each December 31 from 2018 through 2022. At the end of the six-year lease term ending December 31, 2023, the equipment will be returned to the lessor and is expected to have a residual value of $60,000. The estimated useful life of the equipment is seven years. The interest rate in these financing arrangements is 10%. CompuDec manufactured the equipment at a cost of $300,000.

Beginning of the Lease (January 1, 2018)

CompuDec Corporation (Lessor)

Lease receivable (PV of lease payments* plus PV of $60,000 residual value**)	479,079	
Cost of goods sold ($300,000 – 33,868**)	266,132	
Sales revenue ($479,079 – 33,868**)		445,211
Equipment (lessor's cost)		300,000

*$92,931 × 4.79079† = $445,211 present value of lease payments
**$60,000 × 0.56447†† = $33,868 present value of residual value
†Present value of $1: $n = 6, i = 10\%$.
††Present value of an annuity due of $1: $n = 6, i = 10\%$.

Sales revenue does not include the residual value because the revenue to be recovered from the lessee is lease payments only. The remainder of the lessor's investment is to be recovered—not from payment by the lessee, but by selling, releasing, or otherwise obtaining value from the asset when it reverts back to the lessor. Think of it this way: The portion of the asset sold is the portion not represented by the residual value. So, both the asset's cost of goods sold and its selling price are reduced by the present value of the portion *not sold.*

When a Cash Payment is Predicted Due to a Lessee-Guaranteed Residual Value. We saw in Illustration 15–4 that without a residual value contributing to the lessor recovering its investment, the amount of the six payments needed to recover the $479,079 investment would have been $100,000. We also saw in Illustration 15–12 that *with* a residual value guaranteed to the lessor at the end of the lease, the payments would be reduced to $92,931. Other than this reduction of lease payments, should the *lessee* (Sans Serif Publishers) be concerned with the residual value of the leased asset? The answer is maybe. It depends on whether the lessee has arranged to guarantee a specific value of the residual asset at the conclusion of the lease and, even then, how that value compares to the prediction of its actual value. We explore that possibility next.

As we discussed earlier, a lease agreement sometimes includes a guarantee by the lessee that the lessor will recover a specified residual value when custody of the asset reverts back to the lessor at the end of the lease term. The lessee promises to return not only the property but also sufficient cash to provide the lessor with a minimum combined value. That doesn't necessarily mean, though, that the lessee will be required to make any cash payment. A cash payment would be expected as of the beginning of a lease only if the guaranteed amount exceeds the estimated residual value of the asset.

If a cash payment under a lessee-guaranteed residual value is predicted, the present value of that payment is added to the present value of the periodic lease payments that the lessee records as both a right-of-use asset and a lease liability. For instance, let's assume that in the situation described in Illustration 15–12 when the estimated residual value was $60,000, negotiations led to Sans Serif guaranteeing an $80,000 residual value. That means that if the property's value is less than $80,000 at the end of the six-year lease term, the lessee will pay cash for the difference. Since that value is expected to be $60,000, the expected *excess* guaranteed residual value is $80,000 − 60,000 = $20,000. The lessee views the expected excess guaranteed residual value as an additional cash flow to be paid to the lessor (addition to lease payments). The present value of the expected excess guaranteed residual is $11,289 ($20,000 × 0.56447), and the lessee would add this amount to the present value of the periodic lease payments to record the right-of-use asset and lease liability at the beginning of the lease.[16]

A cash payment that's predicted because of a lessee-guaranteed residual value is treated the same as another lease payment.

Looking at it from the other side of the transaction, does the lessor also view the expected *excess* guaranteed residual value as an additional amount to be collected? Yes. In fact, the lessor expects to receive that payment ($20,000) *as well as the residual value itself* (60,000). Those two amounts combine to equal the $80,000 guaranteed residual value that, if in a *sales-type* lease, the lessor includes in the lease receivable.[17]

Situations in which the lessee-guaranteed residual value exceeds the estimate of the actual residual value are rare in practice. It makes little economic sense for a lessee to agree to guarantee an amount greater than the estimated residual value, virtually ensuring an additional cash payment at the conclusion of the lease. The requirement to account for it in this way, though, serves as a deterrent to lessees and lessors who might be inclined to manipulate reported numbers by reducing lease payments while creating an excess *lessee-guaranteed* residual value to compensate for the reduced lease payments.

Additional Consideration

If a residual value is not guaranteed by the lessee or is guaranteed by the lessee but the guaranteed amount does not differ from the estimate of the actual fair value at the end of the lease term, it does not affect the lessee's calculation of the right-of-use asset or lease liability, other than influencing the amount of each lease payment as we saw in Illustration 15–12.

EFFECT OF A RESIDUAL VALUE ON LEASE CLASSIFICATION We classify a lease as a finance/sales-type lease if, in substance, the lessor is transferring control of the asset to the lessee. Recall that one of the classification criteria is a comparison of the fair value of an asset with the present value of the payments coming from the lessee. Payments from the lessee are the periodic lease payments plus any portion of the residual value the lessee has guaranteed. That's the basis for classification criterion 4 (Illustration 15–2): If the present value of the lease payments, including any *lessee-guaranteed* residual value, constitutes "substantially all" of the fair value of the asset, it's a finance lease from the lessee's perspective and a sales-type lease from the lessor's perspective.

[16]Present value of $1: $n = 6$, $i = 10\%$.

[17]Remember, in an *operating* lease, the lessor doesn't record a receivable nor remove the asset from its books.

When the lessee does not control substantially all of the remaining benefits of the underlying asset, the lease usually is considered an operating lease.

When control is not transferred to the lessee, but the present value of lease payments constitutes substantially all of the asset's fair value due to a third-party guaranteed residual value and it's probable that the lessor will collect the lease payments, the lease is considered a direct financing lease.

In the unlikely event of a profit in a direct financing lease, the revenue (and profit) must be deferred.

Additional Consideration

Recall that by one of the lease classification criteria, we have a finance/sales-type lease if the sum of the present value of the lease payments and any residual value guaranteed by the lessee amounts to substantially all of the fair value of the underlying asset. When that's the case, the lessee, through its contractually obligated payments, guarantees recovery of substantially all the lessor's investment in the asset, so the lessee controls substantially all of the remaining benefits of the underlying asset. This control is consistent with the principle of a sale in ASC Topic 606: *Revenue from Contracts with Customers* for the lessor to recognize sales revenue on the lease.[18] On the other hand, when the lessee lacks that control, the lease is considered an operating lease.

An exception is when the lease qualifies as a **direct financing lease**. We have a direct financing lease only when a third party (typically an insurance company) is paid to guarantee all or part of the residual value. When that happens, it's possible that the combined present value of (a) the *lessee's* periodic payments, (b) the *lessee*-guaranteed residual value, and (c) the *third-party* guaranteed residual value will constitute substantially all of the asset's fair value, but that the lessee's obligated payments, (a) and (b), are insufficient to do so. That situation would indicate that the lessee *does not* control substantially all of the remaining benefits of the underlying asset, so from the lessee's perspective the lease is an operating lease. However, from the lessor's perspective, the *total* of the obligated payments guarantees recovery of substantially all the lessor's investment in the asset (assuming collection is probable) indicating that it shouldn't be an operating lease, but the lessee's portion of the total is insufficient to indicate control, so it shouldn't be a sales-type lease either.

A lease is considered a direct financing lease if:

1. It doesn't qualify as a sales-type lease.
2. The combined present value of (a) the *lessee's* periodic payments, (b) the *lessee*-guaranteed residual value, and (c) the *third-party* guaranteed residual value will constitute substantially all of the asset's fair value.
3. It's probable that the lessor will collect the lease payments.

When a lease is a direct financing lease rather than a sales-type lease, the lessor's primary involvement in the lease is providing financing of the asset in exchange for interest revenue. The lessor records the lease the same as it would a sales-type lease with no selling profit:

Lease receivable (present value of lease payments*)	xxx	
Asset (carrying value)		xxx

*Including the lessee's periodic payments, any lessee-guaranteed residual value, and the third-party guaranteed residual value.

Although rare, if a direct financing lease gives rise to selling profit, the lessor does not recognize the profit at the beginning of the lease. Instead, the lessor would credit deferred profit (considered a contra asset reduction in the receivable) in the entry above. The lessor then would recognize the profit over the lease term in such a manner that the total of that profit and the interest revenue on the remainder of the lease receivable is a constant periodic rate of return on the lease. This can be accomplished by not recording the "deferred profit" separately, but subtracting it from the lease receivable. Decreasing the receivable causes the implicit rate (the interest rate that causes the present value of the lease payments to equal the receivable) to be higher. Determining interest revenue at this higher rate accomplishes the purpose of increasing interest revenue (actually interest plus a portion of profit) each period by a portion of the deferred revenue.

Purchase Option

A **purchase option** is a provision of some lease contracts that gives the lessee the option to purchase the lease asset during, or at the end of, the lease term at a specified exercise price. If it is "reasonably certain" that the lessee will exercise the purchase option, the accounting

[18]As explained in more detail in Chapter 5, "control" requires that the customer has direct influence over the use of the good or service and obtains its benefits.

for the lease is affected in three ways: (1) the lease is classified as a finance/sales-type lease, (2) both the lessee and the lessor consider the exercise price of the option to be an additional cash payment, and (3) we assume the lease term ends on the date that the option is expected to be exercised. Both the additional cash payment and the shortened lease term impact the calculation of the lessee's right-of-use asset and lease liability and the lessor's lease receivable. Another implication is that, since the lessee is predicted to own the asset after the lease term, the right-of-use asset recognized by the lessee should be amortized over the economic life of the asset, rather than over the lease term.

The exercise price of a purchase option is considered to be an additional cash payment if exercise of the option is "reasonably certain."

In practice, a purchase option whose exercise is reasonably certain is often referred to as a "bargain" purchase option (BPO), and we'll use that term in this book. BPOs are so named because the exercise price of the purchase option is a good deal (a bargain) to the lessee, making it reasonably certain that the lessee will exercise the option. To see the accounting for a BPO, let's again modify Illustration 15–4, this time to assume the lease agreement allows Sans Serif the option to purchase the leased equipment for $60,000 at the end of the lease term. At this time, the fair value is expected to be sufficiently high ($75,000) to indicate reasonable certainty that Sans Serif will exercise the option. This situation is assumed in Illustration 15–14.

Illustration 15–14

Bargain Purchase Option

On January 1, 2018, Sans Serif Publishers leased printing equipment from First LeaseCorp. First LeaseCorp purchased the equipment from CompuDec Corporation at a cost of $479,079.

The lease agreement specifies six annual payments of $92,931 beginning January 1, 2018, the beginning of the lease, and at each December 31 from 2018 through 2022. On December 31, 2023, at the end of the six-year lease term, the equipment is expected to be worth $75,000, and Sans Serif has the option to purchase it for $60,000 on that date. The residual value after seven years is zero.* First LeaseCorp routinely acquires electronic equipment for lease to other firms. The interest rate in these financing arrangements is 10%.

Lessor's calculation of lease payments:

Amount to be recovered (fair value)	$479,079
Less: Present value of the exercise price ($60,000 × 0.56447**)	(33,868)
Amount to be recovered through periodic rental payments	445,211
	÷ 4.79079*
Lease payments at the beginning of each of the six years:	$ 92,931

The lessor *subtracts* the PV of the exercise price to determine lease payments.

Lessee's calculation of PV of lease payments:

Present value of periodic lease payments ($92,931 × 4.79079†)	$445,211
Plus: Present value of the exercise price ($60,000 × 0.56447**)	33,868
Present value of lease payments	$479,079
(Recorded as a leased asset and a lease liability)	

The lessee *adds* the PV of the exercise price to determine its asset and liability.

*Our discussion of the effect of a bargain purchase option (BPO) would be exactly the same if our illustration were of a sales-type lease with a selling profit (for instance, if the lessor's cost were $300,000) except that, of course, sales revenue and cost of goods sold would be recorded.
**Present value of $1: $n = 6, i = 10\%$.
†Present value of an annuity due of $1: $n = 6, i = 10\%$.

The lessor's calculation of periodic lease payments is precisely the same as when we had the $60,000 residual value in the previous illustration. In fact, the amortization schedule is exactly the same as in Illustration 15–12B when we had a residual value. This is because the exercise price is a component of the lease payments for both the lessor and lessee as was the residual value.

A question you might have at this point is: Why do we ignore the residual value now when we have a bargain purchase option? The reason is obvious when you recall an essential characteristic of such an option—it's expected to be exercised. So, when it is exercised, title to the leased asset passes to the lessee and, with title, any residual value also passes. When that happens, the residual value cannot be considered an additional lease payment to the lessor.

If the lessee obtains title, the lessor's computation of rental payments is unaffected by any residual value.

Recording the exercise of the option is similar to recording the periodic lease payments. That is, a portion of the payment covers interest for the year, and the remaining portion reduces the outstanding liability/receivable balance (to zero with this last payment), as shown in Illustration 15–14A.

Illustration 15–14A

Journal Entries—with Purchase Option

The cash payment expected when the BPO is exercised represents part interest and part principal just like the other cash payments.

Exercise of Purchase Option (December 31, 2023)

Sans Serif Publishers (Lessee)		
Interest expense (10% × $54,542*)	5,458	
Lease payable (difference)	54,542	
Cash (exercise price)		60,000
CompuDec Corporation (Lessor)		
Cash (exercise price)	60,000	
Lease receivable (account balance)		54,542
Interest revenue (10% × outstanding balance)		5,458

*$54,542 is the balance of lease payable after all periodic lease payments have been made (see Illustration 15–12B).

Note also that amortization is affected by the BPO. As pointed out earlier, the lessee normally amortizes its right-of-use asset over the term of the lease. But if ownership transfers by contract or by the expected exercise of a purchase option, the lessee will have the asset beyond the lease term, and will amortize it over the longer useful life. This reflects the fact that the lessee anticipates using the leased equipment for its full useful life. In Illustration 15–14B, the lease term is six years but the equipment is expected to be useful for seven years, so amortization each year is $68,440 ($479,079 ÷ 7 years).

Illustration 15–14B

Amortization Expense with Purchase Option

Each December 31 over the life of the asset		
Sans Serif Publishers (Lessee)		
Amortization expense ($479,079* ÷ 7 years)	68,440	
Right-of-use asset		68,440

*The residual value is zero after the full seven-year useful life.

When we have a BPO, the length of the lease term is limited to the time up to when the purchase option becomes exercisable.

PURCHASE OPTION EXERCISABLE BEFORE THE END OF THE LEASE TERM. In Illustration 15–14 we assumed that the purchase option was exercisable on December 31, 2023—the end of the lease term. Sometimes, though, the lease contract specifies that an option becomes exercisable before the designated lease term ends. If the option is reasonably certain to be exercised, *the lease term ends for accounting purposes when the option becomes exercisable.* Lease payments include only the periodic cash payments specified in the agreement that occur prior to the date a BPO becomes exercisable. We assume the option is exercised at that time and the lease ends.

TERMINATION PENALTIES. Similar to a lease with a purchase option, if a lease contract includes a penalty payment if the lessee chooses to terminate the lease at a time specified in the contract, we consider the termination penalty to be an additional cash payment if the lessee is "reasonably certain" to terminate the lease. Again, if termination is predicted, we consider the lease term to be from the beginning of the lease to the expected termination date.

In Illustration 15–15, we see the factors that are included in the lease term and the lease payments used in accounting for leases.

Summary of the Lease Uncertainties

Illustration 15–16 provides a summary of various uncertainties concerning lease arrangements that might influence the way lessees and lessors determine lease payments, the lessee's right-of-use asset and lease liability, and the lessor's lease receivable.

Illustration 15–15

Composition of Lease Term and Payments

LEASE TERM INCLUDES:		LEASE PAYMENTS INCLUDE:	
Noncancelable period		Fixed payments	
PLUS:	Periods covered by renewal options if exercise is "reasonably certain"	*PLUS:*	Exercise price for purchase option if exercise is "reasonably certain"
MINUS:	Periods following date of purchase option if exercise is "reasonably certain"	*PLUS:*	Termination penalty for termination option if exercise is "reasonably certain"
PLUS:	Periods covered by renewal options if *under control of lessor*	*PLUS:*	Variable lease payments only if (a) deemed in-substance fixed payments or (b) based on an index or rate (with any changes in payments included only if and when the lessee remeasures the lease liability for another reason)
PLUS:	Periods following date of termination option if it's "reasonably certain" the option will ***not*** be exercised	*PLUS:*	Excess of guaranteed residual value over expected residual value

Illustration 15–16 Summary of Effects of Uncertainties

The lease term	Noncancelable period for which a lessee has the right to use an underlying asset, modified by any renewal or termination options that are "reasonably certain" to be exercised, or not exercised. Options whose exercise is under the control of the lessor are automatically included. Reassessed only when a significant occurrence indicates a change in the economic incentive.
Variable lease payments	Included only if payments are: • in-substance fixed payments or • based on an index or rate, with changes due to the index or rate considered only if and when the lessee remeasures the lease liability for another reason.
Unguaranteed residual value	Present value (called residual asset): • influences the size of lease payments • added to lease receivable • subtracted from sales revenue and COGS in sales type lease
Lessee guaranteed residual value	Present value: • considered when determining lease classification (criterion 4) • added to lease receivable • added to sales revenue
Excess of guaranteed residual value over expected residual value	Present value: • influences the size of lease payments • added to right-of-use asset and lease liability
Purchase options	If exercise is "reasonably certain:" • limits lease term • PV of exercise price added to right-of-use asset and lease liability • PV of exercise price added to lease receivable
Termination penalties	If exercise is "reasonably certain:" • limits lease term • PV of penalty amount added to right-of-use asset and lease liability • PV of penalty amount added to lease receivable
Modification of a lease	• If a modification grants the lessee an *additional right of use,* the original lease is terminated and a new lease is created • Otherwise, it means adjusting, adding, or deleting accounts to conform with the new terms and perhaps reclassifying it from one type of lease to another

Remeasurement of the Lease Liability

When considering the various uncertainties surrounding leases in the previous sections, we've encountered several situations that cause us to remeasure a lease liability (and right-of-use asset). Illustration 15–17 provides us with a summary.

In each case, we compare the remeasured liability with its current balance to see the adjustment needed, calculating the new amount as the present value of the *remaining* lease payments:

Present value of *remaining* payments	$xxx
Liability balance (current)	xxx
Increase (or decrease) in balance	$xxx

Illustration 15–17 Situations Requiring Remeasurement of the Lease Liability

SITUATIONS REQUIRING REMEASUREMENT OF THE LEASE LIABILITY		**Discount rate** used in present value calculation **updated** from rate used at the beginning of the lease to rate **current** at remeasurement
1. There is a **change in the assessment** of:	• the lease term*	Yes
	• whether exercise of a purchase or termination option is reasonably certain*	Yes
	• any cash payment because of a guaranteed residual value	No
	• whether a variable payment is now a fixed payment	No
2. There is a **modification** of the terms of the lease:†	• not accounted for as a new lease	Yes

*We reassess the lease term or exercise of an option only when some new event, like a leasehold improvement, triggers a reassessment.
†Under prior GAAP, a modification was the only time the lease liability was remeasured.

Ethical Dilemma

"I know we had discussed that they're supposed to be worth $24,000 when our purchase option becomes exercisable," Ferris insisted. "That's why we agreed to the lease terms. But, Jenkins, you know how uncertain technology changes are. We can make a good case that they'll be worth $40,000 in three years."

The computers to which Ferris referred were leased to a customer this week. The lease meets none of the criteria for classification as a sales-type lease except that it contains a purchase option that is reasonably certain to be exercised if the computers could be purchased for $24,000 after three years.

"We could record revenue earlier that way," Jenkins agreed.

How could revenue be recorded earlier?

Do you perceive an ethical problem?

PART C

Other Lease Accounting Issues and Reporting Requirements

● LO15–7

Nonlease Components of Lease Payments

Service contracts, maintenance, hazard insurance, and property taxes are costs often associated with owning and operating an asset. Frequently, for convenience, a lease contract will specify that the lessor is to pay some or all of these costs, but in reality these additional costs are embedded in the periodic payments made by the lessee. The accounting question is whether to include these costs as separate components of the lease contract (to be expensed by the lessee) or, instead, as amounts to be capitalized as part of the right-of-use asset. The determining factor is whether the charge represents a *transfer of a good or service to the lessee.* If so, it qualifies as a "nonlease component" of the payment and is separated from the lease payments.

Illustration 15–18

Lease Payments That Include NonLease Components Paid by the Lessor

On January 1, 2018, Sans Serif Publishers leased equipment from First LeaseCorp. First LeaseCorp purchased the equipment from CompuDec Corporation at a cost of $479,079.

- Six annual payments of $102,000 beginning January 1, 2018.
- Payments include $2,000 which First LeaseCorp will use to pay an annual maintenance fee.
- The interest rate in these financing arrangements is 10%.
- Finance lease to Sans Serif Publishers.
- Sales-type lease to First LeaseCorp.

First Payment (January 1, 2018)

Sans Serif Publishers (Lessee)		
Maintenance expense (2018 fee)	2,000	
Lease payable	100,000	
Cash (lease payment)		102,000
First LeaseCorp (Lessor)		
Cash (lease payment)	102,000	
Lease receivable		100,000
Maintenance fee payable*		2,000

*This assumes the $2,000 maintenance fee hasn't yet been paid to the outside maintenance service.

Nonlease components that are included in periodic lease payments to be paid by the lessor are, in effect, indirectly paid by the lessee—and expensed by the lessee.

For demonstration, let's modify Illustration 15–4A. Recall that the lease payments in that illustration were $100,000 each year. Now, let's assume the periodic lease payments were increased to $102,000 with the provision that the lessor (First LeaseCorp) pays an annual maintenance fee of $2,000 to a third-party maintenance firm. Illustration 15–18 demonstrates how the lessee and lessor would account for the maintenance portion of the lease payment.

Sans Serif receives two separate benefits in the lease contract—the right to use equipment as well as maintenance on that equipment. Thus, payments specified in the lease contract contain a lease component (use of equipment for $100,000) and a nonlease component (maintenance service of $2,000).

At the beginning of the lease, Sans Serif would record a right-of-use asset and lease liability for the present value of the six $100,000 lease payments, $479,079 (see Illustration 15–4A). For the first payment of $102,000, $2,000 is recorded as maintenance expense and the remaining $100,000 reduces the lease liability.

On the other hand, if the $2,000 had been a payment for *hazard insurance or property taxes,* that payment does not transfer to the lessee a separate good or service. Instead, payments for hazard insurance and property taxes are specifically identified in the lease accounting guidance as part of the lease payments rather than nonlease components. So, in that case, the right-of-use asset and lease liability (and the lessor's lease receivable) would be measured as the present value of the $102,000 lease payments, not $100,000.

As a practical expedient, the lessee is given the *option* to elect *not* to exclude nonlease components (like maintenance). For example, the lessee in our illustration could elect to treat the $2,000 maintenance cost, not as maintenance expense as shown, but instead as part of the lease payment like for insurance or taxes. If the amounts are material, the lessee likely will not elect this option because the effect is to increase the lease liability, something most lessees try to avoid.

Initial Direct Costs

The costs that (a) are associated directly with consummating a lease, (b) are essential to acquire the lease, and (c) would not have been incurred had the lease agreement not occurred are referred to as **initial direct costs**. They include legal fees, commisions, and preparing and processing lease documents. While legal and processing fees for executing the lease document are included, legal fees for negotiations and drafting documents are not initial direct costs and are expensed as incurred.

For the lessee, initial direct costs incurred are added to the right-of-use asset. For the lessor, accounting for indirect costs incurred depends on the classification of the lease.

If initial direct costs are incurred by the lessor:
(a) recorded as a *selling expense* in a sales-type lease that *includes selling profit*.
(b) deferred and expensed over the lease term in a *sales-type* lease with *no selling profit*.
(c) deferred and expensed over the lease term in an *operating* lease.

- In a sales-type lease *that includes selling profit,* initial direct costs are expensed in the period of "sale"—that is, at the beginning of the lease. This treatment assumes that in a sales-type lease the primary reason for incurring these costs is to facilitate the sale of the leased asset.
- In a sales-type lease *with no selling profit,* initial direct costs are deferred and expensed over the lease term. This can be accomplished by not recording the "prepaid expense" separately, but including it in the lease receivable. Increasing the receivable causes the implicit rate (the interest rate that causes the present value of the lease payments to equal the receivable) to be lower. Determining interest revenue at this lower rate accomplishes the purpose of reducing interest revenue each period by a portion of the prepaid expense.
- In an operating lease, initial direct costs are deferred and expensed over the lease term, generally on a straight-line basis.

Advance Payments

Often lease agreements call for **advance payments** to be made at the beginning of the lease. Those payments represent prepaid rent (lease costs). Such payments are included with other payments when the lessee determines the present value of lease payments to determine the right-of-use asset and lease liability and when the lessor calculates its lease receivable in a sales-type lease. Remember, though, the lessor doesn't record a lease receivable for an operating lease. So, in that case, these advance payments are recorded as deferred rent revenue and allocated (normally on a straight-line basis) to rent revenue over the lease term. The rent that is periodically reported in those cases consists of the periodic rent payments themselves plus an allocated portion of deferred rent revenue.

Advance payments represent prepaid rent.

Leasehold Improvements

Sometimes a lessee will make improvements to leased property that reverts back to the lessor at the end of the lease. If a lessee constructs a new building or makes modifications to existing structures, that cost represents an asset just like any other capital expenditure. Like other assets, its cost is allocated as amortization or depreciation expense over its useful life to the lessee, which will be the shorter of the lease term or the physical life of the asset. Theoretically, such assets can be recorded in accounts descriptive of their nature, such as buildings or plant. In practice, the traditional account title used is **leasehold improvements**.[19] In any case, the undepreciated cost usually is reported in the balance sheet under the caption *property, plant, and equipment.* Movable assets like office furniture and equipment that are not attached to the leased property are not considered leasehold improvements.

The cost of a *leasehold improvement* is depreciated over its useful life to the lessee.

As discussed previously in Part B of this chapter, the existence of leasehold improvements can affect the determination of the lease term. For instance, let's say a company leased a building for a noncancellable term of six years with a two-year renewal option. Before it takes possession of the building, the company pays for leasehold improvements that are expected to have significant value at the end of six years. Because that value can be realized only through continued occupancy of the leased building, at the beginning of the lease the company would determine that it is reasonably certain to exercise the renewal

[19]Also, traditionally, depreciation sometimes is labeled amortization when in connection with leased assets and leasehold improvements. This is of little consequence. Remember, both depreciation and amortization refer to the process of allocating an asset's cost over its useful life.

option because it would suffer a significant economic penalty if the leasehold improvements were abandoned at the end of the initial lease term. As a result, at the beginning of the lease, the company would conclude that the lease term is eight years. Similarly, if the leasehold improvement is made during the lease term, that additional cost might trigger a reconsideration of whether a purchase or renewal option is reasonably certain to be exercised, and thus a reassessment of the lease term.

Additional Consideration

During 2005, hundreds of companies, particularly in the retail and restaurant industries, underwent one of the most widespread accounting correction events ever. Corrections were required because of the way these companies, including Pep Boys, Ann Taylor, Target, and Domino's Pizza, had allocated the cost of leasehold improvements. Rather than expensing leasehold improvements properly over the lease terms, these firms for years had inappropriately expensed the cost over the longer estimated useful lives of the properties. Prompting the sweeping revisions was a Securities and Exchange Commission letter on February 7, 2005, urging companies to follow long-standing accounting standards in this area. A result of the improper practices was to defer expense, thereby accelerating earnings. For instance, McDonald's Corp. recorded a charge of $139 million to adjust for the difference.

Hundreds of firms in 2005 corrected the way they accounted for leases.

Concept Review Exercise

VARIOUS LEASE ACCOUNTING ISSUES: FINANCE/SALES-TYPE LEASE

(This is an extension of the previous Concept Review Exercise.)

United Cellular Systems leased a satellite transmission device from Satellite Technology Corporation on January 1, 2018. Satellite Technology paid $500,000 for the transmission device. Its retail value is $653,681. The lease qualifies as a finance lease to the lessee and a sales-type lease with a selling profit to the lessor.

Terms of the Lease Agreement and Related Information:

Lease term	3 years (6 semiannual periods)
Semiannual lease payments	$123,000 at the beginning of each period
Economic life of asset	4 years
Interest rate	12%
Unguaranteed residual value	$40,000
Maintenance fees paid by lessor	$3,000/twice each year (included in lease payments)
Lessor's initial direct costs	$4,500
Contingent lease payments	Additional $4,000 if revenues exceed a specified base

Required:

1. Prepare an amortization schedule that describes the pattern of interest expense over the lease term for United Cellular Systems.
2. Prepare an amortization schedule that describes the pattern of interest revenue over the lease term for Satellite Technology.
3. Prepare the appropriate entries for both United Cellular Systems and Satellite Technology on January 1 and June 30, 2018. (Amortization is recorded only at year-end.)
4. Prepare the appropriate entries for both United Cellular Systems and Satellite Technology on December 31, 2020 (the end of the lease term), assuming the device is returned to the lessor and its actual residual value is $14,000 on that date.

Solution:

1. Prepare an amortization schedule that describes the pattern of interest expense over the lease term for United Cellular Systems.

Calculation of the Present Value of Lease Payments:
Present value of periodic lease payments excluding maintenance costs of $3,000:

($120,000 × 5.21236*) = $625,483

*Present value of an annuity due of $1: $n = 6$, $i = 6\%$.
Note: The residual value is excluded from lease payments for both the lessee and lessor but was influential in establishing the size of the lease payments.

Date	Payments	Effective Interest	Decrease in Balance	Outstanding Balance
		(6% × Outstanding balance)		
1/1/18				625,483
1/1/18	120,000		120,000	505,483
6/30/18	120,000	0.06 (505,483) = 30,329	89,671	415,812
1/1/19	120,000	0.06 (415,812) = 24,949	95,051	320,761
6/30/19	120,000	0.06 (320,761) = 19,246	100,754	220,007
1/1/20	120,000	0.06 (220,007) = 13,200	106,800	113,207
6/30/20	120,000	0.06 (113,207) = 6,793*	113,207	0
	720,000	94,517	625,483	

*Adjusted for rounding of other numbers in the schedule.

2. Prepare an amortization schedule that describes the pattern of interest revenue over the lease term for Satellite Technology.

Calculation of the Lessor's Net Investment:

Present value of periodic lease payments excluding maintenance costs of $3,000 ($120,000 × 5.21236*)	$625,483
Plus: Present value of the residual value ($40,000 × 0.70496†)	28,198
Lessor's net investment in lease	$653,681

*Present value of an annuity due of $1: $n = 6$, $i = 6\%$.
†Present value of $1: $n = 6$, $i = 6\%$.
Note: The residual value is excluded from lease payments, but is part of the lessor's gross and net invest ment in the lease.

Date	Payments	Effective Interest	Decrease in Balance	Outstanding Balance
		(6% × Outstanding balance)		
1/1/18				653,681
1/1/18	120,000		120,000	533,681
6/30/18	120,000	0.06 (533,681) = 32,021	87,979	445,702
1/1/19	120,000	0.06 (445,702) = 26,742	93,258	352,444
6/30/19	120,000	0.06 (352,444) = 21,147	98,853	253,591
1/1/20	120,000	0.06 (253,591) = 15,215	104,785	148,806
6/30/20	120,000	0.06 (148,806) = 8,928*	111,072	37,734
12/31/20	40,000	0.06 (37,734) = 2,266*	37,734	0
	760,000	106,319	653,681	

*Adjusted for rounding of other numbers in the schedule.

3. Prepare the appropriate entries for both United Cellular Systems and Satellite Technology on January 1 and June 30, 2018. (Amortization is only recorded at year-end.)

January 1, 2018

United Cellular Systems (Lessee)

Right-of-asset (calculated above)	625,483	
Lease payable (calculated above)		625,483
Lease payable (payment less maintenance costs)	120,000	
Maintenance expense	3,000	
Cash (lease payment)		123,000

(continued)

(concluded)

Satellite Technology (Lessor)		
Lease receivable (PV of lease payments)	653,681	
Cost of goods sold [$500,000 – ($40,000* × 0.70496)]	471,802	
Sales revenue (present value of lease payments)		625,483
Equipment (lessor's cost)		500,000
Selling expense	4,500	
Cash (initial direct costs†)		4,500
Cash (lease payment)	123,000	
Maintenance fee payable (or cash)		3,000
Lease receivable (payment less maintenance costs)		120,000

*This is the unguaranteed residual value.
†If incurred by the lessor, initial direct costs are recorded as a selling expense at the beginning of a sales-type lease.

June 30, 2018		
United Cellular Systems (Lessee)		
Interest expense [6% × ($625,483 – 120,000)]	30,329	
Lease payable (difference)	89,671	
Maintenance expense (annual fee)	3,000	
Cash (lease payment)		123,000
Satellite Technology (Lessor)		
Cash (lease payment)	123,000	
Maintenance fee payable (or cash)		3,000
Lease receivable (to balance)		87,979
Interest revenue [6% × ($653,681 – 120,000)]		32,021

4. Prepare the appropriate entries for both United Cellular Systems and Satellite Technology on December 31, 2020, (the end of the lease term) assuming the device is returned to the lessor and its actual residual value is $14,000 on that date.

December 31, 2020		
United Cellular Systems (Lessee)		
Amortization expense ($625,483 ÷ 3 years)	208,494	
Right-of-use asset		208,494
Satellite Technology (Lessor)		
Equipment (actual residual value)	14,000	
Loss on leased assets ($40,000 – 14,000)	26,000	
Lease receivable (account balance)		37,734
Interest revenue (6% × $37,734: from schedule)		2,266

Statement of Cash Flow Impact

Operating Leases

LO15–8

Remember, lease payments for operating leases represent rent—expense to the lessee, revenue for the lessor. These amounts are included in net income, so both the lessee and lessor report cash payments for operating leases in a statement of cash flows as cash flows from operating activities.

Both the lessee and lessor report cash payments for operating leases as *operating activities.*

Finance Leases–Lessee

The interest portion of a finance lease payment is a cash flow from operating activities and the principal portion is a cash flow from financing activities.

You've learned in this chapter that finance leases are agreements that we identify as being formulated outwardly as leases, but which are in reality installment purchases, so we account for them as such. Each lease payment (except the first if paid at beginning) includes both an amount that represents interest and an amount that represents a reduction of principal. In a statement of cash flows, then, the lessee reports the interest portion as a cash outflow from operating activities and the principal portion as a cash outflow from financing activities.

At the beginning of the lease, the lessee reports the right-of-use asset and lease liability as a noncash investing/financing activity in the disclosure notes to the financial statements.

Sales-Type Leases–Lessor

Cash receipts from a sales-type lease are cash flows from *operating activities*.

In a sales-type lease we assume the lessor is actually selling its product. Consistent with reporting sales of products under installment sales agreements rather than lease agreements, the lessor reports cash receipts from a sales-type lease as cash inflows from operating activities.

At the beginning of the lease, the lessor reports the lease as a noncash investing activity (acquiring one asset and disposing of another) in the disclosure notes to the financial statements.

Lease Disclosures

Lease disclosure requirements are quite extensive for both the lessor and lessee. Virtually all aspects of the lease agreement must be disclosed. The guiding objective is that lessees and lessors provide disclosures that enable users of financial statements to assess the *amount, timing,* and *uncertainty* of cash flows arising from leases. Information disclosed is both qualitative and quantitative.

Qualitative Disclosures

A general description of the leasing arrangement is required, including information about variable lease payments, options, nonlease payments, and residual values. A reason for excluding variable lease payments from the measurement of the lessee's lease liability and the lessor's receivable is that they could result in unreliable measurements in the financial statements. Disclosing information in notes to financial statements about variable lease payments would be more useful than estimating and including the payments in assets and liabilities.

Quantitative Disclosures

LESSEE

- Finance lease costs, with separate disclosure of interest and amortization. (The total of these two is reported together in the income statement as lease expense.)
- Operating lease cost.
- Short term lease cost.
- Variable lease cost.
- Weighted average lease term of operating leases and finance leases.
- Weighted average discount rate.
- A reconciliation of opening and closing balances of the right-of-use asset.
- Contractual obligations (and options that the lessee is "reasonably certain" to exercise) for each of the five succeeding fiscal years, plus a total for the remaining years.
- Table of future lease payments, segregated by type of lease, for each of the next five years, and total of payments for the remaining years, and (for finance leases) reconciled with the balance sheet liabilities.

LESSOR

- Information about lease contracts and significant assumptions and judgments.
- Table of lease revenues received.
- Lease sales disclosed separately from regular sales.

- Table of future lease payments, segregated by type of lease, for each of the next five years, and total of payments thereafter and (for sales-type leases) reconciled with the balance sheet receivables.
- Information about assets under operating lease.
- Information about risks associated with residual values.
- Information about significant changes in unguaranteed residual values.
- The gross investment and net investment in leases.

Financial Reporting Case Solution

© Pressmaster/ Shutterstock

1. **Are there advantages of leasing its equipment that HG should consider?** *(p. 834)* Leasing can offer many benefits. Leasing allows a company to acquire the use of an asset without having to pay the entire purchase price upfront. Leasing also can avoid a time-consuming purchase process. Also, if obsolescence is a concern, as it is for HG, leasing facilitates frequent replacement of assets.
2. **Would the effect on HG's income statement be the same if finance leases replace operating leases?** *(p. 841)* Finance leases involve the "front loading" of lease expense due to the fact that interest expense is higher initially than it is in the later years of a lease, while amortization expense for the right-of-use asset remains the same each period. Straight-line lease expense that occurs with operating leases defers expense recognition, making net income higher in the early years of the lease. ●

The Bottom Line

- **LO15–1** In keeping with the concept of substance over form, a lease is accounted for as either a rental agreement or a purchase/sale accompanied by debt financing. A lessee should classify a lease transaction as a finance lease if one or more of five classification criteria is met, and a lessor should record the lease as a sales-type lease. If none of the five criteria is met, both the lessee and the lessor classify the lease as an operating lease. The criteria are used to identify situations when the lease is economically similar to the purchase of an asset because the lessee obtains control of the underlying asset, meaning the ability to direct the use of the asset and obtain substantially all of its remaining benefits, in contrast to merely obtaining control over the use of the asset for a period of time. *(p. 832)*
- **LO15–2** When a lease is classified as a finance lease from the lessee's perspective and a sales-type lease from the lessor's perspective, (1) the lessee records a right-of-use asset and lease liability for the present value of the lease payments, and (2) the lessor records a lease receivable for the same amount and removes the asset from its books. The lessor recognizes interest revenue and the lessee recognizes interest expense at the effective rate times the outstanding balance. The lessee amortizes the right-of-use asset on a straight line basis. For an operating lease, the two components, interest and amortization, are shown as one lease expense in the income statement *(p. 836)*
- **LO15–3** The lessor records sales revenue and cost of goods sold for a sales-type lease with a selling profit. That happens when the present value of the lease payments exceeds the asset's carrying value. *(p. 841)*
- **LO15–4** In an operating lease, a sale is not recorded by the lessor. Instead, the periodic lease payments are accounted for as rent revenue by the lessor. The lessee records a right-of-use asset and lease liability at the present value of the lease payments. Interest expense is recognized at the effective rate times the outstanding balance. Amortization of the right-of-use asset is determined as the amount needed to cause the total lease expense (interest plus amortization) to be a straight-line amount equal to the lease payment. *(p. 843)*
- **LO15–5** In a lease of 12 months or less, the lessee can elect not to record a right-of-use asset and lease payable at the beginning of the lease term, but instead simply record lease payments as expense as they occur (short-cut method). *(p. 849)*
- **LO15–6** The lease term is the contractual lease term modified by any renewal or termination options that are reasonably certain to be exercised or not exercised. Options whose exercise is under the control of the

lessor are automatically included. Lease payments include payments resulting from those options as well as excess guaranteed residual values. The calculation of the present value of lease payments at the beginning of the lease does not include any variable lease payments, unless those payments are "in-substance fixed payments" or if they are based solely on an index or rate. *(p. 850)*

LO15–7 Nonlease components that are included in periodic lease payments (like maintenance) to be paid by the lessor are, in effect, indirectly paid by the lessee—and are expensed by the lessee. Insurance and property taxes included in periodic lease payments, however, do not transfer a good or service to the lessee and thus are considered part of lease payments. Initial direct costs incurred by the lessee are added to the right-of-use asset. If incurred by the lessor, they are recorded as a selling expense in a sales-type lease with a selling profit or expensed over the lease term in a sales-type lease with no selling profit or in an operating lease. The cost of a leasehold improvement is depreciated over its useful life to the lessee. *(p. 861)*

LO15–8 We report all cash flows as operating cash flows, except the principal portion of each payment in a finance lease, which is a cash flow from financing activities. Extensive disclosure requirements for lessees and lessors are designed to enable users of financial statements to assess the amount, timing, and uncertainty of cash flows arising from leases. *(p. 867)*

LO15–9 Accounting for leases is similar in most respects under U.S. GAAP or IFRS. The primary difference is that IFRS treats all leases as finance leases by the lessee. *(pp. 849* and *853)*

APPENDIX 15 Sale-Leaseback Arrangements

In a sale-leaseback transaction, the owner of an asset sells it and immediately leases it back from the new owner. Sound strange? Maybe, but this arrangement is common. In a sale-leaseback transaction two things happen:

1. The seller-lessee receives cash from the sale of the asset.
2. The seller-lessee pays periodic rent payments to the buyer-lessor to retain the use of the asset.

What motivates this kind of arrangement? The two most common reasons are: (a) if the asset had been financed originally with debt and interest rates have fallen, the sale-leaseback transaction can be used to effectively refinance at a lower rate; or (b) the most likely motivation for a sale-leaseback transaction is to generate cash.

We account for this type of arrangement in one of two ways.

- **Sale-Leaseback Approach.** Record the sale of the asset (with any accompanying gain or loss) and then record a lease for the leaseback portion in accordance with the lease guidance described earlier in this chapter. As we see below, though, if the leaseback qualifies as a finance lease, no sale has occurred and this approach cannot be applied. Thus, the sale-leaseback approach is allowed only if the leaseback qualifies as an operating lease.
- **Financing Arrangement.** View the arrangement, not as a sale, but as a loan by the lessor to the lessee for the "sale" price. The asset remains on the lessee's books, and the leaseback is accounted for as debt. The "lease" payments are deemed to be repayment of the loan.

We apply the sale-leaseback approach only if the usual requirements for revenue recognition (Chapter 5) are met (so the sale can be recorded), and it's not a finance lease, which would indicate the asset is effectively sold back to the lessee.[20]

[20]More specifically, ***none*** of the following conditions can be present if sale-leaseback accounting is to be used:

The seller-lessee has an option to buy back the asset at any price other than fair value (and other similar items must be available to buy).

The buyer-lessor has the option to sell the asset back to the seller-lessee that the buyer-lessor is "reasonably certain" to exercise.

The leaseback term is for 75% of the remaining economic life of the asset.

The present value of the lease payments accounts for 90% of the fair value of the asset.

If the transaction does not qualify for sale-leaseback accounting, both the companies account for it as a financing arrangement. The reasoning for allowing sale-leaseback accounting only for situations in which the leaseback qualifies as an operating lease is quite logical when we remember the primary distinction between a finance lease and an operating lease. A finance lease is substantively a "sale," so if this is the nature of a leaseback, then we have a sale by the lessee and then a sale back to the lessee, so we really have no sale at all. Essentially, the asset still belongs to the lessee, and cash comes to the lessee at the time of the transaction which is paid back in the form of periodic "lease payments." Of course, this is the nature of a loan, so we account for it that way.

Recording a sale-leaseback transaction follows the basic accounting concept of substance over form.

Illustration 15–A1 demonstrates a sale-leaseback involving a leaseback that qualifies as an operating lease.

Illustration 15–A1
Sale-Leaseback

Teledyne Distribution Center was in need of cash. Its solution: sell its four warehouses for $1,000,000, their fair value, and then lease back the warehouses to continue using them. The warehouses had a carrying value on Teledyne's books of $900,000 (original cost $1,200,000). Other information:

1. The sale date is December 31, 2018.
2. The noncancelable lease term is 10 years and requires annual payments of $118,360 beginning December 31, 2018. The estimated remaining useful life of the warehouses is 15 years.
3. The annual lease payments (present value $800,000) provides the lessor with a 10% rate of return on the financing arrangement.*

December 31, 2018

Cash	1,000,000	
Accumulated depreciation ($1,200,000 − 900,000)	300,000	
Warehouses (cost)		1,200,000
Gain on sale-leaseback (difference)		100,000
Right-of-use asset (present value of lease payments)	800,000	
Lease payable (present value of lease payments)		800,000
Lease payable	118,360	
Cash		118,360

December 31, 2019

Interest expense [10% × ($800,000 − 118,360)]	68,164	
Lease payable (difference)	50,196	
Cash (lease payment)		118,360
Amortization expense ($118,360 − 68,164)	50,196	
Right-of-use asset		50,196

*$118,360 lease payments × 6.75902 (from Table 6) $n = 10, i = 10\%$ = $800,000 ($799,997.61 rounded) Present value

The gain (or loss) on a sale-leaseback is recognized at the time of the sale.

In an operating lease, the lessee records interest the normal way and then "plugs" the amortization at whatever amount is needed for interest plus amortization to equal the *straight-line* lease payment.

Since none of the criteria for a finance lease is met, the leaseback is recorded by the lessee as an operating lease.[21] The sale-leaseback, then, is deemed to be two distinct transactions: a legitimate sale creating a $100,000 gain and then an operating lease. On the flip side of the transaction, the lessor would record the purchase of a $1,000,000 asset and then record lease revenue of $118,360 each year over the term of the lease.

But now suppose the remaining useful life is 12 years instead of 15 and that the ten lease payments are $147,950, creating a present value of $1,000,000 instead of $800,000. According to the criteria in Illustration 15–2, either of those circumstances would require that the arrangement be accounted for as a finance lease, instead of an operating lease. As such, the transaction does not qualify for sale-leaseback accounting. We would view the arrangement,

[21]The lease term is less than the major part of the expected useful life of the warehouses (67%). Also, the present value of lease payments ($800,000) is less than substantially all of the fair value of the warehouses ($1,000,000). None of the other three of the five criteria is present.

not as a sale, but as a loan by the lessor to the lessee for the $1,000,000 "sale" price. The asset remains on the lessee's books. The "lease" payments would be considered to be repayment of the loan. It would be recorded as shown in Illustration 15–A2.

Illustration 15–A2

Sale-Leaseback Deemed to Be a Loan

Though structured as a sale and then a lease, in substance, the lessee is actually borrowing $1,000,000.

The "lease" payments would be considered to be repayment of the loan.

December 31, 2018		
Cash	1,000,000	
Note payable		1,000,000
Note payable	147,950	
Cash		147,950
December 31, 2019		
Interest expense [10% × ($1,000,000 – 147,950)]	85,205	
Note payable (difference)	62,745	
Cash (lease payment)		147,950

Questions For Review of Key Topics

Q 15–1 The basic concept of "substance over form" influences lease accounting. Explain.

Q 15–2 How is interest expense determined in a finance lease transaction? How does the approach compare to other forms of debt (such as bonds payable or notes payable)?

Q 15–3 How are leases and installment notes the same? How do they differ?

Q 15–4 A lessee should classify a lease transaction as a finance lease if it is noncancelable and one or more of five classification criteria are met. Otherwise, it is an operating lease. What are these criteria?

Q 15–5 Lukawitz Industries leased non-specialized equipment to Seminole Corporation for a four-year period, at which time possession of the leased asset will revert back to Lukawitz. The equipment cost Lukawitz $4 million and has an expected useful life of six years. Its normal sales price is $5.6 million. The present value of the lease payments for both the lessor and lessee is $5.2 million. The first payment was made at the beginning of the lease. How should this lease be classified (a) by Lukawitz Industries (the lessor) and (b) by Seminole Corporation (the lessee)? Why?

Q 15–6 In accounting for a finance lease/sales-type lease, how are the lessee's and lessor's income statements affected?

Q 15–7 What is selling profit on a sales-type lease? How do we account for a sales-type lease with a selling profit?

Q 15–8 At the beginning of an operating lease, the lessee will record what asset and liability, if any?

Q 15–9 At the beginning of an operating lease, the lessor will record what asset or assets, if any?

Q 15–10 In accounting for an operating lease, how are the lessee's and lessor's income statements affected?

Q 15–11 Briefly describe the conceptual basis for asset and liability recognition under the right-of-use approach used by the lessee in a lease transaction.

Q 15–12 In a financing lease, "front loading" of lease expense and lease revenue occurs. What does this mean, and how is it avoided in an operating lease?

Q 15–13 The discount rate influences virtually every amount reported in connection with a lease by both the lessor and the lessee. What is the lessor's discount rate when determining the present value of lease payments? What is the lessee's discount rate?

Q 15–14 A lease that has a lease term (including any options to terminate or renew that are reasonably certain) of twelve months or less is considered a "short-term lease." How does a lessee record a lease using the short-cut approach available as an option for short-term leases?

Q 15–15 A lease might specify that lease payments may be increased (or decreased) at some future time during the lease term depending on whether or not some specified event occurs such as revenues or profits exceeding some designated level. Under what circumstances are contingent rentals included or excluded from lease payments? If excluded, how are they recognized in income determination?

Q 15–16 What is a purchase option? How does it affect accounting for a lease?

Q 15–17 A six-year lease can be renewed for two additional three-year periods, and it also can be terminated after only three years. How do the lessee and lessor decide the lease term to be used in accounting for the lease?

Q 15–18 Culinary Creations leased kitchen equipment under a five-year lease with an option to renew for three years at the end of five years and an option to renew for an additional three years at the end of eight years. The first three-year renewal option can be exercised for one-half the original and usual rate. What is the length of the lease term that Culinary Creations should assume in recording the transactions related to the lease?

Q 15–19 What situations cause us to remeasure a lease liability and right-of-use asset? How is that accomplished?

Q 15–20 Occasionally, a lease agreement includes a guarantee by the lessee that the lessor will recover a specified residual value when custody of the asset reverts back to the lessor at the end of the lease term. Under what circumstance can the guaranteed residual value influence the amounts recorded by the lessee and lessor? In that circumstance, how are the amounts affected?

Q 15–21 Compare the way a purchase option that is reasonably certain to be exercised and a lessee-guaranteed residual value are treated by the lessee and lessor when determining lease payments.

Q 15–22 What nonlease costs might be included as part of lease payments? How are they accounted for by the lessee in a finance lease when paid by the lessee? When paid by the lessor? Explain.

Q 15–23 The lessor's initial direct costs often are substantial. What are initial direct costs?

Q 15–24 When are initial direct costs recognized in an operating lease? In a sales-type lease with selling profit? In a sales-type lease with no selling profit? Why?

Q 15–25 What is the primary objective of the required lease disclosures for the lessor and lessee?

Q 15–26 Where can we find authoritative guidance for accounting for leases under IFRS?

Q 15–27 Could a finance lease under IFRS be classified as an operating lease under U.S. GAAP? Explain.

Q 15–28 When a company sells an asset and simultaneously leases it back, what criteria must be met to apply sale-leaseback accounting rather than accounting for the transaction as a loan ?

Q 15–29 Zimmern Machines sold equipment with a 10-year economic life to Bourdain Acres, while concurrently entering into an 8-year leaseback. Eight years is considered a major part of the economic life of the equipment. The sale agreement contains no option for Zimmern to repurchase the equipment or any other provision that would prevent its sale. Can Zimmern Machines account for the transaction as a sale-leaseback? Why?

Brief Exercises

connect

BE 15–1
Lease classification
● LO15–1

(Note: Brief Exercises 1 and 2 are two variations of the same basic situation.)
Corinth Co. leased nonspecialized equipment to Athens Corporation for an eight-year period, at which time possession of the equipment will revert back to Corinth. The equipment cost Corinth $16 million and has an expected useful life of 12 years. Its normal sales price is $22.4 million. The present value of the lease payments for both the lessor and lessee is $20.6 million. The first payment was made at the beginning of the lease. How should Corinth classify this lease? Why?

BE 15–2
Lease classification
● LO15–1, LO15–2

Corinth Co. leased nonspecialized equipment to Athens Corporation for an eight-year period, at which time possession of the equipment will revert back to Corinth. The equipment cost Corinth $16 million and has an expected useful life of 12 years. Its normal sales price is $22.4 million. The present value of the lease payments for both the lessor and lessee is $20.6 million. The first payment was made at the beginning of the lease. How should Athens classify this lease? Why?

BE 15–3
Lessee and lessor; calculate interest; finance/sales-type lease
● LO15–2

A finance lease agreement calls for quarterly lease payments of $5,376 over a 10-year lease term, with the first payment on July 1, the beginning of the lease. The annual interest rate is 8%. Both the present value of the lease payments and the cost of the asset to the lessor are $150,000. What would be the amount of interest expense the lessee would record in conjunction with the second quarterly payment on October 1? What would be the amount of interest revenue the lessor would record in conjunction with the second quarterly payment on October 1?

BE 15–4
Finance lease; lessee; balance sheet effects
● LO15–2

(Note: Brief Exercises 4, 5, and 6 are three variations of the same basic situation.)
A lease agreement that qualifies as a finance lease calls for annual lease payments of $26,269 over a six-year lease term (also the asset's useful life), with the first payment at January 1, the beginning of the lease. The interest rate is 5%. If the lessee's fiscal year is the calendar year, what would be the amount of the lease liability that the lessee would report in its balance sheet at the end of the first year? What would be the interest payable?

BE 15–5
Finance lease; lessee; income statement effects
● LO15–2

A lease agreement that qualifies as a finance lease calls for annual lease payments of $26,269 over a six-year lease term (also the asset's useful life), with the first payment at January 1, the beginning of the lease. The interest rate is 5%. If the lessee's fiscal year is the calendar year, what would be the amounts related to the lease that the lessee would report in its income statement for the year ended December 31 (ignore taxes)?

BE 15–6
Sales-type lease; lessor; income statement effects
● LO15–3

A lease agreement that qualifies as a finance lease calls for annual lease payments of $26,269 over a six-year lease term (also the asset's useful life), with the first payment at January 1, the beginning of the lease. The interest rate is 5%. The lessor's fiscal year is the calendar year. The lessor manufactured this asset at a cost of $125,000. What would be the amounts related to the lease that the lessor would report in its income statement for the year ended December 31 (ignore taxes)?

BE 15–7
Sales-type lease; lessor; calculate lease payments
● LO15–3

Manning Imports is contemplating an agreement to lease equipment to a customer for five years. Manning normally sells the asset for a cash price of $100,000. Assuming that 8% is a reasonable rate of interest, what must be the amount of quarterly lease payments (beginning at the commencement of the lease) in order for Manning to recover its normal selling price as well as be compensated for financing the asset over the lease term?

BE 15–8
Operating lease
● LO15–4

(Note: Brief Exercises 8 and 9 are two variations of the same basic situation.)
At the beginning of its fiscal year, Lakeside Inc. leased office space to LTT Corporation under a seven-year operating lease agreement. The contract calls for quarterly rent payments of $25,000 each. The office building was acquired by Lakeside at a cost of $2 million and was expected to have a useful life of 25 years with no residual value. What will be the effect of the lease on LTT's earnings for the first year (ignore taxes)?

BE 15–9
Operating lease
● LO15–4

At the beginning of its fiscal year, Lakeside Inc. leased office space to LTT Corporation under a seven-year operating lease agreement. The contract calls for quarterly rent payments of $25,000 each. The office building was acquired by Lakeside at a cost of $2 million and was expected to have a useful life of 25 years with no residual value. What will be the effect of the lease on Lakeside's earnings for the first year (ignore taxes)?

BE 15–10
Short-term lease
● LO15–5

King Cones leased ice cream-making equipment from Ace Leasing. Ace earns interest under such arrangements at a 6% annual rate. The lease term is eight months with monthly payments of $10,000 due at the end of each month. King Cones elected the short-term lease option. What is the effect of the lease on King Cones' earnings during the eight-month term (ignore taxes)?

BE 15–11
Uncertain lease term
● LO15–6

Java Hut leased a specialty expresso machine for a 10-year noncancelable term. At the end of the 10-year term, Java Hut has four consecutive one-year renewal options. A replacement machine can be acquired, but due to an expensive installation process and Java Hut's lease term for its store, Java Hut expects to lease the machine for 12 years. What is the lease term?

BE 15–12
Uncertain lease payments
● LO15–6

On January 1, Espinoza Moving and Storage leased a truck for a four-year period, at which time possession of the truck will revert back to the lessor. Annual lease payments are $10,000 due on December 31 of each year, calculated by the lessor using a 5% discount rate. If Espinoza's revenues exceed a specified amount during the lease term, Espinoza will pay an additional $4,000 lease payment at the end of the lease. Espinoza estimates a 60% probability of meeting the target revenue amount. What amount, if any, should be added to the right-of-use asset and lease liability under the contingent rent agreement?

BE 15–13
Purchase option; lessor; sales-type lease
● LO15–2, LO15–3, LO15–6

Ace Leasing acquires equipment and leases it to customers under long-term sales-type leases. Ace earns interest under these arrangements at a 6% annual rate. Ace leased a machine it purchased for $600,000 under an arrangement that specified annual payments beginning at the commencement of the lease for five years. The lessee had the option to purchase the machine at the end of the lease term for $100,000 when it was expected to have a residual value of $160,000. Calculate the amount of the annual lease payments.

BE 15–14
Residual value; sales-type lease
● LO15–2, LO15–3, LO15–6

On January 1, James Industries leased equipment to a customer for a four-year period, at which time possession of the leased asset will revert back to James. The equipment cost James $700,000 and has an expected useful life of six years. Its normal sales price is $700,000. The residual value after four years is $100,000. Lease payments are due on December 31 of each year, beginning with the first payment at the end of the first year. The interest rate is 5%. Calculate the amount of the annual lease payments.

BE 15–15
Guaranteed residual value
● LO15–6

On January 1, Garcia Supply leased a truck for a four-year period, at which time possession of the truck will revert back to the lessor. Annual lease payments are $10,000 due on December 31 of each year, calculated by the lessor using a 5% discount rate. Negotiations led to Garcia guaranteeing a $36,000 residual value at the end of the lease term. Garcia estimates that the residual value after four years will be $35,000. What is the amount to be added to the right-of-use asset and lease liability under the residual value guarantee?

BE 15–16
Lessor's initial direct costs; sales-type lease
● LO15–3, LO15–7

Bryant leased equipment that had a retail cash selling price of $600,000 and a useful life of five years with no residual value. The lessor paid $530,000 to acquire the equipment and used an implicit rate of 8% when calculating annual lease payments of $139,142 beginning January 1, the beginning of the lease. Lease payments will be made January 1 each year of the lease. Incremental costs of consummating the lease transaction incurred by the lessor were $15,000. What is the effect of the lease on the lessor's earnings during the first year (ignore taxes)?

BE 15–17
Nonlease payments
● LO15–2, LO15–7

On January 1, 2018, Jasperse Corporation leased equipment under a finance lease designed to earn the lessor a 12% rate of return for providing long-term financing. The lease agreement specified ten annual payments of $75,000 beginning January 1, and each December 31 thereafter through 2026. A 10-year service agreement was scheduled to provide maintenance of the equipment as required for a fee of $5,000 per year. Insurance premiums of $4,000 annually are related to the equipment. Both amounts were to be paid by the lessor and lease payments reflect both expenditures. At what amount will Jasperse record a right-of-use asset?

Exercises

connect

E 15–1
Lease classification
● LO15–1

Each of the four independent situations below describes a lease requiring annual lease payments of $10,000. For each situation, determine the appropriate lease classification by the lessee and indicate why.

	Situation			
	1	2	3	4
Lease term (years)	4	4	4	4
Asset's useful life (years)	6	5	6	6
Asset's fair value	$44,000	$43,000	$41,000	$39,000
Purchase option that is reasonably certain to be exercised?	No	Yes	No	No
Annual lease payments	Beg. of yr.	End of yr.	Beg. of yr.	End of yr.
Lessor's implicit rate (known by lessee)	5%	6%	5%	6%
Lessee's incremental borrowing rate	5%	5%	5%	5%

E 15–2
Finance lease; calculate lease payments
● LO15–2

American Food Services, Inc. leased a packaging machine from Barton and Barton Corporation. Barton and Barton completed construction of the machine on January 1, 2018. The lease agreement for the $4 million (fair value and present value of the lease payments) machine specified four equal payments at the end of each year. The useful life of the machine was expected to be four years with no residual value. Barton and Barton's implicit interest rate was 10%.

Required:

1. Prepare the journal entry for American Food Services at the beginning of the lease on January 1, 2018.
2. Prepare an amortization schedule for the four-year term of the lease.
3. Prepare the appropriate entries related to the lease on December 31, 2018.
4. Prepare the appropriate entries related to the lease on December 31, 2020.

(Note: You may wish to compare your solution to this exercise with that of E 14–18 which deals with a parallel situation in which the packaging machine was acquired with an installment note.)

E 15–3
Finance lease; lessee; balance sheet and income statement effects
● LO15–2

(Note: Exercises 3, 4, and 5 are three variations of the same situation.)

On June 30, 2018, Georgia-Atlantic, Inc. leased a warehouse facility from IC Leasing Corporation. The lease agreement calls for Georgia-Atlantic to make semiannual lease payments of $562,907 over a three-year lease term, payable each June 30 and December 31, with the first payment at June 30, 2018. Georgia-Atlantic's incremental borrowing rate is 10%, the same rate IC uses to calculate lease payment amounts. Depreciation is recorded on a straight-line basis at the end of each fiscal year. The fair value of the warehouse is $3 million.

Required:

1. Determine the present value of the lease payments at June 30, 2018 (to the nearest $000) that Georgia-Atlantic uses to record the right-of-use asset and lease liability.
2. What amounts related to the lease would Georgia-Atlantic report in its balance sheet at December 31, 2018 (ignore taxes)?
3. What amounts related to the lease would Georgia-Atlantic report in its income statement for the year ended December 31, 2018 (ignore taxes)?

E 15–4
Sales-type lease; lessor; balance sheet and income statement effects
● LO15–2

On June 30, 2018, Georgia-Atlantic, Inc. leased warehouse equipment from IC Leasing Corporation. The lease agreement calls for Georgia-Atlantic to make semiannual lease payments of $562,907 over a three-year lease term, payable each June 30 and December 31, with the first payment at June 30, 2018. Georgia-Atlantic's incremental borrowing rate is 10%, the same rate IC used to calculate lease payment amounts. IC purchased the warehouse from Builders, Inc. at a cost of $3 million.

Required:

1. What amounts related to the lease would IC report in its balance sheet at December 31, 2018 (ignore taxes)?
2. What amounts related to the lease would IC report in its income statement for the year ended December 31, 2018 (ignore taxes)?

E 15–5
Sales-type lease; lessor; balance sheet and income statement effects
● LO15–3

On June 30, 2018, Georgia-Atlantic, Inc. leased warehouse equipment from Builders, Inc. The lease agreement calls for Georgia-Atlantic to make semiannual lease payments of $562,907 over a three-year lease term, payable each June 30 and December 31, with the first payment at June 30, 2018. Georgia-Atlantic's incremental borrowing rate is 10%, the same rate Builders used to calculate lease payment amounts. Builders manufactured the equipment at a cost of $2.5 million.

Required:

1. Determine the price at which Builders is "selling" the equipment (present value of the lease payments) at June 30, 2018 (to the nearest $000).
2. What amounts related to the lease would Builders report in its balance sheet at December 31, 2018 (ignore taxes)?
3. What amounts related to the lease would Builders report in its income statement for the year ended December 31, 2018 (ignore taxes)?

E 15–6
Finance lease; lessee
● LO15–2

(Note: Exercises 6, 7, and 8 are three variations of the same basic situation.)
Manufacturers Southern leased high-tech electronic equipment from Edison Leasing on January 1, 2018. Edison purchased the equipment from International Machines at a cost of $112,080.

Related Information:	
Lease term	2 years (8 quarterly periods)
Quarterly rental payments	$15,000 at the beginning of each period
Economic life of asset	2 years
Fair value of asset	$112,080
Implicit interest rate	8%
(Also lessee's incremental borrowing rate)	

Required:

Prepare a lease amortization schedule and appropriate entries for Manufacturers Southern from the beginning of the lease through January 1, 2019. Depreciation is recorded at the end of each fiscal year (December 31) on a straight-line basis.

E 15–7
Sales-type lease with no selling profit; lessor
● LO15–2

Edison Leasing leased high-tech electronic equipment to Manufacturers Southern on January 1, 2018. Edison purchased the equipment from International Machines at a cost of $112,080.

Related Information:	
Lease term	2 years (8 quarterly periods)
Quarterly rental payments	$15,000 at the beginning of each period
Economic life of asset	2 years
Fair value of asset	$112,080
Implicit interest rate	8%
(Also lessee's incremental borrowing rate)	

Required:

Prepare a lease amortization schedule and appropriate entries for Edison Leasing from the beginning of the lease through January 1, 2019. Edison's fiscal year ends December 31.

E 15–8
Sales-type lease with selling profit; lessor; calculate lease payments
● LO15–3

Manufacturers Southern leased high-tech electronic equipment from International Machines on January 1, 2018. International Machines manufactured the equipment at a cost of $85,000. Manufacturers Southern's fiscal year ends December 31.

Related Information:	
Lease term	2 years (8 quarterly periods)
Quarterly rental payments	$15,000 at the beginning of each period
Economic life of asset	2 years
Fair value of asset	$112,080
Implicit interest rate	8%

Required:

1. Show how International Machines determined the $15,000 quarterly lease payments.
2. Prepare appropriate entries for International Machines to record the lease at its beginning, January 1, 2018, and the second lease payment on April 1, 2018.

E 15–9
Lessor calculation of annual lease payments; lessee calculation of asset and liability
● LO15–2

Each of the three independent situations below describes a finance lease in which annual lease payments are payable at the beginning of each year. The lessee is aware of the lessor's implicit rate of return.

	Situation		
	1	2	3
Lease term (years)	10	20	4
Lessor's rate of return (known by lessee)	11%	9%	12%
Lessee's incremental borrowing rate	12%	10%	10%
Fair value of lease asset	$600,000	$980,000	$185,000

Required:

For each situation, determine:

a. The amount of the annual lease payments as calculated by the lessor.
b. The amount the lessee would record as a right-of-use asset and a lease liability.

E 15–10
Lessor calculation of annual lease payments; lessee calculation of asset and liability
● LO15–2

(Note: This is a variation of E 15-9 modified to assume lease payments are at the end of each period.)
Each of the three independent situations below describes a finance lease in which annual lease payments are payable at the *end* of each year. The lessee is aware of the lessor's implicit rate of return.

	Situation		
	1	2	3
Lease term (years)	10	20	4
Lessor's rate of return	11%	9%	12%
Lessee's incremental borrowing rate	12%	10%	10%
Fair value of lease asset	$600,000	$980,000	$185,000

Required:

For each situation, determine:

a. The amount of the annual lease payments as calculated by the lessor.
b. The amount the lessee would record as a right-of-use asset and a lease liability.

E 15–11
Lessee and lessor; sales-type lease with selling profit
● LO15–2, LO15–3

Eye Deal Optometry leased vision-testing equipment from Insight Machines on January 1, 2018. Insight Machines manufactured the equipment at a cost of $200,000 and lists a cash selling price of $250,177. Appropriate adjusting entries are made quarterly.

Related Information:	
Lease term	5 years (20 quarterly periods)
Quarterly lease payments	$15,000 at Jan. 1, 2018, and at Mar. 31, June 30, Sept. 30, and Dec. 31 thereafter
Economic life of asset	5 years
Interest rate charged by the lessor	8%

Required:

1. Prepare appropriate entries for Eye Deal to record the arrangement at its beginning, January 1, 2018, and on March 31, 2018.
2. Prepare appropriate entries for Insight Machines to record the arrangement at its beginning, January 1, 2018, and on March 31, 2018.

E 15–12
Lessee; finance lease; effect on financial statements
● LO15–2

(Note: Exercises 12, 13, 14, and 25 are variations of the same situation.)
At January 1, 2018, Café Med leased restaurant equipment from Crescent Corporation under a nine-year lease agreement. The lease agreement specifies annual payments of $25,000 beginning January 1, 2018, the beginning of the lease, and at each December 31 thereafter through 2025. The equipment was acquired recently by Crescent at a cost of $180,000 (its fair value) and was expected to have a useful life of 12 years with no salvage value at the end of its life. (Because the lease term is only nine years, the asset does have an expected residual value at the end of the lease term of $90,995.) Crescent seeks a 10% return on its lease investments. By this arrangement, the lease is deemed to be a finance lease.

Required:

1. What will be the effect of the lease on Café Med's earnings for the first year (ignore taxes)?
2. What will be the balances in the balance sheet accounts related to the lease at the end of the first year of Café Med (ignore taxes)?

E 15–13
Lessee; operating lease; effect on financial statements
● LO15–4

At January 1, 2018, Café Med leased restaurant equipment from Crescent Corporation under a nine-year lease agreement. The lease agreement specifies annual payments of $25,000 beginning January 1, 2018, the beginning of the lease, and at each December 31 thereafter through 2025. The equipment was acquired recently by Crescent at a cost of $180,000 (its fair value) and was expected to have a useful life of 13 years with no salvage value at the end of its life. (Because the lease term is only nine years, the asset does have an expected residual value at the end of the lease term of $90,995.) Crescent seeks a 10% return on its lease investments. By this arrangement, the lease is deemed to be an operating lease.

Required:

1. What will be the effect of the lease on Café Med's earnings for the first year (ignore taxes)?
2. What will be the balances in the balance sheet accounts related to the lease at the end of the first year for Café Med (ignore taxes)?

E 15–14
Lessor; operating lease; effect on financial statements
● LO15–4

At January 1, 2018, Café Med leased restaurant equipment from Crescent Corporation under a nine-year lease agreement. The lease agreement specifies annual payments of $25,000 beginning January 1, 2018, the beginning of the lease, and at each December 31 thereafter through 2025. The equipment was acquired recently by Crescent at a cost of $180,000 (its fair value) and was expected to have a useful life of 13 years with no salvage value at the end of its life. (Because the lease term is only nine years, the asset does have an expected residual value at the end of the lease term of $90,995.) Crescent seeks a 10% return on its lease investments. By this arrangement, the lease is deemed to be an operating lease.

Required:

1. What will be the effect of the lease on Crescent's (lessor's) earnings for the first year (ignore taxes)?
2. What will be the balances in the balance sheet accounts related to the lease at the end of the first year for Crescent (ignore taxes)?

E 15–15
Sales-type lease; lessor; income statement effects
● LO15–3

King Company leased equipment from Mann Industries. The lease agreement qualifies as a finance lease and requires annual lease payments of $52,538 over a six-year lease term (also the asset's useful life), with the first payment at January 1, the beginning of the lease. The interest rate is 5%. The asset being leased cost Mann $230,000 to produce.

Required:

1. Determine the price at which the lessor is "selling" the asset (present value of the lease payments).
2. What would be the amounts related to the lease that the lessor would report in its income statement for the year ended December 31 (ignore taxes)?

E 15–16
Lessee; operating lease
● LO15–4

Grichuk Power leased high-tech electronic equipment from Kolten Leasing on January 1, 2018. Kolten purchased the equipment from Wong Machines at a cost of $112,080.

Related Information:	
Lease term	2 years (8 quarterly periods)
Quarterly lease payments	$15,000 at Jan. 1, 2018, and at Mar. 31, June 30, Sept. 30, and Dec. 31 thereafter
Economic life of asset	5 years
Interest rate charged by the lessor	8%

Required:

Prepare appropriate entries for Grichuk Power from the beginning of the lease through December 31, 2018. December 31 is the fiscal year end for each company. Appropriate adjusting entries are recorded at the end of each quarter.

E 15–17
Lessee and lessor; operating lease
● LO15–4

On January 1, 2018, Nath-Langstrom Services, Inc. a computer software training firm, leased several computers under a two-year operating lease agreement from ComputerWorld Leasing, which routinely finances equipment for other firms at an annual interest rate of 4%. The contract calls for four rent payments of $10,000 each, payable semiannually on June 30 and December 31 each year. The computers were acquired by ComputerWorld at a cost of $90,000 and were expected to have a useful life of five years with no residual value. Both firms record amortization and depreciation semiannually.

Required:

Prepare the appropriate entries for both (a) the lessee and (b) the lessor from the beginning of the lease through the end of 2018.

E 15–18
Short-term lease
● LO15–5

Chance Enterprises leased equipment from Third Bank Leasing on January 1, 2018. Chance purchased the equipment at a cost of $1,000,000. Chance elected the short-term lease option. Appropriate adjusting entries are made annually.

Related Information:	
Lease term	1 year (4 quarterly periods)
Quarterly lease payments	$40,000 at Jan. 1, 2018, and at Mar. 31, June 30, and Sept. 30
Economic life of asset	5 years
Interest rate charged by the lessor	8%

Required:
Prepare appropriate entries for Chance from the beginning of the lease through December 31, 2018.

E 15–19
Lessee; renewal option
● LO15–2, LO15–6

Natick Industries leased high-tech instruments from Framingham Leasing on January 1, 2018. Natick has the option to renew the lease at the end of two years for an additional three years. Natick is subject to a $45,000 penalty after two years if it fails to renew the lease. Framingham Leasing purchased the equipment from Waltham Machines at a cost of $250,177.

Related Information:	
Lease term	3 years (12 quarterly periods)
Lease renewal option for an additional	2 years (8 quarterly periods)
Quarterly lease payments	$15,000 at Jan. 1, 2018, and at Mar. 31, June 30, Sept. 30, and Dec. 31 thereafter
Economic life of asset	5 years
Interest rate charged by the lessor	8%

Required:
Prepare appropriate entries for Natick Industries from the beginning of the lease through March 31, 2018. Appropriate adjusting entries are made quarterly.

E 15–20
Variable lease payments
● LO15–2, LO15–6

On January 1, 2018, Wetick Optometrists leased diagnostic equipment from Southern Corp., which had purchased the equipment at a cost of $1,437,237. The lease agreement specifies six annual payments of $300,000 beginning January 1, 2018, the beginning of the lease, and at each December 31 thereafter through 2022. The six-year lease term ending December 31, 2023 (a year after the final payment), is equal to the estimated useful life of the equipment. The contract specifies that lease payments for each year will increase on the basis of the increase in the Consumer Price Index for the year just ended. Thus, the first payment will be $300,000, and the second and subsequent payments might be different. The CPI at the beginning of the lease is 120. Southern routinely acquires diagnostic equipment for lease to other firms. The interest rate in these financing arrangements is 10%.

Required:
1. Prepare the appropriate journal entries for Wetick and Southern to record the lease at its beginning.
2. Assuming the CPI is 124 at that time, prepare the appropriate journal entries related to the lease for Wetick at December 31, 2018,.

E 15–21
Lessee; variable lease payments
● LO15–2, LO15–6

On January 1, 2018, QuickStream Communications leased telephone equipment from Digium, Inc. Digium's cash selling price for the equipment is $1,306,578. The lease agreement specifies six annual payments of $300,000 beginning December 31, 2018, and at each December 31 thereafter through 2023. The six-year lease is equal to the estimated useful life of the equipment. The contract specifies that lease payments for each year will increase by the higher of (a) the increase in the Consumer Price Index for the preceding year or (b) 3%. The CPI at the beginning of the lease is 120. Digium routinely leases equipment to other firms. The interest rate in these lease arrangements is 10%.

Required:
Prepare the appropriate journal entries for QuickStream to record the lease at its beginning date of January 1, 2018.

E 15–22
Lessee; variable lease payments
● LO15–2, LO15–6

On January 1, 2018, Taco King leased retail space from Fogelman Properties. The 10-year finance lease requires quarterly variable lease payments equal to 3% of Taco King's sales revenue, with a quarterly sales minimum of $400,000. Payments at the beginning of each quarter are based on previous quarter sales. During the previous 5-year period, Taco King has generated quarterly sales of over $650,000. Fogelman's interest rate, known by Taco King, was 4%.

Required:
1. Prepare the journal entries for Taco King at the beginning of the lease at January 1, 2018.
2. Prepare the journal entries for Taco King at April 1, 2018. First quarter sales were $660,000. Amortization is recorded quarterly.

E 15–23
Lessee; renewal options
● LO15–2, LO15–6

On January 1, 2018, Rick's Pawn Shop leased a truck from Corey Motors for a six-year period with an option to extend the lease for three years. Rick's had no significant economic incentive as of the beginning of the lease to exercise the 3-year extension option. Annual lease payments are $10,000 due on December 31 of each year, calculated by the lessor using a 5% interest rate. The agreement is considered an operating lease.

Required:

1. Prepare Rick's journal entry to record for the right-of-use asset and lease liability at January 1, 2018.
2. Prepare the journal entries to record interest and amortization at December 31, 2018.

E 15–24
Calculation of annual lease payments; residual value
● LO15–2, LO15–6

Each of the four independent situations below describes a finance lease in which annual lease payments are payable at the beginning of each year. The lessee is aware of the lessor's implicit rate of return.

	Situation			
	1	2	3	4
Lease term (years)	4	7	5	8
Lessor's rate of return	10%	11%	9%	12%
Fair value of lease asset	$50,000	$350,000	$75,000	$465,000
Lessor's cost of lease asset	$50,000	$350,000	$45,000	$465,000
Residual value:				
Estimated fair value	0	$ 50,000	$ 7,000	$ 45,000
Guaranteed fair value	0	0	$ 7,000	$ 50,000

Required:

For each situation, determine:

a. The amount of the annual lease payments as calculated by the lessor.
b. The amount the lessee would record as a right-of-use asset and a lease liability.

E 15–25
Lessor; sales-type lease; residual value effect on financial statements
● LO15–2, LO15–6

At January 1, 2018, Café Med leased restaurant equipment from Crescent Corporation under a nine-year lease agreement. The lease agreement specifies annual payments of $25,000 beginning January 1, 2018, the beginning of the lease, and at each December 31 thereafter through 2025. The equipment was acquired recently by Crescent at a cost of $180,000 (its fair value) and was expected to have a useful life of 12 years with no salvage value at the end of its life. (Because the lease term is only 9 years, the asset does have an expected residual value at the end of the lease term of $50,995.). Both (a) the present value of the lease payments and (b) the present value of the residual value (i.e., the residual asset) are included in the lease receivable because the two amounts combine to allow the lessor to recover its net investment. Crescent seeks a 10% return on its lease investments. By this arrangement, the lease is deemed to be a finance lease.

Required:

1. What will be the effect of the lease on Crescent's earnings for the first year (ignore taxes)?
2. What will be the balances in the balance sheet accounts related to the lease at the end of the first year for Crescent (ignore taxes)?

E 15–26
Lease concepts; finance/sales-type leases; guaranteed and unguaranteed residual value
● LO15–2, LO15–6

Each of the four independent situations below describes a sales-type lease in which annual lease payments of $100,000 are payable at the beginning of each year. Each is a finance lease for the lessee. Determine the following amounts at the beginning of the lease:

A. The lessor's:
 1. Lease payments
 2. Gross investment in the lease
 3. Net investment in the lease

B. The lessee's:
 4. Lease payments
 5. Right-of-use asset
 6. Lease liability

	Situation			
	1	2	3	4
Lease term (years)	7	7	8	8
Lessor's and lessee's interest rate	9%	11%	10%	12%
Residual value:				
Estimated fair value	0	$50,000	$8,000	$50,000
Guaranteed by lessee	0	0	$8,000	$60,000

E 15–27
Lessee; lessee guaranteed residual value
● LO15–2, LO15–6

On January 1, 2018, Maywood Hydraulics leased drilling equipment from Aqua Leasing for a four-year period ending December 31, 2021, at which time possession of the leased asset will revert back to Aqua. The equipment cost Aqua $412,184 and has an expected economic life of five years. Aqua expects the residual value at December 31, 2021, to be $50,000. Negotiations led to Maywood guaranteeing a $70,000 residual value.

Equal payments under the lease are $100,000 and are due on December 31 of each year with the first payment being made on December 31, 2018. Maywood is aware that Aqua used a 5% interest rate when calculating lease payments.

Required:

1. Prepare the appropriate entry for Maywood on January 1, 2018, to record the lease.
2. Prepare all appropriate entries for Maywood on December 31, 2018, related to the lease.

E 15–28
Calculation of annual lease payments; purchase option
● LO15–2, LO15–6

For each of the three independent situations below determine the amount of the annual lease payments. Each describes a finance lease in which annual lease payments are payable at the beginning of each year. Each lease agreement contains an option that permits the lessee to acquire the leased asset at an option price that is sufficiently lower than the expected fair value that the exercise of the option appears reasonably certain.

	Situation		
	1	2	3
Lease term (years)	5	5	4
Lessor's rate of return	12%	11%	9%
Fair value of leased asset	$60,000	$420,000	$185,000
Lessor's cost of leased asset	$50,000	$420,000	$145,000
Purchase option:			
Exercise price	$10,000	$ 50,000	$ 22,000
Exercisable at end of year:	5	5	3
Reasonably certain?	yes	no	yes

E 15–29
Finance lease; purchase options; lessee
● LO15–2, LO15–6

Federated Fabrications leased a tooling machine on January 1, 2018, for a three-year period ending December 31, 2020. The lease agreement specified annual payments of $36,000 beginning with the first payment at the beginning of the lease, and each December 31 through 2019. The company had the option to purchase the machine on December 30, 2020, for $45,000 when its fair value was expected to be $60,000, a sufficient difference that exercise seems reasonably certain. The machine's estimated useful life was six years with no salvage value. Federated was aware that the lessor's implicit rate of return was 12%.

Required:

1. Calculate the amount Federated should record as a right-of-use asset and lease liability for this finance lease.
2. Prepare an amortization schedule that describes the pattern of interest expense for Federated over the lease term.
3. Prepare the appropriate entries for Federated from the beginning of the lease through the end of the lease term.

E 15–30
Purchase option; lessor; sales-type lease; no selling profit
● LO15–2, LO15–6

Universal Leasing leases electronic equipment to a variety of businesses. The company's primary service is providing alternate financing by acquiring equipment and leasing it to customers under long-term sales-type leases. Universal earns interest under these arrangements at a 10% annual rate.

The company leased an electronic typesetting machine it purchased for $30,900 to a local publisher, Desktop Inc. on December 31, 2017. The lease contract specified annual payments of $8,000 beginning January 1, 2018, the beginning of the lease, and each December 31 through 2019 (three-year lease term). The publisher had the option to purchase the machine on December 30, 2020, the end of the lease term, for $12,000 when it was expected to have a residual value of $16,000, a sufficient difference that exercise seems reasonably certain.

Required:

1. Show how Universal calculated the $8,000 annual lease payments for this sales-type lease.
2. Prepare an amortization schedule that describes the pattern of interest revenue for Universal Leasing over the lease term.
3. Prepare the appropriate entries for Universal Leasing from the beginning of the lease through the end of the lease term.

E 15–31
Nonlease payments; lessor and lessee
● LO15–2, LO15–7

On January 1, 2018, NRC Credit Corporation leased equipment to Brand Services under a finance/sales-type lease designed to earn NRC a 12% rate of return for providing long-term financing. The lease agreement specified:

a. Ten annual payments of $55,000 beginning January 1, 2018, the beginning of the lease and each December 31 thereafter through 2026.
b. The estimated useful life of the leased equipment is 10 years with no residual value. Its cost to NRC was $316,412.

c. The lease qualifies as a finance lease/sales-type lease.

d. A 10-year service agreement with Quality Maintenance Company was negotiated to provide maintenance of the equipment as required. Payments of $5,000 per year are specified, beginning January 1, 2018. NRC was to pay this cost as incurred, but lease payments reflect this expenditure.

e. A partial amortization schedule, appropriate for both the lessee and lessor, follows:

	Payments	Effective Interest	Decrease in Balance	Outstanding Balance
		(12% × Outstanding balance)		
				316,412
1/1/2018	50,000		50,000	266,412
12/31/2018	50,000	0.12 (266,412) = 31,969	18,031	248,381
12/31/2019	50,000	0.12 (248,381) = 29,806	20,194	228,187

Required:

Prepare the appropriate entries for both the lessee and lessor related to the lease on:

1. January 1, 2018
2. December 31, 2018

E 15–32
Lessor's initial direct costs; sales-type lease
● LO15–2, LO15–7

Terms of a lease agreement and related facts were:

a. Incremental costs of commissions for brokering the lease and consummating the completed lease transaction incurred by the lessor were $4,242.

b. The retail cash selling price of the leased asset was $500,000. Its useful life was three years with no residual value.

c. The lease term is three years and the lessor paid $500,000 to acquire the asset.

d. Annual lease payments at the beginning of each year were $184,330.

e. Lessor's implicit rate when calculating annual rental payments was 11%.

Required:

1. Prepare the appropriate entries for the lessor to record the lease and related payments at its beginning, January 1, 2018.
2. Calculate the effective rate of interest revenue after adjusting the net investment by initial direct costs.
3. Record any entry(s) necessary at December 31, 2018, the fiscal year-end.

E 15–33
Lessor's initial direct costs; sales-type lease
● LO15–3, LO15–7

The lease agreement and related facts indicate the following:

a. Leased equipment had a retail cash selling price of $300,000. Its useful life was five years with no residual value.

b. The lease term is five years and the lessor paid $265,000 to acquire the equipment (thus, selling profit).

c. Lessor's implicit rate when calculating annual lease payments was 8%.

d. Annual lease payments beginning January 1, 2018, the beginning of the lease, were $69,571.

e. Incremental costs of commissions for brokering the lease and consummating the completed lease transaction incurred by the lessor were $7,500.

Required:

Prepare the appropriate entries for the lessor to record:

1. The lease and the initial payment at its commencement.
2. Any entry(s) necessary at December 31, 2018, the fiscal year-end.

E 15–34
Lessor's initial direct costs; operating lease
● LO15–4, LO15–7

The following relate to an operating lease agreement:

a. The lease term is 3 years, beginning January 1, 2018.

b. The leased asset cost the lessor $800,000 and had a useful life of eight years with no residual value. The lessor uses straight-line depreciation for its depreciable assets.

c. Annual lease payments at the beginning of each year were $137,000.

d. Incremental costs of negotiating and consummating the completed lease transaction incurred by the lessor were $2,400.

Required:

Prepare the appropriate entries for the lessor from the beginning of the lease through the end of the lease term.

E 15–35
Concepts; terminology
● LO15–2 through LO15–8

Listed below are several terms and phrases associated with leases. Pair each item from List A with the item from List B (by letter) that is most appropriately associated with it.

List A		List B
_____	1. Effective rate times balance	a. PV of purchase option exercise price
_____	2. Revenue recognition issues	b. Lessor's net investment
_____	3. Lease payments plus residual value	c. Lessor's gross investment
_____	4. Periodic lease payments plus excess lessee-guaranteed residual value	d. Operating lease
		e. Depreciable assets
_____	5. PV of lease payments plus PV of residual value	f. Component of lease payments
_____	6. Initial direct costs	g. Nonlease payments
_____	7. Rent revenue	h. Depreciation longer than lease term
_____	8. Purchase option	i. Disclosure only
_____	9. Leasehold improvements	j. Interest expense
_____	10. Cash expected to satisfy residual value guarantee	k. Control passed to lessee
		l. Lessee's lease payments
_____	11. Finance lease expense	m. Might shorten lease term
_____	12. Deducted in lessor's computation of lease payments	n. Sales-type lease selling expense
_____	13. Title transfers to lessee	
_____	14. Contingent rentals	

E 15–36
FASB codification research; reassessment of lease terms
● LO15–8

The lease term is the noncancelable period for which a lessee has the right to use an underlying asset, modified by any renewal or termination options that are "reasonably certain" to be exercised, or not exercised. Options whose exercise is under the control of the lessor are automatically included. The *FASB Accounting Standards Codification*® represents the single source of authoritative U.S. generally accepted accounting principles.

Required:

1. Obtain the relevant authoritative literature on when the lessee should reassess the term of the lease. Use your institution's Academic Accounting Access to the FASB's Codification Research System (www.fasb.org) or through your school library's subscription to a research database that includes the Codification. What is the specific citation that describes the guidelines for determining when the lessee should reassess the term of the lease?
2. List the disclosure requirements.

E 15–37
FASB codification research
● LO15–8

Access the FASB's Codification Research System at the FASB website (www.fasb.org). Determine the specific citation for accounting for each of the following items:

1. Definition of initial direct costs.
2. When a modification to a contract is reported as a separate contract (that is, separate from the original contract).
3. The disclosures required in the notes to the financial statements for a lessor.
4. The classification criteria for when a lessee classifies a lease as a finance lease and a lessor classifies a lease as a sales-type lease.

E 15–38
Sale-leaseback
Appendix 15

To raise operating funds, Signal Aviation sold an airplane on January 1, 2018, to a finance company for $770,000. Signal immediately leased the plane back for a 13-year period, at which time ownership of the airplane will transfer to Signal. The airplane has a fair value of $800,000. Its cost and its book value were $600,000. Its useful life is estimated to be 15 years. The lease requires Signal to make payments of $102,771 to the finance company each January 1. Signal depreciates assets on a straight-line basis. The lease has an implicit rate of 11%.

Required:

Prepare the appropriate entries for Signal on:

1. January 1, 2018, to record the transaction
2. December 31, 2018, to record necessary adjustments

E 15–39
Sale-leaseback; operating lease
Appendix 15

To raise operating funds, National Distribution Center sold its office building to an insurance company on January 1, 2018, for $800,000 and immediately leased the building back. The operating lease is for the final 12 years of the building's estimated 20-year remaining useful life. The building has a fair value of $800,000 and a book value of $650,000 (its original cost was $1 million). The rental payments of $100,000 are payable to the insurance company each December 31. The lease has an implicit rate of 9%.

Required:
Prepare the appropriate entries for National Distribution Center on:
1. January 1, 2018, to record the sale-leaseback
2. December 31, 2018, to record necessary adjustments

Problems

connect

P 15–1
Integrating problem; bonds; note; lease
● LO15–2

You are the new controller for Moonlight Bay Resorts. The company CFO has asked you to determine the company's interest expense for the year ended December 31, 2018. Your accounting group provided you the following information on the company's debt:
1. On July 1, 2018, Moonlight Bay issued bonds with a face amount of $2,000,000. The bonds mature in 20 years and interest of 9% is payable semiannually on June 30 and December 31. The bonds were issued at a price to yield investors 10%. Moonlight Bay records interest at the effective rate.
2. At December 31, 2017, Moonlight Bay had a 10% installment note payable to Third Mercantile Bank with a balance of $500,000. The annual payment is $60,000, payable each June 30.
3. On January 1, 2018, Moonlight Bay leased a building under a finance lease calling for four annual lease payments of $40,000 beginning January 1, 2018. Moonlight Bay's incremental borrowing rate on the date of the lease was 11% and the lessor's implicit rate, which was known by Moonlight Bay, was 10%.

Required:
Calculate interest expense for the year ended December 31, 2018.

P 15–2
Finance lease
● LO15–2

At the beginning of 2018, VHF Industries acquired a machine with a fair value of $6,074,700 by signing a four-year lease. The lease is payable in four annual payments of $2 million at the end of each year.

Required:
1. What is the effective rate of interest implicit in the agreement?
2. Prepare the lessee's journal entry at the beginning of the lease.
3. Prepare the journal entry to record the first lease payment at December 31, 2018.
4. Prepare the journal entry to record the second lease payment at December 31, 2019.
5. Suppose the fair value of the machine and the lessor's implicit rate were unknown at the time of the lease, but that the lessee's incremental borrowing rate of interest for notes of similar risk was 11%. Prepare the lessee's entry at the beginning of the lease.

(Note: You may wish to compare your solution to Problem 15–2 with that of Problem 14–12, which deals with a parallel situation in which the machine was acquired with an installment note.)

P 15–3
Lease amortization schedule
● LO15–2

On January 1, 2018, Majestic Mantles leased a lathe from Equipment Leasing under a finance lease. Lease payments are made annually. Title does not transfer to the lessee and there is no purchase option or guarantee of a residual value by Majestic. Portions of the Equipment Leasing's lease amortization schedule appear below:

Jan. 1	Payments	Effective Interest	Decrease in Balance	Outstanding Balance
				187,298
2018	20,000		20,000	167,298
2018	20,000	16,730	3,270	164,028
2019	20,000	16,403	3,597	160,431
2020	20,000	16,043	3,957	156,474
2021	20,000	15,647	4,353	152,122
2022	20,000	15,212	4,788	147,334
2023	20,000	14,733	5,267	142,067

—	—	—	—	—
—	—	—	—	—
—	—	—	—	—
2035	20,000	4,974	15,026	34,711
2036	20,000	3,471	16,529	18,182
2037	20,000	1,818	18,182	0

Required:

1. What is Majestic's lease liability at the beginning of the lease (after the first payment)?
2. What amount would Majestic record as a right-of-use asset?
3. What is the lease term in years?
4. What is the effective annual interest rate?
5. What is the total amount of lease payments?
6. What is the total effective interest expense recorded over the term of the lease?

P 15–4
Finance/sales-type lease; lessee and lessor
● LO15–1, LO15–2, LO15–3

Rand Medical manufactures lithotripters. Lithotripsy uses shock waves instead of surgery to eliminate kidney stones. Physicians' Leasing purchased a lithotripter from Rand for $2,000,000 and leased it to Mid-South Urologists Group, Inc. on January 1, 2018.

Lease Description:	
Quarterly lease payments	$130,516—beginning of each period
Lease term	5 years (20 quarters)
No residual value; no purchase option	
Economic life of lithotripter	5 years
Implicit interest rate and lessee's incremental borrowing rate	12%
Fair value of asset	$2,000,000

1. How should this lease be classified by Mid-South Urologists Group and by Physicians' Leasing?
2. Prepare appropriate entries for both Mid-South Urologists Group and Physicians' Leasing from the beginning of the lease through the second rental payment on April 1, 2018. Adjusting entries are recorded at the end of each fiscal year (December 31).
3. Assume Mid-South Urologists Group leased the lithotripter directly from the manufacturer, Rand Medical, which produced the machine at a cost of $1.7 million. Prepare appropriate entries for Rand Medical from the beginning of the lease through the second lease payment on April 1, 2018.

P 15–5
Lessee; operating lease; advance payment; leasehold improvement
● LO15–4

On January 1, 2018, Winn Heat Transfer leased office space under a three-year operating lease agreement. The arrangement specified three annual rent payments of $80,000 each, beginning December 31, 2018, and at each December 31 through 2020. The lessor, HVAC Leasing calculates lease payments based on an annual interest rate of 5%. Winn also paid a $100,000 advance payment at the beginning of the lease in addition to the first $80,000 rent payment. With permission of the owner, Winn made structural modifications to the building before occupying the space at a cost of $180,000. The useful life of the building and the structural modifications were estimated to be 30 years with no residual value.

Required:

Prepare the appropriate entries for Winn Heat Transfer from the beginning of the lease through the end of 2020. Winn's fiscal year is the calendar year.

P 15–6
Operating lease; scheduled rent increases
● LO15–4

On January 1, 2018, Sweetwater Furniture Company leased office space under a 21-year operating lease agreement. The contract calls for annual rent payments on December 31 of each year. The payments are $10,000 the first year and increase by $500 per year. Benefits expected from using the office space are expected to remain constant over the lease term.

Required:

Record Sweetwater's rent payment at December 31, 2022 (the fifth rent payment) and December 31, 2032 (the fifteenth rent payment).

P 15–7
Lease amortization schedule
● LO15–2, LO15–6

On January 1, 2018, National Insulation Corporation (NIC) leased equipment from United Leasing under a finance lease. Lease payments are made annually. Title does not transfer to the lessee and there is no purchase option or guarantee of a residual value by NIC. Portions of the United Leasing's lease amortization schedule appear below:

Jan. 1	Payments	Effective Interest	Decrease in Balance	Outstanding Balance
2018				192,501
2018	20,000		20,000	172,501
2019	20,000	17,250	2,750	169,751
2020	20,000	16,975	3,025	166,726
2021	20,000	16,673	3,327	163,399
2022	20,000	16,340	3,660	159,739
2023	20,000	15,974	4,026	155,713
—	—	—	—	—
—	—	—	—	—
—	—	—	—	—
2035	20,000	7,364	12,636	61,006
2036	20,000	6,101	13,899	47,107
2037	20,000	4,711	15,289	31,818
2038	35,000	3,182	31,818	0

Required:

1. What is the lease term in years?
2. What is the asset's residual value expected at the end of the lease term?
3. What is the effective annual interest rate?
4. What is the total amount of lease payments for United?
5. What is the total amount of lease payments for NIC?
6. What is United's net investment at the beginning of the lease (after the first payment)?
7. What is United's total effective interest revenue recorded over the term of the lease?
8. What amount would NIC record as a right-of-use asset at the beginning of the lease?

P 15–8
Reassessment of lease term
● LO15–2, LO15–4, LO15–6

On January 1, 2018, Rick's Pawn Shop leased a truck from Corey Motors for a six-year period with an option to extend the lease for three years. Rick's had no significant economic incentive as of the beginning of the lease to exercise the 3-year extension option. Annual lease payments are $10,000 due on December 31 of each year, calculated by the lessor using a 5% discount rate. Assume that at the beginning of the third year, January 1, 2020, Rick's had made significant improvements to the truck whose cost could be recovered only if it exercises the extension option, creating an expectation that extension of the lease was "reasonably certain." The relevant interest rate at that time was 6%.

Required:

1. Prepare the journal entry, if any, at the end of the second year for the lessee to account for the reassessment.
2. Prepare the journal entry, if any, at the end of the second year for the lessor to account for the reassessment.

P 15–9
Lease concepts; sales-type leases; guaranteed and unguaranteed residual value
● LO15–2, LO15–6

Each of the four independent situations below describes a sales-type lease in which annual lease payments of $10,000 are payable at the beginning of each year. Each is a finance lease for the lessee. Determine the following amounts at the beginning of the lease.

A. The lessor's:
   1. Lease payments
   2. Gross investment in the lease
   3. Net investment in the lease

B. The lessee's:
   4. Lease payments
   5. Right-of-use asset
   6. Lease liability

	Situation			
	1	2	3	4
Lease term (years)	4	4	4	4
Asset's useful life (years)	4	5	5	7
Lessor's implicit rate (known by lessee)	11%	11%	11%	11%
Residual value:				
Guaranteed by lessee	0	$4,000	$2,000	0
Unguaranteed	0	0	$2,000	$4,000
Purchase option:				
After (years)	none	3	4	3
Exercise price	n/a	$7,000	$1,000	$3,000
Reasonably certain?	n/a	no	no	yes

P 15–10
Sales-type lease; purchase option reasonably certain to be exercised before lease term ends; lessor and lessee
● LO15–3, LO15–6

Mid-South Auto Leasing leases vehicles to consumers. The attraction to customers is that the company can offer competitive prices due to volume buying and requires an interest rate implicit in the lease that is one percent below alternate methods of financing. On September 30, 2018, the company leased a delivery truck to a local florist, Anything Grows.

The lease agreement specified quarterly payments of $3,000 beginning September 30, 2018, the beginning of the lease, and each quarter (December 31, March 31, and June 30) through June 30, 2021 (three-year lease term). The florist had the option to purchase the truck on September 29, 2020, for $6,000 when it was expected to have a residual value of $10,000. The estimated useful life of the truck is four years. Mid-South Auto Leasing's quarterly interest rate for determining payments was 3% (approximately 12% annually). Mid-South paid $25,000 for the truck. Both companies use straight-line depreciation or amortization. Anything Grows' incremental interest rate is 12%.

Hint: A lease term ends for accounting purposes when an option becomes exercisable if it's expected to be exercised (i.e., a BPO).

Required:

1. Calculate the amount of selling profit that Mid-South would recognize in this sales-type lease. (Be careful to note that, although payments occur on the last calendar day of each quarter, since the first payment was at the beginning of the lease, payments represent an annuity due.)
2. Prepare the appropriate entries for Anything Grows and Mid-South on September 30, 2018.
3. Prepare an amortization schedule(s) describing the pattern of interest expense for Anything Grows and interest revenue for Mid-South Auto Leasing over the lease term.
4. Prepare the appropriate entries for Anything Grows and Mid-South Auto Leasing on December 31, 2018.
5. Prepare the appropriate entries for Anything Grows and Mid-South on September 29, 2020, assuming the purchase option was exercised on that date.

P 15–11
Change in lease term; operating lease; lessor
● LO15–4, LO15–6

Universal Leasing leases electronic equipment to a variety of businesses. The company's primary service is providing alternate financing by acquiring equipment and leasing it to customers under long-term leases. Universal earns interest under these arrangements at a 10% annual rate.

Universal purchased an electronic typesetting machine on December 31, 2017, for $90,000 and then leased it to Desktop, Inc. a local publisher. The six-year operating lease term commenced January 1, 2018, and the lease contract specified annual payments of $8,000 beginning December 31, 2018, and on each December 31 through 2023. The machine's estimated useful life is 15 years with no estimated residual value.

The publisher had the option to terminate the lease after four years. At the beginning of the lease, there was no reason to believe the lease would be terminated.

Required:

1. Prepare the appropriate entries for Universal Leasing from the beginning of the lease through the end of 2018.
2. At the beginning of 2019, there was a significant indication that Desktop's economic incentive to terminate the lease had changed causing both companies to believe termination of the lease at the end of four years (three years remaining) is "reasonably certain." Prepare any appropriate entries for Universal Leasing at January 1, 2019, to reflect the change in the lease term.
3. Prepare the appropriate entries pertaining to the lease for Universal Leasing at December 31, 2019.

P 15–12
Lessee; renewal option
● LO15–2, LO15–6

High Time Tours leased rock-climbing equipment from Adventures Leasing on January 1, 2018. High Time has the option to renew the lease at the end of two years for an additional three years for $8,000 per quarter. Adventures purchased the equipment at a cost of $198,375.

Related Information:	
Lease term	2 years (8 quarterly periods)
Lease renewal option for an additional	3 years at $8,000 per quarter
Quarterly lease payments	$15,000 at Jan. 1, 2018, and at Mar. 31, June 30, Sept. 30, and Dec. 31 thereafter
Economic life of asset	5 years
Interest rate charged by the lessor	8%

Required:

1. Prepare appropriate entries for High Time Tours from the beginning of the lease through March 31, 2018. Appropriate adjusting entries are made quarterly.
2. Prepare an amortization schedule for the term of the lease.

P 15–13
Lessee and lessor; lessee guaranteed residual value
● LO15–2, LO15–6

On January 1, 2018, Allied Industries leased a high-performance conveyer to Karrier Company for a four-year period ending December 31, 2021, at which time possession of the leased asset will revert back to Allied. The equipment cost Allied $956,000 and has an expected useful life of five years. Allied expects the residual value at December 31, 2022, will be $300,000. Negotiations led to the lessee guaranteeing a $340,000 residual value.

Equal payments under the finance/sales-type lease are $200,000 and are due on December 31 of each year with the first payment being made on December 31, 2018. Karrier is aware that Allied used a 5% interest rate when calculating lease payments.

Required:

1. Prepare the appropriate entries for both Karrier and Allied on January 1, 2018, to record the lease.
2. Prepare all appropriate entries for both Karrier and Allied on December 31, 2018, related to the lease.

P 15–14
Lessee and lessor; lessor; sales-type lease with selling profit; residual value
● LO15–2, LO15–3

Newton Labs leased chronometers from Brookline Instruments on January 1, 2018. Brookline Instruments manufactured the chronometers at a cost of $200,000. The chronometers have a fair value of $260,000. Appropriate adjusting entries are made quarterly.

Related Information:	
Lease term	5 years (20 quarterly periods)
Quarterly lease payments	$14,547 at Jan. 1, 2018, and at Mar. 31, June 30, Sept. 30, and Dec. 31 thereafter
Economic life of asset	6 years
Estimated residual value of chronometers at end of lease term	$11,228
Interest rate charged by the lessor	8%

Required:

1. Prepare appropriate entries for Newton Labs to record the arrangement at its commencement, January 1, 2018, and on March 31, 2018.
2. Prepare appropriate entries for Brookline Instruments to record the arrangement at its commencement, January 1, 2018, and on March 31, 2018.

P 15–15
Nonlease payments; lessor and lessee
● LO15–2, LO15–7

On January 1, 2018, Lesco Leasing leased equipment to Quality Services under a finance/sales-type lease designed to earn NRC a 12% rate of return for providing long-term financing. The lease agreement specified:

a. Ten annual payments of $56,000 beginning January 1, 2018, the beginning of the lease and each December 31 thereafter through 2026.
b. The estimated useful life of the leased equipment is 10 years with no residual value. Its cost to Lesco was $322,741.
c. The lease qualifies as a finance lease/sales-type lease.
d. A 10-year service agreement with Quality Maintenance Company was negotiated to provide maintenance of the equipment as required. Payments of $5,000 per year are specified, beginning January 1, 2018. Lesco was to pay this cost as incurred, but lease payments reflect this expenditure. Also included in the $56,000 payments is an insurance premium of $4,000 providing coverage for the equipment.

Required:

1. Prepare the appropriate entries for both the lessee and lessor related to the lease on January 1, 2018.
2. Prepare the appropriate entries for both the lessee and lessor related to the lease on December 31, 2018.

P 15–16
Lessor's initial direct costs; operating and sales-type leases
● LO15–2, LO15–3, LO15–4, LO15–7

Terms of a lease agreement and related facts were:

a. The lease asset had a retail cash selling price of $100,000. Its useful life was six years with no residual value (straight-line depreciation).
b. Annual lease payments at the beginning of each year were $20,873, beginning January 1.
c. Lessor's implicit rate when calculating annual rental payments was 10%.
d. Costs of $2,062 for legal fees for the lease execution were the responsibility of the lessor.

Required:

Prepare the appropriate entries for the lessor to record the lease, the initial payment at its beginning, and at the December 31 fiscal year-end under each of the following three independent assumptions:

1. The lease term is three years and the lessor paid $100,000 to acquire the asset (operating lease).

2. The lease term is six years and the lessor paid $100,000 to acquire the asset. Also assume that adjusting the lease receivable (net investment) by initial direct costs reduces the effective rate of interest to 9%.
3. The lease term is six years and the lessor paid $85,000 to acquire the asset.

P 15–17
Nonlease costs; lessor and lessee
● LO15–2, LO15–7

Branif Leasing leases mechanical equipment to industrial consumers under sales-type leases that earn Branif a 10% rate of return for providing long-term financing. A lease agreement with Branson Construction specified 20 annual payments beginning December 31, 2018, the beginning of the lease. The estimated useful life of the leased equipment is 20 years with no residual value. Its cost to Branif was $936,492. The lease qualifies as a finance lease to Branson. Maintenance of the equipment was contracted for through a 20-year service agreement with Midway Service Company requiring 20 annual payments of $3,000 beginning December 31, 2018. Progressive Insurance Company charges Branif $3,000 annually for hazard insurance coverage on the equipment. Both companies use straight-line depreciation or amortization.

Required:
Prepare the appropriate entries for both the lessee and lessor to record the second lease payment and depreciation on December 31, 2019, under each of three independent assumptions:
1. The lessee pays maintenance costs as incurred. The lessor pays insurance premiums as incurred. The lease agreement requires annual payments of $100,000.
2. The contract specifies that the lessor pays maintenance costs as incurred. The lessee's lease payments were increased to $103,000 to include an amount sufficient to reimburse these costs.
3. The lessee's lease payments of $103,000 included $3,000 for hazard insurance on the equipment rather than maintenance.

P 15–18
Lessee-guaranteed residual value; unguaranteed residual value; nonlease costs; different interest rates for lessor and lessee
● LO15–3, LO15–6, LO15–7

On December 31, 2018, Yard Art Landscaping leased a delivery truck from Branch Motors. Branch paid $40,000 for the truck. Its retail value is $45,114.

The lease agreement specified annual payments of $11,000 beginning December 31, 2018, the beginning of the lease, and at each December 31 through 2021. Branch Motors' interest rate for determining payments was 10%. At the end of the four-year lease term (December 31, 2022) the truck was expected to be worth $15,000. The estimated useful life of the truck is five years with no salvage value. Both companies use straight-line amortization or depreciation.

Yard Art guaranteed a residual value of $6,000. Yard Art's incremental borrowing rate is 9% and is unaware of Branch's implicit rate.

A $1,000 per year maintenance agreement was arranged for the truck with an outside service firm. As an expedient, Branch Motors agreed to pay this fee. It is, however, reflected in the $11,000 lease payments.

Required:
1. How should this lease be classified by Yard Art Landscaping (the lessee)? Why?
2. Calculate the amount Yard Art Landscaping would record as a right-of-use asset and a lease liability.
3. How should this lease be classified by Branch Motors (the lessor)? Why?
4. Show how Branch Motors calculated the $11,000 annual lease payments.
5. Calculate the amount Branch Motors would record as sales revenue.
6. Prepare the appropriate entries for both Yard Art and Branch Motors on December 31, 2018.
7. Prepare an amortization schedule that describes the pattern of interest expense over the lease term for Yard Art.
8. Prepare an amortization schedule that describes the pattern of interest revenue over the lease term for Branch Motors.
9. Prepare the appropriate entries for both Yard Art and Branch Motors on December 31, 2019.
10. Prepare the appropriate entries for both Yard Art and Branch Motors on December 31, 2021 (the final lease payment).
11. Prepare the appropriate entries for both Yard Art and Branch Motors on December 31, 2022 (the end of the lease term), assuming the truck is returned to the lessor and the actual residual value of the truck was $4,000 on that date.

P 15–19
Initial direct costs; sales-type lease
● LO15–2, LO15–7

Bidwell Leasing purchased a single-engine plane for its fair value of $645,526 and leased it to Red Baron Flying Club on January 1, 2018.

Terms of the lease agreement and related facts were:

a. Eight annual payments of $110,000 beginning January 1, 2018, the beginning of the lease, and at each December 31 through 2024. Bidwell Leasing's implicit interest rate was 10%. The estimated useful life of the plane is eight years. Payments were calculated as follows:

Amount to be recovered (fair value)	$645,526
Lease payments at the beginning of each of the next eight years: ($645,526 ÷ 5.86842*)	$110,000

*Present value of an annuity due of $1: $n = 8$, $i = 10\%$.

b. Red Baron's incremental borrowing rate is 11%.

c. Incremental costs of negotiating and consummating the completed lease transaction incurred by Bidwell Leasing were $18,099.

Required:

1. How should this lease be classified (a) by Bidwell Leasing (the lessor) and (b) by Red Baron (the lessee)?
2. Prepare the appropriate entries for both Red Baron Flying Club and Bidwell Leasing on January 1, 2018.
3. Prepare an amortization schedule that describes the pattern of interest expense over the lease term for Red Baron Flying Club.
4. Determine the effective rate of interest for Bidwell Leasing for the purpose of recognizing interest revenue over the lease term.
5. Prepare an amortization schedule that describes the pattern of interest revenue over the lease term for Bidwell Leasing.
6. Prepare the appropriate entries for both Red Baron and Bidwell Leasing on December 31, 2018 (the second lease payment). Both companies use straight-line depreciation.
7. Prepare the appropriate entries for both Red Baron and Bidwell Leasing on December 31, 2024 (the final lease payment).

P 15–20
Initial direct costs; sales-type lease with a selling profit
● LO15–3, LO15–7

(Note: This problem is a variation of the preceding problem, modified to cause the lease to be a sales-type lease with a selling profit.)

Bidwell Leasing purchased a single-engine plane for $400,000 and leased it to Red Baron Flying Club for its fair value of $645,526 on January 1, 2018.

Terms of the lease agreement and related facts were:

a. Eight annual payments of $110,000 beginning January 1, 2018, the beginning of the lease, and at each December 31 through 2024. Bidwell Leasing's implicit interest rate was 10%. The estimated useful life of the plane is eight years. Payments were calculated as follows:

Amount to be recovered (fair value)	$645,526
Lease payments at the beginning of each of the next eight years: ($645,526 ÷ 5.86842*)	$110,000

*Present value of an annuity due of $1: $n = 8$, $i = 10\%$.

b. Red Baron's incremental borrowing rate is 11%.

c. Incremental costs of consummating the completed lease transaction incurred by Bidwell Leasing were $18,099.

Required:

1. How should this lease be classified (a) by Bidwell Leasing (the lessor) and (b) by Red Baron (the lessee)?
2. Prepare the appropriate entries for both Red Baron Flying Club and Bidwell Leasing on January 1, 2018.
3. Prepare an amortization schedule that describes the pattern of interest expense over the lease term for Red Baron Flying Club.
4. Prepare the appropriate entries for both Red Baron and Bidwell Leasing on December 31, 2018 (the second lease payment). Both companies use straight-line depreciation.
5. Prepare the appropriate entries for both Red Baron and Bidwell Leasing on December 31, 2024 (the final lease payment).

P 15–21
Guaranteed residual value; sales-type lease
● LO15–2, LO15–5, LO15–6

(Note: Problems 21, 22, and 23 are three variations of the same basic situation.)

On December 31, 2018, Rhone-Metro Industries leased equipment to Western Soya Co. for a four-year period ending December 31, 2022, at which time possession of the leased asset will revert back to Rhone-Metro. The equipment cost Rhone-Metro $365,760 and has an expected useful life of six years. Its normal sales price is $365,760. The lessee-guaranteed residual value at December 31, 2022, is $25,000. Equal payments under the lease are $100,000 and are due on December 31 of each year. The first payment was made on December 31, 2018.

Western Soya's incremental borrowing rate is 12%. Western Soya knows the interest rate implicit in the lease payments is 10%. Both companies use straight-line depreciation.

Required:

1. Show how Rhone-Metro calculated the $100,000 annual lease payments.
2. How should this lease be classified (a) by Western Soya Co. (the lessee) and (b) by Rhone-Metro Industries (the lessor)? Why?
3. Prepare the appropriate entries for both Western Soya Co. and Rhone-Metro on December 31, 2018.
4. Prepare an amortization schedule(s) describing the pattern of interest over the lease term for the lessee and the lessor.
5. Prepare all appropriate entries for both Western Soya and Rhone-Metro on December 31, 2019 (the second lease payment and depreciation).
6. Prepare the appropriate entries for both Western Soya and Rhone-Metro on December 31, 2022 assuming the equipment is returned to Rhone-Metro and the actual residual value on that date is $1,500.

P 15–22

Unguaranteed residual value; nonlease payments; sales-type lease

● LO15–2, LO15–6, LO15–7

Rhone-Metro Industries manufactures equipment that is sold or leased. On December 31, 2018, Rhone-Metro leased equipment to Western Soya Co. for a four-year period ending December 31, 2022, at which time possession of the leased asset will revert back to Rhone-Metro. The equipment cost $300,000 to manufacture and has an expected useful life of six years. Its normal sales price is $365,760. The expected residual value of $25,000 at December 31, 2022, is not guaranteed. Equal payments under the lease are $104,000 (including $4,000 maintenance costs) and are due on December 31 of each year. The first payment was made on December 31, 2018. Western Soya's incremental borrowing rate is 12%. Western Soya knows the interest rate implicit in the lease payments is 10%. Both companies use straight-line depreciation.

Required:

1. Show how Rhone-Metro calculated the $104,000 annual lease payments.
2. How should this lease be classified (a) by Western Soya Co. (the lessee) and (b) by Rhone-Metro Industries (the lessor)? Why?
3. Prepare the appropriate entries for both Western Soya Co. and Rhone-Metro on December 31, 2018.
4. Prepare an amortization schedule(s) describing the pattern of interest over the lease term for the lessee and the lessor.
5. Prepare the appropriate entries for both Western Soya and Rhone-Metro on December 31, 2019 (the second lease payment and amortization).
6. Prepare the appropriate entries for both Western Soya and Rhone-Metro on December 31, 2022, assuming the equipment is returned to Rhone-Metro and the actual residual value on that date is $1,500.

P 15–23

Purchase option reasonably certain to be exercised before lease term ends; nonlease payments; sales-type lease

● LO15–3, LO15–6, LO15–7

Rhone-Metro Industries manufactures equipment that is sold or leased. On December 31, 2018, Rhone-Metro leased equipment to Western Soya Co. for a noncancelable stated lease term of four years ending December 31, 2022, at which time possession of the leased asset will revert back to Rhone-Metro. The equipment cost $300,000 to manufacture and has an expected useful life of six years. Its normal sales price is $365,760. The expected residual value of $25,000 at December 31, 2022, is not guaranteed. Western Soya Co. is reasonably certain to exercise a purchase option on December 30, 2021, at an option price of $10,000. Equal payments under the lease are $134,960 (including $4,000 annual maintenance costs) and are due on December 31 of each year. The first payment was made on December 31, 2018. Western Soya's incremental borrowing rate is 12%. Western Soya knows the interest rate implicit in the lease payments is 10%. Both companies use straight-line depreciation.

Hint: A lease term ends for accounting purposes when an option becomes exercisable if it's expected to be exercised (i.e., a BPO).

Required:

1. Show how Rhone-Metro calculated the $134,960 annual lease payments.
2. How should this lease be classified (a) by Western Soya Co. (the lessee) and (b) by Rhone-Metro Industries (the lessor)? Why?
3. Prepare the appropriate entries for both Western Soya Co. and Rhone-Metro on December 31, 2018.
4. Prepare an amortization schedule(s) describing the pattern of interest over the lease term for the lessee and the lessor.
5. Prepare the appropriate entries for both Western Soya and Rhone-Metro on December 31, 2019 (the second rent payment and depreciation).
6. Prepare the appropriate entries for both Western Soya and Rhone-Metro on December 30, 2021, assuming the purchase option is exercised on that date.

P 15–24
Lessee and lessor; lessee guaranteed residual value
● LO15–2, LO15–7

On January 1, 2018, Nguyen Electronics leased equipment from Nevels Leasing for a four-year period ending December 31, 2021, at which time possession of the leased asset will revert back to Nevels. The equipment cost Nevels $824,368 and has an expected economic life of five years. Nevels expects the residual value at December 31, 2021, will be $100,000. Negotiations led to the lessee guaranteeing a $140,000 residual value.

Equal payments under the lease are $200,000 and are due on December 31 of each year with the first payment being made on December 31, 2018. Nguyen is aware that Nevels used a 5% interest rate when calculating lease payments.

Required:

1. Prepare the appropriate entries for both Nguyen and Nevels on January 1, 2018, to record the lease.
2. Prepare all appropriate entries for both Nguyen and Nevels on December 31, 2018, related to the lease.

P 15–25
Operating lease; uneven lease payments
● LO15–4, LO15–7

On January 1, 2018, Harlon Consulting entered into a three-year lease for new office space agreeing to lease payments of: $5,000 in 2018, $6,000 in 2019 and $7,000 in 2020. Payments are due on December 31 of each year with the first payment being made on December 31, 2018. Harlon is aware that the lessor used a 5% interest rate when calculating lease payments.

Required:

1. Prepare the appropriate entries for Harlon Consulting on January 1, 2018, to record the lease.
2. Prepare all appropriate entries for Harlon Consulting on December 31, 2018, related to the lease.
3. Prepare all appropriate entries for Harlon Consulting on December 31, 2019, related to the lease.
4. Prepare all appropriate entries for Harlon Consulting on December 31, 2020, related to the lease.

P 15–26
Operating lease; uneven lease payments
● LO15–4, LO15–7

On January 1, 2018, Harlon Consulting entered into a three-year lease for new office space agreeing to lease payments of: $7,000 in 2018, $6,000 in 2019 and $5,000 in 2020. Payments are due on December 31 of each year with the first payment being made on December 31, 2018. Harlon is aware that the lessor used a 5% interest rate when calculating lease payments.

Required:

1. Prepare the appropriate entries for Harlon Consulting on January 1, 2018, to record the lease.
2. Prepare all appropriate entries for Harlon Consulting on December 31, 2018, related to the lease.
3. Prepare all appropriate entries for Harlon Consulting on December 31, 2019, related to the lease.
4. Prepare all appropriate entries for Harlon Consulting on December 31, 2020, related to the lease.

P 15–27
Modification of a lease
● LO15–2, LO15–3, LO15–6

On January 1, 2018, Worchester Construction leased International Harvester equipment from Newton LeaseCorp. Newton LeaseCorp purchased the equipment from Wellesley Harvester at a cost of $958,158. Worchester borrowing rate for similar transactions is 10%.

The lease agreement specified four annual payments of $200,000 beginning January 1, 2018, the beginning of the lease, and on each December 31 thereafter through 2020. The useful life of the equipment is estimated to be six years. The present value of those four payments at a discount rate of 10% is $697,370.

On January 1, 2020 (after two years and three payments), Worchester and Newton agreed to extend the lease term by two years. The market rate of interest at that time was 9%.

Required:

1. Prepare the appropriate entries for Worchester Construction on January 1, 2020, to adjust its lease liability for the lease modification.
2. Prepare all appropriate entries for Newton LeaseCorp on January 1, 2020, to record the lease modification.
3. Prepare all appropriate entries for Worchester Construction on December 31, 2020, related to the lease.
4. Prepare all appropriate entries for Newton LeaseCorp on December 31, 2020, related to the lease.

P 15–28
Finance lease; lessee; financial statement effects
● LO15–2, LO15–8

(Note: Problems 28, 29, and 30 are three variations of the same basic situation.) Werner Chemical, Inc. leased a protein analyzer on September 30, 2018. The five-year lease agreement calls for Werner to make quarterly lease payments of $391,548, payable each September 30, December 31, March 31, June 30, with the first payment at September 30, 2018. Werner's incremental borrowing rate is 12%. Amortization is recorded on a straight-line basis at the end of each fiscal year. The useful life of the equipment is five years.

Required:

1. Determine the present value of the lease payments at September 30, 2018 (to the nearest $000).
2. What pretax amounts related to the lease would Werner report in its balance sheet at December 31, 2018?
3. What pretax amounts related to the lease would Werner report in its income statement for the year ended December 31, 2018?
4. What pretax amounts related to the lease would Werner report in its statement of cash flows for the year ended December 31, 2018?

P 15–29
Sales-type lease; lessor; financial statement effects
● LO15–2, LO15–8

Abbott Equipment leased a protein analyzer to Werner Chemical, Inc. on September 30, 2018. Abbott purchased the machine from NutraLabs, Inc. at a cost of $6 million. The five-year lease agreement calls for Werner to make quarterly lease payments of $391,548, payable each September 30, December 31, March 31, and June 30, with the first payment at September 30, 2018. Abbot's implicit interest rate is 12%.

Required:

1. What pretax amounts related to the lease would Abbott report in its balance sheet at December 31, 2018?
2. What pretax amounts related to the lease would Abbott report in its income statement for the year ended December 31, 2018?
3. What pretax amounts related to the lease would Abbott report in its statement of cash flows for the year ended December 31, 2018?

P 15–30
Sales-type lease; lessor; financial statement effects
● LO15–3, LO15–8

NutraLabs, Inc. leased a protein analyzer to Werner Chemical, Inc. on September 30, 2018. NutraLabs manufactured the machine at a cost of $5 million. The five-year lease agreement calls for Werner to make quarterly lease payments of $391,548, payable each September 30, December 31, March 31, June 30, with the first payment at September 30, 2018. NutraLabs' implicit interest rate is 12%.

Required:

1. Determine the price at which NutraLabs is "selling" the equipment (present value of the lease payments) at September 30, 2018 (to the nearest $000).
2. What pretax amounts related to the lease would NutraLabs report in its balance sheet at December 31, 2018?
3. What pretax amounts related to the lease would NutraLabs report in its income statement for the year ended December 31, 2018?
4. What pretax amounts related to the lease would NutraLabs report in its statement of cash flows for the year ended December 31, 2018?

P 15–31
Sale-leaseback
Appendix

To raise operating funds, North American Courier Corporation sold its building on January 1, 2018, to an insurance company for $500,000 and immediately leased the building back. The lease is for a 10-year period ending December 31, 2027, at which time ownership of the building will revert to North American Courier. The building has a carrying amount of $400,000 (original cost $1,000,000). The lease requires North American to make payments of $88,492 to the insurance company each December 31. The building had a total original useful life of 30 years with no residual value and is being depreciated on a straight-line basis. The lease has an implicit rate of 12%.

Required:

1. Prepare the appropriate entries for North American (a) on January 1, 2018, to record the transaction and (b) on December 31, 2018, to record necessary adjustments.
2. Show how North American's December 31, 2018, balance sheet and income statement would reflect the sale-leaseback.

Broaden Your Perspective

Apply your critical-thinking ability to the knowledge you've gained. These cases will provide you an opportunity to develop your research, analysis, judgment, and communication skills. You also will work with other students, integrate what you've learned, apply it in real world situations, and consider its global and ethical ramifications. This practice will broaden your knowledge and further develop your decision-making abilities.

Research Case 15–1
FASB codification; locate and extract relevant information and authoritative support for a financial reporting issue; finance lease; sublease of a leased asset
● LO15–2, LO15–8

"I don't see that in my intermediate accounting text I saved from college," you explain to another member of the accounting division of Dowell Chemical Corporation. "This will take some research." Your comments pertain to the appropriate accounting treatment of a proposed sublease of warehouses Dowell has used for product storage.

Dowell leased the warehouses one year ago on December 31. The five-year lease agreement called for Dowell to make quarterly lease payments of $2,398,303, payable each December 31, March 31, June 30, and September 30, with the first payment at the lease's beginning. As a finance lease, Dowell had recorded the right-of-use asset and liability at $40 million, the present value of the lease payments at 8%. Dowell records depreciation on a straight-line basis at the end of each fiscal year.

Today, Jason True, Dowell's controller, explained a proposal to sublease the underused warehouses to American Tankers, Inc. for the remaining four years of the lease term. American Tankers would be substituted as lessee under the original lease agreement. As the new lessee, it would become the primary obligor under the agreement, and Dowell would not be secondarily liable for fulfilling the obligations under the lease agreement. "Check on how we would need to account for this and get back to me," he had said.

CODE

Required:

1. After the first full year under the warehouse lease, what is the balance in Dowell's lease liability? An amortization schedule will be helpful in determining this amount.
2. After the first full year under the warehouse lease, what is the carrying amount (after accumulated depreciation) of Dowell's leased warehouses?
3. Obtain the relevant authoritative literature on accounting for derecognition of finance leases by lessees using the FASB's Codification Research System. You might gain access from the FASB website (www.fasb.org), from your school library, or some other source. Determine the appropriate accounting treatment for the proposed sublease. What is the specific Codification citation that Dowell would rely on to determine:
   a. if the proposal to sublease will qualify as a termination of a finance lease, and
   b. the appropriate accounting treatment for the sublease?
4. What, if any, journal entry would Dowell record in connection with the sublease?

Communication Case 15–2
Classification issues; lessee accounting; group interaction
● LO15–1, LO15–2, LO15–3, LO15–6, LO15–7

Interstate Automobiles Corporation leased 40 vans to VIP Transport under a four-year noncancelable lease on January 1, 2018. Information concerning the lease and the vans follows:

a. Equal annual lease payments of \$300,000 are due on January 1, 2018, and thereafter on December 31 each year. The first payment was made January 1, 2018. Interstate's implicit interest rate is 10% and known by VIP.
b. VIP has the option to purchase all of the vans at the end of the lease for a total of \$290,000. The vans' estimated residual value is \$300,000 at the end of the lease term and \$50,000 at the end of 7 years, the estimated life of each van.
c. VIP estimates the fair value of the vans to be \$1,240,000. Interstate's cost was \$1,050,000.
d. VIP's incremental borrowing rate is 9%.
e. VIP will pay the maintenance fees not included in the annual lease payments of \$1,000 per year. The depreciation method is straight-line.

Your instructor will divide the class into two to six groups depending on the size of the class. The mission of your group is to assess the proper recording and reporting of the lease described.

Required:

1. Each group member should deliberate the situation independently and draft a tentative argument prior to the class session for which the case is assigned.
2. In class, each group will meet for 10 to 15 minutes in different areas of the classroom. During that meeting, group members will take turns sharing their suggestions for the purpose of arriving at a single group treatment.
3. After the allotted time, a spokesperson for each group (selected during the group meetings) will share the group's solution with the class. The goal of the class is to incorporate the views of each group into a consensus approach to the situation.

Specifically, you should address:

a. Identify potential advantages to VIP of leasing the vans rather than purchasing them.
b. How should the lease be classified by VIP? by Interstate?
c. Regardless of your response to previous requirements, suppose VIP recorded the lease on January 1, 2018, as a finance lease in the amount of \$1,100,000. What would be the appropriate journal entries related to the finance lease for the second lease payment on December 31, 2018?

Ethics Case 15–3
Leasehold improvements
● LO15–3

American Movieplex, a large movie theater chain, leases most of its theater facilities. In conjunction with recent operating leases, the company spent \$28 million for seats and carpeting. The question being discussed over breakfast on Wednesday morning was the length of the depreciation period for these leasehold improvements. The company controller, Sarah Keene, was surprised by the suggestion of Larry Person, her new assistant.

Keene: Why 25 years? We've never depreciated leasehold improvements for such a long period.

Person: I noticed that in my review of back records. But during our expansion to the Midwest, we don't need expenses to be any higher than necessary.

Keene: But isn't that a pretty rosy estimate of these assets' actual life? Trade publications show an average depreciation period of 12 years.

Required:

1. How would increasing the depreciation period affect American Movieplex's earnings?
2. Does revising the estimate pose an ethical dilemma?
3. Who would be affected if Person's suggestion is followed?

Analysis Case 15–4
Lease concepts; Walmart
● LO15–1 through LO15–4
Real World Financials

Walmart Stores, Inc. is the world's largest retailer. A large portion of the premises that the company occupies are leased. Its financial statements and disclosure notes revealed the following information:

Balance Sheet
($ in millions)

	2016	2015
Assets		
Property:		
Property under capital lease	$11,096	$5,239
Less: Accumulated amortization	(4,751)	(2,864)
Liabilities		
Current liabilities:		
Obligations under finance leases due within one year	551	287
Long-term debt:		
Long-term obligations under finance leases	5,816	2,606

Required:

1. Discuss some possible reasons why Walmart leases rather than purchases most of its premises.
2. The net asset "property under finance lease" has a 2016 balance of $6,345 million ($11,096 − 4,751). Liabilities for finance leases total $6,367 ($551 + 5,816). Why do the asset and liability amounts differ?
3. Prepare a 2016 summary entry to record Walmart's lease payments, which were $600 million.
4. What is the approximate average interest rate on Walmart's finance leases? (Hint: See Req. 3)

Communication Case 15–5
Where's the gain?
Appendix

General Tools is seeking ways to maintain and improve cash balances. As company controller, you have proposed the sale and leaseback of much of the company's equipment. As seller-lessee, General Tools would retain the right to essentially all of the remaining use of the equipment. The term of the lease would be six years.

You previously convinced your CFO of the cash flow benefits of the arrangement, but now he doesn't understand the way you will account for the transaction. "I really had counted on that gain on the sale portion of the transaction to bolster this period's earnings. What gives?" he wondered. "Put it in a memo, will you? I'm having trouble following what you're saying to me."

Required:

Write a memo to your CFO. Include discussion of each of these points:

1. How the transaction should be accounted for.
2. Why General Tools will not get the gain the CFO had counted on.

Trueblood Case 15–6
Lease

The following Trueblood case is recommended for use with this chapter. The case provides an excellent opportunity for class discussion, group projects, and writing assignments. The case, along with Professor's Discussion Material, can be obtained from the Deloitte foundation at its website (www.deloitte.com/us/truebloodcases).

Case 15–4: All-in

This case gives students the opportunity to extend their knowledge beyond chapter coverage by determining the accounting for leases when the lessee is involved with construction of the leased asset

IFRS Case 15–7
Lease classification; U.S. GAAP
● LO15–1, LO15–2, LO15–4, LO15–9
IFRS

Security Devices Inc. (SDI) needs additional office space to accommodate expansion. SDI wants to avoid income statement effects that would disrupt its attempts to "smooth" income over time.

Required:

1. Which lease classification would management prefer? Explain.
2. Would meeting its reporting objective be more or less difficult under IFRS? Explain.

Continuing Cases

Target Case
● LO15–2, LO15–4
Real World Financials

Target Corporation prepares its financial statements according to U.S. GAAP. Target's financial statements and disclosure notes for the year ended January 30, 2016, are available in Connect. This material is also available under the Investor Relations link at the company's website (www.target.com).

Required:

In its Analysis of "Financial Condition: New Accounting Pronouncements," Target's financial statements for the year ended January 30, 2016, the company indicates that:

> In February 2016, the FASB issued *ASU No. 2016-02*, Leases, to require organizations that lease assets to recognize the rights and obligations created by those leases on the balance sheet. The new standard is effective in 2019, with early adoption permitted. We are currently evaluating the effect the new standard will have on our financial statements.

Refer to *Note 22: Leases.* When Target applies the new standard, what will be the primary effect on its financial statements? Explain.

Air France–KLM Case

IFRS

● LO15–9

Real World Financials

Air France–KLM (AF), a Franco-Dutch company, prepares its financial statements according to International Financial Reporting Standards. AF's financial statements and disclosure notes for the year ended December 31, 2015, are available in Connect. This material is also available under the Finance link at the company's website (www.airfranceklm.com).

Required:

1. In *Note 4:* Summary of accounting policies, part 4.14: Leases, AF states that "leases are classified as finance leases when the lease arrangement transfers substantially all the risks and rewards of ownership to the lessee. All other leases are classified as operating leases. Is this the policy companies using U.S. GAAP follow?
2. Is this the policy AF will follow when it begins applying the new lease guidance in the 2015 update to *IFRS 16*? Explain.

CPA Exam Questions and Simulations

ROGER CPA Review

Sample CPA Exam questions from Roger CPA Review are available in Connect as support for the topics in this chapter. These Multiple Choice Questions and Task-Based Simulations include expert-written explanations and solutions, and provide a starting point for students to become familiar with the content and functionality of the actual CPA Exam.

LEASES:

GAAP in Effect Prior to ASU No. 2016-02

A Chapter Supplement

PREFACE

Chapter 15 is based on the lease accounting approach established in Accounting Standards Update No. 2016-02: "Leases" (Topic 842), which is effective for fiscal years (and interim periods within those fiscal years) beginning after December 15, 2018. *Early adoption was permitted for all companies and organizations upon issuance of the standard.* In this Supplement we discuss GAAP that is eliminated by the ASU that established Accounting Standards Codification (ASC) 842—"Leases," but will be relevant until ASC 842 becomes effective, and students taking the CPA or CMA exams will be responsible for this GAAP until six months after the effective date of the ASC.

PART A

Accounting by the Lessor and Lessee

Over $3.3 trillion of existing assets were acquired with leases. The vast majority of those assets and the obligations to pay for them are not included in corporate balance sheets.[22] Accounting Standards Update (ASU) No. 2016-02 changes that. The ASU requires lessees to recognize a right-of-use asset and a lease liability for all leases, including operating leases (other than those of 12 months or less). This and other differences between preexisting GAAP and the new lease guidance are summarized in Illustration 15–S1.

Illustration 15–S1 Some Significant Differences between Preexisting Guidance in Lease Accounting and ASC 842

	Preexisting GAAP	New GAAP Under ASC 842
Changes in terminology	Minimum lease payments Bargain purchase option Capital lease Direct financing lease	Lease payments Purchase option the lessee is reasonably certain to exercise Finance lease Sales-type lease with no selling profit
Balance sheet presentation	Lessees recognize a lease asset and a lease liability only for capital leases. Operating leases are off-balance sheet.	Lessees recognize a right-of-use asset and a lease liability for all leases (except those with a lease term of 12 months or less).
Income statement presentation–Lessee	Capital leases: Interest expense and amortization expense Operating leases: Straight-line lease expense	Finance leases: Interest expense and amortization expense Operating leases: Straight-line lease expense (by plugging amortization to cause interest plus amortization to equal the straight-line lease payment)

(continued)

[22]Balance Sheets to Swell $2.8 Trillion as Leasing Rules Tighten," Jon Glover, *Bloomberg.com*, January 12, 2016.

Income statement presentation–Lessor	Direct financing leases: Interest revenue Sales-type leases: Interest revenue and selling profit Operating leases: Straight-line lease revenue	Sales-type leases with no selling profit: Interest revenue Sales-type leases with selling profit: Interest revenue and selling profit Operating leases: Straight-line lease revenue
Definition of a lease	An arrangement can contain a lease even without "control" of the use of the asset if the lessee receives substantially all of the benefits over the term of the arrangement.	An arrangement contains a lease only when it conveys to the lessee the right to "control" the use of an "identified asset."
Lease classification	Four criteria and "bright lines:" 1. The agreement specifies that ownership of the asset transfers to the lessee. 2. The agreement contains a purchase option that the lessee is reasonably certain to exercise. 3. The lease term is for the 75% or more of the remaining economic life of the underlying asset.* 4. The present value of the total of the lease payments† equals or exceeds 90% of the fair value of the underlying asset.	Five criteria and no "bright lines:" 1. The agreement specifies that ownership of the asset transfers to the lessee. 2. The agreement contains a purchase option that the lessee is reasonably certain to exercise. 3. The lease term is for the "major part" of the remaining economic life of the underlying asset.** 4. The present value of the total of the lease payments equals or exceeds "substantially all" of the fair value of the underlying asset. 5. The underlying asset is of such a specialized nature that it is expected to have no alternative use to the lessor at the end of the lease term.
Lessors: Additional conditions to be a capital lease	No important uncertainties surround the amount of unreimbursable costs yet to be incurred by the lessor. The collectibility of the minimum lease payments is reasonably assured (i.e., predictable).	Both of these conditions have been removed from the new guidance.
Sales-type lease or direct financing lease	The difference between a sales-type lease and a direct finance lease is the presence of selling profit.	Equivalents are sales-type leases with a selling profit and sales-type leases without a selling profit. A direct finance lease only if (a) the "substantially all" criterion has been met in part due to a *third-party residual value guarantee* and (b) payments are collectible.

*If the lease begins at or near the end of the economic life of the asset, this criterion shouldn't be used for purposes of classifying the lease.
**Balance Sheets to Swell $2.8 Trillion as Leasing Rules Tighten," Jon Glover, Bloomberg.com, January 12, 2016.
†This total includes any residual value of the asset at the end of the lease term that is guaranteed by the lessee.

Let's take a closer look at these differences.

Classification Criteria

In both preexisting GAAP and new GAAP both the lessee and lessor distinguish between operating leases and non-operating leases. With preexisting GAAP the intent is to determine whether the usual *risks and rewards of ownership* are transferred. Illustration 15–S2a compares the classification possibilities.

Illustration 15–S2a

Basic Lease Classifications: Preexisting GAAP

Lessee	**Lessor**
• Operating lease	• Operating lease
• Capital lease	• Capital lease
	➥ Direct financing lease
	➥ Sales-type lease

The goal is similar under new GAAP, but the essential question is whether the lease is economically similar to the purchase of an asset because the lessee *obtains substantially all of its remaining benefits* by controlling the use of the asset, in contrast to merely obtaining control over the use of the asset for a period of time. Illustration 15–S2b compares the classification possibilities by the new lease guidance.

Lessee	Lessor
• Operating lease	• Operating lease
• Finance lease	• Sales-type lease:
	➡ With no selling profit
	➡ With selling profit

Illustration 15–S2b

Basic Lease Classifications: ASC 842

Leases labeled as capital leases under preexisting GAAP are called finance leases under the new guidance. Direct financing leases under preexisting GAAP are essentially equivalent to *sales-type leases with no selling profit* under the new guidance.[23]

The criteria we use to make the distinction are similar under both approaches. In preexisting lease accounting, a lessee should classify a lease transaction as a *capital lease* if it includes a noncancelable lease term and one or more of the four criteria listed in Illustration 15–S3a are met. Otherwise, it is an *operating lease.*

1. The agreement specifies that ownership of the asset transfers to the lessee.
2. The agreement contains a bargain purchase option.
3. The noncancelable lease term is equal to **75% or more** of the expected economic life of the asset.
4. The present value of the "minimum lease payments"* is **equal to or greater than 90%** of the fair value of the asset.

*Minimum lease payments are referred to simply as lease payments in ASC 842.

Illustration 15–S3a

Criteria for Classification as a Capital Lease: Preexisting GAAP

By ASC 842, classification is based on criteria quite similar to those applied in current lease accounting, but *without explicit "bright lines"* (75%; 90%), and adding a *fifth criterion.* A lease is viewed as a finance lease if any one of the criteria in Illustration 15–S3b is satisfied:

1. The agreement specifies that ownership of the asset transfers to the lessee.
2. The agreement contains a purchase option that the lessee is reasonably certain to exercise.
3. The lease term is for the "major part" of the remaining economic life of the underlying asset.
4. The present value of the sum of the lease payments equals or exceeds "substantially all" of the fair value of the underlying asset.
5. The underlying asset is of such a specialized nature that it is expected to have no alternative use to the lessor at the end of the lease term.

Illustration 15 S3b

Criteria for Classification as a Capital Lease: ASC 842

ADDITIONAL LESSOR CONDITIONS. The four classification criteria listed in Illustration 15–S3a apply to both parties to the transaction, lessees and lessors. However, a fundamental difference is that for a lessor to record the sale side of the transaction, it is necessary also to satisfy the conditions needed for revenue recognition. Preexisting GAAP bases those conditions on revenue recognition criteria prior to the current ASC 606—Revenue from Contracts with Customers discussed in Chapter 5.

In preexisting GAAP, additional lessor conditions for classification as a capital lease are consistent with criteria of the previous revenue realization principle.

[23]While the direct financing label still exists in the new lease guidance, it is used in a different context. It now refers to a situation that happens only when the lease includes a residual value and at least some of the residual value is *guaranteed by a third party* (not the lessee).

Consistent with the *previous* revenue realization principle, preexisting GAAP specifies that for the lessor to record a lease as a direct financing lease or a sales-type lease, two conditions must be met in addition to one of the four classification criteria. These are listed in Illustration 15–S4.

Illustration 15–S4

Additional Conditions for Classification as a Capital Lease by the Lessor

1. The collectibility of the lease payments must be reasonably predictable.
2. If any costs to the lessor have yet to be incurred, they are reasonably predictable. (Performance by the lessor is substantially complete.)

Both of these conditions have been removed from the new guidance.

Financial Statement Presentation

Under preexisting GAAP, a lease is accounted for as either a purchase/sale accompanied by debt financing or as a rental agreement. The accounting method used hinges on the nature of the leasing arrangement.

Accounting for leases attempts to see through the legal form of the agreements to determine their economic substance.

Capital leases (called finance leases in the new guidance) are agreements that we identify as being formulated outwardly as leases, but which are in reality essentially installment purchases. The essential question is whether the usual *risks and rewards of ownership have been transferred* to the lessee. Otherwise it's an operating lease. Our focus here is on the differences in accounting for operating leases because capital (financial) leases are accounted for essentially the same way under preexisting and new GAAP (other than the new label for the lease asset discussed below).

Balance Sheet

The most significant impact of the distinction is its effect on the balance sheet. A capital lease adds to both the asset and liability side of the balance sheet; operating leases don't affect the balance sheet at all.

Most lessees strongly prefer a lease to be an operating lease for this very reason—to keep the liability off the balance sheet. Why? It's because for most analysts, liabilities signify risk. The more obligations to make timely interest and principle payments that a company has, the riskier the company appears. Designing leases to qualify as operating leases as a way to achieve "off balance sheet financing" for decades has been a popular and successful practice. Stopping this practice was the driving force behind the new Accounting Standard Update.

In Illustration 15–S5, we compare preexisting GAAP and the new GAAP as to the way a lessee accounts for an operating lease.

Notice a couple differences. The primary distinction is that we record an asset and a liability when following the new guidance, but not under preexisting GAAP. Note, too, that the lease asset is referred to as a "right-of-use asset." This is consistent with the philosophy of ASC 842 that all leases (finance or operating) convey to the lessee the right to use the asset, and that right meets the definition of an asset. In fact, even for a finance lease, we use the right-of-use asset label under the new GAAP.

Income Statement

Another difference is how we determine lease expense. We see that in Illustration 15–S5a.

By the ASC, amortization is a balancing amount, calculated to cause the total lease expense (interest plus amortization) to be a straight-line amount over the lease term.

Although the operating lease is reported in the balance sheet under the new lease guidance, but not under preexisting GAAP, *by either approach, lease expense is $100,000 in each of the four years.* That is by design. In ASC 842, lease expense is recorded in a manner that's designed to mirror *straight-line rental* of the asset during the lease term, which is the notion of an operating lease under preexisting GAAP as well. However, because we do record a right-of-use asset and a lease liability in the new approach, it's necessary to force that outcome. The way the lessee does that is to determine interest expense in the usual way, and then determine amortization of the right-of-use asset as the amount needed to cause

Illustration 15–S5

Operating Leases: Balance Sheet; Preexisting GAAP and ASC 842

On January 1, 2018, Sans Serif Publishers, Inc. a computer services and printing firm, leased printing equipment from First LeaseCorp. The lease agreement specifies four annual payments of $100,000 beginning January 1, 2018, the beginning of the lease, and at each December 31 thereafter through 2020. The useful life of the copier is estimated to be six years.

Before deciding to lease, Sans Serif considered purchasing the equipment for its cash price of $479,079. The interest rate First LeaseCorp used in establishing lease payments was 10%.

Since none of the classification criteria is met, this is an operating lease.

Preexisting GAAP			ASC 842		
January 1, 2018			**January 1, 2018**		
No entry			Right-of-use asset.............	348,685	
			Lease liability.................		348,685*
Prepaid rent (first payment)....	100,000		Lease liability.....................	100,000	
Cash.......................................		100,000	Cash (lease payment)...		100,000

*Present value of an annuity due of $1: $n = 4$, $i = 10\%$.

Lessees recognize a right-of-use asset and a lease liability for operating leases under ASC 842, but not under preexisting GAAP.

Interest expense	$ 24,869
Amortization exp.	75,131
Lease expense	$100,000

Illustration 15–S5a Operating Leases: Income Statement; Preexisting GAAP and ASC 842

Preexisting GAAP			ASC 842		
December 31, 2018			**December 31, 2018**		
Rent expense	100,000		Interest expense...............................		
Prepaid rent (first payment)........		100,000	[10% × ($348,685 − 100,000)].....	24,869	
			Lease payable....................................	75,131	
Prepaid rent (second payment).....	100,000		Cash (lease payment)....................		100,000
Cash..		100,000			
			Amortization expense		
			($100,000 − 24,869)........................	75,131	
			Right-of-use asset		75,131

the *total* lease expense (interest plus amortization) to be an equal, *straight-line amount over the lease term.* In other words, the lessee records interest and then "plugs" the right-of-use asset amortization at whatever amount is needed for interest plus amortization to equal the straight-line lease payment. So, in Illustration 15–S5a, Sans Serif, having determined interest to be $24,869, plugs an amortization expense of $75,131 to cause the total of the two expenses to be $100,000.

After recording these entries, the lessee will have two lease-related expenses—interest expense and amortization expense. The lessee combines these two accounts into a single *lease expense* and reports a single $100,000 amount each year in its income statement. This is in keeping with the key objective of reporting a straight-line lease expense for an operating lease. In a finance lease, the lessee reports interest expense and amortization expense separately in the income statement.

In an operating lease, the lessee combines interest expense and amortization expense to report a single lease expense in the income statement.

Under preexisting GAAP, the lessee has only a single lease expense account for an operating lease and reports that straight-line amount, $100,000, each year in its income statement. Thus, in keeping with the presumption that an operating lease is considered to be more in the nature of a rental agreement, the lessee reports ***lease expense on a straight-line basis*** over the lease term using both preexisting GAAP and the new ASC. Illustration 15–S6 compares how this occurs under preexisting GAAP and the new guidance.

Illustration 15–S6

Comparison of Lessee's Expense Recognition between Preexisting GAAP and ASC 842 for Operating Leases

	Preexisting GAAP Operating Lease	ASC 842 Operating Lease		
	Lease Expense	Interest Expense	Amortization Expense	Total Expense
2018	100,000	24,869	75,131	100,000
2019	100,000	17,355	82,645	100,000
2020	100,000	9,091	90,909	100,000
2021	100,000	0	100,000	100,000
	400,000	51,315	348,685	400,000

PART B

Additional Differences

Some additional differences between preexisting GAAP and the new lease guidance are summarized in Illustration 15–S7.

Appreciating some of these differences will benefit from the additional discussion that follows.

Lease Term

In both preexisting and new GAAP, we adjust the lease term for periods represented by options that are reasonably certain to be exercised by the lessee.

Under both preexisting GAAP and ASC 842, we reassess the lease term if (a) the provisions of the lease are modified or (b) an option is exercised.

Under ASC 842, though, other "triggering events" also can require reassessment.

Similar to preexisting GAAP, the term of a lease in the new guidance includes the noncancellable lease term, adjusted for periods represented by options that are reasonably certain to be exercised by the lessee or within the control of the lessor.

For instance, a company adjusts the lease term for an option only if it is "reasonably certain" that the lessee will exercise the option after considering the relevant economic factors. Under both preexisting and new GAAP, if the benefits of exercising an option are high enough that we think the lessee will exercise it, we add the additional period that follows a purchase option, or subtract the period that follows a termination option.

Circumstances can change that require reassessment of how long the lease term will be. Under preexisting GAAP, we don't reassess the lease term unless (a) the provisions of the lease are modified by the lessee and lessor or (b) an option is exercised. Following the Accounting Standard Update, either of those would require reassessment as well, but other "triggering events" also can require reassessment. That happens if the event suggests that a lessee now has an economic incentive to exercise an option that extends or terminates the lease. For example, if the lessee has made significant improvements to the asset whose cost could be recovered only if it exercises an extension option, such that extension of the lease is "reasonably certain," the lease term would be adjusted.

Lease Payments

Measurement decisions are made at the *beginning* of the lease under preexisting GAAP and at the *commencement* of the lease under new GAAP.

Sometimes lease payments might be increased (or decreased) at some future time during the lease term, depending on whether or not some specified event occurs. Usually the contingency is related to revenues, profitability, or usage above some designated level. For example, a quarterly report of Dollar General Corporation included the note recreated in Illustration 15–S8.

Using preexisting GAAP, contingent payments are *not* included in the minimum lease payments because they are not determinable at the beginning of the lease. Instead, they are included as components of income when (and if) they occur or when they are considered probable.

Under the new guidance, lease payments generally exclude variable lease payments, except those (a) that are in-substance fixed payments or (b) based on an index (e.g., Consumer Price Index) or rate (e.g., market interest rate). In the second exception, initial measurement of the right-of-use asset, lease liability, and lease receivable are based on the payment amounts prior to any changes due to the index or rate. Payment *changes* are included only if and when the lease is reassessed.

Illustration 15–S7 Additional Differences between Preexisting Guidance in Lease Accounting and ASC 842

	Preexisting GAAP	New GAAP Under ASC 842
Reassessment of lease term	No reassessment unless the lease is modified or an option is exercised.	A lessee is required to reassess the lease term if a triggering event occurs that is under the lessee's control. A change to the lease term will lead to *remeasurement* of the right-of-use asset and liability using the current discount rate changes in lease payments based on an index or rate and might cause *reclassification* of the lease.
Discount rate	Lessee uses the lessor's implicit rate or its own incremental borrowing rate, whichever is lower.	Lessee uses the lessor's implicit rate if known, otherwise its own incremental borrowing rate.
Variable lease payments	Variable payments, such as those based on performance (e.g., a percentage of sales) are recognized in income when they are incurred (lessee) or earned (lessor).	Variable payments (not changes in those payments) that depend on an index or rate or are in-substance fixed payments are included as lease payments. Others, such as those based on performance (e.g., a percentage of sales) are recognized in income when they occur.
Lessee-guaranteed residual value	Total amount of a lessee-guaranteed residual value is included in the lease payments whose present value the lessee records as both a lease asset and a lease liability.	Only if a cash payment is predicted under a lessee-guaranteed residual value, the present value of that payment is added to the present value of the lease payments that the lessee records as both a right-of-use asset and a lease liability.
Lease versus non-lease payments	Property taxes and insurance are considered "executory costs" rather than lease payments. Land is separately classified when the fair value of the land is 25% or more of the combined fair value of the land and building.	Property taxes and insurance are not for a service provided by the lessor to the lessee and are therefore a part of lease payments rather than "nonlease payments." The right to use land is considered a separate lease component.
Commencement date and inception date	Lease-related assets and liabilities are measured on the inception date. The inception date is the date on which the principal terms of the lease are agreed to.	Lease-related assets and liabilities are measured on the commencement date. The lease commencement date is the date on which the lessor makes an underlying asset available for use by the lessee.
Sale-leasebacks (Appendix)	A gain on the sale of an asset in a sale leaseback arrangement is deferred and amortized over the lease term (or asset life if title is expected to transfer to the lessee). The lease portion of the transaction is evaluated and accounted for like any lease.	Sale is recorded only if the usual requirements for revenue recognition (Chapter 5) are met, it's not a financing lease (which would indicate the asset is effectively sold back to the lessee), and no repurchase option, unless the repurchase price is at the asset's fair value at the time of exercise. Any gain or loss is recognized at the time of the sale. If not a sale, transaction is accounted for as a loan.

. . . approximately 35% of our stores had provisions for contingent rentals based upon a percentage of defined sales volume. We recognize contingent rental expense when the achievement of specified sales targets is considered probable.

Illustration 15–S8

Disclosure of Contingent Rentals—Dollar General

Real World Financials

Reassessment of the lease payments may be triggered by a reassessment of the lease term, and requires a remeasurement of the lease liability and right-of-use asset. When remeasuring the lease liability, the lessee will use whatever interest rate prevails on the remeasurement date. Under preexisting GAAP, we don't reassess lease payments unless the lease is modified or an option is exercised.

Residual Value

Lessor accounting for a residual value is the same under either preexisting GAAP or new GAAP.

The lessee-guaranteed residual value of leased property is an estimate of what its commercial value will be at the end of the lease term.

Lessor. From the *lessor's* perspective, the residual value affects lease accounting the *same way under either preexisting GAAP or new GAAP:*

1. It contributes to the total amount to be recovered by the lessor and thus *reduces the amount of the periodic lease payments.*
2. Its present value is included along with the present value of the periodic lease payments as the lessor's net investment (that we record as a lease receivable), and
3. It is a component of *lease payments* when classifying a lease (present value of lease payments constitutes 90% under preexisting GAAP/"substantially all" of the assets fair value under new GAAP) only if it is guaranteed (by either the lessee or a third-party guarantor).

Preexisting GAAP: The lessee considers a guaranteed residual value to be an additional lease payment.

Lessee. The lessee views a residual value the same way under either preexisting GAAP or new GAAP *with one exception.* Sometimes a lease agreement includes a guarantee by the lessee that the lessor will recover a specified residual value when custody of the asset reverts back to the lessor at the end of the lease term. The lessee promises to return not only the property but also sufficient cash to provide the lessor with a minimum combined value. In effect, the guaranteed residual value is an additional lease payment that is to be paid in property, or cash, or both. If the lessee does not guarantee the residual value, it has no effect on lease accounting. If the lessee does guarantee all or part of a residual value:

A. In *preexisting GAAP,* any lessee-guaranteed residual value is included in the minimum lease payments, so its present value is included in the amount the lessee records as both a lease asset and a lease liability. If we assume six annual payments of $100,000 each, a 10% interest rate, and a $60,000 lessee-guaranteed residual value, the lease asset and lease liability are calculated as shown in Illustration 15–S9a.

Illustration 15–S9a

Lessee's Calculation of the Present Value of Minimum Lease Payments Including a Guaranteed Residual Value: Preexisting GAAP

Present value of periodic lease payments ($100,000 × 4.79079*)	$479,079
Plus: Present value of the residual value ($60,000 × 0.56447†)	33,868
Present value of minimum lease payments (recorded as a lease asset and a lease liability)	$512,947

*Present value of an annuity due of $1: $n = 6$, $i = 10\%$.
†Present value of $1: $n = 6$, $i = 10\%$.

New GAAP: The lessee includes an additional lease payment only if a cash payment is predicted.

B. In *new GAAP,* any lessee-guaranteed residual value is *not* included in the lease payments *unless* a cash payment is predicted. In that case, the present value of that cash payment is added to the present value of the periodic lease payments that the lessee records as both a right-of-use asset and a lease liability.

Let's assume that in the situation described in A. above that negotiations led to the lessee guaranteeing an $80,000 residual value. That means that if the property's value is less than $80,000 at the end of the six-year lease term, the lessee will pay cash for the difference. Since that value is expected to be $60,000, the expected excess guaranteed residual value is $80,000 − 60,000 = $20,000. The lessee views the expected excess guaranteed residual value as an additional cash flow to be paid to the lessor (addition to lease payments), and the right-of-use asset and lease liability are calculated as shown in Illustration 15–S9b.

Illustration 15–S9b

Lessee's Calculation of the Present Value of Lease Payments Including an Excess Lessee-Guaranteed Residual Value: ASC 842

Present value of periodic lease payments ($100,000 × 4.79079*)	$479,079
Plus: Present value of the residual value ($20,000 × 0.56447†)	11,289
Present value of minimum lease payments (recorded as a lease asset and a lease liability)	$490,368

*Present value of an annuity due of $1: $n = 6$, $i = 10\%$.
†Present value of $1: $n = 6$, $i = 10\%$.

Executory Costs

Preexisting GAAP: Executory costs
New GAAP: Nonlease payments

Service contracts, maintenance, hazard insurance, and property taxes are costs often associated with owning and operating an asset. Often, for convenience, a lease contract specifies that the lessor is to pay some or all of these costs, when these additional costs actually are embedded in the periodic payments made by the lessee to the lessor. The accounting question is whether to include these costs as separate components of the lease contract (to be expensed by the lessee) or, instead, as amounts to be capitalized as part of the lease asset.

Under preexisting GAAP, these are referred to as **executory costs** and are treated as separate components of the lease contract (to be expensed by the lessee) rather than capitalized as part of the lease asset. Let's say that a $2,000 per year maintenance agreement was arranged with an outside service for some leased equipment. The lessor will pay this amount annually to the maintenance firm. The lessee expenses the $2,000 annually as shown in Illustration 15–S10.

Executory costs that are included in periodic rental payments to be paid by the lessor are, in effect, indirectly paid by the lessee—and expensed by the lessee.

Equipment was leased under a capital lease specifying annual payments of $102,000 that include $2,000 that the lessor will use to pay an annual maintenance fee.

Lessee		
Maintenance expense	2,000	
Lease payable	100,000	
Cash (lease payment)		102,000
Lessor		
Cash (lease payment)	102,000	
Lease receivable		100,000
Maintenance fee payable*		2,000

*This assumes the $2,000 maintenance fee has not yet been paid to the outside maintenance service.

Illustration 15–S10
Lease Payments Including Executory Costs Paid by the Lessor: Preexisting GAAP

The $2,000 executory cost is excluded from the lease payments used to determine the lease asset and lease liability, which would be recorded at the present value of the $100,000 net payments. Other executory costs that are treated this way include repairs, insurance, and taxes.

ASC 842 treats these costs similarly, but with important differences, both conceptual and practical. Conceptually, the determining factor under the new guidance is whether the charge represents a *transfer of a good or service to the lessee.* If so, it qualifies as a "nonlease component" (executory cost under preexisting GAAP) of the payment and is separated from the lease payments as an expense.

Payments for taxes and insurance are executory costs under preexisting GAAP, but do not qualify as nonlease components, under new GAAP and thus must be included in the right-of-use asset and lease liability.

In application, if the $2,000 had been a fixed payment for *hazard insurance or property taxes,* that payment does not transfer to the lessee a separate good or service. Payments for hazard insurance and property taxes are specifically identified in the lease accounting guidance as part of the lease payments rather than nonlease components. So, in that case, the right-of-use asset and lease liability (and the lessor's lease receivable) would be measured as the present value of the *$102,000* lease payments, not $100,000.

Lessor Accounting

Lessor accounting is relatively unchanged by ASC 842 other than the terminology differences and its being updated to align with the new revenue recognition standard as we discussed.

CHAPTER

16 Accounting for Income Taxes

OVERVIEW

In this chapter we explore financial accounting and reporting for the effects of income taxes. The discussion defines and illustrates temporary differences, which are the basis for recognizing deferred tax assets and deferred tax liabilities, as well as permanent differences, which have no deferred tax consequences. You will learn how to adjust deferred tax assets and deferred tax liabilities when tax laws or rates change. We also discuss accounting for net operating loss carrybacks and carryforwards as well as intraperiod tax allocation.

LEARNING OBJECTIVES

After studying this chapter, you should be able to:

- **LO16–1** Describe the types of temporary differences that cause deferred tax liabilities and determine the amounts needed to record periodic income taxes. (*p. 908*)
- **LO16–2** Describe the types of temporary differences that cause deferred tax assets and determine the amounts needed to record periodic income taxes. (*p. 915*)
- **LO16–3** Describe when and how a valuation allowance is recorded for deferred tax assets. (*p. 918*)
- **LO16–4** Explain why permanent differences have no deferred tax consequences. (*p. 922*)
- **LO16–5** Explain how a change in tax rates affects the measurement of deferred tax amounts. (*p. 926*)
- **LO16–6** Determine income tax amounts when multiple temporary differences exist. (*p. 928*)
- **LO16–7** Describe when and how a net operating loss carryforward and a net operating loss carryback are recognized in the financial statements. (*p. 929*)
- **LO16–8** Explain how deferred tax assets and deferred tax liabilities are reported in a classified balance sheet and describe related disclosures. (*p. 934*)
- **LO16–9** Demonstrate how to account for uncertainty in income tax decisions. (*p. 935*)
- **LO16–10** Explain intraperiod tax allocation. (*p. 937*)
- **LO16–11** Discuss the primary differences between U.S. GAAP and IFRS with respect to accounting for income taxes. (*pp. 920* and *924*)

© Image Source

FINANCIAL REPORTING CASE

What's the Difference?

The board of directors for Times-Lehrer Industries is meeting for the first time since Laura Drake was asked to join the board. Laura was the director of the regional office of United Charities. Although she has broad experience with the tax advantages of charitable giving and the vast array of investment vehicles available to donors, her 15 years of experience with not-for-profit organizations has not exposed her to the issues involved with corporate taxation. This gap in her considerable business knowledge causes her to turn to you, Times-Lehrer's CFO and a long-time friend, who recommended Laura for appointment to the board.

"I must say," Laura confided, "I've looked long and hard at these statements, and I can't quite grasp why the amount reported for income tax expense is not the same as the amount of income taxes we paid. What's the difference?"

QUESTIONS

By the time you finish this chapter, you should be able to respond appropriately to the questions posed in this case. Compare your response to the solution provided at the end of the chapter.

1. What's the difference? Explain to Laura how differences between financial reporting standards and income tax rules might cause the income tax expense and the amount of income tax paid to differ. *(p. 907)*
2. What is the conceptual advantage of determining income tax expense as we do? *(p. 908)*
3. Are there differences between financial reporting standards and income tax rules that will not cause a difference between income tax expense and the amount of income taxes paid? *(p. 922)*

PART A

Deferred Tax Assets and Deferred Tax Liabilities

A manufacturer of leather accessories in the Midwest is obligated to pay the Internal Revenue Service $24 million in income taxes as determined by its 2018 income tax return. Another $9 million in income taxes also is attributable to 2018 activities. However, tax laws permit the company to postpone paying the additional $9 million until subsequent tax years because the company reports some revenues and expenses on the tax return in years other than when those amounts are reported in the income statement. In other words, before-tax income on the income statement is different from before-tax income on the company's tax return.

FINANCIAL Reporting Case

Q1, p. 907

Here's the accounting question: Does the company only have a current income tax liability of $24 million? Or does it also have a deferred income tax liability for the other $9 million? To phrase the question differently: Should the company report a 2018 income tax expense of only the $24 million tax payable for the current year, or should it report expense of $33 million to include the future tax effects of events already recognized? For perspective on this question, we should look closer at the circumstances that might create the situation. Such circumstances are called *temporary differences*.

Conceptual Underpinning

FINANCIAL Reporting Case

Q2, p. 907

The goals of financial accounting and tax accounting are not the same.

When a company prepares its tax return for a particular year, the revenues and expenses (and gains and losses) included on the return are, by and large, the same as those reported on the company's income statement for the same year. However, in some instances tax laws and financial accounting standards differ. The reason they differ is that the fundamental objectives of financial reporting and those of taxing authorities are not the same. Financial accounting standards are established to provide useful information to investors and creditors. Congress, on the other hand, establishes tax regulations to allow it to raise funds in a socially acceptable manner, as well as to influence the behavior of taxpayers. In pursuing the latter objective, Congress uses tax laws to encourage activities it deems desirable, such as investment in productive assets, and to discourage activities it deems undesirable, such as violations of law.

Accounting for income taxes is consistent with the accrual concept of accounting.

A consequence of differences between GAAP and tax rules is that tax payments frequently occur in years different from when the revenues and expenses that cause the taxes are generated. For example, in many situations, revenue is not recognized on the tax return until it is collected, but GAAP requires revenue to be recognized when performance obligations are satisfied. One way to deal with these timing differences would be to ignore them, and simply report tax expense in the income statement each period equal to whatever tax is paid in that period. However, that approach would not communicate to investors that the company's current activities have resulted in future tax consequences.

Companies should recognize income tax expense based on the "accrual concept," just like other expenses. That is, income tax expense reported each period should be the amount caused by that period's activities, regardless of *when* the tax laws require that the tax be paid. If tax laws allow a company to avoid a current tax payment by postponing when an amount is included in taxable income, the company must report a **deferred tax liability** based on the **future taxable amount**. On the other hand, if tax laws require the company to wait until a future period to take a tax deduction that *reduces* taxable income, the company reports a **deferred tax asset** reflecting the benefit of that **future deductible amount**. That means that tax expense includes not only current tax payable but also changes in the deferred tax assets and liabilities that represent taxes due in other periods but that resulted from the current period's operations.

To understand how that works, let's consider deferred tax liabilities and deferred tax assets in more detail, as well as the "temporary differences" that give rise to them.

Temporary Differences

● LO16–1

The differences in the rules for computing taxable income and those for financial reporting often cause amounts to be included in taxable income in a year later—or earlier—than the year in which they are recognized for financial reporting purposes. For example, you learned in Chapter 4 that income from selling properties on an installment basis is reported for financial reporting purposes in the year of the sale. But tax laws permit installment income to be reported on the tax return as it actually is received. This means taxable income might be less than accounting income in the year of an installment sale but higher than accounting income in later years when installment income is collected.

Temporary differences arise when tax rules and accounting rules recognize income in different periods.

The situation just described creates what's referred to as a **temporary difference** between pretax *accounting* income and *taxable* income and, consequently, between the amount of an asset or liability that is reported in the financial statements and the equivalent amount, called the *tax basis* of an asset or a liability, that is included in the company's tax records. In our example, the asset for which the temporary difference exists is the installment receivable that's recognized for financial reporting purposes, but not for tax purposes.

Deferred Tax Liabilities

It's important to understand that a temporary difference *originates* in one period and *reverses,* or turns around, in one or more subsequent periods. The temporary difference described above originates in the year the installment sales are made and are reported in the *income statement.* The temporary difference reverses in a future period when the installments are collected and income is reported on the *tax return.* An example is provided in Illustration 16–1.

Illustration 16–1

Revenue Reported on the Tax Return *after* the Income Statement

Kent Land Management reported pretax accounting income in 2018, 2019, and 2020 of $100 million, plus additional 2018 income of $40 million from installment sales of property. However, the installment sales income is reported on the tax return when collected, in 2019 ($10 million) and 2020 ($30 million).* The enacted tax rate is 40% each year.

($ in millions)	2018	2019	2020	Total
Pretax accounting income	$140	$100	$100	$340
Installment sale income on the income statement	(40)	0	0	(40)
Installment sale income on the tax return	0	10	30	40
Taxable income (tax return)	$100	$110	$130	$340

*The installment method is not available to accrual method taxpayers. H.R. 1180, sec. 536, 1999.

In 2018, taxable income is less than accounting income because income from installment sales is not reported on the tax return until 2019–2020.

Notice that pretax accounting income and taxable income total the same amount over the three-year period but are different in each individual year. In 2018, taxable income is $40 million *less* than accounting income because it does not include income from installment sales. The difference is temporary, though. That situation reverses over the next two years. In 2019 and 2020 taxable income is *more* than accounting income because income from the installment sales, reported in the income statement in 2018, becomes taxable during the next two years as installments are collected.

The 2018 deferred tax liability will become tax payable in the next two years.

Because tax laws permit the company to delay reporting this income as part of taxable income, the company is able to defer paying the tax on that income. As shown in Illustration 16–1A, that tax is not avoided, just deferred.

Illustration 16–1A

Determining and Recording Income Taxes—2018

($ in millions)	Current Year 2018	Future Taxable Amounts 2019	Future Taxable Amounts 2020	Future Taxable Amounts (total)
Pretax accounting income	$140			
Temporary difference:				
Installment income	(40)	$10	$30	$40
Taxable income (tax return)	$100			
Enacted tax rate	40%			40%
Tax payable currently	$ 40			

Reported in the income statement, not on the tax return

Deferred Tax Liability

	0 beg. bal.
	16
	16 end. bal.

Deferred Tax Liability	
Desired ending balance	$ 16
Less: Beginning balance	0
Change in balance	$16

Journal Entry at the End of 2018

Income tax expense (to balance)	56	
Income tax payable (determined above)		40
Deferred tax liability (determined above)		16

With **future taxable amounts** of $40 million, taxable at 40%, a $16 million **deferred tax liability** should be recognized as of the end of 2018. Because no previous balance exists, we credit deferred tax liability for the entire $16 million.

Each year, income tax expense comprises both the current and the deferred tax consequences of events and transactions already recognized. This means we:

1. Calculate the income tax that is payable currently.
2. Calculate what the ending balance in the deferred tax liability (or asset) should be.
3. Determine the change (debit or credit) in the deferred tax liability (or asset) necessary to reach that ending balance.
4. Combine that change with tax payable to determine income tax expense.

Tax expense is a "plug" determined by changes in the tax payable, deferred tax assets, and deferred tax liability accounts.

Notice that, under this approach, tax expense is not calculated directly, but rather is the result of the combination of income tax payable and any changes in deferred tax assets and liabilities. In other words, tax expense is a "plug" in the journal entry that is debited or credited to make the rest of the journal entry balance. That perspective will be important throughout this chapter.

Using the 2019 and 2020 income numbers, the change in deferred tax liability and journal entries to record income taxes for those years would be:

Deferred tax liability

1/1/2019	16 beg. bal.
change 4	
12/31/2019	12 ending bal.

2019	($ in millions)	
Income tax expense (to balance)	40	
Deferred tax liability [($30 million × 40%) − 16 million]	4	
Income tax payable ($110 million × 40%)		44

Deferred tax liability

1/1/2020	12 beg. bal.
change 12	
12/31/2020	0 ending bal.

2020		
Income tax expense (to balance)	40	
Deferred tax liability ($0 million − 12 million)	12	
Income tax payable ($130 million × 40%)		52

Now look at the activity in the deferred tax liability account over the life of the installment receivable. See how the temporary difference originates in 2018 and reverses in 2019 and 2020?

Deferred Tax Liability

($ in millions)			
		16	2018 ($40 × 40%)
2019 ($10 × 40%)	4		
2020 ($30 × 40%)	12		
		0	Balance after 3 years

Balance Sheet and Income Statement Perspectives

Deferred tax assets and liabilities can be computed from temporary book-tax differences.

The *tax basis* of an asset or liability is its original value for tax purposes reduced by any amounts included to date on tax returns.

Our perspective in this example so far has centered around the income effects of the installment sales and thus on the changes in the deferred tax liability as the temporary difference reverses. Another perspective starts with the balance sheet effect. An assumption underlying a balance sheet is that assets will be recovered (used or sold to produce cash) and liabilities will be settled (typically paid with cash). So, for example, receivables will be collected, machines will be used or sold, and liabilities will be paid when they are due. Those assets and liabilities typically create taxable or deductible amounts in the future when they are recovered (an installment receivable is collected and taxable income is increased; a machine is used and depreciation is deducted) or settled (a warranty liability is paid and warranty expense is deducted). Before that occurs, there is a temporary difference between the *book value* (also called the *carrying value* or *carrying amount*) of those assets and liabilities on the balance sheet and the tax basis of those assets and liabilities for the tax return. The tax basis of an asset or liability is its original value for tax purposes reduced by any amounts included to date on tax returns. We can calculate the related deferred tax asset or liability balance by multiplying the *temporary book-tax difference* by the applicable tax rate.

In our example, the company reports an installment receivable in the balance sheet in 2018 when it makes an installment sale. However, the tax return doesn't recognize a sale until cash has been collected, so there is no receivable for 2018 tax purposes. Therefore, as shown in Illustration 16–1B, we have a temporary book-tax difference in 2018 between the receivable's book value ($40) and its tax basis ($0), so we recognize a deferred tax liability to reflect the tax that will be paid when that difference reverses in the future. The book-tax difference (and the deferred tax liability) declines in 2019 and 2020 as the receivable is collected.

Illustration 16–1B
Temporary Book-Tax Difference

The deferred tax liability each year is the tax rate times the temporary difference between the financial statement book value of the receivable and its tax basis.

	December 31					
($ in millions)	2018		2019		2020	
Receivable from installment sales:						
Accounting book value	$40	$40	$(10)	$30	$(30)	$0
Tax basis	(0)	(0)	(0)	(0)	(0)	(0)
Temporary difference	$40	$40	$(10)	$30	$(30)	$0
Tax rate	↑ Originating Difference	× 40%	↑ Reversing Differences	× 40%	↑ Reversing Differences	× 40%
Deferred tax liability		$16		$12		$0

Of course, we should get to the same deferred tax asset or liability if we base our calculations on (a) future deductible and taxable amounts or (b) present temporary book-tax differences. They are two different perspectives of the same basic event. We consider both perspectives in subsequent examples in this chapter.

Types of Temporary Differences

Examples of temporary differences are provided in Illustration 16–2.

Illustration 16–2
Types of Temporary Differences

	Revenues (or gains)	Expenses (or losses)
Reported in the income statement now, but on the tax return later	• Installment sales of property (installment method for taxes) • Unrealized gain from recording investments at fair value (taxable when asset is sold)	• Estimated expenses and losses (tax-deductible when paid) • Unrealized loss from recording investments at fair value or inventory at LCM (tax-deductible when asset is sold)
Reported on the tax return now, but in the income statement later	• Rent collected in advance • Subscriptions collected in advance • Other revenue collected in advance	• Accelerated depreciation on the tax return in excess of straight-line depreciation in the income statement • Prepaid expenses (tax-deductible when paid)

- The temporary differences shown in the diagonal purple areas create *deferred tax liabilities* because they result in *taxable* amounts in some future year(s) when the related assets are recovered or the related liabilities are settled (when the temporary differences reverse).
- The temporary differences in the opposite diagonal blue areas create *deferred tax assets* because they result in *deductible* amounts in some future year(s) when the related assets are recovered or the related liabilities are settled (when the temporary differences reverse).

Additional Consideration

As shown in Illustration 16–2, temporary differences between the reported amount of an asset or liability in the financial statements and its tax basis are primarily caused by revenues, expenses, gains, and losses being included in taxable income in a year other than the year in which they are recognized for financial reporting purposes. Other events also can cause temporary differences between the reported amount of an asset or liability in the financial statements and its tax basis. Other such events that are beyond the scope of this textbook are briefly described in FASB ASC 740–10–25: Income Taxes–Overall–Recognition (previously "Accounting for Income Taxes," *Statement of Financial Accounting Standards No. 109* (Norwalk, Conn.: FASB, 1992), par. 11 e–h). Our discussions in this chapter focus on temporary differences caused by the timing of revenue and expense recognition, but it's important to realize that the concept of temporary differences embraces all differences that will result in taxable or deductible amounts in future years.

Be sure to notice that deferred tax liabilities can arise from either (a) a revenue being reported on the tax return after the income statement or (b) an expense being reported on the tax return before the income statement. Illustration 16–1 was of the first type. We look at the second type in Illustration 16–3, which examines deferred tax liabilities associated with depreciation.

Illustration 16–3

Expense Reported on the Tax Return before the Income Statement

To determine taxable income, we add back to accounting income the actual depreciation taken in the income statement and then subtract the depreciation deduction allowed on the tax return.

Courts Temporary Services reported pretax accounting income in 2018, 2019, 2020, and 2021 of $100 million. In 2018, an asset was acquired for $100 million. The asset is depreciated for financial reporting purposes over four years on a straight-line basis (no residual value). For tax purposes the asset's cost is deducted (by MACRS) over 2018–2021 as follows: $33 million, $44 million, $15 million, and $8 million. No other depreciable assets were acquired. The enacted tax rate is 40% each year.

	Temporary Difference				
	Originates		Reverses		
($ in millions)	**2018**	**2019**	**2020**	**2021**	**Total**
Pretax accounting income	$100	$100	$100	$100	$400
Depreciation on the income statement	25	25	25	25	100
Depreciation on the tax return	(33)	(44)	(15)	(8)	(100)
Taxable income (tax return)	$ 92	$ 81	$110	$117	$400

Notice that the temporary difference shown in Illustration 16–3 originates during more than a single year before it begins to reverse. This usually is true when depreciation is the cause of the temporary difference. Tax laws typically permit the cost of a depreciable asset to be deducted on the tax return sooner than it is reported as depreciation in the income statement.[1] This means taxable income will be less than pretax accounting income in the income statement during the years the tax deduction is higher than income statement depreciation, but higher than pretax accounting income in later years when the situation reverses. 2018 income taxes would be recorded as shown in Illustration 16–3A.

Let's follow the determination of income taxes for this illustration all the way through the complete reversal of the temporary difference. We assume accounting income is $100 million each year and that the only difference between pretax accounting income and taxable income is caused by depreciation. 2019 income taxes would be determined as shown in Illustration 16–3B.

[1]The accelerated depreciation method prescribed by the tax code is the modified accelerated cost recovery system (MACRS). The method is described in the Chapter 11 appendix.

Illustration 16–3A

Determining and Recording Income Taxes—2018

($ in millions)	Current Year 2018	Future Taxable Amounts 2019	2020	2021	Future Taxable Amounts (total)
Pretax accounting income	$ 100				
Temporary difference:					
Depreciation	(8)	$(19)	$10	$17	$ 8
Taxable income	$ 92				
Enacted tax rate	40%				40%
Tax payable currently	$36.8				

Tax depreciation is $8 million more than in the income statement.

Deferred Tax Liability	
	0 beg. bal.
3.2	
	3.2 end. bal.

Deferred Tax Liability	
Ending balance needed	$3.2
Less: Beginning balance	0
Change in balance	$3.2

Journal Entry at the End of 2018

Income tax expense (to balance)	40	
Income tax payable (determined above)		36.8
Deferred tax liability (determined above)		3.2

Taxable income is $8 million less than accounting income because that much more depreciation is deducted on the 2018 tax return ($33 million) than is reported in the income statement ($25 million).

Income tax expense is comprised of two components: the amount payable currently and the amount deferred until later.

Illustration 16–3B

Determining and Recording Income Taxes—2019

($ in millions)	2018	Current Year 2019	Future Taxable Amounts 2020	2021	Future Taxable Amounts (total)
Pretax accounting income		$ 100			
Temporary difference:					
Depreciation	$(8)	(19)	$10	$17	$ 27
Taxable income (tax return)		81			
Enacted tax rate		40%			40%
Tax payable currently		$32.4			

Deferred Tax Liability	
	3.2 beg. bal.
7.6	
	10.8 end. bal.

Deferred Tax Liability	
Ending balance needed	$ 10.8
Less: Beginning balance	(3.2)
Change in balance	$ 7.6

Journal Entry at the End of 2019

Income tax expense (to balance)	40	
Income tax payable (determined above)		32.4
Deferred tax liability (determined above)		7.6

The cumulative temporary difference ($27 million) is both (a) the sum of the amounts originating in 2018 ($8 million) and in 2019 ($19 million) and (b) the sum of the amounts reversing in 2020 ($10 million) and in 2021 ($17 million).

Since a balance of $3.2 million already exists, $7.6 million must be added.

Notice that each year the appropriate balance is determined for the deferred tax liability. That amount is compared with any existing balance to determine whether the account must be either increased or decreased.

Income taxes for 2020 would be recorded as shown in Illustration 16–3C.

Illustration 16–3C

Determining and Recording Income Taxes—2020

A credit balance of $6.8 million is needed in the deferred tax liability account.

Since a credit balance of $10.8 million already exists, $4 million must be deducted (debited).

A portion of the tax deferred from 2018 and 2019 is now payable in 2020.

($ in millions)	2018	2019	Current Year 2020	Future Taxable Amounts 2021	Future Taxable Amounts (total)
Pretax accounting income			$100		
Temporary difference:					
Depreciation	$(8)	$(19)	10	$17	$ 17
Taxable income (tax return)			$110		
Enacted tax rate			40%		40%
Tax payable currently			$ 44		

Deferred Tax Liability (T-account)

Debit	Credit
	10.8 beg. bal.
4.0	
	6.8 end. bal.

Deferred Tax Liability	
Ending balance needed	$ 6.8
Less: Beginning balance	(10.8)
Change in balance	$ (4.0)

Journal Entry at the End of 2020

Income tax expense (to balance)	40	
Deferred tax liability (determined above)	4	
Income tax payable (determined above)		44

Income taxes for 2021 would be recorded as shown in Illustration 16–3D.

Illustration 16–3D

Determining and Recording Income Taxes—2021

Because the entire temporary difference has now reversed, there is a zero cumulative temporary difference, and the balance in the deferred tax liability should be zero.

Since a credit balance of $6.8 million exists, that amount must be deducted (debited). The final portion of the tax deferred from 2018 and 2019 is payable in 2021.

($ in millions)	2018	2019	2020	Current Year 2021	Future Taxable Amounts (total)
Pretax accounting income				$ 100	
Temporary difference:					
Depreciation	$(8)	$(19)	$10	17	$ 0
Taxable income (tax return)				$ 117	
Enacted tax rate				40%	40%
Tax payable currently				$46.8	

Deferred Tax Liability (T-account)

Debit	Credit
	6.8 beg. bal.
6.8	
	0 end. bal.

Deferred Tax Liability	
Ending balance needed	$ 0.0
Less: Beginning balance	(6.8)
Change in balance	$(6.8)

Journal Entry at the End of 2021

Income tax expense (to balance)	40.0	
Deferred tax liability (determined above)	6.8	
Income tax payable (determined above)		46.8

The deferred tax liability increases the first two years and becomes tax payable over the next two years.

Notice that the deferred tax liability is increased in 2018–2019 and decreased in 2020–2021.

Deferred Tax Liability

($ in millions)			
		3.2	2018 ($ 8 × 40%)
2020 ($10 × 40%)	4.0	7.6	2019 ($19 × 40%)
2021 ($17 × 40%)	6.8		
		0	Balance after 4 years

We also can calculate this deferred tax liability each year using the alternate perspective of looking at the temporary book–tax difference that exists for the depreciable asset. Its book value is its cost minus accumulated straight-line depreciation. Its tax basis is its cost minus accumulated depreciation deductions taken on its tax return.

	December 31								
($ in millions)			2018		2019		2020		2021
Depreciable asset:									
Accounting book value	$100	$(25)	$75	$(25)	$ 50	$(25)	$ 25	$(25)	$ 0
Tax basis	100	(33)	67	(44)	23	(15)	8	(8)	0
Temporary difference		$ 8	$ 8	$ 19	$ 27	$(10)	$ 17	$(17)	$ 0
Tax rate			40%		40%		40%		40%
Deferred tax liability			$3.2		$10.8		$6.8		$ 0
		Originating Differences				Reversing Differences			

Deferred Tax Assets

The temporary differences illustrated to this point produce future taxable amounts when the temporary differences reverse. Future taxable amounts mean taxable income will be increased relative to pretax accounting income in one or more future years, so we recognize a deferred tax liability to reflect the tax that will be due in those years. Sometimes, though, the future tax consequence of a temporary difference will be to *decrease* taxable income relative to accounting income. Such situations produce what's referred to as **future deductible amounts**. These have favorable future tax consequences that are recognized as **deferred tax assets**. Unlike most assets, management views deferred tax assets to be *less* desirable than deferred tax liabilities. The reason is that deferred tax liabilities result from having lower taxable income (and thus lower tax) now. As we see in this section, deferred tax assets result from taxable income (and tax) being higher now than later. It's more desirable to delay paying taxes as long as possible.

● LO16–2

Deferred tax assets are recognized for the future tax benefits of temporary differences that create future deductible amounts.

As noted in Illustration 16–2, one circumstance that requires recognition of a deferred tax asset is when estimated expenses are recognized in income statements when incurred but deducted on tax returns in later years when the expenses are actually paid. Illustration 16–4 provides an example: a quality-assurance warranty.

RDP Networking reported pretax accounting income in 2018, 2019, and 2020 of $70 million, $100 million, and $100 million, respectively. The 2018 income statement includes a $30 million warranty expense that is deducted for tax purposes when paid in 2019 ($15 million) and 2020 ($15 million). The income tax rate is 40% each year.

	Temporary Difference			
	Originates	**Reverses**		
($ in millions)	**2018**	**2019**	**2020**	**Total**
Pretax accounting income	$ 70	$100	$100	$270
Warranty expense in the income statement	30			30
Warranty expense on the tax return		(15)	(15)	(30)
Taxable income (tax return)	$100	$ 85	$ 85	$270

Illustration 16–4

Expense Reported on the Tax Return after the Income Statement

In 2018, taxable income is more than pretax accounting income because the warranty expense is not deducted on the tax return until paid.

At the end of 2018, the amounts needed to record income tax for 2018 would be determined as shown in Illustration 16–4A.

Illustration 16–4A

Determining and Recording Income Taxes—2018

Because the warranty expense is subtracted in the 2018 income statement but isn't deductible on the 2018 tax return, it is added back to pretax accounting income to find taxable income.

($ in millions)	Current Year 2018	Future Deductible Amounts 2019	Future Deductible Amounts 2020	Future Taxable Amounts (total)
Pretax accounting income	$ 70			
Temporary difference:				
Warranty expense in the income statement	30	$(15)	$(15)	$(30)
Taxable income (tax return)	$100			
Enacted tax rate	40%			40%
Tax payable currently	$ 40			

Deferred Tax Asset	
beg. bal. 0	
12	
end. bal. 12	

Deferred Tax Asset	
Ending balance needed	$ 12
Less: Beginning balance	0
Change in balance	$ 12

The amounts deductible in 2019 and 2020 will later produce tax benefits that are recognized now as a deferred tax asset.

Journal Entry at the End of 2018

Income tax expense (to balance)	28	
Deferred tax asset (determined above)	12	
Income tax payable (determined above)		40

If we continue the assumption of $85 million taxable income in each of 2019 and 2020, income tax those years would be recorded this way:

2019		
Income tax expense (to balance)	40	
Deferred tax asset ($15 million × 40%)		6
Income tax payable ($85 million × 40%)		34
2020		
Income tax expense (to balance)	40	
Deferred tax asset ($15 million × 40%)		6
Income tax payable ($85 million × 40%)		34

At the end of 2018 and 2019, the company reports a deferred tax asset for future income tax benefits. That deferred tax asset is reduced to zero by the end of 2020.

Deferred Tax Asset

			($ in millions)
2018 ($30 × 40%)	12		
		6	2019 ($15 × 40%)
		6	2020 ($15 × 40%)
Balance after 3 years	0		

Income taxes payable in 2019 and 2020 are less because of the taxes prepaid in 2018.

We also can calculate this deferred tax asset each year using the alternative perspective of looking at the "temporary book-tax difference" that exists for the warranty liability. The warranty liability starts with a book value of $30 in the balance sheet, but a tax basis of $0. That temporary book-tax difference of $30 in 2018 falls to $15 in 2019 and then $0 in 2020 as the warranty liability is satisfied.

($ in millions)	2018		2019		2020	
	December 31					
Warranty liability:						
Accounting book value	$30	$30	$(15)	$15	$(15)	$0
Tax basis	(0)	(0)	(0)	(0)	(0)	(0)
Temporary difference	$30	$30	$(15)	$15	$(15)	$0
Tax rate	↑	× 40%	↑	× 40%	↑	× 40%
Deferred tax asset		$12		$ 6		$0
	Originating Difference		Reversing Differences			

A warranty liability is recognized for financial reporting purposes when the product is sold:

2018	Warr. exp	30	
	Liability		30

and reduced when the expense is paid:

2019	Liability	15	
	Cash		15
2020	Liability	15	
	Cash		15

The preceding is an example of an estimated expense that is reported in the income statement when incurred but deducted on tax returns in later years when actually paid. A second type of temporary difference that gives rise to a deferred tax asset is a *revenue* that is taxed when collected but recognized on income statements in later years when actually earned. Illustration 16–5 demonstrates this second type with a common example: deferred revenue.

Illustration 16–5

Revenue Reported on the Tax Return before the Income Statement

Tomorrow Publications reported pretax accounting income in 2018, 2019, and 2020 of $80 million, $115 million, and $105 million, respectively. The 2018 income statement does not include $20 million of magazine subscriptions received that year for one- and two-year subscriptions. The subscription revenue is reported for tax purposes in 2018. The revenue will be recognized in 2019 ($15 million) and 2020 ($5 million). The income tax rate is 40% each year.

	Temporary Difference			
	Originates	Reverses		
($ in millions)	2018	2019	2020	Total
Pretax accounting income	$ 80	$115	$105	$300
Subscription revenue in the income statement		(15)	(5)	(20)
Subscription revenue on the tax return	20	0	0	20
Taxable income (tax return)	$100	$100	$100	$300

In 2018, taxable income is more than accounting income because subscription revenue is not reported in the income statement until 2019 and 2020.

Notice that this temporary difference produces future *deductible* amounts. In 2018, taxable income is $20 million *more* than pretax accounting income because it includes the deferred subscription revenue not yet reported in the income statement. However, in 2019 and 2020 taxable income is *less* than accounting income because the subscription revenue is recognized and reported in the income statements but not on the tax returns of those two years.

A deferred tax asset is recognized when an existing temporary difference will produce future deductible amounts.

In effect, tax laws require the company to prepay the income tax on this revenue, which is a sacrifice now but will benefit the company later when the revenue is recognized but not taxed. In the meantime, the company has an asset representing this future income tax benefit.

At the end of 2018, the amounts needed to record income tax for 2018 would be determined as shown in Illustration 16–5A.

At the end of 2018 and 2019, the company reports a deferred tax asset for future tax benefits. That deferred tax asset is reduced to zero by the end of 2020.

Deferred Tax Asset

			($ in millions)
2018 ($20 × 40%)	8		
		6	2019 ($15 × 40%)
		2	2020 ($ 5 × 40%)
Balance after 3 years	0		

Income taxes payable in 2019 and 2020 are less because of the taxes prepaid in 2018.

Illustration 16–5A

Determining and Recording Income Taxes—2018

($ in millions)	2018	Future Deductible Amounts 2019	2020	Future Deductible Amounts (total)
Pretax accounting income	$ 80			
Temporary difference:				
Subscription revenue	20	$(15)	$(5)	$(20)
Taxable income	$100			
Enacted tax rate	40%			40%
Tax payable currently	$ 40			

$20 million is taxable in 2018, but not yet recognized in the income statement.

Deferred Tax Asset	
beg. bal. 0	
change 8	
end. bal. 8	

Deferred Tax Asset	
Ending balance needed	$ 8
Less: Beginning balance	0
Change in balance	$ 8

Journal Entry at the End of 2018

Income tax expense (to balance)	32	
Deferred tax asset (determined above)	8	
Income tax payable (determined above)		40

Again, we instead could determine the deferred tax asset as the future tax benefit from the reversal of a temporary difference between the balance sheet's book value of the subscription liability (a deferred revenue account) and its tax basis.[2]

A liability is recognized for financial reporting purposes when the cash is received:

2018	Cash	20	
	Liability		20

and reduced when the revenue is recognized:

2019	Liability	15	
	Revenue		15
2020	Liability	5	
	Revenue		5

From a tax perspective, there is no liability.

	December 31					
($ in millions)	2018		2019		2020	
Liability—subscriptions:						
Accounting book value	$20	$20	$(15)	$ 5	$(5)	$ 0
Tax basis	(0)	(0)	(0)	(0)	(0)	(0)
Temporary difference	$20	$20	$(15)	$ 5	$(5)	$ 0
Tax rate		× 40%		× 40%		× 40%
Deferred tax asset		$ 8		$ 2		$ 0
	Originating Difference		Reversing Differences			

Valuation Allowance

● LO16–3

We recognize deferred tax assets for all deductible temporary differences.[3] However, we then reduce a deferred tax asset by a valuation allowance if it is "more likely than not" that some portion or all of the deferred tax asset will not be realized.[4] Remember, a future deductible amount reduces taxable income in the future and saves taxes only if there is taxable income to be reduced when that deduction is available. So, a **valuation allowance** is needed if taxable income is anticipated to be insufficient to realize the tax benefit.

[2]It is less intuitive to view deferred revenue (Illustration 16–5) as producing future deductible amounts when the deferred revenue liability is settled than it is to view the future deductibility of an estimated expense (Illustration 16–4) as a future deductible amount. Nevertheless, the recognition of deferred tax assets for the future tax benefits of deferred revenue liability temporary differences is consistent with GAAP because these deferred revenue liabilities are reported as if they represent future refundable amounts and therefore future deductible amounts.

[3]Unless the deductibility itself is uncertain. In that case, whether we recognize a deferred tax asset (and if so, its amount) is determined in accordance with FASB ASC 740–10–25: Income Taxes–Overall–Recognition (previously FIN 48), discussed later in the chapter.

[4]"More likely than not" means a likelihood of more than 50%, FASB ASC 740–10–30: Income Taxes–Overall–Initial Measurement (previously "Accounting for Income Taxes," Statement of Financial Accounting Standards No. 109 (Norwalk, Conn.: FASB, 1992), par. 17).

For example, let's say that in the previous illustration management determines that it's more likely than not that $3 million of the deferred tax asset ultimately will not be realized. The deferred tax asset would be reduced by the creation of a valuation allowance as follows:

	($ in millions)	
Income tax expense	3	
Valuation allowance—deferred tax asset		3

A valuation allowance is needed if it is more likely than not that some portion or all of a deferred tax asset will not be realized.

The effect is to increase the income tax expense as a result of reduced expectations of future tax savings. In the 2018 balance sheet, the deferred tax asset would be reported at its estimated net realizable value:

Deferred tax asset	$8
Less: Valuation allowance—deferred tax asset	(3)
	$5

This is not a new concept for you. You've reduced assets before using a valuation allowance. Suppose, for example, that you have accounts receivable of $8 million but expect that $3 million of that amount will not ultimately be collected from your customers. You would reduce the asset indirectly using a valuation allowance:

Accounts receivable	$8
Less: Allowance for uncollectible accounts	(3)
	$5

Additional Consideration

The decision as to whether a valuation allowance is needed should be based on the weight of all available evidence. The real question is whether or not there will be sufficient taxable income in future years for the anticipated tax benefit to be realized. The benefit of future deductible amounts can be realized only if future income is at least equal to the deferred deductions. After all, a deduction reduces taxes only if it reduces taxable income.

All evidence—both positive and negative—should be considered. For instance, operating losses in recent years or anticipated circumstances that would adversely affect future operations would constitute negative evidence. On the other hand, a strong history of profitable operations or sizable, existing contracts would constitute positive evidence of sufficient taxable income to be able to realize the deferred tax asset.

Managerial actions that could be taken to reduce or eliminate a valuation allowance when deferred tax assets are not otherwise expected to be realized must be considered. These tax-planning strategies include any prudent and feasible actions management might take to realize a tax benefit while it is available.

This having been said, it should be clear that the decision as to whether or not a valuation allowance is used, as well as how large the allowance should be, rests squarely on managerial judgment. Because that decision directly impacts the amount of income tax expense and therefore reported income, it has obvious implications for earnings quality assessment from an analyst's perspective.

At the end of each reporting period, the valuation allowance is reevaluated. The appropriate balance is decided on and the valuation allowance is adjusted—up or down—to create that balance. For instance, let's say that at the end of the following year, 2019, available evidence now indicates that $500,000 of the deferred tax asset at the end of 2019 ultimately will not be realized. We would adjust the valuation allowance to reflect the indicated amount:

	($ in millions)	
Valuation allowance—deferred tax asset ($3 – 0.5)	2.5	
Income tax expense		2.5

Valuation Allowance—Deferred Tax Asset

	Debit	Credit
1/1/2019		3
	2.5	
12/31/2019		0.5

The disclosure note shown in Illustration 16–6 accompanied the January 30, 2016, annual report of **Sears Holdings Corporation**, which operates a variety of retailers including Sears, Kmart, and Lands' End. Sears disclosed that it had deferred tax assets of $5 billion, offset by a valuation allowance of $4.8 billion. Why such a large valuation allowance? Illustration 16–6 provides Sears's depressing explanation.

Illustration 16–6

Explanation for Valuation Allowance—Sears Holding Corporation

Real World Financials

Note 10 – Income Taxes (in part)

Management assesses the available positive and negative evidence to estimate if sufficient future taxable income will be generated to use the existing deferred tax assets. A significant piece of objective negative evidence evaluated was the cumulative loss incurred over the three-year periods ended January 30, 2016, January 31, 2015, and February 1, 2014.

Given its large recent losses, Sears cannot argue that it's more likely than not that it will have sufficient future income to utilize its deferred tax assets, so it must record a large valuation allowance.

International Financial Reporting Standards

Valuation Allowances. Under U.S. GAAP, companies recognize deferred tax assets and then reduce those assets with an offsetting valuation allowance if it is not "more likely than not" that the asset will be realized. In contrast, under IFRS, deferred tax assets only are recognized if it is probable (defined as "more likely than not") that they will be realized. Thus, while the end result is the same, under U.S. GAAP, gross deferred tax assets may be larger and offset with valuation allowances as compared to how the same company would appear under IFRS.

Disclosures Linking Tax Expense with Changes in Deferred Tax Assets and Liabilities

We've now worked through four examples that illustrate revenue-related and expense-related deferred tax assets and deferred tax liabilities. In each example, the journal entry to recognize tax expense included three items: income tax payable, the change in the deferred tax asset or liability, and (to balance) the debit to tax expense (or credit to tax benefit). We've also seen that changes in the valuation allowance against deferred tax assets have an offsetting effect on tax expenses. Companies provide disclosure in the notes that help investors see these relationships. As an example, let's look at the tax note that appeared in the January 31, 2015, annual report of **Shoe Carnival, Inc.**, a large footwear retailer.

Illustrations 16–7A shows enough of Shoe Carnival's tax note to reproduce a journal entry that summarizes the company's 2014 tax expense. We just have to understand that "total current" in the note refers to income tax payable, "total deferred" refers to the total change in deferred tax assets and liabilities, "valuation allowance" refers to the change in the valuation allowance, and "total provision" refers to income tax expense:

Income tax expense	16,175		
Deferred tax assets and liabilities	2,493		} $2,493 − 1,943 = $550
Valuation allowance		1,943	
Income tax payable		16,725	

We can see from this journal entry that Shoe Carnival's operations caused total deferred tax assets and liabilities to change by a debit of **$2,493** during 2014, and its valuation allowance against deferred tax assets changed by an offsetting credit of **$1,943**, so the total change in these accounts was **$550**. Let's verify that change by comparing the 2014 fiscal year end (January 31, 2015) and 2013 fiscal year end (February 1, 2014) balances of

Illustration 16–7A

Disclosure of Tax Expense—Shoe Carnival, Inc.

Real World Financials

Note 7 – Income Taxes (in part)

The provision for income taxes consisted of:

($ in thousands)	2014	2013	2012
Current:			
Federal	$ 14,575	$15,366	$19,581
State	1,800	1,805	2,601
Puerto Rico	350	185	79
Total current	16,725	17,356	22,261
Deferred:			
Federal	(1,229)	(139)	(2,692)
State	(115)	(138)	(304)
Puerto Rico	(1,149)	(444)	(350)
Total deferred	**(2,493)**	(721)	(3,346)
Valuation allowance	**1,943**	0	0
Total provision	$16,175	$ 16,635	$18,915

Shoe Carnival's deferred tax assets, valuation allowance and deferred tax liabilities, shown in Illustration 16–7B.

Illustration 16–7B

Disclosure of Deferred Tax Assets and Liabilities—Shoe Carnival, Inc.

Real World Financials

Note 7 – Income Taxes (in part)

Deferred income taxes are the result of temporary differences in the recognition of revenue and expense for tax and financial reporting purposes. The sources of these differences and the tax effect of each are as follows:

($ in thousands)	January 31, 2015		February 1, 2014	
Deferred tax assets:				
Accrued rent	$ 4,045		$ 3,543	
Accrued compensation	5,896		5,625	
Accrued employee benefits	523		506	
Inventory	740		411	
Self-insurance reserves	592		593	
Lease incentives	12,073		10,003	
Net operating loss carry forward	1,943		449	
Other	367		396	
Total deferred tax assets	26,179		21,526	
Valuation allowance	(1,943)		0	
Total deferred tax assets—net of valuation allowance	24,236		21,526	
Deferred tax liabilities:				
Depreciation	17,767		15,625	
Capitalized costs	1,284		1,180	
Puerto Rico net operating loss carry forward impact to federal taxes	0		444	
Other	1		3	
Total deferred tax liabilities	19,052		16,892	
Net deferred tax asset	$ 5,184	–	$4,634	= **$550**

We can see from Illustration 16–7B that Shoe Carnival has a net deferred tax asset of $5,184 as of January 31, 2015 (the end of its 2014 fiscal year), equal to its total deferred tax asset of $26,179 less its valuation allowance of $1,943 and its total deferred tax liability of $19,052. Compared to the net deferred tax asset of $4,634 at February 1, 2014, we see that the net deferred tax asset has increased by $5,184 – 4,634 = **$550**. Now look back at our journal entry following

Illustration 16–7A. That entry showed an increase in net deferred tax assets (**$2,493**) with an offsetting increase in valuation allowance (**$1,943**), again totaling **$550**. See how the tax expense journal entry ties to the changes in deferred tax assets, liabilities and valuation allowance?

Additional Consideration

The amount of change in deferred taxes reconciles perfectly between the tables shown in Illustrations 16–7A and 16–7B. That won't always be the case in practice because the table shown in Illustration 16–7A focuses on taxes from *continuing operations,* but the deferred tax assets and liabilities listed in Illustration 16–7B relate to all aspects of the company. For example, if Shoe Carnival had deferred taxes associated with discontinued operations or other comprehensive income items, or if it had added deferred tax assets and liabilities from an acquisition during the year, the change in deferred taxes from continuing operations wouldn't capture everything that affected deferred tax assets and liabilities.

Permanent Differences

LO16–4

So far, we've dealt with temporary differences between the reported amount of an asset or liability in the financial statements and its tax basis. However, some differences aren't temporary. Rather, they are caused by transactions and events that under existing tax law will *never* affect taxable income or taxes payable. Interest received from investments in bonds issued by state and municipal governments, for instance, is exempt from taxation. Interest revenue of this type is, of course, reported as revenue on the recipient's income statement but not on its tax return—not now, not later. So, there is a **permanent difference** between pretax accounting income and taxable income. This situation will *not* reverse in a later year—the tax-free income will *never* be reported on the tax return.

FINANCIAL Reporting Case

Q3, p. 907

Illustration 16–8 provides examples of permanent differences that commonly occur in practice.

Illustration 16–8

Differences without Deferred Tax Consequences

Provisions of the tax laws, in some instances, dictate that the amount of a revenue that is taxable or expense that is deductible permanently differs from the amount reported in the income statement.

- Interest received from investments in bonds issued by state and municipal governments (not taxable).
- Investment expenses incurred to obtain tax-exempt income (not tax deductible).
- Life insurance proceeds on the death of an insured executive (not taxable).
- Premiums paid for life insurance policies when the payer is the beneficiary (not tax deductible).
- Compensation expense pertaining to some employee stock option plans (not tax deductible).
- Expenses due to violations of the law (not tax deductible).
- Difference in tax paid on foreign income permanently reinvested in the foreign country and the amount that would have been paid if taxed at U.S. rates.
- Portion of dividends received from U.S. corporations that is not taxable due to the dividends received deduction.*
- Tax deduction for depletion of natural resources (percentage depletion) that is allowed in excess of an already full-depleted asset's cost.†

*When a corporation owns shares of another U.S. corporation, a percentage of the dividends from those shares is exempt from taxation due to the dividends received deduction. The percentage is 70% if the investor owns less than 20% of the investee's shares, 80% for 20% to 80% ownership, and 100% for more than 80% ownership.
†The cost of natural resources is reported as depletion expense over their extraction period for financial reporting purposes, but tax rules prescribe sometimes different percentages of cost to be deducted for tax purposes. There usually is a difference between the cost depletion and percentage depletion that doesn't eventually reverse.

Accounting for permanent differences is less complex than is accounting for temporary differences. We calculate taxes payable according to the tax law, and, since permanent differences are not temporary, we don't create a deferred tax asset or liability. Therefore, tax expense is determined by tax payable. The term *permanent difference* doesn't refer to a difference between tax payable and tax expense—those are the same with respect to this item. Rather, it refers to a difference between taxable income and pretax accounting income. That's why we adjust pretax accounting income in the illustrations that follow to eliminate permanent differences when calculating tax payable.

To compare temporary and permanent differences, we can modify Illustration 16–1 to include nontaxable income in Kent Land Management's 2019 pretax accounting income. We do this in Illustration 16–9.

Illustration 16–9

Temporary and Permanent Differences

Kent Land Management reported pretax accounting income in 2018 of $100 million except for additional income of $40 million from installment sales of property and $5 million interest from investments in municipal bonds in 2018. The installment sales income is reported for tax purposes in 2019 ($10 million) and 2020 ($30 million). The enacted tax rate is 40% each year.

($ in millions)	Current Year 2018	Future Taxable Amounts 2019	Future Taxable Amounts 2020	Future Taxable Amounts (total)
Pretax accounting income	$145			
Permanent difference:				
Municipal bond interest	(5)			
Temporary difference:				
Installment income	(40)	$10	$30	$40
Taxable income (tax return)	$100			
Enacted tax rate	40%			40%
Tax payable currently	$ 40			

Deferred Tax Liability	
	0 beg. bal.
	16
	16 end. bal.

Deferred Tax Liability	
Ending balance needed	$16
Less: Beginning balance	0
Change in balance	$16

Journal Entry at the End of 2018

Income tax expense (to balance)	56	
Income tax payable (determined above)		40
Deferred tax liability (determined above)		16

Because interest on municipal bonds is tax exempt, it is reported only in the income statement. This difference between pretax accounting income and taxable income does not reverse later.

A company's effective tax rate is calculated by dividing the company's tax expense by its pretax accounting income. Permanent differences affect the effective tax rate because they affect pretax accounting income. Let's look at Illustration 16–9 to understand why that's the case. In Illustration 16–9, the effective tax rate is $56 million ÷ $145 million, or 38.6%. That's with $5 million of municipal bond interest included in the $145 million of pretax accounting income. If, instead, pretax accounting income hadn't included the $5 million of municipal bond interest, it would have been only $140 million, and the effective tax rate would have been $56 million ÷ $140 million, or 40%. Including the municipal bond interest in pretax accounting income increased the denominator of the effective tax rate, so it produced a lower effective tax rate.

The *effective tax rate* equals tax expense divided by pretax accounting income.

More generally, nontaxable revenues and gains like municipal bond interest are permanent differences that result in *higher* pretax accounting income, so they produce effective tax rates that are *lower* than the statutory tax rate. Likewise, nondeductible expenses and losses are permanent differences that result in *lower* pretax accounting income, so they produce effective tax rates that are *higher* than the statutory tax rate. Companies are required to

Permanent differences affect a company's effective tax rate.

report a reconciliation between their effective and statutory tax rates in disclosure notes, as shown in Illustration 16–10's example from Walmart's financial statements for the fiscal year ended January 31, 2016.

Illustration 16–10
Effective Tax Rate—Walmart
Real World Financials

Note 9: Taxes (in part)
Effective Tax Rate Reconciliation

	Fiscal Year Ended January 31,		
	2016	**2015**	**2014**
U.S. statutory tax rate	35.0%	35.0%	35.0%
U.S. state income taxes, net of federal income tax benefit	1.8%	1.8%	2.0%
Income taxed outside the U.S.	(4.0)%	(2.7)%	(2.8)%
Net impact of repatriated international earnings	0.1%	(1.5)%	(1.4)%
Other, net	(2.6)%	(0.4)%	0.1%
Effective income tax rate	30.3%	32.2%	32.9%

Additional Consideration

Accounting for taxes on unrepatriated foreign earnings. The biggest "permanent difference" in many companies' effective tax rate reconciliation relates to taxes on foreign earnings. Companies often seek to minimize their tax bills by arranging their operations so their income is recognized outside the United States in jurisdictions that have low tax rates. Those lower tax bills are viewed as creating permanent differences so long as the company does not intend to "repatriate" the foreign earnings by transferring those earnings back to the United States. A company still must include the foreign income in pretax accounting income on the income statement, but that income is taxed at the lower foreign rate, so income tax payable is lower, tax expense is lower, and the company's effective tax rate is lower.

What if management changes its mind and decides to repatriate foreign earnings? In that case, the company must pay tax at the higher U.S. rate, making up the tax previously avoided. Companies usually don't want to pay that tax, so you will hear companies talk about having cash "trapped" overseas and needing to raise cash in other ways. For example, in 2013 Apple announced that it would be returning $60 billion to shareholders by repurchasing stock. Apple had $145 billion of cash and short-term investments at its disposal, so no problem, right? Wrong. Only $45 billion of Apple's cash was in the United States, so it issued $17 billion in bonds to make up the shortfall instead of paying tax to repatriate cash from foreign operations.

If a company does repatriate foreign earnings and repatriates cash, they have a higher tax bill and higher tax expense. Pretax accounting income is unaffected (remember, that income was recognized in the period in which it was earned), so the higher tax expense results in a higher effective tax rate. The company's original choice not to repatriate created a "permanent" difference that reduced the effective tax rate, and the company's later decision to repatriate creates an offsetting "permanent" difference that goes in the other direction.

International Financial Reporting Standards

LO16–11

Non-Tax Differences Affect Taxes. Despite the similar approaches for accounting for taxation under IAS No. 12, "Income Tax," and U.S. GAAP, differences in reported amounts for deferred taxes are among the most frequent between the two reporting approaches.[5] The reason is that a great many of the nontax differences between IFRS and U.S. GAAP affect deferred taxes as well.

For example, we noted in Chapter 13 that we accrue a loss contingency under U.S. GAAP if it's both probable and can be reasonably estimated and that IFRS guidelines are similar, but the threshold is "more likely than not." This is a lower threshold than "probable." In this

(continued)

[5]"Income Taxes," International Accounting Standard No. 12 (IASCF), as amended effective January 1, 2014.

(concluded)

chapter, we noted that accruing a loss contingency (like warranty expense) in the income statement leads to a deferred tax asset if it can't be deducted on the tax return until a later period. As a result, under the lower threshold of IFRS, we might record a loss contingency and thus a deferred tax asset, but under U.S. GAAP we might record neither. So, even though accounting for deferred taxes is the same, accounting for loss contingencies is different, causing a difference in the reported amounts of deferred taxes under IFRS and U.S. GAAP.

Concept Review Exercise

TEMPORARY AND PERMANENT DIFFERENCES

Mid-South Cellular Systems began operations in 2018. That year the company reported pretax accounting income of $70 million, which included the following amounts:

1. Compensation expense of $3 million related to employee stock option plans granted to organizers was reported in the 2018 income statement. This expense is not deductible for tax purposes.
2. An asset with a four-year useful life was acquired at the beginning of 2018. It is depreciated by the straight-line method in the income statement. MACRS is used on the tax return, causing deductions for depreciation to be more than straight-line depreciation the first two years but less than straight-line depreciation the next two years ($ in millions):

	Depreciation		
	Income Statement	**Tax Return**	**Difference**
2018	$150	$198	$ (48)
2019	150	264	(114)
2020	150	90	60
2021	150	48	102
	$600	$600	$ 0

The enacted tax rate is 40%.

Required:

Prepare the journal entry to record Mid-South Cellular's income taxes for 2018.

Solution

Because the compensation expense is not tax deductible, taxable income does not include the $3 million deduction and is higher than accounting income by that amount.

	Current Year	Future Taxable Amounts			Future Taxable Amounts
($ in millions)	**2018**	**2019**	**2020**	**2021**	**(total)**
Pretax accounting income	$70				
Permanent difference:					
Compensation expense	3				
Temporary difference:					
Depreciation	(48)	$(114)	$60	$102	$ 48
Taxable income (tax return)	$25				
Enacted tax rate	40%				40%
Tax payable currently	$10				↓

Because the compensation expense is not tax deductible, taxable income does not include the $3 million deduction and is higher than accounting income by that amount.

Deferred Tax Liability	
	0 beg. bal.
	19.2
	19.2 end. bal.

Deferred Tax Liability	$19.2
Ending balance needed	0.0
Less: Beginning balance	$19.2
Change in balance	

The necessary journal entry is:

Journal Entry at the End of 2018		
Income tax expense (to balance)	29.2	
Income tax payable (determined above)		10.0
Deferred tax liability (determined above)		19.2

PART B

Other Tax Accounting Issues

Tax Rate Considerations

● LO16–5

To measure the deferred tax liability or asset, we multiply the temporary difference by the currently *enacted* tax rate that will be effective in the year(s) the temporary difference reverses[6] We do not base calculations on *anticipated* legislation that would alter the company's tax rate. A conceptual case can be made that expected rate changes should be anticipated when measuring the deferred tax liability or asset. However, this is one of many examples of the frequent trade-off between relevance and reliability. In this case, the FASB chose to favor reliability by waiting until an anticipated change actually is enacted into law before recognizing its tax consequences.

When Enacted Tax Rates Differ

A deferred tax liability (or asset) is based on enacted tax rates and laws.

Existing tax laws may call for enacted tax rates to be different in future years in which a temporary difference is expected to reverse. When a phased-in change in rates is scheduled to occur, the specific tax rates of each future year are multiplied by the amounts reversing in each of those years. The total is the deferred tax liability or asset.

To illustrate, let's again modify our Kent Land Management illustration, this time to assume a scheduled change in tax rates. See Illustration 16–11.

Illustration 16–11

Scheduled Change in Tax Rates

Kent Land Management reported pretax accounting income in 2018 of $100 million except for additional income of $40 million from installment sales of property and $5 million interest from investments in municipal bonds in 2018. The installment sales income is reported for tax purposes in 2019 ($10 million) and 2020 ($30 million). The enacted tax rates are 40% for 2018 and 2019, and 35% for 2020.

($ in millions)	Current Year 2018	Future Taxable Amounts 2019	2020		(total)
Pretax accounting income	$145				
Permanent difference:					
Municipal bond interest	(5)				
Temporary difference:					
Installment income	(40)	$10	$ 30		
Taxable income (tax return)	$100				
Enacted tax rate	40%	40%	35%		
Tax payable currently	$ 40				
Deferred tax liability		$ 4 +	$10.5	=	$14.5

The tax effects of the future taxable amounts depend on the tax rates at which those amounts will be taxed.

Deferred Tax Liability	
	0 beg. bal.
	14.5
	14.5 end. bal.

Deferred Tax Liability	
Ending balance needed	$14.5
Less: Beginning balance	0.0
Change in balance	$14.5

(continued)

[6]The current U.S. federal corporate tax rate is 35%. Most states tax corporate income at rates less than 10%. We use 40% in most of our illustrations to simplify calculations.

(concluded)

Journal Entry at the End of 2018

Income tax expense (to balance)	54.5	
Income tax payable (determined above)		40.0
Deferred tax liability (determined above)		14.5

Be sure to note that the 2019 rate (40%) as well as the 2020 rate (35%) already is enacted into law as of 2018 when the deferred tax liability is established. In the next section, we discuss how to handle a change resulting from new legislation.

Changes in Tax Laws or Rates

Tax laws sometimes change. If a change in a tax law or rate occurs, any existing tax liability or asset must be adjusted. Remember, the deferred tax liability or asset is meant to reflect the amount to be paid or recovered in the future. When legislation changes that amount, the deferred tax liability or asset also should change. The effect is reflected in operating income in the year of the enactment of the change in the tax law or rate.[7]

For clarification, reconsider the previous illustration. Without a change in tax rates and assuming that pretax accounting income reported in the income statement in 2019 is $100 million (with no additional temporary or permanent differences), the 2019 income tax amounts would be determined as shown in Illustration 16–11A.

Illustration 16–11A

Reversal of Temporary Difference *without* a Tax Rate Change

($ in millions)	2018	Current Year 2019	Future Taxable Amount 2020
Pretax accounting income		$100	
Temporary difference:			
Installment income	(40)	10	$30
Taxable income (tax return)		$110	
Enacted tax rate		40%	35%
Tax payable currently		$ 44	

Deferred Tax Liability	
	14.5 beg. bal.
4	
	10.5 end. bal.

Deferred Tax Liability	
Ending balance needed	$10.5
Less: Beginning balance	(14.5)
Change in balance	$ (4.0)

Journal Entry at the End of 2019

Income tax expense (to balance)	40	
Deferred tax liability (determined above)	4	
Income tax payable (determined above)		44

The 40% 2019 rate and the 35% 2020 rate are established by previously enacted legislation.

Now assume Congress passed a new tax law in 2019 that will cause the 2020 tax rate to be 30% instead of the previously scheduled 35% rate. Because a deferred tax liability was established in 2018 with the expectation that the 2020 taxable amount would be taxed at 35%, it would now be adjusted to reflect taxation at 30%, instead. This is demonstrated in Illustration 16–11B.

Notice that the methods used to determine the deferred tax liability and the change in that balance are the same as without the rate change—the calculation merely uses the new rate (30%) rather than the old rate (35%). So, tax rate changes are automatically taken into

[7]FASB ASC 740–10–35: Income Taxes–Overall–Subsequent Measurement (previously "Accounting for Income Taxes," Statement of Financial Accounting Standards No. 109 (Norwalk, Conn.: FASB, 1992)).

Illustration 16–11B

Reversal of Temporary Difference with a Tax Rate Change

($ in millions)	2018	Current Year 2019	Future Taxable Amount 2020
Pretax accounting income		$100	
Temporary difference:			
Installment income	(40)	10	$ 30
Taxable income (tax return)		$110	
Enacted tax rate		40%	30%*
Tax payable currently		$ 44	

*2020 rate enacted into law in 2016.

Deferred Tax Liability	
	14.5 beg. bal.
5.5	
	9 end. bal.

Deferred Tax Liability	
Ending balance	$ 9.0
Less: Beginning balance	(14.5)
Change in balance	$ (5.5)

Journal Entry at the End of 2019

Income tax expense (to balance)	38.5	
Deferred tax liability (determined above)	5.5	
Income tax payable (determined above)		44.0

The deferred tax liability would have been $10.5 million (30 million × 35%) if the tax rate had not changed.

account by recalculating the balance needed in the deferred tax liability each period and comparing that amount with any previously existing balance.

Also notice that income tax expense ($38.5 million) is $1.5 million less than it would have been without the tax rate change ($40 million). This is highlighted if we separate the previous entry into its component parts: (1) record the income tax expense without the tax rate change, and (2) separately record the adjustment of the deferred tax liability for the change.

Journal Entry at the End of 2019 (in two parts)

1) Journal entry without future tax rate change:	($ in millions)	
Income tax expense	40	
Deferred tax liability	4	
Income tax payable		44
2) Effect of future tax rate change:		
Deferred tax liability [$30 million × (35% − 30%)]	1.5	
Income tax expense		1.5

When a tax rate changes, the deferred tax liability or asset should be adjusted and the effect shown in tax expense in the year of the change.

The tax consequence of a change in a tax law or rate is recognized in the period the change is enacted. In this case, the consequence of a lower tax rate is a reduced deferred tax liability, recognized as a reduction in income tax expense in 2019 when the change occurs.

Multiple Temporary Differences

LO16–6

It would be unusual for any but a very small company to have only a single temporary difference in any given year. Having multiple temporary differences, though, doesn't change any of the principles you've learned so far in connection with single differences. We categorize all temporary differences according to whether they create (a) future taxable amounts or (b) future deductible amounts. The total of the future taxable amounts then is multiplied by the future tax rate to determine the appropriate balance for the deferred tax liability, and the total of the future deductible amounts is multiplied by the future tax rate to determine the appropriate balance for the deferred tax asset. This is demonstrated in Illustration 16–12.

Illustration 16–12

Multiple Temporary Differences

2018

During 2018, its first year of operations, Eli-Wallace Distributors reported pretax accounting income of $200 million, which included the following amounts:

1. Income (net) from installment sales of warehouses in 2018 of $9 million will be reported for tax purposes in 2019 ($5 million) and 2020 ($4 million).
2. Depreciation is reported by the straight-line method on an asset with a four-year useful life. On the tax return, deductions for depreciation will be more than straight-line depreciation the first two years but less than straight-line depreciation the next two years ($ in millions):

	Income Statement	Tax Return	Difference
2018	$ 50	$ 66	$(16)
2019	50	88	(38)
2020	50	30	20
2021	50	16	34
	$200	$200	$ 0

3. Estimated warranty expense will be deductible on the tax return when actually paid during the next two years. Estimated deductions are as follows ($ in millions):

	Income Statement	Tax Return	Difference
2018	$7		$7
2019		$4	(4)
2020		3	(3)
	$7	$7	$0

2019

During 2019, pretax accounting income of $200 million included an estimated loss of $1 million from having accrued a loss contingency. The loss is expected to be paid in 2021, at which time it will be tax deductible.

The enacted tax rate is 40% each year.

Look at Illustration 16–12A to see how Eli-Wallace determines the income tax amounts for 2018. Then look at Illustration 16–12B to see how those amounts are determined for 2019.

Of course, if a phased-in change in rates is scheduled to occur, it would be necessary to determine the total of the future taxable amounts and the total of the future deductible amounts for each future year, as outlined previously. Then the specific tax rates of each future year would be multiplied by the two totals in each of those years. Those annual tax effects then would be summed to find the balances for the deferred tax liability and the deferred tax asset.

Net Operating Losses

● LO16–7

A **net operating loss** (NOL) is negative taxable income: tax-deductible expenses exceed taxable revenues. Of course, there is no tax payable for the year a net operating loss occurs because there's no taxable income. In addition, tax laws permit a net operating loss to be used to reduce taxable income in other, profitable years. Why do the tax laws permit that offsetting? Well, let's consider two imaginary companies. Volatile Co. has negative income some years and positive income other years that averages out to $0 income over time. Stable Co. has $0 income each year. It wouldn't be fair to tax Volatile in the good years and provide no relief in the bad years, while not taxing Stable at all, because Volatile and Stable generate the same total amount of income over time. It's more fair to allow Volatile to offset the income in its good years with the losses in its bad years when determining how much tax it should pay.

Illustration 16–12A

Multiple Temporary Differences—2018

Temporary differences are grouped according to whether they create future *taxable* amounts or future *deductible* amounts.

The balances needed in the deferred tax liability and the deferred tax asset are separately determined.

Income tax expense is composed of three components: (1) the tax payable currently plus (2) the tax deferred until later, reduced by (3) the deferred tax benefit.

($ in millions)	Current Year 2018	Future Taxable (Deductible) Amounts 2019	2020	2021	Future Taxable Amounts (total)	Future Deductible Amounts (total)
Pretax accounting income	$ 200					
Temporary differences:						
Installment sales	(9)	$ 5	$ 4		$ 9	
Depreciation	(16)	(38)	20	$34	16	
Warranty expense	7	(4)	(3)			$ (7)
Taxable income (tax return)	$ 182				$25	(7)
Enacted tax rate	40%				40%	40%
Tax payable currently	$72.8					
		Deferred tax liability			$10	
		Deferred tax asset				$(2.8)

Deferred Tax Liability

	0 beg. bal.
	10
	10 end. bal.

Deferred Tax Asset

beg. bal. 0	
2.8	
end. bal. 2.8	

	Deferred Tax Liability	Deferred Tax Asset
Ending balances:	$10	$ 2.8
Less: Beginning balances:	(0)	(0.0)
Change in balances	$10	$ 2.8

Journal Entry at the End of 2018

Income tax expense (to balance)	80.0	
Deferred tax asset (determined above)	2.8	
Deferred tax liability (determined above)		10.0
Income tax payable (determined above)		72.8

Offsetting operating profits with NOLs is achieved by either a carryback of the NOL to prior years or a carryforward of the NOL to later years, or both. In essence, the tax deductible expenses that can't be deducted this year because they exceed taxable revenues can be deducted in other years. A net operating loss can be carried back 2 years and forward for up to 20 years:

Carryforward → Up to 20 Years

2016	2017	LOSS	2019	2020	2021	→	2037	2038

2 years ← Carryback

Tax laws permit a choice. A company can use a **net operating loss carryback** if taxable income was reported in either of the two previous years.[8] By reducing taxable income of a previous year, the company can receive an immediate refund of taxes paid that year.

If taxable income was not reported in either of the two previous years or higher tax rates are anticipated in the future, a company might elect to forgo the net operating loss carryback and instead carry the NOL forward for up to 20 years to offset taxable income of those years. The carryforward election is a choice that must be made in the year the NOL occurs, and the choice is irrevocable. Even if an NOL carryback is used, any NOL that remains after the two-year carryback can be carried forward. It usually is advantageous to carry back NOLs because a company can realize the benefit much sooner by filing an amended tax return to get a refund, than if the NOL is carried forward.

The accounting question is: When should the tax benefit created by a net operating loss be recognized in the income statement? The answer is: In the year the loss occurs.

[8]Actually, a carryback is automatic unless a company elects to forgo the carryback in favor of a carryforward.

Illustration 16–12B

Multiple Temporary Differences—2019

($ in millions)	2018	Current Year 2019	Future Taxable (Deductible) Amounts 2020	2021	Future Taxable Amounts (total)*	Future Deductible Amounts (total)*
Pretax accounting income		$200				
Temporary differences:						
Installment sales	$ (9)	$ 5	$ 4		$ 4	
Depreciation	(16)	(38)	20	$34	54	
Warranty expense	7	(4)	(3)			$ (3)
Estimated loss		1		(1)		(1)
Taxable income (tax return)		$ 164			$58	$ (4)
Enacted tax rate		40%			40%	40%
Tax payable currently		$ 65.6				
			Deferred tax liability		$23.2	
			Deferred tax asset			$(1.6)

Deferred Tax Liability	
	10.0 beg. bal.
	13.2
	23.2 end. bal.

Deferred Tax Asset	
beg. bal. 2.8	
	1.2
end. bal. 1.6	

	Deferred Tax Liability	Deferred Tax Asset
Ending balance:	$23.2	$ 1.6
Less: Beginning balance:	(10.0)	(2.8)
Change in balances	$13.2	$(1.2)

Journal Entry at the End of 2019

Income tax expense (to balance)	80.0	
Deferred tax asset (determined above)		1.2
Deferred tax liability (determined above)		13.2
Deferred tax payable (determined above)		65.6

*Total future taxable and deductible amounts also are equal to the cumulative temporary differences in the related assets and liabilities.

The future taxable amount of installment sales ($4 million) is equal to the cumulative temporary difference ($9 million − 5 million).

Similarly, the total of other future taxable and deductible amounts is equal to the cumulative temporary differences in the related assets and liabilities.

Analysis indicates that the deferred tax liability should be increased further and the deferred tax asset should be reduced.

Net Operating Loss Carryforward

First consider an NOL carryforward. You have learned in this chapter that a deferred tax asset is recognized for the future tax benefit of temporary differences that create future deductible amounts. A **net operating loss carryforward** also creates future deductible amounts. Logically, then, a deferred tax asset is recognized for a net operating loss carryforward also. This is demonstrated in Illustration 16–13.

The income tax benefit of a net operating loss carryforward is recognized for accounting purposes in the year the net operating loss occurs. Just as we reduce pretax income by tax expense to calculate net income, we reduce a pretax loss by its tax benefit to calculate a net loss. That way, the net after-tax operating loss shown on the income statement reflects the tax savings that the operating loss is expected to create.

Income Statement (partial)

	($ in millions)
Operating loss before income taxes	$(125)
Less: Income tax benefit—net operating loss	50
Net loss	$ (75)

VALUATION ALLOWANCE. Just as for all deductible temporary differences, deferred tax assets are recognized for any net operating loss without regard to the likelihood of having taxable income in future years sufficient to absorb future deductible amounts. However, the deferred tax asset is then reduced by a valuation allowance if it is more likely than not that some portion or all of the deferred tax asset will not be realized. Valuation allowances

The income tax benefit of a net operating loss carryback, like a carryforward, is recognized in the year the net operating loss occurs.

Illustration 16–13
Net Operating Loss Carryforward

A net operating loss (NOL) carryforward can be deducted from taxable income in future years.

The tax benefit of being able to deduct amounts in the future represents a deferred tax asset.

During 2018, its first year of operations, American Laminating Corporation reported an operating loss of $125 million for financial reporting and tax purposes. The enacted tax rate is 40%.

($ in millions)	Current Year 2018	Future Deductible Amounts (total)
Net operating loss	$(125)	
NOL carryforward	125	$(125)
	$ 0	
Enacted tax rate	40%	40%
Tax payable	$ 0	

Deferred Tax Asset	
0 beg. bal.	
50	
50 end. bal.	

Deferred Tax Asset	
Ending balance	$ 50
Less: Beginning balance	0
Change in balance	$ 50

Journal Entry at the End of 2018

Deferred tax asset (determined above)	50	
Income tax benefit—operating loss (to balance)		50

often accompany NOLs because the same problems that give rise to current operating losses also make it less likely the company will earn enough taxable income in the future to be able to utilize its deferred tax assets. Remember, a valuation allowance both reduces the net deferred tax asset and increases the income tax expense, just as if that portion of the deferred tax asset had not been recognized.

Net Operating Loss Carryback

To compare the treatment of a net operating loss carryback, let's modify the illustration to assume that there was taxable income in the two years prior to the net operating loss and that American Laminating will utilize the NOL carryback (see Illustration 16–14). Note that the net operating loss must be applied to the earlier year first and then brought forward to the next year. If any of the NOL remains after reducing taxable income to zero in the two previous years, the remainder is carried forward to future years as a net operating loss carryforward.

	($ in millions)	
Operating loss before income taxes		$(125)
Income tax benefit:		
Tax refund from net operating loss carryback	$29	
Future tax savings from net operating loss carryforward	20	49
Net loss		$ (76)

The income tax benefit of both a net operating loss carryback and a net operating loss carryforward is recognized for accounting purposes in the year the NOL occurs. The net after-tax loss reflects the reduction of past taxes from the NOL carryback and future tax savings that the NOL carryforward is expected to create.

Notice that the income tax benefit ($49 million) is less than it was when we assumed a carryforward only ($50 million). This is because the tax rate in one of the carryback years (2016) was lower than the carryforward rate (40%).

Let's extend the illustration one year (see Illustration 16–14A) and assume a performance turnaround in 2019 resulted in pretax accounting income of $15 million.

Illustration 16–14

Net Operating Loss Carryback and Carryforward

During 2018, American Laminating Corporation reported a net operating loss of $125 million for financial reporting and tax purposes. The enacted tax rate is 40% for 2018. Taxable income, tax rates, and income taxes paid in the two previous years were as follows:

	Taxable Income	Taxable Rates	Income Taxes Paid
2016	$20 million	35%	$ 7 million
2017	55 million	40%	22 million

Here's how the income tax benefit of the net operating loss carryback and the net operating loss carryforward is determined:

	Prior Years		Current Year	Future Deductible Amounts
($ in millions)	2016	2017	2018	(total)
Net operating loss			$(125)	
NOL carryback	$(20)	$(55)	75	
NOL carryforward			50	$(50)
			$ 0	
Enacted tax rate	35%	40%	40%	40%
Tax payable (refundable)	$ (7)	$(22)	$ 0	

Deferred Tax Asset	
beg. bal. 0	
20	
end. bal. 20	

Deferred Tax Asset	
Ending balance	$ 20
Less: Beginning balance	0
Change in balance	$ 20

Journal Entry at the End of 2018

Receivable—income tax refund ($7 + 22)	29	
Deferred tax asset (determined above)	20	
Income tax benefit—operating loss (to balance)		49

A net operating loss (NOL) carryback can be deducted from taxable income in the two prior years, creating a refund of taxes paid for those years.

The portion of a net operating loss that remains after a carryback is carried forward.

The income tax benefit of a net operating loss carryforward is recognized in the year the operating loss occurs.

Illustration 16–14A

Determining and Recording Income Taxes—2019

($ in millions)	2018	Current Year 2019	Future Deductible Amounts (total)
Pretax accounting income		$15	
Temporary difference:			
NOL carryforward	$50	(15)	$(35)
Taxable income (tax return)		$ 0	
Enacted tax rate		40%	40%
Tax payable currently		$ 0	

Deferred Tax Asset	
beg. bal. 20	
	6
end. bal. 14	

Deferred Tax Asset	
Ending balance	$ 14.0
Less: Beginning balance	(20.0)
Change in balance	$ (6.0)

Journal Entry at the End of 2019

Income tax expense (to balance)	6	
Deferred tax asset (determined above)		6

$15 million of the NOL carryforward can be used to offset 2019 income. The remaining $35 million is carried forward up to 19 more years.

The $20 million deferred tax asset is reduced to $14 million.

Financial Statement Presentation

Balance Sheet Classification

LO16–8

All deferred tax liabilities, deferred tax assets, and any valuation allowance against deferred tax assets are classified as noncurrent in the balance sheet.[9] If these deferred tax accounts relate to the same tax-paying component of the company and the same tax jurisdiction, they are netted against each other and shown as a single net number in the balance sheet. For example, a company with a deferred tax liability of $10 million, a deferred tax asset of $5 million, and a valuation allowance of $2 million would show a net noncurrent deferred tax liability of $7 million [$10 million – ($5 million – $2 million)].

Sometimes components of a single company are viewed as different companies for tax purposes, or pay tax in different jurisdictions. If deferred tax liabilities and assets relate to components of a company that are separate for tax purposes, or relate to different tax jurisdictions, they should not be offset. So, in the prior illustration, if the deferred tax assets (and related valuation allowance) applied to a separate tax jurisdiction from the deferred tax liabilities, the company would show a noncurrent deferred tax liability of $10 million and a noncurrent deferred tax asset of $3 million ($5 million – $2 million).

Disclosure Notes

We've already seen many of the disclosures that companies have to present in the tax note, but there are a few we haven't yet covered.

INCOME TAX EXPENSE Illustration 16–7A shows Shoe Carnival's disclosure of current tax payable, deferred tax, and tax expense. More generally, disclosure notes should indicate the following:

- Current portion of the tax expense (or tax benefit); that's new tax payable this period
- Deferred portion of the tax expense (or tax benefit), with separate disclosure of amounts attributable to:
  - Portions that do not include the effect of separately disclosed amounts
  - Operating loss carryforwards
- Adjustments due to changes in tax laws or rates
- Adjustments to the beginning-of-the-year valuation allowance due to revised estimates
- Tax credits

DEFERRED TAX ASSETS AND DEFERRED TAX LIABILITIES Illustration 16–7B shows Shoe Carnival's disclosure of its deferred tax assets and deferred tax liabilities. It shows a total net deferred tax asset of $5,184 thousand, which would appear in its January 31, 2015 balance sheet. More generally, companies must disclose the following:

- Total of all deferred tax liabilities
- Total of all deferred tax assets
- Total valuation allowance recognized for deferred tax assets
- Net change in the valuation allowance
- Approximate tax effect of each type of temporary difference (and carryforward)

EFFECTIVE TAX RATE RECONCILIATION Illustration 16–10 shows Walmart's effective tax rate reconciliation. Companies are required to provide that reconciliation, indicating the amount and nature of each significant reconciling item.

NET OPERATING LOSS (NOL) CARRYFORWARDS The amounts and expiration dates should be revealed for any net operating loss carryforwards. Remember, net operating losses can be carried forward for reduction of future taxable income for 20 years. This potential

[9] Prior to 2017, companies were required to classify deferred tax assets and liabilities as current or noncurrent. To simplify presentation, the FASB required that all deferred tax items be classified as noncurrent when it issued "Balance Sheet Classification of Deferred Taxes," *Accounting Standards Update No. 2015-17: (Topic 740)* (Norwalk, Conn.: FASB, 2015).

tax benefit can foreshadow desirable cash savings for the company if earnings sufficient to absorb the NOL carryforwards are anticipated before their expiration date. The presence of large net operating loss carryforwards also can make an unprofitable company an attractive target for acquisition by a company that could use those NOL carryforwards to shelter its own earnings from taxes with that loss deduction. If the IRS determines that an acquisition is made solely to obtain the tax benefits of net operating loss carryforwards, the deductions will not be allowed. However, motivation is difficult to determine, so it is not uncommon for companies to purchase other companies to obtain their net operating loss carryforwards.

Coping with Uncertainty in Income Taxes

● LO16–9

Few expense items in the income statement rival the size of the income tax expense line, and few are subject to the complexities and differing interpretations inherent in reporting income tax expense. As you might imagine, most companies strive to legitimately reduce their overall tax burden and to reduce or delay cash outflows for taxes.

The IRS frequently disagrees with the position a company takes on its tax return.

Even without additional efforts to reduce taxes, most companies' tax returns will include many tax positions that are subject to multiple interpretations. That is, the position management takes with respect to an element of tax expense might differ from the position the IRS or the tax court might take on that same item. Despite good faith positions taken in preparing tax returns, those judgments may not ultimately prevail if challenged by the IRS. Managements' tax positions frequently are subjected to legal scrutiny before the uncertainty ultimately is resolved.

For example, assume that if Derrick Company claims on its tax return a particular deduction it believes is legitimate, that position will save the company $8 million in 2018 income taxes. Derrick knows that, historically, the IRS has challenged many deductions of this type. Since tax returns usually aren't examined for one, two, or more years, uncertainty exists.

TWO-STEP DECISION PROCESS To deal with that uncertainty, companies are allowed to recognize in the financial statements the tax benefit of a position it takes, such as the reduction in tax expense from Derrick's decision to take the 2018 deduction, only if it is "more likely than not" (greater than 50% chance) to be sustained if challenged.[10] Guidance also prescribes how to *measure* the amount to be recognized if, in fact, it can be recognized. The decision, then, is a "two-step" process.

Step 1. A tax benefit may be reflected in the financial statements only if it is "more likely than not" that the company will be able to sustain the tax return position, based on its technical merits.

Step 2. A tax benefit should be measured as the largest amount of benefit that is "cumulatively greater than 50 percent likely to be realized" (demonstrated later).

For the Step 1 decision as to whether the position can be sustained, companies must assume that the position will be reviewed by the IRS or other taxing authority and litigated to the "highest court possible," and that the taxing authority has knowledge of all relevant facts.

If there's a 50% chance or less of the company's position being sustained on examination, tax expense can't be reduced to reflect the tax benefit.

NOT "MORE LIKELY THAN NOT" Let's say that in the Step 1 decision, Derrick believes the more-likely-than-not criterion is *not* met. This means that none of the tax benefit (reduction in tax expense) can be recorded in 2018. The income tax expense must be recorded at the same amount as if the tax deduction was not taken.

Suppose, for instance, that Derrick's current income tax payable is $24 million after being reduced by the full $8 million tax benefit.[11] However, if it's *more likely than not* that the tax benefit isn't sustainable upon examination, the benefit can't be recognized as a reduction of tax expense. So, Derrick would record (a) current income tax payable that reflects the entire $8 million benefit of the deduction, (b) an additional tax liability that represents the obligation to pay an additional $8 million of taxes under the assumption that the deduction ultimately will not be upheld, and (c) tax expense as if the deduction had never been taken.

[10]FASB ASC 740: Income Taxes–Overall (previously "Accounting for Uncertainty in Income Taxes, an Interpretation of FASB Statement No. 109," FASB Interpretation No. 48 (Norwalk, Conn.: FASB, June 2006)), commonly called FIN 48.

[11]For illustration, if pretax accounting income is $80 million, the tax rate is 40%, and the questionable deduction is $20 million, income tax payable would be ($80 million − 20 million) × 40% = $24 million.

	($ in millions)	
Income tax expense (without $8 tax benefit)	32	
Income tax payable (with $8 tax benefit)		24
Liability—projected additional tax		8

The $8 million liability is recognized to account for the fact that it is probable that tax officials will disallow the tax treatment used to compute income tax payable.

The $8 million difference is the tax that Derrick didn't pay because Derrick took the deduction. That amount is potentially due if the deduction is not upheld later. Because the ultimate outcome probably won't be determined within the upcoming year, the *Liability—projected additional tax* is reported as a long-term liability unless it's known to be current.[12]

MEASURING THE TAX BENEFIT Now, let's say that even though Derrick is aware of the IRS's tendency to challenge deductions of this sort, management believes it *is* more likely than not that the position will be upheld if later challenged. Since Derrick has determined in Step 1 that yes, a tax benefit can be recognized, it now needs to decide how much. That's Step 2.

Suppose the following table represents management's estimates of the likelihood of various amounts of tax benefit that would be upheld:

The largest amount that has a cumulative greater-than-50%-chance of being realized is $6 million (10% + 20% + 25% = 55%).

Likelihood Table	($ in millions)				
Amount of the tax benefit that management expects to be sustained	$8	$7	$6	$5	$4
Percentage likelihood that the tax position will be sustained at this level	10%	20%	25%	25%	20%
Cumulative probability that at least that much tax position will be sustained	10%	30%	55%	80%	100%

The amount of tax benefit that Derrick can recognize in the financial statements (reduce tax expense) is $6 million because it represents the largest amount of benefit that is more likely than not (greater than 50% probability) to be sustained. So, Derrick would record (a) current income tax payable that reflects the entire $8 million benefit of the deduction, (b) an additional tax liability that represents the obligation to pay an additional $2 million of taxes under the assumption that $6 million of tax benefit ultimately will be upheld, and (c) tax expense as if there is a $6 million tax benefit.

	($ in millions)	
Income tax expense (with $6 tax benefit)	26	
Income tax payable (with $8 tax benefit)		24
Liability—projected additional tax ($8 – 6)		2

Only $6 million of the tax benefit is recognized in income tax expense.

In summary, the highest amount Derrick might have to pay is the full $8 million benefit of the 2018 deduction; the least amount, of course, is zero. The most likely amount (the largest amount of benefit that is cumulatively greater than 50 percent likely to be realized) is $6 million.

Because the most likely amount not to be paid is $6 million, the most likely additional liability is $2 million ($8 – 6 = $2). That's the amount we record as a *Liability—projected additional tax,* along with the current income tax payable of $24 million.

RESOLUTION OF THE UNCERTAINTY Now let's consider what happens in the future, when the uncertainty associated with the tax position has been resolved. We'll consider three scenarios. Note that, in each scenario, the "Liability—projected additional tax" gets reduced to zero in the period in which the uncertainty is resolved.

1. **Worst case scenario.** The entire position is disallowed, such that Derrick owes $8 million tax (plus any interest and penalties, which we are ignoring).

	($ in millions)	
Income tax expense	6	
Liability—projected additional tax	2	
Income tax payable (or cash)		8

[12]If a company has any deferred tax assets from net operating loss carryforwards, it generally nets the liability for uncertain tax positions against those deferred tax assets for presentation in the balance sheet, rather than presenting the liability separately. Why? The liability indicates that future tax will be *paid,* and the operating loss carryforward indicates that future tax will be *saved,* so the two are netted.

2. **Best case scenario.** The entire position is upheld, so Derrick owes no additional tax.

	($ in millions)	
Liability—projected additional tax	2	
Income tax expense		2

3. **Expected scenario.** The $6 million position is allowed as expected, so Derrick owes the expected $2 million tax (plus any interest and penalties, which we are ignoring).

	($ in millions)	
Liability—projected additional tax	2	
Income tax payable (or cash)		2

Companies are required to include in the disclosure notes a clear reconciliation of the beginning and ending balance of their liability for unrecognized tax benefits. As an example, Illustration 16–15 includes an excerpt from the tax note of Staples, Inc., for its fiscal year ended January 30, 2016.

Illustration 16–15

Disclosure of Deferred Taxes—Staples, Inc.

Real World Financials

The following summarizes the activity related to the Company's unrecognized tax benefits, including those related to discontinued operations ($ in millions):

	2015	2014	2013
Balance at beginning of fiscal year	$216	$281	$255
Additions for tax positions related to current year	19	22	28
Additions for tax positions of prior years	5	36	4
Reductions for tax positions of prior years	(5)	(88)	—
Reduction for statute of limitations expiration	(69)	(17)	(6)
Settlements	(30)	(18)	—
Balance at end of fiscal year	$136	$216	$281

Intraperiod Tax Allocation

LO16–10

You should recall that an income statement reports discontinued operations separately from income (or loss) from continuing operations to better allow the user of the statement to isolate irregular components of net income from those that represent recurring business operations.[13] This helps the user to more accurately project future operations. Because taxes are an important part of operations, the total income tax expense for a reporting period should be allocated between continuing and discontinued operations.

The related tax effect can be either a tax expense or a tax benefit. A gain on disposal of a discontinued operation increases taxable income, so it produces tax expense, while a loss on disposal reduces taxable income, so it produces a tax benefit.[14] For example, a company with a tax rate of 40% would report $100 million pretax income that includes a $10 million gain on disposal of a discontinued operation this way:

	($ in millions)
Income before tax and discontinued operation ($100 – 10)	$ 90
Less: Income tax expense ($90 × 40%)	(36)
Income before discontinued operation	54
Gain on disposal of discontinued operation (net of $4 income tax expense)	6
Net income	$ 60

[13]Until recently, GAAP included another category, extraordinary items, for which income was shown separately net of tax. The FASB eliminated the concept of extraordinary items starting in 2016 when it issued "Income Statement-Extraordinary and Unusual Items," *Accounting Standards Update No. 2015-01:* (Subtopic 225-20) (Norwalk, Conn.: FASB, 2015).

[14]As discussed in Chapter 4, companies separately report (a) any gain or loss from running a discontinued operation prior to disposal, and (b) any gain or loss on disposal of a discontinued operation's assets. For simplicity we focus on reporting taxes for (b), but the same separate net-of-tax presentation is used for (a).

Additional Consideration

The Balance Sheet Focus of Income Tax Accounting. The way we account for income taxes is a useful example of the FASB's balance sheet emphasis. Rather than calculating tax expense directly, it always is calculated as whatever amount is implied by the combination of income tax payable and the changes that occurred during the period in deferred tax assets, deferred tax liabilities, the valuation allowance for deferred tax assets, and the liability for uncertain tax positions. In fact, we can summarize virtually everything in this chapter by visualizing the journal entry implied by the changes in those accounts. Let's draw some T-accounts to see how that works:

	Deferred Tax Assets		**Val. Allowance—Deferred Tax Assets**		**Deferred Tax Liabilities**		**Liability for Uncertain Tax Positions**	
Beg. bal.	S			U		W		Y
	B	or B	C	or C	D	or D	E	or E
End. Bal.	T			V		X		Z

With these T-accounts in mind, think of a company's tax accounting as including the following steps:

1. Determine income tax payable (tax rate times taxable income). We'll call that number "A."
2. Determine T, V, X, and Z, the ending balances needed in the tax-related balance sheet accounts, as we do in the chapter.
3. Determine whatever changes in those accounts, B, C, D, and E, are needed to reach their required ending balances. We already know the beginning balances in those accounts because they are the same as the ending balances reported in the prior period.
4. Finally, calculate tax expense, F, as the amount necessary to balance the journal entry. For example:

Tax expense (to balance)	F	
Deferred tax asset (amount needed to achieve needed balance)	B	
Deferred tax liability (amount needed to achieve needed balance)		D
Valuation allowance—deferred tax asset (amount needed to achieve needed balance)		C
Liability for uncertain tax positions (amount needed to achieve needed balance)		E
Taxes payable (tax rate × taxable income)		A

Tax expense (F) always is a "plug" figure to make the journal entry balance. Usually the plug is a debit, but sometimes its a credit to recognize a tax benefit. Depending on a company's particular circumstances, a debit or a credit could be required to reach the appropriate ending balance in each of the tax-related balance sheet accounts, B, C, D, and E. To the extent these accounts changed because of other transactions (for example, an acquisition), we would account for those effects first and then determine the amounts necessary to reach the appropriate ending balances.

If the $100 million pretax income included a $10 million loss, the loss would be reported net of associated tax savings:

	($ in millions)
Income before tax and discontinued operation ($100 + 10)	$110
Less: Income tax expense ($110 × 40%)	(44)
Income before discontinued operation	66
Loss on disposal of discontinued operation (net of $4 income tax benefit)	(6)
Net income	$ 60

Additional Consideration

If the gain in the earlier example had been of a type taxable at a capital gains tax rate of 30%, it would have been reported net of the specific tax associated with that gain:

Gain on disposal of discontinued operation (net of $3 income tax expense)	$7

Allocating income taxes among financial statement components in this way within a particular reporting period is referred to as *intraperiod tax allocation.* You should recognize the contrast with *inter* period tax allocation—terminology sometimes used to describe allocating income taxes between two or more reporting periods by recognizing deferred tax assets and liabilities. While interperiod tax allocation is challenging and controversial, intraperiod tax allocation is relatively straightforward and substantially free from controversy.

Allocating income taxes within a particular reporting period is intraperiod tax allocation.

OTHER COMPREHENSIVE INCOME Allocating income tax expense or benefit also applies to components of comprehensive income reported separately from net income. You should recall from our discussions in Chapters 4 and 12 that "comprehensive income" extends our view of income beyond conventional net income to include four types of gains and losses that traditionally haven't been included in income statements. The other comprehensive income (OCI) items relate to investments, postretirement benefit plans, derivatives, and foreign currency translation. When these OCI items are reported in a statement of comprehensive income and then accumulated in shareholders' equity, they are reported net of their respective income tax effects.[15]

Decision Makers' Perspective

Income taxes represent one of the largest expenditures that many firms incur. When state, local, and foreign taxes are considered along with federal taxes, the total bite can easily consume 40% of income. A key factor, then, in any decision that managers make should be the impact on taxes. Decision makers must constantly be alert to options that minimize or delay taxes. During the course of this chapter, we encountered situations that avoid taxes (for example, interest on municipal bonds) and those that delay taxes (for example, using accelerated depreciation on the tax return). Astute managers make investment decisions that consider the tax effect of available alternatives. Similarly, outside analysts should consider how effectively management has managed its tax exposure and monitor the current and prospective impact of taxes on their interests in the company.

Consider an example. Large, capital-intensive companies with significant investments in buildings and equipment often have sizable deferred tax liabilities from temporary differences in depreciation. If new investments cause the level of depreciable assets to at least remain the same over time, the deferred tax liability can be effectively delayed indefinitely. Investors and creditors should be watchful for situations that might cause material paydowns of that deferred tax liability, such as impending plant closings or investment patterns that suggest declining levels of depreciable assets. Unexpected additional tax expenditures can severely diminish an otherwise attractive prospective rate of return.

You also learned in the chapter that deferred tax assets represent future tax benefits. One such deferred tax asset that often reflects sizable future tax deductions is a net operating loss (NOL) carryforward. When a company has a large net operating loss carryforward, a large amount of future income can be earned tax-free. This tax shelter can be a huge advantage, not to be overlooked by careful analysts.

Investment patterns and other disclosures can indicate potential tax expenditures.

[15]This can be accomplished by (a) presenting components of other comprehensive income net of related income tax effects or (b) presenting a single tax amount for all, and individual components shown before income tax effects with disclosure of the income taxes allocated to each component either in a disclosure note or parenthetically in the statement.

Net operating loss carryforwards can indicate significant future tax savings.

Managers and outsiders are aware that increasing debt increases risk. Deferred tax liabilities increase reported debt. As discussed and demonstrated in the previous chapter, financial risk often is measured by the debt to equity ratio, total liabilities divided by shareholders' equity. Other things being equal, the higher the debt to equity ratio, the higher the risk. Should the deferred tax liability be included in the computation of this ratio? Some analysts will argue that it should be excluded, observing that in many cases the deferred tax liability account remains the same or continually grows larger. Their contention is that no future tax payment will be required. Others, though, contend that is no different from the common situation in which long-term borrowings tend to remain the same or continually grow larger. Research supports the notion that deferred tax liabilities are, in fact, viewed by investors as real liabilities and investors appear to discount them according to the timing and likelihood of the liabilities' settlement.[16]

Deferred tax liabilities increase risk as measured by the debt to equity ratio.

Whenever managerial discretion can materially impact reported earnings, analysts should be wary of the implications for earnings quality assessment. We indicated earlier that the decision as to whether or not a valuation allowance is used, as well as the size of the allowance, is largely discretionary. Research indicates that an increase in a valuation allowance provides useful information, signaling that management is pessimistic about its ability to generate enough future income to benefit from the tax deductions provided by deferred tax assets.[17] However, research also indicates that some companies do use the deferred tax asset valuation allowance account to manage earnings upward to meet analyst forecasts.[18] More generally, a recent survey of nearly 600 corporate tax executives provides evidence that most top management care at least as much about tax expense and its effect on earnings per share as they do about the actual cash taxes that are paid by their companies, and that an important consideration in tax planning is increasing earnings per share.[19] Alert investors should not overlook the potential for companies using tax expense to manage their earnings.

In short, managers who make decisions based on estimated pretax cash flows and outside investors and creditors who make decisions based on pretax income numbers are perilously ignoring one of the most important aspects of those decisions. Taxes should be a primary consideration in any business decision.

Concept Review Exercise

MULTIPLE DIFFERENCES AND NET OPERATING LOSS

Mid-South Cellular Systems began operations in 2018. That year, the company reported taxable income of $25 million. In 2019, its second year of operations, pretax accounting income was $88 million, which included the following amounts:

1. Insurance expense of $14 million, representing one-third of a $42 million, three-year casualty and liability insurance policy that is deducted for tax purposes entirely in 2019.
2. Insurance expense for a $1 million premium on a life insurance policy for the company president. This is not deductible for tax purposes.
3. An asset with a four-year useful life was acquired last year. It is depreciated by the straight-line method in the income statement. MACRS is used on the tax return, causing deductions for depreciation to be more than straight-line depreciation the first two years but less than straight-line depreciation the next two years ($ in millions):

	Income Statement	Tax Return	Difference
2018	$150	$198	$ (48)
2019	150	264	(114)
2020	150	90	60
2021	150	48	102
	$600	$600	0

[16]See Dan Givoly and Carla Hayn, "The Valuation of the Deferred Tax Liability: Evidence from the Stock Market," *The Accounting Review*, April 1992, pp. 394–410.

[17]See Greg Miller and Doug Skinner, "Determinants of the Valuation Allowance for Deferred Tax Assets under SFAS No. 109," *The Accounting Review*, April 1998, pp. 213–233.

[18]See Sonia O. Rego and Mary Margaret Frank, "Do Managers Use the Valuation Allowance Account to Manage Earnings Around Certain Earnings Targets?" *Journal of the American Taxation Association 28 (1)*, 2006, pp. 43–65.

[19]See John Graham, Michelle Hanlon, Terry Shevlin, and Nemit Shroff, "Incentives for Tax Planning and Avoidance: Evidence from the Field," *The Accounting Review*, May 2014, pp. 999–1023.

4. Equipment rental revenue of $80 million, which does not include an additional $20 million of advance payment for 2020 rent. $100 million of rental revenue is reported on the 2019 income tax return.

The enacted tax rate is 40%.

Required:

1. Prepare the journal entry to record Mid-South Cellular's income taxes for 2019.
2. What is Mid-South Cellular's 2019 net income?

Solution

1. Prepare the journal entry to record Mid-South Cellular's income taxes for 2019.

($ in millions)	2018	Current Year 2019	Future Taxable (Deductible) Amounts 2020	2021	Future Taxable Amounts (total)	Future Deductible Amounts (total)
Pretax accounting income		$ 88				
Permanent difference:						
Life insurance premium		1				
Temporary differences:						
Prepaid insurance		(28)	$ 14	$ 14	$ 28	
Depreciation	$(48)	(114)	60	102	162	
Advance rent received		20	(20)			$(20)
Net operating loss		$ (33)				
Loss carryback	(25)	← 25				
Loss carryforward		8 →				(8)
		$ 0			$ 190	$(28)
Enacted tax rate	40%	40%			40%	40%
Tax payable (refundable)	$(10)	$ 0				
Deferred tax liability					$ 76.0	
Deferred tax asset						$(11.2)

Differences in tax reporting and financial reporting of both the prepaid insurance and the depreciation create future taxable amounts.

Both the advance rent and the net operating loss carryforward create future deductible amounts.

	Deferred Tax Liability	Deferred Tax Asset
Ending balances:	$ 76.0	$ 11.2
Less: Beginning balance ($48* × 40%)	(19.2)	(0.0)
Change in balances	$ 56.8	$ 11.2

*2018's only temporary difference.

Journal Entry at the End of 2019

Income tax expense (to balance)	35.6	
Receivable—income tax refund (determined above)	10.0	
Deferred tax asset (determined above)	11.2	
Deferred tax liability (determined above)		56.8

Note: Adjusting pretax accounting income by the permanent difference and the three temporary differences creates a negative taxable income, which is a net operating loss.

2. What is Mid-South Cellular's 2019 net income?

Pretax accounting income	$88.0
Income tax expense	(35.6)
Net income	$52.4

Financial Reporting Case Solution

© Image Source

1. **What's the difference? Explain to Laura how differences between financial reporting standards and income tax rules might cause the income tax expense and the amount of income tax paid to differ.** *(p. 907)* The differences in the rules for computing taxable income and those for financial reporting often cause amounts to be included in taxable income in a different year(s) from the year in which they are recognized for financial reporting purposes. Temporary differences result in future taxable or deductible amounts when the temporary differences reverse. As a result, tax payments frequently occur in years different from the years in which the revenues and expenses that cause the taxes are generated.
2. **What is the conceptual advantage of determining income tax expense as we do?** *(p. 908)* Income tax expense is the combination of the current tax effect and the deferred tax consequences of the period's activities. Under the asset-liability approach, the objective of accounting for income taxes is to recognize a deferred tax liability or deferred tax asset for the tax consequences of amounts that will become taxable or deductible in future years as a result of transactions or events that already have occurred. A result is to recognize both the current and the deferred tax consequences of the operations of a reporting period.
3. **Are there differences between financial reporting standards and income tax rules that will not cause a difference between income tax expense and the amount of income taxes paid?** *(p. 922)* Yes. Some differences between accounting income and taxable income are caused by transactions and events that will never affect taxable income or taxes payable. These differences between accounting income and taxable income do not reverse later. These are permanent differences that are disregarded when determining (a) the tax payable currently, (b) the deferred tax effect, and therefore (c) the income tax expense. ●

The Bottom Line

- **LO16–1** Temporary differences produce future taxable amounts when the taxable income will be increased relative to pretax accounting income in one or more future years. These produce deferred tax liabilities for the taxes to be paid on the future taxable amounts. Income tax expense for the year includes an amount for which payment (or receipt) is deferred in addition to the amount for which payment is due currently. The deferred amount is the change in the tax liability (or asset). (*p. 908*)
- **LO16–2** When the future tax consequence of a temporary difference will be to decrease taxable income relative to pretax accounting income, future deductible amounts are created. These have favorable tax consequences that are recognized as deferred tax assets. (*p. 915*)
- **LO16–3** Deferred tax assets are recognized for all deductible temporary differences. However, a deferred tax asset is then reduced by a valuation allowance if it is more likely than not that some portion or all of the deferred tax asset will not be realized. (*p. 918*)
- **LO16–4** Permanent differences between the reported amount of an asset or liability in the financial statements and its tax basis are those caused by transactions and events that under existing tax law will never affect taxable income or taxes payable. These are disregarded when determining both the tax payable currently, the deferred tax effect, and tax expense. (*p. 922*)
- **LO16–5** Deferred tax liabilities (and assets) are calculated by multiplying future taxable (and deductible) amounts by the currently enacted tax rates that will apply to them. If a change in a tax law or rate occurs, the deferred tax liability or asset is adjusted to reflect the change in the amount to be paid or recovered. That effect is reflected in tax expense in the year of the enactment of the change in the tax law or rate. (*p. 926*)
- **LO16–6** When multiple temporary differences exist, the total of the future *taxable* amounts is multiplied by the future tax rate to determine the appropriate balance for the deferred tax liability, and the total of the future *deductible* amounts is multiplied by the future tax rate to determine the appropriate balance for the deferred tax asset. (*p. 928*)

- **LO16–7** Tax laws permit a net operating loss (NOL) to be used to reduce taxable income in other, profitable years by either a carryback of the loss to up to two prior years or a carryforward of the loss to up to 20 later years. The tax benefit of a net operating loss carryback or a net operating loss carryforward is recognized in the year of the loss. *(p. 929)*
- **LO16–8** Deferred tax assets and deferred tax liabilities are classified as noncurrent. If they relate to the same taxable component of the company and the same tax jurisdiction, they are netted against each other and shown as a single noncurrent net deferred tax asset or liability. Otherwise they are not offset against each other for purposes of balance-sheet presentation. Disclosure notes should reveal additional relevant information pertaining to deferred tax amounts reported on the balance sheet, the components of income tax expense, and available operating loss carryforwards. *(p. 934)*
- **LO16–9** A tax benefit associated with an uncertain tax position may be reflected in the financial statements only if it is "more likely than not" that the company will be able to sustain the tax return position, based on its technical merits. It should be measured as the largest amount of benefit that is cumulatively greater than 50 percent likely to be realized. *(p. 935)*
- **LO16–10** Through intraperiod tax allocation, the total income tax expense for a reporting period is allocated among the financial statement items that gave rise to it: specifically income (or loss) from continuing operations, discontinued operations, and prior period adjustments (to the beginning retained earnings balance). *(p. 937)*
- **LO16–11** Despite the similar approaches for accounting for taxation under IFRS and U.S. GAAP, differences in reported amounts for deferred taxes are among the most frequent between the two approaches because a great many of the *nontax* differences between IFRS and U.S. GAAP affect deferred taxes. *(pp. 920 and 924)*

Questions For Review of Key Topics

Q 16–1 A member of the board of directors is concerned that the company's income statement reports income tax expense of $12.3 million, but the income tax obligation to the government for the year is only $7.9 million. How might the corporate controller explain this difference?

Q 16–2 A deferred tax liability (or asset) is described as the tax effect of the temporary difference between the financial statement carrying amount (book value) of an asset or liability and its tax basis. Explain this tax effect of the temporary difference. How might it produce a deferred tax liability? A deferred tax asset?

Q 16–3 Sometimes a temporary difference will produce future deductible amounts. Explain what is meant by future deductible amounts. Describe two general situations that have this effect. How are such situations recognized in the financial statements?

Q 16–4 The benefit of future deductible amounts can be achieved only if future income is sufficient to take advantage of the deferred deductions. For that reason, not all deferred tax assets will ultimately be realized. How is this possibility reflected in the way we recognize deferred tax assets?

Q 16–5 Temporary differences result in future taxable or deductible amounts when the related asset or liability is recovered or settled. Some differences, though, are not temporary. What events create permanent differences? What effect do these have on the determination of income taxes payable? Of deferred income taxes? Of tax expense?

Q 16–6 Identify three examples of differences with no deferred tax consequences.

Q 16–7 The income tax rate for Hudson Refinery has been 35% for each of its 12 years of operation. Company forecasters expect a much-debated tax reform bill to be passed by Congress early next year. The new tax measure would increase Hudson's tax rate to 42%. When measuring this year's deferred tax liability, which rate should Hudson use?

Q 16–8 Suppose a tax reform bill is enacted that causes the corporate tax rate to change from 34% to 36%. How would this affect an existing deferred tax liability? How would the change be reflected in income?

Q 16–9 A net operating loss occurs when tax-deductible expenses exceed taxable revenues. Tax laws permit the net operating loss to be used to reduce taxable income in other, profitable years by either a carryback of the loss to prior years or a carryforward of the loss to later years. How are loss carrybacks and loss carryforwards recognized for financial reporting purposes?

Q 16–10 How are deferred tax assets and deferred tax liabilities reported in a classified balance sheet?

Q 16–11 Additional disclosures are required pertaining to deferred tax amounts reported on the balance sheet. What are the needed disclosures?

Q 16–12 Additional disclosures are required pertaining to the income tax expense reported in the income statement. What are the needed disclosures?

Q 16–13 Accounting for uncertainty in tax positions is prescribed by GAAP in FASB ASC 740–10: Income Taxes–Overall (previously *FASB Interpretation No. 48 (FIN 48))*. Describe the two-step process required by GAAP.

Q 16–14 What is intraperiod tax allocation?

IFRS **Q 16–15** IFRS and U.S. GAAP follow similar approaches to accounting for taxation. Nevertheless, differences in reported amounts for deferred taxes are among the most frequent between IFRS and U.S. GAAP. Why?

Brief Exercises

connect

BE 16–1
Temporary difference
● LO16–1

A company reports *pretax accounting income* of $10 million, but because of a single temporary difference, *taxable income* is only $7 million. No temporary differences existed at the beginning of the year, and the tax rate is 40%. Prepare the appropriate journal entry to record income taxes.

BE 16–2
Temporary difference; determine taxable income; determine prior year deferred tax amount
● LO16–1

Kara Fashions uses straight-line depreciation for financial statement reporting and MACRS for income tax reporting. Three years after its purchase, one of Kara's buildings has a book value of $400,000 and a tax basis of $300,000. There were no other temporary differences and no permanent differences. Taxable income was $4 million and Kara's tax rate is 40%. What is the deferred tax liability to be reported in the balance sheet? Assuming that the deferred tax liability balance was $32,000 the previous year, prepare the appropriate journal entry to record income taxes this year.

BE 16–3
Temporary difference
● LO16–2

A company reports *pretax accounting income* of $10 million, but because of a single temporary difference, *taxable income* is $12 million. No temporary differences existed at the beginning of the year, and the tax rate is 40%. Prepare the appropriate journal entry to record income taxes.

BE 16–4
Temporary difference; income tax payable given
● LO16–2

In 2018, Ryan Management collected rent revenue for 2019 tenant occupancy. For financial reporting, the rent is recorded as deferred revenue and then recognized as income in the period tenants occupy rental property, but for income tax reporting it is taxed when collected. The deferred portion of the rent collected in 2018 was $50 million. Taxable income is $180 million. No temporary differences existed at the beginning of the year, and the tax rate is 40%. Prepare the appropriate journal entry to record income taxes.

BE 16–5
Temporary difference; income tax payable given
● LO16–2

Refer to the situation described in BE 16–4. Suppose the deferred portion of the rent collected was $40 million at the end of 2019. Taxable income is $200 million. Prepare the appropriate journal entry to record income taxes.

BE 16–6
Valuation allowance
● LO16–2, LO16–3

At the end of the year, the deferred tax asset account had a balance of $12 million attributable to a cumulative temporary difference of $30 million in a liability for estimated expenses. Taxable income is $35 million. No temporary differences existed at the beginning of the year, and the tax rate is 40%. Prepare the journal entry(s) to record income taxes, assuming it is more likely than not that one-fourth of the deferred tax asset will not ultimately be realized.

BE 16–7
Valuation allowance
● LO16–2, LO16–3

VeriFone Systems is a provider of electronic card payment terminals, peripherals, network products, and software. In its 2015 annual report, the company reported deferred tax assets totaling about $398 million. The company also reported valuation allowances totaling about $332 million. What would motivate VeriFone to have a valuation allowance almost equal to its deferred tax assets?

BE 16–8
Temporary and permanent differences; determine deferred tax consequences
● LO16–1, LO16–4

Differences between financial statement and taxable income were as follows:

	($ in millions)
Pretax accounting income	$300
Permanent difference	(24)
	276
Temporary difference	(18)
Taxable income	$258

The cumulative temporary difference to date is $40 million (also the future taxable amount). The enacted tax rate is 40%. What is deferred tax asset or liability to be reported in the balance sheet?

BE 16–9
Calculate taxable income
● LO16–1, LO16–4

Shannon Polymers uses straight-line depreciation for financial reporting purposes for equipment costing $800,000 and with an expected useful life of four years and no residual value. For tax purposes, the deduction is 40%, 30%, 20%, and 10% in those years. Pretax accounting income the first year the equipment was used was $900,000, which includes interest revenue of $20,000 from municipal bonds. Other than the two described, there are no differences between accounting income and taxable income. The enacted tax rate is 40%. Prepare the journal entry to record income taxes.

BE 16–10
Multiple tax rates
● LO16–5

J-Matt, Inc., had pretax accounting income of $291,000 and taxable income of $300,000 in 2018. The only difference between accounting and taxable income is estimated product warranty costs for sales this year. Warranty payments are expected to be in equal amounts over the next three years. Recent tax legislation will change the tax rate from the current 40% to 30% in 2020. Determine the amounts necessary to record J-Matt's income taxes for 2018 and prepare the appropriate journal entry.

BE 16–11
Change in tax rate
● LO16–5

Superior Developers sells lots for residential development. When lots are sold, Superior recognizes income for financial reporting purposes in the year of the sale. For some lots, Superior recognizes income for tax purposes when collected. In the *prior* year, income recognized for financial reporting purposes for lots sold this way was $20 million, which would be collected equally over the next two years. The enacted tax rate was 40%. This year, a new tax law was enacted, revising the tax rate from 40% to 35% beginning next year. Calculate the amount by which Superior should reduce its deferred tax liability this year.

BE 16–12
Net operating loss carryforward
● LO16–7

During its first year of operations, Nile.com reported a net operating loss of $15 million for financial reporting and tax purposes. The enacted tax rate is 40%. Prepare the journal entry to recognize the income tax benefit of the net operating loss.

BE 16–13
Net operating loss carryback
● LO16–7

AirParts Corporation reported a net operating loss of $25 million for financial reporting and tax purposes. Taxable income last year and the previous year, respectively, was $20 million and $15 million. The enacted tax rate each year is 40%. Prepare the journal entry to recognize the income tax benefit of the net operating loss. AirParts elects the carryback option.

BE 16–14
Tax uncertainty
● LO16–9

First Bank has some question as to the tax-free nature of $5 million of its municipal bond portfolio. This amount is excluded from First Bank's taxable income of $55 million. Management has determined that there is a 65% chance that the tax-free status of this interest can't withstand scrutiny of taxing authorities. Assuming a 40% tax rate, what amount of income tax expense should the bank report?

BE 16–15
Intraperiod tax allocation
● LO16–10

Southeast Airlines had pretax earnings of $65 million, including a gain on disposal of a discontinued operation of $10 million. The company's tax rate is 40%. What is the amount of income tax expense that Southeast should report in its income statement? How should the gain on disposal of a discontinued operation be reported?

Exercises

connect

E 16–1
Temporary difference; taxable income given
● LO16–1

Alvis Corporation reports *pretax accounting income* of $400,000, but due to a single temporary difference, *taxable income* is only $250,000. At the beginning of the year, no temporary differences existed.

Required:

1. Assuming a tax rate of 35%, what will be Alvis's net income?
2. What will Alvis report in the balance sheet pertaining to income taxes?

E 16–2
Determine taxable income; determine prior year deferred tax amount
● LO16–1

On January 1, 2013, Ameen Company purchased a building for $36 million. Ameen uses straight-line depreciation for financial statement reporting and MACRS for income tax reporting. At December 31, 2017, the book value of the building was $30 million and its tax basis was $20 million. At December 31, 2018, the book value of the building was $28 million and its tax basis was $13 million. There were no other temporary differences and no permanent differences. Pretax accounting income for 2018 was $45 million.

Required:

1. Prepare the appropriate journal entry to record Ameen's 2018 income taxes. Assume an income tax rate of 40%.
2. What is Ameen's 2018 net income?

E 16–3
Taxable income given; calculate deferred tax liability
● LO16–1

Ayres Services acquired an asset for $80 million in 2018. The asset is depreciated for financial reporting purposes over four years on a straight-line basis (no residual value). For tax purposes the asset's cost is depreciated by MACRS. The enacted tax rate is 40%. Amounts for pretax accounting income, depreciation, and taxable income in 2018, 2019, 2020, and 2021 are as follows:

	($ in millions)			
	2018	**2019**	**2020**	**2021**
Pretax accounting income	$330	$350	$365	$400
Depreciation on the income statement	20	20	20	20
Depreciation on the tax return	(25)	(33)	(15)	(7)
Taxable income	$325	$337	$370	$413

Required:
For December 31 of each year, determine (a) the temporary book–tax difference for the depreciable asset and (b) the balance to be reported in the deferred tax liability account.

E 16–4
Temporary difference; income tax payable given
● LO16–2

In 2018, DFS Medical Supply collected rent revenue for 2019 tenant occupancy. For income tax reporting, the rent is taxed when collected. For financial statement reporting, the rent is recorded as deferred revenue and then recognized as income in the period tenants occupy the rental property. The deferred portion of the rent collected in 2018 amounted to $300,000 at December 31, 2018. DFS had no temporary differences at the beginning of the year.

Required:
Assuming an income tax rate of 40% and 2018 income tax payable of $950,000, prepare the journal entry to record income taxes for 2018.

E 16–5
Temporary difference; future deductible amounts; taxable income given
● LO16–2

Lance Lawn Services reports warranty expense by estimating the amount that eventually will be paid to satisfy warranties on its product sales. For tax purposes, the expense is deducted when the cost is incurred. At December 31, 2018, Lance has a warranty liability of $1 million and taxable income of $75 million. At December 31, 2017, Lance reported a deferred tax asset of $435,000 related to this difference in reporting warranties, its only temporary difference. The enacted tax rate is 40% each year.

Required:
Prepare the appropriate journal entry to record Lance's income tax provision for 2018.

E 16–6
Identify future taxable amounts and future deductible amounts
● LO16–1, LO16–2

Listed below are 10 causes of temporary differences. For each temporary difference, indicate (by letter) whether it will create future deductible amounts (D) or future taxable amounts (T).

Temporary Difference

_____ 1. Accrual of loss contingency; tax-deductible when paid
_____ 2. Newspaper subscriptions; taxable when received, recognized for financial reporting when the performance obligation is satisfied
_____ 3. Prepaid rent; tax-deductible when paid
_____ 4. Accrued bond interest expense; tax-deductible when paid
_____ 5. Prepaid insurance; tax-deductible when paid
_____ 6. Unrealized loss from recording investments at fair value; tax-deductible when investments are sold
_____ 7. Warranty expense; estimated for financial reporting when products are sold; deducted for tax purposes when paid
_____ 8. Advance rent receipts on an operating lease as the lessor; taxable when received
_____ 9. Straight-line depreciation for financial reporting; accelerated depreciation for tax purposes
_____ 10. Accrued expense for employee postretirement benefits; tax-deductible when subsequent payments are made

E 16–7
Identify future taxable amounts and future deductible amounts
● LO16–1, LO16–2

(This is a variation of E 16–6, modified to focus on the balance sheet accounts related to the deferred tax amounts.)

Listed below are 10 causes of temporary differences. For each temporary difference indicate the balance sheet account for which the situation creates a temporary difference.

Temporary Difference

_____ 1. Accrual of loss contingency; tax-deductible when paid
_____ 2. Newspaper subscriptions; taxable when received, recognized for financial reporting when the performance obligation is satisfied
_____ 3. Prepaid rent; tax-deductible when paid
_____ 4. Accrued bond interest expense; tax-deductible when paid
_____ 5. Prepaid insurance; tax-deductible when paid

(continued)

(concluded)

_____ 6. Unrealized loss from recording investments at fair value; tax-deductible when investments are sold
_____ 7. Warranty expense; estimated for financial reporting when products are sold; deducted for tax purposes when paid
_____ 8. Advance rent receipts on an operating lease as the lessor; taxable when received
_____ 9. Straight-line depreciation for financial reporting; accelerated depreciation for tax purposes
_____ 10. Accrued expense for employee postretirement benefits; tax-deductible when subsequent payments are made

E 16–8
Calculate income tax amounts under various circumstances
● LO16–1, LO16–2

Four independent situations are described below. Each involves future deductible amounts and/or future taxable amounts produced by temporary differences:

	($ in thousands) Situation			
	1	**2**	**3**	**4**
Taxable income	$85	$215	$195	$260
Future deductible amounts	15		20	20
Future taxable amounts		15	15	30
Balance(s) at beginning of the year:				
Deferred tax asset	2		9	4
Deferred tax liability		2	2	

The enacted tax rate is 40%.

Required:
For each situation, determine the:
a. Income tax payable currently
b. Deferred tax asset—balance
c. Deferred tax asset—change (dr) cr
d. Deferred tax liability—balance
e. Deferred tax liability—change (dr) cr
f. Income tax expense

E 16–9
Determine taxable income
● LO16–1, LO16–2

Eight independent situations are described below. Each involves future deductible amounts and/or future taxable amounts ($ in millions).

	Temporary Differences Reported First on:			
	The Income Statement		The Tax Return	
	Revenue	**Expense**	**Revenue**	**Expense**
1.		$20		
2.	$20			
3.			$20	
4.				$20
5.	15	20		
6.		20	15	
7.	15	20		10
8.	15	20	5	10

Required:
For each situation, determine taxable income, assuming pretax accounting income is $100 million.

E 16–10
Deferred tax asset; taxable income given; valuation allowance
● LO16–3

At the end of 2017, Payne Industries had a deferred tax asset account with a balance of $30 million attributable to a temporary book–tax difference of $75 million in a liability for estimated expenses. At the end of 2018, the temporary difference is $70 million. Payne has no other temporary differences and no valuation allowance for the deferred tax asset. Taxable income for 2018 is $180 million and the tax rate is 40%.

Required:
1. Prepare the journal entry(s) to record Payne's income taxes for 2018, assuming it is more likely than not that the deferred tax asset will be realized.
2. Prepare the journal entry(s) to record Payne's income taxes for 2018, assuming it is more likely than not that one-fourth of the deferred tax asset will ultimately be realized.

E 16–11
Deferred tax asset; income tax payable given; previous balance in valuation allowance
● LO16–3

(This is a variation of E 16–10, modified to assume a previous balance in the valuation allowance.)
At the end of 2017, Payne Industries had a deferred tax asset account with a balance of $30 million attributable to a temporary book-tax difference of $75 million in a liability for estimated expenses. At the end of 2018, the temporary difference is $70 million. Payne has no other temporary differences. Taxable income for 2018 is $180 million and the tax rate is 40%.

Payne has a valuation allowance of $10 million for the deferred tax asset at the beginning of 2018.

Required:
1. Prepare the journal entry(s) to record Payne's income taxes for 2018, assuming it is more likely than not that the deferred tax asset will be realized.
2. Prepare the journal entry(s) to record Payne's income taxes for 2018, assuming it is more likely than not that one-fourth of the deferred tax asset will ultimately be realized.

E 16–12
FASB codification research; valuation allowance
● LO16–3

When a company records a deferred tax asset, it may need to also report a valuation allowance if it is "more likely than not" that some portion or all of the deferred tax asset will not be realized. The *FASB Accounting Standards Codification* represents the single source of authoritative U.S. generally accepted accounting principles.

Required:
1. Obtain the relevant authoritative literature on disclosure requirements pertaining to how a firm should determine whether a valuation allowance for deferred tax assets is needed using the FASB's Codification Research System at the FASB website (www.fasb.org). What is the specific citation that describes the guidelines for determining the disclosure requirements?
2. What are the guidelines?

E 16–13
Multiple differences; calculate taxable income
● LO16–1, LO16–4, LO16–6

Southern Atlantic Distributors began operations in January 2018 and purchased a delivery truck for $40,000. Southern Atlantic plans to use straight-line depreciation over a four-year expected useful life for financial reporting purposes. For tax purposes, the deduction is 50% of cost in 2018, 30% in 2019, and 20% in 2020. Pretax accounting income for 2018 was $300,000, which includes interest revenue of $40,000 from municipal bonds. The enacted tax rate is 40%.

Required:
Assuming no differences between accounting income and taxable income other than those described above:
1. Prepare the journal entry to record income taxes in 2018.
2. What is Southern Atlantic's 2018 net income?

E 16–14
Multiple differences
● LO16–4, LO16–6

For the year ended December 31, 2018, Fidelity Engineering reported pretax accounting income of $977,000. Selected information for 2018 from Fidelity's records follows:

Interest income on municipal bonds	$32,000
Depreciation claimed on the 2018 tax return in excess of depreciation on the income statement	55,000
Carrying amount of depreciable assets in excess of their tax basis at year-end	85,000
Warranty expense reported on the income statement	26,000
Actual warranty expenditures in 2018	16,000

Fidelity's income tax rate is 40%. At January 1, 2018, Fidelity's records indicated balances of zero and $12,000 in its deferred tax asset and deferred tax liability accounts, respectively.

Required:
1. Determine the amounts necessary to record income taxes for 2018, and prepare the appropriate journal entry.
2. What is Fidelity's 2018 net income?

E 16–15
Multiple tax rates
● LO16–2, LO16–5

Allmond Corporation, organized on January 3, 2018, had pretax accounting income of $14 million and taxable income of $20 million for the year ended December 31, 2018. The 2018 tax rate is 35%. The only difference between accounting income and taxable income is estimated product warranty costs. Expected payments and scheduled tax rates (based on recent tax legislation) are as follows:

2019	$2 million	30%
2020	1 million	30%
2021	1 million	30%
2022	2 million	25%

Required:
1. Determine the amounts necessary to record Allmond's income taxes for 2018 and prepare the appropriate journal entry.
2. What is Allmond's 2018 net income?

E 16–16
Change in tax rates; calculate taxable income
● LO16–1, LO16–5

Arnold Industries has pretax accounting income of $33 million for the year ended December 31, 2018. The tax rate is 40%. The only difference between accounting income and taxable income relates to an operating lease in which Arnold is the lessee. The inception of the lease was December 28, 2018. An $8 million advance rent payment at the inception of the lease is tax-deductible in 2018 but, for financial reporting purposes, represents prepaid rent expense to be recognized equally over the four-year lease term.

Required:

1. Determine the amounts necessary to record Arnold's income taxes for 2018, and prepare the appropriate journal entry.
2. Determine the amounts necessary to record Arnold's income taxes for 2019, and prepare the appropriate journal entry. Pretax accounting income was $50 million for the year ended December 31, 2019.
3. Assume a new tax law is enacted in 2019 that causes the tax rate to change from 40% to 30% beginning in 2020. Determine the amounts necessary to record Arnold's income taxes for 2019, and prepare the appropriate journal entry.
4. Why is Arnold's 2019 income tax expense different when the tax rate change occurs from what it would be without the change?

E 16–17
Deferred taxes; change in tax rates
● LO16–1, LO16–5

Bronson Industries reported a deferred tax liability of $8 million for the year ended December 31, 2017, related to a temporary difference of $20 million. The tax rate was 40%. The temporary difference is expected to reverse in 2019, at which time the deferred tax liability will become payable. There are no other temporary differences in 2017–2019. Assume a new tax law is enacted in 2018 that causes the tax rate to change from 40% to 30% beginning in 2019. (The rate remains 40% for 2018 taxes.) Taxable income in 2018 is $30 million.

Required:

Determine the effect of the change and prepare the appropriate journal entry to record Bronson's income tax expense in 2018. What adjustment, if any, is needed to revise retained earnings as a result of the change?

E 16–18
Multiple temporary differences; record income taxes
● LO16–6

The information that follows pertains to Esther Food Products:

a. At December 31, 2018, temporary differences were associated with the following future taxable (deductible) amounts:

Depreciation	$ 60,000
Prepaid expenses	17,000
Warranty expenses	(12,000)

b. No temporary differences existed at the beginning of 2018.

c. Pretax accounting income was $80,000 and taxable income was $15,000 for the year ended December 31, 2018.

d. The tax rate is 40%.

Required:

Determine the amounts necessary to record income taxes for 2018, and prepare the appropriate journal entry.

E 16–19
Multiple temporary differences; record income taxes
● LO16–6

The information that follows pertains to Richards Refrigeration, Inc.:

a. At December 31, 2018, temporary differences existed between the financial statement carrying amounts and the tax bases of the following ($ in millions):

	Carrying Amount	Tax Basis	Future Taxable (Deductible) Amount
Buildings and equipment (net of accumulated depreciation)	$120	$90	$ 30
Prepaid insurance	50	0	50
Liability—loss contingency	25	0	(25)

b. No temporary differences existed at the beginning of 2018.

c. Pretax accounting income was $200 million and taxable income was $145 million for the year ended December 31, 2018. The tax rate is 40%.

Required:

1. Determine the amounts necessary to record income taxes for 2018, and prepare the appropriate journal entry.
2. What is the 2018 net income?

E 16–20
Net operating loss carryforward
● LO16–7

During 2018, its first year of operations, Baginski Steel Corporation reported a net operating loss of $375,000 for financial reporting and tax purposes. The enacted tax rate is 40%.

Required:

1. Prepare the journal entry to recognize the income tax benefit of the net operating loss. Assume the weight of available evidence suggests future taxable income sufficient to benefit from future deductible amounts from the net operating loss carryforward.
2. Show the lower portion of the 2018 income statement that reports the income tax benefit of the net operating loss.

E 16–21
Net operating loss carryback
● LO16–7

Wynn Sheet Metal reported a net operating loss of $100,000 for financial reporting and tax purposes in 2018. The enacted tax rate is 40%. Taxable income, tax rates, and income taxes paid in Wynn's first four years of operation were as follows:

	Taxable Income	Tax Rates	Income Taxes Paid
2014	$60,000	30%	$18,000
2015	70,000	30	21,000
2016	80,000	40	32,000
2017	60,000	45	27,000

Required:

1. Prepare the journal entry to recognize the income tax benefit of the net operating loss. Wynn elects the carryback option.
2. Show the lower portion of the 2018 income statement that reports the income tax benefit of the net operating loss.

E 16–22
Net operating loss carryback and carryforward
● LO16–7

(This exercise is based on the situation described in E 16–21, modified to include a carryforward in addition to a carryback.)

Wynn Sheet Metal reported a net operating loss of $160,000 for financial reporting and tax purposes in 2018. The enacted tax rate is 40%. Taxable income, tax rates, and income taxes paid in Wynn's first four years of operation were as follows:

	Taxable Income	Tax Rates	Income Taxes Paid
2014	$60,000	30%	$18,000
2015	70,000	30	21,000
2016	80,000	40	32,000
2017	60,000	45	27,000

Required:

1. Prepare the journal entry to recognize the income tax benefit of the net operating loss. Wynn elects the carryback option.
2. Show the lower portion of the 2018 income statement that reports the income tax benefit of the net operating loss.

E 16–23
Identifying income tax deferrals
● LO16–1, LO16–2, LO16–4, LO16–7

Listed below are ten independent situations. For each situation indicate (by letter) whether it will create a deferred tax asset (A), a deferred tax liability (L), or neither (N).

Situation

_____ 1. Advance payments on insurance, deductible when paid
_____ 2. Estimated warranty costs; tax deductible when paid
_____ 3. Rent revenue collected in advance; cash basis for tax purposes
_____ 4. Interest received from investments in municipal bonds
_____ 5. Prepaid expenses, tax deductible when paid
_____ 6. Net operating loss carryforward
_____ 7. Net operating loss carryback
_____ 8. Straight-line depreciation for financial reporting; MACRS for tax purposes
_____ 9. Organization costs expensed when incurred; tax deductible over 15 years
_____ 10. Life insurance proceeds received upon the death of the company president

E 16–24
Multiple temporary differences; balance sheet presentation
● LO16–4, LO16–5, LO16–6, LO16–8

At December 31, DePaul Corporation had a $16 million balance in its deferred tax asset account and a $68 million balance in its deferred tax liability account. The balances were due to the following cumulative temporary differences:

1. Estimated warranty expense, $15 million: expense recorded in the year of the sale; tax-deductible when paid (one-year warranty).
2. Depreciation expense, $120 million: straight-line in the income statement; MACRS on the tax return.
3. Income from installment sales of properties, $50 million: income recorded in the year of the sale; taxable when received equally over the next five years.
4. Rent revenue collected in advance, $25 million; taxable in the year collected; recorded as income when the performance obligation is satisfied in the following year.

Required:

Assuming DePaul will show a single noncurrent net amount in its December 31 balance sheet, indicate that amount and whether it is a net deferred tax asset or liability. The tax rate is 40%.

E 16–25
Multiple tax rates
● LO16–1, LO16–4, LO16–5

Case Development began operations in December 2018. When property is sold on an installment basis, Case recognizes installment income for financial reporting purposes in the year of the sale. For tax purposes, installment income is reported by the installment method. 2018 installment income was $600,000 and will be collected over the next three years. Scheduled collections and enacted tax rates for 2019–2021 are as follows:

2019	$150,000	30%
2020	250,000	40
2021	200,000	40

Pretax accounting income for 2018 was $810,000, which includes interest revenue of $10,000 from municipal bonds. The enacted tax rate for 2018 is 30%.

Required:

1. Assuming no differences between accounting income and taxable income other than those described above, prepare the appropriate journal entry to record Case's 2018 income taxes.
2. What is Case's 2018 net income?

E 16–26
Multiple differences; multiple tax rates
● LO16–1, LO16–2, LO16–4, LO16–5, LO16–6

(This exercise is a variation of E 16–25, modified to include a second temporary difference.)
Case Development began operations in December 2018. When property is sold on an installment basis, Case recognizes installment income for financial reporting purposes in the year of the sale. For tax purposes, installment income is reported by the installment method. 2018 installment income was $600,000 and will be collected over the next three years. Scheduled collections and enacted tax rates for 2019–2021 are as follows:

2019	$150,000	30%
2020	250,000	40
2021	200,000	40

Case also had product warranty costs of $80,000 expensed for financial reporting purposes in 2018. For tax purposes, only the $20,000 of warranty costs actually paid in 2018 was deducted. The remaining $60,000 will be deducted for tax purposes when paid over the next three years as follows:

2019	$20,000
2020	25,000
2021	15,000

Pretax *accounting* income for 2018 was $810,000, which includes interest revenue of $10,000 from municipal bonds. The enacted tax rate for 2018 is 30%.

Required:

1. Assuming no differences between accounting income and taxable income other than those described above, prepare the appropriate journal entry to record Case's 2018 income taxes.
2. What is Case's 2018 net income?

E 16–27
Balance sheet classification
● LO16–8

As of December 31, 2016, Lange Company has the following deferred tax assets and liabilities:

Deferred tax assets	
Pension plans	$300,000
Inventory	200,000
Total deferred tax assets	$500,000

(continued)

(concluded)

Deferred tax liabilities	
Property, plant and equipment	$100,000
Unrealized gains on investments	350,000
Total deferred tax liabilities	$450,000

Required:

1. Assume that all of Lange's deferred tax assets and liabilities are in the same tax jurisdiction. How would deferred taxes be shown on Lange's balance sheet?
2. Assume that the deferred tax effects of Lange's pension plans and unrealized gains on investments occurred in a different tax jurisdiction from Lange's other deferred tax effects. How would deferred taxes be shown on Lange's balance sheet?

E 16–28
Concepts; terminology
● LO16–1 through LO16–8

Listed below are several terms and phrases associated with accounting for income taxes. Pair each item from List A with the item from List B (by letter) that is most appropriately associated with it.

List A	List B
_____ 1. No tax consequences	a. Deferred tax liability
_____ 2. Originates, then reverses	b. Deferred tax asset
_____ 3. Revise deferred tax amounts	c. 2 years
_____ 4. Operating loss	d. Current and deferred tax consequence combined
_____ 5. Future tax effect of prepaid expenses; tax deductible when paid	e. Temporary difference
_____ 6. Loss carryback	f. Specific tax rates times amounts reversing each year
_____ 7. Future tax effect of estimated warranty expense	g. Nontemporary differences
_____ 8. Valuation allowance	h. When enacted tax rate changes
_____ 9. Phased-in change in rates	i. Net deferred tax asset or liability
_____ 10. Balance sheet presentation	j. "More likely than not" test
_____ 11. Individual tax consequences of financial statement components	k. Intraperiod tax allocation
_____ 12. Income tax expense	l. Negative taxable income

E 16–29
Tax credit; uncertainty regarding sustainability
● LO16–9

Delta Catfish Company has taken a position in its tax return to claim a tax credit of $10 million (direct reduction in taxes payable) and has determined that its sustainability is "more likely than not," based on its technical merits. Delta has developed the probability table shown below of all possible material outcomes ($ in millions):

Probability Table

Amount of the tax benefit that management expects to receive	$10	$ 8	$ 6	$ 4	$ 2
Percentage likelihood that the tax benefit will be sustained at this level	10%	20%	25%	20%	25%

Delta's taxable income is $85 million for the year. Its effective tax rate is 40%. The tax credit would be a direct reduction in current taxes payable.

Required:

1. At what amount would Delta measure the tax benefit in its income statement?
2. Prepare the appropriate journal entry for Delta to record its income taxes for the year.

E 16–30
Intraperiod tax allocation
● LO16–10

The following income statement does not reflect intraperiod tax allocation.

Required:

Recast the income statement to reflect intraperiod tax allocation.

INCOME STATEMENT
For the Fiscal Year Ended March 31, 2018
($ in millions)

Revenues	$830
Cost of goods sold	(350)
Gross profit	480
Operating expenses	(180)
Income tax expense	(86)
Income before discontinued operations	214
Loss from discontinued operations	(85)
Net income	$129

The company's tax rate is 40%.

E 16–31
FASB codification research
● LO16–5, LO16–8, LO16–10

CODE

Access the *FASB Accounting Standards Codification* at the FASB website (www.fasb.org). Determine the specific citation for accounting for each of the following items:

1. The specific items to which income tax expense is allocated for intraperiod tax allocation.
2. The tax rate used to calculate deferred tax assets and liabilities.
3. The required disclosures in the notes to financial statements for the components of income tax expense.

Problems

connect

P 16–1
Single temporary difference originates each year for four years
● LO16–1

Alsup Consulting sometimes performs services for which it receives payment at the conclusion of the engagement, up to six months after services commence. Alsup recognizes service revenue for financial reporting purposes when the services are performed. For tax purposes, revenue is reported when fees are collected. Service revenue, collections, and pretax accounting income for 2017–2020 are as follows:

	Service Revenue	Collections	Pretax Accounting Income
2017	$650,000	$620,000	$186,000
2018	750,000	770,000	250,000
2019	715,000	700,000	220,000
2020	700,000	720,000	200,000

There are no differences between accounting income and taxable income other than the temporary difference described above. The enacted tax rate for each year is 40%.

Required:

1. Prepare the appropriate journal entry to record Alsup's 2018 income taxes.
2. Prepare the appropriate journal entry to record Alsup's 2019 income taxes.
3. Prepare the appropriate journal entry to record Alsup's 2020 income taxes.

(Hint: You may find it helpful to prepare a schedule that shows the balances in service revenue receivable at December 31, 2017–2020.)

P 16–2
Temporary difference; determine deferred tax amount for three years
● LO16–2

Times-Roman Publishing Company reports the following amounts in its first three years of operation:

($ in thousands)	2018	2019	2020
Pretax accounting income	$250	$240	$230
Taxable income	290	220	260

The difference between pretax accounting income and taxable income is due to subscription revenue for one-year magazine subscriptions being reported for tax purposes in the year received, but reported in the income statement in later years when the performance obligation is satisfied. The income tax rate is 40% each year. Times-Roman anticipates profitable operations in the future.

Required:

1. What is the balance sheet account for which a temporary difference is created by this situation?
2. For each year, indicate the cumulative amount of the temporary difference at year-end.
3. Determine the balance in the related deferred tax account at the end of each year. Is it a deferred tax asset or a deferred tax liability?

P 16–3
Change in tax rate; single temporary difference
● LO16–1, LO16–5

Dixon Development began operations in December 2018. When lots for industrial development are sold, Dixon recognizes income for financial reporting purposes in the year of the sale. For some lots, Dixon recognizes income for tax purposes when collected. Income recognized for financial reporting purposes in 2018 for lots sold this way was $12 million, which will be collected over the next three years. Scheduled collections for 2019–2021 are as follows:

2019	$ 4 million
2020	5 million
2021	3 million
	$12 million

Pretax accounting income for 2018 was $16 million. The enacted tax rate is 40%.

Required:

1. Assuming no differences between accounting income and taxable income other than those described above, prepare the journal entry to record income taxes in 2018.
2. Suppose a new tax law, revising the tax rate from 40% to 35%, beginning in 2020, is enacted in 2019, when pretax accounting income was $15 million. No 2019 lot sales qualified for the special tax treatment. Prepare the appropriate journal entry to record income taxes in 2019.
3. If the new tax rate had not been enacted, what would have been the appropriate balance in the deferred tax liability account at the end of 2019? Why?

P 16–4
Change in tax rate; record taxes for four years
● LO16–1, LO16–5

Zekany Corporation would have had identical income before taxes on both its income tax returns and income statements for the years 2018 through 2021 except for differences in depreciation on an operational asset. The asset cost $120,000 and is depreciated for income tax purposes in the following amounts:

2018	$39,600
2019	52,800
2020	18,000
2021	9,600

The operational asset has a four-year life and no residual value. The straight-line method is used for financial reporting purposes.

Income amounts before depreciation expense and income taxes for each of the four years were as follows:

	2018	2019	2020	2021
Accounting income before taxes and depreciation	$60,000	$80,000	$70,000	$70,000

Assume the average and marginal income tax rate for 2018 and 2019 was 30%; however, during 2019, tax legislation was passed to raise the tax rate to 40% beginning in 2020. The 40% rate remained in effect through the years 2020 and 2021. Both the accounting and income tax periods end December 31.

Required:

Prepare the journal entries to record income taxes for the years 2018 through 2021.

P 16–5
Change in tax rate; record taxes for four years
● LO16–1, LO16–4, LO16–5

The DeVille Company reported pretax accounting income on its income statement as follows:

2018	$350,000
2019	270,000
2020	340,000
2021	380,000

Included in the income of 2018 was an installment sale of property in the amount of $50,000. However, for tax purposes, DeVille reported the income in the year cash was collected. Cash collected on the installment sale was $20,000 in 2019, $25,000 in 2020, and $5,000 in 2021.

Included in the 2020 income was $15,000 interest from investments in municipal bonds.

The enacted tax rate for 2018 and 2019 was 30%, but during 2019, new tax legislation was passed reducing the tax rate to 25% for the years 2020 and beyond.

Required:

Prepare the year-end journal entries to record income taxes for the years 2018–2021.

P 16–6
Multiple differences; temporary difference yet to originate; multiple tax rates
● LO16–5, LO16–6

You are the new accounting manager at the Barry Transport Company. Your CFO has asked you to provide input on the company's income tax position based on the following:

1. Pretax accounting income was $41 million and taxable income was $8 million for the year ended December 31, 2018.
2. The difference was due to three items:
   a. Tax depreciation exceeds book depreciation by $30 million in 2018 for the business complex acquired that year. This amount is scheduled to be $60 million in 2019 and to reverse as ($50 million) and ($40 million) in 2020 and 2021, respectively.
   b. Insurance of $9 million was paid in 2018 for 2019 coverage.
   c. A $6 million loss contingency was accrued in 2018, to be paid in 2018.

3. No temporary differences existed at the beginning of 2018.
4. The tax rate is 40%.

Required:

1. Determine the amounts necessary to record income taxes for 2018, and prepare the appropriate journal entry.
2. Assume the enacted federal income tax law specifies that the tax rate will change from 40% to 35% in 2020. When scheduling the reversal of the depreciation difference, you were uncertain as to how to deal with the fact that the difference will continue to originate in 2019 before reversing the next two years. Upon consulting PricewaterhouseCoopers' *Comperio* database, you found:

   .441 Depreciable and amortizable assets

   Only the reversals of the temporary difference at the balance sheet date would be scheduled. Future originations are not considered in determining the reversal pattern of temporary differences for depreciable assets. *FAS 109* [FASB ASC 740–Income Taxes] is silent as to how the balance sheet date temporary differences are deemed to reverse, but the FIFO pattern is intended.

You interpret that to mean, when future taxable amounts are being scheduled, and a portion of a temporary difference has yet to originate, only the reversals of the *temporary difference at the balance sheet date* can be scheduled and multiplied by the tax rate that will be in effect when the difference reverses. Future originations (like the depreciation difference the second year) are not considered when determining the timing of the reversal. For the existing temporary difference, it is assumed that the difference will reverse the first year the difference begins reversing.

Determine the amounts necessary to record income taxes for 2018, and prepare the appropriate journal entry.

P 16–7
Multiple differences; calculate taxable income; balance sheet classification
● LO16–4, LO16–6, LO16–8

Sherrod, Inc., reported pretax accounting income of $76 million for 2018. The following information relates to differences between pretax accounting income and taxable income:

a. Income from installment sales of properties included in pretax accounting income in 2018 exceeded that reported for tax purposes by $3 million. The installment receivable account at year-end had a balance of $4 million (representing portions of 2017 and 2018 installment sales), expected to be collected equally in 2019 and 2020.
b. Sherrod was assessed a penalty of $2 million by the Environmental Protection Agency for violation of a federal law in 2018. The fine is to be paid in equal amounts in 2018 and 2019.
c. Sherrod rents its operating facilities but owns one asset acquired in 2017 at a cost of $80 million. Depreciation is reported by the straight-line method, assuming a four-year useful life. On the tax return, deductions for depreciation will be more than straight-line depreciation the first two years but less than straight-line depreciation the next two years ($ in millions):

	Income Statement	Tax Return	Difference
2017	$20	$26	$(6)
2018	20	35	(15)
2019	20	12	8
2020	20	7	13
	$80	$80	$ 0

d. Warranty expense of $3 million is reported in 2018. For tax purposes, the expense is deducted when costs are incurred, $2 million in 2018. At December 31, 2018, the warranty liability was $2 million (after adjusting entries). The balance was $1 million at the end of 2017.
e. In 2018, Sherrod accrued an expense and related liability for estimated paid future absences of $7 million relating to the company's new paid vacation program. Future compensation will be deductible on the tax return when actually paid during the next two years ($4 million in 2019; $3 million in 2020).
f. During 2017, accounting income included an estimated loss of $2 million from having accrued a loss contingency. The loss is paid in 2018, at which time it is tax deductible.

Balances in the deferred tax asset and deferred tax liability accounts at January 1, 2018, were $1.2 million and $2.8 million, respectively. The enacted tax rate is 40% each year.

Required:

1. Determine the amounts necessary to record income taxes for 2018, and prepare the appropriate journal entry.

2. What is the 2018 net income?
3. Show how any deferred tax amounts should be classified and reported in the 2018 balance sheet.

P 16–8
Multiple differences; taxable income given; two years; balance sheet classification; change in tax rate
● LO16–4, LO16–6, LO16–8

Arndt, Inc., reported the following for 2018 and 2019 ($ in millions):

	2018	2019
Revenues	$888	$983
Expenses	760	800
Pretax accounting income (income statement)	$128	$183
Taxable income (tax return)	$120	$200
Tax rate: 40%		

a. Expenses each year include $30 million from a two-year casualty insurance policy purchased in 2018 for $60 million. The cost is tax deductible in 2018.
b. Expenses include $2 million insurance premiums each year for life insurance on key executives.
c. Arndt sells one-year subscriptions to a weekly journal. Subscription sales collected and taxable in 2018 and 2019 were $33 million and $35 million, respectively. Subscriptions included in 2018 and 2019 financial reporting revenues were $25 million ($10 million collected in 2017 but not recognized as revenue until 2018) and $33 million, respectively. Hint: View this as two temporary differences—one reversing in 2018; one originating in 2018.
d. 2018 expenses included a $17 million unrealized loss from reducing investments (classified as trading securities) to fair value. The investments were sold in 2019.
e. During 2017, accounting income included an estimated loss of $5 million from having accrued a loss contingency. The loss was paid in 2018, at which time it is tax deductible.
f. At January 1, 2018, Arndt had a deferred tax asset of $6 million and no deferred tax liability.

Required:

1. Which of the five differences described are temporary and which are permanent differences? Why?
2. Prepare a schedule that (a) reconciles the difference between pretax accounting income and taxable income and (b) determines the amounts necessary to record income taxes for 2018. Prepare the appropriate journal entry.
3. Show how any 2018 deferred tax amounts should be classified and reported on the 2018 balance sheet.
4. Prepare a schedule that (a) reconciles the difference between pretax accounting income and taxable income and (b) determines the amounts necessary to record income taxes for 2019. Prepare the appropriate journal entry.
5. Explain how any 2019 deferred tax amounts should be classified and reported on the 2019 balance sheet.
6. Suppose that during 2019, tax legislation was passed that will lower Arndt's effective tax rate to 35% beginning in 2020. Repeat requirement 4.

P 16–9
Determine deferred tax assets and liabilities
● LO16–6

Corning-Howell reported taxable income in 2018 of $120 million. At December 31, 2018, the reported amount of some assets and liabilities in the financial statements differed from their tax bases as indicated below:

	Carrying Amount	Tax Basis
Assets		
Current		
Net accounts receivable	$ 10 million	$ 12 million
Prepaid insurance	20 million	0
Prepaid advertising	6 million	0
Noncurrent		
Investments at fair value with changes in OCI*	4 million	0
Buildings and equipment (net)	360 million	280 million
Liabilities		
Current		
Liability—subscriptions received	14 million	0
Long-term		
Liability—postretirement benefits	594 million	0

*Gains and losses taxable when investments are sold.

The total deferred tax asset and deferred tax liability amounts at January 1, 2018, were $250 million and $40 million, respectively. The enacted tax rate is 40% each year.

Required:

1. Determine the total deferred tax asset and deferred tax liability amounts at December 31, 2018.

2. Determine the increase (decrease) in the deferred tax asset and deferred tax liability accounts at December 31, 2018.
3. Determine the income tax payable currently for the year ended December 31, 2018.
4. Prepare the journal entry to record income taxes for 2018.

P 16–10
Net operating loss carryback and carryforward; multiple differences
● LO16–2, LO16–4, LO16–7

Fores Construction Company reported a pretax operating loss of $135 million for financial reporting purposes in 2018. Contributing to the loss were (a) a penalty of $5 million assessed by the Environmental Protection Agency for violation of a federal law and paid in 2018 and (b) an estimated loss of $10 million from accruing a loss contingency. The loss will be tax deductible when paid in 2019.

The enacted tax rate is 40%. There were no temporary differences at the beginning of the year and none originating in 2018 other than those described above. Taxable income in Fores's two previous years of operation was as follows:

2016	$75 million
2017	30 million

Required:

1. Prepare the journal entry to recognize the income tax benefit of the net operating loss in 2018. Fores elects the carryback option.
2. Show the lower portion of the 2018 income statement that reports the income tax benefit of the net operating loss.
3. Prepare the journal entry to record income taxes in 2019 assuming pretax accounting income is $60 million. No additional temporary differences originate in 2019.

P 16–11
Valuation allowance; Delta Air Lines
● LO16–3
Real World Financials

Delta Air Lines revealed in its 10-K filing that its valuation allowance for deferred tax assets at the end of 2013 was $177 million, dramatically lower than the over $10 billion recorded at the end of 2012. Here is an excerpt from a press report from Bloomberg in January 2014, regarding this allowance:

> Delta Air Lines Inc. (DAL) led shares of U.S. carriers higher after posting fourth-quarter profit that topped analysts' estimates and forecasting an operating margin of as much as 8 percent in this year's initial three months. . . . Airlines are benefiting from lower fuel prices, constraints on capacity growth, controls on operating costs and demand that's keeping planes full, said Ray Neidl of Nexa Capital Partners LLC, a Washington-based aerospace and transportation consulting firm. . . . Net income was $8.48 billion, including an $8 billion non-cash gain from the reversal of a tax valuation allowance.[20]

The following is an excerpt from a disclosure note to Delta's 2013 financial statements:

NOTE 12. INCOME TAXES *(In part)*
Deferred Taxes
The components of deferred tax assets and liabilities at December 31 were as follows ($ in millions):

	December 31,	
	2013	**2012**
Deferred tax assets:		
Net operating loss carryforwards	$ 6,024	$ 6,414
Pension, postretirement and other benefits	4,982	6,415
AMT credit carryforward	378	402
Deferred revenue	1,965	2,133
Other	698	881
Valuation allowance	(177)	(10,963)
Total deferred tax assets	$13,870	$ 5,282
Deferred tax liabilities:		
Depreciation	$ 4,799	$ 4,851
Intangible assets	1,704	1,730
Other	639	285
Total deferred tax liabilities	$ 7,142	$ 6,866

[20] Mary Schlangenstein, "Delta Leads Airline Stock Gains as Profit Beats Estimates," *Bloomberg*, January 21, 2014.

Required:

1. What is a valuation allowance against deferred tax assets? When must such an allowance be recorded? Use Delta's situation to help illustrate your response.
2. Is an amount recorded in a valuation allowance for a deferred tax asset permanent? Explain why Delta is able to reclaim its valuation allowance.
3. Consider the excerpt from Bloomberg's press release. Recalculate the effect on Delta's 2013 net income of the change in Delta's valuation allowance for its deferred tax assets.

P 16–12
Integrating problem—bonds, leases, taxes
● LO16–1, LO16–5, LO16–8

The long-term liabilities section of CPS Transportation's December 31, 2017, balance sheet included the following:

a. A lease liability with 15 remaining lease payments of $10,000 each, due annually on January 1:

Lease liability	$76,061
Less: current portion	2,394
	$73,667

The incremental borrowing rate at the inception of the lease was 11% and the lessor's implicit rate, which was known by CPS Transportation, was 10%.

b. A deferred income tax liability due to a single temporary difference. The only difference between CPS Transportation's taxable income and pretax accounting income is depreciation on a machine acquired on January 1, 2017, for $500,000. The machine's estimated useful life is five years, with no salvage value. Depreciation is computed using the straight-line method for financial reporting purposes and the MACRS method for tax purposes. Depreciation expense for tax and financial reporting purposes for 2018 through 2021 is as follows:

Year	MACRS Depreciation	Straight-line Depreciation	Difference
2018	$160,000	$100,000	$60,000
2019	80,000	100,000	(20,000)
2020	70,000	100,000	(30,000)
2021	60,000	100,000	(40,000)

The enacted federal income tax rates are 35% for 2017 and 40% for 2018 through 2021. For the year ended December 31, 2018, CPS's income before income taxes was $900,000.

On July 1, 2018, CPS Transportation issued $800,000 of 9% bonds. The bonds mature in 20 years, and interest is payable each January 1 and July 1. The bonds were issued at a price to yield the investors 10%. CPS records interest at the effective interest rate.

Required:

1. Determine CPS Transportation's income tax expense and net income for the year ended December 31, 2018.
2. Determine CPS Transportation's interest expense for the year ended December 31, 2018.
3. Prepare the long-term liabilities section of CPS Transportation's December 31, 2018, balance sheet.

P 16–13
Multiple differences; uncertain tax position
● LO16–3, LO16–4, LO16–6, LO16–9

Tru Developers, Inc., sells plots of land for industrial development. Tru recognizes income for financial reporting purposes in the year it sells the plots. For some of the plots sold this year, Tru took the position that it could recognize the income for tax purposes when the installments are collected. Income that Tru recognized for financial reporting purposes in 2018 for plots in this category was $60 million. The company expected to collect 60% of each sale in 2019 and 40% in 2020. This amount over the next two years is as follows:

2019	$36 million
2020	24 million
	$60 million

Tru's pretax accounting income for 2018 was $90 million. In its income statement, Tru reported interest income of $15 million, unrelated to the land sales, for which the company's position is that the interest is not taxable. Accordingly, the interest was not reported on the tax return. There are no differences between accounting income and taxable income other than those described above. The enacted tax rate is 40 percent.

Management believes the tax position taken on the land sales has a greater than 50% chance of being upheld based on its technical merits, but the position taken on the interest has a less than 50% chance of being upheld. It is further believed that the following likelihood percentages apply to the tax treatment of the land sales ($ in millions):

Amount Qualifying for Installment Sales Treatment	Percentage Likelihood of Tax Treatment Being Sustained
$60	20%
50	20%
40	20%
30	20%
20	20%

Required:

1. What portion of the tax benefit of tax-free interest will Tru recognize on its 2018 tax return?
2. What portion of the tax benefit of tax-free interest will Tru recognize on its 2018 financial statements?
3. What portion of the tax on the $60 million income from the plots sold on an installment basis will Tru defer on its 2018 tax return? What portion of the tax on the $60 million income from the plots sold on an installment basis will Tru defer in its 2018 financial statements? How is the difference between these two amounts reported?
4. Prepare the journal entry to record income taxes in 2018, assuming full recognition of the tax benefits in the financial statements of both differences between pretax accounting income and taxable income.
5. Prepare the journal entry to record income taxes in 2018, assuming the recognition of the tax benefits in the financial statements you indicated in requirements 1–3.

Broaden Your Perspective

Apply your critical-thinking ability to the knowledge you've gained. These cases will provide you an opportunity to develop your research, analysis, judgment, and communication skills. You also will work with other students, integrate what you've learned, apply it in real-world situations, and consider its global and ethical ramifications. This practice will broaden your knowledge and further develop your decision-making abilities.

Analysis Case 16–1
Basic concepts
• LO16–1 through LO16–8

One of the longest debates in accounting history is the issue of deferred taxes. The controversy began in the 1940s and has continued, even after the FASB issued *Statement of Financial Accounting Standards No. 109* [FASB ASC 740: Income Taxes] in 1992. At issue is the appropriate treatment of tax consequences of economic events that occur in years other than that of the events themselves.

Required:

1. Distinguish between temporary differences and permanent differences. Provide an example of each.
2. Distinguish between *intraperiod* tax allocation and *interperiod* tax allocation (deferred tax accounting). Provide an example of each.
3. How are deferred tax assets and deferred tax liabilities classified and reported in the financial statements?

Integrating Case 16–2
Postretirement benefits
• LO16–2

FASB ASC 715–60: Compensation–Retirement Benefits–Defined Benefit Plans–Other Postretirement (previously *Statement of Financial Accounting Standards No. 106)* establishes accounting standards for postretirement benefits other than pensions, most notably postretirement health care benefits. Essentially, the standard requires companies to accrue compensation expense each year employees perform services, for the expected cost of providing future postretirement benefits that can be attributed to that service. Typically, companies do not prefund these costs for two reasons: (a) unlike pension liabilities, no federal law requires companies to fund nonpension postretirement benefits, and (b) funding contributions, again unlike for pension liabilities, are not tax deductible. (The costs aren't tax deductible until paid to, or on behalf of, employees.)

Required:

1. As a result of being required to record the periodic postretirement expense and related liability, most companies now report lower earnings and higher liabilities. How might many companies also report higher assets as a result of GAAP for postretirement plans?
2. One objection to current GAAP as cited in the chapter is the omission of requirements to discount deferred tax amounts to their present values. This objection is inappropriate in the context of deferred tax amounts necessitated by accounting for postretirement benefits. Why?

Integrating Case 16–3
Tax effects of accounting changes and error correction; six situations
• LO16–1, LO16–2, LO16–8

Williams-Santana Inc. is a manufacturer of high-tech industrial parts that was started in 2004 by two talented engineers with little business training. In 2018, the company was acquired by one of its major customers. As part of an internal audit, the following facts were discovered. The audit occurred during 2018 before any adjusting entries or closing entries were prepared. The income tax rate is 40% for all years.

a. A five-year casualty insurance policy was purchased at the beginning of 2016 for $35,000. The full amount was debited to insurance expense at the time.
b. On December 31, 2017, merchandise inventory was overstated by $25,000 due to a mistake in the physical inventory count using the periodic inventory system.
c. The company changed inventory cost methods to FIFO from LIFO at the end of 2018 for both financial statement and income tax purposes. The change will cause a $960,000 increase in the beginning inventory at January 1, 2017.
d. At the end of 2017, the company failed to accrue $15,500 of sales commissions earned by employees during 2017. The expense was recorded when the commissions were paid in early 2018.

e. At the beginning of 2016, the company purchased a machine at a cost of $720,000. Its useful life was estimated to be 10 years with no salvage value. The machine has been depreciated by the double declining-balance method. Its carrying amount on December 31, 2017, was $460,800. On January 1, 2018, the company changed to the straight-line method.

f. Additional industrial robots were acquired at the beginning of 2013 and added to the company's assembly process. The $1,000,000 cost of the equipment was inadvertently recorded as repair expense. Robots have 10-year useful lives and no material salvage value. This class of equipment is depreciated by the straight-line method for both financial reporting and income tax reporting.

Required:

For each situation:

1. Identify whether it represents an accounting change or an error. If an accounting change, identify the type of change.
2. Prepare any journal entry necessary as a direct result of the change or error correction, as well as any adjusting entry for 2018 related to the situation described. Any tax effects should be adjusted for through the deferred tax liability account.
3. Briefly describe any other steps that should be taken to appropriately report the situation.

Communication Case 16–4
Deferred taxes; changing rates; write a memo
● LO16–1, LO16–4, LO16–5

You are the new controller for Engineered Solutions. The company treasurer, Randy Patey, believes that as a result of pending legislation, the current 40% income tax rate will be decreased for 2019 to 35% and is uncertain which tax rate to apply in determining deferred taxes for 2018. Patey also is uncertain which differences should be included in that determination and has solicited your help. Your accounting group provided you the following information.

Two items are relevant to the decisions. One is the $50,000 insurance premium the company pays annually for the CEO's life insurance policy, for which the company is the beneficiary. The second is that Engineered Solutions purchased a building on January 1, 2017, for $6,000,000. The building's estimated useful life is 30 years from the date of purchase, with no salvage value. Depreciation is computed using the straight-line method for financial reporting purposes and the MACRS method for tax purposes. As a result, the building's tax basis is $5,200,000 at December 31, 2018.

Required:

Write a memo to Patey that:

a. Identifies the objectives of accounting for income taxes.
b. Differentiates temporary differences and permanent differences.
c. Explains which tax rate to use.
d. Calculates the deferred tax liability at December 31, 2018.

Real World Case 16–5
Disclosure issues; balance sheet classifications; Walmart
● LO16–1, LO16–2, LO16–8

Real World Financials

The income tax disclosure note accompanying the January 31, 2016, financial statements of Walmart is reproduced below:

Note 9. Taxes (in part)
Income from Continuing Operations

	Fiscal Year Ended January 31,		
($ in millions)	**2016**	**2015**	**2014**
Current:			
U.S. federal	$ 5,562	$ 6,165	$ 6,377
U.S. state and local	622	810	719
International	1,400	1,529	1,523
Total current tax provision	7,584	8,504	8,619
Deferred:			
U.S. federal	(704)	(387)	(72)
U.S. state and local	(106)	(55)	37
International	(216)	(77)	(479)
Total deferred tax expense (benefit)	(1,026)	(519)	(514)
Total provision for income taxes	$ 6,558	$ 7,985	$ 8,105

(continued)

(concluded)

Deferred Taxes

The significant components of the Company's deferred tax account balances are as follows:

	January 31,	
($ in millions)	**2016**	**2015**
Deferred tax assets:		
Loss and tax credit carryforwards	$ 3,313	$ 3,255
Accrued liabilities	3,763	3,395
Share-based compensation	192	184
Other	1,390	1,119
Total deferred tax assets	8,658	7,953
Valuation allowances	(1,456)	(1,504)
Deferred tax assets, net of valuation allowance	$ 7,202	$ 6,449
Deferred tax liabilities:		
Property and equipment	$ 5,813	$ 5,972
Inventories	1,790	1,825
Other	1,452	1,618
Total deferred tax liabilities	9,055	9,415
Net deferred tax liabilities	$ 1,853	$ 2,966

Required:

1. Focusing on only the first part of Note 9, relating current, deferred, and total provision for income taxes, prepare a summary journal entry that records Walmart's 2016 tax expense associated with income from continuing operations.
2. Compare the change in deferred taxes you recorded in your summary journal entry to the actual change in Walmart's net deferred tax liability for fiscal 2016. Do they reconcile? What besides continuing operations might affect deferred taxes?

Research Case 16–6
Researching the way tax deductions are reported on a corporation tax return; retrieving a tax form from the Internet
● LO16–1, LO16–2, LO16–3, LO16–8

The U.S. Treasury maintains an information site on the Internet. As part of this site, the Internal Revenue Service provides tax information and services. Among those services is a server for publications and forms which allows a visitor to download a variety of IRS forms and publications.

Required:

1. Access the Treasury site on the Internet. The web address is www.ustreas.gov. After exploring the information available there, navigate to the IRS server for forms and publications via the IRS home page.
2. Download the corporation tax return, Form 1120.
3. Note the specific deductions listed that are deductible from total income to arrive at taxable income. Are any deductions listed that might not also be included among expenses in the income statement?
4. One of the deductions indicated is "net operating loss deduction." Under what circumstances might a company report an amount for this item?
5. Based on how taxable income is determined, how might temporary differences be created between taxable income and pretax income in the income statement?

Analysis Case 16–7
Reporting deferred taxes; Ford Motor Company
● LO16–1, LO16–2, LO16–3, LO16–7
Real World Financials

Access the 2015 financial statements and related disclosure notes of Ford Motor Company from its website at corporate.ford.com.

Required:

1. In Note 21, find Ford's net deferred tax asset or liability. What is that number?
2. Does Ford show a valuation allowance against deferred tax assets? If so, what is the number, and what is Ford's explanation for it?
3. Does Ford have any NOL carryforwards? What is the amount of any carryforward, what deferred tax asset or liability is associated with it, and what effective tax rate does that imply was used to calculate its deferred tax effect?

Analysis Case 16–8
Reporting deferred taxes; Kroger Co.
● LO16–1, LO16–2, LO16–3, LO16–7, LO16–8
Real World Financials

Kroger Co. is one of the largest retail food companies in the United States as measured by total annual sales. The Kroger Co. operates supermarkets, convenience stores, and manufactures and processes food that its supermarkets sell.

Using EDGAR (www.sec.gov) or the company's website, check the company's annual report for the year ended January 30, 2016.

Required:

1. From the income statement, determine the income tax expense for the most recent year. Tie that number to the first table in disclosure Note 5: "Taxes Based on Income," and prepare a summary journal entry that records Kroger's tax expense from continuing operations in the most recent year.

2. In 2015 companies were required to classify their deferred tax assets and liabilities as current or noncurrent. From Kroger's Note 5, calculate the total (current + noncurrent) net deferred tax asset or liability as of January 30, 2016, and January 31, 2015. By how much did that amount change? To what extent did you account for that change in the journal entry you wrote for the first requirement of this case? Speculate as to the explanation of any difference.

Judgment Case 16–9
Analyzing the effect of deferred tax liabilities on firm risk; Macy's, Inc.
● LO16–8
Real World Financials

The following is a portion of the balance sheets of Macy's, Inc. for the years ended January 30, 2016 and January 31, 2015:

	January 30, 2016	January 31, 2015
LIABILITIES AND SHAREHOLDERS' EQUITY		
Current Liabilities:		
Short-term debt	$ 642	$ 76
Merchandise accounts payable	1,526	1,594
Accounts payable and accrued liabilities	3,333	3,109
Income taxes	227	296
Total Current Liabilities	5,728	5,075
Long-Term debt	6,995	7,233
Deferred Income Taxes	1,477	1,443
Other Liabilities	2,123	2,201
Shareholders' Equity		
Common stock (310.3 and 340.6 shares outstanding)	3	4
Additional paid-in capital	621	1,048
Accumulated equity	6,334	7,340
Treasury stock	(1,665)	(1,942)
Accumulated other comprehensive loss	(1,043)	(1,072)
Total Macy's, Inc. Shareholders' Equity	4,250	5,378
Noncontrolling interest	3	—
Total Shareholders' Equity	4,253	5,378
Total Liabilities and Shareholders' Equity	$20,576	$21,330

Macy's debt to equity ratio for the year ended January 30, 2016, was 3.84, calculated as ($20,576 – 4,253) ÷ 4,253. Some analysts argue that long-term deferred tax liabilities should be excluded from liabilities when computing the debt to equity ratio.

Required:

1. What is the rationale for the argument that long-term deferred tax liabilities should be excluded from liabilities when computing the debt to equity ratio?
2. What would be the effect on Macy's debt to equity ratio of excluding deferred tax liabilities from its calculation? What would be the percentage change?
3. What might be the rationale for not excluding long-term deferred tax liabilities from liabilities when computing the debt to equity ratio?

Trueblood Accounting Case 16–10
Valuation allowances against deferred tax assets
● LO16–3

The following Trueblood case is recommended for use with this chapter. The case provides an excellent opportunity for class discussion, group projects, and writing assignments. The case, along with Professor's Discussion material, can be obtained from the Deloitte foundation at its website: www.deloitte.com/us/truebloodcases.

Case 13-10: LOL – Income Taxes

This case gives students an opportunity to better understand how valuation allowances against deferred tax assets are estimated and calculated. Students consider the sources of taxable income that can be used to determine whether a deferred tax asset is more likely than not to be realized in the future.

Trueblood Accounting Case 16–11
Uncertain tax positions
● LO16–9

The following Trueblood case is recommended for use with this chapter. The case provides an excellent opportunity for class discussion, group projects, and writing assignments. The case, along with Professor's Discussion Material, can be obtained from the Deloitte Foundation at its website: www.deloitte.com/us/truebloodcases.

Case 15-9: Settled or Not Settled

This case gives the students an opportunity to better understand accounting for uncertain tax positions. The case illustrates the judgments involved in applying FASB ASC 740 (formerly FIN 48).

Judgment Case 16–12
Intraperiod tax allocation
● LO16–10

Russell-James Corporation is a diversified consumer products company. During 2018, Russell-James discontinued its line of cosmetics, which constituted discontinued operations for financial reporting purposes. As vice president of the food products division, you are interested in the effect of the discontinuance on the company's profitability. One item of information you requested was an income statement. The income statement you received was labeled *preliminary* and *unaudited:*

RUSSELL-JAMES CORPORATION
Income Statement
For the Year Ended December 31, 2018
($ in millions, except per share amounts)

Revenues		$ 300
Cost of goods sold		90
Gross profit		210
Selling and administrative expenses		(60)
Income from continuing operations before income taxes		150
Income taxes		(26)
Income from continuing operations		124
Discontinued operations:		
Loss from operations of cosmetics division	$(100)	
Gain from disposal of cosmetics division	15	(85)
Net income		$ 39
Per Share of Common Stock (100 million shares):		
Income from continuing operations		$1.24
Loss from operations of cosmetics division		(1.00)
Gain from disposal of cosmetics division		0.15
Net income		$0.39

You are somewhat surprised at the magnitude of the loss incurred by the cosmetics division prior to its disposal. Another item that draws your attention is the apparently low tax rate indicated by the statement ($26 ÷ 150 = 17.3%). Upon further investigation, you are told the company's tax rate is 40%.

Required:

1. Recast the income statement to reflect intraperiod tax allocation.
2. How would you reconcile the income tax expense shown on the statement above with the amount your recast statement reports?

Continuing Cases

Target Case
● LO16-1, LO16-2, LO16-4, LO16-8, LO16-9

Real World Financials

Target Corporation prepares its financial statements according to U.S. GAAP. Target's financial statements and disclosure notes for the year ended January 30, 2016, are available in Connect. This material also is available under the Investor Relations link at the company's website (www.target.com).

Required:

1. From the income statement, determine the income tax expense for the most recent year. Tie that number to the second table in disclosure Note 23, "Provision for Income Taxes," and prepare a summary journal entry that records Target's tax expense from continuing operations for the year ended January 30, 2016.
2. Focusing on the third table in disclosure Note 23, "Net Deferred Tax Asset/(Liability)," calculate the change in net deferred tax assets or liability. By how much did that amount change? To what extent did you account for that change in the journal entry you wrote for the first requirement of this case? List possible causes of any difference.
3. Target's Note 23 indicates that "We have not recorded deferred taxes when earnings from foreign operations are considered to be indefinitely invested outside the U.S. These accumulated net earnings relate to certain ongoing operations and were $685 million at January 30, 2016, and $328 million at January 31, 2015." Are these amounts treated as temporary or permanent differences by Target? If Target decides to repatriate earnings in the future, what will be the effect on net income in the year of the repatriation?
4. What is Target's liability for unrecognized tax benefits as of January 30, 2016? If Target were to prevail in court and realize $50 million more in tax savings than it thought more likely than not to occur, what would be the effect on the liability for unrecognized tax benefits and on net income?

Air France–KLM Case

IFRS

● LO16–11

Real World Financials

Air France–KLM (AF), a Franco-Dutch company, prepares its financial statements according to International Financial Reporting Standards. AF's financial statements and disclosure notes for the year ended December 31, 2015, are available in Connect. This material is also available under the Finance link at the company's website (www.airfranceklm.com).

Required:

1. Where in its December 31, 2015, balance sheet does AF report deferred taxes? How does this approach differ from the way deferred taxes are reported using U.S. GAAP? Using the Internet, determine how deferred taxes would be reported using IFRS at the time of your research. Explain why that approach might differ from the way AF reported deferred taxes at December 31, 2015.
2. Here's an excerpt from AF's notes to its financial statements:

   Deferred taxes (in part)
   The Group records deferred taxes using the balance sheet liability method, providing for any temporary differences between the carrying amounts of assets and liabilities for financial reporting purposes and the amounts used for taxation purposes, except for exceptions described in IAS 12 "Income taxes." The tax rates used are those enacted or substantively enacted at the balance sheet date.

   Is this policy consistent with U.S. GAAP? Explain.
3. Here's an excerpt from one of AF's notes to its financial statements:

   Deferred taxes (in part)
   Deferred tax assets related to temporary differences and tax losses carried forward are recognized only to the extent it is probable that a future taxable profit will be available against which the asset can be utilized at the tax entity level.

   Is this policy consistent with U.S. GAAP? Explain.

CPA Exam Questions and Simulations

ROGER CPA Review

Sample CPA Exam questions from Roger CPA Review are available in Connect as support for the topics in this chapter. These Multiple Choice Questions and Task-Based Simulations include expert-written explanations and solutions, and provide a starting point for students to become familiar with the content and functionality of the actual CPA Exam.

CHAPTER

17 Pensions and Other Postretirement Benefits

OVERVIEW

Employee compensation comes in many forms. Salaries and wages, of course, provide direct and current payment for services provided. However, it's commonplace for compensation also to include benefits payable after retirement. We discuss pension benefits and other postretirement benefits in this chapter. Accounting for pension benefits recognizes that they represent deferred compensation for current service. Accordingly, the cost of these benefits is recognized on an accrual basis during the years that employees earn the benefits.

LEARNING OBJECTIVES

After studying this chapter, you should be able to:

- **LO17–1** Explain the fundamental differences between a defined contribution pension plan and a defined benefit pension plan. *(p. 968)*
- **LO17–2** Distinguish among the vested benefit obligation, the accumulated benefit obligation, and the projected benefit obligation (PBO). *(p. 973)*
- **LO17–3** Describe the five events that might change the balance of the PBO. *(p. 974)*
- **LO17–4** Explain how plan assets accumulate to provide retiree benefits and understand the role of the trustee in administering the fund. *(p. 979)*
- **LO17–5** Describe the funded status of pension plans and how that amount is reported. *(p. 981)*
- **LO17–6** Describe how pension expense is a composite of periodic changes that occur in both the pension obligation and the plan assets. *(p. 981)*
- **LO17–7** Record for pension plans the periodic expense and funding as well as new gains and losses and new prior service cost as they occur. *(p. 986)*
- **LO17–8** Understand the interrelationships among the elements that constitute a defined benefit pension plan. *(p. 992)*
- **LO17–9** Describe the nature of postretirement benefit plans other than pensions and identify the similarities and differences in accounting for those plans and pensions. *(p. 997)*
- **LO17–10** Explain how the obligation for postretirement benefits is measured and how the obligation changes. *(p. 999)*
- **LO17–11** Determine the components of postretirement benefit expense. *(p. 1000)*
- **LO17–12** Discuss the primary differences between U.S. GAAP and IFRS with respect to accounting for postretirement benefit plans. *(pp. 987, 989, 993, and 995)*

© Stockbyte/PunchStock

FINANCIAL REPORTING CASE

United Dynamics

You read yesterday that many companies in the United States have pension plans that are severely underfunded in the wake of the recent economic crisis. This caught your attention in part because you have your office interview tomorrow with United Dynamics. You hadn't really thought that much about the pension plan of your potential future employer, in part because your current employer has a defined contribution 401(k) plan, for which funding is not a concern. However, United Dynamics is an older firm with a defined benefit plan, for which funding is the employer's responsibility.

To prepare for your interview, you obtained a copy of United Dynamics' financial statements. Unfortunately, the financial statements themselves are of little help. You are unable to find any pension liability in the balance sheet, but the statement does report a relatively small "pension asset." The income statement reports pension expense for each of the years reported. For help, you search the disclosure notes. In part, the pension disclosure note reads as follows:

Note 7: Pension Plan

United Dynamics has a defined benefit pension plan covering substantially all of its employees. Plan benefits are based on years of service and the employee's compensation during the last three years of employment. The company's funding policy is consistent with the funding requirements of federal law and regulations. The net periodic pension expense for the company included the following components. The company's pension expense was as follows ($ in millions):

	2018	2017	2016
Current service costs	$ 43	$ 47	$ 42
Interest cost on projected benefit obligation	178	164	152
Return on assets	(213)	(194)	(187)
Amortization of prior service cost	43	43	43
Amortization of net gain	(2)	(1)	—
Net pension costs	$ 49	$ 59	$ 50

The following table describes the change in projected benefit obligation for the plan years ended December 31, 2018, and December 31, 2017 ($ in millions):

	2018	2017
Projected benefit obligation at beginning of year	$2,194	$2,121
Service cost	43	47
Interest cost	178	164
Actuarial (gain) loss	319	(40)
Benefits paid	(106)	(98)
Projected benefit obligation at end of year	$2,628	$2,194

The weighted-average discount rate and rate of increase in future compensation levels used in determining the actuarial present value of the projected benefit obligations in the above table were 8.1% and 4.3%, respectively, at December 31, 2018, and 7.73% and 4.7%, respectively, at December 31, 2017. The expected long-term rate of return on assets was 9.1% at December 31, 2018 and 2017.

(continued)

(concluded)

The following table describes the change in the fair value of plan assets for the plan years ended December 31, 2018 and 2017 ($ in millions):

	2018	2017
Fair value of plan assets at beginning of year	$2,340	$ 2,133
Actual return on plan assets	215	178
Employer contributions	358	127
Benefits paid	(106)	(98)
Fair value of plan assets at end of year	$2,807	$2,340

"Ouch! I can't believe how much of my accounting I forgot," you complain to yourself. "I'd better get out my old intermediate accounting book."

QUESTIONS

By the time you finish this chapter, you should be able to respond appropriately to the questions posed in this case. Compare your response to the solution provided at the end of the chapter.

1. Why is pension plan underfunding not a concern in your present employment? *(p. 971)*
2. Were you correct that the pension liability is not reported in the balance sheet? What is the liability? *(p. 973)*
3. What is the amount of the plan assets available to pay benefits? What are the factors that can cause that amount to change? *(p. 979)*
4. What does the "pension asset" represent? Are you interviewing with a company whose pension plan is severely underfunded? *(p. 981)*
5. How is the pension expense influenced by changes in the pension liability and plan assets? *(p. 982)*

PART A

The Nature of Pension Plans

LO17–1

United States pension funds total more than $15 trillion, over three times the size of Japan's gross national product. This powerful investment base now controls a sizable portion of the stock market. At the company level, the enormous size of pension funds is reflected in a periodic pension cost that constitutes one of the largest expenses many companies report. The corporate liability for providing pension benefits is huge. Obviously, then, the financial reporting responsibility for pensions has important social and economic implications.

Pension plans are designed to provide income to individuals during their retirement years. This is accomplished by setting aside funds during an employee's working years so that at retirement the accumulated funds plus earnings from investing those funds are available to replace wages. Actually, an individual who periodically invests in stocks, bonds, certificates of deposit (CDs), or other investments for the purpose of saving for retirement is establishing a personal pension fund. Often, such individual plans take the form of individual retirement accounts (IRAs) to take advantage of tax breaks offered by that arrangement. In employer plans, some or all of the periodic contributions to the retirement fund often are provided by the employer.

Pension plans often enhance productivity, reduce turnover, satisfy union demands, and allow employers to compete in the labor market.

Corporations establish pension plans for a variety of reasons. Sponsorship of pension plans provides employees with a degree of retirement security and fulfills a moral obligation felt by many employers. This security also can induce a degree of job satisfaction and perhaps loyalty that might enhance productivity and reduce turnover. Motivation to sponsor a plan sometimes comes from union demands and often relates to being competitive in the labor market.

Additional Consideration

When established according to tight guidelines, a pension plan gains important tax advantages. Such arrangements are called *qualified plans* because they qualify for favorable tax treatment. In a qualified plan, the employer is permitted an immediate tax deduction for amounts paid into the pension fund (within specified limits). The employees, on the other hand, are not taxed at the time employer contributions are made—only when retirement benefits are received. Moreover, earnings on the funds set aside by the employer are not taxed while in the pension fund, so the earnings accumulate tax free. If you are familiar with the tax advantages of IRAs, you probably recognize the similarity between those individual plans and corporate pension arrangements.

For a pension plan to be qualified for special tax treatment it must meet these general requirements.

1. It must cover at least 70% of employees.
2. It cannot discriminate in favor of highly compensated employees.
3. It must be funded in advance of retirement through contributions to an irrevocable trust fund.
4. Benefits must vest after a specified period of service, commonly five years. (We discuss this in more detail later.)
5. It complies with specific restrictions on the timing and amount of contributions and benefits.

Qualified pension plans offer important tax benefits.

Sometimes, employers agree to annually contribute a specific (defined) amount to a pension fund on behalf of employees but make no commitment regarding benefit amounts at retirement. In other arrangements, employers don't specify the amount of annual contributions but promise to provide determinable (defined) amounts at retirement. These two arrangements describe defined contribution pension plans and defined benefit pension plans, respectively:

- **Defined contribution pension plans** promise fixed annual contributions to a pension fund (say, 5% of the employees' pay or, more often, to match contributions by workers). Employees choose (from designated options) where funds are invested—usually stocks or fixed-income securities. Retirement pay depends on the size of the fund at retirement.
- **Defined benefit pension plans** promise fixed retirement benefits defined by a designated formula. Typically, the pension formula bases retirement pay on the employees' (a) years of service, (b) annual compensation (often final pay or an average for the last few years), and sometimes (c) age. Employers are responsible for ensuring that sufficient funds are available to provide promised benefits.

Today, approximately three-fourths of workers covered by pension plans are covered by defined contribution plans, roughly one-fourth by defined benefit plans. This represents a radical shift from previous years when the traditional defined benefit plan was far more common. However, very few *new* pension plans are of the defined benefit variety. In fact, many companies are terminating long-standing defined benefit plans and substituting defined contribution plans. Why the shift? There are three main reasons:

Virtually all *new* pension plans are defined contribution plans.

1. Government regulations make defined benefit plans cumbersome and costly to administer.
2. Employers are increasingly unwilling to bear the risk of defined benefit plans; with defined contribution plans, the company's obligation ends when contributions are made.
3. There has been a shift among many employers from trying to "buy long-term loyalty" (with defined benefit plans) to trying to attract new talent (with more mobile defined contribution plans).

The two categories of pension plans are depicted in Illustration 17–1.

Illustration 17–1

Defined Contribution and Defined Benefit Pension Plans

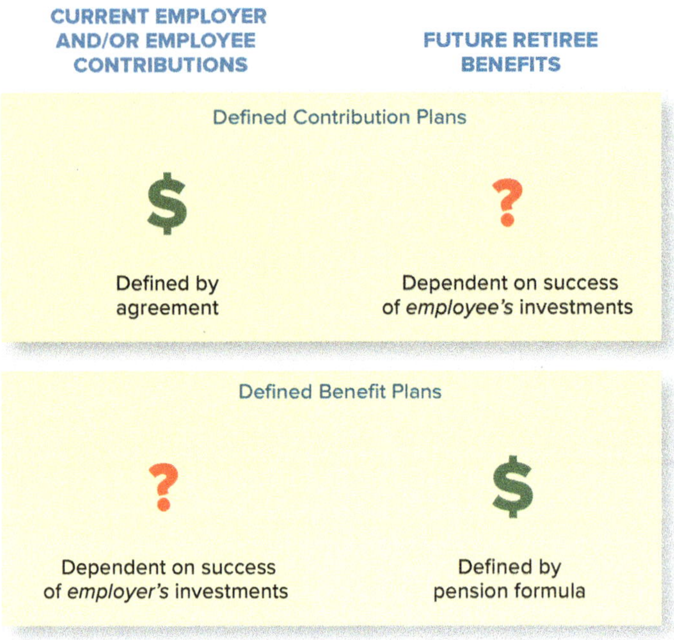

Both types of plans have a common goal: to provide income to employees during their retirement years. Still, the two types of plans differ regarding who bears the risk—the employer or the employees—for whether the retirement objectives are achieved. The two types of plans also have entirely different implications for accounting and financial reporting. Our discussion of defined contribution plans will be brief. Although these are now the most popular type of corporate pension plan, their relative simplicity permits a rather straightforward accounting treatment that requires little explanation. On the other hand, defined benefit plans require considerably more complex accounting treatment and constitute the primary focus of this chapter.

Defined Contribution Pension Plans

***Defined contribution plans* promise defined periodic contributions to a pension fund, without further commitment regarding benefit amounts at retirement.**

Defined contribution pension plans are becoming increasingly popular vehicles for employers to provide retirement income without the paperwork, cost, and risk generated by the more traditional defined benefit plans. Defined contribution plans promise fixed periodic contributions to a pension fund. Retirement income depends on the size of the fund at retirement. No further commitment is made by the employer regarding benefit amounts at retirement.

These plans have several variations. In money purchase plans, employers contribute a fixed percentage of employees' salaries. Thrift plans, savings plans, and 401(k) plans (named after the Tax Code section that specifies the conditions for the favorable tax treatment of these plans) permit voluntary contributions by employees. These contributions typically are matched to a specified extent by employers. Many employers match up to 50% of employee contributions up to the first 5% or 6% of salary.

Approximately two-thirds of American workers participate in 401(k) plans. More than six trillion dollars are invested in these plans.

When plans link the amount of contributions to company performance, labels include profit sharing plans, incentive savings plans, 401(k) profit sharing plans, and similar titles. When employees make contributions to the plan in addition to employer contributions, it's called a *contributory* plan. Sometimes the amount the employer contributes is tied to the amount of the employee contribution.[1] Variations are seemingly endless. An example from a recent annual report of **Microsoft Corporation** is shown in Illustration 17–2.

[1]One popular way for employer companies to provide contributions is with shares of its own common stock. If so, the arrangements usually are designed to comply with government requirements to be designated an employee stock ownership plan (ESOP).

Note 20 (in part)
Savings plan

We have a savings plan in the U.S. that qualifies under Section 401(k) of the Internal Revenue Code, and a number of savings plans in international locations. Participating U.S. employees may contribute up to 75% of their salary, but not more than statutory limits. We contribute fifty cents for each dollar of the first 6% a participant contributes in this plan, with a maximum contribution of the lesser of 3% of a participant's earnings or 3% of the IRS compensation limit for the given year. Matching contributions for all plans were $454 million, $420 million, and $393 million in fiscal years 2015, 2014, and 2013, respectively, and were expensed as contributed.

Illustration 17–2

Defined Contribution Plan—Microsoft Corporation

Real World Financials

Accounting for these plans is quite easy. Each year, the employer simply records pension expense equal to the amount of the annual contribution. Suppose a plan promises an annual contribution equal to 3% of an employee's salary. If an employee's salary is $110,000 in a particular year, the employer would simply recognize pension expense in the amount of the contribution:

FINANCIAL Reporting Case

Q1, p. 968

Pension expense	3,300	
Cash ($110,000 × 3%)		3,300

The employee's retirement benefits are totally dependent upon how well investments perform. Who bears the risk (or reward) of that uncertainty? The employee would bear the risk of uncertain investment returns and, potentially, settle for far less at retirement than at first expected.[2] On the other hand, the employer would be free of any further obligation. Because the actual investments are held by an independent investment firm, the employer is free of that record-keeping responsibility as well.

For defined contribution plans, the employer simply records pension expense equal to the cash contribution.

Risk is reversed in a defined benefit plan. Because specific benefits are promised at retirement, the employer would be responsible for making up the difference when investment performance is less than expected. We look at defined benefit plans next.

Defined Benefit Pension Plans

When setting aside cash to fund a pension plan, the uncertainty surrounding the rate of return on plan assets is but one of several uncertainties inherent in a defined benefit plan. Employee turnover affects the number of employees who ultimately will become eligible for retirement benefits. The age at which employees will choose to retire as well as life expectancies will impact both the length of the retirement period and the amount of the benefits. Inflation, future compensation levels, and interest rates also have obvious influence on eventual benefits.

Defined benefit plans promise fixed retirement benefits defined by a designated formula.

This is particularly true when pension benefits are defined by a pension formula, as usually is the case. A typical formula might specify that a retiree will receive annual retirement benefits based on the employee's years of service and annual pay at retirement (say, pay level in the final year, highest pay achieved, or average pay in the last two or more years). For example, a pension formula might define annual retirement benefits as:

Uncertainties complicate determining how much to set aside each year to ensure that sufficient funds are available to provide promised benefits.

$$1\tfrac{1}{2}\% \times \text{Years of service} \times \text{Final year's salary}$$

By this formula, the annual benefits to an employee who retires after 30 years of service, with a final salary of $100,000, would be:

$$1\tfrac{1}{2}\% \times 30 \text{ years} \times \$100{,}000 = \$45{,}000$$

A pension formula typically defines retirement pay based on the employees' (a) years of service, (b) annual compensation, and sometimes (c) age.

Typically, a firm will hire an **actuary**, a professional trained in a particular branch of statistics and mathematics, to assess the various uncertainties (employee turnover, salary levels, mortality, etc.) and to estimate the company's obligation to employees in connection

Pension gains and losses occur when the *pension obligation* is lower or higher than expected.

[2]Of course, this is not entirely unappealing to the employee. Defined contribution plans allow an employee to select investments in line with his or her own risk preferences and often provide greater retirement benefits and flexibility than defined benefit plans.

with its pension plan. Such estimates are inherently subjective, so regardless of the skill of the actuary, estimates invariably deviate from the actual outcome to one degree or another.[3] For instance, the return on assets can turn out to be more or less than expected. These deviations are referred to as *gains* and *losses* on pension assets. When it's necessary to revise estimates related to the pension obligation because it's determined to be more or less than previously thought, these revisions are referred to as *losses* and *gains,* respectively, on the pension liability. Later, we will discuss the accounting treatment of gains and losses from either source. The point here is that the risk of the pension obligation changing unexpectedly or the pension funds being inadequate to meet the obligation is borne by the employer with a defined benefit pension plan.

The key elements of a defined benefit pension plan are listed below:

Pension gains and losses occur when the return on plan assets is higher or lower than expected.

1. The *employer's obligation* to pay retirement benefits in the future.
2. The *plan assets* set aside by the employer from which to pay the retirement benefits in the future.
3. The *periodic expense* of having a pension plan.

Neither the pension obligation nor the plan assets are reported individually in the balance sheet.

As you will learn in this chapter, the first two of these elements are not reported individually in the employer's financial statements. This may seem confusing at first because it is inconsistent with the way you're accustomed to treating assets and liabilities. Even though they are not separately reported, it's critical that you understand the composition of both the pension obligation and the plan assets because (a) they are reported as a net amount in the balance sheet, and (b) their balances are reported in disclosure notes. And, importantly, the pension expense reported in the income statement is a direct composite of periodic changes that occur in both the pension obligation and the plan assets.

The pension expense is a direct composite of periodic changes that occur in both the pension obligation and the plan assets.

For this reason, we will devote a considerable portion of our early discussion to understanding the composition of the pension obligation and the plan assets before focusing on the derivation of pension expense and required financial statement disclosures. We will begin with a quick overview of how periodic changes that occur in both the pension obligation and the plan assets affect pension expense. Next, we will explore how those changes occur, beginning with changes in the pension obligation followed by changes in plan assets. We'll then return to pension expense for a closer look at how those changes influence its calculation. After that, we will bring together the separate but related parts by using a simple spreadsheet to demonstrate how each element of the pension plan articulates with the other elements.

Pension Expense—An Overview

The annual pension expense reflects changes in both the pension obligation and the plan assets. Illustration 17–3 provides a brief overview of how these changes are included in pension expense. After the overview, we'll look closer at each of the components.

Illustration 17–3

Components of Pension Expense—Overview (More Later)

Components of Pension Expense

+	**Service cost** ascribed to employee service during the period
+	**Interest** accrued on the pension liability
−	**Return** on the plan assets*
	Amortized portion of:
+	**Prior service cost** attributed to employee service before an amendment to the pension plan
+ or (−)	**Losses or (gains)** from revisions in the pension liability or from investing plan assets
=	**Pension expense**

*The actual return is adjusted for any difference between actual and expected return, resulting in the expected return being reflected in pension expense. This loss or gain from investing plan assets is combined with losses and gains from revisions in the pension liability for deferred inclusion in pension expense. (See the last component of pension expense.)

Interest and investment return are financing aspects of the pension cost.

The recognition of some elements of the pension expense is delayed.

[3] We discuss changes in more detail in Chapter 20.

Next we explore each of these pension expense components in the context of its being a part of either (a) the pension obligation or (b) the plan assets. After you learn how the expense components relate to these elements of the pension plan, we'll return to explore further how they are included in the pension expense.

PART B

The Pension Obligation and Plan Assets

The Pension Obligation

FINANCIAL Reporting Case

Q2, p. 968

LO17–2

Now we consider more precisely what is meant by the pension obligation. Unfortunately, there's not just one definition, nor is there uniformity concerning which definition is most appropriate for pension accounting. Actually, three different ways to measure the pension obligation have meaning in pension accounting, as shown in Illustration 17–4.

Illustration 17–4

Ways to Measure the Pension Obligation

1. **Accumulated benefit obligation (ABO)** The actuary's estimate of the total retirement benefits (at their discounted present value) earned so far by employees, applying the pension formula using existing compensation levels.
2. **Vested benefit obligation (VBO)** The portion of the accumulated benefit obligation that plan participants are entitled to receive regardless of their continued employment.
3. **Projected benefit obligation (PBO)** The actuary's estimate of the total retirement benefits (at their discounted present value) earned so far by employees, applying the pension formula using estimated future compensation levels. (If the pension formula does not include future compensation levels, the PBO and the ABO are the same.)

Later you will learn that the projected benefit obligation is the basis for some elements of the periodic pension expense. Remember, there is but one obligation; these are three ways to measure it. The relationship among the three is depicted in Illustration 17–5.

Illustration 17–5

Alternative Measures of the Pension Obligation

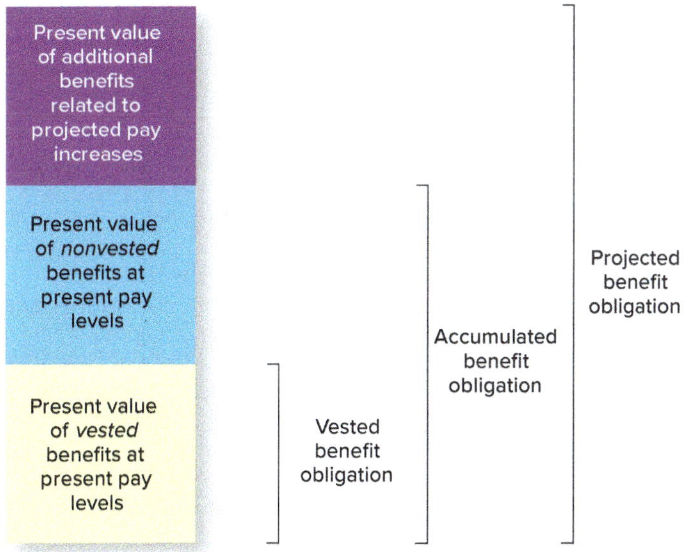

Now let's look closer at how the obligation is measured in each of these three ways. Keep in mind, though, that it's not the accountant's responsibility to actually derive the measurement; a professional actuary provides these numbers. However, for the accountant to effectively use the numbers provided, she or he must understand their derivation.

Accumulated Benefit Obligation

The *accumulated benefit obligation* ignores possible pay increases in the future.

The **accumulated benefit obligation (ABO)** is an estimate of the discounted present value of the retirement benefits earned so far by employees, applying the plan's pension formula using existing compensation levels. When we look at a detailed calculation of the projected benefit obligation later, keep in mind that simply substituting the employee's existing compensation in the pension formula for her projected salary at retirement would give us the accumulated benefit obligation.

Vested Benefit Obligation

Suppose an employee leaves the company to take another job. Will she still get earned benefits at retirement? The answer depends on whether the benefits are vested under the terms of this particular pension plan. If benefits are fully vested—yes. **Vested benefits** are those that employees have the right to receive even if their employment were to cease today.

The benefits of most pension plans vest after five years.

Pension plans typically require some minimum period of employment before benefits vest. Before the Employee Retirement Income Security Act (ERISA) was passed in 1974, horror stories relating to lost benefits were commonplace. It was possible, for example, for an employee to be dismissed a week before retirement and be left with no pension benefits. Vesting requirements were tightened drastically to protect employees. These requirements have been changed periodically since then. Today, benefits must vest (a) fully within five years or (b) 20% within three years with another 20% vesting each subsequent year until fully vested after seven years. Five-year vesting is most common. ERISA also established the Pension Benefit Guaranty Corporation (PBGC) to impose liens on corporate assets for unfunded pension liabilities in certain instances and to administer terminated pension plans. The PBGC provides a form of insurance for employees similar to the role of the FDIC for bank accounts and is financed by premiums from employers equal to specified amounts for each covered employee. It makes retirement payments for terminated plans and guarantees basic vested benefits when pension liabilities exceed assets. The vested benefit obligation is actually a subset of the ABO, the portion attributable to benefits that have vested.

Projected Benefit Obligation

● LO17–3

The *PBO* estimates retirement benefits by applying the pension formula using projected future compensation levels.

As described earlier, when the ABO is estimated, the most recent salary is included in the pension formula to estimate future benefits, even if the pension formula specifies the final year's salary. No attempt is made to forecast what that salary would be the year before retirement. Of course, the most recent salary certainly offers an objective number to measure the obligation, but is it realistic? Since it's unlikely that there will be no salary increases between now and retirement, a more meaningful measurement should include a projection of what the salary might be at retirement.[4] Measured this way, the liability is referred to as the **projected benefit obligation (PBO)**. Hereafter in the chapter, when we mention the "pension obligation," we are referring to the PBO. The PBO measurement may be less reliable than the ABO but is more relevant and representationally faithful.

To understand the concepts involved, it's helpful to look at a numerical example. We'll simplify the example (Illustration 17–6) by looking at how pension amounts would be determined for a single employee. Keep in mind though, that in actuality, calculations would be made (by the actuary) for the entire employee pool rather than on an individual-by-individual basis.

If the actuary's estimate of the final salary hasn't changed, the PBO a year later at the end of 2017 would be $139,715 as demonstrated in Illustration 17–6A.

CHANGES IN THE PBO. Notice that the PBO increased during 2017 (Illustration 17–6A) from $119,822 to $139,715 for two reasons:

1. One more service year is included in the pension formula calculation (service cost).
2. The employee is one year closer to retirement, causing the present value of benefits to increase due to the time value of future benefits (interest cost).

[4]To project future salaries for a group of employees, actuaries usually assume some percentage rate of increase in compensation levels in upcoming years. Recent estimates of the rate of compensation increase have ranged from 0.8% to 5.99% with 4% being the most commonly reported expectation (Pension/OPEB 2015 Assumption and Disclosure Survey, PWC, 2015).

Illustration 17–6

Projected Benefit Obligation

Jessica Farrow was hired by Global Communications at the beginning of 2007. The company has a defined benefit pension plan that specifies annual retirement benefits equal to:

1.5% × Service years × Final year's salary

Farrow is expected to retire at the end of 2046 after 40 years service. Her retirement period is expected to be 20 years. At the end of 2016, 10 years after being hired, her salary is $100,000. The interest rate is 6%. The company's actuary projects Farrow's salary to be $400,000 at retirement.*

What is the company's projected benefit obligation with respect to Jessica Farrow?

Steps to calculate the projected benefit obligation:

1. Use the pension formula (including a projection of future salary levels) to determine the retirement benefits earned to date.
2. Find the present value of the retirement benefits as of the retirement date (end of 2046).
3. Find the present value of retirement benefits as of the current date (end of 2016).

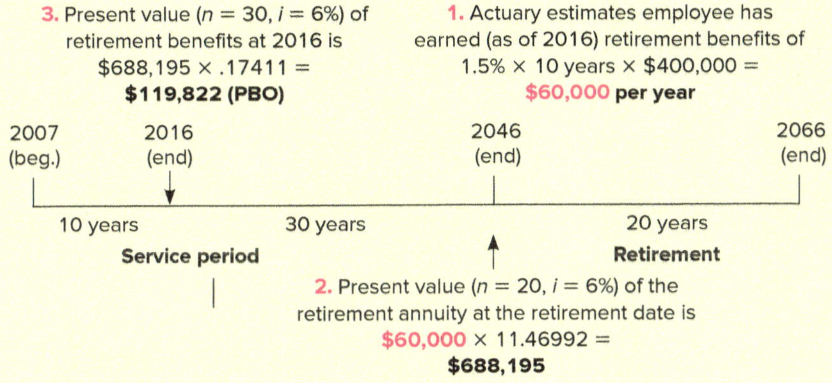

*This salary reflects an estimated compound rate of increase of about 5% and should take into account expectations concerning inflation, promotions, productivity gains, and other factors that might influence salary levels.

The actuary includes projected salaries in the pension formula. The projected benefit obligation is the present value of those benefits.

Using Excel, enter:
=PV(.06,20,–60000)
Output: 688195

Using a calculator:
enter: N 20 I 6 PMT – 60000 FV
Output: PV 688195

Illustration 17–6A

PBO in 2017

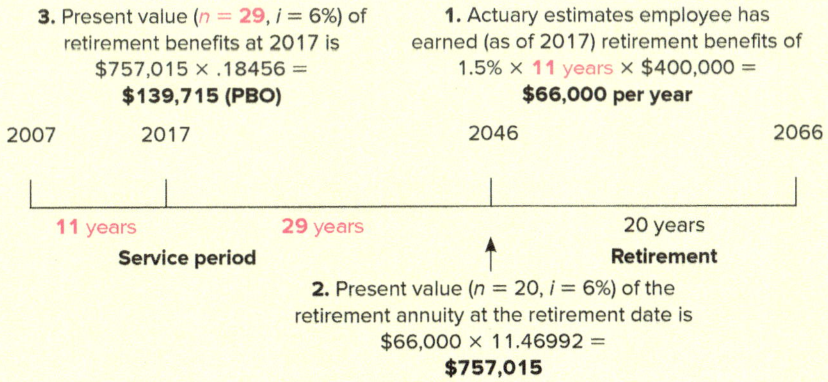

In 2017 the pension formula includes one more service year.

Also, 2017 is one year closer to the retirement date for the purpose of calculating the present value.

These represent two of the events that might possibly cause the balance of the PBO to change. Let's elaborate on these and the three other events that might change the balance of the PBO. The five events are (1) service cost, (2) interest cost, (3) prior service cost, (4) gains and losses, and (5) payments to retired employees.

Each year's service adds to the obligation to pay benefits.

1. Service cost. As we just witnessed in the illustration, the PBO increases each year by the amount of that year's service cost. This represents the increase in the projected benefit obligation attributable to employee service performed during the period. As we explain later, it also is the primary component of the annual pension expense.

Interest accrues on the PBO each year.

2. Interest cost. The second reason the PBO increases is called the interest cost. Even though the projected benefit obligation is not formally recognized as a liability in the company's balance sheet, it is a liability nevertheless. And, as with other liabilities, interest accrues on its balance as time passes. The amount can be calculated directly as the assumed discount rate multiplied by the projected benefit obligation at the beginning of the year.[5]

Additional Consideration

We can verify the increase in the PBO as being caused by the service cost and interest cost as follows:

PBO at the beginning of 2017 (end of 2016)					$119,822
Service cost: (1.5% × 1 yr. × $400,000) Annual retirement benefits from 2017 service	×	11.46992* To discount to 2046	×	0.18456† To discount to 2017	12,701
Interest cost: $119,822 × 6%					7,189
PBO at the end of 2017					$139,712‡

*Present value of an ordinary annuity of $1; $n = 20$, $i = 6\%$.
†Present value of $1; $n = 29$, $i = 6\%$.
‡Differs from $139,715 due to rounding.

3. Prior service cost. Another reason the PBO might change is when the pension plan itself is *amended* to revise the way benefits are determined. For example, Global Communications in our illustration might choose to revise the pension formula by which benefits are calculated. Let's back up and assume the formula's salary percentage is increased in 2017 from 1.5% to 1.7%:

1.7% × Service years × Final year's salary
(revised pension formula)

Obviously, the annual service cost from this date forward will be higher than it would have been without the amendment. This will cause a more rapid future expansion of the PBO. But it also might cause an immediate increase in the PBO as well. Here's why.

When a pension plan is amended, credit often is given for employee service rendered in prior years. The cost of doing so is called *prior service cost.*

Suppose the amendment becomes effective for future years' service only, without consideration of employee service to date. As you might imagine, the morale and dedication of long-time employees of the company could be expected to suffer. So, for economic as well as ethical reasons, most companies choose to make amendments retroactive to prior years. In other words, the more beneficial terms of the revised pension formula are not applied just to future service years, but benefits attributable to all prior service years also are recomputed under the more favorable terms. Obviously, this decision is not without cost to the company. Making the amendment retroactive to prior years adds an extra layer of retirement benefits, increasing the company's benefit obligation. The increase in the PBO attributable to making a plan amendment retroactive is referred to as prior service cost.[6]

[5]Assumed discount rates should reflect rates used currently in annuity contracts. Discount rates recently reported have ranged from 3.5% to 4.52% with 4% being the most commonly assumed rate (Pension/OPEB 2015 Assumption and Disclosure Survey, PWC, 2015).

[6]Prior service cost also is created if a defined benefit pension plan is initially adopted by a company that previously did not have one, and the plan itself is made retroactive to give credit for prior years' service. Prior service cost is created by plan amendments far more often than by plan adoptions because most companies already have pension plans, and new pension plans in recent years have predominantly been defined contribution plans.

For instance, Illustration 17–7 presents an excerpt from an annual report of Ecolab, Inc. describing the increase in its PBO as a result of making an amendment retroactive:

Note 1: Retirement Plans (in part)
. . . The Company amended its U.S. pension plan to change the formula for pension benefits and to provide a more rapid vesting schedule. The plan amendments resulted in a $6 million increase in the projected benefits obligation.

Illustration 17–7
Prior Service Cost—Ecolab, Inc.
Real World Financials

Let's put prior service cost in the context of our illustration.

At the end of 2016, and therefore the beginning of 2017, the PBO is $119,822. If the plan is amended on January 3, 2017, the PBO for that date could be recomputed as:

	PBO without Amendment		PBO with Amendment	
1.	1.5% × 10 yrs. × $400,000	= $ 60,000	1.7% × 10 yrs. × $400,000	= $ 68,000
2.	$60,000 × 11.46992	= 688,195	$68,000 × 11.46992	= 779,955
3.	$688,195 × .17411	= 119,822	$779,955 × .17411	= 135,798

$15,976
Prior service cost

Retroactive benefits from an amendment add additional costs, increasing the company's PBO. This increase is the prior service cost.

The $15,976 increase in the PBO attributable to applying the more generous terms of the amendment to prior service years is the prior service cost. And, because we assumed the amendment occurred at the beginning of 2017, both the 2017 service cost and the 2017 interest cost would change as a result of the prior service cost. This is how:

PBO at the beginning of 2017 (end of 2016)	$119,822
Prior service cost (determined above)	15,976
PBO including prior service cost at the beginning of 2017	135,798
Service cost: (1.7% × 1yr. × $400,000) × 11.46992* × 0.18456† (Annual retirement benefits from 2017 service) (To discount to 2046) (To discount to 2017)	14,395
Interest cost: $135,798‡ × 6%	8,148
PBO at the end of 2017	$158,341

*Present value of an ordinary annuity of $1; $n = 20$, $i = 6\%$.
†Present value of $1; $n = 29$, $i = 6\%$.
‡Includes the beginning balance plus the prior service cost because the amendment occurred at the beginning of the year.

Additional Consideration

We can verify the PBO balance by calculating it directly:

3. Present value ($n = 29$, $i = 6\%$) of retirement benefits at 2017 is $857,950 × .18456 = **$158,341* (PBO)**

1. Actuary estimates employee has earned (as of 2017) retirement benefits of 1.7% × 11 years × $400,000 = **$74,800 per year**

2007 — 2017 — 2046 — 2066

11 years — 29 years — 20 years

Service period — **Retirement**

2. Present value ($n = 20$, $i = 6\%$) of the retirement annuity at the retirement date is $74,800 × 11.46992 = **$857,950**

*Adjusted by $2 to compensate for the rounding of present value factors.

The pension formula reflects the plan amendment.

The plan amendment would affect not only the year in which it occurs, but also each subsequent year because the revised pension formula determines each year's service cost. Continuing our illustration to 2018 demonstrates this:

During 2018, the PBO increased as a result of service cost and interest cost.

PBO at the beginning of 2018 (end of 2017)	$158,341
Service cost: (1.7% × 1yr. × $400,000) × 11.46992* × 0.19563† (Annual retirement benefits from 2018 service; To discount to 2046; To discount to 2018)	15,258
Interest cost: $158,341 × 6%	9,500
PBO at the end of 2018	$183,099

*Present value of an ordinary annuity of $1; $n = 20$, $i = 6\%$.
†Present value of $1; $n = 28$, $i = 6\%$.

Decreases and increases in estimates of the PBO because of periodic re-evaluation of uncertainties are called gains and losses.

4. Gain or loss on the PBO. We mentioned earlier that a number of estimates are necessary to derive the PBO. When one or more of these estimates requires revision, the estimate of the PBO also will require revision. The resulting decrease or increase in the PBO is referred to as a *gain* or *loss,* respectively. Let's modify our illustration to imitate the effect of revising one of the several possible estimates involved. Suppose, for instance, that new information at the end of 2018 about inflation and compensation trends suggests that the estimate of Farrow's final salary should be increased by 5% to $420,000. This would affect the estimate of the PBO as follows:

Changing the final salary estimate changes the PBO.

	PBO *without* Revised Estimate		**PBO *with* Revised Estimate**	
1.	1.7% × 12 yrs. × $400,000	= $ 81,600	1.7% × 12 yrs. × $420,000	= $ 85,680
2.	$81,600 × 11.46992	= 935,945	$85,680 × 11.46992	= 982,743
3.	$935,945 × .19563	= 183,099	$982,743 × .19563	= 192,254

$9,155
Loss on PBO

The difference of $9,155 represents a loss on the PBO because the obligation turned out to be higher than previously expected. Now there would be three elements of the increase in the PBO during 2018.[7]

The revised estimate caused the PBO to increase.

PBO at the beginning of 2018	$158,341
Service cost (calculated above)	15,258
Interest cost (calculated above)	9,500
Loss on PBO (calculated above)	9,155
PBO at the end of 2018	$192,254

If a revised estimate causes the PBO to be lower than previously expected, a gain would be indicated. Consider how a few of the other possible estimate changes would affect the PBO:

- A change in life expectancies might cause the retirement period to be estimated as 21 years rather than 20 years. Calculation of the present value of the retirement annuity would use $n = 21$, rather than $n = 20$. The estimate of the PBO would increase.
- The expectation that retirement will occur two years earlier than previously thought would cause the retirement period to be estimated as 22 years rather than 20 years and the service period to be estimated as 28 years rather than 30 years. The new expectation would probably also cause the final salary estimate to change. The net effect on the PBO would depend on the circumstances.
- A change in the assumed discount rate would affect the present value calculations. A lower rate would increase the estimate of the PBO. A higher rate would decrease the estimate of the PBO.

[7]The increase in the PBO due to amending the pension formula (prior service cost) occurred in 2017.

5. Payment of retirement benefits. We've seen how the PBO will change due to the accumulation of service cost from year to year, the accrual of interest as time passes, making plan amendments retroactive to prior years, and periodic adjustments when estimates change. Another change in the PBO occurs when the obligation is reduced as benefits actually are paid to retired employees.

Payment of retirement benefits reduces the PBO.

The payment of such benefits is not applicable in our present illustration because we've limited the situation to calculations concerning an individual employee who is several years from retirement. Remember, though, in reality the actuary would make these calculations for the entire pool of employees covered by the pension plan. But the concepts involved would be the same. Illustration 17–8 summarizes the five ways the PBO can change.

Illustration 17–8

Components of Change in the PBO

The Projected Benefits Obligation Changes as a Result of:

Cause	Effect	Frequency
Service cost	+	Each period
Interest cost	+	Each period (except the first period of the plan, when no obligation exists to accrue interest)
Prior service cost	+	Only if the plan is amended (or initiated) that period
Loss or gain on PBO	+ or −	Whenever revisions are made in the pension liability estimate
Retiree benefits paid	−	Each period (unless no employees have yet retired under the plan)

Illustration Expanded to Consider the Entire Employee Pool

For our single employee, the PBO at the end of 2018 is $192,254. Let's say now that Global Communications has 2,000 active employees covered by the pension plan and 100 retired employees receiving retirement benefits. Illustration 17–9 expands the numbers to represent all covered employees.

The PBO is not formally recognized in the balance sheet.

Illustration 17–9

The PBO Expanded to Include All Employees

The changes in the PBO for Global Communications during 2018 were as follows:*

	($ in millions)
PBO at the beginning of 2018† (amount assumed)	$400
Service cost, 2018 (amount assumed)	41
Interest cost: $400 × 6%	24
Loss (gain) on PBO (amount assumed)	23
Less: Retiree benefits paid (amount assumed)	(38)
PBO at the end of 2018	$450

*Of course, these expanded amounts are not simply the amounts for Jessica Farrow multiplied by 2,000 employees because her years of service, expected retirement date, and salary are not necessarily representative of other employees. Also, the expanded amounts take into account expected employee turnover and current retirees.

†Includes the prior service cost that increased the PBO when the plan was amended in 2017.

Pension Plan Assets

LO17–4

So far our focus has been on the employer's obligation to provide retirement benefits in the future. We turn our attention now to the resources with which the company will satisfy that obligation—the pension plan assets. Like the PBO, the pension plan assets are not reported separately in the employer's balance sheet but are netted together with the PBO to report either a net pension asset (debit balance) or a net pension liability (credit balance). Its separate balance, too, must be reported in the disclosure notes to the financial statements (as does the separate PBO balance), and as explained below, the return on these assets is included in the calculation of the periodic pension expense.

FINANCIAL Reporting Case

Q3, p. 968

We assumed in the previous section that Global Communications' obligation is $450 million for service performed to date. When employees retire, will there be sufficient funds to provide the anticipated benefits? To ensure sufficient funding, Global will contribute cash each year to a pension fund.

A *trustee* manages pension plan assets.

The assets of a pension fund must be held by a **trustee**. A trustee accepts employer contributions, invests the contributions, accumulates the earnings on the investments, and pays benefits from the plan assets to retired employees or their beneficiaries. The trustee can be an individual, a bank, or a trust company. Plan assets are invested in stocks, bonds, and other income-producing assets. The accumulated balance of the annual employer contributions plus the return on the investments (dividends, interest, market price appreciation) must be sufficient to pay benefits as they come due.

When an employer estimates how much it must set aside each year to accumulate sufficient funds to pay retirement benefits as they come due, it's necessary to estimate the return those investments will produce. This is the **expected return on plan assets**. The higher the return, the less the employer must actually contribute. On the other hand, a relatively low return means the difference must be made up by higher contributions. In practice, recent estimates of the rate of return have ranged from 4.6% to 9%, with 7.3% being the most commonly reported expectation.[8] In Illustration 17–10, we shift the focus of our numerical illustration to emphasize Global's pension plan assets.

Illustration 17–10

How Plan Assets Change

A trustee accepts employer contributions, invests the contributions, accumulates the earnings on the investments, and pays benefits from the plan assets.

Global Communications funds its defined benefit pension plan by contributing each year the year's service cost plus a portion of the prior service cost. Cash of $48 million was contributed to the pension fund at the end of 2018.

Plan assets at the beginning of 2018 were valued at $300 million. The expected rate of return on the investment of those assets was 9%, but the actual return in 2018 was 10%. Retirement benefits of $38 million were paid at the end of 2018 to retired employees.

What is the value of the company's pension plan assets at the end of 2018?

	($ in millions)
Plan assets at the beginning of 2018	$300
Actual return on plan assets (10% × $300)	30
Cash contributions	48
Less: Retiree benefits paid	(38)
Plan assets at the end of 2018	$340

An *underfunded* pension plan means the PBO exceeds plan assets.

Recall that Global's PBO at the end of 2018 is $450 million. Because the plan assets are only $340 million, the pension plan is said to be *underfunded.* One reason is that we assumed Global incurred a $60 million prior service cost from amending the pension plan at the beginning of 2017, and that cost is being funded over several years. Another factor is the loss from increasing the PBO due to the estimate revision, since funding has been based on the previous estimate. Later, we'll assume earlier revisions also have increased the PBO. Of course, actual performance of the investments also impacts a plan's funded status.

An *overfunded* pension plan means plan assets exceed the PBO.

It is not unusual for pension plans today to be underfunded. Historically, the funded status of pension plans has varied considerably. Prior to the Employee Retirement Income Security Act (ERISA) in 1974, many plans were grossly underfunded. The law established minimum funding standards among other matters designed to protect plan participants. The new standards brought most plans closer to full funding. Then the stock market boom of the 1980s caused the value of plan assets for many pension funds to swell to well in excess of their projected benefit obligations. More than 80% of pension plans were overfunded. As a result, managers explored ways to divert funds to other areas of operations. Today, a majority of plans again are underfunded. The economic crisis has taken its toll. Stock market

[8]Pension/OPEB 2015 Assumption and Disclosure Survey, PWC, 2015.

declines reduced the funded status of pension plans from 108% at the end of 2007 to 79% at the end of 2008.[9] Despite positive stock market returns since, the funded status for plans at the 1,500 largest U.S. companies tracked by Standard & Poor's was 89% in 2015. One culprit was low interest rates. Low interest rates hurt plans' funded status because the pension obligation is a present value calculation that increases with a lower discount rate. Even small interest rate changes have big effects on funded status. Many of the underfunded plans are with troubled companies, placing employees at risk. The PBGC guarantees are limited to about $5,000 per month, often less than promised pension benefits.

Reporting the Funded Status of the Pension Plan

● LO17–5

FINANCIAL Reporting Case

Q4, p. 968

A company must report in its balance sheet a liability for the underfunded (or asset for the overfunded) status of its postretirement plans.

A company's PBO is not reported separately among liabilities in the balance sheet. Similarly, the plan assets a company sets aside to pay those benefits are not separately reported among assets in the balance sheet. However, firms do report the net difference between those two amounts, referred to as the "funded status" of the plan.[10] From our previous discussion, we see the funded status for Global to be the following at December 31, 2018, and December 31, 2017:

($ in millions)	2018	2017
Projected benefit obligation (PBO)	$450	$400
Fair value of plan assets	340	300
Underfunded status	$110	$100

Because the plan is underfunded, Global reports a net pension liability of $110 million in its 2018 balance sheet and $100 million in 2017. Be sure to note that the "net pension liability" is not an actual account balance. Instead, it's the PBO account balance and the Plan assets account balance simply reported in the balance sheet as a single net amount. If the plan becomes overfunded in the future, Global will report a net pension asset instead.

Now, let's look at all the ways that changes in the PBO and the pension plan assets affect pension expense.

PART C

Determining Pension Expense

The Relationship between Pension Expense and Changes in the PBO and Plan Assets

● LO17–6

The costs are allocated to the periods the services are performed.

Like wages, salaries, commissions, and other forms of pay, pension expense is part of a company's compensation for employee services each year. Accordingly, the accounting objective is to achieve a matching of the costs of providing this form of compensation with the benefits of the services performed. However, the fact that this form of compensation actually is paid to employees many years after the service is performed means that other elements in addition to the annual service cost will affect the ultimate pension cost. These other elements are related to changes that occur over time in both the pension obligation and the pension plan assets. Illustration 17–11 provides a summary of how some of these changes influence pension expense.

We've examined each of the components of pension expense from the viewpoint of its effect on the PBO or on plan assets, using the Global Communications illustration to demonstrate that effect. Now, let's expand the same illustration to see how these changes affect *pension expense*. Illustration 17–12 provides this expanded example.

[9]Goldman Sachs, "Global Markets Institute Accounting Policy Update: Pension review 2009–Fallout from funded status decline just beginning," Global Markets Institute, June 4, 2009.

[10]FASB 715–30–25: Compensation–Retirement Benefits–Defined Benefit Plans–Pension–Recognition (previously "Employers' Accounting for Defined Benefit Pension and Other Postretirement Plans–an amendment of FASB Statements No. 87, 88, 106, and 132(R)," *Statement of Financial Accounting Standards No. 158* (Stamford, Conn.: FASB, 2006)).

Illustration 17–11

Components of the Periodic Pension Expense

FINANCIAL Reporting Case

Q5, p. 968

The pension expense reported in the income statement is a composite of periodic changes that occur in both the pension obligation and the plan assets.

Changes in the PBO

Service cost—increase in the employer's obligation attributed to employee service during the current period

Interest cost—interest accrued on the obligation during the current period (balance at the beginning of the period multiplied by the interest rate)

Prior service cost—increase in the employer's obligation due to giving credit to employees for years of service provided before the pension plan is amended (or initiated)

Losses or (gains) on the PBO—increases or (decreases) in the estimate of the PBO from revisions in underlying assumptions

Less: Payments to retirees

Pension Expense

Included currently:

Service cost

Interest cost

(Expected return on the plan assets)

Delayed recognition:

Amortized portion of:

Prior service cost

Net loss or (gain)

Changes in Plan Assets

Expected return on the plan assets—estimated long-term return from changes in the value of plan assets, due to dividends, interest, and market price changes, plus (minus):

Gains or (losses) on the plan assets—return on plan assets lower or (higher) than expected

Cash contributions—payments into the fund by the employer

Less: Payments to retirees

Illustration 17–12

Pension Expense

These are the changes in the PBO and in the plan assets we previously discussed (Illustration 17–9 and Illustration 17–10).

Reports from the actuary and the trustee of plan assets indicate the following changes during 2018 in the PBO and plan assets of Global Communications ($ in millions).

	PBO
Beginning of 2018	$400
Service cost	41
Interest cost, 6%	24
Loss (gain) on PBO	23
Less: Retiree benefits	(38)
End of 2018	$450

	Plan Assets
Beginning of 2018	$300
Actual return on plan assets, 10% (9% expected)*	30
Cash contributions	48
Less: Retiree benefits	(38)
End of 2018	$340

Assume a *prior service cost* of $60 million was incurred at the beginning of the previous year (2017) due to a plan amendment increasing the PBO. Also assume that at the beginning of 2018, Global had a *net loss* of $55 million (previous losses exceeded previous gains). The average remaining service life of employees is estimated at 15 years.

2018 Pension Expense

Global's 2018 Pension Expense Is Determined as Follows:	($ in millions)
Service cost	$41
Interest cost	24
Expected return on the plan assets ($30 actual, less $3 gain)	(27)
Amortization of prior service cost (calculated later)	4
Amortization of net loss (calculated later)	1
Pension expense	$43

*Expected rates of return anticipate the performance of various investments of plan assets. This is not necessarily the same as the discount rate used by the actuary to estimate the pension obligation. Assumed rates of return recently reported have ranged from 4.6% to 9%, with 7.3% being the most commonly assumed rate (Pension/OPEB 2015 Assumption and Disclosure Survey, PWC, 2015).

Components of Pension Expense

Illustration 17–12 demonstrates the relationship between some of the changes in the PBO and in plan assets and the components of pension expense: service cost, interest cost, the return on plan assets, prior service cost amortization, and net gain or loss amortization. Let's look at these five components of pension expense one at a time.

1. SERVICE COST. The $41 million service cost represents the increase in the projected benefit obligation attributable to employee service performed during 2018 (benefits earned by employees during the year). Each year, this is the first component of the pension expense.

2. INTEREST COST. The interest cost is calculated as the interest rate (discount rate) multiplied by the projected benefit obligation at the beginning of the year. In 2018, this is 6% times $400 million, or $24 million.

Interest cost is the discount rate times the PBO balance at the beginning of the year.

The PBO balance is not separately reported as a liability in the company's balance sheet, but it is a liability nevertheless.[11] The interest expense that accrues on its balance is not separately reported in the income statement but instead becomes the second component of the annual pension expense.

3. RETURN ON PLAN ASSETS. Remember, plan assets comprise funds invested in stocks, bonds, and other securities that presumably will generate dividends, interest, and capital gains. Each year, these earnings represent the return on plan assets during that year. When accounting for the return, we need to differentiate between its two modes: the *expected* return and the *actual* return.

The return earned on investment securities increases the plan asset balance.

Actual versus expected return. We've assumed Global's expected rate of return is 9%, so its expected return on plan assets in 2018 was 9% times $300 million, or $27 million. But, as previously indicated, the actual rate of return in 2018 was 10%, producing an actual return on plan assets of 10% times $300 million, or $30 million.

Obviously, investing plan assets in income-producing assets lessens the amounts employers must contribute to the fund. So, the return on plan assets reduces the net cost of having a pension plan. Accordingly, the return on plan assets each year *reduces* the amount recorded as pension expense. Just as the interest expense that accrues on the PBO is included as a component of pension expense rather than being separately reported, the investment revenue on plan assets is not separately reported either. In actuality, both the interest and return-on-assets components of pension expense do not directly represent employee compensation. Instead, they are financial items created only because the future obligation to retirees must be funded currently.

The interest and return-on-assets components are financial items created rather than direct employee compensation.

Adjustment for loss or gain. A controversial question is *when* differences between the actual and expected return should be recognized in pension expense. It seems logical that since the net cost of having a pension plan is reduced by the actual return on plan assets, the charge to pension expense should be the actual return on plan assets. However, the FASB concluded that the actual return should first be adjusted by any difference between that return and the return amount that had been expected. So, it's actually the *expected* return that is included in the calculation of pension expense. In our illustration, Global's pension expense is reduced by the expected return of $27 million.

The return on plan assets reduces the net *cost of having a* pension plan.

The difference between the actual and expected return is considered a loss or gain on plan assets. Although we don't include these losses and gains as part of pension expense when they occur, it's possible they will affect pension expense at a later time. Soon, we will discuss how that might happen.

Any loss or gain is not included in pension expense right away.

4. AMORTIZATION OF PRIOR SERVICE COST. Recall that the $60 million increase in Global's PBO due to recalculating benefits employees earned in prior years as a result of a plan amendment is referred to as the prior service cost. Obviously, prior service cost adds to the cost of having a pension plan. But when should this cost be recognized as pension expense? An argument can be made that the cost should be recognized as expense in the year of the amendment when the cost increases the company's pension obligation. In fact,

[11] As we discussed earlier and will revisit later, the PBO is combined with pension assets with the net difference reported in the balance sheet as either a net pension liability or a net pension asset.

some members of the FASB have advocated this approach. At present, though, we amortize the cost gradually to pension expense. Here's the rationalization.

Prior service cost is recognized as pension expense over the future service period of the employees whose benefits are recalculated.

Amending a pension plan, and especially choosing to make that amendment retroactive, typically is done with the idea that future operations will benefit from those choices. For that reason, the cost is not recognized as pension expense in the year the plan is amended. Instead, it is recognized as pension expense over the time that the employees who benefited from the retroactive amendment will work for the company in the future. Presumably, this future service period is when the company will receive the benefits of its actions.

In our illustration, the amendment occurred in 2017, increasing the PBO at that time. For the individual employee, Jessica Farrow, the prior service cost was calculated to be $15,976. Our illustration assumes that, for *all* plan participants, the prior service cost was $60 million at the beginning of 2017. The prior service cost at the beginning of 2018 is $56 million. The following section explains how this amount was computed.

One assumption in our illustration is that the average remaining service life of the active employee group is 15 years. To recognize the $60 million prior service cost in equal annual amounts over this period, the amount amortized as an increase in pension expense each year is **$4 million**:[12]

By the straight-line method, prior service cost is recognized over the average remaining service life of the active employee group.

Amortization of Prior Service Cost	($ in millions)
Service cost	$41
Interest cost	24
Expected return on the plan assets	(27)
Amortization of prior service cost–AOCI	**4**
Amortization of net loss–AOCI	1
Pension expense	$43

Prior service cost is not expensed as it is incurred. Instead, it is reported as a component of AOCI to be amortized over time.

Be sure to note that, even though we're amortizing it, the prior service cost is not an asset, but instead a part of *accumulated other comprehensive income* (AOCI), a shareholders' equity account. This is a result of the FASB's disinclination to treat the cost as an expense as it is incurred. The Board, instead, prefers to consider it to be *other comprehensive income* (OCI) like the handful of losses and gains also categorized the same way and not reported among the gains and losses in the traditional income statement. You first learned about comprehensive income in Chapter 4 and again in Chapter 12. We'll revisit it again later in this chapter.

The prior service cost balance in AOCI declines by $4 million each year:

Prior Service Cost–AOCI	($ in millions)
Prior service cost at the beginning of 2018	$56
Less: 2018 amortization	**(4)**
Prior service cost at the end of 2018	$52

5. AMORTIZATION OF A NET LOSS OR NET GAIN. You learned previously that gains and losses can occur when expectations are revised concerning either the PBO or the return on plan assets. Illustration 17–13 summarizes the possibilities.

We report gains and losses as OCI in the statement of comprehensive income.

Like the prior service cost we just discussed, we don't include these gains and losses as part of pension expense in the income statement, but instead report them as OCI in the statement of comprehensive income as they occur. We then report the gains and losses (net of subsequent amortization) on a cumulative basis as a net loss–AOCI or a net gain–AOCI, depending on whether we have greater losses or gains over time. We report this amount in the balance sheet as a part of *accumulated other comprehensive income* (AOCI), a shareholders' equity account.

There is no conceptual justification for not including losses and gains in earnings. After all, these increases and decreases in either the PBO or plan assets immediately impact the net cost of providing a pension plan and, conceptually, should be included in pension expense as they occur.

Nevertheless, the FASB requires that income statement recognition of gains and losses from either source be delayed. Why? For practical reasons.

[12]An alternative to this straight-line approach, called the *service method,* attempts to allocate the prior service cost to each year in proportion to the fraction of the total remaining service years worked in each of those years. This method is described in the chapter appendix.

Illustration 17–13

Gains and Losses

	Projected Benefit Obligation	Return on Plan Assets
Higher than expected	Loss	Gain
Lower than expected	Gain	Loss

Gains and losses occur when either the PBO or the return on plan assets turns out to be different than expected.

Income Smoothing

The FASB acknowledged the conceptual shortcoming of delaying the recognition of a gain or a loss while opting for this more politically acceptable approach. Delayed recognition was favored by a dominant segment of corporate America that was concerned with the effect of allowing gains and losses to immediately impact reported earnings.

The practical justification for delayed recognition is that, over time, gains and losses might cancel one another out. Given this possibility, why create unnecessary fluctuations in reported income by letting temporary gains and losses decrease and increase (respectively) pension expense? Of course, as years pass there may be more gains than losses, or vice versa, preventing their offsetting one another completely. So, if a net gain or a net loss gets "too large," pension expense must be adjusted.

The FASB defines too large rather arbitrarily as being when a net gain or a net loss at the beginning of a year exceeds an amount equal to 10% of the PBO, or 10% of plan assets, whichever is higher.[13] This threshold amount is referred to as the "corridor." When the corridor is exceeded, the excess is not charged to pension expense all at once. Instead, as a further concession to income smoothing, only a portion of the excess is included in pension expense. The minimum amount that should be included is the excess divided by the average remaining service period of active employees expected to receive benefits under the plan.[14]

In our illustration, we're assuming a net loss–AOCI of $55 million at the beginning of 2018. Also recall that the PBO and plan assets are $400 million and $300 million, respectively, at that time. The amount amortized to 2018 pension expense is **$1 million**, calculated as follows:

A net gain or a net loss affects pension expense only if it exceeds an amount equal to 10% of the PBO, or 10% of plan assets, whichever is higher.

Determining Net Loss Amortization—2018	($ in millions)
Net loss (previous losses exceeded previous gains)	$ 55
10% of $400 ($400 is greater than $300): the "corridor"	(40)
Excess at the beginning of the year	$ 15
Average remaining service period	÷ 15 years
Amount amortized to 2018 pension expense	**$ 1**

Because the net loss exceeds an amount equal to the greater of 10% of the PBO or 10% of plan assets, part of the excess is amortized to pension expense.

The pension expense is increased because a net loss is being amortized. If a net *gain* were being amortized, the amount would be *deducted* from pension expense because a gain would indicate that balance of the net cost of providing the pension plan had decreased.

Amortization of the Net Loss–AOCI	($ in millions)
Service cost	$41
Interest cost	24
Expected return on the plan assets	(27)
Amortization of prior service cost–AOCI	4
Amortization of net loss–AOCI	**1**
Pension expense	$43

Amortization of a net gain would decrease pension expense.

Amortization of a net loss increases pension expense.

[13]For this purpose, the FASB specifies the market-related value of plan assets. This can be either the fair value or a weighted-average fair value over a period not to exceed five years. We will uniformly assume fair value in this chapter.

[14]Companies are permitted to amortize the entire net loss (or gain) rather than just the excess, but few choose that option. (FASB ASC 715–30–35–25: Compensation–Retirement Benefits–Defined Benefit Plans–Pension–Subsequent Measurement–Gains and Losses (previously "Employers' Accounting for Pensions," *Statement of Financial Accounting Standards No. 87* (Stamford, Conn.: FASB, 1985))).

This amortization reduces the net loss–AOCI in 2018 by $1 million. Also recall that Global incurred (a) a $23 million loss in 2018 from revising estimates relating to the PBO and (b) a $3 million gain when the 2018 return on plan assets was higher than expected. These three changes affected the net loss–AOCI in 2018 as follows:

New losses add to a net loss; new gains reduce a net loss.

Net Loss–AOCI	($ in millions)
Net loss–AOCI at the beginning of 2018	$55
Less: 2018 amortization	(1)
Plus: 2018 loss on PBO	23
Less: 2018 gain on plan assets	(3)
Net loss–AOCI at the end of 2018	$74

Additional Consideration

The $74 million balance in net loss–AOCI at the end of 2018 would be the beginning balance in 2019. It would be compared with the 2019 beginning balances in the PBO and plan assets to determine whether amortization would be necessary in 2019. If you were to look back to our analyses of the changes in those two balances, you would see the 2019 beginning balances in the PBO and plan assets to be $450 million and $340 million, respectively. The amount amortized to 2019 pension expense will be $1.93 million, calculated as follows:

	($ in millions)
Net loss (previous losses exceeded previous gains)	$ 74
10% of $450 ($450 is greater than $340)	(45)
Excess at the beginning of the year	$ 29
Average remaining service period	÷ 15 years*
Amount amortized to 2019 pension expense	**$1.93**

*Assumes the average remaining service period of active employees is still 15 years in 2019, due to new employees joining the firm.

PART D

Reporting Issues

Recording Gains and Losses

● LO17–7

As we discussed earlier, gains and losses (either from changing assumptions regarding the PBO or from the return on assets being higher or lower than expected) are deferred and not immediately included in pension expense and net income. Instead, we report them as *other comprehensive income (OCI)* in the statement of comprehensive income. So Global records a *loss–OCI* for the $23 million loss that occurs in 2018 when it revises its estimate of future salary levels causing its PBO estimate to increase. Global also records a $3 million *gain–OCI* that occurred when the $30 million actual return on plan assets exceeded the $27 million expected return. Here's the entry:

Losses and gains (as well as any new prior service cost should it occur) are reported as OCI.

To Record Gains and Losses	($ in millions)	
Loss–OCI (from change in assumption)	23	
PBO		23
Plan assets	3	
Gain–OCI ($30 actual return on assets − $27 expected return)		3

The loss is an increase in the PBO due to a change in an assumption. In this entry, we are recording that increase in the PBO account balance. If the change in assumption had caused the PBO to be reduced instead, we would debit the PBO here and credit a gain–OCI.

Similarly, the gain due to the actual return on plan assets exceeding the expected return is an increase in plan assets. In the next section, we increase plan assets for the expected return (as a component of pension expense) so the two adjustments together cause the plan assets account balance to reflect the actual return (expected increase plus the additional increase represented by the gain). Of course, if the actual return had been less than expected, we would debit a loss–OCI and credit plan assets here.

Additional Consideration

Just as we record new losses and gains as they occur, we also will record a change in the prior service cost account for any new prior service cost should it occur. For instance, if Global revised its pension formula again and recalculated its PBO using the more generous formula, causing a $40 million increase in the PBO, the company would record the new prior service cost this way:

To Record New Prior Service Cost	($ in millions)	
Prior service cost–OCI (increase in PBO due to plan amendment)	40	
PBO		40

If an amendment *reduces* rather than increases the PBO, the *negative prior service cost* would reduce both the prior service cost and pension liability.

International Financial Reporting Standards

● LO17–12

Accounting for Gains and Losses. Accounting for gains and losses in defined benefit plans (called "remeasurement" gains and losses under IFRS) under *IAS No. 19* is similar to U.S. GAAP, but there are two important differences.

The first difference relates to the make-up of the gain or loss on plan assets. As we know from the chapter, this amount under U.S. GAAP is the difference between the actual and expected returns, where the expected return is different from company to company and usually different from the interest rate used to determine the interest cost. Not so under IFRS, which requires that we use the same rate (the rate for "high grade corporate bonds") for both the interest cost on the defined benefit obligation (called projected benefit obligation or PBO under U.S. GAAP) and the interest revenue on the plan assets. In fact, under IFRS, we multiply that rate, say 6%, times the net difference between the defined benefit obligation (DBO) and plan assets and report the **net interest cost/income**:

	($ in millions)	
Net interest cost [6% × ($400 − 300)]	6	
Plan assets (6% × $300: interest income)	18	
DBO (6% × $400: interest cost)		24

As a result, the remeasurement gain (or loss) under IFRS usually is an amount different from the gain (or loss) on plan assets under GAAP:

To Record Gains and Losses

U.S. GAAP

Actual return = 10% — Expected return = 9%

Plan assets	3	
Gain–OCI [(10% − 9%) × $300]		3

IFRS

Plan assets (actual interest income in excess of 6%)	12	
Remeasurement gain–OCI [(10% − 6%) × $300]		12

Actual return = 10% — High grade corporate bond rate = 6%

Under IFRS, we have a *remeasurement* gain when the actual return on plan assets exceeds the "high grade corporate bond rate" we use to determine the net interest cost/income.

(continued)

Remeasurement gains and losses under IFRS are reported as OCI but, unlike under U.S. GAAP, are *not subsequently amortized to expense* and recycled into net income.

(concluded)

A second difference relates to the treatment of gains and losses *after* they are initially recorded in OCI. We've seen that U.S. GAAP requires that gains and losses (either from the actual return exceeding an assumed amount [*entries above*] or from changing assumptions regarding the pension obligation [*entries below*]) are to be (a) included among OCI items in the statement of comprehensive income when they first arise and then (b) gradually amortized or recycled out of OCI and into expense (when the accumulated net gain or net loss exceeds the 10% threshold). Similar to U.S. GAAP, under IFRS these gains and losses are included in OCI when they first arise, but unlike U.S. GAAP those amounts are *not subsequently amortized out of OCI and into expense.** Instead, under IFRS those amounts remain in the balance sheet as accumulated other comprehensive income. The initial entries, then, are the same:

U.S. GAAP

Loss–OCI†	23	
PBO		23

IFRS

Remeasurement loss–OCI††	23	
DBO		23

*"Employee Benefits," *International Accounting Standard No. 19* (IASCF), as amended effective January 1, 2016.
†Subsequently amortized to expense and recycled from other comprehensive income to net income.
††Not subsequently amortized to expense; remains in accumulated other comprehensive income.

Recording the Pension Expense

Recall from Illustration 17–12 that Global's 2018 pension expense is $43 million. The expense includes the $41 million service cost and the $24 million interest cost, both of which, as we learned earlier, add to Global's PBO. Similarly, the expense includes a $27 million expected return on plan assets, which adds to the plan assets.[15] These changes are reflected in the following entry:

Each component of the pension expense is recorded in the journal entry to record pension expense.

Service cost and interest cost increase the PBO. The return on assets increases plan assets.

Service cost	$41
Interest cost	24
Expected return on assets	(27)
Amortization of prior service cost	4
Amortization of net loss	1
Pension expense	$43

To Record Pension Expense	($ in millions)	
Pension expense (total)	43	
Plan assets ($27 expected return on assets)	27	
PBO ($41 Service Cost + $24 Interest Cost)		65
Amortization of prior service cost—OCI (2018 amortization)		4
Amortization of net loss—OCI (2018 amortization)		1

The pension expense also includes the $4 million amortization of the prior service cost and the $1 million amortization of the net loss. As we discussed earlier, we report prior service cost when it arises, as well as gains and losses as they occur as *other comprehensive income (OCI)* in the statement of comprehensive income. These OCI items accumulate as Prior service cost–AOCI and Net loss (or gain)–AOCI. So, when we amortize these AOCI accounts, we report the amortization amounts as OCI items in the statement of comprehensive income as well. These amortized amounts are being "reclassified" from OCI to net income.

New gains and losses and prior service cost are reported as OCI. So is the amortization of their accumulated balances.

Amortization reduces the Prior service cost–AOCI and the Net loss–AOCI. Since these accounts have debit balances, we credit the accounts for the amortization. If we were amortizing a net gain, we would *debit* the account because a net gain has a credit balance.

[15]The increase in plan assets is the $30 million *actual* return, but the $27 million *expected* return is the component of pension expense because the $3 million gain isn't included in expense. We saw in the previous section that the $3 million gain also increases plan assets.

Remember, we report the funded status of the plan in the balance sheet. That's the difference between the PBO and plan assets. In this case, it's a net pension liability since the plan is underfunded; that is, the PBO exceeds plan assets.

Reporting Pension Expense in the Income Statement

The service cost represents benefits earned by employees during the year as part of their compensation. Consistent with that characteristic, companies report the service cost component of pension expense in the income statement as part of the total *compensation costs* arising from services rendered by the employees during the period, separate from the other components of pension expense. This presentation reflects the nature of service cost being different from that of the other elements of pension cost. The other components of pension expense are presented in the income statement also, but separate from the service cost component and outside the subtotal of income from operations.[16] In our illustration, then, Global will report the $41 million service cost as one of the elements of compensation expense and the $2 million net amount of the remaining components of pension expense on a separate line below income from operations.

The service cost component of pension expense is reported separate from the other components of pension expense in the income statement as part of the total compensation costs.

In addition, the components of pension expense are itemized in disclosure notes. For instance, Kellogg Company described the composition of its pension expense in the disclosure note in its annual report for the year ended January 2, 2016, shown in Illustration 17–14.

Illustration 17–14
Disclosure of Pension Expense—Kellogg Company
Real World Financials

The components of pension expense are itemized in the disclosure note.

Components of Pension Expense

($ in millions)	2015	2014	2013
Service cost	$ 114	$106	$133
Interest cost	206	225	203
Expected return on plan assets	(399)	(415)	(359)
Amortization of losses (gains)	303	782	(854)
Amortization of prior service costs (credits)	13	14	16
Curtailment and special termination benefits	(1)	4	34
Net expense	$ 236	$716	$(827)

International Financial Reporting Standards

Prior Service Cost. Under *IAS No. 19*, prior service cost (called past service cost under IFRS) is combined with the current service cost and reported within the income statement rather than as a component of other comprehensive income as it is under U.S. GAAP.[17] For Global, the service cost would be recorded under IFRS in 2017 when the plan amendment occurred as follows ($ in millions):

Service cost (service cost–2017 plus $60)	xxx	
DBO (service cost–2017)		xxx
DBO (past service cost)		60*

*From Illustration 17–12.

● LO17–12

Recording the Funding of Plan Assets

When Global adds its annual cash investment to its plan assets, the value of those plan assets increases by $48 million:

To Record Funding	($ in millions)	
Plan assets	48	
Cash (contribution to plan assets)		48

[16] Accounting Standards Update, *Compensation—Retirement Benefits (Topic 715): Improving the Presentation of Net Periodic Pension Cost and Net Periodic Postretirement Benefit Cost*, FASB: December, 2016).
[17] "Employee Benefits," *International Accounting Standard No. 19* (IASCF), as amended effective January 1, 2016.

It's not unusual for the cash contribution to differ from that year's pension expense. After all, determining the periodic pension expense and the funding of the pension plan are two separate processes. Pension expense is an accounting decision. How much to contribute each year is a financing decision affected by cash flow and tax considerations, as well as minimum funding requirements. The Pension Protection Act of 2006 and the Employee Retirement Income Security Act of 1974 (ERISA) establish the pension funding requirements. Subject to these considerations, cash contributions are actuarially determined with the objective of accumulating (along with investment returns) sufficient funds to provide promised retirement benefits.

We saw earlier that when pension benefits are paid to retired employees, those payments reduce the plan assets established to pay the benefits and also reduce the obligation to pay the benefits, the PBO:

To Record Payment of Benefits	($ in millions)	
PBO	38	
Plan assets (payments to retired employees)		38

Now that we've recorded these entries for the funding of the pension plan and payment of benefits, we have recorded all the changes in the PBO and plan assets:

($ in millions)

PBO (debit)		PBO (credit)		Plan Assets (debit)		Plan Assets (credit)	
		400	Balance	Balance	300		
		23	Loss	Gain	3		
		41	Service cost	Expected return	27		
		24	Interest cost	Funding	48		
Benefits paid	38					38	Benefits paid
		450	Balance	Balance	340		

Remember, though, we don't report either of these balances separately in the balance sheet. Instead, we net the two and report a net pension liability of $450 = 340 − $110 million, the funded status of the pension plan.

Additional Consideration

Rather than recording each of these changes in the PBO and Plan Asset accounts, we could have recorded them in a single Net pension (liability) asset account. For example, we could have recorded the gains and losses, pension expense, and funding as follows:

	($ in millions)	
Loss—OCI (from change in assumption)	23	
Net pension (liability) asset		23
Net pension (liability) asset	3	
Gain—OCI ($30 actual return on assets − $27 expected return)		3
Pension expense	43	
Net pension (liability) asset		38
Amortization of prior service cost—OCI*		4
Amortization of net loss—OCI*		1
Net pension (liability) asset	48	
Cash		48

In fact many companies use this abbreviated approach. However, recording the changes in the accounts they affect (PBO and Plan assets) and then combining the two accounts for balance sheet reporting as we do in our illustrations has two advantages. First, we need the separate balances for the required disclosure in the pension disclosure note. Second, it is a more logical approach. It's easier to see that the return on plan assets is an increase in plan assets than it is to see it as a reduction in Net pension (liability) asset.

*Because Prior service cost—OCI and Net loss—OCI have debit balances, we amortize them with credits. We would amortize a Net gain—OCI (credit balance) with a debit.

Comprehensive Income

Comprehensive income, as you may recall from Chapter 4, is a more expansive view of income than traditional net income. In fact, it encompasses all changes in equity other than from transactions with owners.[18] So, in addition to net income, comprehensive income includes up to four other changes in equity. A statement of comprehensive income is demonstrated in Illustration 17–15, highlighting the presentation of the components of OCI pertaining to Global's pension plan.

Illustration 17–15
Statement of Comprehensive Income

		($ in millions)
Net income		$xxx
Other comprehensive income:		
Unrealized holding gains (losses) on investments*	$ x	
Pension plan:		
Loss—due to revising a PBO estimate†	(23)	
Gain—return on plan assets exceeds expected†	3	
Amortization of net loss	1	
Amortization of prior service cost	4	
Deferred gains (losses) from derivatives	x	
Gains (losses) from foreign currency transactions and exchange rate adjustments	x	xx
Comprehensive income		$xxx

Note: These amounts are shown without considering taxes. Actually each of the elements of comprehensive income should be reported net of tax. For instance, if the tax rate is 40%, the loss would be reported as $13.8 million: $23 million less a $9.2 million tax benefit.

*An unrealized loss also might occur from recording an impairment of a debt security investment as described in Chapter 12 and, as discussed in Chapter 14, applying the "fair value option" to a liability entails reporting in OCI any part of the change in the liability's fair value that's due to the liability's credit risk.

†From Illustration 17–12.

Gains and losses, as well as any new prior service cost should it arise, are among the OCI items reported in the period they occur.

Other comprehensive income (OCI) items are reported both (a) as they occur and then (b) as an accumulated balance within shareholder's equity in the balance sheet as shown in Illustration 17–16.[19]

In addition to reporting the gains or losses (and other elements of comprehensive income) that occur in the current reporting period, we also report these amounts on a *cumulative* basis in the balance sheet. Comprehensive income includes (a) net income and (b) OCI. Remember that we report net income that occurs in the current reporting period in the income statement and also report accumulated net income (that hasn't been distributed as dividends) in the balance sheet as retained earnings. Similarly, we report OCI as it occurs in the current reporting period (see Illustration 17–15) and also report *accumulated other comprehensive income* in the balance sheet. In its 2018 balance sheet, Global will report the amounts as shown in Illustration 17–16.

Reporting OCI as it occurs and also as an accumulated balance is consistent with the way we report net income and its accumulated counterpart, retained earnings.

Look back to the schedule shown earlier to see how the net loss–AOCI increased from $55 million to $74 million during 2018 and another schedule also shown earlier to see how the prior service cost–AOCI decreased from $56 million to $52 million. The pension liability represents the underfunded status of Global's pension plan on the two dates.

Income Tax Considerations

We have ignored the income tax effects of the amounts in order to focus on the core issues. Note, though, that as gains and losses occur, they are reported along with their tax effects (tax expense for a gain, tax savings for a loss) in the statement of comprehensive income. This can be accomplished by presenting components of other comprehensive income either net of related income tax effects or *before* income tax effects with disclosure of the income

OCI items are reported net of tax, in both the (a) statement of comprehensive income and (b) AOCI.

[18]Transactions with owners primarily include dividends and the sale or purchase of shares of the company's stock.

[19]Companies can present net income and other comprehensive income either in a single continuous statement of comprehensive income or in two separate but consecutive statements.

Illustration 17–16

Balance Sheet Presentation of Pension Amounts

If the plan had been overfunded, Global would have reported a pension asset among its assets rather than this pension liability.

The net loss and prior service cost *reduce* shareholders' equity.

Global Communication Balance Sheets For Years Ended December 31	2018	2017
Assets		
Current assets	$xxx	$xxx
Property, plant, and equipment	xxx	xxx
Liabilities		
Current liabilities	$xxx	$xxx
Net pension liability	110	100
Other long-term liabilities	xxx	xxx
Shareholders' Equity		
Common stock	$xxx	$xxx
Retained earnings	xxx	xxx
Accumulated other comprehensive income:		
Net unrealized holding gains and losses on investments—AOCI	xxx	xxx
Net loss—AOCI*	(74)	(55)
Prior service cost—AOCI*	(52)	(56)

*These are debit balances and therefore negative components of accumulated other comprehensive income; a net gain–AOCI would have a credit balance and be a positive component of accumulated other comprehensive income.

taxes allocated to each component either in a disclosure note or parenthetically in the statement.[20] Likewise, AOCI in the balance sheet also is reported net of tax.

Putting the Pieces Together

LO17–8

In preceding sections, we've discussed (1) the projected benefit obligation (including changes due to periodic service cost, accrued interest, revised estimates, plan amendments, and the payment of benefits); (2) the plan assets (including changes due to investment returns, employer contributions, and the payment of benefits); (3) prior service cost; (4) gains and losses; (5) the periodic pension expense (comprising components of each of these); and (6) the funded status of the plan. These elements of a pension plan are interrelated. It's helpful to see how each element relates to the others. One way is to bring each part together in a *pension spreadsheet*. We do this for Global Communications in Illustration 17–17.

You should spend several minutes studying this spreadsheet, focusing on the relationships among the elements that constitute a pension plan. Notice that the first numerical column simply repeats the actuary's report of how the PBO changed during the year, as explained previously (Illustration 17–9). Likewise, the second column reproduces the changes in plan assets we discussed earlier (Illustration 17–10). We've also previously noted the changes in the prior service cost—AOCI and the net loss—AOCI that are duplicated in the third and fourth columns. The fifth column repeats the calculation of the 2018 pension expense we determined earlier, and the cash contribution to the pension fund is the sole item in the next column.

Rather than report the PBO and plan asset balances separately, we combine those balances and report a single net pension liability or net pension asset in the balance sheet.

The last column shows the changes in the funded status of the plan. Be sure to notice that the funded status is the difference between the PBO (column 1) and the plan assets (column 2). That means that each of the changes we see in either of the first two columns also is reflected as a change in the funded status in the last column. The net pension liability (or net pension asset) balance is not carried in company records. Instead, we use this label to report the PBO and plan assets in the balance sheet as a single net amount.

[20]Similarly, if any new prior service cost should arise due to a plan amendment, it too would be reported net of tax or with tax effects shown parenthetically.

Illustration 17–17

Pension Spreadsheet

	Recorded in Accounts						Reported Only
	PBO	**Plan Assets**	**Prior Service Cost —AOCI**	**Net Loss —AOCI**	**Pension Expense**	**Cash**	**Net Pension (Liability)/ Asset**
Balance, Jan. 1, 2018	(400)	300	56	55			(100)
Service cost	(41)				41		(41)
Interest cost	(24)				24		(24)
Expected return on assets		27			(27)		27
Adjust for: Gain on assets		3		(3)			3
Amortization of:							
Prior service cost—AOCI			(4)		4		
Net loss—AOCI				(1)	1		
Loss on PBO	(23)			23			(23)
Prior service cost (new)*	0		0				0
Contributions to fund		48				(48)	48
Retiree benefits paid	38	(38)					
Balance, Dec. 31, 2018	(450)	340	52	74	43		(110)

Note: ( )s represent credits to accounts, not necessarily decreases.
*This amount was $60 million in the 2015 pension spreadsheet.

When the PBO exceeds plan assets, we have a net pension liability. If plan assets exceed the PBO we have a net pension asset.

The net pension liability (or net pension asset) is not recorded in a journal entry but is the amount reported in the balance sheet as the PBO and plan assets combined.

Notice that each change in a formal account (light-shaded columns) is reflected in exactly two of those columns with one debit and one credit.

International Financial Reporting Standards

Reporting Pension Expense. Under IFRS we separately report (a) the service cost component (including past service cost) and (b) the net interest cost/income component in the *income statement* and (c) remeasurement gains and losses as *other comprehensive income.*

● LO17–12

Decision Makers' Perspective

Although financial statement items are casualties of the political compromises of GAAP guidance, information provided in the disclosure notes fortunately makes up for some of the deficiencies.[21] Foremost among the useful disclosures are changes in the projected benefit obligation, changes in the fair value of plan assets, and a breakdown of the components of the annual pension expense. Other information also is made available to make it possible for interested analysts to reconstruct the financial statements with pension assets and liabilities included. We'll look at specific disclosures after we discuss postretirement benefits other than pensions because the two types of plans are reported together.

Investors and creditors must be cautious of the nontraditional treatment of pension information when developing financial ratios as part of an analysis of financial statements. The various elements of pensions that are not reported separately on the balance sheet and income statement (PBO, plan assets, gains and losses) can be included in ratios such as the debt to equity ratio or return on assets, but only by deliberately obtaining those numbers

Pension amounts reported in the disclosure notes fill a reporting gap left by the minimal disclosures in the primary financial statements.

[21]FASB ASC 715–20–50: Compensation–Retirement Benefits–Defined Benefit Plans–General–Disclosure (previously "Employers' Disclosures about Pensions and Other Postretirement Benefits," *Statement of Financial Accounting Standards No. 132* (revised 2003), (Stamford, Conn.: FASB, 2003)).

from the disclosure notes and adjusting the computation of the ratios. Similarly, without adjustment, profitability ratios and the times interest earned ratio will be distorted because pension expense includes the financial components of interest and return on assets.

Earnings quality (as defined in Chapter 4 and discussed in other chapters) also can be influenced by amounts reported in pension disclosures. Companies with relatively sizeable unrecognized pension costs (prior service cost, net gain or loss) can be expected to exhibit a relatively high "temporary" earnings component. Recall that temporary earnings are expected to be less predictive of future earnings than the "permanent" earnings component.

Settlement or Curtailment of Pension Plans

Companies sometimes terminate defined benefit plans to reduce costs and lessen risk.

To cut down on cumbersome paperwork and lessen their exposure to the risk posed by defined benefit plans, many companies are providing defined contribution plans instead. When a plan is terminated, a change in earnings is reported at that time.[22] For instance, Melville Corporation described the termination of its pension plan in the following disclosure note:

Illustration 17–18

Gain on the Termination of a Defined Benefit Plan—Melville Corporation

Real World Financials

Retirement Plans (in part)

. . . As a result of the termination of the defined benefit plans, and after the settlement of the liability to plan participants through the purchase of nonparticipating annuity contracts or lump-sum rollovers into the new 401(k) profit sharing plan, the Company recorded a nonrecurring gain of approximately $4,000,000 which was the amount of plan assets that reverted to the Company. This was accounted for in accordance with Statement of Financial Accounting Standards No. 88, "Employers' Accounting for Settlements and Curtailments of Defined Benefit Pension Plans and for Termination Benefits." (FASB ASC 715–30–35)

Concept Review Exercise

PENSION PLANS

Allied Services, Inc., has a noncontributory, defined benefit pension plan. Pension plan assets had a fair value of $900 million at December 31, 2017.

On January 3, 2018, Allied amended the pension formula to increase benefits for each service year. By making the amendment retroactive to prior years, Allied incurred a prior service cost of $75 million, adding to the previous projected benefit obligation of $875 million. The prior service cost is to be amortized (expensed) over 15 years. The service cost is $31 million for 2018. Both the actuary's discount rate and the expected rate of return on plan assets were 8%. The actual rate of return on plan assets was 10%.

At December 31, 2018, $16 million was contributed to the pension fund and $22 million was paid to retired employees. Also, at that time, the actuary revised a previous assumption, increasing the PBO estimate by $10 million. The net loss AOCI at the beginning of the year was $13 million.

Required:

Determine each of the following amounts as of December 31, 2018, the fiscal year-end for Allied: (1) projected benefit obligation; (2) plan assets; and (3) pension expense.

Solution:

($ in millions)	Projected Benefit Obligation	Plan Assets	Pension Expense
Balances at Jan. 1	$ 875	$900	$ 0
Prior service cost	75		
Service cost	31		31
Interest cost [($875 + 75)* × 8%]	76		76

(continued)

[22]FASB ASC 715–30–35: Compensation–Retirement Benefits–Defined Benefit Plans–Pension–Subsequent Measurement (previously "Employers' Accounting for Settlements and Curtailments of Defined Benefit Pension Plans and for Termination Benefits," *Statement of Financial Accounting Standards No. 88* (Stamford, Conn.: FASB, 1985)).

(concluded)

($ in millions)	Projected Benefit Obligation	Plan Assets	Pension Expense
Return on plan assets:			
Actual ($900 × 10%)		90	
Expected ($900 × 8%)			(72)
Amortization of prior service cost ($75 ÷ 15)			5
Amortization of net loss			0†
Loss on PBO	10		
Cash contribution		16	
Retirement payments	(22)	(22)	
Balance at Dec. 31	$1,045	$984	$40

Note: The $18 million gain on plan assets ($90 − 72 million) is not recognized yet; it is carried forward to be combined with previous and future gains and losses, which will be recognized only if the net gain or net loss exceeds 10% of the higher of the PBO or plan assets.
*Since the plan was amended at the beginning of the year, the prior service cost increased the PBO at that time.
†Since the net loss ($13) does not exceed 10% of $900 (higher than $875), no amortization is required for 2018.

International Financial Reporting Standards

Accounting for pensions and other postretirement benefits under IFRS is specified in a recent IASB amendment to its postemployment benefit standard, *IAS No. 19*.

Under the update, the changes that constitute the components of the net pension cost are separated into (a) the cost of service, (b) the cost of financing that cost, and (c) gains or losses from occasional remeasurement of the cost:

LO17–12

Components	Include:	Recognized immediately in:
Service cost	• Current service costs • Past service costs (if any)	• the balance sheet • income statement
Net interest cost/income	• Net interest cost/income [(Interest rate* × net pension liability) ÷ asset]	• the balance sheet • income statement
Remeasurement cost	• Remeasurements of service costs caused by changes in assumptions (i.e., assumptions like salary expectations, length of service, length of retirement, etc.) • Gains and losses arising from experience differing from what was assumed • Investment gains and losses on plan assets	• the balance sheet • statement of comprehensive income as OCI

*High-quality corporate bond rate.

Classifying the Components of the Net Pension Cost

Using the amounts from our Global Communications illustration, the changes in 2018 would be classified as follows:

Profit & Loss (Income Statement)

	($ in millions)	
Service cost:		
Service cost—2018	$41	
Past service cost	0*	$41
Net interest cost/income:		
Net interest cost [6% × ($400 −300)]		6
		$47

(continued)

(concluded)

Other Comprehensive Income (OCI)

Remeasurement cost:

Loss (gain) on DBO—change in salary estimate	$23	
Loss (gain) on plan assets: (10% − 6%) × $300	(12)	11
Net pension cost		$58

*Last year (2017), this amount was $60 million.

Notice that there is no separate interest cost and there is no "expected" return on plan assets. Instead, those two are essentially combined into a single measure, net interest cost/income. Because they're combined, the same rate (6% in this case) is used for both, rather than having one rate for interest cost and another for expected return on assets.

Recording the Components of the Net Pension Cost

We report the (a) service cost and (b) net interest cost/income in *net income* and (c) remeasurement costs in *OCI,* as each of those amounts occurs. By recording each component, we record the total pension expense. Remember, each component is a change in either plan assets (the return on assets) or the defined benefit obligation (all others), so as we record each component we also record its effect on plan assets and the defined benefit obligation, as follows:

We record (a) individual components of the net pension cost (in net income or OCI) and (b) the balance sheet accounts they affect.

To Record Net Pension Cost	($ in millions)	
Service cost	41	
DBO (service cost-2018)		41
DBO (past service cost: none in 2018)		0
Net interest cost [6% × ($400 − 300)]	6	
Plan assets (6% × $300: interest income)	18	
DBO (6% × $400: interest cost)		24
Plan assets (actual return in excess of 6%)	12	
Remeasurement gain on plan assets—OCI [(10% − 6%) × $300]		12
Remeasurement loss from change in assumption—OCI	23	
DBO (change in future salary estimate)		23

When Global adds its annual cash investment to its plan assets, the value of those plan assets increases by $48 million:

To Record Funding	($ in millions)	
Plan assets	48	
Cash (contribution to plan assets)		48

In our illustration, Global's retired employees were paid benefits of $38 million in 2018. Paying those benefits, of course, reduces the obligation to pay benefits (the DBO), and since the payments are made from the plan assets, that balance is reduced as well:

To Record Payment of Benefits	($ in millions)	
DBO	38	
Plan assets		38

Reporting the Components of the Net Pension Cost

We report the components of the total pension cost in the **statement of comprehensive income** as follows:

We report separately the three costs of having a defined benefit plan:

In net income:
- service cost
- net interest cost

In OCI:
- remeasurement cost

Revenue	$xxx
Operating expenses (including **$41 pension service cost**)	(xx)
Finance costs (including **$6 net interest cost on pensions**)	xx
Profit before tax	$xxx
Tax expense	(xx)
Net income	$xxx
Other comprehensive income	

(continued)

(concluded)

Remeasurement loss arising from change in pension assumption	$ 23
Remeasurement gain from the return on plan assets exceeding the interest rate	(12)
Comprehensive income	$xxx

Notice in the journal entries that we have no "pension expense" being recorded as we had using U.S. GAAP in the chapter. Instead, individual components of the net pension cost are recorded. The reason is that the amendment calls for components, not the net total, to be reported in the income statement and statement of comprehensive income.

PART E

Postretirement Benefits Other Than Pensions

LO17–9

As we just discussed, most companies have pension plans that provide for the future payments of retirement benefits to compensate employees for their current services. Many companies also furnish *other postretirement benefits* to their retired employees. These may include medical coverage, dental coverage, life insurance, group legal services, and other benefits. By far the most common is health care benefits. One of every three U.S. workers in medium- and large-size companies participates in health care plans that provide for coverage that continues into retirement. The aggregate impact is considerable; the total obligation for all U.S. corporations is about $500 billion.

Prior to 1993, employers accounted for postretirement benefit costs on a pay-as-you-go basis, meaning the expense each year was simply the amount of insurance premiums or medical claims paid, depending on the way the company provided health care benefits. The FASB revised GAAP to require a completely different approach. The expected future health care costs for retirees now must be recognized as an expense over the years necessary for employees to become entitled to the benefits.[23] This is the accrual basis that also is the basis for pension accounting.

In fact, accounting for postretirement benefits is similar in most respects to accounting for pension benefits. This is because the two forms of benefits are fundamentally similar. Each is a form of deferred compensation earned during the employee's service life and each can be estimated as the present value of the cost of providing the expected future benefits. General Motors described its plan as shown in Illustration 17–19.

Illustration 17–19
Disclosures—General Motors
Real World Financials

Note 5: Other Postretirement Benefits (in part)

The Corporation and certain of its domestic subsidiaries maintain hourly and salaried benefit plans that provide postretirement medical, dental, vision, and life insurance to retirees and eligible dependents. . . . [GAAP] requires that the cost of such benefits be recognized in the financial statements during the period employees provide service to the Corporation.

Despite the similarities, though, there are a few differences in the characteristics of the benefits that necessitate differences in accounting treatment. Because accounting for the two types of retiree benefits is so nearly the same, our discussion in this portion of the chapter will emphasize the differences. This will allow you to use what you learned earlier in the chapter regarding pension accounting as a foundation for learning how to account for other postretirement benefits, supplementing that common base only when necessary. Focusing on the differences also will reinforce your understanding of pension accounting.

[23]ASB ASC 715–60: Compensation–Retirement Benefits–Defined Benefit Plans–Postretirement (previously "Employers' Accounting for Postretirement Benefits Other Than Pensions," *Statement of Financial Accounting Standards No. 106* (Norwalk, Conn.: FASB, 1990)). The Standard became effective (with some exceptions) in 1993.

What Is a Postretirement Benefit Plan?

Before addressing the accounting ramifications, let's look at a typical retiree health care plan.[24] First, it's important to distinguish retiree health care benefits from health care benefits provided during an employee's working years. The annual cost of providing *preretirement* benefits is simply part of the annual compensation expense. However, many companies offer coverage that continues into retirement. It is the deferred aspect of these *postretirement* benefits that creates an accounting issue.

Eligibility usually is based on age and/or years of service.

Usually a plan promises benefits in exchange for services performed over a designated number of years, or reaching a particular age, or both. For instance, a plan might specify that employees are eligible for postretirement benefits after both working 20 years and reaching age 62 while in service. Eligibility requirements and the nature of benefits usually are specified by a written plan, or sometimes only by company practice.

Postretirement Health Benefits and Pension Benefits Compared

Keep in mind that retiree health benefits differ fundamentally from pension benefits in some important respects:

1. The amount of *pension* benefits generally is based on the number of years an employee works for the company so that the longer the employee works, the higher are the benefits. On the other hand, the amount of *postretirement health care* benefits typically is unrelated to service. It's usually an all-or-nothing plan in which a certain level of coverage is promised upon retirement, independent of the length of service beyond that necessary for eligibility.
2. Although coverage might be identical, the cost of providing the coverage might vary significantly from retiree to retiree and from year to year because of differing medical needs.
3. Postretirement health care plans often require the retiree to share in the cost of coverage through monthly contribution payments. For instance, a company might pay 80% of insurance premiums, with the retiree paying 20%. The net cost of providing coverage is reduced by these contributions as well as by any portion of the cost paid by Medicare or other insurance.
4. Coverage often is provided to spouses and eligible dependents.

Determining the Net Cost of Benefits

To determine the postretirement benefit obligation and the postretirement benefit expense, the company's actuary first must make estimates of what the postretirement benefit costs will be for current employees. Then, as illustrated in Illustration 17–20, contributions to those costs by employees are deducted, as well as Medicare's share of the costs (for retirement years when the retiree will be 65 or older), to determine the estimated net cost of benefits to the employer:

Illustration 17–20

Estimating the Net Cost of Benefits

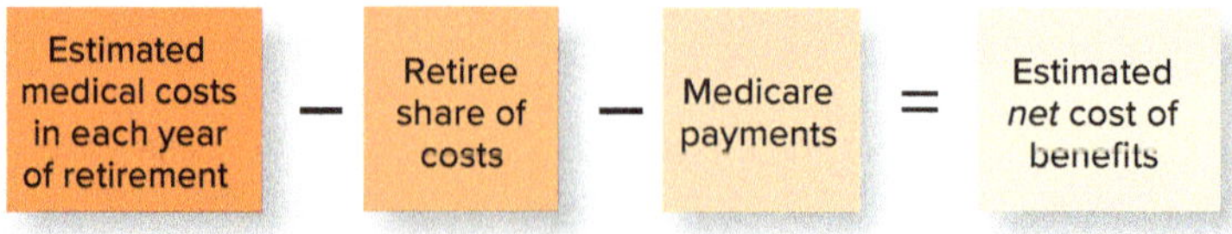

Remember, postretirement health care benefits are anticipated actual costs of providing the promised health care, rather than an amount estimated by a defined benefit formula. This makes these estimates inherently more intricate, particularly because health care costs in general are notoriously difficult to forecast. And, since postretirement health care benefits are partially paid by the retiree and by Medicare, these cost-sharing amounts must be estimated as well.

---

[24]For convenience, our discussion focuses on health care benefits because these are by far the most common type of postretirement benefits other than pensions. But the concepts we discuss apply equally to other forms of postretirement benefits.

On the other hand, estimating postretirement benefits costs is similar in many ways to estimating pension costs. Both estimates entail a variety of assumptions to be made by the company's actuary. Many of these assumptions are the same; for instance, both require estimates of:

Many of the assumptions needed to estimate postretirement health care benefits are the same as those needed to estimate pension benefits.

1. A discount rate
2. Expected return on plan assets (if the plan is funded)
3. Employee turnover
4. Expected retirement age
5. Expected compensation increases (if the plan is pay-related)
6. Expected age of death
7. Number and ages of beneficiaries and dependents

Of course, the relative importance of some estimates is different from that for pension plans. Dependency status, turnover, and retirement age, for example, take on much greater significance. Also, additional assumptions become necessary as a result of differences between pension plans and other postretirement benefit plans. Specifically, it's necessary to estimate:

Some additional assumptions are needed to estimate postretirement health care benefits besides those needed to estimate pension benefits.

1. The current cost of providing health care benefits at each age that participants might receive benefits
2. Demographic characteristics of plan participants that might affect the amount and timing of benefits
3. Benefit coverage provided by Medicare, other insurance, or other sources that will reduce the net cost of employer-provided benefits
4. The expected health care cost trend rate[25]

Taking these assumptions into account, the company's actuary estimates what the net cost of postretirement benefits will be for current employees in each year of their expected retirement. The discounted present value of those costs is the expected postretirement benefit obligation.

The postretirement benefit obligation is the discounted present value of the benefits during retirement.

Postretirement Benefit Obligation

LO17–10

There are two related obligation amounts. As indicated in Illustration 17–21, one measures the total obligation and the other refers to a specific portion of the total:

1. **Expected Postretirement Benefit Obligation (EPBO):** The actuary's estimate of the total postretirement benefits (at their discounted present value) expected to be received by plan participants.
2. **Accumulated Postretirement Benefit Obligation (APBO):** The portion of the EPBO attributed to employee service to date.

Illustration 17–21
Two Views of the Obligation for Postretirement Benefits Other Than Pensions

The accumulated postretirement benefit obligation (APBO) is analogous to the projected benefit obligation (PBO) for pensions. Like the PBO, the APBO is reported in the balance sheet only to the extent that it exceeds plan assets.

Measuring the Obligation

To illustrate, assume the actuary estimates that the net cost of providing health care benefits to Jessica Farrow (our illustration employee from earlier in the chapter) during her retirement years has a present value of $10,842 as of the end of 2016. This is the EPBO. If the

[25]Health care cost trend rates recently reported have ranged from 3% to 8.7%, with 7% being the most commonly assumed rate. (Pension/OPEB 2015 Assumption and Disclosure Survey, PWC, 2015).

benefits (and therefore the costs) relate to an estimated 35 years of service and 10 of those years have been completed, the APBO would be:[26]

$3,098 represents the portion of the EPBO related to the first 10 years of the 35-year service period.

$10,842	×	10⁄35	=	$3,098
EPBO		Fraction attributed to service to date		APBO

If the assumed discount rate is 6%, a year later the EPBO will have grown to $11,493 simply because of a year's interest accruing at that rate ($10,842 × 1.06 = $11,493). Notice that there is no increase in the EPBO for service because, unlike the obligation in most pension plans, the total obligation is not increased by an additional year's service.

The APBO, however, is the portion of the EPBO related to service up to a particular date. Consequently, the APBO will have increased both because of interest and because the service fraction will be higher (service cost):

$3,612 represents the portion of the EPBO related to the first 11 years of the 35-year service period.

$11,493	×	11⁄35	=	$3,612
EPBO		Fraction attributed to service to date		APBO

The two elements of the increase in 2017 can be separated as follows:

The APBO increases each year due to (a) interest accrued on the APBO and (b) the portion of the EPBO attributed to that year.

APBO at the beginning of the year	$3,098
Interest cost: $3,098 × 6%	186
Service cost: ($11,493 × 1⁄35) portion of EPBO attributed to the year	328
APBO at the end of the year	$3,612

Attribution

Attribution is the process of assigning the cost of benefits to the years during which those benefits are assumed to be earned by employees. We accomplish this by assigning an equal fraction of the EPBO to each year of service from the employee's date of hire to the employee's full eligibility date.[27] This is the date the employee has performed all the service necessary to have earned all the retiree benefits estimated to be received by the employee.[28] In our earlier example, we assumed the attribution period was 35 years and accordingly accrued 1⁄35 of the EPBO each year. The amount accrued each year increases both the APBO and the postretirement benefit expense. In Illustration 17–22 we see how the 35-year attribution (accrual) period was determined.

The attribution period does not include years of service beyond the full eligibility date even if the employee is expected to work after that date.

Some critics of this approach feel there is a fundamental inconsistency between the way we measure the benefits and the way we assign the benefits to specific service periods. The benefits (EPBO) are measured with the concession that the employee may work beyond the full eligibility date; however, the attribution period does not include years of service after that date. The counterargument is the fact that at the full eligibility date the employee will have earned the right to receive the full benefits expected under the plan and the amount of the benefits will not increase with service beyond that date.[29]

Accounting for Postretirement Benefit Plans Other Than Pensions

● LO17–11

We account for pensions and for other postretirement benefits essentially the same way.

As we just discussed, it's necessary to attribute a portion of the accumulated postretirement benefit obligation to each year as the service cost for that year as opposed to measuring the actual benefits employees earn during the year as we did for pension plans. That's due to the

[26]Assigning the costs to particular service years is referred to as the *attribution* of the costs to the years the benefits are assumed earned. We discuss attribution in the next section.

[27]If the plan specifically grants credit only for service from a date after employee's date of hire, the beginning of the attribution period is considered to be the beginning of that credited service period, rather than the employee's date of hire.

[28]Or any beneficiaries and covered dependents.

[29]FASB ASC 715–60: Compensation–Retirement Benefits–Defined Benefit Plans–Other Postretirement (previously "Employers' Accounting for Postretirement Benefits Other Than Pensions," *Statement of Financial Accounting Standards No. 106* (Norwalk, Conn.: FASB, 1990), par. 219–239. These specific paragraphs are not codified in the FASB Research System as they contain bases for conclusions and are therefore what codifiers consider "nonessential" material.

Jessica Farrow was hired by Global Communications at age 22 at the beginning of 2007 and is expected to retire at the end of 2046 at age 61. The retirement period is estimated to be 20 years.*

Global's employees are eligible for postretirement health care benefits after both reaching age 56 while in service and having worked 20 years.

Since Farrow becomes fully eligible at age 56 (the end of 2041), retiree benefits are attributed to the 35-year period from her date of hire through that date. Graphically, the situation can be described as follows:

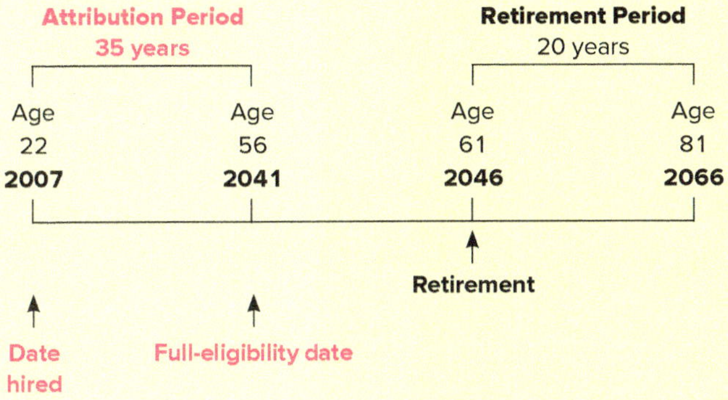

*You probably recognize this as the situation used earlier in the chapter to illustrate pension accounting.

Illustration 17–22

Determining the Attribution Period

The attribution period spans each year of service from the employee's date of hire to the employee's full eligibility date.

fundamental nature of these other postretirement plans under which employees are ineligible for benefits until specific eligibility criteria are met, at which time they become 100% eligible. This contrasts with pension plans under which employees earn additional benefits each year until they retire.

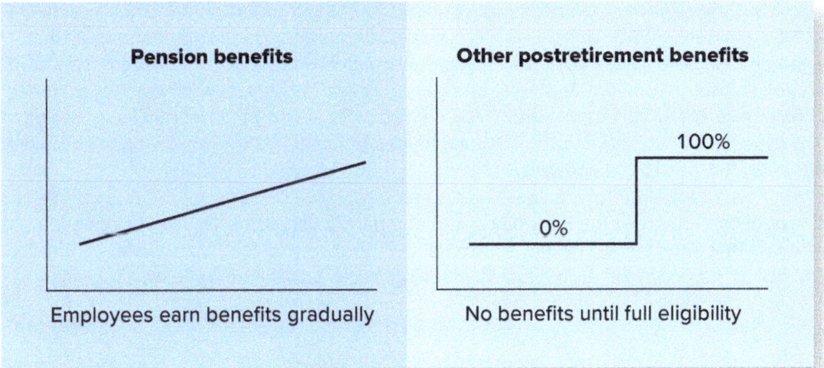

Illustration 17–23

Measuring Service Cost

Measuring the service cost differs, though, due to a fundamental difference in the way employees acquire benefits under the two types of plans.

The way we measure service cost is the primary difference between accounting for pensions and for other postretirement benefits. Otherwise, though, accounting for the two is virtually identical. For example, a company with an underfunded postretirement benefit plan with existing prior service cost and net loss–AOCI would record the following journal entries annually:

We record the annual expense and funding for other postretirement benefit plans the same way we do for pensions.

To Record Postretirement Benefit Expense		
Postretirement benefit expense (total)	xx	
Plan assets (expected return on assets)	xx	
Amortization of net gain—OCI (current amortization)	xx	
APBO (service cost + interest cost)		xx
Amortization of net loss—OCI (current amortization)		xx
Amortization of prior service cost—OCI* (current amortization)		xx

(continued)

(concluded)

To Record Cash Funding of Plan Assets		
Plan assets	xx	
Cash (contribution to plan assets)		xx
To Record Gains and Losses		
Loss—OCI (from change in assumption)	xx	
APBO		xx
or		
APBO	xx	
Gain—OCI (from change in assumption)		xx
Plan assets	xx	
Gain—OCI (actual return on assets − expected return)		xx
or		
Loss—OCI (expected return on assets − actual return)	xx	
Plan assets		xx

*The prior service cost for other postretirement benefits is amortized over the average remaining time until "full eligibility" for employees rather than until retirement, as is the case for pension plans. This is consistent with recording "regular" service cost over the time to full eligibility.

We record losses and gains (as well as any new prior service cost should it occur) the same way we do for pensions.

Ethical Dilemma

Earlier this year, you were elected to the board of directors of Champion International, Inc. Champion has offered its employees postretirement health care benefits for 35 years. The practice of extending health care benefits to retirees began modestly. Most employees retired after age 65, when most benefits were covered by Medicare. Costs also were lower because life expectancies were shorter and medical care was less expensive. Because costs were so low, little attention was paid to accounting for these benefits. The company simply recorded an expense when benefits were provided to retirees. The FASB changed all that. Now, the obligation for these benefits must be anticipated and reported in the annual report. Worse yet, the magnitude of the obligation has grown enormously, almost unnoticed. Health care costs have soared in recent years. Medical technology and other factors have extended life expectancies. Of course, the value to employees of this benefit has grown parallel to the growth of the burden to the company.

Without being required to anticipate future costs, many within Champion's management were caught by surprise at the enormity of the company's obligation. Equally disconcerting was the fact that such a huge liability now must be exposed to public view. Now you find that several board members are urging the dismantling of the postretirement plan altogether.

A Comprehensive Illustration

We assumed earlier that the EPBO at the end of 2016 was determined by the actuary to be $10,842. This was the present value on that date of all anticipated future benefits. Then we noted that the EPBO at the end of the next year would have grown by 6% to $11,493. This amount, too, would represent the present value of the same anticipated future benefits, but as of a year later. The APBO, remember, is the portion of the EPBO attributed to service performed to a particular date. So, we determined the APBO at the end of 2017 to be $11,493 × $^{11}/_{35}$, or $3,612. We determined the $328 service cost noted earlier for 2017 as the portion of the EPBO attributed to that year: $11,493 × $^{1}/_{35}$.

Now, let's review our previous discussion of how the EPBO, the APBO, and the postretirement benefit expense are determined by calculating those amounts a year later, at the end of 2018. Before doing so, however, we can anticipate (a) the EPBO to be $11,493 × 1.06, or $12,182, (b) the APBO to be $^{12}/_{35}$ of that amount, or $4,177, and (c) the 2018 service cost to be $^{1}/_{35}$ of that amount, or $348. In Illustration 17–24 we see if our expectations are borne out by direct calculation.

Illustration 17–24

Determining the Postretirement Benefit Obligation

Assume the actuary has estimated the net cost of retiree benefits in each year of Jessica Farrow's 20-year expected retirement period to be the amounts shown in the calculation below. She is fully eligible for benefits at the end of 2041 and is expected to retire at the end of 2046.

Calculating the APBO and the postretirement benefit expense at the end of 2018, 12 years after being hired, begins with estimating the EPBO. Steps to calculate (a) the EPBO, (b) the APBO, and (c) the annual service cost at the end of 2018, 12 years after being hired, are:

(a). 1. Estimate the cost of retiree benefits in each year of the expected retirement period and deduct anticipated Medicare reimbursements and retiree cost-sharing to derive the net cost to the employer in each year of the expected retirement period.
2. Find the present value of each year's net benefit cost as of the retirement date.
3. Find the present value of the total net benefit cost as of the current date. This is the **EPBO**.

(b). Multiply the EPBO by the attribution factor (service to date/total attribution period). This is the **APBO**. The **service cost** in any year is simply one year's worth of the EPBO.

(c). Multiply the EPBO by 1/total attribution period.

The EPBO is the discounted present value of the total benefits expected to be earned.

The fraction of the EPBO considered to be earned this year is the service cost.

The fraction of the EPBO considered to be earned so far is the APBO.

The steps are demonstrated in Illustration 17–24A.

Illustration 17–24A

EPBO, APBO, and Service Cost in 2016

(a.1). Actuary estimates the net cost of benefits paid during retirement years:

(a.2). Present value [n = 1, 2, 3, 4, . . . 19, 20: i = 6%] of the net benefits as of the retirement date:

Year	Age	Net Benefit	Present Value at 2046
2047	62	5,000	$ 4,717
2048	63	5,600	4,984
2049	64	6,300	5,290
2050	65	3,000	2,376
~	~	~	~
2065	80	9,550	3,156
2066	81	10,300	3,212
			$62,269

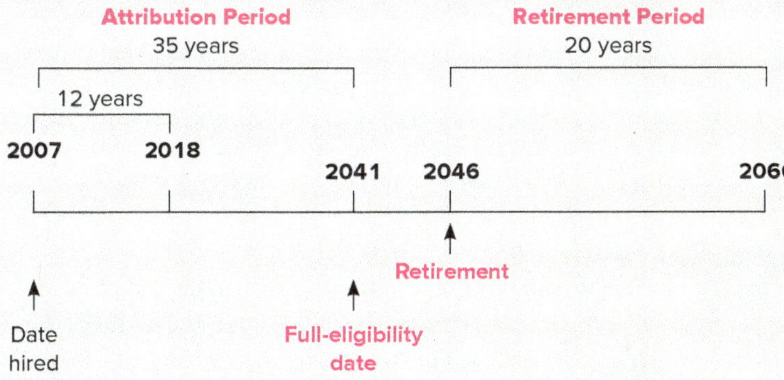

(a.3). Present value (n = 28, i = 6%) of postretirement benefits at 2018 is
$62,269 × 0.19563 = **$12,182** (EPBO)
(b). $12,182 × 12/35 = **$4,177** (APBO)
(c). $12,182 × 1/35 = **$348** (Service Cost)

The actuary estimates the net cost to the employer in each year the retiree is expected to receive benefits.

As of the retirement date, the lump-sum equivalent of the expected yearly costs is $62,269.

The EPBO in 2018 is the present value of those benefits.

The APBO is the portion of the EPBO attributed to service to date.

The service cost is the portion of the EPBO attributed to a particular year's service.

Decision Makers' Perspective

Postretirement benefit amounts reported in the disclosure notes fill a reporting gap left by the minimal disclosures in the primary financial statements.

When they analyze financial statements, investors and creditors should be wary of the non-standard way companies report pension and other postretirement information. Recall that in the balance sheet, firms do not separately report the benefit obligation and the plan assets. Also, companies have considerable latitude in making the several assumptions needed to estimate the components of postretirement benefit plans. Fortunately, information provided in the disclosure notes makes up for some of the deficiency in balance sheet information and makes it possible for interested analysts to modify their analysis. As for pensions, the choices companies make for the discount rate, expected return on plan assets, and the compensation growth rate can greatly impact postretirement benefit expense and earnings quality. The disclosures required are very similar to pension disclosures. In fact, disclosures for the two types of retiree benefits typically are combined.[30] Disclosures include:

- Descriptions of the plans.
- Estimates of the obligations (PBO, ABO, vested benefit obligation, EPBO, and APBO).
- The percentage of total plan assets for each major category of assets (equity securities, debt securities, real estate, other) as well as a description of investment strategies, including any target asset allocations and risk management practices.
- A breakdown of the components of the annual pension and postretirement benefit expenses for the years reported.
- The discount rates, the assumed rate of compensation increases used to measure the PBO, the expected long-term rate of return on plan assets, and the expected rate of increase in future medical and dental benefit costs.
- Estimated benefit payments presented separately for the next five years and in the aggregate for years 6–10.
- Estimate of expected contributions to fund the plan for the next year.
- (a) Any changes to the net gain or net loss and prior service cost arising during the period, (b) the accumulated amounts of these components of accumulated other comprehensive income, and (c) the amounts of those balances expected to be amortized in the next year.
- Other information to make it possible for interested analysts to reconstruct the financial statements with plan assets and liabilities included.

Concept Review Exercise

OTHER POSTRETIREMENT BENEFITS

Technology Group, Inc., has an unfunded retiree health care plan. The actuary estimates the net cost of providing health care benefits to a particular employee during his retirement years to have a present value of $24,000 as of the end of 2018 (the EPBO). The benefits, and therefore the expected postretirement benefit obligation, relate to an estimated 36 years of service, and 12 of those years have been completed. The interest rate is 6%.

Required:

Pertaining to the one employee only:

1. What is the accumulated postretirement benefit obligation at the end of 2018?
2. What is the expected postretirement benefit obligation at the end of 2019?
3. What is the service cost to be included in 2019 postretirement benefit expense?
4. What is the interest cost to be included in 2019 postretirement benefit expense?
5. What is the accumulated postretirement benefit obligation at the end of 2019?

[30]FASB ASC 715–60–50: Compensation–Retirement Benefits–Defined Benefit Plans–Other Postretirement–Disclosure (previously "Employers' Disclosures about Pensions and Other Postretirement Benefits," *Statement of Financial Accounting Standards No. 132* (Stamford, Conn.: FASB, 1998).

6. Show how the APBO changed during 2019 by reconciling the beginning and ending balances.
7. What is the 2019 postretirement benefit expense, assuming no net gains or losses and no prior service cost?

Solution:

1. What is the accumulated postretirement benefit obligation at the end of 2018?

$24,000	×	12/36	=	$8,000
EPBO 2018		Fraction earned		APBO 2018

2. What is the expected postretirement benefit obligation at the end of 2019?

$24,000	×	1.06	=	$25,440
EPBO 2018		To accrue interest		EPBO 2019

3. What is the service cost to be included in 2019 postretirement benefit expense?

$25,440	×	1/36	=	$707
EPBO 2019		Attributed to 2019		Service cost

4. What is the interest cost to be included in 2019 postretirement benefit expense?

$8,000 (beginning APBO) × 6% = $480

5. What is the accumulated postretirement benefit obligation at the end of 2019?

$25,440	×	13/36	=	$9,187
EPBO 2019		Fraction attributed to service to date		APBO 2019

6. Show how the APBO changed during 2019 by reconciling the beginning and ending balances.

APBO at the beginning of 2019 (from req. 1)	$8,000
Service cost (from req. 3)	707
Interest cost (from req. 4)	480
APBO at the end of 2019 (from req. 5)	$9,187

7. What is the 2019 postretirement benefit expense, assuming no net gains or losses and no prior service cost?

Service cost	$ 707
Interest cost	480
Actual return on the plan assets	(not funded)
Adjusted for: gain or loss on the plan assets	(not funded)
Amortization of prior service cost	none
Amortization of net gain or loss	none
Postretirement benefit expense	$1,187

Financial Reporting Case Solution

© Stockbyte/PunchStock

1. **Why is pension plan underfunding not a concern in your present employment?** *(p. 971)* In a defined contribution plan, the employer is not obliged to provide benefits beyond the annual contribution to the employees' plan. No liability is created. Unlike retirement benefits paid in a defined benefit plan, the employee's retirement benefits in a defined contribution plan are totally dependent on how well invested assets perform in the marketplace.
2. **Were you correct that the pension liability is not reported in the balance sheet? What is the liability?** *(p. 973)* Yes and no. The pension liability is not reported separately in the balance sheet. It is, however, combined with pension assets with the net difference reported in the balance sheet. The separate balance is disclosed, though, in the notes. For United Dynamics, the PBO at the end of 2018 is $2,628 million.
3. **What is the amount of the plan assets available to pay benefits? What are the factors that can cause that amount to change?** *(p. 979)* The plan assets at the end of 2018 total $2,807 million. A trustee accepts employer contributions, invests the contributions, accumulates the earnings on the investments, and pays benefits from the plan assets. So the amount is increased each year by employer cash contributions and (hopefully) a return on assets invested. It is decreased by amounts paid out to retired employees.
4. **What does the "pension asset" represent? Are you interviewing with a company whose pension plan is severely underfunded?** *(p. 981)* The pension asset is not the plan assets available to pay pension benefits. Instead, it's the net difference between those assets and the pension obligation. United Dynamics' plan assets exceed the pension obligation in each year presented, and therefore it is one of the few companies whose pension plan is overfunded.
5. **How is the pension expense influenced by changes in the pension liability and plan assets?** *(p. 982)* The pension expense reported on the income statement is a composite of periodic changes that occur in both the pension obligation and the plan assets. For United Dynamics in 2018, the pension expense included the service cost and interest cost, which are changes in the PBO, and the return on plan assets. It also included an amortized portion of prior service costs (a previous change in the PBO) and of net gains (gains and losses result from changes in both the PBO and plan assets). ●

The Bottom Line

- **LO17–1** Pension plans are arrangements designed to provide income to individuals during their retirement years. *Defined contribution* plans promise fixed annual contributions to a pension fund, without further commitment regarding benefit amounts at retirement. *Defined benefit* plans promise fixed retirement benefits defined by a designated formula. The employer sets aside cash each year to provide sufficient funds to pay promised benefits. (*p. 968*)
- **LO17–2** The *accumulated benefit obligation* is an estimate of the discounted present value of the retirement benefits earned so far by employees, applying the plan's pension formula to *existing* compensation levels. The vested benefit obligation is the portion of the accumulated benefit obligation that plan participants are entitled to receive regardless of their continued employment. The *projected benefit obligation* estimates retirement benefits by applying the pension formula to *projected future* compensation levels. (*p. 973*)
- **LO17–3** The PBO can change due to the accumulation of *service cost* from year to year, the accrual of *interest* as time passes, making plan amendments retroactive to prior years (prior service cost), and periodic adjustments when estimates change (gains and losses). The obligation is reduced as benefits actually are paid to retired employees. (*p. 974*)
- **LO17–4** The plan assets consist of the accumulated balance of the annual employer contributions plus the return on the investments less benefits paid to retirees. (*p. 979*)

- **LO17–5** The difference between an employer's obligation (PBO for pensions, APBO for other postretirement benefit plans) and the resources available to satisfy that obligation (plan assets) is the funded status of the pension plan. The employer must report the "funded status" of the plan in the balance sheet as a net pension liability if the obligation exceeds the plan assets or as a net pension asset if the plan assets exceed the obligation. *(p. 981)*
- **LO17–6** The pension expense is a composite of periodic changes in both the projected benefit obligation and the plan assets. Service cost is the increase in the PBO attributable to employee service and is the primary component of pension expense. The interest and return-on-assets components are financial items created only because the pension payment is delayed and the obligation is funded currently. Prior service cost is recognized over employees' future service period. Also, neither a loss (gain) on the PBO nor a loss (gain) on plan assets is immediately recognized in pension expense; they are recognized on a delayed basis to achieve income smoothing. *(p. 981)*
- **LO17–7** Recording pension expense causes the net pension liability/asset to change by the service cost, the interest cost, and the expected return on plan assets. Any amortization amounts included in the expense will reduce the *accumulated other comprehensive income* balances being amortized, e.g., net loss—AOCI and prior service cost—AOCI. Similarly, the plan assets are increased by the annual cash investment. New losses and gains (as well as any new prior service cost should it occur) are recognized as other comprehensive income. *(p. 986)*
- **LO17–8** The various elements of a pension plan—projected benefit obligation, plan assets, prior service cost, gains and losses, pension expense, and the funded status of the plan—are interrelated. One way to see how each element relates to the other is to bring each part together in a *pension spreadsheet. (p. 992)*
- **LO17–9** Accounting for postretirement benefits is similar in most respects to accounting for pension benefits. Like pensions, other postretirement benefits are a form of deferred compensation. Unlike pensions, their cost is attributed to the years from the employee's date of hire to the full eligibility date. *(p. 997)*
- **LO17–10** The expected postretirement benefit obligation (EPBO) is the actuary's estimate of the total postretirement benefits (at their discounted present value) expected to be received by plan participants. The accumulated postretirement benefit obligation (APBO) is the portion of the EPBO attributed to employee service to date. *(p. 999)*
- **LO17–11** The components of postretirement benefit expense are essentially the same as those for pension expense. *(p. 1000)*
- **LO17–12** Under both U.S. GAAP and IFRS we report all changes in the obligation and in the value of plan assets as they occur. The ways the changes are determined and reported are different, though, for some of the changes. The changes that constitute the components of the net pension cost are reported separately as (a) the service cost, (b) the net interest cost/income, and (c) remeasurement gains or losses. Under IFRS, *past service cost* is combined with current service cost and reported as service cost within the income statement rather than as a component of other comprehensive income as it is under U.S. GAAP. Under IFRS, gains and losses are not recycled from other comprehensive income as is required under U.S. GAAP (when the accumulated net gain or net loss exceeds the 10% threshold). Also, the interest cost and return on plan assets are replaced by net interest cost/income (interest rate times the difference between the DBO and plan assets). *(pp. 987, 989, 993,* and *995)*

APPENDIX 17

Service Method of Allocating Prior Service Cost

When amortizing prior service cost, our objective is to match the cost with employee service. The straight-line method described in this chapter allocates an equal amount of the prior service cost to each year of the 15-year average service period of affected employees. But consider this: fewer of the affected employees will be working for the company toward the end of that period than at the beginning. Some probably will retire or quit in each year following the amendment.

An allocation approach that reflects the declining service pattern is called the **service method**. This method allocates the prior service cost to each year in proportion to the fraction of the total remaining service years worked in each of those years. To do this, it's necessary to estimate how many of the 2,000 employees working at the beginning of 2017 when the amendment is made will still be employed in each year after the amendment.

Let's suppose, for example, that the actuary estimates that a declining number of these employees still will be employed in each of the next 28 years as indicated in the abbreviated schedule below. The portion of the prior service cost amortized to pension expense each year is $60 million times a declining fraction. Each year's fraction is that year's service divided by the 28-year total (30,000). This is demonstrated in Illustration 17A–1.

Illustration 17A–1

Service Method of Amortizing Prior Service Cost

By the service method, prior service cost is recognized each year in proportion to the fraction of the total remaining service years worked that year.

Year	Number of Employees Still Employed (assumed for the illustration)	Fraction of Total Service Years		Prior Service Cost ($ in millions)		Amount Cost Amortized ($ in millions)
2017	2,000	2,000/30,000	×	$60	=	$ 4.0
2018	2,000	2,000/30,000	×	60	=	4.0
2019	1,850	1,850/30,000	×	60	=	3.7
2020	1,700	1,700/30,000	×	60	=	3.4
2021	1,550	1,550/30,000	×	60	=	3.1
—	—	—	×	—	=	—
2042	400	400/30,000	×	60	=	0.8
2043	250	250/30,000	×	60	=	0.5
2044	100	100/30,000	×	60	=	0.2
Totals	30,000	30,000/30,000				$60.0
	Total number of service years					Total amount amortized

Conceptually, the service method achieves a better matching of the cost and benefits. In fact, this is the FASB's recommended approach. However, GAAP permits the consistent use of any method that amortizes the prior service cost at least as quickly.[31] The straight-line method meets this condition and is the approach most often used in practice. In our illustration, the cost is completely amortized over 15 years rather than the 28 years required by the service method. The 15-year average service life is simply the total estimated service years divided by the total number of employees in the group:

The service method amortized an equal amount *per employee* each year.

30,000 years	÷	2,000	=	15 years
Total number of service years		Total number of employees		Average service years

Questions For Review of Key Topics

Q 17–1 What is a pension plan? What motivates a corporation to offer a pension plan for its employees?

Q 17–2 Qualified pension plans offer important tax benefits. What is the special tax treatment and what qualifies a pension plan for these benefits?

Q 17–3 Lamont Corporation has a pension plan in which the corporation makes all contributions and employees receive benefits at retirement based on the balance in their accumulated pension fund. What type of pension plan does Lamont have?

Q 17–4 What is the vested benefit obligation?

Q 17–5 Differentiate between the accumulated benefit obligation and the projected benefit obligation.

Q 17–6 Name five events that might change the balance of the PBO.

Q 17–7 Name three events that might change the balance of the plan assets.

[31]FASB ASC 715–30–35–13: Compensation–Retirement Benefits–Defined Benefit Plans–Pension–Subsequent Measurement–Prior Service Costs (previously "Employers' Accounting for Pensions," *Statement of Financial Accounting Standards No. 87* (Stamford, Conn.: FASB, 1985), par. 26).

Q 17–8 What are the components that might be included in the calculation of net pension cost recognized for a period by an employer sponsoring a defined benefit pension plan?

Q 17–9 Define the service cost component of the periodic pension expense.

Q 17–10 Define the interest cost component of the periodic pension expense.

Q 17–11 The return on plan assets is the increase in plan assets (at fair value), adjusted for contributions to the plan and benefits paid during the period. How is the return included in the calculation of the periodic pension expense?

Q 17–12 Define prior service cost. How is it reported in the financial statements? How is it included in pension expense?

Q 17–13 How should gains or losses related to pension plan assets be recognized? How does this treatment compare to that for gains or losses related to the pension obligation?

Q 17–14 Is a company's PBO reported in the balance sheet? Its plan assets? Explain.

Q 17–15 What two components of pension expense may be negative (i.e., reduce pension expense)?

Q 17–16 Which are the components of pension expense that involve delayed recognition?

Q 17–17 Evaluate this statement: The excess of the actual return on plan assets over the expected return decreases the employer's pension cost.

Q 17–18 When accounting for pension costs, how should the payment into the pension fund be recorded? How does it affect the funded status of the plan?

Q 17–19 TFC Inc. revises its estimate of future salary levels, causing its PBO estimate to increase by $3 million. How is the $3 million reflected in TFC's financial statements?

Q 17–20 A pension plan is underfunded when the employer's obligation (PBO) exceeds the resources available to satisfy that obligation (plan assets) and overfunded when the opposite is the case. How is this funded status reported on the balance sheet if plan assets exceed the PBO? If the PBO exceeds plan assets?

Q 17–21 What are two ways to measure the obligation for postretirement benefits other than pensions? Define these measurement approaches.

Q 17–22 How are the costs of providing postretirement benefits other than pensions expensed?

Q 17–23 The components of postretirement benefit expense are similar to the components of pension expense. In what fundamental way does the service cost component differ between these two expenses?

Q 17–24 The EPBO for Branch Industries at the end of 2018 was determined by the actuary to be $20,000 as it relates to employee Will Lawson. Lawson was hired at the beginning of 2004. He will be fully eligible to retire with health care benefits after 15 more years but is expected to retire in 25 years. What is the APBO as it relates to Will Lawson?

IFRS **Q 17–25** The income statement of Mid-South Logistics includes $12 million for amortized prior service cost. Does Mid-South Logistics prepare its financial statements according to U.S. GAAP or IFRS? Explain.

IFRS **Q 17–26** How do U.S. GAAP and IFRS differ with regard to reporting gains and losses from changing assumptions used to measure the pension obligation?

Brief Exercises

connect

BE 17–1
Changes in the projected benefit obligation
● LO17–3

The projected benefit obligation was $80 million at the beginning of the year. Service cost for the year was $10 million. At the end of the year, pension benefits paid by the trustee were $6 million and there were no pension-related other comprehensive income accounts requiring amortization. The actuary's discount rate was 5%. What was the amount of the projected benefit obligation at year-end?

BE 17–2
Changes in the projected benefit obligation
● LO17–3

The projected benefit obligation was $80 million at the beginning of the year and $85 million at the end of the year. At the end of the year, pension benefits paid by the trustee were $6 million and there were no pension-related other comprehensive income accounts requiring amortization. The actuary's discount rate was 5%. What was the amount of the service cost for the year?

BE 17–3
Changes in the projected benefit obligation
● LO17–3

The projected benefit obligation was $80 million at the beginning of the year and $85 million at the end of the year. Service cost for the year was $10 million. At the end of the year, there was no prior service cost and a negligible net loss–AOCI. The actuary's discount rate was 5%. What was the amount of the retiree benefits paid by the trustee?

BE 17–4
Changes in the projected benefit obligation
● LO17–3

The projected benefit obligation was $80 million at the beginning of the year and $85 million at the end of the year. Service cost for the year was $10 million. At the end of the year, pension benefits paid by the trustee were $6 million. The actuary's discount rate was 5%. At the end of the year, the actuary revised the estimate of the percentage rate of increase in compensation levels in upcoming years. What was the amount of the gain or loss the estimate change caused?

BE 17–5
Changes in pension plan assets
● LO17–4

Pension plan assets were $80 million at the beginning of the year. The return on plan assets was 5%. At the end of the year, retiree benefits paid by the trustee were $6 million and cash invested in the pension fund was $7 million. What was the amount of the pension plan assets at year-end?

BE 17–6
Changes in pension plan assets
● LO17–4

Pension plan assets were $80 million at the beginning of the year and $83 million at the end of the year. The return on plan assets was 5%. At the end of the year, cash invested in the pension fund was $7 million. What was the amount of the retiree benefits paid by the trustee?

BE 17–7
Changes in pension plan assets
● LO17–4

Pension plan assets were $100 million at the beginning of the year and $104 million at the end of the year. At the end of the year, retiree benefits paid by the trustee were $6 million and cash invested in the pension fund was $7 million. What was the percentage rate of return on plan assets?

BE 17–8
Reporting the funded status of pension plans
● LO17–5

JDS Foods' projected benefit obligation, accumulated benefit obligation, and plan assets were $40 million, $30 million, and $25 million, respectively, at the end of the year. What, if any, pension liability must be reported in the balance sheet? What would JDS report if the plan assets were $45 million instead?

BE 17–9
Pension expense
● LO17–6

The projected benefit obligation was $80 million at the beginning of the year. Service cost for the year was $10 million. At the end of the year, pension benefits paid by the trustee were $6 million and there were no pension-related other comprehensive income accounts requiring amortization. The actuary's discount rate was 5%. The actual return on plan assets was $5 million although it was expected to be only $4 million. What was the pension expense for the year?

BE 17–10
Pension expense; prior service cost
● LO17–6

The pension plan was amended last year, creating a prior service cost of $20 million. Service cost and interest cost for the year were $10 million and $4 million, respectively. At the end of the year, there was a negligible balance in the net gain–pensions account. The actual return on plan assets was $4 million although it was expected to be $6 million. On average, employees' remaining service life with the company is 10 years. What was the pension expense for the year?

BE 17–11
Net gain
● LO17–6

The projected benefit obligation and plan assets were $80 million and $100 million, respectively, at the beginning of the year. Due primarily to favorable stock market performance in recent years, there also was a net gain of $30 million. On average, employees' remaining service life with the company is 10 years. As a result of the net gain, what was the increase or decrease in pension expense for the year?

BE 17–12
Recording pension expense
● LO17–7

The Warren Group's pension expense is $67 million. This amount includes a $70 million service cost, a $50 million interest cost, a $55 million reduction for the expected return on plan assets, and a $2 million amortization of a prior service cost. How is the net pension liability affected when the pension expense is recorded?

BE 17–13
Recording pension expense
● LO17–7

Andrews Medical reported a net loss–AOCI in last year's balance sheet. This year, the company revised its estimate of future salary levels causing its PBO estimate to decline by $4 million. Also, the $8 million actual return on plan assets fell short of the $9 million expected return. How does this gain and loss affect Andrews' income statement, statement of comprehensive income, and balance sheet?

BE 17–14
Postretirement benefits; determine the APBO and service cost
● LO17–9, LO17–10

Prince Distribution Inc. has an unfunded postretirement benefit plan. Medical care and life insurance benefits are provided to employees who render 10 years service and attain age 55 while in service. At the end of 2018, Jim Lukawitz is 31. He was hired by Prince at age 25 (6 years ago) and is expected to retire at age 62. The expected postretirement benefit obligation for Lukawitz at the end of 2018 is $50,000 and $54,000 at the end of 2019. Calculate the accumulated postretirement benefit obligation at the end of 2018 and 2019 and the service cost for 2018 and 2019, as pertaining to Lukawitz.

BE 17–15
Postretirement benefits; changes in the APBO
● LO17–11

On January 1, 2018, Medical Transport Company's accumulated postretirement benefit obligation was $25 million. At the end of 2018, retiree benefits paid were $3 million. Service cost for 2018 is $7 million. Assumptions regarding the trend of future health care costs were revised at the end of 2018, causing the actuary to revise downward the estimate of the APBO by $1 million. The actuary's discount rate is 8%. Determine the amount of the accumulated postretirement benefit obligation at December 31, 2018.

Exercises

connect

E 17–1
Changes in the PBO
● LO17–3

Indicate by letter whether each of the events listed below increases (**I**), decreases (**D**), or has no effect (**N**) on an employer's projected benefit obligation.

Events

_____ 1. Interest cost
_____ 2. Amortization of prior service cost
_____ 3. A decrease in the average life expectancy of employees
_____ 4. An increase in the average life expectancy of employees
_____ 5. A plan amendment that increases benefits is made retroactive to prior years
_____ 6. An increase in the actuary's assumed discount rate
_____ 7. Cash contributions to the pension fund by the employer
_____ 8. Benefits are paid to retired employees
_____ 9. Service cost
_____ 10. Return on plan assets during the year are lower than expected
_____ 11. Return on plan assets during the year are higher than expected

E 17–2
Determine the projected benefit obligation
● LO17–3

On January 1, 2018, Burleson Corporation's projected benefit obligation was $30 million. During 2018, pension benefits paid by the trustee were $4 million. Service cost for 2018 is $12 million. Pension plan assets (at fair value) increased during 2018 by $6 million as expected. At the end of 2018, there was no prior service cost and a negligible balance in net loss–AOCI. The actuary's discount rate was 10%.

Required:
Determine the amount of the projected benefit obligation at December 31, 2018.

E 17–3
Components of pension expense
● LO17–6

Indicate by letter whether each of the events listed below increases (**I**), decreases (**D**), or has no effect (**N**) on an employer's periodic pension expense in the year the event occurs.

Events

_____ 1. Interest cost
_____ 2. Amortization of prior service cost—AOCI
_____ 3. Excess of the expected return on plan assets over the actual return
_____ 4. Expected return on plan assets
_____ 5. A plan amendment that increases benefits is made retroactive to prior years
_____ 6. Actuary's estimate of the PBO is increased
_____ 7. Cash contributions to the pension fund by the employer
_____ 8. Benefits are paid to retired employees
_____ 9. Service cost
_____ 10. Excess of the actual return on plan assets over the expected return
_____ 11. Amortization of net loss—AOCI
_____ 12. Amortization of net gain—AOCI

E 17–4
Recording pension expense
● LO17–6, LO17–7

Harrison Forklift's pension expense includes a service cost of $10 million. Harrison began the year with a pension liability of $28 million (underfunded pension plan).

Required:
Prepare the appropriate general journal entries to record Harrison's pension expense in each of the following independent situations regarding the other components of pension expense ($ in millions):

1. Interest cost, $6; expected return on assets, $4; amortization of net loss, $2.
2. Interest cost, $6; expected return on assets, $4; amortization of net gain, $2.
3. Interest cost, $6; expected return on assets, $4; amortization of net loss, $2; amortization of prior service cost, $3 million.

E 17–5
Determine pension plan assets
● LO17–4

The following data relate to Voltaire Company's defined benefit pension plan:

	($ in millions)
Plan assets at fair value, January 1	$600
Expected return on plan assets	60
Actual return on plan assets	48
Contributions to the pension fund (end of year)	100
Amortization of net loss	10
Pension benefits paid (end of year)	11
Pension expense	72

Required:
Determine the amount of pension plan assets at fair value on December 31.

E 17–6
Changes in the pension obligation; determine service cost
● LO17–3, LO17–6

Pension data for Millington Enterprises include the following:

	($ in millions)
Discount rate, 10%	
Projected benefit obligation, January 1	$360
Projected benefit obligation, December 31	465
Accumulated benefit obligation, January 1	300
Accumulated benefit obligation, December 31	415
Cash contributions to pension fund, December 31	150
Benefit payments to retirees, December 31	54

Required:
Assuming no change in actuarial assumptions and estimates, determine the service cost component of pension expense for the year ended December 31.

E 17–7
Changes in plan assets; determine cash contributions
● LO17–4

Pension data for Fahy Transportation Inc. include the following:

	($ in millions)
Discount rate, 7%	
Expected return on plan assets, 10%	
Actual return on plan assets, 11%	
Projected benefit obligation, January 1	$730
Plan assets (fair value), January 1	700
Plan assets (fair value), December 31	750
Benefit payments to retirees, December 31	66

Required:
Assuming cash contributions were made at the end of the year, what was the amount of those contributions?

E 17–8
Components of pension expense
● LO17–6

Pension data for Sterling Properties include the following:

	($ in thousands)
Service cost, 2018	$112
Projected benefit obligation, January 1, 2018	850
Plan assets (fair value), January 1, 2018	900
Prior service cost—AOCI (2018 amortization, $8)	80
Net loss—AOCI (2018 amortization, $1)	101
Interest rate, 6%	
Expected return on plan assets, 10%	
Actual return on plan assets, 11%	

Required:
Determine pension expense for 2018.

E 17–9
Components of pension expense; IFRS
● LO17–6, LO17–12
IFRS

Refer to the situation described in E 17–8.

Required:
How might your answer differ if we assume Sterling Properties prepares its financial statements according to International Financial Reporting Standards? 6% is the interest rate on high grade corporate bonds.

E 17–10
Determine pension expense
● LO17–6, LO17–7

Abbott and Abbott has a noncontributory, defined benefit pension plan. At December 31, 2018, Abbott and Abbott received the following information:

Projected Benefit Obligation	($ in millions)
Balance, January 1	$120
Service cost	20
Interest cost	12
Benefits paid	(9)
Balance, December 31	$143

(continued)

(concluded)

Plan Assets	
Balance, January 1	$ 80
Actual return on plan assets	9
Contributions 2018	20
Benefits paid	(9)
Balance, December 31	$100

The expected long-term rate of return on plan assets was 10%. There was no prior service cost and a negligible net loss—AOCI on January 1, 2018.

Required:

1. Determine Abbott and Abbott's pension expense for 2018.
2. Prepare the journal entries to record Abbott and Abbott's pension expense, funding, and payment for 2018.

E 17–11
Components of pension expense; journal entries
● LO17–6, LO17–7

Pension data for Barry Financial Services Inc. include the following:

	($ in thousands)
Discount rate, 7%	
Expected return on plan assets, 10%	
Actual return on plan assets, 9%	
Service cost, 2018	$ 310
January 1, 2018:	
Projected benefit obligation	2,300
Accumulated benefit obligation	2,000
Plan assets (fair value)	2,400
Prior service cost—AOCI (2018 amortization, $25)	325
Net gain—AOCI (2018 amortization, $6)	330
There were no changes in actuarial assumptions.	
December 31, 2018:	
Cash contributions to pension fund, December 31, 2018	245
Benefit payments to retirees, December 31, 2018	270

Required:

1. Determine pension expense for 2018.
2. Prepare the journal entries to record pension expense, gains and losses (if any), funding, and retiree benefits for 2018.

E 17–12
PBO calculations; ABO calculations; present value concepts
● LO17–1, LO17–2, LO17–3

Clark Industries has a defined benefit pension plan that specifies annual retirement benefits equal to:

$$1.2\% \times \text{Service years} \times \text{Final year's salary}$$

Stanley Mills was hired by Clark at the beginning of 1999. Mills is expected to retire at the end of 2043 after 45 years of service. His retirement is expected to span 15 years. At the end of 2018, 20 years after being hired, his salary is $80,000. The company's actuary projects Mills's salary to be $270,000 at retirement. The actuary's discount rate is 7%.

Required:

1. Estimate the amount of Stanley Mills's annual retirement payments for the 15 retirement years earned as of the end of 2018.
2. Suppose Clark's pension plan permits a lump-sum payment at retirement in lieu of annuity payments. Determine the lump-sum equivalent as the present value as of the retirement date of annuity payments during the retirement period.
3. What is the company's projected benefit obligation at the end of 2018 with respect to Stanley Mills?
4. Even though pension accounting centers on the PBO calculation, the ABO still must be disclosed in the pension disclosure note. What is the company's accumulated benefit obligation at the end of 2018 with respect to Stanley Mills?
5. If we assume no estimates change in the meantime, what is the company's projected benefit obligation at the end of 2019 with respect to Stanley Mills?
6. What portion of the 2019 increase in the PBO is attributable to 2019 service (the service cost component of pension expense) and to accrued interest (the interest cost component of pension expense)?

E 17–13
Determining the amortization of net loss or net gain
● LO17–6

Hicks Cable Company has a defined benefit pension plan. Three alternative possibilities for pension-related data at January 1, 2018, are shown below:

	($ in thousands)		
	Case 1	**Case 2**	**Case 3**
Net loss (gain)—AOCI, Jan. 1	$ 320	$ (330)	$ 260
2018 loss (gain) on plan assets	(11)	(8)	2
2018 loss (gain) on PBO	(23)	16	(265)
Accumulated benefit obligation, Jan. 1	(2,950)	(2,550)	(1,450)
Projected benefit obligation, Jan. 1	(3,310)	(2,670)	(1,700)
Fair value of plan assets, Jan. 1	2,800	2,700	1,550
Average remaining service period of active employees (years)	12	15	10

Required:

1. For each independent case, calculate any amortization of the net loss or gain that should be included as a component of pension expense for 2018.
2. For each independent case, determine the net loss—AOCI or net gain—AOCI as of January 1, 2019.

E 17–14
Effect of pension expense components on balance sheet accounts
● LO17–7, LO17–8

Warrick Boards calculated pension expense for its underfunded pension plan as follows:

	($ in millions)
Service cost	$224
Interest cost	150
Expected return on the plan assets ($100 actual, less $10 gain)	(90)
Amortization of prior service cost	8
Amortization of net loss	2
Pension expense	$294

Required:

Which elements of Warrick's balance sheet are affected by the components of pension expense? What are the specific changes in these accounts?

E 17–15
Pension spreadsheet
● LO17–8

A partially completed pension spreadsheet showing the relationships among the elements that comprise the defined benefit pension plan of Universal Products is given below. The actuary's discount rate is 5%. At the end of 2016, the pension formula was amended, creating a prior service cost of $120,000. The expected rate of return on assets was 8%, and the average remaining service life of the active employee group is 20 years in the current year as well as the previous two years.

Required:

Copy the incomplete spreadsheet and fill in the missing amounts.

( )s indicate credits; debits otherwise ($ in thousands)	PBO	Plan Assets	Prior Service Cost	Net Loss	Pension Expense	Cash	Net Pension (Liability)/ Asset
Balance, Jan. 1, 2018	(800)	600	114	80			(200)
Service cost					84		
Interest cost, 5%	(40)						
Expected return on assets					(48)		
Adjust for:							
Loss on assets				6			
Amortization:							
Prior service cost							
Amortization:							
Net loss							
Gain on PBO							12
Prior service cost	0						
Cash funding						(68)	
Retiree benefits							
Balance, Dec. 31, 2018	(862)		108				

E 17–16
Determine and record pension expense and gains and losses; funding and retiree benefits
● LO17–6, LO17–7

Actuary and trustee reports indicate the following changes in the PBO and plan assets of Douglas-Roberts Industries during 2018:

Prior service cost at Jan. 1, 2018, from plan amendment at the beginning of 2015 (amortization: $4 million per year)	$28 million
Net loss—AOCI at Jan. 1, 2018 (previous losses exceeded previous gains)	$80 million
Average remaining service life of the active employee group	10 years
Actuary's discount rate	7%

($ in millions)

PBO			Plan Assets
Beginning of 2018	$600	*Beginning* of 2018	$400
Service cost	80	Return on plan assets,	
Interest cost, 7%	42	8% (10% expected)	32
Loss (gain) on PBO	(14)	Cash contributions	90
Less: Retiree benefits	(38)	Less: Retiree benefits	(38)
End of 2018	$670	*End* of 2018	$484

Required:
1. Determine Douglas-Roberts's pension expense for 2018, and prepare the appropriate journal entries to record the expense.
2. Prepare the appropriate journal entry(s) to record any 2018 gains and losses.
3. Prepare the appropriate journal entry to record the cash contribution to plan assets.
4. Prepare the appropriate journal entry to record retiree benefits.

E 17–17
Concepts; terminology
● LO17–2 through LO17–8

Listed below are several terms and phrases associated with pensions. Pair each item from List A with the item from List B (by letter) that is most appropriately associated with it.

List A	List B
_____ 1. Future compensation levels estimated	a. Actual return exceeds expected
_____ 2. All funding provided by the employer	b. Net gain—AOCI
_____ 3. Credit to OCI and debit to plan assets	c. Vested benefit obligation
_____ 4. Retirement benefits specified by formula	d. Projected benefit obligation
_____ 5. Trade-off between being relevant and representationally faithful	e. Choice between PBO and ABO
	f. Noncontributory pension plan
_____ 6. Cumulative gains in excess of losses	g. Accumulated benefit obligation
_____ 7. Current pay levels implicitly assumed	h. Plan assets
_____ 8. Created by the passage of time	i. Interest cost
_____ 9. Not contingent on future employment	j. Delayed recognition in earnings
_____ 10. Risk borne by employee	k. Defined contribution plan
_____ 11. Increased by employer contributions	l. Defined benefit plan
_____ 12. Caused by plan amendment	m. Prior service cost
_____ 13. Loss on plan assets	n. Amortize net loss—AOCI
_____ 14. Excess over 10% of plan assets or PBO	

E 17–18
IFRS; actuarial gains and losses
● LO17–7, LO17–12
IFRS

Patel Industries has a noncontributory, defined benefit pension plan. Since the inception of the plan, the actuary has used as the discount rate the rate on high quality corporate bonds, which recently has been 7%. During 2018, changing economic conditions caused the rate to change to 6%, and the actuary decided that 6% is the appropriate rate.

Required:
1. Does the change in discount rate create a gain, or does it create a loss for Patel under U.S. GAAP? Why?
2. Assume the magnitude of the change is $13 million. Prepare the appropriate journal entry to record any 2018 gain or loss under U.S. GAAP. If Patel prepares its financial statements according to U.S. GAAP, how will the company report the gain or loss?
3. Would your response to requirement 2 differ if Patel prepares its financial statements according to International Financial Reporting Standards?

E 17–19
Record pension expense, funding, and gains and losses; determine account balances
● LO17–6, LO17–7, LO17–8

Beale Management has a noncontributory, defined benefit pension plan. On December 31, 2018 (the end of Beale's fiscal year), the following pension-related data were available:

Projected Benefit Obligation	($ in millions)
Balance, January 1, 2018	$480
Service cost	82
Interest cost, discount rate, 5%	24
Gain due to changes in actuarial assumptions in 2018	(10)
Pension benefits paid	(40)
Balance, December 31, 2018	$536
Plan Assets	
Balance, January 1, 2018	$500
Actual return on plan assets	40
(Expected return on plan assets, $45)	
Cash contributions	70
Pension benefits paid	(40)
Balance, December 31, 2018	$570
January 1, 2018, balances:	
Pension asset	$ 20
Prior service cost—AOCI (amortization $8 per year)	48
Net gain—AOCI (any amortization over 15 years)	80

Required:
1. Prepare the 2018 journal entry to record pension expense.
2. Prepare the journal entry(s) to record any 2018 gains and losses.
3. Prepare the 2018 journal entries to record the contribution to plan assets and benefit payments to retirees.
4. Determine the balances at December 31, 2018, in the PBO, plan assets, the net gain—AOCI, and prior service cost—AOCI. Show how the balances changed during 2018. [Hint: You might find T-accounts useful.]
5. What amount will Beale report in its 2018 balance sheet as a net pension asset or net pension liability for the funded status of the plan?

E 17–20
Pension spreadsheet
● LO17–8

Refer to the data provided in E 17–19.

Required:
Prepare a pension spreadsheet to show the relationship among the PBO, plan assets, prior service cost, the net gain, pension expense, and the net pension asset.

E 17–21
Determine pension expense; prior service cost
● LO17–6, LO17–7

Lacy Construction has a noncontributory, defined benefit pension plan. At December 31, 2018, Lacy received the following information:

Projected Benefit Obligation	($ in millions)
Balance, January 1	$360
Service cost	60
Prior service cost	12
Interest cost (7.5%)	27
Benefits paid	(37)
Balance, December 31	$422
Plan Assets	
Balance, January 1	$240
Actual return on plan assets	27
Contributions 2018	60
Benefits paid	(37)
Balance, December 31	$290

The expected long-term rate of return on plan assets was 10%. There were no AOCI balances related to pensions on January 1, 2018. At the end of 2018, Lacy amended the pension formula creating a prior service cost of $12 million.

Required:
1. Determine Lacy's pension expense for 2018.
2. Prepare the journal entry(s) to record Lacy's pension expense, gains or losses, prior service cost, funding, and payment of retiree benefits for 2018.

E 17–22
IFRS; prior service cost
● LO17–7, LO17–12
IFRS

Refer to the situation described in E 17–21.

Required:

How might your solution differ if Lacy Construction prepares its financial statements according to International Financial Reporting Standards? Assume the actuary's discount rate is the rate on high quality corporate bonds. Include any appropriate journal entries in your response.

E 17–23
Classifying accounting changes and errors
● LO17–8

Indicate with the appropriate letter the nature of each adjustment described below:

Type of Adjustment

A. Change in principle
B. Change in estimate
C. Correction of an error
D. Neither an accounting change nor an error

_____ 1. Change in actuarial assumptions for a defined benefit pension plan.

_____ 2. Determination that the projected benefit obligation under a pension plan exceeded the fair value of plan assets at the end of the previous year by $17,000. The only pension-related amount on the balance sheet was a net pension liability of $30,000.

_____ 3. Pension plan assets for a defined benefit pension plan achieving a rate of return in excess of the amount anticipated.

_____ 4. Instituting a pension plan for the first time and adopting GAAP for employers' accounting for defined benefit pension and other postretirement plans.

E 17–24
Postretirement benefits; determine APBO, EPBO
● LO17–10

Classified Electronics has an unfunded retiree health care plan. Each of the company's three employees has been with the firm since its inception at the beginning of 2017. As of the end of 2018, the actuary estimates the total net cost of providing health care benefits to employees during their retirement years to have a present value of $72,000. Each of the employees will become fully eligible for benefits after 28 more years of service but aren't expected to retire for 35 more years. The interest rate is 6%.

Required:

1. What is the expected postretirement benefit obligation at the end of 2018?
2. What is the accumulated postretirement benefit obligation at the end of 2018?
3. What is the expected postretirement benefit obligation at the end of 2019?
4. What is the accumulated postretirement benefit obligation at the end of 2019?

E 17–25
Postretirement benefits; determine APBO, service cost, interest cost; prepare journal entry
● LO17–10, LO17–11

The following data are available pertaining to Household Appliance Company's retiree health care plan for 2018:

Number of employees covered	2
Years employed as of January 1, 2018	3 (each)
Attribution period	25 years
Expected postretirement benefit obligation, Jan. 1	$50,000
Expected postretirement benefit obligation, Dec. 31	$53,000
Interest rate	6%
Funding	none

Required:

1. What is the accumulated postretirement benefit obligation at the beginning of 2018?
2. What is interest cost to be included in 2018 postretirement benefit expense?
3. What is service cost to be included in 2018 postretirement benefit expense?
4. Prepare the journal entry to record the postretirement benefit expense for 2018.

E 17–26
Postretirement benefits; determine EPBO; attribution period
● LO17–10, LO17–11

Lorin Management Services has an unfunded postretirement benefit plan. On December 31, 2018, the following data were available concerning changes in the plan's accumulated postretirement benefit obligation with respect to one of Lorin's employees:

APBO at the beginning of 2018	$16,364
Interest cost: ($16,364 × 10%)	1,636
Service cost: ($44,000 × 1/22)	2,000
Portion of EPBO attributed to 2018	
APBO at the end of 2018	$20,000

Required:

1. Over how many years is the expected postretirement benefit obligation being expensed (attribution period)?

2. What is the expected postretirement benefit obligation at the *end* of 2018?
3. When was the employee hired by Lorin?
4. What is the expected postretirement benefit obligation at the *beginning* of 2018?

E 17–27
Postretirement benefits; components of postretirement benefit expense
● LO17–11

Data pertaining to the postretirement health care benefit plan of Sterling Properties include the following for 2018:

	($ in thousands)
Service cost	$124
Accumulated postretirement benefit obligation, January 1	700
Plan assets (fair value), January 1	50
Prior service cost—AOCI	none
Net gain—AOCI (2018 amortization, $1)	91
Retiree benefits paid (end of year)	87
Contribution to health care benefit fund (end of year)	185
Discount rate, 7%	
Return on plan assets (actual and expected), 10%	

Required:
1. Determine the postretirement benefit expense for 2018.
2. Prepare the appropriate journal entries to record the postretirement benefit expense, funding, and retiree benefits for 2018.

E 17–28
Postretirement benefits; amortization of net loss
● LO17–11

Cahal-Michael Company has a postretirement health care benefit plan. On January 1, 2018, the following plan-related data were available:

	($ in thousands)
Net loss—AOCI	$ 336
Accumulated postretirement benefit obligation	2,800
Fair value of plan assets	500
Average remaining service period to retirement	14 years (same in previous 10 years)

The rate of return on plan assets during 2018 was 10%, although it was expected to be 9%. The actuary revised assumptions regarding the APBO at the end of the year, resulting in a $39,000 increase in the estimate of that obligation.

Required:
1. Calculate any amortization of the net loss that should be included as a component of postretirement benefit expense for 2018.
2. Assume the postretirement benefit expense for 2018, not including the amortization of the net loss component, is $212,000. What is the expense for the year?
3. Determine the net loss or gain as of December 31, 2018.

E 17–29
Postretirement benefits; determine and record expense
● LO17–11

Gorky-Park Corporation provides postretirement health care benefits to employees who provide at least 12 years of service and reach age 62 while in service. On January 1, 2018, the following plan-related data were available:

	($ in millions)
Accumulated postretirement benefit obligation	$130
Fair value of plan assets	none
Average remaining service period to retirement	25 years (same in previous 10 years)
Average remaining service period to full eligibility	20 years (same in previous 10 years)

On January 1, 2018, Gorky-Park amends the plan to provide certain dental benefits in addition to previously provided medical benefits. The actuary determines that the cost of making the amendment retroactive increases the APBO by $20 million. Management chooses to amortize the prior service cost on a straight-line basis. The service cost for 2018 is $34 million. The interest rate is 8%.

Required:
1. Calculate the postretirement benefit expense for 2018.
2. Prepare the journal entry to record the expense.

E 17–30
Postretirement benefits; negative plan amendment
● LO17–11

Southeast Technology provides postretirement health care benefits to employees. On January 1, 2018, the following plan-related data were available:

	($ in thousands)
Prior service cost—originated in 2013	$ 50
Accumulated postretirement benefit obligation	530
Fair value of plan assets	none
Average remaining service period to retirement	20 years (same in previous 10 years)
Average remaining service period to full eligibility	15 years (same in previous 10 years)

On January 1, 2018, Southeast amends the plan in response to spiraling health care costs. The amendment establishes an annual maximum of $3,000 for medical benefits that the plan will provide. The actuary determines that the effect of this amendment is to decrease the APBO by $80,000. Management amortizes prior service cost on a straight-line basis. The interest rate is 8%. The service cost for 2018 is $114,000.

Required:

1. Calculate the prior service cost amortization for 2018.
2. Calculate the postretirement benefit expense for 2018.

E 17–31
Prior service cost; service method; straight-line method (Based on Appendix)

Frazier Refrigeration amended its defined benefit pension plan on December 31, 2018, to increase retirement benefits earned with each service year. The consulting actuary estimated the prior service cost incurred by making the amendment retroactive to prior years to be $110,000. Frazier's 100 present employees are expected to retire at the rate of approximately 10 each year at the end of each of the next 10 years.

Required:

1. Using the service method, calculate the amount of prior service cost to be amortized to pension expense in each of the next 10 years.
2. Using the straight-line method, calculate the amount of prior service cost to be amortized to pension expense in each of the next 10 years.

E 17–32
FASB codification research; postretirement benefit plan
● LO17–11

When a company sponsors a postretirement benefit plan other than a pension plan, benefits typically are not earned by employees on the basis of a formula, so assigning the service cost to specific periods is more difficult. The *FASB Accounting Standards Codification* represents the single source of authoritative U.S. generally accepted accounting principles.

Required:

1. Obtain the relevant authoritative literature on how a firm should attribute the expected postretirement benefit obligation to years of service using the *FASB Accounting Standards Codification* at the FASB website (www.fasb.org). Find the specific citations that describe the guidelines for each of the following questions:
   a. What is the objective for attributing expected postretirement benefit obligations to years of service?
   b. When does the attribution period for expected postretirement benefits begin for an employee?
   c. When does the attribution period for expected postretirement benefits end for an employee?
2. What are the guidelines for each?

E 17–33
FASB codification research
● LO17–1, LO17–2, LO17–5

Access the *FASB Accounting Standards Codification* at the FASB website (www.fasb.org). Determine the specific citation for accounting for each of the following items:

1. The disclosure required in the notes to the financial statements for pension plan assets.
2. Recognition of the net pension asset or net pension liability.
3. Disclosures required in the notes to the financial statements for pension cost for a defined contribution plan.

Problems

(Note: Problems 1–5 are variations of the same situation, designed to focus on different elements of the pension plan.)

P 17–1
ABO calculations; present value concepts
● LO17–2, LO17–3

Sachs Brands defined benefit pension plan specifies annual retirement benefits equal to: 1.6% × service years × final year's salary, payable at the end of each year. Angela Davenport was hired by Sachs at the beginning of 2004 and is expected to retire at the end of 2038 after 35 years' service. Her retirement is expected to span

18 years. Davenport's salary is $90,000 at the end of 2018 and the company's actuary projects her salary to be $240,000 at retirement. The actuary's discount rate is 7%.

Required:

1. Draw a time line that depicts Davenport's expected service period, retirement period, and a 2018 measurement date for the pension obligation.
2. Estimate by the accumulated benefits approach the amount of Davenport's annual retirement payments earned as of the end of 2018.
3. What is the company's accumulated benefit obligation at the end of 2018 with respect to Davenport?
4. If no estimates are changed in the meantime, what will be the accumulated benefit obligation at the end of 2021 (three years later), when Davenport's salary is $100,000?

P 17–2
PBO calculations; present value concepts
● LO17–3

Sachs Brands defined benefit pension plan specifies annual retirement benefits equal to: 1.6% × service years × final year's salary, payable at the end of each year. Angela Davenport was hired by Sachs at the beginning of 2004 and is expected to retire at the end of 2038 after 35 years' service. Her retirement is expected to span 18 years. Davenport's salary is $90,000 at the end of 2018 and the company's actuary projects her salary to be $240,000 at retirement. The actuary's discount rate is 7%.

Required:

1. Draw a time line that depicts Davenport's expected service period, retirement period, and a 2018 measurement date for the pension obligation.
2. Estimate by the projected benefits approach the amount of Davenport's annual retirement payments earned as of the end of 2018.
3. What is the company's projected benefit obligation at the end of 2018 with respect to Davenport?
4. If no estimates are changed in the meantime, what will be the company's projected benefit obligation at the end of 2021 (three years later) with respect to Davenport?

P 17–3
Service cost, interest, and PBO calculations; present value concepts
● LO17–3

Sachs Brands defined benefit pension plan specifies annual retirement benefits equal to: 1.6% × service years × final year's salary, payable at the end of each year. Angela Davenport was hired by Sachs at the beginning of 2004 and is expected to retire at the end of 2038 after 35 years' service. Her retirement is expected to span 18 years. Davenport's salary is $90,000 at the end of 2018 and the company's actuary projects her salary to be $240,000 at retirement. The actuary's discount rate is 7%.

Required:

1. What is the company's projected benefit obligation at the beginning of 2018 (after 14 years' service) with respect to Davenport?
2. Estimate by the projected benefits approach the portion of Davenport's annual retirement payments attributable to 2018 service.
3. What is the company's service cost for 2018 with respect to Davenport?
4. What is the company's interest cost for 2018 with respect to Davenport?
5. Combine your answers to requirements 1, 3, and 4 to determine the company's projected benefit obligation at the end of 2018 (after 15 years' service) with respect to Davenport.

P 17–4
Prior service cost; components of pension expense; present value concepts
● LO17–3, LO17–6

Sachs Brands defined benefit pension plan specifies annual retirement benefits equal to: 1.6% × service years × final year's salary, payable at the end of each year. Angela Davenport was hired by Sachs at the beginning of 2004 and is expected to retire at the end of 2038 after 35 years' service. Her retirement is expected to span 18 years. Davenport's salary is $90,000 at the end of 2018 and the company's actuary projects her salary to be $240,000 at retirement. The actuary's discount rate is 7%.

At the beginning of 2019, the pension formula was amended to:

1.75% × Service years × Final year's salary

The amendment was made retroactive to apply the increased benefits to prior service years.

Required:

1. What is the company's prior service cost at the beginning of 2019 with respect to Davenport after the amendment described above?
2. Since the amendment occurred at the *beginning* of 2019, amortization of the prior service cost begins in 2019. What is the prior service cost amortization that would be included in pension expense?
3. What is the service cost for 2019 with respect to Davenport?
4. What is the interest cost for 2019 with respect to Davenport?

5. Calculate pension expense for 2019 with respect to Davenport, assuming plan assets attributable to her of $150,000 and a rate of return (actual and expected) of 10%.

P 17–5
Gain on PBO; present value concepts
● LO17–3, LO17–6

Sachs Brands defined benefit pension plan specifies annual retirement benefits equal to: 1.6% × service years × final year's salary, payable at the end of each year. Angela Davenport was hired by Sachs at the beginning of 2004 and is expected to retire at the end of 2038 after 35 years' service. Her retirement is expected to span 18 years. Davenport's salary is $90,000 at the end of 2018 and the company's actuary projects her salary to be $240,000 at retirement. The actuary's discount rate is 7%.

At the beginning of 2019, changing economic conditions caused the actuary to reassess the applicable discount rate. It was decided that 8% is the appropriate rate.

Required:

Calculate the effect of the change in the assumed discount rate on the PBO at the beginning of 2019 with respect to Davenport.

P 17–6
Determine the PBO; plan assets; pension expense; two years
● LO17–3, LO17–4, LO17–6

Stanley-Morgan Industries adopted a defined benefit pension plan on April 12, 2018. The provisions of the plan were not made retroactive to prior years. A local bank, engaged as trustee for the plan assets, expects plan assets to earn a 10% rate of return. A consulting firm, engaged as actuary, recommends 6% as the appropriate discount rate. The service cost is $150,000 for 2018 and $200,000 for 2019. Year-end funding is $160,000 for 2018 and $170,000 for 2019. No assumptions or estimates were revised during 2018.

Required:

Calculate each of the following amounts as of both December 31, 2018, and December 31, 2019:

1. Projected benefit obligation
2. Plan assets
3. Pension expense
4. Net pension asset or net pension liability

P 17–7
Determining the amortization of net gain
● LO17–6

Herring Wholesale Company has a defined benefit pension plan. On January 1, 2018, the following pension-related data were available:

	($ in thousands)
Net gain—AOCI	$ 170
Accumulated benefit obligation	1,170
Projected benefit obligation	1,400
Fair value of plan assets	1,100
Average remaining service period of active employees (expected to remain constant for the next several years)	15 years

The rate of return on plan assets during 2018 was 9%, although it was expected to be 10%. The actuary revised assumptions regarding the PBO at the end of the year, resulting in a $23,000 decrease in the estimate of that obligation.

Required:

1. Calculate any amortization of the net gain that should be included as a component of net pension expense for 2018.
2. Assume the net pension expense for 2018, not including the amortization of the net gain component, is $325,000. What is pension expense for the year?
3. Determine the net loss—AOCI or net gain—AOCI as of January 1, 2019.

P 17–8
Pension spreadsheet; record pension expense and funding; new gains and losses
● LO17–7, LO17–8

A partially completed pension spreadsheet showing the relationships among the elements that constitute Carney, Inc., defined benefit pension plan follows. Six years earlier, Carney revised its pension formula and recalculated benefits earned by employees in prior years using the more generous formula. The prior service cost created by the recalculation is being amortized at the rate of $5 million per year. At the end of 2018, the pension formula was amended again, creating an additional prior service cost of $40 million. The expected rate of return on assets and the actuary's discount rate were 10%, and the average remaining service life of the active employee group is 10 years.

( )s indicate credits; debits otherwise ($ in millions)	PBO	Plan Assets	Prior Service Cost	Net Loss	Pension Expense	Cash	Net Pension (Liability)/ Asset
Balance, Jan. 1, 2018	(830)	680	20	93			(150)
Service cost	?				74		?

(continued)

(concluded)

Interest cost	?				?		?
Expected return on asset		?					
Adjust for:							
Loss on assets		(7)		?			?
Amortization of:							
Prior service cost			?		?		
Net loss				?	?		
Loss on PBO	?			?			(13)
Prior service cost	?		?				?
Cash funding		?				?	84
Retiree benefits	?	?					
Balance, Dec. 31, 2018	?	775	?	?	?		?

Required:

1. Copy the incomplete spreadsheet and fill in the missing amounts.
2. Prepare the 2018 journal entry to record pension expense.
3. Prepare the journal entry(s) to record any 2018 gains and losses and new prior service cost in 2018.
4. Prepare the 2018 journal entries to record the cash contribution to plan assets and payment of retiree benefits.

P 17–9
Determine pension expense; PBO; plan assets; net pension asset or liability; journal entries
● LO17–3 through LO17–8

U.S. Metallurgical Inc. reported the following balances in its financial statements and disclosure notes at December 31, 2017.

Plan assets	$400,000
Projected benefit obligation	320,000

U.S.M.'s actuary determined that 2018 service cost is $60,000. Both the expected and actual rate of return on plan assets are 9%. The interest (discount) rate is 5%. U.S.M. contributed $120,000 to the pension fund at the end of 2018, and retirees were paid $44,000 from plan assets.

Required:

1. What is the pension expense at the end of 2018?
2. What is the projected benefit obligation at the end of 2018?
3. What is the plan assets balance at the end of 2018?
4. What is the net pension asset or net pension liability at the end of 2018?
5. Prepare journal entries to record the pension expense, funding of plan assets, and retiree benefit payments.

P 17–10
Prior service cost; calculate pension expense; journal entries; determine net pension asset or liability
● LO17–5 through LO17–7

Electronic Distribution has a defined benefit pension plan. Characteristics of the plan during 2018 are as follows:

	($ in millions)
PBO balance, January 1	$480
Plan assets balance, January 1	300
Service cost	75
Interest cost	45
Gain from change in actuarial assumption	22
Benefits paid	(36)
Actual return on plan assets	20
Contributions 2018	60

The expected long-term rate of return on plan assets was 8%. There were no AOCI balances related to pensions on January 1, 2018, but at the end of 2018, the company amended the pension formula, creating a prior service cost of $12 million.

Required:

1. Calculate the pension expense for 2018.
2. Prepare the journal entry to record pension expense, gains or losses, prior service cost, funding, and payment of benefits for 2018.
3. What amount will Electronic Distribution report in its 2018 balance sheet as a net pension asset or net pension liability?

P 17–11
IFRS; calculate pension expense; journal entries; determine net pension asset or liability
- LO17–5 through LO17–7, LO17–12

IFRS

Refer to the situation described in P 17–10. Assume Electronic Distribution prepares its financial statements according to International Financial Reporting Standards (IFRS). Also assume that 10% is the current interest rate on high-quality corporate bonds.

Required:

1. Calculate the net pension cost for 2018, separating its components into appropriate categories for reporting.
2. Prepare the journal entry to record the components of net pension cost, gains or losses, past service cost, funding, and payment of benefits for 2018.
3. What amount will Electronic Distribution report in its 2018 balance sheet as a net pension asset or net pension liability?

P 17–12
Determine pension expense; journal entries; two years
- LO17–3 through LO17–8

The Kollar Company has a defined benefit pension plan. Pension information concerning the fiscal years 2018 and 2019 are presented below ($ in millions):

Information Provided by Pension Plan Actuary:

a. Projected benefit obligation as of December 31, 2017 = $1,800
b. Prior service cost from plan amendment on January 2, 2018 = $400 (straight-line amortization for 10-year average remaining service period)
c. Service cost for 2018 = $520
d. Service cost for 2019 = $570
e. Discount rate used by actuary on projected benefit obligation for 2018 and 2019 = 10%
f. Payments to retirees in 2018 = $380
g. Payments to retirees in 2019 = $450
h. No changes in actuarial assumptions or estimates
i. Net gain—AOCI on January 1, 2018 = $230
j. Net gains and losses are amortized for 10 years in 2018 and 2019

Information Provided by Pension Fund Trustee:

a. Plan asset balance at fair value on January 1, 2018 = $1,600
b. 2018 contributions = $540
c. 2019 contributions = $590
d. Expected long-term rate of return on plan assets = 12%
e. 2018 actual return on plan assets = $180
f. 2019 actual return on plan assets = $210

Required:

1. Calculate pension expense for 2018 and 2019.
2. Prepare the journal entries for 2018 and 2019 to record pension expense.
3. Prepare the journal entries for 2018 and 2019 to record any gains and losses and new prior service cost.
4. Prepare the journal entries for 2018 and 2019 to record the cash contribution to plan assets and benefit payments to retirees.

P 17–13
Determine the PBO, plan assets, pension expense; prior service cost
- LO17–3, LO17–4, LO17–6

Lewis Industries adopted a defined benefit pension plan on January 1, 2018. By making the provisions of the plan retroactive to prior years, Lewis incurred a prior service cost of $2 million. The prior service cost was funded immediately by a $2 million cash payment to the fund trustee on January 2, 2018. However, the cost is to be amortized (expensed) over 10 years. The service cost—$250,000 for 2018—is fully funded at the end of each year. Both the actuary's discount rate and the expected rate of return on plan assets were 9%. The actual rate of return on plan assets was 11%. At December 31, the trustee paid $16,000 to an employee who retired during 2018.

Required:

Determine each of the following amounts as of December 31, 2018, the fiscal year-end for Lewis:

1. Projected benefit obligation
2. Plan assets
3. Pension expense

P 17–14
Relationship among pension elements
● LO17–3 through LO17–8

The funded status of Hilton Paneling Inc.'s defined benefit pension plan and the balances in prior service cost and the net gain–pensions, are given below ($ in thousands):

	2018 Beginning Balances	2018 Ending Balances
Projected benefit obligation	$2,300	$2,501
Plan assets	2,400	2,591
Funded status	100	90
Prior service cost—AOCI	325	300
Net gain—AOCI	330	300

Retirees were paid $270,000, and the employer contribution to the pension fund was $245,000 at the end of 2018. The expected rate of return on plan assets was 10%, and the actuary's discount rate is 7%. There were no changes in actuarial estimates and assumptions regarding the PBO.

Required:

Determine the following amounts for 2018:

1. Actual return on plan assets
2. Loss or gain on plan assets
3. Service cost
4. Pension expense
5. Average remaining service life of active employees (used to determine amortization of the net gain)

P 17–15
Comprehensive—pension elements; spreadsheet
● LO17–8

The following pension-related data pertain to Metro Recreation's noncontributory, defined benefit pension plan for 2018 ($ in thousands):

	Jan. 1	Dec. 31
Projected benefit obligation	$4,100	$4,380
Accumulated benefit obligation	3,715	3,950
Plan assets (fair value)	4,530	4,975
Interest (discount) rate, *7%*		
Expected return on plan assets, 10%		
Prior service cost—AOCI		
(from Dec. 31, 2017, amendment)	840	
Net loss—AOCI	477	
Average remaining service life: 12 years		
Gain due to changes in actuarial assumptions		44
Contributions to pension fund (end of year)		340
Pension benefits paid (end of year)		295

Required:

Prepare a pension spreadsheet that shows the relationships among the various pension balances, shows the changes in those balances, and computes pension expense for 2018.

P 17–16
Comprehensive—reporting a pension plan; pension spreadsheet; determine changes in balances; two years
● LO17–3 through LO17–8

Actuary and trustee reports indicate the following changes in the PBO and plan assets of Lakeside Cable during 2018:

Prior service cost at Jan. 1, 2018, from plan amendment at the beginning of 2016 (amortization: $4 million per year)	$32 million
Net loss-pensions at Jan. 1, 2018 (previous losses exceeded previous gains)	$40 million
Average remaining service life of the active employee group	10 years
Actuary's discount rate	8%

($ in millions)

	PBO		Plan Assets
Beginning of 2018	$300	*Beginning* of 2018	$200
Service cost	48	Return on plan assets,	
Interest cost, 8%	24	7.5% (10% expected)	15
Loss (gain) on PBO	(2)	Cash contributions	45
Less: Retiree benefits	(20)	Less: Retiree benefits	(20)
End of 2018	$350	*End* of 2018	$240

Required:

1. Determine Lakeside's pension expense for 2018, and prepare the appropriate journal entries to record the expense as well as the cash contribution to plan assets and payment of benefits to retirees.
2. Determine the new gains and/or losses in 2018 and prepare the appropriate journal entry(s) to record them.
3. Prepare a pension spreadsheet to assist you in determining end of 2018 balances in the PBO, plan assets, prior service cost—AOCI, the net loss—AOCI, and the pension liability.
4. Assume the following actuary and trustee reports indicating changes in the PBO and plan assets of Lakeside Cable during 2019 ($ in millions):

	PBO		Plan Assets
Beginning of 2019	$350	*Beginning* of 2019	$240
Service cost	38	Return on plan assets, 15% (10% expected)	36
Interest cost at 8%	28	Cash contributions	30
Loss (gain) on PBO	5	Less: Retiree benefits	(16)
Less: Retiree benefits	(16)		
End of 2019	$405	*End* of 2019	$290

Determine Lakeside's pension expense for 2019, and prepare the appropriate journal entries to record the expense, the cash funding of plan assets, and payment of benefits to retirees.

5. Determine the new gains and/or losses in 2019, and prepare the appropriate journal entry(s) to record them.
6. Using T-accounts, determine the balances at December 31, 2019, in the net loss–AOCI and prior service cost–AOCI.
7. Confirm the balances determined in Requirement 6 by preparing a pension spreadsheet.

P 17–17
Integrating Problem—Deferred tax effects of pension entries; integrate concepts learned in Chapter 16
● LO17–7

Reproduced below are the journal entries related to Illustration 17–12 in this chapter that Global Communications used to record its pension expense and funding in 2018 and the new gain and loss that occurred that year. To focus on the core issues, we ignored the income tax effects of the pension amounts.

	($ in millions)	
To Record Pension Expense		
Pension expense (total)	43	
Plan assets (expected return on plan assets)	27	
PBO ($41 service cost + $24 interest cost)		65
Amortization of prior service cost—OCI (2018 amortization)		4
Amortization of net loss—OCI (2018 amortization)		1
To Record Funding		
Plan assets	48	
Cash (contribution to plan assets)		48
To Record Payment of Benefits		
PBO	38	
Plan assets (retiree benefits)		38
To Record Gains and Losses		
Loss—OCI (from change in assumption)	23	
PBO		23
Plan assets	3	
Gain—OCI (from actual return exceeding expected return)		3

Required:

1. Recast these journal entries to include the income tax effects of the events being recorded. Assume that Global's tax rate is 40%. [Hint: Costs are incurred and recognized for financial reporting purposes now, but the tax impact comes much later—when these amounts are deducted for tax purposes as actual payments for retiree benefits occur in the future. As a result, the tax effects are deferred, creating the need to record deferred tax assets and deferred tax liabilities. So, you may want to refer back to Chapter 16 to refresh your memory on these concepts.]
2. Prepare a statement of comprehensive income for 2018, assuming Global's only other sources of comprehensive income were net income of $300 million and a $30 million unrealized holding gain on investments in securities available for sale.

P 17–18
Postretirement benefits; EPBO calculations; APBO calculations; components of postretirement benefit expense; present value concepts
● LO17–9, LO17–10

Century-Fox Corporation's employees are eligible for postretirement health care benefits after both being employed at the end of the year in which age 60 is attained and having worked 20 years. Jason Snyder was hired at the end of 1995 by Century-Fox at age 34 and is expected to retire at the end of 2023 (age 62). His retirement is expected to span five years (unrealistically short in order to simplify calculations). The company's actuary has estimated the net cost of retiree benefits in each retirement year as shown below. The discount rate is 6%. The plan is not prefunded. Assume costs are incurred at the end of each year.

Year	Expected Age	Net Cost
2024	63	$4,000
2025	64	4,400
2026	65	2,300
2027	66	2,500
2028	67	2,800

Required:
1. Draw a time line that depicts Snyder's attribution period for retiree benefits and expected retirement period.
2. Calculate the present value of the net benefits as of the expected retirement date.
3. With respect to Snyder, what is the company's expected postretirement benefit obligation at the end of 2018?
4. With respect to Snyder, what is the company's accumulated postretirement benefit obligation at the end of 2018?
5. With respect to Snyder, what is the company's accumulated postretirement benefit obligation at the end of 2019?
6. What is the service cost to be included in 2019 postretirement benefit expense?
7. What is the interest cost to be included in 2019 postretirement benefit expense?
8. Show how the APBO changed during 2019 by reconciling the beginning and ending balances.

P 17–19
Postretirement benefits; schedule of postretirement benefit costs
● LO17–9 through LO17–11

Stockton Labeling Company has a retiree health care plan. Employees become fully eligible for benefits after working for the company eight years. Stockton hired Misty Newburn on January 1, 2018. As of the end of 2018, the actuary estimates the total net cost of providing health care benefits to Newburn during her retirement years to have a present value of $18,000. The actuary's discount rate is 10%.

Required:
Prepare a schedule that shows the EPBO, the APBO, the service cost, the interest cost, and the postretirement benefit expense for each of the years 2018–2025.

P 17–20
Postretirement benefits; relationship among elements of postretirement benefit plan
● LO17–9 through LO17–11

The information below pertains to the retiree health care plan of Thompson Technologies:

($ in thousands)	2018 Beginning Balances	2018 Ending Balances
Accumulated postretirement benefit obligation	$460	$485
Plan assets	0	75
Funded status	(460)	(410)
Prior service cost—AOCI	120	110
Net gain—AOCI	(50)	(49)

Thompson began funding the plan in 2018 with a contribution of $127,000 to the benefit fund at the end of the year. Retirees were paid $52,000. The actuary's discount rate is 5%. There were no changes in actuarial estimates and assumptions.

Required:
Determine the following amounts for 2018:
1. Service cost
2. Postretirement benefit expense
3. Net benefit liability

P 17–21
Pension disclosure; amortization of actuarial gain or loss; Office Depot, Inc.
● LO17–3 through LO17–7
Real World Financials

Office Depot, Inc. is a leading global provider of products, services, and solutions for workplaces. The following is an excerpt from a disclosure note in the company's annual report for the fiscal year ended December 31, 2015:

NOTE 13. EMPLOYEE BENEFIT PLANS (in part)

	Pension Benefits	
($ in millions)	2015	2014
Changes in projected benefit obligation:		
Obligation at beginning of period	$1,218	$1,122
Service cost	3	3
Interest cost	46	52
Actuarial (gain) loss	(78)	138
Benefits paid	(95)	(97)
Obligation at end of period	$1,094	$1,218
Change in plan assets:		
Fair value of plan assets at beginning of period	$1,039	$ 986
Actual return (loss) on plan assets*	(30)	107
Employer contribution	8	43
Benefits paid	(95)	(97)
Fair value of plan assets at end of period	922	1,039
Net liability recognized at end of period	$ (172)	$ (179)

*Expected return $56 and $62 in 2015 and 2014, respectively

Required:

1. What amount did Office Depot report in its balance sheet related to the pension plan at December 31, 2015?
2. When calculating pension expense at December 31, what amount did Office Depot include as the amortization of unrecognized net actuarial loss (net loss–AOCI), which was $67 million at the beginning of the year and the only AOCI account related to pensions? The average remaining service life of employees was 10 years.
3. What was the pension expense?
4. What were the appropriate journal entries to record Office Depot's pension expense and to record gains and/or losses related to the pension plan?

Broaden Your Perspective

Apply your critical-thinking ability to the knowledge you've gained. These cases will provide you an opportunity to develop your research, analysis, judgment, and communication skills. You also will work with other students, integrate what you've learned, apply it in real-world situations, and consider its global and ethical ramifications. This practice will broaden your knowledge and further develop your decision-making abilities.

Judgment Case 17–1
Choose your retirement option
● LO17–1, LO17–3, LO17–4, LO17–5

"I only get one shot at this?" you wonder aloud. Mrs. Montgomery, human resources manager at Covington State University, has just explained that newly hired assistant professors must choose between two retirement plan options. "Yes, I'm afraid so," she concedes. "But you do have a week to decide."

Mrs. Montgomery's explanation was that your two alternatives are: (1) the state's defined benefit plan and (2) a defined contribution plan under which the university will contribute each year an amount equal to 8% of your salary. The defined benefit plan will provide annual retirement benefits determined by the following formula: 1.5% × years of service × salary at retirement.

"It's a good thing I studied pensions in my accounting program," you tell her. "Now let's see. You say the state is currently assuming our salaries will rise about 3% a year, and the interest rate they use in their calculations is 6%? And, for someone my age, you say they assume I'll retire after 40 years and draw retirement pay for 20 years. I'll do some research and get back to you."

Required:

1. You were hired at the beginning of 2018 at a salary of $100,000. If you choose the state's defined benefit plan and projections hold true, what will be your annual retirement pay? What is the present value of your retirement annuity as of the anticipated retirement date (end of 2057)?
2. Suppose instead that you choose the defined contribution plan. Assuming that the rate of increase in salary is the same as the state assumes and that the rate of return on your retirement plan assets will be 6% compounded annually, what will be the future value of your plan assets as of the anticipated retirement date (end

of 2057)? What will be your annual retirement pay (assuming continuing investment of remaining assets at 6%)?

3. Based on this numerical comparison, which plan would you choose? What other factors must you also consider in making the choice?

Hint: The calculations are greatly simplified using an electronic spreadsheet such as Excel. There are many ways to set up the spreadsheet. One relatively easy way is to set up the first few rows with the formulas as shown below, then use the "fill down" function to fill in the remaining 38 rows, and use the Insert: Name: Define: function to name column B "n". Since contributions are assumed made at the end of each year, there are 39 years remaining to maturity at the end of 2018. Note that multiplying each contribution by $(1.06)^n$, where n equals the remaining number of years to retirement, calculates the future value of each contribution invested at 6% until retirement.

	A	B	C	D	E
1	End of	Years to			Future Value
2	Year	Retirement	Salary	Contribution	at Retirement
3	2018	39	100,000	=C3*0.08	=D3*1.06^n
4	=A3+1	= B3-1	=C3*1.03	=C4*0.08	=D4*1.06^n

Communication Case 17–2
Pension concepts
● LO17–2 through LO17–8

Stacy Persoff is the newly hired assistant controller of Kemp Industries, a regional supplier of hardwood derivative products. The company sponsors a defined benefit pension plan that covers its 420 employees. On reviewing last year's financial statements, Persoff was concerned about some items reported in the disclosure notes relating to the pension plan. Portions of the relevant note follow:

Note 8: Pensions
The company has a defined benefit pension plan covering substantially all of its employees. Pension benefits are based on employee service years and the employee's compensation during the last two years of employment. The company contributes annually the maximum amount permitted by the federal tax code. Plan contributions provide for benefits expected to be earned in the future as well as those earned to date. The following reconciles the plan's funded status and amount recognized in the balance sheet at December 31, 2018 ($ in thousands).

Actuarial Present Value Benefit Obligations:	
Accumulated benefit obligation (including vested benefits of $318)	$(1,305)
Projected benefit obligation	(1,800)
Plan assets at fair value	1,575
Projected benefit obligation in excess of plan assets	$ (225)

Kemp's comparative income statements reported net periodic pension expense of $108,000 in 2018 and $86,520 in 2017. Since employment has remained fairly constant in recent years, Persoff expressed concern over the increase in the pension expense. She expressed her concern to you, a three-year senior accountant at Kemp. "I'm also interested in the differences in these liability measurements," she mentioned.

Required:
Write a memo to Persoff. In the memo, do the following:

1. Explain to Persoff how the composition of the net periodic pension expense can create the situation she sees. Briefly describe the components of pension expense.
2. Briefly explain how pension gains and losses are recognized in earnings.
3. Describe for her the differences and similarities between the accumulated benefit obligation and the projected benefit obligation.
4. Explain how the "Projected benefit obligation in excess of plan assets" is reported in the financial statements.

Judgment Case 17–3
Barlow's wife; relationship among pension elements
● LO17–8

LGD Consulting is a medium-sized provider of environmental engineering services. The corporation sponsors a noncontributory, defined benefit pension plan. Alan Barlow, a new employee and participant in the pension plan, obtained a copy of the 2018 financial statements, partly to obtain additional information about his new employer's obligation under the plan. In part, the pension disclosure note reads as follows:

Note 8: Retirement Benefits

The Company has a defined benefit pension plan covering substantially all of its employees. The benefits are based on years of service and the employee's compensation during the last two years of employment. The company's funding policy is consistent with the funding requirements of federal law and regulations. Generally, pension costs accrued are funded. Plan assets consist primarily of stocks, bonds, commingled trust funds, and cash.

The change in projected benefit obligation for the plan years ended December 31, 2018, and December 31, 2017.

($ in thousands)	2018	2017
Projected benefit obligation at beginning of year	$3,786	$3,715
Service cost	103	94
Interest cost	287	284
Actuarial (gain) loss	302	(23)
Benefits paid	(324)	(284)
Projected benefit obligation at end of year	$4,154	$3,786

The weighted average discount rate and rate of increase in future compensation levels used in determining the actuarial present value of the projected benefit obligations in the above table were 7.0% and 4.3%, respectively, at December 31, 2018, and 7.75% and 4.7%, respectively, at December 31, 2017. The expected long-term rate of return on assets was 10.0% at December 31, 2018 and 2017.

The change in the fair value of plan assets for the plan years ended December 31, 2018 and 2017.

($ in thousands)	2018	2017
Fair value of plan assets at beginning of year	$3,756	$3,616
Actual return on plan assets	1,100	372
Employer contributions	27	52
Benefits paid	(324)	(284)
Fair value of plan assets at end of year	$4,559	$3,756

Included in the Consolidated Balance Sheets are the following components of accumulated other comprehensive income.

($ in thousands)	2018	2017
Net actuarial gain	$(620)	$(165)
Prior service cost	44	46

Net periodic defined benefit pension cost for fiscal 2018, 2017, and 2016 included the following components.

($ in thousands)	2018	2017	2016
Service cost	$ 103	$ 94	$ 112
Interest cost	287	284	263
Expected return on plan assets	(342)	(326)	(296)
Amortization of prior service cost	2	2	1
Recognized net actuarial (gain) loss	(2)	2	4
Net periodic pension cost	$ 48	$ 56	$ 84

In attempting to reconcile amounts reported in the disclosure note with amounts reported in the income statement and balance sheet, Barlow became confused. He was able to find the pension expense on the income statement but was unable to make sense of the balance sheet amounts. Expressing his frustration to his wife, Barlow said, "It appears to me that the company has calculated pension expense as if they have the pension liability and pension assets they include in the note, but I can't seem to find those amounts in the balance sheet. In fact, there are several amounts here I can't seem to account for. They also say they've made some assumptions about interest rates, pay increases, and profits on invested assets. I wonder what difference it would make if they assumed other numbers."

Barlow's wife took accounting courses in college and remembers most of what she learned about pension accounting. She attempts to clear up her husband's confusion.

Required:

Assume the role of Barlow's wife. Answer the following questions for your husband.

1. Is Barlow's observation correct that the company has calculated pension expense on the basis of amounts not reported in the balance sheet?
2. What amount would the company report as a pension liability in the balance sheet?
3. What amount would the company report as a pension asset in the balance sheet?
4. Which of the other amounts reported in the disclosure note would the company report in the balance sheet?
5. The disclosure note reports a net actuarial gain as well as an actuarial loss. How are these related? What do the amounts mean?
6. Which components of the pension expense represent deferred recognition? Where are these deferred amounts reported prior to amortization?

Communication Case 17–4
Barlow's wife; relationship among pension elements
● LO17–8

The focus of this case is question 1 in the previous case. Your instructor will divide the class into two to six groups, depending on the size of the class. The mission of your group is to assess the correctness of Barlow's observation and to suggest the appropriate treatment of the pension obligation. The suggested treatment need not be that required by GAAP.

Required:

1. Each group member should deliberate the situation independently and draft a tentative argument prior to the class session for which the case is assigned.
2. In class, each group will meet for 10 to 15 minutes in different areas of the classroom. During that meeting, group members will take turns sharing their suggestions for the purpose of arriving at a single group treatment.
3. After the allotted time, a spokesperson for each group (selected during the group meetings) will share the group's solution with the class. The goal of the class is to incorporate the views of each group into a consensus approach to the situation.

Real World Case 17–5
Types of pension plans; disclosures
● LO17–1
Real World Financials

Refer to the financial statements and related disclosure notes of Microsoft Corporation (www.microsoft.com).

Required:

1. What type of pension plan does Microsoft sponsor for its employees? Explain.
2. Who bears the "risk" of factors that might reduce retirement benefits in this type of plan? Explain.
3. Assuming that employee and employer contributions vest immediately, suppose a Microsoft employee contributes $1,000 to the pension plan during her first year of employment and directs investments to a bond mutual fund. If she leaves Microsoft early in her second year, after the mutual fund's value has increased by 2%, how much will she be entitled to roll over into an Individual Retirement Account (IRA)?
4. How did Microsoft account for its participation in the pension plan in fiscal 2015?

Ethics Case 17–6
401(k) plan contributions
● LO17–1

You are in your third year as internal auditor with VXI International, manufacturer of parts and supplies for jet aircraft. VXI began a defined contribution pension plan three years ago. The plan is a so-called 401(k) plan (named after the Tax Code section that specifies the conditions for the favorable tax treatment of these plans) that permits voluntary contributions by employees. Employees' contributions are matched with one dollar of employer contribution for every two dollars of employee contribution. Approximately $500,000 of contributions is deducted from employee paychecks each month for investment in one of three employer-sponsored mutual funds.

While performing some preliminary audit tests, you happen to notice that employee contributions to these plans usually do not show up on mutual fund statements for up to two months following the end of pay periods from which the deductions are drawn. On further investigation, you discover that when the plan was first begun, contributions were invested within one week of receipt of the funds. When you question the firm's investment manager about the apparent change in the timing of investments, you are told, "Last year Mr. Maxwell (the CFO) directed me to initially deposit the contributions in the corporate investment account. At the close of each quarter, we add the employer matching contribution and deposit the combined amount in specific employee mutual funds."

Required:

1. What is Mr. Maxwell's apparent motivation for the change in the way contributions are handled?
2. Do you perceive an ethical dilemma?

Real World Case 17–7
Types of pension plans; reporting postretirement plans; disclosures
● LO17–5, LO17–8
Real World Financials

Refer to the 2015 financial statements and related disclosure notes of FedEx Corporation. The financial statements can be found at the company's website (www.fedex.com).

Required:

1. What pension and other postretirement benefit plans does FedEx sponsor for its employees? Explain.
2. What amount does FedEx report in its balance sheet for its pension and other postretirement benefit plans? Explain.
3. FedEx reports three actuarial assumptions used in its pension calculations. Did reported changes in those assumptions from the previous year increase or decrease the projected benefit obligation? Why?

Analysis Case 17–8
Pension amendment
● LO17–5, LO17–8

Charles Rubin is a 30-year employee of Amalgamated Motors. Charles was pleased with recent negotiations between his employer and the United Auto Workers. Among other favorable provisions of the new agreement, the pact also includes a 14% increase in pension payments for workers under 64 with 30 years of service who retire during the agreement. Although the elimination of a cap on outside income earned by retirees has been generally viewed as an incentive for older workers to retire, Charles sees promise for his dream of becoming a part-time engineering consultant after retirement. What has caught Charles's attention is the following excerpt from an article in the financial press:

> **Amalgamated Motors Corp. will record a $240 million charge due to increases in retirement benefits for hourly United Auto Workers employees.**
>
> **The charge stems from AM's new tentative labor contract with the UAW. According to a filing with the Securities and Exchange Commission, the charge amounts to 26 cents a share.**
>
> **The company warned that its "unfunded pension obligation and pension expense are expected to be unfavorably impacted as a result of the recently completed labor negotiations."**

Taking advantage of an employee stock purchase plan, Charles has become an active AM stockholder as well as employee. His stockholder side is moderately concerned by the article's reference to the unfavorable impact of the recently completed labor negotiations.

Required:

1. When a company modifies its pension benefits the way Amalgamated Motors did, what name do we give the added cost? How is it accounted for?
2. What does AM mean when it says its "unfunded pension obligation and pension expense are expected to be unfavorably impacted as a result of the recently completed labor negotiations"?

Analysis Case 17–9
Effect of pensions on earnings
● LO17–7

While doing some online research concerning a possible investment you come across an article that mentions in passing that a representative of Morgan Stanley had indicated that a company's pension plan had benefited its reported earnings. Curiosity piqued, you seek your old Intermediate Accounting text.

Required:

1. Can the net periodic pension "cost" cause a company's reported earnings to increase? Explain.
2. Companies must report the actuarial assumptions used to make estimates concerning pension plans. Which estimate influences the earnings effect in requirement 1? Can any of the other estimates influence earnings? Explain.

Research Case 17–10
Researching the way employee benefits are tested on the CPA Exam; retrieving information from the Internet
● LO17–9, LO17–10, LO17–11

The board of examiners of the American Institute of Certified Public Accountants (AICPA) is responsible for preparing the CPA examination. The boards of accountancy of all 50 states, the District of Columbia, Guam, Puerto Rico, the U.S. Virgin Islands, and the Mariana Islands use the examination as the primary way to measure the technical competence of CPA candidates. The content for each examination section is specified by the AICPA and described in outline form.

Required:

1. Access the AICPA website on the Internet. The web address is www.aicpa.org.
2. Access the CPA exam section within the site. Locate the exam content portion of the section.
3. In which of the four separately graded sections of the exam are postretirement benefits tested?
4. From the AICPA site, access the Board of Accountancy for your state. What are the education requirements in your state to sit for the CPA exam?

Analysis Case 17–11
Pensions and other postretirement benefit plans; analysis of disclosure notes
● LO17–6, LO17–11

Real World Financials

Macy's, Inc., operates about 840 Macy's and Bloomingdale's department stores and furniture galleries in 45 states and U.S. territories as well as Bloomingdale's Outlet stores, macys.com, and bloomingdales.com. Refer to the financial statements for the year ended January 30, 2016 and related disclosure notes of the company. The financial statements can be found at the company's website (www.macys.com).

Required:

1. From the information provided in various portions of Note 9, reconcile the beginning balance ($1,397) and ending balances for Net loss–AOCI associated with Macy's pension plan. Clearly label each reconciling amount.
2. Macy's was required to amortize a portion of its Net loss–AOCI associated with its pension plan in 2015. Based on the calculation of that amount, determine the average remaining service life of the company's employees used in that calculation.
3. From the information provided in various portions of Note 10, reconcile the beginning balance ($349) and ending balances for Net loss–AOCI associated with Macy's *Other postretirement employee benefit plan.* Clearly label each reconciling amount.
4. Suppose you believe that Macy's should have assumed a 1% lower health care cost trend during 2015. What would 2015 net income have been under that assumption? Assume a 35% income tax rate.

Continuing Cases

Target Case

- LO17–3, LO17–4, LO17–5, LO17–6

Target Corporation prepares its financial statements according to U.S. GAAP. Target's financial statements and disclosure notes for the year ended January 30, 2016, are available in Connect. This material also is available under the Investor Relations link at the company's website (www.target.com).

Target has both defined contribution and defined benefit pension plan. In Note 28 "Pension and Postretirement Health Care Plans," Target describes its defined benefit plans.

Required:

1. What were the changes in Target's Projected Benefits Obligation in the fiscal years ended January 30, 2016 (fiscal 2015) and January 31, 2015 (fiscal 2014), for its qualified pension plans?
2. What were the changes in Target's Pension Plan Assets in the fiscal years ended January 30, 2016 and January 31, 2015, for its qualified pension plans?
3. Were these pension plans overfunded or underfunded for the fiscal years ended January 30, 2016 and January 31, 2015?
4. What were the components of Target's Pension Expense in the fiscal years ended January 30, 2016, January 31, 2015, and February 1, 2014?

Air France–KLM Case

IFRS

- LO17–12

Air France–KLM (AF), a Franco-Dutch company, prepares its financial statements according to International Financial Reporting Standards. AF's financial statements and disclosure notes for the year ended December 31, 2015, are available in Connect. This material also is available under the Finance link at the company's website (www.airfranceklm-finance.com).

Required:

1. AF reported past service cost (called prior service cost under U.S. GAAP) in its income statement as part of net periodic pension cost. Is that reporting method the same or different from the way we report prior service cost under U.S. GAAP?
2. Look at note 31.2, "Retirement Benefits." AF incorporates estimates regarding staff turnover, life expectancy, salary increase, retirement age, and discount rates. How did AF report changes in these assumptions? Is that reporting method the same or different from the way we report changes under U.S. GAAP?
3. AF does not report remeasurement gains and losses in its income statement. Where did AF report these amounts? Is that reporting method the same or different from the way we report pension expense under U.S. GAAP?
4. See Note 23. Did AF report net interest cost or net interest income in 2015? How is that amount determined?

CPA Exam Questions and Simulations

Sample CPA Exam questions from Roger CPA Review are available in Connect as support for the topics in this chapter. These Multiple Choice Questions and Task-Based Simulations include expert-written explanations and solutions, and provide a starting point for students to become familiar with the content and functionality of the actual CPA Exam.

CHAPTER

18 Shareholders' Equity

OVERVIEW

We turn our attention from liabilities, which represent the creditors' interests in the assets of a corporation, to the shareholders' residual interest in those assets. The discussions distinguish between the two basic sources of shareholders' equity: (1) *invested capital* and (2) *earned capital.* We explore the expansion of corporate capital through the issuance of shares and the contraction caused by the retirement of shares or the purchase of treasury shares. In our discussions of retained earnings, we examine cash dividends, property dividends, stock dividends, and stock splits.

LEARNING OBJECTIVES

After studying this chapter, you should be able to:

- **LO18–1** Describe the components of shareholders' equity and explain how they are reported in a statement of shareholders' equity. (*p. 1035*)
- **LO18–2** Describe comprehensive income and its components. (*p. 1038*)
- **LO18–3** Understand the corporate form of organization and the nature of stock. (*p. 1039*)
- **LO18–4** Record the issuance of shares when sold for cash and for noncash consideration. (*p. 1046*)
- **LO18–5** Distinguish between accounting for retired shares and for treasury shares. (*p. 1050*)
- **LO18–6** Describe retained earnings and distinguish it from paid-in capital. (*p. 1056*)
- **LO18–7** Explain the basis of corporate dividends, including the similarities and differences between cash and property dividends. (*p. 1056*)
- **LO18–8** Explain stock dividends and stock splits and how we account for them. (*p. 1058*)
- **LO18–9** Discuss the primary differences between U.S. GAAP and IFRS with respect to accounting for shareholders' equity. (*pp. 1040* and *1046*)

© Peathegee Inc/Blend Images

FINANCIAL REPORTING CASE

Nike, Inc.

Finally, you have some uninterrupted time to get back on the net. Earlier today you noticed on the Internet that the market price of Nike's common stock was up almost 10%. You've been eager to look into why this happened, but have had one meeting after another all day.

You've been a stockholder of Nike since the beginning of the year when you bought your last pair of running shoes and saw how much they sell for these days. The dividends that you receive quarterly are nice, but that's not why you bought the stock; you were convinced at the time that the stock price was poised to rise rapidly. A few well-placed clicks of the mouse and you come across the following news article:

BEAVERTON, Ore.--(BUSINESS WIRE) 11/19/2015 -- NIKE, Inc. (NYSE:NKE) announced today that its Board of Directors approved a new four-year, $12 billion program to repurchase shares of NIKE's Class B Common Stock. The Company anticipates that the current $8 billion share repurchase program will be completed before the end of fiscal 2016.

"In a growing sports industry, NIKE is the clear leader," said Mark Parker, President and CEO of NIKE, Inc. "We are built for growth, while also staying committed to creating shareholder value over the long term. We've proven it time and again, having returned over $23 billion to shareholders over the last 14 years through share repurchases and dividends."

The Board of Directors also declared a quarterly cash dividend on the Company's outstanding Class A and Class B Common Stock of $0.32 per share, on a pre-split basis, payable on January 4, 2016 to shareholders of record at the close of business on December 9, 2015. The dividend represents a 14 percent increase over the previous pre-split quarterly rate of $0.28 per share.

The Board of Directors also approved a two-for-one split of both NIKE's Class A and Class B Common shares. The stock split will be in the form of a 100 percent stock dividend payable on December 23, 2015 to shareholders of record at the close of business December 9, 2015.

QUESTIONS

By the time you finish this chapter, you should be able to respond appropriately to the questions posed in this case. Compare your response to the solution provided at the end of the chapter.

1. Do you think the stock price increase is related to Nike's share repurchase plan? *(p. 1050)*
2. What are Nike's choices in accounting for the share repurchases? *(p. 1051)*
3. What effect does the quarterly cash dividend of 32 cents a share have on Nike's assets? Its liabilities? Its shareholders' equity? *(p. 1057)*
4. What effect does the stock split have on Nike's assets? Its liabilities? Its shareholders' equity? *(p. 1060)*

The Nature of Shareholders' Equity

PART A

● LO18–1

A corporation raises money to fund its business operations by some mix of debt and equity financing. In earlier chapters, we examined debt financing in the form of notes, bonds, leases, and other liabilities. Amounts representing those liabilities denote *creditors' interest* in the company's assets. Now we focus on various forms of equity financing. Specifically, in this chapter we consider transactions that affect shareholders' equity—those accounts that represent the *ownership interests* of shareholders.

In principle, shareholders' equity is a relatively straightforward concept. Shareholders' equity is a residual amount—what's left over after creditor claims have been subtracted from assets (in other words, net assets). You probably recall the residual nature of shareholders' equity from the basic accounting equation:

Net assets equal shareholders' equity.

$$\underbrace{\text{Assets} - \text{Liabilities}}_{\text{Net Assets}} = \text{Shareholders' Equity}$$

Shareholders' equity accounts denote the ownership interests of shareholders.

Ownership interests of shareholders arise primarily from two sources: (1) amounts *invested* by shareholders in the corporation and (2) amounts *earned* by the corporation on behalf of its shareholders. These two sources are reported as (1) paid-in capital and (2) retained earnings.

Despite being a seemingly clear-cut concept, shareholders' equity and its component accounts often are misunderstood and misinterpreted. As we explore the transactions that affect shareholders' equity and its component accounts, try not to allow yourself to be overwhelmed by unfamiliar terminology or to be overly concerned with precise account titles. Terminology pertaining to shareholders' equity accounts is notoriously diverse. Every shareholders' equity account has several aliases. Indeed, shareholders' equity itself is often referred to as *stockholders' equity* (WalMart), *shareowners' equity* (General Electric), *shareholders' investment* (Target), *stockholders' investment* (FedEx), *shareholders' equity* (Apple), *equity* (Air France–KLM), and many other similar titles.

Complicating matters, transactions that affect shareholders' equity are influenced by corporation laws of individual states in which companies are located. And, as we see later, generally accepted accounting principles provide companies with considerable latitude when choosing accounting methods in this area.

Legal requirements and disclosure objectives make it preferable to separate a corporation's capital into several separate shareholders' equity accounts.

Keeping this perspective in mind while you study the chapter should aid you in understanding the essential concepts. At a very basic level, each transaction we examine can be viewed simply as an increase or decrease in shareholders' equity, per se, without regard to specific shareholders' equity accounts. In fact, for a business organized as a single proprietorship, all capital changes are recorded in a single owner's equity account. The same concepts apply to a corporation. But for corporations, additional considerations make it desirable to separate owners' equity into several separate shareholders' equity accounts. These additional considerations—legal requirements and disclosure objectives—are discussed in later sections of this chapter. So, as you study the separate effects of transactions on retained earnings and specific paid-in capital accounts, you may find it helpful to ask yourself frequently, "What is the net effect of this transaction on shareholders' equity?" or, equivalently, "By how much are net assets (assets minus liabilities) affected by this transaction?"

Financial Reporting Overview

Before we examine the events that underlie specific shareholders' equity accounts, let's summarize how individual accounts relate to each other. The condensed balance sheet in Illustration 18–1 of Exposition Corporation, a hypothetical company, provides that perspective.

Illustration 18–1 depicts a rather comprehensive situation. It's unlikely that any one company would have shareholders' equity from all of these sources at any one time. Remember that, at this point, our objective is only to get a general perspective of the items constituting shareholders' equity. Although company records would include separate accounts for each of these components of shareholders' equity in the balance sheet, in practice. Exposition would report a more condensed version similar to that in Illustration 18–1A and the one we will see later in the chapter when we look at the presentation by Abercrombie & Fitch (in Illustration 18–3).

The four classifications within shareholders' equity are paid-in capital, retained earnings, accumulated other comprehensive income, and treasury stock. We discuss these now in the context of Exposition Corporation.

Paid-in Capital

Paid-in capital consists primarily of amounts invested by shareholders when they purchase shares of stock from the corporation or arise from the company buying back some of those

Illustration 18–1

Detailed Shareholders' Equity Presentation

EXPOSITION CORPORATION
Balance Sheet
December 31, 2018
($ in millions)
Assets
$3,000
Liabilities
$1,000
Shareholders' Equity

Paid-in capital:		
Capital stock (par):		
Preferred stock, 10%, $10 par, cumulative, nonparticipating	$100	
Common stock, $1 par	55	
Common stock dividends distributable	5	
Additional paid-in capital:		
Paid-in capital—excess of par, preferred	50	
Paid-in capital—excess of par, common	260	
Paid-in capital—share repurchase	8	
Paid-in capital—conversion of bonds	7	
Paid-in capital—stock options	9	
Paid-in capital—restricted stock	5	
Paid-in capital—lapse of stock options	1	
Total paid-in capital		$ 500
Retained earnings		1,670
Accumulated other comprehensive income:		
Net unrealized holding gains (losses) on investments	(85)	
Net unrecognized gain (loss) on pensions	(75)	
Deferred gains (losses) on derivatives*	(4)	
Adjustments from foreign currency translation**	–0–	(164)
Treasury stock (at cost)		(6)
Total shareholders' equity		$2,000

*When a derivative designated as a cash flow hedge is adjusted to fair value, the gain or loss is deferred as a component of other comprehensive income and included in earnings later, at the same time as earnings are affected by the hedged transaction (described in Appendix A at the end of this textbook).

**Changes in foreign currency exchange rates are discussed elsewhere in your accounting curriculum. The amount could be an addition to or reduction in shareholders' equity.

Assets *minus* Liabilities equals Shareholders' Equity.

The primary source of paid-in capital is the investment made by shareholders when buying preferred and common stock.

Several other events also affect paid-in capital.

Retained earnings represents earned capital.

Illustration 18–1A

Typical Shareholders' Equity Presentation

Preferred stock, 10%, $10 par, cumulative, nonparticipating	$ 100
Common stock, $1 par	60
Additional paid-in capital	340
Retained earnings	1,670
Accumulated other comprehensive income:	
Net unrealized holding losses on investments	(85)
Net unrealized loss on pensions	(75)
Deferred losses on derivatives	(4)
Treasury stock	(6)
Total shareholders' equity	$2,000

shares or from share-based compensation activities. Later in this chapter and the next, we consider in more detail the events and transactions that affect paid-in capital.

Retained Earnings

Retained earnings is accumulated on behalf of shareholders and reported as a single amount. We discuss retained earnings in Part C of this chapter.

Treasury Stock

We discuss the final component of shareholders' equity—treasury stock—later in the chapter. It indicates that some of the shares previously sold were bought back by the corporation from shareholders.

● LO18–2

Accumulated Other Comprehensive Income

Comprehensive income includes net income as well as other gains, losses, and adjustments that change shareholders' equity but are not included in traditional net income.

Also notice that shareholders' equity of Exposition Corporation is adjusted for three events that are not included in net income and so don't affect retained earnings but are part of "other comprehensive income" and therefore are included as a separate component of shareholders' equity: accumulated comprehensive income.[1] **Comprehensive income** provides a more expansive view of the change in shareholders' equity than does traditional net income. It is the total *nonowner* change in equity for a reporting period. In fact, it encompasses all changes in equity other than those from transactions with *owners.* Transactions between the corporation and its shareholders primarily include dividends and the issuance or purchase of shares of the company's stock. Most nonowner changes are reported in the income statement. So, the nonowner changes other than those that are part of traditional net income are the ones reported as "other comprehensive income."

Comprehensive income extends our view of income beyond net income reported in an income statement to include four types of gains and losses not included in income statements.

1. Net holding gains (losses) on available-for-sale investments in debt securities
2. Gains (losses) from and amendments to postretirement benefit plans
3. Deferred gains (losses) on derivatives
4. Adjustments from foreign currency translation

The first of these are the gains and losses on some securities that occur when the fair values of these investments increase or decrease. As you learned in Chapters 12 and 14, gains and losses on available-for-sale investments in debt securities aren't included in earnings until they are realized through the sale of the securities but are considered a component of *other comprehensive income (OCI)* in the meantime. Similarly, as we discussed in Chapter 17, net gains and losses as well as "prior service cost" on pensions sometimes affect other comprehensive income rather than net income as they occur. You have not yet studied the third and fourth potential components of other comprehensive income. As described in Appendix A, "Derivatives," at the back of this textbook, when a derivative designated as a "*cash flow hedge*" is adjusted to fair value, the gain or loss is deferred as a component of other comprehensive income and included in earnings later, at the same time as earnings are affected by the hedged transaction. Adjustments from changes in foreign currency exchange rates are discussed elsewhere in your accounting curriculum. These, too, are included in other comprehensive income (OCI) but not net income.

OCI is reported in the statement of comprehensive income.

AOCI is reported in the balance sheet.

OCI shares another trait with net income. Just as net income is reported periodically in the income statement and also on a *cumulative* basis as part of retained earnings, OCI too, is reported periodically in the statement of comprehensive income and also as **accumulated other comprehensive income (AOCI)** in the balance sheet along with retained earnings. In other words, we report two attributes of OCI: (1) components of comprehensive income *created during the reporting period* and (2) the comprehensive income *accumulated* over the current and prior periods.

The first attribute—components of comprehensive income *created during the reporting period*—can be reported either as (a) an expanded version of the income statement or (b) a separate statement immediately following the income statement. Regardless of the placement a company chooses, the presentation is similar. It will report net income, other components of comprehensive income, and total comprehensive income, similar to the presentation in Illustration 18–2. Note that each component is reported net of its related income tax expense or income tax benefit.[2]

[1]Comprehensive income was introduced in Chapter 4 and revisited in Chapters 12 and 17.

[2]This can be accomplished by presenting components of other comprehensive income, either net of related income tax effects (as in this presentation) or before income tax effects with disclosure of the income taxes allocated to each component either in a disclosure note or parenthetically in the statement.

Illustration 18–2
Statement of Comprehensive Income

	($ in millions)	
Net income		$xxx
Other comprehensive income:		
Net unrealized holding gains (losses) on available-for-sale investments in debt securities (net of tax)*	$ x	
Gains (losses) from and amendments to postretirement benefit plans (net of tax)†	(x)	
Deferred gains (losses) on derivatives (net of tax)‡	(x)	
Adjustments from foreign currency translation (net of tax)§	x	xx
Comprehensive income		$xxx

*Changes in the fair value of some investments in debt securities (described in Chapter 12). An unrealized loss also might occur from recording an "other than temporary" impairment in excess of a credit loss for a debt investment. And, as discussed in Chapter 14, applying the "fair value option" to a liability entails reporting in OCI any part of the change in the liability's fair value that's due to the liability's credit risk.
†Gains and losses due to revising assumptions or market returns differing from expectations and prior service cost from amending the plan (described in Chapter 17).
‡When a derivative designated as a cash flow hedge is adjusted to fair value, the gain or loss is deferred as a component of comprehensive income and included in earnings later, at the same time as earnings are affected by the hedged transaction (described in the Derivatives Appendix to the text).
§Changes in foreign currency exchange rates when translating financial statements of foreign subsidiaries to U.S. dollars. The amount could be an addition to or reduction in shareholders' equity. (This item is discussed elsewhere in your accounting curriculum.)

The second measure—the comprehensive income *accumulated* over the current and prior periods—is reported as a separate component of shareholders' equity following retained earnings, similar to the presentation by Exposition Corporation in Illustration 18–1. Note that amounts reported here—accumulated other comprehensive income (AOCI)—represent the *cumulative* sum of the changes in each component of other comprehensive income created during each reporting period (Illustration 18–2) throughout all prior years.

Reporting Shareholders' Equity

You seldom, if ever, will see the numerous list of items shown in Illustration 18–1 reported in the presentation of paid-in capital. Instead, companies keep track of individual additional paid-in capital accounts in company records but ordinarily report these amounts as a single subtotal: additional paid-in capital. Pertinent rights and privileges of various securities outstanding, such as dividend and liquidation preferences, call and conversion information, and voting rights, are summarized in disclosure notes.[3] The shareholders' equity portion of the balance sheet of Abercrombie & Fitch, shown in Illustration 18–3, is a typical presentation format.

The balance sheet reports annual balances of shareholders' equity accounts. However, companies also should disclose the sources of the changes in those accounts.[4] This is the purpose of the statement of shareholders' equity. To illustrate, Illustration 18–4 shows how Walmart reported the changes in its shareholders' equity balances.

A statement of shareholders' equity reports the transactions that cause changes in its shareholders' equity account balances.

The current year changes that Walmart statements of shareholders' equity reveal are net income, other comprehensive income, the purchase of common stock, and dividends declared.

The Corporate Organization

● LO18–3

A company may be organized in any of three ways: (1) a sole proprietorship, (2) a partnership, or (3) a corporation. In your introductory accounting course, you studied each form. In this course, we focus exclusively on the corporate form of organization.

[3]FASB ACS 505–10–50: Equity–Overall–Disclosure (previously "Disclosure of Information about Capital Structure," *Statement of Financial Accounting Standards No. 129* (Norwalk, Conn.: FASB, 1997)).
[4]FASB ASC 505–10–50–2: Equity–Overall–Disclosure (previously "Omnibus Opinion," *APB Opinion No. 12* (New York: AICPA, 1967)).

Illustration 18–3

Typical Presentation Format—Abercrombie & Fitch

Real World Financials

Details of each class of stock are reported on the face of the balance sheet or in disclosure notes.

ABERCROMBIE & FITCH CO.
Consolidated Balance Sheets
($ in thousands, except par value amounts)

	January 30, 2016	January 31, 2015
Stockholders' Equity:		
Class A common stock—$0.01 par value: 150,000 shares authorized and 103,300 shares issued at each of January 30, 2016, and January 31, 2015	1,033	1,033
Paid-in capital	407,029	434,137
Retained earnings	2,530,196	2,550,673
Accumulated other comprehensive (loss), net of tax	(114,619)	(83,580)
Treasury stock, at average cost—35,952 and 33,948 shares at January 30, 2016, and January 31, 2015, respectively	(1,532,576)	(1,512,562)
Total Stockholders' Equity	$1,291,063	$1,389,701

International Financial Reporting Standards

LO18–9

Use of the term "reserves" and other terminology differences. Shareholders' equity is classified under IFRS into two categories: share capital and "reserves." The term reserves is considered misleading and thus is discouraged under U.S. GAAP. Here are some other differences in equity terminology:

U.S. GAAP	IFRS
Capital stock:	Share capital:
Common stock	Ordinary shares
Preferred stock	Preference shares
Paid-in capital—excess of par, common	Share premium, ordinary shares
Paid-in capital—excess of par, preferred	Share premium, preference shares
Accumulated other comprehensive income:	Reserves:
Net gains (losses) on investments—AOCI	Investment revaluation reserve
Net gains (losses) foreign currency translation—AOCI	Translation reserve
{N/A: adjusting P, P, & E to fair value not permitted}	Revaluation reserve
Retained earnings	Retained earnings
Total shareholders' equity	**Total equity**
Presented after Liabilities	Often presented before Liabilities

Corporations are the dominant form of business organization.

Most well-known companies, such as Microsoft, Google, and General Electric, are corporations. Also, many smaller companies—even one-owner businesses—are corporations. Although fewer in number than proprietorships and partnerships, in terms of business volume, corporations are the predominant form of business organization.

Accounting for most transactions is the same regardless of the form of business organization.

In most respects, transactions are accounted for in the same way regardless of the form of business organization. Assets and liabilities are unaffected by the way a company is organized. The exception is the method of accounting for capital, the ownership interest in the company. Rather than recording all changes in ownership interests in a single capital account for each owner, as we do for sole proprietorships and partnerships, we use the several capital accounts described in the previous section to record those changes for a corporation. Before discussing how we account for specific ownership changes, let's look at the characteristics of a corporation that make this form of organization distinctive and require special accounting treatment.

Illustration 18–4 Statement of Shareholders' Equity—Walmart

Real World Financials

($ in millions)	Common Stock Shares	Common Stock Amount	Capital in Excess of Par Value	Retained Earnings	Accumulated Other Comprehensive Income (Loss)	Total Walmart Shareholders' Equity
Balances as of February 1, 2013	3,314	$332	$ 3,620	$72,978	$ (587)	$76,343
Consolidated net income	—	—	—	16,022	—	16,022
Other comprehensive income, net of income taxes	—	—	—	—	(2,409)	(2,409)
Cash dividends declared ($1.88 per share)	—	—	—	(6,139)	—	(6,139)
Purchase of Company stock	(87)	(9)	(294)	(6,254)	—	(6,557)
Redemption value adjustment of redeemable noncontrolling interest	—	—	(1,019)	—	—	(1,019)
Other	6	—	55	(41)	—	14
Balances as of January 31, 2014	3,233	323	2,362	76,566	(2,996)	76,255
Consolidated net income	—	—	—	16,363	—	16,363
Other comprehensive loss, net of income taxes	—	—	—	—	(4,172)	(4,172)
Cash dividends declared ($1.92 per share)	—	—	—	(6,185)	—	(6,185)
Purchase of Company stock	(13)	(1)	(29)	(950)	—	(980)
Other	8	1	129	(17)	—	113
Balances as of January 31, 2015	3,228	323	2,462	85,777	(7,168)	81,394
Consolidated net income	—	—	—	14,694	—	14,694
Other comprehensive income, net of income taxes	—	—	—	—	(4,429)	(4,429)
Cash dividends declared ($1.96 per share)	—	—	—	(6,294)	—	(6,294)
Purchase of Company stock	(65)	(6)	(102)	(4,148)	—	(4,256)
Cash dividend declared to noncontrolling interest	—	—	—	—	—	—
Other	(1)	—	(555)	(8)	—	(563)
Balances as of January 31, 2016	3,162	$317	$ 1,805	$90,021	$(11,597)	$80,546

Limited Liability

The owners are not personally liable for debts of a corporation. Unlike a proprietorship or a partnership, a corporation is a separate legal entity, responsible for its own debts. Shareholders' liability is limited to the amounts they invest in the company when they purchase shares (unless the shareholder also is an officer of the corporation). The limited liability of shareholders is perhaps the single most important advantage of corporate organization. In other forms of business, creditors may look to the personal assets of owners for satisfaction of business debt.

Ease of Raising Capital

A corporation is better suited to raising capital than is a proprietorship or a partnership. All companies can raise funds by operating at a profit or by borrowing. However, attracting equity capital is easier for a corporation. Because corporations sell ownership interest in the

A corporation is a separate legal entity—separate and distinct from its owners.

Ownership interest in a corporation is easily transferred.

Shareholders do not have a mutual agency relationship.

form of shares of stock, ownership rights are easily transferred. An investor can sell his/her ownership interest at any time and without affecting the corporation or its operations.

From the viewpoint of a potential investor, another favorable aspect of investing in a corporation is the lack of mutual agency. Individual partners in a partnership have the power to bind the business to a contract. Therefore, an investor in a partnership must be careful regarding the character and business savvy of fellow co-owners. On the other hand, shareholders' participation in the affairs of a corporation is limited to voting at shareholders' meetings (unless the shareholder also is a member of management). Consequently, a shareholder needn't exercise the same degree of care that partners must in selecting co-owners.

Obviously, then, a corporation offers advantages over the other forms of organization, particularly in its ability to raise investment capital. As you might guess, though, these benefits do not come without a price.

Disadvantages

Corporations are subject to extensive government regulation.

Paperwork! To protect the rights of those who buy a corporation's stock or who loan money to a corporation, the state in which the company is incorporated and the federal government impose extensive reporting requirements. Primarily, the required paperwork is intended to ensure adequate disclosure of information needed by investors and creditors.

Corporations create double taxation.

You read earlier that corporations are separate legal entities. As such, they also are separate taxable entities. Often this causes what is referred to as *double taxation.* Corporations first pay income taxes on their earnings. Then, when those earnings are distributed as cash dividends, shareholders pay personal income taxes on the previously taxed earnings. Proprietorships and partnerships are not taxed at the business level; each owner's share of profits is taxed only as personal income.

Types of Corporations

When referring to corporations in this text, we are referring to corporations formed by private individuals for the purpose of generating profits. These corporations raise capital by selling stock. There are, however, other types of corporations.

Not-for-profit corporations may be owned:
1. By the public sector.
2. By a governmental unit.

Some corporations, such as churches, hospitals, universities, and charities do not sell stock and are not organized for profit. Also, some not-for-profit corporations are government-owned—the **Federal Deposit Insurance Corporation (FDIC)**, for instance. Accounting for not-for-profit corporations is discussed elsewhere in the accounting curriculum.

Corporations organized for profit may be:
1. Publicly held and traded:
   a. On an exchange.
   b. Over-the-counter.
2. Privately held.

Corporations organized for profit may be publicly held or privately (or closely) held. The stock of publicly held corporations is available for purchase by the general public. You can buy shares of **General Electric**, **Ford Motor Company**, or **Walmart** through a stockbroker. These shares are traded on the New York Stock Exchange. Other publicly held stock, like **Intel** and **Microsoft**, are available through Nasdaq (National Association of Securities Dealers Automated Quotations).

On the other hand, shares of privately held companies are owned by only a few individuals (perhaps a family) and are not available to the general public. Corporations whose stock is privately held do not need to register those shares with the Securities and Exchange Commission and are spared the voluminous, annual reporting requirements of the SEC. Of course, new sources of equity financing are limited when shares are privately held, as is the market for selling existing shares.

Privately held companies' shares are held by only a few individuals and are not available to the general public.

Frequently, companies begin as smaller, privately held corporations. Then as success broadens opportunities for expansion, the corporation goes public. For example, in 2012, the shareholders of **Facebook** decided to take public the privately held company. The result was the largest initial public offering since **Visa** in 2008.

Hybrid Organizations

A corporation can elect to comply with a special set of tax rules and be designated an **S corporation**. S corporations have characteristics of both regular corporations and partnerships. Owners have the limited liability protection of a corporation, but income and expenses are passed through to the owners as in a partnership, avoiding double taxation.

Two particular business structures have evolved in response to liability issues and tax treatment—limited liability companies and limited liability partnerships.

A **limited liability company** offers several advantages. Owners are not liable for the debts of the business, except to the extent of their investment. Unlike a limited partnership, all members of a limited liability company can be involved with managing the business without losing liability protection. Like an S corporation, income and expenses are passed through to the owners as in a partnership, avoiding double taxation, but there are no limitations on the number of owners as in an S corporation.

A **limited liability partnership** is similar to a limited liability company, except it doesn't offer all the liability protection available in the limited liability company structure. Partners are liable for their own actions but not entirely liable for the actions of other partners.

The Model Business Corporation Act

Corporations are formed in accordance with the corporation laws of individual states. State laws are not uniform, but share many similarities, thanks to the widespread adoption of the **Model Business Corporation Act**.[5] This act is designed to serve as a guide to states in the development of their corporation statutes. It presently serves as the model for the majority of states.

The *Model Business Corporation Act* serves as the model for the corporation statutes of most states.

State laws regarding the nature of shares that can be authorized, the issuance and repurchase of those shares, and conditions for distributions to shareholders obviously influence actions of corporations. Naturally, differences among state laws affect how we account for many of the shareholders' equity transactions discussed in this chapter. For that reason, we will focus on the normal case, as described by the Model Business Corporation Act, and note situations where variations in state law might require different accounting. Your goal is not to learn diverse procedures caused by peculiarities of state laws, but to understand the broad concepts of accounting for shareholders' equity that can be applied to any specific circumstance.

Variations among state laws influence GAAP pertaining to shareholders' equity transactions.

The process of incorporating a business is similar in all states. The **articles of incorporation** (sometimes called the *corporate charter*) describe (a) the nature of the firm's business activities, (b) the shares to be issued, and (c) the composition of the initial **board of directors**. The board of directors establishes corporate policies and appoints officers who manage the corporation.

The number of shares authorized is the maximum number of shares that a corporation is legally permitted to issue, as specified in its articles of incorporation. The number of authorized shares is determined at the company's creation and can only be increased by a vote of the shareholders. At least some of the shares authorized by the articles of incorporation are sold (issued) at the inception of the corporation. Frequently, the initial shareholders include members of the board of directors or officers (who may be one and the same). Ultimately, it is the corporation's shareholders that control the company. Shareholders are the owners of the corporation. By voting their shares, they determine the makeup of the board of directors—who in turn appoint officers, who in turn manage the company.

Shareholders' investment in a corporation ordinarily is referred to as paid-in capital. In the next section, we examine the methods normally used to maintain records of shareholders' investment and to report such paid-in capital in financial statements.

Paid-in Capital

PART B

Fundamental Share Rights

In reading the previous paragraphs, you noted that corporations raise equity funds by selling shares of the corporation. Shareholders are the owners of a corporation. If a corporation has only one class of shares, no designation of the shares is necessary, but they typically are labeled *common shares*. Ownership rights held by common shareholders, unless specifically withheld by agreement with the shareholders, are as follows:

[5] *Model Business Corporation Act*, the American Bar Association, 2011.

1. The right to vote on matters that come before the shareholders, including the election of corporate directors. Each share represents one vote.
2. The right to share in profits when dividends are declared. The percentage of shares owned by a shareholder determines his/her share of dividends distributed.
3. The right to share in the distribution of assets if the company is liquidated. The percentage of shares owned by a shareholder determines his/her share of assets after creditors and preferred shareholders are paid.

Another right sometimes given to common shareholders is the right to maintain one's percentage share of ownership when new shares are issued. This is referred to as a *preemptive right.* Each shareholder is offered the opportunity to buy a percentage of any new shares issued equal to the percentage of shares he/she owns at the time. In most states, this right must be specifically granted; in others, it is presumed unless contractually excluded.

However, this right usually is not explicitly stated because of the inconvenience it causes corporations when they issue new shares. The exclusion of the preemptive right ordinarily is inconsequential because few shareholders own enough stock to be concerned about their ownership percentage.

Distinguishing Classes of Shares

It is not uncommon for a firm to have more than one, and perhaps several, classes of shares, each with different rights and limitations. To attract investors, companies have devised quite a variety of ownership securities.

If more than one class of shares is authorized by the articles of incorporation, the specific rights of each (for instance, the right to vote, residual interest in assets, and dividend rights) must be stated. Also, some designation must be given to distinguish each class.

Some of the distinguishing designations often used are these:

Terminology varies in the way companies differentiate among share types.

1. Class A, class B, and so on (**Tyson Foods**)
2. Preferred stock, common stock, and class B stock (**Hershey's**)
3. Common and preferred (**HP**)
4. Capital stock (**Reader's Digest**)
5. Common and serial preferred (**Smucker's**)

It often is difficult to predict the rights and privileges of shares on the basis of whether they are labeled *common* or *preferred.*

In your introductory study of accounting, you probably became most familiar with the common stock–preferred stock distinction. That terminology has deep roots in tradition. Early English corporate charters provided for shares that were preferred over others as to dividends and liquidation rights. These provisions were reflected in early American corporation laws. But as our economy developed, corporations increasingly felt the need for innovative ways of attracting investment capital. The result has been a gradual development of a wide range of share classifications that cannot easily be identified by these historical designations.

To reflect the flexibility that now exists in the creation of equity shares, the Model Business Corporation Act, and thus many state statutes, no longer mention the words common and preferred. But the influence of tradition lingers. Most corporations still designate shares as common or preferred. For consistency with practice, the illustrations you study in this chapter use those designations. As you consider the examples, keep in mind that the same concepts apply regardless of the language used to distinguish shares.

Typical Rights of Preferred Shares

An issue of shares with certain preferences or features that distinguish it from the class of shares customarily called common shares may be assigned any of the several labels mentioned earlier. Very often the distinguishing designation is **preferred shares**. The special rights of preferred shareholders usually include one or both of the following:

1. Preferred shareholders typically have a preference to a specified amount of dividends (stated dollar amount per share or % of par value per share). That is, if the board of

directors declares dividends, preferred shareholders will receive the designated dividend before any dividends are paid to common shareholders.

2. Preferred shareholders customarily have a preference (over common shareholders) as to the distribution of assets in the event the corporation is dissolved.

Preferred shareholders sometimes have the **right of conversion**, which allows them to exchange shares of preferred stock for common stock at a specified conversion ratio. For instance, in 2016, **Xerox Corporation** had outstanding 300,000 shares of convertible preferred stock. Alternatively, a **redemption privilege** might allow preferred shareholders the option, under specified conditions, to return their shares for a predetermined redemption price. Preferred shareholders have preference over common stockholders in dividends and liquidation rights. Each Xerox preferred share is convertible into 90 common shares. Similarly, shares may be redeemable at the option of the issuing corporation (sometimes referred to as *callable*).

Shares may be:
1. *Convertible* into a specified number of another class of shares.
2. *Redeemable* at the option of:
   a. Shareholders.
   b. The corporation.

Preferred shares may be **cumulative** or **noncumulative**. Typically, preferred shares are cumulative, which means that if the specified dividend is not paid for a given year, the unpaid dividends (called *dividends in arrears*) accumulate and must be made up in a later dividend year before any dividends are paid on common shares. We see this illustrated in Part B of the chapter.

Preferred shares may be **participating** or **nonparticipating**. A participating feature allows preferred shareholders to receive additional dividends beyond the stated amount. If the preferred shares are fully participating, the distribution of dividends to common and preferred shareholders is a pro rata allocation based on the relative par amounts of common and preferred stock outstanding. Participating preferred stock, previously quite common, is rare today.

Remember that the designations of common and preferred imply no necessary rights, privileges, or limitations of the shares so designated. Such relative rights must be specified by the contract with shareholders. A corporation can create classes of preferred shares that are indistinguishable from common shares in voting rights and/or the right to participate in assets (distributed as dividends or distributed upon liquidation). Likewise, it is possible to devise classes of common shares that possess preferential rights, superior to those of preferred shares.

Is It Equity or Is It Debt?

You probably also can imagine an issue of preferred shares that is almost indistinguishable from a bond issue. Let's say, for instance, that preferred shares call for annual cash dividends of 10% of the par value, dividends are cumulative, and the shares must be redeemed for cash in 10 years. Although the declaration of dividends rests in the discretion of the board of directors, the contract with preferred shareholders can be worded in such a way that directors are compelled to declare dividends each year the company is profitable. For a profitable company, it would be difficult to draw the line between this issue of preferred shares and a 10%, 10-year bond issue. Even in a more typical situation, preferred shares are somewhat hybrid securities—a cross between equity and debt.

The line between debt and equity is hard to draw.

Sometimes the similarity to debt is even more obvious. Suppose shares are mandatorily redeemable—the company is obligated to buy back the shares at a specified future date. The fact that the company is obligated to pay cash (or other assets) at a fixed or determinable date in the future makes this financial instrument tantamount to debt. A mandatorily redeemable financial instrument must be reported in the balance sheet as a liability, not as shareholders' equity.[6] **Extended Stay America**, for instance, reported its mandatorily redeemable preferred shares as a liability in its 2016 balance sheet.

Mandatorily redeemable shares are classified as liabilities.

The Concept of Par Value

Another prevalent practice (besides labeling shares as common and preferred) that has little significance other than historical is assigning a par value to shares. The concept of par value dates back as far as the concept of owning shares of a business. Par value originally indicated the real value of shares. All shares were issued at that price.

We have inherited the archaic concept of par value from early corporate law.

[6]FASB ASC 480–10–25–4: Distinguishing Liabilities from Equity–Overall–Recognition (previously "Accounting for Certain Financial Instruments with Characteristics of Both Liabilities and Equity," *Statement of Financial Accounting Standards No. 150* (Norwalk, Conn.: FASB, 2005)).

International Financial Reporting Standards

LO18–9

Distinction between Debt and Equity for Preferred Stock. Differences in the definitions and requirements can result in the same instrument being classified differently between debt and equity under IFRS and U.S. GAAP. Under U.S. GAAP, preferred stock normally is reported as equity, but is reported as debt with the dividends reported in the income statement as interest expense if it is "mandatorily redeemable" preferred stock. Under IFRS, most non-mandatorily redeemable preferred stock (preference shares) also is reported as debt as well as some preference shares that aren't redeemable. Under IFRS (*IAS No. 32*), the critical feature that distinguishes a liability is if the issuer is or can be required to deliver cash (or another financial instrument) to the holder.[7] Unilever describes such a difference in a disclosure note:

> **Additional Information for U.S. Investors (in part)**
>
> **Preference Shares**
>
> Under IAS 32, Unilever recognizes preference shares that provide a fixed preference dividend as borrowings with preference dividends recognized in the income statement. Under U.S. GAAP such preference shares are classified in shareholders' equity with dividends treated as a deduction to shareholder's equity.

During the late 19th and early 20th centuries, many cases of selling shares for less than par value—known as *watered shares*—received a great deal of attention and were the subject of a number of lawsuits. Investors and creditors contended that they relied on the par value as the permanent investment in the corporation and therefore net assets must always be at least that amount. Not only was par value assumed to be the amount invested by shareholders, but it also was defined by early corporation laws as the amount of net assets not available for distribution to shareholders (as dividends or otherwise).

Shares with nominal par value became common to dodge elaborate statutory rules pertaining to par value shares.

Many companies began turning to par value shares with very low par values—often pennies—to escape the watered shares liability of issuing shares below an arbitrary par value and to limit the restrictions on distributions. This practice is common today.

Accountants and attorneys have been aware for decades that laws pertaining to par value and legal capital not only are bewildering but fail in their intent to safeguard creditors from payments to shareholders. Actually, to the extent that creditors are led to believe that they are afforded protection, they are misled. Like the designations of common and preferred shares, the concepts of par value and legal capital have been eliminated entirely from the Model Business Corporation Act.[8]

Many states already have adopted these provisions of the Model Act. But most established corporations issued shares prior to changes in the state statutes. Consequently, most companies have par value shares outstanding and continue to issue previously authorized par value shares. The evolution will be gradual to the simpler, more meaningful provisions of the Model Act.

Most shares continue to bear arbitrarily designated par values.

In the meantime, accountants must be familiar with the outdated concepts of par value and legal capital in order to properly record and report transactions related to par value shares. For that reason, most of the discussion in this chapter centers on par value shares. Largely, this means only that proceeds from shareholders' investment is allocated between stated capital and additional paid-in capital. Be aware, though, that in the absence of archaic laws that prompted the creation of par value shares, there is no theoretical reason to do so.

Accounting for the Issuance of Shares

Shares Issued For Cash

LO18–4

When shares are sold for cash (see Illustration 18–5), the capital stock account (usually common or preferred) is credited for the amount representing stated capital. When shares have a designated par value, that amount denotes stated capital and is credited to the stock

[7] "Financial Instruments: Presentation," *International Accounting Standard No. 32* (IASCF), as amended effective January 1, 2016.
[8] American Bar Association, official comment to Section 6.21 of the *Model Business Corporation Act*, 2011.

account. Proceeds in excess of this amount are credited to paid-in capital—excess of par (also called additional paid-in capital).

Illustration 18–5
Shares Sold for Cash

Dow Industrial sells 100,000 of its common shares, $1 par per share, for $10 per share:

	($ in thousands)	
Cash (100,000 shares at $10 price per share)	1,000	
Common stock (100,000 shares at $1 par per share)		100
Paid-in capital—excess of par (remainder)		900

The entire proceeds from the sale of no-par stock are deemed stated capital and recorded in the stock account. If the shares are no-par, the entry is as follows:

Cash (100,000 shares at $10 price per share)	1,000	
Common stock		1,000

The total amount received from the sale of no-par shares is credited to the stock account.

Shares Issued for Noncash Consideration

Occasionally, a company might issue its shares for consideration other than cash. It is not uncommon for a new company, yet to establish a reliable cash flow, to pay for promotional and legal services with shares rather than with cash. Similarly, shares might be given in payment for land, or for equipment, or for some other noncash asset.

Shares should be issued at fair value.

Even without a receipt of cash to establish the fair value of the shares at the time of the exchange, the transaction still should be recorded at fair value. Best evidence of fair value might be one or more of the following:

- A quoted market price for the shares
- A selling price established in a recent issue of shares for cash
- The amount of cash that would have been paid in a cash purchase of the asset or service
- An independent appraisal of the value of the asset received
- Other available evidence

Whichever evidence of fair value seems more clearly evident should be used.[9]

Illustration 18–6 demonstrates a situation where the quoted market price is the best evidence of fair value.

Illustration 18–6
Shares Sold for Noncash Consideration

DuMont Chemicals issues 1 million of its common shares, $1 par per share, in exchange for a custom-built factory for which no cash price is available. Today's issue of *The Wall Street Journal* lists DuMont's stock at $10 per share:

	($ in millions)	
Property, plant, and equipment (1 million shares at $10 per share)	10	
Common stock (1 million shares at $1 par per share)		1
Paid-in capital—excess of par (remainder)		9

The quoted market price for the shares issued might be the best evidence of fair value.

More Than One Security Issued for a Single Price

Although uncommon, a company might sell more than one security—perhaps common shares and preferred shares—for a single price. As you might expect, the cash received usually is the sum of the separate market values of the two securities. Of course, each is then recorded at its market value. However, if only one security's value is known, the second security's market value is inferred from the total selling price, as demonstrated in Illustration 18–7.

Because the shares sell for a total of $100 million, and the market value of the common shares is known to be $40 million (4 million × $10), the preferred shares are inferred to have a market value of $60 million.

[9]Although stock issuances are not specifically mentioned in FASB ASC 845–10–30: Nonmonetary Transactions–Overall–Initial Measurement (previously *APB Opinion No. 29*), this treatment is consistent with the general rule for accounting for noncash transactions as described in that pronouncement, pars. 18 and 25.

Illustration 18–7

More than One Security Sold for a Single Price

When only one security's value is known ($40 million), the second security's market value ($60 million) is assumed from the total selling price ($100 million).

AP&P issues 4 million of its common shares, $1 par per share, and 4 million of its preferred shares, $10 par, for $100 million. Today's issue of *The Wall Street Journal* lists AP&P's common at $10 per share. There is no established market for the preferred shares.

	($ in millions)	
Cash	100	
Common stock (4 million shares × $1 par)		4
Paid-in capital—excess of par, common		36
Preferred stock (4 million shares × $10 par)		40
Paid-in capital—excess of par, preferred		20

Additional Consideration

In the unlikely event that the total selling price is not equal to the sum of the two market prices (when both market values are known), the total selling price is allocated between the two securities, in proportion to their relative market values. You should note that this is the same approach we use (a) when more than one asset is purchased for a single purchase price to allocate the single price to the various assets acquired, (b) when detachable warrants and bonds are issued for a single price, and (c) in any other situation when more than one item is associated with a single purchase price or selling price.

Share Issue Costs

Share issue costs reduce the net cash proceeds from selling the shares and thus paid-in capital—excess of par.

When a company sells shares, it obtains the legal, promotional, and accounting services necessary to effect the sale. The cost of these services reduces the net proceeds from selling the shares. Since paid-in capital—excess of par is credited for the excess of the proceeds over the par value of the shares sold, the effect of share issue costs is to reduce the amount credited to that account. For example, in June 2016, **Spark Therapeutics, Inc.** sold 3,025,000 shares of its $0.001 par common stock at $45.00 per share, "for aggregate gross proceeds of $136.1 million. The Company received net proceeds from the public offering of $127.6 million, after deducting underwriting discounts and commissions and other offering expenses." Spark Therapeutics' entry to record the sale was:

The cash proceeds is the net amount received after paying share issue costs.

	($ in millions)	
Cash	127.6	
Common stock (3,025,000 shares at $0.001 par per share)		0.0
Paid-in capital—excess of par (remainder)		127.6

Concept Review Exercise

EXPANSION OF CORPORATE CAPITAL

Situation: The shareholders' equity section of the balance sheet of National Foods, Inc., included the following accounts at December 31, 2016:

Shareholders' Equity	**($ in millions)**
Paid-in capital:	
Common stock, 120 million shares at $1 par	$ 120
Paid-in capital—excess of par	836
Retained earnings	2,449
Total shareholders' equity	$3,405

Required:

1. During 2017, several transactions affected the stock of National Foods. Prepare the appropriate entries for these events.
   a. On March 11, National Foods issued 10 million of its 9.2% preferred shares, $1 par per share, for $44 per share.
   b. On November 22, 1 million common shares, $1 par per share, were issued in exchange for eight labeling machines. Each machine was built to custom specifications so no cash price was available. National Food's stock was listed at $10 per share.
   c. On November 23, 1 million of the common shares and 1 million preferred shares were sold for $60 million. The preferred shares had not traded since March and their market value was uncertain.
2. Prepare the shareholders' equity section of the comparative balance sheets for National Foods at December 31, 2017 and 2016. Assume that net income for 2017 was $400 million and the only other transaction affecting shareholders' equity was the payment of the 9.2% dividend on the 11 million preferred shares ($1 million).

Solution:

1. During 2017 several transactions affected the stock of National Foods. Prepare the appropriate entries for these events.
   a. On March 11, National Foods issued 10 million of its preferred shares, $1 par per share, for $44 per share.

	($ in millions)	
Cash	440	
Preferred stock (10 million shares × $1 par per share)		10
Paid-in capital—excess of par, preferred		430

   b. On November 22, 1 million common shares, $1 par per share, were issued in exchange for eight labeling machines:

	($ in millions)	
Machinery (fair value of shares)	10	
Common stock (1 million shares × $1 par per share)		1
Paid-in capital—excess of par, common (1 million shares × $9)		9

The transaction was recorded at the fair value of the shares exchanged for the machinery.

   c. On November 23, 1 million of the common shares and 1 million preferred shares were sold for $60 million:

	($ in millions)	
Cash	60	
Common stock (1 million shares × $1 par per share)		1
Paid-in capital—excess of par, common		9
Preferred stock (1 million shares × $1 par per share)		1
Paid-in capital—excess of par, preferred (to balance)		49

Since the value of only the common stock was known, the preferred stock's market value ($50 per share) was inferred from the total selling price.

2. Prepare the shareholders' equity section of the comparative balance sheets for National Foods at December 31, 2017 and 2016.

NATIONAL FOODS, INC.
Balance Sheet
(Shareholders' Equity Section)

($ in millions)	2017	2016
Shareholders' Equity		
Preferred stock, 9.2%, $1 par (2017: $10 million + 1 million)	$ 11	$ —
Common stock, $1 par (2017: $120 million + 1 million + 1 million)	122	120
Paid-in capital—excess of par, preferred (2017: $430 million + 49 million)	479	—
Paid-in capital—excess of par, common (2017: $836 million + 9 million + 9 million)	854	836
Retained earnings (2016: $2,449 million + 400 million − 1 million)	2,848	2,449
Total shareholders' equity	$4,314	$3,405

Note: This situation is continued in the next Concept Review Exercise.

Share Buybacks

LO18–5

In the previous section we examined various ways stock might be issued. In this section, we look at situations in which companies reacquire shares previously sold. Most medium- and large-size companies buy back their own shares. Many have formal share repurchase plans to buy back stock over a series of years.

Decision Makers' Perspective

When a company's management feels the market price of its stock is undervalued, it may attempt to support the price by decreasing the supply of stock in the marketplace. A Johnson & Johnson announcement that it planned to buy back up to $5 billion of its outstanding shares triggered a buying spree that pushed the stock price up by more than 3 percent.

Decreasing the supply of shares in the marketplace supports the price of remaining shares.

When announcing plans to expand its stock buyback program to $90 billion, Apple chief executive Tim Cook said it "views its shares as undervalued."[10] Although clearly a company may attempt to increase net assets by buying its shares at a low price and selling them back later at a higher price, that investment is not viewed as an asset. Similarly, increases and decreases in net assets from that activity are not reported as gains and losses in the company's income statement. Instead, buying and selling its shares are transactions between the corporation and its owners, analogous to retiring shares and then selling previously unissued shares. You should note the contrast between a company's purchasing of its own shares and its purchasing of shares in another corporation as an investment.

FINANCIAL Reporting Case

Q1, p. 1035

Unlike an investment in another firm's shares, the acquisition of a company's own shares does not create an asset.

Though not considered an investment, the repurchase of shares often is a judicious use of a company's cash. By increasing per share earnings and supporting share price, shareholders benefit. To the extent this strategy is effective, a share buyback can be viewed as a way to "distribute" company profits without paying dividends. Capital gains from any stock price increase are taxed at lower capital gains tax rates than ordinary income tax rates on dividends.

Companies buy back shares to offset the increase in shares issued to employees.

Perhaps the primary motivation for most stock repurchases is to offset the increase in shares that routinely are issued to employees under stock award and stock option compensation programs. Microsoft reported its stock buyback program designed to offset the effect of its stock option and stock purchase plans, as shown in Illustration 18–8.

[10]Daisuke Wakabayashi, "Apple Boosts Buyback, Splits Stock to Reward Investors," Dow Jones Business Report, www.nasdaq.com, April 23, 2014.

> **Note 11: Stockholders' Equity (in part)**
> Our board of directors has approved a program to repurchase shares of our common stock to reduce the dilutive effect of our stock option and stock purchase plans.

Illustration 18–8

Disclosure of Share Repurchase Program—Microsoft

Real World Financials

Similarly, shares might be reacquired to distribute in a stock dividend, a proposed merger, or as a defense against a hostile takeover.[11]

The usual pattern of stock buybacks was interrupted by the recent economic decline. With corporate profits down and cash in short supply, companies drastically reduced their share repurchases. For some companies, the decision was a choice between cutting buybacks or cutting dividends, and dividend reductions are more obvious and less palatable than curtailing a buyback program.

Whatever the reason shares are repurchased, a company has a choice of how to account for the buyback.

1. The shares can be formally retired.
2. The shares can be called treasury stock.

Unfortunately, the choice is not dictated by the nature of the buyback, but by practical motivations of the company. ●

Shares Formally Retired or Viewed as Treasury Stock

FINANCIAL Reporting Case

Q2, p. 1035

When a corporation retires its own shares, those shares assume the same status as authorized but unissued shares, just the same as if they never had been issued. We saw earlier in the chapter that when shares are sold, both cash (usually) and shareholders' equity are increased; the company becomes larger. Conversely, when cash is paid to retire stock, the effect is to decrease both cash and shareholders' equity; the size of the company literally is reduced.

Reacquired shares are equivalent to authorized but unissued shares.

Out of tradition and for practical reasons, companies usually reacquire shares of previously issued stock without formally retiring them.[12] Shares repurchased and not retired are referred to as treasury stock. Because reacquired shares are essentially the same as shares that never were issued at all, treasury shares have no voting rights nor do they receive cash dividends. As demonstrated in Illustration 18–9, when shares are repurchased as treasury stock, we reduce shareholders' equity with a debit to a negative (or contra) shareholders' equity account labeled treasury stock. That entry is reversed later through a credit to treasury stock when the treasury stock is resold. Like the concepts of par value and legal capital, the concept of treasury shares no longer is recognized in most state statutes.[13] Some companies, in fact, are eliminating treasury shares from their financial statements as corporate statutes are modernized. Microsoft retires the shares it buys back rather than labeling them treasury stock. Still, you will see treasury shares reported in the balance sheets of many companies.

Accounting for Retired Shares

When shares are formally retired, we should reduce precisely the same accounts that previously were increased when the shares were sold, namely, common (or preferred) stock and paid-in capital—excess of par. The first column of Illustration 18–9 demonstrates this.

[11]A corporate takeover occurs when an individual or group of individuals acquires a majority of a company's outstanding common stock from present shareholders. Corporations that are the object of a hostile takeover attempt–a public bid for control of a company's stock against the company's wishes–often take evasive action involving the reacquisition of shares.

[12]The concept of treasury shares originated long ago when new companies found they could sell shares at an unrealistically low price equal to par value to incorporators, who then donated those shares back to the company. Since these shares already had been issued (though not outstanding), they could be sold at whatever the real market price was without adjusting stated capital. Because treasury shares are already issued, different rules apply to their purchase and resale than to unissued shares. Companies can:

1. Issue shares without regard to preemptive rights of shareholders.
2. Distribute shares as a dividend to shareholders even without a balance in retained earnings.

[13]*The Revised Model Business Corporation Act* eliminated the concept of treasury shares in 1984, after 1980 revisions had eliminated the concepts of par value and legal capital. Most state laws have since followed suit.

Illustration 18–9

Comparison of Share Retirement and Treasury Stock Accounting—Share Buybacks

American Semiconductor's balance sheet included the following:

Shareholders' Equity	($ in millions)
Common stock, 100 million shares at $1 par	$ 100
Paid-in capital—excess of par	900
Paid-in capital—share repurchase	2
Retained earnings	2,000

Retirement			**Treasury Stock**		
Reacquired 1 million of its common shares					
Case 1: Shares repurchased at $7 per share					
Common stock ($1 par × 1 million shares)	1		Treasury stock (cost)	7	
Paid-in capital—excess of par ($9 per share)	9				
Paid-in capital—share repurchase (difference)		3			
Cash		7	Cash		7
OR					
Case 2: Shares repurchased at $13 per share					
Common stock ($1 par × 1 million shares)	1		Treasury stock (cost)	13	
Paid-in capital—excess of par ($9 per share)	9				
Paid-in capital—share repurchase	2*				
Retained earnings (difference)	1				
Cash		13	Cash		13

*Because there is a $2 million credit balance.

Formally retiring shares restores the balances in both the Common stock account and Paid-in capital—excess of par to what those balances would have been if the shares never had been issued.

When we view a buyback as treasury stock, the cost of acquiring the shares is debited to the treasury stock account.

The paid-in capital—excess of par account for American Semiconductor shows a balance of $900 million while the common stock account shows a balance of $100 million. Thus the 100 million outstanding shares were originally sold for an average of $9 per share above par, or $10 per share. Consequently, when 1 million shares are retired (regardless of the retirement price), American Semiconductor should reduce its common stock account by $1 per share and its paid-in capital—excess of par by $9 per share. Another way to view the reduction is that because 1% of the shares are retired, both share account balances (common stock and paid-in capital—excess of par) are reduced by 1%.

How we treat the difference between the cash paid to buy the shares and the amount the shares originally sold for (amounts debited to common stock and paid-in capital—excess of par) depends on whether the cash paid is *less* than the original issue price (credit difference) or the cash paid is *more* than the original issue price (debit difference):

1. If a *credit* difference is created (as in Case 1 of Illustration 18–9), we credit paid-in capital—share repurchase.
2. If a *debit* difference is created (as in Case 2 of Illustration 18–9), we debit paid-in capital—share repurchase, but only if that account already has a credit balance. Otherwise, we debit retained earnings. (Reducing the account beyond its previous balance would create a negative balance.)

Paid-in capital—share repurchase is debited to the extent of its credit balance before debiting retained earnings.

Payments made by a corporation to retire its own shares are viewed as a distribution of corporate assets to shareholders.

Why is paid-in capital credited in Case 1 and retained earnings debited in Case 2? The answer lies in the fact that the payments made by a corporation to repurchase its own shares are a distribution of corporate assets to shareholders.

In Case 1, only $7 million is distributed to shareholders to retire shares that originally provided $10 million of paid-in capital. Thus, some of the original investment ($3 million in this case) remains and is labeled *paid-in capital—share repurchase.*

In Case 2, more cash ($13 million) is distributed to shareholders to retire shares than originally was paid in. The amount paid in comprises the original investment of $10 million for the shares being retired, plus $2 million of paid-in capital created by previous repurchase transactions—$12 million total. Thirteen million is returned to shareholders. The additional

$1 million paid is viewed as a dividend on the shareholders' investment, and thus a reduction of retained earnings.[14]

Additional Consideration

Some companies choose to debit retained earnings for the entire debit difference between the cash paid to repurchase shares and the par amount of those shares rather than allocate that difference in the prescribed way. Target Corporation is an example of a company that follows this approach. While this method lacks conceptual merit by itself, it's permitted by ASC 505-30-30-8, which states that "a corporation can always capitalize or allocate retained earnings for such purposes."

Accounting for Treasury Stock

We view the purchase of treasury stock as a temporary reduction of shareholders' equity, to be reversed later when the treasury stock is resold. The cost of acquiring the shares is "temporarily" debited to the treasury stock account (second column of Illustration 18–9). At this point, the shares are considered to be *issued, but not outstanding.*

Recording the effects on specific shareholders' equity accounts is delayed until later when the shares are reissued. In the meantime, the shares assume the fictional status we discussed earlier of being neither unissued nor outstanding. Effectively, we consider the purchase of treasury stock and its subsequent resale to be a "single transaction."

Additional Consideration

The approach to accounting for treasury stock we discuss in this chapter is referred to as the "cost method." Another permissible approach is the "par value method." It is essentially identical to formally retiring shares, which is why it sometimes is referred to as the *retirement method of accounting for treasury stock.* In fact, if we substitute Treasury stock for Common stock in each of the journal entries we used to account for retirement of shares in Illustrations 18–9 and 18–11, we have the par value method. Because the method has virtually disappeared from practice, we do not discuss it further in this chapter.

BALANCE SHEET EFFECT. Formally retiring shares restores the balances in both the Common stock account and Paid-in capital—excess of par to what those balances would have been if the shares never had been issued at all. As discussed above, any net increase in assets resulting from the sale and subsequent repurchase is reflected as Paid-in capital—share repurchase. On the other hand, any net decrease in assets resulting from the sale and subsequent repurchase is reflected as a reduction in retained earnings.

In contrast, when a share repurchase is viewed as treasury stock, the cost of the treasury stock is simply reported as a reduction in total shareholders' equity. Reporting under the two approaches is compared in Illustration 18–10, using the situation described above for American Semiconductor after the purchase of treasury stock in Illustration 18–9 (Case 2). Notice that either way total shareholders' equity is the same.

Resale of Shares

After shares are formally retired, any subsequent sale of shares is simply the sale of new, unissued shares and is accounted for accordingly. This is demonstrated in the first column of Illustration 18–11.

Allocating the cost of treasury shares occurs when the shares are resold.

The resale of treasury shares is viewed as the consummation of the single transaction begun when the treasury shares were repurchased. The effect of the single transaction of

[14]In the next section of this chapter, you will be reminded that dividends reduce retained earnings. (You first learned this in your introductory accounting course.)

Illustration 18–10

Reporting Share Buyback in the Balance Sheet

Retirement reduces common stock and associated shareholders' equity accounts.

($ in millions)	Shares Retired	Treasury Stock
Shareholders' Equity		
Paid-in capital:		
Common stock, 100 million shares at $1 par	$ 99	$ 100
Paid-in capital—excess of par	891	900
Paid-in capital—share repurchase		2
Retained earnings	1,999	2,000
Less: Treasury stock, 1 million shares (at cost)		(13)
Total shareholders' equity	$2,989	$2,989

Illustration 18–11

Comparison of Share Retirement and Treasury Stock Accounting—Subsequent Sale of Shares

After formally retiring shares, we record a subsequent sale of shares exactly like any sale of shares.

The resale of treasury shares is viewed as the consummation of the "single transaction" begun when the treasury shares were purchased.

American Semiconductor sold 1 million shares after reacquiring shares at $13 per share (Case 2 in Illustration 18–9).

Retirement			Treasury Stock		
Sold 1 million shares					
Case A: Shares sold at $14 per share					
Cash	14		Cash	14	
Common stock (par)		1	Treasury stock (cost)		13
Paid-in capital—excess of par		13	Paid-in capital—share repurchase		1
Or					
Case B: Shares sold at $10 per share					
Cash	10		Cash	10	
Common stock (par)		1	Retained earnings (to balance)	1	
Paid-in capital—excess of par		9	Paid-in capital—share repurchase	2*	
			Treasury stock (cost)		13

*Because there is a $2 million credit balance.

purchasing treasury stock and reselling it for more than cost (Case 2 of Illustration 18–9 and Case A of Illustration 18–11) is to *increase* both cash and shareholders' equity (by $1 million). The effect of the single transaction of purchasing treasury stock and reselling it for less than cost (Case 2 of Illustration 18–9 and Case B of Illustration 18–11) is to *decrease* both cash and shareholders' equity (by $3 million).

Note that retained earnings may be debited in a treasury stock transaction, but not credited. Also notice that transactions involving treasury stock have no impact on the income statement. This follows the reasoning discussed earlier that a corporation's buying and selling of its own shares are transactions between the corporation and its owners and not part of the revenue recognition process.

Additional Consideration

Determining the cost of treasury stock sold is similar to determining the cost of goods sold.

Treasury Shares Acquired at Different Costs

Notice that the treasury stock account always is credited for the cost of the reissued shares ($13 million in Illustration 18–11). When shares are reissued, if treasury stock on hand has been purchased at different per share prices, the cost of the shares sold must be determined using a cost flow assumption—FIFO, LIFO, or weighted average—similar to determining the cost of goods sold when inventory items are acquired at different unit costs.

Concept Review Exercise

TREASURY STOCK

Situation: The shareholders' equity section of the balance sheet of National Foods, Inc. included the following accounts at December 31, 2017.

Shareholders' Equity	($ in millions)
Paid-in capital:	
Preferred stock, 11 million shares at $1 par	$ 11
Common stock, 122 million shares at $1 par	122
Paid-in capital—excess of par, preferred	479
Paid-in capital—excess of par, common	854
Retained earnings	2,848
Total shareholders' equity	$4,314

Required:

1. National Foods reacquired common shares during 2018 and sold shares in two separate transactions later that year. Prepare the entries for both the purchase and subsequent sale of shares during 2018, assuming that the shares were (a) retired and (b) considered to be treasury stock.
   a. National Foods purchased 6 million shares at $10 per share.
   b. National Foods sold 2 million shares at $12 per share.
   c. National Foods sold 2 million shares at $7 per share.
2. Prepare the shareholders' equity section of National Foods' balance sheet at December 31, 2018, assuming the shares were both (a) retired and (b) viewed as treasury stock. Net income for 2018 was $400 million, and preferred shareholders were paid $1 million cash dividends.

Solution:

1. National Foods reacquired common shares during 2018 and sold shares in two separate transactions later that year. Prepare the entries for both the purchase and subsequent sale of shares during 2018, assuming that the shares were (a) retired and (b) considered to be treasury stock.
   a. National Foods purchased 6 million shares at $10 per share:

Retirement ($ in millions)			**Treasury Stock** ($ in millions)		
Common stock (6 million shares × $1)	6		Treasury stock (6 million shares × $10)	60	
Paid-in capital—excess of par (6 million shares × $7*)	42		Cash		60
Retained earnings (to balance)	12				
Cash		60			

*$854 million ÷ 122 million shares

   b. National Foods sold 2 million shares at $12 per share ($ in millions):

Cash	24		Cash	24	
Common stock (2 million shares × $1)		2	Treasury stock (2 million shares × $10)		20
Paid-in capital—excess of par		22	Paid-in capital—share repurchase		4

   c. National Foods sold 2 million shares at $7 per share ($ in millions):

Cash	14		Cash	14	
Common stock (2 million shares × $1 par)		2	Paid-in capital—share repurchase	4	
Paid-in capital—excess of par		12	Retained earnings (to balance)	2	
			Treasury stock (2 million shares × $10)		20

2. Prepare the shareholders' equity section of National Foods' balance sheet at December 31, 2018, assuming the shares were both (a) retired and (b) viewed as treasury stock.

NATIONAL FOODS, INC.
Balance Sheet
(Shareholders' Equity Section)
At December 31, 2018

($ in millions)	Shares Retired	Treasury Stock
Shareholders' Equity		
Preferred stock, 11 million shares at $1 par	$ 11	$ 11
Common stock, 122 million shares at $1 par	120	122
Paid-in capital—excess of par, preferred	479	479
Paid-in capital—excess of par, common	846*	854
Retained earnings	3,235†	3,245‡
Treasury stock, at cost; 2 million common shares	—	(20)
Total shareholders' equity	$4,691	$4,691

Note: This situation is continued in the next Concept Review Exercise.

*$854 − 42 + 22 + 12
†$2,848 − 12 + 400 − 1
‡$2,848 − 2 + 400 − 1

PART C

Retained Earnings

Characteristics of Retained Earnings

LO18–6

In the previous section we examined *invested* capital. Now we consider *earned* capital, that is, retained earnings. In general, retained earnings represents a corporation's accumulated, undistributed net income (or net loss). A more descriptive title used by some companies is reinvested earnings. A credit balance in this account indicates a dollar amount of assets previously earned by the firm but not distributed as dividends to shareholders. We refer to a debit balance in retained earnings as a deficit. Microsoft reported a deficit for several years until retained earnings grew to a positive balance in 2013.

You saw in the previous section that the buyback of shares (as well as the resale of treasury shares in some cases) can decrease retained earnings. We examine in this section the effect on retained earnings of dividends and stock splits.[15]

Dividends

LO18–7

Shareholders' initial investments in a corporation are represented by amounts reported as paid-in capital. One way a corporation provides a return to its shareholders on their investments is to pay them a dividend, typically cash.[16]

Dividends are distributions of assets the company has earned on behalf of its shareholders. If dividends are paid that exceed the amount of assets earned by the company, then management is, in effect, returning to shareholders a portion of their investments, rather than providing them a return on that investment. So most companies view retained earnings as the amount available for dividends.[17]

[15]Retained earnings also can be affected by some changes in accounting principles and for some corrections of errors, as we will see in chapter 20. And, too, retained earnings can be affected by the repurchase of shares as we discussed in Part A of this chapter.

[16]Dividends are not the only return shareholders earn; when market prices of their shares rise, shareholders benefit also. Indeed, many companies have adopted policies of never paying dividends but reinvesting all assets they earn. The motivation is to accommodate more rapid expansion and thus, presumably, increases in the market price of the stock.

[17]Ordinarily, this is not the legal limitation. Most states permit a company to pay dividends so long as, after the dividend, its assets would not be "less than the sum of its total liabilities plus the amount that would be needed, if the corporation were to be dissolved at the time of the distribution, to satisfy the preferential rights upon dissolution of shareholders whose preferential rights are superior to those receiving the distribution." (Revised Model Business Corporation Act, American Bar Association, 2011.) Thus, legally, a corporation can distribute amounts equal to total shareholders' equity less dissolution preferences of senior equity securities (usually preferred stock).

Liquidating Dividend

In unusual instances in which a dividend exceeds the balance in retained earnings, the excess is referred to as a **liquidating dividend** because some of the invested capital is being liquidated. This might occur when a corporation is being dissolved and assets (not subject to a superior claim by creditors) are distributed to shareholders. Any portion of a dividend not representing a distribution of earnings should be debited to additional paid-in capital rather than retained earnings.

Any dividend not representing a distribution of earnings should be debited to paid-in capital.

Retained Earnings Restrictions

Sometimes the amount available for dividends purposely is reduced by management. A restriction of retained earnings designates a portion of the balance in retained earnings as being *unavailable for dividends.* A company might restrict retained earnings to indicate management's intention to withhold for some specific purpose the assets represented by that portion of the retained earnings balance. For example, management might anticipate the need for a specific amount of assets in upcoming years to repay a maturing debt, to cover a contingent loss, or to finance expansion of the facilities. Be sure to understand that the restriction itself does not set aside cash for the designated event but merely communicates management's intention not to distribute the stated amount as a dividend.

A restriction of retained earnings communicates management's intention to withhold assets represented by a specified portion of the retained earnings balance.

A restriction of retained earnings normally is indicated by a disclosure note to the financial statements. Although instances are rare, a formal journal entry may be used to reclassify a portion of retained earnings to an "appropriated" retained earnings account.

Normally a restriction of retained earnings is indicated by a disclosure note.

Cash Dividends

You learned in Chapter 14 that paying interest to creditors is a contractual obligation. No such legal obligation exists for paying dividends to shareholders. A liability is not recorded until a company's board of directors votes to declare a dividend. In practice, though, corporations ordinarily try to maintain a stable dividend pattern over time.

When directors declare a cash dividend, we reduce retained earnings and record a liability. Before the payment actually can be made, a listing must be assembled of shareholders entitled to receive the dividend. A specific date is stated as to when the determination will be made of the recipients of the dividend. This date is called the **date of record**. Registered owners of shares of stock on this date are entitled to receive the dividend—even if they sell those shares prior to the actual cash payment. To be a registered owner of shares on the date of record, an investor must purchase the shares before the **ex-dividend date**. This date usually is two business days before the date of record. Shares purchased on or after that date are purchased ex dividend—without the right to receive the declared dividend. As a result, the market price of a share typically will decline by the amount of the dividend, other things being equal, on the ex-dividend date. Consider Illustration 18–12.

FINANCIAL Reporting Case

Q3, p. 1035

Illustration 18–12
Cash Dividends

On June 1, the board of directors of Craft Industries declares a cash dividend of $2 per share on its 100 million shares, payable to shareholders of record June 15, to be paid July 1.

June 1—Declaration Date	($ in millions)	
Retained earnings	200	
Cash dividends payable (100 million shares at $2 per share)		200
June 13—Ex-Dividend Date		
No entry		
June 15—Date of Record		
No entry		
July 1—Payment Date		
Cash dividends payable	200	
Cash		200

At the declaration date, retained earnings is reduced and a liability is recorded.

Registered owners of shares on the date of record are entitled to receive the dividend.

A sufficient balance in retained earnings permits a dividend to be declared. Remember, though, that retained earnings is a shareholders' equity account representing a dollar claim on assets in general, but not on any specific asset in particular. Sufficient retained earnings does not ensure sufficient cash to make payment. These are two separate accounts having no necessary connection with one another. When a dividend is "paid from retained earnings," this simply means there are sufficient assets to pay the dividend without returning invested assets to shareholders.

DIVIDENDS ON PREFERRED SHARES. As mentioned in Part A, preferred shares can be cumulative or noncumulative. Cumulative means that if the specified dividend is not paid for a given year, the unpaid dividends (called *dividends* in *arrears*) accumulate and must be made up in a later dividend year before any dividends are paid on common shares. Illustration 18–13 provides an example.

Illustration 18–13

Distribution of Dividends to Preferred Shareholders

The shareholders' equity section of Corbin Enterprises includes the items shown below. The board of directors declared cash dividends of $360,000, $500,000, and $700,000 in its first three years of operation—2017, 2018, and 2019, respectively.

Common stock	$3,000,000
Paid-in capital—excess of par, common	9,800,000
Preferred stock, 8%	6,000,000
Paid-in capital—excess of par, preferred	780,000

If preferred shares are not cumulative, dividends not declared in any given year need never be paid.

Determine the amount of dividends to be paid to preferred and common shareholders in each of the three years, assuming that the preferred stock is cumulative and nonparticipating.

	Preferred	Common
2017	$360,000*	$0
2018	500,000**	0
2019	580,000†	120,000 (remainder)

*The preferred shareholders are entitled to dividends of $480,000 (8% × $6,000,000), but only $360,000 dividends are declared in 2017 so dividends in arrears are $120,000.
**$120,000 dividends in arrears plus $380,000 of the $480,000 current preference.
†$100,000 dividends in arrears ($480,000 − 380,000) plus the $480,000 current preference

Property Dividends

The *fair value* of the assets to be distributed is the amount recorded for a property dividend.

Because cash is the asset most easily divided and distributed to shareholders, most corporate dividends are cash dividends. In concept, though, any asset can be distributed to shareholders as a dividend. When a noncash asset is distributed, it is referred to as a **property dividend** (often called a *dividend in kind* or a *nonreciprocal transfer to owners*). **Gold Resource Corp.**, a Colorado gold mining company, announced in 2014 that it would make dividend payments in gold bullion instead of cash.

RFM Corporation conferred a property dividend to its shareholders when it distributed shares of **Philipine Townships, Inc.**, stock that RFM was holding as an investment. Securities held as investments are the assets most often distributed in a property dividend due to the relative ease of dividing these assets among shareholders and determining their fair values.

A property dividend should be recorded at the fair value of the assets to be distributed, measured at the date of declaration. This may require revaluing the asset to fair value prior to recording the dividend. If so, a gain or loss is recognized for the difference between book value and fair value. This is demonstrated in Illustration 18–14.

Stock Dividends and Splits

Stock Dividends

LO18–8

A **stock dividend** is the distribution of additional shares of stock to current shareholders of the corporation. Be sure to note the contrast between a stock dividend and either a cash or

Illustration 18–14

Property Dividends

On October 1 the board of directors of Craft Industries declares a property dividend of 2 million shares of Beaman Corporation's preferred stock that Craft had purchased in March as an investment (book value: $9 million). The investment shares have a fair value of $5 per share, $10 million, and are payable to shareholders of record October 15, to be distributed November 1.

	($ in millions)	
October 1—Declaration Date		
Investment in Beaman Corporation preferred stock	1	
Gain on appreciation of investment ($10 − 9)		1
Retained earnings (2 million shares at $5 per share)	10	
Property dividends payable		10
October 15—Date of Record		
No entry		
November 1—Payment Date		
Property dividends payable	10	
Investment in Beaman Corporation preferred stock		10

Before recording the property dividend, the asset first must be written up to fair value.

property dividend. A stock dividend affects neither the assets nor the liabilities of the firm. Also, because each shareholder receives the same percentage increase in shares, shareholders' proportional interest in (percentage ownership of) the firm remains unchanged. For example, if a 5% stock dividend is declared, every shareholder will receive additional shares of stock to equal 5% of the shares they currently own.

The prescribed accounting treatment of a stock dividend requires that shareholders' equity items bc reclassified by reducing one or more shareholders' equity accounts and simultaneously increasing one or more paid-in capital accounts. The amount reclassified depends on the size of the stock dividend. For a small stock dividend, typically less than 25%, the fair value of the additional shares distributed is transferred from retained earnings to paid-in capital, as demonstrated in Illustration 18–15.[18]

Illustration 18–15

Stock Dividend

Craft declares and distributes a 10% common stock dividend (10 million shares) when the market value of the $1 par common stock is $12 per share.

	($ in millions)	
Retained earnings (10 million shares at $12 per share)	120	
Common stock (10 million shares at $1 par per share)		10
Paid-in capital—excess of par (remainder)		110

A small stock dividend requires reclassification to paid-in capital of retained earnings equal to the fair value of the additional shares distributed.

Additional Consideration

The entry above is recorded on the declaration date. Since the additional shares are not yet issued, some accountants would prefer to credit "common stock dividends issuable" at this point, instead of common stock. In that case, when the shares are issued, common stock dividends issuable is debited and common stock credited. The choice really is inconsequential; either way the $10 million amount would be reported as part of paid-in capital on a balance sheet prepared between the declaration and distribution of the shares.

STOCK MARKET REACTION TO STOCK DISTRIBUTIONS. As a Craft shareholder owning 10 shares at the time of the 10% stock dividend, you would receive an 11th share. Since each is worth $12, would you benefit by $12 when you receive the additional share from Craft? Of course not. If the value of each share were to remain $12 when the

[18]FASB ASC 505–20: Equity–Stock Dividends and Stock Splits (previously "Restatement and Revision of Accounting Research Bulletins," *Accounting Research Bulletin No. 43* (New York: AICPA, 1961), Chap. 7, sec. B, pars. 10–14). In this pronouncement, a small stock dividend is defined as one 20% to 25% or less. For filings with that agency, the SEC has refined the definition to comprise stock distributions of less than 25%.

10 million new shares are distributed, the total market value of the company would grow by $120 million (10 million shares × $12 per share).

The market price per share will decline in proportion to the increase in the number of shares distributed in a stock dividend.

A corporation cannot increase its market value simply by distributing additional stock certificates. Because all shareholders receive the same percentage increase in their respective holdings, you, and all other shareholders, still would own the same percentage of the company as before the distribution. Accordingly, the per share value of your shares should decline from $12 to $10.91 so that your 11 shares would be worth $120— precisely what your 10 shares were worth prior to the stock dividend. You might compare Craft Industries to a pizza. Cutting the pizza into 16 slices instead of 12 doesn't create more to eat; you still have the same pizza, just a higher number of smaller slices. Any failure of the stock price to actually adjust in proportion to the additional shares issued probably would be due to information other than the distribution reaching shareholders at the same time.

Early rule-makers felt that per share market prices do not adjust in response to an increase in the number of shares.

Then, what justification is there for recording the additional shares at market value? In 1941 (and reaffirmed in 1953), accounting rule-makers felt that many shareholders are deceived by small stock dividends, believing they benefit by the market value of their additional shares. Furthermore they erroneously felt that these individual beliefs are collectively reflected in the stock market by per share prices that remain unchanged by stock dividends. Consequently, their prescribed accounting treatment is to reduce retained earnings by the same amount as if cash dividends were paid equal to the market value of the shares issued.[19]

This obsolete reasoning is inconsistent with our earlier conclusion that the market price per share *will* decline in approximate proportion to the increase in the number of shares distributed. Our intuitive conclusion is supported also by formal research.[20]

Capitalizing retained earnings for a stock dividend artificially reclassifies earned capital as invested capital.

Besides being based on fallacious reasoning, accounting for stock dividends by artificially reclassifying "earned" capital as "invested" capital conflicts with the reporting objective of reporting shareholders' equity by source. Despite these limitations, this outdated accounting standard still applies.

Companies sometimes declare a stock dividend in lieu of a real dividend.

REASONS FOR STOCK DIVIDENDS. Since neither the corporation nor its shareholders apparently benefits from stock dividends, why do companies declare them?[21] Occasionally, a company tries to give shareholders the illusion that they are receiving a real dividend.

Companies sometimes declare a stock dividend so they can capitalize retained earnings.

Another reason is merely to enable the corporation to take advantage of the accepted accounting practice of capitalizing retained earnings. Specifically, a company might wish to reduce an existing balance in retained earnings—otherwise available for *cash* dividends—so it can reinvest the earned assets represented by that balance without carrying a large balance in retained earnings.

Stock Splits

FINANCIAL Reporting Case

Q4, p. 1035

A frequent reason for issuing a stock dividend is actually to induce the per share market price decline that follows. For instance, after a company declares a 100% stock dividend on 100 million shares of common stock, with a per share market price of $12, it then has 200 million shares, each with an approximate market value of $6. The motivation for reducing the per share market price is to increase the stock's *marketability* by making it attractive to a larger number of potential investors.

A large stock dividend is known as a stock *split*.

A stock distribution of 25% or higher can be accounted for in one of two ways: (1) as a "large" stock dividend or (2) as a **stock split**.[22] Thus, a 100% stock dividend could be labeled a 2-for-1 stock split and accounted for as such. Conceptually, the proper accounting treatment of a stock distribution is to make no journal entry. This, in fact, is the prescribed accounting treatment for a stock split.

[19]FASB ASC 505–20–30–3: Equity–Stock Dividends and Stock Splits–Initial Measurement (previously "Restatement and Revision of Accounting Research Bulletins," *Accounting Research Bulletin No. 43* (New York: AICPA, 1961), chap. 7).

[20]Foster and Vickrey, "The Information Content of Stock Dividend Announcements," *Accounting Review* (April 1978); and Spiceland and Winters, "The Market Reaction to Stock Distributions: The Effect of Market Anticipation and Cash Returns," *Accounting and Business Research* (Summer 1986).

[21]After hitting a high in the 1940s, the number of stock dividends has declined significantly. Currently, about 3% of companies declare stock dividends in any given year.

[22]FASB ASC 505–20–25–2: Equity–Stock Dividends and Stock Splits–Recognition (previously "Restatement and Revision of Accounting Research Bulletins," *Accounting Research Bulletin No. 43* (New York: AICPA, 1961), Chap. 7, sec. B, par. 11).

Additional Consideration

No cash dividends are paid on treasury shares. Usually stock dividends aren't paid on treasury shares either. Treasury shares are essentially equivalent to shares that never have been issued. In some circumstances, though, the intended use of the repurchased shares will give reason for the treasury shares to participate in a stock dividend. For instance, if the treasury shares have been specifically designated for issuance to executives in a stock option plan or stock award plan, it would be appropriate to adjust the number of shares by the stock distribution.

Since the same common stock account balance (total par) represents twice as many shares in a 2-for-1 stock split, the par value per share will be reduced by one-half. In the previous example, if the par were $1 per share before the stock distribution, then after the 2-for-1 stock split, the par would be $0.50 per share.

As you might expect, having the par value per share change in this way is cumbersome and expensive. All records, printed or electronic, that refer to the previous amount must be changed to reflect the new amount. The practical solution is to account for the large stock distribution as a stock dividend rather than a stock split.

Stock Splits Effected in the Form of Stock Dividends (Large Stock Dividends)

To avoid changing the per share par value of the shares, the stock distribution is referred to as a *stock split effected in the form of a stock dividend,* or simply a *stock dividend.* In that case, a journal entry increases the common stock account by the par value of the additional shares. To avoid reducing retained earnings in these instances, most companies reduce (debit) paid-in capital—excess of par to offset the credit to common stock (Illustration 18–16).

Craft declares and distributes a 2-for-1 stock split effected in the form of a 100% stock dividend (100 million shares) when the market value of the $1 par common stock is $12 per share.

	($ in millions)	
Paid-in capital—excess of par	100	
Common stock (100 million shares at $1 par per share)		100

Illustration 18–16

Stock Split Effected in the Form of a Stock Dividend

If a *stock split* is effected in the form of a stock dividend, a journal entry prevents the par per share from changing.

Notice that this entry does not reclassify earned capital as invested capital. Some companies, though, choose to debit retained earnings instead.

	($ in millions)	
Retained earnings	100	
Common stock (10 million shares × $1 par per share)		100

Some companies capitalize retained earnings when recording a stock split effected in the form of a stock dividend.

Netflix described a stock split in its disclosure notes as shown in Illustration 18–17.

Note 8 — Stock Split

On June 23, 2015, the Company's Board of Directors declared a seven-for-one stock split in the form of a stock dividend that was paid on July 14, 2015 to all shareholders of record as of July 2, 2015. Outstanding share and per-share amounts disclosed for all periods presented have been retroactively adjusted to reflect the effects of the stock split.

Illustration 18–17

Stock Split Disclosure—Netflix

Real World Financials

In 2015, Netflix distributed a rare 7-for-1 stock split that dropped the price of Netflix shares from about \$700 all the way down to about \$100.

Additional Consideration

A company choosing to capitalize retained earnings when recording a stock split effected in the form of a stock dividend may elect to capitalize an amount other than par value. Accounting guidelines are vague in this regard, stating only that legal amounts are minimum requirements and do not prevent the capitalization of a larger amount per share.

Source: FASB ASC 505–20–30–4: Equity–Stock Dividends and Stock Splits–Initial Measurement (previously "Restatement and Revision of Accounting Research Bulletins," *Accounting Research Bulletin No. 43* (New York: AICPA, 1961), Chap. 7, sec. B, par. 14).

REVERSE STOCK SPLIT. A **reverse stock split** occurs when a company decreases, rather than increases, its outstanding shares. After a 1-for-4 reverse stock split, for example, 100 million shares, \$1 par per share, would become 25 million shares, \$4 par per share. No journal entry is necessary. Of course the market price per share theoretically would quadruple, which usually is the motivation for declaring a reverse stock split. Companies that reverse split their shares frequently are struggling companies trying to accomplish with the split what the market has been unwilling to do—increase the stock price. Often this is to prevent the stock's price from becoming so low that it is delisted from a market exchange. Reverse splits are not unusual occurrences, particularly during stock market downturns. In 2014, Great American Group declared a 1-for-20 reverse split.

FRACTIONAL SHARES. Typically, a stock dividend or stock split results in some shareholders being entitled to fractions of whole shares. For example, if a company declares a 25% stock dividend, or equivalently a 5-for-4 stock split, a shareholder owning 10 shares would be entitled to 2½ shares. Another shareholder with 15 shares would be entitled to 3¾ shares.

Cash payments usually are made when shareholders are entitled to fractions of whole shares.

Cash payments usually are made to shareholders for *fractional* shares and are called "cash in lieu of payments." In the situation described above, for instance, if the market price at declaration is \$12 per share, the shareholder with 15 shares would receive 3 additional shares and \$9 in cash (\$12 × ¾).

Decision Maker's Perspective

The return on shareholders' equity is a popular measure of profitability.

Profitability is the key to a company's long-run survival. A summary measure of profitability often used by investors and potential investors, particularly common shareholders, is the return on shareholders' equity. This ratio measures the ability of company management to generate net income from the resources that owners provide. The ratio is computed by dividing net income by average shareholders' equity. A variation of this ratio often is used when a company has both preferred and common stock outstanding. The return to common shareholders' equity is calculated by subtracting dividends to preferred shareholders from the numerator and using average common shareholders' equity as the denominator. The modified ratio focuses on the profits generated on the assets provided by common shareholders.

Book value measures have limited use in financial analysis.

Although the ratio is useful when evaluating the effectiveness of management in employing resources provided by owners, analysts must be careful not to view it in isolation or without considering how the ratio is derived. Keep in mind that shareholders' equity is a measure of the book value of equity, equivalent to the book value of net assets. Book value measures quickly become out of line with market values. An asset's book value usually equals its market value on the date it's purchased; the two aren't necessarily the same after that. Equivalently, the market value of a share of stock (or of total shareholders' equity) usually is different from its book value. As a result, to supplement the return on shareholders' equity ratio, analysts often relate earnings to the market value of equity, calculating the earnings-price ratio. This ratio is simply the earnings per share divided by the market price per share.

To better understand the differences between the book value ratio and the market value ratio, let's consider the following condensed information reported by Sharp-Novell Industries for 2018 and 2017:

($ in thousands, except per share amounts)	2018	2017
Sales	$3,500	$3,100
Net income	125	114
Current assets	$ 750	$ 720
Property, plant, and equipment (net)	900	850
Total assets	$1,650	$1,570
Current liabilities	$ 550	$ 530
Long-term liabilities	540	520
Paid-in capital	210	210
Retained earnings	350	310
Liabilities and shareholders' equity	$1,650	$1,570
Shares outstanding	50,000	50,000
Stock price (average)	$42.50	$42.50

The 2018 return on shareholders' equity is computed by dividing net income by average shareholders' equity:

$$\$125 \div [(\$560 + 520) \div 2] = \underline{\underline{23.1\%}}$$

The earnings-price ratio is the earnings per share divided by the market price per share:

$$\text{Earnings per share (2018)} = \$125 \div 50 = \$2.50$$
$$\text{Earnings-price ratio} = \$2.50 \div 42.50 = \underline{\underline{5.9\%}}$$

Obviously, the return on the market value of equity is much lower than on the book value of equity. This points out the importance of looking at more than a single ratio when making decisions. While 23.1% may seem like a desirable return, 5.9% is not nearly so attractive. Companies often emphasize the return on shareholders' equity in their annual reports. Alert investors should not accept this measure of achievement at face value. For some companies this is a meaningful measure of performance; but for others, the market-based ratio means more, particularly for a mature firm whose book value and market value are more divergent.

Share retirement and treasury stock transactions can affect the return to owners.

Decisions managers make with regard to shareholders' equity transactions can significantly impact the return to shareholders. For example, when a company buys back shares of its own stock, the return on shareholders' equity goes up. Net income is divided by a smaller amount of shareholders' equity. On the other hand, the share buy-back uses assets, reducing the resources available to earn net income in the future. So, managers as well as outside analysts must carefully consider the decision to reacquire shares in light of the current economic environment, the firm's investment opportunities, and cost of capital to decide whether such a transaction is in the long-term best interests of owners. Investors should be wary of buybacks during down times because the resulting decrease in shares and increase in earnings per share can be used to mask a slowdown in earnings growth.

Dividend decisions should be evaluated in light of prevailing circumstances.

The decision to pay dividends requires similar considerations. When earnings are high, are shareholders better off receiving substantial cash dividends or having management reinvest those funds to finance future growth (and future dividends)? The answer, of course, depends on the particular circumstances involved. Dividend decisions should reflect managerial strategy concerning the mix of internal versus external financing, alternative investment opportunities, and industry conditions. High dividends often are found in mature industries and low dividends in growth industries. ●

Ethical Dilemma

Interworld Distributors has paid quarterly cash dividends since 1985. The dividends have steadily increased from $.25 per share to the latest dividend declaration of $2.00 per share. The board of directors is eager to continue this trend despite the fact that revenues fell significantly during recent months as a result of worsening economic conditions and increased competition. The company founder and member of the board proposes a solution. He suggests a 5% stock dividend in lieu of a cash dividend to be accompanied by the following press announcement:

"In lieu of our regular $2.00 per share cash dividend, Interworld will distribute a 5% stock dividend on its common shares, currently trading at $40 per share. Changing the form of the dividend will permit the Company to direct available cash resources to the modernization of physical facilities in preparation for competing in the 21st century."

What do you think?

Concept Review Exercise

CHANGES IN RETAINED EARNINGS

Situation: The shareholders' equity section of the balance sheet of National Foods, Inc., included the following accounts at December 31, 2018:

Shareholders' Equity	($ in millions)
Paid-in capital	
Preferred stock, 9.09%, 11 million shares at $1 par	$ 11
Common stock, 122 million shares at $1 par	122
Paid-in capital—excess of par, preferred	479
Paid-in capital—excess of par, common	854
Retained earnings	3,245
Treasury stock, at cost, 2 million common shares	(20)
Total shareholders' equity	$4,691

Required:

1. During 2019, several events and transactions affected the retained earnings of National Foods. Prepare the appropriate entries for these events.
   a. On March 1, the board of directors declared a cash dividend of $1 per share on its 120 million outstanding shares (122 million − 2 million treasury shares), payable on April 3 to shareholders of record March 11.
   b. On March 5, the board of directors declared a property dividend of 120 million shares of Kroger common stock that National Foods had purchased in February as an investment (book value: $900 million). The investment shares had a fair value of $8 per share and were distributed March 30 to shareholders of record March 15.
   c. On April 13, a 3-for-2 stock split was declared and distributed. The stock split was effected in the form of a 50% stock dividend. The market value of the $1 par common stock was $20 per share.
   d. On October 13, a 10% common stock dividend was declared and distributed when the market value of the $1 par common stock was $12 per share. Cash in lieu of payments was distributed for fractional shares equivalent to 1 million whole shares.
   e. On December 1, the board of directors declared the 9.09% cash dividend on the 11 million preferred shares, payable on December 23 to shareholders of record December 11.
2. Prepare a statement of shareholders' equity for National Foods reporting the changes in shareholders' equity accounts for 2017, 2018, and 2019. Refer to the previous two Concept Reviews in this chapter for the 2017 and 2018 changes. For 2018, assume that shares were reacquired as treasury stock. Also, look back to the statement of shareholders' equity in Illustration 18–4 for the format of the statement. Assume that net income for 2019 is $225 million.

Solution:

1. During 2019, several events and transactions affected the retained earnings of National Foods. Prepare the appropriate entries for these events.

a. Cash dividend of $1 per share on its 120 million *outstanding* common shares (122 million − 2 million treasury shares), payable on April 3 to shareholders of record March 11. (Note: Dividends aren't paid on treasury shares.)

	($ in millions)	
March 1—Declaration Date		
Retained earnings	120	
Cash dividends payable (120 million shares at $1 per share)		120
March 11—Date of Record		
No entry		
April 3—Payment Date		
Cash dividends payable	120	
Cash		120

The declaration of a dividend reduces retained earnings and creates a liability.

b. Property dividend of 120 million shares of Kroger common stock:

	($ in millions)	
March 5—Declaration Date		
Investment in Kroger common stock	60	
Gain on appreciation of investment ($960 − 900)		60
Retained earnings (fair value of asset to be distributed)	960	
Property dividends payable		960
March 15—Date of Record		
No entry		
March 30—Payment Date		
Property dividends payable	960	
Investment in Kroger common stock		960

The investment first must be written up to the $960 million fair value ($8 × 120 million shares).

The liability is satisfied when the Kroger shares are distributed to shareholders.

c. 3-for-2 stock split effected in the form of a 50% stock dividend:

	($ in millions)	
April 13		
Paid-in capital—excess of par*	60	
Common stock (60 million shares at $1 par per share)		60

*Alternatively, retained earnings may be debited.

120 million shares times 50% equals 60 million new shares—recorded at par.

d. 10% common stock dividend—with cash in lieu of payments for shares equivalent to 1 million whole shares:

	($ in millions)	
October 13		
Retained earnings (18 million shares* at $12 per share)	216	
Common stock (17 million shares at $1 par per share)		17
Paid-in capital—excess of par (17 million shares at $11 per share above par)		187
Cash (1 million equivalent shares at $12 market price per share)		12

*(120 million + 60 million) × 10% = 18 million shares

The stock dividend occurs after the 3-for-2 stock split; thus 18 million shares are distributed.

The $12 fair value of the additional shares is capitalized in this small stock dividend.

e. 9.09% cash dividend on the 11 million preferred shares, payable on December 23 to shareholders of record December 11:

	($ in millions)	
December 1—Declaration Date		
Retained earnings	1	
Cash dividends payable ($11 million par × 9.09%)		1
December 11—Date of Record		
No entry		
December 23—Payment Date		
Cash dividends payable	1	
Cash		1

Preferred shareholders annually receive the designated percentage (9.09%) of the preferred's par value ($1 million), if dividends are declared.

f. Prepare a statement of shareholders' equity for National Foods reporting the changes in shareholders' equity accounts for 2017, 2018, and 2019.

NATIONAL FOODS
Statement of Shareholders' Equity
For the Years Ended December 31, 2019, 2018, and 2017
($ in millions)

These are the transactions from Concept Review Exercise—Expansion of Corporate Capital.

These are the transactions from Concept Review Exercise—Treasury Stock.

These are the transactions from Concept Review Exercise—Changes in Retained Earnings.

	Preferred Stock	Common Stock	Additional Paid-In Capital	Retained Earnings	Treasury Stock (at cost)	Total Shareholders' Equity
Balance at January 1, 2017		120	836	2,449		3,405
Sale of preferred shares	10		430			440
Issuance of common shares		1	9			10
Issuance of common and preferred shares	1	1	58			60
Net income				400		400
Cash dividends, preferred	—	—	—	(1)	—	(1)
Balance at December 31, 2017	11	122	1,333	2,848		4,314
Purchase of treasury shares					(60)	(60)
Sale of treasury shares			4		20	24
Sale of treasury shares			(4)	(2)	20	14
Net income				400		400
Cash dividends, preferred	—	—	—	(1)	—	(1)
Balance at December 31, 2018	11	122	1,333	3,245	(20)	4,691
Cash dividends, common				(120)		(120)
Property dividends, common				(960)		(960)
3-for-2 split effected in the form of a stock dividend		60	(60)			
10% stock dividend		17	187	(216)		(12)
Cash dividends, preferred				(1)		(1)
Net income	—	—	—	225	—	225
Balance at December 31, 2019	11	199	1,460	2,173	(20)	3,823

Financial Reporting Case Solution

© Peathegee Inc/Blend Images

1. **Do you think the stock price increase is related to Nike's share repurchase plan?** *(p. 1050)* The stock price increase probably is related to Nike's buyback plan. The marketplace realizes that decreasing the supply of shares supports the price of remaining shares. However, the repurchase of shares is not necessarily the best use of a company's cash. Whether it is in the shareholders' best interests depends on what other opportunities the company has for the cash available.
2. **What are Nike's choices in accounting for the share repurchases?** *(p. 1051)* When a corporation reacquires its own shares, those shares assume the same status as authorized but unissued shares, just as if they never had been issued. However, for exactly the same transaction, companies can choose between two accounting alternatives: (a) formally retiring them or (b) accounting for the shares repurchased as treasury stock. In actuality, Nike uses alternative (a).
3. **What effect does the quarterly cash dividend of 32 cents share have on Nike's assets? Its liabilities? Its shareholders' equity?** *(p. 1057)* Each quarter, when directors declare a cash dividend, retained earnings are reduced and a liability is recorded. The liability is

paid with cash on the payment date. So, the net effect is a decrease in Nike's assets and its shareholders' equity. The effect on liabilities is temporary.

4. **What effect does the stock split have on Nike's assets? Its liabilities? Its shareholders' equity?** *(p. 1060)* Conceptually, the proper accounting treatment of a stock split is to make no journal entry. However, since Nike refers to the stock distribution as a stock split "in the form of a 100% stock dividend," a journal entry would increase the common stock account by the par value of the additional shares and would reduce paid-in capital—excess of par. This merely moves an amount from one part of shareholders' equity to another. Regardless of the accounting method, there is no change in Nike's assets, liabilities, or total shareholders' equity.

The Bottom Line

- **LO18–1** Shareholders' equity is the owners' residual interest in a corporation's assets. It arises primarily from (1) amounts invested by shareholders and (2) amounts earned by the corporation on behalf of its shareholders. These are reported as (1) paid-in capital and (2) retained earnings in a balance sheet. A statement of shareholders' equity reports the sources of the changes in individual shareholders' equity accounts. (*p. 1035*)
- **LO18–2** Comprehensive income encompasses all changes in equity except those caused by transactions with owners (like dividends and the sale or purchase of shares). It includes traditional net income as well as "other comprehensive income." (*p. 1038*)
- **LO18–3** A corporation is a separate legal entity—separate and distinct from its owners. A corporation is well suited to raising capital and has limited liability. However, it gives rise to "double taxation." Common shareholders usually have voting rights; preferred shareholders usually have a preference to a specified amount of dividends and to assets in the event of liquidation. (*p. 1039*)
- **LO18–4** Shares sold for consideration other than cash (maybe services or a noncash asset) should be recorded at the fair value of the shares or the noncash consideration, whichever seems more clearly evident. (*p. 1046*)
- **LO18–5** When a corporation retires previously issued shares, those shares assume the same status as authorized but unissued shares—just the same as if they had never been issued. Payments made to retire shares are viewed as a distribution of corporate assets to shareholders. When reacquired shares are viewed as treasury stock, the cost of acquiring the shares is temporarily debited to the treasury stock account. Recording the effects on specific shareholders' equity accounts is delayed until later when the shares are reissued. (*p. 1050*)
- **LO18–6** Retained earnings represents, in general, a corporation's accumulated, undistributed, or reinvested net income (or net loss). Distributions of assets are dividends. (*p. 1056*)
- **LO18–7** Most corporate dividends are paid in cash. When a noncash asset is distributed, it is referred to as a property dividend. The fair value of the assets to be distributed is the amount recorded for a property dividend. (*p. 1056*)
- **LO18–8** A stock dividend is the distribution of additional shares of stock to current shareholders. For a small stock dividend (25% or less), the fair value of the additional shares distributed is transferred from retained earnings to paid-in capital. For a stock distribution of 25% or higher, the par value of the additional shares is reclassified within shareholders' equity if referred to as a stock split effected in the form of a stock dividend, but if referred to merely as a stock split, no journal entry is recorded. (*p. 1058*)
- **LO18–9** U.S. GAAP and IFRS are generally compatible with respect to accounting for shareholders' equity. Some differences exist in presentation format and terminology. (*pp. 1040* and *1046*)

APPENDIX 18

Quasi Reorganizations

A firm undergoing financial difficulties, but with favorable future prospects, may use a **quasi reorganization** to write down inflated asset values and eliminate an accumulated deficit (debit balance in retained earnings). To effect the reorganization, these procedures are followed:

1. The firm's assets (and perhaps liabilities) are revalued (up or down) to reflect fair values, with corresponding credits or debits to retained earnings. This process typically increases the deficit.

2. The debit balance in retained earnings (deficit) is eliminated against additional paid-in capital. If additional paid-in capital is not sufficient to absorb the entire deficit, a reduction in stock may be necessary (with an appropriate restating of the par amount per share).
3. Retained earnings is dated. That is, disclosure is provided to indicate the date the deficit was eliminated and when the new accumulation of earnings began.

The procedure is demonstrated in Illustration 18A–1. The shareholders approved the quasi reorganization effective January 1, 2018. The plan was to be accomplished by a reduction of inventory by $75 million, a reduction in property, plant, and equipment (net) of $175 million, and appropriate adjustments to shareholders' equity.

Illustration 18A–1
Quasi Reorganization

The Emerson-Walsch Corporation has incurred operating losses for several years. A newly elected board of directors voted to implement a quasi reorganization, subject to shareholder approval. The balance sheet, on December 31, 2017, immediately prior to the restatement, includes the data shown below.

	($ in millions)
Cash	$ 75
Receivables	200
Inventory	375
Property, plant, and equipment (net)	400
	$1,050
Liabilities	$ 400
Common stock (800 million shares at $1 par)	800
Additional paid-in capital	150
Retained earnings (deficit)	(300)
	$1,050

When assets are revalued to reflect fair values, the process often increases the deficit.

To Revalue Assets:		
Retained earnings	75	
Inventory		75
Retained earnings	175	
Property, plant, and equipment		175
To Eliminate a Portion of the Deficit against Available Additional Paid-In Capital:		
Additional paid-in capital	150	
Retained earnings		150
To Eliminate the Remainder of the Deficit against Common Stock:		
Common stock	400	
Retained earnings		400

The deficit, $550 ($300 + 75 + 175), can be only partially absorbed by the balance of additional paid-in capital.

The remaining deficit, $400 ($300 + 75 + 175 − 150), must be absorbed by reducing the balance in common stock.

The balance sheet immediately after the restatement would include the following:

	($ in millions)
Cash	$ 75
Receivables	200
Inventory	300
Property, plant, and equipment (net)	225
	$800
Liabilities	$400
Common stock (800 million shares at $0.50 par)	400
Additional paid-in capital	0
Retained earnings (deficit)	0
	$800

Assets and liabilities reflect current values.

Because a reduced balance represents the same 800 million shares, the par amount per share must be reduced.

The deficit is eliminated.

Note A: Upon the recommendation of the board of directors and approval by shareholders, a quasi reorganization was implemented January 1, 2018. The plan was accomplished by a reduction of inventory by $75 million, a reduction in property, plant, and equipment (net) of $175 million, and appropriate adjustments to shareholders' equity. The balance in retained earnings reflects the elimination of a $300 million deficit on that date.

Questions For Review of Key Topics

Q 18–1 Identify and briefly describe the two primary sources of shareholders' equity.

Q 18–2 Identify the three common forms of business organization and the primary difference between the way they are accounted for.

Q 18–3 Corporations offer the advantage of limited liability. Explain what is meant by that statement.

Q 18–4 Distinguish between not-for-profit and for-profit corporations.

Q 18–5 Distinguish between publicly held and privately (or closely) held corporations.

Q 18–6 How does the Model Business Corporation Act affect the way corporations operate?

Q 18–7 The owners of a corporation are its shareholders. If a corporation has only one class of shares, they typically are labeled common shares. Indicate the ownership rights held by common shareholders, unless specifically withheld by agreement.

Q 18–8 What is meant by a shareholder's preemptive right?

Q 18–9 Terminology varies in the way companies differentiate among share types. But many corporations designate shares as common or preferred. What are the two special rights usually given to preferred shareholders?

Q 18–10 Most preferred shares are cumulative. Explain what this means.

Q 18–11 The par value of shares historically indicated the real value of shares and all shares were issued at that price. The concept has changed with time. Describe the meaning of par value as it has evolved to today.

Q 18–12 What is comprehensive income? How does comprehensive income differ from net income? Where do companies report it in a balance sheet?

Q 18–13 How do we report components of comprehensive income *created during the reporting period?*

Q 18–14 The balance sheet reports the balances of shareholders' equity accounts. What additional information is provided by the statement of shareholders' equity?

Q 18–15 At times, companies issue their shares for consideration other than cash. What is the measurement objective in those cases?

Q 18–16 Companies occasionally sell more than one security for a single price. How is the issue price allocated among the separate securities?

Q 18–17 The costs of legal, promotional, and accounting services necessary to effect the sale of shares are referred to as share issue costs. How are these costs recorded? Compare this approach to the way debt issue costs are recorded.

Q 18–18 When a corporation acquires its own shares, those shares assume the same status as authorized but unissued shares, as if they never had been issued. Explain how this is reflected in the accounting records if the shares are formally retired.

Q 18–19 Discuss the conceptual basis for accounting for a share buyback as treasury stock.

Q 18–20 The prescribed accounting treatment for stock dividends implicitly assumes that shareholders are fooled by small stock dividends and benefit by the market value of their additional shares. Explain this statement. Is it logical?

Q 18–21 Brandon Components declares a 2-for-1 stock split. What will be the effects of the split, and how should it be recorded?

Q 18–22 What is a reverse stock split? What would be the effect of a reverse stock split on one million $1 par shares? On the accounting records?

Q 18–23 Suppose you own 80 shares of Facebook common stock when the company declares a 4% stock dividend. What will you receive as a result?

Q 18–24 (Based on Appendix 18) A quasi reorganization is sometimes employed by a firm undergoing financial difficulties but with favorable future prospects. What are two objectives of this procedure? Briefly describe the procedural steps.

Brief Exercises

connect

BE 18–1
Comprehensive income
● LO18–1

Schaeffer Corporation reports $50 million accumulated other comprehensive income in its balance sheet as a component of shareholders' equity. In a related statement reporting comprehensive income for the year, the company reveals net income of $400 million and other comprehensive income of $15 million. What was the balance in accumulated other comprehensive income in last year's balance sheet?

BE 18–2
Stock issued
● LO18–4

Penne Pharmaceuticals sold 8 million shares of its $1 par common stock to provide funds for research and development. If the issue price is $12 per share, what is the journal entry to record the sale of the shares?

BE 18–3
Stock issued
● LO18–4

Lewelling Company issued 100,000 shares of its $1 par common stock to the Michael Morgan law firm as compensation for 4,000 hours of legal services performed. Morgan's usual rate is $240 per hour. By what amount should Lewelling's paid-in capital—excess of par increase as a result of this transaction?

BE 18–4
Stock issued
● LO18–4

Hamilton Boats issued 175,000 shares of its no par common stock to Sudoku Motors in exchange for 1,000 four-stroke outboard motors that normally sell in quantity for $3,500 each. By what amount should Hamilton's shareholders' equity increase as a result of this transaction?

BE 18–5
Retirement of shares
● LO18–5

Horton Industries' shareholders' equity included 100 million shares of $1 par common stock and a balance in paid-in capital—excess of par of $900 million. Assuming that Horton retires shares it reacquires (restores their status to that of authorized but unissued shares), by what amount will Horton's total paid-in capital decline if it reacquires 2 million shares at $8.50 per share?

BE 18–6
Retirement of shares
● LO18–5

Agee Storage issued 35 million shares of its $1 par common stock at $16 per share several years ago. Last year, for the first time, Agee reacquired 1 million shares at $14 per share. Assuming that Agee retires shares it reacquires (restores their status to that of authorized but unissued shares), by what amount will Agee's total paid-in capital decline if it now reacquires 1 million shares at $19 per share?

BE 18–7
Treasury stock
● LO18–5

The Jennings Group reacquired 2 million of its shares at $70 per share as treasury stock. Last year, for the first time, Jennings sold 1 million treasury shares at $71 per share. By what amount will Jennings' retained earnings decline if it now sells the remaining 1 million treasury shares at $67 per share?

BE 18–8
Treasury stock
● LO18–5

In previous years, Cox Transport reacquired 2 million treasury shares at $20 per share and, later, 1 million treasury shares at $26 per share. By what amount will Cox's paid-in capital—share repurchase increase if it now sells 1 million treasury shares at $29 per share and determines cost as the weighted-average cost of treasury shares?

BE 18–9
Treasury stock
● LO18–5

Refer to the situation described in BE 18–9. By what amount will Cox's paid-in capital—share repurchase increase if it determines the cost of treasury shares by the FIFO method?

BE 18–10
Cash dividend
● LO18–8
Real World Financials

Following is a recent Microsoft press release:

REDMOND, Wash.—March 16, 2016 —Microsoft today announced that its board of directors have declared a quarterly dividend of $0.36 per share. The dividend will be payable on June 9, 2016, to shareholders of record on May 19, 2016. The ex-dividend date will be May 17, 2016.

Prepare the journal entries Microsoft used to record the declaration and payment of the cash dividend for its 7,870 million shares.

BE 18–11
Effect of preferred stock on dividends
● LO18–7

The shareholders' equity of MLS Enterprises includes $200 million of no par common stock and $400 million of 6% cumulative preferred stock. The board of directors of MLS declared cash dividends of $50 million in 2018 after paying $20 million cash dividends in both 2017 and 2016. What is the amount of dividends common shareholders will receive in 2018?

BE 18–12
Property dividend
● LO18–7

Adams Moving and Storage, a family-owned corporation, declared a property dividend of 1,000 shares of GE common stock that Adams had purchased in February for $37,000 as an investment. GE's shares had a market value of $35 per share on the declaration date. Prepare the journal entries to record the property dividend on the declaration and payment dates.

BE 18–13
Stock dividend
● LO18–8

On June 13, the board of directors of Siewert Inc. declared a 5% stock dividend on its 60 million, $1 par, common shares, to be distributed on July 1. The market price of Siewert common stock was $25 on June 13. Prepare the journal entry to record the stock dividend.

BE 18–14
Stock split
● LO18–8

Refer to the situation described in BE 18–13, but assume a 2-for-1 stock split instead of the 5% stock dividend. Prepare the journal entry to record the stock split if it is *not* to be effected in the form of a stock dividend. What is the par per share after the split?

BE 18–15
Stock split
● LO18–8

Refer to the situation described in BE 18–13, but assume a 2-for-1 stock split instead of the 5% stock dividend. Prepare the journal entry to record the stock split if it is to be effected in the form of a 100% stock dividend. What is the par per share after the split?

BE 18–16
IFRS; reporting shareholders' equity
● LO18–9
IFRS

Nestlé S.A., the largest food and beverage company in the world, prepares its financial statements according to International Financial Reporting Standards. Its financial statements include ordinary share capital, translation reserve, and share premium. If Nestlé used U.S. GAAP, what would be the likely account titles for these accounts?

Exercises

connect

E 18–1
Comprehensive income
● LO18–2

The following is from the 2018 annual report of Kaufman Chemicals, Inc.:

Statements of Comprehensive Income	**Years Ended December 31**		
	2018	**2017**	**2016**
Net income	$856	$766	$594
Other comprehensive income:			
Change in net unrealized gains on investments, net of tax of $22, ($14), and $15 in 2018, 2017, and 2016, respectively	34	(21)	23
Other	(2)	(1)	1
Total comprehensive income	$888	$744	$618

Kaufman reports accumulated other comprehensive income in its balance sheet as a component of shareholders' equity as follows:

($ in millions)	2018	2017
Shareholders' equity:		
Common stock	355	355
Additional paid-in capital	8,567	8,567
Retained earnings	6,544	5,988
Accumulated other comprehensive income	107	75
Total shareholders' equity	$15,573	$14,985

Required:

1. What is comprehensive income and how does it differ from net income?
2. How is comprehensive income reported in a balance sheet?
3. Why is Kaufman's 2018 balance sheet amount different from the 2018 amount reported in the disclosure note? Explain.
4. From the information provided, determine how Kaufman calculated the $107 million accumulated other comprehensive income in 2018.

E 18–2
FASB codification research; reporting other comprehensive income in shareholders' equity
● LO18–2
CODE

Companies are required to transfer "other comprehensive income" each period to shareholders' equity. The *FASB Accounting Standards Codification* represents the single source of authoritative U.S. generally accepted accounting principles.

Required:

1. Obtain the relevant authoritative literature on reporting other comprehensive income in shareholders' equity using the *FASB Accounting Standards Codification* at the FASB website (www.fasb.org). What is the specific citation that describes the guidelines for reporting that component of shareholders' equity?
2. What is the specific citation that describes the guidelines for presenting accumulated other comprehensive income on the statement of shareholders' equity?

E 18–3
Earnings or OCI?
● LO18–2

Indicate by letter whether each of the items listed below most likely is reported in the income statement as Net Income (**NI**) or in the statement of comprehensive income as Other Comprehensive Income (**OCI**).

	Items
_____	1. Increase in the fair value of available-for-sale debt securities
_____	2. Gain on sale of land
_____	3. Loss on pension plan assets (actual return less than expected)
_____	4. Adjustment for foreign currency translation
_____	5. Increase in the fair value of investments in common stock securities
_____	6. Loss from revising an assumption related to a pension plan
_____	7. Loss on sale of patent
_____	8. Prior service cost in defined benefit pension plan
_____	9. Increase in the fair value of bonds outstanding due to change in general interest rates; fair value option
_____	10. Gain on postretirement plan assets (actual return more than expected)

E 18–4
Stock issued for cash; Wright Medical Group
● LO18–4
Real World Financials

The following is a news item reported by Reuters:

WASHINGTON, Jan 29 (Reuters)—**Wright Medical Group**, a maker of reconstructive implants for knees and hips, on Tuesday filed to sell 3 million shares of common stock.

In a filing with the U.S. Securities and Exchange Commission, it said it plans to use the proceeds from the offering for general corporate purposes, working capital, research and development, and acquisitions.

After the sale there will be about 31.5 million shares outstanding in the Arlington, Tennessee-based company, according to the SEC filing.

Wright shares closed at $17.15 on Nasdaq.

The common stock of Wright Medical Group has a par of $0.01 per share.

Required:
Prepare the journal entry to record the sale of the shares assuming the price existing when the announcement was made and ignoring share issue costs.

E 18–5
Issuance of shares; noncash consideration
● LO18–4

During its first year of operations, Eastern Data Links Corporation entered into the following transactions relating to shareholders' equity. The articles of incorporation authorized the issue of 8 million common shares, $1 par per share, and 1 million preferred shares, $50 par per share.

Required:
Prepare the appropriate journal entries to record each transaction.

Feb. 12	Sold 2 million common shares, for $9 per share.
13	Issued 40,000 common shares to attorneys in exchange for legal services.
13	Sold 80,000 of its common shares and 4,000 preferred shares for a total of $945,000.
Nov. 15	Issued 380,000 of its common shares in exchange for equipment for which the cash price was known to be $3,688,000.

E 18–6
Redeemable shares
● LO18–4

Williams Industries has outstanding 30 million common shares, 20 million Class A shares, and 20 million Class B shares. Williams has the right but not the obligation to repurchase the Class A shares if a change in ownership of the voting common shares causes J. P. Williams, founder and CEO, to have less than 50% ownership. Williams has the unconditional obligation to repurchase the Class B shares upon the death of J. P. Williams.

Required:
Which, if any, of the shares should be reported in Williams's balance sheet as liabilities? Explain.

E 18–7
Share issue costs; issuance
● LO18–4

ICOT Industries issued 15 million of its $1 par common shares for $424 million on April 11. Legal, promotional, and accounting services necessary to effect the sale cost $2 million.

Required:
1. Prepare the journal entry to record the issuance of the shares.
2. Explain how recording the share issue costs differs from the way debt issue costs are recorded.

E 18–8
Reporting preferred shares
● LO18–4, LO18–7

Ozark Distributing Company is primarily engaged in the wholesale distribution of consumer products in the Ozark Mountain regions. The following disclosure note appeared in the company's 2018 annual report:

Note 5. Convertible Preferred Stock (in part):
The Company has the following Convertible Preferred Stock outstanding as of September 2018:

Date of issuance:	June 17, 2015
Optionally redeemable beginning:	June 18, 2017
Par value (gross proceeds):	$2,500,000
Number of shares:	100,000
Liquidation preference per share:	$25.00
Conversion price per share:	$30.31
Number of common shares in which to be converted:	82,481
Dividend rate:	6.785%

The Preferred Stock is convertible at any time by the holders into a number of shares of Ozark's common stock equal to the number of preferred shares being converted times a fraction equal to $25.00 divided by the conversion price. The conversion prices for the Preferred Stock are subject to customary adjustments in the event of stock splits, stock dividends and certain other distributions on the Common Stock. Cumulative dividends for the Preferred Stock are payable in arrears, when, as, and if declared by the Board of Directors, on March 31, June 30, September 30, and December 31 of each year.

The Preferred Stock is optionally redeemable by the Company beginning on various dates, as listed above, at redemption prices equal to 112% of the liquidation preference. The redemption prices decrease 1% annually thereafter until the redemption price equals the liquidation preference, after which date it remains the liquidation preference.

Required:

1. What amount of dividends is paid annually to a preferred shareholder owning 100 shares of the Series A preferred stock?
2. If dividends are not paid in 2019 and 2020, but are paid in 2021, what amount of dividends will the shareholder receive?
3. If the investor chooses to convert the shares in 2019, how many shares of common stock will the investor receive for his/her 100 shares?
4. If Ozark chooses to redeem the shares on June 18, 2019, what amount will the investor be paid for his/her 100 shares?

E 18–9
New equity issues; offerings announcements
● LO18–4

When companies offer new equity security issues, they publicize the offerings in the financial press and on Internet sites. Assume the following were among the equity offerings reported in December 2018:

New Securities Issues

Equity

American Materials Transfer Corporation (AMTC)—7.5 million common shares, $.001 par, priced at $13.546 each through underwriters led by Second Tennessee Bank N.A. and Morgan, Dunavant & Co., according to a syndicate official.

Proactive Solutions Inc. (PSI)—Offering of 9 million common shares, $0.01 par, was priced at $15.20 a share via lead manager Stanley Brothers, Inc., according to a syndicate official.

Required:
Prepare the appropriate journal entries to record the sale of both issues to underwriters. Ignore share issue costs.

E 18–10
Retirement of shares
● LO18–5

Borner Communications' articles of incorporation authorized the issuance of 130 million common shares. The transactions described below effected changes in Borner's outstanding shares. Prior to the transactions, Borner's shareholders' equity included the following:

Shareholders' Equity	($ in millions)
Common stock, 100 million shares at $1 par	$100
Paid-in capital—excess of par	300
Retained earnings	210

Required:

Assuming that Borner Communications retires shares it reacquires (restores their status to that of authorized but unissued shares), record the appropriate journal entry for each of the following transactions:

1. On January 7, 2018, Borner reacquired 2 million shares at $5 per share.
2. On August 23, 2018, Borner reacquired 4 million shares at $3.50 per share.
3. On July 25, 2019, Borner sold 3 million common shares at $6 per share.

E 18–11
Retirement of shares
● LO18–5

In 2018, Borland Semiconductors entered into the transactions described below. In 2015, Borland had issued 170 million shares of its $1 par common stock at $34 per share.

Required:

Assuming that Borland retires shares it reacquires, record the appropriate journal entry for each of the following transactions:

1. On January 2, 2018, Borland reacquired 10 million shares at $32.50 per share.
2. On March 3, 2018, Borland reacquired 10 million shares at $36 per share.
3. On August 13, 2018, Borland sold 1 million shares at $42 per share.
4. On December 15, 2018, Borland sold 2 million shares at $36 per share.

E 18–12
Treasury stock
● LO18–5

In 2018, Western Transport Company entered into the treasury stock transactions described below. In 2016, Western Transport had issued 140 million shares of its $1 par common stock at $17 per share.

Required:

Prepare the appropriate journal entry for each of the following transactions:

1. On January 23, 2018, Western Transport reacquired 10 million shares at $20 per share.
2. On September 3, 2018, Western Transport sold 1 million treasury shares at $21 per share.
3. On November 4, 2018, Western Transport sold 1 million treasury shares at $18 per share.

E 18–13
Treasury stock; weighted-average and FIFO cost
● LO18–5

At December 31, 2017, the balance sheet of Meca International included the following shareholders' equity accounts:

Shareholders' Equity	($ in millions)
Common stock, 60 million shares at $1 par	$ 60
Paid-in capital—excess of par	300
Retained earnings	410

Required:

Assuming that Meca International views its share buybacks as treasury stock, record the appropriate journal entry for each of the following transactions:

1. On February 12, 2018, Meca reacquired 1 million common shares at $13 per share.
2. On June 9, 2019, Meca reacquired 2 million common shares at $10 per share.
3. On May 25, 2020, Meca sold 2 million treasury shares at $15 per share. Determine cost as the weighted-average cost of treasury shares.
4. For the previous transaction, assume Meca determines the cost of treasury shares by the FIFO method.

E 18–14
Reporting shareholders' equity after share repurchase
● LO18–5

On two previous occasions, the management of Dennison and Company, Inc., repurchased some of its common shares. Between buyback transactions, the corporation issued common shares under its management incentive plan. Shown below is shareholders' equity following these share transactions, as reported by two different methods of accounting for reacquired shares.

($ in millions)	Method A	Method B
Shareholders' equity		
Paid-in capital:		
Preferred stock, $10 par	$ 150	$ 150
Common stock, $1 par	200	197
Additional paid-in capital	1,204	1,201
Retained earnings	2,994	2,979
Less: Treasury stock	(21)	
Total shareholders' equity	$4,527	$4,527

Required:

1. Infer from the presentation which method of accounting for reacquired shares is represented by each of the two columns.
2. Explain why presentation formats are different and why some account balances are different for the two methods.

E 18–15
Change from treasury stock to retired stock
● LO18–5

In keeping with a modernization of corporate statutes in its home state, UMC Corporation decided in 2018 to discontinue accounting for reacquired shares as treasury stock. Instead, shares repurchased will be viewed as having been retired, reassuming the status of unissued shares. As part of the change, treasury shares held were reclassified as retired stock. At December 31, 2017, UMC's balance sheet reported the following shareholders' equity:

	($ in millions)
Common stock, $1 par	$ 200
Paid-in capital—excess of par	800
Retained earnings	956
Treasury stock (4 million shares at cost)	(25)
Total shareholders' equity	$1,931

Required:

Identify the type of accounting change this decision represents, and prepare the journal entry to effect the reclassification of treasury shares as retired shares.

E 18–16
Stock buyback; Ford press announcement
● LO18–5
Real World Financials

The following excerpt is from an article reported in an online issue of Bloomberg.

(Bloomberg) Ford Motor Co. (F) said it will repurchase $1.8 billion of its shares to reduce dilution from recent stock grants to executives.

The par amount per share for Ford's common stock is $0.01. Paid-in capital—excess of par is $5.39 per share on average. The market price was $16.

Required:

1. Suppose Ford reacquires 112 million shares through repurchase on the open market at $16 per share. Prepare the appropriate journal entry to record the purchase. Ford considers the shares it buys back to be treasury stock.
2. Suppose Ford considers the shares it buys back to be retired rather than treated as treasury stock. Prepare the appropriate journal entry to record the purchase.
3. What does the company mean by saying that the buyback will serve "to offset dilution from executive compensation?"

E 18–17
Transactions affecting retained earnings
● LO18–6, LO18–7

Shown below in T-account format are the changes affecting the retained earnings of Brenner-Jude Corporation during 2018. At January 1, 2018, the corporation had outstanding 105 million common shares, $1 par per share.

Retained Earnings ($ in millions)

	Debit	Credit	
		90	Beginning balance
Retirement of 5 million common shares for $22 million	2		
		88	Net income for the year
Declaration and payment of a $0.33 per share cash dividend	33		
Declaration and distribution of a 4% stock dividend	20		
		123	Ending balance

Required:

1. From the information provided by the account changes, you should be able to recreate the transactions that affected Brenner-Jude's retained earnings during 2018. Prepare the journal entries that Brenner-Jude must have recorded during the year for these transactions.
2. Prepare a statement of retained earnings for Brenner-Jude for the year ended 2018.

E 18–18
Effect of cumulative, nonparticipating preferred stock on dividends—3 years
● LO18–7

The shareholders' equity of ILP Industries includes the items shown below. The board of directors of ILP declared cash dividends of $8 million, $20 million, and $150 million in its first three years of operation—2018, 2019, and 2020, respectively.

	($ in millions)
Common stock	$100
Paid-in capital—excess of par, common	980
Preferred stock, 8%	200
Paid-in capital—excess of par, preferred	555

Required:
Determine the amount of dividends to be paid to preferred and common shareholders in each of the three years, assuming that the preferred stock is cumulative and nonparticipating.

	Preferred	Common
2018		
2019		
2020		

E 18–19
Stock dividend
● LO18–8

The shareholders' equity of Core Technologies Company on June 30, 2017, included the following:

Common stock, $1 par; authorized, 8 million shares; issued and outstanding, 3 million shares	$ 3,000,000
Paid-in capital—excess of par	12,000,000
Retained earnings	14,000,000

On April 1, 2018, the board of directors of Core Technologies declared a 10% stock dividend on common shares, to be distributed on June 1. The market price of Core Technologies' common stock was $30 on April 1, 2018, and $40 on June 1, 2018.

Required:
Prepare the journal entry to record the declaration and distribution of the stock dividend on the declaration date.

E 18–20
Stock split; Hanmi Financial Corporation
● LO18–8
Real World Financials

Hanmi Financial Corporation is the parent company of Hanmi Bank. The company's stock split was announced in the following wire:

LOS ANGELES Jan. 20 *BUSINESS WIRE* —Hanmi Financial Corporation (Nasdaq), announced that the Board of Directors has approved a two-for-one stock split, to be effected in the form of a 100 percent common stock dividend. Hanmi Financial Corporation stockholders of record at the close of business on January 31 will receive one additional share of common stock for every share of common stock then held. Distribution of additional shares issued as a result of the split is expected to occur on or about February 15.

At the time of the stock split, 24.5 million shares of common stock, $.001 par per share, were outstanding.

Required:
1. Prepare the journal entry, if any, that Hanmi recorded at the time of the stock split.
2. What is the probable motivation for declaring the 2-for-1 stock split to be effected by a dividend payable in shares of common stock?
3. If Hanmi's stock price had been $36 at the time of the split, what would be its approximate value after the split (other things equal)?

E 18–21
Cash in lieu of fractional share rights
● LO18–8

Douglas McDonald Company's balance sheet included the following shareholders' equity accounts at December 31, 2017:

	($ in millions)
Paid-in capital:	
Common stock, 900 million shares at $1 par	$ 900
Paid-in capital—excess of par	15,800
Retained earnings	14,888
Total shareholders' equity	$31,588

On March 16, 2018, a 4% common stock dividend was declared and distributed. The market value of the common stock was $21 per share. Fractional share rights represented 2 million equivalent whole shares. Cash was paid in lieu of the fractional share rights.

Required:

1. What is a fractional share right?
2. Prepare the appropriate entries for the declaration and distribution of the stock dividend.

E 18–22
FASB codification research
LO18–1, LO18–5, LO18–8

Access the *FASB Accounting Standards Codification* at the FASB website (www.fasb.org). Determine the specific citation for accounting for each of the following items:

1. Requirements to disclose within the financial statements the pertinent rights and privileges of the various securities outstanding.
2. Requirement to record a "small" stock dividend at the fair value of the shares issued.
3. Requirement to exclude from the determination of net income gains and losses on transactions in a company's own stock.

E 18–23
Transactions affecting retained earnings
LO18–6 through LO18–8

The balance sheet of Consolidated Paper, Inc., included the following shareholders' equity accounts at December 31, 2017:

	($ in millions)
Paid-in capital:	
Preferred stock, 8.8%, 90,000 shares at $1 par	$ 90,000
Common stock, 364,000 shares at $1 par	364,000
Paid-in capital—excess of par, preferred	1,437,000
Paid-in capital—excess of par, common	2,574,000
Retained earnings	9,735,000
Treasury stock, at cost; 4,000 common shares	(44,000)
Total shareholders' equity	$14,156,000

During 2018, several events and transactions affected the retained earnings of Consolidated Paper.

Required:

1. Prepare the appropriate entries for these events:
   a. On March 3, the board of directors declared a property dividend of 240,000 shares of Leasco International common stock that Consolidated Paper had purchased in January as an investment (book value: $700,000). The investment shares had a fair value of $3 per share and were distributed March 31 to shareholders of record March 15.
   b. On May 3, a 5-for-4 stock split was declared and distributed. The stock split was effected in the form of a 25% stock dividend. The market value of the $1 par common stock was $11 per share.
   c. On July 5, a 2% common stock dividend was declared and distributed. The market value of the common stock was $11 per share.
   d. On December 1, the board of directors declared the 8.8% cash dividend on the 90,000 preferred shares, payable on December 28 to shareholders of record December 20.
   e. On December 1, the board of directors declared a cash dividend of $0.50 per share on its common shares, payable on December 28 to shareholders of record December 20.
2. Prepare the shareholders' equity section of the balance sheet for Consolidated Paper, Inc., at December 31, 2018. Net income for the year was $810,000.

E 18–24
Profitability ratio
LO18–1

Comparative balance sheets for Softech Canvas Goods for 2018 and 2017 are shown below. Softech pays no dividends and instead reinvests all earnings for future growth.

Comparative Balance Sheets
($ in thousands)

	December 31	
	2018	**2017**
Assets:		
Cash	$ 50	$ 40
Accounts receivable	100	120
Short-term investments	50	40
Inventory	200	140
Property, plant, and equipment (net)	600	550
	$1,000	$890

(continued)

(concluded)

Liabilities and Shareholders' Equity:		
Current liabilities	$ 240	$210
Bonds payable	160	160
Paid-in capital	400	400
Retained earnings	200	120
	$1,000	$890

Required:

1. Determine the return on shareholders' equity for 2018.
2. What does the ratio measure?

E 18–25
IFRS; equity terminology
● LO18–9
IFRS

Indicate by letter whether each of the terms or phrases listed below is more associated with financial statements prepared in accordance with U.S. GAAP (**U**) or International Financial Reporting Standards (**I**).

Terms and phrases

_____ 1. Common stock
_____ 2. Preference shares
_____ 3. Liabilities often listed before equity in the balance sheet (statement of financial position)
_____ 4. Asset revaluation reserve
_____ 5. Accumulated other comprehensive income
_____ 6. Share premium
_____ 7. Equity often listed before liabilities in the balance sheet (statement of financial position)
_____ 8. Translation reserve
_____ 9. Ordinary shares
_____ 10. Paid-in capital—excess of par
_____ 11. Net gains (losses) on investments—AOCI
_____ 12. Investment revaluation reserve
_____ 13. Preferred stock

Problems

connect

P 18–1
Various stock transactions; correction of journal entries
● LO18–4
IFRS

Part A

During its first year of operations, the McCollum Corporation entered into the following transactions relating to shareholders' equity. The corporation was authorized to issue 100 million common shares, $1 par per share.

Required:

Prepare the appropriate journal entries to record each transaction.

Jan. 9	Issued 40 million common shares for $20 per share.
Mar. 11	Issued 5,000 shares in exchange for custom-made equipment. McCollum's shares have traded recently on the stock exchange at $20 per share.

Part B

A new staff accountant for the McCollum Corporation recorded the following journal entries during the second year of operations. McCollum retires shares that it reacquires (restores their status to that of authorized but unissued shares).

		($ in millions)	
Jan. 12	Land	2	
	Paid-in capital—donation of land		2
Sept. 1	Common stock	2	
	Retained earnings	48	
	Cash		50
Dec. 1	Cash	26	
	Common stock		1
	Gain on sale of previously issued shares		25

Required:

Prepare the journal entries that should have been recorded for each of the transactions.

P 18–2
Share buyback—comparison of retirement and treasury stock treatment
● LO18–5

The shareholders' equity section of the balance sheet of TNL Systems Inc. included the following accounts at December 31, 2017:

Shareholders' Equity	($ in millions)
Common stock, 240 million shares at $1 par	$ 240
Paid-in capital—excess of par	1,680
Paid-in capital—share repurchase	1
Retained earnings	1,100

Required:

1. During 2018, TNL Systems reacquired shares of its common stock and later sold shares in two separate transactions. Prepare the entries for both the purchase and subsequent resale of the shares assuming the shares are (a) retired and (b) viewed as treasury stock.
   a. On February 5, 2018, TNL Systems purchased 6 million shares at $10 per share.
   b. On July 9, 2018, the corporation sold 2 million shares at $12 per share.
   c. On November 14, 2020, the corporation sold 2 million shares at $7 per share.
2. Prepare the shareholders' equity section of TNL Systems' balance sheet at December 31, 2020, comparing the two approaches. Assume all net income earned in 2018–2020 was distributed to shareholders as cash dividends.

P 18–3
Reacquired shares—comparison of retired shares and treasury shares
● LO18–5

National Supply's shareholders' equity included the following accounts at December 31, 2017:

Shareholders' Equity	($ in millions)
Common stock, 6 million shares at $1 par	$ 6,000,000
Paid-in capital—excess of par	30,000,000
Retained earnings	86,500,000

Required:

1. National Supply reacquired shares of its common stock in two separate transactions and later sold shares. Prepare the entries for each of the transactions under each of two separate assumptions: the shares are (a) retired and (b) accounted for as treasury stock.

February 15, 2018	Reacquired 300,000 shares at $8 per share.
February 17, 2019	Reacquired 300,000 shares at $5.50 per share.
November 9, 2020	Sold 200,000 shares at $7 per share (assume FIFO cost).

2. Prepare the shareholders' equity section of National Supply's balance sheet at December 31, 2020, assuming the shares are (a) retired and (b) accounted for as treasury stock. Net income was $14 million in 2018, $15 million in 2019, and $16 million in 2020. No dividends were paid during the three-year period.

P 18–4
Statement of retained earnings
● LO18–5, LO18–7

Comparative statements of retained earnings for Renn-Dever Corporation were reported in its 2018 annual report as follows.

RENN-DEVER CORPORATION
Statements of Retained Earnings
For the Years Ended December 31

	2018	2017	2016
Balance at beginning of year	**$6,794,292**	**$5,464,052**	**$5,624,552**
Net income (loss)	3,308,700	2,240,900	(160,500)
Deductions:			
Stock dividend (34,900 shares)	242,000		
Common shares retired (110,000 shares)		212,660	
Common stock cash dividends	889,950	698,000	0
Balance at end of year	**$8,971,042**	**$6,794,292**	**$5,464,052**

At December 31, 2015, common shares consisted of the following:

Common stock, 1,855,000 shares at $1 par	$1,855,000
Paid-in capital—excess of par	7,420,000

Required:

Infer from the reports the events and transactions that affected Renn-Dever Corporation's retained earnings during 2016, 2017, and 2018. Prepare the journal entries that reflect those events and transactions.

P 18–5
Shareholders' equity transactions; statement of shareholders' equity
● LO18–6 through LO18–8

Listed below are the transactions that affected the shareholders' equity of Branch-Rickie Corporation during the period 2018–2020. At December 31, 2017, the corporation's accounts included:

	($ in thousands)
Common stock, 105 million shares at $1 par	$105,000
Paid-in capital—excess of par	630,000
Retained earnings	970,000

a. November 1, 2018, the board of directors declared a cash dividend of $0.80 per share on its common shares, payable to shareholders of record November 15, to be paid December 1.

b. On March 1, 2019, the board of directors declared a property dividend consisting of corporate bonds of Warner Corporation that Branch-Rickie was holding as an investment. The bonds had a fair value of $1.6 million, but were purchased two years previously for $1.3 million. Because they were intended to be held to maturity, the bonds had not been previously written up. The property dividend was payable to shareholders of record March 13, to be distributed April 5.

c. On July 12, 2019, the corporation declared and distributed a 5% common stock dividend (when the market value of the common stock was $21 per share). Cash was paid in lieu of fractional shares representing 250,000 equivalent whole shares.

d. On November 1, 2019, the board of directors declared a cash dividend of $0.80 per share on its common shares, payable to shareholders of record November 15, to be paid December 1.

e. On January 15, 2020, the board of directors declared and distributed a 3-for-2 stock split effected in the form of a 50% stock dividend when the market value of the common stock was $22 per share.

f. On November 1, 2020, the board of directors declared a cash dividend of $0.65 per share on its common shares, payable to shareholders of record November 15, to be paid December 1.

Required:

1. Prepare the journal entries that Branch-Rickie recorded during the three-year period for these transactions.
2. Prepare comparative statements of shareholders' equity for Branch-Rickie for the three-year period ($ in 000s). Net income was $330 million, $395 million, and $455 million for 2018, 2019, and 2020, respectively.

P 18–6
Statement of shareholders' equity
● LO18–1, LO18–3 through LO18–8

Comparative statements of shareholders' equity for Anaconda International Corporation were reported as follows for the fiscal years ending December 31, 2018, 2019, and 2020.

ANACONDA INTERNATIONAL CORPORATION
Statements of Shareholders' Equity
For the Years Ended Dec. 31, 2018, 2019, and 2020
($ in millions)

	Preferred Stock $10 par	Common Stock $1 par	Additional Paid-In Capital	Retained Earnings	Total Shareholders' Equity
Balance at January 1, 2018		55	495	1,878	2,428
Sale of preferred shares	10		470		480
Sale of common shares		7	63		70
Cash dividend, preferred				(1)	(1)
Cash dividend, common				(16)	(16)
Net income				290	290
Balance at December 31, 2018	10	62	1,028	2,151	3,251
Retirement of shares		(3)	(27)	(20)	(50)
Cash dividend, preferred				(1)	(1)
Cash dividend, common				(20)	(20)
3-for-2 split effected in the form of a dividend	5		(5)		
Net income				380	380
Balance at December 31, 2019	15	59	996	2,490	3,560
Common stock dividend		6	59	(65)	
Cash dividend, preferred				(1)	(1)
Cash dividend, common				(22)	(22)
Net income				412	412
Balance at December 31, 2020	15	65	1,055	2,814	3,949

Required:

1. Infer from the statements the events and transactions that affected Anaconda International Corporation's shareholders' equity during 2018, 2019, and 2020. Prepare the journal entries that reflect those events and transactions.
2. Prepare the shareholders' equity section of Anaconda's comparative balance sheets at December 31, 2020 and 2019.

P 18–7
Reporting shareholders' equity; comprehensive income; Cisco Systems
- LO18–1 through LO18–4

Real World Financials

The following is a portion of the Statement of Shareholders' Equity from Cisco Systems' January 23, 2016, quarterly report.

CISCO SYSTEMS, INC.
Consolidated Statements of Equity (in part)

($ in millions)	Shares of Common Stock	Common Stock and Additional Paid-In Capital	Retained Earnings	Accumulated Other Comprehensive Income	Total Shareholder' Equity
Balance at July 25, 2015	**5,085**	**$43,592**	**$16,045**	**$ 61**	**$59,698**
Net income			5,577		5,577
Other comprehensive income (loss)				(868)	(868)
Issuance of common stock	76	701			701
Repurchase of common stock	(93)	(801)	(1,668)		(2,469)
Shares repurchased for tax withholdings on vesting of restricted stock units	(16)	(412)			(412)
Cash dividends declared ($0.42 per common share)			(2,133)		(2,133)
Tax effects from employee stock incentive plans		28			28
Share-based compensation expense		706			706
Purchase acquisitions		43			43
Balance at January 23, 2016	**5,052**	**$43,857**	**$17,821**	**$(807)**	**$60,871**

Required:

1. What is the purpose of the statement of shareholders' equity?
2. How does Cisco account for its share buybacks?
3. For its share buybacks in the period shown, was the price Cisco paid for the shares repurchased more or less than the average price at which Cisco had sold the shares previously? Reconstruct the journal entry Cisco used to record the buyback. The par amount of Cisco's shares is $0.001.
4. What is comprehensive income? What is other comprehensive income?
5. What caused the change in Cisco's comprehensive income for the period shown? What was the amount of Accumulated other comprehensive income (loss) that Cisco reported in its January 23, 2016, balance sheet? Be specific.

P 18–8
Share issue costs; issuance; dividends; early retirement
- LO18–3, LO18–4, LO18–7

During its first year of operations, Cupola Fan Corporation issued 30,000 of $1 par Class B shares for $385,000 on June 30, 2018. Share issue costs were $1,500. One year from the issue date (July 1, 2019), the corporation retired 10% of the shares for $39,500.

Required:

1. Prepare the journal entry to record the issuance of the shares.
2. Prepare the journal entry to record the declaration of a $2 per share dividend on December 1, 2018.
3. Prepare the journal entry to record the payment of the dividend on December 31, 2018.
4. Prepare the journal entry to record the retirement of the shares.

(Note: You may wish to compare your solution to this problem with that of P 14–16, which deals with parallel issues of debt issue costs and the retirement of debt.)

P 18–9
Effect of preferred stock characteristics on dividends
● LO18–7

The shareholders' equity of Kramer Industries includes the data shown below. During 2019, cash dividends of $150 million were declared. Dividends were not declared in 2017 or 2018.

	($ in millions)
Common stock	$200
Paid-in capital—excess of par, common	800
Preferred stock, 10%, nonparticipating	100
Paid-in capital—excess of par, preferred	270

Required:
Determine the amount of dividends payable to preferred shareholders and to common shareholders under each of the following two assumptions regarding the characteristics of the preferred stock.

Assumption A —The preferred stock is noncumulative.
Assumption B —The preferred stock is cumulative.

P 18–10
Transactions affecting retained earnings
● LO18–4 through LO18–8

Indicate by letter whether each of the transactions listed below increases (**I**), decreases (**D**), or has no effect (**N**) on retained earnings. Assume the shareholders' equity of the transacting company includes only common stock, paid-in capital—excess of par, and retained earnings at the time of each transaction. (Some transactions have two possible answers. Indicate both.)

	Transactions
N	1. Sale of common stock
____	2. Purchase of treasury stock at a cost *less* than the original issue price
____	3. Purchase of treasury stock at a cost *greater* than the original issue price
____	4. Declaration of a property dividend
____	5. Sale of treasury stock for *more* than cost
____	6. Sale of treasury stock for *less* than cost
____	7. Net income for the year
____	8. Declaration of a cash dividend
____	9. Payment of a previously declared cash dividend
____	10. Issuance of convertible bonds for cash
____	11. Declaration and distribution of a 5% stock dividend
____	12. Retirement of common stock at a cost *less* than the original issue price
____	13. Retirement of common stock at a cost *greater* than the original issue price
____	14. A stock split effected in the form of a stock dividend
____	15. A stock split in which the par value per share is reduced (not effected in the form of a stock dividend)
____	16. A net loss for the year

P 18–11
Stock dividends received on investments; integrative problem
● LO18–8

Ellis Transport Company acquired 1.2 million shares of stock in L&K Corporation at $44 per share. They are classified by Ellis as "available for sale." Ellis sold 200,000 shares at $46, received a 10% stock dividend, and then later in the year sold another 100,000 shares at $43.

Hint: There is no entry for the stock dividend, but a new investment per share must be calculated for use later when the shares are sold.

Required:
Prepare journal entries to record these transactions.

P 18–12
Various shareholders' equity topics; comprehensive
● LO18–1, LO18–4 through LO18–8

Part A
In late 2017, the Nicklaus Corporation was formed. The corporate charter authorizes the issuance of 5,000,000 shares of common stock carrying a $1 par value, and 1,000,000 shares of $5 par value, noncumulative, nonparticipating preferred stock. On January 2, 2018, 3,000,000 shares of the common stock are issued in exchange for cash at an average price of $10 per share. Also on January 2, all 1,000,000 shares of preferred stock are issued at $20 per share.

Required:
1. Prepare journal entries to record these transactions.
2. Prepare the shareholders' equity section of the Nicklaus balance sheet as of March 31, 2018. (Assume net income for the first quarter 2018 was $1,000,000.)

Part B

During 2018, the Nicklaus Corporation participated in three treasury stock transactions:

a. On June 30, 2018, the corporation reacquires 200,000 shares for the treasury at a price of $12 per share.

b. On July 31, 2018, 50,000 treasury shares are reissued at $15 per share.

c. On September 30, 2018, 50,000 treasury shares are reissued at $10 per share.

Required:

1. Prepare journal entries to record these transactions.
2. Prepare the Nicklaus Corporation shareholders' equity section as it would appear in a balance sheet prepared at September 30, 2018. (Assume net income for the second and third quarter was $3,000,000.)

Part C

On October 1, 2018, Nicklaus Corporation receives permission to replace its $1 par value common stock (5,000,000 shares authorized, 3,000,000 shares issued, and 2,900,000 shares outstanding) with a new common stock issue having a $0.50 par value. Since the new par value is one-half the amount of the old, this represents a 2-for-1 stock split. That is, the shareholders will receive two shares of the $0.50 par stock in exchange for each share of the $1 par stock they own. The $1 par stock will be collected and destroyed by the issuing corporation.

On November 1, 2018, the Nicklaus Corporation declares a $0.05 per share cash dividend on common stock and a $0.25 per share cash dividend on preferred stock. Payment is scheduled for December 1, 2018, to shareholders of record on November 15, 2018.

On December 2, 2018, the Nicklaus Corporation declares a 1% stock dividend payable on December 28, 2018, to shareholders of record on December 14. At the date of declaration, the common stock was selling in the open market at $10 per share. The dividend will result in 58,000 (0.01 × 5,800,000) additional shares being issued to shareholders.

Required:

1. Prepare journal entries to record the declaration and payment of these stock and cash dividends.
2. Prepare the December 31, 2018, shareholders' equity section of the balance sheet for the Nicklaus Corporation. (Assume net income for the fourth quarter was $2,500,000.)
3. Prepare a statement of shareholders' equity for Nicklaus Corporation for 2018.

P 18–13
Quasi reorganization (based on Appendix 18)
● Appendix

A new CEO was hired to revive the floundering Champion Chemical Corporation. The company had endured operating losses for several years, but confidence was emerging that better times were ahead. The board of directors and shareholders approved a quasi reorganization for the corporation. The reorganization included devaluing inventory for obsolescence by $105 million and increasing land by $5 million. Immediately prior to the restatement, at December 31, 2018, Champion Chemical Corporation's balance sheet appeared as follows (in condensed form):

CHAMPION CHEMICAL CORPORATION
Balance Sheet
At December 31, 2018
($ in millions)

Cash	$ 20
Receivables	40
Inventory	230
Land	40
Buildings and equipment (net)	90
	$ 420
Liabilities	$ 240
Common stock (320 million shares at $1 par)	320
Additional paid-in capital	60
Retained earnings (deficit)	(200)
	$ 420

Required:

1. Prepare the journal entries appropriate to record the quasi reorganization on January 1, 2019.
2. Prepare a balance sheet as it would appear immediately after the restatement.

Broaden Your Perspective

Apply your critical-thinking ability to the knowledge you've gained. These cases will provide you an opportunity to develop your research, analysis, judgment, and communication skills. You also will work with other students, integrate what you've learned, apply it in real-world situations, and consider its global and ethical ramifications. This practice will broaden your knowledge and further develop your decision-making abilities.

Real World Case 18–1
Initial public offering of common stock; Dolby Laboratories
● LO18–4

Real World Financials

Ray Dolby started Dolby Laboratories and since then has been a leader in the entertainment industry and consumer electronics. Closely held since its founding in 1965, Dolby decided to go public. Here's an AP news report:

DOLBY'S IPO EXPECTED TO PLAY SWEET MUSIC—The initial public offering market is hoping for a big bang this week from Dolby Laboratories Inc. The San Francisco company, whose sound systems and double-D logo are ubiquitous in the movie industry as well as in consumer electronics, plans to sell 27.5 million shares for $13.50 to $15.50 each. Founded by Cambridge-trained scientist Ray Dolby 39 years ago, the company started out manufacturing noise-reduction equipment for the music industry that eliminated the background "hiss" on recordings, and has since expanded to encompass everything from digital audio systems to Dolby Surround sound. The company's IPO, which is lead-managed by underwriters Morgan Stanley and Goldman Sachs Group Inc., is expected to do well not only because of its brand recognition, but also because of its strong financials. (*AP*)

Required:

1. Assuming the shares are issued at the midpoint of the price range indicated, how much capital did the IPO raise for Dolby Laboratories before any underwriting discount and offering expenses?
2. If the par amount is $.01 per share, what journal entry did Dolby use to record the sale?

Analysis Case 18–2
Statement of shareholders' equity
● LO18–1, LO18–3, LO18–6, LO18–7

The shareholders' equity portion of the balance sheet of Sessel's Department Stores, Inc., a large regional specialty retailer, is as follows:

SESSEL'S DEPARTMENT STORES, INC.
Comparative Balance Sheets
Shareholders' Equity Section

($ in thousands, except per share amounts)	Dec. 31, 2019	Dec. 31, 2018
Shareholders' Equity		
Preferred stock—$1 par value; 20,000 total shares authorized, Series A—600 shares authorized, issued, and outstanding,	$ 57,700	$ —
$50 per share liquidation preference		
Series B—33 shares authorized, no shares outstanding		
Common stock—$0.10 par; 200,000 shares authorized, 19,940 and 18,580 shares issued and outstanding at Dec. 31, 2019, and Dec. 31, 2018, respectively	1,994	1,858
Additional paid-in capital	227,992	201,430
Retained income	73,666	44,798
Total shareholders' equity	$361,352	$248,086

Disclosures elsewhere in Sessel's annual report revealed the following changes in shareholders' equity accounts for 2019, 2018, 2017:

2019:

1. The only changes in retained earnings during 2019 were preferred dividends on preferred stock of $3,388,000 and net income.
2. The preferred stock is convertible. During the year, 6,592 shares were issued. All shares were converted into 320,000 shares of common stock. No gain or loss was recorded on the conversion.
3. Common shares were issued in a public offering and upon the exercise of stock options. On the statement of shareholders' equity, Sessel's reports these two items on a single line entitled: "Issuance of shares."

2018:

1. Net income: $12,126,000.
2. Issuance of common stock: 5,580,000 shares at $112,706,000.

2017:

1. Net income: $13,494,000.
2. Issuance of common stock: 120,000 shares at $826,000.

Required:

From these disclosures, prepare comparative statements of shareholders' equity for 2019, 2018, and 2017.

Communication Case 18–3
IFRS; Is preferred stock debt or equity?; Group interaction
● LO18–1, LO18–9
IFRS

An unsettled question in accounting for stock is this: Should preferred stock be recognized as a liability, or should it be considered equity? Under International Financial Reporting Standards, preferred stock (preference shares) often is reported as debt with the dividends reported in the income statement as interest expense. Under U.S. GAAP, that is the case only for "mandatorily redeemable" preferred stock.

Two opposing viewpoints are:

View 1: Preferred stock should be considered equity.

View 2: Preferred stock should be reported as a liability.

In considering this question, focus on conceptual issues regarding the practicable and theoretically appropriate treatment, unconstrained by GAAP.

Required:

1. Which view do you favor? Develop a list of arguments in support of your view prior to the class session for which the case is assigned.
2. In class, your instructor will pair you (and everyone else) with a classmate (who also has independently developed an argument).
   a. You will be given three minutes to argue your view to your partner. Your partner likewise will be given three minutes to argue his or her view to you. During these three-minute presentations, the listening partner is not permitted to speak.
   b. Then after each person has had a turn attempting to convince his or her partner, the two partners will have a three-minute discussion in which they will decide which view is more convincing and arguments will be merged into a single view for each pair.
3. After the allotted time, a spokesperson for each of the two views will be selected by the instructor. Each spokesperson will field arguments from the class in support of that view's position and list the arguments on the board. The class then will discuss the merits of the two lists of arguments and attempt to reach a consensus view, though a consensus is not necessary.

Research Case 18–4
FASB codification; comprehensive income; locate and extract relevant information and authoritative support for a financial reporting issue; integrative; Cisco Systems
● LO18–2
CODE
Real World Financials

Titan Networking became a public company through an IPO (initial public offering) two weeks ago. You are looking forward to the challenges of being assistant controller for a publicly owned corporation. One such challenge came in the form of a memo in this morning's in-box. "We need to start reporting comprehensive income in our financials," the message from your boss said. "Do some research on that, will you? That concept didn't exist when I went to school." In response, you sought out the financial statements of Cisco Systems, the networking industry leader. The following are excerpts from disclosure notes from Cisco's 2015 annual report:

	Years Ended		
	July 25, 2015	July 26, 2014	July 27, 2013
Net income	$8,981	$7,853	$9,983
Other comprehensive income (loss):			
Available-for-sale investments:			
Change in net unrealized gains, net of tax	(12)	233	(6)
Net gains reclassified into earnings, net of tax	(100)	(189)	(31)
	(112)	44	(37)
Cash flow hedging instruments:			
Change in unrealized gains and losses, net of tax	(158)	48	73
Net (gains) losses reclassified into earnings	154	(68)	(12)
	(4)	(20)	61
Net change in cumulative translation adjustment and actuarial gains and losses, net of tax	(498)	44	(84)
Other comprehensive income (loss)	(614)	68	(60)
Comprehensive income	$8,367	$7,921	$9,923

Required:

1. Locate the financial statements of Cisco at www.sec.gov or Cisco's website. Search the 2015 annual report for information about how Cisco accounts for comprehensive income. What does Cisco report in its balance sheet regarding comprehensive income?

2. Access the *FASB Accounting Standards Codification* at the FASB website (www.fasb.org). Identify the specific citation from the authoritative literature that describes the two alternative formats for reporting comprehensive income.
3. What is comprehensive income? How does it differ from net income? Where is it reported in a balance sheet?
4. One component of Other comprehensive income for Cisco is "net unrealized gains on investments." What does this mean? From the information Cisco's financial statements provide, determine how the company calculated the $61 million accumulated other comprehensive income at the end of fiscal 2015.
5. What might be possible causes for the "Other" component of Cisco's Other comprehensive income?

Judgment Case 18–5
Treasury stock; stock split; cash dividends; Alcoa
● LO18–5 through LO18–8
Real World Financials

Alcoa is the world's leading producer of primary aluminum, fabricated aluminum, and alumina. The following is a press release from the company:

ALCOA ANNOUNCES 33% INCREASE IN BASE DIVIDEND, 2-FOR-1 STOCK SPLIT
PITTSBURGH—Alcoa today announced that its Board of Directors approved a base quarterly dividend increase of 33.3%.

Alcoa's announcement indicated that the new quarterly dividend would be $0.25 per share. It also stated that the Board of Directors declared a two-for-one stock split and reaffirmed its commitment to a share repurchase program.

Required:

1. What are the two primary reporting alternatives Alcoa has in accounting for the repurchase of its shares? What would be the effect of the optional courses of action on total shareholders' equity? Explain. What would be the effect of the optional courses of action on how stock would be presented in Alcoa's balance sheet? If the shares are later resold for an amount greater than cost, how should Alcoa account for the sale?
2. What are the two primary courses of action Alcoa has in accounting for the stock split, and how would the choice affect Alcoa's shareholders' equity? Why?
3. How should Alcoa account for the cash dividend, and how would it affect Alcoa's balance sheet? Why?

Communication Case 18–6
Issuance of shares; share issue costs; prepare a report
● LO18–4

You are the newest member of the staff of Brinks & Company, a medium-size investment management firm. You are supervised by Les Kramer, an employee of two years. Les has a reputation as being technically sound but has a noticeable gap in his accounting education. Knowing you are knowledgeable about accounting issues, he requested you provide him with a synopsis of accounting for share issue costs.

"I thought the cost of issuing securities is recorded separately and expensed over time," he stated in a handwritten memo. "But I don't see that for IBR's underwriting expenses. What gives?"

He apparently was referring to a disclosure note on a page of a prospective investee's annual report, photocopied and attached to his memo. To raise funds for expansion, the company sold additional shares of its $0.10 par common stock. The following disclosure note appeared in the company's most recent annual report:

NOTES TO CONSOLIDATED FINANCIAL STATEMENTS
Note 10—Stock Transactions (in part)
In February and March, the Company sold 2,395,000 shares of Common Stock at $22.25 per share in a public offering. Net proceeds to the Company were approximately $50.2 million after the underwriting discount and offering expenses.

Required:

Write a formal memo to your supervisor. Briefly explain how share issue costs are accounted for and how that accounting differs from that of debt issue costs. To make sure your explanation is understood in context of the footnote, include in your memo the following:

a. At what total amount did the shares sell to the public? How is the difference between this amount and the $50.2 million net proceeds accounted for?
b. The appropriate journal entry to record the sale of the shares.

Analysis Case 18–7
Analyzing financial statements; price-earnings ratio; dividend payout ratio
● LO18–1

AGF Foods Company is a large, primarily domestic, consumer foods company involved in the manufacture, distribution, and sale of a variety of food products. Industry averages are derived from Troy's *The Almanac of Business and Industrial Financial Ratios* and Dun and Bradstreet's *Industry Norms and Key Business Ratios*. Following are the 2018 and 2017 comparative income statements and balance sheets for AGF. The market price of AGF's common stock is $47 during 2018. (The financial data we use are from actual financial statements of a well-known corporation, but the company name used in our illustration is fictitious and the numbers and dates have been modified slightly to disguise the company's identity.)

Profitability is the key to a company's long-run survival. Profitability measures focus on a company's ability to provide an adequate return relative to resources devoted to company operations.

AGF FOODS COMPANY
Years Ended December 31, 2018 and 2017

($ in millions)	2018	2017
Comparative Income Statements		
Net sales	$ 6,440	$ 5,800
Cost of goods sold	(3,667)	(3,389)
Gross profit	2,773	2,411
Operating expenses	(1,916)	(1,629)
Operating income	857	782
Interest expense	(54)	(53)
Income from operations before tax	803	729
Income taxes	(316)	(287)
Net income	$ 487	$ 442
Average shares outstanding	181 million	181 million
Comparative Balance Sheets		
Assets		
Current assets:		
Cash	$ 48	$ 142
Accounts receivable	347	320
Marketable securities	358	—
Inventories	914	874
Prepaid expenses	212	154
Total current assets	1,879	1,490
Property, plant, and equipment (net)	2,592	2,291
Intangibles (net)	800	843
Other assets	74	60
Total assets	$ 5,345	$ 4,684
Liabilities and Shareholders' Equity		
Current liabilities:		
Accounts payable	$ 254	$ 276
Accrued liabilities	493	496
Notes payable	518	115
Current portion of long-term debt	208	54
Total current liabilities	1,473	941
Long-term debt	534	728
Deferred income taxes	407	344
Total liabilities	2,414	2,013
Shareholders' equity:		
Common stock, $1 par	180	180
Additional paid-in capital	21	63
Retained earnings	2,730	2,428
Total shareholders' equity	2,931	2,671
Total liabilities and shareholders' equity	$ 5,345	$ 4,684

Required:

1. Calculate the return on shareholders' equity for AGF. The average return for the stocks listed on the New York Stock Exchange in a comparable period was 18.8%. What information does your calculation provide an investor?
2. Calculate AGF's earnings per share and earnings-price ratio. The average return for the stocks listed on the New York Stock Exchange in a comparable time period was 5.4%. What does your calculation indicate about AGF's earnings?

Ethics Case 18–8
The Swiss label maker; value of shares issued for equipment
● LO18–4

Bricker Graphics is a privately held company specializing in package labels. Representatives of the firm have just returned from Switzerland, where a Swiss firm is manufacturing a custom-made high speed, color labeling machine. Confidence is high that the new machine will help rescue Bricker from sharply declining profitability. Bricker's chief operating officer, Don Benson, has been under fire for not reaching the company's performance goals of achieving a rate of return on assets of at least 12%.

The afternoon of his return from Switzerland, Benson called Susan Sharp into his office. Susan is Bricker's Controller.

Benson: I wish you had been able to go. We have some accounting issues to consider.
Sharp: I wish I'd been there, too. I understand the food was marvelous. What are the accounting issues?
Benson: They discussed accepting our notes at the going rate for a face amount of $12.5 million. We also discussed financing with stock.
Sharp: I thought we agreed; debt is the way to go for us now.
Benson: Yes, but I've been thinking. We can issue shares for a total of $10 million. The labeler is custom made and doesn't have a quoted selling price, but the domestic labelers we considered went for around $10 million. It sure would help our rate of return if we keep the asset base as low as possible.

Required:
1. How will Benson's plan affect the return measure? What accounting issue is involved?
2. Is the proposal ethical?
3. Who would be affected if the proposal is implemented?

Research Case 18–9
Researching the way shareholders' equity transactions are reported; retrieving financial statements from the Internet
● LO18–1, LO18–6

EDGAR, the Electronic Data Gathering, Analysis, and Retrieval system, performs automated collection, validation, indexing, and forwarding of submissions by companies and others who are required by law to file forms with the U.S. Securities and Exchange Commission (SEC). All publicly traded domestic companies use EDGAR to make the majority of their filings. (Filings by foreign companies are not required to be filed on EDGAR, but some of these companies do so voluntarily.) Form 10-K, which includes the annual report, is required to be filed on EDGAR. The SEC makes this information available on the Internet.

Required:
1. Access EDGAR on the Internet at www.sec.gov.
2. Search for a public company with which you are familiar. Access its most recent 10-K filing. Search or scroll to find the statement of shareholders' equity and related note(s). If a statement of shareholders' equity is not provided, try another company.
3. Determine from the statement the transactions that occurred during the most recent three years that affected retained earnings.
4. Determine from the statement the transactions that occurred during the most recent three years that affected common stock. Were any of these transactions identified in requirement 3 also?
5. Cross-reference your findings with amounts reported on the balance sheet. How do these two statements articulate with one another?

Communication Case 18–10
Should the present two-category distinction between liabilities and equity be retained? Group interaction.
● LO18–1

The current conceptual distinction between liabilities and equity defines liabilities independently of assets and equity, with equity defined as a residual amount. The present proliferation of financial instruments that combine features of both debt and equity and the difficulty of drawing a distinction have led many to conclude that the present two-category distinction between liabilities and equity should be eliminated. Two opposing viewpoints are:

View 1: The distinction should be maintained.
View 2: The distinction should be eliminated and financial instruments should instead be reported in accordance with the priority of their claims to enterprise assets.

One type of security that often is mentioned in the debate is convertible bonds. Although stock in many ways, such a security also obligates the issuer to transfer assets at a specified price and redemption date. Thus it also has features of debt. In considering this question, focus on conceptual issues regarding the practicable and theoretically appropriate treatment, unconstrained by GAAP.

Required:
1. Which view do you favor? Develop a list of arguments in support of your view prior to the class session for which the case is assigned.
2. In class, your instructor will pair you (and everyone else) with a classmate (who also has independently developed an argument).
   a. You will be given three minutes to argue your view to your partner. Your partner likewise will be given three minutes to argue his or her view to you. During these three-minute presentations, the listening partner is not permitted to speak.
   b. Then after each person has had a turn attempting to convince his or her partner, the two partners will have a three-minute discussion in which they will decide which view is more convincing and arguments will be merged into a single view for each pair.
3. After the allotted time, a spokesperson for each of the two views will be selected by the instructor. Each spokesperson will field arguments from the class in support of that view's position and list the arguments on

the board. The class then will discuss the merits of the two lists of arguments and attempt to reach a consensus view, though a consensus is not necessary.

Continuing Cases

Target Case

- LO18–1, LO18–5

Target Corporation prepares its financial statements according to U.S. GAAP. Target's financial statements and disclosure notes for the year ended January 30, 2016, are available in Connect. This material also is available under the Investor Relations link at the company's website (www.target.com). Target refers to its Shareholders' Equity as Shareholders' Investment.

Required:

1. Refer to Target's Consolidated Statements of Shareholders' Investment. What are the five types of events and transactions that affected one or more of the Shareholders' Investment accounts in the year ended January 30, 2016?
2. Note 25, "Share Repurchase," provides the information we need to reconstruct the journal entry that summarizes Target's share repurchases in the year ended January 30, 2016. Provide that entry. Does Target account for share repurchases as treasury stock or retired shares? Explain.

Air France–KLM Case

IFRS

- LO18–9

Air France–KLM (AF), a Franco-Dutch company, prepares its financial statements according to International Financial Reporting Standards. AF's financial statements and disclosure notes for the year ended December 31, 2015, are available in Connect. This material is also available under the Finance link at the company's website (www.airfranceklm.com).

Required:

1. AF lists four items in the shareholders' equity section of its balance sheet. If AF used U.S. GAAP, what would be the likely account titles for the first and fourth of those components?
2. Locate Note 29.5 in AF's financial statements. What items comprise "Reserves and retained earnings" as reported in the balance sheet? If AF used U.S. GAAP, what would be different for the reporting of these items?
3. Describe the apparent differences in the order of presentation of the components of liabilities and shareholders' equity between IFRS as applied by AF and a typical balance sheet prepared in accordance with U.S. GAAP.

CPA Exam Questions and Simulations

ROGER CPA Review

Sample CPA Exam questions from Roger CPA Review are available in Connect as support for the topics in this chapter. These Multiple Choice Questions and Task-Based Simulations include expert-written explanations and solutions, and provide a starting point for students to become familiar with the content and functionality of the actual CPA Exam.

Additional Financial Reporting Issues

CHAPTER

19 Share-Based Compensation and Earnings Per Share

OVERVIEW

We've discussed a variety of employee compensation plans in prior chapters, including pension and other postretirement benefits in Chapter 17. In this chapter we look at some common forms of compensation in which the amount of the compensation employees receive is tied to the market price of company stock. We will see that these *share-based* compensation plans—restricted stock awards, restricted stock units, stock options, and stock appreciation rights—create shareholders' equity, which was the topic of the previous chapter, and which also often affects the way we calculate earnings per share, the topic of the second part of the current chapter. Specifically, we view these as *potential common shares* along with convertible securities, and we calculate earnings per share as if the securities already had been exercised or converted into additional common shares.

LEARNING OBJECTIVES

After studying this chapter, you should be able to:

- **LO19–1** Explain and implement the accounting for restricted stock plans. (*p. 1092*)
- **LO19–2** Explain and implement the accounting for stock options. (*p. 1094*)
- **LO19–3** Explain and implement the accounting for employee share purchase plans. (*p. 1104*)
- **LO19–4** Distinguish between a simple and a complex capital structure. (*p. 1106*)
- **LO19–5** Describe what is meant by the weighted-average number of common shares. (*p. 1107*)
- **LO19–6** Differentiate the effect on EPS of the sale of new shares, a stock dividend or stock split, and the reacquisition of shares. (*p. 1108*)
- **LO19–7** Describe how preferred dividends affect the calculation of EPS. (*p. 1110*)
- **LO19–8** Describe how options, rights, and warrants are incorporated in the calculation of EPS. (*p. 1111*)
- **LO19–9** Describe how convertible securities are incorporated in the calculation of EPS. (*p. 1113*)
- **LO19–10** Determine whether potential common shares are antidilutive. (*p. 1116*)
- **LO19–11** Describe the two components of the proceeds used in the treasury stock method and how restricted stock is incorporated in the calculation of EPS. (*p. 1120*)
- **LO19–12** Explain the way contingently issuable shares are incorporated in the calculation of EPS. (*p. 1122*)
- **LO19–13** Describe the way EPS information should be reported in an income statement. (*p. 1124*)
- **LO19–14** Discuss the primary differences between U.S. GAAP and IFRS with respect to accounting for share-based compensation and earnings per share. (*pp. 1099, 1101, and 1106*)

© Cultura RM/Alamy Stock Photo

FINANCIAL REPORTING CASE

Proper Motivation?

The coffee room discussion Thursday morning was particularly lively. Yesterday's press release describing National Electronic Ventures' choice of Sandra Veres as its president and chief operating officer was today's hot topic in all the company's departments. The press release noted that Ms. Veres's compensation package includes elements beyond salary that are intended to not only motivate her to accept the offer, but also to remain with the company and work to increase shareholder value. Excerpts from the release follow:

National Electronic Ventures, Inc., today announced it had attracted G. Sandra Veres, respected executive from the wireless communications industry, to succeed chairman Walter Kovac. Veres will assume the new role as CEO on Jan. 1, 2018. Ms. Veres will receive a compensation package at NEV of more than $1 million in salary, stock options to buy more than 800,000 shares of NEV stock and a grant of restricted stock.

QUESTIONS

By the time you finish this chapter, you should be able to respond appropriately to the questions posed in this case. Compare your response to the solution provided at the end of the chapter.

1. How can a compensation package such as this serve as an incentive to Ms. Veres? *(p. 1091)*
2. Ms. Veres received a "grant of restricted stock." How should NEV account for the grant? *(p. 1092)*
3. Included were stock options to buy more than 800,000 shares of NEV stock. How will the options affect NEV's compensation expense? *(p. 1094)*
4. How will the presence of these and other similar stock options affect NEV's earnings per share? *(p. 1111)*

Share-Based Compensation

PART A

Employee compensation plans frequently include share-based awards. These awards are forms of payment whose value is dependent on the value of the company's stock. These may be outright awards of shares, stock options, or cash payments tied to the market price of shares. Sometimes only key executives participate in a stock benefit plan. Typically, an executive compensation plan is tied to performance in a strategy that uses compensation to motivate its recipients. Some firms pay their directors entirely in shares. Actual compensation depends on the market value of the shares. Obviously, that's quite an incentive to act in the best interests of shareholders.

Although the variations of share-based compensation plans are seemingly endless, each shares common goals. Whether the plan is a stock award plan, a stock option plan, a stock appreciation rights (SARs) plan, or one of the several similar plans, the goals are to provide compensation to designated employees, while sometimes providing those employees with some sort of performance incentive. Likewise, our goals in accounting for each of these plans are the same for each: (1) to determine the fair value of the compensation and (2) to expense that compensation over the periods in which participants perform services. The issue is not trivial. Salary often is a minor portion of executive pay relative to stock awards and stock options.

FINANCIAL Reporting Case

Q1, p. 1091

The accounting objective is to record compensation expense over the periods in which related services are performed.

Restricted Stock Plans

● LO19–1

Executive compensation sometimes includes a grant of shares of stock or the right to receive shares. Usually, such shares are restricted in such a way as to provide some incentive to the recipient. Typically, restricted stock award plans are tied to continued employment. The two primary types of restricted stock plans are (a) restricted stock awards and (b) restricted stock units. Let's compare the two.

Restricted Stock Awards

Usually, restricted shares are subject to forfeiture if the employee doesn't remain with the company.

In a **restricted stock award**, shares actually are awarded in the name of the employee, although the company might retain physical possession of the shares. The employee has all rights of a shareholder, subject to certain restrictions or forfeiture. Ordinarily, the shares are subject to forfeiture by the employee if employment is terminated within some specified number of years from the date of grant. The employee usually is not free to sell the shares during the restriction period, and a statement to that effect often is inscribed on the stock certificates. These restrictions give the employee incentive to remain with the company until rights to the shares vest.

FINANCIAL Reporting Case

Q2, p. 1091

The compensation associated with a share of restricted stock is the market price at the grant date of an unrestricted share of the same stock. This amount is accrued as compensation expense with a credit to paid-in capital—restricted stock, over the service period for which participants receive the shares, usually from the date of grant to when restrictions are lifted (the vesting date).[1] Once the shares vest and the restrictions are lifted, paid-in capital—restricted stock is replaced by common stock and paid-in capital—excess of par. Any market price changes that might occur after that don't affect the total compensation. This is essentially the same as accounting for restricted stock units to be settled in shares, as demonstrated in the next section.

Restricted Stock Units

An increasingly popular variation of **restricted stock** awards is **restricted stock units (RSUs)**. In fact, RSUs have become a much more popular form of compensation than their restricted stock award cousins. A restricted stock unit is a right to receive a specified number of shares of company stock. It could be a performance bonus, a signing bonus, or regular compensation. The employee doesn't receive the stock right away. Instead, the shares are distributed as the recipient of RSUs satisfies the vesting requirement.[2] So, like restricted stock awards, the recipient benefits by the value of the shares at the end of the vesting period. Unlike restricted stock awards, though, the shares are not issued at the time of the grant. Delaying the increase in outstanding shares is more acceptable to other shareholders. As part of its share-based compensation plan, **Apple Inc.** provides compensation to executives in the form of RSUs as we see in Illustration 19–1.

Illustration 19–1

Restricted Stock Units (RSUs); Apple Inc.

Real World Financials

Share-Based Compensation (in part)

Share-based compensation cost for RSUs is measured based on the closing fair market value of the Company's common stock on the date of grant . . . The Company recognizes share-based compensation cost over the award's requisite service period on a straight-line basis.

Terms of RSUs vary.[3] Sometimes, the recipient is given the *cash equivalent* of the number of shares used to value the RSUs. Or, the terms might stipulate that either the recipient or the company is allowed to choose whether to settle in stock or cash.

[1]Restricted stock plans usually are designed to comply with Tax Code Section 83 to allow employee compensation to be nontaxable to the employee until the date the shares become substantially vested, which is when the restrictions are lifted. Likewise, the employer gets no tax deduction until the compensation becomes taxable to the employee.

[2]Sometimes, the shares to be issued depend upon achieving specific performance targets.

[3]Typically, but not always, RSUs have no voting privileges and receive no dividends until the shares are issued at vesting. Sometimes, restricted stock does have voting privileges and receives dividends during the vesting period even though recipients are restricted from selling the shares until vesting.

Although RSUs delay the issuance of shares and avoid some administrative complexities of outright awards of restricted stock, accounting for RSUs to be settled in stock is essentially the same as for restricted stock awards. We see accounting for award plans or units of restricted stock demonstrated in Illustration 19–2.

Illustration 19–2

Restricted Stock Award Plans or Restricted Stock Units (RSUs)

Under its restricted stock unit (RSU) plan, Universal Communications grants RSUs representing 5 million of its $1 par common shares to certain key executives at January 1, 2018. The shares are subject to forfeiture if employment is terminated within four years. Shares have a current market price of $12 per share.

January 1, 2018

No entry

Calculate total compensation expense:

$12
× 5 million
= $60 million

The total compensation is to be allocated to expense over the four-year service (vesting) period: 2018–2021.

$60 million ÷ 4 years = $15 million per year

	($ in millions)	
December 31, 2018, 2019, 2020, 2021		
Compensation expense ($60 million ÷ 4 years)	15	
Paid-in capital—restricted stock		15
December 31, 2021		
Paid-in capital—restricted stock (5 million shares at $12)	60	
Common stock (5 million shares at $1 par)		5
Paid-in capital—excess of par (difference)		55

The total compensation is the market value of the shares ($12) times 5 million shares.

The $60 million is accrued to compensation expense over the four-year service period.

When restrictions are lifted, paid-in capital—restricted stock, is replaced by common stock and paid-in capital—excess of par.

On the other hand, *if the employee will receive cash* or can elect to receive cash, we consider the award to be a *liability* rather than equity, as is the case in Illustration 19–2. When an RSU is considered to be a liability, we determine its fair value at the grant date and recognize that amount as compensation expense over the requisite service period consistent with the way we account for restricted stock awards, RSUs, and other share-based compensation. However, because these plans are considered to be liabilities payable in cash, the credit portion of the entry as we recognize compensation expense each year is to Liability—restricted stock. And, it's necessary to periodically adjust the liability (and corresponding compensation) based on the change in the stock's fair value until the liability is paid. Note that this is consistent with the way we account for other liabilities. Accounting for share-based compensation that's considered to be a liability is demonstrated in Appendix B of the chapter.

If restricted stock shares or RSUs are forfeited because, say, the employee leaves the company, entries previously made related to that specific employee would simply be reversed. This would result in a decrease in compensation expense in the year of forfeiture. The total compensation, adjusted for the forfeited amount, is then allocated over the remaining service period.

Additional Consideration

An alternative way of accomplishing the same result is to debit deferred compensation for the full value of the RSUs ($60 million in the illustration) on the date they are granted.

	($ in millions)	
Deferred compensation (5 million shares at $12)	60	
Common stock (5 million shares at $1 par)		5
Paid-in capital—excess of par (difference)		55

If so, deferred compensation (a term used for delayed recognition of compensation expense) is reported as a reduction in shareholders' equity, resulting in a zero net effect on shareholders' equity. Then, deferred compensation is credited when compensation expense is debited over the service period. Just as in Illustration 19–2, the result is an increase in both compensation expense and shareholders' equity each year over the vesting period.

Stock Option Plans

Often, employees aren't actually awarded shares, but rather are given the option to buy shares in the future. In fact, stock options have become an integral part of the total compensation package for key officers of most medium and large companies. As with any compensation plan, the accounting objective is to report compensation expense during the period of service for which the compensation is given.

LO19–2

Expense—The Great Debate

Stock option plans give employees the option to purchase (a) a specified number of shares of the firm's stock, (b) at a specified price, (c) during a specified period of time. One of the most heated controversies in standard-setting history has been the debate over the amount of compensation to be recognized as expense for stock options. At issue is how the value of stock options is measured, which for most options determines whether any expense at all is recognized.

Historically, options were measured at their intrinsic values—the simple difference between the market price of the shares and the option price at which they can be acquired. For instance, an option that permits an employee to buy a $25-per-share stock for $10 per share has an intrinsic value of $15. However, plans in which the exercise price equals the market value of the underlying stock at the date of grant (which describes most executive stock option plans) have no intrinsic value and therefore result in zero compensation when measured this way, even though the fair value of the options can be quite significant. Facebook CEO Mark Zuckerberg reaped a $3.3 billion gain in 2013 alone by exercising stock options.[4] To many, it seems counterintuitive to not recognize compensation expense for plans that routinely provide executives with a substantial part of their total compensation.

FINANCIAL Reporting Case

Q3, p. 1091

After lengthy debate, the FASB consented to encourage, rather than require, that the fair value of options be recognized as expense.

FAILED ATTEMPT TO REQUIRE EXPENSING. This is where the controversy ensues. In 1993, the FASB issued an Exposure Draft of a new standard that would have required companies to measure options at their *fair values* at the time they are granted and to expense that amount over the appropriate service period. To jump straight to the punch line, the FASB bowed to public pressure and agreed to withdraw the requirement before it became a standard. The FASB consented to encourage, rather than require, that fair value compensation be recognized as expense. Companies were permitted to continue accounting under prior GAAP (the intrinsic value method referred to in the previous paragraph).[5] Before we discuss the details of accounting for stock options, it's helpful to look back at what led the FASB to first propose fair value accounting and later rescind that proposal.

As the 1990s began, the public was becoming increasingly aware of the enormity of executive compensation in general and compensation in the form of stock options in particular. The lack of accounting for this compensation was apparent, prompting the SEC to encourage the FASB to move forward on its stock option project. Even Congress got into the fray when, in 1992, a bill was introduced that would require firms to report compensation expense based on the fair value of options. Motivated by this encouragement, the FASB issued its exposure draft in 1993. The real disharmony began then. Opposition to the proposed standard was broad and vehement, and that perhaps is an understatement. Critics based their opposition on one or more of these three objections:

1. *Options with no intrinsic value at issue have zero fair value and should not give rise to expense recognition.* The FASB, and even some critics of the proposal, were adamant that options provide valuable compensation at the grant date to recipients.
2. *It is impossible to measure the fair value of the compensation on the grant date.* The FASB argued vigorously that value can be approximated using one of several option pricing models. These are statistical models that use computers to incorporate

[4] *San Jose Mercury News*, April 1, 2014.

[5] "Accounting for Stock Issued to Employees," *Opinions of the Accounting Principles Board No. 25* (New York: AICPA, 1972). This pronouncement is superseded and therefore is not codified in the *FASB Accounting Standards Codification*.

information about a company's stock and the terms of the stock option to estimate the options' fair value. We might say the FASB position is that it's better to be approximately right than precisely wrong.

3. *The proposed standard would have unacceptable economic consequences.* Essentially, this argument asserted that requiring this popular means of compensation to be expensed would cause companies to discontinue the use of options.

The opposition included corporate executives, auditors, members of Congress, and the SEC.[6] Ironically, the very groups that provided the most impetus for the rule change initially—the SEC and Congress—were among the most effective detractors in the end. The only group that offered much support at all was the academic community, and that was by-and-large nonvocal support. In reversing its decision, the FASB was not swayed by any of the specific arguments of any opposition group. Dennis Beresford, chair of the FASB at the time, indicated that it was fear of government control of the standard-setting process that prompted the Board to modify its position. The Board remained steadfast that the proposed change was appropriate.

There were consistent criticisms of the FASB's requirement to expense option compensation.

VOLUNTARY EXPENSING. Prior to 2002, only two companies—Boeing and Winn-Dixie—reported stock option compensation expense at fair value. However, in 2002, public outrage mounted amid high-profile accounting scandals at Enron, WorldCom, Tyco, and others. Some degree of consensus emerged that greed on the part of some corporate executives contributed to the fraudulent and misleading financial reporting at the time. In fact, many in the media were pointing to the proliferation of stock options as a primary form of compensation as a culprit in fueling that greed. An episode of the PBS series *Frontline* argued that not expensing the value of stock options contributed to the collapse of Enron. For these reasons, renewed interest surfaced in requiring stock option compensation to be reported in income statements.

CURRENT REQUIREMENT TO EXPENSE. Emerging from the rekindled debate was a GAAP revision that now requires fair value accounting for employee stock options, eliminating altogether the intrinsic value approach.[7] As you might expect, the proposal did not come without opposition. Many of the same groups that successfully blocked the FASB from enacting a similar requirement in 1995 led the opposition. Not surprisingly, at the forefront of the resistance were the high-tech companies that extensively use stock options as a primary form of compensating employees and thus are most susceptible to a reduction in reported earnings when that compensation is included in income statements. For example, consider Apple Inc.'s earnings for the 12 months ending March 27, 2004. Reported net income of $179 million would have been only $56 million, or 69% less, if the GAAP revision had been in effect then.[8]

Current GAAP now requires companies to record the value of options in their income statements.

It's important to note that the way we account for stock options has no effect whatsoever on cash flows, only on whether the value of stock options is included among expenses. This is not to say that companies haven't altered their compensation strategies. Already, we have seen a shift in the way some companies compensate their employees. Partly due to the negative connotation that has become associated with executive stock options, we've seen fewer options and more bonuses and restricted stock awards. Let's examine the way stock options are accounted for now.

We've witnessed a discernable shift in the way executives are compensated—fewer options, more stock awards and bonuses.

Recognizing the Fair Value of Options

Accounting for stock options parallels the accounting for restricted stock we discussed in the first part of this chapter. That is, we measure compensation as the fair value of the stock options at the grant date and then record that amount as compensation expense over the

[6]All of the then "Big Six" CPA firms lobbied against the proposal. Senator Lieberman of Connecticut introduced a bill in Congress that, if passed, would have forbidden the FASB from passing a requirement to expense stock option compensation.

[7]FASB ASC 718–Compensation (previously "Share-Based Payment," *Statement of Financial Accounting Standards No. 123 (revised 2004)*, (Norwalk, Conn.: FASB 2004)).

[8]Alex Salkever, "What Could Crunch Apple Shares," *BusinessWeek*, July 12, 2004, p. 11.

The fair value of a stock option can be determined by employing a recognized option pricing model.

service period for which employees receive the options. Estimating the fair value requires the use of one of several option pricing models. These mathematical models assimilate a variety of information about a company's stock and the terms of the stock option to estimate the option's fair value. The model should take into account the following:

An option pricing model takes into account several variables.

- Exercise price of the option
- Expected term of the option
- Current market price of the stock
- Expected dividends
- Expected risk-free rate of return during the term of the option
- Expected volatility of the stock

The techniques for estimating fair value have been among the most controversial issues in the debate.

The current GAAP for accounting for employee stock options modified the way companies actually measure fair value. It calls for using models that permit greater flexibility in modeling the ways employees are expected to exercise options and their expected employment termination patterns after options vest.[9] Option-pricing theory, on which the pricing models are based, is a topic explored in depth in finance courses and is subject to active empirical investigation and development. A simplified discussion is provided in Appendix 19A.[10]

The total compensation, as estimated by the options' fair value, is reported as compensation expense over the period of service for which the options are given. Recipients normally are not allowed to exercise their options for a specified number of years. This delay provides added incentive to remain with the company. The time between the date options are granted and the first date they can be exercised is the vesting period and usually is considered to be the service period over which the compensation expense is reported. The process is demonstrated in Illustration 19–3.

Illustration 19–3
Stock Options

At January 1, 2018, Universal Communications grants 10 million options that permit key executives to acquire 10 million of the company's $1 par common shares within the next eight years, but not before December 31, 2021 (the vesting date). The exercise price is the market price of the shares on the date of grant, $35 per share. The fair value of the options, estimated by an appropriate option pricing model, is $8 per option.

January 1, 2018
No entry

Fair value is estimated at the date of grant.

Calculate total compensation expense:

$ 8	Estimated fair value per option
× 10 million	Options granted
= $80 million	Total compensation

The value of the award is expensed over the service period for which the compensation is provided.

The total compensation is allocated to expense over the four-year service (vesting) period: 2018–2021.

$80 million ÷ 4 years = $20 million per year

December 31, 2018, 2019, 2020, 2021	($ in millions)	
Compensation expense ($80 million ÷ 4 years)	20	
Paid-in capital—stock options		20

Option compensation expense is based on the number of options expected to vest.

FORFEITURES. If previous experience indicates that a material number of the options will be forfeited before they vest (due to employee turnover or violation of other terms of the options), we adjust the amount of compensation recorded (a) by estimating forfeitures or (b) as forfeitures occur.

[9]FASB ASC 718–10–55–30 to 32: Compensation–Stock Compensation–Overall–Implementation and Guidance Illustrations–Selecting or Estimating the Expected Term (previously "Share-Based Payment," *Statement of Financial Accounting Standards No. 123 (revised 2004)*, (Norwalk, Conn.: FASB 2004), par. A27–A29)).

[10]An expanded discussion is provided in FASB ASC 718–10–55: Compensation–Stock Compensation–Overall–Implementation and Guidance Illustrations (previously *SFAS No. 123 (revised 2004)*).

The default approach is to *estimate the percentage* of options that will be forfeited and adjust grant date calculation of the fair value of the options to reflect that expectation. For instance, if a forfeiture rate of 5% is expected, Universal's estimated total compensation would be 95% of $80 million, or $76 million. In that case, the annual compensation expense in Illustration 19–3 would have been **$19 million** ($76 ÷ 4) instead of $20 million. We see the effect of that possibility in Illustration 19–3A.

What if that expectation changes later? Universal should adjust the cumulative amount of compensation expense recorded to date in the year the estimate changes. Suppose, for instance, that during the third year, Universal revises its estimate of forfeitures from 5% to 10%. The new estimate of total compensation would then be $80 million × 90%, or $72 million. For the first three years, the portion of the total compensation that should have been reported would be $72 million × ¾, or $54 million, and since $38 million ($19 × 2) of that was recorded in 2018–2019 before the estimate changed, an additional $16 million would now be recorded in 2020. Then if the estimate isn't changed again, the remaining $18 million ($72 − 54) would be recorded in 2021.

When forfeiture estimates change, the cumulative effect on compensation is reflected in current earnings.

Illustration 19–3A

Default Approach: Forfeiture Estimates with Revisions

	($ in millions)	
Initial Expectation:		
2018		
Compensation expense ([$80 × 95%] ÷ 4)	19	
Paid-in capital—stock options		19
2019		
Compensation expense ([$80 × 95%] ÷ 4)	19	
Paid-in capital—stock options		19
Estimate Revision after 2 Years:		
2020		
Compensation expense [($80 × 90% × ¾) − ($19 + 19)]	16	
Paid-in capital—stock options		16
2021		
Compensation expense [($80 × 90% × ¾) − ($19 + 19 + 16)]	18	
Paid-in capital—stock options		18

The value of the compensation is originally estimated to be $76 million, or $19 million per year.

The expense each year is the current estimate of total compensation that should have been recorded to date less the amount already recorded.

Additional Consideration

Notice that the $18 million in 2021 is the amount that would have been reported in each of the four years if Universal had assumed a 10% forfeiture rate from the beginning. Also be aware that this approach is contrary to the usual way companies account for changes in estimates. For instance, assume a company acquires a four-year depreciable asset having an estimated residual value of 5% of cost. The $76 million depreciable cost would be depreciated straight line at **$19 million** over the four-year useful life. If the estimated residual value changes after two years to 10%, the new estimated depreciable cost of $72 would be reduced by the $38 million depreciation recorded the first two years, and the remaining $34 million would be depreciated equally, $17 million per year, over the remaining two years.

In an alternative approach, as a practical expedient, companies can elect to account for forfeitures of stock options (or restricted stock) when forfeitures actually occur, rather than estimate forfeitures that will occur during the vesting period. So rather than recording compensation expense and paid-in capital for the *net* amount of awards expected to vest, companies can choose to initially record compensation based on the total amount and then reduce compensation expense and paid-in capital only if and when forfeitures occur.[11] Once a

Companies can elect to account for forfeitures when forfeitures actually occur rather than estimate them.

[11]Accounting Standards Update 2016-09: Compensation—Stock Compensation (Topic 718), Improvements to Employee Share-Based Payment Accounting (Norwalk, CT: FASB, March 2016).

forfeiture occurs, we adjust the cumulative amount of compensation expense recorded to date in the year the forfeiture occurs and thereafter in a manner similar to the way estimates are adjusted as demonstrated in Illustration 19–3A.

This election applies only to forfeitures related to employee turnover. A company must disclose its policy election for forfeitures (estimated or recorded as they occur). To demonstrate the alternative approach, let's say Universal Communications recorded compensation of $20 million in both 2018 and 2019 based on the $80 million fair value of the stock options issued at the beginning of 2018. Then, in 2020, options with a fair value of $8 million when granted are forfeited due to executive turnover. Universal's journal entries would look like those in Illustration 19–3B.

Illustration 19–3B
Optional Approach: Revisions as Forfeitures Occur

December 31, 2018	($ in millions)	
Compensation expense ($80 million ÷ 4 years)	20	
Paid-in capital—stock options		20
December 31, 2019 ($ in millions)		
Compensation expense ($80 million ÷ 4 years)	20	
Paid-in capital—stock options		20
When Actual Forfeitures Occur in the Third Year:		
December 31, 2020 ($ in millions)		
Compensation expense [($80 – $8 × ¾) – 20 – 20]	14	
Paid-in capital—stock options		14
December 31, 2021 ($ in millions)		
Compensation expense [($80 – $8 × 4⁄4) – 20 – 20 – 14]	18	
Paid-in capital—stock options		18

This election applies only to forfeitures related to employee *turnover*. For share-based plans with performance conditions (which we discuss later), companies must assess the probability that such conditions will be achieved. A company must disclose its policy election for forfeitures (estimated, or recorded as they occur).

When Options are Exercised

If half the options in Illustration 19–3 (for 5 million shares) are exercised on July 11, 2024, when the market price is $50 per share, the following journal entry is recorded:

Recording the exercise of options is not affected by the market price on the exercise date.

July 11, 2024	($ in millions)	
Cash ($35 exercise price × 5 million shares)	175	
Paid-in capital—stock options (½ account balance)	40	
Common stock (5 million shares at $1 par per share)		5
Paid-in capital—excess of par (to balance)		210

Notice that the market price at exercise is irrelevant. Changes in the market price of underlying shares do not influence the previously measured fair value of options.

When Unexercised Options Expire

If options that have vested expire without being exercised, the following journal entry is made (assuming the remaining 5 million options in our illustration are allowed to expire):

Paid-in capital—stock options becomes *paid-in capital—expiration of stock options* when options expire without being exercised.

	($ in millions)	
Paid-in capital—stock options (account balance)	40	
Paid-in capital—expiration of stock options		40

In effect, we rename the paid-in capital attributable to the stock option plan. Compensation expense for the four years' service, as of the measurement date, is not affected.

Additional Consideration

Tax Consequences of Stock-Based Compensation Plans. In Illustration 19–3 we ignored the tax effect. To illustrate the effect of taxes, let's assume Universal Communications' income tax rate is 40%.

For tax purposes, plans can either qualify as "incentive stock option plans" under the Tax Code or be "nonqualified plans." Among the requirements of a qualified option plan is that the exercise price be equal to the market price at the grant date. Under a qualified incentive plan, the recipient pays no income tax until any shares acquired from exercise of stock options are subsequently sold. On the other hand, the company gets no tax deduction at all. With a nonqualified plan the employee can't delay paying income tax, but the employer is permitted to deduct the difference between the exercise price and the market price at the exercise date. Let's consider both.

Tax treatment favors the employer in a nonqualified stock option plan.

Case 1. With an incentive plan, the employer receives no tax deduction at all. If Universal's plan qualifies as an incentive plan, the company will receive no tax deduction upon exercise of the options and thus no tax consequences.

Because an incentive plan provides no tax deduction, it has no deferred tax consequences.

Case 2. On the other hand, if we assume the plan does not qualify as an incentive plan, Universal will deduct from taxable income the difference between the exercise price and the market price at the exercise date. Recall from Chapter 16 that this creates a temporary difference between accounting income (for which compensation expense is recorded currently) and taxable income (for which the tax deduction is taken later upon the exercise of the options). We assume the temporary difference is the cumulative amount expensed for the options. The following entries would be recorded on the dates shown:

December 31, 2018, 2019, 2020, 2021	($ in millions)	
Compensation expense ($80 million ÷ 4 years)	20	
Paid-in capital—stock options		20
Deferred tax asset (40% × $20 million)	8	
Income tax expense		8

A deferred tax asset is recognized now for the future tax savings from the tax deduction when the nonqualified stock options are exercised.

The after-tax effect on earnings is thus $12 million each year ($20 − 8).

If all of the options (for 10 million shares) are exercised on April 4, 2023, when the stock's market price is $50 per share:

Cash ($35 exercise price × 10 million shares)	350	
Paid-in capital—stock options (account balance)	80	
Common stock (10 million shares at $1 par per share)		10
Paid-in capital—excess of par (to balance)		420
Income taxes payable [($50 − 35) × 10 million shares × 40%]	60	
Deferred tax asset (4 years × $8 million)		32
Income tax expense (remainder)*		28

*This treatment is consistent with ASU 2016-09, "Improvements to Employee Share-Based Payment Accounting," which amends ASC Topic 718, Compensation – Stock Compensation.

The difference between the market price at exercise and the eventual tax savings is recognized in income tax expense.

The tax consequences of all nonqualifying stock options as well as restricted stock plans also are accounted for in the manner demonstrated above.

International Financial Reporting Standards

● LO19–14

Recognition of Deferred Tax Asset for Stock Options. Under U.S. GAAP, a deferred tax asset (DTA) is created for the cumulative amount of the fair value of the options the company has recorded for compensation expense. The DTA is the tax rate times the amount of compensation.

(continued)

(concluded)

Under IFRS, the deferred tax asset isn't created until the award is "in the money;" that is, it has intrinsic value. When it is in the money, the addition to the DTA is the portion of the intrinsic value earned to date times the tax rate.

IFRS ILLUSTRATION

For illustration, refer to Case 2 in the Additional Consideration example above. Now assume the share price, which was equal to the $35 exercise price on January 1, 2018, was $35, $37, $37, and $37.50 on December 31, 2018, 2019, 2020, and 2021, respectively. We need this information to determine the intrinsic value for IFRS.

The addition to the DTA and reduction in the tax expense (tax benefit) is calculated in the following table for both U.S. GAAP and IFRS ($ in millions):

Dec. 31	Compensation expense	Addition to DTA and reduction in tax expense at 40% U.S. GAAP	Cumulative reduction in tax expense	Intrinsic value (price − $35) × 10M shares	Cumulative percent of services received	Percent × Intrinsic value	Addition to DTA and reduction in tax expense at 40%* IFRS
2018	$20	$ 8	$ 8	$ 0	25%	$ 0	$ 0
2019	20	8	16	20	50	10	4
2020	20	8	24	20	75	15	2
2021	20	8	32	25	100	25	4

December 31, 2018, 2019, 2020, 2021 ($ in millions)	U.S. GAAP		IFRS	
Compensation expense ($80 million ÷ 4 years)	20		20	
Paid-in capital—stock options		20		20
Deferred tax asset	8		0	
Income tax expense		8		0
Deferred tax asset	8		4	
Income tax expense		8		4
Deferred tax asset	8		2	
Income tax expense		8		2
Deferred tax asset	8		4	
Income tax expense		8		4

*The tax benefit recorded in earnings (cumulative amount in this column) cannot exceed the cumulative tax effect of the compensation (4th column). Any tax benefit in excess of that amount is recorded in equity. In 2021, $10 ($0 + 4 + 2 + 4) does not exceed $32.

Plans with Graded Vesting

The stock option plans we've discussed so far vest (become exercisable) on one single date (e.g., four years from date of grant). This is referred to as *cliff vesting*. More frequently, though, awards specify that recipients gradually become eligible to exercise their options rather than all at once. This is called *graded vesting*. For instance, a company might award stock options that vest 25% the first year, 25% the second year, and 50% the third year, or maybe 25% each year for four years.

In such a case, the company can choose to account for the options essentially the same as the cliff-vesting plans we've discussed to this point. It can estimate a single fair value for each of the options, even though they vest over different time periods, using a single weighted-average expected life of the options. The company then allocates that total compensation cost (fair value per option times number of options) over the entire vesting period.

Most companies, though, choose a slightly more complex method because it usually results in a lower expense.[12] In this approach, we view each vesting group (or tranche) separately, as if it were a separate award. See Illustration 19–4.

Illustration 19–4 Stock Options; Graded Vesting; Separate Valuation Approach

At January 1, 2018, Taggart Mobility issued 10 million executive stock options permitting executives to buy 10 million shares of stock for $25. The vesting schedule is 20% the first year, 30% the second year, and 50% the third year (graded-vesting). The value of the options that vest over the 3-year period is estimated at January 1, 2018, by separating the total award into three groups (or tranches) according to the year in which they vest (because the expected life for each group differs). The fair value of the options as of January 1, 2018 is *estimated* as follows:

Vesting Date	Amount Vesting	Fair Value per Option
Dec. 31, 2018	20%	$3.50
Dec. 31, 2019	30%	$4.00
Dec. 31, 2020	50%	$6.00

We allocate the compensation cost for each of the three groups (tranches) evenly over its *individual* vesting (service) period:

	Compensation Expense in ($ in millions)				
Shares Vesting at	**2018**	**2019**	**2020**	**Total**	
Dec. 31, 2018	$ 7			$ 7	(10 M × 20% × $3.50)
Dec. 31, 2019	6	$ 6		12	(10 M × 30% × $4.00)
Dec. 31, 2020	10	10	$10	30	(10 M × 50% × $6.00)
Expensed	$23	$16	$10	= $49	

At any given date, a company must have recognized at least the amount vested by that date. The allocation in this instance meets that constraint:

- The $23 million recognized in 2018 exceeds the $7 million vested.
- The $39 million ($23 + $16) recognized by 2019 exceeds the $19 million ($7 + $12) vested by the same time.

Companies also can choose to use the straight-line method, which would allocate the $49 million total compensation cost equally to 2018, 2019, and 2020 at $16.333 million per year.

International Financial Reporting Standards

● LO19–14

When options have graded vesting, U.S. GAAP permits companies to account for each vesting amount separately, for instance as if there were three separate awards as in the previous illustration, but also allows companies the option to account for the entire award on

(continued)

[12]The fair value of the options usually is higher when estimated using a single weighted-average expected life of the options rather than when estimated as the total of fair values of the multiple vesting groups.

(concluded)

a straight-line basis over the entire vesting period. Either way, the company must recognize at least the amount of the award that has vested by that date.

Under IFRS, the straight-line choice is not permitted. Also, there's no requirement that the company must recognize at least the amount of the award that has vested by each reporting date.

Plans with Performance or Market Conditions

The terms of performance options vary with some measure of performance that ties rewards to productivity.

Stock option (and other share-based) plans often specify a performance condition or a market condition that must be satisfied before employees are allowed the benefits of the award. The objective is to provide employees with additional incentive for managerial achievement. For instance, an option might not be exercisable until a performance target is met. The target could be divisional revenue, earnings per share, sales growth, or rate of return on assets. The possibilities are limitless. On the other hand, the target might be market-related, perhaps a specified stock price or a stock price change exceeding a particular index. The way we account for such plans depends on whether the condition is performance-based or market-based.

If compensation from a stock option depends on meeting a performance target, compensation is recorded only if we feel it's probable the target will be met.

PLANS WITH PERFORMANCE CONDITIONS. Whether we recognize compensation expense for performance-based options depends (a) initially on whether it's probable[13] that the performance target will be met and (b) ultimately on whether the performance target actually is met. Accounting is as described earlier for other stock options. Initial estimates of compensation cost, as well as subsequent revisions of that estimate, take into account the likelihood of both forfeitures and achieving performance targets. For example, in Illustration 19–3, if the options described also had included a condition that the options would become exercisable only if sales increase by 10% after four years, we would estimate the likelihood of that occurring; specifically, is it probable? Let's say we initially estimate that it is probable that sales will increase by 10% after four years. Then, our initial estimate of the total compensation would have been unchanged at

10 million	×	\$8	=	\$80 million
Options expected to vest		Fair value per option		Estimated total compensation

Suppose, though, that after two years, we estimate that it is *not* probable that sales will increase by 10% after four years. Then, our new estimate of the total compensation would change to

If it later becomes probable that a performance target will not be met, we reverse any compensation expense already recorded.

0	×	\$8	=	0
Options expected to vest		Fair value per option		Estimated total compensation

When we revise our estimate of total compensation because our expectation of probability changes, we record the effect of the change in the current period.

In that case, we would reverse the \$40 million expensed in 2018–2019. No compensation can be recognized for options that don't vest due to performance targets not being met, and that's our expectation.

Conversely, assume that our initial expectation is that it is *not* probable that sales will increase by 10% after four years and so we record no annual compensation expense. But then, in the third year, we estimate that it *is* probable that sales will increase by 10% after four years. At that point, our revised estimate of the total compensation would change to

[13]"Probable" means the same as it did in Chapter 13, when we were estimating the likelihood that payment would be made for a loss contingency, and elsewhere when making accounting estimates. Probable is a matter of professional judgement (often 70–75%).

$80 million, and we would reflect the cumulative effect on compensation in 2020 earnings and record compensation thereafter:

2020		
Compensation expense [($80 × 3/4) − $0]	60	
Paid-in capital—stock options		60
2021		
Compensation expense [($80 × 4/4) − $60]	20	
Paid-in capital—stock options		20

If we had begun with our new estimate of total compensation, $20 million would have been expensed in each of the first three years.

Additional Consideration

Suppose an executive who is granted some of the performance-based options in this example is eligible to retire on January 1, 2018. So, when the options are granted she would be eligible to receive the options even if the performance target (sales increase by 10%) is met after she retires. In that case, the service period needed to receive compensation effectively is one day. Should compensation for her be measured and expensed over the vesting period as in the example, or should that compensation be measured and recorded all at once (full amount if probable, zero otherwise) on the grant date?

It should be treated the same as the compensation for the other options. It should be treated as a performance condition consistent with those for which the requisite service period is not met prior to the performance target being met. So, we would record no compensation expense until meeting the performance target is probable, even if this is not until *after* the requisite vesting period is completed. An important secondary benefit of this treatment is that the employer doesn't need to assess at the grant date whether certain employees are retirement-eligible or will become retirement-eligible during the performance period in order to value the awards.[14]

This treatment differs from that of International Financial Reporting Standards, which specifies that if the performance target can be met *after* the requisite vesting period is completed, compensation should be measured and recorded all at once (full amount if probable, zero otherwise) on the grant date.

PLANS WITH MARKET CONDITIONS. If the award contains a market condition (e.g., a share option with an exercisability requirement based on the stock price reaching a specified level), then no special accounting is required. The fair value estimate of the share option already implicitly reflects market conditions due to the nature of share option pricing models. So, we recognize compensation expense regardless of when, if ever, the market condition is met.

If the target is based on changes in the market rather than on performance, we record compensation as if there were no target.

DECLINE IN POPULARITY OF OPTIONS. Recent years have witnessed a steady shift in the way companies compensate their top executives. At their peak in 1999, stock options represented about 78% of the average executive's incentive pay. In 2013, they accounted for just 31%, expected to shrink to 25% by 2015.[15] In the wake of recent accounting scandals, the image of stock options has been tarnished in the view of many who believe that the potential to garner millions in stock option gains created incentives for executives to boost company stock prices through risky or fraudulent behavior. That image has motivated many firms to move away from stock options in favor of other forms of share-based compensation, particularly restricted stock awards and, increasingly, restricted stock units. Also

[14]FASB Emerging Issues Task Force, *Accounting Standards Update No. 2014-12,* "Compensation–Stock Compensation (Topic 718): Accounting for Share-Based Payments When the Terms of an Award Provide That a Performance Target Could Be Achieved after the Requisite Service Period," June 2014.

[15]According to an analysis of the 200 largest U.S. public companies by compensation consulting firm James F. Reda & Associates, as reported by Emily Chasan, "Last Gasp for Stock Options?" *USA Today,* August 26, 2013.

contributing to the rise of restricted stock is the feeling by many that it better aligns pay with performance. From the executive's perspective, restricted stock is a more certain, though potentially less lucrative, form of compensation.

Employee Share Purchase Plans

LO19–3

Share purchase plans permit employees to buy shares directly from the corporation.

Employee share purchase plans often permit all employees to buy shares directly from their company at favorable terms. The primary intent of these plans is to encourage employee ownership of the company's shares. Presumably loyalty is enhanced among employee-shareholders. The employee also benefits because, typically, these plans allow employees to buy shares from their employer without brokerage fees and, perhaps, at a slight discount. Some companies even encourage participation by matching or partially matching employee purchases.

When accounting for employee share purchase plans (ESPPs), we need to determine whether or not they provide compensation to employees. If not, we simply record the sale of new shares as employees buy them and do not record compensation expense. An ESPP is considered noncompensatory as long as:

1. substantially all employees can participate,
2. employees have no longer than one month after the price is fixed to decide whether to participate, and
3. the discount is no greater than 5% (or can be justified as reasonable).

If these criteria for the plan being noncompensatory are *not* met, say the discount is 15%, accounting is similar to other share-based plans. The 15% discount to employees, then, is considered to be compensation, and that amount is recorded as expense.[16] Compensation expense replaces the cash debit for any employer-provided portion. Say an employee buys shares (no par) under the plan for $850 rather than the current market price of $1,000. The $150 discount is recorded as compensation expense.

Cash (discounted price)	850	
Compensation expense ($1,000 × 15%)	150	
Common stock (market value)		1,000

Decision Makers' Perspective

Analysts should be aware of the possibility of earnings management as a way to increase managers' compensation.

In several previous chapters, we have revisited the concept of "earnings quality" (as first defined in Chapter 4). We also have noted that one rather common practice that negatively influences earnings quality is earnings management, which refers to companies' use of one or more of several techniques designed to artificially increase (or decrease) earnings. A frequent objective of earnings management is to meet analysts' expectations regarding projections of income. The share-based compensation plans we discuss in this chapter suggest another motive managers sometimes have to manipulate income. If a manager's personal compensation includes company stock, stock options, or other compensation based on the value of the firm's stock, it's not hard to imagine an increased desire to ensure that market expectations are met and that reported earnings have a positive effect on stock prices. In fact, as we discussed earlier, that is precisely the reaction these incentive compensation plans are designed to elicit. Investors and creditors, though, should be alert to indications of attempts to artificially manipulate income and realize that the likelihood of earnings management is probably higher for companies with generous share-based compensation plans.

[16]FASB ASC 718–50–25–1 and 2: Compensation–Stock Compensation–Employee Share Purchase Plans–Recognition (previously "Share-Based Payment," *Statement of Financial Accounting Standards No. 123 (revised 2004)*, (Norwalk, Conn.: FASB 2004), par. 12–13).

One way managers might manipulate numbers is to low-ball the data that go into the option-pricing models. The models used to estimate fair value are built largely around subjective assumptions. That possibility emphasizes the need for investors to look closely at the assumptions reported in the stock option disclosure note, and particularly at how those assumptions change from year to year. ●

Concept Review Exercise

SHARE-BASED COMPENSATION PLANS

Listed below are transactions dealing with various stock benefit plans of Fortune-Time Corporation during the period 2018–2020. The market price of the stock is $45 at January 1, 2018.

a. On January 1, 2018, the company issued 10 million common shares to divisional managers under its restricted stock award plan. The shares are subject to forfeiture if employment is terminated within three years.

b. On January 1, 2018, the company granted incentive stock options to its senior management, exercisable for 1.5 million common shares. The options must be exercised within five years, but not before January 1, 2020. The exercise price of the stock options is equal to the fair value of the common stock on the date the options are granted. An option pricing model estimates the fair value of the options to be $4 per option. All recipients are expected to remain employed through the vesting date.

c. Recorded compensation expense on December 31, 2018.

d. A divisional manager holding 1 million of the restricted shares left the company to become CEO of a competitor on September 15, 2019, before the required service period ended.

e. Recorded compensation expense on December 31, 2019.

Required:

Prepare the journal entries that Fortune-Time recorded for each of these transactions. (Ignore any tax effects.)

Solution:

January 1, 2018

Restricted Stock Award Plan

No entry.

Total compensation is measured as 10 million shares × $45 = $450 million.

Stock Options

No entry.

Total compensation is measured as 1.5 million shares × $4 = $6 million.

December 31, 2018

	($ in millions)	
Restricted Stock		
Compensation expense ($450 million ÷ 3 years)	150	
Paid-in capital—restricted stock		150
Stock Options		
Compensation expense ($6 million ÷ 2 years)	3	
Paid-in capital—stock options		3

September 15, 2019

Restricted Stock		
Paid-in capital—restricted stock (10% × $150)	15	
Compensation expense		15

(continued)

(concluded)

December 31, 2019

Restricted Stock

Compensation expense [$450 − (0.10 × $450) − 150 + 15] ÷ 2 years	135	
Paid-in capital—restricted stock		135

Stock Options

Compensation expense ($6 million ÷ 2 years)	3	
Paid-in capital—stock options		3

PART B

Earnings Per Share

Earnings per share is the single accounting number that receives the most media attention.

Comparability is an enhancing characteristic of relevant accounting information *(Conceptual Framework)*.

A typical corporate annual report contains four comparative financial statements, an extensive list of disclosure notes and schedules, and several pages of charts, tables, and textual descriptions. Of these myriad facts and figures, the single accounting number that is reported most frequently in the media and receives by far the most attention by investors and creditors is **earnings per share** (EPS). The reasons for the considerable attention paid to earnings per share certainly include the desire to find a way to summarize the performance of business enterprises into a single number.

Summarizing performance in a way that permits comparisons is difficult because the companies that report the numbers are different from one another. And yet, the desire to condense performance to a single number has created a demand for EPS information. The profession has responded with rules designed to maximize the comparability of EPS numbers by minimizing the inconsistencies in their calculation from one company to the next.[17]

Keep in mind as you study the requirements that a primary goal is comparability. As a result, many of the rules devised to achieve consistency are unavoidably arbitrary, meaning that other choices the FASB might have made in many instances would be equally adequate.

International Financial Reporting Standards

LO19–14

Earnings per Share. The earnings per share requirements of U.S. GAAP, *FASB ASC 260: Earnings per Share,* are a result of the FASB's cooperation with the IASB to narrow the differences between IFRS and U.S. GAAP. A few differences remain. The differences that remain are the result of differences in the application of the treasury stock method, the treatment of contracts that may be settled in shares or cash, and contingently issuable shares.

Basic Earnings Per Share

A firm has a simple capital structure if it has no *potential common shares.*

LO19–4

A firm is said to have a **simple capital structure** if it has no outstanding securities that could potentially dilute earnings per share. In this context, to dilute means to *reduce* earnings per share. For instance, if a firm has convertible bonds outstanding and those bonds are converted, the resulting increase in common shares could decrease (or dilute) earnings per share. That is, the new shares replaced by the converted bonds might participate in future earnings. So convertible bonds are referred to as **potential common shares**. Other potential common shares are convertible preferred stock, stock options, and contingently issuable shares. We will see how the potentially dilutive effects of these securities are included in the calculation of EPS later in this chapter. Now, though, our focus is on the calculation of EPS for a simple capital structure—when no potential common shares are present. In these cases,

[17]FASB ASC 260: Earnings per Share (previously "Earnings per Share," *Statement of Financial Accounting Standards No. 128* (Norwalk, Conn.: FASB, 1997)). The guidance is applicable only for public companies.

the calculation is referred to as basic EPS, and is simply earnings available to common shareholders divided by the weighted-average number of common shares outstanding.

Basic EPS reflects no dilution, only shares now outstanding.

In the most elemental setting, earnings per share (or net loss per share) is merely a firm's net income (or net loss) divided by the number of shares of common stock outstanding throughout the year. The calculation becomes more demanding (a) when the number of shares has changed during the reporting period, (b) when the earnings available to common shareholders are diminished by dividends to preferred shareholders, or (c) when we attempt to take into account the impending effect of potential common shares (which we do in a later section of the chapter). To illustrate the calculation of EPS in each of its dimensions, we will use only one example in this chapter. We'll start with the most basic situation and then add one new element at a time until we have considered all the principal ways the calculation can be affected. In this way, you can see the effect of each component of earnings per share, not just in isolation, but in relation to the effects of other components as well. The basic calculation is shown in Illustration 19–5.

EPS expresses a firm's profitability on a per share basis.

Illustration 19–5

Fundamental Calculation

Sovran Financial Corporation reported net income of $154 million in 2018 (tax rate 40%). Its capital structure consisted of the following:

Common Stock

Jan. 1 — 60 million common shares were outstanding

($ in millions, except per share amount)

Basic EPS:

$$\frac{\overset{\text{Net income}}{\$154}}{\underset{\text{Shares outstanding}}{60}} = \$2.57$$

In the most elemental setting, earnings per share is simply a company's earnings divided by the number of shares outstanding.

Issuance of New Shares

Because the shares discussed in Illustration 19–5 remained unchanged throughout the year, the denominator of the EPS calculation is simply the number of shares outstanding. But if the number of shares has changed, it's necessary to find the *weighted average* of the shares outstanding during the period the earnings were generated. For instance, if an additional 12 million shares had been issued on March 1 of the year just ended, we calculate the weighted-average number of shares to be 70 million, as demonstrated in Illustration 19–6.

Because the new shares were outstanding only 10 months, or $^{10}/_{12}$ of the year, we increase the 60 million shares already outstanding by the additional shares—weighted by the fraction

● LO19–5

Illustration 19–6

Weighted Average

Sovran Financial Corporation reported net income of $154 million for 2018 (tax rate 40%). Its capital structure included the following:

Common Stock

Jan. 1 — 60 million common shares were outstanding

Mar. 1 — 12 million new shares were sold

($ in millions, except per share amount)

Basic EPS:

$$\frac{\overset{\text{Net income}}{\$154}}{\underset{\text{Shares at Jan. 1}}{60} + \underset{\text{New shares}}{12\,(^{10}/_{12})}} = \frac{\$154}{70} = \$2.20$$

Any new shares issued are time-weighted by the fraction of the period they were outstanding and then added to the number of shares outstanding for the entire period.

of the year ($^{10}/_{12}$) they were outstanding. The weighted average is 60 + 12 ($^{10}/_{12}$) = 60 + 10 = 70 shares. The reason for time-weighting the shares issued is that the resources the stock sale provides the company are available for generating income only after the date the shares are sold. So, weighting is necessary to make the shares in the fraction's denominator consistent with the income in its numerator (see Illustration 19–6).

Stock Dividends and Stock Splits

LO19–6

Recall that a stock dividend or a stock split is a distribution of additional shares to existing shareholders. But there's an important and fundamental difference between the increase in shares caused by a stock dividend and an increase from selling new shares. When new shares are sold, both assets and shareholders' equity are increased by an additional investment in the firm by shareholders. On the other hand, a stock dividend or stock split merely increases the number of shares without affecting the firm's assets. In effect, the same pie is divided into more pieces. The result is a larger number of less valuable shares. This fundamental change in the nature of the shares is reflected in a calculation of EPS by simply increasing the number of shares.

In Illustration 19–7, notice that the additional shares created by the stock dividend are *not* weighted for the time period they were outstanding. Instead, the increase is treated as if it occurred at the beginning of the year.

Illustration 19–7

Stock Dividends and Stock Splits

Shares outstanding prior to the stock dividend are retroactively restated to reflect the 10% increase in shares— that is, treated as if the distribution occurred at the beginning of the period.

Sovran Financial Corporation reported net income of $154 million in 2018 (tax rate 40%). Its capital structure included the following:

Common Stock

Jan. 1	60 million common shares were outstanding
Mar. 1	12 million new shares were sold
June 17	A 10% stock dividend was distributed
	($ in millions, except per share amount)

Basic EPS:

Net income

$$\frac{\$154}{60\ (1.10) + 12\ (^{10}/_{12})\ (1.10)} = \frac{\$154}{77} = \$2.00$$

Shares at Jan. 1 — New shares — Stock dividend adjustment

The number of shares outstanding after a 10% stock dividend is 1.10 times higher than before. This multiple is applied to both the beginning shares and the new shares sold before the stock distribution. If this had been a 25% stock dividend, the multiple would have been 1.25; a 2-for-1 stock split means a multiple of 2, and so on.

Notice that EPS without the 10% stock dividend ($2.20) is 10% more than it is with the stock distribution ($2). This is caused by the increase in the number of shares. But, unlike a sale of new shares, this should not be interpreted as a "dilution" of earnings per share. Shareholders' interests in their company's earnings have not been diluted. Instead, each shareholder's interest is represented by more—though less valuable—shares.

A simplistic but convenient way to view the effect is to think of the predistribution shares as having been "blue." After the stock dividend, the more valuable "blue" shares are gone, replaced by a larger number of, let's say, "green" shares. From now on, we compute the earnings per "green" share, whereas we previously calculated earnings per "blue" share. We restate the number of shares retroactively to reflect the stock dividend, as if the shares always had been "green." After all, our intent is to let the calculation reflect the fundamental change in the nature of the shares.

Additional Consideration

When last year's EPS is reported in the current year's comparative income statements, it too should reflect the increased shares from the stock dividend. For instance, suppose EPS was \$2.09 for 2017: \$115 million net income divided by 55 million weighted-average shares. When reported again for comparison purposes in the 2018 comparative income statements, that figure would be restated to reflect the 10% stock dividend [\$115 ÷ (55 × 1.10) = \$1.90], as shown:

Earnings per Share:	**2018**	**2017**
	\$2.00	\$1.90

The EPS numbers now are comparable—both reflect the stock dividend. Otherwise we would be comparing earnings per "green" share with earnings per "blue" share; this way both are earnings per "green" share.

Reacquired Shares

If shares were reacquired during the period (either retired or as treasury stock), the weighted-average number of shares is reduced. The number of reacquired shares is time-weighted for the *fraction of the year they were **not** outstanding,* prior to being *subtracted* from the number of shares outstanding during the period. Let's modify our continuing illustration to assume 8 million shares were reacquired on October 1 as treasury stock (Illustration 19–8).

Illustration 19–8

Reacquired Shares

Sovran Financial Corporation reported net income of \$154 million in 2018 (tax rate 40%). Its capital structure included the following:

Common Stock

Jan. 1	60 million common shares outstanding
Mar. 1	12 million new shares were sold
June 17	A 10% stock dividend was distributed
Oct. 1	8 million shares were reacquired as treasury stock

($ in millions, except per share amounts)

Basic EPS:

$$\frac{\overset{\text{Net income}}{\$154}}{60\ (1.10) + 12\ (^{10}/_{12})\ (1.10) - 8\ (^{3}/_{12})} = \frac{\$154}{75} = \$2.05$$

60 = Shares at Jan. 1; 12 (10/12) = New shares; 8 (3/12) = Treasury shares; (1.10) = Stock dividend adjustment*

*Not necessary for the treasury shares since they were reacquired after the stock dividend and thus already reflect the adjustment (that is, the shares repurchased are 8 million "new green" shares).

The 8 million shares reacquired as treasury stock are weighted by (3/12) to reflect the fact they were not outstanding the last three months of the year.

Compare the adjustment for treasury shares with the adjustment for new shares sold. Each is time-weighted for the fraction of the year the shares were or were not outstanding. But also notice two differences. The new shares are added, while the reacquired shares are subtracted. The second difference is that the reacquired shares are not multiplied by 1.10 to adjust for the 10% stock dividend. The reason is the shares were repurchased after the June 17 stock dividend; the reacquired shares are 8 million of the new post-distribution shares. (To use our earlier representation, these are 8 million "green" shares.) To generalize, when a stock distribution occurs during the reporting period, any sales or purchases of shares that occur *before* the distribution are increased by the distribution. But the stock distribution does not increase the number of shares sold or purchased, if any, *after* the distribution.

The adjustment for reacquired shares is the same as for new shares sold, except the shares are deducted rather than added.

Any sales or purchases of shares that occur before, but not after, a stock dividend or split are affected by the distribution.

Earnings Available to Common Shareholders

● LO19–7 The denominator in an EPS calculation is the weighted-average number of common shares outstanding. Logically, the numerator should similarly represent earnings available to common shareholders. This was automatic in our illustrations to this point because the only shares outstanding were common shares. But when a senior class of shareholders (like preferred shareholders) is entitled to a specified allocation of earnings (like preferred dividends), those amounts are subtracted from earnings before calculating earnings per share.[18] This is demonstrated in Illustration 19–9.

Illustration 19–9
Preferred Dividends

Sovran Financial Corporation reported net income of $154 million in 2018 (tax rate 40%). Its capital structure included the following:

Common Stock

January 1	60 million common shares were outstanding
March 1	12 million new shares were sold
June 17	A 10% stock dividend was distributed
October 1	8 million shares were reacquired as treasury stock

Preferred Stock Nonconvertible

January 1–December 31	5 million shares 8%, $10 par

($ in millions, except per share amount)

Basic EPS:

$$\frac{\$154 - \$4^{*}}{60\ (1.10) + 12\ (^{10}/_{12})\ (1.10) - 8\ (^{3}/_{12})} = \frac{\$150}{75} = \$2.00$$

Net income: $154; Preferred dividends: −$4*
Shares at Jan. 1; New shares; Treasury shares
Stock dividend adjustment

*8% × $10 par × 5 million shares.

Preferred dividends are subtracted from net income so that "earnings available to common shareholders" is divided by the weighted-average number of common shares.

Preferred dividends reduce earnings available to common shareholders unless the preferred stock is noncumulative and no dividends were declared that year.

Suppose no dividends were declared for the year. Should we adjust for preferred dividends? Yes, if the preferred stock is cumulative—and most preferred stock is. This means that when dividends are not declared, the unpaid dividends accumulate to be paid in a future year when (if) dividends are subsequently declared. Obviously, the presumption is that although the year's dividend preference isn't distributed this year, it eventually will be paid.

We have encountered no potential common shares to this point in our continuing illustration. As a result, we have what is referred to as a simple capital structure. (Although, at this point, you may question this label.) For a simple capital structure, a single presentation of basic earnings per common share is appropriate. We turn our attention now to situations described as complex capital structures. In these situations, two separate presentations are required: basic EPS and diluted EPS.

Diluted Earnings Per Share

Potential Common Shares

Imagine a situation in which convertible bonds are outstanding that will significantly increase the number of common shares if bondholders exercise their options to exchange their bonds for shares of common stock. Should these potential shares be ignored when

[18]You learned in Chapter 18 that when dividends are declared, preferred shareholders have a preference (over common shareholders) to a specified amount.

earnings per share is calculated? After all, they haven't been converted as yet, so to assume an increase in shares for a conversion that may never occur might mislead investors and creditors. On the other hand, if conversion is imminent, not taking into account the dilutive effect of the share increase might mislead investors and creditors. The profession's solution to the dilemma is to calculate earnings per share twice.

Securities such as these convertible bonds, while not being common stock, may become common stock through their exercise or conversion. Therefore, they may dilute (reduce) earnings per share and are called **potential common shares**. A firm is said to have a **complex capital structure** if potential common shares are outstanding. Besides convertible bonds, other potential common shares are convertible preferred stock, stock options, and contingently issuable securities. (We'll discuss each of these shortly.) A firm with a complex capital structure reports two EPS calculations. **Basic EPS** ignores the dilutive effect of such securities; **diluted EPS** incorporates the dilutive effect of all potential common shares.

In a complex capital structure, a second EPS computation takes into account the assumed effect of *potential common shares*, essentially a "worst case scenario."

Options, Rights, and Warrants

LO19–8

Stock options, stock rights, and stock warrants are similar. Each gives its holders the right to exercise their option to purchase common stock, usually at a specified exercise price. The dilution that would result from their exercise should be reflected in the calculation of diluted EPS, but not basic EPS.

To include the dilutive effect of a security means to calculate EPS *as if* the potential increase in shares already has occurred (even though it hasn't yet). So, for stock options (or rights, or warrants), we pretend the options have been exercised. In fact, we assume the options were exercised at the beginning of the reporting period, or when the options were issued if that's later. We then assume the cash proceeds from selling the new shares at the exercise price are used to buy back as many shares as possible at the shares' average market price during the year. This is demonstrated in Illustration 19–10.

Stock options are assumed to have been exercised when calculating diluted EPS.

When we simulate the exercise of the stock options, we calculate EPS as if 15 million shares were sold at the beginning of the year. This obviously increases the number of shares in the denominator by 15 million shares. But it is insufficient to simply add the additional shares without considering the accompanying consequences. Remember, if this hypothetical scenario had occurred, the company would have had $300 million cash proceeds from the exercise of the options (15 million shares × $20 exercise price per share). What would have been the effect on earnings per share? This depends on what the company would have done with the $300 million cash proceeds. Would the proceeds have been used to buy more equipment? Increase the sales force? Expand facilities? Pay dividends?

FINANCIAL Reporting Case

Q4, p. 1091

Obviously, there are literally hundreds of choices, and it's unlikely that any two firms would spend the $300 million exactly the same way. But remember, our objective is to create some degree of uniformity in the way firms determine earnings per share so the resulting numbers are comparable. So, standard-setters decided on a single assumption for all firms to enhance comparability.

For diluted EPS, we assume the proceeds from exercise of the options were used to reacquire shares as treasury stock at the average market price of the common stock during the reporting period. Consequently, the weighted-average number of shares is increased by the difference between the shares assumed issued and those assumed reacquired. In our illustration, 15 million shares issued minus 12 million shares reacquired ($300 million × $25 per share) equals 3 million net increase in shares.

The way we take into account the dilutive effect of stock options is called the *treasury stock method* because of our assumption that treasury shares are purchased with the cash proceeds of the exercise of the options. Besides providing comparability, this assumption actually is plausible because, if the options were exercised, more shares would be needed to issue to option-holders. And, as discussed in the previous chapter, many firms routinely buy back shares either to issue to option-holders or, equivalently, to offset the issuance of new shares.

Illustration 19–10
Stock Options

Stock options give their holders (company executives in this case) the right to purchase common stock at a specified exercise price ($20 in this case).

The stock options do not affect the calculation of *basic EPS.*

The calculation of diluted EPS assumes that the shares specified by stock options were issued at the exercise price and that the proceeds were used to buy back (as treasury stock) as many of those shares as can be purchased at the market price during the period.

Sovran Financial Corporation reported net income of $154 million in 2018 (tax rate 40%). Its capital structure included the following:

Common Stock

January 1	60 million common shares outstanding
March 1	12 million new shares were sold
June 17	A 10% stock dividend was distributed
October 1	8 million shares were reacquired as treasury stock

(The average market price of the common shares during 2018 was $25 per share.)

Preferred Stock Nonconvertible

January 1–December 31 5 million shares 8%, $10 par

Incentive Stock Options

Executive stock options granted in 2013, exercisable after 2017 for 15 million common shares* at an exercise price of $20 per share

($ in millions, except per share amounts)

Basic EPS (unchanged)

$$\frac{\underset{\text{Net income}}{\$154} \quad \underset{\text{Preferred dividends}}{-\$4}}{\underset{\text{Shares at Jan. 1}}{60}(1.10) + \underset{\text{New shares}}{12\left(^{10}\!/_{12}\right)}(1.10) - \underset{\text{Treasury shares}}{8\left(^{3}\!/_{12}\right)}} = \frac{150}{78} = \$2.00$$

(1.10) = Stock dividend adjustment

Diluted EPS

$$\frac{\underset{\text{Net income}}{\$154} \quad \underset{\text{Preferred dividends}}{-\$4}}{\underset{\text{Shares at Jan. 1}}{60}(1.10) + \underset{\text{New shares}}{12\left(^{10}\!/_{12}\right)}(1.10) - \underset{\text{Treasury shares}}{8\left(^{3}\!/_{12}\right)} + \underset{\text{Exercise of options}}{(15^{*} - 12^{\dagger})}} = \frac{150}{78} = \$1.92$$

(1.10) = Stock dividend adjustment

*Adjusted for the stock dividend. Prior to the stock dividend, the options were exercisable for 13⁷⁄₁₁ million of the "old" shares. Upon the stock dividend, the new equivalent of 13⁷⁄₁₁ became 15 million (13⁷⁄₁₁ × 1.10) of the "new" shares.

†Shares Assumed Reacquired for Diluted EPS

15	million shares
× $ 20	(exercise price)
$300	million
÷ $ 25	(average market price)
12	million shares reacquired

Additional Consideration

Actual Exercise of Options. What if options are actually exercised during the reporting period? In that case, we include in the denominator of both basic and diluted EPS the actual shares issued upon the exercise of the options, time-weighted for the fraction of the year the new shares actually are outstanding. This is consistent with the way we include new shares sold under any circumstances.

In addition, we include in diluted EPS only the incremental shares that would have been issued prior to the actual exercise of the options if we pretend the options were exercised

(continued)

(concluded)

at the beginning of the period. We time-weight those shares by the fraction of the year the shares would be outstanding prior to the actual exercise of the options.

Let's say the options in our illustration were exercised on September 1 and that the average per-share price of the stock from the beginning of the year until September 1 was $24. In that case, we add 5 million shares to the denominator of both basic and diluted EPS: the 15 million shares actually issued × 4/12 of the year actually outstanding = 5 million shares. Then, for *diluted EPS only*, we add the incremental shares that would have been issued *prior to* the actual exercise of the options if we pretend the options were exercised at the beginning of the period. We assume the proceeds (15 million shares × $20 = $300 million) are used to buy shares back at $24.

15	million shares
× $ 20	(exercise price)
$300	million
÷ $ 24	(average market price prior to exercise)
12.5	million shares

The incremental number of shares to be included in the computation of diluted EPS, then, is weighted for the period the options were outstanding prior to exercise, the 8 months from January 1 to September 1, or 8/12 of a year.

$$\frac{\text{No adjustment to the numerator}}{+ (15 - 12.5)(8/12)}$$

Convertible Securities

● LO19–9

Sometimes corporations include a conversion feature as part of a bond offering, a note payable, or an issue of preferred stock. Convertible securities can be converted into (exchanged for) shares of stock at the option of the holder of the security. For that reason, convertible securities are potentially dilutive. EPS will be affected if and when such securities are converted and new shares of common stock are issued. In the previous section you learned that the potentially dilutive effect of stock options is reflected in diluted EPS calculations by assuming the options were exercised. Similarly, the potentially dilutive effect of convertible securities is reflected in diluted EPS calculations by assuming they were converted.

When we assume conversion, the denominator of the EPS fraction is increased by the additional common shares that would have been issued upon conversion.

By the *if converted method,* as it's called, we assume the conversion into common stock occurred at the beginning of the period (or at the time the convertible security is issued, if that's later). We increase the denominator of the EPS fraction by the additional common shares that would have been issued upon conversion. We increase the numerator by the interest (after-tax) on bonds or other debt or the preferred dividends that would have been avoided if the convertible securities had not been outstanding due to having been converted.

The numerator is increased by the after-tax interest that would have been avoided.

CONVERTIBLE BONDS. Now, let's return to our continuing illustration and modify it to include the existence of convertible bonds (Illustration 19–11).

Illustration 19–11
Convertible Bonds

Sovran Financial Corporation reported net income of $154 million in 2018 (tax rate 40%). Its capital structure included the following:

Common Stock

Jan. 1	60 million common shares were outstanding
Mar. 1	12 million new shares were sold
June 17	A 10% stock dividend was distributed
Oct. 1	8 million shares were reacquired as treasury stock

(The average market price of the common shares during 2018 was $25 per share.)

(continued)

Illustration 19–11
(concluded)

Preferred Stock, Nonconvertible

January 1–December 31 5 million shares 8%, $10 par

Incentive Stock Options

Executive stock options granted in 2013, exercisable after 2017 for 15 million common shares* at an exercise price of $20 per share

Convertible Bonds

10%, $300 million face amount issued in 2017, convertible into 12 million common shares

($ in millions, except per share amounts)

Basic EPS (unchanged)

The convertible bonds do not affect the calculation of *basic EPS.*

Net income: $154; Preferred dividends: −$4

$$\frac{\$154 - \$4}{60\,(1.10) + 12\,(^{10}/_{12})\,(1.10) - 8\,(^{3}/_{12})} = \frac{\$150}{75} = \$2.00$$

Shares at Jan. 1; New shares; Treasury shares; Stock dividend adjustment (1.10)

Diluted EPS

If the bonds had been converted, 12 million more common shares would have been issued, and net income would have been higher by the interest saved (after tax) from not having the bonds outstanding.

Net income: $154; Preferred dividends: −$4; After-tax interest savings: + 30 − 40% (30)

$$\frac{\$154 - \$4 + 30 - 40\%\,(30)}{60\,(1.10) + 12\,(^{10}/_{12})\,(1.10) - 8\,(^{3}/_{12}) + (15^{*} - 12) + 12^{*}} = \frac{\$168}{90} = \$1.87$$

Shares at Jan. 1; New shares; Treasury shares; Exercise of options; Conversion of bonds; Stock dividend adjustment (1.10)

*Adjusted for the stock dividend. For example, prior to the stock dividend, the bonds were exercisable for $10^{10}/_{11}$ million of the "old" shares, which became 12 million ($10^{10}/_{11}$ × 1.10) of the "new" shares after the stock dividend.

We increase the denominator by the 12 million shares that would have been issued if the bonds had been converted. However, if that hypothetical conversion had occurred, the bonds would not have been outstanding during the year. What effect would the absence of the bonds have had on income? Obviously, the bond interest expense (10% × $300 million = $30 million) would have been saved, causing income to be higher. But saving the interest paid would also have meant losing a $30 million tax deduction on the income tax return. With a 40% tax rate that would mean paying $12 million more income taxes. So, to reflect in earnings the $18 million after-tax interest that would have been avoided in the event of conversion, we add back the $30 million of interest expense, but deduct 40% × $30 million for the higher tax expense.

Additional Consideration

The $300 million of convertible bonds in our illustration were issued at face value. Suppose the bonds had been issued for $282 million. In that case, the adjustment to earnings would be modified to include the amortization of the $18 million bond discount. Assuming straight-line amortization and a 10-year maturity, the adjustment to the diluted EPS calculation would have been

$$\frac{+[\$30 + (\$18 \div 10 \text{ years})] \times (1 - 40\%)^{*}}{+12}$$

(continued)

(concluded)

to reflect the fact that the interest expense would include the $30 million stated interest plus one-tenth of the bond discount.[19]

*This is an alternative way to represent the after-tax adjustment to interest since subtracting 40% of the interest expense is the same as multiplying interest expense by 60%.

Our illustration describes the treatment of convertible bonds. The same treatment pertains to other debt that is convertible into common shares such as convertible notes payable. Remember from our discussion of debt in earlier chapters that all debt is similar, whether in the form of bonds, notes, or other configurations.

Additional Consideration

Notice that we assumed the bonds were converted at the beginning of the reporting period since they were outstanding all year. However, if the convertible bonds had been issued during the reporting period, we would assume their conversion occurred on the date of issue. It would be illogical to assume they were converted before they were issued. If the convertible bonds in our illustration had been sold on **September 1**, for instance, the adjustment to the EPS calculation would have been

$$\frac{+\ [\$30 - 40\%(\$30)]\ (4/12)}{+12\ (4/12)}$$

to reflect the fact that the net increase in shares would have been effective for only four months of the year.

We assume convertible securities were converted (or options exercised) at the beginning of the reporting period or at the time the securities are issued, if later.

CONVERTIBLE PREFERRED STOCK. The potentially dilutive effect of convertible preferred stock is reflected in EPS calculations in much the same way as convertible debt. That is, we calculate EPS as if conversion already had occurred. Specifically, we add shares to the denominator of the EPS fraction. We do not subtract the preferred dividends in the numerator because those dividends would have been avoided if the preferred stock had been converted. In Illustration 19–12, we assume our preferred stock is convertible into 3 million shares of common stock.

Illustration 19–12
Convertible Preferred Stock

Sovran Financial Corporation reported net income of $154 million in 2018 (tax rate 40%). Its capital structure included the following:

Common Stock

Jan. 1	60 million common shares were outstanding
Mar. 1	12 million new shares were sold
June 17	A 10% stock dividend was distributed
Oct. 1	8 million shares were reacquired as treasury stock

(The average market price of the common shares during 2018 was $25 per share.)

Preferred Stock, Convertible into 3 million common shares*

January 1–December 31 **5 million shares 8%, $10 par**

Incentive Stock Options

Executive stock options granted in 2013, exercisable after 2017 for 15 million common shares* at an exercise price of $20 per share

(continued)

[19]See Chapter 14 if you need to refresh your memory about bond discount amortization.

Illustration 19–12
(concluded)

Convertible Bonds

10%, $300 million face amount issued in 2017, convertible into 12 million common shares

($ in millions, except per share amounts)

Basic EPS

$$\frac{\underset{\text{Net income}}{\$154} \quad \underset{\text{Preferred dividends}}{-\$4}}{\underset{\text{Shares at Jan. 1}}{60}\ (1.10) + \underset{\text{New shares}}{12\ (^{10}/_{12})}\ (1.10) - \underset{\text{Treasury shares}}{8\ (^{3}/_{12})}} = \frac{\$150}{75} = \$2.00$$

(1.10): Stock dividend adjustment

Diluted EPS

$$\frac{\underset{\text{Net income}}{\$154} \quad \cancel{\underset{\text{Preferred dividends}}{-\$4}} \quad \underset{\text{After-tax interest savings}}{+ \$30 - 40\%\ (30)}}{\underset{\text{Shares at Jan. 1}}{60}\ (1.10) + \underset{\text{New shares}}{12\ (^{10}/_{12})}\ (1.10) - \underset{\text{Treasury shares}}{8\ (^{3}/_{12})} + \underset{\text{Exercise of options}}{(15 - 12)} \underset{\text{Conversion of bonds}}{+12} \underset{\text{Conversion of preferred shares}}{+3^{*}}} = \frac{\$172}{93} = \$1.85$$

(1.10): Stock dividend adjustment

*Adjusted for the stock dividend. For example, prior to the stock dividend, the preferred shares were convertible into 2$^{8}/_{11}$ million of the "old" shares, which became 3 million (2$^{8}/_{11}$ × 1.10) of the "new" shares after the stock dividend.

Since diluted EPS is calculated as if the preferred shares had been converted, there are no dividends.

The adjustment for the conversion of the preferred stock is applied only to diluted EPS computations. Basic EPS is unaffected.

However, when diluted EPS is calculated, we hypothetically assume the convertible preferred stock was *not* outstanding. Accordingly, no preferred dividends on these shares would have been paid.

Antidilutive Securities

At times, the effect of the conversion or exercise of potential common shares would be to increase, rather than decrease, EPS. These we refer to as **antidilutive securities**. Such securities are ignored when calculating both basic and diluted EPS.

● LO19–10

Options, Warrants, Rights

For illustration, recall the way we treated the stock options in our continuing illustration. In applying the treasury stock method, the number of shares assumed repurchased is fewer than the number of shares assumed sold. This is the case any time the buyback (average market) price is higher than the exercise price. Consequently, there will be a net increase in the number of shares, so earnings per share will decline.

Antidilutive securities are ignored when calculating both basic and diluted EPS.

On the other hand, when the exercise price is *higher* than the market price, to assume shares are sold at the exercise price and repurchased at the market price would mean buying back *more* shares than were sold. This would produce a net decrease in the number of shares. So EPS would increase, not decrease. These would have an antidilutive effect and would not be considered exercised. In fact, a rational investor would not exercise options at an exercise price higher than the current market price anyway. Let's look at the example provided by Illustration 19–13.

To assume 4 million shares were sold at the $32.50 exercise price and repurchased at the lower market price ($25) would mean reacquiring 5.2 million shares. That's *more* shares than were assumed sold. Because the effect would be antidilutive, we would simply ignore the warrants in the calculations.

Illustration 19–13
Antidilutive Warrants

Sovran Financial Corporation reported net income of $154 million in 2018 (tax rate 40%). Its capital structure included the following:

Common Stock

Jan. 1	60 million common shares were outstanding
Mar. 1	12 million new shares were sold
June 17	A 10% stock dividend was distributed
Oct. 1	8 million shares were reacquired as treasury stock

(The average market price of the common shares during 2018 was $25 per share.)

Preferred Stock, Convertible into 3 million common shares

January 1–December 31 5 million shares 8%, $10 par

Incentive Stock Options

Executive stock options granted in 2013, exercisable after 2017 for 15 million common shares at an exercise price of $20 per share

Convertible Bonds

10%, $300 million face amount issued in 2017, convertible into 12 million common shares

Stock Warrants

Warrants granted in 2017, exercisable for 4 million common shares* at an exercise price of $32.50 per share

Calculations

The calculations of both basic and diluted EPS are unaffected by the warrants because the effect of exercising the warrants would be antidilutive

*Adjusted for the stock dividend. For example, prior to the stock dividend, the warrants were exercisable for $3\frac{7}{11}$ million of the "old" shares, which became 4 million ($3\frac{7}{11}$ × 1.10) of the "new" shares after the stock dividend.

The $32.50 exercise price is higher than the market price, $25, so to assume shares are sold at the exercise price and repurchased at the market price would mean reacquiring more shares than were sold.

In our continuing illustration, only the stock warrants were antidilutive. The other potential common shares caused EPS to decline when we considered them exercised or converted. In the case of the executive stock options, it was readily apparent that their effect would be dilutive because the exercise price was less than the market price, indicating that fewer shares could be repurchased (at the average market price) than were assumed issued (at the exercise price). As a result, the denominator increased. When only the denominator of a fraction increases, the fraction itself decreases. On the other hand, in the case of the warrants, it was apparent that their effect would be antidilutive because the exercise price was higher than the market price, which would have decreased the denominator and therefore increased the fraction.

When a company has a *net loss,* rather than net income, it reports a loss per share. In that situation, stock options that otherwise are dilutive will be antidilutive. Here's why. Suppose we have a loss per share of $2.00 calculated as ($150 million) ÷ 75 million shares = ($2.00). Now suppose stock options are outstanding that, if exercised, will increase the number of shares by 5 million. If that increase is included in the calculation, the loss per share will be $1.88 calculated as ($150 million) ÷ 80 million shares = ($1.88). The *loss* per share *declines.* This represents an *increase* in performance—not a dilution of performance. The options would be considered antidilutive, then, and not included in the calculation of the net loss per share. Any potential common shares not included in dilutive EPS because they are antidilutive should be revealed in the disclosure notes.

Convertible Securities

For convertible securities, though, it's not immediately obvious whether the effect of their conversion would be dilutive or antidilutive because the assumed conversion would affect both the numerator and the denominator of the EPS fraction. We discovered each was dilutive only after including the effect in the calculation and observing the result—a decline in EPS. But there's an easier way.

To determine whether convertible securities are dilutive and should be included in a diluted EPS calculation, we can compare the "incremental effect" of the conversion (expressed as a fraction) with the EPS fraction before the effect of any convertible security is considered. This, of course is our basic EPS. Recall from Illustration 19–12 that basic EPS is $2.00.

For comparison, we determine the "earnings per incremental share" of the two convertible securities.

The incremental effect (of conversion) of the bonds is the after-tax interest saved divided by the additional common shares from conversion.

Conversion of bonds

After-tax interest savings

$$\frac{+\$30 - 40\%\ (\$30)}{+12} = \frac{\$18}{12} = \$1.50$$

Conversion of bonds

The incremental effect (of conversion) of the preferred stock is the dividends that wouldn't be paid divided by the additional common shares from conversion.

Conversion of preferred stock

Preferred dividends

$$\frac{+\$4}{+3} = \$1.33$$

Conversion of preferred shares

If the incremental effect of a security is *higher* than basic EPS, it is antidilutive. That's not the case in our illustration.

Order of Entry for Multiple Convertible Securities

A convertible security might seem to be dilutive when looked at individually but, in fact, may be antidilutive when included in combination with other convertible securities. This is because the *order of entry* for including their effects in the EPS calculation determines by how much, or even whether, EPS decreases as a result of their assumed conversion. Because our goal is to reveal the maximum potential dilution that might result, theoretically we should calculate diluted EPS using every possible combination of potential common shares to find the combination that yields the lowest EPS. But that's not necessary.

We can use the earnings per incremental share we calculated to determine the sequence of including securities' effects in the calculation. We include the securities in reverse order, beginning with the lowest incremental effect (that is, most dilutive), followed by the next lowest, and so on. This is, in fact, the order in which we included the securities in our continuing illustration.

Additional Consideration

Actually, the order of inclusion made no difference in our example, but would in many instances. For example, suppose the preferred stock had been convertible into 2.1 million shares, rather than 3 million shares. The incremental effect of its conversion would have been as follows:

Conversion of Preferred Stock

Preferred dividends

$$\frac{+\$4}{+2.1} = \$1.90$$

Conversion of preferred shares

(continued)

(concluded)

On the surface, the effect would seem to be dilutive because $1.90 is less than $2.00, basic EPS. In fact, if this were the only convertible security, it would be dilutive. But, after the convertible bonds are assumed converted first, then the assumed conversion of the preferred stock would be *antidilutive*.

With Conversion of Bonds

$$\frac{\underset{\text{Net income}}{\$154} \;\; \underset{\text{Preferred dividends}}{-\$4} \;\; \underset{\text{After-tax interest savings}}{+\$30 - 40\%(\$30)}}{\underset{\text{Shares at Jan. 1}}{60}\,(1.10) + \underset{\text{New shares}}{12\left(\tfrac{10}{12}\right)}\,(1.10) - \underset{\text{Treasury shares}}{8\left(\tfrac{3}{12}\right)} + \underset{\text{Exercise of options}}{(15-12)} + \underset{\text{Conversion of bonds}}{12}} = \frac{\$168}{90} = \$1.867$$

(1.10): Stock dividend adjustment

With Conversion of Preferred Stock

$$\frac{\underset{\text{Net income}}{\$154} \;\; \cancel{\underset{\text{Preferred dividends}}{-\$4}} \;\; \underset{\text{After-tax interest savings}}{+\$30 - 40\%(\$30)}}{\underset{\text{Shares at Jan. 1}}{60}\,(1.10) + \underset{\text{New shares}}{12\left(\tfrac{10}{12}\right)}\,(1.10) - \underset{\text{Treasury shares}}{8\left(\tfrac{3}{12}\right)} + \underset{\text{Exercise of options}}{(15-12)} + \underset{\text{Conversion of bonds}}{12} \;\; \underset{\text{Conversion of preferred shares}}{+2.1}} = \frac{\$172}{92.1} = \$1.868$$

(1.10): Stock dividend adjustment

Although the incremental effect of the convertible preferred stock ($1.90) is lower than basic EPS ($2.00), when included in the calculation after the convertible bonds, the effect is antidilutive (EPS increases).

Because the incremental effect of the convertible bonds ($1.50) is lower than the incremental effect of the convertible preferred stock ($1.90), it is included first.

A convertible security might seem to be dilutive when looked at individually but may be antidilutive when included in combination with other convertible securities.

Concept Review Exercise

BASIC AND DILUTED EPS

At December 31, 2018, the financial statements of Clevenger Casting Corporation included the following:

Net income for 2018	$500 million
Common stock, $1 par:	
Shares outstanding on January 1	150 million shares
Shares retired for cash on February 1	24 million shares
Shares sold for cash on September 1	18 million shares
2-for-1 split on July 23	
Preferred stock, 10%, $70 par, cumulative, nonconvertible	$ 70 million
Preferred stock, 8%, $50 par, cumulative, convertible into 4 million shares of common stock	$100 million
Incentive stock options outstanding, fully vested, for 4 million shares of common stock; the exercise price is $15	
Bonds payable, 12.5%, convertible into 20 million shares of common stock	$200 million

Additional data:

The market price of the common stock averaged $20 during 2018.

The convertible preferred stock and the bonds payable had been issued at par in 2016. The tax rate for the year was 40%.

Required:

Compute basic and diluted earnings per share for the year ended December 31, 2018.

($ in millions, except per share amounts)

Solution:

Basic EPS

$$\frac{\underset{\text{Net income}}{\$500} \quad \underset{\text{Preferred dividends}}{-\$7^{a}} \quad \underset{\text{Preferred dividends}}{-\$8^{b}}}{\underset{\text{Shares at Jan. 1}}{150}\ (2.00) - \underset{\text{Retired shares}}{24\ (11/12)}\ (2.00) + \underset{\text{New shares}}{18\ (4/12)}} = \frac{\$485}{262} = \$1.85$$

(2.00) = Stock split adjustment

Diluted EPS

$$\frac{\underset{\text{Net income}}{\$500} \quad \underset{\text{Preferred dividends}}{-\$7^{a}} \quad \underset{\text{Preferred dividends}}{-\$8^{b}} \quad \underset{\text{After-tax interest savings}}{+\ 25^{d} - 40\%\ (\$25^{d})}}{\underset{\text{Shares at Jan. 1}}{150}\ (2.00) - \underset{\text{Retired shares}}{24\ (11/12)}\ (2.00) + \underset{\text{New shares}}{18\ (4/12)} + \underset{\text{Exercise of warrants}}{(4-3)^{c}} \quad \underset{\text{Conversion of bonds}}{+\ 20}} = \frac{\$500}{283} = \$1.77$$

(2.00) = Stock split adjustment

[a] 10% × $70 million = $7 million
[b] 8% × $100 million = $8 million

[c] Exercise of warrants:

	4 million shares
×	$15 (exercise price)
	$60 million
÷	$20 (average market price)
	3 million shares

[d] 12.5% × $200 million = $25 million

Dilution:

Conversion of Bonds

$$\frac{\underset{\text{After-tax interest savings}}{+\ \$25 - 40\%\ (\$25)}}{\underset{\text{Conversion of bonds}}{+\ 20}} = \$0.75$$

Conversion of 8% Preferred Stock

$$\frac{\underset{\text{Preferred dividends}}{+\ \$8}}{\underset{\text{Conversion of preferred shares}}{+\ 4}} = \$2.00^{*}$$

*Because the incremental effect of conversion of the preferred stock ($2) is higher than EPS without the conversion of the preferred stock, the conversion would be *antidilutive* and is *not* considered in the calculation of diluted EPS.

Additional EPS Issues

Components of the "Proceeds" in the Treasury Stock Method

LO19–11

In calculating diluted EPS when stock options are outstanding, we assume the options have been exercised. That is, we pretend the company sold the shares specified by the options at the exercise price and that the "proceeds" were used to buy back (as treasury stock) as many shares as can be purchased at the average market price of the stock during the year. The proceeds for the calculation should include the amount received from the hypothetical exercise of the options ($300 million in Illustration 19–10). But that's only the first of two possible components.

The second component of the proceeds is the total compensation from the award that's *not yet expensed.* If the fair value of an option had been $4 at the grant date, the total compensation would have been 15 million shares times $4, or $60 million. In our illustration, though, we assumed the options were fully vested before 2018, so all $60 million already had been expensed and this second component of the proceeds was zero. If the options had been only half vested, half the compensation would have been unexpensed and $30 million would have been added to the $300 million proceeds. This would have been the case, for instance, if our calculation was made after two years of a four-year vesting period.

For the treasury stock method, "proceeds" include:

1. The amount, if any, received from the hypothetical exercise of options or vesting of restricted stock.

2. The total compensation from the award that's not yet expensed.

Why do the proceeds include these two components? We might think of it like this. The "proceeds" include everything the firm will receive from the award: (1) cash, if any, at exercise and (2) services from the recipient (value of award given as compensation). The reason we *exclude the expensed portion* is that, when it's expensed, earnings are reduced, so that portion of the dilution already is reflected in EPS. Excluding that expensed portion from the proceeds avoids the additional dilution that would occur if we included those additional proceeds in our hypothetical buyback of shares. Hence, we avoid double-counting the dilutive effect of the compensation.

Restricted Stock Awards in EPS Calculations

As we discussed earlier, restricted stock awards and their cousins, restricted stock units (RSUs), have replaced stock options as the share-based compensation plan of choice. Like stock options, they represent potential common shares and their dilutive effect is included in diluted EPS. In fact, they too are included using the treasury stock method. That is, the shares are added to the denominator and then reduced by the number of shares that can be bought back with the "proceeds" at the average market price of the company's stock during the year. Unlike stock options, though, the first component of the proceeds usually is absent; employees don't pay to acquire their shares.

Also, only *unvested* restricted stock award shares and RSU shares are included in EPS calculations; fully vested shares are actually distributed and thus outstanding. The proceeds for the EPS calculation include the total compensation from the unvested restricted stock that's not yet expensed, the second component. For an example, refer back to the restricted stock in Illustration 19–2. The total compensation for the award is $60 million ($12 market price per share × 5 million shares). Because the restricted stock vests over four years, it is expensed as $15 million each year for four years. At the end of 2018, the first year, $45 million remains unexpensed, so $45 million would be the assumed proceeds in an EPS calculation. If we assume the average market price that year was, say, $15, the $45 million will buy back 3 million shares and we would add to the denominator of diluted EPS 2 million common shares:

$$\frac{\text{No adjustment to the numerator}}{5 \text{ million} - 3^{*} \text{ million} = 2 \textit{ million}}$$

*Assumed purchase of treasury shares

$45	million
÷ $15	average market price
3	million shares

At the end of 2019, the *second* year, $30 million remains unexpensed, so assuming the average market price that year was, say, $12, we would add to the denominator of diluted EPS 2.5 million common shares:

$$\frac{\text{No adjustment to the numerator}}{5 \text{ million} - 2.5^{*} \text{ million} = 2.5 \textit{ million}}$$

*Assumed purchase of treasury shares

$30	million
÷ $12	average market price
2.5	million shares

Contingently Issuable Shares

LO19–12

Sometimes an agreement specifies that additional shares of common stock will be issued, contingent on the occurrence of some future circumstance. For instance, in the disclosure note reproduced in Illustration 19–14, **Hunt Manufacturing Co.** reported contingent shares in connection with its acquisition of **Feeny Manufacturing Company**.

Illustration 19–14
Contingently Issuable Shares—Hunt Manufacturing Company

Real World Financials

> **Note 12: Acquisitions (in part)**
> The Company acquired Feeny Manufacturing Company of Muncie, Indiana, for 135,000 shares of restricted common stock with a value of $7.71 per share. Feeny Manufacturing Company is a manufacturer of kitchen storage products. The purchase agreement calls for the issuance of up to 135,000 additional shares of common stock in the next fiscal year based on the earnings of Feeny Manufacturing Company. . . .

At times, contingent shares are issuable to shareholders of an acquired company, certain key executives, or others in the event a certain level of performance is achieved. Contingent performance may be a desired level of income, a target stock price, or some other measurable activity level.

Contingently issuable shares are considered outstanding in the computation of diluted EPS.

When calculating EPS, **contingently issuable shares** are considered to be outstanding in the computation of diluted EPS if the target performance level already is being met (assumed to remain at existing levels until the end of the contingency period). For example, if shares will be issued at a future date if a certain level of income is achieved and that level of income or more was already reported this year, those additional shares are simply added to the denominator of the diluted EPS fraction.[20]

For clarification, refer to our continuing illustration of diluted EPS and assume 3 million additional shares will become issuable to certain executives in the following year (2019) if net income that year is $150 million or more. Recall that net income for Sovran Finanical in 2018 was $154 million, so the additional shares would be considered outstanding in the computation of diluted EPS by simply adding 3 million additional shares to the denominator of the EPS fraction. Obviously, the 2019 condition ($150 million net income or more) has not been met yet since it's only 2018. But because that level of income was achieved in 2018, the presumption is that it's likely to be achieved in 2019 as well.

If a level of income must be attained before the shares will be issued, and income already is that amount or more, the additional shares are simply added to the denominator.

Assumed Issuance of Contingently Issuable Shares (diluted EPS):

$$\frac{\text{No adjustment to the numerator}}{\begin{array}{c}+3\\ \text{Additonal shares}\end{array}}$$

On the other hand, if the target income next year is $160 million, the contingent shares would simply be ignored in our calculation.

Summary of the Effect of Potential Common Shares on Earnings Per Share

You have seen that under certain circumstances, securities that have the potential of reducing earnings per share by becoming common stock are assumed already to have become common stock for the purpose of calculating EPS. The table in Illustration 19–15 summarizes the circumstances under which the dilutive effect of these securities is reflected in the calculation of basic and diluted EPS.

Illustration 19–16 summarizes the specific effects on the diluted EPS fraction when the dilutive effect of a potentially dilutive security is reflected in the calculation.

[20]The shares should be included in both basic and diluted EPS if all conditions have actually been met so that there is no *circumstance* under which those shares would not be issued. In essence, these *are no longer contingent shares.*

Potential Common Shares	Is the Dilutive Effect Reflected in the Calculation of EPS?*	
	Basic EPS	**Diluted EPS**
• Stock options (or warrants, rights)	no	yes
• Restricted stock	no	yes
• Convertible securities (bonds, notes, preferred stock)	no	yes
• Contingently issuable shares	no	yes†

*The effect is not included for any security if its effect is antidilutive.
†Unless shares are contingent upon some level of performance not yet achieved.

Illustration 19–15

When Potential Common Shares Are Reflected in EPS

Potential Common Shares	Modification to the Diluted EPS Fractions	
	Numerator	**Denominator**
• Stock options (or warrants, rights)	None	Add the shares that would be created by their exercise,* reduced by shares repurchased at the average share price.
• Restricted stock	None	Add shares that would be created by their vesting,* reduced by shares repurchased at the average share price.
• Convertible bonds (or notes)	Add the interest (after-tax) that would have been avoided if the debt had been converted.	Add shares that would be created by the conversion* of the bonds (or notes).
• Convertible preferred stock	Do not deduct the dividends that would have been avoided if the preferred stock had been converted.	Add shares that would have been created by the conversion* of the preferred stock.
• Contingently issuable shares: Issuable when specified conditions are met, and those conditions currently are being met	None	Add shares that are issuable.
• Contingently issuable shares: Issuable when specified conditions are met, and those conditions are not currently being met	None	None

*At the beginning of the year or when potential common shares were issued, whichever is later (time-weight the increase in shares if assumed exercised or converted in midyear).

Illustration 19–16

How Potential Common Shares Are Reflected in a Diluted EPS Calculation

Actual Conversions

When calculating EPS in our example, we "pretended" the convertible bonds had been converted at the beginning of the year. What if they actually had been converted, let's say on November 1? Interestingly, diluted EPS would be precisely the same. Here's why:

1. The actual conversion would cause an actual increase in shares of 12 million on November 1. These would be time-weighted so the denominator would increase by 12 ($^2/_{12}$). Also, the numerator would be higher because net income actually would be

increased by the after-tax interest saved on the bonds for the last two months, [\$30 − 40% (\$30)] × (2/12). Be sure to note that this would not be an adjustment in the EPS calculation. Instead, net income would actually have been higher by [\$30 − 40% (\$30)] × (2/12) = \$3. That is, reported net income would have been \$157 rather than \$154.

2. We would assume conversion for the period before November 1 because they were potentially dilutive during that period. The 12 million shares assumed outstanding from January 1 to November 1 would be time-weighted for that 10-month period: 12 (10/12). Also, the numerator would be increased by the after-tax interest assumed saved on the bonds for the first 10 months, [\$30 − 40% (\$30)] × (10/12).

Notice that the incremental effect on diluted EPS is the same either way.

EPS would be precisely the same whether convertible securities were actually converted or not.

Not Actually Converted:		Converted on November 1:		
Assumed after-tax interest savings		Actual after-tax interest savings		Assumed after-tax interest savings
+ \$30 − 40% (\$30)	=	+[\$30 − 40% (\$30)] × (2/12)	+	[\$30 − 40% (\$30)] × (10/12)
+ 12		+ 12 (2/12)		+ 12 (10/12)
Assumed conversion of bonds		Actual conversion of bonds		Assumed conversion of bonds
\$18	=	\$3	+	\$15
12		2	+	10

Illustration 19–17 shows the disclosure note Clorox Company reported after the conversion of convertible notes during the year.

Illustration 19–17
Conversion of Notes—The Clorox Company

Real World Financials

Note 1: Significant Accounting Policies—Earnings Per Common Share (in part)
A \$9,000,000 note payable to Henkel Corporation was converted into 1,200,000 shares of common stock on August 1. . . . Earnings per common share and weighted-average shares outstanding reflect this conversion as if it were effective during all periods presented.

LO19–13

Financial Statement Presentation of Earnings Per Share Data

Recall from Chapter 4 that if a company disposes of a component of its operations, the company will report "discontinued operations" as a separate item within the income statement as follows:

Income from Continuing Operations
Discontinued operations
Net income

When the income statement includes discontinued operations, EPS data (both basic and diluted) must also be reported separately for income from continuing operations and net income. Per share amounts for discontinued operations would be disclosed either on the face of the income statement or in the notes to financial statements. Presentation on the face of the income statement is illustrated by the partial income statements of H&R Block, Inc., from its annual report for the year ended April 30, 2016, and exhibited in Illustration 19–18.

Basic and diluted EPS data should be reported on the face of the income statement for all reporting periods presented in the comparative statements. Businesses without potential common shares present basic EPS only. Disclosure notes should provide additional disclosures including:

1. A reconciliation of the numerator and denominator used in the basic EPS computations to the numerator and the denominator used in the diluted EPS computations.
   An example of this is presented in Illustration 19–19 using the situation described previously in Illustration 19–12.

Illustration 19–18

EPS Disclosure—H&R Block

Real World Financials

Consolidated Income Statements (partial)
For the Years Ended April 30, 2016 and 2015

	2016	2015
Net income from continuing operations	$383,553	$486,744
Net loss from discontinued operations	(9,286)	(13,081)
Net income	$374,267	$473,663
Basic Earnings (Loss) Per Share:		
Continuing operations	$ 1.54	$ 1.77
Discontinued operations	(0.04)	(0.05)
Consolidated	$ 1.50	$ 1.72
Diluted Earnings (Loss) Per Share:		
Continuing operations	$ 1.53	$ 1.75
Discontinued operations	(0.04)	(0.04)
Consolidated	$ 1.49	$ 1.71

2. Any adjustments to the numerator for preferred dividends.
3. Any potential common shares that weren't included because they were antidilutive.
4. Any transactions that occurred after the end of the most recent period that would materially affect earnings per share.

Illustration 19–19

Reconciliation of Basic EPS Computations to Diluted EPS Computations

Earnings per Share Reconciliation

($ in millions)	Income (Numerator)	Share (Denominator)	Per Share Amount
Net income	$ 154		
Preferred dividends	(4)		
Basic earnings per share	150	75	$2.00
Stock options	None	3*	
Convertible debt	18	12	
Convertible preferred stock	4	3	
Diluted earnings per share	$ 172	93	$1.85

Note: Stock warrants to purchase an additional 4 million shares at $32.50 per share were outstanding throughout the year but were not included in diluted EPS because the warrants' exercise price is greater than the average market price of the common shares.

*15 million − [(15 million × $20) ÷ $25] = 3 million net additional shares.

Additional Consideration

It's possible that potential common shares would have a dilutive effect on one component of net income but an antidilutive effect on another. When the inclusion of the potential common shares has a dilutive effect on "income from continuing operations," the effect should be included in all calculations of diluted EPS. In other words, the same number of potential common shares used in computing the diluted per-share amount for income from continuing operations is used in computing all other diluted per-share amounts, even when amounts are antidilutive to the individual per-share amounts.

Decision Makers' Perspective

We noted earlier in the chapter that investors and creditors pay a great deal of attention to earnings per share information. Because of the importance analysts attach to earnings announcements, companies are particularly eager to meet earnings expectations. As we first noted in Chapter 4, this desire has contributed to a relatively recent trend, especially among technology firms, to report pro forma earnings per share. What exactly are pro forma earnings? Unfortunately there is no answer to that question. Essentially, pro forma earnings are actual (GAAP) earnings reduced by any expenses the reporting company feels are unusual and should be excluded. Always, though, the pro forma results of a company look better than the real results. **Broadcom Corporation**, a provider of broadband and network products, reported pro forma *earnings* of $0.49 per share. However on a GAAP basis, it actually had a *loss* of $3.29 per share. This is not an isolated example.

Make sure you pay lots of attention to the man behind the curtain. If any earnings figure says pro forma, you should immediately look for a footnote or explanation telling you just what is and is not included in the calculation.

When companies report pro forma results, they argue they are trying to help investors by giving them numbers that more accurately reflect their normal business activities, because they exclude unusual expenses. Analysts should be skeptical, though. Because of the purely discretionary nature of pro forma reporting and several noted instances of abuse, analysts should, at a minimum, find out precisely what expenses are excluded and what the actual GAAP numbers are.

Another way management might enhance the appearance of EPS numbers is by massaging the denominator of the calculation. Reducing the number of shares increases earnings *per share.* Some companies judiciously use share buyback programs to manipulate the number of shares and therefore EPS. There is nothing inherently wrong with share buybacks and, as we noted in Chapter 18, they can benefit shareholders. The motivation for buybacks, though, can sometimes be detected in the year-to-year pattern of net income and EPS. Companies whose growth rates in earnings per share routinely exceed their growth in net income may be using buybacks to artificially increase EPS.

One way analysts use EPS data is in connection with the price-earnings ratio. This ratio is simply the market price per share divided by the earnings per share. It measures the market's perception of the quality of a company's earnings by indicating the price multiple the capital market is willing to pay for the company's earnings. Presumably, this ratio reflects the information provided by all financial information in that the market price reflects analysts' perceptions of the company's growth potential, stability, and relative risk. The price-earnings ratio relates these performance measures with the external judgment of the marketplace concerning the value of the firm.

The price-earnings ratio measures the quality of a company's earnings.

The ratio measures the quality of earnings in the sense that it represents the market's expectation of future earnings as indicated by current earnings. Caution is called for in comparing price-earnings ratios. For instance, a ratio might be low, not because earnings expectations are low, but because of abnormally elevated current earnings. On the contrary, the ratio might be high, not because earnings expectations are high, but because the company's current earnings are temporarily depressed. Similarly, an analyst should be alert to differences among accounting methods used to measure earnings from company to company when making comparisons.

The dividend payout ratio indicates the percentage of earnings that is distributed to shareholders as dividends.

Another ratio frequently calculated by shareholders and potential shareholders is the dividend payout ratio. This ratio expresses the percentage of earnings that is distributed to shareholders as dividends. The ratio is calculated by dividing dividends per common share by the earnings per share.

This ratio provides an indication of a firm's reinvestment strategy. A low payout ratio suggests that a company is retaining a large portion of earnings for reinvestment for new facilities and other operating needs. Low payouts often are found in growth industries and high payouts in mature industries. Often, though, the ratio is merely a reflection of managerial strategy concerning the mix of internal versus external financing. The ratio also is considered by investors who, for tax or other reasons, prefer current income over market price appreciation, or vice versa. ●

Concept Review Exercise

ADDITIONAL EPS ISSUES

At December 31, 2018, the financial statements of Bahnson General, Inc., included the following:

Net income for 2018 (including a net-of-tax loss from discontinued operations of \$10 million)	\$180 million
Common stock, \$1 par:	
Shares outstanding on January 1	44 million
The share price was \$25 and \$28 at the beginning and end of the year, respectively.	

Additional data:

- At January 1, 2018, \$200 million of 10% convertible notes were outstanding. The notes were converted on April 1 into 16 million shares of common stock.
- An agreement with company executives calls for the issuance of up to 12 million additional shares of common stock in 2019 and 2020 based on Bahnson's net income in those years. Executives will receive 2 million shares at the end of each of those two years if the company's stock price is at least \$26 and another 4 million shares each year if the stock price is at least \$29.50.

  The tax rate is 40%.

Required:

Compute basic and diluted earnings per share for the year ended December 31, 2018.

Solution:

(\$ in millions, except per share amounts)

Basic EPS

$$\frac{\overset{\text{Net income}}{\$180}}{\underset{\text{Shares at Jan. 1}}{44} + \underset{\text{Actual conversion of notes}}{16\left(\tfrac{9}{12}\right)}} = \frac{\$180}{56} = \$3.21$$

Diluted EPS

$$\frac{\overset{\text{Net income}}{\$180} + [\$20 - 40\%(\$20)] \times \left(\tfrac{3}{12}\right)}{\underset{\text{Shares at Jan. 1}}{44} + \underset{\text{Actual conversion of notes}}{16\left(\tfrac{9}{12}\right)} + \underset{\text{Assumed conversion of notes}}{16\left(\tfrac{3}{12}\right)} + \underset{\text{Contingent shares}}{(2+2)}} = \frac{\$183}{64} = \$2.86$$

Convertible Notes: Notice that the effect on diluted EPS would be precisely the same whether the convertible notes were actually converted or not.

Converted on April 1:

$$\frac{\overset{\text{Net income including actual after-tax interest savings}}{\$180} + \overset{\text{Assumed after-tax interest savings}}{[\$20 - 40\%(\$20)] \times \left(\tfrac{3}{12}\right)}}{\underset{\text{Shares at Jan. 1}}{44} + \underset{\text{Actual conversion of notes}}{16\left(\tfrac{9}{12}\right)} + \underset{\text{Assumed conversion of notes}}{16\left(\tfrac{3}{12}\right)}} = \frac{\$183}{60}$$

Not Actually Converted:

Net income without actual after-tax interest savings — Assumed after-tax interest savings

$$\frac{\$171^* + [\$20 - 40\%\,(\$20)]}{44 + 16} = \frac{\$183}{60}$$

Shares at Jan. 1 — Assumed conversion of notes

*$180 – {[$20 – 40% ($20)] × (9/12)} = $171; after-tax interest from Apr. 1 to Dec. 31.

Contingently Issuable Shares:
Because the conditions are met for issuing 4 million shares (2 million for each of two years), those shares are simply added to the denominator of diluted EPS. The current share price ($28) is projected to remain the same throughout the contingency period, so the other 8 million shares (4 million for each of two years) are excluded.

Income Statement Presentation:
To determine the per share amounts for income before discontinued operations, we substitute that amount for net income in the numerator (in this case, that means adding back the $10 million loss from discontinued operations):

$$\textbf{Basic: } \frac{\$180 + 10}{56} = \$3.39 \qquad \textbf{Diluted: } \frac{\$183 + 10}{56} = \$3.02$$

Earnings per Share:	**Basic***	**Diluted**
Income before discontinued operations	$3.39	$3.02
Loss from discontinued operations	(0.18)	(0.16)
Net income	$3.21	$2.86

*Only diluted EPS is required on the face of the income statement. Basic EPS is reported in the EPS reconciliation shown in the disclosure note (below).

Disclosure Note:
Earnings per Share Reconciliation:

	Income (Numerator)	**Shares (Denominator)**	**Per Share Amount**
Basic Earnings per Share			
Income before discontinued operations	$190	56	$3.39
Loss from discontinued operations	(10)	56	(0.18)
Net income	$180	56	$3.21
Convertible debt	3	4	
Contingently issuable shares	—	4	
Diluted Earnings per Share			
Income before discontinued operations	$193	64	$3.02
Loss from discontinued operations	(10)	64	(0.16)
Net income	$183	64	$2.86

Financial Reporting Case Solution

© Cultura RM/Alamy Stock Photo

1. **How can a compensation package such as this serve as an incentive to Ms. Veres?** *(p. 1091)* Stock-based plans like the restricted stock and stock options that Ms. Veres is receiving are designed to motivate recipients. If the shares awarded are restricted so that Ms. Veres is not free to sell the shares during the restriction period, she has an incentive to remain with the company until rights to the shares vest. Likewise, stock options can be made exercisable only after a specified period of employment. An additional incentive

of stock-based plans is that the recipient will be motivated to take actions that will maximize the value of the shares.

2. **Ms. Veres received a "grant of restricted stock." How should NEV account for the grant?** *(p. 1092)* The compensation associated with restricted stock is the market price of unrestricted shares of the same stock. NEV will accrue this amount as compensation expense over the service period from the date of grant to when restrictions are lifted.
3. **Included were stock options to buy more than 800,000 shares of NEV stock. How will the options affect NEV's compensation expense?** *(p. 1094)* Similar to the method used for restricted stock, the value of the options is recorded as compensation over the service period, usually the vesting period.
4. **How will the presence of these and other similar stock options affect NEV's earnings per share?** *(p. 1111)* If outstanding stock options were exercised, the resulting increase in shares would reduce or dilute EPS. If we don't take into account the dilutive effect of the share increase, we might mislead investors and creditors. So, in addition to basic EPS, we also calculate diluted EPS to include the dilutive effect of options and other potential common shares. This means calculating EPS as if the potential increase in shares already has occurred (even though it hasn't yet). ●

The Bottom Line

- **LO19–1** We measure the fair value of stock issued in a restricted stock plan and expense it over the service period, usually from the date of grant to the vesting date. (*p. 1092*)
- **LO19–2** Similarly, we estimate the fair value of stock options at the grant date and expense it over the service period, usually from the date of grant to the vesting date. Fair value is estimated at the grant date using an option-pricing model that considers the exercise price and expected term of the option, the current market price of the underlying stock and its expected volatility, expected dividends, and the expected risk-free rate of return. (*p. 1094*)
- **LO19–3** Employee share purchase plans allow employees to buy company stock under convenient or favorable terms. Most such plans are considered compensatory and require any discount to be recorded as compensation expense. (*p. 1104*)
- **LO19–4** A company has a simple capital structure if it has no outstanding securities that could potentially dilute earnings per share. For such a firm, EPS is simply earnings available to common shareholders divided by the weighted-average number of common shares outstanding. When potential common shares are outstanding, the company is said to have a complex capital structure. In that case, two EPS calculations are reported. Basic EPS assumes no dilution. Diluted EPS assumes maximum potential dilution. (*p. 1106*)
- **LO19–5** EPS calculations are based on the weighted-average number of shares outstanding during the period. Any new shares issued during the period are time-weighted by the fraction of the period they were outstanding and then added to the number of shares outstanding for the period. (*p. 1107*)
- **LO19–6** For a stock dividend or stock split, shares outstanding prior to the stock distribution are retroactively restated to reflect the increase in shares. When shares are reacquired, as treasury stock or to be retired, they are time-weighted for the fraction of the period they were not outstanding, prior to being subtracted from the number of shares outstanding during the reporting period. (*p. 1108*)
- **LO19–7** The numerator in the EPS calculation should reflect earnings available to common shareholders. So, any dividends on preferred stock outstanding should be subtracted from reported net income. This adjustment is made for cumulative preferred stock whether or not dividends are declared that period. (*p. 1110*)
- **LO19–8** For diluted EPS, it is assumed that stock options, rights, and warrants are exercised at the beginning of the period (or at the time the options are issued, if later) and the cash proceeds received are used to buy back (as treasury stock) as many of those shares as can be acquired at the average market price during the period. (*p. 1111*)
- **LO19–9** To incorporate convertible securities into the calculation of diluted EPS, the conversion is assumed to have occurred at the beginning of the period (or at the time the convertible security is issued, if later). The denominator of the EPS fraction is adjusted for the additional common shares assumed, and the numerator

is increased by the interest (after-tax) on bonds and not reduced by the preferred dividends that would have been avoided in the event of conversion. (*p. 1113*)

- **LO19–10** If including potential common shares in the EPS calculation causes EPS to *increase* rather than decrease, then those potential common shares are considered *antidilutive* and are omitted from the calculation. (*p. 1116*)
- **LO19–11** For the treasury stock method, "proceeds" include (1) the amount, if any, received from the hypothetical exercise of options or vesting of restricted stock and (2) the total compensation from the award that's not yet expensed. (*p. 1120*)
- **LO19–12** Contingently issuable shares are considered outstanding in the computation of diluted EPS when they will later be issued upon the mere passage of time or because of conditions that currently are met. (*p. 1122*)
- **LO19–13** EPS data (both basic and diluted) must be reported for (a) income before any discontinued operations, (b) the discontinued operations, and (c) net income. Disclosures also should include a reconciliation of the numerator and denominator used in the computations. (*p. 1124*)
- **LO19–14** When options have graded vesting, unlike under U.S. GAAP, IFRS does not permit the straight-line method for allocating compensation or require that the company recognize at least the amount of the award that has vested by each reporting date. The earnings per share requirements of IFRS and U.S. GAAP are similar. The few differences that remain are the result of differences in the application of the treasury stock method, the treatment of contracts that may be settled in shares or cash, and contingently issuable shares. (*pp. 1099, 1101,* and *1106*)

APPENDIX 19A Option-Pricing Theory

Option values have two essential components: (1) intrinsic value and (2) time value.

Intrinsic Value

Intrinsic value is the benefit the holder of an option would realize by exercising the option rather than buying the underlying stock directly. An option that permits an employee to buy $25 stock for $10 has an intrinsic value of $15. An option that has an exercise price equal to or exceeding the market price of the underlying stock has zero intrinsic value.

Time Value

In addition to their intrinsic value, options also have a time value due to the fact that (a) the holder of an option does not have to pay the exercise price until the option is exercised and (b) the market price of the underlying stock may yet rise and create additional intrinsic value. All options have time value so long as time remains before expiration. The longer the time until expiration, other things being equal, the greater the time value. For instance, the option described above with an intrinsic value of $15, might have a fair value of, say, $22 if time still remains until the option expires. The $7 difference represents the time value of the option. Time value can be subdivided into two components: (1) the effects of time value of money and (2) volatility value.

TIME VALUE OF MONEY

An option's value is enhanced by the delay in paying cash for the shares.

The time value of money component arises because the holder of an option does not have to pay the exercise price until the option is exercised. Instead, the holder can invest funds elsewhere while waiting to exercise the option. For measurement purposes, the time value of money component is assumed to be the rate of return available on risk-free U.S. Treasury Securities. The higher the time value of money, the higher the value of being able to delay payment of the exercise price.

When the underlying stock pays no dividends, the time value of money component is the difference between the exercise price (a future amount) and its discounted present value. Let's say the exercise price is $30. If the present value (discounted at the risk-free rate) is $24, the time value of money component is $6. On the other hand, if the stock pays a dividend (or is expected to during the life of the option), the time value of money component is lower. The value of being able to delay payment of the exercise price would be partially off-set by the cost of forgoing the dividend in the meantime. For instance, if the stock underlying the options just described were expected to pay dividends and the discounted present value of the expected dividends were $2, the time value of money component in that example would be reduced from $6 to $4.

The time value of money component is the difference between the exercise price and its discounted present value minus the present value of expected dividends.

VOLATILITY VALUE

The volatility value represents the possibility that the option holder might profit from market price appreciation of the underlying stock while being exposed to the loss of only the value of the option, rather than the full market value of the stock. For example, fair value of an option to buy a share at an exercise price of $30 might be measured as $7. The potential profit from market price appreciation is conceptually unlimited. And yet, the potential loss from the stock's value failing to appreciate is only $7.

A stock's volatility is the amount by which its price has fluctuated previously or is expected to fluctuate in the future. The greater a stock's volatility, the greater the potential profit. It usually is measured as one standard deviation of a statistical distribution. Statistically, if the expected annualized volatility is 25%, the probability is approximately 67% that the stock's year-end price will fall within roughly plus or minus 25% of its beginning-of-year price. Stated differently, the probability is approximately 33% that the year-end stock price will fall outside that range.

Volatility enhances the likelihood of stock price appreciation.

Option-pricing models make assumptions about the likelihood of various future stock prices by making assumptions about the statistical distribution of future stock prices that take into account the expected volatility of the stock price. One popular option pricing model, the Black–Scholes model, for instance, assumes a log-normal distribution. This assumption posits that the stock price is as likely to fall by half as it is to double and that large price movements are less likely than small price movements. The higher a stock's volatility, the higher the probability of large increases or decreases in market price. Because the cost of large decreases is limited to the option's current value, but the profitability from large increases is unlimited, an option on a highly volatile stock has a higher probability of a large profit than does an option on a less volatile stock.

Summary

In summary, the fair value of an option is (a) its intrinsic value plus (b) its time value of money component plus (c) its volatility component. The variables that affect an option's fair value and the effect of each are indicated in Illustration 19A–1.

All Other Factors Being Equal, If the:	The Option Value Will Be:
Exercise price is higher	Lower
Term of the option is longer	Higher
Market price of the stock is higher	Higher
Dividends are higher	Lower
Risk-free rate of return is higher	Higher
Volatility of the stock is higher	Higher

Illustration 19A–1

Effect of Variables on an Option's Fair Value

APPENDIX 19B

Stock Appreciation Rights

Stock appreciation rights (SARs) overcome a major disadvantage of stock option plans that require employees to actually buy shares when the options are exercised. Even though the options' exercise price may be significantly lower than the market value of the shares, the employee still must come up with enough cash to take advantage of the bargain. This can be quite a burden if the award is sizable. In a nonqualified stock option plan, income taxes also would have to be paid when the options are exercised.[21]

SARs offer a solution. Unlike stock options, these awards enable an employee to benefit by the amount that the market price of the company's stock rises without having to buy shares. Instead, the employee is awarded the share appreciation, which is the amount by which the market price on the exercise date exceeds a prespecified price (usually the market price at the date of grant). For instance, if the share price rises from $35 to $50, the employee receives $15 cash for each SAR held. The share appreciation usually is payable in cash or the recipient has the choice between cash and shares. A plan of this type offered by IBM is described in Illustration 19B–1.

In an SAR plan, the employer pays compensation equal to the increase in share price from a specified level.

Illustration 19B–1

Stock Appreciation Rights—IBM Corporation

Real World Financials

Long-Term Performance Plan (in part)

SARs offer eligible optionees the alternative of electing not to exercise the related stock option, but to receive payment in cash and/or stock, equivalent to the difference between the option price and the average market price of IBM stock on the date of exercising the right.

IS IT DEBT OR IS IT EQUITY?

In some plans, the employer chooses whether to issue shares or cash at exercise. In other plans, the choice belongs to the employee.[22] Who has the choice determines the way it's accounted for. More specifically, the accounting treatment depends on whether the award is considered an equity instrument or a liability. If the employer can elect to settle in shares of stock rather than cash, the award is considered to be equity. On the other hand, if the employee will receive cash or can elect to receive cash, the award is considered to be a liability.

If an employer can elect to settle in shares of stock rather than cash, the award is considered to be equity.

The distinction between share-based awards that are considered equity and those that are considered liabilities is based on whether the employer is obligated to transfer assets to the employee. A cash SAR requires the transfer of assets, and therefore is a liability. A stock option, on the other hand, is an equity instrument if it requires only the issuance of stock. This does not mean that a stock option whose issuer may later choose to settle in cash is not an equity instrument. Instead, cash settlement would be considered equivalent to repurchasing an equity instrument for cash.

If an employee can elect to receive cash, the award is considered to be a liability.

SARS PAYABLE IN SHARES (EQUITY)

The cash settlement of an equity award is considered the repurchase of an equity instrument.

When a SAR is considered to be equity (because the employer can elect to settle in shares of stock rather than cash), we estimate the fair value of the SARs at the grant date and accrue that compensation to expense over the service period. Normally, the fair value of a SAR is the same as the fair value of a stock option with the same terms. The fair value is determined at the grant date and accrued to compensation expense over the service period the same way as for other share-based compensation plans. The total compensation is not revised for subsequent changes in the price of the underlying stock. This is demonstrated in Case 1 of Illustration 19–B2.

SARS PAYABLE IN CASH (LIABILITY)

Compensation expense reported to date is the estimated total compensation multiplied by the fraction of the service period that has expired.

When a SAR is considered to be a liability (because the employee can elect to receive cash upon settlement), we estimate the fair value of the SARs and recognize that amount as compensation expense over the requisite service period consistent with the way we account for options and other share-based compensation. However, because these plans are considered to be liabilities, it's necessary to periodically re-estimate the fair value in order to continually adjust the liability (and corresponding compensation) until it is paid. Be sure to note that this is consistent with the way we account for other liabilities. Recall from our discussions in Chapter 16, for instance, that when a tax rate change causes a change in the eventual liability for deferred income taxes, we adjust that liability.

[21]The tax treatment of share-based plans is discussed an earlier Additional Consideration box.

[22]Many such plans are called tandem plans and award an employee both a cash SAR and an SAR that calls for settlement in an equivalent amount of shares. The exercise of one cancels the other.

The periodic expense (and adjustment to the liability) is the fraction of the total compensation earned to date by recipients of the SARs (based on the elapsed fraction of the service period) reduced by any amounts expensed in prior periods. For example, if the fair value of SARs at the end of a period is $8, the total compensation would be $80 million if 10 million SARs are expected to vest. Let's say two years of a four-year service period have elapsed, and $21 million was expensed the first year. Then, compensation expense the second year would be $19 million, calculated as (2/4 of $80 million) minus $21. An example spanning several years is provided in Illustration 19B–2, Case 2.

We make up for incorrect previous estimates by adjusting expense in the period the estimate is revised.

Illustration 19B–2

Stock Appreciation Rights
Case 1: Equity

At January 1, 2018, Universal Communications issued SARs that, upon exercise, entitle key executives to receive compensation equal in value to the excess of the market price at exercise over the share price at the date of grant. The SARs vest at the end of 2021 (cannot be exercised until then) and expire at the end of 2025. The fair value of the SARs, estimated by an appropriate option pricing model, is $8 per SAR at January 1, 2018. The fair value re-estimated at December 31, 2018, 2019, 2020, 2021, and 2022, is $8.40, $8, $6, $4.30, and $5, respectively.

Case 1: SARs considered to be equity because Universal can elect to settle in shares of Universal stock at exercise

January 1, 2018
No entry
Calculate total compensation expense:

$ 8	Estimated fair value per SAR
× 10 million	SARs granted
= $80 million	Total compensation

Fair value is estimated at the date of grant.

The total compensation is allocated to expense over the four-year service (vesting) period: 2018–2021

$80 million ÷ 4 years = $20 million per year

The value of the award is expensed over the service period for which the compensation is provided.

December 31, 2018, 2019, 2020, 2021	($ in millions)	
Compensation expense ($80 million ÷ 4 years)	20	
Paid-in capital—SAR plan		20

Case 2: SARs considered to be a liability because employees can elect to receive cash at exercise

The value of the compensation is estimated each year at the fair value of the SARs.

January 1, 2018
No entry

	($ in millions)	
December 31, 2018		
Compensation expense ($8.40 × 10 million × ¼)	21	
Liability—SAR plan		21
December 31, 2019		
Compensation expense [($8 × 10 million × 2/4) − 21]	19	
Liability—SAR plan		19
December 31, 2020		
Compensation expense [($6 × 10 million × ¾) − 21 − 19]	5	
Liability—SAR plan		5
December 31, 2021		
Liability—SAR plan	2	
Compensation expense [($4.30 × 10 million × 4/4) − 21 − 19 − 5]		2

The expense each year is the current estimate of total compensation that should have been recorded to date less the amount already recorded.

If the fair value falls below the amount expensed to date, both the liability and expense are reduced.

Note that the way we treat changes in compensation estimates entails a catch-up adjustment in the period of change, *inconsistent* with the usual treatment of a change in estimate.

Remember that for most changes in estimate, revisions are allocated over remaining periods, rather than all at once in the period of change. The treatment is, however, consistent with the way we treat changes in forfeiture rate estimates, as we discussed earlier in the chapter.

The liability continues to be adjusted after the service period if the rights haven't been exercised yet.

Compensation expense and the liability continue to be adjusted until the SARs expire or are exercised.

December 31, 2022	($ in millions)	
Compensation expense [($5 × 10 million × all) − 21 − 19 − 5 + 2]	7	
Liability—SAR plan		7

It's necessary to continue to adjust both compensation expense and the liability until the SARs ultimately either are exercised or lapse.[23] Assume, for example, that the SARs are exercised on October 11, 2023, when their fair value is $4.50, and executives choose to receive the market price appreciation in cash.

Adjustment continues after the service period if the SARs have not yet been exercised.

October 11, 2023	($ in millions)	
Liability—SAR plan	5	
Compensation expense [($4.50 × 10 million × all) − 50]		5
Liability—SAR plan (balance)	45	
Cash		45

Let's look at the changes in the liability—SAR plan account during the 2018–2023 period:

The liability is adjusted each period as changes in the fair value estimates cause changes in the liability.

Liability—SAR Plan

			($ in millions)
		21	2018
		19	2019
		5	2020
2021	2		
		7	2022
2023	5		
2023	45		
		0	Balance after exercise

RESTRICTED STOCK UNITS PAYABLE IN CASH (LIABILITY)

Accounting for RSUs payable in cash is essentially the same as accounting for the SARs payable in cash.

Recall from our discussion in the chapter that restricted stock units (RSUs) give the recipient the right to receive a set number of shares of company stock after the vesting requirement is satisfied. But, sometimes the recipient is given the *cash equivalent* of those shares instead. *If the employee will receive cash* or can elect to receive cash, as in the case of an SAR, we consider the award to be a *liability*. We determine its fair value at the grant date and recognize that amount as compensation expense over the requisite service period and, like SARs payable in cash, we periodically adjust the liability (and corresponding compensation) based on the change in the stock's fair value until the liability is paid. Accounting for RSUs payable in cash (sometimes called phantom shares or phantom performance shares) is quite similar to accounting for the SARs payable in cash in case 2 of Illustration 19B–2. Of course, though, we would label the liability "Liability—restricted stock." And, we would determine the periodic value of the liability (and compensation) as the actual fair value of the shares, rather than an *estimated* fair value as is necessary when valuing SARs.

[23] Except that the cumulative compensation expense cannot be negative; that is, the liability cannot be reduced below zero.

Questions For Review of Key Topics

Q 19–1 What is restricted stock? How do restricted stock awards differ from restricted stock units (RSUs)? Describe how compensation expense is determined and recorded for a restricted stock award plan.

Q 19–2 Stock option plans provide employees the option to purchase: (a) a specified number of shares of the firm's stock, (b) at a specified price, (c) during a specified period of time. One of the most controversial aspects of accounting for stock-based compensation is how the fair value of stock options should be measured. Describe the general approach to measuring fair value.

Q 19–3 The Tax Code differentiates between qualified option plans, including incentive plans, and nonqualified plans. What are the major differences in tax treatment between incentive plans and nonqualified plans?

Q 19–4 Stock option (and other share-based) plans often specify a performance condition or a market condition that must be satisfied before employees are allowed the benefits of the award. Describe the general approach we use to account for performance-based options and options with market-related conditions.

Q 19–5 What is a simple capital structure? How is EPS determined for a company with a simple capital structure?

Q 19–6 When calculating the weighted average number of common shares, how are stock dividends and stock splits treated? Compare this treatment with that of additional shares sold for cash at midyear.

Q 19–7 Blake Distributors had 100,000 common shares outstanding at the beginning of the year, January 1. On May 13, Blake distributed a 5% stock dividend. Blake retired 1,200 shares on August 1. What is the weighted average number of shares for calculating EPS?

Q 19–8 Why are preferred dividends deducted from net income when calculating EPS? Are there circumstances when this deduction is not made?

Q 19–9 Distinguish between basic and diluted EPS.

Q 19–10 The treasury stock method is used to incorporate the dilutive effect of stock options, stock warrants, and similar securities. Describe this method as it applies to diluted EPS.

Q 19–11 The potentially dilutive effect of convertible securities is reflected in EPS calculations by the if-converted method. Describe this method as it relates to convertible bonds.

Q 19–12 How is the potentially dilutive effect of convertible preferred stock reflected in EPS calculations by the if-converted method? How is this different from the way convertible bonds are considered?

Q 19–13 A convertible security may appear to be dilutive when looked at individually but might be antidilutive when included in combination with other convertible securities. How should the order be determined for inclusion of convertible securities in an EPS calculation to avoid including an antidilutive security?

Q 19–14 If stock options and restricted stock are outstanding when calculating diluted EPS, what are the components of the "proceeds" available for the repurchase of shares under the treasury stock method?

Q 19–15 Wiseman Electronics has an agreement with certain of its division managers that 50,000 contingently issuable shares will be issued next year in the event operating income exceeds $2.1 million that year. In what way, if any, is the calculation of EPS affected by these contingently issuable shares, assuming this year's operating income was $2.2 million? $2.0 million?

Q 19–16 Diluted EPS would be precisely the same whether convertible securities were actually converted or not. Why?

Q 19–17 When the income statement includes discontinued operations, which amounts require per share presentation?

Q 19–18 In addition to EPS numbers themselves, what additional disclosures should be provided concerning the EPS information?

Q 19–19 (Based on Appendix A) The fair value of stock options can be considered to comprise two main components. What are they?

Q 19–20 (Based on Appendix B) LTV Corporation grants SARs to key executives. Upon exercise, the SARs entitle executives to receive either cash or stock equal in value to the excess of the market price at exercise over the share price at the date of grant. How should LTV account for the awards?

Brief Exercises

connect

BE 19–1
Restricted stock award
● LO19–1

First Link Services granted 8 million of its $1 par common shares to executives, subject to forfeiture if employment is terminated within three years. The common shares have a market price of $6 per share on the grant date of the restricted stock award. Ignoring taxes, what is the total compensation cost pertaining to the restricted shares? What is the effect on earnings in the year after the shares are granted to executives?

BE 19–2
Restricted stock units
● LO19–1

Second Link Services granted restricted stock units (RSUs) representing 16 million of its $1 par common shares to executives, subject to forfeiture if employment is terminated within four years. After the recipients of the RSUs satisfy the vesting requirement, the company will distribute the shares. The common shares had a market price of $10 per share on the grant date. Ignoring taxes, what is the total compensation cost pertaining to the restricted stock units? What is the effect on earnings in the year after the shares are granted to executives?

BE 19–3
Stock options
● LO19–2

Under its executive stock option plan, National Corporation granted 12 million options on January 1, 2018, that permit executives to purchase 12 million of the company's $1 par common shares within the next six years, but not before December 31, 2020 (the vesting date). The exercise price is the market price of the shares on the date of grant, $17 per share. The fair value of the options, estimated by an appropriate option pricing model, is $5 per option. No forfeitures are anticipated. Ignoring taxes, what is the total compensation cost pertaining to the stock options? What is the effect on earnings in the year after the options are granted to executives?

BE 19–4
Stock options; forfeiture
● LO19–2

Refer to the situation described in BE 19–3. Suppose that unexpected turnover during 2019 caused the forfeiture of 5% of the stock options. What is the effect on earnings in 2019? In 2020?

BE 19–5
Stock options; forfeitures
● LO19–2

On January 1, 2018, Hugh Morris Comedy Club (HMCC) granted 1 million stock options to key executives exercisable for 1 million shares of the company's common stock at $20 per share. The stock options are intended as compensation for the next three years. The options are exercisable within a four-year period beginning January 1, 2021, by the executives still in the employ of the company. No options were terminated during 2018. The market price of the common stock was $25 per share at the date of the grant. HMCC estimated the fair value of the options at $9 each. 1% of the options are forfeited during 2019 due to executive turnover. What amount should HMCC record as compensation expense for the year ended December 31, 2019, assuming HMCC chooses the option to record forfeitures as they actually occur?

BE 19–6
Stock options; exercise
● LO19–2

Refer to the situation described in BE 19–3. Suppose that the options are exercised on April 3, 2021, when the market price is $19 per share. What journal entry will National record?

BE 19–7
Stock options; expiration
● LO19–2

Refer to the situation described in BE 19–3. Suppose that the options expire without being exercised. What journal entry will National record?

BE 19–8
Performance-based options
● LO19–2

On October 1, 2018, Farmer Fabrication issued stock options for 100,000 shares to a division manager. The options have an estimated fair value of $6 each. To provide additional incentive for managerial achievement, the options are not exercisable unless divisional revenue increases by 5% in three years. Farmer initially estimates that it is probable the goal will be achieved. How much compensation will be recorded in each of the next three years?

BE 19–9
Performance-based options
● LO19–2

Refer to the situation described in BE 19–8. Suppose that after one year, Farmer estimates that it is *not* probable that divisional revenue will increase by 5% in three years. What action will be taken to account for the options in 2019?

BE 19–10
Performance-based options
● LO19–2

Refer to the situation described in BE 19–8. Suppose that Farmer initially estimates that it is *not* probable the goal will be achieved, but then after one year, Farmer estimates that it *is* probable that divisional revenue will increase by 5% by the end of 2020. What action will be taken to account for the options in 2019 and thereafter?

BE 19–11
Options with market-based conditions
● LO19–2

On October 1, 2018, Farmer Fabrication issued stock options for 100,000 shares to a division manager. The options have an estimated fair value of $6 each. To provide additional incentive for managerial achievement, the options are not exercisable unless Farmer Fabrication's stock price increases by 5% in three years. Farmer initially estimates that it is not probable the goal will be achieved. How much compensation will be recorded in each of the next three years?

BE 19–12
EPS; shares issued; shares retired
● LO19–5, LO19–6

McDonnell-Myer Corporation reported net income of $741 million. The company had 544 million common shares outstanding at January 1 and sold 36 million shares on Feb. 28. As part of an annual share repurchase plan, 6 million shares were retired on April 30 for $47 per share. Calculate McDonnell-Myer's earnings per share for the year.

BE 19–13
EPS; nonconvertible preferred shares
● LO19–7

At December 31, 2017 and 2018, Funk & Noble Corporation had outstanding 820 million shares of common stock and 2 million shares of 8%, $100 par value cumulative preferred stock. No dividends were declared on either the preferred or common stock in 2017 or 2018. Net income for 2018 was $426 million. The income tax rate is 40%. Calculate earnings per share for the year ended December 31, 2018.

BE 19–14
EPS; stock options
● LO19–8

Fully vested incentive stock options exercisable at $50 per share to obtain 24,000 shares of common stock were outstanding during a period when the average market price of the common stock was $60 and the ending market price was $60. By how many shares will the assumed exercise of these options increase the weighted-average number of shares outstanding when calculating diluted earnings per share?

BE 19–15
EPS; convertible preferred shares
● LO19–9

Ahnberg Corporation had 800,000 shares of common stock issued and outstanding at January 1. No common shares were issued during the year, but on January 1, Ahnberg issued 100,000 shares of convertible preferred stock. The preferred shares are convertible into 200,000 shares of common stock. During the year Ahnberg paid $60,000 cash dividends on the preferred stock. Net income was $1,500,000. What were Ahnberg's basic and diluted earnings per share for the year?

BE 19–16
EPS; restricted stock award
● LO19–11

Niles Company granted 9 million of its no par common shares to executives, subject to forfeiture if employment is terminated within three years. The common shares have a market price of $5 per share on January 1, 2017, the grant date of the restricted stock award. When calculating diluted EPS at December 31, 2018, what will be the net increase in the denominator of the EPS fraction if the market price of the common shares averaged $5 per share during 2018?

Exercises

connect

E 19–1
Restricted stock award plan
● LO19–1

Allied Paper Products, Inc. offers a restricted stock award plan to its vice presidents. On January 1, 2018, the company granted 16 million of its $1 par common shares, subject to forfeiture if employment is terminated within two years. The common shares have a market price of $5 per share on the grant date.

Required:

1. Determine the total compensation cost pertaining to the restricted shares.
2. Prepare the appropriate journal entries related to the restricted stock through December 31, 2019.

E 19–2
Restricted stock units
● LO19–1

On January 1, 2018, VKI Corporation awarded restricted stock units (RSUs) representing 12 million of its $1 par common shares to key personnel, subject to forfeiture if employment is terminated within three years. After the recipients of the RSUs satisfy the vesting requirement, the company will distribute the shares. On the grant date, the shares had a market price of $2.50 per share.

Required:

1. Determine the total compensation cost pertaining to the RSUs.
2. Prepare the appropriate journal entry to record the award of RSUs on January 1, 2018.
3. Prepare the appropriate journal entry to record compensation expense on December 31, 2018.
4. Prepare the appropriate journal entry to record compensation expense on December 31, 2019.
5. Prepare the appropriate journal entry to record compensation expense on December 31, 2020.
6. Prepare the appropriate journal entry to record the lifting of restrictions on the RSUs and issuing shares at December 31, 2020.

E 19–3
Restricted stock units; Facebook
● LO19–1

Real World Financials

Facebook Inc. included the following disclosure note in an annual report:

Share-Based Compensation (in part)

. . . . compensation expense related to these grants is based on the grant date fair value of the RSUs and is recognized on a straight-line basis over the applicable service period.

The following table summarizes the activities for our unvested RSUs for the year ended December 31, 2015:

	Number of Shares	Weighted Average Grant Date Fair Value
Unvested at December 31, 2014	138,055	$ 55.89
Granted	28,164	79.85
Vested	(28,455)	41.55
Forfeited	(5,625)	49.50
Unvested at September 30, 2015	132,139	$ 64.36

Required:

1. Assuming a four-year vesting period, how much compensation expense did Facebook report in the year ended December 31, 2016, for the restricted stock units granted during the year ended December 31, 2015? (Round dollar amounts to the nearest million.)
2. Based on the information provided in the disclosure note, prepare the journal entry that summarizes the vesting of RSUs during the year ended December 31, 2015. (Facebook's common shares have a par amount per share of $0.000006. Round dollar amounts to the nearest million.)

E 19–4
Restricted stock units; forfeitures anticipated
● LO19–1

Magnetic-Optical Corporation offers a variety of share-based compensation plans to employees. Under its restricted stock unit plan, the company on January 1, 2018, granted restricted stock units (RSUs) representing 4 million of its $1 par common shares to various division managers. The shares are subject to forfeiture if employment is terminated within three years. The common shares have a market price of $22.50 per share on the grant date. Management's policy is to estimate forfeitures.

Required:

1. Determine the total compensation cost pertaining to the RSUs.
2. Prepare the appropriate journal entry to record the RSUs on January 1, 2018.
3. Prepare the appropriate journal entry to record compensation expense on December 31, 2018.
4. Suppose Magnetic-Optical expected a 10% forfeiture rate on the RSUs prior to vesting. Determine the total compensation cost.

E 19–5
Restricted stock units; forfeitures
● LO19–1

On January 1, 2018, David Mest Communications granted restricted stock units (RSUs) representing 30 million of its $1 par common shares to executives, subject to forfeiture if employment is terminated within three years. After the recipients of the RSUs satisfy the vesting requirement, the company will distribute the shares. The common shares had a market price of $12 per share on the grant date. At the date of grant, Mest anticipated that 6% of the recipients would leave the firm prior to vesting. On January 1, 2019, 5% of the RSUs are forfeited due to executive turnover. Mest chooses the option to account for forfeitures when they actually occur.

Required:

1. Prepare the appropriate journal entry to record compensation expense on December 31, 2018.
2. Prepare the appropriate journal entry to record compensation expense on December 31, 2019.
3. Prepare the appropriate journal entry to record compensation expense on December 31, 2020.

E 19–6
Stock options
● LO19–2

American Optical Corporation provides a variety of share-based compensation plans to its employees. Under its executive stock option plan, the company granted options on January 1, 2018, that permit executives to acquire 4 million of the company's $1 par common shares within the next five years, but not before December 31, 2019 (the vesting date). The exercise price is the market price of the shares on the date of grant, $14 per share. The fair value of the 4 million options, estimated by an appropriate option pricing model, is $3 per option. No forfeitures are anticipated. Ignore taxes.

Required:

1. Determine the total compensation cost pertaining to the options.
2. Prepare the appropriate journal entry to record the award of options on January 1, 2018.

3. Prepare the appropriate journal entry to record compensation expense on December 31, 2018.
4. Prepare the appropriate journal entry to record compensation expense on December 31, 2019.

E 19–7
Stock options; forfeiture of options
● LO19–2

On January 1, 2018, Adams-Meneke Corporation granted 25 million incentive stock options to division managers, each permitting holders to purchase one share of the company's $1 par common shares within the next six years, but not before December 31, 2020 (the vesting date). The exercise price is the market price of the shares on the date of grant, currently $10 per share. The fair value of the options, estimated by an appropriate option pricing model, is $3 per option. Management's policy is to estimate forfeitures. No forfeitures are anticipated. Ignore taxes.

Required:
1. Determine the total compensation cost pertaining to the options on January 1, 2018.
2. Prepare the appropriate journal entry to record compensation expense on December 31, 2018.
3. Unexpected turnover during 2019 caused an estimate of the forfeiture of 6% of the stock options. Determine the adjusted compensation cost, and prepare the appropriate journal entry(s) on December 31, 2019 and 2020.

E 19–8
Stock options exercise; expirations
● LO19–2

Walters Audio Visual Inc. offers an incentive stock option plan to its regional managers. On January 1, 2018, options were granted for 40 million $1 par common shares. The exercise price is the market price on the grant date—$8 per share. Options cannot be exercised prior to January 1, 2020, and expire December 31, 2024. The fair value of the 40 million options, estimated by an appropriate option pricing model, is $1 per option.

Required:
1. Determine the total compensation cost pertaining to the incentive stock option plan.
2. Prepare the appropriate journal entry to record compensation expense on December 31, 2018.
3. Prepare the appropriate journal entry to record compensation expense on December 31, 2019.
4. Prepare the appropriate journal entry to record the exercise of 75% of the options on March 12, 2020, when the market price is $9 per share.
5. Prepare the appropriate journal entry on December 31, 2024, when the remaining options that have vested expire without being exercised.

E 19–9
Stock options; exercise
● LO19–2

SSG Cycles manufactures and distributes motorcycle parts and supplies. Employees are offered a variety of share-based compensation plans. Under its nonqualified stock option plan, SSG granted options to key officers on January 1, 2018. The options permit holders to acquire 12 million of the company's $1 par common shares for $11 within the next six years, but not before January 1, 2021 (the vesting date). The market price of the shares on the date of grant is $13 per share. The fair value of the 12 million options, estimated by an appropriate option pricing model, is $3 per option.

Required:
1. Determine the total compensation cost pertaining to the incentive stock option plan.
2. Prepare the appropriate journal entries to record compensation expense on December 31, 2018, 2019, and 2020.
3. Record the exercise of the options if all of the options are exercised on May 11, 2022, when the market price is $14 per share.

E 19–10
Employee share purchase plan
● LO19–3

In order to encourage employee ownership of the company's $1 par common shares, Washington Distribution permits any of its employees to buy shares directly from the company through payroll deduction. There are no brokerage fees and shares can be purchased at a 15% discount. During March, employees purchased 50,000 shares at a time when the market price of the shares on the New York Stock Exchange was $12 per share.

Required:
Prepare the appropriate journal entry to record the March purchases of shares under the employee share purchase plan.

E 19–11
Employee share purchase plan; Tesla Motors
● LO19–3
Real World Financials

Tesla Motor's disclosure notes for the year ending December 31, 2015, included the following regarding its $0.001 par common stock:

EMPLOYEE STOCK PURCHASE PLAN—Employees are eligible to purchase common stock through payroll deductions of up to 15% of their eligible compensation, subject to any plan limitations. The purchase price of the shares on each purchase date is equal to 85% of the lower of the fair market value of our common stock on the first and last trading days of each six-month offering period. During the years ended December 31, 2015, 2014 and 2013, 220,571, 163,600 and 518,743 shares were issued under the ESPP for $37.5 million, $28.6 million and $13.8 million, respectively. A total of 3,615,749 shares of common stock have been reserved for issuance under the ESPP, and there were 2,115,851 shares available for issuance under the ESPP as of December 31, 2015.

Required:

Describe the way compensation expense for employee stock purchase plans is recognized. Include in your explanation the journal entry that summarizes employee share purchases for the year ending December 31, 2015.

E 19–12
EPS; shares issued; stock dividend
• LO19–5, LO19–6

For the year ended December 31, 2018, Norstar Industries reported net income of $655,000. At January 1, 2018, the company had 900,000 common shares outstanding. The following changes in the number of shares occurred during 2018:

Apr. 30	Sold 60,000 shares in a public offering
May 24	Declared and distributed a 5% stock dividend
June 1	Issued 72,000 shares as part of the consideration for the purchase of assets from a subsidiary

Required:

Compute Norstar's earnings per share for the year ended December 31, 2018.

E 19–13
EPS; treasury stock; new shares; stock dividends; two years
• LO19–5, LO19–6

The Alford Group had 202,000 shares of common stock outstanding at January 1, 2018. The following activities affected common shares during the year. There are no potential common shares outstanding.

2018	
Feb. 28	Purchased 6,000 shares of treasury stock
Oct. 31	Sold the treasury shares purchased on February 28
Nov. 30	Issued 24,000 new shares
Dec. 31	Net income for 2018 is $400,000
2019	
Jan. 15	Declared and issued a 2-for-1 stock split
Dec. 31	Net income for 2019 is $400,000

Required:

1. Determine the 2018 EPS.
2. Determine the 2019 EPS.
3. At what amount will the 2018 EPS be presented in the 2019 comparative financial statements?

E 19–14
EPS; stock dividend; nonconvertible preferred stock
• LO19–5, LO19–6, LO19–7

Hardaway Fixtures' balance sheet at December 31, 2017, included the following:

Shares issued and outstanding:	
Common stock, $1 par	$800,000
Nonconvertible preferred stock, $50 par	20,000

On July 21, 2018, Hardaway issued a 25% stock dividend on its common stock. On December 12, it paid $50,000 cash dividends on the preferred stock. Net income for the year ended December 31, 2018, was $2,000,000.

Required:

Compute Hardaway's earnings per share for the year ended December 31, 2018.

E 19–15
EPS; net loss; nonconvertible preferred stock; shares sold
• LO19–5, LO19–6, LO19–7

At December 31, 2017, Albrecht Corporation had outstanding 373,000 shares of common stock and 8,000 shares of 9.5%, $100 par value cumulative, nonconvertible preferred stock. On May 31, 2018, Albrecht sold for cash 12,000 shares of its common stock. No cash dividends were declared for 2018. For the year ended December 31, 2018, Albrecht reported a net loss of $114,000.

Required:

Calculate Albrecht's net loss per share for the year ended December 31, 2018.

E 19–16
EPS; stock dividend; nonconvertible preferred stock; treasury shares; shares sold
• LO19–5, LO19–6, LO19–7

On December 31, 2017, Berclair Inc. had 200 million shares of common stock and 3 million shares of 9%, $100 par value cumulative preferred stock issued and outstanding. On March 1, 2018, Berclair purchased 24 million shares of its common stock as treasury stock. Berclair issued a 5% common stock dividend on July 1, 2018. Four million treasury shares were sold on October 1. Net income for the year ended December 31, 2018, was $150 million.

Required:

Compute Berclair's earnings per share for the year ended December 31, 2018.

E 19–17
EPS; stock dividend; nonconvertible preferred stock; treasury shares; shares sold; stock options
● LO19–5 through LO19–8

(Note: This is a variation of E 19–16, modified to include stock options.) On December 31, 2017, Berclair Inc. had 200 million shares of common stock and 3 million shares of 9%, $100 par value cumulative preferred stock issued and outstanding. On March 1, 2018, Berclair purchased 24 million shares of its common stock as treasury stock. Berclair issued a 5% common stock dividend on July 1, 2018. Four million treasury shares were sold on October 1. Net income for the year ended December 31, 2018, was $150 million.

Also outstanding at December 31 were 30 million incentive stock options granted to key executives on September 13, 2013. The options were exercisable as of September 13, 2017, for 30 million common shares at an exercise price of $56 per share. During 2018, the market price of the common shares averaged $70 per share.

Required:
Compute Berclair's basic and diluted earnings per share for the year ended December 31, 2018.

E 19–18
EPS; stock dividend; nonconvertible preferred stock; treasury shares; shares sold; stock options exercised
● LO19–5 through LO19–8

(Note: This is a variation of E 19–16, modified to include the exercise of stock options.)

On December 31, 2017, Berclair Inc. had 200 million shares of common stock and 3 million shares of 9%, $100 par value cumulative preferred stock issued and outstanding. On March 1, 2018, Berclair purchased 24 million shares of its common stock as treasury stock. Berclair issued a 5% common stock dividend on July 1, 2018. Four million treasury shares were sold on October 1. Net income for the year ended December 31, 2018, was $150 million.

Also outstanding at December 31 were 30 million incentive stock options granted to key executives on September 13, 2013. The options were exercisable as of September 13, 2017, for 30 million common shares at an exercise price of $56 per share. During 2018, the market price of the common shares averaged $70 per share.

The options were exercised on September 1, 2018.

Required:
Compute Berclair's basic and diluted earnings per share for the year ended December 31, 2018.

E 19–19
EPS; stock dividend; nonconvertible preferred stock; treasury shares; shares sold; stock options; convertible bonds
● LO19–5 through LO19–9

(Note: This is a variation of E 19–17 modified to include convertible bonds).

On December 31, 2017, Berclair Inc. had 200 million shares of common stock and 3 million shares of 9%, $100 par value cumulative preferred stock issued and outstanding. On March 1, 2018, Berclair purchased 24 million shares of its common stock as treasury stock. Berclair issued a 5% common stock dividend on July 1, 2018. Four million treasury shares were sold on October 1. Net income for the year ended December 31, 2018, was $150 million. The income tax rate is 40%.

Also outstanding at December 31 were incentive stock options granted to key executives on September 13, 2013. The options are exercisable as of September 13, 2017, for 30 million common shares at an exercise price of $56 per share. During 2018, the market price of the common shares averaged $70 per share.

In 2014, $62.5 million of 8% bonds, convertible into 6 million common shares, were issued at face value.

Required:
Compute Berclair's basic and diluted earnings per share for the year ended December 31, 2018.

E 19–20
EPS; shares issued; stock options
● LO19–6 through LO19–9

Stanley Department Stores reported net income of $720,000 for the year ended December 31, 2018.

Additional Information:

Common shares outstanding at Jan. 1, 2018	80,000
Incentive stock options (vested in 2017) outstanding throughout 2018	24,000
(Each option is exercisable for one common share at an exercise price of $37.50.)	
During the year, the market price of Stanley's common stock averaged $45 per share.	
On Aug. 30, Stanley sold 15,000 common shares.	
Stanley's only debt consisted of $50,000 of 10% short term bank notes.	
The company's income tax rate is 40%.	

Required:
Compute Stanley's basic and diluted earnings per share for the year ended December 31, 2018.

E 19–21
EPS; convertible preferred stock; convertible bonds; order of entry
● LO19–7, LO19–9

Information from the financial statements of Ames Fabricators, Inc., included the following:

	December 31	
	2018	**2017**
Common shares	100,000	100,000
Convertible preferred shares (convertible into 32,000 shares of common)	12,000	12,000
10% convertible bonds (convertible into 30,000 shares of common)	$1,000,000	$1,000,000

Ames's net income for the year ended December 31, 2018, is $500,000. The income tax rate is 40%. Ames paid dividends of $5 per share on its preferred stock during 2018.

Required:

Compute basic and diluted earnings per share for the year ended December 31, 2018.

E 19–22
EPS; restricted stock
● LO19–11

As part of its executive compensation plan, Vertovec Inc. granted 54,000 of its no par common shares to executives, subject to forfeiture if employment is terminated within three years. Vertovec's common shares have a market price of $5 per share on January 1, 2017, the grant date of the restricted stock award, as well as on December 31, 2018. 800,000 shares were outstanding at January 1, 2018. Net income for 2018 was $120,000.

Required:

Compute Vertovec's basic and diluted earnings per share for the year ended December 31, 2018.

E 19–23
Record restricted stock; effect on EPS
● LO19–1, LO19–11

PHN Foods granted 18 million of its no par common shares to executives, subject to forfeiture if employment is terminated within three years. The common shares have a market price of $5 per share on January 1, 2017, the grant date.

Required:

1. What journal entry will PHN Foods prepare to record executive compensation regarding these restricted shares at December 31, 2017 and December 31, 2018?
2. When calculating diluted EPS at December 31, 2018, what will be the net increase in the denominator of the EPS fraction if the market price of the common shares averages $5 per share during 2018?

E 19–24
New shares; contingently issuable shares
● LO19–6, LO19–12

During 2018, its first year of operations, McCollum Tool Works entered into the following transactions relating to shareholders' equity. The corporation was authorized to issue 100 million common shares, $1 par per share.

Jan. 2	Issued 35 million common shares for cash.
3	Entered an agreement with the company president to issue up to 2 million additional shares of common stock in 2019 based on the earnings of McCollum in 2019. If net income exceeds $140 million, the president will receive 1 million shares; 2 million shares if net income exceeds $150 million.
Mar. 31	Issued 4 million shares in exchange for plant facilities.

Net income for 2018 was $148 million.

Required:

Compute basic and diluted earnings per share for the year ended December 31, 2018.

E 19–25
EPS; new shares; contingent agreements
● LO19–6, LO19–12

Anderson Steel Company began 2018 with 600,000 shares of common stock outstanding. On March 31, 2018, 100,000 new shares were sold at a price of $45 per share. The market price has risen steadily since that time to a high of $50 per share at December 31. No other changes in shares occurred during 2018, and no securities are outstanding that can become common stock. However, there are two agreements with officers of the company for future issuance of common stock. Both agreements relate to compensation arrangements reached in 2017. The first agreement grants to the company president a right to 10,000 shares of stock each year the closing market price is at least $48. The agreement begins in 2019 and expires in 2022. The second agreement grants to the controller a right to 15,000 shares of stock if she is still with the firm at the end of 2026. Net income for 2018 was $2,000,000.

Required:

Compute Anderson Steel Company's basic and diluted EPS for the year ended December 31, 2018.

E 19–26
EPS; concepts; terminology
● LO19–5 through LO19–13

Listed below are several terms and phrases associated with earnings per share. Pair each item from List A with the item from List B (by letter) that is most appropriately associated with it.

List A	List B
_____ 1. Subtract preferred dividends	a. Options exercised
_____ 2. Time-weighted by $\frac{5}{12}$	b. Simple capital structure
_____ 3. Time-weighted shares assumed issued plus time-weighted actual shares	c. Basic EPS
	d. Convertible preferred stock
_____ 4. Midyear event treated as if it occurred at the beginning of the reporting period	e. Earnings available to common shareholders
	f. Antidilutive
_____ 5. Preferred dividends do not reduce earnings	g. Increased marketability
_____ 6. Single EPS presentation	h. Discontinued operations
_____ 7. Stock split	i. Stock dividend
_____ 8. Potential common shares	j. Add after-tax interest to numerator
_____ 9. Exercise price exceeds market price	k. Diluted EPS
_____ 10. No dilution assumed	l. Noncumulative, undeclared preferred dividends

(continued)

(concluded)

List A	List B
_____ 11. Convertible bonds	m. Common shares retired at the beginning of August
_____ 12. Contingently issuable shares	n. Include in diluted EPS when conditions for issuance are met
_____ 13. Maximum potential dilution	
_____ 14. Shown between per share amounts for net income and for income from continuing operations	

E 19–27
FASB codification research
● LO19–2

The *FASB Accounting Standards Codification* represents the single source of authoritative U.S. generally accepted accounting principles.

Required:

1. Obtain the relevant authoritative literature on stock compensation using the *FASB Accounting Standards Codification* at the FASB website (www.fasb.org). What is the specific citation that describes the information that companies must disclose about the exercise prices for their stock option plans?
2. List the disclosure requirements.

E 19–28
FASB codification research
● LO19–2, LO19–3, LO19–7, LO19–13

Access the *FASB Accounting Standards Codification* at the FASB website (www.fasb.org). Determine the specific citation for accounting for each of the following items:

1. Initial measurement of stock options.
2. The measurement date for share-based payments classified as liabilities.
3. The formula to calculate diluted earnings per share.
4. The way stock dividends or stock splits in the current year affect the presentation of EPS in the income statement.

E 19–29
Stock appreciation rights; settlement in shares
● Appendix B

As part of its stock-based compensation package, International Electronics granted 24 million stock appreciation rights (SARs) to top officers on January 1, 2018. At exercise, holders of the SARs are entitled to receive stock equal in value to the excess of the market price at exercise over the share price at the date of grant. The SARs cannot be exercised until the end of 2021 (vesting date) and expire at the end of 2023. The $1 par common shares have a market price of $46 per share on the grant date. The fair value of the SARs, estimated by an appropriate option pricing model, is $3 per SAR at January 1, 2018. The fair value reestimated at December 31, 2018, 2019, 2020, 2021, and 2022, is $4, $3, $4, $2.50, and $3, respectively. All recipients are expected to remain employed through the vesting date.

Required:

1. Prepare the appropriate journal entry to record the award of SARs on January 1, 2018. Will the SARs be reported as debt or equity?
2. Prepare the appropriate journal entries pertaining to the SARs on December 31, 2018–December 31, 2021.
3. The SARs remain unexercised on December 31, 2022. Prepare the appropriate journal entry on that date.
4. The SARs are exercised on June 6, 2023, when the share price is $50. Prepare the appropriate journal entry(s) on that date.

E 19–30
Stock appreciation rights; cash settlement
● Appendix B

(Note: This is a variation of E 19–29, modified to allow settlement in cash.)

As part of its stock-based compensation package, International Electronics granted 24 million stock appreciation rights (SARs) to top officers on January 1, 2018. At exercise, holders of the SARs are entitled to receive cash or stock equal in value to the excess of the market price at exercise over the share price at the date of grant. The SARs cannot be exercised until the end of 2021 (vesting date) and expire at the end of 2023. The $1 par common shares have a market price of $46 per share on the grant date. The fair value of the SARs, estimated by an appropriate option pricing model, is $3 per SAR at January 1, 2018. The fair value re-estimated at December 31, 2018, 2019, 2020, 2021, and 2022, is $4, $3, $4, $2.50, and $3, respectively. All recipients are expected to remain employed through the vesting date.

Required:

1. Prepare the appropriate journal entry to record the award of SARs on January 1, 2018.
2. Prepare the appropriate journal entries pertaining to the SARs on December 31, 2018–December 31, 2021.
3. The SARs remain unexercised on December 31, 2022. Prepare the appropriate journal entry on that date.
4. The SARs are exercised on June 6, 2023, when the share price is $50, and executives choose to receive the market price appreciation in cash. Prepare the appropriate journal entry(s) on that date.

E 19–31
Restricted stock units; cash settlement
● Appendix B

As part of its stock-based compensation package, on January 1, 2018, International Electronics granted restricted stock units (RSUs) representing 50 million $1 par common shares. At exercise, holders of the RSUs are entitled to receive cash or stock equal in value to the market price of those shares at exercise. The RSUs cannot be exercised until the end of 2021 (vesting date) and expire at the end of 2023. The $1 par common shares have a market price of $6 per share on the grant date. The fair value at December 31, 2018, 2019, 2020, 2021, and 2022, is $8, $6, $8, $5, and $6, respectively. All recipients are expected to remain employed through the vesting date. After the recipients of the RSUs satisfy the vesting requirement, the company will distribute the shares.

Required:

1. Prepare the appropriate journal entry to record the award of RSUs on January 1, 2018.
2. Prepare the appropriate journal entries pertaining to the RSUs on December 31, 2018–December 31, 2021.
3. The RSUs remain unexercised on December 31, 2022. Prepare the appropriate journal entry on that date.
4. The RSUs are exercised on June 6, 2023, when the share price is $6.50, and executives choose to receive cash. Prepare the appropriate journal entry(s) on that date.

Problems

connect

P 19–1
Stock options; forfeiture; exercise
● LO19–2

On October 15, 2017, the board of directors of Ensor Materials Corporation approved a stock option plan for key executives. On January 1, 2018, 20 million stock options were granted, exercisable for 20 million shares of Ensor's $1 par common stock. The options are exercisable between January 1, 2021, and December 31, 2023, at 80% of the quoted market price on January 1, 2018, which was $15. The fair value of the 20 million options, estimated by an appropriate option pricing model, is $6 per option. Ensor chooses the option to recognize forfeitures only when they occur.

Ten percent (2 million) of the options were forfeited when an executive resigned in 2019. All other options were exercised on July 12, 2022, when the stock's price jumped unexpectedly to $19 per share.

Required:

1. When is Ensor's stock option measurement date?
2. Determine the compensation expense for the stock option plan in 2018. (Ignore taxes.)
3. What is the effect of forfeiture of the stock options on Ensor's financial statements for 2019 and 2020?
4. Is this effect consistent with the general approach for accounting for changes in estimates? Explain.
5. How should Ensor account for the exercise of the options in 2022?

P 19–2
Stock options; graded vesting
● LO19–2

Pastner Brands is a calendar-year firm with operations in several countries. As part of its executive compensation plan, at January 1, 2018, the company issued 400,000 executive stock options permitting executives to buy 400,000 shares of Pastner stock for $34 per share. One-fourth of the options vest in each of the next four years beginning at December 31, 2018 (graded vesting). Pastner elects to separate the total award into four groups (or tranches) according to the year in which they vest and measures the compensation cost for each vesting date as a separate award. The fair value of each tranche is estimated at January 1, 2018, as follows:

Vesting Date	Amount Vesting	Fair Value per Option
Dec. 31, 2018	25%	$3.50
Dec. 31, 2019	25%	$4.00
Dec. 31, 2020	25%	$4.50
Dec. 31, 2021	25%	$5.00

Required:

1. Determine the compensation expense related to the options to be recorded each year 2018–2021, assuming Pastner allocates the compensation cost for each of the four groups (tranches) separately.
2. Determine the compensation expense related to the options to be recorded each year 2018–2021, assuming Pastner uses the straight-line method to allocate the total compensation cost.

P 19–3
Stock options; graded vesting; measurement using a single fair value per option
● LO19–2

Refer to the situation described in P 19–2. Assume Pastner measures the fair value of all options on January 1, 2018, to be $4.50 per option using a single weighted-average expected life of the options assumption.

Required:

1. Determine the compensation expense related to the options to be recorded each year 2018–2021, assuming Pastner allocates the compensation cost for each of the four groups (tranches) separately.
2. Determine the compensation expense related to the options to be recorded each year 2018–2021, assuming Pastner uses the straight-line method to allocate the total compensation cost.

P 19–4
Stock options; graded vesting; IFRS
● LO19–2, LO19–14
IFRS

Refer to the situation described in P 19–2. Assume Pastner prepares its financial statements using International Financial Reporting Standards (IFRS).

Required:

How might your responses to requirement 1 and requirement 2 differ using IFRS? Explain.

P 19–5
Stock option plan; deferred tax effect recognized
● LO19–2

Walters Audio Visual, Inc. offers a stock option plan to its regional managers. On January 1, 2018, 40 million options were granted for 40 million $1 par common shares. The exercise price is the market price on the grant date, $8 per share. Options cannot be exercised prior to January 1, 2020, and expire December 31, 2024. The fair value of the options, estimated by an appropriate option pricing model, is $2 per option. Because the plan does not qualify as an incentive plan, Walters will receive a tax deduction upon exercise of the options equal to the excess of the market price at exercise over the exercise price. The income tax rate is 40%.

Required:

1. Determine the total compensation cost pertaining to the stock option plan.
2. Prepare the appropriate journal entries to record compensation expense and its tax effect on December 31, 2018.
3. Prepare the appropriate journal entries to record compensation expense and its tax effect on December 31, 2019.
4. Record the exercise of the options and their tax effect if *all* of the options are exercised on March 20, 2023, when the market price is $12 per share.
5. Assume the option plan qualifies as an incentive plan. Prepare the appropriate journal entries to record compensation expense and its tax effect on December 31, 2018.
6. Assuming the option plan qualifies as an incentive plan, record the exercise of the options and their tax effect if *all* of the options are exercised on March 20, 2023, when the market price is $11 per share.

P 19–6
Stock option plan; deferred tax effect of a nonqualifying plan
● LO19–2

JBL Aircraft manufactures and distributes aircraft parts and supplies. Employees are offered a variety of share-based compensation plans. Under its nonqualified stock option plan, JBL granted options to key officers on January 1, 2018. The options permit holders to acquire 6 million of the company's $1 par common shares for $22 within the next six years, but not before January 1, 2021 (the vesting date). The market price of the shares on the date of grant is $26 per share. The fair value of the 6 million options, estimated by an appropriate option pricing model, is $6 per option. Because the plan does not qualify as an incentive plan, JBL will receive a tax deduction upon exercise of the options equal to the excess of the market price at exercise over the exercise price. The tax rate is 40%.

Required:

1. Determine the total compensation cost pertaining to the incentive stock option plan.
2. Prepare the appropriate journal entries to record compensation expense and its tax effect on December 31, 2018, 2019, and 2020.
3. Record the exercise of the options and their tax effect if *all* of the options are exercised on August 21, 2022, when the market price is $27 per share.

P 19–7
Performance option plan
● LO19–2

LCI Cable Company grants 1 million performance stock options to key executives at January 1, 2018. The options entitle executives to receive 1 million of LCI $1 par common shares, subject to the achievement of specific financial goals over the next four years. Attainment of these goals is considered probable initially and throughout the service period. The options have a current fair value of $12 per option.

Required:

1. Prepare the appropriate entry when the options are awarded on January 1, 2018.
2. Prepare the appropriate entries on December 31 of each year 2018–2021.
3. Suppose at the beginning of 2020, LCI decided it is not probable that the performance objectives will be met. Prepare the appropriate entries on December 31 of 2020 and 2021.

P 19–8
Net loss; stock dividend; nonconvertible preferred stock; treasury shares; shares sold; discontinued operations
● LO19–5 through LO19–7, LO19–13

On December 31, 2017, Ainsworth, Inc., had 600 million shares of common stock outstanding. Twenty million shares of 8%, $100 par value cumulative, nonconvertible preferred stock were sold on January 2, 2018. On April 30, 2018, Ainsworth purchased 30 million shares of its common stock as treasury stock. Twelve million treasury shares were sold on August 31. Ainsworth issued a 5% common stock dividend on June 12, 2018. No cash dividends were declared in 2018. For the year ended December 31, 2018, Ainsworth reported a net loss of $140 million, including an after-tax loss from discontinued operations of $400 million.

Required:

1. Determine Ainsworth's net loss per share for the year ended December 31, 2018.
2. Determine the per share amount of income or loss from continuing operations for the year ended December 31, 2018.
3. Prepare an EPS presentation that would be appropriate to appear on Ainsworth's 2018 and 2017 comparative income statements. Assume EPS was reported in 2017 as $0.75, based on net income (no discontinued operations) of $450 million and a weighted-average number of common shares of 600 million.

P 19–9
EPS from statement of retained earnings
● LO19–4 through LO19–6

(Note: This problem is based on the same situation described in P 18–4 in Chapter 18, modified to focus on EPS rather than recording the events that affected retained earnings.)

Comparative Statements of Retained Earnings for Renn-Dever Corporation were reported as follows for the fiscal years ending December 31, 2016, 2017, and 2018.

RENN-DEVER CORPORATION
Statements of Retained Earnings

	For the Years Ended December 31		
	2018	**2017**	**2016**
Balance at beginning of year	$6,794,292	$5,464,052	$5,624,552
Net income (loss)	3,308,700	2,240,900	(160,500)
Deductions:			
Stock dividend (34,900 shares)	242,000		
Common shares retired, September 30 (110,000 shares)		212,660	
Common stock cash dividends	889,950	698,000	0
Balance at end of year	$8,971,042	$6,794,292	$5,464,052

At December 31, 2015, paid-in capital consisted of the following:

Common stock, 1,855,000 shares at $1 par	$1,855,000
Paid in capital—excess of par	7,420,000

No preferred stock or potential common shares were outstanding during any of the periods shown.

Required:

Compute Renn-Dever's earnings per share as it would have appeared in income statements for the years ended December 31, 2016, 2017, and 2018.

P 19–10
EPS from statement of shareholders' equity
● LO19–4 through LO19–6

Comparative Statements of Shareholders' Equity for Locke Intertechnology Corporation were reported as follows for the fiscal years ending December 31, 2016, 2017, and 2018.

LOCKE INTERTECHNOLOGY CORPORATION
Statements of Shareholders' Equity
For the Years Ended Dec. 31, 2016, 2017, and 2018
($ in millions)

	Preferred Stock, $10 par	Common Stock, $1 par	Additional Paid-in Capital	Retained Earnings	Total Shareholders' Equity
Balance at January 1, 2016		$ 55	$ 495	$1,878	$2,428
Sale of preferred shares	10		470		480
Sale of common shares, 7/1		9	81		90
Cash dividend, preferred				(1)	(1)
Cash dividend, common				(16)	(16)
Net income				290	290
Balance at December 31, 2016	10	64	1,046	2,151	3,271
Retirement of common shares, 4/1		(4)	(36)	(20)	(60)

(continued)

(concluded)

LOCKE INTERTECHNOLOGY CORPORATION
Statements of Shareholders' Equity
For the Years Ended Dec. 31, 2016, 2017, and 2018
($ in millions)

	Preferred Stock, $10 par	Common Stock, $1 par	Additional Paid-in Capital	Retained Earnings	Total Shareholders' Equity
Cash dividend, preferred				(1)	(1)
Cash dividend, common				(20)	(20)
3-for-2 split effected in the form of a common stock dividend, 8/12		30	(30)		
Net income				380	380
Balance at December 31, 2017	10	90	980	2,490	3,570
10% common stock dividend, 5/1		9	90	(99)	
Sale of common shares, 9/1		3	31		34
Cash dividend, preferred				(2)	(2)
Cash dividend, common				(22)	(22)
Net income				412	412
Balance at December 31, 2018	$10	$102	$1,101	$2,779	$3,992

Required:
Infer from the statements the events and transactions that affected Locke Intertechnology Corporation's shareholders' equity and compute earnings per share as it would have appeared on the income statements for the years ended December 31, 2016, 2017, and 2018. No potential common shares were outstanding during any of the periods shown.

P 19–11
EPS; nonconvertible preferred stock; treasury shares; shares sold; stock dividend
- LO19–4 through LO19–7

On December 31, 2017, Dow Steel Corporation had 600,000 shares of common stock and 300,000 shares of 8%, noncumulative, nonconvertible preferred stock issued and outstanding. Dow issued a 4% common stock dividend on May 15 and paid cash dividends of $400,000 and $75,000 to common and preferred shareholders, respectively, on December 15, 2018.

On February 28, 2018, Dow sold 60,000 common shares. In keeping with its long-term share repurchase plan, 2,000 shares were retired on July 1. Dow's net income for the year ended December 31, 2018, was $2,100,000. The income tax rate is 40%.

Required:
Compute Dow's earnings per share for the year ended December 31, 2018.

P 19–12
EPS; nonconvertible preferred stock; treasury shares; shares sold; stock dividend; options
- LO19–4 through LO19–8, LO19–10

(Note: This is a variation of P 19–11, modified to include stock options.)
On December 31, 2017, Dow Steel Corporation had 600,000 shares of common stock and 300,000 shares of 8%, noncumulative, nonconvertible preferred stock issued and outstanding. Dow issued a 4% common stock dividend on May 15 and paid cash dividends of $400,000 and $75,000 to common and preferred shareholders, respectively, on December 15, 2018.

On February 28, 2018, Dow sold 60,000 common shares. In keeping with its long-term share repurchase plan, 2,000 shares were retired on July 1. Dow's net income for the year ended December 31, 2018, was $2,100,000. The income tax rate is 40%.

As part of an incentive compensation plan, Dow granted incentive stock options to division managers at December 31 of the current and each of the previous two years. Each option permits its holder to buy one share of common stock at an exercise price equal to market value at the date of grant and can be exercised one year from that date. Information concerning the number of options granted and common share prices follows:

Date Granted	Options Granted (adjusted for the stock dividend)	Share Price
December 31, 2016	8,000	$24
December 31, 2017	3,000	$33
December 31, 2018	6,500	$32

The market price of the common stock averaged $32 per share during 2018.

Required:
Compute Dow's earnings per share for the year ended December 31, 2018.

P 19–13
EPS; nonconvertible preferred stock; treasury shares; shares sold; stock dividend; options; convertible bonds; contingently issuable shares
- LO19–4 through LO19–11

(Note: This is a variation of P 19–12, modified to include convertible bonds and contingently issuable shares.) On December 31, 2017, Dow Steel Corporation had 600,000 shares of common stock and 300,000 shares of 8%, noncumulative, nonconvertible preferred stock issued and outstanding. Dow issued a 4% common stock dividend on May 15 and paid cash dividends of $400,000 and $75,000 to common and preferred shareholders, respectively, on December 15, 2018.

On February 28, 2018, Dow sold 60,000 common shares. In keeping with its long-term share repurchase plan, 2,000 shares were retired on July 1. Dow's net income for the year ended December 31, 2018, was $2,100,000. The income tax rate is 40%. Also, as a part of a 2017 agreement for the acquisition of Merrill Cable Company, another 23,000 shares (already adjusted for the stock dividend) are to be issued to former Merrill shareholders on December 31, 2019, if Merrill's 2019 net income is at least $500,000. In 2018, Merrill's net income was $630,000.

As part of an incentive compensation plan, Dow granted incentive stock options to division managers at December 31 of the current and each of the previous two years. Each option permits its holder to buy one share of common stock at an exercise price equal to market value at the date of grant and can be exercised one year from that date. Information concerning the number of options granted and common share prices follows:

Date Granted	Options Granted	Share Price
	(adjusted for the stock dividend)	
December 31, 2016	8,000	$24
December 31, 2017	3,000	$33
December 31, 2018	6,500	$32

The market price of the common stock averaged $32 per share during 2018.

On July 12, 2016, Dow issued $800,000 of convertible 10% bonds at face value. Each $1,000 bond is convertible into 30 common shares (adjusted for the stock dividend).

Required:
Compute Dow's basic and diluted earnings per share for the year ended December 31, 2018.

P 19–14
EPS; convertible preferred stock; convertible bonds; order of entry
- LO19–7, LO19–9, LO19–10

Information from the financial statements of Henderson-Niles Industries included the following at December 31, 2018:

Common shares outstanding throughout the year	100 million
Convertible preferred shares (convertible into 32 million shares of common)	60 million
Convertible 10% bonds (convertible into 13.5 million shares of common)	$900 million

Henderson-Niles's net income for the year ended December 31, 2018, is $520 million. The income tax rate is 40%. Henderson-Niles paid dividends of $2 per share on its preferred stock during 2018.

Required:
Compute basic and diluted earnings per share for the year ended December 31, 2018.

P 19–15
EPS; antidilution
- LO19–4 through LO19–10, LO19–13

Alciatore Company reported a net income of $150,000 in 2018. The weighted-average number of common shares outstanding for 2018 was 40,000. The average stock price for 2018 was $33. Assume an income tax rate of 40%.

Required:
For each of the following independent situations, indicate whether the effect of the security is antidilutive for diluted EPS.

1. 10,000 shares of 7.7% of $100 par convertible, cumulative preferred stock. Each share may be converted into two common shares.
2. 8% convertible 10-year, $500,000 of bonds, issued at face value. The bonds are convertible to 5,000 shares of common stock.
3. Stock options exercisable at $30 per share after January 1, 2020.
4. Warrants for 1,000 common shares with an exercise price of $35 per share.
5. A contingent agreement to issue 5,000 shares of stock to the company president if net income is at least $125,000 in 2019.

P 19–16
EPS; convertible bonds; treasury shares
• LO19–4 through LO19–6, LO19–9

At December 31, 2018, the financial statements of Hollingsworth Industries included the following:

Net income for 2018	$560 million
Bonds payable, 10%, convertible into 36 million shares of common stock	$300 million
Common stock:	
Shares outstanding on January 1	400 million
Treasury shares purchased for cash on September 1	30 million

Additional data:
The bonds payable were issued at par in 2016. The tax rate for 2018 was 40%.

Required:
Compute basic and diluted EPS for the year ended December 31, 2018.

P 19–17
EPS; options; convertible preferred; additional shares
• LO19–4 through LO19–9

On January 1, 2018, Tonge Industries had outstanding 440,000 common shares ($1 par) that originally sold for $20 per share, and 4,000 shares of 10% cumulative preferred stock ($100 par), convertible into 40,000 common shares.

On October 1, 2018, Tonge sold and issued an additional 16,000 shares of common stock at $33. At December 31, 2018, there were 20,000 incentive stock options outstanding, issued in 2017, and exercisable after one year for 20,000 shares of common stock at an exercise price of $30. The market price of the common stock at year-end was $48. During the year, the price of the common shares had averaged $40.

Net income was $650,000. The tax rate for the year was 40%.

Required:
Compute basic and diluted EPS for the year ended December 31, 2018.

P 19–18
EPS; stock options; nonconvertible preferred; convertible bonds; shares sold
• LO19–4 through LO19–9

At January 1, 2018, Canaday Corporation had outstanding the following securities:

600 million common shares
20 million 6% cumulative preferred shares, $50 par
8% convertible bonds, $2,000 million face amount, convertible into 80 million common shares

The following additional information is available:

- On September 1, 2018, Canaday sold 72 million additional shares of common stock.
- Incentive stock options to purchase 60 million shares of common stock after July 1, 2017, at $12 per share, were outstanding at the beginning and end of 2018. The average market price of Canaday's common stock was $18 per share during 2018.
- Canaday's net income for the year ended December 31, 2018, was $1,476 million. The effective income tax rate was 40%.

Required:
1. Calculate basic earnings per common share for the year ended December 31, 2018.
2. Calculate the diluted earnings per common share for the year ended December 31, 2018.

P 19–19
EPS; options; restricted stock; additional components for "proceeds" in treasury stock method
• LO19–1, LO19–2, LO19–4, LO19–8, LO19–11

Witter House is a calendar-year firm with 300 million common shares outstanding throughout 2018 and 2019. As part of its executive compensation plan, at January 1, 2017, the company had issued 30 million executive stock options permitting executives to buy 30 million shares of stock for $10 within the next eight years, but not prior to January 1, 2020. The fair value of the options was estimated on the grant date to be $3 per option.

In 2018, Witter House began granting employees stock awards rather than stock options as part of its equity compensation plans and granted 15 million restricted common shares to senior executives at January 1, 2018. The shares vest four years later. The fair value of the stock was $12 per share on the grant date. The average price of the common shares was $12 and $15 during 2018 and 2019, respectively.

The stock options qualify for tax purposes as an incentive plan. The restricted stock does not. The company's net income was $150 million and $160 million in 2018 and 2019, respectively. Its income tax rate is 40%.

Required:
1. Determine basic and diluted earnings per share for Witter House in 2018.
2. Determine basic and diluted earnings per share for Witter House in 2019.

Broaden Your Perspective

Apply your critical-thinking ability to the knowledge you've gained. These cases will provide you an opportunity to develop your research, analysis, judgment, and communication skills. You also will work with other students, integrate what you've learned, apply it in real-world situations, and consider its global and ethical ramifications. This practice will broaden your knowledge and further develop your decision-making abilities.

Real World Case 19–1
Restricted stock awards; Microsoft
● LO19–1

Real World Financials

Microsoft provides compensation to executives in the form of a variety of incentive compensation plans, including restricted stock award grants. The following is an excerpt from a disclosure note from Microsoft's 2015 annual report:

Note 20 Employee Stock and Savings Plans (in part)
Stock awards are grants that entitle the holder to shares of common stock as the award vests. Our stock awards generally vest over a five-year period . . . During fiscal year 2015, the following activity occurred under our plans:

	Shares ($ in millions)	**Weighted Average Grant-Date Fair Value**
Stock awards:		
Nonvested balance, beginning of year	259	$ 27.88
Granted	75	42.36
Vested	(94)	27.47
Forfeited	(24)	31.81
Nonvested balance, end of year	**216**	**$32.72**

Required:
1. What is the "incentive" provided by Microsoft's restricted stock grants?
2. If all awards are granted, vested, and forfeited evenly throughout the year, what is the compensation expense in fiscal 2015 pertaining to the previous and current stock awards? Explain. Assume forfeited shares were granted evenly throughout the three previous years.

Communication Case 19–2
Stock options; basic concepts; prepare a memo
● LO19–2

You are assistant controller of Stamos & Company, a medium-size manufacturer of machine parts. On October 22, 2017, the board of directors approved a stock option plan for key executives. On January 1, 2018, a specific number of stock options were granted. The options were exercisable between January 1, 2020, and December 31, 2024, at 100% of the quoted market price at the grant date. The service period is for 2018 through 2020.

Your boss, the controller, is one of the executives to receive options. Neither he nor you have had occasion to deal with GAAP on accounting for stock options. He and you are aware of the traditional approach your company used years ago but do not know the newer method. Your boss understands how options might benefit him personally but wants to be aware also of how the options will be reported in the financial statements. He has asked you for a one-page synopsis of accounting for stock options under the fair value approach. He instructed you, "I don't care about the effect on taxes or earnings per share—just the basics, please."

Required:
Prepare such a report that includes the following:
1. At what point should the compensation cost be measured? How should it be measured?
2. How should compensation expense be measured for the stock option plan in 2018 and later?
3. If options are forfeited because an executive resigns before vesting, what is the effect of that forfeiture of the stock options on the financial statements?
4. If options are allowed to lapse after vesting, what is the effect on the financial statements?

Ethics Case 19–3
Stock options
● LO19–2

You are in your second year as an auditor with Dantly and Regis, a regional CPA firm. One of the firm's long-time clients is Mayberry-Cleaver Industries, a national company involved in the manufacturing, marketing, and sales of hydraulic devices used in specialized manufacturing applications. Early in this year's audit, you discover that Mayberry-Cleaver has changed its method of determining inventory from LIFO to FIFO. Your client's explanation is that FIFO is consistent with the method used by some other companies in the industry. Upon further investigation, you discover an executive stock option plan whose terms call for a significant increase in the shares available to executives if net income this year exceeds $44 million. Some quick calculations convince you that without the change in inventory methods, the target will not be reached; with the change, it will.

Required:

Do you perceive an ethical dilemma? What would be the likely impact of following the controller's suggestions? Who would benefit? Who would be injured?

Trueblood Accounting Case 19–4
Share-based awards
● LO19–1, LO19–2

The following Trueblood case is recommended for use with this chapter. The case provides an excellent opportunity for class discussion, group projects, and writing assignments. The case, along with Professor's Discussion Material, can be obtained from the Deloitte Foundation at its website: www.deloitte.com/us/truebloodcases.

Case 13-5: ***Occupy Mall Street***

This case gives students the opportunity to consider the accounting treatment for different aspects of a share-based compensation plan.

Real World Case 19–5
Share-based plans; Walmart
● LO19–1, LO19–2

Real World Financials

Walmart offers its employees a variety of share-based compensation plans including stock options, performance share awards, restricted stock, and restricted stock units. The following is an excerpt from a disclosure note from Walmart's 2015 financial statements:

Share-Based Compensation

The Company has awarded share-based compensation to associates and nonemployee directors of the Company. The compensation expense recognized for all plans was $448 million, $462 million and $388 million for fiscal 2016, 2015 and 2014, respectively. Share-based compensation expense is included in operating, selling, general and administrative expenses in the Company's Consolidated Statements of Income. The total income tax benefit recognized for share-based compensation was $151 million, $173 million and $145 million for fiscal 2016, 2015 and 2014, respectively. The following table summarizes the Company's share-based compensation expense by award type:

	Fiscal Years Ended January 31,		
($ in millions)	2016	2015	2014
Restricted stock and performance share units	$134	$157	$141
Restricted stock units	292	277	224
Other	22	28	23
Share-based compensation expense	$448	$462	$388

Required:

1. Walmart's share-based compensation includes stock options, restricted stock units, restricted stock awards, and performance-based awards. What is the general financial reporting objective when recording compensation expense for these forms of compensation?
2. Walmart reported share-based expense of $448 million in 2015. Without referring to specific numbers and ignoring other forms of share-based compensation, describe how this amount reflects the value of stock options.

Ethics Case 19–6
International Network Solutions
● LO19–6

International Network Solutions provides products and services related to remote access networking. The company has grown rapidly during its first 10 years of operations. As its segment of the industry has begun to mature, though, the fast growth of previous years has begun to slow. In fact, this year revenues and profits are roughly the same as last year.

One morning, nine weeks before the close of the fiscal year, Rob Mashburn, CFO, and Jessica Lane, controller, were sharing coffee and ideas in Lane's office.

Lane:	About the Board meeting Thursday. You may be right. This may be the time to suggest a share buyback program.
Mashburn:	To begin this year, you mean?
Lane:	Right! I know Barber will be lobbying to use the funds for our European expansion. She's probably right about the best use of our funds, but we can always issue more notes next year. Right now, we need a quick fix for our EPS numbers.
Mashburn:	Our shareholders are accustomed to increases every year.

Required:

1. How will a buyback of shares provide a "quick fix" for EPS?
2. Is the proposal ethical?
3. Who would be affected if the proposal is implemented?

Real World Case 19–7
Per share data; stock options; antidilutive securities; Best Buy Co.
● LO19–8

Real World Financials

The 2016 annual report of **Best Buy Co., Inc.** reported profitable operations for the most recent three years. However, the company suffered a net loss in 2012. Best Buy reported the following for the twelve months ended March 3, 2012:

Basic (loss) earnings per share:	
Continuing operations	$(2.89)
Discontinued operations	(0.47)
Basic (loss) earnings per share	$(3.36)
Diluted (loss) earnings per share:	
Continuing operations	$(2.89)
Discontinued operations	(0.47)
Diluted (loss) earnings per share	$(3.36)
Dividends declared per Best Buy Co., Inc. common share	$ 0.62
Weighted average common shares outstanding (in millions)	
Basic	366.3
Diluted	366.3

Note: The calculation of diluted earnings per share assumes the conversion of the company's previously outstanding convertible debentures due in 2024 into 8.8 million shares common stock . . . and adds back the related after-tax interest expense of $1.5. . . . The calculation of diluted (loss) per share for the twelve months ended March 3, 2012, does not include potential dilutive shares of common stock because their inclusion would be antidilutive (i.e., reduce the net loss per share).

Required:

1. The note indicates that Best Buy does not include potentially dilutive shares when calculating EPS for the twelve months ended March 3, 2012. What are potentially dilutive shares?
2. The note indicates that "diluted earnings per share assumes the conversion of the company's *previously outstanding* convertible debentures due in 2024 into 8.8 million shares common stock . . . and adds back the related after-tax interest expense of $1.5." Apparently, these bonds were actually converted during the year. Would diluted EPS have been different if the bonds had not been converted and were still outstanding? Explain.
3. Best Buy does not include potentially dilutive shares when calculating EPS for the twelve months ended March 3, 2012. Why not? Assume Best Buy had 40 million common equivalent shares and included them in the calculation, what would have been the amount of diluted loss per share for the twelve months ended March 3, 2012?

Analysis Case 19–8
EPS concepts
● LO19–4 through LO19–8

The shareholders' equity of Proactive Solutions, Inc., included the following at December 31, 2018:

Common stock, $1 par
Paid-in capital—excess of par on common stock
7% cumulative convertible preferred stock, $100 par value
Paid-in capital—excess of par on preferred stock
Retained earnings

Additional Information:

- Proactive had 7 million shares of preferred stock authorized of which 2 million were outstanding. All 2 million shares outstanding were issued in 2012 for $112 a share. The preferred stock is convertible into common stock on a two-for-one basis until December 31, 2020, after which the preferred stock no longer is convertible. None of the preferred stock has been converted into common stock at December 31, 2018. There were no dividends in arrears.
- Of the 13 million common shares authorized, there were 8 million shares outstanding at January 1, 2018. Proactive also sold 3 million shares at the beginning of September 2018 at a price of $52 a share.
- The company has an employee stock option plan in which certain key employees and officers may purchase shares of common stock at the market price at the date of the option grant. All options are exercisable beginning one year after the date of the grant and expire if not exercised within five years of the grant date. On January 1, 2018, options for 2 million shares were outstanding at prices ranging from $45 to $53 a share. Options for 1 million shares were exercised at $49 a share at the end of June 2018. No options expired during 2018. Additional options for 1.5 million shares were granted at $55 a share during the year. The 2.5 million options outstanding at December 31, 2018, were exercisable at $45 to $55 a share.

The only changes in the shareholders' equity for 2018 were those described above, 2018 net income, and cash dividends paid.

Required:

Explain how each of the following amounts should be determined when computing earnings per share for presentation in the income statements. For each, be specific as to the treatment of each item.

1. Numerator for basic EPS
2. Denominator for basic EPS
3. Numerator for diluted EPS
4. Denominator for diluted EPS

Analysis Case 19–9
EPS
● LO19–5 through LO19–8

"I guess I'll win that bet!" you announced to no one in particular.

"What bet?" Renee asked. Renee Patey was close enough to overhear you.

"When I bought my REC stock last year Randy insisted it was a mistake, that they were going to collapse. I bet him a Coke he was wrong. This press release says they have positive earnings," you bragged. Renee was looking over your shoulder now at the article you were pointing at:

> CHICAGO (ACCOUNTING WIRE)—July 1, 2018—Republic Enterprise Companies, Inc. (REC) today reported net income attributable to REC of $3.6 billion for the quarter ended May 31, 2018 . . . Diluted earnings per share attributable to REC were $1.52 for the second quarter of 2018, compared with $1.21 for the second quarter of 2017.
>
> Our Board of Directors . . . authorized the repurchase of shares of REC Common Stock, with an aggregate purchase price of up to $2.0 billion.

"A dollar fifty-two a share, huh?" Renee asked. "How many shares do you have? When do you get the check?"

Required:

1. Renee's questions imply that she thinks you will get cash dividends of $1.52 a share. What does earnings per share really tell you?
2. A previous press release indicated that "Share and per share amounts prior to the second quarter of 2016 have been restated to reflect the 1-for-20 reverse stock split effective June 30, 2016." What does that mean?
3. The press release indicates plans to repurchase shares of its own stock. Would the reduction in shares from a stock repurchase be taken into account when EPS is calculated? How?

Judgment Case 19–10
Where are the profits?
● LO19–4 through LO19–7, LO19–9

Del Conte Construction Company has experienced generally steady growth since its inception in 1953. Management is proud of its record of having maintained or increased its earnings per share in each year of its existence.

The economic downturn has led to disturbing dips in revenues the past two years. Despite concerted cost-cutting efforts, profits have declined in each of the two previous years. Net income in 2016, 2017, and 2018 was as follows:

2016	$145 million
2017	$134 million
2018	$ 95 million

A major shareholder has hired you to provide advice on whether to continue her present investment position or to curtail that position. Of particular concern is the declining profitability, despite the fact that earnings per share has continued a pattern of growth:

	Basic	Diluted
2016	$2.15	$1.91
2017	$2.44	$2.12
2018	$2.50	$2.50

She specifically asks you to explain this apparent paradox. During the course of your investigation you discover the following events:

- For the decade ending December 31, 2015, Del Conte had 60 million common shares and 20 million shares of 8%, $10 par nonconvertible preferred stock outstanding. Cash dividends have been paid quarterly on both.
- On July 1, 2017, half the preferred shares were retired in the open market. The remaining shares were retired on December 30, 2017.
- $55 million of 8% nonconvertible bonds were issued at the beginning of 2018, and a portion of the proceeds were used to call and retire $50 million of 10% debentures (outstanding since 2013) that were convertible into 9 million common shares.
- In 2016, management announced a share repurchase plan by which up to 24 million common shares would be retired. 12 million shares were retired on March 1 of both 2016 and 2017.
- Del Conte's income tax rate is 40% and has been for the last several years.

Required:

Explain the apparent paradox to which your client refers. Include calculations that demonstrate your explanation.

Communication Case 19–11
Dilution
● LO19–9

"I thought I understood earnings per share," lamented Brad Dawson, "but you're telling me we need to pretend our convertible bonds have been converted! Or maybe not?"

Dawson, your boss, is the new manager of the Fabricating division of BVT Corporation. His background is engineering and he has only a basic understanding of earnings per share. Knowing you are an accounting graduate, he asks you to explain the questions he has about the calculation of the company's EPS. His reaction is to your explanation that the company's convertible bonds might be included in this year's calculation.

"Put it in a memo!" he grumbled as he left your office.

Required:

Write a memo to Dawson. Explain the effect on earnings per share of each of the following:

1. Convertible securities.
2. Antidilutive securities.

Real World Case 19–12
Reporting EPS; discontinued operations; Kaman Corporation
● LO19–13

Real World Financials

Kaman Corporation, headquartered in Bloomfield, Connecticut, was incorporated in 1945. It is a diversified company that conducts business in the aerospace and distribution markets. The following is an excerpt from the comparative income statements (beginning with earnings from continuing operations) from Kaman's 2015 annual report ($ in thousands). A disclosure note from Kaman's 2015 annual report is shown below.

An income statement sometimes includes discontinued operations. Kaman Corporation reports income from discontinued operations.

17. COMPUTATION OF EARNINGS PER SHARE (in part)

The computation of basic earnings per share is based on net earnings divided by the weighted average number of shares of common stock outstanding for each year. The computation of diluted earnings per share includes the common stock equivalency of dilutive options granted to employees under the Stock Incentive Plan.

Excluded from the diluted earnings per share calculation for the years ended December 31, 2015, 2014 and 2013, respectively, are 487,071, 342,994 and 391,717 shares associated with equity awards granted to employees that are anti-dilutive based on the average stock price. Convertible Notes for the years ended December 31, 2015, 2014 and 2013, shares issuable under the Convertible Notes that were dilutive during the period were included in the calculation of earnings per share as the conversion price for the Convertible Notes was less than the average share price of the Company's stock. Warrants excluded from the diluted earnings per share calculation for the years ended December 31, 2015, 2014 and 2013, respectively were 3,422,477, 3,411,539, and 3,404,626 shares, issuable under the warrants sold in connection with the Company's Convertible Note offering as they would be anti-dilutive.

	For the year ended December 31,		
($ in thousands, except per share amounts)	2015	2014	2013
Earnings from continuing operations	$60,438	$65,780	$59,066
Loss from discontinued operations, net of tax	—	(2,924)	(2,386)
Gain (loss) on disposal of discontinued operations, net of tax	—	(4,984)	420
Net earnings	$60,438	$57,872	$57,100
Basic:			
Weighted average number of shares outstanding	27,177	27,053	26,744
Diluted:			
Weighted average number of shares outstanding	27,177	27,053	26,744
Weighted average shares issuable on exercise of dilutive stock options	133	147	159
Weighted average shares issuable on exercise of convertible notes	588	577	240
Total	27,868	27,777	27,143

Required:

1. The disclosure note shows adjustments for "shares issuable under the Convertible Notes that were dilutive during the period were included in the calculation of earnings per share." What other adjustments might be needed? Explain why and how these adjustments are made to the weighted-average shares outstanding.
2. The disclosure note indicates that the effect of some of the equity awards granted to employees were not included because they would be antidilutive. What does that mean? Why not include antidilutive securities?
3. Based on the information provided, prepare the presentation of basic and diluted earnings per share for 2015, 2014, and 2013 that Kaman reports in its 2015 annual report.

Analysis Case 19–13
Analyzing financial statements; price-earnings ratio; dividend payout ratio
● LO19–13

IGF Foods Company is a large, primarily domestic, consumer foods company involved in the manufacture, distribution, and sale of a variety of food products. Industry averages are derived from Troy's *The Almanac of Business and Industrial Financial Ratios* and Dun and Bradstreet's *Industry Norms and Key Business Ratios.* Following are the 2018 and 2017 comparative income statements and balance sheets for IGF. The market price of IGF's common stock is $47 during 2018. (The financial data we use are from actual financial statements of a well-known corporation, but the company name used in our illustration is fictitious and the numbers and dates have been modified slightly to disguise the company's identity.)

IGF FOODS COMPANY
Years Ended December 31, 2018 and 2017

($ in millions)	2018	2017
Comparative Income Statements		
Net sales	$6,440	$5,800
Cost of goods sold	(3,667)	(3,389)
Gross profit	2,773	2,411
Operating expenses	(1,916)	(1,629)
Operating income	857	782
Interest expense	(54)	(53)
Income from operations before tax	803	729
Income taxes	(316)	(287)
Net income	$ 487	$ 442
Net income per share	$ 2.69	$ 2.44
Average shares outstanding	181 million	181 million

($ in millions)	2018	2017
Comparative Balance Sheets		
Assets		
Total current assets	$1,879	$1,490
Property, plant, and equipment (net)	2,592	2,291
Intangibles (net)	800	843
Other assets	74	60
Total assets	$5,345	$4,684
Liabilities and Shareholders' Equity		
Total current liabilities	$1,473	$ 941
Long term debt	534	728
Deferred income taxes	407	344
Total liabilities	2,414	2,013
Shareholders' equity:		
Common stock	180	180
Additional paid-in capital	21	63
Retained earnings	2,730	2,428
Total shareholders' equity	2,931	2,671
Total liabilities and shareholders' equity	$5,345	$4,684

Some ratios express income, dividends, and market prices on a per share basis. As such, these ratios appeal primarily to common shareholders, particularly when weighing investment possibilities. These ratios focus less on the fundamental soundness of a company and more on its investment characteristics.

Required:

1. Earnings per share expresses a firm's profitability on a per share basis. Calculate 2018 earnings per share for IGF.
2. Calculate IGF's 2018 price-earnings ratio. The average price-earnings ratio for the stocks listed on the New York Stock Exchange in a comparable time period was 18.5. What does your calculation indicate about IGF's earnings?
3. Calculate IGF's 2018 dividend payout ratio. What information does the calculation provide an investor?

Research Case 19–14
Determining and comparing price-earnings ratios; retrieving stock prices and earnings per share numbers from the Internet
● LO19–13

Many sites on the Internet allow the retrieval of current stock price information. Among those sites are Marketwatch (marketwatch.com) and Quicken (www.quicken.com).

Required:

1. Access any site on the Internet that permits you to get a current stock quote. Determine the current price of Microsoft Corporation's common stock (MSFT) and that of Intel Corporation (INTC).
2. Access EDGAR on the Internet at www.sec.gov. Search for Microsoft and access its most recent 10-K filing. Search or scroll to find the income statement and related note(s). Determine the most recent earnings per share. Repeat this step for Intel.
3. Calculate the price-earnings ratio for each company.
4. Compare the PE ratios of Microsoft and Intel. What information might be gleaned from your comparison?

Analysis Case 19–15
Kellogg's EPS; PE ratio; dividend payout
● LO19–13

Real World Financials

While eating his Kellogg's Frosted Flakes one January morning, Tony noticed the following article in his local paper:

Kellogg Company Reports Fourth-Quarter and Full-Year Results and Provides Guidance For 2016 (in part)

BATTLE CREEK, Mich., Feb. 11, 2016 /PRNewswire/—Kellogg Company (NYSE: K) Reported full-year 2015 net earnings $614 million, or $1.72 per share.

As a shareholder, Tony is well aware that Kellogg pays a regular cash dividend of $0.50 per share quarterly. A quick click on a price quote service indicated that Kellogg's shares closed at $72.27 on December 31.

Required:

1. Using the numbers provided, determine the price-earnings ratio for Kellogg Company for 2015. What information does this ratio impart?
2. What is the dividend payout ratio for Kellogg? What does it indicate?

Research Case 19–16
FASB codification; locate and extract relevant information and cite authoritative support for a financial reporting issue; change in classification of a share-based compensation instrument
● LO19–13

"Now what do I do?" moaned your colleague, Matt. "This is a first for me," he confided. You and Matt are recent hires in the Accounting Division of National Paper. A top executive in the company has been given share-based incentive instruments that permit her to receive shares of National Paper equal in value to the amount the company shares rise above the shares' value two years ago when the instruments were issued to her as compensation. The instruments vest in three years. A clause was included in the compensation agreement that would permit her to receive cash rather than shares upon exercise if sales revenue in her division were to double by that time. Because that contingency was considered unlikely, the instruments have been accounted for as equity, with the grant date fair value being expensed over the five-year vesting period.

Now, though, surging sales of her division indicate that the contingent event has become probable, and the instruments should be accounted for as a liability rather than equity. The fair value of the award was estimated at $5 million on the grant date, but now is $8 million. Matt has asked your help in deciding what to recommend to your controller as the appropriate action to take at this point.

Required:

1. Obtain the relevant authoritative literature on accounting for a change in classification due to a change in probable settlement outcome using the *FASB Accounting Standards Codification* at the FASB website (www.fasb.org). Explain to Matt the basic treatment of the situation described. What is the specific citation that you would rely on in applying that accounting treatment?
2. Prepare the journal entry to record the change in circumstance.

Continuing Cases

Target Case
● LO3–2, LO3–3, LO3–8

Target Corporation prepares its financial statements according to U.S. GAAP. Target's financial statements and disclosure notes for the year ended January 30, 2016, are available in Connect. This material is also available under the Investor Relations link at the company's website (www.target.com). Target's share-based compensation includes several long-term incentive plans.

Required:

1. Over how many years is the compensation associated with Target's share-based awards expensed?
2. Based on the fair value of the awards, what was Target's primary form of share-based compensation for the year ended January 30, 2016?

3. If projecting Target's earnings per share based solely on EPS reported over the most recent three years, would you project increasing or decreasing EPS?
4. How many shares were included in diluted earnings per share but not basic earnings per share due to share-based compensation awards?

Air France–KLM Case

IFRS

● LO19–9

Air France–KLM (AF), a Franco-Dutch company, prepares its financial statements according to International Financial Reporting Standards. AF's financial statements and disclosure notes for the year ended December 31, 2015, are available in Connect. This material is also available under the Finance link at the company's website (www.airfranceklm-finance.com).

Required:

1. AF provides share-based compensation in the form of PPSs, Phantom Performance Shares. Recipients receive compensation in what form? How are such plans reported in the balance sheet? [Hint: See Note 30: "Share-Based Compensation."] Are AF's PPSs cliff vesting or graded vesting? How does accounting differ between U.S. GAAP and IFRS for graded-vesting plans?
2. What amount(s) of earnings per share did AF report in its income statement for the year ended December 31, 2015? If AF used U.S. GAAP, would it have reported EPS using the same classification?

CPA Exam Questions and Simulations

ROGER CPA Review

Sample CPA Exam questions from Roger CPA Review are available in Connect as support for the topics in this chapter. These Multiple Choice Questions and Task-Based Simulations include expert-written explanations and solutions, and provide a starting point for students to become familiar with the content and functionality of the actual CPA Exam.

CHAPTER

20 Accounting Changes and Error Corrections

OVERVIEW

Chapter 4 provided a brief overview of accounting changes and error correction. Later, we discussed changes encountered in connection with specific assets and liabilities as we dealt with those topics in subsequent chapters.

Here we revisit accounting changes and error correction to synthesize the way these are handled in a variety of situations that might be encountered in practice. We see that most changes in accounting principle are reported retrospectively. Changes in estimates are accounted for prospectively. A change in depreciation methods is considered a change in estimate resulting from a change in principle. Both changes in reporting entities and the correction of errors are reported retrospectively.

LEARNING OBJECTIVES

After studying this chapter, you should be able to:

- **LO20–1** Differentiate among the three types of accounting changes and distinguish among the retrospective, modified retrospective, and prospective approaches to accounting for and reporting accounting changes. *(p. 1160)*
- **LO20–2** Describe how changes in accounting principle typically are reported. *(p. 1162)*
- **LO20–3** Explain how and why some changes in accounting principle are reported prospectively. *(p. 1166)*
- **LO20–4** Explain how and why changes in estimates are reported prospectively. *(p. 1168)*
- **LO20–5** Describe the situations that constitute a change in reporting entity. *(p. 1171)*
- **LO20–6** Understand and apply the four-step process of correcting and reporting errors, regardless of the type of error or the timing of its discovery. *(p. 1174)*
- **LO20–7** Discuss the primary differences between U.S. GAAP and IFRS with respect to accounting changes and error corrections. *(pp. 1167, 1174, and 1181)*

© REUTERS/Alamy Stock Photo

FINANCIAL REPORTING CASE

In a Jam

"What the heck!" Martin yelped as he handed you the annual report of J.M. Smucker he'd received in the mail today. "It looks like Smucker found a bunch of lost jelly. It says here that their inventory was $54 million last year. I distinctly remember them reporting that number last year as $52 million because my dad was born in '52, and I did a little wordplay in my mind about him 'taking inventory' of his life when he bought the red Mustang." He had circled the number in the comparative balance sheets. "When I bought Smucker shares last year, I promised myself I would monitor things pretty closely, but it's not as easy as I thought it would be."

As an accounting graduate, you can understand Martin's confusion. Flipping to the disclosure note on accounting changes, you proceed to clear things up for him.

QUESTIONS

By the time you finish this chapter, you should be able to respond appropriately to the questions posed in this case. Compare your response to the solution provided at the end of the chapter.

1. How can an accounting change cause a company to increase a previously reported inventory amount? *(p. 1163)*
2. Are all accounting changes reported this way? *(p. 1169)*

You learned early in your study of accounting that two of the qualitative characteristics of accounting information that contribute to its relevance and representational faithfulness are *consistency* and *comparability*. Though we strive to achieve and maintain these financial reporting attributes, we cannot ignore the forces of change. Ours is a dynamic business environment. The economy is increasingly a global one. Technological advances constantly transform both day-to-day operations and the flow of information about those operations. The accounting profession's response to the fluid environment often means issuing new standards that require companies to change accounting methods. Often, developments within an industry or the economy will prompt a company to voluntarily switch methods of accounting or to revise estimates or expectations. In short, change is inevitable. The question then becomes a matter of how best to address change when reporting financial information from year to year.

In the first part of this chapter, we differentiate among the various types of accounting changes that businesses face, with a focus on the most meaningful and least disruptive ways to report those changes. Then, in the second part of the chapter, we direct our attention to a closely related circumstance—the correction of errors.

PART A

Accounting Changes

Accounting changes fall into one of the three categories listed in Illustration 20–1.[1]

[1]FASB ASC 250: Accounting Changes and Error Corrections (previously "Accounting Changes and Error Corrections–A Replacement of APB Opinion No. 20 and FASB Statement No. 3," *Statement of Financial Accounting Standards No. 154* (Norwalk, Conn.: FASB, 2005)).

Illustration 20–1
Types of Accounting Changes

● LO20–1

Type of Change	Description	Examples
Change in accounting principle	Change from one generally accepted accounting principle to another.	• Adopt a new Accounting Standard. • Change methods of inventory costing. • Change from cost method to equity method, or vice versa.
Change in accounting estimate	Revise an estimate because of new information or new experience.	• Change depreciation methods.* • Change estimate of useful life of depreciable asset. • Change estimate of residual value of depreciable asset. • Change estimate of periods benefited by intangible assets. • Change actuarial estimates pertaining to a pension plan.
Change in reporting entity	Change from reporting as one type of entity to another type of entity.	• Consolidate a subsidiary not previously included in consolidated financial statements. • Report consolidated financial statements in place of individual statements.

*A change in depreciation methods is a change in estimate that is achieved by a change in accounting principle.

The correction of an error is another adjustment sometimes made to financial statements that is not actually an accounting change but is accounted for similarly. Errors occur when transactions are either recorded incorrectly or not recorded at all, as shown in Illustration 20–2.

Illustration 20–2
Correction of Errors

Type of Change	Description	Examples
Error correction	Correct an error caused by a transaction being recorded incorrectly or not at all.	• Mathematical mistakes. • Inaccurate physical count of inventory. • Change from the cash basis of accounting to the accrual basis. • Failure to record an adjusting entry. • Recording an asset as an expense, or vice versa. • Fraud or gross negligence.

Three approaches to reporting accounting changes and error corrections are used, depending on the situation.

The retrospective approach offers consistency and comparability.

1. Using the **retrospective approach**, financial statements issued prior to the change are adjusted to reflect the impact of the change whenever those statements are presented again for comparative purposes (comparative financial statements). For each year reported in the comparative statements, the balance of each account affected is adjusted to incorporate the change. So for the first period presented in the comparative statements, the adjusted balances include the cumulative effect of the change prior to that date. In other words, those statements are made to appear as if the newly adopted accounting method had been applied all along or that the error had never occurred. Then, a journal entry is created to adjust all account balances affected to what those amounts would have been. In addition, if retained earnings is one of the accounts that requires adjustment, that adjustment is made

to the beginning balance of retained earnings for the earliest period reported in the comparative statements of shareholders' equity. An advantage of this approach is that it achieves comparability among financial statements. All financial statements presented are prepared on the same basis. However, some argue that public confidence in the integrity of financial data suffers when numbers previously reported as correct are later superseded. On the other hand, proponents argue the opposite—that it's impossible to maintain public confidence unless the financial statements are comparable.

2. The **modified retrospective approach** requires application of the new standard only to the adoption period (that is, the current period) as well as adjustment of the balance of retained earnings at the beginning of the adoption period to capture the cumulative effects of prior periods without actually adjusting the numbers in the prior periods reported.
3. The **prospective approach** requires neither a modification of prior years' financial statements nor a journal entry to adjust account balances. Instead, the change is simply implemented in the period of the change, and its effects are reflected in the financial statements of the period of the change and future periods only.

The effects of a change are reflected in the financial statements of only the in the year of the change and future years under the *prospective approach*.

Now, let's look at each type of accounting change, one at a time, focusing on the selective application of these approaches.

Change in Accounting Principle

Accounting is not an exact science. Professional judgment is required to apply a set of principles, concepts, and objectives to specific sets of circumstances. This means choices must be made. In your study of accounting to date, you've encountered many areas where choices are necessary. For example, management must choose whether to use accelerated or straight-line depreciation. Is FIFO, LIFO, or average cost most appropriate to measure inventories? Should we adopt a new accounting standard early or wait until it's mandatory? These are but a few of the accounting choices management makes.

Although consistency and comparability are desirable, changing to a new method sometimes is appropriate.

You also probably recall that comparability is an enhancing qualitative characteristic of financial reporting. To achieve this attribute of information, accounting choices, once made, should be consistently followed from year to year. This doesn't mean, though, that methods can never be changed. Changing circumstances might make a new method more appropriate. A change in economic conditions, for instance, might prompt a company to change accounting methods. The most extensive voluntary accounting change ever—a switch by hundreds of companies from FIFO to LIFO in the mid-1970s, for example—was a result of heightened inflation. Changes within a specific industry, too, can lead a company to switch methods, often to adapt to new technology or to be consistent with others in the industry. And, of course, a change might be mandated when the FASB codifies a new accounting standard. For these reasons, it's not uncommon for a company to switch from one accounting method to another. This is called a **change in accounting principle**.

Decision Makers' Perspective—Motivation for Accounting Choices

It would be nice to think that all accounting choices are made by management in the best interest of fair and consistent financial reporting. Unfortunately, other motives influence the choices among accounting methods and whether to change methods. It has been suggested that the effect of choices on management compensation, on existing debt agreements, and on union negotiations each can affect management's selection of accounting methods.[2] For instance, research has suggested that managers of companies with bonus plans are more likely to choose accounting methods that maximize their bonuses (often those that increase net income).[3] Other research has indicated that the existence and nature of debt agreements

[2]R. L. Watts and J. L. Zimmerman, "Towards a Positive Theory of the Determination of Accounting Standards," *The Accounting Review*, January 1978, and "Positive Accounting Theory: A Ten Year Perspective," *The Accounting Review*, January 1990.

[3]For example, see P. M. Healy, "The Effect of Bonus Schemes on Accounting Decisions," *Journal of Accounting and Economics*, April 1985; and D. Dhaliwal, G. Salamon, and E. Smith, "The Effect of Owner versus Management Control on the Choice of Accounting Methods," *Journal of Accounting and Economics*, July 1992.

and other aspects of a firm's capital structure can influence accounting choices.[4] Whether a company is forbidden from paying dividends if retained earnings fall below a certain level, for example, can affect the choice of accounting methods.

A financial analyst must be aware that different accounting methods used by different firms, and by the same firm in different years, complicate comparisons. Financial ratios, for example, will differ when different accounting methods are used, even when there are no differences in attributes being compared.

Investors and creditors also should be alert to instances in which companies change accounting methods. They must consider not only the effect on comparability but also possible hidden motivations for making the changes. Are managers trying to compensate for a downturn in actual performance with a switch to methods that artificially inflate reported earnings? Is the firm in danger of violating debt covenants or other contractual agreements regarding financial position? Are executive compensation plans tied to reported performance measures? Fortunately, the nature and effect of changes are reported in the financial statements. Although a justification for a change is provided by management, analysts should be wary of accepting the reported justification at face value without considering a possible hidden agenda.

Choices are not always those that tend to increase income. As you learned in Chapter 8, many companies use the LIFO inventory method because it reduces income and therefore reduces the amount of income taxes that must be paid currently. Also, some very large and visible companies might be reluctant to report high income that might render them vulnerable to union demands, government regulations, or higher taxes.[5]

Another reason managers sometimes choose accounting methods that don't necessarily increase earnings was mentioned earlier. Most managers tend to prefer to report earnings that follow a regular, smooth trend from year to year. The desire to "smooth" earnings means that any attempt to manipulate earnings by choosing accounting methods is not always in the direction of higher income. Instead, the choice might be to avoid irregular earnings, particularly those with wide variations from year to year, a pattern that might be interpreted by analysts as denoting a risky situation.

Obviously, any time managers make accounting choices for any of the reasons discussed here, when the motivation is an objective other than to provide useful information, earnings quality suffers. As mentioned frequently throughout this text, earnings quality refers to the ability of reported earnings (income) to predict a company's future earnings.

A notable example of alleged "cooking the books" involved General Electric. The company was often suspected of using "cookie jar accounting," the practice of using unrealistic estimates and strategic choices of accounting methods to smooth out its earnings. In 2009, GE appeared to get its hand caught in the cookie jar for going beyond acceptable limits. GE paid a $50 million civil penalty to settle charges by the Securities and Exchange Commission accusing the company of violating U.S. securities laws four times between 2002 and 2003 to help it maintain a succession of earnings reports that beat Wall Street expectations each quarter from 1995 through 2004.

Let's turn our attention now to situations involving changes in methods and how we account for those changes. ●

The Retrospective Approach: Most Changes in Accounting Principle

● LO20–2

We report most voluntary changes in accounting principles retrospectively.[6] This means reporting all previous period's financial statements as if the new method had been used in all prior periods. An example is provided in Illustration 20–3.

---

[4]R. M. Bowen, E. W. Noreen, and J. M. Lacy, "Determinants of the Corporate Decision to Capitalize Interest," *Journal of Accounting and Economics,* August 1981.

[5]This political cost motive is suggested by R. L. Watts and J. L. Zimmerman, "Positive Accounting Theory: A Ten Year Perspective," *The Accounting Review,* January 1990, and M. Zmijewski and R. Hagerman, "An Income Strategy Approach to the Positive Theory of Accounting Standard Setting/Choice," *Journal of Accounting and Economics,* August 1981.

[6]FASB ASC 250–10–45: Accounting Changes and Error Corrections–Overall–Other Presentation Matters (previously "Accounting Changes and Error Corrections–A Replacement of APB Opinion No. 20 and FASB Statement No. 3," *Statement of Financial Accounting Standards No. 154* (Norwalk, Conn.: FASB, 2005)).

Air Parts Corporation used the LIFO inventory costing method. At the beginning of 2018, Air Parts decided to change to the FIFO method. Income components for 2018 and prior years were as follows:

($ in millions)	2018	2017	2016	Previous Years
Cost of goods sold (LIFO)	$430	$420	$405	$2,000
Cost of goods sold (FIFO)	370	365	360	1,700
Difference	$ 60	$ 55	$ 45	$ 300
Revenues	$950	$900	$875	$4,500
Operating expenses	230	210	205	1,000

Air Parts has paid dividends of $40 million each year beginning in 2011. Its income tax rate is 40%. Retained earnings on January 1, 2016, was $700 million; inventory was $500 million.

Illustration 20–3
Change in Accounting Principle

LIFO usually produces higher cost of goods sold than does FIFO because more recently purchased goods (usually higher priced) are assumed sold first.

1. REVISE COMPARATIVE FINANCIAL STATEMENTS. For each year reported in the comparative statements, Air Parts makes those statements appear as if the newly adopted accounting method (FIFO) had been applied all along. As you learned in Chapter 1, comparability is one of the important qualitative characteristics of accounting information.

When accounting changes occur, the usefulness of the comparative financial statements is enhanced with retrospective application of those changes.

FINANCIAL Reporting Case

Q1, p. 1159

Income Statements

($ in millions)	2018	2017	2016
Revenues	$950	$900	$875
Cost of goods sold (FIFO)	(370)	(365)	(360)
Operating expenses	(230)	(210)	(205)
Income before tax	350	325	310
Income tax expense (40%)	(140)	(130)	(124)
Net income	$210	$195	$186

The company recasts the comparative statements to appear as if the accounting method adopted in 2018 (FIFO) had been used in 2017 and 2016 as well.

Earnings per share each year, of course, also will be based on the revised net income numbers.

Balance Sheets

Inventory. In its comparative balance sheets, Air Parts will report 2018 inventory by its newly adopted method, FIFO, and also will revise the amounts it reported last year for its 2017 and 2016 inventory. Each year, inventory will be higher than it would have been by LIFO. Here's why:

Since the cost of goods *available for sale* each period is the sum of the cost of goods *sold* and the cost of goods *unsold* (inventory), a difference in cost of goods sold resulting from having used LIFO rather than FIFO means there also is an opposite difference in inventory. Because cost of goods sold by the FIFO method is *less* than by LIFO, inventory by FIFO is *greater* than by LIFO. The amounts of the differences and also the cumulative differences over the years are calculated in Illustration 20–3A.

FIFO usually produces *lower* cost of goods sold and thus *higher* inventory than does LIFO.

Retained earnings. Similarly, Air Parts will report retained earnings by FIFO each year as well. Retained earnings is different because the two inventory methods affect income differently. Because cost of goods sold by FIFO is *less* than by LIFO, income and therefore retained earnings by FIFO are *greater* than by LIFO.

Comparative balance sheets, then, will report retained earnings for 2018, 2017, and 2016 at amounts $276, $240, and $207 million higher than would have been reported if the switch from LIFO had not occurred. These are the cumulative net income differences shown in Illustration 20–3A.

When costs are rising, FIFO produces *lower* cost of goods sold than does LIFO and thus *higher* net income and retained earnings.

Retained earnings is revised each year to reflect FIFO.

Illustration 20–3A

Effects of Switch to FIFO

By FIFO, cost of goods sold is lower.

The cumulative income effect increases each year by the annual after-tax difference in COGS.

Inventory, pretax income, income taxes, net income, and retained earnings all are higher.

($ in millions)	2018	2017	2016	Previous Years
	Years Ending Dec. 31			
Cost of goods sold (LIFO)	$430	$420	$405	$2,000
Cost of goods sold (FIFO)	370	365	360	1,700
Differences	$ 60	$ 55	$ 45	$ 300
Cumulative differences:				
Cost of goods sold	$460	$400	$345	$ 300
Income taxes (40%)	184	160	138	120
Net income and retained earnings	$276	$240	$207	$ 180

Comparative balance sheets, then, will report 2016 inventory $345 million higher than it was reported in last year's statements. Likewise, 2017 inventory will be increased by $400 million. Inventory for 2018, being reported for the first time, is $460 million higher than it would have been if the switch from LIFO had not occurred.

Statements of shareholders' equity. Recall that a statement of shareholders' equity reports changes that occur in each shareholders' equity account starting with the beginning balances in the earliest year reported.

Because it's the earliest year reported, 2016's beginning retained earnings is increased by the $180 million cumulative income effect of the difference in inventory methods that occurred before 2016.

So, if retained earnings is one of the accounts whose balance requires adjustment due to a change in accounting principle (and it usually is), we must adjust the beginning balance of retained earnings for the earliest period reported in the comparative statements of shareholders' equity. The amount of the revision is the cumulative effect of the change on years prior to that date. Air Parts will revise its 2016 beginning retained earnings since that's the earliest year in its comparative statements. That balance had been reported in prior statements as $700 million. If FIFO had been used for inventory rather than LIFO, that amount would have been higher by $180 million, as calculated in Illustration 20–3A. The disclosure note pertaining to the inventory change should point out the amount of the adjustment. The January 1, 2016, retained earnings balance reported in the comparative statements of shareholders' equity in Illustration 20–3B has been adjusted from $700 million to $880 million.

Illustration 20–3B

Comparative Statements of Shareholders' Equity

A disclosure note should indicate that the beginning retained earnings balance has been increased by $180 million, from $700 million to $880 million.

($ in millions)	Common Stock	Additional Paid-In Capital	Retained Earnings	Total Shareholders' Equity
Jan. 1, 2016			$ 880	
Net income (*revised* to FIFO)			186	
Dividends			(40)	
Dec. 31, 2016			$1,026	
Net income (*revised* to FIFO)			195	
Dividends			(40)	
Dec. 31, 2017			$1,181	
Net income (*using* FIFO)			210	
Dividends			(40)	
Dec. 31, 2018			$1,351	

2. ADJUST ACCOUNTS FOR THE CHANGE. Besides reporting revised amounts in the comparative financial statements, Air Parts must also adjust the book balances of affected accounts. It does so by creating a journal entry to change those balances from their current amounts (from using LIFO) to what those balances would have been using the newly adopted method (FIFO). As discussed in the previous section, differences in cost of goods sold and income are reflected in retained earnings, as are the income tax effects of changes in income. So, the journal entry updates inventory, retained earnings, and the income tax liability for revisions resulting from differences in the LIFO and FIFO methods prior to the switch, pre-2018. Repeating a portion of the calculation we made in Illustration 20–3A, we determine the difference in cost of goods sold and therefore in inventory.

($ in millions)	2017	2016	Cumulative Difference pre-2016	Cumulative Difference pre-2018
Cost of goods sold (LIFO)	$420	$405	$1,000	
Cost of goods sold (FIFO)	365	360	700	
Difference	$ 55	$ 45	$ 300	$400

Cost of goods sold would have been $400 million less if FIFO rather than LIFO had been used in years before the change.

The $400 million cumulative difference in cost of goods sold also is the difference between the balance in inventory and what that balance would have been if the FIFO method, rather than LIFO, had been used before 2018. Inventory must be increased by that amount. Retained earnings must be increased also, but by only 60% of that amount because income taxes would have been higher by 40% of the change in pretax income.

Journal entry to record the change in principle

January 1, 2018		
Inventory (additional inventory if FIFO had been used)	400	
Retained earnings (additional net income if FIFO had been used)		240
Income tax payable ($400 × 40%)		160

Inventory would have been $400 million more and cumulative prior earnings $240 more if FIFO rather than LIFO had been used.

Notice that the income tax effect is reflected in the income tax payable account. The reason is that, unlike for other accounting method changes, the Internal Revenue Code requires that the inventory costing method used for tax purposes must be the same as that used for financial reporting. For that reason, the tax code allows a retrospective change in an inventory method, but then requires that taxes saved previously ($160 million in this case) from having used another inventory method must now be repaid. However, taxpayers are given up to six years to pay the tax due. As a result, this liability has both a current portion (payable within one year) and a noncurrent portion (payable after one year), but is not a deferred tax liability.

Additional Consideration

What if the tax law did not require a recapture of the tax difference? Then there would be a credit to a deferred tax liability. That's because retrospectively increasing accounting income, but not taxable income, creates a temporary difference between the two that will reverse over time as the unsold inventory becomes cost of goods sold. Recall from Chapter 16 that in the meantime, there is a temporary difference, reflected in the deferred tax liability.

If we were switching from FIFO to, say, the average method, we would record a deferred tax asset instead. For financial reporting purposes, but not for tax, we would be retrospectively decreasing accounting income, but not taxable income. This creates a temporary difference between the two that will reverse over time as the unsold inventory becomes cost of goods sold. When that happens, taxable income will be less than accounting income. When taxable income will be less than accounting income as a temporary difference reverses, we have a "future deductible amount" and record a deferred tax asset.

3. DISCLOSURE NOTES. To achieve consistency and comparability, accounting choices once made should be consistently followed from year to year. Any change, then, requires that the new method be justified as clearly more appropriate. In the first set of financial statements after the change, a disclosure note is needed to provide that justification. The note also should point out that comparative information has been revised, or that retrospective revision has not been made because it is impracticable, and report any per share amounts affected for the current period and all prior periods presented. Disclosure of a recent change

Note disclosure explains why the change was needed as well as its effects on items not reported on the face of the primary statements.

by **Abercrombie & Fitch** in a recent annual report provides us the example shown in Illustration 20–4.

Illustration 20–4

Disclosure of a Change in Inventory Method—Abercrombie & Fitch

Real World Financials

> **4. CHANGE IN ACCOUNTING PRINCIPLE**
>
> The Company elected to change its method of accounting for inventory from the lower of cost or market utilizing the retail method to the weighted average cost method. . . . In accordance with generally accepted accounting principles, all periods have been retroactively adjusted to reflect the period-specific effects of the change to the weighted average cost method. The Company believes that accounting under the weighted average cost method is preferable as it better aligns with the Company's focus on realized selling margin and improves the comparability of the Company's financial results with those of its competitors. Additionally, it will improve the matching of cost of goods sold with the related net sales and reflect the acquisition cost of inventory outstanding at each balance sheet date. The cumulative adjustment . . . was an increase in its inventory of $73.6 million and an increase in retained earnings of $47.3 million.

The Modified Retrospective Approach

When a new FASB accounting standard update mandates a change in accounting principle, the Board typically specifies the way companies should implement the change and often allows companies to choose among multiple ways of accounting for the change. One approach usually allowed is the retrospective approach we discussed for voluntary changes in accounting principle, by which the new standard is applied retrospectively to all periods presented in the financial statements. And, as we discuss in the next section, sometimes the prospective approach is allowed or mandated for a new standard. A third approach the FASB sometimes allows is a *modified retrospective approach.* By this approach, we apply the new standard only to the adoption period (that is, the current period) and then adjust the balance of retained earnings at the beginning of the adoption period to capture the cumulative effects of prior periods without actually adjusting the numbers in the prior periods reported.

The Prospective Approach

● LO20–3

Although we usually report voluntary changes in accounting principles retrospectively, it's not always practicable or appropriate to do so.

THE PROSPECTIVE APPROACH: WHEN RETROSPECTIVE APPLICATION IS IMPRACTICABLE. For some changes in principle, insufficient information is available for retrospective application to be practicable. Revising balances in prior years means knowing what those balances should be. But suppose we're switching from the FIFO method of inventory costing to the LIFO method. Recall from your study of inventory costing methods that LIFO inventory consists of "layers" added in prior years at costs existing in those years. If another method has been used, though, the company likely hasn't kept track of those costs. So, accounting records of prior years usually are inadequate to report the change retrospectively. In that case, a company changing *to* LIFO usually reports the change prospectively, and the beginning inventory in the year the LIFO method is adopted becomes the base year inventory for all future LIFO calculations. A disclosure note should indicate reasons why retrospective application was impracticable. Prospective changes usually are accounted for as of the beginning of the year of change.

Sometimes a lack of information makes it impracticable to report a change retrospectively so the new method is simply applied prospectively.

When **Books A Million, Inc.**, adopted the LIFO cost flow assumption for valuing its inventories, the change was reported in a disclosure note as shown in Illustration 20–5.

When it is impracticable to determine some period-specific effects. A company may have some, but not all, the information it needs to account for a change retrospectively. For instance, let's say a company changes to the LIFO inventory method effective as of the beginning of 2018. It has information that would allow it to revise all assets and liabilities on the basis of the newly adopted method for 2017 in its comparative

If it's impracticable to adjust each year reported, the change is applied retrospectively as of the earliest year practicable.

Inventories (in part)

. . . the Company changed from the first-in, first-out (FIFO) method of accounting for inventories to the last-in, first-out (LIFO) method. Management believes this change was preferable in that it achieves a more appropriate matching of revenues and expenses. The impact of this accounting change was to increase "Costs of Products Sold" in the consolidated statements of operations by $0.7 million for the fiscal year. . . . The cumulative effect of a change in accounting principle from the FIFO method to LIFO method is not determinable. Accordingly, such change has been accounted for prospectively.

Illustration 20–5

Disclosure of a Change to LIFO—Books A Million, Inc.

Real World Financials

statements, but not for 2016. In that case, the company should report 2017 statement amounts (revised) and 2018 statement amounts (reported without restatement for the first time) based on LIFO, but not revise 2016 numbers. Then, account balances should be retrospectively adjusted at the beginning of 2017 since that's the earliest date it's practicable to do so.

When it is impracticable to determine the cumulative effect of prior years. Another possibility is that the company doesn't have the information necessary to retrospectively adjust retained earnings, but does have information that would allow it to revise all assets and liabilities for one or more specific years. Let's say the records of inventory purchases and sales are not available for some previous years, which would have allowed it to determine the cumulative effect of applying this change to LIFO retrospectively. However, it does have all of the information necessary to apply the LIFO method on a prospective basis beginning in, say, 2016. In that case, the company should report numbers for years beginning in 2016 as if it had carried forward the 2015 ending balance in inventory (measured on the previous inventory costing basis) and then had begun applying LIFO as of January 1, 2016. Of course there would be no adjustment to retained earnings for the cumulative income effect of not using LIFO prior to that.

If full retrospective application isn't possible, the new method is applied prospectively beginning in the earliest year practicable.

THE PROSPECTIVE APPROACH: WHEN MANDATED BY AUTHORITATIVE ACCOUNTING LITERATURE. Another exception to retrospective application of voluntary changes in accounting principle is when authoritative literature requires prospective application for specific changes in accounting methods. For instance, for a change from the equity method to another method of accounting for long-term investments, GAAP requires the prospective application of the new method.[7] Recall from Chapter 12 that when an investor's level of influence changes, it may be necessary to change from the equity method to another method. This could happen, for instance, if a sale of shares causes the investor's ownership interest to fall from, say, 25% to 15%, resulting in the equity method no longer being appropriate. When this situation happens, no adjustment is made to the remaining book value, sometimes called carrying value or carrying amount of the investment. Instead, the equity method is simply discontinued and the new method applied from then on. The balance in the investment account when the equity method is discontinued would serve as the new "cost" basis for writing the investment up or down to fair value on the next set of financial statements.

If a new accounting standards update specifically requires prospective accounting, that requirement is followed.

International Financial Reporting Standards

In previous chapters we discussed the possibility that U.S. companies will be required to or may choose to switch from U.S. GAAP to international financial reporting standards. When a company moves for the first time from U.S. GAAP to IFRS it should follow the requirements of *IFRS No. 1:* "First-time Adoption of International Financial Reporting Standards."

(continued)

● LO20–7

[7]FASB ACS 323–10–35–36: Investments–Equity Method and Joint Ventures–Overall–Subsequent Measurement–Decrease in Level of Ownership or Degree of Influence (previously "The Equity Method of Accounting for Investments in Common Stock," *Accounting Principles Board Opinion No. 18* (New York: AICPA, 1971)).

(concluded)

The basic requirement is full retrospective application of IFRS for the company's first IFRS financial statements. A company's first IFRS financial statements must include at least three balance sheets and two of each of the other financial statements. For instance, if the company's first IFRS reporting period is for the year ended December 31, 2020, the first balance sheet will be the opening balance sheet of 2019, which is the ending balance sheet of 2018. The other two balance sheets and each of the other statements—income statement, statement of comprehensive income, statement of cash flows, statements of changes in equity—are for the years ended December 31, 2019, and December 31, 2020. The date of transition to IFRS is the date of the opening balance sheet, January 1, 2019, in this situation.

First-time application of IFRS entails:

- Recording some assets and liabilities not permitted under U.S. GAAP, such as some provisions (contingent liabilities) permitted under IFRS but not U.S. GAAP.
- *Not* recording (derecognizing) some assets and liabilities, for example, an intangible asset for research expenditures, permitted under U.S. GAAP but not IFRS.
- Reclassifying items that are classified differently under the two sets of standards, for instance, reclassifying some preferred shares from shareholder equity classification under U.S. GAAP to liability classification under IFRS.
- Providing disclosures (in notes to the financial statements) required under IFRS but not U.S. GAAP.
- Providing extensive disclosures to explain how the transition to IFRS affected the company's financial position, financial performance, and cash flows. These disclosures include (a) providing explanations of material adjustments to the balance sheet, income statement, and cash flow statement; and (b) reconciliations of equity and total comprehensive income reported under previous GAAP to equity under IFRS.

THE PROSPECTIVE APPROACH: CHANGING DEPRECIATION, AMORTIZATION, AND DEPLETION METHODS. A change in depreciation methods is considered to be a change in accounting estimate that is achieved by a change in accounting principle. As a result, we account for such a change prospectively—precisely the way we account for changes in estimates. We discuss that approach in the next section.

Change in Accounting Estimate

LO20–4

You've encountered many instances during your study of accounting in which it's necessary to make estimates of uncertain future events. Depreciation, for example, entails estimates not only of the useful lives of depreciable assets, but their anticipated residual values as well. Anticipating uncollectible accounts receivable, predicting warranty expenses, amortizing intangible assets, and making actuarial assumptions for pension benefits are but a few of the accounting tasks that require estimates.

Revisions are viewed as a natural consequence of making estimates.

Accordingly, estimates are an inherent aspect of accounting. Unfortunately, though, estimates routinely turn out to be wrong. No matter how carefully known facts are considered and forecasts are prepared, new information and experience frequently force the revision of estimates. Of course, if the original estimate was based on erroneous information or calculations or was not made in good faith, the revision of that estimate constitutes the correction of an error.

A change in estimate is reflected in the financial statements of the current period and future periods.

Changes in accounting estimates are accounted for prospectively. When a company revises a previous estimate, prior financial statements are *not* revised. Instead, the company merely incorporates the new estimate in any related accounting determinations from then on. So, it usually will affect some aspects of both the balance sheet and the income statement in the current period and future periods. A disclosure note should describe the effect of a change in estimate on income from continuing operations, net income, and related per share amounts for the current period.

When Owens-Corning Fiberglass revised estimates of the useful lives of some of its depreciable assets, the change was disclosed in its annual report as shown in Illustration 20–6.

Illustration 20–6

Change in Estimate—Owens-Corning Fiberglass Corporation

Real World Financials

Note 6: Depreciation of Plant and Equipment (in part)

. . . the Company completed a review of its fixed asset lives. The Company determined that as a result of actions taken to increase its preventative maintenance and programs initiated with its equipment suppliers to increase the quality of their products, actual lives for certain asset categories were generally longer than the useful lives for depreciation purposes. Therefore, the Company extended the estimated useful lives of certain categories of plant and equipment, effective. . . . The effect of this change in estimate reduced depreciation expense for the year ended . . . , by $14 million and increased income before cumulative effect of accounting change by $8 million ($.19 per share).

An example of another change in estimate is provided in Illustration 20–7.

Illustration 20–7

Change in Accounting Estimate

Universal Semiconductors estimates warranty expense as 2% of sales. After a review during 2018, Universal determined that 3% of sales is a more realistic estimate of its payment experience. Sales in 2018 are $300 million. The effective income tax rate is 40%.

No account balances are adjusted. The cumulative effect of the estimate change is not reported in current income. Rather, in 2018 and later years, the adjusting entry to record warranty expense simply will reflect the new percentage. In 2018, the entry would be:

	($ in millions)	
Warranty expense (3% × $300 million)	9	
Warranty liability		9

The after-tax effect of the change in estimate is $1.8 million [$300 million × (3% – 2%) = $3 million, less 40% of $3 million]. Assuming 100 million outstanding shares of common stock, the effect is described in a disclosure note to the financial statements as follows:

Note A: Warranties

In 2018, the company revised the percentage used to estimate warranty expense. The change provides a better indication of cost experience. The effect of the change was to decrease 2018 net income by $1.8 million, or $0.018 per share.

Changing Depreciation, Amortization, and Depletion Methods

FINANCIAL Reporting Case

Q2, p. 1159

When a company acquires an asset that will provide benefits for several years, it allocates the cost of the asset over the asset's useful life. If the asset is a building, equipment, or other tangible asset, the allocation process is called *depreciation.* It's referred to as *amortization* if an intangible asset or *depletion* if a natural resource. In each case, estimates are essential to the allocation process. How long will benefits accrue? What will be the value of the asset when its use is discontinued? Will the benefits be realized evenly over the asset's life or will they be higher in some years than in others?

An exception to retrospective application of a change in accounting principle is a change in the method of depreciation (or amortization or depletion).

The choice of depreciation method and application reflects these estimates. Likewise, when a company changes the way it depreciates an asset in midstream, the change would be made to reflect a change in (a) estimated future benefits from the asset, (b) the pattern of receiving those benefits, or (c) the company's knowledge about those benefits. For instance, suppose Universal Semiconductors originally chose an accelerated depreciation method because it expected greater benefits in the earlier years of an asset's life. Then, two years later, when it became apparent that remaining benefits would be realized approximately evenly over the remaining useful life, Universal Semiconductor switched to straight-line depreciation. Even though the company is changing its depreciation method, it is doing so to reflect changes in its estimates of future benefits. As a result, we report a change in depreciation method as a change in estimate, rather than as a change in accounting principle.

Companies report a change in depreciation prospectively.

For this reason, a company reports a change in depreciation method (say to straight-line) prospectively; previous financial statements are not revised. Instead, the company simply employs the straight-line method from then on. The undepreciated cost remaining at the time of the change would be depreciated straight-line over the remaining useful life. Illustration 20–8 provides an example.

Illustration 20–8
Change in Depreciation Methods

Universal Semiconductors switched from the SYD depreciation method to straight-line depreciation in 2018. The change affects its precision equipment purchased at the beginning of 2016 at a cost of $63 million. The machinery has an expected useful life of five years and an estimated residual value of $3 million.

The depreciation prior to the change is as follows:

Sum-of-the-Years'-Digits Depreciation	($ in millions)
2016 depreciation	$20 ($60 × 5/15)
2017 depreciation	16 ($60 × 4/15)
Accumulated depreciation	$36

A change in depreciation method is considered a change in accounting estimate resulting from a change in accounting principle. So, Universal Semiconductors reports the change prospectively; previous financial statements are not revised. Instead, the company simply employs the straight-line method from 2018 on. The undepreciated cost remaining at the time of the change is depreciated straight-line over the remaining useful life.

Calculation of Straight-Line Depreciation	($ in millions)
Asset's cost	$63
Accumulated depreciation to date (calculated above)	(36)
Undepreciated cost, Jan. 1, 2018	$27
Estimated residual value	(3)
To be depreciated over remaining 3 years	$24
	3 years
Annual straight-line depreciation 2018–2020	$ 8

The $24 million depreciable cost not yet depreciated is spread over the asset's remaining three years.

Adjusting entry (2018, 2019, and 2020 depreciation)	($ in millions)	
Depreciation expense (calculated above)	8	
Accumulated depreciation		8

A company must justify any change in principle as preferable to the previous method.

Is a change in depreciation method a change in accounting principle, or is it a change in estimate? As we've seen, it's both. Even though it's considered to reflect a change in estimate and is accounted for as such, a change to a new depreciation method requires the company to justify the new method as being preferable to the previous method, just as for any other change in principle. A disclosure note should justify that the change is preferable and describe the effect of a change on any financial statement line items and per share amounts affected for all periods reported.

In practice, the situation arises infrequently. Most companies changing depreciation methods do not apply the change to existing assets, but instead to assets placed in service after that date. In those cases, of course, the new method is simply applied prospectively (see Illustration 20–9).

Illustration 20–9
Change in Depreciation Method for Newly Acquired Assets—Rohm and Haas Company
Real World Financials

Note 12: Land, Buildings, and Equipment, Net (in part)
. . . the company changed its method of depreciation for newly acquired buildings and equipment to the straight-line method. The change had no cumulative effect on prior years' earnings but did increase [current year] net earnings by $9 million, or $0.14 per share . . .

When it's not possible to distinguish between a change in principle and a change in estimate, the change should be treated as a change in estimate.

Sometimes, it's not easy to distinguish between a change in principle and a change in estimate. For example, if a company begins to capitalize rather than expense the cost of tools because their benefits beyond one year become apparent, the change could be construed as either a change in principle or a change in the estimated life of the asset. When the distinction is not possible, the change should be treated as a change in estimate. This treatment also is appropriate when both a change in principle and a change in estimate occur simultaneously.

Change in Reporting Entity

● LO20–5

A reporting entity can be a single company, or it can be a group of companies that reports a single set of financial statements. For example, the consolidated financial statements of **PepsiCo Inc.** report the financial position and results of operations not only for the parent company, but also for its subsidiaries which include **Frito-Lay** and **Gatorade**. A **change in reporting entity** occurs as a result of (1) presenting consolidated financial statements in place of statements of individual companies or (2) changing specific companies that constitute the group for which consolidated or combined statements are prepared.[8]

Some changes in reporting entity are a result of changes in accounting rules. For example, companies like **Ford**, **General Motors**, and **General Electric** must consolidate their manufacturing operations with their *financial* subsidiaries, creating a new entity that includes them both.[9] For those changes in entity, the prior-period financial statements that are presented for comparative purposes must be restated to appear as if the new entity existed in those periods.

However, the more frequent change in entity occurs when one company acquires another one. In those circumstances, the financial statements of the acquirer include the acquiree as of the date of acquisition, and the acquirer's prior-period financial statements that are presented for comparative purposes are not restated. This makes it difficult to make year-to-year comparisons for a company that frequently acquires other companies. Acquiring companies are required to provide a footnote that presents key financial statement information as if the acquisition had occurred before the beginning of the previous year. At a minimum, the supplemental pro forma information should display revenue, income from continuing operations, net income, and earnings per share.

A change in reporting entity is reported by recasting all previous periods' financial statements as if the new reporting entity existed in those periods.[10] In the first set of financial statements after the change, a disclosure note should describe the nature of the change and the reason it occurred. Also, the effect of the change on net income, income from continuing operations, and related per share amounts should be indicated for all periods presented. These disclosures aren't necessary in subsequent financial statements. **Hartford Life Insurance Company**, a financial services company, changed the composition of its reporting entity and described it this way (see Illustration 20–10):

A change in reporting entity requires that financial statements of prior periods be retrospectively revised to report the financial information for the new reporting entity in all periods.

1. Basis of Presentation and Accounting Policies (In part)

Hartford Life changed its reporting entity structure to contribute certain wholly owned subsidiaries, including Hartford Life's European insurance operations, several broker dealer entities and investment advisory and service entities from Hartford Life and Accident to the Company. The contribution of subsidiaries was effected to more closely align servicing entities with the writing company issuing the business they service as well as to more efficiently deploy capital across the organization. The change in reporting entity was retrospectively applied to the financial statements of the Company for all periods presented. The contributed subsidiaries resulted in an increase in stockholder's equity of approximately $1.3 billion.

Illustration 20–10

Change in Reporting Entity Hartford Life Insurance

Real World Financials

Errors

The correction of an error is not actually an accounting change but is accounted for similarly. In fact, it's accounted for retrospectively, like a change in reporting entity and like most changes in accounting principle.

[8]FASB ASC 810: Consolidation (previously "Consolidation of All Majority-Owned Subsidiaries," *Statement of Financial Accounting Standards No. 94* (Stamford, Conn.: FASB, 1987)).

[9]The issuance of *SFAS No. 94*, "Consolidation of All Majority-Owned Subsidiaries," [FASB ASC 810: Consolidation and 840: Leases] resulted in hundreds of entities consolidating previously unconsolidated finance subsidiaries.

[10]Any prior periods' statements are recast when those statements are presented again for comparative purposes.

Previous years' financial statements are retrospectively restated to reflect the correction of an error.

More specifically, previous years' financial statements that were incorrect as a result of the error are retrospectively restated to reflect the correction. And, of course, any account balances that are incorrect as a result of the error are corrected by a journal entry. If retained earnings is one of the incorrect accounts, the correction is reported as a prior period adjustment to the beginning balance in a statement of shareholders' equity (or statement of retained earnings if that's presented instead).[11] And, as for accounting changes, a disclosure note is needed to describe the nature of the error and the impact of its correction on operations. We discuss the correction of errors in more detail in Part B of this chapter. But first, let's compare the two approaches for reporting accounting changes and error corrections (see Illustration 20–11).

Illustration 20–11

Approaches to Reporting Accounting Changes and Error Corrections

Previous Years	Current Year	Later Years

← Retrospective

Most changes in accounting principle

Change in reporting entity

Corrections of errors

Prospective →

Changes in estimate including changes in depreciation method

Changes in accounting principle when retrospective application is impractical

Changes in accounting principle when prospective application is mandated

A comparison of accounting treatments is provided by Illustration 20–12.

Illustration 20–12 Accounting Changes and Errors: A Summary

	Change in Accounting Principle		Change in Estimate (including depreciation changes)	Change in Reporting Entity	Error
	Most Changes*	Exceptions†			
Method of accounting:	Retrospective	Prospective	Prospective	Retrospective	Retrospective
• Restate prior years' statements?	Yes	No	No	Yes	Yes
• Cumulative effect on prior years' income reported:	As adjustment to retained earnings of earliest year reported‡	Not reported	Not reported	As adjustment to retained earnings** of earliest year reported‡	As adjustment to retained earnings of earliest year reported‡
• Journal entry:	To adjust affected balances to new method	None, but subsequent accounting is affected by the change	None, but subsequent accounting is affected by the new estimate	Involves consolidated financial statements discussed in other courses	To correct any balances that are incorrect as a result of the error
• Disclosure note?	Yes	Yes	Yes	Yes	Yes

*Changes in depreciation, amortization, and depletion methods are considered changes in estimates.
†When retrospective application is impracticable, such as most changes to LIFO and certain mandated changes.
‡In the statement of shareholders' equity or statement of retained earnings.
**Except when one company acquires another one. Then the acquirer's prior-period financial statements that are presented for comparative purposes are not restated.

[11]FASB ASC 250–10–45: Accounting Changes and Error Corrections–Overall–Other Presentation Matters (previously "Prior Period Adjustments," *Statement of Financial Accounting Standards No. 16* (Stamford, Conn.: FASB, 1977)).

Concept Review Exercise

ACCOUNTING CHANGES

Modern Business Machines recently conducted an extensive review of its accounting and reporting policies. The following accounting changes are an outgrowth of that review:

1. MBM has a patent on a copier design. The patent has been amortized on a straight-line basis since it was acquired at a cost of $400,000 in 2015. During 2018, MBM decided that the benefits from the patent would be experienced over a total of 13 years rather than the 20-year legal life now being used to amortize its cost.
2. At the beginning of 2018, MBM changed its method of valuing inventory from the FIFO cost method to the average cost method. At December 31, 2017 and 2016, MBM's inventories were $560 and $540 million, respectively, on a FIFO cost basis but would have totaled $500 and $490 million, respectively, if determined on an average cost basis. MBM's income tax rate is 40%.

Required:

Prepare all journal entries needed in 2018 related to each change. Also, briefly describe any other measures MBM would take in connection with reporting the changes.

Solution:

1. **Change in estimate**

	($ in millions)	
Patent amortization expense (determined below)	34	
Patent		34

Calculation of Annual Amortization after the Estimate Change

	$400,000	Cost
$20,000		Old annual amortization ($400,000 ÷ 20 years)
× 3 years	(60,000)	Amortization to date (2015, 2016, 2017)
	340,000	Unamortized cost
	÷ 10	Estimated remaining life (13 years − 3 years)
	$ 34,000	New annual amortization

A disclosure note should describe the effect of a change in estimate on income from continuing operations, net income, and related per share amounts for the current period.

2. **Change in principle**

MBM creates a journal entry to bring up to date all account balances affected.

	($ in millions)	
Retained earnings (the difference in net income before 2018)	36	
Deferred tax asset ($60 million × 40%)	24	
Inventory ($560 million − 500 million)		60

For financial reporting purposes, but not for tax, MBM is retrospectively *decreasing* accounting income, but not taxable income. This creates a temporary difference between the two that will reverse over time as the unsold inventory becomes cost of goods sold. When that happens, taxable income will be less than accounting income. When taxable income will be less than accounting income as a temporary difference reverses, we have a "future deductible amount" and record a deferred tax asset.

Prior years' financial statements are revised to reflect the use of the new accounting method.

Also, MBM will revise all previous periods' financial statements (in this case 2017) as if the new method (average cost) were used in those periods. In other words, for each year in the comparative statements reported, the balance of each account affected will be revised to appear as if the average method had been applied all along.

Since it's the earliest year reported, 2017's beginning retained earnings is adjusted for the portion of the cumulative income effect of the change attributable to prior years.

Since retained earnings is one of the accounts whose balance requires adjustment (and it usually is), MBM makes an adjustment to the beginning balance of retained earnings for the earliest period (2017) reported in the comparative statements of shareholders' equity. Also, in the first set of financial statements after the change, a *disclosure note* describes the nature of the change, justifies management's decision to make the change, and indicates its effect on each item affected in the financial statements.

International Financial Reporting Standards

LO20–7

The FASB and the International Accounting Standards Board have a continuing commitment to converge their accounting standards. As part of their short-term convergence effort, they identified how companies report accounting changes as an area in which the FASB could improve its guidance by converging it with the provisions of *IAS No. 8*, "Accounting Policies, Changes in Accounting Estimates and Errors."[12] The product of this effort was new FASB guidance issued in 2005.[13] Few differences remain, so it's unlikely we will see much change in this area.

PART B

Correction of Accounting Errors

LO20–6

Nobody's perfect. People make mistakes, even accountants. When errors are discovered, they should be corrected.[14] Illustration 20–13 describes the steps to be taken to correct an error, if the effect of the error is material.[15]

Illustration 20–13
Steps to Correct an Error

Step 1	A journal entry is made to correct any account balances that are incorrect as a result of the error.
Step 2	Previous years' financial statements that were incorrect as a result of the error are retrospectively restated to reflect the correction (for all years reported for comparative purposes).
Step 3	If retained earnings is one of the accounts incorrect as a result of the error, the correction is reported as a prior period adjustment to the beginning balance in a statement of shareholders' equity (or statement of retained earnings if that's presented instead).
Step 4	A disclosure note should describe the nature of the error and the impact of its correction on net income.

The retrospective approach is used for the correction of errors.

The correction of an error is treated as a prior period adjustment.

Prior Period Adjustments

Before we see these steps applied to the correction of an error, one of the steps requires elaboration. As discussed in Chapter 4, the correction of errors is the situation that creates prior period adjustments. A prior period adjustment refers to an addition to or reduction in the beginning retained earnings balance in a statement of shareholders' equity (or statement of retained earnings if that's presented instead).

In an earlier chapter we saw that a statement of shareholders' equity is the most commonly used way to report the events that cause components of shareholders' equity to

[12]"Accounting Policies, Changes in Accounting Estimates and Errors," *International Accounting Standard No. 8* (IASCF), as amended effective January 1, 2011.

[13]FASB ASC 250: Accounting Changes and Error Corrections (previously "Accounting Changes and Error Corrections–A Replacement of APB Opinion No. 20 and FASB Statement No. 3," *Statement of Financial Accounting Standards No. 154* (Norwalk, Conn.: FASB, 2005)).

[14]Interestingly, it appears that not all accounting errors are unintentional. Research has shown that firms with errors that overstate income are more likely "to have diffuse ownership, lower growth in earnings and fewer income-increasing GAAP alternatives available, and are less likely to have audit committees," suggesting that "overstatement errors are the result of managers responding to economic incentives." M. L. DeFond and J. Jiambaolvo, "Incidence and Circumstances of Accounting Errors," *The Accounting Review*, July 1991.

[15]In practice, the vast majority of errors are not material with respect to their effect on the financial statements and are, therefore, simply corrected in the year discovered (step 1 only).

change during a particular reporting period. Some companies, though, choose to report the changes that occur in the balance of retained earnings separately in a statement of retained earnings. When it's discovered that the ending balance of retained earnings in the period prior to the discovery of an error was incorrect as a result of that error, the balance must be corrected when it appears as the beginning balance the following year. However, simply reporting a corrected amount might cause misunderstanding for someone familiar with the previously reported amount. Explicitly reporting a prior period adjustment on the statement itself avoids this confusion. Assume, for example, the following comparative statements of retained earnings:

STATEMENTS OF RETAINED EARNINGS
For the Years Ended December 31, 2017 and 2016

	2017	2016
Balance at beginning of year	$600,000	$450,000
Net income	400,000	350,000
Less: Dividends	(200,000)	(200,000)
Balance at end of year	$800,000	$600,000

A statement of retained earnings reports the events that cause changes in retained earnings.

Now suppose that in 2018 it's discovered that an error in 2016 caused that year's net income to be overstated by $20,000 (it should have been $330,000). This means retained earnings in both prior years were overstated. Because comparative financial statements are presented and the current year is the year in which the error was discovered, the prior year would include a prior period adjustment as shown below:

STATEMENTS OF RETAINED EARNINGS
For the Years Ended December 31, 2018 and 2017

	2018	2017
Balance at beginning of year	$ 780,000	$600,000
Prior period adjustment		(20,000)
Corrected balance		$580,000
Net Income	500,000	400,000
Less: Dividends	(200,000)	(200,000)
Balance at end of year	$1,080,000	$780,000

The incorrect balance as previously reported is corrected by the prior period adjustment.

At least two years' (as in our example) and often three years' statements are reported in comparative financial statements. The prior period adjustment is applied to beginning retained earnings for the year following the error, or for the earliest year being reported in the comparative financial statements when the error occurs prior to the earliest year presented.[16]

Error Correction Illustrated

Now, let's discuss these procedures to correct errors in the context of a variety of the most common types of errors. Since there are literally thousands of possibilities, it's not practical to describe every error in every stage of its discovery. However, by applying the process to the situations described below, you should become sufficiently comfortable with the *process* that you could apply it to whatever situation you might encounter.

You shouldn't try to memorize how specific errors are corrected; you should learn the process needed to analyze whatever errors you might encounter.

As you study these examples, be sure to notice that it's significantly more complicated to deal with an error if (a) it affected net income in the reporting period in which it occurred and (b) it is not discovered until a later period.

Error Discovered in the Same Reporting Period That It Occurred

If an accounting error is made and discovered in the same accounting period, the original erroneous entry should simply be reversed and the appropriate entry recorded. The possibilities are limitless. Let's look at the one in Illustration 20–14.

[16]The retained earnings balances in years after the first year also are adjusted to what those balances would be if the error had not occurred, but a company may choose not to explicitly report those adjustments as separate line items.

Illustration 20–14

Error Discovered in the Same Reporting Period That It Occurred

G. H. Little, Inc., paid $3 million for replacement computers and recorded the expenditure as maintenance expense. The error was discovered a week later.

To Reverse Erroneous Entry	($ in millions)	
Cash	3	
Maintenance expense		3
To Record Correct Entry		
Equipment	3	
Cash		3

Note: These entries can, of course, be combined.

Error Affecting Previous Financial Statements, but Not Net Income

If an error did *not* affect net income in the year it occurred, it's relatively easy to correct. Examples are incorrectly recording salaries payable as accounts payable, recording a loss as an expense, or classifying a cash flow as an investing activity rather than a financing activity on the statement of cash flows. The 2015 financial statements of **Barnes & Noble** reported that "the SEC's New York Regional office notified the Company that it had commenced an investigation into the. . . . Company's restatement of earnings announced on July 29, 2013. The disclosure note reporting that restatement is reproduced in Illustration 20–15.

Illustration 20–15

Error Correction; Barnes & Noble

Real World Financials

2. Restatement of Prior Period Financial Statements (in part)

The Company has restated its previously reported consolidated financial statements for the years ended April 28, 2012 and April 30, 2011, including the opening stockholders' equity balance, in order to correct certain previously reported amounts.

In fiscal 2013, management determined that the Company had incorrectly overstated certain accruals for the periods prior to April 27, 2013, as a result of inadequate controls over its Distribution Center accrual reconciliation process . . . the Company recorded an adjustment to decrease cost of sales by $6,700 ($4,027 after tax) and $8,460 ($5,084 after tax) to correctly present the statement of operations for fiscal 2012 and 2011, respectively. The Company also decreased accounts payable by $89,500 and $96,200 at April 30, 2011 and April 28, 2012, respectively; increased income taxes payable included in Accrued Liabilities in the consolidated Balance Sheets by $14,939 and $18,598 at April 30, 2011 and April 28, 2012, respectively; and increased retained earnings by $74,561 and $78,588, net of tax at April 30, 2011 and April 28, 2012, respectively.

Illustration 20–16 provides another example.

Illustration 20–16

Error Affecting Previous Financial Statements, but Not Net Income

MDS Transportation incorrectly recorded a $2 million note receivable as accounts receivable. The error was discovered a year later.

To Correct Incorrect Accounts	($ in millions)	
Note receivable	2	
Accounts receivable		2

Step 1

When reported for comparative purposes in the current year's annual report, last year's balance sheet would be restated to report the note as it should have been reported last year.

Step 2

Since last year's net income was not affected by the error, the balance in retained earnings was not incorrect. So no prior period adjustment to that account is necessary.

Step 3

A disclosure note would describe the nature of the error, but there would be no impact on net income, income from continuing operations, and earnings per share to report.

Step 4

Error Affecting a Prior Year's Net Income

Most errors affect net income in some way. When they do, they affect the balance sheet as well. Both statements must be retrospectively restated; the statement of cash flows sometimes is affected, too. As with any error, all incorrect account balances must be corrected. Because these errors affect income, one of the balances that will require correction is retained earnings. Complicating matters, income taxes often are affected by income errors. In those cases, amended tax returns are prepared either to pay additional taxes or to claim a tax refund for taxes overpaid.

In Illustration 20–17, except as indicated, we ignore the tax effects of the errors and their correction to allow us to focus on the errors themselves rather than their tax aspects.

Illustration 20–17

Error Affecting Net Income: Recording an Asset as an Expense

In 2018, internal auditors discovered that Seidman Distribution, Inc., had debited an expense account for the $7 million cost of sorting equipment purchased at the beginning of 2016. The equipment's useful life was expected to be five years with no residual value. Straight-line depreciation is used by Seidman.

Analysis

Sometimes, the analysis is easier if you re-create the entries actually recorded incorrectly and those that would have been recorded if the error hadn't occurred and then compare them.

Correct (Should have been recorded)	($ in millions)		**Incorrect** (As recorded)	($ in millions)	
2016 Equipment	7.0		Expense	7.0	
Cash		7.0	Cash		7.0
2016 Expense	1.4		*Depreciation entry omitted*		
Accum. deprec.		1.4			
2017 Expense	1.4		*Depreciation entry omitted*		
Accum. deprec.		1.4			

During the two-year period, depreciation expense was understated by $2.8 million, but other expenses were overstated by $7 million, so net income during the period was understated by $4.2 million. This means retained earnings is currently understated by that amount.

Accumulated depreciation is understated by $2.8 million.

Step 1

To Correct Incorrect Accounts	($ in millions)	
Equipment	7.0	
Accumulated depreciation		2.8
Retained earnings		4.2

Step 2

The 2016 and 2017 financial statements that were incorrect as a result of the error are retrospectively restated to report the equipment acquired and to reflect the correct amount of depreciation expense and accumulated depreciation, assuming both statements are reported again for comparative purposes in the 2018 annual report.

Step 3

Because retained earnings is one of the accounts that is incorrect as a result of the error, a correction to that account of $4.2 million is reported as a prior period adjustment to the 2018 beginning retained earnings balance in Seidman's comparative statements of shareholders' equity. A correction would be made also to the 2017 beginning retained earnings balance. That prior period adjustment, though, would be for the pre-2017 difference: $7 million – 1.4 million = $5.6 million. If 2016 statements also are included in the comparative report, no adjustment would be necessary for that period because the error didn't occur until after the beginning of 2016.

Step 4

Also, a disclosure note accompanying Seidman's 2018 financial statements should describe the nature of the error and the impact of its correction on each year's net income (understated by $5.6 million in 2016 and overstated by $1.4 million in 2017), income from continuing operations (same as net income), and earnings per share.

The effect of most errors is different, depending on *when* the error is discovered. For example, if the error in Illustration 20–17 is not discovered until 2019, rather than 2018, accumulated depreciation would be understated by another $1.4 million, or a total of $4.2 million. If not discovered until 2021 or after, no correcting entry at all would be needed. By then, the sum of the omitted depreciation amounts ($1.4 million × 5 years) would equal the expense incorrectly recorded in 2016 ($7 million), so the retained earnings balance would be the same as if the error never had occurred. Also, the asset may have been disposed of—if the useful life estimate was correct—so neither the equipment nor accumulated depreciation would need to be recorded. Of course, any statements of prior years that were affected and are reported again in comparative statements still would be restated, and a disclosure note would describe the error.

Most errors, in fact, eventually self-correct. An example of an uncommon instance in which an error never self-corrects would be an expense account debited for the cost of land. Because land doesn't depreciate, the error would continue until the land is sold.

Additional Consideration

We ignored the tax impact of the error and its correction in Illustration 20–17. To consider taxes, we need to know whether depreciation was also omitted from the tax return and the depreciation methods used for tax reporting. Let's say that depreciation was omitted from the tax return also, and that straight-line depreciation is used by Seidman for both tax and financial reporting. The tax rate is 40%.

Total operating expenses (nontax) still would have been overstated by $4.2 million over the two-year period. But that would have caused taxable income to be understated and the tax liability and income tax expense to be understated by 40% of $4.2 million, or $1.68 million. So net income and retained earnings would have been understated by only $2.52 million.

Operating expenses *overstated*	$4.20 million
Income tax expense *understated*	(1.68) million
Net income (and retained earnings) *understated*	$ 2.52 million

To Correct Incorrect Accounts	($ in millions)	
Equipment	7.00	
Accumulated depreciation		2.80
Income tax payable (40% × $4.2 million)		1.68
Retained earnings		2.52

If depreciation had been omitted from the income statement but not from the tax return, or if accelerated depreciation was used for tax reporting but straight-line depreciation for financial reporting, the credit to income tax payable in the correcting entry would be replaced by a credit to deferred tax liability.

Even errors that eventually correct themselves cause financial statements to be misstated in the meantime.

Some errors correct themselves the following year. For instance, if a company's ending inventory is incorrectly counted or otherwise misstated, the income statement would be in error for the year of the error and the following year, but the balance sheet would be incorrect only for the year the error occurs. After that, all account balances will be correct. This is demonstrated in Illustration 20–18.

Other error corrections that benefit from a similar analysis are the overstatement of ending inventory, the overstatement or understatement of beginning inventory, and errors in recording merchandise purchases (or returns).

An error also would occur if a revenue or an expense is recorded in the wrong accounting period. Illustration 20–19 offers an example.

In early 2018, Overseas Wholesale Supply discovered that $1 million of inventory had been inadvertently excluded from its 2016 ending inventory count.

Analysis:
U = Understated O = Overstated

2016		**2017**	
Beginning inventory		→ Beginning inventory	U
Plus: Net purchases		Plus: Net purchases	
Less: Ending inventory	U →	Less: Ending inventory	
Cost of goods sold	O	Cost of goods sold	U
Revenues		Revenues	
Less: Cost of goods sold	O	Less: Cost of goods sold	U
Less: Other expenses		Less: Other expenses	
Net income	U	Net income	O
↓		↓	
Retained earnings	U	Retained earnings	*corrected*

If Error Is Discovered in 2017 (before closing) ($ in millions)

Inventory	1	
Retained earnings		1

If Error Discovered in 2018 or Later
No correcting entry needed.

If the error is discovered in 2017, the 2016 financial statements that were incorrect as a result of the error are retrospectively restated to reflect the correct inventory amounts, cost of goods sold, and retained earnings when those statements are reported again for comparative purposes in the 2017 annual report. If the error is discovered in 2018, the 2017 financial statements also are retrospectively restated to reflect the correct inventory amounts and cost of goods sold (retained earnings would not require adjustment), even though no correcting entry would be needed at that point.

Because retained earnings is one of the accounts incorrect if the error is discovered in 2017, the correction to that account is reported as a prior period adjustment to the 2017 beginning retained earnings balance in Overseas' statement of shareholders' equity. Of course, no prior period adjustment is needed if the error isn't discovered until 2019 or later.

Also, a disclosure note in Overseas' annual report should describe the nature of the error and the impact of its correction on each year's net income (understated by $1 million in 2016, overstated by $1 million in 2017), income from continuing operations (same as net income), and earnings per share.

Illustration 20–18

Error Affecting Net Income: Inventory Misstated

When analyzing inventory errors or other errors that affect cost of goods sold, you may find it helpful to visualize the determination of cost of goods sold, net income, and retained earnings.

Step 1

Step 2

Step 3

Step 4

In 2018, General Paper Company discovered that $3,000 of merchandise (credit) sales the last week of 2017 were not recorded until the first week of 2018. The merchandise sold was appropriately excluded from 2017 ending inventory.

Analysis

Correct (Should have been recorded)	($ in thousands)		Incorrect (As recorded)	($ in thousands)	
2017 Accounts receivable	3		No entry		
Sales revenue		3			
2018 No entry			Accounts receivable	3	
			Sales revenue		3

(continued)

Illustration 20–19

Error Affecting Net Income: Failure to Record Sales Revenue

Illustration 20–19
(concluded)

2017 sales revenue was incorrectly recorded in 2018, so 2017 net income was understated. Retained earnings is currently understated in 2018. 2018 sales revenue is overstated.

Step 1

To Correct Incorrect Accounts	($ in thousands)	
Sales revenue	3	
Retained earnings		3

Note: If the sales revenue had not been recorded at all, the correcting entry would include a debit to accounts receivable rather than sales revenue.

Step 2 The 2017 financial statements that were incorrect as a result of the error are retroactively restated to reflect the correct amount of sales revenue and accounts receivable when those statements are reported again for comparative purposes in the 2018 annual report.

Step 3 Because retained earnings is one of the accounts incorrect as a result of the error, the correction to that account is reported as a prior period adjustment to the 2018 beginning retained earnings balance in General Paper's comparative statements of shareholders' equity.

Step 4 Also, a disclosure note in General Paper's 2018 annual report should describe the nature of the error and the impact of its correction on each year's net income ($3,000 in 2017), income from continuing operations ($3,000 in 2017), and earnings per share.

Ethical Dilemma

As a second-year accountant for McCormack Chemical Company, you were excited to be named assistant manager of the Agricultural Chemicals Division. After two weeks in your new position, you were supervising the year-end inventory count when the senior manager mentioned that two carloads of herbicides were omitted from the count and should be added. Upon checking, you confirm your understanding that the inventory in question had been deemed to be unsalable. "Yes," your manager agreed, "but we'll write that off next year when our bottom line won't be so critical to the continued existence of the Agricultural Chemicals Division. Jobs and families depend on our division showing well this year."

Hertz Global Holding, Inc. operates car rental businesses through the Hertz, Dollar, Thrifty and Firefly brands. Illustration 20–20 reports information from a disclosure note in Hertz's annual report issued July 16, 2015. It shows how Hertz corrected its financial statements primarily because of depreciation errors on the sale of vehicles at retail locations.

Illustration 20–20
Error Correction; Hertz
Real World Financials

Note 2—Restatement (in part)

During the fourth quarter of 2013, the Company identified certain out of period misstatements totaling $46 million, of which $35 million ($21 million, net of tax) related to its previously issued consolidated financial statements for the years ended December 31, 2012 and prior. While these misstatements did not, individually or in the aggregate, result in a material misstatement of the Company's previously issued consolidated financial statements, correcting these misstatements in the fourth quarter of 2013 would have been material to that quarter . . . this Note 2 to the consolidated financial statements discloses the nature of the restatement matters and adjustments and shows the impact of the restatement matters on revenues, expenses, income, assets, liabilities, equity, and cash flows from operating activities, investing activities, and financing activities, and the cumulative effects of these adjustments on the consolidated statement of operations, balance sheet, and cash flows for 2012 and 2013. In addition, this Note shows the effects of the adjustment to opening retained earnings as of January 1, 2012, which adjustment reflects the impact of the restatement on periods prior to 2012. The cumulative impact of the out of period misstatements for all previously reported periods through December 31, 2013, including amounts associated with the revision previously reported in the 2013 Form 10-K/A, was approximately a $349 million reduction in pre-tax income and $231 million reduction in net income.

As mentioned at the outset, we've made no attempt to demonstrate the correction process for every kind of error in every stage of its discovery. However, after seeing the process applied to the few situations described, you should feel comfortable that the process is the same regardless of the specific situation you might encounter.

International Financial Reporting Standards

Accounting Changes and Error Corrections. U.S. GAAP and International standards are largely converged regarding accounting changes and error corrections, but one difference concerns error corrections. When correcting errors in previously issued financial statements, IFRS (*IAS No. 8*) permits the effect of the error to be reported in the current period if it's not considered practicable to report it retrospectively, as is required by U.S. GAAP.[17]

● LO20–7

Concept Review Exercise

CORRECTION OF ERRORS

In 2018, the following errors were discovered by the internal auditors of Development Technologies, Inc.

1. 2017 accrued wages of $2 million were not recognized until they were paid in 2018.
2. A $3 million purchase of merchandise in 2018 was recorded in 2017 instead. The physical inventory count at the end of 2017 was correct.

Required:

Prepare the journal entries needed in 2018 to correct each error. Also, briefly describe any other measures Development Technologies would take in connection with correcting the errors. (Ignore income taxes.)

Solution:

Step 1:

1. To reduce 2018 wages expense and reduce retained earnings to what it would have been if the expense had reduced net income in 2017.

	($ in millions)	
Retained earnings	2	
Wages expense		2

2. To include the $3 million in 2018 purchases and increase retained earnings to what it would have been if 2017 cost of goods sold had not included the $3 million purchases.

Analysis

U = Understated O = Overstated

2017		**2018**	
Beginning inventory		Beginning inventory	
Purchases	O	Purchases	U
Less: Ending inventory			
Cost of goods sold	O		
Revenues			
Less: Cost of goods sold	O		
Less: Other expenses			
Net income	U		
Retained earnings	U		

[17]"Accounting Policies, Changes in Accounting Estimates and Errors," *International Accounting Standard No. 8* (IASCF), as amended effective January 1, 2014.

	($ in millions)	
Purchases	3	
Retained earnings		3

Step 2:
The 2017 financial statements that were incorrect as a result of the errors would be *retrospectively restated* to reflect the correct wages expense, cost of goods sold (income tax expense if taxes are considered), net income, and retained earnings when those statements are reported again for comparative purposes in the 2018 annual report.

Step 3:
Because retained earnings is one of the accounts that is incorrect, the correction to that account is reported as a "*prior period adjustment*" to the 2018 beginning retained earnings balance in the comparative Statements of Shareholders' Equity.

Step 4:
Also, a *disclosure note* should describe the nature of the error and the impact of its correction on each year's net income, income from continuing operations, and earnings per share.

Financial Reporting Case Solution

1. **How can an accounting change cause a company to increase a previously reported inventory amount?** *(p. 1163)* Smucker didn't find any lost jelly. The company increased last year's inventory number by $2 million to reflect its change from *LIFO* to *FIFO* this year. If it had not revised the number, last year's inventory would be based on *LIFO* and this year's inventory on *FIFO*. Analysts would be comparing apples and oranges (or apple jelly and orange jelly). Retrospective application of an accounting change provides better comparability in accounting information.
2. **Are all accounting changes reported this way?** *(p. 1169)* Not all accounting changes are reported retrospectively. Besides most changes in accounting principle, changes in reporting entity and the correction of errors are reported that way, but some changes are reported prospectively instead. Changes in depreciation method, changes in accounting estimate, and some changes for which retrospective application is either impracticable or prohibited are reported prospectively in current and future periods only.

The Bottom Line

- **LO20–1** Accounting changes are categorized as (a) changes in *principle,* (b) changes in *estimates,* or (c) changes in *reporting entity.* Accounting changes can be accounted for retrospectively (prior years revised) or prospectively (only year of change and future years affected), or by the modified retrospective approach (apply a new standard only to the adoption period). *(p. 1160)*
- **LO20–2** Most voluntary changes in accounting principles are reported retrospectively. This means for each year reported in the comparative statements, we make those statements appear as if the newly adopted accounting method had been applied all along. A journal entry is created to adjust all account balances affected as of the date of the change. In the first set of financial statements after the change, a disclosure note describes the change and justifies the new method as preferable. It also describes the effects of the change on all items affected, including the fact that the retained earnings balance was revised in the statement of shareholders' equity. *(p. 1162)*

- **LO20–3** Some changes are reported prospectively. These include (a) changes in the method of depreciation, amortization, or depletion, (b) some changes in principle for which retrospective application is impracticable, and (c) a few changes for which an authoritative pronouncement requires prospective application. (*p. 1166*)
- **LO20–4** Changes in estimates are accounted for prospectively. When a company revises a previous estimate, prior financial statements are not revised. Instead, the company merely incorporates the new estimate in any related accounting determinations from then on. (*p. 1168*)
- **LO20–5** A change in reporting entity requires that financial statements of prior periods be retrospectively revised to report the financial information for the new reporting entity in all periods. (*p. 1171*)
- **LO20–6** When errors are discovered, they should be corrected and accounted for retrospectively. Previous years' financial statements that were incorrect as a result of an error are retrospectively restated, and any account balances that are incorrect are corrected by a journal entry. If retained earnings is one of the incorrect accounts, the correction is reported as a prior period adjustment to the beginning balance in a statement of shareholders' equity. And, a disclosure note should describe the nature of the error and the impact of its correction on operations. (*p. 1174*)
- **LO20–7** U.S. GAAP and International standards are largely converged with respect to accounting changes and error corrections. One remaining difference is that when correcting errors in previously issued financial statements, IFRS permits the effect of the error to be reported in the current period if it's not considered practicable to report it retrospectively, as is required by U.S. GAAP. (*pp. 1167, 1174,* and *1181*)

Questions For Review of Key Topics

Q 20–1 For accounting purposes, we classify accounting changes into three categories. What are they? Provide a short description of each.

Q 20–2 There are three basic accounting approaches to reporting accounting changes. What are they?

Q 20–3 We report most changes in accounting principle retrospectively. Describe this general way of recording and reporting changes in accounting principle.

Q 20–4 Lynch Corporation changes from the sum-of-the-years'-digits method of depreciation for existing assets to the straight-line method. How should the change be reported? Explain.

Q 20–5 Sugarbaker Designs Inc. changed from the FIFO inventory costing method to the average cost method during 2018. Which items from the 2017 financial statements should be restated on the basis of the average cost method when reported in the 2018 comparative financial statements?

Q 20–6 Most changes in accounting principles are recorded and reported retrospectively. In a few situations, though, the changes should be reported prospectively. When is prospective application appropriate? Provide examples.

Q 20–7 Southeast Steel, Inc., changed from the FIFO inventory costing method to the LIFO method during 2017. How would this change likely be reported in the 2018 comparative financial statements?

Q 20–8 Direct Assurance Company revised the estimates of the useful life of a trademark it had acquired three years earlier. How should Direct account for the change?

Q 20–9 It's not easy sometimes to distinguish between a change in principle and a change in estimate. In these cases, how should the change be accounted for?

Q 20–10 For financial reporting, a reporting entity can be a single company, or it can be a group of companies that reports a single set of financial statements. When changes occur that cause the financial statements to be those of a different reporting entity, we account for the situation as a change in reporting entity. What are the situations deemed to constitute a change in reporting entity?

Q 20–11 The issuance of FASB guidance regarding consolidation of all majority-owned subsidiaries required Ford Motors to include a previously unconsolidated finance subsidiary as part of the reporting entity. How did Ford report the change?

Q 20–12 Describe the process of correcting an error when it's discovered in a subsequent reporting period.

Q 20–13 If merchandise inventory is understated at the end of 2017, and the error is not discovered, how will net income be affected in 2018?

Q 20–14 If it is discovered that an extraordinary repair in the previous year was incorrectly debited to repair expense, how will retained earnings be reported in the current year's statement of shareholders' equity?

Q 20–15 What action is required when it is discovered that a five-year insurance premium payment of $50,000 two years ago was debited to insurance expense? (Ignore taxes.)

Q 20–16 Suppose the error described in the previous question is not discovered until six years later. What action will the discovery of this error require?

IFRS **Q 20–17** With regard to the correction of accounting errors, what is the difference between U.S. GAAP and IFRS?

Brief Exercises

connect

BE 20–1
Change in inventory methods; FIFO method to the average cost method
● LO20–2

In 2018, the Barton and Barton Company changed its method of valuing inventory from the FIFO method to the average cost method. At December 31, 2017, B & B's inventories were $32 million (FIFO). B & B's records indicated that the inventories would have totaled $23.8 million at December 31, 2017, if determined on an average cost basis. Ignoring income taxes, what journal entry will B & B use to record the adjustment in 2018? Briefly describe other steps B & B should take to report the change.

BE 20–2
Change in inventory methods; average cost method to the FIFO method
● LO20–2

In 2018, Adonis Industries changed its method of valuing inventory from the average cost method to the FIFO method. At December 31, 2017, Adonis's inventories were $47.6 million (average cost). Adonis's records indicated that the inventories would have totaled $64 million at December 31, 2017, if determined on a FIFO basis. Ignoring income taxes, what journal entry will Adonis use to record the adjustment in 2018?

BE 20–3
Change in inventory methods; FIFO method to the LIFO method
● LO20–3

In 2018, J J Dishes changed its method of valuing inventory from the FIFO method to the LIFO method. At December 31, 2017, J J's inventories were $96 million (FIFO). J J's records were insufficient to determine what inventories would have totaled if determined on a LIFO cost basis. Briefly describe the steps J J should take to report the change.

BE 20–4
Change in depreciation methods
● LO20–3

Irwin, Inc., constructed a machine at a total cost of $35 million. Construction was completed at the end of 2014 and the machine was placed in service at the beginning of 2015. The machine was being depreciated over a 10-year life using the sum-of-the-years'-digits method. The residual value is expected to be $2 million. At the beginning of 2018, Irwin decided to change to the straight-line method. Ignoring income taxes, what journal entry(s) should Irwin record relating to the machine for 2018?

BE 20–5
Change in depreciation methods
● LO20–3

Refer to the situation described in BE 20–4. Suppose Irwin has been using the straight-line method and switches to the sum-of-the-years'-digits method. Ignoring income taxes, what journal entry(s) should Irwin record relating to the machine for 2018?

BE 20–6
Book royalties
● LO20–4

Three programmers at Feenix Computer Storage, Inc., write an operating systems control manual for Hill-McGraw Publishing, Inc., for which Feenix receives royalties equal to 12% of net sales. Royalties are payable annually on February 1 for sales the previous year. The editor indicated to Feenix on December 31, 2016, that book sales subject to royalties for the year just ended are expected to be $300,000. Accordingly, Feenix accrued royalty revenue of $36,000 at December 31 and received royalties of $36,500 on February 1, 2019. What adjustments, if any, should be made to retained earnings or to the 2016 financial statements? Explain.

BE 20–7
Warranty expense
● LO20–4

In 2017, Quapau Products introduced a new line of hot water heaters that carry a one-year warranty against manufacturer's defects. Based on industry experience, warranty costs were expected to approximate 5% of sales revenue. First-year sales of the heaters were $300,000. An evaluation of the company's claims experience in late 2018 indicated that actual claims were less than expected—4% of sales rather than 5%. Assuming sales of the heaters in 2018 were $350,000 and warranty expenditures in 2018 totaled $12,000, what is the 2018 warranty expense?

BE 20–8
Change in estimate; useful life of patent
● LO20–4

Van Frank Telecommunications has a patent on a cellular transmission process. The company has amortized the $18 million cost of the patent on a straight-line basis since it was acquired at the beginning of 2014. Due to rapid technological advances in the industry, management decided that the patent would benefit the company over a total of six years rather than the nine-year life being used to amortize its cost. The decision was made at the end of 2018 (before adjusting and closing entries). What is the appropriate adjusting entry for patent amortization in 2018 to reflect the revised estimate?

BE 20–9
Error correction
● LO20–6

When DeSoto Water Works purchased a machine at the end of 2017 at a cost of $65,000, the company debited Buildings and credited Cash $65,000. The error was discovered in 2018. What journal entry will DeSoto use to correct the error? What other step(s) would be taken in connection with the error?

BE 20–10
Error correction
● LO20–6

In 2018, internal auditors discovered that PKE Displays, Inc., had debited an expense account for the $350,000 cost of a machine purchased on January 1, 2015. The machine's useful life was expected to be five years with no residual value. Straight-line depreciation is used by PKE. Ignoring income taxes, what journal entry will PKE use to correct the error?

BE 20–11
Error correction
● LO20–6

Refer to the situation described in BE 20–10. Assume the error was discovered in 2020, after the 2019 financial statements are issued. Ignoring income taxes, what journal entry will PKE use to correct the error?

BE 20–12
Error correction
● LO20–6

In 2018, the internal auditors of Development Technologies, Inc., discovered that (a) 2017 accrued wages of $2 million were not recognized until they were paid in 2018, and (b) a $3 million purchase of merchandise in 2018 was recorded in 2017 instead. The physical inventory count at the end of 2017 was correct. Ignoring income taxes, what journal entries are needed in 2018 to correct each error? Also, briefly describe any other measures Development Technologies would take in connection with correcting the errors.

Exercises

connect

E 20–1
Change in principle; change in inventory methods
● LO20–2

During 2016 (its first year of operations) and 2017, Batali Foods used the FIFO inventory costing method for both financial reporting and tax purposes. At the beginning of 2018, Batali decided to change to the average method for both financial reporting and tax purposes.

Income components before income tax for 2018, 2017, and 2016 were as follows:

($ in millions)	2018	2017	2016
Revenues	$ 420	$ 390	$ 380
Cost of goods sold (FIFO)	(46)	(40)	(38)
Cost of goods sold (average)	(62)	(56)	(52)
Operating expenses	(254)	(250)	(242)

Dividends of $20 million were paid each year. Batali's fiscal year ends December 31.

Required:

1. Prepare the journal entry at the beginning of 2018 to record the change in accounting principle. (Ignore income taxes.)
2. Prepare the 2018–2017 comparative income statements.
3. Determine the balance in retained earnings at January 1, 2017, as Batali reported previously using the FIFO method.
4. Determine the adjustment to the January 1, 2017, balance in retained earnings that Batali would include in the 2018–2017 comparative statements of retained earnings or retained earnings column of the statements of shareholders' equity to revise it to the amount it would have been if Batali had used the average method.

E 20–2
Change in principle; change in inventory methods
● LO20–2

Aquatic Equipment Corporation decided to switch from the LIFO method of costing inventories to the FIFO method at the beginning of 2018. The inventory as reported at the end of 2017 using LIFO would have been $60,000 higher using FIFO. Retained earnings at the end of 2017 was reported as $780,000 (reflecting the LIFO method). The tax rate is 40%.

Required:

1. Calculate the balance in retained earnings at the time of the change (beginning of 2018) as it would have been reported if FIFO had been used in prior years.
2. Prepare the journal entry at the beginning of 2018 to record the change in accounting principle.

E 20–3
Change from the treasury stock method to retired stock
● LO20–2

In keeping with a modernization of corporate statutes in its home state, UMC Corporation decided in 2018 to discontinue accounting for reacquired shares as treasury stock. Instead, shares repurchased will be viewed as having been retired, reassuming the status of unissued shares. As part of the change, treasury shares held were reclassified as retired stock. At December 31, 2017, UMC's balance sheet reported the following shareholders' equity:

	($ in millions)
Common stock, $1 par	$ 200
Paid-in capital—excess of par	800
Retained earnings	956
Treasury stock (4 million shares at cost)	(25)
Total shareholders' equity	$1,931

Required:
Identify the type of accounting change this decision represents and prepare the journal entry to effect the reclassification of treasury shares as retired shares.

E 20–4
Change in principle; change to the equity method
● LO20–2

The Crump Companies, Inc., has ownership interests in several public companies. At the beginning of 2018, the company's ownership interest in the common stock of Silken Properties increased to the point that it became appropriate to begin using the equity method of accounting for the investment. The balance in the investment account was $31 million at the time of the change. Accountants working with company records determined that the balance would have been $48 million if the account had been adjusted to reflect the equity method.

Required:
1. Prepare the journal entry to record the change in accounting principle. (Ignore income taxes.)
2. Briefly describe other steps Crump should take to report the change.
3. Suppose Crump is changing *from* the equity method rather than *to* the equity method. How would your answers to requirements 1 and 2 differ?

E 20–5
FASB codification research; change in accounting for investments
● LO20–2

Companies often invest in the common stock of other corporations. The way we report these investments depends on the nature of the investment and the investor's motivation for the investment. The *FASB Accounting Standards Codification* represents the single source of authoritative U.S. generally accepted accounting principles.

Required:
1. Obtain the relevant authoritative literature on the disclosure of accounting policies using the *FASB Accounting Standards Codification* at the FASB website (www.fasb.org).
2. What is the specific citation that describes how to account for a change in the level of ownership to a percentage that will mandate use of the equity method for investments in common stock?
3. What are the specific requirements?

E 20–6
FASB codification research
● LO20–2

Access the *FASB Accounting Standards Codification* at the FASB website (www.fasb.org). Determine the specific citation for accounting for each of the following items:
1. Reporting most changes in accounting principle.
2. Disclosure requirements for a change in accounting principle.
3. Illustration of the application of a retrospective change in the method of accounting for inventory.

E 20–7
Change in principle; change in inventory cost method
● LO20–2

Millington Materials is a leading supplier of building equipment, building products, materials and timber for sale, with over 200 branches across the Mid-South. On January 1, 2018, management decided to change from the average inventory costing method to the FIFO inventory costing method at each of its outlets.

The following table presents information concerning the change. The income tax rate for all years is 40%.

	Income before Income Tax		
	FIFO	Average Cost	Difference
Before 2017	$15 million	$8 million	$7 million
2017	8 million	5 million	3 million
2018	10 million	9 million	1 million

Required:
1. Prepare the journal entry to record the change in accounting principle.
2. Determine the net income to be reported in the 2018–2017 comparative income statements.
3. Which other 2017 amounts would be reported differently in the 2018–2017 comparative income statements and 2018–2017 comparative balance sheets than they were reported the previous year?

4. How would the change be reflected in the 2018–2017 comparative statements of shareholders' equity? Cash dividends were $1 million each year. Assume no dividends were paid prior to 2017.

E 20–8
Change in inventory methods; FIFO method to the LIFO method
● LO20–3

Flay Foods has always used the FIFO inventory costing method for both financial reporting and tax purposes. At the beginning of 2018, Flay decided to change to the LIFO method. As a result of the change, net income in 2018 was $80 million. If the company had used LIFO in 2017, its cost of goods sold would have been higher by $6 million that year. Flay's records of inventory purchases and sales are not available for 2016 and several previous years. Last year, Flay reported the following net income amounts in its comparative income statements:

($ in millions)	2017	2016	2015
Net income	$84	$82	$80

Required:
1. Prepare the journal entry at the beginning of 2018 to record the change in accounting principle. (Ignore income taxes.)
2. Briefly describe other steps Flay will take to report the change.
3. What amounts will Flay report for net income in its 2018–2016 comparative income statements?

E 20–9
Change in inventory methods; FIFO method to the LIFO method
● LO20–3

Wolfgang Kitchens has always used the FIFO inventory costing method for both financial reporting and tax purposes. At the beginning of 2018, Wolfgang decided to change to the LIFO method. Net income in 2018 was correctly stated as $90 million. If the company had used LIFO in 2017, its cost of goods sold would have been higher by $7 million that year. Company accountants are able to determine that the cumulative net income for all years prior to 2017 would have been lower by $23 million if LIFO had been used all along, but have insufficient information to determine specific effects of using LIFO in 2016. Last year, Wolfgang reported the following net income amounts in its comparative income statements:

($ in millions)	2017	2016	2015
Net income	$94	$92	$90

Required:
1. Prepare the journal entry at the beginning of 2018 to record the change in accounting principle. (Ignore income taxes.)
2. Briefly describe other steps Wolfgang will take to report the change.
3. What amounts will Wolfgang report for net income in its 2018–2016 comparative income statements?

E 20–10
Change in depreciation methods
● LO20–3

For financial reporting, Clinton Poultry Farms has used the declining-balance method of depreciation for conveyor equipment acquired at the beginning of 2015 for $2,560,000. Its useful life was estimated to be six years with a $160,000 residual value. At the beginning of 2018, Clinton decides to change to the straight-line method. The effect of this change on depreciation for each year is as follows:

	($ in thousands)		
Year	Straight-Line	Declining Balance	Difference
2015	$ 400	$ 853	$453
2016	400	569	169
2017	400	379	(21)
	$1,200	$1,801	$601

Required:
1. Briefly describe the way Clinton should report this accounting change in the 2017–2018 comparative financial statements.
2. Prepare any 2018 journal entry related to the change.

E 20–11
Change in depreciation methods
● LO20–3

The Canliss Milling Company purchased machinery on January 2, 2016, for $800,000. A five-year life was estimated and no residual value was anticipated. Canliss decided to use the straight-line depreciation method and recorded $160,000 in depreciation in 2016 and 2017. Early in 2018, the company changed its depreciation method to the sum-of-the-years'-digits (SYD) method.

Required:
1. Briefly describe the way Canliss should report this accounting change in the 2017–2018 comparative financial statements.
2. Prepare any 2018 journal entry related to the change.

E 20–12
Book royalties
● LO20–4

Dreighton Engineering Group receives royalties on a technical manual written by two of its engineers and sold to William B. Irving Publishing, Inc. Royalties are 10% of net sales, receivable on October 1 for sales in January through June and on April 1 for sales in July through December of the prior year. Sales of the manual began in July 2017, and Dreighton accrued royalty revenue of $31,000 at December 31, 2017, as follows:

Receivable—royalty revenue	31,000	
Royalty revenue		31,000

Dreighton received royalties of $36,000 on April 1, 2018, and $40,000 on October 1, 2018. Irving indicated to Dreighton on December 31 that book sales subject to royalties for the second half of 2018 are expected to be $500,000.

Required:

1. Prepare any journal entries Dreighton should record during 2018 related to the royalty revenue.
2. What adjustments, if any, should be made to retained earnings or to the 2017 financial statements? Explain.

E 20–13
Loss contingency
● LO20–4

The Commonwealth of Virginia filed suit in October 2016, against Northern Timber Corporation seeking civil penalties and injunctive relief for violations of environmental laws regulating forest conservation. When the financial statements were issued in 2017, Northern had not reached a settlement with state authorities, but legal counsel advised Northern Timber that it was probable the ultimate settlement would be $1,000,000 in penalties. The following entry was recorded:

Loss—litigation	1,000,000	
Liability—litigation		1,000,000

Late in 2018, a settlement was reached with state authorities to pay a total of $600,000 to cover the cost of violations.

Required:

1. Prepare any journal entries related to the change.
2. Briefly describe other steps Northern should take to report the change.

E 20–14
Warranty expense
● LO20–4

Woodmier Lawn Products introduced a new line of commercial sprinklers in 2017 that carry a one-year warranty against manufacturer's defects. Because this was the first product for which the company offered a warranty, trade publications were consulted to determine the experience of others in the industry. Based on that experience, warranty costs were expected to approximate 2% of sales. Sales of the sprinklers in 2017 were $2,500,000. Accordingly, the following entries relating to the contingency for warranty costs were recorded during the first year of selling the product:

Accrued liability and expense		
Warranty expense (2% × $2,500,000)	50,000	
Estimated warranty liability		50,000
Actual expenditures (summary entry)		
Estimated warranty liability	23,000	
Cash, wages payable, parts and supplies, etc		23,000

In late 2018, the company's claims experience was evaluated and it was determined that claims were far more than expected—3% of sales rather than 2%.

Required:

1. Assuming sales of the sprinklers in 2018 were $3,600,000 and warranty expenditures in 2018 totaled $88,000, prepare any journal entries related to the warranty.
2. Assuming sales of the sprinklers were discontinued after 2017, prepare any journal entries in 2018 related to the warranty.

E 20–15
Deferred taxes; change in tax rates
● LO20–4

Bronson Industries reported a deferred tax liability of $8 million for the year ended December 31, 2017, related to a temporary difference of $20 million. The tax rate was 40%. The temporary difference is expected to reverse in 2019, at which time the deferred tax liability will become payable. There are no other temporary differences in 2017–2019. Assume a new tax law is enacted in 2018 that causes the tax rate to change from 40% to 30% beginning in 2019. (The rate remains 40% for 2018 taxes.) Taxable income in 2018 is $30 million.

Required:

1. Determine the effect of the change and prepare the appropriate journal entry to record Bronson's income tax expense in 2018.
2. What adjustment, if any, is needed to revise retained earnings as a result of the change?

E 20–16
Accounting change
● LO20–4

The Peridot Company purchased machinery on January 2, 2016, for $800,000. A five-year life was estimated and no residual value was anticipated. Peridot decided to use the straight-line depreciation method and recorded $160,000 in depreciation in 2016 and 2017. Early in 2018, the company revised the total estimated life of the machinery to eight years.

Required:

1. What type of change is this?
2. Briefly describe the accounting treatment for this change.
3. Determine depreciation for 2018.

E 20–17
Change in estimate; useful life and residual value of equipment
● LO20–4

Wardell Company purchased a mini computer on January 1, 2016, at a cost of $40,000. The computer has been depreciated using the straight-line method over an estimated five-year useful life with an estimated residual value of $4,000. On January 1, 2018, the estimate of useful life was changed to a total of 10 years, and the estimate of residual value was changed to $900.

Required:

1. Prepare the appropriate adjusting entry for depreciation in 2018 to reflect the revised estimate.
2. Repeat requirement 1, assuming that the company uses the sum-of-the-years'-digits method instead of the straight-line method.

E 20–18
Classifying accounting changes
● LO20–1 through LO20–5

Indicate with the appropriate letter the nature of each situation described below:

Type of Change	
PR	Change in principle reported retrospectively
PP	Change in principle reported prospectively
E	Change in estimate
EP	Change in estimate resulting from a change in principle
R	Change in reporting entity
N	Not an accounting change

_____ 1. Change from declining balance depreciation to straight-line
_____ 2. Change in the estimated useful life of office equipment
_____ 3. Technological advance that renders worthless a patent with an unamortized cost of $45,000
_____ 4. Change from determining lower of cost or net realizable value (LCNRV) for the inventories by the individual item approach to the aggregate approach
_____ 5. Change from LIFO inventory costing to the weighted-average inventory costing
_____ 6. Settling a lawsuit for less than the amount accrued previously as a loss contingency
_____ 7. Including in the consolidated financial statements a subsidiary acquired several years earlier that was appropriately not included in previous years
_____ 8. Change by a retail store from reporting warranty expense on a pay-as-you-go basis to estimating the expense in the period of sale
_____ 9. A shift of certain manufacturing overhead costs to inventory that previously were expensed as incurred to more accurately measure cost of goods sold (Either method is generally acceptable)
_____ 10. Pension plan assets for a defined benefit pension plan achieving a rate of return in excess of the amount anticipated

E 20–19
Error correction; inventory error
● LO20–6

During 2018, WMC Corporation discovered that its ending inventories reported on its financial statements were misstated by the following amounts:

2016	understated by	$120,000
2017	overstated by	150,000

WMC uses the periodic inventory system and the FIFO cost method.

Required:

1. Determine the effect of these errors on retained earnings at January 1, 2018, before any adjustments. Explain your answer. (Ignore income taxes.)
2. Prepare a journal entry to correct the error.
3. What other steps would be taken in connection with the error?

E 20–20
Error corrections; investment
● LO20–6

On December 12, 2018, an investment costing $80,000 was sold for $100,000. The total of the sale proceeds was credited to the investment account.

Required:

1. Prepare the journal entry to correct the error, assuming it is discovered before the books are adjusted or closed in 2018. (Ignore income taxes.)

2. Prepare the journal entry to correct the error assuming it is not discovered until early 2019. (Ignore income taxes.)

E 20–21
Error in amortization schedule
● LO20–6

Wilkins Food Products Inc. acquired a packaging machine from Lawrence Specialists Corporation. Lawrence completed construction of the machine on January 1, 2016. In payment for the machine Wilkins issued a three-year installment note to be paid in three equal payments at the end of each year. The payments include interest at the rate of 10%. Lawrence made a conceptual error in preparing the amortization schedule, which Wilkins failed to discover until 2018. As a result of the error, Wilkins understated interest expense by $45,000 in 2016 and $40,000 in 2017.

Required:

1. Determine which accounts are incorrect as a result of these errors at January 1, 2018, before any adjustments. Explain your answer. (Ignore income taxes.)
2. Prepare a journal entry to correct the error.
3. What other steps would be taken in connection with the error?

E 20–22
Error correction; accrued interest on bonds
● LO20–6

At the end of 2017, Majors Furniture Company failed to accrue $61,000 of interest expense that accrued during the last five months of 2017 on bonds payable. The bonds mature in 2029. The discount on the bonds is amortized by the straight-line method. The following entry was recorded on February 1, 2018, when the semiannual interest was paid:

Interest expense	73,200	
Discount on bonds payable		1,200
Cash		72,000

Required:

Prepare any journal entry necessary to correct the error, as well as any adjusting entry for 2018 related to the situation described. (Ignore income taxes.)

E 20–23
Error correction; three errors
● LO20–6

Below are three independent and unrelated errors.

a. On December 31, 2017, Wolfe-Bache Corporation failed to accrue office supplies expense of $1,800. In January 2018, when it received the bill from its supplier, Wolfe-Bache made the following entry:

Office supplies expense	1,800	
Cash		1,800

b. On the last day of 2017, Midwest Importers received a $90,000 prepayment from a tenant for 2018 rent of a building. Midwest recorded the receipt as rent revenue.

c. At the end of 2017, Dinkins-Lowery Corporation failed to accrue interest of $8,000 on a note receivable. At the beginning of 2018, when the company received the cash, it was recorded as interest revenue.

Required:

For each error:

1. What would be the effect of each error on the income statement and the balance sheet in the 2017 financial statements?
2. Prepare any journal entries each company should record in 2018 to correct the errors.

E 20–24
Inventory errors
● LO20–6

For each of the following inventory errors occurring in 2018, determine the effect of the error on 2018's cost of goods sold, net income, and retained earnings. Assume that the error is not discovered until 2019 and that a periodic inventory system is used. Ignore income taxes.

U = Understated O = Overstated NE = No effect

		Cost of Goods Sold	Net Income	Retained Earnings
1.	Overstatement of ending inventory	U	O	O
2.	Overstatement of purchases			
3.	Understatement of beginning inventory			
4.	Freight-in charges are understated			
5.	Understatement of ending inventory			
6.	Understatement of purchases			
7.	Overstatement of beginning inventory			
8.	Understatement of purchases and understatement of ending inventory, by the same amount			

E 20–25
Classifying accounting changes and errors
● LO20–1 through LO20–6

Indicate with the appropriate letter the nature of each adjustment described below:

Type of Adjustment

A. Change in accounting principle (reported retrospectively)
B. Change in accounting principle (exception reported prospectively)
C. Change in estimate
D. Change in estimate resulting from a change in principle
E. Change in reporting entity
F. Correction of an error

_____ 1. Change from expensing extraordinary repairs to capitalizing the expenditures
_____ 2. Change in the residual value of machinery
_____ 3. Change from FIFO inventory costing to LIFO inventory costing
_____ 4. Change in the percentage used to determine warranty expense
_____ 5. Change from LIFO inventory costing to FIFO inventory costing
_____ 6. Change from reporting an investment by the equity method due to a reduction in the percentage of shares owned
_____ 7. Change in the composition of a group of firms reporting on a consolidated basis
_____ 8. Change from sum-of-the-years'-digits depreciation to straight-line
_____ 9. Change from FIFO inventory costing to average inventory costing
_____ 10. Change in actuarial assumptions for a defined benefit pension plan

Problems

connect

P 20–1
Change in inventory costing methods; comparative income statements
● LO20–2

The Cecil-Booker Vending Company changed its method of valuing inventory from the average cost method to the FIFO cost method at the beginning of 2018. At December 31, 2017, inventories were $120,000 (average cost basis) and were $124,000 a year earlier. Cecil-Booker's accountants determined that the inventories would have totaled $155,000 at December 31, 2017, and $160,000 at December 31, 2016, if determined on a FIFO basis. A tax rate of 40% is in effect for all years.

One hundred thousand common shares were outstanding each year. Income from continuing operations was $400,000 in 2017 and $525,000 in 2018. There were no discontinued operations either year.

Required:

1. Prepare the journal entry to record the change in accounting principle. (All tax effects should be reflected in the deferred tax liability account.)
2. Prepare the 2018–2017 comparative income statements beginning with income from continuing operations. Include per share amounts.

P 20–2
Change in principle; change in method of accounting for long-term construction
● LO20–2

The Pyramid Company has used the LIFO method of accounting for inventory during its first two years of operation, 2016 and 2017. At the beginning of 2018, Pyramid decided to change to the average cost method for both tax and financial reporting purposes. The following table presents information concerning the change for 2016–2018. The income tax rate for all years is 40%.

	Income before Income Tax				
	Average Cost Method	**LIFO Method**	**Difference**	**Income Tax Effect**	**Difference after Tax**
2016	$ 90,000	$60,000	$30,000	$12,000	$18,000
2017	45,000	36,000	9,000	3,600	5,400
Total	$135,000	$96,000	$39,000	$15,600	$23,400
2018	$ 51,000	$46,000	$ 5,000	$ 2,000	$ 3,000

Pyramid issued 50,000 $1 par, common shares for $230,000 when the business began, and there have been no changes in paid-in capital since then. Dividends were not paid the first year, but $10,000 cash dividends were paid in both 2017 and 2018.

Required:

1. Prepare the journal entry to record the change in accounting principle.
2. Prepare the 2018–2017 comparative income statements beginning with income before income taxes.
3. Prepare the 2018–2017 comparative statements of shareholders' equity. [Hint: The 2016 statements reported retained earnings of $36,000. This is $60,000 − ($60,000 × 40%).]

P 20–3
Change in inventory costing methods; comparative income statements
● LO20–2, LO20–3

Shown below are net income amounts as they would be determined by Weihrich Steel Company by each of three different inventory costing methods ($ in thousands).

	FIFO	Average Cost	LIFO
Pre-2017	$2,800	$2,540	$2,280
2017	750	600	540
	$3,550	$3,140	$2,820

Required:

1. Assume that Weihrich used FIFO before 2018, and then in 2018 decided to switch to average cost. Prepare the journal entry to record the change in accounting principle and briefly describe any other steps Weihrich should take to appropriately report the situation. (Ignore income tax effects.)
2. Assume that Weihrich used FIFO before 2018, and then in 2018 decided to switch to LIFO. Assume accounting records are inadequate to determine LIFO information prior to 2018. Therefore, the 2017 ($540) and pre-2017 ($2,280) data are not available. Prepare the journal entry to record the change in accounting principle and briefly describe any other steps Weihrich should take to appropriately report the situation. (Ignore income tax effects.)
3. Assume that Weihrich used FIFO before 2018, and then in 2018 decided to switch to LIFO cost. Weihrich's records of inventory purchases and sales are not available for several previous years. Therefore, the pre-2017 LIFO information ($2,280) is not available. However, Weihrich does have the information needed to apply LIFO on a prospective basis beginning in 2017. Prepare the journal entry to record the change in accounting principle, and briefly describe any other steps Weihrich should take to appropriately report the situation. (Ignore income tax effects.)

P 20–4
Change in inventory methods
● LO20–2

The Rockwell Corporation uses a periodic inventory system and has used the FIFO cost method since inception of the company in 1979. In 2018, the company decided to change to the average cost method. Data for 2018 are as follows:

Beginning inventory, FIFO (5,000 units @ $30.00)		$150,000
Purchases:		
5,000 units @ $36.00	$180,000	
5,000 units @ $40.00	200,000	380,000
Cost of goods available for sale		$530,000
Sales for 2018 (8,000 units @ $70.00)		$560,000

Additional Information:

1. The company's effective income tax rate is 40% for all years.
2. If the company had used the average cost method prior to 2018, ending inventory for 2017 would have been $130,000.
3. 7,000 units remained in inventory at the end of 2018.

Required:

1. Prepare the journal entry at the beginning of 2018 to record the change in principle.
2. In the 2018–2016 comparative financial statements, what will be the amounts of cost of goods sold and inventory reported for 2018?

P 20–5
Change in inventory methods
● LO20–2

Fantasy Fashions had used the LIFO method of costing inventories, but at the beginning of 2018 decided to change to the FIFO method. The inventory as reported at the end of 2017 using LIFO would have been $20 million higher using FIFO.

Retained earnings reported at the end of 2016 and 2017 was $240 million and $260 million, respectively (reflecting the LIFO method). Those amounts reflecting the FIFO method would have been $250 million and $272 million, respectively. 2017 net income reported at the end of 2017 was $28 million (LIFO method) but would have been $30 million using FIFO. After changing to FIFO, 2018 net income was $36 million. Dividends of $8 million were paid each year. The tax rate is 40%.

Required:

1. Prepare the journal entry at the beginning of 2018 to record the change in accounting principle.
2. In the 2018–2017 comparative income statements, what will be the amounts of net income reported for 2017 and 2018?
3. Prepare the 2018–2017 retained earnings column of the comparative statements of shareholders' equity.

P 20–6
Change in principle; change in depreciation methods
● LO20–3

During 2016 and 2017, Faulkner Manufacturing used the sum-of-the-years'-digits (SYD) method of depreciation for its depreciable assets, for both financial reporting and tax purposes. At the beginning of 2018, Faulkner decided to change to the straight-line method for both financial reporting and tax purposes. A tax rate of 40% is in effect for all years.

For an asset that cost $21,000 with an estimated residual value of $1,000 and an estimated useful life of 10 years, the depreciation under different methods is as follows:

Year	Straight Line	SYD	Difference
2016	$2,000	$3,636	$1,636
2017	2,000	3,273	1,273
	$4,000	$6,909	$2,909

Required:

1. Describe the way Faulkner should account for the change described. Include in your answer any journal entry Faulkner will record in 2018 related to the change and any required footnote disclosures.
2. Suppose instead that Faulkner previously used straight-line depreciation and changed to sum-of-the-years'-digits in 2018. Describe the way Faulkner should account for the change. Include in your answer any journal entry Faulkner will record in 2018 related to the change and any required note disclosures.

P 20–7
Depletion; change in estimate
● LO20–4

In 2018, the Marion Company purchased land containing a mineral mine for $1,600,000. Additional costs of $600,000 were incurred to develop the mine. Geologists estimated that 400,000 tons of ore would be extracted. After the ore is removed, the land will have a resale value of $100,000.

To aid in the extraction, Marion built various structures and small storage buildings on the site at a cost of $150,000. These structures have a useful life of 10 years. The structures cannot be moved after the ore has been removed and will be left at the site. In addition, new equipment costing $80,000 was purchased and installed at the site. Marion does not plan to move the equipment to another site, but estimates that it can be sold at auction for $4,000 after the mining project is completed.

In 2018, 50,000 tons of ore were extracted and sold. In 2019, the estimate of total tons of ore in the mine was revised from 400,000 to 487,500. During 2019, 80,000 tons were extracted.

Required:

1. Compute depletion and depreciation of the mine and the mining facilities and equipment for 2018 and 2019. Marion uses the units-of-production method to determine depreciation on mining facilities and equipment.
2. Compute the book value of the mineral mine, structures, and equipment as of December 31, 2019.

P 20–8
Accounting changes; six situations
● LO20–1, LO20–3, LO20–4

Described below are six independent and unrelated situations involving accounting changes. Each change occurs during 2018 before any adjusting entries or closing entries were prepared. Assume the tax rate for each company is 40% in all years. Any tax effects should be adjusted through the deferred tax liability account.

a. Fleming Home Products introduced a new line of commercial awnings in 2017 that carry a one-year warranty against manufacturer's defects. Based on industry experience, warranty costs were expected to approximate 3% of sales. Sales of the awnings in 2017 were $3,500,000. Accordingly, warranty expense and a warranty liability of $105,000 were recorded in 2017. In late 2018, the company's claims experience was evaluated, and it was determined that claims were far fewer than expected: 2% of sales rather than 3%. Sales of the awnings in 2018 were $4,000,000, and warranty expenditures in 2018 totaled $91,000.

b. On December 30, 2014, Rival Industries acquired its office building at a cost of $1,000,000. It was depreciated on a straight-line basis assuming a useful life of 40 years and no salvage value. However, plans were finalized in 2018 to relocate the company headquarters at the end of 2022. The vacated office building will have a salvage value at that time of $700,000.

c. Hobbs-Barto Merchandising, Inc., changed inventory cost methods to LIFO from FIFO at the end of 2018 for both financial statement and income tax purposes. Under FIFO, the inventory at January 1, 2018, is $690,000.

d. At the beginning of 2015, the Hoffman Group purchased office equipment at a cost of $330,000. Its useful life was estimated to be 10 years with no salvage value. The equipment was depreciated by the sum-of-the-years'-digits method. On January 1, 2018, the company changed to the straight-line method.

e. In November 2016, the State of Minnesota filed suit against Huggins Manufacturing Company, seeking penalties for violations of clean air laws. When the financial statements were issued in 2017, Huggins had not reached a settlement with state authorities, but legal counsel advised Huggins that it was probable the company would have to pay $200,000 in penalties. Accordingly, the following entry was recorded:

Loss—litigation	200,000	
Liability—litigation		200,000

Late in 2018, a settlement was reached with state authorities to pay a total of $350,000 in penalties.

f. At the beginning of 2018, Jantzen Specialties, which uses the sum-of-the-years'-digits method, changed to the straight-line method for newly acquired buildings and equipment. The change increased current year net earnings by $445,000.

Required:

For each situation:

1. Identify the type of change.
2. Prepare any journal entry necessary as a direct result of the change, as well as any adjusting entry for 2018 related to the situation described.
3. Briefly describe any other steps that should be taken to appropriately report the situation.

P 20–9
Accounting changes; identify type and reporting approach
● LO20–1 through LO20–4

At the beginning of 2018, Wagner Implements undertook a variety of changes in accounting methods, corrected several errors, and instituted new accounting policies.

Required:

Indicate for each item 1 to 10 below the type of change and the reporting approach Wagner would use.

Type of Change (choose one)	Reporting Approach (choose one)
P. Change in accounting principle	R. Retrospective approach
E. Change in accounting estimate	P. Prospective approach
EP. Change in estimate resulting from a change in principle	
X. Correction of an error	
N. Neither an accounting change nor an accounting error	

Change:

1. By acquiring additional stock, Wagner increased its investment in Wise, Inc., from a 12% interest to 25% and changed its method of accounting for the investment to the equity method.
2. Wagner instituted a postretirement benefit plan for its employees in 2018. Wagner did not previously have such a plan.
3. Wagner changed its method of depreciating computer equipment from the SYD method to the straight-line method.
4. Wagner determined that a liability insurance premium it both paid and expensed in 2017 covered the 2017–2019 period.
5. By selling shares in Launch Corp, Wagner decreased its investment in the company from a 23% interest to 15% and changed its method of accounting for the investment from the equity method to the fair value through net income method.
6. Due to an unexpected relocation, Wagner determined that its office building, previously depreciated using a 45-year life, should be depreciated using an 18-year life.
7. Wagner offers a three-year warranty on the farming equipment it sells. Manufacturing efficiencies caused Wagner to reduce its expectation of warranty costs from 2% of sales to 1% of sales.
8. Wagner changed from LIFO to FIFO to account for its materials and work-in-process inventories.
9. Wagner changed from FIFO to average cost to account for its equipment inventory.
10. Wagner sells extended service contracts on some of its equipment sold. Wagner performs services related to these contracts over several years, so in 2018, Wagner changed from recognizing revenue from these service contracts on a cash basis to the accrual basis.

P 20–10
Inventory errors
● LO20–6

You have been hired as the new controller for the Ralston Company. Shortly after joining the company in 2018, you discover the following errors related to the 2016 and 2017 financial statements:

a. Inventory at 12/31/2016 was understated by $6,000.
b. Inventory at 12/31/2017 was overstated by $9,000.
c. On 12/31/2017, inventory was purchased for $3,000. The company did not record the purchase until the inventory was paid for early in 2018. At that time, the purchase was recorded by a debit to purchases and a credit to cash.

The company uses a periodic inventory system.

Required:

1. Assuming that the errors were discovered after the 2017 financial statements were issued, analyze the effect of the errors on 2017 and 2016 cost of goods sold, net income, and retained earnings. (Ignore income taxes.)
2. Prepare a journal entry to correct the errors.
3. What other step(s) would be taken in connection with the error?

P 20–11
Error correction; change in depreciation method
● LO20–6

The Collins Corporation purchased office equipment at the beginning of 2016 and capitalized a cost of $2,000,000. This cost included the following expenditures:

Purchase price	$1,850,000
Freight charges	30,000
Installation charges	20,000
Annual maintenance charge	100,000
Total	$2,000,000

The company estimated an eight-year useful life for the equipment. No residual value is anticipated. The double-declining-balance method was used to determine depreciation expense for 2016 and 2017.

In 2018, after the 2017 financial statements were issued, the company decided to switch to the straight-line depreciation method for this equipment. At that time, the company's controller discovered that the original cost of the equipment incorrectly included one year of annual maintenance charges for the equipment.

Required:

1. Ignoring income taxes, prepare the appropriate correcting entry for the equipment capitalization error discovered in 2018.
2. Ignoring income taxes, prepare any 2018 journal entries related to the change in depreciation methods.

P 20–12
Accounting changes and error correction; seven situations; tax effects ignored
● LO20–1 through LO20–4, LO20–6

Williams-Santana Inc. is a manufacturer of high-tech industrial parts that was started in 2006 by two talented engineers with little business training. In 2018, the company was acquired by one of its major customers. As part of an internal audit, the following facts were discovered. The audit occurred during 2018 before any adjusting entries or closing entries were prepared.

a. A five-year casualty insurance policy was purchased at the beginning of 2016 for $35,000. The full amount was debited to insurance expense at the time.
b. Effective January 1, 2018, the company changed the salvage value used in calculating depreciation for its office building. The building cost $600,000 on December 29, 2007, and has been depreciated on a straight-line basis assuming a useful life of 40 years and a salvage value of $100,000. Declining real estate values in the area indicate that the salvage value will be no more than $25,000.
c. On December 31, 2017, merchandise inventory was overstated by $25,000 due to a mistake in the physical inventory count using the periodic inventory system.
d. The company changed inventory cost methods to FIFO from LIFO at the end of 2018 for both financial statement and income tax purposes. The change will cause a $960,000 increase in the beginning inventory at January 1, 2019.
e. At the end of 2017, the company failed to accrue $15,500 of sales commissions earned by employees during 2017. The expense was recorded when the commissions were paid in early 2018.
f. At the beginning of 2016, the company purchased a machine at a cost of $720,000. Its useful life was estimated to be 10 years with no salvage value. The machine has been depreciated by the double declining balance method. Its book value on December 31, 2017, was $460,800. On January 1, 2018, the company changed to the straight-line method.
g. Warranty expense is determined each year as 1% of sales. Actual payment experience of recent years indicates that 0.75% is a better indication of the actual cost. Management effects the change in 2018. Credit sales for 2018 are $4,000,000; in 2017 they were $3,700,000.

Required:

For each situation

1. Identify whether it represents an accounting change or an error. If an accounting change, identify the type of change.
2. Prepare any journal entry necessary as a direct result of the change or error correction, as well as any adjusting entry for 2018 related to the situation described. (Ignore tax effects.)
3. Briefly describe any other steps that should be taken to appropriately report the situation.

P 20–13
Accounting changes and error correction; seven situations; tax effects considered
● LO20–1 through LO20–4, LO20–6

(Note: This problem is a variation of P 20–12, modified to consider income tax effects.) Williams-Santana Inc. is a manufacturer of high-tech industrial parts that was started in 2006 by two talented engineers with little business training. In 2018, the company was acquired by one of its major customers. As part of an internal audit, the following facts were discovered. The audit occurred during 2018 before any adjusting entries or closing entries were prepared. The income tax rate is 40% for all years.

a. A five-year casualty insurance policy was purchased at the beginning of 2016 for $35,000. The full amount was debited to insurance expense at the time.
b. Effective January 1, 2018, the company changed the salvage values used in calculating depreciation for its office building. The building cost $600,000 on December 29, 2007, and has been depreciated on a

straight-line basis assuming a useful life of 40 years and a salvage value of $100,000. Declining real estate values in the area indicate that the salvage value will be no more than $25,000.

c. On December 31, 2017, merchandise inventory was overstated by $25,000 due to a mistake in the physical inventory count using the periodic inventory system.

d. The company changed inventory cost methods to FIFO from LIFO at the end of 2018 for both financial statement and income tax purposes. The change will cause a $960,000 increase in the beginning inventory at January 1, 2019.

e. At the end of 2017, the company failed to accrue $15,500 of sales commissions earned by employees during 2017. The expense was recorded when the commissions were paid in early 2018.

f. At the beginning of 2016, the company purchased a machine at a cost of $720,000. Its useful life was estimated to be ten years with no salvage value. The machine has been depreciated by the double-declining balance method. Its book value on December 31, 2017, was $460,800. On January 1, 2018, the company changed to the straight-line method.

g. Warranty expense is determined each year as 1% of sales. Actual payment experience of recent years indicates that 0.75% is a better indication of the actual cost. Management effects the change in 2018. Credit sales for 2018 are $4,000,000; in 2017 they were $3,700,000.

Required:

For each situation

1. Identify whether it represents an accounting change or an error. If an accounting change, identify the type of change.
2. Prepare any journal entry necessary as a direct result of the change or error correction, as well as any adjusting entry for 2018 related to the situation described. Any tax effects should be adjusted for through Income tax payable or Refund income tax.
3. Briefly describe any other steps that should be taken to appropriately report the situation.

P 20–14
Errors; change in estimate; change in principle; restatement of previous financial statements
● LO20–1, LO20–3, LO20–4, LO20–6

Whaley Distributors is a wholesale distributor of electronic components. Financial statements for the years ended December 31, 2016 and 2017, reported the following amounts and subtotals ($ in millions):

	Assets	Liabilities	Shareholders' Equity	Net Income	Expenses
2016	$740	$330	$410	$210	$150
2017	820	400	420	230	175

In 2018, the following situations occurred or came to light:

a. Internal auditors discovered that ending inventories reported on the financial statements the two previous years were misstated due to faulty internal controls. The errors were in the following amounts:

2016 inventory	Overstated by $12 million
2017 inventory	Understated by $10 million

b. A liability was accrued in 2016 for a probable payment of $7 million in connection with a lawsuit ultimately settled in December 2018 for $4 million.

c. A patent costing $18 million at the beginning of 2016, expected to benefit operations for a total of six years, has not been amortized since acquired.

d. Whaley's conveyer equipment was depreciated by the sum-of-the-years'-digits (SYD) basis since it was acquired at the beginning of 2016 at a cost of $30 million. It has an expected useful life of five years and no expected residual value. At the beginning of 2018, Whaley decided to switch to straight-line depreciation.

Required:

For each situation

1. Prepare any journal entry necessary as a direct result of the change or error correction, as well as any adjusting entry for 2018 related to the situation described. (Ignore tax effects.)
2. Determine the amounts to be reported for each of the five items shown above from the 2016 and 2017 financial statements when those amounts are reported again in the 2016–2018 comparative financial statements.

P 20–15
Correction of errors; six errors
● LO20–6

Conrad Playground Supply underwent a restructuring in 2018. The company conducted a thorough internal audit, during which the following facts were discovered. The audit occurred during 2018 before any adjusting entries or closing entries are prepared.

a. Additional computers were acquired at the beginning of 2016 and added to the company's office network. The $45,000 cost of the computers was inadvertently recorded as maintenance expense. Computers have five-year useful lives and no material salvage value. This class of equipment is depreciated by the straight-line method.

b. Two weeks prior to the audit, the company paid $17,000 for assembly tools and recorded the expenditure as office supplies. The error was discovered a week later.

c. On December 31, 2017, merchandise inventory was understated by $78,000 due to a mistake in the physical inventory count. The company uses the periodic inventory system.

d. Two years earlier, the company recorded a 4% stock dividend (2,000 common shares, $1 par) as follows:

Retained earnings	2,000	
Common stock		2,000

The shares had a market price at the time of $12 per share.

e. At the end of 2017, the company failed to accrue $104,000 of interest expense that accrued during the last four months of 2017 on bonds payable. The bonds, which were issued at face value, mature in 2022. The following entry was recorded on March 1, 2018, when the semiannual interest was paid, as well as on September 1 of each year:

Interest expense	156,000	
Cash		156,000

f. A three-year liability insurance policy was purchased at the beginning of 2017 for $72,000. The full premium was debited to insurance expense at the time.

Required:

For each error, prepare any journal entry necessary to correct the error, as well as any year-end adjusting entry for 2018 related to the situation described. (Ignore income taxes.)

P 20–16
Integrating problem; errors; deferred taxes; contingency; change in tax rates
● LO20–6

You are internal auditor for Shannon Supplies, Inc., and are reviewing the company's preliminary financial statements. The statements, prepared after making the adjusting entries, but before closing entries for the year ended December 31, 2018, are as follows:

SHANNON SUPPLIES, INC.
Balance Sheet
December 31, 2018

Assets	($ in thousands)
Cash	$2,400
Investments	250
Accounts receivable, net	810
Inventory	1,060
Property, plant, and equipment	1,240
Less: Accumulated depreciation	(560)
Total assets	$5,200
Liabilities and Shareholders' Equity	
Accounts payable and accrued expenses	$3,320
Income tax payable	220
Common stock, $1 par	200
Additional paid-in capital	750
Retained earnings	710
Total liabilities and shareholders' equity	$5,200

SHANNON SUPPLIES, INC.
Income Statement
For the Year Ended December 31, 2018

Sales revenue		$3,400
Operating expenses:		
Cost of goods sold	$1,140	
Selling and administrative	896	
Depreciation	84	2,120
Income before income tax		1,280
Income tax expense		(512)
Net income		$ 768

Shannon's income tax rate was 40% in 2018 and previous years. During the course of the audit, the following additional information (not considered when the above statements were prepared) was obtained:

a. Shannon's investment portfolio consists of blue chip stocks held for long-term appreciation. To raise working capital, some of the shares with an original cost of $180,000 were sold in May 2018. Shannon accountants debited cash and credited investments for the $220,000 proceeds of the sale.

b. At December 31, 2018, the fair value of the remaining securities in the portfolio was $274,000.

c. The state of Alabama filed suit against Shannon in October 2016, seeking civil penalties and injunctive relief for violations of environmental regulations regulating emissions. Shannon's legal counsel previously believed that an unfavorable outcome was not probable, but based on negotiations with state attorneys in 2018, now believe eventual payment to the state of $130,000 is probable, most likely to be paid in 2021.

d. The $1,060,000 inventory total, which was based on a physical count at December 31, 2018, was priced at cost. Based on your conversations with company accountants, you determined that the inventory cost was overstated by $132,000.

e. Electronic counters costing $80,000 were added to the equipment on December 29, 2017. The cost was charged to repairs.

f. Shannon's equipment, on which the counters were installed, had a remaining useful life of four years on December 29, 2017, and is being depreciated by the straight-line method for both financial and tax reporting.

g. A new tax law was enacted in 2018 which will cause Shannon's income tax rate to change from 40% to 35% beginning in 2019.

Required:

Prepare journal entries to record the effects on Shannon's accounting records at December 31, 2018, for each of the items described above. Show all calculations.

P 20–17
Integrating problem; error; depreciation; deferred taxes
● LO20–6

George Young Industries (GYI) acquired industrial robots at the beginning of 2015 and added them to the company's assembly process. During 2018, management became aware that the $1 million cost of the machinery was inadvertently recorded as repair expense on GYI's books and on its income tax return. The industrial robots have 10-year useful lives and no material salvage value. This class of equipment is depreciated by the straight-line method for financial reporting purposes and for tax purposes it is considered to be MACRS 7-year property. Cost deducted over 7 years by the modified accelerated recovery system as follows:

Year	MACRS Deductions
2015	$ 142,900
2016	244,900
2017	174,900
2018	124,900
2019	89,300
2020	89,200
2021	89,300
2022	44,600
Totals	$1,000,000

The tax rate is 40% for all years involved.

Required:

1. Prepare any journal entry necessary as a direct result of the error described.
2. Briefly describe any other steps GYI would take to appropriately report the situation.
3. Prepare the adjusting entry for 2018 depreciation.

Broaden Your Perspective

Apply your critical-thinking ability to the knowledge you've gained. These cases will provide you an opportunity to develop your research, analysis, judgment, and communication skills. You also will work with other students, integrate what you've learned, apply it in real-world situations, and consider its global and ethical ramifications. This practice will broaden your knowledge and further develop your decision-making abilities.

Integrating Case 20–1
Change to dollar-value LIFO
● LO20–3

Webster Products, Inc., adopted the dollar-value LIFO method of determining inventory costs for financial and income tax reporting on January 1, 2018. Webster continues to use the FIFO method for internal decision-making purposes. Webster's FIFO inventories at December 31, 2018, 2019, and 2020, were $300,000, $412,500, and $585,000, respectively. Internally generated cost indexes are used to convert FIFO inventory amounts to dollar-value LIFO amounts. Webster estimated these indexes as follows:

2018	1.00
2019	1.25
2020	1.50

Required:

1. Determine Webster's dollar-value LIFO inventory at December 31, 2019 and 2020.
2. Describe how the change should have been reported in Webster's 2018 financial statements.

Communication Case 20–2
Change in inventory method; disclosure note
● LO20–2

Mayfair Department Stores operates over 30 retail stores in the Pacific Northwest. Prior to 2018, the company used the FIFO method to value its inventory. In 2018, Mayfair decided to switch to the dollar-value LIFO retail inventory method. One of your responsibilities as assistant controller is to prepare the disclosure note describing the change in method that will be included in the company's 2018 financial statements. Kenneth Meier, the controller, provided the following information:

- Internally developed retail price indexes are used to adjust for the effects of changing prices.
- If the change had not been made, cost of goods sold for the year would have been $22 million lower. The company's income tax rate is 40% and there were 100 million shares of common stock outstanding during 2018.
- The cumulative effect of the change on prior years' income is not determinable.
- The reasons for the change were (a) to provide a more consistent matching of merchandise costs with sales revenue, and (b) the new method provides a more comparable basis of accounting with competitors that also use the LIFO method.

Required:

1. Prepare for Kenneth Meier the disclosure note that will be included in the 2018 financial statements.
2. Explain why the "cumulative effect of the change on prior years' income is not determinable."

Ethics Case 20–3
Softening the blow
● LO20–1, LO20–2, LO20–3

Late one Thursday afternoon, Joy Martin, a veteran audit manager with a regional CPA firm, was reviewing documents for a long-time client of the firm, AMT Transport. The year-end audit was scheduled to begin Monday.

For three months, the economy had been in a down cycle and the transportation industry was particularly hard hit. As a result, Joy expected AMT's financial results would not be pleasant news to shareholders. However, what Joy saw in the preliminary statements made her sigh aloud. Results were much worse than she feared.

"Larry (the company president) already is in the doghouse with shareholders," Joy thought to herself. "When they see these numbers, they'll hang him out to dry."

"I wonder if he's considered some strategic accounting changes," she thought, after reflecting on the situation. "The bad news could be softened quite a bit by changing inventory methods from LIFO to FIFO or reconsidering some of the estimates used in other areas."

Required:

1. How would the actions contemplated contribute toward "softening" the bad news?
2. Do you perceive an ethical dilemma? What would be the likely impact of following up on Joy's thoughts? Who would benefit? Who would be injured?

Analysis Case 20–4
Change in inventory methods; concepts
● LO20–2, LO20–3

Generally accepted accounting principles should be applied consistently from period to period. However, changes within a company, as well as changes in the external economic environment, may force a company to change an accounting method. The specific reporting requirements when a company changes from one generally accepted inventory method to another depend on the methods involved.

Required:

Explain the accounting treatment for a change in inventory method (a) not involving LIFO, (b) from the LIFO method, and (c) to the LIFO method. Explain the logic underlying those treatments. Also, describe how disclosure requirements are designed to address the departure from consistency and comparability of changes in accounting principle.

Communication Case 20–5
Change in loss contingency; write a memo
● LO20–4

Late in 2018, you and two other officers of Curbo Fabrications Corporation just returned from a meeting with officials of the City of Jackson. The meeting was unexpectedly favorable even though it culminated in a settlement with city authorities that your company pay a total of $475,000 to cover the cost of violations of city construction codes. Jackson filed suit in November 2016 against Curbo Fabrications Corporation, seeking civil penalties and injunctive relief for violations of city construction codes regulating earthquake damage standards. Alleged violations involved several construction projects completed during the previous three years. When the financial statements were issued in 2017, Curbo had not reached a settlement with state authorities, but legal counsel had advised the company that it was probable the ultimate settlement would be $750,000 in penalties. The following entry was recorded:

Loss—litigation	750,000	
Liability—litigation		750,000

The final settlement, therefore, was a pleasant surprise. While returning from the meeting, conversation turned to reporting the settlement in the 2018 financial statements. You drew the short straw and were selected to write a memo to Janet Zeno, the financial vice president, advising the proper course of action.

Required:

Write the memo. Include descriptions of any journal entries related to the change in amounts. Briefly describe other steps Curbo should take to report the settlement.

Analysis Case 20–6
Two wrongs make a right?
● LO20–4

Early one Wednesday afternoon, Ken and Larry studied in the dormitory room they shared at Fogelman College. Ken, an accounting major, was advising Larry, a management major, regarding a project for Larry's Business Policy class. One aspect of the project involved analyzing the 2018 annual report of Craft Paper Company. Though not central to his business policy case, a footnote had caught Larry's attention.

Depreciation and Cost of Timber Harvested (in part)

($ in millions)	2018	2017	2016
Depreciation of buildings, machinery and equipment	$260.9	$329.8	$322.5
Cost of timber harvested and amortization of logging roads	4.9	4.9	4.9
	$265.8	$334.7	$327.4

Beginning in 2018, the Company revised the estimated average useful lives used to compute depreciation for most of its pulp and paper mill equipment from 16 years to 20 years and for most of its finishing and converting equipment from 12 years to 15 years. These revisions were made to more properly reflect the true economic lives of the assets and to better align the Company's depreciable lives with the predominant practice in the industry. The change had the effect of increasing net income by approximately $55 million.

"If I understand this right, Ken, the company is not going back and recalculating a lower depreciation for earlier years. Instead they seem to be leaving depreciation overstated in earlier years and making up for that by understating it in current and future years," Larry mused. "Is that the way it is in accounting? Two wrongs make a right?"

Required:

What are the two wrongs to which Larry refers? Is he right?

Research Case 20–7
FASB codification; researching the way changes in postretirement benefit estimates are reported; retrieving disclosures from the Internet
● LO20–4

It's financial statements preparation time at Center Industries, where you have been assistant controller for two months. Ben Huddler, the controller, seems to be pleasant but unpredictable. Today, although your schedule is filled with meetings with internal and outside auditors and two members of the board of directors, Ben made a request. "As you know, we're decreasing the rate at which we assume health care costs will rise when measuring our postretirement benefit obligation. I'd like to know how others have reported similar changes. Can you find me an example?" he asked. "I'd bet you could get one off the Internet." As a matter of fact, you often use EDGAR, the Electronic Data Gathering, Analysis, and Retrieval system (www.sec.gov), to access financial statements filed with the U.S. Securities and Exchange Commission (SEC).

Required:

1. Access EDGAR on the Internet. Access a recent 10-K filing of a firm you think might have a postretirement health care plan. You may need to look up several companies before you find what you're looking for. Older, established companies are most likely to have such benefit plans.

   (Note: You may be able to focus your search by searching with key words and phrases in Google on the Internet.)
2. Find the portion of the disclosures that reports the effect of a change in health care cost trends.
3. What information is provided about the effect of the change on the company's estimated benefit obligation?
4. Obtain the relevant authoritative literature on the disclosure of accounting policies using the *FASB Accounting Standards Codification* at the FASB website (www.fasb.org). What authoritative literature do companies rely on when disclosing the effect of a change in health care cost trends?

Analysis Case 20–8
Various changes
● LO20–1 through LO20–4

DRS Corporation changed the way it depreciates its computers from the sum-of-the-year's-digits method to the straight-line method beginning January 1, 2018. DRS also changed its estimated residual value used in computing depreciation for its office building. At the end of 2018, DRS changed the specific subsidiaries constituting the group of companies for which its consolidated financial statements are prepared.

Required:

1. For each accounting change DRS undertook, indicate the type of change and how DRS should report the change. Be specific.
2. Why should companies disclose changes in accounting principles?

Analysis Case 20–9
Various changes
● LO20–1 through LO20–4

Ray Solutions decided to make the following changes in its accounting policies on January 1, 2018:

a. Changed from the cash to the accrual basis of accounting for recognizing revenue on its service contracts.
b. Adopted straight-line depreciation for all future equipment purchases, but continued to use accelerated depreciation for all equipment acquired before 2018.
c. Changed from the LIFO inventory method to the FIFO inventory method.

Required:

For each accounting change Ray undertook, indicate the type of change and how Ray should report the change. Be specific.

Judgment Case 20–10
Accounting changes; independent situations
● LO20–1 through LO20–5

Sometimes a business entity will change its method of accounting for certain items. The change may be classified as a change in accounting principle, a change in accounting estimate, or a change in reporting entity. Listed below are three independent, unrelated sets of facts relating to accounting changes.

Situation I: A company determined that the depreciable lives of its fixed assets are presently too long to fairly match the cost of the fixed assets with the revenue produced. The company decided at the beginning of the current year to reduce the depreciable lives of all of its existing fixed assets by five years.

Situation II: On December 31, 2017, Gary Company owned 51% of Allen Company, at which time Gary reported its investment on a nonconsolidated basis due to political uncertainties in the country in which Allen was located. On January 2, 2018, the management of Gary Company was satisfied that the political uncertainties were resolved and the assets of the company were in no danger of nationalization. Accordingly, Gary will prepare consolidated financial statements for Gary and Allen for the year ended December 31, 2018.

Situation III: A company decides in January 2018 to adopt the straight-line method of depreciation for plant equipment. The straight-line method will be used for new acquisitions as well as for previously acquired plant equipment, for which depreciation had been provided on an accelerated basis.

Required:

For each of the situations described above, provide the information indicated below. Complete your discussion of each situation before going on to the next situation.

1. Type of accounting change
2. Manner of reporting the change under current generally accepted accounting principles, including a discussion, where applicable, of how amounts are computed
3. Effect of the change on the balance sheet and income statement
4. Footnote disclosures that would be necessary

Judgment Case 20–11
Inventory errors
● LO20–6

Some inventory errors are said to be "self-correcting," in that the error has the opposite financial statement effect in the period following the error, thereby "correcting," the original account balance errors.

Required:

Despite this self correcting feature, discuss why these errors should not be ignored and describe the steps required to account for the error correction.

Ethics Case 20–12
Overstatement of ending inventory
● LO20–6

Danville Bottlers is a wholesale beverage company. Danville uses the FIFO inventory method to determine the cost of its ending inventory. Ending inventory quantities are determined by a physical count. For the fiscal year-end June 30, 2018, ending inventory was originally determined to be $3,265,000. However, on July 17, 2018, John Howard, the company's controller, discovered an error in the ending inventory count. He determined that the correct ending inventory amount should be $2,600,000.

Danville is a privately owned corporation with significant financing provided by a local bank. The bank requires annual audited financial statements as a condition of the loan. By July 17, the auditors had completed their review of the financial statements which are scheduled to be issued on July 25. They did not discover the inventory error.

John's first reaction was to communicate his finding to the auditors and to revise the financial statements before they are issued. However, he knows that his and his fellow workers' profit-sharing plans are based on annual pretax earnings and that if he revises the statements, everyone's profit sharing bonus will be significantly reduced.

Required:

1. Why will bonuses be negatively affected? What is the effect on pretax earnings?
2. If the error is not corrected in the current year and is discovered by the auditors during the following year's audit, how will the error be reported in the company's financial statements?
3. Discuss the ethical dilemma Howard faces.

Continuing Cases

Target Case

● LO20–2, LO20–4

Target Corporation prepares its financial statements according to U.S. GAAP. Target's financial statements and disclosure notes for the year ended January 30, 2016, are available in Connect. This material is also available under the Investor Relations link at the company's website (www.target.com). Target's share-based compensation includes several long-term incentive plans.

Required:

1. Refer to Target's financial statements for the year ended January 30, 2016. Note 12 provides information on Target's inventories. What method does Target use to report most of its inventories? If Target changed that method to another method, what are the steps Target would take to account for and report the change?
2. Suppose that Target uses FIFO costing method but decided to change to the LIFO method. What are the steps Target would take to account for and report the change?

Air France–KLM Case

IFRS

● LO20–2

Air France–KLM (AF), a Franco-Dutch company, prepares its financial statements according to International Financial Reporting Standards. AF's financial statements and disclosure notes for the year ended December 31, 2015, are available in Connect. This material also is available under the Finance link at the company's website (www.airfranceklm-finance.com).

Required:

1. Refer to AF's disclosure notes, in particular Note 2: Restatement of Accounts 2014. For the three changes in accounting principle reported in the note, does AF account for the changes prospectively or retrospectively? Is this the same approach AF would follow if using U.S. GAAP?
2. For the change described in 2.1, which if any account balances required adjustment?

CPA Exam Questions and Simulations

ROGER CPA Review

Sample CPA Exam questions from Roger CPA Review are available in Connect as support for the topics in this chapter. These Multiple Choice Questions and Task-Based Simulations include expert-written explanations and solutions, and provide a starting point for students to become familiar with the content and functionality of the actual CPA Exam.

CHAPTER

21 The Statement of Cash Flows Revisited

OVERVIEW

The objective of financial reporting is to provide investors and creditors with useful information, primarily in the form of financial statements. The balance sheet and the income statement—the focus of your study in earlier chapters—do not provide all the information needed by these decision makers. Here you will learn how the statement of cash flows fills the information gap left by the other financial statements.

The statement lists all cash inflows and cash outflows, and classifies them as cash flows from (a) operating, (b) investing, or (c) financing activities. Investing and financing activities that do not directly affect cash also are reported.

LEARNING OBJECTIVES

After studying this chapter, you should be able to:

- **LO21–1** Explain the usefulness of the statement of cash flows. *(p. 1205)*
- **LO21–2** Define cash equivalents. *(p. 1209)*
- **LO21–3** Determine cash flows from operating activities by the direct method. *(p. 1210)*
- **LO21–4** Determine cash flows from operating activities by the indirect method. *(p. 1211)*
- **LO21–5** Identify transactions that are classified as investing activities. *(p. 1212)*
- **LO21–6** Identify transactions that are classified as financing activities. *(p. 1213)*
- **LO21–7** Identify transactions that represent noncash investing and financing activities. *(p. 1215)*
- **LO21–8** Prepare a statement of cash flows with the aid of a spreadsheet or T-accounts. *(p. 1215)*
- **LO21–9** Discuss the primary differences between U.S. GAAP and IFRS with respect to the statement of cash flows. *(p. 1235)*

© Jose Luis Pelaez Inc./Blend Images LLC

FINANCIAL REPORTING CASE

Where's the Cash?

"What do you mean you can't afford a wage increase?" union negotiator Vince Barr insisted. "We've all seen your income statement. You had record earnings this year."

This is the first day of company negotiations with union representatives. As company controller, you know it's going to be up to you to explain the company's position on the financial aspects of the negotiations. In fact, you've known for some time that a critical point of contention would be the moderate increase in this year's profits after three years of level or slightly declining earnings. Not helping the situation is that the company has always used accelerated depreciation on its equipment, which it began replacing this year at considerably higher prices than it cost several years back.

QUESTIONS

By the time you finish this chapter, you should be able to respond appropriately to the questions posed in this case. Compare your response to the solution provided at the end of the chapter.

1. What are the cash flow aspects of the situation that Mr. Barr may be overlooking in making his case for a wage increase? How can a company's operations generate a healthy profit and yet produce meager or even negative cash flows? (*p. 1210*)
2. What information can a statement of cash flows provide about a company's investing activities that can be useful in decisions such as this? (*p. 1212*)
3. What information can a statement of cash flows provide about a company's financing activities that can be useful in decisions such as this? (*p. 1213*)

The Content and Value of the Statement of Cash Flows

PART A

Decision Makers' Perspective—Usefulness of Cash Flow Information

A fund manager of a major insurance company, considering investing $8,000,000 in the common stock of The Coca-Cola Company, asks herself, "What are the prospects of future dividends and market-price appreciation? Will we get a return commensurate with the cost and risk of our investment?" A bank officer, examining an application for a business loan, asks himself, "If I approve this loan, what is the likelihood of the borrower making interest payments on time and repaying the loan when due?" Investors and creditors continually face these and similar decisions that require projections of the relative ability of a business to generate future cash flows and of the risk associated with those forecasts.

LO21–1

To make these projections, decision makers rely heavily on the information reported in periodic financial statements. In the final analysis, cash flows into and out of a business enterprise are the most fundamental events on which investors and creditors base their decisions. Naturally, these decisions focus on the prospects of the decision makers receiving cash returns from their dealings with the firm. However, it is the ability of the firm to

Investors and creditors require cash flows from the corporation.

Cash flows to investors and creditors depend on the corporation generating cash flows to itself.

generate cash flows to itself that ultimately determines the potential for cash flows from the firm to investors and creditors.

The financial statements that have been the focus of your study in earlier chapters—the income statement and the balance sheet—offer information helpful in forecasting future cash-generating ability. Some important questions, however, are not easily answered from the information these statements provide. For example, meaningful projections of a company's future profitability and risk depend on answers to such questions as:

- In what types of activities is the company investing?
- Are these activities being financed with debt? With equity? By cash generated from operations?
- Are facilities being acquired to accommodate future expansion?
- How does the amount of cash generated from operations compare with net income over time?
- Why isn't the increase in retained earnings reflected as an increase in dividends?
- What happens to the cash received from the sale of assets?
- By what means is debt being retired?

Many decisions benefit from information about the company's underlying cash flow process.

The information needed to answer these and similar questions is found in the continuous series of cash flows that the income statement and the balance sheet describe only indirectly. This underlying cash flow process is considered next. ●

Cash Inflows and Outflows

Cash continually flows in and out of an active business. Businesses disburse cash to acquire property and equipment to maintain or expand productive capacity. When no longer needed, these assets may be sold for cash. Cash is paid to produce or purchase inventory for resale, as well as to pay for the expenses of selling these goods. The ultimate outcome of these selling activities is an inflow of cash. Cash might be invested in securities of other firms. These investments provide cash inflows during the investment period in the form of dividends or interest and at the end of the investment period when the securities are sold. To raise cash to finance their operations, firms sell stock and/or acquire debt. Cash payments are made as dividends to shareholders and interest to creditors. When debt is repaid or stock repurchased, cash flows out of the firm. To help you visualize the continual process of cash receipts and cash payments, that process is diagrammed in Illustration 21–1. The diagram also previews the way we will later classify the cash flows in a statement of cash flows.

Illustration 21–1

Cash Inflows and Cash Outflows

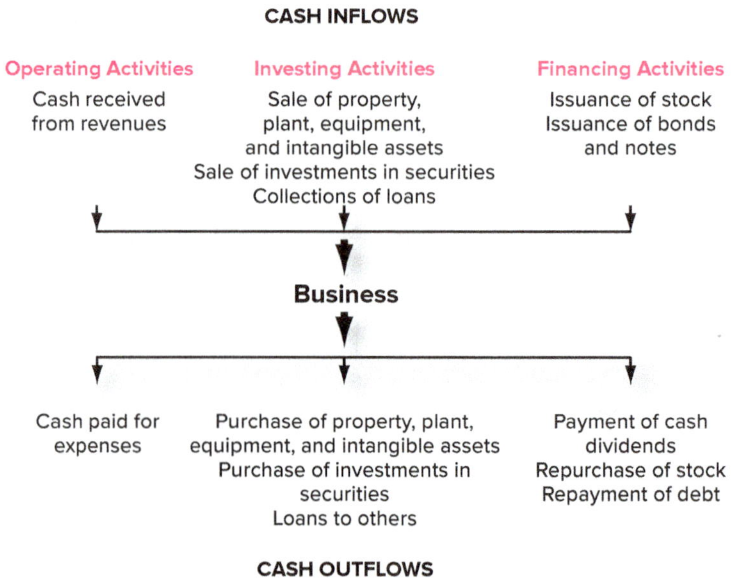

Embodied in this assortment of cash flows is a wealth of information that investors and creditors require to make educated decisions. Much of the value of the underlying information provided by the cash flows is lost when reported only indirectly by the balance sheet and the income statement. Each cash flow eventually impacts decision makers by affecting the balances of various accounts in the balance sheet. Also, many of the cash flows—those related to income-producing activities—are represented in the income statement. However, they are not necessarily reported in the period the cash flows occur because the income statement measures activities on an accrual basis. The statement of cash flows fills the information gap by reporting the cash flows directly.

The statement of cash flows provides information about cash flows that is lost when reported only indirectly by the balance sheet and the income statement.

Structure of the Statement of Cash Flows

A statement of cash flows is shown in Illustration 21–2. The statement lists all cash inflows and cash outflows during the reporting period. To enhance the informational value of the presentation, the cash flows are classified according to the nature of the activities that bring about the cash flows. The three primary categories of cash flows are (1) cash flows from operating activities, (2) cash flows from investing activities, and (3) cash flows from financing activities. Classifying each cash flow by source (operating, investing, or financing activities) is more informative than simply listing the various cash flows. Notice, too, that the noncash investing and financing activities—investing and financing activities that do not directly increase or decrease cash—also are reported. The GAAP requirement for the statement of cash flows was issued in direct response to *FASB Concept Statement 1,* which stated that the primary objective of financial reporting is to "provide information to help investors and creditors, and others assess the amounts, timing, and uncertainty of prospective net cash inflows to the related enterprise."[1]

Many companies suffered bankruptcy because they were unable to generate sufficient cash to satisfy their obligations. Doubtless, many investors in the stock of these firms would have been spared substantial losses if the financial statements had been designed to foresee the cash flow problems the companies were experiencing. A noted illustration is the demise of W. T. Grant during the 1970s. Grant, a general retailer in the days before malls, was a blue chip stock of its time. Grant's statement of changes in financial position (the predecessor of the statement of cash flows) reported working capital from operations of $46 million in 1972. Yet, if presented, a statement of cash flows would have reported cash flows from operating activities of negative $10 million. In fact, the unreported cash flow deficiency grew to $114 million in 1973, while working capital from operations was reported as having increased by $1 million. That year, without the benefit of cash flow information, investors were buying Grant's stock at prices that represented up to 20 times its earnings.[2]

More recently, even with cash flow information available, cash flow problems can go unnoticed. An example is the rapid growth and subsequent bankruptcy of the Wicks 'N' Sticks franchise. The company's drive for rapid growth led to a dependence on the sale of new franchises in order to generate cash flow instead of doing so in a more healthy way internally through its operations. As we see shortly, a statement of cash flows can indicate not just the amount of cash flows, but also whether those cash flows are coming from internal operations or from outside sources. Wicks 'N' Sticks was able to emerge from bankruptcy through restructuring and a new perspective on cash flow management.

Realize, too, that an unprofitable company with good cash flow can survive. Amazon.com provides an excellent example. Founded as an online seller of books in 1995, Amazon didn't actually make a profit for a decade, but it did raise huge amounts of cash by selling stock, so much so that it was able to weather 10 years of sizable losses. The financing cash inflows funded expansion into many new lines of business and made up for the continual losses. Amazon now has positive operating cash flows and is profitable.

[1]FASB Concepts Statement No. 8, Conceptual Framework for Financial Reporting–Chapter 1, *The Objective of General Purpose Financial Reporting,* and Chapter 3, *Qualitative Characteristics of Useful Financial Information* (a replacement of FASB Concepts Statements No. 1 and No. 2), *September 2010.*

[2]Cheryl A. Zega, "The New Statement of Cash Flows," *Management Accounting,* September 1988.

Illustration 21–2

Statement of Cash Flows

UNITED BRANDS CORPORATION
Statement of Cash Flows
For Year Ended December 31, 2018

Cash Flows from Operating Activities	($ in millions)	
Cash inflows:		
From customers	$ 98	
From investment revenue	3	
Cash outflows:		
To suppliers of goods	(50)	
To employees	(11)	
For interest	(3)	
For insurance	(4)	
For income taxes	(11)	
Net cash flows from operating activities		$ 22
Cash Flows from Investing Activities		
Purchase of land	(30)	
Purchase of short-term investment	(12)	
Sale of land	18	
Sale of equipment	5	
Net cash flows from investing activities		(19)
Cash Flows from Financing Activities		
Sale of common shares	26	
Retirement of bonds payable	(15)	
Payment of cash dividends	(5)	
Net cash flows from financing activities		6
Net increase in cash		9
Cash balance, January 1		20
Cash balance, December 31		$ 29

Note X:
Noncash Investing and Financing Activities

Acquired $20 million of equipment by issuing a 12%, 5-year note	$ 20

Reconciliation of Net Income to Cash Flows from Operating Activities:

Net income	$ 12
Adjustments for noncash effects:	
Gain on sale of land	(8)
Depreciation expense	3
Loss on sale of equipment	2
Changes in operating assets and liabilities:	
Increase in accounts receivable	(2)
Decrease in inventory	4
Increase in accounts payable	6
Increase in salaries payable	2
Discount on bonds payable	2
Decrease in prepaid insurance	3
Decrease in income tax payable	(2)
Net cash flows from operating activities	$ 22

The Importance of Cash Flows in an Economic Decline

The near-collapse of Bear Stearns in the Spring of 2008 likely will be remembered as the single most dramatic event in exposing the fragility of Wall Street and precipitating the most severe financial crisis since the Great Depression. At the heart of Bear's calamity and the subsequent worldwide economic decline was a shortage of cash flows. First Bear

Stearns; then Lehman Brothers; then AIG, Citigroup, Fannie Mae, and Freddie Mac. As we know, it didn't stop there. Each of these meltdowns involved a lack of measuring and monitoring the ebb and flow of cash.

When the financial industry is burdened with enormous amounts of uncollectible debt, as during the recent credit crisis, banks and others are reluctant to lend money. Cash becomes scarce. It's critical for companies to monitor their cash flows.

Let's say Lucky Strike Lures, Inc. manufactures fishing lures and sells them to a distributor. The distributor warehouses them before selling them to Bubba's Bait Shop, where they are put on display awaiting customers to buy them. During an economic downturn, the customers may delay buying the lures or not buy them at all. So, the lures stay in the store gathering dust, and Bubba's Bait can't pay for the lures that haven't sold. The distributor is then slow to pay Lucky Strike. Lucky Strike has bills to pay but no cash. In normal times, the company would go to the bank and borrow money. But in hard times, the bank is reluctant to lend. There is no quick fix as normal financing options are closed. Lucky Strike has cash flowing out but not flowing in.

The survival and success of every business depends on its ability to create or otherwise attain cash. You can be profitable and still go broke. Companies must closely plan and monitor their cash flows to stay in business. During the recent economic decline, even some of the most well-known companies suffered the consequences of not following this principle.

Cash is king! Especially during an economic downturn.

The statement of cash flows for United Brands Corporation (UBC), shown in Illustration 21–2, is intended at this point in the discussion to illustrate the basic structure and composition of the statement. Later, we will see how the statement of cash flows for UBC is prepared from the information typically available for this purpose. We will refer to UBC's statement of cash flows frequently throughout the chapter as the discussion becomes more specific regarding the criteria for classifying cash flows in the three primary categories and as we identify the specific cash flows to be reported on the statement. We will examine the content of the statement in more detail following a look at how this relatively recent financial statement has evolved to its present form over the course of the last several decades.

Cash, Cash Equivalents, and Restricted Cash

● LO21–2

Skilled cash managers will invest temporarily idle cash in short-term investments to earn interest on those funds, rather than maintain an unnecessarily large balance in a checking account. The FASB views short-term, highly liquid investments that can be readily converted to cash, with little risk of loss, as cash equivalents. Amounts held as investments of this type are essentially equivalent to cash because they are quickly available for use as cash. Therefore, on the statement of cash flows there is no differentiation between amounts held as cash (e.g., currency and checking accounts) and amounts held in cash equivalent investments. Similarly, sometimes companies might have contractual agreements that require specific amounts to be set aside for designated purposes, like debt repayment or workers' compensation claims. Those restricted cash amounts also are part of reported cash balances. So, when we refer in this chapter to cash, we are referring to the total of cash, cash equivalents, and restricted cash.

There is no differentiation between amounts held as cash and amounts held in cash equivalent investments or as restricted cash.

Examples of cash equivalents are money market funds, Treasury bills, and commercial paper. To be classified as cash equivalents, these investments must have a maturity date not longer than three months from the date of purchase. Flexibility is permitted in designating cash equivalents. Each company must establish a policy regarding which short-term, highly liquid investments it classifies as cash equivalents. The policy should be consistent with the company's customary motivation for acquiring various investments and should be disclosed in the notes to the statement.[3] A recent annual report of ExxonMobil Corporation provides this description of its cash equivalents (Illustration 21–3):

Each firm's policy regarding which short-term, highly liquid investments it classifies as cash equivalents should be disclosed in the notes to the financial statements.

Note 4: Cash Flow Information (in part)

The consolidated statement of cash flows provides information about changes in cash and cash equivalents. Highly liquid investments with maturities of three months or less when acquired are classified as cash equivalents.

Illustration 21–3

Disclosure of Cash Equivalents—ExxonMobil Corporation

Real World Financials

[3]A change in that policy is treated as a change in accounting principle.

Transactions that involve merely transfers from cash to cash equivalents (such as the purchase of a three-month Treasury bill), or from cash equivalents to cash (such as the sale of a Treasury bill), should not be reported on the statement of cash flows. The total of cash and cash equivalents is not altered by such transactions.[4] The cash balance reported in the balance sheet also represents the total of cash and cash equivalents, which allows us to compare the change in that balance with the net increase or decrease in the cash flows reported on the statement of cash flows.

● LO21–3

Primary Elements of the Statement of Cash Flows

This section describes the three primary activity classifications: (1) operating activities, (2) investing activities, and (3) financing activities. It also describes two other requirements of the statement of cash flows: (4) the reconciliation of the net increase or decrease in cash with the change in the balance of the cash account and (5) noncash investing and financing activities.

FINANCIAL Reporting Case

Q1, p. 1205

CASH FLOWS FROM OPERATING ACTIVITIES. The income statement reports the success of a business in generating a profit from its operations. Net income (or loss) is the result of netting together the revenues recognized during the reporting period, regardless of when cash is received, and the expenses incurred in generating those revenues, regardless of when cash is paid. This is the accrual concept of accounting that has been emphasized throughout your study of accounting. Information about net income and its components, measured by the accrual concept, generally provides a better indication of current operating performance than does information about current cash receipts and payments.[5] Nevertheless, as indicated earlier, the cash effects of earning activities also provide useful information that is not directly accessible from the income statement. The first cash flow classification in the statement of cash flows reports that information.

The cash effects of the elements of net income are reported as cash flows from operating activities.

Cash flows from operating activities are both inflows and outflows of cash that result from activities reported in the income statement. In other words, this classification of cash flows includes the elements of net income, but reported on a cash basis. The components of this section of the statement of cash flows, and their relationship with the elements of the income statement, are illustrated in Illustration 21–4.

Illustration 21–4

Relationship between the Income Statement and Cash Flows from Operating Activities (Direct Method)

Income Statement	Cash Flows from Operating Activities
Revenues:	Cash inflows:
Sales and service revenue	Cash received from customers
Investment revenue	Cash revenue received (e.g., dividends, interest)
Noncash revenues and gains (e.g., gain on sale of assets)	(Not reported)
Less: Expenses:	Less: Cash outflows:
Cost of goods sold	Cash paid to suppliers of inventory
Salaries expense	Cash paid to employees
Noncash expenses and losses (e.g., depreciation, amortization, loss on sale of assets)	(Not reported)
Interest expense	Cash paid to creditors
Other operating expenses	Cash paid to insurance companies and others
Income tax expense	Cash paid to the government
Net income	*Net cash flows from operating activities*

[4]An exception is the sale of a cash equivalent at a gain or loss. This exception is described in more detail later in the chapter.

[5]FASB Concepts Statement No. 8, *Conceptual Framework for Financial Reporting*–Chapter 1, "*The Objective of General Purpose Financial Reporting*," and Chapter 3, "*Qualitative Characteristics of Useful Financial Information*" (a replacement of FASB Concepts Statements No. 1 and No. 2), September 2010.

To see the concept applied, let's look again at the cash flows from operating activities reported by United Brands Corporation. That section of the statement of cash flows is extracted from Illustration 21–2 and reproduced in Illustration 21–5.

Illustration 21–5

Cash Flows from Operating Activities; Direct Method

Cash Flows from Operating Activities:		
Cash inflows:		
From customers	$ 98	
From investment revenue	3	
Cash outflows:		
To suppliers of goods	(50)	
To employees	(11)	
For interest	(3)	
For insurance	(4)	
For income taxes	(11)	
Net cash flows from operating activities		$22

Cash flows from operating activities are the elements of net income, but reported on a cash basis.

Cash inflows from operating activities exceeded cash outflows for expenses by $22 million. We'll see later (in Illustration 21–9) that UBC's net income from the same operating activities was only $12 million. Why did operating activities produce net cash inflows greater than net income? The reason will become apparent when we determine, in a later section, the specific amounts of these cash flows.

You also should be aware that the generalization stated earlier that cash flows from operating activities include the elements of net income reported on a cash basis is not strictly true for all elements of the income statement. Notice in Illustration 21–5 that no cash effects are reported for depreciation and amortization of property, plant, and equipment, and intangibles, nor for gains and losses from the sale of those assets. Cash outflows occur when these assets are acquired, and cash inflows occur when the assets are sold. However, as described later, the acquisition and subsequent resale of these assets are classified as investing activities rather than as operating activities.

Quite the opposite, the purchase and the sale of inventory are considered operating activities. The cash effects of these transactions—namely, (1) cash payments to suppliers and (2) cash receipts from customers—are included in the determination of cash flows from operating activities. Why are inventories treated differently from property, plant, equipment, and intangible assets when classifying their cash effects if they all are acquired for the purpose of producing revenues? The essential difference is that inventory typically is purchased for the purpose of being sold as part of the firm's current operations, while the other assets are purchased as investments to benefit the business over a relatively long period of time.

DIRECT METHOD OR INDIRECT METHOD OF REPORTING CASH FLOWS FROM OPERATING ACTIVITIES. The presentation by UBC of cash flows from operating activities illustrated in Illustration 21–2 and reproduced in Illustration 21–5 is referred to as the **direct method**. The method is named for the fact that the cash effect of each operating activity (i.e., income statement item) is reported *directly* in the statement of cash flows. For instance, UBC reports "cash received from customers" as the cash effect of sales activities, "cash paid to suppliers" as the cash effect of cost of goods sold, and so on. Then, UBC simply omits from the presentation any income statement items that do not affect cash at all, such as depreciation expense.

● LO21–4

Another way UBC might have reported cash flows from operating activities is by the **indirect method**. By this approach, the net cash increase or decrease from operating activities ($22 million in our example) would be derived *indirectly* by starting with reported net income and working backwards to convert that amount to a cash basis. As we see later in the chapter, UBC's net income is $12 million. Using the indirect method, UBC would replace the previous presentation of net cash flows from operating activities with the one shown in Illustration 21–6.

Illustration 21–6

Cash Flows from Operating Activities; Indirect Method

By the indirect method, UBC derives the net cash increase or decrease from operating activities indirectly, by starting with reported net income and working backwards to convert that amount to a cash basis.

Cash Flows from Operating Activities		
Net income	$12	
Adjustments for noncash effects:		
Gain on sale of land	(8)	
Depreciation expense	3	
Loss on sale of equipment	2	
Changes in operating assets and liabilities:		
Increase in accounts receivable	(2)	
Decrease in inventory	4	
Increase in accounts payable	6	
Increase in salaries payable	2	
Decrease in discount on bonds payable	2	
Decrease in prepaid insurance	3	
Decrease in income tax payable	(2)	
Net cash flows from operating activities		$22

Be sure to note that the indirect method generates the same $22 million net cash flows from operating activities as the direct method. Rather than directly reporting only the components of the income statement that *do* represent increases or decreases in cash, by the indirect method we begin with net income—which includes both cash and noncash components—and back out all amounts that *don't* reflect increases or decreases in cash. Later in the chapter, we explore the specific adjustments made to net income to achieve this result. At this point, it is sufficient to realize that two alternative methods are permitted for reporting net cash flows from operating activities. Either way, we convert accrual-based income to cash flows produced by those same operating activities.

Notice also that the indirect method presentation is identical to what UBC reported earlier as the "Reconciliation of Net Income to Cash Flows from Operating Activities" in Note X of Illustration 21–2. Whether cash flows from operating activities are reported by the direct method or by the indirect method, the financial statements must reconcile the difference between net income and cash flows from operating activities. When a company uses the *direct method,* the company presents the reconciliation in a separate schedule, as UBC does. That presentation is precisely the same as the presentation of net cash flows from operating activities by the indirect method. On the other hand, a company choosing to use the indirect method is not required to provide a separate reconciliation schedule because the "cash flows from operating activities" section of the statement of cash flows serves that purpose. Most companies use the indirect method.[6]

It's important to understand, too, that regardless of which method a company chooses to report *operating* activities, that choice has no effect on the way it identifies and reports cash flows from *investing* and *financing* activities. We turn our attention now to those two sections of the statement of cash flows. Later, in Part C, we'll return for a more thorough discussion of the alternative methods of reporting the operating activities section.

FINANCIAL Reporting Case

Q2, p. 1205

CASH FLOWS FROM INVESTING ACTIVITIES. Companies periodically invest cash to replace or expand productive facilities such as property, plant, and equipment. Investments might also be made in other assets, such as securities of other firms, with the expectation of a return on those investments. Information concerning these investing activities can provide valuable insight to decision makers regarding the nature and magnitude of assets being acquired for future use, as well as provide clues concerning the company's ambitions for the future.

LO21–5

Cash flows from investing activities are both outflows and inflows of cash caused by the acquisition and disposition of assets. Included in this classification are cash payments to acquire (1) property, plant, and equipment and other productive assets (except inventories);

[6]According to the *AICPA, U.S. GAAP Financial Statements–Best Practices in Presentation and Disclosure–2013,* a survey of 500 companies showed that 495 companies chose to use the indirect method, only 5 the direct method.

(2) investments in securities (except cash equivalents and trading securities); and (3) nontrade receivables.[7,8] When these assets later are liquidated, any cash receipts from their disposition also are classified as investing activities. For instance, cash received from the sale of the assets or from the collection of a note receivable (principal amount only) represents cash inflows from investing activities. Be sure to realize that, unlike what the label might imply, any investment revenue like interest, dividends, or other cash return from these investments is not an investing activity. The reason, remember, is that investment revenue is an income statement item and therefore is an operating activity.

Cash outflows and cash inflows due to the acquisition and disposition of assets (other than inventory and assets classified as cash equivalents) are reported as cash flows from investing activities.

For illustration, notice the cash flows reported as investing activities by UBC. That section of the statement of cash flows is extracted from the complete statement in Illustration 21–2 and reproduced in Illustration 21–7.

Illustration 21–7

Cash Flows from Investing Activities

Cash flows from investing activities include investments in assets and their subsequent sale.

Cash Flows from Investing Activities:		
Purchase of land	$(30)	
Purchase of short-term investment	(12)	
Sale of land	18	
Sale of equipment	5	
Net cash flows from investing activities		$(19)

UBC reports as investing activities the cash paid to purchase both land and a short-term investment. The other two investing activities reported are cash receipts for the sale of assets—equipment and land—that were acquired in earlier years. The specific transactions creating these cash flows are described in a later section of this chapter.

The purchase and sale of inventories are not considered investing activities. Inventories are purchased for the purpose of being sold as part of the firm's primary operations, so their purchase and sale are classified as operating activities.

Also, the purchase and sale of assets classified as cash equivalents are not reported as investing activities. In fact, these activities usually are not reported on the statement of cash flows. For example, when temporarily idle cash is invested in a money market fund considered to be a cash equivalent, the total of cash and cash equivalents does not change. Likewise, when the cash is later withdrawn from the money market fund, the total remains unchanged. The exception is when cash equivalents are sold at a gain or a loss. In that case, the total of cash and cash equivalents actually increases or decreases in the process of transferring from one cash equivalent account to another cash equivalent account. As a result, the change in cash would be reported as a cash flow from operating activities. This is illustrated later in the chapter.

CASH FLOWS FROM FINANCING ACTIVITIES. Not only is it important for investors and creditors to be informed about how a company is investing its funds, but also how its investing activities are being financed. Hopefully, the primary operations of the firm provide a source of internal financing. Information revealed in the cash flows from operating activities section of the statement of cash flows lets statement users know the extent of available internal financing. However, a major portion of financing for many companies is provided by external sources, specifically by shareholders and creditors.

FINANCIAL Reporting Case

Q3, p. 1205

● LO21–6

Cash flows from financing activities are both inflows and outflows of cash resulting from the external financing of a business. We include in this classification cash inflows from (a) the sale of common and preferred stock and (b) the issuance of bonds and other debt securities. Subsequent transactions related to these financing transactions, such as a buyback of stock (to retire the stock or as treasury stock), the repayment of debt, and the payment of cash dividends to shareholders, also are classified as financing activities.

Cash inflows and cash outflows due to the external financing of a business are reported as cash flows from financing activities.

[7]Inflows and outflows of cash from buying and selling trading securities typically are considered operating activities because financial institutions that routinely transact in trading securities consider them an appropriate part of their normal operations.

[8]A nontrade receivable differs from a trade receivable in that it is not one associated with the company's normal trade; that is, it's not received from a customer. A trade receivable, or accounts receivable, is an *operating asset.* A nontrade receivable, on the other hand, might be a loan to an affiliate company or to an officer of the firm. To understand how the creation of a nontrade receivable is an *investing* activity, you might view such a loan as an investment in the receivable.

For illustration, refer to Illustration 21–8 excerpted from the complete statement of cash flows of UBC in Illustration 21–2.

Illustration 21–8

Cash Flows from Financing Activities

Cash flows from financing activities include the sale or repurchase of shares, the issuance or repayment of debt securities, and the payment of cash dividends.

Cash Flows from Financing Activities:		
Sale of common shares	$ 26	
Retirement of bonds payable	(15)	
Payment of cash dividends	(5)	
Net cash flows from financing activities		$6

The cash received from the sale of common stock is reported as a financing activity. Since the sale of common stock is a financing activity, providing a cash return (dividend) to common shareholders also is a financing activity. Similarly, when the bonds being retired were issued in a prior year, that cash inflow was reported as a financing activity. In the current year, when the bonds are retired, that same amount of the resulting cash outflow is likewise classified as a financing activity.

Interest, unlike dividends, is a determinant of net income and therefore an operating activity.

At first glance, it may appear inconsistent to classify the payment of cash dividends to shareholders as a financing activity when, as stated earlier, paying interest to creditors is classified as an operating activity. But remember, cash flows from operating activities should reflect the cash effects of items that enter into the determination of net income. Interest expense is a determinant of net income. A dividend, on the other hand, is a distribution of net income and not an expense.

Additional Consideration

Sometimes a cash receipt or a cash payment relates to more than one type of activity. For instance, proceeds from an insurance policy might be for a fire loss for a building that contained both equipment in use and inventory for sale. In that case, the cash proceeds pertaining to the building and the equipment is an investing activity and the part pertaining to inventory is an operating activity. It's not always clear how a cash flow should be allocated. When the "nature of the cash flows" cannot be determined using reasonable judgment, the classification should be based on the "predominance principle"—that is, the activity that is likely to be the predominant source or use of cash flows.

RECONCILIATION WITH CHANGE IN CASH BALANCE. One of the first items you may have noticed about UBC's statement of cash flows is that there is a net change in cash of $9 million. Is this a significant item of information provided by the statement? The primary objective of the statement of cash flows is not to tell us that cash increased by $9 million. We can readily see the increase or decrease in cash by comparing the beginning and ending balances in the cash account in comparative balance sheets. Instead, the purpose of the statement of cash flows is to explain *why* cash increased by $9 million.

To reinforce the fact that the net amount of cash inflows and outflows explains the change in the cash balance, the statement of cash flows includes a reconciliation of the net increase (or decrease) in cash with the company's beginning and ending cash balances. Notice, for instance, that on UBC's statement of cash flows, the reconciliation appears as:

The net amount of cash inflows and outflows reconciles the change in the company's beginning and ending cash balances.

Net increase in cash	$ 9
Cash balance, January 1	20
Cash balance, December 31	$29

NONCASH INVESTING AND FINANCING ACTIVITIES. Suppose UBC were to borrow $20 million cash from a bank, issuing a long-term note payable for that amount. This transaction would be reported on a statement of cash flows as a financing activity. Now suppose UBC used that $20 million cash to purchase new equipment. This second transaction would be reported as an investing activity.

Instead of two separate transactions, as indicated by Illustration 21–2, UBC acquired $20 million of new equipment by issuing a $20 million long-term note payable in a single transaction. Undertaking a significant investing activity and a significant financing activity as two parts of a single transaction does not diminish the value of reporting these activities. For that reason, transactions that do not increase or decrease cash, but which result in significant investing and financing activities, must be reported in related disclosures.

● LO21–7

These **noncash investing and financing activities**, such as UBC's acquiring equipment (an investing activity) by issuing a long-term note payable (a financing activity), are reported in a separate disclosure schedule or note. UBC reported this transaction in the following manner:

Significant noncash investing and financing activities are reported also.

Noncash Investing and Financing Activities:

Acquired $20 million of equipment by issuing a 12%, 5-year note.

It's convenient to report noncash investing and financing activities on the same page as the statement of cash flows, as did UBC, only if there are few such transactions. Otherwise, precisely the same information would be reported in disclosure notes to the financial statements.[9]

Examples of noncash transactions that would be reported in this manner are as follows:

1. Acquiring an asset by incurring a debt payable to the seller
2. Acquiring use of an asset by entering into a lease agreement
3. Converting debt into common stock or other equity securities
4. Exchanging noncash assets or liabilities for other noncash assets or liabilities

Noncash transactions that do not affect a company's assets or liabilities, such as the distribution of stock dividends, are not considered investing or financing activities and are not reported. Recall from Chapter 18 that stock dividends merely increase the number of shares of stock owned by existing shareholders. From an accounting standpoint, the stock dividend causes a dollar amount to be transferred from one part of shareholders' equity (retained earnings) to another part of shareholders' equity (paid-in capital). Neither assets nor liabilities are affected; therefore, no investing or financing activity has occurred.

Preparation of the Statement of Cash Flows

The objective in preparing the statement of cash flows is to identify all transactions and events that represent operating, investing, or financing activities and to list and classify those activities in proper statement format. A difficulty in preparing a statement of cash flows is that typical accounting systems are not designed to produce the specific information we need for the statement. At the end of a reporting cycle, balances exist in accounts reported in the income statement (sales revenue, cost of goods sold, etc.) and the balance sheet (accounts receivable, common stock, etc.). However, the ledger contains no balances for cash paid to acquire equipment, or cash received from sale of land, or any other cash flow needed for the statement. As a result, it's necessary to find a way of using available information to reconstruct the various cash flows that occurred during the reporting period. Typically, the information available to assist the statement preparer includes an income statement for the year and balance sheets for both the current and preceding years (comparative statements). The accounting records also can provide additional information about transactions that caused changes in account balances during the year.

● LO21–8

Additional Consideration

A transaction involving an investing and financing activity may be part cash and part noncash. For example, a company might pay cash for a part of the purchase price of new equipment and issue a long-term note for the remaining amount. In our previous illustration, UBC issued a note payable for the $20 million cost of the equipment it acquired.

(continued)

[9]FASB ASC 230–10–50–6: Statement of Cash Flows–Overall–Disclosure–Noncash Investing and Financing Activities (previously "Statement of Cash Flows," *Statement of Financial Accounting Standards No. 95* (Stamford, Conn.: FASB, 1987), par. 74).

(concluded)

Suppose the equipment were purchased in the following manner:

Equipment	20	
Cash		6
Note payable		14

In that case, $6 million would be reported under the caption "Cash flows from investing activities," and the noncash portion of the transaction—issuing a $14 million note payable for $14 million of equipment—would be reported as a "noncash investing and financing activity." UBC's statement of cash flows, if modified by the assumption of a part cash/part noncash transaction, would report these two elements of the transaction as follows:

Cash Flows from Investing Activities:		
Purchase of land	$(30)	
Purchase of short-term investments	(12)	
Sale of land	18	
Sale of equipment	5	
Purchase of equipment	(6)	
Net cash flows from investing activities		$(25)

Noncash Investing and Financing Activities:

Acquired $20 million of equipment by paying cash and issuing a 12%, 5-year note as follows:

Cost of equipment	$20 million
Cash paid	(6 million)
Note issued	$14 million

The typical year-end data is provided for UBC in Illustration 21–9. We have referred frequently to the statement of cash flows of UBC to illustrate the nature of the activities the statement reports. Now we'll see how that statement is developed from the data provided in that illustration.

In situations involving relatively few transactions, it's possible to prepare the statement of cash flows by merely inspecting the available data and logically determining the reportable activities. Few real-life situations are sufficiently simple to be solved this way. Usually, it is more practical to use some systematic method of analyzing the available data to ensure that all operating, investing, and financing activities are detected. A common approach is to use either a manual or electronic spreadsheet to organize and analyze the information used to prepare the statement.[10]

Reconstructing the events and transactions that occurred during the period helps identify the operating, investing, and financing activities to be reported.

Whether the statement of cash flows is prepared by an unaided inspection and analysis or with the aid of a systematic technique such as spreadsheet analysis, the analytical process is the same. To identify the activities to be reported in the statement, we use available data to reconstruct the events and transactions that involved operating, investing, and financing activities during the year. It is helpful to reproduce the journal entries that were recorded at the time of the transaction. Examining reconstructed journal entries makes it easier to visualize whether a reportable activity is involved and how that activity is to be classified.

Next, in Part B, we see how a spreadsheet simplifies the process of preparing a statement of cash flows. Even if you choose not to use a spreadsheet, the summary entries described can be used to help you find the cash inflows and outflows you need to prepare a statement of cash flows. For this demonstration, we assume the direct method is used to determine and report cash flows from operating activities. Appreciation of the direct method provides the backdrop for a thorough understanding of the indirect method that we explore in Part C.

[10]The T-account method is a second systematic approach to the preparation of the statement of cash flows. This method is identical in concept and similar in application to the spreadsheet method. The T-account method is used to prepare the statement of cash flows for UBC in Appendix 21B.

Illustration 21–9

Comparative Balance Sheets and Income Statement

UNITED BRANDS CORPORATION
Comparative Balance Sheets
December 31, 2018 and 2017
($ in millions)

	2018	2017
Assets		
Cash	$ 29	$ 20
Accounts receivable	32	30
Short-term investments	12	0
Inventory	46	50
Prepaid insurance	3	6
Land	80	60
Buildings and equipment	81	75
Less: Accumulated depreciation	(16)	(20)
	$267	$221
Liabilities		
Accounts payable	$ 26	$ 20
Salaries payable	3	1
Income tax payable	6	8
Notes payable	20	0
Bonds payable	35	50
Less: Discount on bonds	(1)	(3)
Shareholders' Equity		
Common stock	130	100
Paid-in capital—excess of par	29	20
Retained earnings	19	25
	$267	$221

Income Statement

Revenues		
Sales revenue	$100	
Investment revenue	3	
Gain on sale of land	8	$111
Expenses		
Cost of goods sold	60	
Salaries expense	13	
Depreciation expense	3	
Bond interest expense	5	
Insurance expense	7	
Loss on sale of equipment	2	
Income tax expense	9	99
Net income		$ 12

Additional information from the accounting records:

a. Company land, purchased in a previous year for $10 million, was sold for $18 million.

b. Equipment that originally cost $14 million, and which was one-half depreciated, was sold for $5 million cash.

c. The common shares of Mazuma Corporation were purchased for $12 million as a short-term investment.

d. Property was purchased for $30 million cash for use as a parking lot.

e. On December 30, 2018, new equipment was acquired by issuing a 12%, five-year, $20 million note payable to the seller.

f. On January 1, 2018, $15 million of bonds (issued 20 years ago at their face amount) were retired at maturity.

g. The increase in the common stock account is attributable to the issuance of a 10% stock dividend (1 million shares) and the subsequent sale of 2 million shares of common stock. The market price of the $10 par value common stock was $13 per share on the dates of both transactions.

h. Cash dividends of $5 million were paid to shareholders.

PART B

Preparing the SCF: Direct Method of Reporting Cash Flows from Operating Activities

Using a Spreadsheet

There can be no cash inflow or cash outflow without a corresponding change in a noncash account.

An important advantage gained by using a spreadsheet is that it ensures that no reportable activities are inadvertently overlooked. Spreadsheet analysis relies on the fact that, in order for cash to increase or decrease, there must be a corresponding change in an account other than cash. Therefore, if we can identify the events and transactions that caused the change in each noncash account during the year, we will have identified all the operating, investing, and financing activities that are to be included in the statement of cash flows.

Recording spreadsheet entries that explain account balance changes simultaneously identifies and classifies the activities to be reported on the statement of cash flows.

The beginning and ending balances of each account are entered on the spreadsheet. Then, as journal entries are reconstructed in our analysis of the data, those entries are recorded on the spreadsheet so that the debits and credits of the spreadsheet entries explain the changes in the account balances. Only after spreadsheet entries have explained the changes in all account balances can we feel confident that all operating, investing, and financing activities have been identified. The spreadsheet is designed in such a way that, as we record spreadsheet entries that explain account balance changes, we are simultaneously identifying and classifying the activities to be reported on the statement of cash flows.

We begin by transferring the comparative balance sheets and income statement to a blank spreadsheet. For illustration, refer to the 2018 and 2017 balances in the completed spreadsheet for UBC, shown in Illustration 21–9A. Notice that the amounts for elements of the income statement are ending balances resulting from accumulations during the year. Beginning balances in each of these accounts are always zero.

Following the balance sheets and income statement, we allocate space on the spreadsheet for the statement of cash flows. Although at this point we have not yet identified the specific cash flow activities shown in the completed spreadsheet, we can include headings for the major categories of activities: cash flows from operating activities, cash flows from investing activities, and cash flows from financing activities. Leaving several lines between headings allows adequate space to include the specific cash flows identified in subsequent analysis.

Spreadsheet entries duplicate the actual journal entries used to record the transactions as they occurred during the year.

The spreadsheet entries shown in the two changes columns, which separate the beginning and ending balances, explain the increase or decrease in each account balance. You will see in the next section how these entries were reconstructed. Although spreadsheet entries are in the form of debits and credits like journal entries, they are entered on the spreadsheet only. They are not recorded in the formal accounting records. In effect, these entries duplicate, frequently in summary form, the actual journal entries used to record the transactions as they occurred during the year.

To reconstruct the journal entries, we analyze each account, one at a time, deciding at each step what transaction or event caused the change in that account. Often, the reason for the change in an account balance is readily apparent from viewing the change in conjunction with that of a related account elsewhere in the financial statements. Sometimes it is necessary to consult the accounting records for additional information to help explain the transaction that resulted in the change.

You may find it helpful to diagram in T-account format the relationship between accounts to better visualize certain changes, particularly in your initial study of the chapter. The analysis that follows is occasionally supplemented with such diagrams to emphasize *why,* rather than merely *how,* specific cash flow amounts emerge from the analysis.

Although there is no mandatory order in which to analyze the accounts, it is convenient to begin with the income statement accounts, followed by the balance sheet accounts. We analyze the accounts of UBC in that order below. Although our analysis of each account culminates in a spreadsheet entry, keep in mind that the analysis described also is appropriate to identify reportable activities when a spreadsheet is not used.[11]

[11]The spreadsheet entries also are used to record the same transactions when the T-account method is used. We refer again to these entries when that method is described in Appendix 21B.

Illustration 21–9A

Spreadsheet—Direct Method

UNITED BRANDS CORPORATION
Spreadsheet for the Statement of Cash Flows

	Dec. 31, 2017	Changes				Dec. 31, 2018
		Debits		Credits		
Balance Sheet						
Assets:						
Cash	20	(19)	9			29
Accounts receivable	30	(1)	2			32
Short-term investments	0	(12)	12			12
Inventory	50			(4)	4	46
Prepaid insurance	6			(8)	3	3
Land	60	(13)	30	(3)	10	80
Buildings and equipment	75	(14)	20X	(9)	14	81
Less: Accumulated depreciation	(20)	(9)	7	(6)	3	(16)
	221					267
Liabilities:						
Accounts payable	20			(4)	6	26
Salaries payable	1			(5)	2	3
Income tax payable	8	(10)	2			6
Notes payable	0			(14)	20X	20
Bonds payable	50	(15)	15			35
Less: Discount on bonds	(3)			(7)	2	(1)
Shareholders' Equity:						
Common stock	100			(16)	10	
				(17)	20	130
Paid-in capital—excess of par	20			(16)	3	
				(17)	6	29
Retained earnings	25	(16)	13			
		(18)	5	(11)	12	19
	221					267
Income Statement						
Revenues:						
Sales revenue				(1)	100	100
Investment revenue				(2)	3	3
Gain on sale of land				(3)	8	8
Expenses:						
Cost of goods sold		(4)	60			(60)
Salaries expense		(5)	13			(13)
Depreciation expense		(6)	3			(3)
Bond interest expense		(7)	5			(5)
Insurance expense		(8)	7			(7)
Loss on sale of equipment		(9)	2			(2)
Income tax expense		(10)	9			(9)
Net income		(11)	**12**			**12**
Statement of Cash Flows						
Operating Activities:						
Cash inflows:						
From customers		(1)	98			
From investment revenue		(2)	3			
Cash outflows:						
To suppliers of goods				(4)	50	
To employees				(5)	11	
To bondholders				(7)	3	
For insurance expense				(8)	4	
For income taxes				(10)	11	
Net cash flows						22

(continued)

Illustration 21–9A
(concluded)

	Dec. 31, 2017	Changes				Dec. 31, 2018
		Debits		Credits		
Investing Activities:						
Sale of land		(3)	18			
Sale of equipment		(9)	5			
Purchase of S-T investment				(12)	12	
Purchase of land				(13)	30	
Net cash flows						(19)
Financing Activities:						
Retirement of bonds payable				(15)	15	
Sale of common shares		(17)	26			
Payment of cash dividends				(18)	5	
Net cash flows						6
Net increase in cash				(19)	9	**9**
Totals			376		376	

X: As explained later, the Xs serve as a reminder to report this noncash transaction.

Income Statement Accounts

Amounts reported in the income statement usually are not the same as the cash effects of the items reported.

As described in an earlier section, cash flows from operating activities are inflows and outflows of cash that result from activities reported in the income statement. Thus, to identify those cash inflows and outflows, we begin by analyzing the components of the income statement. It is important to keep in mind that the amounts reported in the income statement usually do not represent the cash effects of the items reported. For example, UBC reports sales revenue of $100 million. This does not mean, however, that it collected $100 million cash from customers during the year. In fact, by referring to the beginning and ending balances in accounts receivable, we see that cash received from customers could not have been $100 million. Since accounts receivable increased during the year, some of the sales revenue recognized must not yet have been collected. This is explained further in the next section.

The cash effects of other income statement elements can be similarly discerned by referring to changes in the balances of the balance sheet accounts that are directly related to those elements. So, to identify cash flows from operating activities, we examine, one at a time, the elements of the income statement in conjunction with any balance sheet accounts affected by each element.

1. SALES REVENUE. Accounts receivable is the balance sheet account that is affected by sales revenue. Specifically, accounts receivable is increased by credit sales and is decreased as cash is received from customers. We can compare sales and the change in accounts receivable during the year to determine the amount of cash received from customers. This relationship can be viewed in T-account format as follows:

Accounts Receivable

Beginning balance	30		
Credit sales *(increases A/R)*	100	?	Cash received *(decreases A/R)*
Ending balance	32		

We see from this analysis that cash received from customers must have been $98 million. Note that even if some of the year's sales were cash sales, say $40 million cash sales and $60 million credit sales, the result is the same:

Accounts Receivable

Beginning balance	30		Cash sales	$40
Credit sales	60	58 →	Received on account	58
Ending balance	32		Cash received	$98

Thus, cash flows from operating activities should include cash received from customers of $98 million. The net effect of sales revenue activity during the year can be summarized in the following entry:

	($ in millions)	
Entry (1) Cash (received from customers)	98	
Accounts receivable (given)	2	
Sales revenue ($100 − 0)		100

Relating sales and the *change* in accounts receivable during the period helps determine the amount of cash received from customers.

The entry above appears as entry (1) in the completed spreadsheet for UBC, shown in Illustration 21–9A. The entry explains the changes in two account balances—accounts receivable and sales revenue. Since the entry affects cash, it also identifies a cash flow to be reported on the statement of cash flows. The $98 million debit to cash is therefore entered in the statement of cash flows section of the spreadsheet under the heading of cash flows from operating activities.

Additional Consideration

The preceding discussion describes the most common situation—companies recognize revenue by selling goods and services, increase accounts receivable, and then collect the cash and decrease accounts receivable later. Some companies, though, often collect the cash in advance of satisfying performance obligations and thus record revenue and decrease deferred revenue. In those cases, we need to analyze any changes in the deferred revenue account for differences between revenue reported and cash collected. For instance, if UBC also had a $1 million increase in deferred revenue, the summary entry would be modified as follows:

	($ in millions)	
Entry (1) Cash (received from customers)	99	
Accounts receivable (given)	2	
Deferred revenue (given)		1
Sales revenue ($100 − 0)		100

Notice that we enter the cash portion of entry (1) as one of several cash flows on the statement of cash flows rather than as a debit to the cash account. Only after all cash inflows and outflows have been identified will the net change in cash be entered as a debit to the cash account. In fact, the entry to reconcile the $9 million increase in the cash account and the $9 million net increase in cash on the statement of cash flows will serve as a final check of the accuracy of our spreadsheet analysis.

Additional Consideration

Notice that bad debt expense does not appear in the income statement and allowance for uncollectible accounts does not appear in the balance sheet. We have assumed that bad debts are immaterial for UBC. When this is not the case, it's necessary to consider the write-off of bad debts as we determine cash received from customers. Here's why.

When using the allowance method to account for bad debts, a company estimates the dollar amount of customer accounts that will ultimately prove uncollectible and records both bad debt expense and allowance for uncollectible accounts for that estimate.

Bad debt expense	xxx	
Allowance for uncollectible accounts		xxx

(continued)

(concluded)

Then, when accounts actually prove uncollectible, accounts receivable and the allowance are reduced.

Allowance for uncollectible accounts	xxx	
Accounts receivable		xxx

In our illustration, we concluded that UBC received $2 million less cash ($98 million) than sales for the year ($100 million) because accounts receivable increased by that amount. However, if a portion of the change in accounts receivable had been due to write-offs of bad debts, that conclusion would be incorrect. Let's say, for instance, that UBC had bad debt expense of $2 million and its allowance for uncollectible accounts had increased by $1 million. Because the allowance for uncollectible accounts would be credited by $2 million in the adjusting entry for bad debts expense, necessarily there also would have been a $1 million debit to the account in order for there to have been a net increase (credit) in its balance of only $1 million. That debit would occur due to write-offs of bad debts totaling $1 million.

	($ in millions)	
Allowance for uncollectible accounts	1	
Accounts receivable		1

This would indicate that a portion ($1 million credit) of the total change in accounts receivable ($2 million debit) would have been due to write-offs of bad debts, and the remaining change ($3 million debit) would have been due to cash collections being less than sales revenue. Cash received from customers would have been only $97 million in that case. We can view this in the framework of our T-account analysis as follows:

Accounts Receivable

Beginning balance	30		
Credit sales	100	97	Cash received
		1	Bad debt write-offs
Ending balance	32		

The effect of write-offs of bad debts can be explicitly considered by combining all the accounts related to sales and collection activities into a single summary spreadsheet entry:

	($ in millions)	
Cash (received from customers)	97	
Accounts receivable ($32 − 30)	2	
Bad debt expense (from income statement)	2	
Allowance for uncollectible accounts ($3 − 2)		1
Sales revenue ($100 − 0)		100

This single entry summarizes all transactions related to sales, bad debt expense, write-offs of accounts receivable, and cash collections from sales.

The remaining summary entries are described in subsections 2 through 19. When including the entries on the spreadsheet, it is helpful to number the entries sequentially to provide a means of retracing the steps taken in the analysis if the need arises. You also may find it helpful to put a check mark (✓) to the right of the ending balance when the change in that balance has been explained. Then, once you have check marks next to every noncash account, you will know you are finished.

2. INVESTMENT REVENUE. The income statement reports investment revenue of $3 million. Before concluding that this amount was received in cash, we first refer to the balance sheets to see whether a change in an account there indicates otherwise. A change in either of two balance sheet accounts, (a) investment revenue receivable or (b) long-term investments, might indicate that cash received from investment revenue differs from the amount reported in the income statement.

Changes in related accounts might indicate that investment revenue reported in the income statement is a different amount from cash received from the investment.

a. If we observe either an increase or a decrease in an *investment revenue receivable* account (e.g., interest receivable, dividends receivable), we would conclude that the amount of cash received during the year was less than (if an increase) or more than (if a decrease) the amount of revenue reported. The analysis would be identical to that of sales revenue and accounts receivable.

b. Also, an unexplained increase in a *long-term investment* account might indicate that a portion of investment revenue has not yet been received in cash. Recall from Chapter 12 that when using the equity method to account for investments in the stock of another corporation, investment revenue is recognized as the investor's percentage share of the investee's income, whether or not the revenue is received currently as cash dividends. For example, assume the investor owns 25% of the common stock of a corporation that reports net income of $12 million and pays dividends of $4 million. This situation would have produced a $2 million increase in long-term investments, which can be demonstrated by reconstructing the journal entries for the recognition of investment and the receipt of cash dividends:

	($ in millions)	
Long-term investments	3	
Investment revenue ($12 × 25%)		3
Cash ($4 × 25%)	1	
Long-term investments		1

A combined entry would produce the same results:

Long-term investments	2	
Cash ($4 × 25%)	1	
Investment revenue ($12 × 25%)		3

The $2 million net increase in long-term investments would represent the investment revenue not received in cash. This would also explain why there is a $3 million increase (credit) in investment revenue. If these events had occurred, we would prepare a spreadsheet entry identical to the combined entry above. The spreadsheet entry would (a) explain the $2 million increase in long-term investments, (b) explain the $3 million increase in investment revenue, and (c) identify a $1 million cash inflow from operating activities.

However, because neither an investment revenue receivable account nor a long-term investment account appears on the comparative balance sheets, we can conclude that $3 million of investment revenue was collected in cash. Entry (2) on the spreadsheet is as follows:

Because no other transactions are apparent that would have caused a change in investment revenue, we can conclude that $3 million of investment revenue was collected in cash.

	($ in millions)	
Entry (2) Cash (received from investment revenue)	3	
Investment revenue ($3 − 0)		3

3. GAIN ON SALE OF LAND. The third item reported in the income statement is an $8 million gain on the sale of land. Recall that our objective in analyzing each element of the statement is to determine the cash effect of that element. To do so, we need additional information about the transaction that caused this gain. The accounting records—item (a) in Illustration 21–9—indicate that land that originally cost $10 million was sold for $18 million. The entry recorded in the journal when the land was sold also serves as our summary entry:

A gain (or loss) is simply the difference between cash received in the sale of an asset and the book value of the asset—not a cash flow.

	($ in millions)	
Entry (3) Cash (received from sale of land)	18	
Land (given)		10
Gain on sale of land ($8 − 0)		8

The cash effect of this transaction is a cash increase of $18 million. We therefore include the debit as a cash inflow in the statement of cash flows section of the spreadsheet. However, unlike the cash effect of the previous two spreadsheet entries, it is not reported as an operating activity. The sale of land is an *investing* activity, so this cash inflow is listed under that heading of the spreadsheet. The entry also accounts for the $8 million gain on sale of land. The $10 million credit to land does not, by itself, explain the $20 million increase in that account. As we will later discover, another transaction also affected the land account.

It is important to understand that the gain is simply the difference between cash received in the sale of land (reported as an investing activity) and the book value of the land. To report the $8 million gain as a cash flow from operating activities, in addition to reporting $18 million as a cash flow from investing activities, would be to report the $8 million twice.

4. COST OF GOODS SOLD. During the year, UBC sold goods that had cost $60 million. This does not necessarily indicate that $60 million cash was paid to suppliers of those goods. To determine the amount of cash paid to suppliers, we look to the two current accounts affected by merchandise purchases—inventory and accounts payable. The analysis can be viewed as a two-step process.

First, we compare cost of goods sold with the change in inventory to determine the cost of goods *purchased* (not necessarily cash paid) during the year. To facilitate our analysis, we can examine the relationship in T-account format:

Inventory

Beginning balance	50		
Cost of goods purchased *(increases inventory)*	?	60	Cost of goods sold *(decreases inventory)*
Ending balance	46		

Determining the amount of cash paid to suppliers means looking at not only the cost of goods sold, but also the changes in both inventory and accounts payable.

From this analysis, we see that $56 million of goods were *purchased* during the year. It is not necessarily true, though, that $56 million cash was paid to suppliers of these goods. By looking in accounts payable, we can determine the cash paid to suppliers:

Accounts Payable

		20	Beginning balance
Cash paid to suppliers *(decreases A/P)*	?	56	Cost of goods purchased *(increases A/P)*
		26	Ending Balance

We now see that cash paid to suppliers was $50 million. The entry that summarizes merchandise acquisitions is as follows:

Although $60 million of goods were sold during the year, only $50 million cash was paid to suppliers of these goods.

	($ in millions)	
Entry (4) Cost of goods sold ($60 − 0)	60	
Inventory ($46 − 50)		4
Accounts payable ($26 − 20)		6
Cash (paid to suppliers of goods)		50

5. SALARIES EXPENSE. The balance sheet account affected by salaries expense is salaries payable. By analyzing salaries expense in relation to the change in salaries payable, we can determine the amount of cash paid to employees:

Salaries Payable

		1	Beginning balance
Cash paid to employees *(decreases salaries payable)*	?	13	Salaries expense *(increases salaries payable)*
		3	Ending Balance

This analysis indicates that only $11 million cash was paid to employees; the remaining $2 million of salaries expense is reflected as an increase in salaries payable.

Viewing the relationship in journal entry format provides the same conclusion and also gives us the entry in our spreadsheet analysis:

	($ in millions)	
Entry (5) Salaries expense ($13 − 0)	13	
Salaries payable ($3 − 1)		2
Cash (paid to employees)		11

Although salaries expense was $13 million, only $11 million cash was paid to employees.

6. DEPRECIATION EXPENSE. The income statement reports depreciation expense of $3 million. The entry used to record depreciation, which also serves as our summary entry, is:

	($ in millions)	
Entry (6) Depreciation expense ($3 − 0)	3	
Accumulated depreciation		3

Depreciation expense does not require a current cash expenditure.

Depreciation is a noncash expense. It is merely an allocation in the current period of a prior cash expenditure (for the depreciable asset). Therefore, unlike the other entries to this point, the depreciation entry has no effect on the statement of cash flows. However, it does explain the change in the depreciation expense account and a portion of the change in accumulated depreciation.

7. INTEREST EXPENSE. Recall from Chapter 14 that bond interest expense differs from the amount of cash paid to bondholders when bonds are issued at either a premium or a discount. The difference between the two amounts is the reduction of the premium or discount. By referring to the balance sheet, we see that UBC's bonds were issued at a discount. Since we know that bond interest expense is $5 million and that $2 million of the discount was reduced in 2018, we can determine that $3 million cash was paid to bondholders by recreating the entry that summarizes the recording of bond interest expense.

	($ in millions)	
Entry (7) Interest expense ($5 − 0)	5	
Discount on bonds payable ($1 − 3)		2
Cash (paid to bondholders)		3

Bond interest expense is not the same as the amount of cash paid to bondholders when bonds are issued at either a premium or a discount.

Recording this entry on the spreadsheet explains the change in both the bond interest expense and discount on bonds payable accounts. It also provides us with another cash outflow from operating activities. Of course, if a premium were being reduced, rather than a discount, the cash outflow would be *greater* than the expense.

8. INSURANCE EXPENSE. A decrease of $3 million in the prepaid insurance account indicates that cash paid for insurance coverage was $3 million less than the $7 million insurance expense for the year. Viewing prepaid insurance in T-account format clarifies this point.

Additional Consideration

If the balance sheet had revealed an increase or decrease in an accrued bond interest payable account, the entry calculating cash paid to bondholders would require modification. For example, if UBC had a bond interest payable account, and that account had increased (a credit) by $1 million, the entry would have been as follows:

	($ in millions)	
Entry (7) Interest expense	5	
(revised) Discount on bonds payable		2
Interest payable		1
Cash (paid to bondholders)		2

(continued)

(concluded)

If the amount owed to bondholders increased by $1 million, they obviously were paid $1 million less cash than if there had been no change in the amount owed them. Similarly, if bond interest payable decreased by $1 million, the opposite would be true; that is, cash paid to them would have been $1 million more.

Prepaid Insurance

Beginning balance	6		
Cash paid for insurance *(increases prepaid insurance)*	?	7	Insurance expense *(decreases prepaid insurance)*
Ending balance	3		

From this analysis, we can conclude that $4 million was paid for insurance. We reach the same conclusion by preparing the following spreadsheet entry:

Since $3 million of prepaid insurance was allocated to insurance expense, only $4 million of the expense was paid in cash during the period.

	($ in millions)	
Entry (8) Insurance expense ($7 − 0)	7	
Prepaid insurance ($3 − 6)		3
Cash (paid for insurance)		4

The entry accounts for the change in both the insurance expense and prepaid insurance accounts and also identifies a cash outflow from operating activities.

9. LOSS ON SALE OF EQUIPMENT. A $2 million loss on the sale of equipment is the next item reported in the income statement. To determine the cash effect of the sale of equipment, we need additional information about the transaction. The information we need is provided in item (b) of Illustration 21–9. Recreating the journal entry for the transaction described gives us the following entry:

Recreating the journal entry for the sale of equipment reveals a $5 million cash inflow from investing activities.

	($ in millions)	
Entry (9) Cash (from the sale of equipment)	5	
Loss on sale of equipment ($2 − 0)	2	
Accumulated depreciation ($14 × 50%)	7	
Buildings and equipment (given)		14

The $5 million cash inflow is entered in the statement of cash flows section of the spreadsheet as an investing activity. The $2 million debit to the loss on sale of equipment explains the change in that account balance. Referring to the spreadsheet, we see that a portion of the change in accumulated depreciation was accounted for in entry (6). The debit to accumulated depreciation in the entry above completes the explanation for the change in that account. However, the credit to buildings and equipment only partially justifies the change in that account. We must assume that the analysis of a subsequent transaction will account for the unexplained portion of the change.

Recognize too that the loss, like the gain in entry (3), has no cash effect in the current period. Therefore, it is not reported in the statement of cash flows when using the direct method.

10. INCOME TAX EXPENSE. The final expense reported in the income statement is income tax expense. Since income taxes payable is the balance sheet account affected by this expense, we look to the change in that account to help determine the cash paid for income taxes. A T-account analysis can be used to find the cash effect as follows:

Income Tax Payable

		8	Beginning balance
Cash paid for income tax *(decreases the liability)*	?	9	Income tax expense
		6	Ending Balance

This analysis reveals that $11 million cash was paid for income taxes, $2 million more than the year's expense. The overpayment explains why the liability for income taxes decreased by $2 million.

The same conclusion can be reached from the following summary entry, which represents the net effect of income taxes on UBC's accounts.

	($ in millions)	
Entry (10) Income tax expense ($9 – 0)	9	
Income tax payable ($6 – 8)	2	
Cash (paid for income taxes)		11

Additional Consideration

Entry (10) would require modification in the situation described below.

Note that UBC does not have a deferred income tax account. Recall from Chapter 16 that temporary differences between taxable income and pretax accounting income give rise to deferred taxes. If temporary differences had been present, which would be evidenced by a change in a deferred income taxes account, the calculation of cash paid for income taxes would require modification. Assume, for example, that a deferred income tax liability account had experienced a credit change of $1 million for the year. In that case, the previous spreadsheet entry would be revised as follows:

	($ in millions)	
Entry (10) Interest tax expense	9	
(revised) Income tax payable	2	
Deferred income tax liability		1
Cash (paid for income taxes)		10

As the revised entry indicates, only $10 million cash would have been paid in this situation, rather than $11 million. The $1 million difference represents the portion of the income tax expense whose payment is deferred to a later year.

11. NET INCOME. The balance in the retained earnings account at the end of the year includes an increase due to net income. If we are to account for all changes in each of the accounts, we must include the following entry on the spreadsheet, which represents the closing of net income to retained earnings.

	($ in millions)	
Entry (11) Net income	12	
Retained earnings		12

This entry partially explains the change in the retained earnings account.

This entry does not affect amounts reported on the statement of cash flows. We include the entry on the spreadsheet analysis only to help explain account balance changes.

Balance Sheet Accounts

To identify all the operating, investing, and financing activities when using a spreadsheet, we must account for the changes in each account for both the income statement and the balance sheet. Thus far, we have explained the change in each income statement account. Since the transactions that gave rise to some of those changes involved balance sheet accounts as well, some changes in balance sheet accounts have already been explained. We now reconstruct the transactions that caused changes in the remaining balances.

With the exception of the cash account, the accounts are analyzed in the order of their presentation in the balance sheet. As noted earlier, we save the entry that reconciles the change in the cash account with the net change in cash from the statement of cash flows as a final check on the accuracy of the spreadsheet.

12. SHORT-TERM INVESTMENTS. Since the change in accounts receivable was explained previously [in entry (1)], we proceed to the next asset in the balance sheet. The balance in short-term investments increased from zero to $12 million. In the absence of evidence to the contrary, we could assume that the increase is due to the purchase of short-term investments during the year. This assumption is confirmed by item (c) of Illustration 21–9.

The entry to record the investment and our summary entry is as follows:

The $12 million increase in the short-term investments account is due to the purchase of short-term investments during the year.

	($ in millions)	
Entry (12) Short-term investment ($12 − 0)	12	
Cash (purchase of short-term investment)		12

The $12 million cash outflow is entered in the statement of cash flows section of the spreadsheet as an investing activity. An exception is when an investment is classified as a "trading security," in which case the cash outflow is reported as an operating activity.

Additional Consideration

Recall that some highly liquid, short-term investments such as money market funds, Treasury bills, or commercial paper might be classified as cash equivalents. If the short-term investment above were classified as a cash equivalent, its purchase would have no effect on the total of cash and cash equivalents. In other words, since cash would include this investment, its purchase would constitute both a debit and a credit to cash. We would neither prepare a spreadsheet entry nor report the transaction on the statement of cash flows.

Likewise, a sale of a cash equivalent would not affect the total of cash and cash equivalents and would not be reported.

An exception would be if the cash equivalent investment were sold for either more or less than its acquisition cost. For example, assume a Treasury bill classified as a cash equivalent was sold for $1 million more than its $2 million cost. The sale would constitute both a $3 million increase and a $2 million decrease in cash. We see the effect more clearly if we reconstruct the transaction in journal entry format:

	($ in millions)	
Cash	3	
Gain on sale of cash equivalent		1
Cash (cash equivalent investment)		2

The spreadsheet entry to reflect the net increase in cash would be:

Entry (X) Cash (from sale of cash equivalents)	1	
Gain on sale of cash equivalent		1

The $1 million net increase in cash and cash equivalents would be reported as a cash inflow from *operating* activities.

When we discuss the "indirect method" of reporting operating activities later in the chapter, we will be adding noncash losses and subtracting noncash gains when adjusting net income for noncash income items. Unlike most losses and gains, though, we would not add a loss or deduct a gain on cash equivalents because they *do* affect "cash" as defined.

13. LAND. The changes in the balances of both inventory and prepaid insurance were accounted for in previous summary entries (4) and (8). Land is the next account whose change has yet to be fully explained. We discovered in a previous transaction that a sale of land caused a $10 million reduction in the account. Yet, the account shows a net *increase* of $20 million. It would be logical to assume that the unexplained increase of $30 million was due to a purchase of land. The transaction described in item (d) of Illustration 21–9 supports that assumption and is portrayed in the following summary entry:

A $30 million purchase of land accounts for the portion of the $20 million increase in the account that was not previously explained by the sale of land.

	($ in millions)	
Entry (13) Land (given)	30	
Cash (purchase of land)		30

The $30 million payment is reported as a cash outflow from investing activities.

14. BUILDINGS AND EQUIPMENT. When examining a previous transaction [entry (9)], we determined that the buildings and equipment account was reduced by $14 million from the sale of used equipment. And yet the account shows a net *increase* of $6 million for the year. The accounting records [item (e) of Illustration 21–9] reveal the remaining unexplained cause of the net increase. New equipment costing $20 million was purchased by issuing a $20 million note payable. Recall from the discussion in a previous section of this chapter that, although this is a noncash transaction, it represents both a significant investing activity (investing in new equipment) and a significant financing activity (financing the acquisition with long-term debt).

The journal entry used to record the transaction when the equipment was acquired also serves as our summary entry:

	($ in millions)	
Entry (14) Buildings and equipment (given)	20	
Note payable (given)		20

Investing in new equipment is a significant investing activity and financing the acquisition with long-term debt is a significant financing activity.

Remember that the statement of cash flows section of the spreadsheet will serve as the basis for our preparation of the formal statement. But the noncash entry above will not affect the cash flows section of the spreadsheet. Because we want to report this noncash investing and financing activity when we prepare the statement of cash flows, it is helpful to "mark" the spreadsheet entry as a reminder not to overlook this transaction when the statement is prepared. Crosses (*X*) serve this purpose on the spreadsheet in Illustration 21–9A.

Additional Consideration

Leases

When a lessee acquires an asset and related liability as a result of a lease agreement, there is no inflow or outflow of cash. However, because a primary purpose of the statement of cash flows is to report significant operating, investing, and financing activities, the initial transaction is reported in the disclosure notes as a significant noncash investing activity (investing in the asset) and financing activity (financing it with debt). Then, the lessee's cash payments for leases are classified as financing activities in its statement of cash flows and presented separately from other financing cash flows. The lessor classifies its cash receipts from lease payments as operating activities in its statement of cash flows, after initially reporting its acquisition of a lease receivable and derecognition of the asset under lease as a significant noncash investing and financing activity in its cash flow disclosure note.

15. BONDS PAYABLE. The balance in the bonds payable account decreased during the year by $15 million. Illustration 21–9, item (f), reveals the cause. Cash was paid to retire $15 million face value of bonds. The spreadsheet entry that duplicates the journal entry that was recorded when the bonds were retired is:

	($ in millions)	
Entry (15) Bonds payable ($35 – 50)	15	
Cash (retirement of bonds payable)		15

The cash outflow is reported as a financing activity.

Additional Consideration

Statement of Cash Flows: Reporting a Bond Discount or Premium

Conceptually, the way we report cash flows for bonds depends on whether the bonds were issued at face amount, at a discount, or at a premium.[12] As we look at these three possibilities, note that in each case:

- The same total amount that is borrowed (lent) and reported as a financing (investing) activity is the amount that should be reported later as a *financing* (*investing*) activity as the loan is repaid.
- All other amounts paid during or at the end of the term to maturity represent interest and should be reported among *operating* activities.

Though not codified in the *FASB Accounting Standards Codification*, this treatment is a preference of the SEC, though anecdotal evidence suggests that many firms do not follow this procedure in practice.

Bonds Issued at Face Amount

If bonds are issued at their face amount, the cash inflow at issuance ($15 million in the illustration) is a financing activity, as is the cash outflow at maturity to repay the amount borrowed ($15 million in the illustration). The periodic cash interest payments in the meantime are operating activities.

Bonds Issued at a Discount

If bonds are issued at a discount, the cash inflow at issuance is a financing activity, but that discounted price is less than the cash outflow for the face amount at maturity. The portion of the face amount paid at maturity to be reported as a financing activity, then, is limited to the amount borrowed (discounted price at issuance). The remaining portion of the payment (equal to the discount) represents interest and thus should be reported as an operating activity. This "extra" amount paid at maturity, together with the periodic cash interest payments during the term to maturity, comprise the total interest paid to borrow the cash received at issuance. This total amount of interest reported among operating activities is equal to the total interest expense reported during the term to maturity.

In Chapter 14's Illustration 14–3, for instance, $700,000 of bonds were issued at $666,633. That discounted price is the amount the issuer borrowed and the amount reported as a financing activity. When the $700,000 face amount is paid at maturity, $666,633 of that amount represents repayment of the borrowing and also is reported as a financing activity. The remaining $33,367 (the discount) represents interest (as do the periodic cash payments) and is reported among operating activities.

(continued)

[12]Lisa Koonce, "SCF Insights," Financial Accounting Standards Research Initiative, October 6, 2011.

(concluded)

We can better visualize this if we look again at the amortization schedule we saw earlier for the bonds issued at a discount:

Date	Cash Interest	Effective Interest	Increase in Balance	Outstanding Balance
	(6% × Face amount)	(7% × Outstanding balance)	(Discount reduction)	
1/1/18				666,633
6/30/18	42,000	.07 (666,633) = 46,664	4,664	671,297
12/31/18	42,000	.07 (671,297) = 46,991	4,991	676,288
6/30/19	42,000	.07 (676,288) = 47,340	5,340	681,628
12/31/19	42,000	.07 (681,628) = 47,714	5,714	687,342
6/30/20	42,000	.07 (687,342) = 48,114	6,114	693,456
12/31/20	42,000	.07 (693,456) = 48,544	6,544	700,000
	252,000	**285,367**	33,367	

Operating

$700,000	Payment
− 33,367	Operating
$666,633	Financing

You may remember from Chapter 14 that the *total* interest, $285,367, is the $252,000 *cash* interest paid during the term to maturity plus the "extra" amount paid at maturity. The $33,367 extra amount is necessary for the bonds to pay an effective interest rate equal to what the market demanded when the bonds were purchased (which was higher than the rate at which the bonds made periodic interest payments).

To summarize, bonds issued at a discount are treated as follows on a statement of cash flows:

	Financing Activities	Operating Activities
INFLOWS:		
At issuance	Face Amount minus Discount	
OUTFLOWS:		
During term to maturity		Cash Interest Payments
At maturity	Face Amount minus Discount	Discount

Bonds Issued at a Premium

If the bonds are issued at a premium, the cash repaid at maturity is less than the cash received at issuance. So, when does the rest of the amount received at issuance get repaid? To see the answer, remember that when bonds are issued at a premium, it's because the stated interest rate at issuance is higher than the market interest rate. That means that the cash interest payments each period are higher than the interest expense amounts reported each period. The remainder of each payment is a repayment of the extra amount received at issuance. Similar to installment payments that include both (a) an amount for interest and (b) an amount that reduces the debt, we can think of these bond interest payments the same way. The cash payments cover the interest expense, and the remainder of each payment (the premium amortization) goes toward paying a portion of the amount borrowed. The interest expense portions of the cash payments are operating activities and the repayment portions are reported as financing activities each period. That means that the total amount of financing *outflows*, including payment of the face amount at maturity and the premium amortization over the life of the bonds, equals the total amount of financing *inflow* received when the bonds are issued.

(continued)

(concluded)

To see this more clearly, let's look again at the amortization schedule we saw in Chapter 14 for bonds issued at a premium:

Date	Cash Interest	Effective Interest	Decrease in Balance	Outstanding Balance
	(6% × Face amount)	(5% × Outstanding balance)	(Premium reduction)	
1/1/18				735,533
6/30/18	42,000	0.05 (735,533) = 36,777	5,223	730,310
12/31/18	42,000	0.05 (730,310) = 36,516	5,484	724,826
6/30/19	42,000	0.05 (724,826) = 36,241	5,759	719,067
12/31/19	42,000	0.05 (719,067) = 35,953	6,047	713,020
6/30/20	42,000	0.05 (713,020) = 35,651	6,349	706,671
12/31/20	42,000	0.05 (706,671) = 35,329	6,671	700,000
	252,000	216,467	35,533	

Operating

$700,000	Payment
+ 35,533	Financing
$735,633	Financing

To summarize, bonds issued at a premium are treated as follows on a statement of cash flows:

	Financing Activities	Operating Activities
INFLOWS:		
At issuance	Face Amount plus Premium	
OUTFLOWS:		
During term to maturity	Premium Amortization	Interest Expense
At maturity	Face Amount	

Remember that when using the indirect method, we add any discount amortization back to net income each period. That's in order to adjust the interest expense that's subtracted within net income to cash interest paid, which is the amount we want to report as an operating activity. When we have a premium, though, the amount we want to report as an operating activity is interest expense, as we just saw. As a result, we do *not* adjust net income for premium amortization as we do for discount amortization.

Early Extinguishment of Debt

The description of the transaction stipulated that $15 million of bonds were retired at their maturity on the first day of the year. Thus, any discount or premium on the bonds would have been completely amortized before the start of the year. If bonds are retired prior to their scheduled maturity, any unamortized discount or premium would be removed from the accounts at that time. For instance, assume that the bonds above were callable at $16 million and that $1 million of unamortized discount remained when they were retired by a call at that price. The summary entry would be revised as follows:

		($ in millions)	
Entry (15)	Bonds payable	15	
(revised)	Loss on early extinguishment of bonds	2	
	Discount on bonds payable		1
	Cash (retirement of bonds payable)		16

The loss would not be reported in the statement of cash flows (direct method). The amortization of the discount, however, would affect a previous summary entry. In entry (7), we concluded that the decrease in discount on bonds payable was due to the amortization of $2 million of the discount when recording bond interest expense. However, if the early

(continued)

(concluded)

retirement assumed above had occurred, that transaction would have accounted for $1 million of the $2 million decrease in the discount. Entry (7) would be modified as follows:

		($ in millions)	
Entry (7)	Interest expense	5	
(revised)	Discount on bonds payable		1
	Cash (paid to bondholders)		4

16–17. COMMON STOCK. The comparative balance sheets indicate that the common stock account balance increased by $30 million. We look to the accounting records—Illustration 21–9, item (g)—for an explanation. Two transactions, a stock dividend and a sale of new shares of common stock, combined to cause the increase. To create the summary entries for our analysis, we replicate the journal entries for the two transactions as described below.

Remember from Chapter 18 that to record a small stock dividend, we capitalize retained earnings for the market value of the shares distributed—in this case, 1 million shares times $13 per share, or $13 million. The entry is as follows:

		($ in millions)	
Entry (16)	Retained earnings (1 million shares × $13)	13	
	Common stock (1 million shares × $10 par)		10
	Paid-in capital—excess of par (difference)		3

Although this transaction does not identify a cash flow, nor does it represent an investing or financing activity, we include the summary entry to help explain changes in the three account balances affected.

Also recall from the discussion of noncash investing and financing activities earlier in the chapter that stock dividends do not represent a significant investing or financing activity. Therefore, this transaction is not reported in the statement of cash flows. We include the entry in our spreadsheet analysis only to help explain changes in the account balances affected.

The sale of 2 million shares of common stock at $13 per share is represented by the following spreadsheet entry:

		($ in millions)	
Entry (17)	Cash (from sale of common stock)	26	
	Common stock ([$130 − 100] − 10)		20
	Paid-in capital—excess of par ([$29 − 20] − 3)		6

The sale of common shares explains the remaining increase in the common stock account and the remaining increase in paid-in capital—excess of par.

The cash inflow is reported in the statement of cash flows as a financing activity.

Additional Consideration

If cash is paid to retire outstanding shares of stock or to purchase those shares as treasury stock, the cash outflow would be reported in a statement of cash flows as a financing activity.

Together, the two entries above account for both the $30 million increase in the common stock account and the $9 million increase in paid-in capital—excess of par.

18. RETAINED EARNINGS. The stock dividend in entry (16) above includes a $13 million reduction of retained earnings. Previously, we saw in entry (11) that net income increased retained earnings by $12 million. The net reduction of $1 million accounted for by these two entries leaves $5 million of the $6 million net decrease in the account unexplained.

Retained Earnings

		25	Beginning balance
(16) Stock dividend	13	12	Net income (11)
(18) ?	?		
		19	Ending balance

Without additional information about the $5 million decrease in retained earnings, we might assume it was due to a $5 million cash dividend. This assumption is unnecessary, though, because the cash dividend is described in Illustration 21–9, item (h).

Retained Earnings

		25	Beginning balance
(16) Stock dividend	13	12	Net income (11)
(18) Cash dividend	5		
		19	Ending balance

The summary entry for the spreadsheet is as follows:

The cash dividend accounts for the previously unexplained change in retained earnings.

	($ in millions)	
Entry (18) Retained earnings	5	
Cash (payment of cash dividends)		5

19. COMPLETING THE SPREADSHEET. In preparing the spreadsheet to this point, we have analyzed each noncash account on both the income statement and the balance sheet. Our purpose was to identify the transactions that, during the year, had affected each account. By recreating each transaction in the form of a summary entry—in effect, duplicating the journal entry that had been used to record the transaction—we were able to explain the change in the balance of each account. That is, the debits and credits in the changes columns of the spreadsheet account for the increase or decrease in each noncash account. When a transaction being entered on the spreadsheet included an operating, investing, or financing activity, we entered that portion of the entry under the corresponding heading of the statement of cash flows section of the spreadsheet. Since, as noted earlier, there can be no operating, investing, or financing activity without a corresponding change in one or more of the noncash accounts, we should feel confident at this point that we have identified all of the activities that should be reported on the statement of cash flows.

To check the accuracy of the analysis, we compare the change in the balance of the cash account with the net change in cash flows produced by the activities listed in the statement of cash flows section of the spreadsheet. The net increase or decrease in cash flows from each of the statement of cash flows categories is extended to the extreme right column of the spreadsheet. By reference to Illustration 21–9A, we see that net cash flows from operating, investing, and financing activities are: $22 million, ($19 million), and $6 million, respectively. Together these activities provide a net increase in cash of $9 million. This amount corresponds to the increase in the balance of the cash account from $20 million to $29 million. To complete the spreadsheet, we include the final summary entry:

The cash flows section of the spreadsheet provides the information to be reported in the statement of cash flows.

	($ in millions)	
Entry (19) Cash	9	
Net increase in cash (from statement of cash flows activities)		9

As a final check of accuracy, we can confirm that the total of the debits is equal to the total of the credits in the changes columns of the spreadsheet.[13]

[13]The mechanical and computational aspects of the spreadsheet analysis are simplified greatly when performed on an electronic spreadsheet such as Microsoft Excel.

Ethical Dilemma

"We must get it," Courtney Lowell, president of Industrial Fasteners, roared. "Without it, we're in big trouble." The "it" Mr. Lowell referred to is the renewal of a $14 million loan with Community First Bank. The big trouble he fears is the lack of funds necessary to repay the existing debt and few, if any, prospects for raising the funds elsewhere.

Mr. Lowell had just hung up the phone after a conversation with a bank vice-president in which it was made clear that this year's statement of cash flows must look better than last year's. Mr. Lowell knows that improvements are not on course to happen. In fact, cash flow projections were dismal.

Later that day, Tim Cratchet, assistant controller, was summoned to Mr. Lowell's office. "Cratchet," Lowell barked, "I've looked at our accounts receivable. I think we can generate quite a bit of cash by selling or factoring most of those receivables. I know it will cost us more than if we collect them ourselves, but it sure will make our cash flow picture look better."

Is there an ethical question facing Cratchet?

International Financial Reporting Standards

LO21–9

Classification of Cash Flows. Like U.S. GAAP, international standards also require a statement of cash flows. Consistent with U.S. GAAP, cash flows are classified as operating, investing, or financing. However, the U.S. standard designates cash outflows for interest payments and cash inflows from interest and dividends received as operating cash flows. Dividends paid to shareholders are classified as financing cash flows.

IAS No. 7, on the other hand, allows more flexibility. Companies can report interest and dividends paid as either operating or financing cash flows and interest and dividends received as either operating or investing cash flows. Interest and dividend payments usually are reported as financing activities. Interest and dividends received normally are classified as investing activities.

Typical Classification of Cash Flows from Interest and Dividend

U.S. GAAP	IFRS
Operating Activities	***Operating Activities***
Dividends received	
Interest received	
Interest paid	
Investing Activities	***Investing Activities***
	Dividends received
	Interest received
Financing Activities	***Financing Activities***
Dividends paid	Dividends paid
	Interest paid

The spreadsheet is now complete. The statement of cash flows can now be prepared directly from the spreadsheet simply by presenting the items included in the statement of cash flows section of the spreadsheet in the appropriate format of the statement.

The statements of cash flows from an annual report of CVS Health Corp. are shown in Illustration 21–10. Notice that the reconciliation schedule was reported by CVS in the statement of cash flows itself. Many companies report the schedule separately in the disclosure notes.

Illustration 21–10 Statement of Cash Flows—CVS Health Corp.

Real World Financials

CVS HEALTH CORP.
Consolidated Statements of Cash Flows

	Year Ended December 31,		
($ in millions)	**2015**	**2014**	**2013**
Cash flows from operating activities:			
Cash receipts from customers	$148,954	$ 132,406	$114,993
Cash paid for inventory and prescriptions dispensed by retail network pharmacies	(122,498)	(105,362)	(91,178)
Cash paid to other suppliers and employees	(14,162)	(15,344)	(14,295)
Interest received	21	15	8
Interest paid	(629)	(647)	(534)
Income taxes paid	(3,274)	(2,931)	(3,211)
Net cash provided by operating activities	8,412	8,137	5,783
Cash flows from investing activities:			
Purchases of property and equipment	(2,367)	(2,136)	(1,984)
Proceeds from sale-leaseback transactions	411	515	600
Proceeds from sale of property and equipment and other assets	35	11	54
Acquisitions (net of cash acquired) and other investments	(11,475)	(2,439)	(415)
Purchase of available-for-sale investments	(267)	(157)	(226)
Maturity of available-for-sale investments	243	161	136
Net cash used in investing activities	$ (13,420)	(4,045)	(1,835)
Cash flows from financing activities:			
Increase (decrease) in short-term debt	(685)	685	(690)
Proceeds from issuance of long-term debt	14,805	1,483	3,964
Repayments of long-term debt	(2,902)	(3,100)	—
Payment of contingent consideration	(58)	—	—
Dividends paid	(1,576)	(1,288)	(1,097)
Proceeds from exercise of stock options	299	421	500
Excess tax benefits from stock-based compensation	127	106	62
Repurchase of common stock	(5,001)	(4,001)	(3,976)
Other	(3)	—	—
Net cash provided by (used in) financing activities	5,006	(5,694)	(1,237)
Effect of exchange rate changes on cash and cash equivalents	$ (20)	(6)	3
Net increase (decrease) in cash and cash equivalents:	(22)	(1,608)	2,714
Cash and cash equivalents at the beginning of the year	2,481	4,089	1,375
Cash and cash equivalents at the end of the year	$ 2,459	$ 2,481	$ 4,089
Reconciliation of net income to net cash provided by operating activities:			
Net income	5,239	$ 4,644	$ 4,592
Adjustments required to reconcile net income to net cash provided by operating activities:			
Depreciation and amortization	2,092	1,931	1,870
Stock-based compensation	230	165	141
Loss on early extinguishment of debt	—	521	—
Deferred income taxes and other noncash Items	(266)	(58)	(86)
Change in operating assets and liabilities, net of effects from acquisitions:			
Accounts receivable, net	(1,594)	(737)	(2,210)
Inventories	(1,141)	(770)	12
Other current assets	355	(383)	105
Other assets	2	9	(135)
Accounts payable and claims and discounts payable	2,834	1,742	1,024
Accrued expenses	765	1,060	471
Other long-term liabilities	(104)	13	(1)
Net cash provided by operating activities	$ 8,412	$ 8,137	$ 5,783

Concept Review Exercise

COMPREHENSIVE REVIEW

The comparative balance sheets for 2018 and 2017 and the income statement for 2018 are given below for Beneficial Drill Company. Additional information from Beneficial Drill's accounting records is provided also.

Required:

Prepare the statement of cash flows of Beneficial Drill Company for the year ended December 31, 2018. Present cash flows from operating activities by the direct method and use a spreadsheet to assist in your analysis.

BENEFICIAL DRILL COMPANY
Comparative Balance Sheets
December 31, 2018 and 2017
($ in millions)

Assets	2018	2017
Cash	$ 24	$ 41
Accounts receivable	94	96
Investment revenue receivable	3	2
Inventory	115	110
Prepaid insurance	2	3
Long-term investments	77	60
Land	110	80
Buildings and equipment	220	240
Less: Accumulated depreciation	(35)	(60)
Patent	15	16
	$625	$588
Liabilities		
Accounts payable	$ 23	$ 30
Salaries payable	2	5
Bond interest payable	4	2
Income tax payable	6	8
Deferred income tax liability	5	4
Notes payable	15	0
Bonds payable	150	130
Less: Discount on bonds	(9)	(10)
Shareholders' Equity		
Common stock	210	200
Paid-in capital—excess of par	44	40
Retained earnings	182	179
Less: Treasury stock (at cost)	(7)	0
	$625	$588

BENEFICIAL DRILL COMPANY
Income Statement
For Year Ended December 31, 2018
($ in millions)

Revenues		
Sales revenue	$200	
Investment revenue	6	
Investment revenue—sale of treasury bills	1	$207

(continued)

(concluded)

Expenses and losses		
Cost of goods sold	110	
Salaries expense	30	
Depreciation expense	5	
Patent amortization expense	1	
Insurance expense	3	
Bond interest expense	14	
Loss on destruction of equipment	10	
Income tax expense	7	(180)
Net income		$ 27

Additional information from the accounting records:

a. Investment revenue includes Beneficial Drill Company's $3 million share of the net income of Hammer Company, an equity method investee.

b. Treasury bills were sold during 2018 at a gain of $1 million. Beneficial Drill Company classifies its investments in Treasury bills as cash equivalents.

c. Equipment that originally cost $60 million and was one-half depreciated was rendered unusable by a bolt of lightning. Most major components of the machine were unharmed and were sold for $20 million.

d. Temporary differences between pretax accounting income and taxable income caused the deferred income tax liability to increase by $1 million.

e. The common stock of Wrench Corporation was purchased for $14 million as a long-term investment.

f. Land costing $30 million was acquired by paying $15 million cash and issuing a 13%, seven-year, $15 million note payable to the seller.

g. New equipment was purchased for $40 million cash.

h. $20 million of bonds were sold at face value.

i. On January 19, Beneficial issued a 5% stock dividend (1 million shares). The market price of the $10 par value common stock was $14 per share at that time.

j. Cash dividends of $10 million were paid to shareholders.

k. In November, 500,000 common shares were repurchased as treasury stock at a cost of $7 million.

Solution:

BENEFICIAL DRILL COMPANY
Spreadsheet for the Statement of Cash Flows

	Dec. 31 2017	Changes: Debits		Changes: Credits		Dec. 31 2018
Balance Sheet						
Assets						
Cash	41			(20)	17	24
Accounts receivable	96			(1)	2	94
Investment revenue receivable	2	(2)	1			3
Inventory	110	(4)	5			115
Prepaid insurance	3			(8)	1	2
Long-term investments	60	(2)	3			
		(13)	14			77
Land	80	(14)	30X			110
Buildings and equipment	240	(15)	40	(10)	60	220
Less: Accumulated depreciation	(60)	(10)	30	(6)	5	(35)
Patent	16			(7)	1	15
	588					625

(continued)

(concluded)

BENEFICIAL DRILL COMPANY
Spreadsheet for the Statement of Cash Flows

	Dec. 31 2017	Changes: Debits	Changes: Credits	Dec. 31 2018
Liabilities				
Accounts payable	30	(4) 7		23
Salaries payable	5	(5) 3		2
Bond interest payable	2		(9) 2	4
Income tax payable	8	(11) 2		6
Deferred income tax liability	4		(11) 1	5
Notes payable	0		(14) 15X	15
Bonds payable	130		(16) 20	150
Less: Discount on bonds	(10)		(9) 1	(9)
Shareholders' Equity				
Common stock	200		(17) 10	210
Paid-in capital—excess of par	40		(17) 4	44
Retained earnings	179	(17) 14		
		(18) 10	(12) 27	182
Less: Treasury stock	0	(19) 7		(7)
	588			625
Income Statement				
Revenues:				
Sales revenue			(1) 200	200
Investment revenue			(2) 6	6
Investment revenue—sale of Treasury bills			(3) 1	1
Expenses:				
Cost of goods sold		(4) 110		(110)
Salaries expense		(5) 30		(30)
Depreciation expense		(6) 5		(5)
Patent amortization expense		(7) 1		(1)
Insurance expense		(8) 3		(3)
Bond interest expense		(9) 14		(14)
Loss on destruction of equipment		(10) 10		(10)
Income tax expense		(11) 7		(7)
Net income		(12) 27		27
Statement of Cash Flows				
Operating Activities:				
Cash inflows:				
From customers		(1) 202		
From investment revenue		(2) 2		
From sale of Treasury bills		(3) 1		
Cash outflows:				
To suppliers of goods			(4) 122	
To employees			(5) 33	
For insurance expense			(8) 2	
For bond interest expense			(9) 11	
For income taxes			(11) 8	
Net cash flows				29
Investing Activities:				
Sale of equipment		(10) 20		
Purchase of LT investments			(13) 14	
Purchase of land			(14) 15	
Purchase of equipment			(15) 40	
Net cash flows				(49)
Financing Activities:				
Sale of bonds payable		(16) 20		
Payment of cash dividends			(18) 10	
Purchase of treasury stock			(19) 7	
Net cash flows				3
Net decrease in cash		(20) 17		(17)
Totals		635	635	

BENEFICIAL DRILL COMPANY
Statement of Cash Flows
For Year Ended December 31, 2018
($ in millions)

Cash Flows from Operating Activities		
Cash inflows:		
From customers	$ 202	
From investment revenue	2	
From sale of Treasury bills	1	
Cash outflows:		
To suppliers of goods	(122)	
To employees	(33)	
For insurance expense	(2)	
For bond interest expense	(11)	
For income taxes	(8)	
Net cash flows from operating activities		$ 29
Cash Flows from Investing Activities		
Sale of equipment	$ 20	
Purchase of long-term investments	(14)	
Purchase of land	(15)	
Purchase of equipment	(40)	
Net cash flows from investing activities		(49)
Cash Flows from Financing Activities		
Sale of bonds payable	$ 20	
Payment of cash dividends	(10)	
Purchase of treasury stock	(7)	
Net cash flows from financing activities		3
Net decrease in cash		$(17)
Cash balance, January 1		41
Cash balance, December 31		$ 24
Noncash Investing and Financing Activities		
Acquired $30 million of land by paying cash and issuing a 13%, 7-year note as follows:		
Cost of land	$ 30	
Cash paid	15	
Note issued	$ 15	

PART C

Preparing the SCF: Indirect Method of Reporting Cash Flows from Operating Activities

Getting There through the Back Door

The presentation of cash flows from operating activities illustrated in Part B is referred to as the *direct method.* By this method, the cash effect of each operating activity (i.e., income statement item) is reported directly on the statement of cash flows. For instance, cash received from customers is reported as the cash effect of sales activities, and cash paid to suppliers is reported as the cash effect of cost of goods sold. Income statement items that have *no* cash effect, such as depreciation expense, gains, and losses, are simply not reported.

As we discussed previously, a permissible alternative is the *indirect method,* by which the net cash increase or decrease from operating activities is derived indirectly by starting with reported net income and working backwards to convert that amount to a cash basis. The derivation by the indirect method of net cash flows from operating activities for UBC is shown in Illustration 21–9B. For the adjustment amounts, you may wish to refer back to UBC's balance sheets and income statement presented in Illustration 21–9.

Illustration 21–9B

Indirect Method

Cash Flows from Operating Activities—Indirect Method
and
Reconciliation of Net Income to
Net Cash Flows from Operating Activities

Net Income	$12
Adjustments for noncash effects:	
Gain on sale of land	(8)
Depreciation expense	3
Loss on sale of equipment	2
Changes in operating assets and liabilities:	
Increase in accounts receivable	(2)
Decrease in inventory	4
Increase in accounts payable	6
Increase in salaries payable	2
Decrease in discount on bonds payable	2
Decrease in prepaid insurance	3
Decrease in income tax payable	(2)
Net cash flows from operating activities	$22

The indirect method derives the net cash increase or decrease from operating activities indirectly, by starting with reported net income and "working backwards" to convert that amount to a cash basis.

Notice that the indirect method yields the same $22 million net cash flows from operating activities as does the direct method. This is understandable when you consider that the indirect method simply reverses the differences between the accrual-based income statement and cash flows from operating activities. We accomplish this as described in the next two sections.

Components of Net Income That Do Not Increase or Decrease Cash

Amounts that were subtracted in determining net income but did not reduce cash are *added back* to net income to reverse the effect of their having been subtracted. For example, depreciation expense and the loss on sale of equipment are added back to net income. Other things being equal, this restores net income to what it would have been had depreciation and the loss not been subtracted at all.

Similarly, amounts that were added in determining net income but did not increase cash are subtracted from net income to reverse the effect of their having been added. For example, UBC's gain on sale of land is deducted from net income. Here's why. UBC sold for $18 million land that originally cost $10 million. Recording the sale produced a gain of $8 million, which UBC appropriately included in its income statement. But did this gain increase UBC's cash? No. Certainly selling the land increased cash—by $18 million. We therefore include the $18 million as a cash inflow in the statement of cash flows. However, the sale of land is an investing activity. The gain itself, though, is simply the difference between cash received in the sale of land (reported as an investing activity) and the original cost of the land. If UBC also reported the $8 million gain as a cash flow from operating activities, in addition to reporting $18 million as a cash flow from investing activities, UBC would report the $8 million twice. So, because UBC added the gain in determining its net income but the gain had no effect on cash, the gain must now be subtracted from net income to reverse the effect of its having been added.

Components of Net Income That Do Increase or Decrease Cash

For components of net income that increase or decrease cash, but by an amount different from that reported in the income statement, net income is adjusted for changes in the balances of related balance sheet accounts to *convert the effects of those items to a cash basis.*

For example, sales of $100 million are included in the income statement as a component of net income, and yet, since accounts receivable increased by $2 million, only $98 million cash was collected from customers during the reporting period. Sales are converted to a cash basis by subtracting the $2 million increase in accounts receivable.

Here's another example. The income statement reports salaries expense as $13 million. Just because employees earned $13 million during the reporting period, though, doesn't necessarily mean UBC paid those employees $13 million in cash during the same period. In fact, we see in the comparative balance sheets that salaries payable increased from $1 million to $3 million; UBC owes its employees $2 million more than before the year started. The company must not have paid the entire $13 million expense. By analyzing salaries expense in relation to the change in salaries payable, we can determine the amount of cash paid to employees, as shown next:

Salaries Payable

		1	Beginning balance
Cash paid to employees *(decreases salaries payable)*	?	13	Salaries expense *(increases salaries payable)*
		3	Ending balance

This inspection indicates that UBC paid only $11 million cash to its employees; the remaining $2 million of salaries expense is reflected as an increase in salaries payable. From a cash perspective, then, by subtracting $13 million for salaries in the income statement, UBC has subtracted $2 million more than the reduction in cash. Adding back the $2 million leaves UBC in the same position as if it had deducted only the $11 million cash paid to employees.

Following a similar analysis of the cash effects of the remaining components of net income, those items are likewise converted to a cash basis by adjusting net income for increases and decreases in related accounts.

For components of net income that increase or decrease cash by an amount exactly the same as that reported in the income statement, no adjustment of net income is required. For example, investment revenue of $3 million is included in UBC's $12 million net income amount. Because $3 million also is the amount of cash received from that activity, this element of net income already represents its cash effect and needs no adjustment.[14]

Comparison with the Direct Method

The indirect method is compared with the direct method in Illustration 21–11, using the data of UBC. To better illustrate the relationship between the two methods, the adjustments to net income using the indirect method are presented parallel to the related cash inflows and cash outflows of the direct method. The income statement is included in the graphic to demonstrate that the indirect method also serves to reconcile differences between the elements of that statement and the cash flows reported by the direct method.

As a practical consideration, you might notice that the adjustments to net income using the indirect method follow a convenient pattern. *Increases* in related assets are deducted from net income (i.e., the increase in accounts receivable) when converting to cash from operating activities. Conversely, *decreases* in assets are added (inventory and prepaid insurance in this case). Changes in related liabilities are handled in just the opposite way. Increases in related liabilities are *added* to net income (i.e., the increases in accounts payable and salaries payable) while decreases in liabilities are subtracted (i.e., decrease in income tax payable).[15]

Of course, these are adjustments to net income that effectively convert components of income from reported accrual amounts to a cash basis. The other adjustments to net income (gain, depreciation, loss), as pointed out earlier, are to remove the three income statement components that have no effect at all on cash. This pattern is summarized in Illustration 21–12.

[14]We determined in Part B (subsection 2) that there is no evidence that cash received from investments differs from investment revenue.

[15]The adjustment for the decrease in bond discount is logically consistent with this pattern as well. Bond discount is a contra liability. It's logical, then, that an adjustment for a decrease in this account be added–the opposite of the way a decrease in a liability is treated.

Illustration 21–11 Comparison of the Indirect Method and the Direct Method of Determining Cash Flows from Operating Activities

Income Statement		Cash Flows from Operating Activities: Indirect Method		Direct Method	
		Net income	$12		
		Adjustments:			
Sales	$100	Increase in accounts receivable	(2)	Cash received from customers	$ 98
Investment revenue	3	*(No adjustment—no investment revenue receivable or long-term investments)*		Cash received from investments	3
Gain on sale of land	8	Gain on sale of land	(8)	*(Not reported—no cash effect)*	
Cost of goods sold	(60)	Decrease in inventory	4		
		Increase in accounts payable	6	Cash paid to suppliers	(50)
Salaries expense	(13)	Increase in salaries payable	2	Cash paid to employees	(11)
Depreciation expense	(3)	Depreciation expense	3	*(Not reported—no cash effect)*	
Interest expense	(5)	Decrease in bond discount	2	Cash paid for interest	(3)
Insurance expense	(7)	Decrease in prepaid insurance	3	Cash paid for insurance	(4)
Loss on sale of equipment	(2)	Loss on sale of equipment	2	*(Not reported—no cash effect)*	
Income tax expense	(9)	Decrease in income tax payable	(2)	Cash paid for income taxes	(11)
Net Income	$ 12	**Net cash flows from operating activities**	**$22**	**Net cash flows from operating activities**	**$ 22**

Illustration 21–12
Adjustments to Convert Net Income to a Cash Basis—Indirect Method

Type of Adjustment	To Adjust for Noncash Effect
Adjustments for Noncash Effects:	
Income statement components that have *no effect* at all on cash but are additions to income	Deduct from net income
Income statement components that have *no effect* at all on cash but are deductions from income	Add to net income
Changes in Operating Assets and Liabilities:	
Increases in assets related to an income statement component	Deduct from net income
Decreases in assets related to an income statement component	Add to net income
Increases in liabilities related to an income statement component	Add to net income
Decreases in liabilities related to an income statement component	Deduct from net income

Although either the direct method or the indirect method is permitted, the FASB strongly encourages companies to report cash flows from operating activities by the direct method. The obvious appeal of this approach is that it reports specific operating cash receipts and operating cash payments, which is consistent with the primary objective of the statement of cash flows. Investors and creditors gain additional insight into the specific sources of cash receipts and payments from operating activities revealed by this reporting method. Also, statement users can more readily interpret and understand the information presented because the direct method avoids the confusion caused by reporting noncash items and other reconciling adjustments under the caption *cash flows from operating activities.* Nonetheless, the vast majority of companies choose to use the indirect method. Reasons for this choice range from longstanding tradition to the desire to withhold as much information as possible from competitors.[16]

[16]As indicated earlier, a recent Staff Draft of an Exposure Draft from the IASB and FASB advocates requiring the direct method and disallowing the indirect method for the proposed new Financial Statement Presentation format.

Reconciliation of Net Income to Cash Flows from Operating Activities

As we discussed earlier, whether cash flows from operating activities are reported by the direct method or by the indirect method, the financial statements must report a reconciliation of net income to net cash flows from operating activities. When the direct method is used, the reconciliation is presented in a separate schedule and is identical to the presentation of net cash flows from operating activities by the indirect method. In other words, Illustration 21–9B also serves as the reconciliation schedule to accompany a statement of cash flows using the direct method. Obviously, a separate reconciliation schedule is not required when using the indirect method because the cash flows from operating activities section of the statement of cash flows *is* a reconciliation of net income to net cash flows from operating activities.[17]

Remember that the direct and indirect methods are alternative approaches to deriving net cash flows from *operating* activities only. The choice of which method is used for that purpose does not affect the way cash flows from *investing* and *financing* activities are identified and reported.

The statements of cash flows from the annual report of Toys "R" Us, Inc., which uses the indirect method, are shown in Illustration 21–13.

Illustration 21–13 Statement of Cash Flows—Indirect Method; Toys "R" Us, Inc. Real World Financials

TOYS "R" US, INC. AND SUBSIDIARIES
Consolidated Statements of Cash Flows

($ in millions)	Fiscal Years Ended January 30, 2016	January 31, 2015	February 1, 2014
Cash flows from operating activities:			
Net loss	**$ (124)**	$ (288)	$ (1,036)
Adjustments to reconcile net loss to net cash provided by operating activities:			
Depreciation and amortization	**343**	377	388
Amortization and write-off of debt issuance costs and debt discount	**28**	59	73
Net gains on sales of properties	**(20)**	(5)	(8)
Deferred income taxes	**17**	(1)	133
Non-cash portion of asset impairments and other charges	**20**	20	49
Goodwill impairment	**—**	—	378
Proceeds from settlement of derivatives	**—**	9	—
Unrealized losses (gains) on foreign exchange	**10**	15	(1)
Other	**(1)**	23	16
Changes in operating assets and liabilities:			
Accounts and other receivables	**(2)**	(6)	(1)
Merchandise inventories	**(256)**	(16)	13
Prepaid expenses and other operating assets	**18**	14	21
Accounts payable, accrued expenses and other liabilities	**190**	283	160
Income taxes payable, net	**15**	(8)	(41)
Net cash provided by operating activities	**238**	476	144
Cash flows from investing activities:			
Capital expenditures	**(219)**	(207)	(238)
Increase in restricted cash	**(2)**	(5)	(34)
Proceeds from sales of fixed assets	**13**	18	35
Acquisitions	**(2)**	(1)	—
Property insurance recovery	**—**	2	—
Purchases of debt securities	**—**	—	(20)
Proceeds from redemption of debt securities	**—**	—	52
Net cash used in investing activities	**(210)**	(193)	(205)

(continued)

[17]It is permissible to present the reconciliation in a separate schedule and to report the net cash flows from operating activities as a single line item on the statement of cash flows.

Illustration 21–13 (concluded)

($ in millions)	Fiscal Years Ended January 30, 2016	January 31, 2015	February 1, 2014
Cash Flows from financing activities:			
Long-term debt borrowings	**1,451**	2,866	3,159
Long-term debt repayments	**(1,472)**	(3,010)	(3,491)
Short-term debt borrowings, net	**—**	(12)	(2)
Capitalized debt issuance costs	**(6)**	(35)	(47)
Other	**—**	—	(7)
Net cash used in financing activities	**(27)**	(191)	(388)
Effect of exchange rate changes on cash and cash equivalents	**(19)**	(38)	(25)
Cash and cash equivalents:			
Net (decrease) increase during period	**(18)**	54	(474)
Cash and cash equivalents at beginning of period	**698**	644	1,118
Cash and cash equivalents at end of period	**$ 680**	$ 698	$ 644
Supplemental disclosures of cash flow information:			
Interest paid	**$ 393**	$ 380	$ 458
Net income tax payments	**$ 39**	$ 43	$ 71
Non-cash operating information:			
Purchases of property and equipment included in accounts payable, Accrued expenses and other current liabilities	**$ 56**	$ 42	$ 24

For most companies, expenditures for interest and for taxes are significant. Cash payments for interest and for taxes usually are specifically indicated when the direct method is employed, as is the case for CVS Health Corp. reported earlier in Illustration 21–10. When the indirect method is used, those amounts aren't readily apparent and must be *separately reported,* either on the face of the statement or in an accompanying disclosure note as Toys "R" Us does.

We use a spreadsheet to help prepare a statement of cash flows by the indirect method in Appendix 21A.

Decision Makers' Perspective—Cash Flow Ratios

We have emphasized the analysis of financial statements from a decision maker's perspective throughout this text. Often that analysis included the development and comparison of financial ratios. Ratios based on income statement and balance sheet amounts enjoy a long tradition of acceptance, from which several standard ratios, including those described in earlier chapters, have evolved. To gain another viewpoint, some analysts supplement their investigation with cash flow ratios. Some cash flow ratios are derived by simply substituting cash flow from operations (CFFO) from the statement of cash flows in place of net income in many ratios, not to replace those ratios, but to complement them. For example, the times interest earned ratio can be modified to reflect the number of times the cash outflow for interest is provided by cash inflow from operations, and any of the profitability ratios can be modified to determine the cash generated from assets, shareholders' equity, sales, etc. Illustration 21–14 summarizes the calculation and usefulness of several representative cash flow ratios.

Cash flow ratios have received limited acceptance to date, due in large part to the long tradition of accrual-based ratios coupled with the relatively brief time that all companies have published statements of cash flows. A lack of consensus on cash flow ratios by which to make comparisons also has slowed their acceptance. In fact, companies are prohibited from

Illustration 21–14

Cash Flow Ratios

	Calculation	Measures
Performance Ratios		
Cash flow to sales	$\frac{\text{CFFO}}{\text{Net sales}}$	Cash generated by each sales dollar
Cash return on assets	$\frac{\text{CFFO}}{\text{Average total assets}}$	Cash generated from all resources
Cash return on shareholders' equity	$\frac{\text{CFFO}}{\text{Average shareholders' equity}}$	Cash generated from owner-provided resources
Cash to income	$\frac{\text{CFFO}}{\text{Income from continuing operations}}$	Cash-generating ability of continuing operations
Cash flow per share	$\frac{\text{CFFO} - \text{preferred dividends}}{\text{Weighted-average shares}}$	Operating cash flow on a per share basis
Sufficiency Ratios		
Debt coverage	$\frac{\text{Total liabilities}}{\text{CFFO}}$	Financial risk and financial leverage
Interest coverage	$\frac{\text{CFFO} + \text{interest} + \text{taxes}}{\text{Interest}}$	Ability to satisfy fixed obligations
Reinvestment	$\frac{\text{CFFO}}{\text{Cash outflow for noncurrent assets}}$	Ability to acquire assets with operating cash flows
Debt payment	$\frac{\text{CFFO}}{\text{Cash outflow for LT debt repayment}}$	Ability to pay debts with operating cash flows
Dividend payment	$\frac{\text{CFFO}}{\text{Cash outflow for dividends}}$	Ability to pay dividends with operating cash flows
Investing and financing activity	$\frac{\text{CFFO}}{\text{Cash outflows for investing and financing activities}}$	Ability to acquire assets, pay debts, and make distributions to owners

reporting cash flow per share in the statement of cash flows. Nevertheless, cash flow ratios offer insight in the evaluation of a company's profitability and financial strength.[18]

Financial Reporting Case Solution

© Jose Luis Pelaez Inc./ Blend Images LLC

1. **What are the cash flow aspects of the situation that Mr. Barr may be overlooking in making his case for a wage increase? How can a company's operations generate a healthy profit and yet produce meager or even negative cash flows?** *(p. 1210)* Positive net income does not necessarily indicate a healthy cash position. A statement of cash flows provides information about cash flows not seen when looking only at the balance sheet and the income statement. Although cash flows from operating activities result from the same activities that are reported in the income statement, the income statement reports the activities on an accrual basis. That is, revenues reported are those earned during the reporting period, regardless of when cash is received, and the expenses incurred in generating those revenues, regardless of when cash is paid. Thus, the very same operations can generate a healthy profit and yet produce meager or even negative cash flows.
2. **What information can a statement of cash flows provide about a company's investing activities that can be useful in decisions such as this?** *(p. 1212)* Cash flows from investing activities result from the acquisition and disposition of assets. Information about investing activities is useful to decision makers regarding the nature and magnitude of

[18]Proposals for informative sets of cash flow ratios are offered by Charles Carslaw and John Mills, "Developing Ratios for Effective Cash Flow Analysis," *Journal of Accountancy,* November 1991; Don Giacomino and David Mielke, "Cash Flows: Another Approach to Ratio Analysis," *Journal of Accountancy,* March 1993; and John Mills and Jeanne Yamamura, "The Power of Cash Flows Ratios," *Journal of Accountancy,* October 1998.

productive assets being acquired for future use. In the union negotiations, for instance, Mr. Barr may not be aware of the substantial investments under way to replace and update equipment and the cash requirements of those investments. Relatedly, the relatively low depreciation charges accelerated depreciation provides in the later years of assets' lives may cause profits to seem artificially high given the necessity to replace those assets at higher prices.

3. **What information can a statement of cash flows provide about a company's financing activities that can be useful in decisions such as this?** *(p. 1213)* Information about financing activities provides insights into sources of a company's external financing. Recent debt issues, for instance, might indicate a need for higher cash flows to maintain higher interest charges. Similarly, recent external financing activity may suggest that a company might be near its practical limits from external sources and, therefore, may need a greater reliance on internal financing through operations.

The Bottom Line

- **LO21–1** Decision makers focus on the prospects of receiving a cash return from their dealings with a firm. But it is the ability of the firm to generate cash flows to itself that ultimately determines the potential for cash flows to investors and creditors. The statement of cash flows fills an information gap left by the balance sheet and the income statement by presenting information about cash flows that the other statements either do not provide or provide only indirectly. (*p. 1205*)
- **LO21–2** Cash includes cash equivalents. These are short-term, highly liquid investments that can readily be converted to cash with little risk of loss. (*p. 1209*)
- **LO21–3** Cash flows from operating activities are both inflows and outflows of cash that result from activities reported in the income statement. (*p. 1210*)
- **LO21–4** Unlike the direct method, which directly lists cash inflows and outflows, the indirect method derives cash flows indirectly, by starting with reported net income and working backwards to convert that amount to a cash basis. (*p. 1211*)
- **LO21–5** Cash flows from investing activities are related to the acquisition and disposition of assets, other than inventory and assets classified as cash equivalents. (*p. 1212*)
- **LO21–6** Cash flows from financing activities result from the external financing of a business. (*p. 1213*)
- **LO21–7** Noncash investing and financing activities, such as acquiring equipment (an investing activity) by issuing a long-term note payable (a financing activity), are reported in a related disclosure schedule or note. (*p. 1215*)
- **LO21–8** A spreadsheet provides a systematic method of preparing a statement of cash flows by analyzing available data to ensure that all operating, investing, and financing activities are detected. Recording spreadsheet entries that explain account balance changes simultaneously identifies and classifies the activities to be reported on the statement of cash flows. (*p. 1215*)
- **LO21–9** IFRS allows more flexibility than U.S. GAAP in the classification of cash flows. Companies can report interest and dividends paid as either operating or financing cash flows and interest and dividends received as either operating or investing cash flows. (*p. 1235*)

Spreadsheet for the Indirect Method

APPENDIX 21A

A spreadsheet is equally useful in preparing a statement of cash flows whether we use the direct or the indirect method of determining cash flows from operating activities. The format of the spreadsheet differs only with respect to operating activities. The analysis of transactions for the purpose of identifying cash flows to be reported is the same. To illustrate, Illustration 21A–1 provides a spreadsheet analysis of the data for UBC.

Two differences should be noted between the spreadsheet in Illustration 21A–1 and the spreadsheet we used earlier for the direct method. First, in the statement of cash flows section of the spreadsheet, under the heading of "cash flows from operating activities," specific

Illustration 21A–1

Indirect Method

UNITED BRANDS CORPORATION
Spreadsheet for the Statement of Cash Flows

	Dec. 31, 2017	Changes				Dec. 31, 2018
		Debits		Credits		
Balance Sheet						
Assets						
Cash	20	(19)	9			29
Accounts receivable	30	(5)	2			32
Short-term investments	0	(12)	12			12
Inventory	50			(6)	4	46
Prepaid insurance	6			(8)	3	3
Land	60	(13)	30	(2)	10	80
Buildings and equipment	75	(14)	20X	(3)	14	81
Less: Accumulated depreciation	(20)	(3)	7	(4)	3	(16)
	221					267
Liabilities						
Accounts payable	20			(7)	6	26
Salaries payable	1			(9)	2	3
Income tax payable	8	(11)	2			6
Notes payable	0			(14)	20X	20
Bonds payable	50	(15)	15			35
Less: Discount on bonds	(3)			(10)	2	(1)
Shareholders' Equity						
Common stock	100			(16)	10	
				(17)	20	130
Paid-in capital—excess of par	20			(16)	3	
				(17)	6	29
Retained earnings	25	(16)	13			
		(18)	5	(1)	12	19
	221					267
Statement of Cash Flows						
Operating activities:						
Net income		(1)	12			
Adjustments for noncash effects:						
Gain on sale of land				(2)	8	
Depreciation expense		(4)	3			
Loss on sale of equipment		(3)	2			
Increase in accounts receivable				(5)	2	
Decrease in inventory		(6)	4			
Decrease in prepaid insurance		(8)	3			
Increase in accounts payable		(7)	6			
Increase in salaries payable		(9)	2			
Decrease in income tax payable				(11)	2	
Amortization of discount		(10)	2			
Net cash flows						22
Investing activities:						
Purchase of land				(13)	30	
Purchase of S-T investment				(12)	12	
Sale of land		(2)	18			
Sale of equipment		(3)	5			
Net cash flows						(19)
Financing activities:						
Sale of common shares		(17)	26			
Retirement of bonds payable				(15)	15	
Payment of cash dividends				(18)	5	
Net cash flows						6
Net increase in cash				(19)	9	9
Totals			198		198	

cash inflows and cash outflows are replaced by net income and the required adjustments for noncash effects. Second, we do not include an income statement section. This section is unnecessary because, using the indirect method, we are not interested in identifying specific operating activities that cause increases and decreases in cash. Instead, we need from the income statement only the amount of net income, which is converted to a cash basis by adjusting for any noncash amounts included in net income. The spreadsheet entries in journal entry form for the indirect method are illustrated in Illustration 21A–2.

Remember that there is no mandatory order in which the account changes must be analyzed. However, since we determine net cash flows from operating activities by working backwards from net income when using the indirect method, it is convenient to start with the spreadsheet entry that represents the credit to retained earnings due to net income. This entry corresponds to summary entry (11) using the direct method. By entering the debit portion of the entry as the first item under the cash flows from operating activities (CFOA), we establish net income as the initial amount of cash flows from operating activities, which is then adjusted to a cash basis by subsequent entries. Entries (2)–(4) duplicate the transactions that involve noncash components of net income. Changes in current assets and current liabilities that represent differences between revenues and expenses and the cash effects of those revenues and expenses are accounted for by entries (5)–(11). Summary entries (12)–(19) explain the changes in the balance sheet not already accounted for by previous entries, and are identical to entries (12)–(19) recorded using the direct method.

Illustration 21A–2

Spreadsheet Entries for the Indirect Method

Entry (1)	Net income—CFOA	12	
	Retained earnings		12
	Establishes net income as the initial amount of cash flows from operating activities, to be adjusted to a cash basis by subsequent entries.		
Entry (2)	Cash (received from sale of land)	18	
	Land		10
	Gain on sale of land—CFOA		8
	Deducts the noncash gain added in determining net income, explains a portion of the change in land, and identifies a cash inflow from investing activities.		
Entry (3)	Cash (received from sale of equipment)	5	
	Loss on sale of equipment—CFOA	2	
	Accumulated depreciation	7	
	Buildings and equipment		14
	Adds back the noncash loss subtracted in determining net income, explains portions of the changes in accumulated depreciation and buildings and equipment, and identifies a cash inflow from investing activities.		
Entry (4)	Depreciation expense—CFOA	3	
	Accumulated depreciation		3
	Adds back the noncash expense subtracted in determining net income.		
Entry (5)	Accounts receivable	2	
	Increase in accounts receivable—CFOA		2
	Reduces net income to reflect $98 million cash received from customers rather than $100 million sales.		
Entry (6)	Decrease in inventory—CFOA	4	
	Inventory		4
	Increases net income to reflect a deduction of $56 million cost of goods purchased rather than $60 million cost of goods sold.		
Entry (7)	Increase in accounts payable—CFOA	6	
	Accounts payable		6
	Increases net income to reflect a deduction of $50 million cash paid to suppliers rather than $56 million cost of goods purchased.		

(continued)

Illustration 21A–2
(concluded)

Entry (8)	Decrease in prepaid insurance—CFOA	3	
	Prepaid insurance		3
	Increases net income to reflect a deduction of $4 million cash paid for insurance rather than $7 million insurance expense.		
Entry (9)	Increase in salaries payable—CFOA	2	
	Salaries payable		2
	Increases net income to reflect a deduction of $11 million cash paid to employees rather than $13 million salaries expense.		
Entry (10)	Amortization of discount on bonds—CFOA	2	
	Discount on bonds		2
	Increases net income to reflect a deduction of $3 million cash paid for bond interest rather than $5 million bond interest expense.		
Entry (11)	Income taxes payable	2	
	Decrease in income taxes payable—CFOA		2
	Reduces net income to reflect a deduction of $11 million cash paid for income taxes rather than $9 million income tax expense.		
Entry (12)	Short-term investment	12	
	Cash (purchase of short-term investment)		12
	Explains the increase in the short-term investment account and identifies a cash outflow from investing activities.		
Entry (13)	Land	30	
	Cash (purchase of land)		30
	Explains a portion of the change in the land account and identifies a cash outflow from investing activities.		
Entry (14)	Buildings and equipment	20	
	Note payable		20
	Partially explains the changes in the buildings, equipment, and notes payable accounts and identifies a significant noncash investing and financing activity.		
Entry (15)	Bonds payable	15	
	Cash (retirement of bonds payable)		15
	Explains the decrease in the bonds payable account and identifies a cash outflow from financing activities.		
Entry (16)	Retained earnings	13	
	Common stock		10
	Paid-in capital—excess of par		3
	Partially explains the changes in the retained earnings, common stock, and paid-in capital—excess of par accounts.		
Entry (17)	Cash (from sale of common stock)	26	
	Common stock		20
	Paid-in capital—excess of par		6
	Partially explains the changes in the common stock and paid-in capital—excess of par accounts and identifies a cash inflow from financing activities.		
Entry (18)	Retained earnings	5	
	Cash (payment of cash dividends)		5
	Partially explains the change in the retained earnings account and identifies a cash outflow from financing activities.		
Entry (19)	Cash	9	
	Net increase in cash (from statement of cash flows activities)		9
	Reconciles the net increase in cash from operating, investing, and financing activities to the increase in the cash balance.		

The statement of cash flows presenting net cash flows from operating activities by the indirect method is illustrated in Illustration 21A–3.

Illustration 21A–3

Statement of Cash flows—Indirect Method

All parts of the statement of cash flows except operating activities are precisely the same as in the direct method.

UNITED BRANDS CORPORATION
Statement of Cash Flows
For Year Ended December 31, 2018
($ in millions)

Cash Flows from Operating Activities		
Net income	$ 12	
Adjustments for noncash effects:		
Gain on sale of land	(8)	
Depreciation expense	3	
Loss on sale of equipment	2	
Changes in operating assets and liabilities:		
Increase in accounts receivable	(2)	
Decrease in inventory	4	
Decrease in prepaid insurance	3	
Increase in accounts payable	6	
Increase in salaries payable	2	
Decrease in income tax payable	(2)	
Decrease in discount on bonds payable	2	
Net cash flows from operating activities		$ 22
Cash Flows from Investing Activities		
Purchase of land	(30)	
Purchase of short-term investment	(12)	
Sale of land	18	
Sale of equipment	5	
Net cash from investing activities		(19)
Cash Flows from Financing Activities		
Sale of common shares	26	
Retirement of bonds payable	(15)	
Payment of cash dividends	(5)	
Net cash flows from financing activities		6
Net increase in cash		9
Cash balance, January 1		20
Cash balance, December 31		$ 29
Note X:		
Noncash Investing and Financing Activities		
Acquired $20 million of equipment by issuing a 12%, 5-year note		$ 20

APPENDIX 21B

The T-Account Method of Preparing the Statement of Cash Flows

The T-account method serves the same purpose as a spreadsheet in assisting in the preparation of a statement of cash flows.

This appendix demonstrates the use of a spreadsheet to prepare the statement of cash flows. A second systematic approach to the preparation of the statement is referred to as the T-account method. The two methods are identical in concept. Both approaches reconstruct the transactions that caused changes in each account balance during the year, simultaneously identifying the operating, investing, and financing activities to be reported on the statement of cash flows. The form of the two methods differs only by whether the entries for those transactions are recorded on a spreadsheet or in T-accounts. In both cases, entries are recorded until the net change in each account balance has been explained.

Some accountants feel that the T-account method is less time-consuming than preparing a spreadsheet but accomplishes precisely the same goal. Since both methods are simply analytical techniques to assist in statement preparation, the choice is a matter of personal preference. The following five steps outline the T-account method:

1. Draw T-accounts for each income statement and balance sheet account.
2. The T-account for cash should be drawn considerably larger than other T-accounts because more space is required to accommodate the numerous debits and credits to cash. Also, the cash T-account will serve the same purpose as the statement of cash flows section of the spreadsheet in that the formal statement of cash flows is developed from the cash flows reported there. Therefore, it is convenient to partition the cash T-account with headings for "Operating Activities," "Investing Activities," and "Financing Activities" before entries are recorded.
3. Enter each account's net change on the appropriate side (debit or credit) of the uppermost portion of each T-account. These changes will serve as individual check figures for determining whether the increase or decrease in each account balance has been explained. These first three steps establish the basic work form for the T-account method.
4. Reconstruct the transactions that caused changes in each account balance during the year and record the entries for those transactions directly in the T-accounts. Again using UBC as an example, the entries we record in the T-accounts are exactly the same as the spreadsheet entries we created in the chapter when using the spreadsheet method. The analysis we used in creating those spreadsheet entries is equally applicable to the T-account method. For that reason, that analysis is not repeated here. The complete T-account work form for UBC is presented below. Account balance changes are provided from balances given in Illustration 21–9.
5. After all account balances have been explained by T-account entries, prepare the statement of cash flows from the cash T-account, being careful also to report noncash investing and financing activities. The statement of cash flows for UBC appears in Illustration 21–2.

BALANCE SHEET ACCOUNTS

Cash (statement of cash flows)

		Debit	Credit		
		9			
Operating Activities:					
From customers	(1)	98	50	(4)	To suppliers of goods
From investment revenue	(2)	3	11	(5)	To employees
			3	(7)	For interest
			4	(8)	For insurance
			11	(10)	For income taxes
Investing Activities:					
Sale of land	(3)	18	12	(12)	Purchase of short-term investment
Sale of equipment	(9)	5	30	(13)	Purchase of land
Financing Activities:					
Sale of common stock	(17)	26	15	(15)	Retirement of bonds payable
			5	(18)	Payment of cash dividends

Accounts Receivable

	2		
(1)	2		

Short-Term Investments

	12		
(12)	12		

Inventory

	Debit	Credit	
		4	
		4	(4)

Prepaid Insurance

		3	
		3	(8)

Land

	Debit	Credit	
	20		
(13)	30	10	(3)

(continued)

(concluded)

Buildings and Equipment

	Debit	Credit	
	6		
X(14)	20	14	(9)

Accumulated Depreciation

	Debit	Credit	
	4		
(9)	7	3	(6)

Accounts Payable

	Debit	Credit	
		6	
		6	(4)

Salaries Payable

	Debit	Credit	
		2	
		2	(5)

Income Tax Payable

	2		
(10)	2		

Notes Payable

	Debit	Credit	
		20	
		20	(14)X

Bonds Payable

	Debit	Credit	
	15		
(15)	15		

Discount on Bonds

		2	
		2	(7)

Common Stock

		30	
		10	(16)
		20	(17)

Paid-in Capital—excess of par

	Debit	Credit	
		9	
		3	(16)
		6	(17)

Retained Earnings

	Debit	Credit	
	6		
(16)	13		
(18)	5	12	(11)

X Noncash Investing and Financing Activity

INCOME STATEMENT ACCOUNTS

Sales Revenue

	Debit	Credit	
		100	
		100	(1)

Investment Revenue

		3	
		3	(2)

Gain on Sale of Land

	Debit	Credit	
		8	
		8	(3)

Cost of Goods Sold

	60		
(4)	60		

Salaries Expense

	13		
(5)	13		

Depreciation Expense

	3		
(6)	3		

Interest Expense

	5		
(7)	5		

Insurance Expense

	7		
(8)	7		

Loss on Sale of Equipment

	2		
(9)	2		

Income Tax Expense

	9		
(10)	9		

Net Income (Income Summary)

	12		
(11)	12		

Questions For Review of Key Topics

Q 21–1 Effects of all cash flows affect the balances of various accounts reported in the balance sheet. Also, the activities that cause some of these cash flows are reported in the income statement. What, then, is the need for an additional financial statement that reports cash flows?

Q 21–2 The statement of cash flows provides a list of all the cash inflows and cash outflows during the reporting period. To make the list more informative, the cash flows are classified according to the nature of the activities that create the cash flows. What are the three primary classifications?

Q 21–3 Is an investment in Treasury bills always classified as a cash equivalent? Explain.

Q 21–4 Transactions that involve merely purchases or sales of cash equivalents generally are not reported in a statement of cash flows. Describe an exception to this generalization. What is the essential characteristic of the transaction that qualifies as an exception?

Q 21–5 What are the differences between cash flows from operating activities and the elements of an income statement?

Q 21–6 Do cash flows from operating activities report all the elements of the income statement on a cash basis? Explain.

Q 21–7 Investing activities include the acquisition and disposition of assets. Provide three specific examples. Identify two exceptions.

Q 21–8 The sale of stock and the sale of bonds are reported as financing activities. Are payments of dividends to shareholders and payments of interest to bondholders also reported as financing activities? Explain.

Q 21–9 Does the statement of cash flows report only transactions that cause an increase or a decrease in cash? Explain.

Q 21–10 How would the acquisition of a building be reported on a statement of cash flows if purchased by issuing a mortgage note payable in addition to a significant cash down payment?

Q 21–11 Perhaps the most noteworthy item reported on an income statement is net income—the amount by which revenues exceed expenses. The most noteworthy item reported on a statement of cash flows is *not* the amount of net cash flows. Explain.

Q 21–12 What is the purpose of the "changes" columns of a spreadsheet to prepare a statement of cash flows?

Q 21–13 Given sales revenue of $200,000, how can it be determined whether or not $200,000 cash was received from customers?

Q 21–14 When an asset is sold at a gain, why is the gain not reported as a cash inflow from operating activities?

Q 21–15 When determining the amount of cash paid for income taxes, what would be indicated by an increase in the deferred income tax liability account?

Q 21–16 When using the indirect method of determining net cash flows from operating activities, how is warranty expense reported? Why? What other expenses are reported in a like manner?

Q 21–17 When using the indirect method of determining net cash flows from operating activities, how are revenues and expenses reported on the statement of cash flows if their cash effects are identical to the amounts reported in the income statement?

Q 21–18 Why does the FASB recommend the direct method over the indirect method?

Q 21–19 Compare the manner in which investing activities are reported on a statement of cash flows prepared by the direct method and by the indirect method.

IFRS **Q 21–20** Where can we find authoritative guidance for the statement of cash flows under IFRS?

IFRS **Q 21–21** U.S. GAAP designates cash outflows for interest payments and cash inflows from interest and dividends received as operating cash flows. Dividends paid to shareholders are classified as financing cash flows. How are these cash flows reported under IFRS?

Brief Exercises

connect

BE 21–1
Determine cash received from customers
● LO21–3

Horton Housewares' accounts receivable decreased during the year by $5 million. What is the amount of cash Horton received from customers during the reporting period if its sales were $33 million? Prepare a summary entry that represents the net effect of the selling and collection activities during the reporting period.

BE 21–2
Determine cash received from customers
● LO21–3

April Wood Products' accounts receivable increased during the year by $4 million. What is the amount of cash April Wood Products received from customers during the reporting period if its sales were $44 million? Prepare a summary entry that represents the net effect of the selling and collection activities during the reporting period.

BE 21–3
Determine cash paid to suppliers
● LO21–3

LaRoe Lawns' inventory increased during the year by $6 million. Its accounts payable increased by $5 million during the same period. What is the amount of cash LaRoe paid to suppliers of merchandise during the reporting period if its cost of goods sold was $25 million? Prepare a summary entry that represents the net effect of merchandise purchases during the reporting period.

BE 21–4
Determine cash paid to employees
● LO21–3

Sherriane Baby Products' salaries expense was $17 million. What is the amount of cash Sherriane paid to employees during the reporting period if its salaries payable increased by $3 million? Prepare a summary entry that represents the net effect of salaries expense incurred and paid during the reporting period.

BE 21–5
Bond interest and discount
● LO21–3, LO21–6

Agee Technology, Inc., issued 9% bonds, dated January 1, with a face amount of $400 million on July 1, 2018, at a price of $380 million. For bonds of similar risk and maturity, the market yield is 10%. Interest is paid semi-annually on June 30 and December 31. Prepare the journal entry to record interest at the effective interest rate at December 31. What would be the amount(s) related to the bonds that Agee would report in its statement of cash flows for the year ended December 31, 2018, if it uses the direct method?

BE 21–6
Bond interest and discount
● LO21–4, LO21–6

Refer to the situation described in BE 21–5. What would be the amount(s) related to the bonds that Agee would report in its statement of cash flows for the year ended December 31, 2018, if it uses the indirect method?

BE 21–7
Installment note
● LO21–3, LO21–6

On January 1, 2018, the Merit Group issued to its bank a $41 million, five-year installment note to be paid in five equal payments at the end of each year. Installment payments of $10 million annually include interest at the rate of 7%. What would be the amount(s) related to the note that Merit would report in its statement of cash flows for the year ended December 31, 2018?

BE 21–8
Sale of land
● LO21–3, LO21–4, LO21–5

On July 15, 2018, M.W. Morgan Distribution sold land for $35 million that it had purchased in 2013 for $22 million. What would be the amount(s) related to the sale that Morgan would report in its statement of cash flows for the year ended December 31, 2018, using the direct method? The indirect method?

BE 21–9
Investing activities
● LO21–5

Carter Containers sold marketable securities, land, and common stock for $30 million, $15 million, and $40 million, respectively. Carter also purchased treasury stock, equipment, and a patent for $21 million, $25 million, and $12 million, respectively. What amount should Carter report as net cash from investing activities?

BE 21–10
Financing activities
● LO21–6

Refer to the situation described in BE 21–9. What amount should Carter report as net cash from financing activities?

BE 21–11
Indirect method
● LO21–4

Sheen Awnings reported net income of $90 million. Included in that number were depreciation expense of $3 million and a loss on the sale of equipment of $2 million. Records reveal increases in accounts receivable, accounts payable, and inventory of $1 million, $4 million, and $3 million, respectively. What were Sheen's cash flows from operating activities?

BE 21–12
Indirect method
● LO21–4

Sunset Acres reported net income of $60 million. Included in that number were trademark amortization expense of $2 million and a gain on the sale of land of $1 million. Records reveal decreases in accounts receivable, accounts payable, and inventory of $2 million, $5 million, and $4 million, respectively. What were Sunset's cash flows from operating activities?

Exercises

connect

E 21–1
Classification of cash flows
● LO21–3 through LO21–6

Listed below are several transactions that typically produce either an increase or a decrease in cash. Indicate by letter whether the cash effect of each transaction is reported on a statement of cash flows as an operating (**O**), investing (**I**), or financing (**F**) activity.

	Transactions
F	1. Sale of common stock
____	2. Sale of land
____	3. Purchase of treasury stock
____	4. Merchandise sales
____	5. Issuance of a long-term note payable
____	6. Purchase of merchandise
____	7. Repayment of note payable

(continued)

(concluded)

_____ 8. Employee salaries
_____ 9. Sale of equipment at a gain
_____ 10. Issuance of bonds
_____ 11. Acquisition of bonds of another corporation
_____ 12. Payment of semiannual interest on bonds payable
_____ 13. Payment of a cash dividend
_____ 14. Purchase of a building
_____ 15. Collection of nontrade note receivable (principal amount)
_____ 16. Loan to another firm
_____ 17. Retirement of common stock
_____ 18. Income taxes
_____ 19. Issuance of a short-term note payable
_____ 20. Sale of a copyright

E 21–2
Determine cash paid to suppliers of merchandise
● LO21–3, LO21–6

Shown below in T-account format are the beginning and ending balances ($ in millions) of both inventory and accounts payable.

Inventory

Beginning balance	90		
Ending balance	93		

Accounts Payable

		14	Beginning balance
		16	Ending balance

Required:

1. Use a T-account analysis to determine the amount of cash paid to suppliers of merchandise during the reporting period if cost of goods sold was $300 million.
2. Prepare a summary entry that represents the net effect of merchandise purchases during the reporting period.

E 21–3
Determine cash received from customers
● LO21–3

Determine the amount of cash received from customers for each of the three independent situations below. All dollars are in millions.

Situation	Sales Revenue	Accounts Receivable Increase (Decrease)	Cash Received from Customers
1	100	-0-	?
2	100	5	?
3	100	(5)	?

E 21–4
Summary entries for cash received from customers
● LO21–3

For each of the three independent situations below, prepare journal entries that summarize the selling and collection activities for the reporting period in order to determine the amount of cash received from customers and to explain the change in each account shown. All dollars are in millions.

Situation	Sales Revenue	Accounts Receivable Increase (Decrease)	Cash Received from Customers
1	200	-0-	?
2	200	10	?
3	200	(10)	?

E 21–5
Determine cash paid to suppliers of merchandise
● LO21–3

Determine the amount of cash paid to suppliers of merchandise for each of the nine independent situations below. All dollars are in millions.

Situation	Cost of Goods Sold	Inventory Increase (Decrease)	Accounts Payable Increase (Decrease)	Cash Paid to Suppliers
1	100	0	0	?
2	100	3	0	?
3	100	(3)	0	?
4	100	0	7	?
5	100	0	(7)	?
6	100	3	7	?
7	100	3	(7)	?
8	100	(3)	(7)	?
9	100	(3)	7	?

E 21–6
Summary entries for cash paid to suppliers of merchandise
● LO21–3

For each of the five independent situations below, prepare a journal entry that summarizes the purchases, sales, and payments related to inventories in order to determine the amount of cash paid to suppliers and explain the change in each account shown. All dollars are in millions.

Situation	Cost of Goods Sold	Inventory Increase (Decrease)	Accounts Payable Increase (Decrease)	Cash Paid to Suppliers
1	200	0	0	?
2	200	6	0	?
3	200	0	14	?
4	200	6	14	?
5	200	(6)	(14)	?

E 21–7
Determine cash paid for bond interest
● LO21–3

Determine the amount of cash paid to bondholders for bond interest for each of the six independent situations below. All dollars are in millions.

Situation	Bond Interest Expense	Bond Interest Payable Increase (Decrease)	Unamortized Discount Increase (Decrease)	Cash Paid for Interest
1	10	0	0	?
2	10	2	0	?
3	10	(2)	0	?
4	10	0	(3)	?
5	10	2	(3)	?
6	10	(2)	(3)	?

E 21–8
Determine cash paid for bond interest
● LO21–3

For each of the four independent situations below, prepare a single journal entry that summarizes the recording and payment of interest in order to determine the amount of cash paid for bond interest and explain the change (if any) in each of the accounts shown. All dollars are in millions.

Situation	Bond Interest Expense	Bond Interest Payable Increase (Decrease)	Unamortized Discount Increase (Decrease)	Cash Paid for Interest
1	20	0	0	?
2	20	4	0	?
3	20	0	(6)	?
4	20	(4)	(6)	?

E 21–9
Determine cash paid for income taxes
● LO21–3

Determine the amount of cash paid for income taxes in each of the nine independent situations below. All dollars are in millions.

Situation	Income Tax Expense	Income Tax Payable Increase (Decrease)	Deferred Tax Liability Increase (Decrease)	Cash Paid for Taxes
1	10	0	0	?
2	10	3	0	?
3	10	(3)	0	?
4	10	0	2	?
5	10	0	(2)	?
6	10	3	2	?
7	10	3	(2)	?
8	10	(3)	(2)	?
9	10	(3)	2	?

E 21–10
Summary entries for cash paid for income taxes
● LO21–3

For each of the five independent situations below, prepare a single journal entry that summarizes the recording and payment of income taxes in order to determine the amount of cash paid for income taxes and explain the change (if any) in each of the accounts shown. All dollars are in millions.

Situation	Income Tax Expense	Income Tax Payable Increase (Decrease)	Deferred Tax Liability Increase (Decrease)	Cash Paid for Taxes
1	10	0	0	?
2	10	3	0	?
3	10	0	(2)	?
4	10	3	2	?
5	10	(3)	(2)	?

E 21–11
Bonds; statement of cash flow effects
● LO21–3

Most Solutions, Inc., issued 10% bonds, dated January 1, with a face amount of $640 million on January 1, 2018. The bonds mature in 2028 (10 years). For bonds of similar risk and maturity the market yield is 12%. Interest expense is recorded at the effective interest rate. Interest is paid semiannually on June 30 and December 31. Most recorded the sale as follows:

January 1, 2018		
Cash (price)	566,589,440	
Discount on bonds (difference)	73,410,560	
Bonds payable (face amount)		640,000,000

Required:
What would be the amount(s) related to the bonds that Most would report in its statement of cash flows for the year ended December 31, 2018?

E 21–12
Installment note; statement of cash flow effects
● LO21–3, LO21–6

National Food Services, Inc., borrowed $4 million from its local bank on January 1, 2018, and issued a 4-year installment note to be paid in four equal payments at the end of each year. The payments include interest at the rate of 10%. Installment payments are $1,261,881 annually.

Required:
What would be the amount(s) related to the note that National would report in its statement of cash flows for the year ended December 31, 2018?

E 21–13
Identifying cash flows from investing activities and financing activities
● LO21–5, LO21–6

In preparation for developing its statement of cash flows for the year ended December 31, 2018, Rapid Pac, Inc., collected the following information:

	($ in millions)
Fair value of shares issued in a stock dividend	$ 65
Payment for the early extinguishment of long-term bonds (book value: $97 million)	102
Proceeds from the sale of treasury stock (cost: $17 million)	22
Gain on sale of land	4
Proceeds from sale of land	12
Purchase of Microsoft common stock	160
Declaration of cash dividends	44
Distribution of cash dividends declared in 2017	40

Required:
1. In Rapid Pac's statement of cash flows, what were net cash inflows (or outflows) from investing activities for 2018?
2. In Rapid Pac's statement of cash flows, what were net cash inflows (or outflows) from financing activities for 2018?

E 21–14
Identifying cash flows from investing activities and financing activities
● LO21–5, LO21–6

In preparation for developing its statement of cash flows for the year ended December 31, 2018, Millennium Solutions, Inc. collected the following information:

	($ in millions)
Payment for the early extinguishments of long-term notes (book value: $50 million)	$ 54
Sale of common shares	176
Retirement of common shares	122
Loss on sale of equipment	2
Proceeds from sale of equipment	8
Issuance of short-term note payable for cash	10
Acquisition of building for cash	7
Purchase of marketable securities (not a cash equivalent)	5
Purchase of marketable securities (considered a cash equivalent)	1
Cash payment for 3-year insurance policy	3
Collection of note receivable with interest (principal amount, $11)	13
Declaration of cash dividends	33
Distribution of cash dividends declared in 2017	30

Required:

1. In Millennium's statement of cash flows, what were net cash inflows (or outflows) from investing activities for 2018?
2. In Millennium's statement of cash flows, what were net cash inflows (or outflows) from financing activities for 2018?

E 21–15
Lease; lessee; statement of cash flows effects
● LO21–3, LO21–5, LO21–6

Wilson Foods Corporation leased a commercial food processor on September 30, 2018. The five-year finance lease agreement calls for Wilson to make quarterly lease payments of $195,774, payable each September 30, December 31, March 31, June 30, with the first payment at September 30, 2018. Wilson's incremental borrowing rate is 12%. Wilson records amortization on a straight-line basis at the end of each fiscal year. Wilson recorded the lease as follows:

September 30, 2018		
Right-of-use asset (calculated below)	3,000,000	
Lease payable (calculated below)		3,000,000
Lease payable	195,774	
Cash (first payment)		195,774

Calculation of the present value of lease payments

$195,774 × 15.32380* = $3,000,000
(rounded)

*Present value of an annuity due of $1: $n = 20$, $i = 3\%$ (from Table 6).

Required:

What would be the pretax amounts related to the lease that Wilson would report in its statement of cash flows for the year ended December 31, 2018?

E 21–16
Equity method investment; statement of cash flow effects
● LO21–3, LO21–5

On January 1, 2018, Beilich Enterprises bought 20% of the outstanding common stock of Wolfe Construction Company for $600 million cash. Wolfe's net income for the year ended December 31, 2018, was $300 million. During 2018, Wolfe declared and paid cash dividends of $60 million. Beilich recorded the investment as follows:

	($ in millions)	
Purchase		
Investment in Wolfe Construction shares	600	
Cash		600
Net income		
Investment in Wolfe Construction shares (20% × $300 million)	60	
Investment revenue		60
Dividends		
Cash (20% × $60 million)	12	
Investment in Wolfe Construction shares		12

Required:

What would be the pretax amounts related to the investment that Beilich would report in its statement of cash flows for the year ended December 31, 2018?

E 21–17
Indirect method; reconciliation of net income to net cash flows from operating activities
● LO21–4

The accounting records of EZ Company provided the data below. Prepare a reconciliation of net income to net cash flows from operating activities.

Net income	$50,000
Depreciation expense	7,000
Increase in inventory	1,500
Decrease in salaries payable	800
Decrease in accounts receivable	2,000
Amortization of patent	500
Amortization of premium on bonds	1,000
Increase in accounts payable	4,000
Cash dividends	12,000

E 21–18
Spreadsheet entries from statement of retained earnings
● LO21–3 through LO21–8

The statement of retained earnings of Gary Larson Publishers is presented below.

GARY LARSON PUBLISHERS
Statement of Retained Earnings
For the Year Ended December 31, 2018
($ in millions)

Retained earnings, January 1		$200
Add:	Net income	75
Deduct:	Cash dividend	(25)
	Stock dividend (1 million shares of $1 par common stock)	(16)
	Property dividend (Garfield Company preferred stock held as a short-term investment)	(12)
	Sale of treasury stock (cost $53 million)	(10)
Retained earnings, December 31		$212

Required:
For the transactions that affected Larson's retained earnings, reconstruct the journal entries that can be used to determine cash flows to be reported in a statement of cash flows. Also indicate any investing and financing activities you identify from this analysis that should be reported on the statement of cash flows.

E 21–19
Relationship between the income statement and cash flows from operating activities (direct method and indirect method)
● LO21–3, LO21–4

The following schedule relates the income statement with cash flows from operating activities, derived by both the direct and indirect methods, in the format illustrated by Illustration 21–11 in the chapter. The amounts for income statement elements are missing.

Income Statement		Cash Flows from Operating Activities: Indirect Method		Cash Flows from Operating Activities: Direct Method	
		Net income	$?		
		Adjustments:			
Sales	$?	Decrease in accounts receivable	12	Cash received from customers	$ 612
Cost of goods sold	?	Increase in inventory	(24)		
		Decrease in accounts payable	(36)	Cash paid to suppliers	(420)
Salaries expense	?	Increase in salaries payable	12	Cash paid to employees	(66)
Depreciation expense	?	Depreciation expense	18	(Not reported—no cash effect)	
Insurance expense	?	Decrease in prepaid insurance	18	Cash paid for insurance	(24)
Loss on sale of land	?	Loss on sale of land	12	(Not reported—no cash effect)	
Income tax expense	?	Increase in income tax payable	12	Cash paid for income taxes	(42)
Net income	**$?**	**Net cash flows from operating activities**	$ 60	**Net cash flows from operating activities**	$ 60

Required:
Deduce the missing amounts and prepare the income statement.

E 21–20
Reconciliation of net cash flows from operating activities to net income
● LO21–3, LO21–4

The income statement and the cash flows from the operating activities section of the statement of cash flows are provided on the next page for Syntric Company. The merchandise inventory account balance neither increased nor decreased during the reporting period. Syntric had no liability for insurance, deferred income taxes, or interest at any time during the period.

SYNTRIC COMPANY
Income Statement
For the Year Ended December 31, 2018
($ in thousands)

Sales		$ 312
Cost of goods sold		(188)
Gross margin		124
Salaries expense	$41	
Insurance expense	22	
Depreciation expense	11	
Depletion expense	5	
Bond interest expense	10	(89)
Gains and losses:		
Gain on sale of equipment		25
Loss on sale of land		(8)
Income before tax		52
Income tax expense		(26)
Net income		$ 26
Cash Flows from Operating Activities:		
Cash received from customers		$ 258
Cash paid to suppliers		(175)
Cash paid to employees		(37)
Cash paid for interest		(9)
Cash paid for insurance		(16)
Cash paid for income taxes		(14)
Net cash flows from operating activities		$ 7

Required:
Prepare a schedule to reconcile net income to net cash flows from operating activities.

E 21–21
Cash flows from operating activities (direct method) derived from an income statement; cash flows from operating activities (indirect method)
● LO21–3, LO21–4

The income statement and a schedule reconciling cash flows from operating activities to net income are provided below ($ in thousands) for Peach Computers.

PEACH COMPUTERS
Income Statement
For the Year Ended December 31, 2018

Sales		$305
Cost of goods sold		185
Gross margin		120
Salaries expense	$41	
Insurance expense	19	
Depreciation expense	11	
Loss on sale of land	5	76
Income before tax		44
Income tax expense		22
Net income		$ 22

Reconciliation of Net Income
To Net Cash Flows from Operating Activities

Net income	$ 22
Adjustments for Noncash Effects	
Depreciation expense	11
Loss on sale of land	5
Changes in operating assets and liabilities:	
Decrease in accounts receivable	6
Increase in inventory	(13)
Decrease in accounts payable	(8)
Increase in salaries payable	5
Decrease in prepaid insurance	9
Increase in income tax payable	20
Net cash flows from operating activities	$ 57

Required:
1. Calculate each of the following amounts for Peach Computers:
   a. Cash received from customers during the reporting period
   b. Cash paid to suppliers of goods during the reporting period
   c. Cash paid to employees during the reporting period
   d. Cash paid for insurance during the reporting period
   e. Cash paid for income taxes during the reporting period
2. Prepare the cash flows from operating activities section of the statement of cash flows (direct method).

E 21–22
Indirect method; reconciliation of net income to net cash flows from operating activities
● LO21–4

The accounting records of Baddour Company provided the data below. Prepare a reconciliation of net income to net cash flows from operating activities.

Net loss	$5,000
Depreciation expense	6,000
Increase in salaries payable	500
Decrease in accounts receivable	2,000
Increase in inventory	2,300
Amortization of patent	300
Reduction in discount on bonds	200

E 21–23
Cash flows from operating activities (direct method)
● LO21–3

Portions of the financial statements for Myriad Products are provided below.

MYRIAD PRODUCTS COMPANY
Income Statement
For the Year Ended December 31, 2018
($ in millions)

Sales		$660
Cost of goods sold		250
Gross margin		410
Salaries expense	$110	
Depreciation expense	90	
Patent amortization expense	5	
Interest expense	20	
Loss on sale of land	3	228
Income before taxes		182
Income tax expense		91
Net Income		$ 91

MYRIAD PRODUCTS COMPANY
Selected Accounts from Comparative Balance Sheets
December 31, 2018 and 2017
($ in millions)

	Year		
	2018	**2017**	**Change**
Cash	$102	$100	$ 2
Accounts receivable	220	232	(12)
Inventory	440	450	(10)
Accounts payable	140	134	6
Salaries payable	80	86	(6)
Interest payable	25	20	5
Income taxes payable	15	10	5

Required:
Prepare the cash flows from operating activities section of the statement of cash flows for Myriad Products Company using the *direct method.*

E 21–24
Cash flows from operating activities (indirect method)
● LO21–4

Refer to the data provided in E 21–23 for Myriad Products Company.

Required:
Prepare the cash flows from operating activities section of the statement of cash flows for Myriad Products Company using the *indirect method.*

E 21–25
Cash flows from operating activities (direct method)—includes sale of cash equivalent
● LO21–3

Portions of the financial statements for Clear Transmissions Company are provided on the following page.

CLEAR TRANSMISSIONS COMPANY
Income Statement
For the Year Ended December 31, 2018 ($ in thousands)

Sales		$1,320
Cost of goods sold		500
Gross margin		820
Salaries expense	$220	
Depreciation expense	180	
Patent amortization expense	10	
Interest expense	40	
Loss on sale of cash equivalents	6	456
Income before taxes		364
Income tax expense		182
Net Income		$ 182

CLEAR TRANSMISSIONS COMPANY
Selected Accounts from Comparative Balance Sheets
December 31, 2018 and 2017 ($ in thousands)

	Year		
	2018	**2017**	**Change**
Cash	$102	$100	$ 2
Accounts receivable	220	232	(12)
Inventory	440	450	(10)
Accounts payable	140	134	6
Salaries payable	80	86	(6)
Interest payable	25	20	5
Income taxes payable	15	10	5

Required:
Prepare the cash flows from operating activities section of the statement of cash flows for Clear Transmissions Company using the *direct method.*

E 21–26
Cash flows from operating activities (indirect method)—includes sale of cash equivalent
● LO21–4

Refer to the data provided in E 21–25 for Clear Transmissions Company.

Required:
Prepare the cash flows from operating activities section of the statement of cash flows for Clear Transmissions Company using the *indirect method.*

E 21–27
Statement of cash flows; direct method
● LO21–3, LO21–5, LO21–6, LO21–8

Comparative balance sheets for 2018 and 2017, a statement of income for 2018, and additional information from the accounting records of Red, Inc., are provided below.

RED, INC.
Comparative Balance Sheets
December 31, 2018 and 2017 ($ in millions)

	2018	**2017**
Assets		
Cash	$ 24	$ 110
Accounts receivable	178	132
Prepaid insurance	7	3
Inventory	285	175
Buildings and equipment	400	350
Less: Accumulated depreciation	(119)	(240)
	$ 775	$ 530
Liabilities		
Accounts payable	$ 87	$ 100
Accrued expenses payable	6	11
Notes payable	50	0
Bonds payable	160	0
Shareholders' Equity		
Common stock	400	400
Retained earnings	72	19
	$ 775	$ 530

RED, INC.
Statement of Income
For Year Ended December 31, 2018
($ in millions)

Revenues		
Sales revenue		$2,000
Expenses		
Cost of goods sold	$1,400	
Depreciation expense	50	
Operating expenses	447	1,897
Net income		$ 103

Additional information from the accounting records:

a. During 2018, $230 million of equipment was purchased to replace $180 million of equipment (95% depreciated) sold at book value.

b. In order to maintain the usual policy of paying cash dividends of $50 million, it was necessary for Red to borrow $50 million from its bank.

Required:

Prepare the statement of cash flows of Red, Inc., for the year ended December 31, 2018. Present cash flows from operating activities by the direct method. (You may omit the schedule to reconcile net income with cash flows from operating activities.)

E 21–28
Pension plan funding
● LO21–3

Mayer Corporation has a defined benefit pension plan. Mayer's policy is to fund the plan annually, cash payments being made at the end of each year. Data relating to the pension plan for 2018 are as follows:

	December 31 ($ in millions)	
	2018	**2017**
Plan assets	$1,080	$900
Net pension expense for 2018:		
Service cost	$ 112	
Interest cost (6% × $850)	51	
Actual return on the plan assets (11% × $900 = $99)		
Adjusted for: $9 gain on the plan assets*	(90)	
Amortization of prior service cost	8	
Amortization of net loss	1	
	$ 82	

*(11% × $900) − (10% − $900)

Required:

Recreate the journal entries used to record Mayer's 2018 pension expense, gain on plan assets, and funding of plan assets in order to determine the cash paid to the pension trustee as reported in the statement of cash flows.

E 21–29
FASB codification research
● LO21–2

The statement of cash flows (as well as the balance sheet) includes within cash the notion of cash equivalents. The *FASB Accounting Standards Codification* represents the single source of authoritative U.S. generally accepted accounting principles.

Required:

1. Obtain the relevant authoritative literature on cash equivalents using the *FASB Accounting Standards Codification* at the FASB website (www.fasb.org). What is the specific citation that describes the guidelines for determining what items should be deemed cash equivalents?
2. List the guidelines.

E 21–30
FASB codification research
● LO21–1, LO21–4, LO21–7

Access the *FASB Accounting Standards Codification* at the FASB website (www.fasb.org). Determine the specific citation for accounting for each of the following items:

1. Disclosure of interest and income taxes paid if the indirect method is used
2. Primary objectives of a statement of cash flows
3. Disclosure of noncash investing and financing activities

E 21–31
Statement of cash flows; indirect method
● LO21–4, LO21–5, LO21–6, LO21–8, Appendix A

Refer to the data provided in E 21–27 for Red, Inc.

Required:
Prepare the statement of cash flows for Red, Inc., using the indirect method to report operating activities.

E 21–32
Statement of cash flows; T-account method
● LO21–8, Appendix B

Refer to the data provided in E 21–27 for Red, Inc.

Required:
Prepare the statement of cash flows (direct method) for Red, Inc. Use the T-account method to assist in your analysis.

Problems

connect

P 21–1
Classification of cash flows from investing and financing activities
● LO21–2, LO21–5 through LO21–7

Listed below are transactions that might be reported as investing and/or financing activities on a statement of cash flows. Possible reporting classifications of those transactions are provided also.

Required:
Indicate the reporting classification of each transaction by entering the appropriate classification code.

Classifications	
+I	Investing activity (cash inflow)
–I	Investing activity (cash outflow)
+F	Financing activity (cash inflow)
–F	Financing activity (cash outflow)
N	Noncash investing and financing activity
X	Not reported as an investing and/or a financing activity

Transactions

+I	1. Sale of land
____	2. Issuance of common stock for cash
____	3. Purchase of treasury stock
____	4. Conversion of bonds payable to common stock
____	5. Lease of equipment
____	6. Sale of patent
____	7. Acquisition of building for cash
____	8. Issuance of common stock for land
____	9. Collection of note receivable (principal amount)
____	10. Issuance of bonds
____	11. Issuance of stock dividend
____	12. Payment of property dividend
____	13. Payment of cash dividends
____	14. Issuance of short-term note payable for cash
____	15. Issuance of long-term note payable for cash
____	16. Purchase of marketable securities ("available for sale")
____	17. Payment of note payable
____	18. Cash payment for five-year insurance policy
____	19. Sale of equipment
____	20. Issuance of note payable for equipment
____	21. Acquisition of common stock of another corporation
____	22. Repayment of long-term debt by issuing common stock
____	23. Payment of semiannual interest on bonds payable
____	24. Retirement of preferred stock
____	25. Loan to another firm
____	26. Sale of inventory to customers
____	27. Purchase of marketable securities (cash equivalents)

P 21–2
Statement of cash flows; direct method
● LO21–3, LO21–8

The comparative balance sheets for 2018 and 2017 and the statement of income for 2018 are given below for Wright Company. Additional information from Wright's accounting records is provided also.

WRIGHT COMPANY
Comparative Balance Sheets
December 31, 2018 and 2017
($ in thousands)

	2018	2017
Assets		
Cash	$ 42	$ 30
Accounts receivable	73	75
Short-term investment	40	15
Inventory	75	70
Land	50	60
Buildings and equipment	550	400
Less: Accumulated depreciation	(115)	(75)
	$ 715	$575
Liabilities		
Accounts payable	$ 28	$ 35
Salaries payable	2	5
Interest payable	5	3
Income tax payable	9	12
Notes payable	0	30
Bonds payable	160	100
Shareholders' Equity		
Common stock	250	200
Paid-in capital—excess of par	126	100
Retained earnings	135	90
	$ 715	$575

WRIGHT COMPANY
Income Statement
For Year Ended December 31, 2018
($ in thousands)

Revenues:		
Sales revenue		$380
Expenses:		
Cost of goods sold	$130	
Salaries expense	45	
Depreciation expense	40	
Interest expense	12	
Loss on sale of land	3	
Income tax expense	70	300
Net income		$ 80

Additional information from the accounting records:

a. Land that originally cost $10,000 was sold for $7,000.
b. The common stock of Microsoft Corporation was purchased for $25,000 as a short-term investment not classified as a cash equivalent.
c. New equipment was purchased for $150,000 cash.
d. A $30,000 note was paid at maturity on January 1.
e. On January 1, 2018, bonds were sold at their $60,000 face value.
f. Common stock ($50,000 par) was sold for $76,000.
g. Net income was $80,000 and cash dividends of $35,000 were paid to shareholders.

Required:
Prepare the statement of cash flows of Wright Company for the year ended December 31, 2018. Present cash flows from operating activities by the direct method. (You may omit the schedule to reconcile net income with cash flows from operating activities.)

P 21–3
Statement of cash flows; direct method
LO21–3, LO21–8

The comparative balance sheets for 2018 and 2017 and the statement of income for 2018 are given below for National Intercable Company. Additional information from NIC's accounting records is provided also.

NATIONAL INTERCABLE COMPANY
Comparative Balance Sheets
December 31, 2018 and 2017
($ in millions)

	2018	2017
Assets		
Cash	$ 57	$ 55
Accounts receivable	181	170
Less: Allowance for uncollectible accounts	(8)	(6)
Prepaid insurance	7	12
Inventory	170	165
Long-term investment	66	90
Land	150	150
Buildings and equipment	290	270
Less: Accumulated depreciation	(85)	(75)
Trademark	24	25
	$852	$856
Liabilities		
Accounts payable	$ 30	$ 45
Salaries payable	3	8
Deferred income tax liability	18	15
Lease liability	68	0
Bonds payable	145	275
Less: Discount on bonds	(22)	(25)
Shareholders' Equity		
Common stock	310	290
Paid-in capital—excess of par	95	85
Preferred stock	50	0
Retained earnings	155	163
	$852	$856

NATIONAL INTERCABLE COMPANY
Income Statement
For Year Ended December 31, 2018
($ in millions)

Revenues		
Sales revenue	$320	
Investment revenue	15	
Gain on sale of investments	5	$340
Expenses		
Cost of goods sold	125	
Salaries expense	55	
Depreciation expense	25	
Trademark amortization expense	1	
Bad debt expense	7	
Insurance expense	13	
Bond interest expense	30	
Loss on building fire	42	298
Income before tax		42
Income tax expense		20
Net income		$ 22

Additional information from the accounting records:

a. Investment revenue includes National Intercable Company's $6 million share of the net income of Central Fiber Optics Corporation, an equity method investee.
b. A long-term investment in bonds, originally purchased for $30 million, was sold for $35 million.
c. Pretax accounting income exceeded taxable income, causing the deferred income tax liability to increase by $3 million.

d. A building that originally cost $60 million, and which was one-fourth depreciated, was destroyed by fire. Some undamaged parts were sold for $3 million.
e. The right to use a building was acquired with a seven-year lease agreement; present value of lease payments, $80 million. Annual lease payments of $12 million are paid at Jan. 1 of each year starting in 2018.
f. $130 million of bonds were retired at maturity.
g. $20 million par value of common stock was sold for $30 million, and $50 million of preferred stock was sold at par.
h. Shareholders were paid cash dividends of $30 million.

Required:
1. Prepare a spreadsheet for preparation of the statement of cash flows (direct method) of National Intercable Company for the year ended December 31, 2018.
2. Prepare the statement of cash flows. (A reconciliation schedule is not required.)

P 21–4
Statement of cash flows; direct method
● LO21–3, LO21–8

The comparative balance sheets for 2018 and 2017 and the statement of income for 2018 are given below for Dux Company. Additional information from Dux's accounting records is provided also.

DUX COMPANY
Comparative Balance Sheets
December 31, 2018 and 2017
($ in thousands)

	2018	2017
Assets		
Cash	$ 33	$ 20
Accounts receivable	48	50
Less: Allowance for uncollectible accounts	(4)	(3)
Dividends receivable	3	2
Inventory	55	50
Long-term investment	15	10
Land	70	40
Buildings and equipment	225	250
Less: Accumulated depreciation	(25)	(50)
	$420	$369
Liabilities		
Accounts payable	$ 13	$ 20
Salaries payable	2	5
Interest payable	4	2
Income tax payable	7	8
Notes payable	30	0
Bonds payable	95	70
Less: Discount on bonds	(2)	(3)
Shareholders' Equity		
Common stock	210	200
Paid-in capital—excess of par	24	20
Retained earnings	45	47
Less: Treasury stock	(8)	0
	$420	$369

DUX COMPANY
Income Statement
For the Year Ended December 31, 2018
($ in thousands)

Revenues		
Sales revenue	$200	
Dividend revenue	3	$203
Expenses		
Cost of goods sold	120	
Salaries expense	25	
Depreciation expense	5	
Bad debt expense	1	
Interest expense	8	
Loss on sale of building	3	
Income tax expense	16	178
Net income		$ 25

Additional information from the accounting records:

a. A building that originally cost $40,000, and which was three-fourths depreciated, was sold for $7,000.
b. The common stock of Byrd Corporation was purchased for $5,000 as a long-term investment.
c. Property was acquired by issuing a 13%, seven-year, $30,000 note payable to the seller.
d. New equipment was purchased for $15,000 cash.
e. On January 1, 2018, bonds were sold at their $25,000 face value.
f. On January 19, Dux issued a 5% stock dividend (1,000 shares). The market price of the $10 par value common stock was $14 per share at that time.
g. Cash dividends of $13,000 were paid to shareholders.
h. On November 12, 500 shares of common stock were repurchased as treasury stock at a cost of $8,000.

Required:

Prepare the statement of cash flows of Dux Company for the year ended December 31, 2018. Present cash flows from operating activities by the direct method. (You may omit the schedule to reconcile net income to cash flows from operating activities.)

P 21–5
Statement of cash flows; direct method
LO21–3, LO21–8

Comparative balance sheets for 2018 and 2017 and a statement of income for 2018 are given below for Metagrobolize Industries. Additional information from the accounting records of Metagrobolize also is provided.

METAGROBOLIZE INDUSTRIES
Comparative Balance Sheets
December 31, 2018 and 2017
($ in thousands)

	2018	2017
Assets		
Cash	$ 580	$ 375
Accounts receivable	600	450
Inventory	900	525
Land	675	600
Building	900	900
Less: Accumulated depreciation	(300)	(270)
Equipment	2,850	2,250
Less: Accumulated depreciation	(525)	(480)
Patent	1,200	1,500
	$6,880	$5,850
Liabilities		
Accounts payable	$ 750	$ 450
Accrued expenses payable	300	225
Lease liability—land	130	0
Shareholders' Equity		
Common stock	3,150	3,000
Paid-in capital—excess of par	750	675
Retained earnings	1,800	1,500
	$6,880	$5,850

METAGROBOLIZE INDUSTRIES
Income Statement
For the Year Ended December 31, 2018
($ in thousands)

Revenues		
Sales revenue	$2,645	
Gain on sale of land	90	$2,735
Expenses		
Cost of goods sold	600	
Depreciation expense—building	30	
Depreciation expense—equipment	315	
Loss on sale of equipment	15	
Amortization of patent	300	
Operating expenses	500	1,760
Net income		$ 975

Additional information from the accounting records:

a. Annual payments of $20,000 on the finance lease liability are paid each January 1, beginning in 2018.

b. During 2018, equipment with a cost of $300,000 (90% depreciated) was sold.

c. The statement of shareholders' equity reveals reductions of $225,000 and $450,000 for stock dividends and cash dividends, respectively.

Required:

Prepare the statement of cash flows of Metagrobolize for the year ended December 31, 2018. Present cash flows from operating activities by the direct method. (You may omit the schedule to reconcile net income to cash flows from operating activities.)

P 21–6
Cash flows from operating activities (direct method) derived from an income statement and cash flows from operating activities (indirect method)
● LO21–3, LO21–4

The income statement and a schedule reconciling cash flows from operating activities to net income are provided below for Mike Roe Computers.

MIKE ROE COMPUTERS
Income Statement
For the Year Ended December 31, 2018
($ in millions)

Sales		$150
Cost of goods sold		90
Gross margin		60
Salaries expense	$20	
Insurance expense	12	
Depreciation expense	5	
Interest expense	6	(43)
Gains and losses:		
Gain on sale of equipment		12
Loss on sale of land		(3)
Income before tax		26
Income tax expense		(13)
Net income		$ 13

Reconciliation of Net Income to Net Cash Flows from Operating Activities

Net income	$ 13
Adjustments for noncash effects:	
Decrease in accounts receivable	5
Gain on sale of equipment	(12)
Increase in inventory	(6)
Increase in accounts payable	9
Increase in salaries payable	3
Depreciation expense	5
Decrease in bond discount	3
Decrease in prepaid insurance	2
Loss on sale of land	3
Increase in income tax payable	6
Net cash flows from operating activities	$ 31

Required:

1. Calculate each of the following amounts for Mike Roe Computers:
   a. Cash received from customers during the reporting period
   b. Cash paid to suppliers of goods during the reporting period
   c. Cash paid to employees during the reporting period
   d. Cash paid for interest during the reporting period
   e. Cash paid for insurance during the reporting period
   f. Cash paid for income taxes during the reporting period
2. Prepare the cash flows from operating activities section of the statement of cash flows (direct method).

P 21–7
Cash flows from operating activities (direct method) derived from an income statement and cash flows from operating activities (indirect method)
● LO21–3, LO21–4

The income statement and a schedule reconciling cash flows from operating activities to net income are provided below for Macrosoft Corporation.

MACROSOFT CORPORATION
Income Statement
For the Year Ended December 31, 2018
($ in millions)

Revenues and gains:		
Sales	$310	
Gain on sale of cash equivalents	2	
Gain on sale of investments	24	$336
Expenses and loss:		
Cost of goods sold	120	
Salaries	40	
Interest expense	12	
Insurance	20	
Depreciation	10	
Patent amortization	4	
Loss on sale of land	6	212
Income before tax		124
Income tax expense		62
Net income		$ 62

Reconciliation of Net Income to Net Cash Flows from Operating Activities

Net income	$ 62
Adjustments for noncash effects:	
Depreciation expense	10
Patent amortization expense	4
Loss on sale of land	6
Gain on sale of investment	(24)
Decrease in accounts receivable	6
Increase in inventory	(12)
Increase in accounts payable	18
Decrease in bond discount	1
Increase in salaries payable	6
Decrease in prepaid insurance	4
Increase in income tax payable	10
Net cash flows from operating activities	$ 91

Required:

Prepare the cash flows from operating activities section of the statement of cash flows (direct method).

P 21–8
Cash flows from operating activities (direct method and indirect method)—deferred income tax liability and amortization of bond discount
● LO21–3, LO21–4

Portions of the financial statements for Parnell Company are provided below.

PARNELL COMPANY
Income Statement
For the Year Ended December 31, 2018
($ in thousands)

Revenues and gains:		
Sales	$800	
Gain on sale of buildings	11	$811
Expenses and loss:		
Cost of goods sold	300	
Salaries	120	
Insurance	40	
Depreciation	123	
Interest expense	50	
Loss on sale of machinery	12	645
Income before tax		166
Income tax expense		78
Net income		$ 88

PARNELL COMPANY
Selected Accounts from Comparative Balance Sheets
December 31, 2018 and 2017
($ in thousands)

	Year		
	2018	**2017**	**Change**
Cash	$134	$100	$ 34
Accounts receivable	324	216	108
Inventory	321	425	(104)
Prepaid insurance	66	88	(22)
Accounts payable	210	117	93
Salaries payable	102	93	9
Deferred income tax liability	60	52	8
Bond discount	190	200	(10)

Required:

1. Prepare the cash flows from operating activities section of the statement of cash flows for Parnell Company using the direct method.
2. Prepare the cash flows from operating activities section of the statement of cash flows for Parnell Company using the indirect method.

P 21–9
Cash flows from operating activities (direct method and indirect method)—cash equivalent
● LO21–3, LO21–4

Portions of the financial statements for Hawkeye Company are provided below.

HAWKEYE COMPANY
Income Statement
For the Year Ended December 31, 2018
($ in millions)

Sales		$900
Cost of goods sold		350
Gross margin		550
Operating expenses:		
Salaries	$232	
Depreciation	190	
Loss on sale of land	12	
Total operating expenses		434
Operating income		116
Other income (expense):		
Gain on sale of cash equivalents		4
Interest expense		(40)
Income before tax		80
Income tax expense		40
Net income		$ 40

HAWKEYE COMPANY
Selected Accounts from Comparative Balance Sheets
December 31, 2018 and 2017

	Year		
	2018	**2017**	**Change**
Cash	$212	$200	$ 12
Accounts receivable	395	421	(26)
Inventory	860	850	10
Accounts payable	210	234	(24)
Salaries payable	180	188	(8)
Interest payable	55	50	5
Income taxes payable	90	104	(14)

Required:

1. Prepare the cash flows from operating activities section of the statement of cash flows for Hawkeye Company using the direct method.
2. Prepare the cash flows from operating activities section of the statement of cash flows for Hawkeye Company using the indirect method.

P 21–10
Relationship between the income statement and cash flows from operating activities (direct method and indirect method)
● LO21–3, LO21–4

The following schedule relates the income statement with cash flows from operating activities, derived by both the direct and indirect methods, in the format illustrated by Illustration 21–11 in the chapter. Some elements necessary to complete the schedule are missing.

Cash Flows from Operating Activities

Income Statement		Indirect Method		Direct Method	
		Net income	$?		
		Adjustments:			
Sales	$300	Decrease in accounts receivable	6	Cash received from customers	$?
Gain on sale of equipment	24	Gain on sale of equipment	(24)	(Not reported—no cash effect)	
		Increase in inventory	(12)		
Cost of goods sold	(?)	Increase in accounts payable	18	Cash paid to suppliers	(174)
Salaries expense	(42)	? in salaries payable	6	Cash paid to employees	(36)
Depreciation expense	(9)	Depreciation expense	9	Cash paid for depreciation	?
Interest expense	(?)	Decrease in bond discount	3	Cash paid for interest	(9)
Insurance expense	(21)	Decrease in prepaid insurance	9	Cash paid for insurance	(?)
Loss on sale of land	(6)	Loss on sale of land	6	(Not reported—no cash effect)	
Income tax expense	(27)	Increase in income tax payable	?	Cash paid for income taxes	(21)
Net Income	$?	**Net cash flows from operating activities**	**$ 54**	**Net cash flows from operating activities**	**$ 54**

Required:

Complete the schedule by determining each of the following missing elements:

1. Cash received from customers
2. Cost of goods sold
3. ? in salaries payable (Increase? Or decrease?)
4. Cash paid for depreciation
5. Interest expense
6. Cash paid for insurance
7. Increase in income tax payable
8. Net income

P 21–11
Prepare a statement of cash flows; direct method
LO21–3, LO21–8

The comparative balance sheets for 2018 and 2017 and the income statement for 2018 are given below for Arduous Company. Additional information from Arduous's accounting records is provided also.

ARDUOUS COMPANY
Comparative Balance Sheets
December 31, 2018 and 2017
($ in millions)

	2018	2017
Assets		
Cash	$ 109	$ 81
Accounts receivable	190	194
Investment revenue receivable	6	4
Inventory	205	200
Prepaid insurance	4	8
Long-term investment	156	125
Land	196	150
Buildings and equipment	412	400
Less: Accumulated depreciation	(97)	(120)
Patent	30	32
	$1,211	$1,074
Liabilities		
Accounts payable	$ 50	$ 65
Salaries payable	6	11
Bond interest payable	8	4
Income tax payable	12	14
Deferred income tax liability	11	8
Notes payable	23	0
Lease liability	75	0
Bonds payable	215	275
Less: Discount on bonds	(22)	(25)
Shareholders' Equity		
Common stock	430	410
Paid-in capital—excess of par	95	85
Preferred stock	75	0
Retained earnings	242	227
Less: Treasury stock	(9)	0
	$1,211	$1,074

ARDUOUS COMPANY
Income Statement
For Year Ended December 31, 2018
($ in millions)

Revenues and gain:		
Sales revenue	$410	
Investment revenue	11	
Gain on sale of Treasury bills	2	$423
Expenses and loss:		
Cost of goods sold	180	
Salaries expense	73	
Depreciation expense	12	
Patent amortization expense	2	
Insurance expense	7	
Bond interest expense	28	
Loss on machine damage	18	
Income tax expense	36	356
Net income		$ 67

Additional information from the accounting records:

a. Investment revenue includes Arduous Company's $6 million share of the net income of Demur Company, an equity method investee.

b. Treasury bills were sold during 2018 at a gain of $2 million. Arduous Company classifies its investments in Treasury bills as cash equivalents.

c. A machine originally costing $70 million that was one-half depreciated was rendered unusable by a flood. Most major components of the machine were unharmed and were sold for $17 million.

d. Temporary differences between pretax accounting income and taxable income caused the deferred income tax liability to increase by $3 million.

e. The preferred stock of Tory Corporation was purchased for $25 million as a long-term investment.

f. Land costing $46 million was acquired by issuing $23 million cash and a 15%, four-year, $23 million note payable to the seller.

g. The right to use a building was acquired with a 15-year lease agreement; present value of lease payments, $82 million. Annual lease payments of $7 million are paid at the beginning of each year starting January 1, 2018.

h. $60 million of bonds were retired at maturity.

i. In February, Arduous issued a 4% stock dividend (4 million shares). The market price of the $5 par value common stock was $7.50 per share at that time.

j. In April, 1 million shares of common stock were repurchased as treasury stock at a cost of $9 million.

Required:

Prepare the statement of cash flows of Arduous Company for the year ended December 31, 2018. Present cash flows from operating activities by the direct method. (A reconciliation schedule is not required.)

P 21–12
Transactions affecting retained earnings
● LO21–5, LO21–6, LO21–8

Shown below in T-account format are the changes affecting the retained earnings of Brenner-Jude Corporation during 2018. At January 1, 2018, the corporation had outstanding 105 million common shares, $1 par per share.

Retained Earnings ($ in millions)

		90	Beginning balance
Retirement of 5 million common shares for $22 million	2		
		88	Net income for the year
Declaration and payment of a $0.33 per share cash dividend	33		
Declaration and distribution of a 4% stock dividend	20		
		123	Ending balance

Required:

1. From the information provided by the account changes you should be able to re-create the transactions that affected Brenner-Jude's retained earnings during 2018. Reconstruct the journal entries which can be used as spreadsheet entries in the preparation of a statement of cash flows. Also indicate any investing and financing activities you identify from this analysis that should be reported on the statement of cash flows.
2. Prepare a statement of retained earnings for Brenner-Jude for the year ended 2018. (You may wish to compare your solution to this problem with the parallel situation described in Exercise 18–18.)

P 21–13
Various cash flows
● LO21–3 through LO21–8

Following are selected balance sheet accounts of Del Conte Corp. at December 31, 2018 and 2017, and the increases or decreases in each account from 2017 to 2018. Also presented is selected income statement information for the year ended December 31, 2018, and additional information.

Selected Balance Sheet Accounts	2018	2017	Increase (Decrease)
Assets			
Accounts receivable	$ 34,000	$ 24,000	$10,000
Property, plant, and equipment	277,000	247,000	30,000
Accumulated depreciation	(178,000)	(167,000)	11,000
Liabilities and Stockholders' Equity			
Bonds payable	49,000	46,000	3,000
Dividends payable	8,000	5,000	3,000
Common stock, $1 par	22,000	19,000	3,000
Additional paid-in capital	9,000	3,000	6,000
Retained earnings	104,000	91,000	13,000

Selected Income Statement Information for the Year Ended December 31, 2018

Sales revenue	$ 155,000
Depreciation	33,000
Gain on sale of equipment	13,000
Net income	28,000

Additional Information:

a. Accounts receivable relate to sales of merchandise.

b. During 2018, equipment costing $40,000 was sold for cash.

c. During 2018, bonds payable with a face value of $20,000 were issued in exchange for property, plant, and equipment. There was no amortization of bond discount or premium.

Required:

Items 1 through 5 represent activities that will be reported in Del Conte's statement of cash flows for the year ended December 31, 2018. The following two responses are required for each item:

a. Determine the amount that should be reported in Del Conte's 2018 statement of cash flows.

b. Using the list below, determine the category in which the amount should be reported in the statement of cash flows.

O. Operating activity

I. Investing activity

F. Financing activity

	Amount	Category
1. Cash collections from customers (direct method).	____	____
2. Payments for purchase of property, plant, and equipment.	____	____
3. Proceeds from sale of equipment.	____	____
4. Cash dividends paid.	____	____
5. Redemption of bonds payable.	____	____

(AICPA adapted)

P 21–14

Statement of cash flows; indirect method; limited information

LO21–4, LO21–8

The comparative balance sheets for 2018 and 2017 are given below for Surmise Company. Net income for 2018 was $50 million.

SURMISE COMPANY
Comparative Balance Sheets
December 31, 2018 and 2017
($ in millions)

	2018	2017
Assets		
Cash	$ 36	$ 40
Accounts receivable	92	96
Less: Allowance for uncollectible accounts	(12)	(4)
Prepaid expenses	8	5
Inventory	145	130
Long-term investment	80	40
Land	100	100
Buildings and equipment	420	300
Less: Accumulated depreciation	(142)	(120)
Patent	16	17
	$ 743	$ 604
Liabilities		
Accounts payable	$ 13	$ 32
Accrued liabilities	2	10
Notes payable	35	0
Lease liability	111	0
Bonds payable	65	125
Shareholders' Equity		
Common stock	60	50
Paid-in capital—excess of par	245	205
Retained earnings	212	182
	$ 743	$ 604

Required:

Prepare the statement of cash flows of Surmise Company for the year ended December 31, 2018. Use the indirect method to present cash flows from operating activities because you do not have sufficient information to use the direct method. You will need to make reasonable assumptions concerning the reasons for changes in some account balances. A spreadsheet or T-account analysis will be helpful. (Hint: The right to use a building was acquired with a seven-year lease agreement. Annual lease payments of $9 million are paid at January 1 of each year starting in 2018.)

P 21–15
Integrating problem; bonds; lease transactions; lessee and lessor; statement of cash flow effects
● LO21–3, LO21–5, LO21–6

Digital Telephony issued 10% bonds, dated January 1, with a face amount of $32 million on January 1, 2018. The bonds mature in 2028 (10 years). For bonds of similar risk and maturity the market yield is 12%. Interest is paid semiannually on June 30 and December 31. Digital recorded the issue as follows:

Cash	28,329,472	
Discount on bonds	3,670,528	
Bonds payable		32,000,000

Digital also leased switching equipment to Midsouth Communications, Inc., on September 30, 2018. Digital purchased the equipment from MDS Corp. at a cost of $6 million. The five-year lease agreement calls for Midsouth to make quarterly lease payments of $391,548, payable each September 30, December 31, March 31, and June 30, with the first payment on September 30, 2018. Digital's implicit interest rate is 12%.

Required:

1. What would be the amount(s) related to the bonds that Digital would report in its statement of cash flows for the year ended December 31, 2018, if Digital uses the direct method? The indirect method?
2. What would be the amounts related to the lease that *Midsouth* would report in its statement of cash flows for the year ended December 31, 2018?
3. What would be the amounts related to the lease that *Digital* would report in its statement of cash flows for the year ended December 31, 2018?
4. Assume MDS manufactured the equipment at a cost of $5 million and that Midsouth leased the equipment directly from MDS. What would be the amounts related to the lease that *MDS* would report in its statement of cash flows for the year ended December 31, 2018?

P 21–16
Statement of cash flows; indirect method
● LO21–4, LO21–8

Refer to the data provided in the P 21–4 for Dux Company.

Required:

Prepare the statement of cash flows for Dux Company using the *indirect method.*

P 21–17
Statement of cash flows; indirect method
● LO21–4, LO21–8

Refer to the data provided in the P 21–5 for Metagrobolize Industries.

Required:

Prepare the statement of cash flows for Metagrobolize Industries using the *indirect method.*

P 21–18
Statement of cash flows; indirect method
● LO21–4, LO21–8

Refer to the data provided in the P 21–11 for Arduous Company.

Required:

Prepare the statement of cash flows for Arduous Company using the *indirect method.*

(Note: The following problems use the technique learned in Appendix 21B.)

P 21–19
Statement of cash flows; T-account method
● LO21–3, LO21–8

Refer to the data provided in the P 21–4 for Dux Company.

Required:

Prepare the statement of cash flows for Dux Company. Use the T-account method to assist in your analysis.

P 21–20
Statement of cash flows; T-account method
LO21–3, LO21–8

Refer to the data provided in the P 21–5 for Metagrobolize Industries.

Required:

Prepare the statement of cash flows for Metagrobolize Industries. Use the T-account method to assist in your analysis.

P 21–21
Statement of cash flows; T-account method
LO21–3, LO21–8

Refer to the data provided in the P 21–11 for Arduous Company.

Required:

Prepare the statement of cash flows for Arduous Company. Use the T-account method to assist in your analysis.

Broaden Your Perspective

Apply your critical-thinking ability to the knowledge you've gained. These cases will provide you an opportunity to develop your research, analysis, judgment, and communication skills. You also will work with other students, integrate what you've learned, apply it in real-world situations, and consider its global and ethical ramifications. This practice will broaden your knowledge and further develop your decision-making abilities.

Communication Case 21–1
Distinguish income and cash flows
LO21–1, LO21–3, LO21–4

"Why can't we pay our shareholders a dividend?" shouted your new boss. "This income statement you prepared for me says we earned $5 million in our first half-year!"

You were hired last month as the chief accountant for Enigma Corporation, which was organized on July 1 of the year just ended. You recently prepared the financial statements below.

ENIGMA CORPORATION
Income Statement
For the Six Months Ended December 31, 2018
($ in millions)

Sales revenue	$ 75
Cost of goods sold	(30)
Depreciation expense	(5)
Remaining expenses	(35)
Net income	$ 5

ENIGMA CORPORATION
Balance Sheet
December 31, 2018
($ in millions)

Cash	$ 1
Accounts receivable (net)	20
Merchandise inventory	15
Machinery (net)	44
Total	$80
Accounts payable	$ 2
Accrued expenses payable	7
Notes payable	36
Common stock	30
Retained earnings	5
Total	$80

You have just explained to your boss, Robert James, that although net income was $5 million, operating activities produced a net decrease in cash. Unable to understand your verbal explanation, he has asked you to prepare a written report.

Required:

Prepare a report explaining the apparent discrepancy between Enigma's profitability and its cash flows. To increase the chances of your boss's understanding the situation, include in your report a determination of net cash flows from operating activities by both the direct and indirect methods. Your report should also include a narrative explanation of how it is possible for operating activities to simultaneously produce a positive net income and negative net cash flows.

Judgment Case 21–2
Distinguish income and cash flows
- LO21–3, LO21–8

You are a loan officer for First Benevolent Bank. You have an uneasy feeling as you examine a loan application from Daring Corporation. The application included the following financial statements.

DARING CORPORATION
Income Statement
For the Year Ended December 31, 2018

Sales revenue	$100,000
Cost of goods sold	(50,000)
Depreciation expense	(5,000)
Remaining expenses	(25,000)
Net income	$ 20,000

DARING CORPORATION
Balance Sheet
December 31, 2018

Cash	$ 5,000
Accounts receivable	25,000
Inventory	20,000
Operational assets	55,000
Accumulated depreciation	(5,000)
Total	$100,000
Accounts payable	$ 10,000
Interest payable	5,000
Note payable	45,000
Common stock	20,000
Retained earnings	20,000
Total	$100,000

It is not Daring's profitability that worries you. The income statement submitted with the application shows net income of $20,000 in Daring's first year of operations. By referring to the balance sheet, you see that this net income represents a 20% rate of return on assets of $100,000. Your concern stems from the recollection that the note payable reported on Daring's balance sheet is a two-year loan you approved earlier in the year.

You also recall another promising new company that, just last year, defaulted on another of your bank's loans when it failed due to its inability to generate sufficient cash flows to meet its obligations. Before requesting additional information from Daring, you decide to test your memory of the intermediate accounting class you took in night school by attempting to prepare a statement of cash flows from the information available in the loan application.

Research Case 21–3
Information from cash flow activities; FedEx
- LO21–3 through LO21–8

Real World Financials

Locate the 2015 financial statements and related disclosure notes of FedEx Corporation. You can locate the report online at www.fedex.com.

Required:

1. From the information provided in the statement of cash flows, explain what allows FedEx Corporation to expand its business, as evidenced by the investing activities, while at the same time not raising as much cash through financing activities.
2. Describe the activities listed under financing activities for the most recent fiscal year. [*Hint:* FedEx's Statement of Changes in Common Stockholders' Investment (statement of shareholders' equity) will help you determine the nature of the stock activity.] What is the most notable financing activity reported?
3. What are the cash payments FedEx made for interest and for income taxes in the three years reported? (*Hint:* See the disclosure notes.)
4. Obtain the relevant authoritative literature on disclosure of interest and income taxes using the *FASB Accounting Standards Codification.* You might gain access at the FASB website (www.fasb.org). What is the specific citation that specifies the way FedEx reports interest and income taxes separately that enabled you to answer requirement 3?

Trueblood Accounting Case 21–4
Presentation issues
- LO21–5, LO21–6

The following Trueblood case is recommended for use with this chapter. The case provides an excellent opportunity for class discussion, group projects, and writing assignments. The case, along with Professor's Discussion Material, can be obtained from the Deloitte Foundation at its website: www.deloitte.com/us/truebloodcases.

Case 13-2: Buck's Dilemma: Gross or Net

This case gives students the opportunity to consider when borrowings and payments under a revolving line of credit may be presented on a net (versus gross) basis within the statement of cash flows.

Analysis Case 21–5
Smudged ink; find missing amounts
- LO21–3, LO21–4

"Be careful with that coffee!" Your roommate is staring in disbelief at the papers in front of her. "This was my contribution to our team project," she moaned. "When you spilled your coffee, it splashed on this page. Now I can't recognize some of these numbers, and Craig has my source documents."

Knowing how important this afternoon's presentation is to your roommate, you're eager to see what can be done. "Let me see that," you offer. "I think we can figure this out." The statement of cash flows and income statement are intact. The reconciliation schedule and the comparative balance sheets are coffee casualties.

DISTINCTIVE INDUSTRIES
Statement of Cash Flows
For the Year Ended December 31, 2018
($ in millions)

Cash Flows from Operating Activities:		
Collections from customers	$213	
Payment to suppliers	(90)	
Payment of general & administrative expenses	(54)	
Payment of income taxes	(27)	
Net cash flows from operating activities		$ 42
Cash Flows from Investing Activities:		
Sale of equipment		120
Cash Flows from Financing Activities:		
Issuance of common stock	30	
Payment of dividends	(9)	
Net cash flows from financing activities		21
Net increase in cash		$183
Reconciliation of net income to cash flows from operating activities:		
Net income	$ 84	
Adjustments for noncash items:		
Depreciation expense	□	
□	□	
□	□	
□	□	
□	□	
□	□	
Net cash flows from operating activities		□

DISTINCTIVE INDUSTRIES
Income Statement
For the Year Ended December 31, 2018
($ in millions)

Sales revenue		$240
Cost of goods sold		96
Gross profit		144
Operating expenses:		
General and administrative	$54	
Depreciation	30	
Total operating expenses		84
Operating income		60
Other income:		
Gain on sale of equipment		45
Income before income taxes		105
Income tax expense		21
Net income		$ 84

DISTINCTIVE INDUSTRIES
Comparative Balance Sheets
At December 31
($ in millions)

	2018	2017
Assets:		
Cash	$ 360	□
Accounts receivable (net)	□	252
Inventory	180	□
Property, plant, and equipment	450	600
Less: Accumulated depreciation	(120)	□
Total assets	□	□
Liabilities and shareholders' equity:		
Accounts payable	$ 120	$ 90
General and administrative expenses payable	27	27
Income taxes payable	66	□
Common stock	720	690
Retained earnings	□	141
Total liabilities and shareholders' equity	□	□

Required:

1. Determine the missing amounts.
2. Reconstruct the reconciliation of net income to cash flows from operating activities (operating cash flows using the indirect method).

Real World Case 21–6
Analyze cash flow activities; Staples, Inc.
● LO21–1 through LO21–8
Real World Financials

Staples, Inc., is the world's leading office products company. Locate the statement of cash flows of Staples for the fiscal year ended January 30, 2016, on the Internet.

Required:

1. In the three years reported, what was Staples' primary investing activity? How was this activity financed? Be specific.
2. During the most recent fiscal year, Staples purchased certificates of deposit. How were these purchases reported in the statement of cash flows? (Note: This is not an investing activity.)
3. How are issuances of debt securities and issuances of equity securities classified in a statement of cash flows?
4. How are payments to investors in debt securities (interest) and payments to investors in equity securities (dividends) classified in a statement of cash flows? Is this a conceptual inconsistency? Explain.
5. Staples' statement of cash flows reports expenditures for acquisition of businesses. It also reports additions to long-term debt. Suppose the businesses had been acquired not with cash, but by exchange for debt securities. Would such a transaction be reported? Explain.

Ethics Case 21–7
Where's the cash?
● LO21–1, LO21–3

After graduating near the top of his class, Ben Naegle was hired by the local office of a Big 4 CPA firm in his hometown. Two years later, impressed with his technical skills and experience, Park Electronics, a large regional consumer electronics chain, hired Ben as assistant controller. This was last week. Now Ben's initial excitement has turned to distress.

The cause of Ben's distress is the set of financial statements he's stared at for the last four hours. For some time prior to his recruitment, he had been aware of the long trend of moderate profitability of his new employer. The reports on his desk confirm the slight, but steady, improvements in net income in recent years. The trend he was just now becoming aware of, though, was the decline in cash flows from operations.

Ben had sketched out the following comparison ($ in millions):

	2018	2017	2016	2015
Income from operations	$140.0	$132.0	$127.5	$127.0
Net income	38.5	35.0	34.5	29.5
Cash flow from operations	1.6	17.0	12.0	15.5

Profits? Yes. Increasing profits? Yes. The cause of his distress? The ominous trend in cash flow which is consistently lower than net income.

Upon closer review, Ben noticed three events in the last two years that, unfortunately, seemed related:

a. Park's credit policy had been loosened; credit terms were relaxed and payment periods were lengthened.
b. Accounts receivable balances had increased dramatically.
c. Several of the company's compensation arrangements, including that of the controller and the company president, were based on reported net income.

Required:

1. What is so ominous about the combination of events Ben sees?
2. What course of action, if any, should Ben take?

Analysis Case 21–8
Information from cash flow activities; Kroger
- LO21–3 through LO21–8

Real World Financials

Refer to the financial statements and related disclosure notes of The Kroger Company for the fiscal year ending January 30, 2016. You can locate the report online from "investor relations" at www.kroger.com.

Notice that Kroger's net income has increased over the three years reported. To supplement their analysis of profitability, many analysts like to look at "free cash flow." A popular way to measure this metric is "structural free cash flow" (or as Warren Buffett calls it, "owner's earnings"), which is calculated as net income from operations, plus depreciation and amortization, minus capital expenditures.

Required:

Determine free cash flows for Kroger in each of the three years reported. Compare that amount with net income each year. What pattern do you detect?

Research Case 21–9
FASB codification; locate and extract relevant information and cite authoritative support for a financial reporting issue; cash flow classification
- LO21–4 through LO21–6

CODE

"This one's got me stumped," you say to no one in particular. "First day on the job; I'd better get it right." It's the classification of notes payable in the statement of cash flows that has you in doubt. Having received an "A" in Intermediate Accounting, you know that a note payable representing a bank loan is a financing activity, but this one is a note payable to your employer's primary merchandise supplier. "I wonder if the accounting is the same."

Required:

1. Obtain the relevant authoritative literature on cash flow classification using the *FASB Accounting Standards Codification*. You might gain access at the FASB website (www.fasb.org). What is the specific citation that specifies the classification of notes payable to suppliers?
2. Is accounting the same as for notes payable to banks? Explain.
3. Is accounting the same for both short-term and long-term notes payable to suppliers?

IFRS Case 21–10
Statement of cash flows presentation, British Telecommunications
- LO21 3 through LO21–6, LO21–9

IFRS

Real World Financials

British Telecommunications Plc (BT), a U.K. company, is the world's oldest communications company. The company prepares its financial statements in accordance with International Financial Reporting Standards. Locate BT's statement of cash flows from it's website at www.btplc.com.

Required:

1. What are the primary classifications into which BT's cash inflows and cash outflows are separated? Is this classification the same as or different from cash flow statements prepared in accordance with U.S. GAAP?
2. How are cash inflows from dividends and interest and cash outflows for dividends and interest classified in BT's cash flow statements? Is this classification the same as or different from cash flow statements prepared in accordance with U.S. GAAP?

Continuing Cases

Target Case
- LO21–2, LO21–3, LO21–4, LO21–5, LO21–6, LO21–7

Target Corporation prepares its financial statements according to U.S. GAAP. Target's financial statements and disclosure notes for the year ended January 30, 2016, are available in Connect. This material is also available under the Investor Relations link at the company's website (www.target.com).

Required:

1. Target's cash flows from its operations over the previous three years has significantly exceeded its net income. Without regard to Target specifically, explain the difference between net income and the cash flows from operating activities.
2. Why did Target add $2,213 million in the determination of cash flows from operating activities for depreciation and amortization for the year ended January 30, 2016?
3. A contributor to the difference in Target's net income and cash flows from operating activities and net income in each of the three years presented is a sizable increase in the amount Target owes its suppliers. If Target had used the direct rather than the indirect method of reporting operating activities, how would this reduction in accounts payable have affected cash from operating activities?

4. Cash outflows for financing activities during each of the three years presented exceeded cash inflows from financing activities. In fact, investing activities also produced net cash outflows in two of the three years. How is that possible? What is the major contributor from year to year in the amount of cash used in financing activities? What are the next two highest contributors to that difference?
5. Some transactions that don't increase or decrease cash must be reported in conjunction with a statement of cash flows. What activity of this type did Target report during each of the three years presented? What are two other such activities that some companies might report?

Air France–KLM Case

● LO21–9

IFRS

Air France–KLM (AF), a Franco-Dutch company, prepares its financial statements according to International Financial Reporting Standards. AF's financial statements and disclosure notes for the year ended December 31, 2015, are provided in Connect. This material is also available under the Finance link at the company's website (www.airfranceklm-finance.com).

Required:

1. What are the primary classifications into which AF's cash inflows and cash outflows are separated? Is this classification the same as or different from cash flow statements prepared in accordance with U.S. GAAP?
2. How are cash inflows from dividends and interest and cash outflows for dividends and interest classified in AF's cash flow statements? Is this classification the same as or different from cash flow statements prepared in accordance with U.S. GAAP?

CPA Exam Questions and Simulations

ROGER CPA Review

Sample CPA Exam questions from Roger CPA Review are available in Connect as support for the topics in this chapter. These Multiple Choice Questions and Task-Based Simulations include expert-written explanations and solutions, and provide a starting point for students to become familiar with the content and functionality of the actual CPA Exam.

APPENDIX

A

Derivatives

"... derivatives are financial weapons of mass destruction ..."

— Warren Buffett, Berkshire Hathaway CEO

"... the growing use of complex financial instruments known as derivatives does not pose a threat to the country's financial system ..."

— Alan Greenspan, Federal Reserve Chairman

"Total world derivatives are $1000 trillion or 19 times the total world GDP of $54 trillion."

— Chuck Burr, *Culture Change*

In today's global economy and evolving financial markets, businesses are increasingly exposed to a variety of risks, which, unmanaged, can have major impacts on earnings or even threaten a company's very existence. Risk management, then, has become critical. Derivative financial instruments have become the key tools of risk management.[1]

Derivatives are financial instruments that "derive" their values or contractually required cash flows from some other security or index. For instance, a contract allowing a company to buy a particular asset (say steel, gold, or flour) at a designated future date at a predetermined price is a financial instrument that derives its value from expected and actual changes in the price of the underlying asset. Financial futures, forward contracts, options, and interest rate swaps are the most frequently used derivatives. Derivatives are valued as tools to manage or hedge companies' increasing exposures to risk, including interest rate risk, price risk, and foreign exchange risk. The variety, complexity, and magnitude of derivatives have grown rapidly in recent years. Accounting standard-setters have scrambled to keep pace.

Derivatives are financial instruments that "derive" their values from some other security or *index*.

A persistent stream of headline stories has alerted us to multimillion-dollar losses by many companies and the financial collapse of Bear Stearns and AIG.[2] Focusing on these headlines, it would be tempting to conclude that derivatives are risky business indeed. Certainly they can be quite risky if misused, but the fact is, these financial instruments exist to lessen, not increase, risk. Properly used, they serve as a form of "insurance" against risk. In fact, if a company is exposed to a substantial risk and does not hedge that risk, it is taking a gamble. On the other hand, if a derivative is used improperly, it can be a huge gamble itself.

Derivatives serve as a form of "insurance" against risk.

The notional amount of the derivatives market vastly exceeds the total value of the assets they are intended to mimic or mirror. This implies that firms are using derivatives for purposes other than risk management. Many observers are fearful that the size of the derivatives market poses significant risk to the economy. Some caution that the vast derivatives market could even cause the entire global financial system to crash. Why? If interest rates rise, then many speculative interest rate swaps would incur losses. But it's the size of the interest rate swap market, and thus the size of the resultant losses, that prompts the anxiety. At the start of 2014, the over-the-counter derivatives market was $702 trillion. Yes, that's 702 with twelve zeroes ($702,000,000,000,000). And, that's over 30 times the U.S. Gross Domestic Product. Eighty-two percent of those derivatives ($584 trillion) are interest rate swaps.[3] Our focus here, though, is not on the risk posed by the speculative use of derivatives, but instead on the use of derivatives to reduce company risk.

[1]Almost all financial institutions and over half of all nonfinancial companies use derivatives.

[2]Bear Sterns has since been sold at a bargain basement price to JP Morgan, and AIG has since recovered from its difficulties.

[3]Bank for International Settlements, *BIS Quarterly Review*, June 2014.

Derivatives Used to Hedge Risk

Hedging means taking a risk position that is opposite to an actual position that is exposed to risk.

Hedging means taking an action that is expected to produce exposure to a particular type of risk that is precisely the *opposite* of an actual risk to which the company already is exposed. For instance, the volatility of interest rates creates exposure to interest-rate risk for companies that issue debt—which, of course, includes most companies. So, a company that frequently arranges short-term loans from its bank under a floating (variable) interest rate agreement is exposed to the risk that interest rates might increase and adversely affect borrowing costs. Similarly, a company that regularly reissues commercial paper as it matures faces the possibility that new rates will be higher and cut into forecasted income. When borrowings are large, the potential cost can be substantial. So, the firm might choose to hedge its position by entering into a transaction that would produce a *gain* of roughly the same amount as the potential loss if interest rates do, in fact, increase.

Hedging is used to deal with three areas of risk exposure: fair value risk, cash flow risk, and foreign currency risk. Let's look at some of the more common derivatives.

A *futures contract* allows a firm to sell (or buy) a financial instrument at a designated future date, at today's price.

FINANCIAL FUTURES A futures contract is an agreement between a seller and a buyer that requires the seller to deliver a particular commodity (say corn, gold, or pork bellies) at a designated future date, at a *predetermined* price. These contracts are actively traded on regulated futures exchanges. When the "commodity" is a *financial instrument,* such as a Treasury bond, Treasury bill, commercial paper, or a certificate of deposit, the agreement is referred to as a *financial futures contract.*[4]

To appreciate the way these hedges work, you need to remember that when interest rates rise, the market price of interest-bearing securities goes down. For instance, if you have an investment in a 10% bond and market interest rates go up to, say, 12%, your 10% bond is less valuable relative to other bonds paying the higher rate. Conversely, when interest rates decline, the market price of interest-bearing securities goes up. This risk that the investment's value might change is referred to as *fair value risk.* The company that issued the securities is faced with fair value risk also. If interest rates decline, the fair value of that company's debt would rise, a risk the borrower may want to hedge against. Later in this section, we'll look at an illustration of how the borrower would account for and report such a hedge.

The seller in a financial futures contract realizes a gain (loss) when interest rates rise (decline).

Now let's look at the effect on a contract to sell or buy securities (or any asset for that matter) at preset prices. One who is contracted to *sell* securities at a *preset* price after their market price has fallen benefits from the rise in interest rates. Consequently, the value of the contract that gives one the right to sell securities at a preset price goes up as the market price declines. The seller in a futures contract derives a gain (loss) when interest rates rise (decline).[5] Conversely, the one obligated to buy securities at a preset price experiences a loss. This risk of having to pay more cash or receive less cash is referred to as *cash flow risk.*

Another example of cash flow risk would be borrowing money by issuing a variable (floating) rate note. If market interest rates rise, the borrower would have to pay more interest. Similarly, the lender (investor) in the variable (floating) rate note transaction would face cash flow risk that interest rates would decline, resulting in lower cash interest receipts.

Let's look closer at how a futures contract can mitigate cash flow risk. Consider a company in April that will replace its $10 million of 8.5% bank notes with a bond issue when the notes mature in June. The company is exposed to the risk that interest rates in June will have risen, increasing borrowing costs. To counteract that possibility, the firm might enter a contract in April to deliver (sell) bonds in June at their *current* price. Since there are no corporate bond futures contracts, the company buys Treasury bond futures, which will accomplish essentially the same purpose. In essence, the firm agrees to sell Treasury bonds in June at a price established now (April). Let's say it's April 6 and the price of Treasury bond futures on the International Monetary Market of the Chicago Mercantile Exchange is quoted as 95.24.[6] Since the trading unit of Treasury bond futures is a 15-year, $100,000, 8% Treasury bond,

[4]Note that a financial futures contract meets the definition of a financial instrument because it entails the exchange of financial instruments (cash for Treasury bonds, for instance). But, a futures contract for the sale or purchase of a nonfinancial commodity like corn or gold does not meet the definition because one of the items to be exchanged is not a financial instrument.

[5]The seller of a futures contract is obligated to sell the bonds at a future date. The buyer of a futures contract is obligated to buy the bonds at a future date. The company in our example, then, is the seller of the futures contract.

[6]Price quotes are expressed as a percentage of par.

the company might sell 105 Treasury bond futures to hedge the June issuance of debt. This would effectively provide a hedge of 105 × \$100,000 × 95.24% = \$10,000,200.[7]

Here's what happens then. If interest rates rise, borrowing costs will go up for our example company because it will have to sell debt securities at a higher interest cost (or lower price). But that loss will be offset (approximately) by the gain produced by being in the opposite position on Treasury bond futures. Take note, though, this works both ways. If interest rates go down causing debt security prices to rise, the potential benefit of being able to issue debt at that lower interest rate (higher price) will be offset by a loss on the futures position.

A very important point about futures contracts is that the seller does not need to have actual possession of the commodity (the Treasury bonds, in this case), nor is the purchaser of the contract required to take possession of the commodity. In fact, virtually all financial futures contracts are "netted out" before the actual transaction is to take place. This is simply a matter of reversing the original position. A seller closes out his transaction with a purchase. Likewise, a purchaser would close out her transaction with a sale. After all, the objective is not to actually buy or sell Treasury bonds (or whatever the commodity might be), but to incur the financial impact of movements in interest rates as reflected in changes in Treasury bond prices. Specifically, it will buy at the lower price (to reverse the original seller position) at the same time it's selling its new bond issue at that same lower price. The financial futures market is an "artificial" exchange in that its reason for existing is to provide a mechanism to transfer risk from those exposed to it to those willing to accept the risk, not to actually buy and sell the underlying financial instruments.

If the impending debt issue being hedged is a short-term issue, the company may attain a more effective hedge by selling Treasury *bill* futures since Treasury bills are 90-day securities, or maybe certificate of deposit (CD) futures that also are traded in futures markets. The object is to get the closest association between the financial effects of interest rate movements on the actual transaction and the effects on the financial instrument used as a hedge.

The effectiveness of a hedge is influenced by the closeness of the match between the item being hedged and the financial instrument chosen as a hedge.

FINANCIAL FORWARD CONTRACTS A **forward contract** is similar to a futures contract but differs in three ways:

1. A forward contract calls for delivery on a specific date, whereas a futures contract permits the seller to decide later which specific day within the specified month will be the delivery date (if it gets as far as actual delivery before it is closed out).
2. Unlike a futures contract, a forward contract usually is not traded on a market exchange.
3. Unlike a futures contract, a forward contract does not call for a daily cash settlement for price changes in the underlying contract. Gains and losses on forward contracts are paid only when they are closed out.

OPTIONS **Options** frequently are purchased to hedge exposure to the effects of changing interest rates. Options serve the same purpose as futures in that respect but are fundamentally different. An option on a financial instrument—say a Treasury bill—gives its holder the right either to buy or to sell the Treasury bill at a specified price and within a given time period. Importantly, though, the option holder has no obligation to exercise the option. On the other hand, the holder of a futures contract must buy or sell within a specified period unless the contract is closed out before delivery comes due.

FOREIGN CURRENCY FUTURES Foreign loans frequently are denominated in the currency of the lender (Japanese yen, Swiss franc, Euro, and so on). When loans must be repaid in foreign currencies, a new element of risk is introduced. This is because if exchange rates change, the dollar equivalent of the foreign currency that must be repaid differs from the dollar equivalent of the foreign currency borrowed.

To hedge against "foreign exchange risk" exposure, some firms buy or sell **foreign currency futures** contracts. These are similar to financial futures except specific foreign

Foreign exchange risk often is hedged in the same manner as interest rate risk.

[7]This is a simplification of the more sophisticated way financial managers determine the optimal number of futures.

currencies are specified in the futures contracts rather than specific debt instruments. They work the same way to protect against foreign exchange risk as financial futures protect against fair value or cash flow risk.

Interest rate swaps exchange fixed interest payments for floating rate payments, or vice versa, without exchanging the underlying notional amounts.

INTEREST RATE SWAPS Over 82% of derivatives are interest rate contracts, of which 75% are **interest rate swaps**. These contracts exchange fixed interest payments for floating rate payments, or vice versa, without exchanging the underlying principal amounts. For example, suppose you owe $100,000 on a 10% fixed rate home loan. You envy your neighbor who also is paying 10% on her $100,000 mortgage, but hers is a floating rate loan, so if market rates fall, so will her loan rate. To the contrary, she is envious of your fixed rate, fearful that rates will rise, increasing her payments. A solution would be for the two of you to effectively swap interest payments using an interest rate swap agreement. The way a swap works, you both would continue to actually make your own interest payments, but you would exchange the net cash difference between payments at specified intervals. So, in this case, if market rates (and thus floating payments) increase, you would pay your neighbor; if rates fall, she pays you. The net effect is to exchange the consequences of rate changes. In other words, you have effectively converted your fixed-rate debt to floating-rate debt; your neighbor has done the opposite.

Of course, this technique is not dependent on happening into such a fortuitous pairing of two borrowers with opposite philosophies on interest rate risk. Instead, banks or other intermediaries offer, for a fee, one-sided swap agreements to companies desiring to be either fixed-rate payers or variable-rate payers. Intermediaries usually strive to maintain a balanced portfolio of matched, offsetting swap agreements.

Theoretically, the two parties to such a transaction exchange principal amounts, say the $100,000 amount above, in addition to the interest on those amounts. It makes no practical sense, though, for the companies to send each other $100,000. So, instead, the principal amount is not actually exchanged, but serves merely as the computational base for interest calculations and is called the *notional amount.* Similarly, the fixed-rate payer doesn't usually send the entire fixed interest amount (say 10% × $100,000 = $10,000) and receive the entire variable interest amount (say 9% × $100,000 = $9,000). Generally, only the net amount ($1,000 in this case) is exchanged. This is illustrated in Illustration A–1.

Illustration A–1
Interest Rate Swap—Shortcut Method

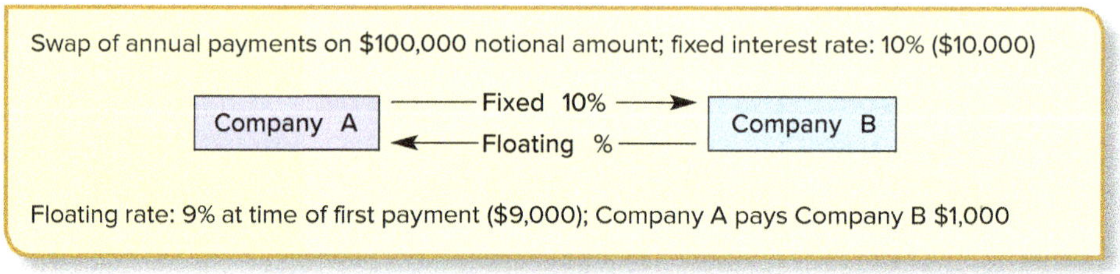

From an accounting standpoint, the central issue is not the operational differences among various hedge instruments, but their similarities in functioning as hedges against risk.

Accounting for Derivatives

A key to accounting for derivatives is knowing the purpose for which a company holds them and whether the company is effective in serving that purpose. Derivatives, for instance, may be held for risk management (hedging activities). The desired effect, and often the real effect, is a reduction in risk. On the other hand, derivatives sometimes are held for speculative position taking, hoping for large profits. The effect of this activity usually is to *increase* risk. Perhaps more important, derivatives acquired as hedges and intended to reduce risk may, in fact, unintentionally increase risk instead.

Derivatives not serving as hedges are extremely speculative due to the high leverage inherent in such investments.

It's important to understand that, serving as investments rather than as hedges, derivatives are extremely speculative. This is due to the high leverage inherent in derivatives. Here's why. The investment outlay usually is negligible, but the potential gain or loss on the investment usually is quite high. A small change in interest rates or another underlying event can trigger a large change in the fair value of the derivative. Because the initial investment was minimal, the change in value relative to the investment itself represents a huge percentage gain or loss. Their extraordinarily risky nature prompted Warren Buffett, one of the country's most celebrated financiers, to refer to derivatives as "financial weapons of mass destruction." Accounting for derivatives is designed to treat differently (a) derivatives designated as hedges and those not designated as hedges as well as (b) the effective portion and the ineffective portion of gains and losses from intended hedges.

The basic approach to accounting for derivatives is fairly straightforward, although implementation can be quite cumbersome. All derivatives, no exceptions, are carried on the balance sheet as either assets or liabilities at fair (or market) value.[8] The reasoning is that (a) derivatives create either rights or obligations that meet the definition of assets or liabilities, and (b) fair value is the most meaningful measurement.

Each derivative contract has a "fair value," which is an amount that one side owes the other at a particular moment.

Accounting for the gain or loss on a derivative depends on how it is used. Specifically, if the derivative is not designated as a hedging instrument or doesn't qualify as one, any gain or loss from fair value changes is recognized immediately in earnings. On the other hand, if a derivative is used to hedge against exposure to risk, any gain or loss from fair value changes is either (a) recognized immediately in earnings along with an offsetting loss or gain on the item being hedged or (b) deferred in comprehensive income until it can be recognized in earnings at the same time as earnings are affected by a hedged transaction. Which way depends on whether the derivative is designated as a (a) fair value hedge, (b) cash flow hedge, or (c) foreign currency hedge. Let's look now at each of the three hedge designations.

FAIR VALUE HEDGES A company can be adversely affected when a change in either prices or interest rates causes a change in the fair value of one of its assets, its liabilities, or a commitment to buy or sell assets or liabilities. If a derivative is used to hedge against the exposure to changes in the fair value of an asset, liability, or a firm commitment, it can be designated as a **fair value hedge**. In that case, when the derivative is adjusted to reflect changes in fair value, the other side of the entry recognizes a gain or loss to be included *currently* in earnings. At the same time, though, the loss or gain from changes in the fair value (due to the risk being hedged)[9] of the item being hedged also is included currently in earnings. This means that, to the extent the hedge is effective in serving its purpose, the gain or loss on the derivative will be offset by the loss or gain on the item being hedged. In fact, this is precisely the concept behind the procedure.

A gain or loss from a *fair value hedge* is recognized immediately in earnings, along with the loss or gain from the item being hedged.

The reasoning is that as interest rates or other underlying events change, a hedge instrument will produce a gain approximately equal to a loss on the item being hedged (or vice versa). These income effects are interrelated and offsetting, so it would be improper to report the income effects in different periods. More critically, the intent and effect of having the hedge instrument is to *lessen* risk. And yet, recognizing gains in one period and counter balancing losses in another period would tend to cause fluctuations in income that convey an *increase* in risk. However, to the extent that a hedge is ineffective and produces gains or losses different from the losses or gains being hedged, the ineffective portion is recognized in earnings immediately.

The income effects of the hedge instrument and the income effects of the item being hedged should affect earnings at the same time.

Some of the more common fair value hedges use as follows:

- An interest rate swap to synthetically convert fixed-rate debt (for which interest rate changes could change the fair value of the debt) into floating-rate debt
- A futures contract to hedge changes in the fair value (due to price changes) of aluminum, sugar, or some other type of inventory
- A futures contract to hedge the fair value (due to price changes) of a firm commitment to sell natural gas or some other asset

ILLUSTRATION Because interest rate swaps comprise the majority of derivatives in use, we will use swaps to illustrate accounting for derivatives. Let's look at the example in Illustration A–2.

[8]FASB ASC 815–10: Derivatives and Hedging–Overall (previously "Accounting for Derivative Instruments and Hedging Activities," *Statement of Financial Accounting Standards No. 133* (Norwalk, Conn.: FASB, 1998)).

[9]The fair value of a hedged item might also change for reasons other than from effects of the risk being hedged. For instance, the hedged risk may be that a change in interest rates will cause the fair value of a bond to change. The bond price might also change, though, if the market perceives that the bond's default risk has changed.

Illustration A–2

Interest Rate Swap—Shortcut Method

Wintel Semiconductors issued $1 million of 18-month, 10% bank notes on January 1, 2018. Wintel is exposed to the risk that general interest rates will decline, causing the fair value of its debt to rise. (If the fair value of Wintel's debt increases, its effective borrowing cost is higher relative to the market.) To hedge against this fair value risk, the firm entered into an 18-month interest rate swap agreement on January 1 and designated the swap as a hedge against changes in the fair value of the note. The swap calls for the company to receive payment based on a 10% fixed interest rate on a notional amount of $1 million and to make payment based on a floating interest rate tied to changes in general rates.* As the Illustration will show, this effectively converts Wintel's fixed-rate debt to floating-rate debt. Cash settlement of the net interest amount is made semiannually at June 30 and December 31 of each year, with the net interest being the difference between the $50,000 fixed interest [$1 million × (10% × ½)] and the floating interest rate, times $1 million at those dates.

Floating (market) settlement rates were 9% at June 30, 2018, 8% at December 31, 2018, and 9% at June 30, 2019. Net interest receipts can be calculated as shown below. Fair values of both the derivative and the note resulting from those market rate changes are assumed to be quotes obtained from securities dealers.

	1/1/18	6/30/18	12/31/18	6/30/19
Fixed rate	10%	10%	10%	10%
Floating rate	10%	9%	8%	9%
Fixed payments [$1 million × (10% × ½)]		$ 50,000	$ 50,000	$ 50,000
Floating payments ($1 million × ½ floating rate)		45,000	40,000	45,000
Net interest receipts		$ 5,000	$ 10,000	$ 5,000
Fair value of interest rate swap	0	$ 9,363	$ 9,615	0
Fair value of note payable	$1,000,000	$1,009,363	$1,009,615	$1,000,000

*A common measure for benchmarking variable interest rates is LIBOR, the London Interbank Offered Rate, a base rate at which large international banks lend funds to each other.

When the floating rate declined from 10% to 9%, the fair values of both the derivative (swap) and the note increased. This created an offsetting gain on the derivative and a holding loss on the note. Both are recognized in earnings at the same time (at June 30, 2018).

The interest rate swap is designated as a fair value hedge on this note at issuance.

The swap settlement is the difference between the fixed interest (5%) and variable interest (4.5%).

The fair value of derivatives is recognized in the balance sheet.

The hedged liability (or asset) is adjusted to fair value as well.

	Debit	Credit
January 1, 2018		
Cash	1,000,000	
Notes payable		1,000,000
To record the issuance of the note.		
June 30, 2018		
Interest expense (10% × ½ × $1 million)	50,000	
Cash		50,000
To record interest.		
Cash [$50,000 – (9% × ½ × $1 million)]	5,000	
Interest expense		5,000
To record the net cash settlement.		
Interest rate swap* ($9,363 – 0)	9,363	
Holding gain—interest rate swap		9,363
To record change in fair value of the derivative.		
Holding loss—hedged note	9,363	
Note payable ($1,009,363 – 1,000,000)		9,363
To record change in fair value of the note due to interest rate changes.		

*This would be a liability rather than an investment (asset) if the fair value had declined.

The net interest settlement on June 30, 2018, is $5,000 because the fixed rate is 5% (half of the 10% annual rate) and the floating rate is 4.5% (half of the 9% annual rate).

December 31, 2018		
Interest expense	50,000	
Cash (10% × ½ × $1,000,000)		50,000
To record interest.		
Cash [$50,000 − (8% × ½ × $1 million)]	10,000	
Interest expense		10,000
To record the net cash settlement.		
Interest rate swap ($9,615 − 9,363)	252	
Holding gain—interest rate swap		252
To record the change in fair value of the derivative.		
Holding loss—hedged note	252	
Note payable ($1,009,615 − 1,009,363)		252
To record the change in fair value of the note due to interest rate changes.		

As with any debt, interest expense is the effective rate times the outstanding balance.

The settlement is the difference between the fixed interest (5%) and variable interest (4%).

The derivative is increased by the change in fair value. The note is increased by the change in fair value.

The fair value of the swap increased by $252 (from $9,363 to $9,615). Similarly, we adjust the note's book value by the amount necessary to increase it to fair value. This produces a holding loss on the note that exactly offsets the gain on the swap. This result is the hedging effect that motivated Wintel to enter the fair value hedging arrangement in the first place.

At June 30, 2019, Wintel repeats the process of adjusting to fair value both the derivative investment and the note being hedged.

June 30, 2019		
Interest expense	50,000	
Cash (10% × ½ × $1,000,000)		50,000
To record interest.		
Cash [$50,000 − (9% × ½ × $1 million)]	5,000	
Interest expense		5,000
To record the net cash settlement.		
Holding loss—interest rate swap	9,615	
Interest rate swap ($0 − 9,615)		9,615
To record the change in fair value of the derivative.		
Note payable ($1,000,000 − 1,009,615)	9,615	
Holding gain—hedged note		9,615
To record the change in fair value of the note due to interest rate changes.		
Note payable	1,000,000	
Cash		1,000,000
To repay the loan.		

The net interest received is the difference between the fixed interest (5%) and floating interest (4.5%).

The swap's fair value now is zero.

The net interest received is the difference between the fixed rate (5%) and floating rate (4.5%) times $1 million. The fair value of the swap decreased by $9,615 (from $9,615 to zero).[10] That decline represents a holding *loss* that we recognize in earnings. Similarly, we record an offsetting holding gain on the note for the change in its fair value.

Now let's see how the book values changed for the swap account and the note:

	Swap (Debit)	Swap (Credit)	Note (Debit)	Note (Credit)
Jan. 1, 2018				1,000,000
June 30, 2018	9,363			9,363
Dec. 31, 2018	252			252
June 30, 2019		9,615	9,615	
			1,000,000	
	0			0

[10]Because there are no future cash receipts from the swap arrangement at this point, the fair value of the swap is zero.

The income statement is affected as follows:

	Income Statement + (−)	
June 30, 2018	(50,000)	Interest expense—fixed payment
	5,000	Interest expense—net cash settlement
	9,363	Holding gain—interest rate swap
	(9,363)	Holding loss—hedged note
	(45,000)	Net effect—same as floating interest payment
Dec. 31, 2018	(50,000)	Interest expense—fixed payment
	10,000	Interest expense—net cash settlement
	252	Holding gain—interest rate swap
	(252)	Holding loss—hedged note
	(40,000)	Net effect—same as floating interest payment
June 30, 2019	(50,000)	Interest expense—fixed payment
	5,000	Interest expense—net cash settlement
	9,615	Holding gain—interest rate swap
	(9,615)	Holding loss—hedged note
	(45,000)	Net effect—same as floating interest payment

As this demonstrates, the swap effectively converts fixed-interest debt to floating-interest debt.

Additional Consideration

Fair Value of the Swap

The fair value of a derivative typically is based on a quote obtained from a derivatives dealer. That fair value will approximate the present value of the expected net interest settlement receipts for the remaining term of the swap. In fact, we can actually calculate the fair value of the swap that we accepted as given in our illustration.

Since the June 30, 2018, floating rate of 9% caused the cash settlement on that date to be $5,000, it's reasonable to look at 9% as the best estimate of future floating rates and therefore assume the remaining two cash settlements also will be $5,000 each. We can then calculate at June 30, 2018, the present value of those expected net interest settlement receipts for the remaining term of the swap.

Fixed interest	10% × ½ × $1 million	$ 50,000
Expected floating interest	9% × ½ × $1 million	45,000
Expected cash receipts for both Dec. 31, 2018 and June 30, 2019		$ 5,000
		× 1.87267*
Present value		$ 9,363

*Present value of an ordinary annuity of $1: $n = 2$, $i = 4.5\%$ (½ of 9%) (from Table 4)

Fair Value of the Notes

The fair value of the note payable will be the present value of principal and remaining interest payments discounted at the market rate. The market rate will vary with the designated floating rate but might differ due to changes in default (credit) risk and the term structure of interest rates. Assuming it's 9% at June 30, 2018, we can calculate the fair value (present value) of the notes.

Interest	$50,000* × 1.87267† =	$ 93,633
Principal	$1,000,000 × 0.91573‡ =	915,730
		$1,009,363

*½ of 10% × $1,000,000
†Present value of an ordinary annuity of $1: $n = 2$, $i = 4.5\%$ (from Table 4)
‡Present value of $1: $n = 2$, $i = 4.5\%$ (from Table 2)

(continued)

(concluded)

Note: Often the cash settlement rate is "reset" as of each cash settlement date. Thus, the floating rate actually used at the end of each period to determine the payment is the floating market rate as of the beginning of the same period. In our illustration, for instance, there would have been no cash settlement at June 30, 2018, since we would use the beginning floating rate of 10% to determine payment. Similarly, we would have used the 9% floating rate at June 30, 2018, to determine the cash settlement six months later at December 31. In effect, each cash settlement would be delayed six months. Had this arrangement been in effect in the current illustration, there would have been one fewer cash settlement payment (two rather than three), but would not have affected the fair value calculations above because, either way, our expectation would be cash receipts of $5,000 for both Dec. 31, 2018, and June 30, 2019.

CASH FLOW HEDGES The risk in some transactions or events is the risk of a change in cash flows, rather than a change in fair values. We noted earlier, for instance, that *fixed-rate* debt subjects a company to the risk that interest rate changes could change the fair value of the debt. On the other hand, if the obligation is *floating-rate* debt, the fair value of the debt will not change when interest rates do, but cash flows will. If a derivative is used to hedge against the exposure to changes in cash inflows or cash outflows of an asset or liability or a forecasted transaction (like a future purchase or sale), it can be designated as a cash flow hedge. In that case, when the derivative is adjusted to reflect changes in fair value, the other side of the entry is a gain or loss to be deferred as a component of other comprehensive income and included in earnings later, at the same time as earnings are affected by the hedged transaction. Once again, the effect is matching the earnings effect of the derivative with the earnings effect of the item being hedged, precisely the concept behind hedge accounting.

A gain or loss from a *cash flow hedge* is deferred as other comprehensive income until it can be recognized in earnings along with the earnings effect of the item being hedged.

To understand the deferral of the gain or loss, we need to revisit the concept of comprehensive income. Comprehensive income, as you may recall from Chapters 4, 12, 17, and 18, is a more expansive view of the change in shareholders' equity than traditional net income. In fact, it encompasses all changes in equity other than from transactions with owners.[11] So, in addition to net income itself, comprehensive income includes up to four other changes in equity that don't (yet) belong in net income, namely, net holding gains (losses) on investments in debt securities (Chapter 12), gains (losses) from and amendments to postretirement benefit plans (Chapter 17), gains (losses) from foreign currency translation, and deferred gains (losses) from derivatives designated as cash flow hedges.[12]

Some of the more commonly used cash flow hedges are:

- An interest rate swap to synthetically convert floating rate debt (for which interest rate changes could change the cash interest payments) into fixed rate debt.
- A futures contract to hedge a forecasted sale (for which price changes could change the cash receipts) of natural gas, crude oil, or some other asset.

FOREIGN CURRENCY HEDGES Today's economy is increasingly a global one. The majority of large "U.S." companies are, in truth, multinational companies that may receive only a fraction of their revenues from U.S. operations. Many operations of those companies are located abroad. Foreign operations often are denominated in the currency of the foreign country (the Euro, Japanese yen, Russian rubles, and so on). Even companies without foreign operations sometimes hold investments, issue debt, or conduct other transactions denominated in foreign currencies. As exchange rates change, the dollar equivalent of the

The possibility that foreign currency exchange rates might change exposes many companies to foreign currency risk.

[11]Transactions with owners primarily include dividends and the sale or purchase of shares of the company's stock.

[12]FASB ASC 220–10–55–2: Comprehensive Income–Overall–Implementation Guidance and Illustrations (previously "Reporting Comprehensive Income," *Statement of Financial Accounting Standards No. 130* (Norwalk, Conn.: FASB, 1997)).

foreign currency changes. The possibility of currency rate changes exposes these companies to the risk that some transactions require settlement in a currency other than the entities' functional currency or that foreign operations will require translation adjustments to reported amounts.

A **foreign currency hedge** can be a hedge of foreign currency exposure of the following:

- A firm commitment—treated as a fair value hedge
- An available-for-sale security—treated as a fair value hedge
- A forecasted transaction—treated as a cash flow hedge
- A company's net investment in a foreign operation—the gain or loss is reported in *other comprehensive income* as part of unrealized gains and losses from foreign currency translation[13]

To qualify as a hedge, the hedging relationship must be highly effective in achieving offsetting changes in fair values or cash flows.

HEDGE EFFECTIVENESS When a company elects to apply hedge accounting, it must establish at the inception of the hedge the method it will use to assess the effectiveness of the hedging derivative, as well as the measurement approach it will use to determine the ineffective portion of the hedge.[14] The key criterion for qualifying as a hedge is that the hedging relationship must be "highly effective" in achieving offsetting changes in fair values or cash flows based on the hedging company's specified risk management objective and strategy.

An assessment of this effectiveness must be made at least every three months and whenever financial statements are issued. There are no precise guidelines for assessing effectiveness, but it generally means a high correlation between changes in the fair value or cash flows of the derivative and of the item being hedged, not necessarily a specific reduction in risk. Hedge accounting must be terminated for hedging relationships that no longer are highly effective.

HEDGE INEFFECTIVENESS In Illustration A–2, the loss on the hedged note exactly offset the gain on the swap. This is because the swap in this instance was highly effective in hedging the risk due to interest rate changes. However, the loss and gain would not have exactly offset each other if the hedging arrangement had been ineffective. For instance, suppose the swap's term had been different from that of the note (say a three-year swap term compared with the 18-month term of the note) or if the notional amount of the swap differed from that of the note (say $500,000 rather than $1 million). In that case, changes in the fair value of the swap and changes in the fair value of the note would not be the same. The result would be a greater (or lesser) amount recognized in earnings for the swap than for the note. Because there would not be an exact offset, earnings would be affected, an effect resulting from hedge ineffectiveness. That is a desired effect of hedge accounting; to the extent that a hedge is effective, the earnings effect of a derivative cancels out the earnings effect of the item being hedged. However, even if a hedge is highly effective, all ineffectiveness is recognized currently in earnings.

Imperfect hedges result in part of the derivative gain or loss being included in current earnings.

FAIR VALUE CHANGES UNRELATED TO THE RISK BEING HEDGED In Illustration A–2, the fair value of the hedged note and the fair value of the swap changed by the same amounts each year because we assumed the fair values changed only due to interest rate changes. It's also possible, though, that the note's fair value would change by an amount different from that of the swap for reasons unrelated to interest rates. Remember from our earlier discussion that the market's perception of a company's creditworthiness,

[13]This is the same treatment previously prescribed for these translation adjustments by FASB ASC 830: Foreign Currency Matters (previously *Statement of Financial Accounting Standards No. 52*).

[14]Remember, if a derivative is not designated as a hedge, any gains or losses from changes in its fair value are recognized immediately in earnings.

and thus its ability to pay interest and principal when due, also can affect the value of debt, whether interest rates change or not. In hedge accounting, we ignore those changes. We recognize only the fair value changes in the hedged item that we can attribute to the risk being hedged (interest rate risk in this case). For example, if a changing perception of default risk had caused the note's fair value to increase by an additional, say $5,000, our journal entries in Illustration A–2 would have been unaffected. Notice, then, that although we always mark a *derivative* to fair value, the reported amount of the *item being hedged* may not be its fair value. We mark a hedged item to fair value only to the extent that its fair value changed due to the risk being hedged.

Fair value changes unrelated to the risk being hedged are ignored.

Disclosure of Derivatives and Risk

To be adequately informed about the effectiveness of a company's risk management, investors and creditors need information about strategies for holding derivatives and specific hedging activities. Toward that end, extensive disclosure requirements provide information that includes the following:

- Objectives and strategies for holding and issuing derivatives
- A description of the items for which risks are being hedged
- For forecasted transactions: a description, time before the transaction is expected to occur, the gains and losses accumulated in other comprehensive income, and the events that will trigger their recognition in earnings
- Beginning balance of, changes in, and ending balance of the derivative component of other comprehensive income
- The net amount of gain or loss reported in earnings (representing aggregate hedge ineffectiveness)
- Qualitative and quantitative information about failed hedges: canceled commitments or previously hedged forecasted transactions no longer expected to occur

The intent is to provide information about the company's success in reducing risks and, consequently, about risks not managed successfully. Remember, too, that when derivatives are employed ineffectively, risks can escalate. Ample disclosures about derivatives are essential to maintain awareness of potential opportunities and problems with risk management.

In addition, GAAP requires companies to provide enhanced disclosures indicating (a) how and why the company uses derivative instruments, (b) how the company accounts for derivative instruments and related hedged items, and (c) how derivative instruments and related hedged items affect the company's balance sheet, income statement, and cash flows.[15] The required disclosures include two tables, one that highlights the location and fair values of derivative instruments in the balance sheet, and another that indicates the location and amounts of gains and losses on derivative instruments in the income statement. The two tables distinguish between derivative instruments that are designated as hedging instruments and those that are not. The tables also categorize derivative instruments by each major type—interest rate contracts, foreign exchange contracts, equity contracts, commodity contracts, credit contracts, and other types of contracts.

Even for some traditional liabilities, the amounts reported on the face of the financial statements provide inadequate disclosure about the degree to which a company is exposed to risk of loss. To provide adequate disclosure about a company's exposure to risk, additional information must be provided about (a) concentrations of credit risk and (b) the fair value of all financial instruments.[16]

[15]FASB ASC 815: Derivatives and Hedging (previously "Disclosures about Derivative Instruments and Hedging Activities—an amendment of FASB Statement No. 133," *Statement of Financial Accounting Standards No. 161* (Stamford, Conn.: FASB, 2008)).

[16]FASB ASC 825–10–50–1: Financial Instruments–Overall–Disclosure (previously "Disclosures About Fair Values of Financial Instruments," *Statement of Financial Accounting Standards No. 107* (Norwalk, Conn.: FASB, 1991), as amended by *Statement of Financial Accounting Standards No. 133,* "Accounting for Derivative Instruments and Hedging Activities" (Norwalk, Conn.: FASB, 1998)).

Extended Method for Interest Rate Swap Accounting

A shortcut method for accounting for an interest rate swap is permitted when a hedge meets certain criteria. In general, the criteria are designed to see if the hedge supports the assumption of "no ineffectiveness." Illustration A–2 of a fair value hedge met those criteria, in particular, (a) the swap's notional amount matches the note's principal amount, (b) the swap's expiration date matches the note's maturity date, (c) the fair value of the swap is zero at inception, and (d) the floating payment is at the market rate.[17] Because Wintel can conclude that the swap will be highly effective in offsetting changes in the fair value of the debt, it can use the changes in the fair value of the swap to measure the offsetting changes in the fair value of the debt. That's the essence of the shortcut method used in Illustration A–2. The extended method required when the criteria are *not* met for the short-cut method is described in this section (Illustration A–3 begins by describing the same scenario as in Illustration A–2). It produces the same effect on earnings and in the balance sheet as does the procedure shown in Illustration A–2.

Illustration A–3

Interest Rate Swap—Extended Method

Wintel Semiconductors issued $1 million of 18-month, 10% bank notes on January 1, 2018. Wintel is exposed to the risk that general interest rates will decline, causing the fair value of its debt to rise. (If the fair value of Wintel's debt increases, its effective borrowing cost is higher relative to the market.) To hedge against this fair value risk, the firm entered into an 18-month interest rate swap agreement on January 1 and designated the swap as a hedge against changes in the fair value of the note. The swap calls for the company to receive payment based on a 10% fixed interest rate on a notional amount of $1 million and to make payment based on a floating interest rate tied to changes in general rates. Cash settlement of the net interest amount is made semiannually at June 30 and December 31 of each year, with the net interest being the difference between the $50,000 fixed interest [$1 million × (10% × ½)] and the floating interest rate, times $1 million at those dates.

Floating (market) settlement rates were 9% at June 30, 2018, 8% at December 31, 2018, and 8% at June 30, 2019. Net interest receipts can be calculated as shown below. Fair values of both the derivative and the note resulting from those market rate changes are assumed to be quotes obtained from securities dealers.

	1/1/18	6/30/18	12/31/18	6/30/19
Fixed rate	10%	10%	10%	10%
Floating rate	10%	9%	8%	9%
Fixed payments				
[$1 million × (10% × ½)]		$ 50,000	$ 50,000	$ 50,000
Floating payments				
($1 million × ½ floating rate)		45,000	40,000	45,000
Net interest receipts		$ 5,000	$ 10,000	$ 5,000
Fair value of interest rate swap	0	$ 9,363	$ 9,615	0
Fair value of note payable	$1,000,000	$1,009,363	$1,009,615	$1,000,000

When the floating rate declined in Illustration A–3 from 10% to 9%, the fair values of both the derivative (swap) and the note increased. This created an offsetting gain on the derivative and holding loss on the note. Both are recognized in earnings the same period (June 30, 2018).

The interest rate swap is designated as a fair value hedge on this note at issuance.

January 1, 2018		
Cash	1,000,000	
Notes payable		1,000,000
To record the issuance of the note.		

[17]There is no precise minimum interval, though it generally is three to six months or less. Other criteria are specified by FASB ASC 815-20-25-104: Derivatives and Hedging–Hedging-General–Recognition–Shortcut Method, *SFAS No. 133* (para. 68), in addition to the key conditions listed here.

June 30, 2018		
Interest expense (10% × ½ × $1 million)	50,000	
Cash		50,000
To record interest.		
Cash [$50,000 − (9% × ½ × $1 million)]	5,000	
Interest rate swap ($9,363 − 0)	9,363	
Interest revenue (10% × ½ × $0)		0
Holding gain—interest rate swap (to balance)		14,363
To record the net cash settlement, accrued interest on the swap, and change in the fair value of the derivative.		
Holding loss—hedged note	9,363	
Notes payable ($1,009,363 − 1,000,000)		9,363
To record change in fair value of the note due to interest rate changes.		

The swap settlement is the difference between the fixed interest (5%) and variable interest (4.5%).

The fair value of derivatives is recognized in the balance sheet.

The hedged liability (or asset) is adjusted to fair value as well.

The net interest settlement on June 30, 2018, is $5,000 because the fixed rate is 5% (half of the 10% annual rate) and the floating rate is 4.5% (half of the 9% annual rate). A holding gain ($14,363) is produced by holding the derivative security during a time when an interest rate decline caused an increase in the value of that asset. A portion ($5,000) of the gain was received in cash, and another portion ($9,363) is reflected as an increase in the value of the asset.

We also have a holding loss of the same amount. This is because we also held a liability during the same time period, and the interest rate change caused its fair value to increase as well.

December 31, 2018		
Interest expense (9% × ½ × $1,009,363)	45,421	
Notes payable (difference)*	4,579	
Cash (10% × ½ × $1,000,000)		50,000
To record interest.		
Cash [$50,000 − (8% × ½ × $1 million)]	10,000	
Interest rate swap ($9,615 − 9,363)	252	
Interest revenue (9% × ½ × $9,363)		421
Holding gain—interest rate swap (to balance)		9,831
To record the net cash settlement, accrued interest on the swap, and change in the fair value of the derivative.		
Holding loss—hedged note	4,831	
Notes payable ($1,009,615 − 1,009,363 + 4,579)		4,831
To record the change in fair value of the note due to interest rate changes.		

*We could use a premium on the note to adjust its book value.

As with any debt, interest expense is the effective rate times the outstanding balance.

The cash settlement is the difference between the fixed interest (5%) and variable interest (4%).

Interest ($421) accrues on the asset.

The note is increased by the change in fair value.

We determine interest on the note the same way we do for any liability, as you learned earlier—at the effective rate (9% × ½) times the outstanding balance ($1,009,363). This results in reducing the note's book value for the cash interest paid in excess of the interest expense.

The fair value of the swap increased due to the interest rate decline by $252 (from $9,363 to $9,615). The holding gain we recognize in earnings consists of that increase (a) plus the $10,000 cash settlement also created by the interest rate decline and (b) minus the $421 increase that results not from the interest rate decline, but from interest accruing on the asset.[18] Similarly, we adjust the note's book value by the amount necessary to increase it to fair value, allowing for the $4,579 reduction in the note in the earlier entry to record interest.

At June 30, 2019, Wintel repeats the process of adjusting to fair value both the derivative investment and the note being hedged.

[18]The investment in the interest rate swap represents the present value of expected future net interest receipts. As with other such assets, interest accrues at the effective rate times the outstanding balance. You also can think of the accrued interest mathematically as the increase in present value of the future cash flows as we get one period nearer to the dates when the cash will be received.

Interest expense is the effective rate times the outstanding balance.

June 30, 2019		
Interest expense (8% × ½ × $1,009,615)	40,385	
Notes payable (difference)	9,615	
Cash (10% × ½ × $1,000,000)		50,000
To record interest.		

The net interest received is the difference between the fixed interest (5%) and floating interest (4.5%).

Cash [$50,000 − (9% × ½ × $1 million)]	5,000	
Holding loss—interest rate swap (to balance)	5,000	
Interest rate swap ($0 − $9,615)		9,615
Interest revenue (8% × ½ × $9,615)		385
To record the net cash settlement, accrued interest on the swap, and change in the fair value of the derivative.		

The swap's fair value now is zero.

Notes payable ($1,000,000 − 1,009,615 + 9,615)	0	
Holding gain—hedged note		0
To record the change in fair value of the note due to interest rate changes.		
Note payable	1,000,000	
Cash		1,000,000
To repay the loan.		

The net interest received is the difference between the fixed rate (5%) and floating rate (4.5%), times $1 million. The fair value of the swap decreased by $9,615 (from $9,615 to zero).[19] The holding loss we recognize in earnings consists of that decline (a) minus the $5,000 portion of the decline resulting from it being realized in cash settlement and (b) plus the $385 increase that results not from the interest rate change, but from interest accruing on the asset.

Now let's see how the book values changed for the swap account and the note.

	Swap		Note	
Jan. 1, 2018				1,000,000
June 30, 2018	9,363			9,363
Dec. 31, 2018	252		4,579	4,831
June 30, 2019		9,615	9,615	
			1,000,000	
	0			0

The income statement is affected as follows:

	Income Statement + (—)	
June 30, 2018	(50,000)	Interest expense
	0	Interest revenue (no time has passed)
	14,363	Holding gain interest rate swap
	(9,363)	Holding loss—hedged note
	(45,000)	Net effect—same as floating interest payment
Dec. 31, 2018	(45,421)	Interest expense
	421	Interest revenue
	9,831	Holding gain—interest rate swap
	(4,831)	Holding loss—hedged note
	(40,000)	Net effect—same as floating interest payment
June 30, 2019	(40,385)	Interest expense
	385	Interest revenue
	(5,000)	Holding gain—interest rate swap
	0	Holding loss—hedged note
	(45,000)	Net effect—same as floating interest payment

As this demonstrates, the swap effectively converts Wintel's fixed-interest debt to floating interest debt.

[19]Because there are no future cash receipts or payments from the swap arrangement at this point, the fair value of the swap is zero.

Additional Consideration

Private Company GAAP – Derivatives and Hedging. The Private Company Council (PCC) sought feedback from private company stakeholders and found that most users of private company financial statements find it difficult to obtain fixed-rate borrowing and often enter into an interest rate swap to economically convert their variable-rate borrowing into a fixed-rate borrowing, which under GAAP caused significant variability in the income statements. As a result, the PCC concluded that the cost and complexity of hedge accounting outweigh the benefits for private companies.

In response to the PCC's conclusion, the FASB issued an Accounting Standards Update in 2014 that allows an accounting alternative to make it easier for certain interest rate swaps to qualify for hedge accounting for private companies that is quite different from what is required for public companies.[20] This alternative allows a nonpublic company (that's not a financial institution) to apply hedge accounting to its interest rate swaps as long as the terms of the swap and the related debt are aligned. If the conditions are met, the company can assume the cash flow hedge is fully effective. Those applying the simplified hedge accounting approach will be able to recognize the swap at its settlement value, instead of at its fair value.

This alternative should significantly reduce the cost and complexity of accounting for derivatives and hedging transactions of private companies.

Where We're Headed

One phase of the FASB's *Financial Instruments* project aspires to improve, simplify, and converge the financial reporting requirements for hedging activities. In May 2010, the FASB proposed revisions of standards for hedge accounting in its proposed Accounting Standards Update, *Accounting for Financial Instruments and Revisions to the Accounting for Derivative Instruments and Hedging Activities—Financial Instruments (Topic 825) and Derivatives and Hedging (Topic 815).*

In July 2014, the International Accounting Standards Board (IASB) issued a revision of IFRS 9 *Financial Instruments.* This guidance differs significantly from the FASB's proposal.

At the time this textbook was written, the FASB was actively developing a proposed new standard intended to make hedge accounting easier for companies to apply and for users of the financial statements to understand. The FASB had reached several tentative decisions that included:

- Helping companies take advantage of the favorable accounting treatment that reduces income-statement volatility.
- Changing language that currently can result in restating financial statements.
- Allowing companies to defer the recognition of ineffectiveness for cash flow hedges until the hedged item affects earnings.
- Allowing companies to hedge contractually specified components of nonfinancial items.
- Expanding the types of interest rates that could be designated as the hedged risk in cash flow and fair value hedges.
- Relaxing certain hedge effectiveness assessment requirements.
- Eliminating the burden to complete ongoing analysis associated with the long-haul method (when the short-cut method is not allowed) for fair value hedges of financial items.

[20] *Accounting Standards Update No. 2014-03,* "Derivatives and Hedging (Topic 815): Accounting for Certain Receive-Variable, Pay-Fixed Interest Rate Swaps—Simplified Hedge Accounting Approach (a consensus of the Private Comapny Council)," (Norwalk, Conn.: FASB, January 2014).

The Bottom Line

- **LOA–1** All derivatives are reported in the balance sheet at fair value.
- **LOA–2** *Hedging* means taking a risk position that is opposite to an actual position that is exposed to risk. For a derivative used to hedge against exposure to risk, treatment of any gain or loss from fair value changes depends on whether the derivative is designated as (a) a fair value hedge, (b) a cash flow hedge, or (c) a foreign currency hedge.
- **LOA–3** We recognize a gain or loss from a *fair value hedge* immediately in earnings along with the loss or gain from the item being hedged. This is so the income effects of the hedge instrument and the income effects of the item being hedged will affect earnings at the same time.
- **LOA–4** We defer a gain or loss from a *cash flow hedge* as part of other comprehensive income until it can be recognized in earnings along with the earnings effect of the item being hedged.
- **LOA–5** Imperfect hedges result in part of the derivative gain or loss being included in current earnings. We ignore market value changes unrelated to the risk being hedged.
- **LOA–6** Extensive disclosure requirements about derivatives are designed to provide investors and creditors information about the adequacy of a company's risk management and the company's success in reducing risks, including risks not managed successfully.

Questions For Review of Key Topics

Q A–1 Some financial instruments are called derivatives. Why?

Q A–2 Should gains and losses on a fair value hedge be recorded as they occur, or should they be recorded to coincide with losses and gains on the item being hedged?

Q A–3 Hines Moving Company held a fixed-rate debt of $2 million. The company wanted to hedge its fair value exposure with an interest rate swap. However, the only notional available at the time, on the type of swap it desired, was $2.5 million. What will be the effect of any gain or loss on the $500,000 notional difference?

Q A–4 What is a futures contract?

Q A–5 What is the effect on interest of an interest rate swap?

Q A–6 How are derivatives reported on the balance sheet? Why?

Q A–7 When is a gain or a loss from a cash flow hedge reported in earnings?

Exercises

connect

E A–1
Derivatives; hedge classification

Indicate (by abbreviation) the type of hedge each activity described below would represent.

Hedge Type

FV	Fair value hedge
CF	Cash flow hedge
FC	Foreign currency hedge
N	Would not qualify as a hedge

Activity

____ 1. An options contract to hedge possible future price changes of inventory
____ 2. A futures contract to hedge exposure to interest rate changes prior to replacing bank notes when they mature
____ 3. An interest rate swap to synthetically convert floating rate debt into fixed rate debt
____ 4. An interest rate swap to synthetically convert fixed rate debt into floating rate debt
____ 5. A futures contract to hedge possible future price changes of timber covered by a firm commitment to sell
____ 6. A futures contract to hedge possible future price changes of a forecasted sale of tin
____ 7. ExxonMobil's net investment in a Kuwait oil field
____ 8. An interest rate swap to synthetically convert floating rate interest on a stock investment into fixed rate interest
____ 9. An interest rate swap to synthetically convert fixed rate interest on a held-to-maturity debt investment into floating rate interest

(continued)

(concluded)

_____10. An interest rate swap to synthetically convert floating rate interest on a held-to-maturity debt investment into fixed rate interest

_____11. An interest rate swap to synthetically convert fixed rate interest on a stock investment into floating rate interest

E A–2
Derivatives; interest rate swap; fixed rate debt

On January 1, 2018, LLB Industries borrowed $200,000 from Trust Bank by issuing a two-year, 10% note, with interest payable quarterly. LLB entered into a two-year interest rate swap agreement on January 1, 2018, and designated the swap as a fair value hedge. Its intent was to hedge the risk that general interest rates will decline, causing the fair value of its debt to increase. The agreement called for the company to receive payment based on a 10% fixed interest rate on a notional amount of $200,000 and to pay interest based on a floating interest rate. The contract called for cash settlement of the net interest amount quarterly.

Floating (LIBOR) settlement rates were 10% at January 1, 8% at March 31, and 6% June 30, 2018. The fair values of the swap are quotes obtained from a derivatives dealer. Those quotes and the fair values of the note are as indicated below.

	January 1	March 31	June 30
Fair value of interest rate swap	0	$ 6,472	$ 11,394
Fair value of note payable	$200,000	$206,472	$211,394

Required:

1. Calculate the net cash settlement at March 31 and June 30, 2018.
2. Prepare the journal entries through June 30, 2018, to record the issuance of the note, interest, and necessary adjustments for changes in fair value.

E A–3
Derivatives; interest rate swap; fixed rate investment

(This is a variation of E A–2, modified to consider an investment in debt securities.)

On January 1, 2018, S&S Corporation invested in LLB Industries' negotiable two-year, 10% notes, with interest receivable quarterly. The company classified the investment as available-for-sale. S&S entered into a two-year interest rate swap agreement on January 1, 2018, and designated the swap as a fair value hedge. Its intent was to hedge the risk that general interest rates will decline, causing the fair value of its investment to increase. The agreement called for the company to make payment based on a 10% fixed interest rate on a notional amount of $200,000 and to receive interest based on a floating interest rate. The contract called for cash settlement of the net interest amount quarterly.

Floating (LIBOR) settlement rates were 10% at January 1, 8% at March 31, and 6% June 30, 2018. The fair values of the swap are quotes obtained from a derivatives dealer. Those quotes and the fair values of the investment in notes are as follows:

	January 1	March 31	June 30
Fair value of interest rate swap	0	$ 6,472	$ 11,394
Fair value of the investment in notes	$200,000	$206,472	$211,394

Required:

1. Calculate the net cash settlement at March 31 and June 30, 2018.
2. Prepare the journal entries through June 30, 2018, to record the investment in notes, interest, and necessary adjustments for changes in fair value.

E A–4
Derivatives; interest rate swap; fixed rate debt; fair value change unrelated to hedged risk

(This is a variation of E A–2, modified to consider fair value change unrelated to hedged risk.)

LLB Industries borrowed $200,000 from Trust Bank by issuing a two-year, 10% note, with interest payable quarterly. LLB entered into a two-year interest rate swap agreement on January 1, 2018, and designated the swap as a fair value hedge. Its intent was to hedge the risk that general interest rates will decline, causing the fair value of its debt to increase. The agreement called for the company to receive payment based on a 10% fixed interest rate on a notional amount of $200,000 and to pay interest based on a floating interest rate.

Floating (LIBOR) settlement rates were 10% at January 1, 8% at March 31, and 6% at June 30, 2018. The fair values of the swap are quotes obtained from a derivatives dealer. Those quotes and the fair values of the note are as indicated below. The additional rise in the fair value of the note (higher than that of the swap) on June 30 was due to investors' perceptions that the creditworthiness of LLB was improving.

	January 1	March 31	June 30
Fair value of interest rate swap	0	$ 6,472	$ 11,394
Fair value of note payable	$200,000	$206,472	$220,000

Required:

1. Calculate the net cash settlement at June 30, 2018.
2. Prepare the journal entries on June 30, 2018, to record the interest and necessary adjustments for changes in fair value.

E A–5
Derivatives; interest rate swap; fixed rate debt; extended method

(This is a variation of Exercise A–2, modified to consider the extended method.)

On January 1, 2018, LLB Industries borrowed $200,000 from Trust Bank by issuing a two-year, 10% note, with interest payable quarterly. LLB entered into a two-year interest rate swap agreement on January 1, 2018, and designated the swap as a fair value hedge. Its intent was to hedge the risk that general interest rates will decline, causing the fair value of its debt to increase. The agreement called for the company to receive payment based on a 10% fixed interest rate on a notional amount of $200,000 and to pay interest based on a floating interest rate. The contract called for cash settlement of the net interest amount quarterly.

Floating (LIBOR) settlement rates were 10% at January 1, 8% at March 31, and 6% at June 30, 2018. The fair values of the swap are quotes obtained from a derivatives dealer. Those quotes and the fair values of the note are as follows:

	January 1	March 31	June 30
Fair value of interest rate swap	0	$ 6,472	$ 11,394
Fair value of note payable	$200,000	$206,472	$211,394

Required:

Prepare the journal entries through June 30, 2018, to record the issuance of the note, interest, and necessary adjustments for changes in fair value. Use the extended method demonstrated in Illustration A–3.

E A–6
Derivatives; interest rate swap; fixed-rate debt; fair value change unrelated to hedged

(Note: This is a variation of Exercise A–5, modified to consider fair value change unrelated to hedged risk.)

On January 1, 2018, LLB Industries borrowed $200,000 from Trust Bank by issuing a two-year, 10% note, with interest payable quarterly. LLB entered into a two-year interest rate swap agreement on January 1, 2018, and designated the swap as a fair value hedge. Its intent was to hedge the risk that general interest rates will decline, causing the fair value of its debt to increase. The agreement called for the company to receive payment based on a 10% fixed interest rate on a notional amount of $200,000 and to pay interest based on a floating interest rate. The contract called for cash settlement of the net interest amount quarterly.

Floating (LIBOR) settlement rates were 10% at January 1, 8% at March 31, and 6% June 30, 2018. The fair values of the swap are quotes obtained from a derivatives dealer. Those quotes and the fair values of the note are as indicated below. The additional rise in the fair value of the note (higher than that of the swap) on June 30 was due to investors' perceptions that the creditworthiness of LLB was improving.

	January 1	March 31	June 30
Fair value of interest rate swap	0	$ 6,472	$ 11,394
Fair value of note payable	$200,000	206,472	220,000

Required:

1. Calculate the net cash settlement at June 30, 2018.
2. Prepare the journal entries on June 30, 2018, to record the interest and necessary adjustments for changes in fair value. Use the extended method demonstrated in Illustration A–3.

Problems

connect

P A–1
Derivatives; interest rate swap

On January 1, 2018, Labtech Circuits borrowed $100,000 from First Bank by issuing a three-year, 8% note, payable on December 31, 2020. Labtech wanted to hedge the risk that general interest rates will decline, causing the fair value of its debt to increase. Therefore, Labtech entered into a three-year interest rate swap agreement on January 1, 2018, and designated the swap as a fair value hedge. The agreement called for the company to receive payment based on an 8% fixed interest rate on a notional amount of $100,000 and to pay interest based on a floating interest rate tied to LIBOR. The contract called for cash settlement of the net interest amount on December 31 of each year.

Floating (LIBOR) settlement rates were 8% at inception and 9%, 7%, and 7% at the end of 2018, 2019, and 2020, respectively. The fair values of the swap are quotes obtained from a derivatives dealer. These quotes and the fair values of the note are as follows:

	January 1	December 31		
	2018	2018	2019	2020
Fair value of interest rate swap	0	$ (1,759)	$ 935	0
Fair value of note payable	$100,000	$98,241	$100,935	$100,000

Required:

1. Calculate the net cash settlement at the end of 2018, 2019, and 2020.
2. Prepare the journal entries during 2018 to record the issuance of the note, interest, and necessary adjustments for changes in fair value.
3. Prepare the journal entries during 2019 to record interest, net cash interest settlement for the interest rate swap, and necessary adjustments for changes in fair value.
4. Prepare the journal entries during 2020 to record interest, net cash interest settlement for the interest rate swap, necessary adjustments for changes in fair value, and repayment of the debt.
5. Calculate the book values of both the swap account and the note in each of the three years.
6. Calculate the net effect on earnings of the hedging arrangement in each of the three years. (Ignore income taxes.)
7. Suppose the fair value of the note at December 31, 2018, had been $97,000 rather than $98,241, with the additional decline in fair value due to investors' perceptions that the creditworthiness of Labtech was worsening. How would that affect your entries to record changes in the fair values?

P A–2
Derivatives; interest rate swap; comprehensive

CMOS Chips is hedging a 20-year, $10 million, 7% bond payable with a 20-year interest rate swap and has designated the swap as a fair value hedge. The agreement called for CMOS to receive payment based on a 7% fixed interest rate on a notional amount of $10 million and to pay interest based on a floating interest rate tied to LIBOR. The contract calls for cash settlement of the net interest amount on December 31 of each year.

At December 31, 2018, the fair value of the derivative and of the hedged bonds has increased by $100,000 because interest rates declined during the reporting period.

Required:

1. Does CMOS have an unrealized gain or loss on the derivative for the period? On the bonds? Will earnings increase or decrease due to the hedging arrangement? Why?
2. Suppose interest rates increased, rather than decreased, causing the fair value of both the derivative and of the hedged bonds to decrease by $100,000. Would CMOS have an unrealized gain or loss on the derivative for the period? On the bonds? Would earnings increase or decrease due to the hedging arrangement? Why?
3. Suppose the fair value of the bonds at December 31, 2018, had increased by $110,000 rather than $100,000, with the additional increase in fair value due to investors' perceptions that the creditworthiness of CMOS was improving. Would CMOS have an unrealized gain or loss on the derivative for the period? On the bonds? Would earnings increase or decrease due to the hedging arrangement? Why?
4. Suppose the notional amount of the swap had been $12 million, rather than the $10 million principal amount of the bonds. As a result, at December 31, 2018, the swap's fair value had increased by $120,000 rather than $100,000. Would CMOS have an unrealized gain or loss on the derivative for the period? On the bonds? Would earnings increase or decrease due to the hedging arrangement? Why?
5. Suppose BIOS Corporation is an investor, having purchased all $10 million of the bonds issued by CMOS as described in the original situation above. BIOS is hedging its investment, classified as available-for-sale, with a 20-year interest rate swap and has designated the swap as a fair value hedge. The agreement called for BIOS to make *payment* based on a 7% fixed interest rate on a notional amount of $10 million and to *receive* interest based on a floating interest rate tied to LIBOR. Would BIOS have an unrealized gain or loss on the derivative for the period due to interest rates having declined? On the bonds? Would earnings increase or decrease due to the hedging arrangement? Why?

P A–3
Derivatives; interest rate swap; fixed rate debt; extended method

(Note: This is a variation of P A–1, modified to consider the extended method demonstrated in Illustration A–3.)

On January 1, 2018, Labtech Circuits borrowed $100,000 from First Bank by issuing a three-year, 8% note, payable on December 31, 2020. Labtech wanted to hedge the risk that general interest rates will decline, causing the fair value of its debt to increase. Therefore, Labtech entered into a three-year interest rate swap agreement on January 1, 2018, and designated the swap as a fair value hedge. The agreement called for the company to receive payment based on an 8% fixed interest rate on a notional amount of $100,000 and to pay interest based on a floating interest rate tied to LIBOR. The contract called for cash settlement of the net interest amount on December 31 of each year.

Floating (LIBOR) settlement rates were 8% at inception and 9%, 7%, and 7% at the end of 2018, 2019, and 2020, respectively. The fair values of the swap are quotes obtained from a derivatives dealer. Those quotes and the fair values of the note are as follows:

	January 1	December 31		
	2018	2018	2019	2020
Fair value of interest rate swap	0	$ (1,759)	$ 935	0
Fair value of note payable	$100,000	$ 98,241	100,935	$100,000

Required:

Use the extended method demonstrated in Illustration A–3.

1. Calculate the net cash settlement at the end of 2018, 2019, and 2020.
2. Prepare the journal entries during 2018 to record the issuance of the note, interest, and necessary adjustments for changes in fair value.
3. Prepare the journal entries during 2019 to record interest, net cash interest settlement for the interest rate swap, and necessary adjustments for changes in fair value.
4. Prepare the journal entries during 2020 to record interest, net cash interest settlement for the interest rate swap, necessary adjustments for changes in fair value, and repayment of the debt.
5. Calculate the book values of both the swap account and the note in each of the three years.
6. Calculate the net effect on earnings of the hedging arrangement in each of the three years. (Ignore income taxes.)
7. Suppose the fair value of the note at December 31, 2018, had been $97,000 rather than $98,241, with the additional decline in fair value due to investors' perceptions that the creditworthiness of Labtech was worsening. How would that affect your entries to record changes in the fair values?

Broaden Your Perspective

Apply your critical-thinking ability to the knowledge you've gained. These cases will provide you an opportunity to develop your research, analysis, judgment, and communication skills. You also will work with other students, integrate what you've learned, apply it in real-world situations, and consider its global and ethical ramifications. This practice will broaden your knowledge and further develop your decision-making abilities.

Real World Case A–1

Derivative losses; recognition in earnings

The following is an excerpt from a disclosure note of Johnson & Johnson:

---

6. Fair Value Measurements (in part)

As of January 3, 2016, the balance of deferred net losses on derivatives included in accumulated other comprehensive income was $36 million after-tax. The Company expects that substantially all of the amounts related to forward foreign exchange contracts will be reclassified into earnings over the next 12 months as a result of transactions that are expected to occur over that period.

Required:

1. Johnson & Johnson indicates that it expects that substantially all of the balance of deferred net losses on derivatives will be reclassified into earnings over the next 12 months as a result of transactions that are expected to occur over that period. What is meant by "reclassified into earnings"?
2. What type(s) of hedging transaction might be accounted for in this way?

Communication Case A–2

Derivatives; hedge accounting

A conceptual question in accounting for derivatives is this: Should gains and losses on a hedge instrument be recorded as they occur, or should they be recorded to coincide (match) with income effects of the item being hedged?

ABI Wholesalers plans to issue long-term notes in May that will replace its $20 million of 9.5% bonds when they mature in July. ABI is exposed to the risk that interest rates in July will have risen, increasing borrowing costs (reducing the selling price of its notes). To hedge that possibility, ABI entered a (Treasury bond) futures contract in May to deliver (sell) bonds in July at their *current* price.

As a result, if interest rates rise, borrowing costs will go up for ABI because it will sell notes at a higher interest cost (or lower price). But that loss will be offset (approximately) by the gain produced by being in the opposite position on Treasury bond futures.

Two opposing viewpoints are:

View 1: Gains and losses on instruments designed to hedge anticipated transactions should be recorded as they occur.

View 2: Gains and losses on instruments designed to hedge anticipated transactions should be recorded to coincide (match) with income effects of the item being hedged.

In considering this question, focus on conceptual issues regarding the practicable and theoretically appropriate treatment, unconstrained by GAAP. Your instructor will divide the class into two to six groups, depending on the size of the class. The mission of your group is to reach consensus on the appropriate accounting for the gains and losses on instruments designed to hedge anticipated transactions.

Required:

1. Each group member should deliberate the situation independently and draft a tentative argument prior to the class session for which the case is assigned.
2. In class, each group will meet for 10 to 15 minutes in different areas of the classroom. During that meeting, group members will take turns sharing their suggestions for the purpose of arriving at a single group treatment.
3. After the allotted time, a spokesperson for each group (selected during the group meetings) will share the group's solution with the class. The goal of the class is to incorporate the views of each group into a consensus approach to the situation.

Real World Case A–3
Researching the way interest rate futures prices are quoted on the Chicago Mercantile Exchange; retrieving information from the Internet

The Chicago Mercantile Exchange, or Merc, at 30 S. Wacker Drive in Chicago, is the world's largest financial exchange, an international marketplace enabling institutions and businesses to trade futures and options contracts including currencies, interest rates, stock indexes, and agricultural commodities.

Required:

1. Access the Merc on the Internet. The web address is www.cmegroup.com.
2. Access the daily settlements within the site. In the Search box, enter "U.S. Treasury Bond." Choose U.S. Treasury Bond.
3. What are the settlement prices for September futures contracts?

Research Case A–4
Issue related to the derivatives standard; research an article

In an effort to keep up with the rapidly changing global financial markets, the FASB issued standards on accounting for and disclosure of derivative financial instruments. A *Journal of Accountancy* article that discusses this standard is "The Decision on Derivatives," by Arlette C. Wilson, Gary Waters, and Barry J. Bryan, November 1998.

Required:

On the Internet, go to the AICPA site at www.aicpa.org and find the article mentioned.

1. What are the primary problems or issues the FASB attempts to address regarding accounting for derivative financial instruments?
2. In considering the issues, the FASB made four fundamental decisions that became the cornerstones of the statement issued in 1998. What are those fundamental decisions? Which do you think is most critical to fair financial reporting?

APPENDIX

B GAAP Comprehensive Case

Target Corporation prepares its financial statements according to U.S. GAAP. Target's financial statements and disclosure notes for the year ended January 30, 2016, are available in Connect. This material is also available under the Investor Relations link at the company's website (www.target.com). This case addresses a variety of characteristics of financial statements prepared using U.S. GAAP. Questions are grouped in parts according to various sections of the textbook.

Part A: Financial Statements, Income Measurement, and Current Assets

A1. By what name does Target label its balance sheet?

A2. What amounts did Target report for the following items on January 30, 2016?

- a. Current assets
- b. Long-term assets
- c. Total assets
- d. Current liabilities
- e. Long-term liabilities
- f. Total liabilities
- g. Total shareholders' equity

A3. What was Target's largest current asset? What was its largest current liability?

A4. Compute Target's current ratio and debt to equity ratio in 2016?

A5. Assuming Target's industry had an average current ratio of 1.0 and an average debt to equity ratio of 2.5, comment on Target's liquidity and long-term solvency.

A6. Why do you think Target has chosen to have its fiscal year end on January 30, as opposed to December 31?

A7. Regarding Target's audit report:

- a. Who is Target's auditor?
- b. Did Target receive a "clean" (unmodified) audit opinion?

A8. By what name does Target label its income statement?

A9. What amounts did Target report for the following items for the year ended January 30, 2016?

- a. Sales
- b. Gross margin
- c. Earnings from continuing operations before income taxes
- d. Net earnings from continuing operations
- e. Net earnings

A10. What was Target's basic earnings per share for the year ended January 30, 2016?

A11. What additional items, if any, does Target report as part of its comprehensive income?

A12. Does Target prepare the statement of cash flows using the direct method or the indirect method?

A13. Which is higher, net earnings or operating cash flows? Which line item is the biggest reason for this difference? Explain why.

A14. Note 13 provides information on Target's current assets. Assume all prepaid expenses are for prepaid insurance and that insurance expense comprises $50 million of the $14,665 million of Selling, general and administrative expenses reported in the income statement for the year ended January 30, 2016. How much cash did Target pay for insurance coverage during the year? Prepare the adjusting entry Target would make to record all insurance expense for the year. What would be the effect on the income statement and balance sheet if Target didn't record an adjusting entry for prepaid expenses?

A15. What are the largest investing cash flow and the largest financing cash flow reported by the company for the year ended January 30, 2016?

A16. On what line of Target's income statement is revenue reported? What was the amount of revenue Target reported for the fiscal year ended January 30, 2016?

A17. Disclosure Note 2 indicates that Target generally records revenue in retail stores at the point of sale. Does that suggest that Target generally records revenue at a point in time or over a period of time? Explain.

A18. Disclosure Note 2 indicates that customers ("guests") can return some merchandise within 90 days of purchase and can return other merchandise within a year of purchase. How are Target's revenue and net income affected by returns, given that it does not know at the time a sale is made which items will be returned?

A19. Disclosure Note 2 indicates that "Commissions earned on sales generated by leased departments are included within sales and were $37 million . . . in 2015. . ." Do you think it likely that Target is accounting for those sales as a principal or an agent? Explain.

A20. Disclosure Note 2 discusses Target's accounting for gift card sales. Does Target recognize revenue when it sells a gift card to a customer? If not, when does it recognize revenue? Explain.

A21. Disclosure Note 4 discussed how Target accounts for consideration received from vendors, which they call "vendor income." Does that consideration produce revenue for Target? Does that consideration produce revenue for Target's vendors? Explain.

A22. What is Target's policy for designating investments as cash equivalents?

A23. What is Target's balance of cash equivalents for the fiscal year ended January 30, 2016?

A24. What is Target's policy with respect to accounting for merchandise returns?

A25. Does Target have accounts receivable? Speculate as to why it has the balance that it has. (Hint, see Disclosure Notes 9, 11 and 13.)

A26. What inventory method(s) does Target use to value its inventories?

A27. In addition to the purchase price, what additional expenditures does the company include in the initial cost of merchandise?

A28. Calculate the gross profit ratio and the inventory turnover ratio for the fiscal year ended January 30, 2016. Compare Target's ratios with the industry averages of 24.5% and 7.1 times.

A29. What indexes does Target use to measure the LIFO provision?

A30. Why does Target feel that the retail inventory method will result in inventory being valued at the lower of cost or market?

A31. How does Target account for inventory when arrangements are made with vendors whereby Target does not purchase or pay for merchandise until the merchandise is ultimately sold to a customer?

Part B: Property, Plant, and Equipment and Intangible Assets

B1. What categories of property, plant, equipment, and intangible assets does Target report in its January 30, 2016, balance sheet?

B2. How much cash was used in the fiscal year ended January 30, 2016, to purchase property and equipment? How does this compare with purchases in previous years?

B3. Do you think a company like Target would have significant research and development costs or capitalized interest related to self-constructed assets? Explain.

B4. What is Target's fixed-asset turnover ratio for the fiscal year ended January 30, 2016? What is the ratio intended to measure?

B5. Compare the property and equipment listed in the balance sheet with the list in Note 14. What are the estimated useful lives for recording depreciation? Why is land not listed in Note 14?

B6. Which depreciation method does Target use for property and equipment for financial reporting? Which depreciation method is used for tax purposes? Why might these methods be chosen?

B7. How does Target record repairs and maintenance expense?

B8. How does Target account for impairment of property and equipment? Were any impairments recorded for the year ended January 30, 2016? If so, what was the amount, and what were the reasons for the impairments?

B9. From Notes 15 and 16, what was the amount of intangible assets for the year ended January 30, 2016? Were any impairments related to intangible assets recorded for the year ended January 30, 2016? If so, what was the amount and, what were the reasons for the impairments?

Part C: Investments

Target does not have investments in stock or bonds. However, **CVS Health Corp.**, which purchased Target's pharmacy and clinical business during 2015, does have some investments. Access CVS's 2015 10K (issued on February 9, 2016) at **investors.cvshealth.com** to answer the following questions:

C1. CVS indicates in Note 1 that it has some short-term investments that consist of certificates of deposit (CDs).
   a. How has CVS classified those CDs for accounting purposes?
   b. Per CVS's balance sheet, what was the balance in CVS's short-term investments as of December 31, 2015 and December 31, 2014?
   c. Per CVS's statement of cash flows, what cash transactions affected short-term investments during 2015?
   d. Prepare a T-account that summarizes transactions affecting CVS's short-term investments during 2015. Speculate as to the explanation for any "plug" figure necessary to make the T-account balance.

C2. Per Note 1, CVS has equity-method investments in SureScripts, LLC and in Heartland Healthcare Services. CVS indicates that those investments are immaterial for the year ended December 31, 2015. Assuming that the Heartland investment is material:
   a. How would Heartland's earnings affect CVS's income statement?
   b. How would Heartland's earnings affect CVS's balance sheet?

Part D: Liabilities

D1. Target's Consolidated Statement of Financial Position (its balance sheet) discloses its current assets and current liabilities.
   a. What are the four components of Target's current liabilities?
   b. Are current assets sufficient to cover current liabilities? What is the current ratio for the year ended January 30, 2016? How does the ratio compare with the prior year?
   c. Why might a company want to avoid having its current ratio be too low? Too high?

D2. Disclosure Note 2 discusses Target's accounting for gift card sales. Disclosure Note 18 indicates the amount of gift card liability that is recognized in Target's balance sheet.
   a. By how much did Target's gift card liability change between January 30, 2016 and January 31, 2015?

b. How would the following affect Target's gift card liability (indicate "increase," "decrease," or "no change" for each):
   i. Sale of a gift card
   ii. Redemption of a gift card (the holder using it to acquire goods or services)
   iii. Increase in breakage estimated for gift cards already sold

D3. Disclosure Note 19 discusses Target's accounting for a data breach in 2013, when "an intruder stole certain payment card and other guest information from our network."
   a. What is Target's approach for accruing losses for litigation claims associated with the data breach? Is their approach appropriate?
   b. Prepare a journal entry to record Target's recognition of new expenses associated with the data breach litigation for the fiscal year ended January 30, 2016.
   c. Prepare a journal entry to record Target's reduction of its liability associated with the data breach litigation for the fiscal year ended January 30, 2016.

D4. Calculate the debt to equity ratio for Target at January 30, 2016. The average ratio for companies in the General Retailers industry sector in a comparable time period was 1.6. What information does your calculation provide an investor?

D5. Calculate Target's times interest earned ratio for the year ended January 30, 2016. The coverage for companies in the General Retailers industry sector in a comparable time period was 10.6. What does your calculation indicate about Target's risk?

Part E: Leases, Income Taxes, and Pensions

E1. Refer to Disclosure Note 22 following Target's financial statements. What is the amount reported for "capital" leases (shown as the present value of minimum lease payments)? What is the total of those lease payments? What accounts for the difference between the two amounts?

E2. What is the total of the operating lease payments? New lease accounting guidance (discussed in Chapter 15) will require companies to report operating leases at present value, as well as capital leases (now called finance leases). If Target had used the new lease accounting guidance in its 2016 financial statements, what would be the amount reported for operating leases? Hint: Assume the payments "after 2020" are to be paid evenly over a 16 years period and all payments are at the end of years indicated. Target indicates elsewhere in its financial statements that 6% is an appropriate discount rate for its leases.

E3. In its Analysis of "Financial Condition: New Accounting Pronouncements," Target's financial statements for the year ended January 30, 2016, the company indicates that:

> In February 2016, the FASB issued ASU No. 2016-02, Leases, to require organizations that lease assets to recognize the rights and obligations created by those leases on the balance sheet. The new standard is effective in 2019, with early adoption permitted. We are currently evaluating the effect the new standard will have on our financial statements.

Refer to Note 22: Leases. When Target applies the new standard, what will be the primary effect on its financial statements? Explain.

E4. From the income statement, determine the income tax expense for the most recent year. Tie that number to the second table in Disclosure Note 23, "Provision for Income Taxes," and prepare a summary journal entry that records Target's tax expense from continuing operations for the year ended January 30, 2016.

E5. Focusing on the third table in Disclosure Note 23, "Net Deferred Tax Asset/ (Liability)," calculate the change in net deferred tax assets or liability. By how much did that amount change? To what extent did you account for that change in the journal entry you wrote for the first requirement of this case? List possible causes of any difference.

E6. Target's Note 23 indicates that "We have not recorded deferred taxes when earnings from foreign operations are considered to be indefinitely invested outside the U.S. These accumulated net earnings relate to certain ongoing operations and were

$685 million at January 30, 2016 and $328 million at January 31, 2015." Are these amounts treated as temporary or permanent differences by Target? If Target decides to repatriate earnings in the future, what will be the effect on net income in the year of the repatriation?

E7. What is Target's liability for unrecognized tax benefits as of January 30, 2016? If Target were to prevail in court and realize $50 million more in tax savings than it thought more likely than not to occur, what would be the effect on the liability for unrecognized tax benefits and on net income?

E8. What were the changes in Target's Projected Benefits Obligation in the fiscal years ended January 30, 2016 (fiscal 2015) and January 31, 2015 (fiscal 2014), for its qualified pension plans?

E9. What were the changes in Target's Pension Plan Assets in the fiscal years ended January 30, 2016 and January 31, 2015, for its qualified pension plans?

E10. Were these pension plans overfunded or underfunded for the fiscal years ended January 30, 2016 and January 31, 2015?

E11. What were the components of Target's Pension Expense in the fiscal years ended January 30, 2016, January 31, 2015, and February 1, 2014?

Part F: Shareholders' Equity and Additional Financial Reporting Issues

F1. Refer to Target's Consolidated Statements of Shareholders' Investment. What are the five types of events and transactions that affected one or more of the Shareholders' Investment accounts in the year ended January 30, 2016?

F2. Note 25, "Share Repurchase," provides the information we need to reconstruct the journal entry that summarizes Target's share repurchases in the year ended January 30, 2016. Provide that entry. Does Target account for share repurchases as treasury stock or retired shares? Explain.

F3. Over how many years is the compensation associated with Target's share-based awards expensed?

F4. Based on the fair value of the awards, what was Target's primary form of share-based compensation for the year ended January 30, 2016?

F5. If projecting Target's earnings per share based solely on EPS reported over the most recent three years, would you project increasing or decreasing EPS?

F6. How many shares were included in diluted earnings per share, but not basic earnings per share, due to share-based compensation awards?

F7. Refer to Target's financial statements for the year ended January 30, 2016. Note 12 provides information on Target's inventories. What method does Target use to report most of its inventories? If Target changed that method to another method, what are the steps Target would take to account for and report the change?

F8. Suppose that Target uses FIFO costing method but decided to change to the LIFO method. What are the steps Target would take to account for and report the change?

F9. Target's cash flows from its operations over the previous three years have significantly exceeded its net income. Without regard to Target specifically, explain the difference between net income and the cash flows from operating activities.

F10. Why did Target add $2.213 million in the determination of cash flows from operating activities for depreciation and amortization for the year ended January 30, 2016?

F11. A contributor to the difference in Target's net income and cash flows from operating activities and net income in each of the three years presented is a sizable increase in the amount Target owes its suppliers. If Target had used the direct rather than the indirect method of reporting operating activities, how would this reduction in accounts payable have affected cash from operating activities?

F12 Cash outflows for financing activities during each of the three years presented exceeded cash inflows from financing activities. In fact, investing activities also produced net cash outflows in two of the three years. How is that possible? What is the major contributor from year to year in the amount of cash used in financing activities? What are the next two highest contributors to that difference?

F13. Some transactions that don't increase or decrease cash must be reported in conjunction with a statement of cash flows. What activity of this type did Target report during each of the three years presented? What are two other such activities that some companies might report?

APPENDIX C

IFRS Comprehensive Case

Air France–KLM (AF), a Franco-Dutch company, prepares its financial statements according to International Financial Reporting Standards. AF's financial statements and disclosure notes for the year ended December 31, 2013, are available in Connect. This material is also available under the Finance link at the company's website (www.airfranceklm.com). This case addresses a variety of characteristics of financial statements prepared using IFRS, often comparing and contrasting those attributes of statements prepared under U.S. GAAP. Questions are grouped in parts according to various sections of the textbook.

Part A: Financial Statements, Income Measurement, and Current Assets

A1. What amounts did AF report for the following items for the fiscal year ended December 31, 2015?

a. Total revenues
b. Income from current operations
c. Net income or net loss (AF equity holders)
d. Total assets
e. Total equity

A2. What was AF's basic earnings or loss per share for the year ended December 31, 2015?

A3. Examine Note 4.1.1 of AF's annual report. What accounting principles were used to prepare AF's financial statements? Under those accounting principles, could AF's financial information differ from that of a company that exactly followed IFRS as published by the IASB? Explain.

A4. Refer to AF's balance sheet and compare it to the balance sheet presentation in Illustration 2–14. What differences do you see in the format of the two balance sheets?

A5. What differences do you see in the terminology used in the two balance sheets?

A6. How does AF classify operating expenses in its income statement? How are these expenses typically classified in a U.S. company's income statement?

A7. How does AF classify interest paid, interest received, and dividends received in its statement of cash flows? What other alternatives, if any, does the company have for the classification of these items? How are these items classified under U.S. GAAP?

A8. In Note 4.6, AF indicates that "Sales related to air transportation are recognized when the transportation service is provided so passenger and freight tickets are consequently recorded as 'Deferred revenue upon issuance.'"

a. Examine AF's balance sheet. What is the total amount of deferred revenue on ticket sales as of December 31, 2015?
b. When transportation services are provided with respect to the deferred revenue on ticket sales, what journal entry would AF make to reduce deferred revenue?
c. Does AF's treatment of deferred revenue under IFRS appear consistent with how these transactions would be handled under U.S. GAAP? Explain.

A9. AF has a frequent flyer program, "Flying Blue," which allows members to acquire "miles" as they fly on Air France or partner airlines that are redeemable for free flights or other benefits.

a. How does AF account for these miles?

b. Does AF report any liability associated with these miles as of December 31, 2015?
c. Although AF's 2015 annual report was issued prior to the effective date of ASU No. 2014-09, consider whether the manner in which AF accounts for its frequent flier program appears consistent with the revenue recognition guidelines included in the ASU.

A10. In Note 4.11, AF describes how it values trade receivables. How does the approach used by AF compare to U.S. GAAP?

A11. In Note 26, AF reconciles the beginning and ending balances of its valuation allowance for trade accounts receivable. Prepare a T-account for the valuation allowance and include entries for the beginning and ending balances and any reconciling items that affected the account during 2015.

A12. Examine Note 28. Does AF have any bank overdrafts? If so, are the overdrafts shown in the balance sheet the same way they would be shown under U.S. GAAP?

A13. What method does the company use to value its inventory? What other alternatives are available under IFRS? Under U.S. GAAP?

A14. AF's inventories are valued at the lower of cost or net realizable value. Does this approach differ from U.S. GAAP?

Part B: Property, Plant, and Equipment and Intangible Assets

B1. AF's property, plant, and equipment is reported at cost. The company has a policy of not revaluing property, plant, and equipment. Suppose AF decided to revalue its flight equipment on December 31, 2015, and that the fair value of the equipment on that date was €10,000 million. Prepare the journal entry to record the revaluation, assuming that the journal entry to record annual depreciation had already been recorded. (Hint: you will need to locate the original cost and accumulated depreciation of the equipment at the end of the year in the appropriate disclosure note.)

B2. Under U.S. GAAP, what alternatives do companies have to value their property, plant, and equipment?

B3. AF calculates depreciation of plant and equipment on a straight-line basis, over the useful life of the asset. Describe any differences between IFRS and U.S. GAAP in the calculation of depreciation.

B4. When does AF test for the possible impairment of fixed assets? How does this approach differ from U.S. GAAP?

B5. Describe the approach AF uses to determine fixed asset impairment losses. (Hint: see Note 4.14.) How does this approach differ from U.S. GAAP?

B6. The following is included in AF's Disclosure Note 4.13: "Intangible assets are recorded at initial cost less accumulated amortization and any accumulated impairment losses." Assume that on December 31, 2015, AF decided to revalue its Other intangible assets (see Note 18), and that the fair value on that date was determined to be €500 million. Amortization expense for the year already has been recorded. Prepare the journal entry to record the revaluation.

Part C: Investments

C1. Read Notes 24 and 36.4. Focusing on investments accounted for at fair value through profit and loss (FVTPL):
a. As of December 31, 2015, what is the total balance of those investments in the balance sheet?
b. How much of that balance is classified as current and how much as noncurrent?
c. How much of the fair value of those investments is accounted for using level 1, level 2, and level 3 inputs of the fair value hierarchy? Given that information, assess the reliability (representational faithfulness) of this fair value estimate.

C2. Complete C1 again, but for investments accounted for as available for sale.

C3. Read Notes 4.3. and 22.

a. When AF can exercise significant influence over an investee, what accounting approach does it use to account for the investment? How does AF determine if it can exercise significant influence?

b. If AF is involved in a joint venture, what accounting approach does it use to account for the investment?

c. What is the carrying value of AF's equity-method investments in its December 31, 2015, balance sheet?

d. How did AF's equity-method investments affect AF's 2015 net income from continuing operations?

Part D: Liabilities

D1. Read Notes 4.6 and 35. What do you think gave rise to total deferred income of €249 as of the end of fiscal 2015? Would transactions of this type be handled similarly under U.S. GAAP?

D2. Is the threshold for recognizing a provision under IFRS different than it is under U.S. GAAP? Explain.

D3. Note 32 lists "other provisions."

a. Do the beginning and ending balances of total provisions and retirement benefits shown in Note 32 for fiscal 2015 tie to the balance sheet? By how much has the total amount of AF's "other provisions" increased or decreased during fiscal 2015?

b. Write journal entries for the following changes in the litigation provision that occurred during fiscal 2015, assuming any amounts recorded on the income statement are recorded as "provision expense" and any use of provisions is paid for in cash. In each case, provide a brief explanation of the event your journal entry is capturing.

i. New provision.

ii. Use of provision.

c. Is AF's treatment of litigation provision under IFRS similar to how it would be treated under U.S. GAAP?

D4. Note 32.2 lists a number of contingent liabilities. Are amounts for those items recognized as a liability on AF's balance sheet? Explain.

D5. Examine the long-term borrowings in AF's balance sheet and the related note (33.2.2). Note that AF has convertible bonds outstanding that it issued in 2013. Prepare the journal entry AF would use to record the issue of convertible bonds. Prepare the journal entry AF would use to record the issue of the convertible bonds if AF used U.S. GAAP.

D6. AF does not elect the fair value option (FVO) to report its financial liabilities. Examine Note 36.3, "Market value of financial instruments." If the company had elected the FVO for all of its debt measured at amortized cost, what would be the balance at December 31, 2015, in the fair value adjustment account?

Part E: Leases, Income Taxes, and Pensions

E1. In Note 4, "Summary of accounting policies," part 4.14, "Leases," AF states that "leases are classified as finance leases when the lease arrangement transfers substantially all the risks and rewards of ownership to the lessee." Is this the policy companies using U.S. GAAP follow?

E2. Is this the policy AF will follow when it begins applying the new lease guidance in the 2015 update to *IFRS 17*? Explain.

E3. Where in its December 31, 2015, balance sheet does AF report deferred taxes? How does this approach differ from the way deferred taxes are reported using U.S. GAAP? Using the Internet, determine how deferred taxes would be reported using IFRS at the time of your research. Explain why that approach might differ from the way AF reported deferred taxes at December 31, 2015.

E4. Here's an excerpt from one of AF's notes to its financial statements:

> **Deferred taxes (in part)**
> The Group records deferred taxes using the balance sheet liability method, providing for any temporary differences between the carrying amounts of assets and liabilities for financial reporting purposes and the amounts used for taxation purposes, except for exceptions described in IAS 12 "Income taxes." The tax rates used are those enacted or substantively enacted at the balance sheet date.

Is this policy consistent with U.S. GAAP? Explain.

E5. Below is an excerpt from one of AF's notes to its financial statements:

> **Deferred taxes (in part)**
> Deferred tax assets related to temporary differences and tax losses carried forward are recognized only to the extent it is probable that a future taxable profit will be available against which the asset can be utilized at the tax entity level.

Is this policy consistent with U.S. GAAP? Explain.

E6. Look at Note 31.2, "Retirement Benefits." AF incorporates estimates regarding staff turnover, life expectancy, salary increase, retirement age, and discount rates. How did AF report changes in these assumptions? Is that reporting method the same or different from the way we report changes under U.S. GAAP?

E7. AF does not report remeasurement gains and losses in its income statement. Where did AF report these amounts? Is that reporting method the same or different from the way we report pension expense under U.S. GAAP?

E8. See Note 23. Did AF report Net interest cost or Net interest income in 2015? How is that amount determined?

Part F: Shareholders' Equity and Additional Financial Reporting Issues

F1. AF lists four items in the shareholders' equity section of its balance sheet. If AF used U.S. GAAP, what would be the likely account titles for the first and fourth of those components?

F2. Locate Note 29.5 in AF's financial statements. What items comprise "Reserves and retained earnings," as reported in the balance sheet? If Air France-KLM used U.S. GAAP, what would be different for the reporting of these items?

F3. Describe the apparent differences in the order of presentation of the components of liabilities and shareholders' equity between IFRS as applied by AF and a typical balance sheet prepared in accordance with U.S. GAAP.

F4. AF provides share-based compensation in the form of PPSs, Phantom Performance Shares. Recipients receive compensation in what form? How are such plans reported in the balance sheet? 2015? [Hint: See Note 30, "Share-Based Compensation."] Are AF's share PPSs cliff vesting or graded vesting? How does accounting differ between U.S. GAAP and IFRS for graded-vesting plans?

F5. What amount(s) of earnings per share did AF report in its income statement for the year ended December 31, 2015? If AF used U.S. GAAP, would it have reported EPS using the same classification?

F6. Refer to AF's disclosure notes, in particular Note 2, "Restatement of Accounts 2014." For the three changes in accounting principle reported in the note, does AF account for the changes prospectively or retrospectively? Is this the same approach AF would follow if using U.S. GAAP?

F7. For the change described in 2.1, which, if any, account balances required adjustment?

F8. What are the primary classifications into which AF's cash inflows and cash outflows are separated? Is this classification the same as or different from cash flow statements prepared in accordance with U.S. GAAP?

F9. How are cash inflows from dividends and interest and cash outflows for dividends and interest classified in AF's cash flow statements? Is this classification the same as or different from cash flow statements prepared in accordance with U.S. GAAP?

Glossary

Accounting equation the process used to capture the effect of economic events; Assets = Liabilities + Owner's Equity.

Accounting Principles Board (APB) the second private sector body delegated the task of setting accounting standards.

Accounts storage areas used to keep track of increases and decreases in financial position elements.

Accounts payable obligations to suppliers of merchandise or of services purchased on open account.

Accounts receivable aging schedule calculating the necessary allowance for uncollectible accounts by applying different percentages to accounts receivable balances depending on the length of time outstanding.

Accounts receivable receivables resulting from the sale of goods or services on account.

Accretion expense the increase in an asset retirement obligation that accrues as an operating expense.

Accrual accounting measurement of the entity's accomplishments and resource sacrifices during the period, regardless of when cash is received or paid.

Accruals when the cash flow comes after either expense or revenue recognition.

Accrued interest interest that has accrued since the last interest date.

Accrued liabilities expenses already incurred but not yet paid (accrued expenses).

Accrued receivables recognition of revenue earned before cash is received.

Accumulated benefit obligation (ABO) the discounted present value of estimated retirement benefits earned so far by employees, applying the plan's pension formula using existing compensation levels.

Accumulated other comprehensive income amount of other comprehensive income (nonowner changes in equity other than net income) accumulated over the current and prior periods.

Acid-test ratio current assets, excluding inventories and prepaid items, divided by current liabilities.

Acquisition costs the amounts paid to acquire the rights to explore for undiscovered natural resources or to extract proven natural resources.

Activity-based method allocation of an asset's cost base using a measure of the asset's input or output.

Actuary a professional trained in a particular branch of statistics and mathematics to assess the various uncertainties and to estimate the company's obligation to employees in connection with its pension plan.

Additions the adding of a new major component to an existing asset.

Adjusted trial balance trial balance after adjusting entries have been recorded.

Adjusting entries internal transactions recorded at the end of any period when financial statements are prepared.

Advance payment payment made at the beginning of the lease that represents prepaid rent

Agent facilitates transfers of goods and services between sellers and customers.

Allocation method the pattern in which the allocation base is expected to be consumed.

Allowance for sales returns contra account to accounts receivable that reduces the receivables balance for estimated future returns.

Allowance for uncollectible accounts contra account that reduces accounts receivable to the net amount expected to be collected. Also called the allowance for bad debts, the allowance for doubtful accounts, or the allowance for credit losses.

Allowance method recording bad debt expense and reducing accounts receivable indirectly by crediting a contra account (allowance for uncollectible accounts) to accounts receivable for an estimate of the amount that eventually will prove uncollectible.

American Institute of Accountants (AIA) national organization of professional public accountants.

American Institute of Certified Public Accountants (AICPA) national organization of professional public accountants.

Amortization cost allocation for intangibles.

Annual bonuses one-time payments in addition to normal salary, typically tied to performance of the individual or company during a period

Annuity cash flows received or paid in the same amount each period.

Annuity due cash flows occurring at the beginning of each period.

Antidilutive securities the effect of the conversion or exercise of potential common shares would be to increase, rather than decrease, EPS.

Articles of incorporation statement of the nature of the firm's business activities, the shares to be issued, and the composition of the initial board of directors.

Asset retirement obligations (AROs) obligations associated with the disposition of an operational asset.

Asset turnover ratio measure of a company's efficiency in using assets to generate revenue.

Asset/liability approach recognition and measurement of assets and liabilities drives revenue and expense recognition.

Assigning using receivables as collateral for loans; nonpayment of a debt will require the proceeds from collecting the assigned receivables to go directly toward repayment of the debt.

Auditors independent intermediaries who help ensure that management has appropriately applied GAAP in preparing the company's financial statements.

Auditor's report report issued by CPAs who audit the financial statements that informs users of the audit findings.

Average collection period indication of the average age of accounts receivable.

Average cost method assumes cost of goods sold and ending inventory consist of a mixture of all the goods available for sale.

Average days in inventory indicates the average number of days it normally takes to sell inventory.

Balance sheet a position statement that presents an organized list of assets, liabilities, and equity at a particular point in time.

Balance sheet approach determining bad debt expense by estimating the appropriate carrying value of accounts receivable to be reported in the balance sheet and then adjusting the allowance for uncollectible accounts as necessary to reach that carrying value.

Bank reconciliation comparison of the bank balance with the balance in the company's own records.

Basic EPS computed by dividing income available to common stockholders (net income less any preferred stock dividends) by the weighted-average number of common shares outstanding for the period.

Bill-and-hold A *bill-and-hold* arrangement occurs when a customer purchases goods but requests that the seller retain physical possession of the goods until a later date.

Billings on construction contract contra account to the asset construction in progress recognizing that a customer has been billed for work performed; subtracted from construction in progress to determine balance sheet presentation.

Board of directors establishes corporate policies and appoints officers who manage the corporation.

Bond indenture document that describes specific promises made to bondholders.

Bonds a form of debt consisting of separable units (bonds) that obligates the issuing corporation to repay a stated amount at a specified maturity date and to pay interest to bondholders between the issue date and maturity.

Book value assets minus liabilities as shown in the balance sheet.

Callable allows the issuing company to buy back, or call, outstanding bonds from the bondholders before their scheduled maturity date.

Capital budgeting the process of evaluating the purchase of operational assets.

Capital leases installment purchases/sales that are formulated outwardly as leases.

Capital markets mechanisms that foster the allocation of resources efficiently.

Cash currency and coins, balances in checking accounts, and items acceptable for deposit in these accounts, such as checks and money orders received from customers.

Cash basis accounting/net operating cash flow difference between cash receipts and cash disbursements during a reporting period from transactions related to providing goods and services to customers.

Cash disbursements journal record of cash disbursements.

Cash discounts sales discounts; represent reductions not in the selling price of a good or service but in the amount to be paid by a credit customer if paid within a specific period of time.

Cash equivalents short-term, highly liquid investments that can be readily converted to cash with little risk of loss.

Cash flows from financing activities both inflows and outflows of cash resulting from the external financing of a business.

Cash flows from investing activities both outflows and inflows of cash caused by the acquisition and disposition of assets.

Cash flows from operating activities both inflows and outflows of cash that result from activities reported on the income statement.

Cash receipts journal record of cash receipts.

Certified Public Accountants (CPAs) licensed individuals who can represent that the financial statements have been audited in accordance with generally accepted auditing standards.

Change in accounting estimate a change in an estimate when new information comes to light.

Change in accounting principle switch by a company from one accounting method to another.

Change in reporting entity presentation of consolidated financial statements in place of statements of individual companies, or a change in the specific companies that constitute the group for which consolidated or combined statements are prepared.

Closing process the temporary accounts are reduced to zero balances, and these temporary account balances are closed (transferred) to retained earnings to reflect the changes that have occurred in that account during the period.

Commercial paper unsecured notes sold in minimum denominations of $25,000, with maturities ranging from 30 to 270 days.

Committee on Accounting Procedure (CAP) first private sector body that was delegated the task of setting accounting standards.

Comparability the ability to help users see similarities and differences among events and conditions.

Comparative financial statements corresponding financial statements from the previous years accompanying the issued financial statements.

Compensating balance specified balance (usually some percentage of the committee amount) a borrower of a loan is asked to maintain in a low-interest or noninterest-bearing account at the bank.

Complete depiction is complete if it includes all information necessary for faithful representation.

Complex capital structure potential common shares are outstanding.

Composite depreciation method physically dissimilar assets are aggregated to gain the convenience of group depreciation.

Compound interest interest computed not only on the initial investment but also on the accumulated interest in previous periods.

Comprehensive income traditional net income plus other nonowner changes in equity.

Conceptual framework deals with theoretical and conceptual issues and provides an underlying structure for current and future accounting and reporting standards.

Confirmatory value confirmation of investor expectations about future cash-generating ability.

Conservatism practice followed in an attempt to ensure that uncertainties and risks inherent in business situations are adequately considered.

Consignment the consignor physically transfers the goods to the other company (the consignee), but the consignor retains legal title.

Consistency permits valid comparisons between different periods.

Consolidated financial statements combination of the separate financial statements of the parent and subsidiary each period into a single aggregate set of financial statements, as if there were only one company.

Construction in progress asset account equivalent to the asset work-in-progress inventory in a manufacturing company.

Contingently issuable shares additional shares of common stock to be issued, contingent on the occurrence of some future circumstance.

Contract an agreement that creates legally enforceable rights and obligations; can be explicit or implicit.

Contract asset asset recognizing that a seller has a conditional right to receive payment after satisfying a performance obligation.

Contract liability a label given to deferred revenue or unearned revenue accounts.

Control usually an investor can control the investee if it owns more than 50% of the investee's voting shares.

Conventional retail method applying the retail inventory method in such a way that LCM is approximated.

Convertible bonds bonds for which bondholders have the option to convert the bonds into shares of stock.

Copyright exclusive right of protection given to a creator of a published work, such as a song, painting, photograph, or book.

Corporation dominant form of business organization that acquires capital from investors in exchange for ownership interest and from creditors by borrowing.

Correction of an error an adjustment a company makes due to an error made.

Cost effectiveness the perceived benefit of increased decision usefulness exceeds the anticipated cost of providing that information.

Cost of goods sold cost of the inventory sold during the period.

Cost recovery method deferral of all gross profit recognition until the cost of the item sold has been recovered.

Cost-to-retail percentage ratio found by dividing goods available for sale at cost by goods available for sale at retail.

Coupon bonds name of the owner was not registered; the holder actually clipped an attached coupon and redeemed it in accordance with instructions on the indenture.

Credit losses losses due to failure by customers to pay amounts owed for purchase of goods or services; also called bad debts, impairments of receivables, and uncollectible accounts.

Credits represent the right side of the account.

Cumulative if the specified dividend is not paid in a given year, the unpaid dividends accumulate and must be made up in a later dividend year before any dividends are paid on common shares.

Current assets includes assets that are cash, will be converted into cash, or will be used up within one year or the operating cycle, whichever is longer.

Current costs the costs that would be incurred to purchase or reproduce an asset.

Current expected credit loss (CECL) model a model used to estimate credit losses (bad debts) for receivables and for debt investments that are accounted for as held to maturity or available for sale.

Current liabilities expected to require the use of current assets for payment, and usually are payable within one year.

Current maturities of long-term debt current installment due on long-term debt, reported as a current liability.

Current ratio current assets divided by current liabilities.

Date of record specific date stated as to when the determination will be made of the recipient of the dividend.

Debenture bond secured only by the "full faith and credit" of the issuing corporation.

Debits represent the left side of the account.

Debt issue costs costs of issuing debt securities are called "debt issue costs" and are accounted for the same way as bond discount.

Debt to equity ratio compares resources provided by creditors with resources provided by owners.

Decision usefulness the quality of being useful to decision making.

Default risk a company's ability to pay its obligations when they come due.

Deferred annuity first cash flow occurs more than the one period after the date the agreement begins.

Deferred revenues cash received from a customer for goods or services to be provided in a future period.

Deferred tax asset taxes to be saved in the future when future deductible amounts reduce taxable income (when the temporary differences reverse).

Deferred tax liability taxes to be paid in the future when future taxable amounts become taxable (when the temporary differences reverse).

Deficit debit balance in retained earnings.

Defined benefit pension plans fixed retirement benefits defined by a designated formula, based on employees' years of service and annual compensation.

Defined contribution pension plans fixed annual contributions to a pension fund; employees choose where funds are invested—usually stocks or fixed-income securities.

Depletion allocation of the cost of natural resources.

Depreciable base cost of the asset expected to be consumed during its service life.

Depreciation cost allocation for plant and equipment.

Derivatives financial instruments usually created to hedge against risks created by other financial instruments or by transactions that have yet to occur but are anticipated and that "derive" their values or contractually required cash flows from some other security or index.

Detachable stock purchase warrants the investor has the option to purchase a stated number of shares of common stock at a specified option price, within a given period of time.

Development costs for natural resources, costs incurred after the resource has been discovered but before production begins.

Diluted EPS incorporates the dilutive effect of all potential common shares in the calculation of EPS.

Direct financing lease lease in which the lessor finances the asset for the lessee and earns interest revenue over the lease term.

Direct method cash effect of each operating activity (i.e., income statement item) is reported directly on the statement of cash flows.

Direct write-off method an allowance for uncollectible accounts is not used; instead, bad debts that do arise are written off as bad debt expense.

Disclosure including pertinent information in the financial statements and accompanying notes.

Disclosure notes additional insights about company operations, accounting principles, contractual agreements, and pending litigation written in notes that accompany the financial statements.

Discontinued operations the discontinuance of a component of an entity whose operations and cash flows can be clearly distinguished from the rest of the entity.

Discount arises when bonds are sold for less than face amount.

Discounting the transfer of a note receivable to a financial institution.

Distinct a good or service is *distinct* if it is both *capable of being distinct* (the customer could use the good or service on its own or in combination with other goods and services it could obtain elsewhere), and *separately identifiable from other goods or services in the contract* (the good or service is distinct in the context of the contract because it is not highly interrelated with other goods and services in the contract). Distinct goods and services are accounted for as separate performance obligations.

Dividend distribution to shareholders of a portion of assets earned.

Dollar-value LIFO (DVL) inventory is viewed as a quantity of value instead of a physical quantity of goods. Instead of layers of units from different purchases, the DVL inventory pool is viewed as comprising layers of dollar value from different years.

Dollar-value LIFO retail method LIFO retail method combined with dollar-value LIFO.

Double-declining-balance (DDB) method 200% of the straight-line rate is multiplied by book value.

Double-entry system dual effect that each transaction has on the accounting equation when recorded.

DuPont framework depict return on equity as determined by profit margin (representing profitability), asset turnover (representing efficiency), and the equity multiplier (representing leverage).

Early extinguishment of debt debt is retired prior to its scheduled maturity date.

Earnings per share (EPS) the amount of income earned by a company expressed on a per share basis.

Earnings quality refers to the ability of reported earnings (income) to predict a company's future earnings.

Economic entity assumption presumes that economic events can be identified specifically with an economic entity.

Economic entity assumption The economic entity assumption presumes that economic events can be identified with a particular economic entity.

Economic event any event that directly affects the financial position of the company.

Effective interest method calculates interest revenue as the market rate of interest multiplied by the outstanding balance of the investment.

Effective rate the actual rate at which money grows per year.

Effective tax rate equals tax expense divided by pretax accounting income.

Emerging Issues Task Force (EITF) responsible for providing more timely responses to emerging financial reporting issues.

Employee share purchase plans permit all employees to buy shares directly from their company, often at favorable terms.

Equity method used when an investor can't control, but can significantly influence, the investee. Under the equity method, the investor recognizes on its own income statement its proportionate share of the investee's income.

Estimates prediction of future events.

Ethics a code or moral system that provides criteria for evaluating right and wrong.

Ex-dividend date date usually two business days before the date of the record and is the first day the stock trades without the right to receive the declared dividend.

Executory costs maintenance, insurance, taxes, and any other costs usually associated with ownership.

Expected cash flow approach adjusts the cash flows, not the discount rate, for the uncertainty or risk of those cash flows.

Expected return on plan assets estimated long-term return on invested assets.

Expenses outflows or other using up of assets or incurrences of liabilities during a period from delivering or producing goods, rendering services, or other activities that constitute the entity's ongoing major, or central, operations.

Exploration costs for natural resources, expenditures such as drilling a well, excavating a mine, or any other costs of searching for natural resources.

Extended warranties additional, extended service that covers new problems arising after the buyer takes control of the product.

External events exchange between the company and a separate economic entity.

F.O.B. (free on board) destination the seller is responsible for shipping and the legal title does not pass until the goods arrive at their destination.

F.O.B. (free on board) shipping point legal title to the goods changes hands at the point of shipment when the seller delivers the goods to the common carrier, and the purchaser is responsible for shipping costs and transit insurance.

Factor financial institution that buys receivables for cash, handles the billing and collection of the receivables, and charges a fee for this service.

Fair value bases measurements on the price that would be received to sell assets or transfer liabilities in an orderly market transaction.

Fair value hedge a derivative is used to hedge against the exposure to changes in the fair value of an asset or liability or a firm commitment.

Fair value option allows companies to report specified financial assets and liabilities at fair value.

Faithful representation exists when there is agreement between a measure or description and the phenomenon it purports to represent.

Finance leases lessee has, in substance, purchased the lease asset; assumed when one of five classification criteria is met.

Financial Accounting Foundation (FAF) responsible for selecting the members of the FASB and its Advisory Council, ensuring adequate funding of FASB activities, and exercising general oversight of the FASB's activities.

Financial Accounting Standards Board (FASB) the current private sector body that has been delegated the task of setting accounting standards.

Financial accounting provides relevant financial information to various external users.

Financial instrument cash; evidence of an ownership interest in an entity; a contract that imposes on one entity an obligation to deliver cash or another financial instrument, and conveys to the second entity a right to receive cash or another financial instrument; and a contract that imposes on one entity an obligation to exchange financial instruments on potentially unfavorable terms and conveys to a second entity a right to exchange other financial instruments on potentially favorable terms.

Financial leverage by earning a return on borrowed funds that exceeds the cost of borrowing the funds, a company can provide its shareholders with a total return higher than it could achieve by employing equity funds alone.

Financial reporting process of providing financial statement information to external users.

Financial statements primary means of communicating financial information to external parties.

Finished goods costs that have accumulated in work-in-process are transferred to finished goods once the manufacturing process is completed.

First-in, first-out (FIFO) method assumes that items sold are those that were acquired first.

Fixed-asset turnover ratio used to measure how effectively managers used PP&E.

$$\text{Fixed-asset turnover ratio} = \frac{\text{Net sales}}{\text{Average-fixed assets}}$$

Foreign currency futures contract agreement that requires the seller to deliver a specific foreign currency at a designated future date at a specific price.

Foreign currency hedge if a derivative is used to hedge the risk that some transactions require settlement in a currency other than the entities' functional currency or that foreign operations will require translation adjustments to reported amounts.

Forward contract calls for delivery on a specific date; is not traded on a market exchange; does not call for a daily cash settlement for price changes in the underlying contract.

Franchise contractual arrangement under which the franchisor grants the franchisee the exclusive right to use the franchisor's trademark or tradename within a geographical area, usually for specified period of time.

Franchisee individual or corporation given the right to operate a business involving the franchisor's products or services and use its name and other symbols for a specific period of time.

Franchisor grants to the franchisee the right to operate a business involving the franchisor's products or services and use its name and other symbols for a specific period of time.

Fraud an intentional act by one or more individuals among management, those charged with governance, employees, or third parties, involving the use of deception that results in a misstatement in the financial statements that are the subject of an audit.

Free from error information is free from error if it contains no errors or omissions.

Freight-in transportation-in; in a periodic system, freight costs generally are added to this temporary account, which is added to purchases in determining net purchases.

Full-cost method allows costs incurred in searching for oil and gas within a large geographical area to be capitalized as assets and expensed in the future as oil and gas from the successful wells are removed from that area.

Full-disclosure principle financial reports should include any information that could affect the decisions made by external users.

Functional intellectual property property, like software, drug formulas, and completed media content, that performs a function or task, or can be played or aired, so it transfers a right of use for which the seller typically recognizes revenue at the point in time the customer can start using the intellectual property.

Future deductible amounts the future tax consequence of a temporary difference will be to decrease taxable income relative to accounting income.

Future taxable amounts the future tax consequence of temporary difference will be to increase taxable income relative to accounting income.

Future value amount of money that a dollar will grow to at some point in the future.

Gains increases in equity from peripheral, or incidental, transactions of an entity.

General journal used to record any type of transaction.

General ledger collection of accounts.

Generally Accepted Accounting Principles (GAAP) set of both broad and specific guidelines that companies should follow when measuring and reporting the information in their financial statements and related notes.

Gift card transferable prepayments for a specified dollar value of goods or services to be delivered at a future date; gift cards give rise to deferred revenue liabilities until they are redeemed or viewed as not going to be redeemed (broken).

Going concern assumption in the absence of information to the contrary, it is anticipated that a business entity will continue to operate indefinitely.

Governmental Accounting Standards Board (GASB) responsible for developing accounting standards for governmental units such as states and cities.

Gross method for the buyer, views a discount not taken as part of the cost of inventory; for the seller, views a discount not taken by the customer as part of sales of revenue.

Gross profit method (gross margin method) estimates cost of goods sold, which is then subtracted from cost of goods available for sale to estimate ending inventory.

Gross profit/ratio highlights the important relationship between net sales revenue and cost of goods sold.

$$\text{Gross profit ratio} = \frac{\text{Gross profit}}{\text{Net sales}}$$

Group depreciation method collection of assets defined as depreciable assets that share similar service lives and other attributes.

Half-year convention record one-half of a full year's depreciation in the year of acquisition and another half year in the year of disposal.

Hedging taking an action that is expected to produce exposure to a particular type of risk that is precisely the opposite of an actual risk to which the company already is exposed.

Historical costs original transaction value.

Horizontal analysis comparison by expressing each item as a percentage of that same item in the financial statements of another year (base amount) in order to more easily see year-to-year changes.

Illegal acts violations of the law, such as bribes, kickbacks, and illegal contributions to political candidates.

Implicit rate of interest rate implicit in the agreement.

Improvements replacement of a major component of an operational asset.

Income from continuing operations revenues, expenses (including income taxes), gain, and losses, excluding those related to discontinued operations and extraordinary items.

Income statement statement of operations or statement of earnings that is used to summarize the profit-generating activities that occurred during a particular reporting period.

Income statement approach estimating bad debt expense as a percentage of each period's net credit sales; usually determined by reviewing the company's recent history of the relationship between credit sales and actual bad debts.

Income summary account that is a bookkeeping convenience used in the closing process that provides a check that all temporary accounts have been properly closed.

Indirect method the net cash increase or decrease from operating activities is derived indirectly by starting with reported net income and working backwards to convert that amount to a cash basis.

Initial direct costs costs incurred by the lessor that are associated directly with originating a lease and are essential to acquire the lease.

Initial market transactions provide for new cash by the issuance of stocks and bonds by the corporation.

Installment sales method recognizes revenue and costs only when cash payments are received.

Institute of Internal Auditors national organization of accountants providing internal auditing services for their own organizations.

Institute of Management Accountants (IMA) primary national organization of accountants working in industry and government.

Intangible assets operational assets that lack physical substance; examples include patents, copyrights, franchises, and goodwill.

Interest "rent" paid for the use of money for some period of time.

Interest cost interest accrued on the projected benefit obligation calculated as the discount rate multiplied by the projected benefit obligation at the beginning of the year.

Interest rate swap agreement to exchange fixed interest payments for floating rate payments, or vice versa, without exchanging the underlying principal amounts.

Interest-bearing note receivable notes that state a principal and interest rate to be paid by a debtor to a creditor.

Internal control a company's plan to encourage adherence to company policies and procedures, promote operational efficiency, minimize errors and theft, and enhance the reliability and accuracy of accounting data.

Internal events events that directly affect the financial position of the company but don't involve an exchange transaction with another entity.

International Accounting Standards Board (IASB) objectives are to develop a single set of high-quality, understandable global accounting standards, to promote the use of those standards, and to bring about the convergence of national accounting standards and International Accounting Standards.

International Accounting Standards Committee (IASC) umbrella organization formed to develop global accounting standards.

International Financial Reporting Standards (IFRS) developed by the IASB and used by more than 100 countries.

Intrinsic value difference between the market price of the shares and the option price at which they can be acquired.

Inventories goods awaiting sale (finished goods), goods in the course of production (work in process), and goods to be consumed directly or indirectly in production (raw materials).

Inventory goods acquired, manufactured, or in the process of being manufactured for sale.

Inventory turnover ratio measures a company's efficiency in managing its investment in inventory.

Investing activities involve the acquisition and sale of long-term assets used in the business and non-operating investment assets.

Journal a chronological record of all economic events affecting financial position.

Journal entry captures the effect of a transaction on financial position in debit/credit form.

Just-in-time (JIT) system a system used by a manufacturer to coordinate production with suppliers so that raw materials or components arrive just as they are needed in the production process.

Land improvements the cost of parking lots, driveways, and private roads and the costs of fences and lawn and garden sprinkler systems.

Last-in, first-out (LIFO) method assumes units sold are the most recent units purchased.

Lease payments payments the lessee is required to make in connection with the lease.

Leasehold improvement account title when a lessee makes improvements to leased property that reverts back to the lessor at the end of the lease.

Lessee user of a leased asset.

Lessor owner of a leased asset.

Liabilities probable future sacrifices of economic benefits arising from present obligations of a particular entity to transfer assets or provide services to other entities in the future as a result of past transactions or events.

Licenses allow the customer to use the seller's intellectual property.

LIFO conformity rule if a company uses LIFO to measure taxable income, the company also must use LIFO for external financial reporting.

LIFO inventory pools simplifies recordkeeping and reduces the risk of LIFO liquidation by grouping inventory units into pools based on physical similarities of the individual units.

LIFO liquidation the decline in inventory quantity during the period.

LIFO reserve contra account to inventory used to record the difference between the internal method and LIFO.

Limited liability company (LLC) owners are not liable for the debts of the business, except to the extent of their investment; all members can be involved with managing the business without losing liability protection; no limitations on the number of owners.

Limited liability partnership similar to a limited liability company, except it doesn't offer all the liability protection available in the limited liability company structure.

Line of credit allows a company to borrow cash without having to follow formal loan procedures and paperwork.

Liquidating dividend when a dividend exceeds the balance in retained earnings and returns invested capital to owners

Liquidity period of time before an asset is converted to cash or until a liability is paid.

Long-term solvency the riskiness of a company with regard to the amount of liabilities in its capital structure.

Loss contingency existing, uncertain situation involving potential loss depending on whether some future event occurs.

Losses decreases in equity from peripheral, or incidental, transactions of the entity.

Lower of cost or market subsequent measurement of inventory applied by companies that use LIFO or the retail inventory method. This approach requires companies to report ending inventory at the lower of cost or market.

Lower of cost or net realizable value (LCNRV) subsequent measurement of inventory applied by companies that use FIFO, average cost, or any other method besides LIFO or the retail inventory method. This approach requires companies to report ending inventory at the lower of cost or net realizable value.

Management discussion and analysis (MDA) provides a biased but informed perspective of a company's operations, liquidity, and capital resources.

Material has qualitative or quantitative characteristics that make it matter for decision making.

Measurement process of associating numerical amounts to the elements.

Model Business Corporation Act designed to serve as a guide to states in the development of their corporation statutes.

Modified accelerated cost recovery system (MACRS) federal income tax code allows taxpayers to compute depreciation for their tax returns using this method.

Modified retrospective approach accounting change is applied only to the adoption period with adjustment of the balance of retained earnings at the beginning of the adoption period to capture the cumulative effects of prior periods.

Monetary assets money and claims to receive money, the amount of which is fixed or determinable.

Monetary liabilities obligations to pay amounts of cash, the amount of which is fixed or determinable.

Monetary unit assumption states that financial statement elements should be measured in a particular monetary unit (in the United States, the U.S. dollar).

Mortgage bond backed by a lien on specified real estate owned by the issuer.

Multiple-step income statement format that includes a number of intermediate subtotals before arriving at income from continuing operations.

Natural resources oil and gas deposits, timber tracts, and mineral deposits.

Net income income statement bottom line.

Net markdown net effect of the change in selling price (increase, decrease, increase).

Net markup net effect of the change in selling price (increase, increase, decrease).

Net method For the buyer, considers the cost of inventory to include the net, after-discount amount, and any discounts not taken are reported as interest expense. For the seller, considers sales revenue to be the net amount, after discount, and any discounts not taken by the customer as interest revenue.

Net operating loss negative taxable income because tax-deductible expenses exceed taxable revenues.

Net operating loss carryforward offsets future taxable income with an NOL to provide a reduction of taxes payable in that future period; therefore, gives rise to a deferred tax asset because it is a future deductible amount.

Net realizable value the amount of cash the company expects to actually collect from customers.

Neutral implies freedom from bias.

Non-GAAP earnings actual (GAAP) earnings reduced by any expenses the reporting company feels are unusual and should be excluded.

Noncash investing and financing activities transactions that do not increase or decrease cash but that result in significant investing and financing activities.

Noncumulative if the specified dividend is not declared in any given year, it need never be paid.

Noninterest-bearing note notes for which the interest is deducted from the face amount of the note to determine the cash proceeds made available to the borrower at the outset.

Nonoperating income includes gains, losses, revenues, and expenses related to peripheral or incidental activities of the company.

Nonparticipating preferred shareholder dividends are limited to the stated amount.

Notes payable promissory notes (essentially an IOU) that obligate the issuing corporation to repay a stated amount at or by a specified maturity date and to pay interest to the lender between the issue date and maturity.

Notes receivable receivables supported by a formal agreement or note that specifies payment terms.

Objectives-oriented/principles-based accounting standards approach to standard setting stresses professional judgment, as opposed to following a list of rules.

Operating activities inflows and outflows of cash related to transactions entering into the determination of net income.

Operating cycle period of time necessary to convert cash to raw materials, raw materials to finished product, the finished product to receivables, and then finally receivables back to cash.

Operating income includes revenues and expenses directly related to the principal revenue-generating activities of the company.

Operating leases fundamental rights and responsibilities of ownership are retained by the lessor and the lessee merely is using the asset temporarily.

Operating segment a component of an enterprise that engages in business activities from which it may earn revenues and incur expenses (including revenues and expenses relating to transactions with other companies of the same enterprise); whose operating results are regularly reviewed by the enterprise's chief operating decision maker to make decisions about resources to be allocated to the segment and assess its performance; for which discrete financial information is available.

Operational risk how adept a company is at withstanding various events and circumstances that might impair its ability to earn profits.

Option gives the holder the right either to buy or sell a financial instrument at a specified price.

Option pricing models statistical models that incorporate information about a company's stock and the terms of the stock option to estimate the option's fair value.

Ordinary annuity cash flows occur at the end of each period.

Other comprehensive income certain gains and losses that are excluded from the calculation of net income, but included in the calculation of comprehensive income.

Paid-in capital invested capital consisting primarily of amounts invested by shareholders when they purchase shares of stock from the corporation.

Parenthetical comments/modifying comments supplemental information disclosed on the face of financial statements.

Participating preferred shareholders are allowed to receive additional dividends beyond the stated amount.

Patent exclusive right to manufacture a product or to use a process.

Pension plan assets employer contributions and accumulated earnings on the investment of those contributions to be used to pay retirement benefits to retired employees.

Performance obligations promises to transfer goods and services to a customer; satisfied when the seller transfers *control* of goods or services to the customer.

Periodic inventory system the merchandise inventory account balance is not adjusted as purchases and sales are made but only periodically at the end of a reporting period when a physical count of the period's ending inventory is made and costs are assigned to the quantities determined.

Periodicity assumption allows the life of a company to be divided into artificial time periods to provide timely information.

Permanent accounts represent assets, liabilities, and shareholders' equity at a point in time.

Permanent difference difference between pretax accounting income and taxable income and, consequently, between the reported amount of an asset or liability in the financial statements and its tax basis that will not "reverse," resulting from transactions and events that under existing tax law will never affect taxable income or taxes payable.

Perpetual inventory system account inventory is continually adjusted for each change in inventory, whether it's caused by a purchase, a sale, or a return of merchandise by the company to its supplier.

Pledging trade receivables in general rather than specific receivables are pledged as collateral; the responsibility for collection of the receivables remains solely with the company.

Post-closing trial balance verifies that the closing entries were prepared and posted correctly and that the accounts are now ready for next year's transactions.

Posting transferring debits and credits recorded in individual journal entries to the specific accounts affected.

Potential common shares securities that, while not being common stock, may become common stock through their exercise, conversion, or issuance and therefore dilute (reduce) earnings per share.

Predictive value confirmation of investor expectations about future cash-generating ability.

Preferred stock typically has a preference (a) to a specified amount of dividends (stated dollar amount per share or percentage of par value per share) and (b) to distribution of assets in the event the corporation is dissolved.

Premium arises when bonds are sold for more than face amount.

Prepaid expense represents an asset recorded when an expense is paid in advance, creating benefits beyond the current period.

Prepayments/deferrals the cash flow precedes either expense or revenue recognition.

Present value today's equivalent to a particular amount in the future, after backing out the time value of money.

Principal controls goods or services and is responsible for providing them to the customer.

Prior period adjustment addition to or reduction in the beginning retained earnings balance in a statement of shareholders' equity due to a correction of an error.

Prior service cost the cost of credit given for an amendment to a pension plan to employee service rendered in prior years.

Product costs costs associated with products and expensed as cost of goods sold only when the related products are sold.

Profit margin on sales net income divided by net sales; measures the amount of net income achieved per sales dollar.

Projected benefit obligation (PBO) the discounted present value of estimated retirement benefits earned so far by employees, applying the plan's pension formula using projected future compensation levels.

Property dividend when a noncash asset is distributed.

Property, plant, and equipment land, buildings, equipment, machinery, autos, and trucks.

Proxy statement contains disclosures on compensation to directors and executives; sent to all shareholders each year.

Purchase commitments contracts that obligate a company to purchase a specified amount of merchandise or raw materials at specified prices on or before specified dates.

Purchase discounts reductions in the amount to be paid if remittance is made within a designated period of time.

Purchase option a provision of some lease contracts that gives the lessee the option of purchasing the leased property during, or at the end of, the lease term at a specified price.

Purchase return a reduction in both inventory and accounts payable (if the account has not yet been paid) at the time of the return.

Purchases journal records the purchase of merchandise on account.

Quality-assurance warranty obligation by the seller to make repairs or replace products that are later demonstrated to be defective for some period of time after the sale.

Quasi reorganization a firm undergoing financial difficulties, but with favorable future prospects, may use a quasi reorganization to write down inflated asset values and eliminate an accumulated deficit.

Rate of return on stock investment

$$\frac{\text{Dividends} + \text{Share price appreciation}}{\text{Initial investment}}$$

Ratio analysis comparison of accounting numbers to evaluate the performance and risk of a firm.

Raw materials cost of components purchased from suppliers that will become part of the finished product.

Realization principle revenue recognition on completion of the earnings process and reasonable certainty about collectibility.

Rearrangements expenditures made to restructure an asset without addition, replacement, or improvement.

Receivables a company's claims to the future collection of cash, other assets, or services.

Receivables turnover ratio indicates how quickly a company is able to collect its accounts receivable.

Recognition process of admitting information into the basic financial statements.

Redemption privilege might allow preferred shareholders the option, under specified conditions, to return their shares for a predetermined redemption price.

Related-party transactions transactions with owners, management, families of owners or management, affiliated companies, and other parties that can significantly influence or be influenced by the company.

Relevance one of the primary decision-specific qualities that make accounting information useful; made up of predictive value and/or feedback value and timeliness.

Replacement depreciation method depreciation is recorded when assets are replaced.

Residual asset carrying amount of a leased asset not transferred to the lessee.

Residual value or salvage value, the amount the company expects to receive for the asset at the end of its service life, less any anticipated disposal costs.

Restoration costs costs to restore land or other property to its original condition after extraction of the natural resource ends.

Restricted stock shares issued in the name of the employee, subject to forfeiture by the employee if employment is terminated within some specified number of years from the date of grant.

Restricted stock units right to receive shares, subject to forfeiture by the employee if employment is terminated within some specified number of years from the date of grant.

Restructuring costs costs associated with plans by management to materially change either the scope or manner in which its company's operations are conducted.

Retained earnings amounts earned by the corporation on behalf of its shareholders and not (yet) distributed to them as dividends.

Retired stock shares repurchased and not designated as treasury stock.

Retirement depreciation method records depreciation when assets are disposed of and measures depreciation as the difference between the proceeds received and cost.

Retrospective approach financial statements issued in previous years are revised to reflect the impact of an accounting change whenever those statements are presented again for comparative purpose.

Return on assets (ROA) indicates a company's overall profitability.

Return on shareholders' equity (ROE) amount of profit management can generate from the assets that owners provide.

Revenue/expense approach recognition and measurement of revenues and expenses are emphasized.

Revenues inflows or other enhancements of assets of an entity or settlements of its liabilities (or a combination of both) from delivering or producing goods, rendering services, or other activities that constitute the entity's ongoing major or central operations.

Reverse stock split when a company decreases, rather than increases, its outstanding shares.

Reversing entries optional entries that remove the effects of some of the adjusting entries made at the end of the previous reporting period for the sole purpose of simplifying journal entries made during the new period.

Right of conversion shareholders' right to exchange shares of preferred stock for common stock at specified conversion ratio.

Right of return customers' right to return merchandise to retailers if they are not satisfied.

Rules-based accounting standards a list of rules for choosing the appropriate accounting treatment for a transaction.

S corporation characteristics of both regular corporations and partnerships.

SAB No. 101 *Staff Accounting Bulletin 101* summarizes SEC's views on revenue recognition.

Sale-leaseback transaction the owner of an asset sells it and immediately leases it back from the new owner.

Sales journal records credit sales.

Sales return the return of merchandise for a refund or for credit to be applied to other purchases.

Sales-type lease lessor transfers control of lease asset to lessee, with or without a selling profit on the sale of the asset.

Secondary market transactions provide for the transfer of stocks and bonds among individuals and institutions.

Securities and Exchange Commission (SEC) responsible for setting accounting and reporting standards for companies whose securities are publicly traded.

Securities available-for-sale debt securities the investor acquires for purposes other than active trading or to be held to maturity.

Securities to be held-to-maturity debt securities for which the investor has the "positive intent and ability" to hold the securities to maturity.

Securitization the company creates a special purpose entity (SPE), usually a trust or a subsidiary; the SPE buys a pool of trade receivables, credit card receivables, or loans from the company and then sells related securities.

Selling profit when the fair value of the asset (usually the present value of the lease payments, or "selling price") exceeds the cost or carrying value of the asset sold.

Separation of duties an internal control technique in which various functions are distributed amongst employees to provide cross-checking that encourages accuracy and discourages fraud.

Serial bonds more structured (and less popular) way to retire bonds on a piecemeal basis.

Service cost increase in the projected benefit obligation attributable to employee service performed during the period.

Service life (useful life) the estimated use that the company expects to receive from the asset.

Service method allocation approach that reflects the declining service pattern of the prior service cost.

Short-term investments investments not classified as cash equivalents that will be liquidated in the coming year or operating cycle, whichever is longer.

Significant influence effective control is absent but the investor is able to affect the operating and financial policies of the investee (usually is the case when investor holds between 20% and 50% of the investee's voting shares).

Simple capital structure a firm that has no potential common shares (outstanding securities that could potentially dilute earnings per share).

Simple interest computed by multiplying an initial investment times both the applicable interest rate and the period of time for which the money is used.

Single-step income statement format that groups all revenues and gains together and all expenses and losses together.

Sinking fund debentures bonds that must be redeemed on a prespecified year-by-year basis; administered by a trustee who repurchases bonds in the open market.

Source documents relay essential information about each transaction to the accountant, e.g., sales invoices, bills from suppliers, cash register tapes.

Special journal record of a repetitive type of transaction, e.g., a sales journal.

Specific identification method each unit sold during the period or each unit on hand at the end of the period to be matched with its actual cost.

Specific interest method for interest capitalization, rates from specific construction loans, to the extent of specific borrowings are used before using the average rate of other debt.

Stand-alone selling price the amount at which the good or service is sold separately under similar circumstances.

Start-up costs whenever a company introduces a new product or service, or commences business in a new territory or with a new customer, it incurs one-time costs that are expensed in the period incurred.

Statement of cash flows change statement summarizing the transactions that caused cash to change during the period.

Statement of shareholders' equity statement disclosing the source of changes in the shareholders' equity accounts.

Stock appreciation rights (SARs) awards that enable an employee to benefit by the amount that the market price of the company's stock rises above a specified amount, without having to buy shares.

Stock dividend distribution of additional shares of stock to current shareholders of the corporation.

Stock options employees aren't actually awarded shares, but rather are given the option to buy shares at a specified exercise price within some specified number of years from the date of grant.

Stock split stock distribution of 25% or higher, sometimes called a *large* stock dividend.

Straight line an equal amount of depreciable base is allocated to each year of the asset's service life.

Straight-line method recording interest each period at the same dollar amount.

Subordinated debenture the holder is not entitled to receive any liquidation payments until the claims of other specified debt issues are satisfied.

Subsequent event a significant development that takes place after the company's fiscal year-end but before the financial statements are issued.

Subsidiary ledger record of a group of subsidiary accounts associated with a particular general ledger control account.

Successful efforts method requires that exploration costs that are known not to have resulted in the discovery of oil or gas be included as expense in the period the expenditures are made.

Sum-of-the-years'-digits (SYD) method systematic acceleration of depreciation by multiplying the depreciable base by a fraction that declines each year.

Supplemental schedules and tables reports containing more detailed information than is shown in the primary financial statements.

Symbolic intellectual property property, like trademarks, logos, brand names and franchise rights, has usefulness to the customer that depends on the seller's ongoing activities, so it transfers a right of access for which the seller recognizes revenue over the period of time the customer accesses the IP.

T-account account with space at the top for the account title and two sides for recording increases and decreases.

Tax basis of an asset or liability is its original value for tax purposes reduced by any amounts included to date on tax returns.

Technological feasibility established when the enterprise has completed all planning, designing, coding, and testing activities that are necessary to establish that the product can be produced to meet its design specifications, including functions, features, and technical performance requirements.

Temporary accounts represent changes in the retained earnings component of shareholders' equity for a corporation caused by revenue, expense, gain, and loss transactions.

Temporary difference difference between pretax accounting income and taxable income and, consequently, between the reported amount of an asset or liability in the financial statements and its tax basis, which will "reverse" in later years.

Time value of money money can be invested today to earn interest and grow to a larger dollar amount in the future.

Time-based methods allocates the cost base according to the passage of time.

Timeliness information that is available to users early enough to allow its use in the decision process.

Times interest earned ratio a way to gauge the ability of a company to satisfy its fixed debt obligations by comparing interest charges with the income available to pay those charges.

Trade discounts percentage reduction from the list price.

Trade notes payable formally recognized by a written promissory note.

Trademark (tradename) exclusive right to display a word, a slogan, a symbol, or an emblem that distinctively identifies a company, a product, or a service.

Trading securities equity or debt securities the investor (usually a financial institution) acquires principally for the purpose of selling in the near term.

Transaction analysis process of reviewing the source documents to determine the dual effect on the accounting equation and the specific elements involved.

Transaction price the amount the seller expects to be entitled to receive from the customer in exchange for providing goods and services.

Transactions economic events.

Treasury stock shares repurchased and not retired.

Troubled debt restructuring the original terms of a debt agreement are changed as a result of financial difficulties experienced by the debtor (borrower).

Trustee person who accepts employer contributions, invests the contributions, accumulates the earnings on the investments, and pays benefits from the plan assets to retired employees or their beneficiaries.

Unadjusted trial balance a list of the general ledger accounts and their balances at a particular date.

Understandability users must understand the information within the context of the decision being made.

Units-of-production method computes a depreciation rate per measure of activity and then multiplies this rate by actual activity to determine periodic depreciation.

Unrealized holding gains and losses gains and losses that arise from holding an investment during a period in which its fair value changes.

Valuation allowance indirect reduction (contra account) in a deferred tax asset when it is more likely than not that some portion or all of the deferred tax asset will not be realized.

Variable consideration transaction price is uncertain because it includes an amount that varies depending on the occurrence or nonoccurrence of a future event.

Verifiability implies a consensus among different measurers.

Vertical analysis expression of each item in the financial statements as a percentage of an appropriate corresponding total, or base amount, but within the same year.

Vested benefits benefits that employees have the right to receive even if their employment were to cease today.

Weighted-average interest method for interest capitalization, weighted-average rate on all interest-bearing debt, including all construction loans, is used.

With recourse the seller retains the risk of uncollectibility.

Without recourse the buyer assumes the risk of bad debts.

Work-in-process inventory products that are not yet complete in the manufacturing process.

Working capital differences between current assets and current liabilities.

Worksheet used to organize the accounting information needed to prepare adjusting and closing entries and the financial statements.

Subject Index

Notes: Page numbers followed by *n* indicate material in footnotes. General information about standards and standard-setting organizations may be found in this index. Specific standards and pronouncements are listed in the Accounting Standards Index.

E

O

Q

R

S

U

Accounting Standards Index

Notes: Page numbers followed by *n* indicate material in footnotes. Specific standards and pronouncements are found in this index; general information about standards and standard-setting organizations is found in the Subject Index. Unless otherwise noted, standards will be found under the name of the issuing organization.

Present and Future Value Tables

This table shows the future value of $1 at various interest rates (i) and time periods (n). It is used to calculate the future value of any single amount.

TABLE 1 Future Value of $1

$FV = \$1\,(1 + i)^n$

n/i	1.0%	1.5%	2.0%	2.5%	3.0%	3.5%	4.0%	4.5%	5.0%	5.5%	6.0%	7.0%	8.0%	9.0%	10.0%	11.0%	12.0%	20.0%
1	1.01000	1.01500	1.02000	1.02500	1.03000	1.03500	1.04000	1.04500	1.05000	1.05500	1.06000	1.07000	1.08000	1.09000	1.10000	1.11000	1.12000	1.20000
2	1.02010	1.03022	1.04040	1.05063	1.06090	1.07123	1.08160	1.09203	1.10250	1.11303	1.12360	1.14490	1.16640	1.18810	1.21000	1.23210	1.25440	1.44000
3	1.03030	1.04568	1.06121	1.07689	1.09273	1.10872	1.12486	1.14117	1.15763	1.17424	1.19102	1.22504	1.25971	1.29503	1.33100	1.36763	1.40493	1.72800
4	1.04060	1.06136	1.08243	1.10381	1.12551	1.14752	1.16986	1.19252	1.21551	1.23882	1.26248	1.31080	1.36049	1.41158	1.46410	1.51807	1.57352	2.07360
5	1.05101	1.07728	1.10408	1.13141	1.15927	1.18769	1.21665	1.24618	1.27628	1.30696	1.33823	1.40255	1.46933	1.53862	1.61051	1.68506	1.76234	2.48832
6	1.06152	1.09344	1.12616	1.15969	1.19405	1.22926	1.26532	1.30226	1.34010	1.37884	1.41852	1.50073	1.58687	1.67710	1.77156	1.87041	1.97382	2.98598
7	1.07214	1.10984	1.14869	1.18869	1.22987	1.27228	1.31593	1.36086	1.40710	1.45468	1.50363	1.60578	1.71382	1.82804	1.94872	2.07616	2.21068	3.58318
8	1.08286	1.12649	1.17166	1.21840	1.26677	1.31681	1.36857	1.42210	1.47746	1.53469	1.59385	1.71819	1.85093	1.99256	2.14359	2.30454	2.47596	4.29982
9	1.09369	1.14339	1.19509	1.24886	1.30477	1.36290	1.42331	1.48610	1.55133	1.61909	1.68948	1.83846	1.99900	2.17189	2.35795	2.55804	2.77308	5.15978
10	1.10462	1.16054	1.21899	1.28008	1.34392	1.41060	1.48024	1.55297	1.62889	1.70814	1.79085	1.96715	2.15892	2.36736	2.59374	2.83942	3.10585	6.19174
11	1.11567	1.17795	1.24337	1.31209	1.38423	1.45997	1.53945	1.62285	1.71034	1.80209	1.89830	2.10485	2.33164	2.58043	2.85312	3.15176	3.47855	7.43008
12	1.12683	1.19562	1.26824	1.34489	1.42576	1.51107	1.60103	1.69588	1.79586	1.90121	2.01220	2.25219	2.51817	2.81266	3.13843	3.49845	3.89598	8.91610
13	1.13809	1.21355	1.29361	1.37851	1.46853	1.56396	1.66507	1.77220	1.88565	2.00577	2.13293	2.40985	2.71962	3.06580	3.45227	3.88328	4.36349	10.69932
14	1.14947	1.23176	1.31948	1.41297	1.51259	1.61869	1.73168	1.85194	1.97993	2.11609	2.26090	2.57853	2.93719	3.34173	3.79750	4.31044	4.88711	12.83918
15	1.16097	1.25023	1.34587	1.44830	1.55797	1.67535	1.80094	1.93528	2.07893	2.23248	2.39656	2.75903	3.17217	3.64248	4.17725	4.78459	5.47357	15.40702
16	1.17258	1.26899	1.37279	1.48451	1.60471	1.73399	1.87298	2.02237	2.18287	2.35526	2.54035	2.95216	3.42594	3.97031	4.59497	5.31089	6.13039	18.48843
17	1.18430	1.28802	1.40024	1.52162	1.65285	1.79468	1.94790	2.11338	2.29202	2.48480	2.69277	3.15882	3.70002	4.32763	5.05447	5.89509	6.86604	22.18611
18	1.19615	1.30734	1.42825	1.55966	1.70243	1.85749	2.02582	2.20848	2.40662	2.62147	2.85434	3.37993	3.99602	4.71712	5.55992	6.54355	7.68997	26.62333
19	1.20811	1.32695	1.45681	1.59865	1.75351	1.92250	2.10685	2.30786	2.52695	2.76565	3.02560	3.61653	4.31570	5.14166	6.11591	7.26334	8.61276	31.94800
20	1.22019	1.34686	1.48595	1.63862	1.80611	1.98979	2.19112	2.41171	2.65330	2.91776	3.20714	3.86968	4.66096	5.60441	6.72750	8.06231	9.64629	38.33760
21	1.23239	1.36706	1.51567	1.67958	1.86029	2.05943	2.27877	2.52024	2.78596	3.07823	3.39956	4.14056	5.03383	6.10881	7.40025	8.94917	10.80385	46.00512
25	1.28243	1.45095	1.64061	1.85394	2.09378	2.36324	2.66584	3.00543	3.38635	3.81339	4.29187	5.42743	6.84848	8.62308	10.83471	13.58546	17.00006	95.39622
30	1.34785	1.56308	1.81136	2.09757	2.42726	2.80679	3.24340	3.74532	4.32194	4.98395	5.74349	7.61226	10.06266	13.26768	17.44940	22.89230	29.95992	237.37631
40	1.48886	1.81402	2.20804	2.68506	3.26204	3.95926	4.80102	5.81636	7.03999	8.51331	10.28572	14.97446	21.72452	31.40942	45.25926	65.00087	93.05097	1469.77160

This table shows the present value of $1 at various interest rates (i) and time periods (n). It is used to calculate the present value of any single amount.

TABLE 2 Present Value of $1

$$PV = \frac{\$1}{(1+i)^n}$$

n/i	1.0%	1.5%	2.0%	2.5%	3.0%	3.5%	4.0%	4.5%	5.0%	5.5%	6.0%	7.0%	8.0%	9.0%	10.0%	11.0%	12.0%	20.0%
1	0.99010	0.98522	0.98039	0.97561	0.97087	0.96618	0.96154	0.95694	0.95238	0.94787	0.94340	0.93458	0.92593	0.91743	0.90909	0.90090	0.89286	0.83333
2	0.98030	0.97066	0.96117	0.95181	0.94260	0.93351	0.92456	0.91573	0.90703	0.89845	0.89000	0.87344	0.85734	0.84168	0.82645	0.81162	0.79719	0.69444
3	0.97059	0.95632	0.94232	0.92860	0.91514	0.90194	0.88900	0.87630	0.86384	0.85161	0.83962	0.81630	0.79383	0.77218	0.75131	0.73119	0.71178	0.57870
4	0.96098	0.94218	0.92385	0.90595	0.88849	0.87144	0.85480	0.83856	0.82270	0.80722	0.79209	0.76290	0.73503	0.70843	0.68301	0.65873	0.63552	0.48225
5	0.95147	0.92826	0.90573	0.88385	0.86261	0.84197	0.82193	0.80245	0.78353	0.76513	0.74726	0.71299	0.68058	0.64993	0.62092	0.59345	0.56743	0.40188
6	**0.94205**	**0.91454**	**0.88797**	**0.86230**	**0.83748**	**0.81350**	**0.79031**	**0.76790**	**0.74622**	**0.72525**	**0.70496**	**0.66634**	**0.63017**	**0.59627**	**0.56447**	**0.53464**	**0.50663**	**0.33490**
7	0.93272	0.90103	0.87056	0.84127	0.81309	0.78599	0.75992	0.73483	0.71068	0.68744	0.66506	0.62275	0.58349	0.54703	0.51316	0.48166	0.45235	0.27908
8	0.92348	0.88771	0.85349	0.82075	0.78941	0.75941	0.73069	0.70319	0.67684	0.65160	0.62741	0.58201	0.54027	0.50187	0.46651	0.43393	0.40388	0.23257
9	0.91434	0.87459	0.83676	0.80073	0.76642	0.73373	0.70259	0.67290	0.64461	0.61763	0.59190	0.54393	0.50025	0.46043	0.42410	0.39092	0.36061	0.19381
10	0.90529	0.86167	0.82035	0.78120	0.74409	0.70892	0.67556	0.64393	0.61391	0.58543	0.55839	0.50835	0.46319	0.42241	0.38554	0.35218	0.32197	0.16151
11	**0.89632**	**0.84893**	**0.80426**	**0.76214**	**0.72242**	**0.68495**	**0.64958**	**0.61620**	**0.58468**	**0.55491**	**0.52679**	**0.47509**	**0.42888**	**0.38753**	**0.35049**	**0.31728**	**0.28748**	**0.13459**
12	0.88745	0.83639	0.78849	0.74356	0.70138	0.66178	0.62460	0.58966	0.55684	0.52598	0.49697	0.44401	0.39711	0.35553	0.31863	0.28584	0.25668	0.11216
13	0.87866	0.82403	0.77303	0.72542	0.68095	0.63940	0.60057	0.56427	0.53032	0.49856	0.46884	0.41496	0.36770	0.32618	0.28966	0.25751	0.22917	0.09346
14	0.86996	0.81185	0.75788	0.70773	0.66112	0.61778	0.57748	0.53997	0.50507	0.47257	0.44230	0.38782	0.34046	0.29925	0.26333	0.23199	0.20462	0.07789
15	0.86135	0.79985	0.74301	0.69047	0.64186	0.59689	0.55526	0.51672	0.48102	0.44793	0.41727	0.36245	0.31524	0.27454	0.23939	0.20900	0.18270	0.06491
16	**0.85282**	**0.78803**	**0.72845**	**0.67362**	**0.62317**	**0.57671**	**0.53391**	**0.49447**	**0.45811**	**0.42458**	**0.39365**	**0.33873**	**0.29189**	**0.25187**	**0.21763**	**0.18829**	**0.16312**	**0.05409**
17	0.84438	0.77639	0.71416	0.65720	0.60502	0.55720	0.51337	0.47318	0.43630	0.40245	0.37136	0.31657	0.27027	0.23107	0.19784	0.16963	0.14564	0.04507
18	0.83602	0.76491	0.70016	0.64117	0.58739	0.53836	0.49363	0.45280	0.41552	0.38147	0.35034	0.29586	0.25025	0.21199	0.17986	0.15282	0.13004	0.03756
19	0.82774	0.75361	0.68643	0.62553	0.57029	0.52016	0.47464	0.43330	0.39573	0.36158	0.33051	0.27651	0.23171	0.19449	0.16351	0.13768	0.11611	0.03130
20	0.81954	0.74247	0.67297	0.61027	0.55368	0.50257	0.45639	0.41464	0.37689	0.34273	0.31180	0.25842	0.21455	0.17843	0.14864	0.12403	0.10367	0.02608
21	**0.81143**	**0.73150**	**0.65978**	**0.59539**	**0.53755**	**0.48557**	**0.43883**	**0.39679**	**0.35894**	**0.32486**	**0.29416**	**0.24151**	**0.19866**	**0.16370**	**0.13513**	**0.11174**	**0.09256**	**0.02174**
24	0.78757	0.69954	0.62172	0.55288	0.49193	0.43796	0.39012	0.34770	0.31007	0.27666	0.24698	0.19715	0.15770	0.12640	0.10153	0.08170	0.06588	0.01258
25	0.77977	0.68921	0.60953	0.53939	0.47761	0.42315	0.37512	0.33273	0.29530	0.26223	0.23300	0.18425	0.14602	0.11597	0.09230	0.07361	0.05882	0.01048
28	0.75684	0.65910	0.57437	0.50088	0.43708	0.38165	0.33348	0.29157	0.25509	0.22332	0.19563	0.15040	0.11591	0.08955	0.06934	0.05382	0.04187	0.00607
29	0.74934	0.64936	0.56311	0.48866	0.42435	0.36875	0.32065	0.27902	0.24295	0.21168	0.18456	0.14056	0.10733	0.08215	0.06304	0.04849	0.03738	0.00506
30	**0.74192**	**0.63976**	**0.55207**	**0.47674**	**0.41199**	**0.35628**	**0.30832**	**0.26700**	**0.23138**	**0.20064**	**0.17411**	**0.13137**	**0.09938**	**0.07537**	**0.05731**	**0.04368**	**0.03338**	**0.00421**
31	0.73458	0.63031	0.54125	0.46511	0.39999	0.34423	0.29646	0.25550	0.22036	0.19018	0.16425	0.12277	0.09202	0.06915	0.05210	0.03935	0.02980	0.00351
40	0.67165	0.55126	0.45289	0.37243	0.30656	0.25257	0.20829	0.17193	0.14205	0.11746	0.09722	0.06678	0.04603	0.03184	0.02209	0.01538	0.01075	0.00068

This table shows the future value of an ordinary annuity of $1 at various interest rates (i) and time periods (n). It is used to calculate the future value of any series of equal payments made at the *end* of each compounding period.

TABLE 3 Future Value of an Ordinary Annuity of $1

$$FVA = \frac{(1+i)^n - 1}{i}$$

n/i	1.0%	1.5%	2.0%	2.5%	3.0%	3.5%	4.0%	4.5%	5.0%	5.5%	6.0%	7.0%	8.0%	9.0%	10.0%	11.0%	12.0%	20.0%
1	1.0000	1.0000	1.0000	1.0000	1.0000	1.0000	1.0000	1.0000	1.0000	1.0000	1.0000	1.0000	1.0000	1.0000	1.0000	1.0000	1.0000	1.0000
2	2.0100	2.0150	2.0200	2.0250	2.0300	2.0350	2.0400	2.0450	2.0500	2.0550	2.0600	2.0700	2.0800	2.0900	2.1000	2.1100	2.1200	2.2000
3	3.0301	3.0452	3.0604	3.0756	3.0909	3.1062	3.1216	3.1370	3.1525	3.1680	3.1836	3.2149	3.2464	3.2781	3.3100	3.3421	3.3744	3.6400
4	4.0604	4.0909	4.1216	4.1525	4.1836	4.2149	4.2465	4.2782	4.3101	4.3423	4.3746	4.4399	4.5061	4.5731	4.6410	4.7097	4.7793	5.3680
5	5.1010	5.1523	5.2040	5.2563	5.3091	5.3625	5.4163	5.4707	5.5256	5.5811	5.6371	5.7507	5.8666	5.9847	6.1051	6.2278	6.3528	7.4416
6	6.1520	6.2296	6.3081	6.3877	6.4684	6.5502	6.6330	6.7169	6.8019	6.8881	6.9753	7.1533	7.3359	7.5233	7.7156	7.9129	8.1152	9.9299
7	7.2135	7.3230	7.4343	7.5474	7.6625	7.7794	7.8983	8.0192	8.1420	8.2669	8.3938	8.6540	8.9228	9.2004	9.4872	9.7833	10.0890	12.9159
8	8.2857	8.4328	8.5830	8.7361	8.8923	9.0517	9.2142	9.3800	9.5491	9.7216	9.8975	10.2598	10.6366	11.0285	11.4359	11.8594	12.2997	16.4991
9	9.3685	9.5593	9.7546	9.9545	10.1591	10.3685	10.5828	10.8021	11.0266	11.2563	11.4913	11.9780	12.4876	13.0210	13.5795	14.1640	14.7757	20.7989
10	10.4622	10.7027	10.9497	11.2034	11.4639	11.7314	12.0061	12.2882	12.5779	12.8754	13.1808	13.8164	14.4866	15.1929	15.9374	16.7220	17.5487	25.9587
11	11.5668	11.8633	12.1687	12.4835	12.8078	13.1420	13.4864	13.8412	14.2068	14.5835	14.9716	15.7836	16.6455	17.5603	18.5312	19.5614	20.6546	32.1504
12	12.6825	13.0412	13.4121	13.7956	14.1920	14.6020	15.0258	15.4640	15.9171	16.3856	16.8699	17.8885	18.9771	20.1407	21.3843	22.7132	24.1331	39.5805
13	13.8093	14.2368	14.6803	15.1404	15.6178	16.1130	16.6268	17.1599	17.7130	18.2868	18.8821	20.1406	21.4953	22.9534	24.5227	26.2116	28.0291	48.4966
14	14.9474	15.4504	15.9739	16.5190	17.0863	17.6770	18.2919	18.9321	19.5986	20.2926	21.0151	22.5505	24.2149	26.0192	27.9750	30.0949	32.3926	59.1959
15	16.0969	16.6821	17.2934	17.9319	18.5989	19.2957	20.0236	20.7841	21.5786	22.4087	23.2760	25.1290	27.1521	29.3609	31.7725	34.4054	37.2797	72.0351
16	17.2579	17.9324	18.6393	19.3802	20.1569	20.9710	21.8245	22.7193	23.6575	24.6411	25.6725	27.8881	30.3243	33.0034	35.9497	39.1899	42.7533	87.4421
17	18.4304	19.2014	20.0121	20.8647	21.7616	22.7050	23.6975	24.7417	25.8404	26.9964	28.2129	30.8402	33.7502	36.9737	40.5447	44.5008	48.8837	105.9306
18	19.6147	20.4894	21.4123	22.3863	23.4144	24.4997	25.6454	26.8551	28.1324	29.4812	30.9057	33.9990	37.4502	41.3013	45.5992	50.3959	55.7497	128.1167
19	20.8109	21.7967	22.8406	23.9460	25.1169	26.3572	27.6712	29.0636	30.5390	32.1027	33.7600	37.3790	41.4463	46.0185	51.1591	56.9395	63.4397	154.7400
20	22.0190	23.1237	24.2974	25.5447	26.8704	28.2797	29.7781	31.3714	33.0660	34.8683	36.7856	40.9955	45.7620	51.1601	57.2750	64.2028	72.0524	186.6880
21	23.2392	24.4705	25.7833	27.1833	28.6765	30.2695	31.9692	33.7831	35.7193	37.7861	39.9927	44.8652	50.4229	56.7645	64.0025	72.2651	81.6987	225.0256
30	34.7849	37.5387	40.5681	43.9027	47.5754	51.6227	56.0849	61.0071	66.4388	72.4355	79.0582	94.4608	113.2832	136.3075	164.4940	199.0209	241.3327	1181.8816
40	48.8864	54.2679	60.4020	67.4026	75.4013	84.5503	95.0255	107.0303	120.7998	136.6056	154.7620	199.6351	259.0565	337.8824	442.5926	581.8261	767.0914	7343.8578

This table shows the future value of an annuity due of $1 at various interest rates (i) and time periods (n). It is used to calculate the future value of any series of equal payments made at the *beginning* of each compounding period.

TABLE 4 Present Value of an Ordinary Annuity of $1

$$PVA = \frac{1 - \frac{1}{(1+i)^n}}{i}$$

n/i	1.0%	1.5%	2.0%	2.5%	3.0%	3.5%	4.0%	4.5%	5.0%	5.5%	6.0%	7.0%	8.0%	9.0%	10.0%	11.0%	12.0%	20.0%
1	0.99010	0.98522	0.98039	0.97561	0.97087	0.96618	0.96154	0.95694	0.95238	0.94787	0.94340	0.93458	0.92593	0.91743	0.90909	0.90090	0.89286	0.83333
2	1.97040	1.95588	1.94156	1.92742	1.91347	1.89969	1.88609	1.87267	1.85941	1.84632	1.83339	1.80802	1.78326	1.75911	1.73554	1.71252	1.69005	1.52778
3	2.94099	2.91220	2.88388	2.85602	2.82861	2.80164	2.77509	2.74896	2.72325	2.69793	2.67301	2.62432	2.57710	2.53129	2.48685	2.44371	2.40183	2.10648
4	3.90197	3.85438	3.80773	3.76197	3.71710	3.67308	3.62990	3.58753	3.54595	3.50515	3.46511	3.38721	3.31213	3.23972	3.16987	3.10245	3.03735	2.58873
5	4.85343	4.78264	4.71346	4.64583	4.57971	4.51505	4.45182	4.38998	4.32948	4.27028	4.21236	4.10020	3.99271	3.88965	3.79079	3.69590	3.60478	2.99061
6	**5.79548**	**5.69719**	**5.60143**	**5.50813**	**5.41719**	**5.32855**	**5.24214**	**5.15787**	**5.07569**	**4.99553**	**4.91732**	**4.76654**	**4.62288**	**4.48592**	**4.35526**	**4.23054**	**4.11141**	**3.32551**
7	6.72819	6.59821	6.47199	6.34939	6.23028	6.11454	6.00205	5.89270	5.78637	5.68297	5.58238	5.38929	5.20637	5.03295	4.86842	4.71220	4.56376	3.60459
8	7.65168	7.48593	7.32548	7.17014	7.01969	6.87396	6.73274	6.59589	6.46321	6.33457	6.20979	5.97130	5.74664	5.53482	5.33493	5.14612	4.96764	3.83716
9	8.56602	8.36052	8.16224	7.97087	7.78611	7.60769	7.43533	7.26879	7.10782	6.95220	6.80169	6.51523	6.24689	5.99525	5.75902	5.53705	5.32825	4.03097
10	9.47130	9.22218	8.98259	8.75206	8.53020	8.31661	8.11090	7.91272	7.72173	7.53763	7.36009	7.02358	6.71008	6.41766	6.14457	5.88923	5.65022	4.19247
11	**10.36763**	**10.07112**	**9.78685**	**9.51421**	**9.25262**	**9.00155**	**8.76048**	**8.52892**	**8.30641**	**8.09254**	**7.88687**	**7.49867**	**7.13896**	**6.80519**	**6.49506**	**6.20652**	**5.93770**	**4.32706**
12	11.25508	10.90751	10.57534	10.25776	9.95400	9.66333	9.38507	9.11858	8.86325	8.61852	8.38384	7.94269	7.53608	7.16073	6.81369	6.49236	6.19437	4.43922
13	12.13374	11.73153	11.34837	10.98319	10.63496	10.30274	9.98565	9.68285	9.39357	9.11708	8.85268	8.35765	7.90378	7.48690	7.10336	6.74987	6.42355	4.53268
14	13.00370	12.54338	12.10625	11.69091	11.29607	10.92052	10.56312	10.22283	9.89864	9.58965	9.29498	8.74547	8.24424	7.78615	7.36669	6.98187	6.62817	4.61057
15	13.86505	13.34323	12.84926	12.38138	11.93794	11.51741	11.11839	10.73955	10.37966	10.03758	9.71225	9.10791	8.55948	8.06069	7.60608	7.19087	6.81086	4.67547
16	**14.71787**	**14.13126**	**13.57771**	**13.05500**	**12.56110**	**12.09412**	**11.65230**	**11.23402**	**10.83777**	**10.46216**	**10.10590**	**9.44665**	**8.85137**	**8.31256**	**7.82371**	**7.37916**	**6.97399**	**4.72956**
17	15.56225	14.90765	14.29187	13.71220	13.16612	12.65132	12.16567	11.70719	11.27407	10.86461	10.47726	9.76322	9.12164	8.54363	8.02155	7.54879	7.11963	4.77463
18	16.39827	15.67256	14.99203	14.35336	13.75351	13.18968	12.65930	12.15999	11.68959	11.24607	10.82760	10.05909	9.37189	8.75563	8.20141	7.70162	7.24967	4.81219
19	17.22601	16.42617	15.67846	14.97889	14.32380	13.70984	13.13394	12.59329	12.08532	11.60765	11.15812	10.33560	9.60360	8.95011	8.36492	7.83929	7.36578	4.84350
20	18.04555	17.16864	16.35143	15.58916	14.87747	14.21240	13.59033	13.00794	12.46221	11.95038	11.46992	10.59401	9.81815	9.12855	8.51356	7.96333	7.46944	4.86958
21	**18.85698**	**17.90014**	**17.01121**	**16.18455**	**15.41502**	**14.69797**	**14.02916**	**13.40472**	**12.82115**	**12.27524**	**11.76408**	**10.83553**	**10.01680**	**9.29224**	**8.64869**	**8.07507**	**7.56200**	**4.89132**
25	22.02316	20.71961	19.52346	18.42438	17.41315	16.48151	15.62208	14.82821	14.09394	13.41393	12.78336	11.65358	10.67478	9.82258	9.07704	8.42174	7.84314	4.94759
30	25.80771	24.01584	22.39646	20.93029	19.60044	18.39205	17.29203	16.28889	15.37245	14.53375	13.76483	12.40904	11.25778	10.27365	9.42691	8.69379	8.05518	4.97894
40	32.83469	29.91585	27.35548	25.10278	23.11477	21.35507	19.79277	18.40158	17.15909	16.04612	15.04630	13.33171	11.92461	10.75736	9.77905	8.95105	8.24378	4.99660

This table shows the future value of an annuity due of $1 at various interest rates (i) and time periods (n). It is used to calculate the future value of any series of equal payments made at the *beginning* of each compounding period.

TABLE 5 Future Value of an Annuity Due of $1

$$FVAD = \left[\frac{(1+i)^n - 1}{i}\right] \times (1+i)$$

n/i	1.0%	1.5%	2.0%	2.5%	3.0%	3.5%	4.0%	4.5%	5.0%	5.5%	6.0%	7.0%	8.0%	9.0%	10.0%	11.0%	12.0%	20.0%
1	1.0100	1.0150	1.0200	1.0250	1.0300	1.0350	1.0400	1.0450	1.0500	1.0550	1.0600	1.0700	1.0800	1.0900	1.1000	1.1100	1.1200	1.2000
2	2.0301	2.0452	2.0604	2.0756	2.0909	2.1062	2.1216	2.1370	2.1525	2.1680	2.1836	2.2149	2.2464	2.2781	2.3100	2.3421	2.3744	2.6400
3	3.0604	3.0909	3.1216	3.1525	3.1836	3.2149	3.2465	3.2782	3.3101	3.3423	3.3746	3.4399	3.5061	3.5731	3.6410	3.7097	3.7793	4.3680
4	4.1010	4.1523	4.2040	4.2563	4.3091	4.3625	4.4163	4.4707	4.5256	4.5811	4.6371	4.7507	4.8666	4.9847	5.1051	5.2278	5.3528	6.4416
5	5.1520	5.2296	5.3081	5.3877	5.4684	5.5502	5.6330	5.7169	5.8019	5.8881	5.9753	6.1533	6.3359	6.5233	6.7156	6.9129	7.1152	8.9299
6	6.2135	6.3230	6.4343	6.5474	6.6625	6.7794	6.8983	7.0192	7.1420	7.2669	7.3938	7.6540	7.9228	8.2004	8.4872	8.7833	9.0890	11.9159
7	7.2857	7.4328	7.5830	7.7361	7.8923	8.0517	8.2142	8.3800	8.5491	8.7216	8.8975	9.2598	9.6366	10.0285	10.4359	10.8594	11.2997	15.4991
8	8.3685	8.5593	8.7546	8.9545	9.1591	9.3685	9.5828	9.8021	10.0266	10.2563	10.4913	10.9780	11.4876	12.0210	12.5795	13.1640	13.7757	19.7989
9	9.4622	9.7027	9.9497	10.2034	10.4639	10.7314	11.0061	11.2882	11.5779	11.8754	12.1808	12.8164	13.4866	14.1929	14.9374	15.7220	16.5487	24.9587
10	10.5668	10.8633	11.1687	11.4835	11.8078	12.1420	12.4864	12.8412	13.2068	13.5835	13.9716	14.7836	15.6455	16.5603	17.5312	18.5614	19.6546	31.1504
11	11.6825	12.0412	12.4121	12.7956	13.1920	13.6020	14.0258	14.4640	14.9171	15.3856	15.8699	16.8885	17.9771	19.1407	20.3843	21.7132	23.1331	38.5805
12	12.8093	13.2368	13.6803	14.1404	14.6178	15.1130	15.6268	16.1599	16.7130	17.2868	17.8821	19.1406	20.4953	21.9534	23.5227	25.2116	27.0291	47.4966
13	13.9474	14.4504	14.9739	15.5190	16.0863	16.6770	17.2919	17.9321	18.5986	19.2926	20.0151	21.5505	23.2149	25.0192	26.9750	29.0949	31.3926	58.1959
14	15.0969	15.6821	16.2934	16.9319	17.5989	18.2957	19.0236	19.7841	20.5786	21.4087	22.2760	24.1290	26.1521	28.3609	30.7725	33.4054	36.2797	71.0351
15	16.2579	16.9324	17.6393	18.3802	19.1569	19.9710	20.8245	21.7193	22.6575	23.6411	24.6725	26.8881	29.3243	32.0034	34.9497	38.1899	41.7533	86.4421
16	17.4304	18.2014	19.0121	19.8647	20.7616	21.7050	22.6975	23.7417	24.8404	25.9964	27.2129	29.8402	32.7502	35.9737	39.5447	43.5008	47.8837	104.9306
17	18.6147	19.4894	20.4123	21.3863	22.4144	23.4997	24.6454	25.8551	27.1324	28.4812	29.9057	32.9990	36.4502	40.3013	44.5992	49.3959	54.7497	127.1167
18	19.8109	20.7967	21.8406	22.9460	24.1169	25.3572	26.6712	28.0636	29.5390	31.1027	32.7600	36.3790	40.4463	45.0185	50.1591	55.9395	62.4397	153.7400
19	21.0190	22.1237	23.2974	24.5447	25.8704	27.2797	28.7781	30.3714	32.0660	33.8683	35.7856	39.9955	44.7620	50.1601	56.2750	63.2028	71.0524	185.6880
20	22.2392	23.4705	24.7833	26.1833	27.6765	29.2695	30.9692	32.7831	34.7193	36.7861	38.9927	43.8652	49.4229	55.7645	63.0025	71.2651	80.6987	224.0256
21	23.4716	24.8376	26.2990	27.8629	29.5368	31.3289	33.2480	35.3034	37.5052	39.8643	42.3923	48.0057	54.4568	61.8733	70.4027	80.2143	91.5026	270.0307
25	28.5256	30.5140	32.6709	35.0117	37.5530	40.3131	43.3117	46.5706	50.1135	53.9660	58.1564	67.6765	78.9544	92.3240	108.1818	126.9988	149.3339	566.3773
30	35.1327	38.1018	41.3794	45.0003	49.0027	53.4295	58.3283	63.7524	69.7608	76.4194	83.8017	101.0730	122.3459	148.5752	180.9434	220.9132	270.2926	1418.2579
40	49.3752	55.0819	61.6100	69.0876	77.6633	87.5095	98.8265	111.8467	126.8398	144.1189	164.0477	213.6096	279.7810	368.2919	486.8518	645.8269	859.1424	8812.6294

This table shows the present value of an annuity due of $1 at various interest rates (i) and time periods (n). It is used to calculate the present value of any series of equal payments made at the *beginning* of each compounding period.

TABLE 6 Present Value of an Annuity Due of $1

$$PVAD = \left[\frac{1 - \frac{1}{(1+i)^n}}{i}\right] \times (1+i)$$

n/i	1.0%	1.5%	2.0%	2.5%	3.0%	3.5%	4.0%	4.5%	5.0%	5.5%	6.0%	7.0%	8.0%	9.0%	10.0%	11.0%	12.0%	20.0%
1	1.00000	1.00000	1.00000	1.00000	1.00000	1.00000	1.00000	1.00000	1.00000	1.00000	1.00000	1.00000	1.00000	1.00000	1.00000	1.00000	1.00000	1.00000
2	1.99010	1.98522	1.98039	1.97561	1.97087	1.96618	1.96154	1.95694	1.95238	1.94787	1.94340	1.93458	1.92593	1.91743	1.90909	1.90090	1.89286	1.83333
3	2.97040	2.95588	2.94156	2.92742	2.91347	2.89969	2.88609	2.87267	2.85941	2.84632	2.83339	2.80802	2.78326	2.75911	2.73554	2.71252	2.69005	2.52778
4	3.94099	3.91220	3.88388	3.85602	3.82861	3.80164	3.77509	3.74896	3.72325	3.69793	3.67301	3.62432	3.57710	3.53129	3.48685	3.44371	3.40183	3.10648
5	4.90197	4.85438	4.80773	4.76197	4.71710	4.67308	4.62990	4.58753	4.54595	4.50515	4.46511	4.38721	4.31213	4.23972	4.16987	4.10245	4.03735	3.58873
6	**5.85343**	**5.78264**	**5.71346**	**5.64583**	**5.57971**	**5.51505**	**5.45182**	**5.38998**	**5.32948**	**5.27028**	**5.21236**	**5.10020**	**4.99271**	**4.88965**	**4.79079**	**4.69590**	**4.60478**	**3.99061**
7	6.79548	6.69719	6.60143	6.50813	6.41719	6.32855	6.24214	6.15787	6.07569	5.99553	5.91732	5.76654	5.62288	5.48592	5.35526	5.23054	5.11141	4.32551
8	7.72819	7.59821	7.47199	7.34939	7.23028	7.11454	7.00205	6.89270	6.78637	6.68297	6.58238	6.38929	6.20637	6.03295	5.86842	5.71220	5.56376	4.60459
9	8.65168	8.48593	8.32548	8.17014	8.01969	7.87396	7.73274	7.59589	7.46321	7.33457	7.20979	6.97130	6.74664	6.53482	6.33493	6.14612	5.96764	4.83716
10	9.56602	9.36052	9.16224	8.97087	8.78611	8.60769	8.43533	8.26879	8.10782	7.95220	7.80169	7.51523	7.24689	6.99525	6.75902	6.53705	6.32825	5.03097
11	**10.47130**	**10.22218**	**9.98259**	**9.75206**	**9.53020**	**9.31661**	**9.11090**	**8.91272**	**8.72173**	**8.53763**	**8.36009**	**8.02358**	**7.71008**	**7.41766**	**7.14457**	**6.88923**	**6.65022**	**5.19247**
12	11.36763	11.07112	10.78685	10.51421	10.25262	10.00155	9.76048	9.52892	9.30641	9.09254	8.88687	8.49867	8.13896	7.80519	7.49506	7.20652	6.93770	5.32706
13	12.25508	11.90751	11.57534	11.25776	10.95400	10.66333	10.38507	10.11858	9.86325	9.61852	9.38384	8.94269	8.53608	8.16073	7.81369	7.49236	7.19437	5.43922
14	13.13374	12.73153	12.34837	11.98318	11.63496	11.30274	10.98565	10.68285	10.39357	10.11708	9.85268	9.35765	8.90378	8.48690	8.10336	7.74987	7.42355	5.53268
15	14.00370	13.54338	13.10625	12.69091	12.29607	11.92052	11.56312	11.22283	10.89864	10.58965	10.29498	9.74547	9.24424	8.78615	8.36669	7.98187	7.62817	5.61057
16	**14.86505**	**14.34323**	**13.84926**	**13.38138**	**12.93794**	**12.51741**	**12.11839**	**11.73955**	**11.37966**	**11.03758**	**10.71225**	**10.10791**	**9.55948**	**9.06069**	**8.60608**	**8.19087**	**7.81086**	**5.67547**
17	15.71787	15.13126	14.57771	14.05500	13.56110	13.09412	12.65230	12.23402	11.83777	11.46216	11.10590	10.44665	9.85137	9.31256	8.82371	8.37916	7.97399	5.72956
18	16.56225	15.90765	15.29187	14.71220	14.16612	13.65132	13.16567	12.70719	12.27407	11.86461	11.47726	10.76322	10.12164	9.54363	9.02155	8.54879	8.11963	5.77463
19	17.39827	16.67256	15.99203	15.35336	14.75351	14.18968	13.65930	13.15999	12.68959	12.24607	11.82760	11.05909	10.37189	9.75563	9.20141	8.70162	8.24967	5.81219
20	18.22601	17.42617	16.67846	15.97889	15.32380	14.70984	14.13394	13.59329	13.08532	12.60765	12.15812	11.33560	10.60360	9.95011	9.36492	8.83929	8.36578	5.84350
21	**19.04555**	**18.16864**	**17.35143**	**16.58916**	**15.87747**	**15.21240**	**14.59033**	**14.00794**	**13.46221**	**12.95038**	**12.46992**	**11.59401**	**10.81815**	**10.12855**	**9.51356**	**8.96333**	**8.46944**	**5.86958**
25	22.24339	21.03041	19.91393	18.88499	17.93554	17.05837	16.24696	15.49548	14.79864	14.15170	13.55036	12.46933	11.52876	10.70661	9.98474	9.34814	8.78432	5.93710
30	26.06579	24.37608	22.84438	21.45355	20.18845	19.03577	17.98371	17.02189	16.14107	15.33310	14.59072	13.27767	12.15841	11.19828	10.36961	9.65011	9.02181	5.97472
40	33.16303	30.36458	27.90259	25.73034	23.80822	22.10250	20.58448	19.22966	18.01704	16.92866	15.94907	14.26493	12.87858	11.72552	10.75696	9.93567	9.23303	5.99592

Online Supplements

McGraw Hill Education **connect**®

Connect Online Access for Intermediate Accounting, Ninth Edition

McGraw-Hill Connect is a digital teaching and learning environment that improves performance over a variety of critical outcomes. With Connect, instructors can deliver assignments, quizzes and tests easily online. Students can practice important skills at their own pace and on their own schedule.

HOW TO REGISTER

Using a Print Book?
To register and activate your Connect account, simply follow these easy steps:

1. **Go to the Connect course web address provided by your instructor or visit the Connect link set up on your instructor's course within your campus learning management system.**
2. **Click on the link to register.**
3. **When prompted, enter the Connect code found on the inside back cover of your book and click Submit. Complete the brief registration form that follows to begin using Connect.**

Using an eBook?
To register and activate your Connect account, simply follow these easy steps:

1. **Upon purchase of your eBook, you will be granted automatic access to Connect.**
2. **Go to the Connect course web address provided by your instructor or visit the Connect link set up on your instructor's course within your campus learning management system.**
3. **Sign in using the same email address and password you used to register on the eBookstore. Complete your registration and begin using Connect.**

**Note: Access Code is for one use only. If you did not purchase this book new, the access code included in this book is no longer valid.*

Need help? Visit mhhe.com/support